A COMPANION TO WITTGENSTEIN'S "PHILOSOPHICAL INVESTIGATIONS"

A COMPANION TO WITTGENSTEIN'S "PHILOSOPHICAL INVESTIGATIONS"

GARTH HALLETT

CORNELL UNIVERSITY PRESS

ITHACA AND LONDON

First published 1977 by Cornell University Press.
Published in the United Kingdom by Cornell University Press Ltd.,
2–4 Brook Street, London W1Y 1AA.

International Standard Book Number 0–8014–0997–7
Library of Congress Catalog Card Number 76-28014
Printed in the United States of America by Vail-Ballou Press, Inc.
*Librarians: Library of Congress cataloging information appears
on the last page of the book.*

This may be compared to the way a chartered accountant precisely investigates and clarifies the conduct of a business undertaking. The aim is a synoptic comparative account of all the applications, illustrations, conceptions of the calculus. The complete survey of everything that may produce unclarity. And this survey must extend over a wide domain, for the roots of our ideas reach a long way.

Wittgenstein, Zettel

What is most difficult here is to put this indefiniteness, correctly and unfalsified, into words.

Wittgenstein, Investigations

CONTENTS

8   Contents

PREFACE

In 1938, while he was working on the *Investigations,* Wittgenstein predicted the difficulties of many a reader, and explained in advance the utility of a commentary, when he wrote: "If this book is written as it should be, everything I say must be easy to understand, indeed trivial; but it will be hard to understand *why* I say it" (Manuscript 160; cf. Manuscript 166). As a result of this policy the work is in its own way quite as difficult as the *Tractatus* and as much in need of detailed explication. To assist in the close study the book richly deserves, I provide both information and interpretation, of the following kinds.

Information: (a) correlations with other parts of the *Investigations* and with other works of Wittgenstein, published and unpublished; (b) citations of or quotations from authors Wittgenstein knew and perhaps was influenced by; (c) identification of passages cited, people and things referred to; (d) references to helpful secondary sources, including books, articles, and passages treating a given point or part of the *Investigations.*

Interpretation: (a) of his thought as a whole; of individual parts and sections and statements, with special attention to explanatory background (authors, problems, and so forth); (b) alternative explanations offered by commentators and objections raised.

This material is organized on three levels: first, a general introduction to the *Investigations* as a whole; second, introductions to whole sections; third, detailed comments on individual expressions, statements, and paragraphs in the sections of Part One and the pages of Part Two. Use of paragraph numbers in my General Introduction and in the sectional introductions permits ready reference downward, for detailed development or illustration of a general observation, or upward, from a particular point to its wider context. Hence the most illuminating observations on a passage are frequently not those in the commentary on it, but those indicated by such a reference. Another device by which I have avoided duplication is the Appendix, which lists authors Wittgenstein knew and, by describing the nature and extent of his contact, explains as well why I cite or quote them and what importance should be attached to a given citation. I have saved further space by choosing illustrative quotations almost solely from these authors, since their writings both clarify the sense of Wittgenstein's remarks and suggest their possible genesis, and by passing over many others who held similar views. Bibliographical data, too, I have shortened by citing works fully only once, in the Bibliography, and using abbreviated references in the text. And the references are selective; I mention only works and passages I consider particularly helpful, not all those which treat a given topic. Furthermore, realizing that a commentary equally suitable for beginners and for specialists is not feasible, I have presupposed that the reader has at least some familiarity with Wittgenstein's life, thought, and writings, say through an introduction such as Norman Malcolm's article in the *Encyclopedia of Philosophy*. Since, however, knowledge of dates, situating works in Wittgenstein's early, transitional, or later period, is so crucially important for the proper use and interpretation of the many quotations given, I have provided a list of the manuscripts cited, with the sure or probable date of composition, and have furnished similar information concerning published works in the List of Abbreviations.

Long though it is, the book would have been much longer had I thought fit to discuss fully all debatable positions I have taken and to document completely every statement made. I have preferred the clarity and availability of a more concise treatment. If the reader feels that the evidence adduced for some point is meager, more probably could have been provided; if he recalls some interpretation at variance with mine, to which I make no reference, the chances are good that I was aware of it but either thought it not worth attention or answered it through the arguments for my own view. As far as possible, I have avoided polemics.

Yet there is one challenge so basic that I cannot overlook it. Having written a book on Wittgenstein's "definition of meaning" and then been told repeatedly that Wittgenstein gave no definition, I may now write a commentary on his book only to hear that he wrote no book, but only a workbook or "album" (see his Preface), which "does not lend itself to the possibility of formulating a commentary, outline, or summary of its views, or even a Wittgensteinian philosophy" (High, *Language*, 19). If Wittgenstein wrote in a way that he knew would puzzle his readers, didn't he perhaps have good reasons and isn't a commentary a mistake?

Kierkegaard, too, believed in indirect communication, of a sort and for reasons analogous to Wittgenstein's; but he lived long enough to compare the theory with the results, so repented and stated explicitly the underlying aim of his writings. I suspect that Wittgenstein too would have been driven to greater explicitness about why he said what he did, had he lived to see how badly he was misunderstood for lack of such guidance. My own experience in preparing this commentary was surprise at how much I had not seen or understood, even when I was thoroughly familiar with at least Wittgenstein's published works. And usually to understand Wittgenstein better was to understand the matter better. In communicating the results of my research, I hope to speed others along the same road I traveled so slowly—and beyond, to the point where, having studied individual topics more fully than I was able to do, they can detect which of my remarks are inadequate, misleading, or even false. Some such there will inevitably be.

My debts are wide and great: to Wittgenstein's literary executors—G. E. M. Anscombe, Rush Rhees, and G. H. von Wright—for permitting me to quote from his unpublished writings; to the Gregorian University for providing time for research; to my fellow Jesuits—Vincent Cooke, Filippo Selvaggi, John Stacer, Xavier Tilliette, S. Youree Watson—for constant helpfulness; to numerous Wittgenstein experts—G. E. M. Anscombe, Max Black, Peter Geach, A. C. Jackson, Brian McGuinness, Norman Malcolm, Rush Rhees, G. H. von Wright, Eddy Zemach—who willingly shared their expertise; but most particularly to Professor Geach, whose generosity was exceptional. To these, and to others whom I have not named, sincere thanks.

The texts of the *Philosophical Investigations, The Blue and Brown Books, Zettel, On Certainty, Remarks on the Foundations of Mathematics, Notebooks 1914–1916,* and *Lectures and Conversations on Aesthetics, Psychology and Religious Belief* have been used by courtesy of the publisher, Basil Blackwell, Oxford. Quotations have been made from Norman Malcolm's *Ludwig Wittgenstein: A Memoir* (© 1962, Oxford University Press) by permission of the Oxford University Press, Oxford; and from G. E. Moore's *Philosophical Papers* and Bertrand Russell's *Logic and Knowledge* by permission of Allen & Unwin Ltd., London. I am grateful also to Dell Publishing Company for permission to quote from K. T. Fann, *Ludwig Wittgenstein: The Man and His Philosophy* (New York, 1967).

As far as possible, I have used published translations in quoting Wittgenstein's German writings. However, Anthony Kenny's translation (Oxford, 1974) of *Philosophische Grammatik* and Raymond Hargreaves and Roger White's translation (Oxford, 1975) of *Philosophische Bemerkungen,* though available in time for consultation, appeared after my text, with its dozens of quotations from both works, was prepared. Fortunately the pagination in both English editions is identical with that in the editions I cite, save for a few slight departures in the latter work. The translations of passages from Wittgenstein's unpublished writings are also my own. Though some errors and infelicities doubtless remain, their number has been greatly reduced by the assistance of Rush Rhees and Carlo Huber, S.J., who separately examined half the translations, and of Joseph Macha, S.J., who checked the other half. I am specially thankful for their labors.

Garth L. Hallett

Rome, Italy

LIST OF ABBREVIATIONS

LE	1929–1930	"A Lecture on Ethics", *Philosophical Review*, 74 (1965), 3–12.
LF	1929	"Some Remarks on Logical Form", in I. Copi and R. Beard, eds., *Essays on Wittgenstein's 'Tractatus'* (New York, 1966), 31–38; reprinted from *Proceedings of the Aristotelian Society* (suppl.), 9 (1929), 162–71.
LO	1922–1933	*Letters to C. K. Ogden with Comments*, ed. by G. H. von Wright (Oxford, 1972).
LR	1912–1948	*Letters to Russell, Keynes, and Moore*, ed. by G. H. von Wright (Oxford, 1974).
Man.	See the List of Manuscripts	This abbreviation indicates one of the manuscripts or other items in Wittgenstein's *Nachlass*, which is available in microfilm or Xerox copy from Cornell University Libraries in Ithaca, New York. The number given after the abbreviation refers to an entry in von Wright's list ("Special Supplement: The Wittgenstein Papers", *Philosophical Review*, 78 [1969], 483–503) or, in a few cases, to a manuscript since entered in the corresponding Cornell list. Where no page number is added to the manuscript number, none is found in the manuscript. Where a manuscript uses one number for two facing pages, I add the letter "A" or "B" to indicate the side. All quotations are translations from Wittgenstein's German, save where otherwise indicated.
NB	1914–1916	*Notebooks 1914–1916*, ed. by G. H. von Wright and G. E. M. Anscombe, with an English translation by G. E. M. Anscombe (Oxford, 1961).
NL	Approximately 1934–1936	"Notes for Lectures on 'Private Experience' and 'Sense Data' ", *Philosophical Review*, 77 (1968), 275–320.
NT	1929–1930	F. Waismann, "Notes on Talks with Wittgenstein", *Philosophical Review*, 74 (1965), 12–16.
OC	1949–1951	*On Certainty*, ed. by G. E. M. Anscombe and G. H. von Wright, with an English translation by Denis Paul and G. E. M. Anscombe (Oxford, 1969).
PB	1929–1930	*Philosophische Bemerkungen*, ed. by R. Rhees (Oxford, 1964).
PG	1932–1934	*Philosophische Grammatik*, ed. by R. Rhees (Frankfort on the Main, 1969).

PP	1930–1933	"Wittgenstein's Lectures in 1930–33", in G. E. Moore, *Philosophical Papers* (London, 1959), 252–324; reprinted from *Mind*, 63 (1954), 1–15, 289–316; 64 (1955), 1–27.
Prototractatus	Completed in 1918	*Prototractatus: An Early Version of Tractatus Logico-Philosophicus*, ed. by B. McGuinness, T. Nyberg, and G. H. von Wright, with an English translation by D. Pears and B. McGuinness, introduction by G. H. von Wright (Ithaca, 1971).
RFM	1937–1944	*Remarks on the Foundations of Mathematics*, ed. by G. H. von Wright, R. Rhees, and G. E. M. Anscombe, with an English translation by G. E. M. Anscombe (Oxford, 1956). For her corrections, see *British Journal for the Philosophy of Science*, 9 (1958), 158.
Tractatus	Completed in 1918	*Tractatus Logico-Philosophicus*, with an English translation by D. Pears and B. McGuinness, introduction by B. Russell (London, 1961).
Z	Mostly 1945–1948	*Zettel*, ed. by G. E. M. Anscombe and G. H. von Wright, with an English translation by G. E. M. Anscombe (Oxford, 1967).

LIST OF MANUSCRIPTS

Since the unpublished manuscripts cited in the commentary and listed below represent different stages in Wittgenstein's thought, their dates are important. For further information about them, see the List of Abbreviations: Man.

Manuscript	Year(s) of composition	Manuscript	Year(s) of composition
105	1929	160	1938
106	1929	161	1939
107	Completed 1930	163	1941
108	1929–1930	164	1941–1944
109	1930–1931	166	Date unknown
110	1930–1931	167	Date unknown
111	1931	168	1947–1949
112	1931	169	Probably first half of 1949
113	1931–1932		
115	1933–1936	170	Probably 1949
116	1936—; May 1945	172	Probably 1950
117	1937; 1938; 1940	173	1950; part undated
119	1937	174	1950
121	1938–1939	175	1950–1951
122	1939–1940	176	1950–1951
123	1940–1941	177	1951
125	1941–1942	178	Undated
127	1943–1944	179	Approximately 1945
128	Approximately 1944	180a	Approximately 1945
129	Begun in 1944	180b	Approximately 1945
130	1946	213	1933
131	1946	219	Probably 1932 or 1933
132	1946	220	1937 or 1938
133	1946–1947	221	1938
134	1947	225	1938
135	1947	226	1937 or 1938
138	1949	227	Probably 1945
159	1938	228	Probably 1945 or 1946

Manuscript	*Year(s) of composition*	Manuscript	*Year(s) of composition*
229	Probably 1945 or 1946	FW	Notes taken by Y. Smythies; probably 1945–1946
232	1947–1948		
302	Approximately 1932–1933 (Dictation)		

NOTE ON REFERENCES

Investigations: Numbers or pages cited without further identification (e.g. §363 or p. 175) are in the *Investigations.* Small letters indicate paragraphs within a section or within a page, starting from the top of the page (these are not so lettered in the *Investigations*). I refer to an insert at the bottom of a page in Part One by giving the page number followed by "n" (e.g. p. 147n).

Other works of Wittgenstein: See the List of Abbreviations. Numbers indicate numbered sections in *OC, Prototractatus,* and *Z;* and pages in all other published works, save the *Tractatus,* whose distinctive decimals (e.g. 4.5) are given without further identification. In references to manuscripts, a number after the manuscript number indicates the page, unless the sign § is used, to designate a numbered section (e.g. Man. 228, §81).

Other parts of this commentary: The letters "GI" followed by a number indicate a numbered paragraph in the General Introduction. A roman numeral and following arabic numeral (e.g. IV, 5) indicate section and paragraph of a sectional introduction (e.g. paragraph 5 of the introduction to section IV).

Secondary sources: With few exceptions, references to articles and books by authors other than Wittgenstein include the author's last name, an abbreviation of the title or description, and the page number; the Bibliography provides fuller data. In the case of certain classical authors (Plato, Augustine, Scotus) standard references seemed preferable; the translations of Scotus and Augustine are mine, but in quoting Plato I have relied on A. Taylor's translation of the *Sophist* (New York, 1961) and B. Jowett's translations of the other dialogues (Oxford, 1875).

Cp. and see: The abbreviation "cp." indicates relevant passages less directly connected with the commented point or passage than are passages indicated by "see" (for example: similar treatment of a different point or different treatment of the same point).

Small letters after page numbers: These indicate indented paragraphs where there is indentation (e.g. in *NB* and *RFM*) and separated paragraphs where there is just separation (e.g. in *PB*), starting from the top of the page.

Use of single and double quotation marks: In my text double quotation marks enclose words to indicate passages quoted from others, a manner of expression, or something said; single quotation marks enclose words used in an idiosyncratic sense.

A COMPANION TO WITTGENSTEIN'S "PHILOSOPHICAL INVESTIGATIONS"

GENERAL INTRODUCTION

(1)   At a time when his judgment was certainly not biased in Wittgenstein's favor, Bertrand Russell wrote: "During the period since 1914 three philosophies have successively dominated the British philosophical world: first that of Wittgenstein's *Tractatus,* second that of the Logical Positivists, and third that of Wittgenstein's *Philosophical Investigations*" (*Development,* 216). If one wishes to characterize ordinary-language philosophy, varied though it is, by naming one book, it is hard to fault Russell's choice; the *Investigations* is the classic of the movement. And though Wittgenstein viewed his own likely influence with misgivings (Malcolm, *Memoir,* 62–63), there is no doubt as to which of his works he considered intrinsically most important. "Wittgenstein refrained from publishing the *Investigations* during his lifetime, but his explicit wish was that it be published posthumously, a wish that he probably did not have with respect to any of the rest of the voluminous work he produced between 1929 and 1951," the year of his death (Malcolm, "Wittgenstein", 334).

(2)   The *Tractatus,* too, he considered important, though mistaken (Malcolm, *Memoir,* 69), and the interest of the *Investigations* is heightened by the fact that it takes so considerable a work as its target. Much of the *Investigations* "is an attack, either explicit or implicit, on the earlier work. This development is probably unique in the history of philosophy—a thinker producing, at different periods of his life, two highly original systems of thought, each system the result of many years of intensive labors, each expressed in an elegant and powerful style, each greatly influencing contemporary philosophy, and the second being a criticism and rejection of the first" (Malcolm, "Wittgenstein", 334).

(3)   Consequently, whoever would fully understand the *Investigations* must relate it to the *Tractatus.* Doubtless Wittgenstein included himself when he wrote: "To every thinker there cling bits of the shell from which he hatched. People can tell *what* you fought against as you grew up. What views your own bear witness to; from which ones you had later to free yourself" (Man. 229, §1791). This parallels his remark that

the *Investigations* "could be seen in the right light only by contrast with and against the background of my old way of thinking" (Preface). The repeated distinction between views rejected and background of another sort suggests both continuity and discontinuity between Wittgenstein's earlier and later thought. The continuity may be less evident, but it is there, and important. (See Drury, *Danger*, ix; Kenny, *Wittgenstein*, 219–32.)

(4)   Indeed it might seem that the author of the *Investigations* disagreed still more with Russell than he did with his own former positions. For the *Tractatus* says little about the psychological concepts which occupy Wittgenstein's attention throughout the *Investigations*, whereas Russell's works treat these matters fully, in addition to the logical atomism he shared with Wittgenstein, and contain views in both areas such as Wittgenstein later criticized. However, the notebooks which preceded the *Tractatus* and especially the transitional manuscripts which followed it reveal unmistakably that the *Investigations* is chiefly concerned with the totality of Wittgenstein's own antecedent thought—the twists and turns, the passing temptations and temporary solutions, all the frenzied buzzings of the fly in the fly-bottle (§309) —and not just those positions which he momentarily assumed or explicitly stated in the *Tractatus*. Accordingly, as I now follow Wittgenstein's advice and consider first continuity between the *Investigations* and the *Tractatus*, then discontinuity, I shall treat the early work as the firm, visible nucleus of a larger body of thought, without trying to determine in every case whether a view belonging to that earlier period, or some ramification in Russell, coincides with Wittgenstein's thinking in the *Tractatus*.

Continuity with the *Tractatus*

(5)   Perhaps the most important agreement of all between the *Tractatus* and the *Investigations*, yet easily overlooked, is the large area of their common silence. I am not referring to the significant fact that both touch only slightly on mathematics, which Wittgenstein treated so profusely elsewhere, nor to their studied neglect of science (Carnap, "Autobiography", 37; Man. 138, 5B), but to the absence of the great questions of politics, history, art, ethics, religion and metaphysics. This is a principal reason why Wittgenstein's writings have not received still wider attention, not only outside the English-speaking world (Williams and Montefiore, *Philosophy*, 12), but also within it. And it readily leads to fundamental misconceptions about Wittgenstein's position, as is evidenced by the logical positivists' interpretation of the *Tractatus*. Only personal contact with Wittgenstein finally revealed to them how dif-

ferent from their own was his attitude toward religion and metaphysics (Carnap, "Autobiography", 36).

(6)   "A whole generation of disciples was able to take Wittgenstein for a positivist because he has something of enormous importance in common with the positivists: he draws the line between what we can speak about and what we must be silent about just as they do. The difference is only that they have nothing to be silent about. Positivism holds—and this is its essence—that what we can speak about is all that matters in life. *Whereas Wittgenstein passionately believes that all that really matters in human life is precisely what, in his view, we must be silent about*" (Engelmann, *Memoir*, 97). This judgment about the *Tractatus*, from an intimate friend, is borne out by Wittgenstein's own words in a letter to Von Ficker: "My work consists of two parts: the one presented here plus all that I have *not* written. And it is precisely this second part that is the important one" (ibid., 143). His attitude was basically similar at the time he wrote the *Investigations*. A man who reads and rereads the *Confessions* of Saint Augustine, who looks on music as a world in itself (Drury, "Symposium", 68), who regards Kierkegaard as the greatest philosopher of the last century (ibid., 70), is no logical positivist, even though he says hardly a word about literature, art, music, ethics, or religion in the writings he prepares for publication. (See Drury, *Danger*, xiv.)

(7)   The motives for Wittgenstein's silence appear to have varied little through the years. He agreed with Kierkegaard that the most important things are best shown, not said, and that the gifted artist is the one who can show them best. For "art is a kind of expression," and "good art is complete expression" (*NB* 83), whereas the propositions of the philosopher can express nothing of what is higher (6.42). Ethics, for instance, "cannot be put into words" (6.421). All attempts to explain morality, to describe, ground, or teach it, are mistaken (*Kreis*, 69, 93, 115–18). In like manner he held that "the doctrines of religion in their various forms had no theoretical content" (Carnap, "Autobiography", 35) and that efforts to prove the existence of God (Malcolm, *Memoir*, 71; Man. 174, 2) or to establish religion on a rational, quasi-scientific basis (*LC* 57–59; end of Man. 118) are misconceived. For as "the world in itself is neither good nor evil" (*NB* 79) so "God does not reveal himself *in* the world" (6.432; see Man. 107, 202). "Only from the consciousness of the *uniqueness of my life* arises religion—science—and art" (*NB* 79). And this consciousness all may have but only the artist can convey. "Only the artist can so represent the particular that it seems a work of art" (Man. 109, 29–30, quoted for §122b); only he can present objects "from outside", "in such a way that they have the whole world as background" (*NB* 83). Thus Wittgenstein remarked that "when Tolstoy just

tells a story he impresses me infinitely more than when he addresses the reader" (Malcolm, *Memoir*, 43). And he epitomized his attitude toward art, life, and religion, and toward aesthetics, ethics, and theology, when he observed of a poem by Uhland: "If only you do not try to utter what is unutterable then *nothing* gets lost. But the unutterable will be—unutterably—*contained* in what has been uttered!" (Engelmann, *Memoir*, 7). (On the topic of this paragraph see also: the commentary on §373; Z 144; LE 4b, 9; NT 16; 6.41–6.45; *NB* 77, 79, 83, 86; *PP* 313–15; Man. 110, 198–99; Man. 107, 196, 202; Griffiths, "Ethics".)

(8) What, then, is the task of philosophy? "The clarification of thoughts," said the *Tractatus* (4.112). That is, philosophy has no content of its own (for qualifications, see GI 28–29) but clears up thinking wherever it is murkiest. The later Wittgenstein agreed that "philosophy is not a body of doctrine but an activity" (4.112), and stressed still more strongly the therapeutic function of the activity. Having read Plato on essences, Augustine on time, James on the flow of thought, and having come to realize that the body of doctrine *de facto* contained in the *Tractatus* was just one more sickness of the mind (Maslow, *Study*, x), he declared still more categorically: "Philosophy is a battle against the bewitchment of our intelligence by means of language" (§109).

(9) Language is not merely the object of misunderstanding but its source. Of the *Tractatus* Wittgenstein had said: "The book deals with the problems of philosophy, and shows, I believe, that the reason why these problems are posed is that the logic of our language is misunderstood" (Preface; see 4.003–4.0031). These misunderstandings are explained in turn by the fact that language disguises the thought it expresses (4.002). In the *Blue Book* Wittgenstein offered other explanations besides the linguistic one (*BB* 17–18; cp. *LC* 24–28, 36, 48), and in the *Investigations*, though these additional explanations have disappeared, he sometimes speaks instead of the misleading influence of "pictures", in the sense of false conceptions of how things are or must be (§§191, 305, 352, 402, 426–27). However, as we shall see in detail, such pictures themselves have a linguistic origin, so that for the later Wittgenstein as for the earlier, language is the primal source of philosophical puzzlement and confusion. "What interests us," he said, "is the contrast between the real state of affairs and that which our mode of expression inclines us to expect" (*EPB* 230). "Such hypotheses or pictures . . . are embodied in many of the forms of expression of our everyday language" (*BB* 40; see commentary on §89c; §§94, 115; *Z* 111–13; *EPB* 216–19; *BB* 23b, 37d, 43c, 144b; Man. 228, §160; Man. 213, 427).

(10) A full and coherent account of how language bewitches our intelligence emerges from Wittgenstein's works. Considering the amount

of disagreement between his earlier and later views, it is also a remarkably consistent one. In the *Tractatus* he stressed the difference between the "apparent logical form of a proposition" and its "real one" (4.0031); in the *Investigations* he made much the same distinction in terms of "surface grammar" versus "depth grammar". "Surface grammar" is "what immediately impresses itself upon us about the use of a word", "the way it is used in the construction of the sentence, the part of its use—one might say—that can be taken in by the ear" (§664). "Depth grammar", on the other hand, is far more difficult to discern (ibid.; 4.002; *NB* 95d–96a, 96c); "we do not *command a clear view* of the use of our words" (§122), of "the game with these words, their employment in the linguistic intercourse that is carried on by their means" (§182; see commentary on §122a). Hence we easily fall victim to the misleading influence of surface grammar. It is to Wittgenstein's analyses of such errors, in individual cases (GI 13–23), that one should turn for clear understanding of the distinction between surface and depth.

(11)   Wittgenstein's account of how the surface of language misleads us never changed: "When words in our ordinary language have prima facie analogous grammars we are inclined to try to interpret them analogously; i.e. we try to make the analogy hold throughout" (*BB* 7; see *PP* 257b; Man. 109, 174; Man. 110, 86–87, quoted for §255; Man. 213, 409). It is not merely that the expressions thus falsely assimilated have different meanings, in the sense that they signify different things. No, the very mode of signification varies. For instance, "in the proposition, 'Green is green'—where the first word is the proper name of a person and the last an adjective—these words do not merely have different meanings: they are *different symbols*" (3.323). They "are of utterly different kinds, but look exactly alike" (*BB* 56). "In this way the most fundamental confusions are easily produced (the whole of philosophy is full of them)" (3.324).

(12)   "When we say that by our method we try to counteract the misleading effect of certain analogies," Wittgenstein warned, "it is important that you should understand that the idea of an analogy being misleading is nothing sharply defined" (*BB* 28). Sometimes, as when we are convinced that one and the same word must have the same meaning on the various occasions of its use, the surface alone may mislead us. Other times we have some notion as well of how one of the parallel expressions functions, and we model the other use on that one—the less known on the better known, the complex on the simpler. And the errors induced in these diverse ways differ in kind, forming recognizable groups within the overall family. Four of these clusters deserve special attention, since between them they account for most of the errors with which Wittgenstein was concerned in the *Investigations*.

Even at this more detailed level, continuity with the *Tractatus* will appear in every case.

(13)   Roughly speaking, two of the errors have to do with the interpretation of whole sentences, and two concern individual words or phrases. A brief listing may help at the start, before detailed exposition. The labels, though mine, are inspired by Wittgenstein's own terminology. (a) *Sense Fallacy:* a meaningless word-group which superficially resembles meaningful sentences is taken to have sense (most prominent in Sections X, XI, XIV, XVII, XXX, XXXIII, XXXV). (b) *Description Fallacy:* an utterance which sounds like many a description or identification is mistakenly taken for one (most prominent in Sections IX, X, XIII, XV, XXII, XXIII, XXV, XXVI, XXVII, XXIX, XXXIII–XXXVIII). (c) *Reference Fallacy:* an expression which parallels referring ones is provided with a nonexistent reference (most prominent in Sections II, III, XI, XIV, XV, XXII–XXVIII, XXXII, XXXIII, XXXV, XXXVII, XL). (d) *Essence Fallacy:* the same term, used on different occasions, is mistakenly thought to pick out the same "essence" each time (most prominent in Sections I–V, VIII, IX, XXXVII). As further explanation will make clear, such errors are not practical but speculative; they do not affect our ordinary intercourse by means of words, but our theorizing (4.002; §§109–12, 122–24, 194c).

(14)   Unlike the other three the Sense Fallacy (see Hallett, "Bottle", 88–89, and "Contrast", 686–92) is not only a speculative error but concerns speculative sayings. According to the *Tractatus,* the "correct method in philosophy" would consist in this: "Whenever someone else wanted to say something metaphysical, to demonstrate to him that he had failed to give a meaning to certain signs in his propositions" (6.53), and was therefore talking nonsense. In like vein the *Investigations* reminds the metaphysician that the meaning of a word is not an atmosphere, as it were, accompanying the word into every kind of application (§117); "only in the stream of thought and life do words have meaning" (Z 173; cp. 3.3, 3.314). English expressions and English grammar may produce an English sentence, but that does not guarantee meaning (§516). For "it is not every sentence-like formation that we know how to do something with, not every technique has an application in our life; and when we are tempted in philosophy to count some quite useless thing as a proposition, that is often because we have not considered its application sufficiently" (§520; cp. 3.328, 6.211). Wittgenstein's preoccupation with this temptation (§§47, 216, 345–52, 398, 420, 513–17, pp. 221–22; OC 347–50; BB 7–11; PP 319) exemplifies a still larger concern: "If I had to say what is the main mistake made by philosophers of the present generation, including Moore, I would say that it is that when language is looked at, what is looked at is

a form of words and not the use made of the form of words" (*LC* 2).
(15)   As the mere ring of a sentence does not suffice to give connections of words a sense (*RFM* 54a), so the mere ring of a description or identification does not suffice to turn a sentence into a report of fact. Against one instance of the Description Fallacy Wittgenstein argued in the *Tractatus* that "all theories that make a proposition of logic appear to have content are false" (6.111); logical propositions are not statements of fact, yet neither are they nonsensical (4.4611), but possess "a unique status among all propositions" (6.112). Later, in his mathematical writings, he insisted that the propositions of mathematics are equally void of factual content; to call them "mathematical truths" is to veil their true status as rules (Hallett, "Contrast", 695–97). In the *Investigations* he focused instead on sentences using psychological predicates with the first-person singular, for example: "Now I know how to go on" (§§154–55, 179–80, 323; see p. 218); "I am in pain" (§§404–5, p. 189; see §§244, 290–92, 410); "I remember" (see §343, pp. 217–18); "I am afraid" (pp. 188–89); "I meant to" (§§645–46); "I believe" (pp. 190, 192); "I wish" (see §§440–41); "I hope he'll come" (§585); "I'm longing to see him" (§586); "I am leaving the room because you tell me to" (§487). "Here we are coerced not by just one or two analogies, but by four, each closer than the last, so that we find it difficult to conceive that the expression in question is not a description, identification, or report. . . . So many other expressions are descriptions, and they look much the same. Closer still, some of these descriptions vary only the verb or the adjective. . . . Still others have the same predicate and differ only in subject. Most insidious of all, the identical set of words may actually be used on some occasions to give a report or description" (Hallett, "Bottle", 93). For example, "the words 'I am afraid' may approximate more, or less, to being a cry. They may come quite close to this and also be *far* removed from it" (p. 189; cp. §§585–86, 441). We do not usually take notice of ourselves as others do, listen to ourselves talking, and draw conclusions about our feelings, beliefs, intentions, or capacities (§441, p. 192). Such first-person expressions, therefore, tend to resemble a cry (§244) or a groan (§404), an instinctive sound (§323), a signal (§180, p. 218), or a mere reaction (§343, p. 218).

(16)   Yet there is a difference. In his "plan for the treatment of psychological concepts" (*Z* 472) Wittgenstein summarized thus: "Psychological verbs characterized by the fact that the third person of the present is to be verified by observation, the first person not. Sentences in the third person of the present: information. In the first person present: expression [*Äusserung*]. ((Not quite right.))" The *Investigations* suggests some necessary nuances. On the one hand, first-person psychological utterances in the present tense do indeed inform, but after

the manner of a cry or a glad start (p. 189): gestures, tones, facial expressions, instinctive utterances, and the like are not mere clues or symptoms of grief, joy, pleasure, or pain; such expressions of an emotion or state belong to the very concept of the emotion or state; they are the outer criteria of which the "inner" has need (§580; X, 22). On the other hand, verbal *Äusserungen* are akin to (Z 472) but not strictly on a par with the others; for we learn them. A cry is natural pain behavior, whereas "I am in pain" is acquired pain behavior (§244). "By nature and by a particular training, a particular education, we are disposed to give expression to wishes [fears, sorrows, expectations, hopes, etc.] in certain circumstances" (§441). Thus it will not do to call these first-person expressions simply *Äusserungen* and leave it at that; they have their own unique status, to be reduced neither to that of reports nor to that of natural expressions. (See Malcolm, "Other Minds", 383.) The term *avowal* serves as well as any to suggest this status.

(17)   Equally prominent in Wittgenstein's thinking, and closely related to the Description Fallacy, was the Reference Fallacy. Logical statements would have been genuine descriptive propositions had their logical terms had referents; for "the possibility of propositions," said the author of the *Tractatus*, "is based on the principle that objects have signs as their representatives," but "my fundamental idea is that the 'logical constants' are not representatives" (4.0312). It is because words like *if, or,* and *not,* and even terms such as *object, relation,* and *property,* refer to no logical objects, that the propositions of logic differ totally from those of any other science (*NB* 119). In like manner, were hope a feeling or meaning an act or knowing a conscious state, that is, did psychological predicates such as *hope, mean,* and *understand* have the sort of references we are inclined to suppose, first-person psychological utterances would more regularly be reports of what a person has just done or experienced. Many a philosopher has peopled the world with just such referents. Moore, for instance, had written: "One of the chief things which we mean, by saying we have minds, is, I think, this: namely, that we perform certain mental acts or acts of consciousness. That is to say, we see and hear and feel and remember and imagine and think and believe and desire and like and dislike and will and love and are angry and afraid, etc. These things that we do are all of them mental acts—acts of mind or acts of consciousness: whenever we do any of them, we are conscious of something" (*Problems*, 4). Russell's *Analysis of Mind* is full of similar thinking. Concerning this whole tradition in the interpretation of psychological verbs, the later Wittgenstein observed: "A false—falsely simplified—conception of their meaning, that is of their grammar, seduces us into thinking that a specific, characteristic

experience must correspond to the word" (*EPB* 219). "Thus we are inclined to look for an activity when we are to give an account of the meaning of a verb & if some activity is closely connected with it we tend to think that the verb stands for this activity" (Man. 166; W.'s English; see GI 19). Wittgenstein would have made similar comments, notice, had Moore spoken for instance of "the bodily acts of growing up, growing radishes, and growing a beard: whenever we perform them, we use our body." Wittgenstein was not a behaviorist (GI 45; XI, 1).

(18) The *Blue Book* speaks more explicitly about the causes of this fallacy than does the *Investigations,* where Wittgenstein was more hesitant to advance any causal hypotheses which might possibly be questioned (§109). "One of the great sources of philosophical bewilderment," he there remarks, is this: "A substantive makes us look for a thing that corresponds to it." Asked "What is length?", "What is meaning?", "What is the number one?", and the like, "we feel that we can't point to anything in reply . . . and yet ought to point to something" (*BB* 1; see *PP* 258c). Philosophical problems "about mental processes and states and about behaviourism" arise in the same way (§308): "We say that understanding is a 'psychological process', and in this case, as in numberless others, this label is misleading. It compares understanding to a specific *process*—such as translation from one language into another; and it suggests a similar conception of thinking, knowing, believing, wishing, intending, and so on" (*PG* 74). With regard to both substantives and verbs, the error amounts to this: "We are looking at words as though they all were proper names" (*BB* 18; see §§1, 304). The temptation is understandable: some substantives do name objects, and some verbs do name activities; and this simpler, more perspicuous use acts as a natural paradigm. The temptation is strengthened by parallel forms of expression which seem to refer to two parallel processes, for instance: "to say something" and "to mean something" (*BB* 35), "He speaks without thinking," "Think before you speak!", "He says one thing and thinks another," "He doesn't mean a word he says" (*BB* 148; *EPB* 231).

(19) Instances treated in the *Investigations* reveal typical forms the fallacy may take: (a) A reference may be provided by seizing on some actual item of experience, in which case the error does not consist merely in supposing the item to be constantly correlated with the word, but in overlooking the circumstances—what went before and after— without which the word would not be applicable. No one characteristic experience constitutes pointing (§35), understanding (§§152–53, 321, 541–42, p. 181), reading (§156), deliberating (§174), thinking (§§316, 332, pp. 217–18), intending (§§337, 588, 633, 635–38, 646, pp. 217, 219), the self (§413), consciousness (§417), meaning (§§557, 592,

675–76, 678, p. 176), expecting (§577), believing (§578, p. 225), loving (§§583, 587), hoping (§§583–84, p. 174), looking for someone (§685), speaking of someone (§689, p. 177), grieving (p. 174), fearing (p. 188), being struck (p. 211), remembering (pp. 217, 231), being certain (p. 225). (b) The inadequacy of observed phenomena may lead us to suppose an unobserved reference, whether in the brain (§§149, 156, 158) or in the fleeting, elusive (§§435–36, 456) phenomena of consciousness (§§322, 607, 645). We "hypostatize feelings where there are none," so as to explain our thoughts (§598). (c) Since no mere phenomenon, actual or supposed, could satisfy our requirements (p. 218), we tend to etherealize the referent, in a Platonic manner. Because we cannot specify any one action or event to which we might attach the desired term, "we say that a *spiritual* [mental, intellectual] activity corresponds to these words" (§36). Guidance, for instance, is then an "ethereal, intangible influence" (§175), remembering an "inner process" (§305), thinking an "incorporeal process" (§339), pointing a "hocus-pocus which can be performed only by the soul" (§§36, 454), recognition a magic look into the past as if down a spyglass (§604), conviction a "special atmosphere" (§607), an "intangible" state of mind (§608). For similar reasons, willing cannot be a mere phenomenon (§176), but is "an immediate non-causal bringing-about" (§613). Meaning, too, is an "intangible *something;* only comparable to consciousness itself" (§358); it is the act "that gives the sentence life" (§592), parading word meanings before the mind (p. 176). The fallacy makes no analytical pretensions: "Whether I say that in the first case they have depth; or that something goes on in me, inside my mind, as I utter them; or that they have an atmosphere—it always comes to the same thing" (§§594, 308). It amounts to the Reference Fallacy.

(20) Were some single act or experience constantly, prominently present in all cases of meaning or willing or expecting or grieving (and so on), then talk of such a "reference" would not be so misleading; but Wittgenstein argued that in these cases neither introspective reflection nor scientific research reveals a common core. And even if it did, the hidden something we found would not have been guiding our use of the word; it would not have figured as a criterion, or have belonged to the concept (GI 60). The items that actually enter into our experience and might serve as guides—the feelings, ideas, gestures, surroundings, tones, purposes—form no constant constellation but a "pattern which recurs, with different variations, in the weave of our life" (p. 174). Thus there is an intimate connection between the Reference Fallacy and the Essence Fallacy, another main simplification of language and reality which the *Investigations* sought to cure. (See e.g. §§156–64; *BB* 121c; *PG* 75; Man. 302, 21.)

(21)   Yet the two errors are not identical. The sort of misconception I have loosely labeled the Reference Fallacy consists, for instance, in taking meaning for an act or grief for a sensation. But what *is* an activity, and what *is* a sensation? Running, for instance, and the sensation of pain, and neither running nor pain has an 'essence'. Running varies, and so do pains. Marking the distinction between reference and essence in this way highlights the importance of the Essence Fallacy: Whereas the reference error is possible only where there is no 'reference', the Essence Fallacy is possible in all the other cases too. Nonreferring expressions get assimilated to the simpler, referring paradigms; but these in turn can be simplistically conceived through the supposition of nonexistent essences.

(22)   The temptation is as general as the danger. For what surface parallel is closer, more evident, or more universal than that between instances of one and the same word in its repeated occurrences? Thus "it is sometimes almost impossible for a child to believe that one word can have two meanings" (*BB* 26). The persuasive strength of the analogy becomes still more evident when a grown philosopher argues, "But why would we use the *same word* if there weren't something in common?" (*PG* 75a; *EPB* 220). What also misleads us "is the uniform appearance of words when we hear them spoken or meet them in script and print" (§11); this accounts for the fact that, when doing philosophy, we are quite capable of assimilating all words to some simple paradigm, especially to proper names (§§1, 10, 383; *BB* 18, 82). And proper names have a relatively constant, uniform reference (*BB* 61d).

(23)   As widespread as the temptation is the fall. The whole of philosophy, said Wittgenstein in the *Tractatus* (3.324), abounds in confusions resulting from just this source. The diversity hiding beneath a single expression is a conspicuous theme in the *Investigations*, recurring in innumerable cases, especially near the start of the book: *signify* (§§10, 13); *word* and *sentence* (§23); *description* (§§24, 291); *talk about* (§27); *point to, attend to* (§§33–37); *name* (§§37, 41, 116); *simple, composite* (§47); *rule* (§§54, 82, 208–10); *language* (§§65, 108); *proposition* (§§65, 108, 116, 135); *game* (§§66–67, 69–70, 75–76); *number* (§§67–68); *Moses* (§79); *red, dark, sweet* (§87); *exact* (§88); *knowledge, being, object, I* (§116); *applying a picture* (§140); *derive* (§§162–64); *read* (§§156ff); *guided* (§§172–78); *being influenced* (§176); *know how to go on* (§§179–81, 183); *fit, be able, understand* (§182); *determine* (§189); *order, regular, uniform, and so on* (§§208–10); *same* (§215); and others. "I cannot characterize my standpoint better," Wittgenstein explained, "than by saying that it is opposed to that which Socrates represents in the Platonic dialogues. For if asked what knowledge is I would list examples of knowledge, and add the words 'and the like'. No common element is to be found in them all"

(Man. 302, 14). That is, no one feature is found in all the cases covered by the term, and in them alone, so that the presence of this feature accounts for our use of the term (*BB* 17–18). (See GI 59.)

(24)   These many illustrations, pointing constantly to misleading surface analogies as the source of error and confusion, show how mistaken is the common account which has Wittgenstein trace most philosophical ills to deviant uses of language. The sayings of philosophers may reveal mental maladies, and may perpetuate them, but are not generally their root cause. "*Language* is the bottle, the labyrinth in which we lose our way. Not this or that statement, tucked away in a tome of Hegel, or uttered in a classroom. Nothing that isolated or that infrequent, and therefore nothing that superficial or limited in its effects. No, the source of our difficulties is the whole conceptual system in which we live and move and have our being from the moment we are born; this second nature; this air we breathe. The difficulties with which Wittgenstein deals are correspondingly widespread, deep-rooted, and tenacious. 'They are deep disquietudes; their roots are as deep in us as the forms of our language and their significance is as great as the importance of our language' (§111)" (Hallett, "Bottle", 85; italics added).

(25)   Yet Wittgenstein never supposed that ordinary language, like a bumpy road on which travelers tend to trip, ought to be leveled or straightened out. Philosophers stumble, but other people don't, and language wasn't introduced for philosophical purposes (4.002). An improvement in our terminology designed to prevent misunderstandings is, of course, perfectly possible (§§132, 577); but for ordinary purposes "every sentence in our language 'is in order as it is' " (§98; also §81 and 5.5563). What philosophers need is a perspicuous representation of the use of our words (§122; 3.325, 4.1213; cp. Frege, *Funktion*, 95). Though Wittgenstein, like Frege (ibid., 92), first supposed that this should take the form of analytic translation into a completely unambiguous notation (3.325) and later abandoned this method, preferring instead the simple samples he called "language-games" (GI 56–57), a basic affinity remains, nonetheless, "between the *Tractatus* method of laying out in minute detail the grammar, the structure, of an expression and thereby *revealing* (not stating) its structure, and the later technique of citing a list of concrete examples and thereby *revealing* (not stating) the grammar of an expression" (Hallett, *Definition*, 191; cp. GI 7).

(26)   This underlying affinity between the method of Wittgenstein's more "analytic" period and that of his later, "linguistic" period points to an important similarity uniting various philosophers and philosophies to which these labels are applied. A pronounced characteristic of "analytic" or "linguistic" philosophy is concern for the distinction be-

tween "apparent logic" and "real logic", "surface grammar" and "depth grammar". The terminology may differ, and the reasons for concern, the remedies employed, and the results of their application, but they all overlap in such a way as to make quite clear to what "family" Wittgenstein belonged. Russell's treatment of definite descriptions; Moore's analysis of philosophers' "real meaning"; Carnap's translations from "material" to "formal mode"; Ayer's interpretation of ethical sayings; Ryle's discussion of category mistakes; Austin's treatment of sense-data—these all show kinship, with the *Tractatus* program on the one hand and with the *Investigations'* practice on the other.

(27) The dissimilarities, though, are often profound—and instructive. For clear understanding of what Wittgenstein was about, a comparison of the *Investigations* with Russell's *Analysis of Mind* is almost as revealing as a comparison with the *Tractatus*. Turning like the later Wittgenstein to questions of psychology, Russell set out "to analyse . . . what it is that really takes place when we, e.g. believe or desire" (p. 9). This very positive undertaking is vitiated from start to finish by Russell's disregard of the truth, *"Essence* is expressed by grammar" (§371). He forgets that things are what we call them, that belief and desire, for instance, are what we call belief and desire, if indeed we may be said to call anything by those names. In his examination of the "objects" designated by substantives and the "objects" designated by verbs (*Logic,* 107), he is untroubled by the possibility that the verbs he examines have uses in the language but no unitary referents, or that their referents are but one aspect of the overall meaning of the verbs and thus do not justify their use in any and every context. Thus he can assert without qualms that "there is no *logical* impossibility in walking occurring as an isolated phenomenon, not forming part of any such series as we call a 'person'" (*Mind,* 195). For anyone aware of the linguistic problems which Russell ignores, a book like *Analysis of Mind* is an impossibility. Either one must resolutely and lucidly cut loose from the conceptual bonds of ordinary language and do empirical psychology or one must adopt a fully conceptual approach such as that of the *Investigations;* for between the empirical regularities studied by science and the conceptual patterns of our language there exists no preestablished harmony (GI 70). On this point the *Investigations* differs most basically from Wittgenstein's own *Tractatus* as well as from Russell's book.

Discontinuity with the *Tractatus*

(28) "The conclusion of the greatest modern philosopher," wrote Frank Ramsey after the *Tractatus,* "is that there is no such subject as philosophy; that it is an activity, not a doctrine; and that, instead of answering questions, it aims merely at curing headaches" (*Foundations,*

288). The same might be said with still more truth of Wittgenstein's later teaching, but even then it would not be the whole truth. Our difficulty, he said, is that we don't know our way about (§123). So he described his procedure as follows: "In teaching you philosophy I'm like a guide showing you how to find your way round London. I have to take you through the city from north to south, from east to west, from Euston to the embankment and from Piccadilly to the Marble Arch. After I have taken you many journeys through the city, in all sorts of directions, we shall have passed through any given street a number of times—each time traversing the street as part of a different journey. At the end of this you will know London; you will be able to find your way about like a born Londoner" (Gasking and Jackson, "Wittgenstein", 51). Thus in the *Investigations* Wittgenstein was not merely dispelling puzzles or confusions, nor just enabling the reader to shift for himself when he encountered conceptual difficulties (p. 206), but gave him as well some acquaintance with the landscape (Preface, ix). Numbers such as 133 and 309 may suggest that Wittgenstein was interested in the landscape only for its therapeutic value; but both his remarks (e.g. *RFM* 157h and §92a) and his practice (e.g. pp. 193–95 and *Z* 472–88) sometimes suggest more positive motivation. He did want to "know London".

(29)   What remains, then, of Wittgenstein's assertions that philosophy merely knocks down houses of cards and leaves nothing standing, that its results are "the uncovering of one or another piece of plain nonsense and of bumps that the understanding has got by running its head up against the limits of language" (§119; see §118)? The answer is that philosophy, as Wittgenstein later conceived it, leaves no *system* standing; it offers no theory (§109) or complete classification (p. 206; *Z* 465), no "universal pronouncements about the world and language" (Man. 110, 201–2). For the philosopher's problems are conceptual, and that means he approaches reality through language. But language is a labyrinth (§203); it resembles "a maze of little streets and squares, of old and new houses, and of houses with additions from various periods; and this surrounded by a multitude of new boroughs with straight regular streets and uniform houses" (§18). Consequently, "only in scattered cases can one arrive at a correct and fruitful judgment, establish a fruitful connexion. And the most general remarks yield at best what looks like the fragments of a system" (p. 228; see quotations for §89c).

(30)   Such was Wittgenstein's final answer to the burning question of his youth: "The great problem round which everything that I write turns is: Is there an order in the world *a priori*, and if so what does it consist in?" (*NB* 53). An *a priori* order would be one that held regardless of what was the case, one required by sheer logic before all exami-

nation of contingent states of affairs. But that would be the order which founded the possibility of propositions as such, whether true or false. "My *whole* task," Wittgenstein concluded, "consists in explaining the nature of the proposition" (*NB* 39). From language to the world, from logic to ontology—that would be the line of inquiry (*NB* 39, 42–43, 79q; 5.4711; *PB* 85d). Thus the title of the resulting book was apt even in the ordering of the words: *Tractatus Logico-Philosophicus.*

(31)   Because it treats the same questions (§§92a, 108a) and follows the same order (§§370–73), the *Investigations* might go by the same name. But what a difference in the execution, and how different the results! In his youth Wittgenstein felt certain that "the solutions of the problems of logic must be simple. . . . Men have always had a presentiment that there must be a realm in which the answers to questions are symmetrically combined—*a priori*—to form a self-contained system. A realm subject to the law: "*Simplex sigillum veri*'"(5.4541). And that, therefore, is what he found. Once he had discovered the secret of the proposition and thereby of language, thought and language appeared to him "as the unique correlate, picture, of the world. These concepts: proposition, language, thought, world, stand in line one behind the other, each equivalent to each" (§96). If we would recognize the "bits of stone and rubble" (§118) that litter the *Investigations,* here is the main structure to examine in detail. For it is the one Wittgenstein there demolished.

(32)   According to the *Tractatus,* even the ancient, tangled center of language (§18) is merely well-camouflaged suburbs (4.013–4.0141). Beneath the deceptive surface there lies this uniform grid: All propositions are pictures of reality (4.01), and the totality of propositions are language (4.001; see *PB* 113a). Propositions are *logical* pictures, that is, pictures in a sense that applies to "a gramophone record, the musical idea, the written notes, and the sound-waves", which "all stand to one another in the same internal relation of depicting that holds between language and the world" (4.014). As there is a mark on the score for each note in the mind, and a sound-wave for each mark on the score, so in a proposition it will be found, upon analysis, that there is a name for each object referred to (4.0311) and a rule by which a person gets from one to the other (4.0141). "One name stands for one thing, another for another thing, and they are combined with one another. In this way the whole group—like a *tableau vivant*—presents a state of affairs" (4.0311).

(33)   But what of questions and commands and various other nonassertive uses of words? Are they such pictures, saying, "This is how things stand" (4.5)? And if not, how justify Wittgenstein's identification of language with the "totality of propositions"? The kernel of the an-

swer, I would suggest (see Hallett, "Picture"), is provided by the note on page eleven of the *Investigations* (cp. *NB* 27fg): "Imagine a picture representing a boxer in a particular stance. Now, this picture can be used to tell someone how he should stand, should hold himself; or how he should not hold himself; or how a particular man did stand in such-and-such a place; and so on." That is, it could be used to give a command, make a prohibition, state a fact, request information, and so on. Replace the visual picture with the logical and you have the explanation of 4.001. "Judgment, command and question all stand on the same level; but all have in common the propositional form, and that alone interests us. What interests logic are only the unasserted propositions" (*NB* 96). In a purely logical sense, it is true, a complete proposition does assert (5.124–5.1241); thus whereas the "p" in "~p" or "p ⊃ q" merely shows how things stand if it is true, the "p" in a conjunction or "p" by itself says as well that they do so stand (4.022). But in the ordinary sense, assertion, like question and command, is merely "psychological" (*NB* 96). "Every proposition must *already* have a sense: it cannot be given a sense by affirmation. Indeed its sense is just what is affirmed. And the same applies to negation, etc." (4.064; see 4.442).

(34)   This theory of the logical picture at the heart of every assertion, question, or command, portraying the state of affairs asserted, questioned, or commanded, seemed to provide a solution to the question which had vexed a generation of Austrian philosophers (Haller, "Österreichische Philosophie", 83) and which began to obsess Wittgenstein once he gave more serious consideration to other forms of thought—to willing, wishing, desiring, hoping, expecting, meaning, intending, fearing, understanding, and so on. We wish, desire, expect, fear, hope for things which do not yet exist, in fact which may never exist. How is that possible (*BB* 4a, 31–32)? Granted, we should not assimilate these acts to riding a nonexistent horse or shooting a nonexistent pheasant. But if we do not actually sit on the object of our act, or drill it with a bullet, how *is* the contact made? How is it established that just *this* and not that is what I foresaw, predicted, or dreaded? It will not do to answer, as Russell did, that the thing I wish for is the thing that gives me satisfaction; for of course I might find satisfaction in an apple though I desired a pear (*PB* 63–65; *BB* 22a; *LC* 66; Man. 108, 196; cp. §§440, 460). What, then, determines that it is a *pear* that I desired?

(35)   A similar problem had arisen earlier with regard to propositions (cp. Russell, *Problems*, chap. 12). For a propositional picture "can present relations that do not exist! How is that possible?" (*NB* 8). How can a picture be a picture of *reality*, yet fail to portray things as they *really* are? What is the difference between a false picture and a picture of

nothing, between a false proposition and a fable? The *Tractatus* answer, simply put, is that the fable does not name real things whereas a statement about the real world does. A proposition is a *picture* of reality in virtue of the way its elements are arranged, its logical form; it is a picture of *reality* in virtue of its names (*NB* 53; 2.1515). Even when a proposition corresponds to no existing state of affairs, its names still have reference. This solution would not work were the names in question those of ordinary language, designating complex and therefore destructible objects; but the true names required by the *Tractatus* theory would stand for absolutely simple, so indestructible objects. It is because the analysis of a proposition like "The Eiffel Tower is in Paris" reveals such names for such objects that the proposition continues to picture the world, though falsely, even when the Eiffel Tower has been dismantled and sold for scrap. The elements would still exist, though in different configurations than those asserted.

(36)   This solution Wittgenstein could then extend to all linguistic and psychological acts (5.542; *PB* 67e). Just as a command says that *you*, and no other, should close *this* door, and no other, foreshadowing the whole thing through its logical form and naming names (Man. 108, 192–93; *PP* 262b, 264; *PB* 63–64; *PG* 103; cp. *BB* 39abc), so too in expectation the picture is already there before the event (see the commentary on §442). And "the wish or will to do something is of the same sort as expecting, believing, and so on"' (Man. 108, 250; see *PB* 69g–70a). "It is as though the thought were a shadow of the event" (Man. 108, 230). The names show *where* to look, the form shows *what* to look for (cp. §448), and it thereby becomes possible to determine whether an assertion is verified, a command obeyed, an expectation met, a wish fulfilled. If the indestructible objects are lined up as represented by their names within the assertion, command, expectation, or wish, then the answer is affirmative, there is correspondence; otherwise not (Man. 108, 229, 236). Such is the crucial role required of names in a consistent extension of the picture theory; they solve the problem of falsehood, which, in a system that puts a proposition at the heart of every linguistic and psychological act and requires of every proposition that it be capable of falsehood, is all-pervasive.

(37)   This generalized, simplified account of content led naturally to an equally general, simplistic conception of the act. If at the very moment words are spoken or mental pictures are formed they unmistakably represent reality, then doubtless the act which gives the dead signs such life occurs simultaneously with them. Thus Wittgenstein tended to agree with Russell when he said, for instance: "What a man is believing at a given moment is wholly determinate if we know the contents of his mind at that moment" (*Mind*, 234; see Man. 108, 271, quoted for §452).

His agreement and the reasons for it appear clearly in *NB* 67–68, a fascinating passage where young Wittgenstein envisaged the two basic options, that of the *Tractatus* and that of the *Investigations,* and spurned the latter. If a proposition is to be definitely true or false in every case, he said, then its names must pick out their objects with pinpoint precision; there can be no fuzziness in the meaning. Yet ordinary statements such as "The book is lying on the table" appear to be vague. There could very well occur cases in which we should not be able to say straight off whether the book is still to be called "lying on the table" (cp. §§68–71, 76). For the expression's "use in the language" (§43) does not possess the necessary precision (cp. §88). In the circumstances, only one solution remained: "It seems clear that what we MEAN must always be *'sharp'* " (cp. §81b). Yes, there is the answer: The personal act of meaning goes beyond mere language and adds the requisite definiteness (cp. *NB* 9c). "When I say, e.g., that the table is a yard long, it is extremely questionable what I mean by this. But I presumably mean that the distance between THESE two points is a yard, and that the points belong to the table." "A proposition," therefore, "is a model of reality as we think it" (4.01; translation slightly altered; see 3.11), with the precision that thought alone can give (*NB* 70; cp. §431; *PB* 136c). "At the bottom of all my considerations lies the insight that thought has an inner, not an outer connection with the world. That we *mean* what we say" (Man. 108, 194; see ibid., 218; commentary on §120b). "When we eliminate the element of intention from language, its whole functioning breaks down" (*PB* 63).

(38)   Nonlinguistic forms of thought require a similar projective act to relate the picture with reality, but this does not account for their specificity. Intention, which is common to fear, hope, desire, will, and so on, may explain their common objectivity or their possessing one object rather than another, but not their being fear rather than hope, desire rather than will, and so on. "We must distinguish," said Russell, "between believing and what is believed. I may believe that Columbus crossed the Atlantic, that all Cretans are liars, that two and two are four, or that nine times six is fifty-six; in all these cases the believing is just the same, and only the contents believed are different. I may remember my breakfast this morning, my lecture last week, or my first sight of New York. In all these cases the feeling of memory-belief is just the same, and only what is remembered differs. Exactly similar remarks apply to expectations. Bare assent, memory and expectation are forms of belief; all three are different from what is believed, and each has a constant character which is independent of what is believed" (*Mind,* 232–33). If anything, Wittgenstein would be still more inclined than Russell to discriminate act from act through some difference in

the mind; for that is where the picture was. "Expectation," it was natural for him to suggest, "is of course not the picture, but the attitude I take towards the picture, & this constitutes the difference between expectation, fear, hope, belief, unbelief" (Man. 108, 249; see ibid., 250). Someone looking into the mind of a believer at the moment of belief would see not only what he believed, but that he believed it. Once again, the simple, uniform account of content tends to induce a simple, uniform account of the state or act.

(39)   Such was the direction Wittgenstein's thinking took momentarily when he pondered the implications of the picture theory and tried to work them out in detail. At the time he wrote the *Tractatus* his reflection on psychological questions seems to have been more rudimentary (see, however, XXXVII, 2–6). He spoke of thought and of thinking, but left the detailed description of mental processes to psychologists. Just as it was not his business as a logician "to try to decide whether this thing or that was a simple thing or a complex thing, that being a purely *empirical* matter" (Malcolm, *Memoir*, 86), so too he neither knew nor cared to know just how the necessary processes of thought take place (4.1121; Man. 108, 217, 241–42; Man. 110, 1–2; *BB* 39c; §§89b, 92, 97a, 308). This particular brand of antipsychologism, which he shared with Russell ("Introduction", xix-xx) and Frege (*Foundations*, v–vi), made Wittgenstein dismiss as irrelevant the particular cases and concrete details (*BB* 19) which alone could have enabled him to resolve the problems which tormented him (§109).

(40)   People frequently fail to notice how limited and superficial Wittgenstein's antipsychologism was and suppose that he placed little or no reliance on psychological acts. His true attitude is perfectly revealed in a letter to Russell: " 'Does a Gedanke consist of words?' No! But of psychical constituents that have the same sort of relation to reality as words. What those constituents are I don't know" (*NB* 130; see X, 2). Not knowing, he said even less about psychical contents than he did about the vagaries of written or spoken symbolism; as he could leave Sanskrit to the attention of linguists, so he could leave mental processes to the attention of psychologists (*NB* 129). As a logician he was interested only in the essential, *a priori* structure of language and of thought. Rather than read our own antipsychologism into the *Tractatus*, we should instead reflect on the fact that if "psychical constituents" have the same relation to reality as words (see also 5.542), then words have the same relation to reality as "psychical constituents". And how are these projectively related to objects in the world? Certainly not by custom or convention (cp. *NB* 6oh). Equally unmistakable are the implications of Wittgenstein's remark to Norman Malcolm, "that in the *Tractatus* he had provided a perfected account of a view that is the *only* al-

ternative to the viewpoint of his later work" (*Memoir*, 69). From the very start of the *Investigations* (see §32) the great adversary is a mentalistic account of meaning, understanding, and thinking, and therefore of language (§§81b, 102). This is not some third view, relegating the *Tractatus* alternative to the sidelines, but the way Wittgenstein himself once thought (ibid.). Passages such as *BB* 3, 5, 42a leave no doubt on the matter: *Non datur tertium*.

(41)   The point is worth stressing, for two reasons. For one thing, only when we take the step from language to thought does the full target of the *Investigations* come into view. Wittgenstein's criticisms are like arrows in flight which, if we look at them alone, create an impression of confusion, coming as they do from so many different directions. But if we look at their target, order returns. On page after page, his barbs wing towards the same fortress, this beautiful, simple, all-embracing plan of our linguistic and mental operations: "Proposition, language, thought, world, stand in line one behind the other, each equivalent to each" (§96). Because in this scheme the acts all have a "constant character", both generic and specific, Wittgenstein's reaction was, "I'll teach you differences" (Drury, "Symposium", 69). Because they take place in the moment, and within the narrow confines of the mind, he insisted equally, "Take a wider look around." These are the *Investigations'* two leitmotifs. The central problem of correspondence and foreshadowing appears most explicitly in Sections IX, XV, XXV, XXVI, XXIX, and XXXVIII, yet is dealt with still more decisively elsewhere. Since atomic names seemed to provide the only solution to the problem of falsehood (GI 34–37) and they would have to be private (X, 3–10), Wittgenstein deals first with atomism (Sections II-V) and shortly thereafter with private meanings (Section X). When he is through, nothing remains of the picture theory, or of representationalism in general.

(42)   Here is a second reason for stressing Wittgenstein's true position. Without its refined psychologism the *Tractatus* is no longer representative of the dominant tradition in philosophy, and Wittgenstein is no longer what he was, a critic who possessed the sort of understanding that can come only from having actually held the opposing view and made every effort to make it work. The problems with which he wrestled in his youth are such as any representationalist must face; the *Tractatus* provides answers to difficulties many of his predecessors had not even noticed. Representationalists may take the *Investigations* more seriously if they realize that Wittgenstein was once one of them; when he said that in the *Tractatus* he had provided a perfected account of a view that is the only alternative to his later position, he was not ignoring the mentalistic, representationalist viewpoint which dominated western thought for two millennia.

(43)   What then is the viewpoint of his later work? How, for instance, does it solve the great problem about the agreement of language and thought with the world? Can we say quite generally that "it is in language that an expectation and its fulfilment make contact" (§445)? And might we say something similar about intention (§197), desire (§441), belief (p. 226h), meaning (§§669, 683, 689, 692), hope (p. 174ac), fear (§650), and thought in general (§429; *LC* 68; XV, 3–4), as Wittgenstein did momentarily in Man. 179: "Thus you would like to say that whatever can be called a thought-act is such only through a technique to which it belongs. And only in this way can the question be answered as to how we can think about an object. How can I hope, expect, fear, believe that such-and-such a man will come through the door? Is it experiential, and will experience teach me whether I really expected (wished) this or that? (As it teaches me whether a walk was what I really needed in order to dissipate my dull feeling.). . . . The connection of thought with things is that of language" (see *PG* 142bc). As the passages cited reveal, such a trend is noticeable in the *Investigations:* it is one of those "fruitful connections" of which Wittgenstein spoke (p. 228; see *PG* 140c). But the attempt to state such a universal thesis, specifying exactly both the connection and the class, would soon lead to an impasse (GI 70). The thesis might hold for meaning, but what of imagining (p. 18n)? Had we learned no language and no word for red, would we be incapable of imagining red (Man. 179)? And may not a dog, despite his lack of language, fear that his master will beat him (§650) or believe that his master is at the door (p. 174b)? In Wittgenstein's thinking there was now a still stronger trend: "I fight continually—whether successfully or not I do not know—against the tendency in my own mind to set up (construct) rules in philosophy, and to make assumptions (hypotheses) instead of simply seeing what is there" (Man. 108, 160; see *PG* 256a). "The rule, not the exception, is the incurable illness" (Man. 168, 3). *Simplex sigillum falsi!* (Man. 229, §1575). (See §§338, 641, 680.)

(44)   Might we at least substitute a negative rule for the positive one and assert that the connection with reality is never made by a momentary occurrence in the mind? But what would that mean? Would it mean, for instance, that understanding is never brought about by a momentary thought? No; for thinking of a formula, say, might indeed justify someone in declaring, "Now I understand" (§179). Likewise, "in many cases some direction of the attention will correspond to your meaning one thing or another" (§666). This, though, is true: The 'inner' never suffices by itself to make the connection (ibid.; §580); for no inner act, process, or experience is a sufficient criterion of thinking, meaning, understanding, or the like (X, 22). Thus Wittgenstein was

neither a behaviorist nor an introspectionist; his position was closer to—though still far from (*BB* 45, 48a)—the neutral monism of James (*Essays*, 9–10), Russell (*Logic*, 326), and Mach (*Analyse*, 17). Our language-games, and the corresponding concepts, and the "natures" thus determined (§§370–73) incorporate the most varied elements, in a wide variety of patterns (*BB* 102–3). Thinking, for instance, does frequently involve having images and sensations (*BB* 43), but these alone are not the thinking, nor are they always present when one thinks (ibid.). Now the inner is prominent, now the outer, but no one element is essential. "Even what goes on within has meaning only in the stream of life" (Man. 169).

(45)   Wittgenstein's later position may be seen (*Kreis*, 103–5, 150; Man. 108, 170; Man. 112, 29; *PG* 292–93; *BB* 4de; Hacker, "Consequences", 285–87) as the synthetic solution in a dialectical movement, of which the first two steps are suggested succinctly in Frege's remarks on number: "We are driven to the conclusion that number is neither spatial and physical, like Mill's piles of pebbles and gingersnaps, nor yet subjective like ideas, but non-sensible and objective" (*Foundations*, 38). As we have seen (GI 39–40), the *Tractatus* moved in equally sublime regions far above the confusion of empirical detail. When Wittgenstein finally came down to earth and examined the facts of language and thought which underlie logic, he did not simply revert to the empiricism and psychologism against which Frege had reacted, but advanced to the balanced view expressed in §108: "We are talking about the spatial and temporal phenomenon of language, not about some non-spatial, non-temporal phantasm. . . . But we talk about it as we do about the pieces in chess when we are stating the rules of the game, not describing their physical properties." (See the commentary on §108bcd.)

Method, Composition, and Structure

(46)   Wittgenstein predicted that people would not understand why he wrote what he did; he might have added that they would be still slower to grasp why he wrote *as* he did, and would frequently be repelled or mystified by his unorthodox style and apparent disorderliness. "Something could have been made of his ideas," they may say with Lichtenberg, "if an angel had organized them for him." The situation is understandable, for to a considerable extent Wittgenstein's method of presentation follows from "the very nature of the investigation" (Preface), and this in turn cannot become clear till Wittgenstein's motives and conclusions are assimilated. Readers habituated to works such as Kant's *Critique of Pure Reason* or Moore's *Principia Ethica*, who therefore find it incomprehensible that a serious philosopher should write a book

like the *Investigations,* without chapters or other clear divisions and without any systematic order, should reflect that those authors had a theory to propound, and so could arrange their ideas in a unified, coherent manner without falsifying the content. But in Wittgenstein's case, as I have just indicated, theory and unity lay in the past, in the *Tractatus* which was the *Investigations'* target. A disease is an organic whole; a handfull of pills is not.

(47)   Wittgenstein's own comparison makes the situation still clearer. Language, he said (GI 28), is like a great, unfamiliar city, of which people need a description, not a definition or causal explanation. Now were the city laid out like central Manhattan, an orderly description in general terms would be possible. But how would one describe the center of London or Rome? Could anything systematic or coherent result? Would there be chapters? A solution I have seen is a book of aerial photos, so arranged that the overlapping and continuity could be noticed as one passed from page to page, though the series sometimes broke off so as to take up again at a different point in the city or come back over the same terrain from a different direction. Such is the plan Wittgenstein adopted in the first part of the *Investigations* and in individual sections of Part Two, and the sort of discontinuity he sometimes found forced on him.

(48)   Since words cause our difficulties (GI 9), they and their uses are what we must describe. And word uses are not introspectible items, even when the words are psychological. Hence "it shews a fundamental misunderstanding, if I am inclined to study the headache I have now in order to get clear about the philosophical problem of sensation" (§314), or the present contents of my mind in order to get clear about thinking (§316), or an image or inner process in order to determine the nature of imagination (§370). "It would be as if without knowing how to play chess, I were to try and make out what the word 'mate' meant by close observation of the last move of some game of chess" (§316; see GI 17–20, 27, 37–38, 41, 44–45). Thus whereas James had insisted that *"introspective observation is what we have to rely on first and foremost and always"* (*Principles,* I, 185), Wittgenstein relied on it hardly at all, especially in the sense of searching out phenomena "that are hard to get hold of, the present experience that slips quickly by, or something of the kind" (§436). That could at most reveal "what is *now* going on in *me*" (p. 219a), not the troubling concept (GI 60; X, 22; p. 187c and commentary).

(49)   An introspectible item may, of course, be causally connected with expressions of fear, pain, hope, desire, and so on, including the verbal ones; and the influence of cerebral and neurological events may be still more decisive. But Wittgenstein was interested in the rules of language,

not its causes (GI 45; §126, pp. 193f, 201j, 203h, 230a). "Scientific questions can interest me," he confessed, "but never really grip me. Only conceptual and aesthetic questions do that. The solution of scientific problems is, at bottom, a matter of indifference to me; but not the solution of the other questions" (Man. 138, 5B). These words suggest why Wittgenstein left science for philosophy, but more than temperament or personal preference accounts for his refusal to bring science into his philosophy. Given his conception of philosophy as therapy, and his conviction that philosophical problems are conceptual not scientific, there is nothing arbitrary about his declaration: "We must do away with all *explanation*, and description alone must take its place" (§109). If there is any arbitrariness, it is in his limitation on the role of philosophy.

(50)   As one might expect in a disciple of Schopenhauer (see *World*, 81–82), then of Frege (*Foundations*, 90–91) and Russell ("Method", 84), already in the *Tractatus* Wittgenstein showed little interest in causal explanation (see *NB* 93b) or in introspection. There, as later, he urged attention to words' application (though generally in a narrowly logical sense) and called for examination of concrete cases. But his early motivation differed decisively from the later. "Again and again," he said, "the individual case turns out to be unimportant, but the possibility of each individual case discloses something about the essence of the world" (3.3421; see Man. 112, 21). Picture writing, for instance, is one of the least-used forms of communication, yet "it must be possible to demonstrate everything essential by considering this case" (*NB* 7; see §92a; *Z* 444). As Wittgenstein later remarked, "Impressed by the possibility of a comparison, we think we are perceiving a state of affairs of the highest generality" (§104). Convinced that there must be a form common to all propositions and so to all language (§65), we rest content with a meager sampling (§593) and dogmatically assert what *must* be the case instead of simply taking the sample for what it is, an object of comparison (§131). Convinced that the sense of every proposition *must* be clear and precise (*NB* 61, 67), we conclude that what we mean must always be "sharp" (*NB* 68; see GI 37). All of this is obvious to the "uncaptive mind"! (*NB* 5, 7, 69).

(51)   Such preconceived ideas, said the later Wittgenstein, "can only be removed by turning our whole examination round" (§108). The really interesting case is the one which shows there is no uniform rule (*BB* 12a). This new approach appears with special clarity in §66, where Wittgenstein uses the humble concept *game* to cast light on the supposed super-concepts with which the *Tractatus* grappled (§97). Employing pointed questions and simple but varied samples, in a perspicuous array of intermediate cases, with the exhortation to "look and see"

replacing general definitions and theorizing, Wittgenstein shows that the word *game* designates no essence, and thereby destroys not only the conviction that there must be something common to all games, but the corresponding prejudice with regard to all other general terms, including the ones that trouble philosophers. Each of these characteristic traits of Wittgenstein's later methodology merits special attention.

(52)   "Don't think, but look!" (§66). This exhortation, so characteristic of the *Investigations*, derives its full significance from passages like those just cited from the *Notebooks*, where Wittgenstein's thinking had already determined what he had to find or, having spotted something interesting, forthwith spun a theory to cover all other cases. The *Tractatus* was a tissue of "musts" and of corresponding essences, brought forth as though by magic from the rags and dust of "inessential" cases (§52). So Wittgenstein later insisted: "Don't say: 'There *must* be something common . . . but *look and see* whether there is anything common to all" (§66).

(53)   Wittgenstein grew increasingly doubtful about standard alternatives to the mere injunction "Look!" In the *Blue Book* (26b) he still thought that a definition is a good way to clear up the 'grammar' of a word, but in the *Investigations* he was far less sanguine (§182). And he experienced enduring doubts about the effectiveness even of description. At the time he was writing the *Investigations* he warned: "How words are understood is not told by words alone" (Z 144); "the verbal expression casts only a dim general glow over the calculation: but the calculation a brilliant light on the verbal expression" (*RFM* 54). Later he wondered: "Am I not getting closer and closer to saying that in the end logic cannot be described? You must look at the practice of language, then you will see it" (*OC* 501; cp. *PG* 40f). Quite similar misgivings had caused Wittgenstein to characterize the *Tractatus* as a mere ladder, to be cast aside once the reader had come, by its means, to "see the world aright" (6.54; cp. §144). The ladder simile fits the *Investigations* better still, for there the reader does not mount on rungs of solid, though "unsayable" doctrine, but by means of mere questions, and simple samples well displayed, many of them imaginary.

(54)   Wittgenstein's penchant for questions is thus more than a stylistic legacy from Frege (see for instance *Writings*, 108, 110, 159). A question is an invitation to look, which specifies the spot. If the spot is well chosen and aptly indicated, the resulting look may be decisive (e.g. §§442b, 545, 621; see Man. 221, 244). Sometimes Wittgenstein answers his own questions, but often not. The preceding paragraph suggests one main reason for this (see also GI 69), but there are others: The question may be a mere prod in the right direction (e.g. §394), or it may in fact be an answer, in undogmatic, nonpolemical form (e.g.

§§270, 505, 682); the missing reply may be evident (e.g. §§82, 448ab), or it may be impossible, recognition of this impossibility being the aim of the question (e.g. §§215b, 262, 335b, 488; cp. Anscombe, *Introduction*, 151a). "In philosophy it is always good to put a *question*," Wittgenstein further explained, "instead of an answer to a question. For an answer to the philosophical question may easily be unfair; disposing of it by means of another question is not" (*RFM* 68; see Man. 119, 65). And it avoids all quibbling about words. Furthermore, he "held that no answer to a philosophical question was any good unless it came to a man when he needed it. This involved an attempt to make you see that you really did need such an answer" (Gasking and Jackson, "Wittgenstein", 52; see Wisdom, "Wittgenstein", 47), so called for unanswered questions, perhaps a barrage of them in quick succession, as in §§153–54, 439, 442. Thus Wittgenstein suggested seriously "that a philosophical treatise might contain nothing but questions (without answers)" (Malcolm, *Memoir*, 29), and in fact momentarily envisaged something similar for the *Investigations* (Man. 164, 161; cp. Man. 109, 288). As it is, "the *Investigations* contain 784 questions. Only 110 of these are answered; and seventy of the answers are *meant* to be wrong" (Kenny, "Aquinas", 235).

(55)   These last occur in the dialogues which have led so many readers astray, where the "voice of temptation" alternates with the "voice of correctness" (Cavell, "Availability", 92). Since it is sometimes difficult to be sure which voice is speaking, people have often attributed to the later Wittgenstein the very thoughts he combated, much as though one were to conclude that Socrates held the views of those he interrogated. Wittgenstein himself frequently alerts the reader by enclosing the suspect view in quotation marks, but not always. So I shall sometimes need to provide further guidance, and would advise the reader here in advance to beware the pronouns *I* and *we*. They do not always signal an expression of Wittgenstein's own views at the time of writing. Contrast, for example, the "I want to say" of §452 with that in §494.

(56)   Pointed questions may penetrate the haze which makes clear vision difficult. It also disperses the fog "to study the phenomena of language in primitive kinds of application in which one can command a clear view of the aim and functioning of the words" (§5). "If we want to study the problems of truth and falsehood, of the agreement and disagreement of propositions with reality, of the nature of assertion, assumption, and question, we shall with great advantage look at primitive forms of language in which these forms of thinking appear without the confusing background of highly complicated processes of thought. When we look at such simple forms of language the mental mist which seems to enshroud our ordinary use of language disappears. We see ac-

tivities, reactions, which are clear-cut and transparent. On the other hand we recognize in these simple processes forms of language not separated by a break from our more complicated ones" (*BB* 17). For example, having raised the question what language is ("what is common to all these activities, and what makes them into language or parts of language"), Wittgenstein moved from this complex case to a simpler, more perspicuous one and asked (§66): What is common to the activities we call games? How do we use that word? He referred to such linguistic samples, whether real or imaginary, as "language-games". (For further information about his use of this expression, see the commentary on §7.)

(57)   In the *Investigations* as in the *Tractatus* Wittgenstein attached great importance to the structure a representation must have if it is to reveal clearly the genuine logic of our language, but his new understanding of linguistic fact and his new diagnosis of the ills to be cured resulted in a totally different arrangement. The author of the *Tractatus* knew that the vagaries of individual words can cause difficulties, but he did not realize that a simplistic reading of words like *mean* and *understand* underlay his own theories (§81b). So he envisaged therapy through the analysis of this or that troublesome proposition. The *Investigations,* on the contrary, focuses on troublesome concepts, such as led Wittgenstein himself astray, so makes no use of analytic translation. Perspicuous representation now "consists in describing a selection of examples exhibiting characteristic features, some examples showing these features in exaggeration, others showing transitions, certain series of examples showing the trailing off of such features" (*BB* 125). "A perspicuous representation produces just that understanding which consists in 'seeing connexions'. Hence the importance of finding and inventing *intermediate cases*" (§122). Our paradigm, §66, illustrates this method of intermediate cases more clearly than any other passage in the *Investigations*. First we look at board games, then pass to card games, where both similarities and dissimilarities appear (§130), then to ball games, where much that is common to card games is retained, but much lost. It is as though to unravel a rope and learn its construction we passed from fiber to overlapping fiber (*BB* 87).

(58)   For purposes of generalization or system-building, such a result, for one trivial concept, has little significance. But for purposes of falsification and therapy its significance may be great. The mesh that strains the gnat strains the camel too. Thus if someone believes that there *must* be something common to the members of every class covered by a general term (GI 22), and that therefore there *is* something common to the members of every class, and that therefore the term *game,* for instance, designates something common to all games, a total

cure can be effected by getting him to recognize that in this case, at least, there is no essence. For then the inference unrolls in reverse; he sees the falsehood of both the generalization and the supposed necessity. No countergeneralization is legitimate; we cannot conclude from the one case that no terms designate essences, any more than we could conclude from one essence that all general terms designate essences. But against the *a priori* requirement, and against *a priori* requirements in general, a single example like that in §66 is decisive (*BB* 12a; Malcolm, *Memoir*, 69). Wittgenstein was not replacing one theory with another, but eliminating *a priori* theorizing.

(59)   In order to demonstrate the impossibility of a definition applicable to all and only the members of a given class, one might indicate instances where the supposed essence is found but the class term is not, as well as those where the term is applied but the candidate essence is missing. Thus in §66 Wittgenstein could easily have mentioned that traits such as amusement, winning, competition, and skill, though characteristic of games, are found in many other activities as well (cp. §§ 156g, 591, p. 182e). But that was not his usual way. He was more likely to point out that the words used to indicate "common" traits are themselves used in as varied ways as the word to be defined (*BB* 41b). Thus "when we say: 'Every word in language signifies something' we have so far said *nothing whatever*" (§13). And if we are tempted to theorize that every sentence is a description, we should "think how many different kinds of things are called 'description' " (§24). Similarly, guidance is no uniform trait of reading (§§170–78), nor attention of pointing (§33), nor meaning of correctness (§§186–90), nor regularity of rules (§208). (See §87a.)

(60)   Besides, even a constant correlation would not justify a definition; for that, knowledge would be necessary. The essence would have to be known. Thus it may be true that all human beings and only human beings have a specific number of vertebrae, and that a constant correlation therefore exists between this number and the application of terms such as *man, woman, chieftain, child, president, truck driver,* and so on. But the people who apply these terms do not know that number, nor therefore does it guide their speech, nor therefore does it belong to these various concepts. So, failing to find any other constant, we may not conclude: A man, a woman, a truck driver, and so on, is simply any creature with this number of vertebrae. In like manner, Wittgenstein insisted that facts which we learn only through attentive introspection or neurological experimentation do not belong in an account of the concept. If, for instance, it were discovered through introspection that "a particular tickle accompanied every one of my intentions," that would not prove that intention is a tickle. "*Essence* is

expressed by grammar" (§371), and these phenomena do not belong to the grammar. Wittgenstein never elucidated in a positive or general way the role of cognition in determining what belongs to a language-game and what not, nor, more specifically, its role in determining what counts as a 'criterion' and what as a mere 'symptom' (§354). But when we compare his repeated assertion that "what is hidden . . . is of no interest to us" (§126) with his equally firm insistence that concepts and language-games *are* his concern, the importance of knowledge becomes evident. And in his discussion of cases this cognitive criterion sometimes rises so clearly to the surface (e.g. §§153, 293, 376, p. 181bc) that we can legitimately extend it to similar instances where he does not mention knowledge. (Cp. Russell, *Logic,* 194–95.)

(61)   The question of knowledge was delicate, and not merely because the concept of knowledge is so problematic (§30). To adopt knowledge as a general norm of what belongs to a language-game might suggest that knowledge of some kind regularly guides a speaker in his statements, whereas a major theme of the *Investigations* is the absence of such guidance in many instances. When employing psychological predicates in the present tense with the first person singular, we do not generally base ourselves on observation (GI 15); knowledge does not guide us (X, 25). But it does when we switch to the second or third person. Here there are criteria, and these criteria belong to the concept; indeed it seems unlikely that we would speak of the concept *pain* or the concept *fear* if there were no such criteria, but only first-person utterances resembling cries of fear or pain (*RFM* 195). We do not talk of a concept *hurrah*. In summary, then, we can say that in Wittgenstein's conceptual studies, so throughout the *Investigations,* the knowledge which guides people in their use of a term determines the boundaries of that concept, even when such guidance does not characterize some uses of the term.

(62)   Systematic cognitive analysis along these lines would have entangled Wittgenstein in the kind of scientific hypotheses he sought to avoid. His interest was therapy. And for that, imaginary cases could serve as well as real ones. In the abstract, this strategy of inventing samples, and often bizarre, improbable ones at that (*BB* 28), may seem puzzling; for how can mere figments of the imagination refute factual theories? The answer is that the theories to be dealt with were not merely factual or scientific, but restricted "the order of possibilities" (§97). So imaginary cases, if accepted as at least possible, could loosen the restrictions. Thus, to dispel the idea that we *must* envisage the act before obeying a command, Wittgenstein imagined an order which has rarely if ever been given, "Imagine a yellow patch," then asked: "Would you still be inclined to assume that he first imagines a yellow

patch, just *understanding* my order, and then imagines a yellow patch to match the first? (Now I don't say that this is not possible. Only, putting it in this way immediately shows you that it need not happen. This, by the way, illustrates the method of philosophy.)" (*BB* 12; see §451, p. 230a; *BB* 42a, 43c; Man. 108, 232).

(63) In accordance with this method, Wittgenstein first envisaged a far fuller, more systematic use of imaginary language-games; spread out perspicuously, case after connecting case, they were to form a continuous series, merging gradually into more complex, realistic samples, thus permitting him to make one therapeutic point after another without sacrificing continuity. In this way he might perhaps achieve the unity which the lack of a system denied him. The seed of this strategy appears already in the *Blue Book*: "We recognize in these simple processes forms of language not separated by a break from our more complicated ones. We see that we can build up the complicated forms from the primitive ones by gradually adding new forms" (*BB* 17; cp. Preface). This is what he set out to do in the *Brown Book*, the first draft of the eventual *Investigations* (*BB* v; *EPB* 10; Man. 159; Man. 225, 1); the first part consists of 73 numbered language-games, some with long commentary, some with none. After dictating the *Brown Book* in 1934–1935, "he started more than once," Rush Rhees recounts, "to make revisions of a German version of it. The last was in August, 1936. He brought this, with some minor changes and insertions, to the beginning of the discussion of voluntary action—about page 154 in our text" (*BB* v–vi). In this version, which now bore the title "Philosophical Investigations" (though it has been given a different one for publication), the basic structure is still more strongly accentuated: throughout the pages which correspond to Part One of the *Brown Book*, not only are numbers given to the language-games, but the description of each language-game is indented, the appended comments not. Well into the second part Wittgenstein broke off in disgust and wrote in heavy strokes: "This whole attempt at a revision, from the start right up to this point, is *worthless*" (cp. *LR* 169). That was when he began what we now have (with minor revisions) as the first part of the *Philosophical Investigations* (*BB* vi). He had not given up the method of language-games, nor even of connecting them in series now and then; but apparently he found the fetters of a uniform system too restricting (Preface). By numbering the thought units instead of the language-games, he freed himself to develop his comments more fully and to space the concrete samples, real or imaginary, as he pleased. The *Bemerkung* (see Preface, ix) replaced the language-game as structural unit. Only attentive reading reveals the dozens of language-games, old and new, scattered one after another throughout Part One, vestigial vertebrae of the continuous

backbone which once held this part together. The only lengthy break comes in §§89–133, where Wittgenstein pauses to reflect on his own philosophizing, past and present.

(64) This interruption marks a basic division in the book, corresponding to stages in Wittgenstein's intellectual history. The sections preceding the break treat linguistic and logical topics that were both fundamental to the *Tractatus* and explicitly considered by its author: the uniformity of language, the doctrine of names and simples, the question of precision—that is, the basics of logical atomism (GI 32–33, 35, 37). The subsequent self-critique, in Section VI, might be termed the confessions of a logical atomist, who describes his former feverish thinking on these matters before writing his own prescription for the malady (Section VII). Thereafter Wittgenstein turns to more psychological questions. For "all of this," he announces already in §81—this whole view of language as a precise calculus—"can only appear in the right light when one has attained greater clarity about the concepts of understanding, meaning, and thinking" (see GI 37); that is, about psychological topics such as Wittgenstein tended to ignore when he wrote the *Tractatus* (GI 39–40), but to which he devotes the rest of Part One, following the interlude. These subsequent numbers (§§134–693) are concerned with the scheme of our mental life described in GI 36–38, that is, with the *full* picture theory, whose beginnings are discernible in the *Notebooks* and in the *Tractatus* but which Wittgenstein gave more thought to later, as he turned his attention to psychology. The overall rationale of these numbers becomes clearer still by contrast with Part Two.

(65) Reading in the Editors' Note that Wittgenstein completed Part One in 1945 and wrote Part Two between 1947 and 1949, someone might suppose that the latter was an afterthought. Glancing through its sections, he might imagine they were all fragments which Wittgenstein did not manage to fit into Part One. However, as the germinal idea of Part Two appears already near the start of the *Blue Book*, so the general conception of Part Two appears past the middle of the same work: "The reason I postponed talking about personal experience was that thinking about this topic raises a host of philosophical difficulties which threaten to break up all our commonsense notions about what we should commonly call the objects of our experience. And if we were struck by these problems it might seem to us that all we have said about signs and about the various objects we mentioned in our examples may have to go into the melting-pot" (*BB* 44). Thus, whereas the examples in the first part of the *Brown Book* treat principally "forms of language" and "forms of thought" (*BB* 17), the second part focuses on "personal experiences" (*BB* 44) and "the concepts of experience" (p. 193g; see *LC*

1c); and whereas the structural unit of the first part is the numbered language-game, the structural unit of the second part is the numbered topic, with personal experiences predominating. So also in the German draft. So too in Part Two of the *Investigations* (though now the sections have been broken up into clusters which resemble the *Bemerkungen* of Part One). It is perhaps significant that Wittgenstein's dissatisfaction finally reached the breaking point precisely in those central numbers in Part Two of the *Brown Book* which depart most notably from this rationale. In the *Investigations* most of the offending material has been relocated in Part One, with the result that Part Two conforms more closely to the initial description in *BB* 44; it discusses emotions (i, ix), word-feelings (ii, vi), images (iii), attitudes (iv), sense-impressions (v), kinesthetic sensations (viii), feelings and states of mind (ix), aspect and meaning experiences (xi), memory-experiences (xiii). Thus whereas Part One covers the area of the full picture theory, Part Two takes up other aspects of our mental life. "Thought" versus nonthought—that is the very general dividing line between the end of Part One and the start of Part Two (cp. Man. 108, 186–87).

(66)   The considerable overlapping, which obscures this division and perhaps raises doubts about the connection with *BB* 44, turns out, on closer examination, to clarify that passage in the *Blue Book* and so to establish the connection. The particular "odd-job" word which occasioned Wittgenstein's remarks and which illustrates his misgivings is the term *meaning* (*BB* 43–44), whose prominence in both parts of the *Investigations* mirrors similar continuity in the *Brown Book*. In both works, after insisting in the first part that the word *meaning* does not refer to any simple item at the moment of speaking, Wittgenstein felt obliged to recognize another use which seems to do just that and which therefore might give the impression "that all we have said about signs and about the various objects we mentioned in our examples may have to go into the melting-pot" (*BB* 44). Appropriately, it is in Part Two that he discusses this experiential sense of the word, at great length (Section XXXVII). The main example of overlapping in the other direction is equally explicable: though pain, as a sensation, would seem to belong in Part Two, its presence in Part One is explained by its utility in treating the question of private meanings and private languages (Section X). Thus, though several sections of Part Two are simply pieces which do not fit elsewhere, the part as a whole retains the role Wittgenstein conceived for it from the start.

(67)   It can hardly be maintained, however, that the layout of the *Investigations,* or the development of each section, is perspicuous. What reader does not feel as Wittgenstein's students did: "Nearly every single thing said was easy to follow and was usually not the sort of thing any-

one would wish to dispute. . . . The considerable difficulty in following the lectures arose from the fact that it was hard to see where all this often rather repetitive concrete detailed talk was leading to—how the examples were interconnected and how all this bore on the problem which one was accustomed to put oneself in abstract terms" (Gasking and Jackson, "Wittgenstein", 51). Wittgenstein knew this (Man. 108, 238; LE 4). He predicted it. What's more, he apparently wanted it (Man. 166; Man. 159). Why? Why, if he recognized that "whoever doesn't understand why we are talking about these matters will necessarily regard what we are saying as mere tomfoolery" (PG 174), did he not say straight out what errors he had in mind? Why, for instance, in the section on private language, which has been criticized and misunderstood for want of just such guidance, did he not say plainly, "My target is the kind of private language Schlick envisaged"?

(68)   We might as well ask: Why didn't Wittgenstein take the fly by the wings and lead it back out through the hole in the fly-bottle (§309)? The fly is disinclined to go that way (see Gasking and Jackson, "Wittgenstein", 52, quoted for §309), and it resists restraint. Just try pointing out to the average philosopher where he went wrong (cp. Man. 112, 221). Just try to set matters straight in words he will accept. So even when Wittgenstein's observations conflict rather directly with the statements of some philosopher, he seldom names the philosopher or quotes the statements. And even when he does both (§§1, 46), he does not simply contradict the statements (§§2–5, 47–50). The sense is generally too indeterminate, and the admixture of truth too important, to make that advisable (§§79d, 423–24; commentary on §255; Z 463; Man. 220, 83; Man. 108, 136, quoted for §306; Gasking and Jackson, "Wittgenstein", 51; Wisdom, "Wittgenstein", 47, quoted for §79d). Nor should we seek to refute. For refutation would require an intelligible target and valid premises, whereas the difficulties Wittgenstein deals with are mere "pictures" (§§192–94, 374, 423–26) or veiled nonsense (§§119, 464), not intelligible hypotheses (e.g. §§47f, 398, 412); and he disposes of no general theories or definitions with which to construct a formal argument (GI 70). "The philosopher *treats* a question," he observed, "—like an illness" (§255; italics mine; translation slightly altered). The feverish question (e.g. §§65, 92, 428, 435), the delirious demand (e.g. §§39, 55, 97, 101–7), the consequent hypotheses and theories (e.g. §110)—all these are mere surface symptoms (GI 9–24; §§122–23; PG 193d). The therapist must treat the root cause, the underlying picture or mind-set, so as to work a radical change in outlook (§§108a, 144, 308; Man. 112, 141; Man. 110, 58; Warnock, *English Philosophy*, 54–55).

(69)   The trouble is that as long as this conversion has not taken place,

readers will expect and demand the very things Wittgenstein refused to give them, for the very reasons, or in virtue of the very assumptions, which he sought to remove, and so will suffer withdrawal symptoms at every turn (Man. 112, 59). Thus his refusal to state countertheses, or to clearly identify his targets, or to make explicit the premises supposedly operative in his supposed refutations, has contributed to the widespread impression that though the *Tractatus* was perhaps mistaken, it was at least rigorous and precise, whereas the *Investigations* is regrettably woolly. This is the reverse of the truth. Wittgenstein's later language-games are incomparably sharper than the nebulous theories of his youth. A doctrine of names, objects, and elementary propositions for which its author can provide not a single illustration (*PP* 296) is not to be compared for definiteness with the discussion of "blocks, pillars, slabs and beams" (§2) or of "red, green, white and black squares" (§48). The mist evaporates (§5). As for real-life cases and all their varied complexity, the very accuracy of the *Investigations* creates the impression of vagueness. For who can do a bright, crisp painting of a foggy day (pp. 200a, 227k)? The ultimate in such precision is the pinpoint question (GI 54), which replaces words with the reader's own eyes. There is no falsification or distortion in a mere look, but there may be in a formula. "Ramsey was quite right," said Wittgenstein, "that in philosophy we must be neither 'woolly' nor scholastic. But I don't think he saw how that is to be achieved, for the solution is not: to be scientific" (Man. 163; see Man. 128, 47; *BB* 84c; cp. Ramsey, *Foundations*, 269).

(70) Perhaps the most momentous development in Wittgenstein's later thought is his critique—penetrating but largely implicit, so seldom fully appreciated—of all "scientific" philosophy, including contemporary analytic, linguistic varieties (*OC* 321; *LC* 28). Plato's Socrates was the acutest thinker of his day and spotted the flaws in every definition offered him; but he failed to question the possibility and desirability of definitions. So the plucking went on and on, leaf after leaf, and no artichoke was found (§164). In Wittgenstein's view, the agelong search for theories and theses is a basically similar enterprise and has failed for the same reasons; the history of western philosophy might be compared to a protracted Socratic dialogue, in which one thesis has followed another and each has been found wanting, yet the interlocutors have never stopped to consider whether theses, theories, principles, definitions, and the rest are either possible or necessary (*BB* 26–27; cp. *PG* 120a). And this is understandable. For one thing, "philosophers constantly see the method of science before their eyes, and are irresistibly tempted to ask and answer questions in the way science does" (*BB* 18; see *PG* 296b; *BB* 25–26). They fail to reflect that: (a) "only in the stream of thought and life do words have meaning" (*Z* 173); (b) a very

special stream of thought and life—precise measures, standard procedures and instruments, rigid mathematical calculi, and the like—has formed through the centuries, within which it is feasible, though difficult, to fashion general formulae which are fairly accurate; (c) neither the definitions of old nor the philosophical theories of today have any such semantic backing (*BB* 25; Man. 111, 134); (d) nor, therefore, can they be expected to satisfy the scientific aspirations of those who formulate them (Hallett, "Contrast", 684–86). Precise definition of one's terms cannot alter this situation; it is not possible to pull oneself up by one's verbal bootstraps (§§87a, 120, 261). (See VII, 1–10.)

(71)   The Wittgensteinian alternative, already indicated, is the method of models. A single well-chosen sample may cast its light as far as any principle, without falsification. And a well-ordered series of samples may cover the landscape (GI 28; §122). Thus may be achieved the generality and clarity of vision which philosophers have sought, and which they are likely still to seek by means of precise, general formulae, despite all difficulties and objections, as long as they envisage no alternative. As Hacker has observed (*Insight*, 99), "Those who thirst for knowledge will not discard their only cup just because it is cracked." Now this situation seems typical. I suspect that in most cases, if a reader were to figure out why Wittgenstein does not provide what seems to be lacking, or why he says what appears objectionable, that would be one of the most valuable things he could learn from the book. Such, at least, has been my own experience; my difficulties have generally resulted from faulty understanding of Wittgenstein or from poor understanding of the problem, usually both. For progress in thought obeys this inexorable law, that people are slow to accept a really important advance, precisely because it is a truth they sorely need.

COMMENTARY

THE TITLE

Wittgenstein's revision of the *Brown Book,* in 1936, already bore the title *Philosophische Untersuchungen* (GI 63), on which Z 458 throws some light: "Philosophical investigations: conceptual investigations. The essential thing about metaphysics: it obliterates the distinction between factual and conceptual investigations" (see Man. 130, 51–52). The proper concern of the philosopher, as distinct from the scientist (GI 48–49), is sense, not truth (*PB* 256b). Still: "We were discussing a suitable title for the book which later he called *Philosophical Investigations.* I foolishly suggested he should just call it 'Philosophy'. He was indignant. 'How could I take a word like that which has meant so much in the history of mankind; as if my writings were anything more than a small fragment of philosophy?' " (Drury, "Symposium", 68).

THE MOTTO

"He expounded and defended his ideas in argument with confidence and power. He did not think of the central conceptions of his philosophy as *possibly* in error. He certainly believed, most of the time, that he had produced an important advance in philosophy. Yet I think that he was inclined to feel that the importance of this advance might be exaggerated by those who were too close to it. This feeling is probably reflected in his choice of Nestroy's remark [in Act 4 of *Schützling*] for the motto of the *Investigations:* ". . . 'It is in the nature of every advance, that it appears much greater than it actually is' " (Malcolm, *Memoir,* 60; cp. *BB* 44d). Wittgenstein himself had declared "that there was now, in philosophy, a 'kink' in the 'development of human thought,' comparable to that which occurred when Galileo and his contemporaries invented dynamics; that a 'new method' had been discovered, as had happened when 'chemistry was developed out of alchemy' " (*PP* 322). This was to oversimplify and overdramatize the situation. "There is not *a* philosophical method" (§133). For still deeper roots of the motto, compare the final remarks of Wittgenstein's Preface; the similar motto of the *Tractatus* and the concluding paragraph of its preface; his lifelong conviction that the most important matters are not susceptible of philosophical exposition (GI 5–7); his favorite quotation: "Und Spass beiseite, meine Freunde, nur wer ein Herz hat, kann so recht fühlen, und zwar von Herzen, dass er nichts taugt" (W. Kraft, "Wittgenstein", 818).

THE PREFACE

From 1938 to 1945 Wittgenstein wrote many versions of this preface (in Manuscripts 117, 128, 129, 159, 163, 180a, 225, and 227, some of which contain several drafts); yet the final one (in Man. 227) agrees about 90 percent with the early effort in Man. 225 (1938). The only paragraphs of the published preface which are not found, substantially the same, in that early version are the third paragraph on p. ix and the first and last full paragraphs on p. x. The fact that Wittgenstein finished the preface in 1945 but wrote the second part of the *Investigations* several years later suggests that the preface be considered an introduction just to Part One. And indeed a number of the remarks do obviously apply only to that part. Yet Part Two was no afterthought (GI 65–66).

DETAILED COMMENTARY

(a) are the precipitate: the expression is apt; *PB* and *PG* consist largely of cuttings from earlier manuscripts, and the *Investigations* retains numerous passages from *PB* and *PG*, so that the final *Bemerkungen* date from all these sixteen (and subsequent) years, a number deriving, sometimes verbatim, from the transitional manuscripts of 1930–1931.

the last sixteen years: that is, since W.'s return to Cambridge and to philosophy in 1929.

the concepts: therefore the uses of words (§383). Cp. *LC* 1: "An intelligent way of dividing up a book on philosophy would be into parts of speech, kinds of words. Where in fact you would have to distinguish far more parts of speech than an ordinary grammar does" (cp. Man. 108, 99).

remarks: "A *Bemerkung*," explains Miss Anscombe, "might be a single short sentence, or might be over a page long; it might itself be divided into several paragraphs. It is the form in which Wittgenstein composed most of what he himself wrote" ("Form", 373). "A great many of them are separate in the sense that one could read each of them without looking before or after; and someone who heard that the author made two quite different arrangements of a lot of the same material might guess that they were all like that. But that is far from being the case. There is very often a necessary connexion between one remark and its predecessor, say in the form of a demonstrative whose reference is, or is given in, the predecessor. Whatever the arrangement of the material as a whole, such connexions were preserved. So that the building blocks for the different structures are *not* quite generally the separate *Bemerkungen*, but may be these or may be short runs of them" (ibid., 376).

pictured differently: see GI 63.

in a natural order and without breaks: two distinct aims; if a person wanders aimlessly over the landscape, his path is still continuous. The full significance and perfect aptness of these words are suggested in GI 63, which traces Part One back to *BB* 17. Simple language-games, W. said there, are "forms of language not separated by a break from our more complicated ones," and in building up "the complicated forms from the primitive ones by gradually adding new forms" he would have followed a natural, not a logical, order. For "language games are the forms of language with which a child begins to make use of words" (cp. §§5, 7).

(b) After several unsuccessful attempts: in 1938 (Man. 159) W. wrote more specifically: "Four years ago I made the first attempt at such a compilation [the *Brown Book*] and after I had made efforts in this direction for two years [when he broke off *EPB*, in 1936]. . . ." See GI 63; Man. 159; cp. Man. 225, 1.

I should never succeed: W. seems to have had most difficulty with the "natural order"—the step-by-step procedure—he at first envisaged (GI 63). "The form of presentation I started with," he complained in 1937 (Man. 118), "is not *elastic* enough. The chance connections of the exposition are too stiff & do not leave room for many others which are also present." Concerning the second aim, continuity, and W.'s overall dissatisfaction Miss Anscombe makes the following observations ("Form", 374–75): (1) "One is much more likely to be jolted and puzzled by a transition from one *Bemerkung* to the next, both being on the very same point, than by the transition to a different subject matter—and in such cases, puzzlement can usually be resolved by philosophical reflection." (2) "It is only in about the last 150 *Bemerkungen* that I find some jerky transitions of topic. . . . And indeed he expressed a particular dissatisfaction to me in Dublin in 1949, with this part of the book." (3) "What can be said is this: Wittgenstein would have liked to write a book that was as great a work of art as his *Tractatus*." (4) "What the *Tractatus* has, and the *Investigations* lacks in this matter of order, is completeness of treatment of each matter before moving on to the next." (See GI 47.)

over a wide field: "A singular 'holisticity' and integratedness characterizes Wittgenstein's philosophy. Everything in it is connected with everything else. This is true of the *Tractatus*, and to an even greater extent of the *Investigations*. This, I think, is *one* reason why Wittgenstein never succeeded in giving to his later philosophy the shape of one completed literary achievement" (von Wright, "Probability", 259).

(c) being approached afresh: "Many a problem we must first get familiar with, by running into it countless times. We then come to recognize
its flavor" (Man. 109, 276).

from different directions: see GI 28, 46–47; §203. "The 'big', difficult problems of philosophy are not such because they treat some
tremendously subtle and mysterious matter which we must investigate
but because in *this* spot a great many misleading forms of expression in-
tersect" (Man. 228, §160; see §191, p. 211j; Z 569). "The situation in a
way is typical in the study of philosophy; and one sometimes has described it by saying that no philosophical problem can be solved until
all philosophical problems are solved; which means that as long as they
aren't all solved every new difficulty renders all our previous results
questionable. To this statement we can only give a rough answer if we
are to speak about philosophy in such general terms. It is, that every
new problem which arises may put in question the *position* which our
previous partial results are to occupy in the final picture. One then
speaks of having to reinterpret these previous results; and we should
say: they have to be placed in a different surrounding" (*BB* 44).

sketches: "A few good epigrams about the use of a word are better
than my long-winded explanations. A philosophical thinker wants to
sketch a portrait of the use of language. And as in the case of every
portrait, the important thing is not to draw many lines, but ones that
are right, characteristic, that hit it exactly. Many free strokes do not
result in one that is just right" (Man. 302, 27; see Man. 132, Oct. 19).
This is important. The reader may often ask himself: Couldn't W. have
explained himself more fully and clearly on this point? Why is he so
elusive, so concise and epigrammatic? One answer is: He was constitu-
tionally incapable of writing in the manner of G. E. Moore (*LR* 9);
when he wrote, he was artist as well as pedagogue.

See GI 46–47, and the paragraph from Man. 228 quoted for §122.

a picture of the landscape: "I strive *not* after *exactness*, but after a
synoptic view" (Z 464). "I am basically a painter, and often a very bad
one" (Man. 138, 31A). See GI 46–47, 51, 56–57.

only an album: perhaps, but an ordered album (see e.g. GI 47,
63–65). Contrast the *Investigations* with Man. 130, where, after making
this remark, W. simply ticks off the themes of the *Investigations*, page
after page, without sequence, elaboration, or connection.

(d) Up to a short time ago: the same words occur in the 1938 version
of this preface (Man. 225).

given up the idea: "With respect to philosophical work his standards
were inexorable. Of a young friend who was preparing a paper to read
to the Moral Science Club of Cambridge he remarked that he ought to
write it for a hundred years from now and not just for next week. This

he said of a paper that was intended merely for a discussion group, not for publication" (Malcolm, "Symposium", 73). See another reason suggested by von Wright, in the quotation given for (*h*) below.

in lectures: to his students; his public lectures (e.g. LE) were extremely rare.

typescripts: the dictated *Blue Book* and *Brown Book*.

discussions: for instance at meetings of the Moral Science Club, at Moore's at-homes, and in meetings with members of the Vienna Circle.

mangled or watered down: "He once exclaimed to me with vehemence that he would gladly see all of his writings destroyed if along with them would vanish the publications of his pupils and disciples" (Malcolm, *Memoir,* 58).

stung my vanity: see the incidents recounted by Malcolm (*Memoir,* 56–57, 59), on which he comments: "Although considerations of reputation were certainly not unknown to his nature, and could even become violent, as in the episodes just related, it must be remembered, on the other hand, that Wittgenstein purposely lived in obscurity, discouraging all attempts to make him into a celebrity or public figure, which otherwise he would certainly have become" (59). There was also humility in thus publicly acknowledging his vanity.

(e) See GI 2–4.

Four years ago: "This sentence makes reference to conversations which Wittgenstein had been having in 1943 with Nicholas Bachtin (linguist and classical scholar, d. 1950). The text, as printed, is here in error and the words 'four years' ought to be corrected to 'two years' " (von Wright, "Papers", 497). On the topic of this paragraph, see GI 2–45. The entry at the end of Man. 128 (1944) may be a contemplated title for the book: "Philosophical Investigations contrasted with the *Tractatus Logico-Philosophicus.*"

(f) grave mistakes: see GI 28–45.

Frank Ramsey: see the Appendix.

during the last two years: "I think this must be a mistake. I imagine that Wittgenstein, trusting to memory alone, had magnified into a series of discussions continuing for two years, a series which in fact only continued for a single year" (*PP* 253).

Mr. P. Sraffa: see Malcolm, *Memoir,* 69, and von Wright, "Sketch", 15–16; Man. 213, 242; Man. 117, 172; Man. 113, 48.

(g) For more than one reason: the German italicizes *one.* "He was sometimes visited by the fear that when his work was finally published posthumously the learned world might believe that he had obtained his ideas from philosophers whom he had taught, because there might be some resemblances between his work and those writings of theirs that had been published before his own" (Malcolm, *Memoir,* 58).

(h) doubtful feelings: "With regard to the question of what the future would hold for his work—whether it would disappear without leaving a mark, or whether, if it continued to live, it would prove any help to mankind—he was in doubt. Freud once remarked in a letter: 'As to the question of the value of my work and its influence on the future development of science I myself find it very hard to form an opinion. Sometimes I believe in it; sometimes I doubt. I don't think there is any way of predicting it; perhaps God himself doesn't yet know'. . . . I think that these sentences would also serve very well to express Wittgenstein's attitude towards his own work, with the exception that his inclination to pessimism was stronger than Freud's. I do not believe that Wittgenstein ever thought of his work as *great*" (Malcolm, *Memoir*, 60). "He was of the opinion—justified, I believe—that his ideas were usually misunderstood and distorted even by those who professed to be his disciples. He doubted that he would be better understood in the future. He once said that he felt as though he were writing for people who would think in a quite different way, breathe a different air of life, from that of present-day men. For people of a different culture, as it were. That was *one* reason why he did not himself publish his later works" (von Wright, "Sketch", 1–2; see Man. 109, 204–6, 209).

It is not impossible: " 'I also believe that much of what I wrote in the past 15 or 20 years may be of interest to people when it's published' " (Malcolm, *Memoir*, 97).

the darkness of this time: W. did not mean merely World War II, then impending or under way. "Modern times were to him a dark age" (von Wright, "Sketch", 20; see Man. 117, 115), an era without a culture or integrating set of goals, at least any he shared (Man. 109, 205–6). "He once remarked that since this is the age of popular science it cannot be a time for philosophy" (Malcolm, "Symposium", 73). Of Frazer's *Golden Bough* he observed: "Frazer is much more of a savage than most of his savages, for they won't be as far from an understanding of spiritual matters as is a twentieth-century Englishman" (BUF 241).

to bring light: in both his pessimism and his attitude towards philosophy, W.'s thinking reflects Schopenhauer's early influence on him: "If anything in the world is desirable, so desirable that even the dull and uneducated herd in its more reflective moments would value it more than silver and gold, it is that a ray of light should fall on the obscurity of our existence, and that we should obtain some information about this enigmatical life of ours, in which nothing is clear except its misery and vanity" (*World*, II, 164; cp. *NB* 81e). From another book W. read and admired: "It is my desire that you may, in your turn, be good enough for comparison with a candle; that you may, like it, be a light to those about you" (Faraday, *History,* 152). A friend recounts: "One evening not long before his death Wittgenstein quoted to me the inscription that Bach wrote on the title page of his *Little Organ Book:* 'To the glory of the most high God, and that my neighbor may be benefited thereby.' Pointing to his own pile of manuscript, he said: 'That is what I would have liked to have been able to say about my own work'" (Drury, "Symposium", 71; cp. *PB* 7).

not likely: "I must live among men," W. often reflected, "to whom I cannot make myself understood" (Man. 107, 154). "The typical western scientific man . . . does not understand the spirit in which I write" (Man. 109, 206; see *PB* 7; cp. GI 69–70; §122b). "Perhaps more importantly, he believed that his influence as a teacher was largely harmful. He was disgusted and pained by what he observed of the half-understanding of his philosophical ideas, and of a tendency towards a shallow cleverness in his students. He felt himself to be a failure as a teacher. This, I believe, was a source of constant torment to him. . . . He once concluded a year's lectures with this sentence: 'The only seed that I am likely to sow is a certain jargon'" (Malcolm, *Memoir,* 62–63).

(i) to stimulate someone: "'I intend to dictate the stuff that I've been writing since last autumn, & *if* I do, I'll send you a copy. May it act as manure on your field'" (Malcolm, *Memoir,* 81). "(Concerning my philosophical remarks) In matters of the intellect an undertaking generally cannot be protracted, and indeed should not be. May *these* thoughts fertilize the ground for new ones" (Man. 168, 4). See Man. 119, 64; Lewy, "Moore", 45.

(j) has not come about: "This remark was not an affectation of modesty. He certainly believed that the work might have been made better, although not by himself" (Malcolm, *Memoir,* 59–60). "He said that it was not in a completely finished state, but that he did not think that he could give the final polish to it in his lifetime. This plan would have the merit that he could put in parentheses after a remark, expressions of dissatisfaction, like 'This is not quite right' or 'This is fishy'" (ibid., 93). In a letter W. said: "And the truth is: it's pretty lousy. (Not that I could improve on it essentially if I tried for another 100 years.) This, however, doesn't worry me" (ibid., 43). See the comments on the motto of the *Investigations.*

the time is past: W. wrote these words in 1944 (Man. 128, 49) and perhaps earlier, yet kept working on the book for years.

I. The Overture: Language as a Game
(§§1–25)

(1) Wittgenstein opens the *Investigations* with an overall treatment of language, touching numerous themes, especially that of diversity, which he repeats or develops later in the book. The work thus resembles the *Tractatus* more closely than did the original draft in the *Brown Book,* where Wittgenstein moved on after the point corresponding to §9 and presented further language-games in rapid succession. In the *Investigations,* as in the *Tractatus,* he proceeds more gradually and systematically, laying the foundations for subsequent sections, and employing for this purpose a comparison between language and games which in its origin and scope closely resembles the contrasting comparison, between language and pictures, with which he opened the *Tractatus.* That early simile goes back to Wittgenstein's reading "an article which recounted that, in a Paris court case concerning a traffic accident, the accident was reenacted by means of dolls and tiny buses" (Man. 108, 203; cp. von Wright, "Sketch", 7; Malcolm, *Memoir,* 68–69). Illumined by this paradigm, he sketched a pair of fencing figures, and declared: "It must be possible to demonstrate everything essential by considering this case" (*NB* 7; see GI 50). Later he would speak in somewhat similar, though less dogmatic vein (*LC* 1e–2a; *BB* 17a) about the simple language-games suggested to him by another incident: "One day when Wittgenstein was passing a field where a football game was in progress the thought first struck him that in *language* we play *games* with *words*. A central idea of his philosophy, the notion of a 'language-game', apparently had its genesis in this incident" (Malcolm, *Memoir,* 65).

(2) The result of this well-prepared inspiration (see the comments on §7b) was not another theory, replacing the previous one, but rather a terminology, incorporating a comparison. "For we can avoid ineptness or emptiness in our assertions only by presenting the model as what it is, as an object of comparison—as, so to speak, a measuring-rod; not as a preconceived idea to which reality *must* correspond" (§131). There are indeed dissimilarities between language and games—far more complex ones than are captured by the facile assertion that language is serious and games are not (see *Kreis,* 170; *BB* 81d); but the similarities

seem more numerous and important (cp. *PG* 289–95). Wittgenstein had the following points particularly in mind when he spoke of "language-games". Language, like many an individual game or games as a class: (a) is autonomous, (b) requires no justification, (c) is not a product of ratiocination, (d) nor constantly accompanied by parallel thought processes, (e) but is rather a comprehensive form of life combining the most diverse elements, (f) according to rules, which are (g) flexible, and (h) varied, so reveal no essence. For the sake of future reference, I shall develop these points rather fully here, in the order indicated. All are suggested already by remarks of the present section.

(3)   The logical-atomist view of meaning (III, 4) put Russell in the rather ludicrous position of having to postulate infinitely many objects if nonfinite mathematics was to be meaningful. Wittgenstein felt equally dependent on a host of atomic objects (GI 35), none of which he had ever identified. Against this background, we can understand the statement which Moore found so queer, that "the idea of meaning is in a way obsolete" (*PP* 258). The comparison with games, with chess the favorite example (see the commentary on §31), makes much the same point. "The analogies of language with chess are useful in that they illustrate the autonomy of language. Thus in the case of chess there is no temptation to think that it is essential to point outside to some object as the meaning" (Man. 219, 8). Winning occurs *within* the game (Z 165). Thus "understanding a sentence is much more akin to understanding a theme in music than one may think" (§527; see §531, p. 182g). If the atomist asks, "But in that case what is the meaning?" we may reply: "What is it in music?" (§529). "Music," we might say, "conveys to us *itself!*" (*BB* 178). So too, in the case of a picture, "its telling me something consists in its own structure, in *its* own lines and colours" (§523). It is in this sense that good architecture, too, "expresses a thought" (Man. 219, 22). "I shall never forget the emphasis," says Drury, "with which he quoted Schopenhauer's dictum: 'Music is a world in itself'" ("Symposium", 68). The terminology of the *Investigations*, especially the expression *language-game*, encapsulates a similar view of language: "*Alles war im Wortspiel*" (see W. Kraft, "Wittgenstein", 829).

(4)   Language, therefore, requires no justification in terms of an ulterior purpose or criterion (XVI, 8–10). Its rules are not read off from reality (p. 230b; cp. 5.4732). In this sense they are arbitrary, like the rules of games (Z 320; *PG* 184e, 192d, 469a; *Kreis*, 103), their aim being simply that of language itself (§497 and commentary). This difference between linguistic rules and scientific laws, which require verification (*Kreis*, 126–28), has important implications (*PB* 322). It eliminates any investigation into the "foundations of language" similar to the inquiries that have been made into the "foundations of mathemat-

ics" (§124). In the philosophical study of language, as in the philosophical study of mathematics (§125, p. 232), we must simply acknowledge the language-game (§§109, 217, 599, 654–56, pp. 200b, 226d), then describe it (§§109, 126–28, 486, 496) in the way required by our problems (§§109, 118, 132–33). Justifications (§§217, 289, 483–85, p. 200b) and explanations (§§1, 5, 29, 87), like reasons (§§211, 326), must finally end, in an agreed way of life (§§240–42, 325, 355). Language itself is the *a priori* (§372; Hallett, "Bottle", 85–86).

(5)   That is, it is the basis of reasoning, the system within which we explain, argue, and test, not the product of such procedures (Z 391). True, the system is not a platonic realm distinct from the actual proceedings (OC 248). True also, we may invent a language or a new terminology for some particular purpose (§§132b, 577), just as we may think up a new game. But language as a whole is not the result of ratiocination (OC 474; Z 391). It is simply part of our natural history, on a par with walking, eating, drinking, playing (§25). And what is true of language and the race as a whole is true also of the individual person. When a child first learns to talk, it does not pass from prelinguistic thought to a linguistic translation (§§32, 342) by a process of guessing meanings (§§71b, 208–10, 363). As a person may learn very simple games at first, by watching (§31), so in the learning of language there is a stage before all definition (§6a), where the child simply watches, imitates, reacts to training (§§5, 146, 211; II, 10). "We talk, we utter words, and only *later* get a picture of their life" (p. 209).

(6)   We should not suppose, though, that what starts as instinct (Z 545) later becomes a much more rational, reflective process. We do, of course, quite frequently reflect on what we say. But not on the language-game itself; that remains obscure (GI 10). Furthermore, understanding the words one speaks is not some inner process accompanying the words (§6c; IX, 2, 11–13) any more than understanding how to play chess is an inner process accompanying the moves (pp. 59n, 181). The same holds for meaning our words (EPB 225–30; XXVI, 5–7; XXVIII, 2; XXXVII, 11, 21) or thinking as we talk (XI, 2). "Our *language-game* is behaviour" (Z 545; see PG 182b); "the term 'language-*game*' is meant to bring into prominence the fact that the *speaking* of language is part of an activity, or of a form of life" (§23; see §§1d, 7d, 206, 241, 432, p. 226d). It is not the mere sensible correlate of a projective mental act (3.1–3.11; GI 37). Nor is its sole purpose the transfer of thoughts to other minds (§§1–8, 23–24, 304b, 317, 363, 449, 501). Granted, as there is a game of guessing thoughts (p. 223) so there might be a use of words for the excitation of images (§6b), but it would be as atypical as the game (p. 181).

(7)   There is an obvious objection to saying that language, like music

or chess, is autonomous and self-contained: with language we refer to objects, communicate information, build roads and machines, order merchandise, and so on (§491). However, the objection supposes that language is mere words and their arrangement, whereas such objects and such results also belong to the complex pattern we call "language". They are pieces with which we play the game, the board on which we move. "What characterizes an order as such, or a description as such, or a question as such, etc., is—as we have said—the role which the utterance of these signs plays in the whole practice of the language"; likewise, what characterizes an individual word is the role which it plays in the whole of life, "the occasions on which it is used, the expressions of emotion by which it is generally accompanied, the ideas which it generally awakens or which prompt its saying, etc., etc." (*BB* 102–3). Thus it is part of the grammar of the word *chair* that *this* is what we call a chair, and *this* is what we call "to sit on a chair" (*BB* 24). There is an idea that once a person has grasped the sense of a sentence, has taken it into his mind, the linguistic exchange is complete; "if he then does something further with it as well, that is no part of the immediate purpose of language" (§363). To remedy such shortsightedness Wittgenstein presented primitive forms of language in which "we see activities, reactions, which are clear-cut and transparent" (*BB* 17) and which are obviously the whole point of the game: "The children are brought up to perform *these* actions, to use *these* words as they do so, and to react in *this* way to the words of others" (§6). All this is the language-game (§7d): "Just as a move in chess doesn't consist simply in moving a piece in such-and-such a way on the board—nor yet in one's thoughts and feelings as one makes the move: but in the circumstances that we call 'playing a game of chess', 'solving a chess problem', and so on" (§33). Thus in the *Investigations* as in the *Tractatus* Wittgenstein might have said: "*The limits of my language* indicate the limits of my world" (5.6; translation slightly altered). For not only does language pervade all our lives (*BB* 59a), in the broad sense suggested by *NB* 77, but what it pervades it also includes (*LC* 8). So if his philosophy gives many people an impression of narrowness, that is due largely, if not entirely (VII, 9), to a narrowly syntactical or mentalistic conception of speech, that is, to their cramped horizons, not Wittgenstein's.

(8)   It may be objected that language is obviously not coextensive with the whole world. But neither, in the same sense, is chess coextensive with pieces, board, and players. Yet when we talk about chess, these are the things we are talking about. Likewise, in linguistic discussions "we are talking about the spatial and temporal phenomenon of language, not about some non-spatial, non-temporal phantasm. But we talk about it as we do about the pieces in chess when we are stating the rules of

the game, not describing their physical properties" (§108). The pattern is partial, not its extension; and the pattern is the rules. Thus a central aspect of the comparison between language and games is their possession of rules (*PG* 187c). Just as chess is not merely the pieces and their configurations (syntax) nor even players moving pieces on a board (§316), but an ordered form of life (§§33c, 199, 345, 567), so too a certain regularity characterizes language (§207). Without rules, its signs have no meaning (§§41–43, p. 147n); with different rules they have a different meaning (ibid.), much as different rules make a different game (§§136, 197, 205).

(9) The analogy becomes still more enlightening (*PG* 187c) when the detailed similarities between the rules of language and the rules of games are noted (see also Cavell, "Availability", 157–58): (a) In both cases these distinctions apply: "The rule may be an aid in teaching the game. The learner is told it and given practice in applying it.—Or it is an instrument of the game itself.—Or a rule is employed neither in the teaching nor in the game itself; nor is it set down in a list of rules," but is rather to be discovered by observing the game, "like a natural law governing the play" (§54; see §31). (b) In both cases, moreover, Wittgenstein was inclined to distinguish between essential and inessential rules (§§562–68). For "the game, one would like to say, has not only rules but also a *point*" (§564). (c) Yet in another sense, as we have seen, linguistic rules, like those of games, are arbitrary. It is the game itself which determines what is the point. It is language itself which determines what is the aim of grammar (§497). The rules, like the game which they form, require no justification (*PB* 322). (d) Hence they are flexible (§81). The rules of tennis, for example, do not specify how high one throws the ball or how hard (§§68, 100); nor are we compelled to maintain the existing rules just as they stand (§83). And we can start entirely new games at will (ibid.). Similarly, "new types of language, new language-games, as we may say, come into existence, and others become obsolete and get forgotten" (§23; see §18). Thus the concept *language* (§§65, 494), like the concept *game* (§§68–70, 200), is shifting and indefinite.

(10)   And it is diversified. For the *Tractatus* as for the *Investigations*, language pervaded the world; but the monotonous logic of picturing pervaded language (5.61). In the later work, Wittgenstein used the comparison with games to illustrate the rich heterogeneity of symbolism. As there are board games, card games, ball games, and countless others (§66), so too there are "countless different kinds of use of what we call 'symbols', 'words', 'sentences' " (§23; see §§1, 11–13, 17–18, 27a, 304b, 494, 501, p. 189e); and what makes us use the same word, *language* or *game,* for all these things is not a common essence of language or of

games, but "a complicated network of similarities overlapping and criss-crossing; sometimes overall similarities, sometimes similarities of detail" (§66). Word uses, like games, form a family (§§67, 108). Or rather, a family of families. For just as board games, for instance, differ not only from ball games and card games, but also among themselves (§66), so it is with language (§24): The *Tractatus* erred not only in reducing all language to description (GI 32–33) but also in overlooking how many different sorts of thing are called "description" (§§24, 291), or "talking about a thing" (§27). Its treatment, therefore, could be straightforward and systematic, whereas in the *Investigations*, both between sections and within, there is "overlapping and criss-crossing" as Wittgenstein traces the true logic which pervades the world: not the "great mirror" (5.511), but the linguistic labyrinth (§§18, 203; GI 47).

DETAILED COMMENTARY

§1   See I, 10; *BB* 69a, 77; *EPB* 117; Man. 111, 15–18; cp. Schlick, *Aufsätze*, 154.

(a) W. here carries out his early intention: "I would like to start with what is given in philosophy, with the written and spoken sentences, almost with the books" (Man. 110, 10). As for his choice of text: "He revered the writings of St. Augustine. He told me he decided to begin his *Investigations* with a quotation from the latter's *Confessions*, not because he could not find the conception expressed in that quotation stated as well by other philosophers, but because the conception *must* be important if so great a mind held it" (Malcolm, *Memoir*, 71). "What Augustine says has importance for us because it is the conception of a naturally clear-thinking man" (Man. 111, 15). Augustine's own criticism, in *De Magistro*, of such a primitive view shows that too much should not be made of one isolated passage. See Kretzmann, "Semantics", 366.

(b) "This roughly means, we are looking at words as though they all were proper names, and we then confuse the bearer of a name with the meaning of the name" (*BB* 18). See §§40, 120f, 264, 304; *BB* 1, 5b, 162b; *PG* 89d; *PP* 260b–261a. For a similar view in Plato, see §46 ("the essence of speech is the composition of names"). Of his own earlier thought W. said: "The concept of meaning, as I took it over into my philosophical discussions, derives from a primitive philosophy of language" (*PG* 56). More specifically, it was influenced by Frege, who said for instance: "Signs are mere proxies for their content, and thus any phrase they occur in just expresses a relation between their various contents" (*Writings*, 10). Similarly, in *Principles of Mathematics* Russell supposed that every word must refer to or "stand for" something—"a man, a moment, a number, a class, a relation, a chimaera" (43). Like them both W. spoke of a name's *Bedeutung* or meaning as the object correlated with it. Yet the *Tractatus* viewpoint is not identical with the one here criticized. As Stenius observes: "This remark can be considered polemical against the Tractatus—because in the Tractatus sentences are considered 'combinations of names'. But if one interprets it so, one must remember that there is at least a strong tendency toward a conception of language much more radically of this kind than that of the Tractatus. This is the idea that *all* words—not only words which occur in elementary sentences—are names, and that this is also true of all other significant expressions, including sentences [as in Frege]: the essential function of language is one of naming" (*Tractatus*, 119).

As evidence that such "Name Theories" are still in vogue, see e.g. Reach, "Name Relation", 97; Langacker, *Language,* 72; Ullmann, *Semantics,* 57.

(c) A reworking of *PG* 56e, which adds in parentheses: "And Plato says that a sentence consists of nouns and verbs" (*Sophist,* 261E, 262A).

In *PB* 118a, *BB* 82b, and *PG* 63cd W. stressed the great differences among names and substantives themselves.

Concerning Augustine he added, in *BB* 77: "He does not primarily think of such words as 'today', 'not', 'but', 'perhaps'."

Nor did Russell when he wrote: "When we examine common words, we find that, broadly speaking, proper names stand for particulars, while other substantives, adjectives, prepositions, and verbs stand for universals. Pronouns stand for particulars, but are ambiguous: it is only by the context or the circumstances that we know what particulars they stand for. The word 'now' stands for a particular, namely the present moment; but like pronouns, it stands for an ambiguous particular, because the present is always changing" (*Problems,* 53; see idem, *Logic,* 196).

In the *Tractatus,* cp. e.g. 3.202 and 4.025.

(d) See I, 6. Compare with this the somewhat different aim and setting of the similar language-game in *BB* 16c.

It is in this and similar ways: in lecture notes, Peter Geach observes: "Even as regards the primitive language-game with numerals, supposing that there is only a limited stock of them as exists in some primitive cultures, notice that the order of the operations in the grocer's shop is determinate: it would be hopeless for the grocer to take the colour chart first and look around for red things until he found some that were also apples, and it would be still more hopeless for him to recite the numerals up to five in his language first of all—this would be a completely idle performance. Frege said that a number attaches to a concept. . . . What Frege of course meant was that a number is a number of a kind of things—a kind of things expressed by a general term; and that until you have fixed upon the kind of thing that you are counting, you can't count, you can't attach a number." (See *BB* 172b; Man. 105, 19, 113, 115.) Thus even this language-game is not as simple as it looks to the accustomed eye.

one operates with words: see §449; *BB* 16c.

"But how does he know . . .": cp. W.'s former attitude: "The characteristic thing is that what we count is designated by substantives. So we must provide a general justification for the use of substantives in the language" (Man. 105, 19).

he *acts:* see I, 6. "For these people the centre of gravity . . . is found *wholly* in *doing*" (*RFM* 118, which parallels this number).

Explanations come to an end: see I, 4–5; *Z* 318–19; *EPB* 129, 216; *BB* 15b; cp. *PB* 51d; 3.261, 3.263; *NB* 46f.

"I cannot describe how (in general) to employ rules, except by *teaching* you, *training* you to employ rules" (*Z* 318).

"A reason is a step which precedes that of choice. But why should every step be preceded by another?" (*EPB* 129).

"If on the other hand you realize that the chain of *actual* reasons has a beginning, you will no longer be revolted by the idea of a case in which there is *no* reason for the way you obey the order. At this point, however, another confusion sets in, that between reason and cause" (*BB* 15).

"A language-game does not have its origin in *consideration*. Consideration is part of a language-game" (*Z* 391).

No such thing: "Thus we are not supposing that the examples call forth something in the learner, that they present an essence to his mind, the meaning of the concept-word, the concept" (*PG* 118; see Man. 111, 95; cp. §73a, p. 54n). "The meaning of a word does not consist in my being able to call its content to mind (vividly representing it, hallucinating it) but in my knowing what road to take in order to reach the object" (*Kreis*, 88n; see §449). In the ordinary sense (§43a) the word does, no doubt, have a meaning (*BB* 69a); but, as the context requires, the imaginary interlocutor to whom W. replies is spokesman for a "philosophical concept of meaning" (§2). See I, 3; cp. *PG* 69c, 144a. In this first unmarked dialogue the alternation is easy to follow: the two sentences beginning with "but" belong to W.'s interlocutor.

§2 See *EPB* 117; *BB* 77; *PG* 57ab.

(a) "We might reword Wittgenstein's remark about 'that philosophical conception of meaning' in two ways. Either: 'That definition of meaning (as the object referred to) fits a language more primitive than ours'; or: 'That philosophical conception of the way words are used (meaning as defined by Wittgenstein) fits a language more primitive than ours.' Some authors have understood his words in the first way and so have concluded that in such primitive uses of language, 'the meaning of the words is the thing to which they refer.' However, I think that Pole and Strawson are clearly right in giving the other interpretation" (Hallett, *Definition,* 97–98; see further discussion there, and in Pole, *Later Philosophy,* 18–19). Notice that, in accordance with Augustine's description, the words of W.'s imagined language do not just statically "signify" objects but serve uniquely to express desires ("in seeking, having, rejecting, or avoiding something").

(b) Concerning "the method of §2", and its present application, see the commentary on §48. There is more in this simple game than straightway meets the eye: (1) Whereas W. had earlier contrasted terms such as *block* and *slab,* which occur in some sentences, with logical constants, which occur in all (Man. 109, 121; see *NB* 29 j), here the tables are more than reversed: *No* logical constants occur in this language. (2) Whereas he and Russell had argued that analysis would reveal "real names", designating atomic "objects", in every meaningful utterance, here ordinary, audible signs are "applied to what in ordinary life we call 'objects', 'things' ('building stones')" (*BB* 81a; see *EPB* 121). Metaphysics is banished (§116). This is rock-bottom (I, 3). (3) Whereas for the *Tractatus* every meaningful use of signs was descriptive (GI 32–33), saying "This is how things stand" (4.5), here there are commands and no descriptions, yet the language is complete (§18). (4) Whereas W. had once insisted that a meaningful sentence must be "logically articulated", so composite (4.032; *Kreis,* 90d; commentary on §19b), here there is no composition, no articulation (§19b). As for actual speech, "the signal 'Stop' is also a one-word sentence, and where is the *composition* here?" (Man. 109, 24; cp. *PP* 261b). (5) Granted, replied W. in his transitional period, but at least the signal belongs to a system (*PP* 261b; Man. 109, 175, 219); the truth in the old doctrine, he suggested, may be restated thus: "Every sentence is an instance of a general rule for the construction of signs" (*Kreis,* 107), for instance for the construction of one-word commands (like "Stop!") from verbs. "It is essential to language that the word occur in various sentences" (Man. 110, 100; see Man. 111, 111). However, here in §2 there is no such construction rule and no such diversity of appearances, but a limited set of mutually independent signals (cp. *PG* 195b; *BB* 94c). (6) But " 'could a language consist of mere disconnected signals?' We might ask instead: Do we still want to call a series of disconnected signals [in contrast to §1 or §8] a language?" (*PG* 194–95). W. does, for the reason indicated in §494. See King-Farlow, "Constructor", 101–6.

On the question of completeness, see §18 and the references there, and §§6a, 19a. For comments on this primitive language, besides those in subsequent numbers of the *Investigations* and their antecedents, see

RFM 103f (the pattern, versus the effects); *RFM* 195h (are there concepts in this language?); *Z* 98–99 (do these people think?); *OC* 396, 566 (how much do they know?); and Man. 232, 655–56 (should we call it a language?).

§3 See I, 10. This is a reworked version of *PG* 57b, which derives in turn from Man. 111, 17.

(a) See §593 and the commentary on §23c ("logicians have said").

in many cases: e.g., "The rules for 'and', 'or', 'not', etc. which I represented by means of the T-F notation are *a part* of these words' grammar but not *the whole*" (Man. 108, 52; *PB* 111). See *BB* 25.

(b) See *EPB* 117; *BB* 77b; Man. 220, 2.

§4 From Man. 111, 18–19, via *PG* 57c. Cp. *BB* 44a.

Augustine's conception: once again, W.'s remark does not seem justified, even by the one text cited.

§5(a) See GI 51, 56, 63; §§7, 122; *EPB* 119; *BB* 17a, 79c–80a; NL 306g; Man. 302, 27; Man. 112, 218 (e.g.: "In philosophy, treat the clear cases, not the unclear ones. The latter will be resolved when the former are").

"One thing we always do when discussing a word is to ask how we were taught it. Doing this on the one hand destroys a variety of misconceptions, on the other hand gives you a primitive language in which the word is used. Although this language is not what you talk when you are twenty, you get a rough approximation to what kind of language game is going to be played" (*LC* 1–2).

Nicod used an analogous technique in "Geometry in the Sensible World". However, the similarity with Köhler (XLI, 3–4) and especially with Mauthner is more obvious. As Weiler has pointed out (*Critique,* 110), both Mauthner's examples and his comments on them are strongly reminiscent of passages like the present one. Citing similar causes, Mauthner observed that "a fog covers all words, all groups of words" (*Beiträge,* I, 94). Accordingly he suggested: "Let us place ourselves with our complicated language back into the most simple conditions, where the accompanying circumstances are transparent to everyone, where the intonation has an immediate effect and we shall use spontaneously again one-word sentences" (ibid., II, 145–46). For a simple situation, similar to that in §2, see the quotation under §6b, from *Beiträge,* II, 255.

It disperses the fog . . . : see GI 69.

(b) See I, 4–5; Man. 110, 121–22.

when it learns to talk: for reflections on this, see *OC* 290.

"It is quite evident that children first learn to use isolated words, then a way of joining them" (Mauthner, *Beiträge,* II, 292). See also K. Bühler, *Development,* chs. 2 and 6, e.g. p. 131: "Whatever the explanation may be, it is at any rate certain that at this stage the child expresses everything that is on its mind by means of single words." For a stage similar to that of §2, see ibid., p. 135.

not explanation, but training: see §31b; *OC* 538; *PG* 191ab; cp. §§6b, 145a, 208; *PG* 187d. The quotations for §32 provide contrast and suggest the significance of this remark.

"The child learns this language from the grown-ups by being trained to its use. I am using the word 'trained' in a way strictly analogous to that in which we talk of an animal being trained to do certain things. It is done by means of example, reward, punishment, and suchlike" (*BB* 77; see *EPB* 117). "The pupil responds, and responds in a particular way. Imagine the gestures, sounds, etc., of encouragement you use when you teach a dog to retrieve" (*BB* 90). "If a child does not respond to the suggestive gesture, it is separated from the others and treated as a lunatic" (*BB* 93).

W. is proffering neither the untenable thesis that explanations never occur in teaching children to speak, nor the mere platitude that explanation sometimes is missing in teaching. Rather: "Any explanation has its foundation in training" (*Z* 419); for "explanation comes to an end" (I, 5; §1d and commentary). Thus there is a difference between first learning to speak and learning, say, to play tennis, by following an instructor's explanations. Whereas in tennis reflection precedes habit, in speech we first play the language-game and only afterward get a view of how it is done—if then (p. 209c; see II, 10; Hallett, "Bottle", 102–3). "But there is no sharp boundary between primitive forms and more complicated ones. I wouldn't know what I can still call 'explanation' [or 'definition'], what not" (*PG* 62).

§6(a) *whole:* see §§2b, 18, 19a; *PG* 112c; Man. 302, 28; cp. Man. 108, 152. "The important thing is that their language, and their thinking too, may be rudimentary, that there is such a thing as 'primitive thinking' which is to be described via primitive *behaviour*" (*Z* 99).

(b) See I, 6; *BB* 12bcd, 14b.

An important part . . . : see *EPB* 117; *BB* 77.

I do not want: the denial is less categorical than that in §5b. For *hinweisende Erklärung* is not simply a species of *Erklärung*. And where usage gives no clear verdict, it is all the same to W. whether we speak one way or the other, "provided we don't let the use of the general term divert us from examining each particular case that we wish to decide" (*PG* 62) or prevent us from seeing things as they are (§§16, 48b, 79d).

It was in fact quite misleading to assert that "the meanings of simple signs (words) must be explained to us if we are to understand them"

(4.026), and for Schlick to suggest that "the only explanation which can work without any previous knowledge is the ostensive definition. We conclude that there is no way of understanding any meaning without ultimate reference to ostensive definitions" ("Meaning", 148). At the very beginning, W. replies, there is not definition or explanation of any sort.

Cp. similar hesitation to speak of "understanding", in §146a.

because the child . . . : though a learner does not always first ask "What is (an) X?" when a teacher points and says "This is (an) X," and the actual question is therefore only "characteristic" (§35) of the game of ostensive definition, the person with whom we use this method is regularly someone who *could* ask that question. To suppose that a beginner could ask it would suggest the error treated in §32.

cannot as yet *ask:* see *OC* 535–38, 540–43, 547–48; and especially §§30b–31d. In *BB* 81f–82a and *EPB* 122, W. introduces asking for the name as a new, distinct language-game; likewise, if the child learns to say "I know that this is called 'a slab'," "the original language-game has been *expanded*" (*OC* 566).

not because it could not be imagined otherwise: cp. §§143–44 and the comments on pp. 14n (a) and 18n (b). "This would be similar to the case of a man who did not naturally follow an order given by a pointing gesture by moving in the direction shoulder to hand, but in the opposite direction. And understanding here means the same as reacting" (*BB* 141; cp. *Z* 187).

establish an association: "If you are asked what is the relation between a name and the thing it names, you will be inclined to answer that the relation is a psychological one, and perhaps when you say this you think in particular of the mechanism of association" (*BB* 3; cp. §53b). Those quoted below did so think.

one very likely thinks: "Russell's causal theory of the symbol" (Man. 109, 198) is doubtless the chief paradigm in W.'s mind (see *PP* 260, below). See e.g. *Logic*, 296–99, 302–3, 315; *Mind*, 201. "Thus speech is a means of producing in our hearers the images which are in us. Also, by a telescoped process, words come in time to produce directly the effects which would have been produced by the images with which they were associated" (*Mind*, 206). W. encountered the same tendency elsewhere, e.g.:

"We must first have images of concrete things and ideas of abstract qualities and relations; we must next have the memory of words and then the capacity so to associate each idea or image with a particular word that, when the word is heard, the idea shall forthwith enter our mind. We must conversely, as soon as the idea arises in our mind, associate with it a mental image of the word, and by means of this image we must innervate our articulatory apparatus so as to reproduce the word as physical sound" (James, *Principles*, I, 29).

"Now when the locksmith calls out to his apprentice 'the pincer,' then he imagines a particular pincer; through the state of affairs and the common state of mind the same image is awakened in the apprentice and he hands the master the right pincer" (Mauthner, *Beiträge*, II, 255).

I can imagine such a use: see *PG* 71b; cp. *LC* 34j.

keyboard of the imagination: see *PG* 152c.

it is *not* the purpose: see I, 6. W. felt that views such as those just quoted exaggerate both the frequency and the importance of images. See XII, 1–6; §§139, 395–97; *EPB* 130; *Z* 243; *BB* 4b, 89bc; *PG* 171c; Man. 302, 3; Man. 115, 13; *Kreis*, 88n (quoted for §1d). Though in the *Tractatus* W. placed no such reliance on images, *BB* 36d suggests a close connection between the simpler image account and the *Tractatus* picture theory (see XXXVII, 2–9). Still, the agnosticism of *NB* 130 concerning the contents of thought contrasts sharply with the assurance of Russell and James, above.

It may, of course . . . : "The first of these mistakes was . . . the view that the meaning of a word was some image which it calls up by association—a view to which he seemed to refer as the 'causal' theory of meaning. He admitted that sometimes you cannot understand a word unless it calls up an image, but insisted that, even where this is the case, the image is just as much a 'symbol' as the word is" (*PP* 260). W.'s attitude towards images therefore bore some resemblance to Frege's: "Time and time again we are led by our thought beyond the scope of our imagination, without thereby forfeiting the support we need for our inferences. Even if, as seems to be the case, it is impossible for men such as we are to think without ideas, it is still possible for their connexion with what we are thinking of to be entirely superficial, arbitrary and conventional" (*Foundations*, 71). See §53b.

(c) Don't you understand . . . : "No interpreting activity takes place in me, but I simply react to what I see and hear" (*PG* 47d). " 'To understand a word' can mean: to *know* how it is used; to *be able* to use it" (*PG* 47). "I could also say of a small child: 'he can use the word, he knows how it is used.' But I can see what that means only by asking: What is the criterion of this knowledge? Here it is not the ability to state rules" (*PG* 62). See IX, 5, 11–13; *BB* 141d (quoted for §6b); *PG* 64c–65a; Man. 112, 145, 148; cp. §146a; Man. 112, 147.

but only together with . . . : notice that in (*b*) W. adopts the appellation "ostensive teaching" for just that "important part of the training" which consists in pointing, directing the child's attention, and uttering the word. Training is also done "by means of example, reward, punishment, and suchlike" (*BB* 77). And it is training to *do* something (§23b). Thus this remark is directed against simplistic notions such as those in II, 3–8; as a person could supposedly attach a name by attending to an object and uttering the name, so he could teach another by directing the person's attention to the object, by means of pointing, and saying the name. "*What* is it a preparation *for*?" (§26).

§7 See *EPB* 121; *BB* 81d.

(a) In instruction: not "in the practice of the use"; cp. §49b: "Naming is so far not a move in the language-game."

    names the objects: a likely reason for W.'s stress on the word *names* is suggested by *EPB* 121 where, commenting on the language-game in which he takes this step, he draws the following contrast with his previous position: "Think of Russell's notion of an 'individual' or mine of 'objects' and their 'names' (*Tractatus Log.-Phil.*); these objects were to be the fundamental constituents of reality; something which could not be said to exist or to not exist. (*Theaetetus*) What these elements of reality are it seemed difficult to say. I thought it was the job of further logical analysis to discover them. In (4), on the contrary, we have introduced names for things, objects, in the ordinary sense of the word."

(b) games: see I, 1–10. We may not infer that W. would call language a game (I, 2). Cp. *PG* 292: "No, the word 'arithmetic' is not the name of a game. (Naturally this is another triviality.)—But the meaning of the word 'arithmetic' can be clarified through the relation of arithmetic to an arithmetical game."

    As in the case of the *Tractatus* picture theory of language, which was similarly triggered by a single incident (I, 1), one can discern influences which doubtless disposed W. to the sudden thought that language is similar to games (ibid.). In 1930 he said: "I have been reflecting on what Weyl can mean when he says that formalists regard the axioms of mathematics as similar to the rules of chess. I would like to say: Not only the axioms of mathematics but all syntax is arbitrary" (*Kreis*, 103). In his *Grundgesetze* Frege discussed at length this same comparison, as made by Thomae, between mathematics and a game such as chess (*Writings*, 183ff). In the same vein, see Hardy, "Proof", 20–21. The comparison is extended in Schlick's article of 1927, "Vom Sinn des Lebens", pp. 334–35, e.g.: "There really are such activities. To be consistent, we should call them *games,* for that is the name for free, purposeless activity (that is, in fact, activity whose purpose is contained in itself)." See also Karl Kraus's poem, "Abenteuer der Arbeit" (in W. Kraft, "Wittgenstein", 829). These references not only suggest the comparison with games, but stress points which motivated W. to make the same comparison (see I, 3–4).

    "language-games": see *BB* viii, 17a, 81d; *LC* 1e–2a. Here, as often, the German italics are omitted. Concerning W.'s application of this expression, see Specht, *Foundations*, 41–47, where he distinguishes its use for: (a) "certain primitive and simplified forms of language"; (b) "ordinary everyday language together with all the activities and performances indissolubly belonging to it"; (c) "certain individual partial language systems", for instance: (1) linguistic acts or performances, e.g. "ordering, requesting, thanking, cursing, greeting, reporting an event, telling a story, making a joke, lying, telling a dream, admitting the motive of an action (P.I. 23, 249, p. 184, p. 224)"; (2) "language-games which would not readily be called linguistic acts, but in which language plays a decisive role: translating, reading, making up a story, acting on order (P.I. 23)"; (3) "activities in which speaking and the use of language withdraw considerably into the background." On these last subdivisions, see also Pitcher, *Philosophy*, 239.

Concerning W.'s employment of language-games, see GI 51, 56–58, 62–64; §§5, 130–31.

(c) See *EPB* 118; *BB* 77c.

(d) See I, 6–7; cp. commentary on §19a; *RFM* 133.

"Our talk gets its meaning from the rest of our proceedings" (*OC* 229). "Only in the stream of thought and life do words have meaning" (*Z* 173).

§8   The language-game no longer consists of "mere disconnected signals" (see the comments on §2b). There is interdependence and order (see the comments on §1d), and general rules permit the construction of combinations which do not occur in the training.

W. advances more rapidly here than in *BB* and *EPB*. The general aim of these developments is evident in §10: we cannot assimilate all words. Sample errors of the sort whose treatment is begun with this number were Frege's concept of number (see §10) and the logical-atomist idea that *this* is a name, an idea which is discussed in §38, with reference to this game. The refutation offered there and in §45 is anticipated in §9.

series of letters: an improvement on *BB* 79b; the use of ordinary numerals would surround this simple game with the kind of haze W. wishes to dissipate (§5).

because this roughly . . . : cp. *BB* 102c.

§9   See *PG* 61d; cp. §208e.

(a) Contrast with this Russell's fantastic account in *Principles*, 133c.

by heart: see *BB* 79bc.

ostensive teaching: see §6b. For the therapeutic significance of this query, see II, 8.

Children do learn: see §§28–29. W. does not say "*only* in this way".

(b) See §§38, 45; *EPB* 119, 121; *BB* 1g, 79d–80a, 80d; cp. *PB* 118b.

§10 See *EPB* 122; *BB* 82b.

In this number W. traces a middle path between sheer formalism on the one hand and Frege's reaction on the other (see GI 45), with the latter more directly in his sights. Frege's position is summarized in *Writings*, 215: "By the number zero we do not mean a certain round figure; for the latter is only a sign for that which we mean and recognize as existing, although not as a physical body nor a property of such a body. So, however much we agree that arithmetic must beware of any concern with sensible things and that the numerical signs accordingly stand for nothing sensible, we equally emphasize that these signs are not therefore without reference and we decline to call the signs themselves numbers." He argues for the existence of mathematical objects as follows: "Let us try to make the nature of formal arithmetic more precise. The obvious question is 'How does it differ from a mere game?' Thomae answers by alluding to the services it could render to natural science. The reason can only be that numerical signs have reference and chess pieces have not. There is no other ground for attributing a higher value to arithmetic than to chess" (*Writings*, 185). To this argument W. replied: "Frege ridiculed the formalist conception of mathematics by saying that the formalists confused the unimportant thing, the sign, with the important, the meaning. . . . But if we had to name anything which is the life of the sign, we should have to say that it was its *use*" (*BB* 4). To realize this, one must look at the whole language-game—e.g. blocks, slabs, gestures, building—and not just at word combinations, as is the formalist tendency. It then becomes clear in what sense numbers are objective. See §§430–32; *RFM* 133–34, 160, 166.

(a) *signify:* see §§13–15.

(d) See *EPB* 119; *BB* 79c; cp. *PG* 57.

Frege, *Foundations*, ii: "Yet surely the number one looks like a definite particular object, with properties that can be specified, for example that of remaining unchanged when multiplied by itself?" For Mill's different assimilation, attacked by Frege, see ibid., 9ff.

§11 See *OC* 351; *BB* 79c; *PB* 118a; *LF* 33ab; 3.323; Russell, *Logic*, 269a, 332b.

(a) See I, 10; *BB* 67–68; *PG* 67b; *LC* 1d; Man. 108, 269.

tools: one would not naturally refer to all these items as tools, but the German term (*Werkzeug*) is broader.

similarities: see §§65–67.

(b) See I, 6; *PG* 193e–194a, 204–5; *PB* 118c–119a; 3.143, 4.002; Man. 138, 24A; Man. 110, 118; cp. *PG* 58c; *NB* 96, 99c.

the uniform appearance: see §167.

is not presented to us so clearly: though of basic importance for the whole of philosophy (GI 9–10), this is one of those familiar facts we tend to overlook (§129). Words generally are and need to be spectacles we look through, not at.

Especially when . . . : for then "language goes on holiday" (§38; see §132b; *BB* 175–80).

§12   A reworked version of *PG* 58a, as that is of *PB* 58g–59a. See also *PG* 58e, 59b, and Kenny, *Wittgenstein*, 120–21. The source of the present comparison is suggested in von Wright's "Sketch", 3: "Throughout his life he was extremely interested in machinery. While a small boy he constructed a sewing machine that aroused much admiration. Even in his last years he could spend a whole day with his beloved steam-engines in the South Kensington Museum."

§13   When we say: cp. V. Kraft, *Circle*, 28: "Signs have a meaning, this is what makes them signs rather than noises or shapes. They refer beyond themselves, to conceptual and propositional meanings which they represent." Russell, *Principles*, 47: *"Words* all have meaning, in the simple sense that they are symbols which stand for something other than themselves."

nothing whatever: one reason might be that the declaration is tautologous, words being by definition meaningful signs (cp. §491; 4.461; *PP* 272–74). "Says nothing" would then mean "adds nothing" (cp. §174; commentary on §251; *RFM* 164i; *BB* 135f, 176d). Another reason would be the vagueness of the term *signify* (cp. §§47, 227, 509a; *Z* 338; *LC* 49f; see below). Within the present discussion of diversity, the latter complaint seems foremost.

exactly *what* distinction: even if taken as a forceful mode of expression and not *ad litteram* (cp. §10d: "absolutely unlike"), these words may seem at variance with W.'s later insistence that speech need not be precise (see Section IV). However, there were limits to the imprecision he would tolerate, especially on the part of philosophers with scientific pretensions (cp. *OC* 387, 406–8). "That's granted," he said of a similar claim, "but it still doesn't give us any special theory of meaning" (Man. 109, 282). The need for explanation or contextual determination (§§117, 514, 520) is especially great when, as in the case of a word like *bezeichnen* (Gätschenberger, *Symbola*, chap. 17), the vague conceptual borders of ordinary use have been further blurred by theoretical discussion.

in Lewis Carroll's poems: that is, in ones like "Jabberwocky" (" 'Twas brillig, and the slithy toves did gyre and gimble in the wabe"), not like the White Rabbit's verses.

§14   Cp. §67c. W. not only announces the start of the dialogue, but conveniently marks both interventions of his imaginary interlocutor by putting them within quotation marks.

§15   See §26; *BB* 172b–173b; *PG* 125d; *Kreis,* 168–70.

(a) most straightforward: the connection between name and thing is made most directly—much more directly, say, than when a child's name is entered in a baptismal register. There name and thing do not come directly into contact with one another.

marked with the sign: "To the question 'How are names and things related?' the answer is: as the house number is related to the house" (Man. 112, 193; cp. ibid., 206). "We get a very similar use of names when labels are stuck on things, like 'Poison' on a bottle or the name-labels worn at conferences" (Geach, lecture notes; see *Kreis*, 169a).

he brings the tool: not "*a* tool". Hence W.'s observation that "in §15 we introduced proper names into language (8)" (§41). The move is made with much less fanfare than in *BB* 80 and *EPB* 120, for W. will not discuss proper names till Section III.

(b) See Man. 110, 146; cp. §73a; Man. 109, 23–24.

and more or less similar ways: for instance, N. signs his checks "N" (*PG* 103), or "N" is written under his portrait (*PG* 102) or is pronounced as someone points to him (§37; *BB* 173a; III, 7). W. is countering the mentality mentioned in §38 ("*the* relation between name and thing").

a name means: puzzlement may arise from the fact that a label has no use without a bearer, whereas a name usually does (§41). How can W. present a spatial conjunction of word and thing as typical, then suggest (III, 6–7) that it is in language that word and thing make contact? The answer, briefly: The *spoken* word, the one used to e.g. request the labeled object, is not attached to it; and only in virtue of the language-game is the uttered sound the "same word" as the written mark.

"Imagine it were the usual thing that the objects around us carried labels with words on them by means of which our speech referred to the objects. Some of these words would be proper names of the objects, others generic names (like table, chair, etc.), others again, names of colours, names of shapes, etc. That is to say, a label would only have a meaning to us in so far as we made a particular use of it. Now we could easily imagine ourselves to be impressed by merely seeing a label on a thing, and to forget that what makes these labels important is their use" (*BB* 69).

and is given to a thing: "The exceedingly interesting account which Dr. Howe gives of the education of his various blind-deaf mutes illustrates this point admirably. He began to teach Laura Bridgman by gumming raised letters on various familiar articles" (James, *Principles*, II, 358).

prove useful: negatively, it may counteract "the conception of naming as, so to speak, an occult process" (§38) performed in and by the mind (§36; *PG* 97e; cp. §§457, 689; *BB* 4). Positively, it may point toward a solution (III, 2, 7; XV, 3–4) of the great problem concerning the connection between language, thought, and world (GI 31–43).

"The relation of name and object, we may say, consists in a scribble being written on an object (or some other such very trivial relation), and that's all there is to it. But we are not satisfied with that, for we feel that a scribble written on an object in itself is of no importance to us, and interests us in no way. And this is true; the whole importance lies in the particular use we make of the scribble written on the object, and we, in a sense, simplify matters by saying that the name has a peculiar relation to its object, a relation other than that, say, of being written on the object, or of being spoken by a person pointing to an object with his finger. A primitive philosophy condenses the whole usage of the name into the idea of a relation, which thereby becomes a mysterious relation" (*BB* 172–73).

§16   See Schlick, *Aufsätze*, 172–73; cp. *PG* 88–89, 131d; *BB* 98e; Man. 112, 166–67; Man. 108, 242; Waismann, *Principles*, 278.

(a)   See *Z* 334–37 and especially *BB* 84–85 and *EPB* 124–25 on "transitions between word and pattern," and the variety of ways in which we use patterns.

   that A shews to B: in §8.

   are they part of the *language*?: "He pointed out very early something which he expressed by saying 'Much of language needs outside help,' giving as an example your use of a specimen of a colour in order to explain what colour you want a wall painted; but he immediately went on to say (using 'language' in a different sense) that in such a case the specimen of a colour is 'a part of your language' " (*PP* 262). He spoke similarly in Man. 107, 281; Man. 109, 99; Man. 112, 214; Man. 220, 39 (source of §50c); *PB* 73b; *PG* 143d; *BB* 98c; and §669. Yet already in 1933 "he expressly said that the answer to the question whether, when you say 'A unicorn looks like this' and point at a picture of a unicorn, the picture is or is not a part of the proposition you are making, was 'You can say which you please' " (*PP* 263). "I was unclear about the distinction between sample & word & their use. The same sample & the same word can have various applications; this sample can be used in different ways as a sample, this word can be used in different ways as a word. To this extent sample and word are similar, but they are different nonetheless" (Man. 112, 174).

To understand W.'s concern with this apparently trifling question, see the notes on p. 18n ("crucial superstition") and on §32b, concerning himself.

   They do not belong among the words: W. had written in 1931: "Mustn't everything by which a word is defined, *ipso facto* be a word, operate as a word, even when it is a colored slip of paper (& so could also function otherwise)? Isn't it true, therefore, that color samples, the minute they define words, are words?" (Man. 112, 169). Yet he also noted: "If (in the statement 'I want you to go there') the speaker, the person addressed, and the arrow which indicates the direction all belong to the symbolism, still they play an entirely different role from that of the words" (Man. 109, 137).

has a role just like . . . : cp. Man. 112, 211.

(b) See *BB* 84c; *PB* 78g, 143d; *PP* 262b.

(c) *"this* **sentence":** *PB* 207i and *Z* 691 (note the similar italics) suggest that the Cretan Liar might have written "This proposition is false," rather than "I am lying." Closer to the examples in (*a*) would be, for instance, the self-referring statement, "This sentence illustrates correct English word order." Without further indication of the case and corresponding remark W. had in mind, it is not clear whether "sentence" (as here) or "proposition" (as in *Z* 691) is a better translation.

§17 See XXI, 4; Man. 138, 14B; Ramsey, *Foundations,* 131–32; Waismann, *Principles,* 96–98; cp. *PB* 181d; James, *Principles,* II, 333–35, 485. *BB* 58b (on "same" versus "different") links this number with the discussion of sameness or difference of meaning, in Sections XX and XXI, and especially with §556.

(a) **different** *kinds:* see *Z* 472, 488; *EPB* 119, 123–24; *BB* 79c, 83bcd; *PG* 61cd, 67c; *LC* 1 (quoted re Preface, *a*); cp. *BB* 19b.

are more alike . . . : cp. *PG* 61c.

But how we group . . . : W. was inclined to group words as one groups chess pieces, according to their rules (Man. 108, 169–71), but he recognized there were other possibilities (§108c), say this one: "Before considering the meaning of words, let us examine them first as occurrences in the sensible world. From this point of view, words are of four sorts: spoken, heard, written, and read" (Russell, *Inquiry,* 23).

the aim: e.g. "Think of the reasons for and against classifying 'o' with the other cardinals" (*BB* 83). Cp. §499.

our own inclination: see *BB* 58b; Ramsey, *Foundations,* 131–32; cp. *BB* 29d–30b. "The only wrong classification is a hasty, stupid one, based on a misunderstanding of our task. (Braithwaite)" (Man. 116, 43).

(b) **tools:** see *PG* 67b.

chess-men: see *BB* 84a.

§18 Reworked from *BB* 81de, *EPB* 121–22. See I, 9–10; Man. 302, 27–28.

only of orders: contrast Man. 109, 175: "When I give an order I must also be able, in the same language, to describe the act which contravenes the order." Cp. GI 36.

incomplete: see *BB* 19b; Man. 229, §§1314–15; cp. I, 3–4.

"We are not, however, regarding the language games which we describe as incomplete parts of a language, but as languages complete in themselves, as complete systems of human communication. To keep this point of view in mind, it very often is useful to imagine such a simple language to be the entire system of communication of a tribe in a primitive state of society. Think of primitive arithmetics of such tribes" (*BB* 81; *EPB* 121). They might, for instance, have just the numbers 1 to 5, plus *many* (Man. 108, 152). See §§2b, 6a, 19a.

"The contempt for what seems the less general case in logic springs from the idea that it is incomplete. It is in fact confusing to talk of cardinal arithmetic as something special as opposed to something more general. Cardinal arithmetic bears no mark of incompleteness; nor does an arithmetic which is cardinal and finite" (*BB* 19).

Contrast Ogden and Richards, *Meaning*, 19: "As we proceed to examine the conditions of communication we shall see why any symbolic apparatus which is in general use is liable to incompleteness and defect."

town . . . city: cp. the quotation in GI 28.

a maze: see §§203, 664; *BB* 28b, 44a; 3.323, 4.002.

"The picture we have of the language of the grown-up is that of a nebulous mass of language, his mother tongue, surrounded by discrete and more or less clear-cut language-games, the technical languages" (*BB* 81; see *Z* 113).

with additions: see I, 9.

with straight regular streets: earlier, when W. stressed the importance of a perspicuous notation, this contrast would have implied a value judgment, but not in the *Investigations* (§§81b, 87–88). *Any* language can lead philosophers astray, for depth grammar is never evident.

§19(a) consisting only . . . : see *PG* 112c.

form of life: see Drury, *Danger*, x. To call a language a "form of life" "means I want to conceive it as something that lies beyond being justified or unjustified; as it were, as something animal" (*OC* 359); "as much a part of our natural history as walking, eating, drinking, playing" (§25). "I mean: it is not based on grounds. It is not reasonable (or unreasonable). It is there—like our life" (*OC* 559). As comes out in the rest of §19 and in §20, this expression also serves to contrast language with a rigid, uniform, mental calculus (§§81, 102). Thus its force is much the same as that of W.'s comparison with games (§23b; see I, 2–7, 10). Later occurrences of the expression *Lebensform* (§§23b, 241, p. 226d) have the same thrust.

As Toulmin has suggested ("Wittgenstein", 71), W. may have borrowed this expression, for his own purposes, from a popular book by

Eduard Spranger. The thought reflected by the title, *Lebensformen*, shows limited similarity with W.'s; Spranger was interested in structures rather than elements, but conceived the structures quite differently (see e.g. p. 38). See Kaplan, "Considerations", 81–82.

Cp. *PG* 65, e.g.: "So is the meaning really just the word's use? Isn't it the way this use connects with our life? But isn't its use part of our life?!" "The gestures, facial expressions, words, and activities [and why not also sensations and feelings?] that constitute pitying and comforting a person or a dog are, I think, a good example of what Wittgenstein means by a 'form of life' " (Malcolm, "Investigations", 202–3). Cp. §7d.

(b) Developed from *BB* 77d–78a, *EPB* 118. See *PG* 122b; cp. §555.

Though one of the most sustained dialogues in the *Investigations*, this is also one of the easiest to follow: after W. himself puts the opening question, every long dash indicates an alternation between him and his *alter ego*—the voice of confusion, rebuttal, or temptation. Thus it is W. who says, for reasons which §20b makes explicit: "In fact it *is* our 'elliptical' sentence."

Like the following number, this paragraph initiates themes developed at length later, especially in Section XI, on thought, and in Section XXVI, on meaning. Here, though, the target is not the "parade of the meanings before one's mind," one for each word (p. 176), but the logical-atomist requirement that any complete expression be articulated, if not in the sensible signs themselves, then at least in thought. "Of course," said Russell, "sometimes you get a proposition expressed by a single word but if it is expressed fully it is bound to contain several words" (*Logic*, 192); "the full expression of a fact will always involve a sentence" (ibid., 183). "A proposition," said the *Tractatus*, "is articulated" (3.141). "There must be exactly as many distinguishable parts as in the situation that it represents" (4.04). True, a single word may do duty for a sentence, but in that case the thought must still be articulated (*NB* 8–9). Especially in such instances, "there is enormously much added in thought to each sentence and not said" (*NB* 70; translation slightly altered). A reaction to this viewpoint similar to that in the present paragraph can be found in §§60 and 63.

a sentence or a word: see §49b; *EPB* 123, 171; *BB* 82d–83b, 118b–119a; *PG* 112c–113b; 2.0122. W. had once believed: " 'Surely I have a definite concept of what I call a "*Satz*" ' " (*PG* 112), from which I can learn the essence of language, thought, and the world (GI 30–33). For " 'surely I know a *Satz* when I see one, so must be able to draw the boundaries of the concept precisely.' But is a doubt really not possible?!" (*PG* 112). What of a game like that in §2, or in *PG* 112–13? W. is anticipating §§65–76.

For similar remarks on an ordinary expression, see Man. 229, §1166:

"Do 'Help!' and 'I need help' have a different sense; is it only the crudeness of our conceptions which makes us treat them as synonymous? Does it always make sense to say: 'Strictly speaking, what I meant was not 'Help!' but 'I want help'? Here the worst enemy of our understanding is the idea, the picture, of a 'sense' of what we say, in our minds."

a degenerate hyperbola: as the lines still satisfy the formula of the hyperbola (in a sense, though they no longer form the sort of figure we call a hyperbola) when the curve, coinciding with the asymptotes, becomes two straight lines, so the utterance still performs the sentential function (in a sense, though it is no longer a word-grouping such as we call a sentence) when but a single word does the job.

Do you say the unshortened sentence: see XXVI, 4–5, and the preceding quotation; cp. §§187, 677, 693, pp. 33n, 192l.

'wanting this': see §334.

§20   An expansion of *BB* 78, *EPB* 118–19. Cp. §607a; *Z* 150, 154; *BB* 73c; *PG* 131cd, 195b–196b; *PB* 59e. W. pursues his former thought, step by step. In the transitional manuscripts he began to move away from the Tractarian position probed in the preceding number. "It is wrong," he decided, "to say 'The proposition must be composite,' for it can in fact be non-composite, at least in a verbal sense.—Its composition consists rather in this, that it is a particular instance of a general rule for the construction of signs" (Man. 108, 289). "That a word is not a proposition, that the proposition—as I used to say—must be composite, means only that the sentence must be part of a grammatical symbolism (mechanism)" (Man. 109, 219). "The utterance of a sentence is not a portrait unless I use my words in a system, so that it can be said I choose *them* rather than others" (Man. 109, 289; see *PG* 131c).

(a) But now it looks . . . : W. drew this inference in Man. 110, 202.

when we use it in contrast . . . : see §607a.

But what does using . . . : W. here gives only half the answer (the language); for the other half (the context), see e.g. §49.

rather tempts us: W. had written: "This combination of sounds or of new words is a proposition only if it is thought within a system in contrast to other propositions of the same system" (Man. 109, 220). "And this answer reveals most clearly the nature of understanding. For when the other person suddenly understands what is meant, he now sees one thing rather than another in the sign. If he interprets it, then he interprets it *so*, as opposed to otherwise" (Man. 110, 294). "We are tempted to imagine this calculus, as it were, as a permanent background to every sentence which we say" (*BB* 42; see IX, 2).

contains the possibility: see *Z* 138.

a foreigner: on this foreigner, cp. Man. 228, §347.

which contains those other sentences: thus translated, the clause is more reminiscent of 4.001 and more open to objection than the precedent rendering of the same idea: "contains the possibility of those other sentences".

having a mastery: see §150.

something that *happens:* see §§148–49, p. 59n; cp. Russell, *Mind,* 9 (in GI 27).

need **not lie:** see GI 58; I, 6; cp. §§151–52.

(b) But doesn't the fact . . . : see Baker and Hacker, Notice, 277–78; cp. *PB* 59f; *NB* 42; Ambrose, "Metamorphoses", 69. This sentence and others like it cause two misgivings, one about the propriety of referring to the "use" of a sentence, the other about identifying the sense of a sentence with its use.

(1)   When, in his defense of W.'s way of speaking, Malcolm says, "A significant sentence is a tool with which a certain job is done" ("Wittgenstein", 336), he makes the very comparison which tends to cause misgivings. A tool, it has been said, is something that preexists its use. So too, in a certain sense, does a word, though even here the distinction between token and type weakens the analogy enough to make some people uneasy. But a sentence does not preexist as part of the language even in the way a word does; we make up new sentences using old words. So it seems still less appropriate to speak of "using" a sentence. However, such objections arise from too limited a diet of examples; in ordinary speech we quite readily speak of using a new approach, or putting every moment to good use, or using a compliment to smooth someone's feathers, and so on, though none of these things precedes its use. W.'s terminology, therefore, seems neither improper nor misleading.

(2)   According to the *Tractatus,* a proposition's sense is what it represents (2.221), that is, a possible state of affairs (3.02). Later, W. defined sense in terms of use, but use in terms of verification (Man. 108, 1; commentary on §353). Once he recognized other aspects of use (§353) and other uses of words besides the propositional (§23), he needed a sufficiently vague and inclusive terminology to cover all these aspects and varieties of sense. *Verwendung* and *Rolle* are such blanket terms. Though rough, W.'s later identifications of sense with use are frequent (see §§47c, 421–22, pp. 184f, 190e, 226h; *RFM* 165abc; Malcolm, *Memoir,* 90e) and sometimes quite explicit (e.g. *PG* 130–31, and Man. 160: "We must understand that the meaning of a proposition lies in the use we make of it"). He would apparently justify them much as he did the more carefully stated equivalence in §43, between a word's meaning and its use in the language: to explain a sentence's sense is to explain its use (*PG* 131b; cp. *BB* 1; *PG* 59–60, 68).

the same *use:* to be equated neither with utility (see §498 and the commentary on §61), nor with "use in the language" (§43).

In Russian . . . : see Man. 110, 188 (similar remarks on "he good").
§21   See commentary on §19b; *EPB* 149; *BB* 102c–103a. Still probing the supposition that we have a definite idea of what a proposition is (GI 32; commentary on §19), W. now considers the distinction between proposition and command—as he will soon study that between proposition and question (§24)—after examining that between proposition and word in the preceding numbers. If usage is our norm (§116), it is an oversimplification to say, for instance, that "a proposition . . . is a sentence in the indicative, a sentence asserting something, not questioning or commanding or wishing" (Russell, *Logic,* 185). According to the first criterion, "Isn't the weather glorious today?" is not a proposition; according to the second it is. The border is not sharp (§§65, 76).

the difference between the report . . . : not "between *a* report and *a* command", in general, but between these two. The instance cited in parentheses shows that no one feature is decisive in all cases. There is no essence of commands or of propositions, but family resemblances among the members of each group.

it is the part . . . : think how one would describe the use of a chess piece, what one would include, for instance moves (cp. §§345, 365), and what one would omit, for instance "the tone of voice and the look".

although it is used as a statement: paraphrasing brings out the similarity with the final sentence in §134: "Thus it illustrates the fact that *one* feature of our concept of a question is, *sounding like a question.*" W. was wont to stress how strongly we are impressed by the mere appearance of words (GI 10ff).

in which *all* statements: that is, all the expressions so used, taking the place of what we presently call statements.
§22   See *NB* 29, 38abc; Man. 116, 321–22; Britton, "Portrait", 61; cp. 4.442; *NB* 96b. "It is quite right," observed Moore, "to say 'A question is not a prop.; a command is not a prop.': = to ask a question is not to make a prop.; to give a command is not. But isn't it also right to say that when you ask *the sort* of question which can be answered by 'Yes' or 'no', & when you give a command you are contemplating a prop.? *What* you ask is whether a certain prop. is true; & *what* you command is that a certain prop. should become true" (*Commonplace,* 246). W. felt that such thinking, common to Moore, Frege, Russell, and the author of the *Tractatus* (GI 33–38), blindly extends the terms *Satz, sentence, proposition* (see *a*), and conjures up mental acts where there are none, with these contents as their objects (*c*). As in the preceding number, he would turn our attention to the way words function (*b, d*).

(a) Frege's idea: and Meinong's, according to Man. 109, 26. See Man.

229, §1168. In the *Tractatus*, W. misunderstood both Frege's use of the word *Annahme* and the doctrine expressed (Anscombe, *Introduction*, 105–6); here only the terminological error clearly reappears. Frege had said: "If we write down an equation or inequality, e.g. $5>4$, we ordinarily wish at the same time to express a judgment; in our example, we want to assert that 5 is greater than 4. According to the view I am here presenting, '$5>4$' and '$1+3=5$' just give us expressions for truth-values, without making any assertion. This separation of the act from the subject-matter of judgment seems to be indispensable: for otherwise we could not express a mere supposition [*Annahme*]—the putting of a case without a simultaneous judgment as to its arising or not. We thus need a special sign in order to be able to assert something" (*Writings*, 34). If we compare this with W.'s present statement (not with 4.063, which reveals fuller misunderstanding), we can say that, apparently under the influence of Russell (Anscombe, ibid.), W. took the *Annahme* to be the case put or asserted, whereas for Frege it was "the putting of a case without a simultaneous judgment". This slip does not affect the validity of W.'s remarks here, which seem readily applicable to Frege's position as summarized by Black (*Companion*, 182–83): "Frege seldom uses *Annahme* and never in a technical sense. According to him, an unasserted proposition expresses a *thought* (the sense of the unasserted proposition) and refers to a *truth-value* (either the True or the False). A judgement is 'the acknowledgement of the truth of a thought' (*Translations*, p. 156). Thus the form of words 'Venus is larger than Mars' is, according to Frege, an 'acknowledgement' that the expression 'that Venus is larger than Mars' refers to the True. This acknowledgement or assertion is symbolized in Frege's ideography by '⊢ (that Venus is larger than Mars)'."

What W. opposed here (cp. §§19–20), as in Moore (*Commonplace*, 375) or in his own picture theory (GI 33–35), was Frege's conception of the "thought" or "sense of the sentence" (*PG* 106c) as something contained in the statement or in the mind of the speaker (*PG* 40a). The aim of (*a*) is to show that this notion is not justified by the surface grammar which suggests it; the words after "it is asserted" do not indicate any such object of an asserting act.

is *not* a sentence: cp. §49b. Russell had a tendency to cast "propositions" in this form. See e.g. *Analysis of Mind*, 241: "A proposition is a series of words (or sometimes a single word) expressing the kind of thing that can be asserted or denied. 'That all men are mortal', 'that Columbus discovered America', 'that Charles I died in his bed', 'that all philosophers are wise', are propositions." To this W. would reply: Such expressions are not used for assertions, but within reports of assertions. As an interesting study of the metamorphosis of W.'s own thinking, trace the development of the present paragraph from *NB* 96, via Man. 109, 199.

(b) For a doctrine somewhat similar to the one suggested here, see Stout, *Psychology*, II, 214 (the predicate answers a question in the subject). However, as the quotation below indicates, W. still has Frege in mind.

(c) two actions: see GI 38; the quotation from Moore, above; *RFM* 49d; Russell's *Principia*, I, 44 ("when I judge 'Socrates is human,' the meaning is completed by the act of judging"), and *Mind*, 247a, 251b; Frege, "Thought", 294, e.g.: "Consequently we may distinguish: (1) the apprehension of a thought—thinking, (2) the recognition of the truth of a thought—judgment, (3) the manifestation of this judgment—assertion. We perform the first act when we form a sentence-question. An advance in science usually takes place in this way, first a thought is apprehended, such as can perhaps be expressed in a sentence-question, and, after appropriate investigations, this thought is finally recognized to be true."

Z 246 links the present discussion with §513.

roughly as we sing . . . : W. himself had frequently compared speech with singing or playing from notes. In these cases too, he said, "I am guided by a general rule" (Man. 109, 256; see 250–51, 257, 264–65). "The rule is 'contained' in the intention" (*PP* 264). Cp. IX, 9; XXVI, 3; XXXVII, 1–8; Man. 110, 5.

(d) Differs importantly from Man. 220, 15. See *Z* 684; 4.022; Man. 109, 199c; Russell, *Principia*, 8c.

§23 This is the number in which W. insists most fully and forcefully on the variety of language (see I, 10). It has been prepared for by his critique of the "only alternative" (Malcolm, *Memoir*, 69), that is, recourse to uniform mental activity underlying the external diversity. (See GI 32–37.)

(a) assertion, question, and command: the limited sampling W. himself previously considered (GI 33), so the object of special scrutiny in the preceding and following numbers.

use of what we call . . . "sentences": see §20b and commentary.

not something fixed: see I, 9; *OC* 63, 256; Mauthner, *Beiträge*, I, 7–9. The misinterpretation discussed in GI 24 leads to the idea that W. insisted on obeying the rules and sticking close to established use. Since passages like the present stress the elasticity of language, this interpretation leads in turn to talk of "tension" or "hidden contradiction" in his thought, as other misunderstandings have. See Hallett, "Bottle", 84–86.

language-games: see I, 1–10; §7.

changes in mathematics: see §67b; *RFM* 47fg.

(b) See I, 6.

form of life: see §19a and commentary. "What belongs to a language-game is a whole culture" (*LC* 8; see *BB* 134; *EPB* 202).

(c) See *EPB* 124; *BB* 68a, 83d. Strawson comments: "There follows a list of activities which involve the use of language. When we look at the items in the list, it becomes clear that the shift from 'kinds of sentence' in the question to 'kinds of use' in the answer was an important one. The list includes, for example, as separate uses, the activities of reading a story, play-acting, and translating from one language to another. The sentence 'It was raining' might occur in the course of any one of these activities; as it might in a factual narration. It would be absurd to speak of different *sentences* here, let alone of different kinds of sentences. We *might* speak of different uses of the sentence, though it would be better to speak of different linguistic activities in each of which the sentence occurred" ("Review", 25–26). Though nothing in the present number implies that W. would speak in the way Strawson considers questionable, *BB* 67–68 comes close: "A great variety of games is played with the sentences of our language: Giving and obeying orders; asking questions. . . ." Only someone more concerned with verbal niceties than W. was, and less with substantive issues, would quibble at *this* way of speaking. Cp. the commentary on §20b.

tools in language: see §§11a, 14, 360, 559; *RFM* 165b.

logicians have said: on Russell and the *Tractatus*, see GI 32–33; I, 10; *PB* 111e, quoted for §3. "The fundamental error of Russell's logic as also of mine in the *Tractatus Logico-Philosophicus* is that the nature of a sentence [*Satz*] is illustrated by means of a few commonplace examples and then is presumed to be generally understood" (Man. 229, §706; see ibid., §707). "We take one *particular* game & make it into *the* game always played. 'The logical structure of the universe' " (Man. 159; W.'s English; cp. §§104–5). "Russellian logic says nothing about kinds of *propositions*—I don't mean *logical* propositions—and their employment: and yet logic gets its whole sense simply from its presumed application to propositions" (*RFM* 118).

On the Vienna Circle, see V. Kraft, *Circle*, 27–28; and Man. 229, §1587: "Indeed there are far more language-games than Carnap and others let themselves dream of."

On the connection with Aristotelian logic, see *RFM* 156c.

Insert, p. 11   The passage derives from *NB* 29 (cp. *NB* 38abc) and ties in with §22a. Though both here and in *NB* 29 W. speaks only of Frege, it is clear (for example from *NB* 7) that W. himself once conceived of *Sätze* or logical pictures in the same way (see GI 32–33). Cp. §663; *RFM* 49e; *PG* 131d; Man. 228, §209.

how he should not hold himself: see §447; *NB* 27fgh; Russell, *Logic*, 317b.

using the language of chemistry: the relevant sense of *radical* would be: "a group of atoms that is capable of remaining unchanged during a series of reactions".

§24 See I, 10; *RFM* 49ab. Such questions as those in the first paragraph would inevitably arise in the mind of anyone who held that: (1) "The totality of propositions is language" (4.001); (2) "A proposition is a description of a state of affairs" (4.023); and therefore, (3) "To give the essence of a proposition means to give the essence of all description" (5.4711). The number contests both the idea that there is an essence of description (*b*) and that description is the essence of language. Rather: "According to the role which propositions [read: sentences] play in a language game, we distinguish between orders, questions, explanations, descriptions, and so on" (*BB* 82; see §21; *EPB* 148–49; *BB* 102c–103a). Similarly, descriptions themselves vary widely in their function (§291, p. 200a; *BB* 181; Malcolm, *Memoir*, 50).

(a) See §304b; cp. §459, pp. 187i–189e, 192lm; *Z* 283.

If you do not keep . . . : more specifically, if you take all meaningful uses of language for statements, descriptions, as the author of the *Tractatus* did—though apparently for none of the reasons suggested here (see GI 33).

the statement that I wish: there is some slight evidence of W.'s having himself once thought this way (Man. 108, 189, 235; Hallett, "Picture", 318–19), but this does not seem the likeliest explanation for his having identified language with the totality of propositions, without mentioning questions and commands (4.001). See GI 33. The view criticized appears clearly at the start of Augustine's *De Magistro* (quoted in Pitcher, *Philosophy*, 216).

the cry "Help!": see Man. 229, §1166 (quoted for §19b) and §1132 (quoted for p. 189b).

(b) See the references above.

(c) it is possible: not personally, on the spur of the moment, but in the language as a whole or by private agreement. Even then the suggestion may cause difficulties: If the form becomes the same, how are we to tell statements from questions, or vice versa? The answer is implicit in this number, this section, and the whole book: As it is, we repeatedly do use an identical form of words in very different ways.

(d) See §317b and commentary; NL 283b; cp. *Z* 21. "Such possibilities of transformation" are the subject of long discussions in *BB* 57–60, 63–65, 71–72, of which §§402–3 (the "other place" here referred to) are the residue in the *Investigations*.

"I think": cp. Moore, *Ethics*, 125: "Whenever we make any assertion whatever (unless we do not mean what we say) we are always *expressing* one or other of two things—namely, either that we *think* the thing in question to be so, or that we *know* it to be so."

"I believe": cp. Russell, *Logic*, 308–9: "A form of words, unless ar-
tificially constructed, usually expresses not only the content of a proposition, but also what may be called a 'propositional attitude'—memory,
expectation, desire, etc."; "for the present I shall define a 'proposition'
as the *content of a belief*, except when, if ever, the content is simple."

into descriptions of *my* inner life: see §317b and commentary.

Solipsism: see X, 6–10.

§25   See I, 5; IX, 6; §415; *OC* 358–59, 559; *Z* 522, 545; *PG* 108b; Man.
116, 325; cp. §§284b, 329–30; *Z* 99, 121; *NB* 82hij; Man. 109, 282; V.
Kraft, *Circle*, 38.

It is sometimes said: talk on these matters tends to be a tissue of
tautologies (§491; *EPB* 216–17; *BB* 143f–144a). Acquisition of even the
barest rudiments of language, it is said, is quite beyond the capacities of
the ape. Yet isn't it also true that retrieving is "quite beyond the capacities" of a cat, though not of a dog (*BB* 90a; *EPB* 131)? W. is not denying human intelligence, but disagrees with the standard demonstration
(Hallett, "Bottle", 102–3), which looks on language as a clever invention
(§§241, 487–97) or the reflective manipulation of a logical calculus
(§81b) rather than as a form of life which characterizes the human
species. "Language did not emerge from some kind of ratiocination"
(*OC* 475). But of course people do ratiocinate, do develop calculi, do invent things. "Our mistake," here as elsewhere, "is to look for an explanation where . . . we ought to have said: *this language-game is played*"
(§654). On this topic W. disagreed with all the philosophers whose
thought he knew best—including the author of the *Tractatus* (GI 37;
3.1–3.12).

Schopenhauer: "The animal communicates his feelings and moods
by gesture and sound; man communicates thought to another, or con-
ceals it from him, by language. Speech is the first product and the necessary instrument of his faculty of reason" (*World*, I, 37). "It is reason
speaking to reason that keeps within its province, and what it communicates and receives are abstract concepts, non-perceptive representations, formed once for all and relatively few in number, but nevertheless embracing, containing, and representing all the innumerable
objects of the actual world. From this alone is to be explained the fact
that an animal can never speak and comprehend, although it has in
common with us the organs of speech, and also the representations of
perception. But just because words express this quite peculiar class of
representations, whose subjective correlative is reason, they are for the
animal without sense and meaning" (ibid., 40).

Frege: "How could man create language without reason?" ("Justification", 160).

James: "The dog whom this similarity could strike would have
grasped the sign *per se* as such, and would probably thereupon become

a general sign-maker, or speaker in the human sense . . . not unless the 'yelp' of the dog at the moment it occurs *recalls* to him his 'beg' by the delicate bond of their subtle similarity of use—not till then can this thought flash through his mind: 'Why, yelp and beg, in spite of all their unlikeness, are yet alike in this: that they are actions, signs, which lead to important boons. Other boons, *any* boons, may then be got by other signs!' This reflection made, the gulf is passed. Animals probably never make it" (*Principles*, II, 357; see 355–57).

Moore: "Animals have no language because they never express judgments—only feelings & desires, or perceptions or images. They perceive things as having certain characters; & their cries may express the fact that they are perceiving a thing having that character; but they don't know or judge of any character *that* anything has it" (*Commonplace*, 45).

See Stout, *Manual*, 459 ("the earliest communication could only take place between minds capable of a certain kind of mental process"); cp. XII, 3; commentary on §363b.

part of our natural history: contrast this with the quotations from Man. 108, under §108bc. "Language is a characteristic part of a large group of activities—talking, writing, travelling on a bus, meeting a man, etc." (*LC* 2). Likewise in mathematics: "I *go through* the proof and then accept its result.—I mean: this is simply what we *do*. This is use and custom among us, or a fact of our natural history" (*RFM* 20). Cp. Mauthner, *Beiträge*, I, 15–16: "We must count language as just another human activity, like walking or breathing. . . . We shall then find the notion 'capacity for speech' just as absurd as, say, a special 'capacity for walking' or a special 'capacity for breathing'." In *BB* 12b–13e, *EPB* 142, and §54 W. draws a contrast somewhat similar to the present one, between rules "involved in the processes of understanding, obeying, etc." (*BB* 12) and rules which resemble natural laws.

II. Naming (§§26–38)

GENERAL COMMENTARY

(1) The overall rationale of this and subsequent sections, already sketched in GI 41 and 63, may also be stated thus: Having stressed the richness and diversity of language, slighted by logical atomists and others, Wittgenstein now demonstrates that even within the narrow boundaries he and Russell set for language, their account was inade-

quate. The *Tractatus*, in particular, erred not only in identifying language with propositions (GI 32–33), but in its account of propositions. "It was with regard to 'elementary' propositions and their connection with truth-functions or 'molecular' propositions," Wittgenstein told Moore in 1930–1931, "that he had had to change his opinions most; and . . . this subject was connected with the use of the words 'thing' and 'name' " (*PP* 296).

(2)   The atomist doctrine of names derived from a primitive conception, common to many thinkers, in which *"naming* seems to be the foundation and be-all and end-all of language" (*PG* 56) and to consist "in correlating in a peculiar and rather mysterious way a sound (or other sign) with something. How we make use of this peculiar correlation then seems to be almost a secondary matter" (*BB* 172; see §38). The quotation at the start of the preceding overture, whose first movement Wittgenstein now develops, illustrates this syndrome (*PG* 56).

(3)   "When they named some object," said Augustine, "and accordingly moved towards something, I saw this and I grasped that the thing was called by the sound they uttered" (§1). The object and the movement were all he needed in order to guess what thing was called by what name. But how did he know about calling and names? Augustine seems not to have noticed this difficulty, for two reasons. First, he did not see language as a rich and varied form of life, with naming just one pattern among many, so did not realize how unrealistic it was to suppose innate acquaintance with the parts of speech. Anyone who sees no difference between kinds of word (§1c) may easily take the naming function for granted. Furthermore, he may conceive naming so simplistically that it appears a natural activity of the human mind. If naming amounts to an immediate hookup between thought and thing, effected by fixing one's attention while uttering or thinking the word, the game need hardly be learned.

(4)   What is merely implicit in Augustine becomes explicit in Russell: "In order to understand a name for a particular, the only thing necessary is to be acquainted with that particular. When you are acquainted with that particular, you have a full, adequate, and complete understanding of the name, and no further information is required" (*Logic*, 202; see 204–5). He recognized that more was necessary in the case of general predicates such as *red* (ibid., 205), but it was vitally important for him to maintain that the learning of proper names is different. For on that difference depended his conception of names as mere pointers, and from that conception stemmed the whole of logical atomism (III, 4). To the complexity of the learning corresponds the complexity of the sign, and the names of logical atomism were to be absolutely simple.

(5) A typical expedient, frequently envisaged in the *Investigations*, is recourse to a laserlike act of attention, pinpointing the object and attaching the sign. "At any moment of my conscious life," wrote Russell in a characteristic passage, "there is one object (or at most some very small number of objects) to which I am attending. All knowledge of particulars radiates out from this object. This object is not intrinsically distinguishable from other objects—it just happens (owing to causes which do not concern us) that I am attending to it. Since I am attending to it, I can name it; I may give it any name I choose, but when inventiveness gives out, I am apt to name it 'this'. By the help of reflection and special experiences, it becomes evident that there is such a relation as 'attention', and that there is always a subject attending to the object called 'this'. The subject attending to 'this' is called 'I', and the time of the things which have to 'I' the relation of presence is called the present time. 'This' is the point from which the whole process starts, and 'this' itself is not defined, but simply given" (*Logic*, 168).

(6) Wittgenstein's early thought followed similar lines: "The naming of complexes presupposes propositions, while propositions presuppose the naming of simples. In this way the naming of simples is shown to be what is logically first in logic" (Russell, Introduction to the *Tractatus*, xiii). But it could not be logically first if the names were verbally defined (3.26). So their meaning must be grasped from their use, in actual propositions (3.261–3.3; cp. p. 18n), much as the rule of a series is intuited in actual members exemplifying the rule (IX, 3). The referent is before one's eyes, perhaps (cp. the end of 3.263), and somebody says, "This is red." Whether he intends his words as a description, or means to teach the word's meaning, the logical form is the same (Man. 112, 151–52, quoted for p. 18n). And if mere words do not suffice, he can use the natural language of gesture (see commentary on §32b) and point to the thing he means (again, cp. end of 3.263).

(7) In any case, the crucial, final step is taken by the mind, connecting word and thing (cp. §362). "It is quite clear," Wittgenstein wrote in the *Notebooks*, "that I can in fact correlate a name with this watch just as it lies here ticking in front of me, and that this name will have reference outside any proposition in the very sense I have always given that word" (*NB* 60). In the *Tractatus*, though he now maintained that "only in the nexus of a proposition does a name have reference" (3.3; Hallett, *Definition*, 9–14), it was still the mind that effected the hookup. For ordinary usage lacks the requisite precision (GI 37).

(8) Waismann and Schlick echoed this atomistic doctrine. "The signs which appear in elementary propositions," wrote Waismann, "are called *primitive signs* (elementary signs). They cannot be dissected by means of definitions. The meaning of primitive signs can only be

pointed out. Primitive signs are the ones which signify directly; all other signs signify indirectly, *via* the primitive signs" (*Kreis*, 250). But how can their meaning be "pointed out"? "It is clear," argued Schlick, "that in order to understand a verbal definition we must know the signification of the explaining words beforehand, and that the only explanation which can work without any previous knowledge is the ostensive definition. We conclude that there is no way of understanding any meaning without ultimate reference to ostensive definitions" ("Meaning", 148).

(9) If the hookup really could be effected "without any previous knowledge", as all these thinkers supposed, the consequences would be incalculable. For example, people could turn their gaze within and, guided by external clues on a par with pointing, label what their gaze revealed: images, feelings, sensations, mental acts and processes of every description. And psychology would become the introspective study of these inner referents (X, 22). Or, if the barrier between mind and mind appeared insurmountable, other-minds skepticism might result (X, 24). And if tables and chairs were analyzed into personal sense-data, they would become subject to similar doubts. And if it were then recognized that knowledge of other people and things was logically precluded, solipsism might seem the final, unsayable truth (5.62); or more radically still: "All that is real is the experience of the present moment" (*PP* 311). (For further implications, see II, 13.)

(10) So how can Schlick's dilemma be resolved? How *do* we break out of language and make contact with reality? Well, how do we break out of swimming and make contact with water? How do we learn to *swim*? Bit by bit, immersed in the water. Such a comparison brings out the fact that language is a form of life, not a mental calculus pairing signs, thoughts, and things. But the comparison with games is closer. For in language too there are right and wrong, rules and customs, which require observation (§31). However, the observation begins the day a child is born. For months, "light dawns gradually over the whole" (*OC* 141). Then one day the child speaks; that is, "one day he begins to *do* something" (Man. 138, 20A). It is as though, having been led dozens of times through the streets adjoining his house, he took a small trip on his own (I, 5).

(11) Definition comes later. It is itself a language-game which has to be learned (§27), and one which presupposes familiarity with the type of word defined. Thus the sort of presuppositionless ostensive definition Schlick thought necessary is not even possible. For "the ostensive definition explains the use—the meaning—of the word when the overall role of the word in language is clear," and only then (§30).

(12) The need of previous linguistic knowledge comes out clearly in

the following illustration, aimed directly at views like Schlick's: "If the definition explains the meaning of a word, surely it can't be essential that you should have heard the word before. It is the ostensive definition's business to *give* it a meaning. Let us then explain the word 'tove' by pointing to a pencil and saying 'this is tove.' . . . Now the ostensive definition 'this is tove' can be interpreted in all sorts of ways. I will give a few such interpretations and use English words with well established usage. The definition then can be interpreted to mean: 'This is a pencil,' 'This is round,' 'This is wood,' 'This is one,' 'This is hard,' etc. etc." (*BB* 2; see §28). If we come to the rescue with an extra word and say, "This color is tove," the person will be helped only if he knows how color words are used. And if he manages without such assistance, that is because he already possesses the kind of knowledge it would have provided.

(13)   Any account which traces thought and language to primitive simples, converting analytic levels into genetic stages, is implicated in Wittgenstein's critique. It applies not only to logical atomism, logical positivism, and classical British empiricism, but also to the ancient, widespread trend of thought revealed in the writings of Plato (§46), or of Scotus: "First the sense is moved by some simple and not complex object, and through the movement of the sense the intellect is moved and apprehends simple objects: this is the intellect's first act. Secondly, after the apprehension of simple objects there follows another act, that of bringing together simple objects, and after this composition the intellect is able to assent to the truth of the complex, if it is a first principle" (*Quaestiones subtilissimae super libros Metaphysicorum*, 2, 1, no. 2). To the extent that talk of concept-formation as "first act of the intellect" is given a temporal or causal sense, it conflicts with Wittgenstein's views, according to which such an act is as mythical as Rousseau's social contract. There is no first act, either for the individual or for the race (§§242, 381). "Light dawns gradually over the whole."

DETAILED COMMENTARY

§26   One thinks . . . : W. once did. Reflection on his early views helps to dissipate the double strangeness in this equation of learning with giving and of learning language with learning names for objects. According to the *Tractatus*, whereas names must be explained to us, thereafter we can use them to make ourselves understood, in propositions (4.026). And in the process of explanation, the prime requisite is that we be acquainted with the referent, pick it out, and connect the name with it (II, 6–7). This, of course, the teacher's words or gestures cannot do. "In the end the pupil is brought to the point of giving himself the correct ostensive definition" (§362; see §§32, 210, 262–63, 380).

to pains: "We say we call something 'toothache', and think that the word has received a definite function in the dealings we carry out with language when, under certain circumstances, we have pointed to our cheek and said: 'This is toothache' " (*BB* 69).

To repeat: see §15b.

this is preparatory: see §49b. "There is an unfortunate ambiguity in the English verb 'to name' which is absent from the German. *Benennen* in German means 'to give a thing a name' and Wittgenstein rightly says that *benennen*, 'giving a thing a name', is not yet language; it is related to language as setting the men in the right position on the board is related to chess" (Geach, lecture notes).

§27(a) See I, 10; §244a.

As if what we did next . . . : see *BB* 69a; cp. Schlick, *Aufsätze*, 154.

(b) no such thing: see §§6b, 31cd.

inventing a name: cp. §31e.

how singular: see Man. 229, §1667, quoted for §524bc. On the motivation of such a remark, cp. §524. If we take a chair as our paradigm "object" or *red* as our paradigm name (*PG* 118), it may indeed seem strange that we should use a name to *call* someone! How would a chair react? Russell suggests that we define the vocative as "the use of a proper name to indicate desire for the presence of the person named" (*Inquiry*, 26). But in that case what a strange metamorphosis the name has undergone! It no longer refers to the person named, but describes the namer! And is all this missing multiplicity really hidden in the mind? (See §§19–20.) If, however, the call is a command and not a self-description, how odd that it should make no mention of the action commanded (GI 33–35)! And in any case what is this word doing by itself (2.0122)? The more narrowly we examine actual language, the sharper becomes the conflict between it and our requirements (§107).

§28   See *BB* 2a (quoted in II, 12); *PG* 60e, 61d; Man. 302, 4; Man. 112, 142; cp. §§9, 143–44; *Kreis*, 51; Frege, *Foundations*, 28–29.

define a proper name: since this way of speaking (cp. §79) is as deviant as W.'s references to the "meanings" of proper names (see III, 10), no doubt it too should be traced to his *Tractatus* days. See Strawson, "Review", 77.

the number two: Hacker notes that according to Brouwer "mathematical abstraction involves abstracting from temporal succession and causal correlation to the bare notion of difference or 'two-oneness' from which the whole series of natural numbers, and ultimately all of pure mathematics can be constructed" (*Insight*, 100).

is perfectly exact: it does not mean, for instance (in the terms of Mill), that we shall call all such *parcels* Twos (see Frege, *Foundations*, 9).

"One difficulty which strikes us is that for many words in our language there do not seem to be ostensive definitions; e.g. for such words as 'one', 'number', 'not', etc." (*BB* 1). Cp. Frege, *Foundations*, 9–12, 115.

He *may* suppose this: see Ogden and Richards (*Meaning*, 77–78) for Congolese responses to the question "What is this?"

in *every* case: see II, 12; §71b, p. 14n; *PG* 439d; cp. §§139–40, 433. A passage like the following from Schlick helps to explain W.'s emphasis: "When I ask somebody, 'What is the meaning of this or that?' he must answer by a sentence that would try to describe the meaning. But he cannot ultimately succeed in this, for his answering sentence would be but another proposition and I would be perfectly justified in asking 'What do you mean by *this*?' We would perhaps go on defining what he meant by using different words, and repeat his thought over and over again by using new sentences. I could always go on asking, 'But what does this new proposition mean?' You see, there would never be any end to this kind of inquiry, the meaning could never be clarified, if there were no other way of arriving at it than by a series of propositions" ("Future", 49–50; see II, 8). Clearly Schlick needed to be reminded that even the purely ostensive, nonverbal definition which he envisaged would be as capable of misinterpretation as those he rejected.

§29   See I, 4; II, 11–12; *PG* 60–61; Man. 112, 142–43; cp. *PB* 54c; Man. 112, 172; the preceding quotation from Schlick.

(a) See *PP* 260b; cp. §86. The paragraph forms a dialogue, with two suggestions and two rejoinders, each separated by a dash.

place: italicized in the German. See §31b, §508a (note the identical stress); *PG* 61b; Man. 125, 1–2. Cp. *PP* 257: "something which he expressed by saying that every significant word or symbol must essentially belong to a 'system'; and (metaphorically) by saying that the meaning of a word is its 'place' in a 'grammatical system' ". On W.'s preoccupation with 'logical space' when he first returned to philosophy, a preoccupation which explains his comparisons of "grammar" with geometry (e.g. *PG* 52–53; *BB* 61c) and links the present expression to 3.4, 3.42, 4.463, etc., see Russell, *Autobiography*, II, 198–200.

in grammar: W.'s use of the terms *grammar* (*Grammatik*) and *grammatical* (*grammatisch*) is broad and varied. By the "grammar" of an individual word he meant its use in the language, the rules of its employment (*BB* 23d; §§187, 199, 492, p. 18n). Here in §29, as in §§497, 520, 664, and p. 230a, grammar is the complex of rules which constitute a language (see I, 8). In §§304, 353, 371, 373, and 496, grammar is the account we give of such rules. Though, as W. realized (Man. 110, 194–95; *PP* 276b), these uses of the term are more inclusive than the ordinary sense, they are continuous with it. See VI, 3; the commentary on §108c; Hacker, *Insight*, 150–53.

is there only *one* way: "are black and white colours? for some purpose—yes, for others—no" (Baker and Hacker, Notice, 276).

(b) Cp. §85.

(c) See the commentary on §34.

Insert, p. 14   Cp. *PG* 91a. The discussion in Man. 112 from which this insert derives (via *PG* 135d–136a) indicates that by reinforcing the central point of §§28–29 in a striking manner it counteracts the Tractarian doctrine that: (1) "Elucidations are propositions that contain the primitive signs" (3.263); (2) though "propositions can only say *how* things are, not *what* they are" (3.221), they can "*show* the logical form of reality" (4.121); (3) "the definition is the paradigm of the step taken in the description" (Man. 112, 151–52, quoted for p. 18n). See II, 6.

(a) See *RFM* 103abc; Man. 112, 152–54, 163, 167, 169–71, 199; cp. *Z* 317; *RFM* 15b; *NB* 23i; Man. 112, 171.

(b) See §§6b, 31bc; Man. 228, §§34, 41; cp. §498; *RFM* 99h, 172c; *BB* 12d; *PG* 187b.

it might well be asked: in Man. 112, 154, W. had written: "It will be objected: 'But such an explanation could not be used to explain the meaning of the word 'red'. To this I can only reply: I don't know; we should have to try it & see whether after this explanation of the sign the person reacts with understanding." He overlooked the conceptual difficulty, not the causal one. Later, "in one lecture he talked about the notion of an *explanation* of the uses of an expression: In supposing that the colour red (and also the phenomenon of thinking something to oneself) is something specific and indescribable, one supposes that one could learn what red is simply by seeing a red image. But what if I hit you on the head, and thereafter you were able to use the word 'red' correctly? Would this be an explanation of what red is? Of course not. An explanation is not *anything* that produces understanding. A key is not *anything* which opens a door" (Malcolm, *Memoir*, 47).

§30(a) the use—the meaning: see §43a.

all sorts of problems: not in using the expressions, but in giving an account of their use. Cp. W.'s own problems in Man. 112, 154–55.

"to know": "One is often bewitched by a word. For example, by the word 'know'" (*OC* 435). Thus: (1) In addition to the simple expression "I know . . . ," "there is also *this* use of the word 'to know': we say 'Now I know!'" (§151). This reference to a point of time (cp. p. 175ab) gives the impression that the declaration is a report of something observed at the moment (see GI 15–17), that knowing is therefore a conscious state or process (§§148, 363c, p. 176f; *PG* 71d, 371c–372a), into which the whole calculus or future development is somehow bundled (*BB* 42a, 142a; §187). (2) If we opt instead for a hypothetical disposition existing in the moment, again we ignore the actual criteria of knowledge (*PG* 118a). (3) These are bewilderingly complex (§31c; *OC* 555), "much more complicated than might appear at first sight" (§182). And the speaker who says "I know" need not consult criteria of his ability (IX, 13). (4) Nor is he always indicating an ability (Z 406). (5) The Platonic problem about the essence of knowledge is therefore a false one (§116; *BB* 20a; Man. 302, 14, quoted in GI 24). (6) The skeptic often reveals similar confusion when he denies we have genuine knowledge, as opposed to "mere belief" (X, 19; XVI, 5–6). (7) Moore's contrary use of *know*, in defense of common sense, seemed as problematic to W. as the skeptic's doubts; there are problems as to *what* things one may be said to know (X, 25; commentary on §246 and p. 221). (8) In the present context W. was specially concerned to distinguish between unreflective mastery of a technique and the ability to state the rules learned (*Kreis*, 78a; Man. 110, 109–10; *PG* 62b; §31b). (9) More precisely still, here in §30 the focus is on the contrast between the child who can ask for the name (§30b) and "the child who is just learning to speak" (*OC* 536; see §§5–6). Knowing, W. was inclined to say, begins only at the later level (*OC* 534–38).

(b) One has already . . . : see *OC* 535–48, 566.

But what. . . . : this question, which returns in §31d, is evidently understood to require the same answer as the question just raised in (*a*) and discussed in the following paragraphs (namely, what one needs to know in order to understand an ostensive definition, as opposed to mere ostensive training).

§31   See Man. 109, 287–88.

(a) See *PG* 61b; NL 291b; cp. *RFM* 60a; *PB* 320b–321a; Frege, *Grundgesetze*, II, 113.

chess: an extremely common comparison in W., as in many authors he read (see commentary on §7b). On it, see Stegmüller, *Hauptströmungen*, 593–94.

W. compared: the *arbitrariness* of chess with the arbitrariness of language (*Kreis*, 103–5); the *autonomy* of chess with the autonomy of language (Z 320; *Kreis*, 103, 150; Man. 219, 8); *describing* chess with describing language (§108; *EPB* 117; *BB* 77b; *PG* 121b, 216d); the *differences* between chess pieces, or between the pieces and the board, with the differences between different words or kinds of words (*EPB* 124; *BB* 84a; *PG* 59b; Man. 108, 169–70); the characteristic *feelings* of words with those of chess pieces (Man. 116, 40–41; see Section XXXII); chess with language in *general* (*BB* 72a; *PG* 170g); *intention* in chess with intention in language (§§197, 337; *EPB* 225, 229–30; *BB* 147a; Man. 110, 226–27, 233); *learning* chess with learning language (§§31, 33–35; *BB* 13e); the "meaning" of chess pieces with the *meaning* of words (§563; Z 143; *PG* 107a); *mistakes* in chess with mistakes in language (*BB* 67a);

naming with putting a piece on the board (§49); *private* chess with private language (NL 292); the *rules* of chess with the rules of language (§§108, 136, 199–200, 205, 563–68; *Z* 320, 440; *BB* 13; *PG* 125d, 184–85, 192d; *Kreis,* 103, 134); winning and losing in chess with *true* and *false* in language (*RFM* 49d, 51a; *PG* 293f); *understanding* chess, knowing how to play, with understanding language, knowing how to speak (§ 197, pp. 59n, 181c; *Z* 348; *RFM* 40f; *BB* 183–84; *PG* 49–51); chess pieces with *words,* signs (§§31, 108, 136; *EPB* 124; *BB* 7c, 65b, 83–84; *PG* 56a, 67c, 121a; *PB* 61d, 328; *Kreis,* 134a). Similar comparisons occur in W.'s discussion of other topics, especially in his treatment of mathematics. For Frege's negative reactions to such comparisons, see e.g. *Basic Laws,* 10b–11a, and *Writings,* 185ff.

You could imagine . . . : contrast this with Frege, *Writings,* 196: "In the game of chess we must first acquaint ourselves with the chessmen in order to understand the rules."

(b) See I, 5; §54; *OC* 95; *PG* 62; cp. *Z* 295.

without ever learning . . . rules: "Does he learn the game only by being told the rules, and not also simply by watching when the game is played? Doubtless he will often say to himself while watching: 'Oh, so that's the rule,' and he might perhaps write down the rules as he observes them; but there is certainly such a thing as learning the game without explicit rules" (*PG* 62; cp. p. 209c; Man. 116, 34, quoted for p. 185gh).

Or even . . . : the move is from a merely factual hypothesis to a conceptual point similar to that raised at the end of the insert on p. 14 and in the next paragraph of §31.

the place: see §29a and commentary.

in another sense: see *PG* 62, quoted for §6c ("Don't you understand"). Cp. §208.

(c) Cp. *PB* 327–328a; Frege, *Writings,* 202a.

only if: see the preceding paragraph ("Or even") and the end of p. 14n.

and similar things: the emphasis is explained by §30a and §69.

only under these conditions: see §6b and comments.

ask relevantly: that is, ask for the name of this *piece,* not simply of this object, as he might in the case of anything he came across (cp. §35c). Here the possibilities are as limitless as in the correlative case of ostensive definition (*BB* 2a). To the mere request, "What is this called?" a perfectly good reply would be: "A piece of wood," or, "A black object," or, "A pawn," or, "A chess piece." Such conditions as those W. has mentioned would be required to turn the words "What do you call this?" into a request for the name of the piece (cp. p. 14n). Hence the words "will he be able" refer to logical, not merely causal possibility.

(d) Again, see §6b and comments.

can significantly: similarly, contrast a move in chess with the same displacement of a piece made by a child who doesn't play chess (§33c). The mere words would not constitute a request for the name.

(e) Cp. §27b; *BB* 90b, 95b, 105b. *PG* 88b (here corrected) reveals the point of the suggestion: "If I say 'The color of this object is called "violet"', I must already have indicated the color, already have presented it for christening, with the designation 'the color of this object', if the naming is to be possible. For I could also say: 'The name of this color is for you to decide'; and the one who gave the name would have to know already what he was to give it to."

§32   See *Z* 324; *PG* 108b; cp. *BB* 131b.

(a) *guess:* similar guessing in the case of a child learning language is suggested by the quotations from Augustine in §1a and below, and is criticized in *BB* 105: "We regard the case as though the child already possessed a language in which it thought and that the teacher's job is to induce it to guess his meaning in the realm of meanings before the child's mind, as though the child could in his own private language ask himself such a question as, 'Does he want me to continue, or repeat what he said, or something else?' " (See I, 5.) *EPB* continues: "Thus the matter is represented as though the child never learned *language,* so never learned to think, but only to translate a language it already knows into another" (152). The need of infant guessing is suggested by the quotations below from Russell and from Ogden and Richards, and in James, *Principles,* II, 357: "The child in each case makes the discovery for himself. No one can help him except by furnishing him with the conditions."

(b) See II, 3; Man. 232, 633. In particular, notice that in Augustine's account he "grasped that the thing was called by the sound", as though knowledge of naming and calling were innate in a child and required no training or acquaintance with the language-game (think how much stage-setting was required in the case of Helen Keller). The whole of Section II up to this point may be viewed as a critique of that phrase in the *Confessions.* The notion of a natural language of the mind, preceding all spoken forms (X, 2), emerges still more clearly in the passage from *Confessions,* I, 6, 8, quoted in *EPB* 152: "Thus little by little I sensed where I was, and wished to reveal my desires to those who could satisfy them, and I could not, for the desires were within me. . . . So I flung out limbs and sounds, making signs similar to my desires." Innumerable authors have spoken in the way here criticized. See for instance:

W. himself: "It is not possible to learn a language without already understanding one" (Man. 110, 186). "Even a child merely learns one language by means of another. He learns a word language through a gesture language. But his understanding of this is something the adult must presume in him or await" (Man. 110, 153; cp. *PG* 88–90). "That is, if the thought were not already articulated, how could the expression of it in language make it articulate? But the articulated thought is in all essentials a proposition" (Man. 108, 279). "We don't have thought and *also* language" (Man. 108, 278; see ibid., 271; *EPB* 152; *NB* 82n).

Augustine: "For of necessity, when we say what is true—i.e. say what we know—the knowledge itself, which we retain in memory, gives birth to a word that is altogether of the same kind as the knowledge from which it is born. For the thought formed by the thing that we know is a word spoken in the heart, which is neither Greek nor Latin nor of any other language. But since it is necessary to convey it into the knowledge of those with whom we speak, some sign is adopted by which it is signified" (*De Trinitate*, XV, 10, 19; cp. Plato, *Cratylus*).

Plato: "*Soc.*—I mean the conversation which the soul holds with herself in considering of anything. I speak of what I scarcely know: but the soul when thinking appears to me to be just talking—asking questions of herself and answering them, affirming and denying" (*Theaetetus*, 189–90; see *Sophist*, 263; Man. 229, §846).

Russell: "When a child learns the meaning of the word 'yellow', there is first an object (or rather a set of objects) which is yellow by definition, and then a perception that other objects are similar in colour. Thus when we say to a child 'this is yellow,' what (with luck) we convey to him is: 'this resembles in colour the object which is yellow by definition' " (*Inquiry*, 35).

Ogden and Richards: "In what precise fashion we first come to know that there are words, or to take some sounds as words but not others, is still to be experimentally investigated, but as infants we do not make this step by guessing straight off that people are talking to us. Long before this surmise could become possible we have developed an extensive private language through the fact that certain sounds have come into contexts with certain other experiences in such a way that the occurrence of the sound is a sign interpreted by a response similar to that aroused by the other associated experience" (*Meaning*, 210).

James: see the quotations (above, and for §25) from *Principles*, II, 357.

In Section X, W. deals with the idea of a private language, recurrent in these quotations, and in Section XI passes to the corresponding conception of thought as a nonverbal, international language of the mind (§§329–30, 342, 597; *BB* 41c; *PB* 53–54; *LC* 30a) which gets translated into spoken or written expressions (§597; *Z* 191; *BB* 41c).

"talk to itself": that is, it is often so conceived, as for example in the quotations from Plato and from *BB* 105 above. In this there is a double error (see the comments on "I do not say *'to* oneself'," p. 211k).

§33 See §§666–76; *EPB* 120; *BB* 80c; cp. *EPB* 233; *BB* 150ab.

(a) Suppose, however . . . : concerning this objection, see §264 and commentary. W. has already indicated the answer (§§26–32; see §34). Here he turns instead to the vague, simplistic notions of pointing, meaning, attending which underlie the suggestion.

'pointing to': see II, 8; §§669–70; *BB* 69; Man. 116, 31; cp. *NB* 100 ("Naming is like pointing").

How did you do it?: pointing to objects may be less problematic, but if we call this familiar paradigm to our assistance and define pointing to a property as pointing to the object which possesses it (*PG* 63), it would follow that we point to color, shape, and countless other properties, simultaneously, any time we point to an object (cp. II, 12; *PG* 60e).

'meant': see §§674–76, p. 18n; *Z* 12.

concentrated your attention: see II, 5; §§411 (end), 666–67; cp. §§275–76; Stout, *Psychology,* II, 197.

how is *that* done?: see *BB* 176fg and James, *Principles,* I, 403–4: "Everyone knows what attention is. It is the taking possession by the mind, in clear and vivid form, of one out of what seem several simultaneously possible objects or trains of thought. Focalization, concentration, of consciousness are of its essence." Contrast not only this answer, but also James's approach to the question, with what follows in §33.

(c) You attend . . . : see *Z* 673–74.

Just as a move in chess . . . : see §316; *EPB* 225, 229–30; *BB* 147cd. Concerning W.'s comparisons with chess, see the commentary on §31a.

§34 From pointing or meaning, the previous number passed to attending as the simple explanation of ostensive definition; after questioning the supposed simplicity of attention, W. now notes its irrelevance as an explanation, even if simplistically conceived, since the intention of the teacher and interpretation of the learner, generally considered decisive, do not consist in any such simple experience. On the irrelevance of attention for definition, see §268.

"intend": see *Z* 236; *PG* 148b.

"interpret": see *BB* 2bc, 36c.

a process which accompanies the giving: as in Waismann's *Thesen:* "The ostension consists essentially of two acts: of an external act, the pointing to various facts, and of a mental operation, namely the internalization of what is common" (*Kreis,* 246). W. had written: "The interpretation is made generally, as preparation for any application. It occurs in *language instruction* & not in language use" (Man. 110, 221).

§35 Implicit in the previous two numbers is the conclusion: If atten-

tion is essential to pointing (§33a), and it turns out that there is no essence of attention (§§33ab, 34), then neither is there an essence of
pointing. However, the first premise is unacceptable; so W. develops
the conclusion independently, repeating for pointing the remarks just
made about attention. Pointing, like attending, is a complex, varying
weave in the pattern of our lives. (See GI 20–23.)

(a) **"characteristic":** see *EPB* 218; cp. §67.

   Besides . . . : see GI 60.

(b) See *EPB* 119; *BB* 79d. The most obvious difference is that in one
case you point in different directions, in the other not, so that words
play a larger role in determining the referent.

   we *learn:* if differently learned, then differently used. See III, 1–2;
cp. §§77b, 376.

(c) *as a piece in a game:* W. would pass from this "patent nonsense to
something which is disguised nonsense" (§524), the previous hypothetical experiences. Cp. *BB* 64b; Man. 112, 152: "I cannot point to the
meaning of a word. (At most to the bearer of a name.)"

   All the same . . . : that is, the hypothesis of such pointing makes
sense, nonetheless, despite the absence of a characteristic experience.

   Recognizing, wishing . . . : "A primitive philosophy condenses the
whole usage of the name into the idea of a relation, which thereby
becomes a mysterious relation. (Compare the ideas of mental activities,
wishing, believing, thinking, etc., which for the same reason have something mysterious and inexplicable about them.)" (*BB* 173). Note the link
with §36.

§36(a) **what we do:** countless philosophers, including Plato (GI 23;
§518; *BB* 20a); Frege (GI 45); Russell (commentary on §598); young W.
(e.g. GI 37–38). "The tendency has always been strong," wrote J. S.
Mill, "to believe that whatever receives a name must be an entity or
being, having an independent existence of its own: and if no real entity
answering to the name could be found, men did not for that reason
suppose that none existed, but imagined that it was something peculiarly abstruse and mysterious, too high to be an object of sense"
(quoted in Ogden and Richards, *Meaning*, xxiv).

   a host of similar cases: instances of the Essence Fallacy or Reference
Fallacy or both (GI 17–23), occasioned by misleading analogies (GI
10–13). The similarity is closest when a mental activity is provided for a
verb (see GI 17–19; Z 86; *EPB* 165, 173, 219; *BB* 7, 42a, 113b,
119c–120a, 144ad; *PG* 74–75; Ambrose, "Universals", 341). Other examples belong at least to the same genus, for instance: "We say 'Surely
two sentences of different languages can have the same sense'; and we
argue, 'therefore the sense is not the same as the sentence,' and ask the
question 'What is the sense?' And we make of 'it' a shadowy being, one

of the many which we create when we wish to give meaning to substantives to which no material objects correspond" (*BB* 36; see *EPB* 134; *BB* 4d). "The mental world in fact is liable to be imagined as gaseous, or rather, aethereal. But let me remind you here of the queer role which the gaseous and the aethereal play in philosophy,—when we perceive that a substantive is not used as what in general we should call the name of an object, and when therefore we can't help saying to ourselves that it is the name of an aethereal object. I mean, we already know the idea of 'aethereal objects' as a subterfuge, when we are embarrassed about the grammar of certain words, and when all we know is that they are not used as names for material objects. This is a hint as to how the problem of the two materials, *mind* and *matter,* is going to dissolve" (*BB* 47; cp. *Z* 552; *BB* 172–73, quoted for §15b and §35c).

(b) Besides the above, see also *BB* 69 (quoted for §398), 73b, 74b; *PB* 287e; Man. 302, 19; Man. 138, 32B; cp. Man. 213, 435; Schopenhauer, *World,* II, 67b.

§37 See III, 7, 9, 13; commentary on §15. The discussion starts to shift from learning a name to using it.

  the picture: see §6b; *BB* 103a; cp. §301 and commentary.

  written on the thing: see §15 and commentary.

  is pointed at: especially in learning the name (§§7, 9, 28–36, 43b, 44, 51a, 429), perhaps also in using it (§8).

Insert, p. 18   The insert seems most closely related to §38a—the first paragraph with "that is called" and the second with "produce confusion"—though the third paragraph connects with §33a.

(a) Cp. §§19–20; Frege, *Writings,* 204.

(b) what was intended . . . : W. is not referring to instances in which the speaker, using the material mode of speech to state a grammatical fact, supposes that he is stating some necessary truth about the world, but to the simpler fact that when one person describes a thing as blue another person may thereby learn how the word *blue* is used. Cp. *Z* 294; *PB* 59c, 249a.

  a crucial superstition: a sampling of errors W. may have had in mind:

(1)   "We can call *Satz* what is taken now this way, now that; but also this or that way of taking it. Here is a source of confusions" (*PG* 43). For instance, we conceive the proposition as a shadowy something distinct from the sentence (*PP* 265, quoted for §94).

(2)   "We confuse the word 'green' with the proposition 'a is green.' (Hence too our difficulty in explaining it in the proposition 'a is not green.')" (Man. 109, 213; cp. §447).

(3)   "This error is akin to that of believing that an ostensive definition

says something about the object to which it directs our attention" (*BB* 175; see *BB* 2; cp. §49b).

(4) "For didn't I say that a sign can be explained only through another sign?" (Man. 112, 214; see II, 6). Thus "color samples, the minute they define words, are words" (Man. 112, 169).

(5) Hence "it is not possible to learn a language without already understanding one" (Man. 110, 186; see commentary on §32b).

(6) And "what a word means, no sentence can say" (*PG* 208; see §46 and commentary). It has to be shown (3.221, 4.121, 4.1212).

(7) Thus from individual uses of a word one might 'intuit' its meaning, somewhat as from initial samples one might intuit the rule of a series (IX, 3). "Even if we understand that the expression 'That is red' can have two entirely different functions—on the one hand as an ostensive definition ('I call the color of this patch "red" ') and on the other as an assertion that the patch is red—still the formal kinship of the two expressions is striking. . . . The kinship lies in this that the definition is the paradigm of the step taken in the description $\left(\begin{array}{cc} 1=0 & 1-11 \\ -=\times, & 0\times 00 \end{array}\right)$ " (Man. 112, 151–52; cp. ibid., 153, 165; 3.262).

(8) "Existence cannot be attributed to an element, for if it did not *exist*, one could not even name it" (§50; cp. Man. 112, 185).

(c) See §508; Z 5–6; cp. §511, pp. 195cd, 206b, 213f; *PG* 176c; Man. 108, 246. In Man. 228 this paragraph occurs after §659 and before §689. For veiled nonsense of the sort this obvious nonsense is aimed at, see *PB* 55f–56; GI 37. Geach, in lecture notes, cites the Humpty Dumpty passage in *Alice* as "a very good specimen of this reducing of concealed nonsense to patent nonsense. 'The question is,' said Alice, 'whether you *can* mean all that by one word.' 'The question is,' said Humpty Dumpty, 'who is to be master, that's all.' " A logical impossibility explains Alice's query, as W.'s parallel one.

the expression "to imagine": on this contrast between meaning and imagining, its important implications and its explanation, see GI 43.

§38(a) The move in this number, from the preceding discussion of "the name of a colour, the name of a material, a numeral", and so on (§28), to discussion of *this*, corresponds to a development in Russell's thought (Hallett, *Definition*, 11–12). Having so defined a name that it was meaningless without a referent, he decided that the word *this*, since regularly used in the presence of a referent and void of all descriptive content, was not only a name (*Logic*, 167–68, 222; *Inquiry*, 41), but the closest thing to a genuine name to be found in ordinary language: "The only words one does use as names in the logical sense are words like 'this' or 'that'. One can use 'this' as a name to stand for a particular with which one is acquainted at the moment" (*Logic*, 201); "we may even go so far as to say that, in all such knowledge as can be expressed in words—with the exception of 'this' and 'that' and a few other words of which the meaning varies on different occasions—no names, in the strict sense, occur, but what seem like names are really descriptions" (*Introduction*, 178). (On the reasons for this final clause, see §39.) Though W. once shared Russell's conception of names and drew similar consequences from it, I have found no clear evidence that he agreed with Russell's conclusion concerning the word *this* (cp. *NB* 61a; Man. 112, 193; *PB* 118b). For a more inclusive denial than the present one, see *BB* 80–81; *EPB* 121; §410.

(b) a tendency to sublime . . . : the context suggests both the tendency to seek or suppose "something purely logical—something independent of the history of a living thing" (Man. 108, 217; see III, 4; §94; Man. 228, §503, quoted for §94), and the tendency to regard this something as an ideal not fully attained in actual language (see III, 4; §§81, 120, 426).

very different things: see §§28, 53a; *EPB* 122; *BB* 82ab; *PB* 118b; *NB* 59j. Contrast Russell, e.g.: "A name can just name a particular, or, if it does not, it is not a name at all, it is a noise. It cannot be a name without having just that one particular relation of naming a certain thing" (*Logic*, 187). So note the italics in the German.

is not among them: "What can be compared with a name is not the word 'this' but, if you like, the symbol consisting of this word, the gesture and the sample" (*BB* 109). See §45; cp. *PP* 260b.

(c) See *BB* 109a, and §45, where another important difference is indicated. See §9b; *EPB* 121; *BB* 80d; *PP* 260b; Man. 229, §707.

(d) See II, 5; cp. *BB* 173, quoted for §35c.

occult process: see GI 19; §36.

by staring . . . and repeating: cp. §§295c, 398b, 412–14; *BB* 66a, 150b; Malcolm, *Memoir*, 90. "When these things cause us philosophical difficulties, we as it were make the experiment of 'naming a color', to see what happens when we do so. We perhaps stare fixedly at some definite object in front of us and keep repeating the name of the color, with the same tone and gesture; we try to read the name off, as it were, from the thing's color. And it is no wonder that we are then inclined to say that something quite definite occurs when we name a color" (*EPB* 233; see the commentary on §413).

on holiday: either in the philosopher's own statements (GI 14; §520) or in his examination of language outside any particular language-game (above; §§47, 96; Man. 219, 24), often both together (e.g. §116; *BB* 56b; *Kreis*, 48b; Malcolm, *Memoir*, 90). Listen, for instance, to W. (in a transitional manuscript) puzzling about the possibility of a "primary language" (X, 8): "Suppose that the world consisted of a single, unchanging visual field. Wouldn't it then be possible to describe it?" But who would do the talking, to whom, with what words, for what purpose? "We feel as though we could give an experience a name without at the same time committing ourselves about its use, and in fact without any intention to use it at all" (*BB* 159; see §380). See §132b; Man. 213, 427–28; Cook, "Solipsism", 54–63; Hallett, "Bottle", 101; cp. *PB* 83d; Mauthner, *Beiträge,* I, 40.

some remarkable act of mind: see II, 7; NL 288b, 290j; cp. *NB* 53d.

address the object as "this": see *BB* 175g; cp. II, 5; *NB* 61a.

III. Names and Their Meanings (§§39–64)

GENERAL COMMENTARY

(1)   Wittgenstein's interest in meaning is well known, and his recommendation to determine an expression's meaning by observing its use. Less attention has been given to his other standard proposal, to consider how the expression is learned or explained. "I used at one time to say," he remarked at the Moral Science Club, "that, in order to get clear how a certain sentence is used, it was a good idea to ask oneself the question: 'How would one try to verify such an assertion?' But that's just one way among others of getting clear about the use of a word or sentence. For example, another question which it is often very useful to ask oneself is: 'How is this word learned?' 'How would one set about teaching a child to use this word?' " (Gasking and Jackson, "Wittgenstein", 54; see §77b; *BB* 11a; *LC* 1–2). This approach, amply illustrated in the previous two sections, is more problematic than the first. For the way an expression is imparted or learned often differs notably from the way it is then used. To grasp accurately the connection between Section Two, on learning names, and Section Three, on using them, it is necessary to reflect on the continuity and discontinuity between learning and use, in the paradigm case of names.

(2)   The history of an expression, the causal antecedents of its present use, form no part of the language-game in which it now occurs (*PG* 80c, 88a, 166c), and need not resemble it. Imagine, for instance, that color words are taught by means of a chart which the learner first consults, then merely calls to mind, then forgets entirely, though he continues to speak as before. The chart has disappeared from the game (*PG* 85–86; §54). Yet the best way to get a synoptic view of the game

now played is to look at the chart used to learn it. Again, the ostensive definition of a name requires the presence of a bearer, but later use does not. So to understand why the name is still said to 'refer' to such-and-such, though no such thing may exist, consult (for instance) the ostensive definition; and to understand why the meaning of the name cannot be identified with the bearer, consider this difference between definition and use. Other differences might be noted, for instance the use of pointing in teaching a name and the absence of pointing in using the name (§§9, 38c, 45); but the chief disparity is the need of a referent to point to at the defining stage, and the possible absence or nonexistence of a referent thereafter (§§40, 43–45).

(3)   Though the one query "How did we learn the meaning of this word?" may lead to information either about the concept *meaning* (cp. §560) or about the word in question (§77), the conceptual issue and the factual must be kept distinct. Similarly, with regard to the resultant language-game we must distinguish, for example, between: "(a) the doctrine of the simplicity of the proper name, and of its contributing to the meaning of the sentence precisely by standing for its bearer; and (b) the idea that the meaning of a name just *is* its bearer, or the meaning of a simple sign like 'red' just *is* the quality with which we have immediate acquaintance" (Anscombe, *Introduction*, 44–45). That is, we must distinguish the factual question (how such names are used) from the conceptual question (what meaning is, how the word *meaning* is used). By the time he wrote the *Investigations*, Wittgenstein had sorted out these issues; but earlier, as Miss Anscombe notes, "these elements were inextricably conflated into one theory."

(4)   The very label *logical atomism* proclaims the centrality of names. The logical atoms of Russell and young Wittgenstein were simple objects corresponding to proper names; they were the names' 'meanings'. To discern the origin of this doctrine, one must go back to Russell's famous Theory of Descriptions, where the same notion of proper names was already operative, but the meanings were not yet atomic. Russell's conception of names as mere pointers, requiring a referent if they were to point at all, gave rise to this principle: "Whenever the grammatical subject of a proposition can be supposed not to exist without rendering the proposition meaningless, it is plain that the grammatical subject is not a proper name, *i.e.* not a name directly representing some object" (*Principia*, I, 66). Since definite descriptions such as "the author of Waverley" or "the present king of France" do not satisfy this requirement, they must be sharply distinguished from proper names such as *Socrates* or *Scott* (ibid.). Later Russell decided that the same condition eliminated all ordinary 'proper names' as well. " 'Romulus',," for instance, "is not really a name but a sort of truncated description. It

stands for a person who did such-and-such things, who killed Remus, and founded Rome, and so on" (*Logic*, 243). This discovery did not greatly discomfit Russell, or suggest to him that his conception of names was mistaken. Ordinary language was at fault. Undoubtedly suitable objects do exist, to which we might refer without giving any description. However, "the whole question of what particulars you actually find in the real world is a purely empirical one which does not interest the logician as such. The logician as such never gives instances, because it is one of the tests of a logical proposition that you need not know anything whatsoever about the real world in order to understand it" (ibid., 199). Thus Russell could simply declare *a priori:* "A name, in the narrow logical sense of a word whose meaning is a particular, can only be applied to a particular with which the speaker is acquainted, because you cannot name anything you are not acquainted with" (ibid., 201)—as you cannot point to anything that is not there before you. Accordingly, the meanings of genuine names would be "such things as little patches of colour or sounds, momentary things" (ibid., 179).

(5)   The author of the *Tractatus* stressed acquaintance less than did Russell (but see X, 6–7), simplicity more. An object's absolute, logical simplicity would guarantee its existence and thereby its name's reference (GI 35) and would distinguish the name from a proposition; for with complexity and composition there enters the possibility of truth and falsehood, and that dichotomy characterizes propositions. Thus there could be no genuine name, as Russell supposed, for such a thing as a patch of color or a sound; these are too complex, having multiple traits of time, place, hue, pitch, timbre, volume, and so on. The sign for such a bundle designates something which might not be: it is conceivable, for instance, that some other hue might occupy this spot at this moment. As for the spot alone or the color alone, were they really simple objects of the kind Wittgenstein stipulated, their union would yield an elementary state of affairs, statable in an atomic proposition. But atomic propositions were supposed to be logically independent of one another, whereas "the statement that a point in the visual field has two different colours at the same time is a contradiction" (6.3751). And this difficulty is typical. Wittgenstein's consequent failure to produce a single elementary proposition, formed from appropriate names, was one of the things which made him suspect, eventually (cp. Malcolm, *Memoir*, 86), that all was not well with logical atomism, particularly its notion of names (*PP* 296).

(6)   As has already been explained (GI 34–42), more was at stake than an odd new form of Platonism, postulating simples as meanings whereas Plato had postulated essences. Without such names for such objects, the whole picture theory crumbled, and with it the hoped-for

solution to the great problem of correspondence between language, thought, and world. Indestructible objects had assured reference even for false propositions and for unsatisfied wishes, hopes, expectations, and the like. Consequently, to deny the simple, indestructible meanings was to reopen the whole issue of correspondence and to make it seem doubtful whether any form of representationalism could succeed.

(7) Section Three suggests a radically new line of solution: If you would find the connection between proposition and verifying fact, look to the words in the proposition and not to any 'picture' in the mind (§429); and if you would discover the connection between the individual words and things, look to the use of the words or the way they are learned (§43), not to projective acts of the mind. The difficulties which doom any correspondence theory that attempts to make the correspondence hold at the very instant of speech disappear the moment correspondence is sought in language as a whole. A word, and therefore the statement in which it occurs, may lack a reference, but any word has a use in the language, with which the present use may be compared, for truth as for meaning (§241). Such are the positive implications of Wittgenstein's new views about the meanings of names (III, 2). They are spelled out more fully in Section XV with respect to propositions. The close connection between that section and this appears most perspicuously in the parallel between §43 and §429, and in the observations of §51.

(8) The structure of Wittgenstein's argument in Section Three, and its relation to the next two sections, are summarized succinctly in *EPB* 158, where, after a passage which corresponds to §39, Wittgenstein says: "This reasoning rests on various errors: a) the idea that a word must 'correspond to' an object in order to have meaning, the confusion of the meaning with the bearer of a name, b) a false concept of the philosophical or logical analysis of a statement, as though it were similar to physical or chemical analysis, c) a false conception of 'logical exactness', ignorance of the notion of 'family'." In the present section, immediately after §39, Wittgenstein treats the two points in (a), then passes to (b), and finally, in Sections Four and Five, to (c). Thus *EPB* indicates the overall organization of §§39–88, with §39 the focal starting point.

(9) To show that names can get along without bearers Wittgenstein envisages a series of possibilities, ranging from a hypothetical language-game which requires the presence of a bearer (§41) to another which requires no bearer, past or present (§42). Our actual use of names is intermediate, being characterized by connection with a referent, for instance at the moment of learning (§43), but also by the possible lack of any referent at the moment of use. Since even then the name has

meaning, the referent is not its meaning (§40). To say that a word has meaning is to say merely that it has a use in the language (§43).

(10)   As a matter of fact we do not generally say that proper names, as such, have meaning or *Bedeutung*. Wittgenstein's terminology, like Russell's, was deviant. But this does not invalidate his argument or save logical atomism. Replace the principle "Every name must have a meaning" with "Every sign must point to *something* if it is going to point at all," and the tautologous nature of the claim becomes still more evident. Such a statement does not reveal the basis of all language (4.0312) or require an immutable substance of the universe (2.021–2.023).

(11)   Atomists were, of course, well aware that ordinary referents like Mr. N. are perishable; that is why the *Tractatus* insisted on the need for simple, therefore indestructible, objects if any picturing, whether graphic, linguistic, or mental, was to be possible (2.02–2.0271). Accordingly, the later Wittgenstein, after criticizing the atomist theory at the level on which it started in Russell's *Principia* (III, 4), turns next to the refined version, which substituted mysterious simples for unreliable people and chairs (III, 5). He points out first that the sense of the word *simple* was left so vague as to render the theory meaningless (§47). Furthermore, no matter how simple an object is and no matter where it is located, it may perish (§§50–59). To state or deny its existence, therefore, is neither a contradiction nor a senseless tautology (§§50, 58).

(12)   Even when the object referred to (for instance a broom) does have parts and the parts are plainly included in the reference (the person who asks for the broom wants both brush and handle), atomic analysis is mistaken. For the presupposition of such analysis was ultimate exactness—the inclusion of just these atomic objects and relations, the exclusion of those—which only the projective activity of the mind could achieve (GI 37). In the *Investigations* Wittgenstein argues first that no such thinking takes place (§§60, 63), then, in Sections IV and V, that the supposition of precision, which required pinpoint thinking, is illusory. As for the words' use in the language, it may (§61) or may not (§64) justify the claim that a more detailed version is equivalent to the original proposition. Talk about sameness of meaning, like talk about simplicity, has no clear, univocal sense (§62) which might serve as a guide in analysis.

(13)   The details of Wittgenstein's argument deserve close attention, for from them emerges something quite impressive. In logical atomism, the reaction to Hegelians' "Truth is the whole" swung to its farthest, most opposed extreme. Neither the materialistic reaction of a Marx, nor the pragmatic reaction of a Dewey, nor even the existentialist revolt of a Kierkegaard took a form so paradigmatically non-Hegelian as the

atomist doctrine of names whose meanings were logical atoms, linked in elementary propositions whose truth was completely independent of the truth of all others (4.211). Now the *Investigations,* rejecting all such meanings and names and therefore all such propositions, swings far in the opposite direction. Yet the result is dialectical: Here meaning, not truth, is the whole. To know a word's meaning is to know its use in the language as a whole (§43); to understand a single sentence in which it occurs is to understand a language (§199c). "Only in the stream of thought and life do words have meaning" (Z 173).

DETAILED COMMENTARY

§39 See III, 8; §55; cp. *BB* 31; *PB* 79e; Man. 109, 164.

Logical atomists really did reason this way (GI 35; III, 4–5). Even in 1940, Russell said: "In the case of a true proper name, the name is meaningless unless it names something, and if it names something, that something must occur" (*Inquiry,* 32). One might suggest the saving qualification: "occur now or in the past, not necessarily at the moment the word is spoken". But Russell and W. frequently failed to make this qualification, and it is often implicitly ruled out (e.g. in 2.0271). For Russell's thought, see his *Introduction,* 178–79; *Logic,* 189, 200–201. For W.'s similar thinking, see *NB* 48f, 52mno, 116f; 2.0211–2.0212, 3.24. Waismann's *Thesen* reveal their influence (*Kreis,* 253).

That is just the reason: to be what is ordinarily called a name is to be no genuine name (III, 4).

"Excalibur": in German, *Nothung,* the mystic sword, whose unusual history in Wagner's *Ring des Nibelungen* probably suggested this illustration. Broken on Wotan's spear, it was later reduced to filings by Siegfried, then forged anew, without loss of identity (see "Siegfried", Act 1, Scene 3).

corresponding: in §§51 and 53a W. discusses the meaning of this expression.

the real names: see §105b for the kind of problems this view generates.

§40 See §120f; *PG* 63g–64a (contrast with *PG* 311e); *PP* 260; Man. 112, 152, 184; Man. 111, 115; Man. 109, 140; cp. Man. 109, 32. The number deals with the first set of errors which, according to *EPB* 158, underlie the reasoning in §39 (see III, 8). Such thinking was common to Russell (III, 4) and to young W. (III, 5), e.g.: "The possibility of propositions is based on the principle that objects have signs as their representatives" (4.0312); "a name means an object. The object is its meaning" (3.203).

that a word . . . : the German permits "that the word", and what follows requires it. Otherwise the third sentence ("That is to confound

. . .") makes an unexplained leap from words in general to just names, and to proper names at that.

That is to confound . . . : it may be suggested that this "is not a sin the *Tractatus* committed, since the reference (*Bedeutung*) *is* the bearer" (Baker and Hacker, Notice, 280). Were the term *Bedeutung* reserved there for the reference, or were meaning and reference clearly distinguished (e.g. in 3.263), the defense might succeed, but as it is the terminology of the *Tractatus* reflects that of Russell (X, 4–6), and his readiness to assert, for example, that "in order to understand a name for a particular, the only thing necessary is to be acquainted with that particular" (II, 4). See *PG* 56.

§41 See *Z* 715; *PG* 143d; cp. *PB* 342a. In successive hypotheses—(1) broken tool and meaningless name (because the *use* has also perished); (2) whole tool yet meaningless name; (3) broken tool yet meaningful name—W. seeks to sever the meaning-object equivalence. For the larger picture, see III, 9.

one *might* say: see *Z* 715; cp. §§499, 556.

§42 See Man. 112, 184–85; cp. Frege, *Writings*, 104b. On the place of this number, too, see III, 9. Its general target: "that one particular relation of naming" (Russell, *Logic*, 187, quoted for §38b). Its particular point: The thesis of §40 is not rendered acceptable by this modification: "A name has no meaning if nothing corresponds to it *at some time.*" Think of names like *Hercules,* and the temptation to say that zero is not really a number (*BB* 83).

sort of joke: cp. *OC* 463: "This is certainly true, that the information 'That is a tree,' when no one could doubt it, might be a kind of joke and as such have meaning. A joke of this kind was in fact made once by Renan."

§43 For the relation between this and the preceding numbers, see III, 9.

(a) See *PG* 87b; *PP* 258; *Kreis,* 20; Man. 164, 126; Hallett, *Definition* and "Did Wittgenstein". Cp. *EPB* 137; *BB* 94a; *Kreis,* 169, 246b; Man. 112, 146–47; James, *Pragmatism,* 273: "Universal conceptions, as things to take account of, may be as real for pragmatism as particular sensations are. They have, indeed, no meaning and no reality if they have no use. But if they have any use they have that amount of meaning." Concerning anticipations in the *Tractatus* (e.g. 3.326, 3.328), see Hallett, *Definition,* 126–27.

large **class:** this is willfully indefinite. Anything precise—even supposing it were possible (GI 70) and useful (GI 29)—would have required pages. It is clear, though, that the class is not of words, but of occasions on which we employ the word *Bedeutung* (cp. p. 216b; *PG* 41c). A frequent and important error is to suppose that W. made an exception for certain words; from the start of the *Investigations* (§1) the meaning of even the most obviously referring or object-related word is the word's use, not the object it refers to (see commentary on §2a; *PP* 260b; Hallett, *Definition*, 97–98). It is also clear that the contexts W. has in mind are the ones of prime philosophical interest, for instance those in which we speak of learning the meaning of a word (*RFM* 7), explaining it (§§30, 247; *BB* 1; *PG* 59–60), understanding it (§§138ff, 191–97), forgetting it (p. 176e), or in which we discuss whether a word has a meaning (p. 147n; *BB* 69) or the same or different meanings (*BB* 79a; Man. 229, §723).

not for all: W. recognized one other important use of the term *meaning* (*Bedeutung*) in the discussion of individual words; see GI 66; XXX-VII, 15; pp. 215–16. We speak too of a word's meaning in a given statement, or in a given author.

we employ: that is, the general population does, not just W. or a narrow circle of philosophers. W. said earlier: "Indeed it is 'the meaning of meaning' that we are looking for, namely the grammar of the word 'meaning'" (Man. 110, 157). It is clear from e.g. GI 9–24 why he attached importance to the actual, ordinary employment of a term (§116).

can be: in *BB* 1 and *PG* 59–60, 68, W. suggests the following justification for the identification: The meaning of a word is whatever we learn or explain when we learn or explain the word's meaning; but what we then learn or explain is not an object, say, but the word's use in the language. That is how we use the expressions *meaning, explain the meaning, learn the meaning,* and so on.

defined: though this translation of *erklären* is faithful to W.'s terminology, both English and German (see e.g. *PG* 60d; *BB* 1f, 82a; cp. §79a with §82), objections have been raised against it. Two deserve attention: (a) "The word *definition,*" it has been argued, "should be reserved for formulae indicating identity of sense and not merely of reference." *De facto* the word *definition* is not used in this restricted way, either within or without the philosophical community (think of *ostensive definition*). Furthermore, there are indications that for W. the *definiens* expression (*use in the language*) did have roughly the same sense as the *definiendum,* in this "large class of cases" (see Hallett, "Did Wittgenstein", 297). (b) An equally common but more important misconception is the idea that W. was not here suggesting how the word *meaning* or *Bedeutung* is actually used, but was directing our attention to what he considered important. His explanation (if such it could still be called) would then resemble §15 or §421, or his famous injunction, "Don't ask for the meaning, ask for the use." In view of the actual wording of §43a; of the reasoning behind W.'s statement (see above); of his explicitly stated interest in how the word *meaning* and other key terms are actually used (see above); of the whole program of the *Investigations* and W.'s enduring conception of philosophy (GI 8–24, 28), this interpretation seems clearly untenable (see Hallett, "Did Wittgenstein"). As for the value of a definition as opposed to the mere injunction to look at the use: "If someone rightly believes that the important thing about a word is its meaning, yet has confused or erroneous notions about meaning, he can be brought to follow the advice to look for the use only by being shown that meaning is use" (Hallett, *Definition*, 161).

of a word: not of a sentence, for in the *Investigations*, as in the *Tractatus* (cp. *Kreis*, 237b), W. never speaks of a sentence's *Bedeutung*, but only of its *Sinn;* and sentences are not repeated the way words are, so could less readily be said to have uses "in the language" (cp. commentary on §20b). For a similar reason one would hesitate to say that proper names, in general, have uses in the language. This suggests why they are not generally said to have meaning, so reveals the error in this argument: If W.'s account were correct, we would say that proper names have "meaning"; but we do not say that; therefore his account is wrong. The first premise is false.

is its: not merely "is determined by", which even the *Tractatus* recognized to some extent. Cp. *PP* 257–258c. For other indications of the same identification, many quite explicit, see: §§30a, 120f, 138, 197, 247, 454a, 508a, 532a, 557, pp. 147n, 175a, 176e; *OC* 61; *RFM* 7ab, 133e, 179h; *EPB* 149; *BB* 1, 69b, 73c, 79a, 103; *PG* 59–60, 68; Man. 112, 198; Ambrose, "Metamorphoses", 69.

use: the vagueness of this term is not a defect but a virtue (GI 70), for the *definiendum* is equally vague (*BB* 19c; *Z* 154). Thus W. would not identify a word's meaning simply with its effects or its purpose (*PG* 69a) nor, on the other hand, with the rules of its use (§§562–64; *BB* 65b; *PP* 258c; Hallett, *Definition*, 78–80), though he came close (p. 147n; *OC* 65; *PB* 178e; cp. *Kreis*, 150). Concerning this rule-result dichotomy, see §§492–93, 555–56, and Hallett, *Definition*, 102–15. The term *use* is broad and unqualified, so should not be narrowed to cover just syntactic features (*PG* 65bc; *BB* 108d; §664) or just external behavior (*BB* 103: "Whether a word of the language of our tribe is rightly translated into a word of the English language depends upon the role this word plays in the whole life of the tribe; the occasions on which it is used, the expressions of emotion by which it is generally accompanied, the ideas which it generally awakens or which prompt its saying, etc., etc."). See I, 7–8.

in the language: contrast this with the doctrine of Frege (e.g. *Foundations*, 71: "Only in a proposition have the words really a meaning") and the *Tractatus* (3.314: "An expression has meaning only in a proposition"). "The expression 'in the language' means no more than it says.

We should not read into these words what is probably true in most cases and what Wittgenstein once extended to all cases: the dependence of the word on the rest of the verbal system" (Hallett, *Definition*, 83). See, for instance, §2, where words are used singly and only singly. For the breadth of the term *language*, see §23. Since misgivings on this score run parallel for *meaning* and for *language*, they constitute no objection to the equivalence here stated between the meaning of a word and its use in the language. Reference to "the language", rather than to "speech", at least leaves out personal or occasional idiosyncracies and errors, and many customary activities conducted in language, but does not exclude asking, asserting, describing, and the like, which we might hesitate to include in the meaning of a word. On this difficulty, see Hallett, *Definition*, 134–35.

(b) Here it is necessary to keep in mind W.'s deviant use of *Bedeutung* (III, 10) for proper names as well as for words in the dictionary; otherwise his suggestion will seem unrealistic. On the significance of this remark, and the parallel with §429, see III, 7. The observation may also serve to suggest one origin of the idea that the meaning is an object, and to suggest a kernel of truth it contains. Cp. Man. 229, §1277.

§44   We said: in §39.

But we can imagine . . . : the implicit point is that of §3a.

§45   See III, 2, and references there; Man. 220, 31–32; cp. *PG* 202–3, where W. notes that for "N" there are criteria of identity, whereas we need not bother about such criteria when we point to a thing and say "this". The difference he indicates here in §45 may seem trivial, but it too is connected with the fact that in terms of the principal, informative function of language proper names lie at the opposite extreme from *this*; whereas proper names are typically more informative than descriptive expressions, *this* is less informative. *PG* 88–89 open broad vistas behind these apparently banal remarks on pointing.

§46(a) The answer in (*b*), giving general background rather than an argument, reveals the sense of the question here in (*a*).

(b) Number 39 answers a similar question in more linear fashion and emphasizes the necessity of reference, whereas the present answer stresses the difference between names and other expressions. For W.'s similar reasoning, see e.g. *PB* 117c and 119: "In a certain sense an object cannot be described. That is, the description should not ascribe to the object any property whose absence would negate the existence of the object itself. That is, the description may not express what would be essential for the existence of the object." This eliminates both the statement that the object exists and the ascription of the simple content which constitutes the object's whole nature. Such existential and essential assertions are ruled out both by Occam's razor (the predicate would be redundant) and by the *Tractatus* principle that "what expresses *itself* in language [for instance the existence of named objects], *we* cannot express by means of language" (4.121). See 4.122–4.124; Hallett, *Definition*, 19–21.

Shortly after he wrote *PB* 119, W. commented: " 'In a certain sense an object cannot be described' (so too Plato: 'it cannot be explained, but only named'). Here 'object' means 'reference of a word which cannot be further defined', and 'description' or 'explanation' means in fact: definition. For of course it is not denied that the object can be 'externally described', that properties can be ascribed to it and so on.

"Thus when we make a declaration like that above we are thinking of a calculus with indefinable—or, more accurately, undefined—signs, the names, and we are saying that no account can be given of them.

" 'What a word means, no sentence can say' " (*PG* 208).

in the Theaetetus: 201–2.

(c) See *EPB* 121 (quoted for §7a); *BB* 81a; Malcolm, *Memoir*, 86.

Russell spoke of simple objects sometimes as 'individuals', sometimes as 'particulars': "We might state our definition compendiously as follows: An 'individual' is anything that can be the subject of an atomic proposition" (*Principia*, I, xix). "The atoms that I wish to arrive at as the sort of last residue in analysis are logical atoms and not physical atoms. Some of them will be what I call 'particulars'—such things as little patches of colour or sounds, momentary things—and some of them will be predicates or relations and so on" (*Logic*, 179). "I confess it seems obvious to me (as it did to Leibniz) that what is complex must be composed of simples, though the number of constituents may be infinite. It is also obvious that the logical uses of the old notion of substance (i.e. those uses which do not imply temporal duration) can only be applied, if at all, to simples; objects of other types do not have that kind of being which one associates with substances. The essence of a substance, from the symbolic point of view, is that it can only be named—in old-fashioned language, it never occurs in a proposition except as the subject or as one of the terms of a relation" (ibid., 337). See also Russell's *Principles*, 43–44; *Logic*, 199, 270, 274b; *Matter*, 277; *Mind*, 193.

For W.'s similar early views see *NB* 51ij; 3.221 ("Objects can only be *named*. Signs are their representatives. I can only speak *about* them: I cannot *put them into words*. Propositions can only say *how* things are, not *what* they are"). W., however, would not accept "little patches of colour or sounds" as genuine logical simples (III, 5).

For Waismann's derivative expression of similar views, see *Kreis*, 236 ("What red is or the nature of sweetness cannot be said. Whatever can be described is always already complex") and 250–52. Cp. Frege, *Writings,* 42–43 ("What is simple cannot be decomposed, and what is logically simple cannot have a proper definition").

§47 See *Z* 338; Man. 220, 86–87; Man. 105, 7, 9; Bogen, *Philosophy,* 64–65. Cp. Frege, *Foundations,* 30b; Russell, *Logic,* 190, 197a. W.'s remarks in this number are a valid criticism of logical atomism; he and Russell did in fact leave the sense of *simple* and *composite* undecided, with the result that W. could never find a simple which satisfied him. After much wrestling with the question, he remarked in the *Notebooks:* "Our difficulty was that we kept on speaking of simple objects and were unable to mention a single one" (*NB* 68). See *NB* 45h–n, 47e, 49m–50, 51b, 59l–60i, 62, 69. W.'s target appears most clearly in *NB* 60d, quoted for §101.

(a) **not composite:** on the requirement of contrast for a statement to be meaningful, see the commentary on §251, and Hallett, "Contrast", especially p. 684 (for examples similar to the present one, e.g. §§13, 174a, 227; *LC* 69).

  absolutely: without any clarification from context (*d*) or explanations (*c*). See the comments on §13. Cp. *Kreis,* 234 (Waismann's *Thesen*): "Every state of affairs is complex. It can be analysed in only *one* way."

(b) **my visual image:** behind this shift from object to image, maintained for the rest of the number, lies W.'s former preoccupation with a "phenomenological language" (X, 8). See also *NB* 3: "Let's take a question quite like that one, which however is simpler and more fundamental, namely the following: Is a point in our visual field a *simple object,* a *thing*? Up to now I have always regarded such questions as the real philosophical ones: and so for sure they are in some sense—but once more what evidence could settle a question of this sort at all? Is there not a mistake in formulation here, for it looks as if *nothing at all* were self-evident to me on this question; it looks as if I could say definitively that these questions could never be settled at all." They can't (*a, f*)—unless the sense is sharpened (*c*), and then they are no longer philosophical (*c*).

(c) **"there are all sorts of things":** see *BB* 168c.

  a clear use: on the equivalence of sense and use, see §20b.

  grammatical: see the commentary on §29a.

  "called": italicized in the German.

(d) **isn't a chessboard . . . :** see §48a.

  could we not also . . . : in *PG* 58 W. was ready to speak "of *combinations of colors with shapes* (say of the colors red and blue with the shapes square and circle), just as we speak of combinations of different shapes or bodies", but in *PB* 302 and *PG* 200 he wrote: "To say that a red circle is *composed* of redness and circularity, or is a complex with these component parts, is a misuse of these words and misleading. (Frege knew this and told me so.)"

like what a boy once did: the point of the comparison is not that the verbs, e.g. *sleep*, were not being used; for even if they had been considered in concrete applications, an answer would have been equally impossible until the questioner made clear what language-game *he* was playing.

(e) See *BB* 168c; Man. 229, §1271.

opposite direction: cp. §48a. Compare this with the positive and negative content of color predications, noted by W. (e.g. 6.3751; *LF* 34–35).

(f) See the citations for (*a*).

philosophical: see §38d; *OC* 467; *Z* 455 ("The philosopher is not a citizen of any community of ideas. That is what makes him into a philosopher"); *NB* 3, quoted for (*b*).

the correct answer is: "In philosophy it is always good to put a *question* instead of an answer to a question. For an answer to the philosophical question may easily be unfair; disposing of it by means of another question is not" (*RFM* 68).

rejection: any attempt at greater precision, or even the realization that it was needed, would have destroyed the mentality that gave rise to the question; with the 'essence' gone, young W. would have lost interest in this "further logical analysis" (*EPB* 121).

§48   Contrast the variety of possibilities suggested here with 3.25 ("A proposition has one and only one complete analysis"); and with Moore, *Commonplace,* 51b, 207 ("A prop. can only have one set of *ultimate* constituents, but it can have many different sets of *constituents*"). For the origins of this number, see Man. 105, 7 (distant) and 43 (nearer); and *PB* 252–53. Cp. Man. 106, 47, 49.

(a) the method of §2: W.'s reference may be taken broadly (as in most of my allusions elsewhere to "the method of §2") or narrowly. Remarks like the following, indicating traits shared by many treatments besides §2 and §48, open the larger perspective. "When I correct a philosophical error & say that people have always conceived the matter thus but it isn't so, I always have to indicate an analogy which they followed but didn't recognize as an analogy" (Man. 110, 193; cp. GI 11; §104). "In philosophy we are deceived by an illusion. But the illusion too is something & I must get it clearly in view before I can say that it is only an illusion" (Man. 110, 239; see §51b, p. 181a; Man. 168, 3; Man. 108, 193). "We can reach no solution of the philosophical difficulty until we draw the blood, so to speak, from the sentences which hold us captive, by attending to the source of our mode of representation; so to whatever served as a model for it" (Man. 116, 220; see Man. 220, 83–84; cp.

§115). Some examples in the *Investigations:* attention, the supposedly simple essence of defining (§§33–34); *this*, the only genuine name (§§38, 45); broom and chair, typical 'composite' objects (§§59–63); a rule, like an arrow or a signpost (§§85–86); a cube and its projection, clear cases of 'fitting' (§§138–41); understanding a series, a paradigm of 'intuition' (§§143–55, 179–92); reading, model of guidance (§§156–78); machinery, model of logical precontainment (§§193–94); pain, most "private" of sensations (Section X; see commentary on §244); imagining, paradigm of thought (Section XII; see *Z* 94) and of privacy (§§398–402); the typical feeling of familiarity (§§594–96); arm movements, standard actions (§§612–27; see XXIV, 4, 6, 8); pointing and attending, models of meaning (§§669–74); "if-feelings", paradigm Jamesian meanings (Section XXXII; cf. XXXII, 1); finger feelings, typical kinesthetic evidence (p. 185; see *BB* 51; XXXIV, 2); aspect-seeing, privileged case of intentional presence (Section XXXVII; see XXXVII, 2–9); mathematics, paradigm of absolute correctness and objectivity (pp. 225–27; see XXXVIII, 4). Numbers 258 (on private language) and 293 (on private meanings) approximate still more closely to §2 and §48; in these four cases W. invents a game for his purposes, rather than imagining an instance or variation of an existing game. These many examples indicate the importance of the method in the *Investigations.*

The present number is a paradigm illustration. W. had envisaged elementary propositions as requiring the use of numbers in a coordinate system. "Imagine a system of rectangular axes, as it were, cross wires, drawn in our field of vision and an arbitrary scale fixed. It is clear that we then can describe the shape and position of every patch of colour in our visual field" (LF 33; see *Kreis,* 74–76, 261a; Man. 105, 74). "However, in this notation how could it be shown that a patch cannot have two colors at the same time" (Man. 105, 70; see *Kreis,* 79), as proper representation requires (Man. 105, 88)? "Our symbolism, which allows us to form the sign of the logical product of 'RPT' and 'BPT' gives here no correct picture of reality" (LF 36). To a certain extent W. now answers that difficulty, by proposing "a system of description which cannot assign two different coordinate-values to reality" (*Kreis,* 76; see 241a); the sign for that logical product can no longer be formed. Thus the language-game of §48 is not only an elegant simplification of the earlier model, but an improvement on it. And the *Tractatus* would have approved the elimination of numbers. An elementary proposition, it declared, consists solely of names. "It is a nexus, a concatenation, of names" (4.22). And there as here the fact that the elements of a picture are related to one another in a determinate way represents that things are related to one another in a determinate way (2.15). No relation sign is used. Thus W. did indeed do his best to "imagine a language for which the description . . . is right" (§2)—both Socrates' description and his own.

However, as the method of §2 requires, the account "is really valid" only to a certain point. Here as in §2 the description of the workings of language is applicable ("the sentence is a complex of names, to which corresponds a complex of elements"), but not the dogmas. From the description it does not follow, for instance, that the colored squares cannot be said to exist (§50), or that they cannot be described (§49); though the language-game cited makes no provision for such propositions, it does not exclude them (cp. §3). Only if this game or the like were all we ever called speech might we agree that "the essence of speech is the composition of names" (§46; cp. §3).

combinations of coloured squares: cp. *PB* 108–9: "What holds for colors is no different from what holds for notes or electrical charges. It is always a question of the description of a certain state at one point or at the same time."

squares on a surface: cp. Man. 111, 30: "One could believe that the visual field is composed of *minima visibilia,* say of clear little squares which are seen as indivisible areas. Nonsense."

what would be more natural: cp. *PB* 252b.

But under other circumstances . . . : see §47d.

or of the elements colour and shape: cp. *PB* 169e.

and another one subtracted from it: see §47e; *PB* 252a.

'composition of forces': for example, the force with which a book presses on a table might be analyzed as the sum of a greater gravitational pull towards the center of the Earth and a slight centrifugal pull in the opposite direction. "Any force exerted on a system, or by a system, can be conceived as a sum of any number of forces, namely, of any number of forces the sum of which, regarded as vector quantities with regard to the system, is equal to that original force" (Hertz, *Principles,* 473).

'division' of a line: a point *c*, beyond the line *ab*, may be regarded as dividing it into the positive segment *ac* and the negative segment *bc* (see §47e).

(b) There is an implicit correction here of *BB* 83b.

of four or of nine elements: four colors, nine squares. Compare the idea with which logical atomists toyed, of taking red or blue as objects, distinct from their location, so that three green spots would be three states of affairs involving four objects, viz. one color and three spots.

of four letters or of nine: RGWB or RRBGGGRWW.

Does it matter which: see the commentary on §6b ("I do not want") and on §79d.

§49 Concerning the preceding number and the use here made of it, the reader may feel that W. wins an easy victory over his earlier views by considering sample objects far more complex than any he would have accepted as genuine *Gegenständen*. However, logical atomists never hit on any true *Gegenständen* which he might have put to the test; concerning any objects the world provides W. might have made much the same remarks as he here makes about colored squares.

(a) **what does it mean to say . . . :** as in §46b.

This might mean . . . : in which case the doctrine loses its metaphysical appearance and becomes a matter of grammar (cp. *Z* 458); we choose not to call this move a description (for such is the implication of "this might mean"). Cp. *PG* 208, quoted for §46b.

a limiting case: of this type of game. The game described in §48 makes no provision for such a move, whose details we are therefore left to fill in as we please.

(b) **all kinds of philosophical superstition:** particularly that discussed in §§19–20. Cp. also p. 18n and commentary ("a crucial superstition").

sometimes a word: see §§19–20 and commentary (especially on §19b).

depends on the situation: cp. *PP* 261.

but it would be queer to . . . : rather: "but accordingly it would be odd here to say that the element can *only* be named" (cp. 3.221). The language-game has not yet even got under way.

For naming and describing . . . : "To be sure, rules for signs, for instance definitions, can be viewed as propositions about signs. But they *need* not be viewed as propositions. They are instruments of language. Instruments of a different kind from the propositions of language" (*PB* 143).

nothing **has so far been done:** cp. *PB* 202d; 4.461–4.462; contrast with Man. 112, 169, quoted for §16a. In the sense which makes it true, this is of course a tautology.

This was what Frege meant . . . : see *Foundations*, 71, 73; Hallett, *Definition*, 10–14; cp. 3.3, 3.314. The equivalence is more readily recognizable if we connect Frege's remark (about words) with more than just the preceding sentence (about things) and note that for four sentences W. has been talking about language in general and not just about the language-game of §48.

§50 See §58ab.

(a) **to say that we can attribute . . . :** W. introduces another doctrine of §46b, common to the *Theaetetus* and the *Tractatus*, and continues as in §49 to counteract such metaphysics by indicating its conceptual, grammatical character (Z 458).

if everything that we call . . . : cp. 2.06: "The existence and non-existence of states of affairs is reality."

(b) See *PG* 209f; Waismann, *Principles*, 278; cp. §215c; Man. 109, 243–44; Moore, *Problems*, 334a, 361b.

One would . . . like to say: cp. §§40–45, and §55a, where the tautology is not so evident.

analogous case: the parallel with the *Tractatus* doctrine is general, not specific or close. "Wittgenstein's point seems to be simply that what cannot be said of a thing cannot be said relative to a specific linguistic practice. If a game does not allow us to say that X exists or fails to exist, all that shows is that X enters into that game in such a way that we would have to play another one to talk about its existence. The point is that we could construct another game for this purpose if we wanted to" (Bogen, *Philosophy*, 88).

one can say neither . . . : without a very special setting, the assertion or denial here envisaged would be as nonsensical as saying that W. was or was not a Wittgensteinian philosopher. Cp. §216; *RFM* 15 ("A thing cannot be at the same time the measure and the thing measured"); *OC* 205 ("If the true is what is grounded, then the ground is not *true*, nor yet false").

Let us imagine . . . : cp. Russell, *Logic*, 206: "You can then define the things which are red, as all the things that have colour-likeness to this standard thing. That is practically the treatment that Berkeley and Hume recommended." For Russell's similar approach, see also *Inquiry*, 35 (quoted for §32b).

Then it will make no sense . . . : see Man. 112, 223–24; cp. §215c (if *sepia* means "having the same color as the standard sample", and *same* has the sense established by comparing distinct objects, then it is senseless to affirm or deny that the standard sample is sepia).

(c) is an instrument: on this shift of terminology from *PG* 143d, predecessor of the present passage, see §16 and commentary.

when we name it: rather than speak about it by means of a sign already defined, as in §48.

it is now a *means* of representation: whether because "used in teaching the language and . . . appealed to in certain disputed cases" (§53a; see §51a) or because "a tool in the use of the language" (§53b). Though the context suggests the former and the wording the latter, doubtless W. wished to remain noncommittal at this stage (see §51).

§51(a) W. now passes to a third point in his discussion of §48: after description and existence, now 'correspondence' (see III, 2) and the problem of falsehood (GI 34–37, 43; III, 7). Cp. 3.2: "In a proposition a thought can be expressed in such a way that elements of the propositional sign correspond to the objects of the thought."

in the *technique of using* . . . : on the reasons for W.'s emphasis here, see III, 2, 7; cp. *NB* 99: "To this correlation corresponds the correlation of name and meaning. Both are psychological."

what is the criterion . . . : see §145b ("he continues the series correctly, that is, as we do it"); cp. §54b.

comes before their minds: see §449; 3.2 (above); cp. §6b.

(b) See GI 50–52; *BB* 17–19; Man. 110, 239, quoted for §48a.

as in countless similar cases: see §645 and references there.

§52(a) As one illustration of these remarks, suggesting why they occur here, we might paraphrase thus: "If someone is inclined, like the author of the *Tractatus,* to think that at the moment one speaks and by means of something that then occurs, the words unmistakably refer to present or future objects (GI 37), he would do well to examine in detail (as in §§51, 53) what this connection might conceivably consist in. But if a person is already convinced that this idea of correspondence-in-the-moment is a mistake, he need not go to the trouble." See GI 52; §109 ("this description gets its light, that is its purpose, from the philosophical problems") and references there.

(b) See GI 39–40; §§92, 94, 340; *BB* 17–19.

§53 See Man. 112, 154–62. After the interruption in §52, W. starts to carry out the injunction of §51b, developing in greater detail the remarks of §51a.

(a) On the variety of names, see §38b.

(b) See *BB* 4bc, 85; Man. 109, 244.

We can also imagine . . . : see §86a; cp. §§1, 8; *BB* 4b, 13, 82c, 89–91, 98, 122–24.

may also use a table . . . : cp. §§449b, 459.

This table might be said . . . : see *BB* 4b.

We do not usually . . . : see *BB* 3abc.

(c) See §82; *EPB* 132, 143–44; *BB* 9od, 98cd. This paragraph provides an intermediate step from correspondence to rules.

expression of a rule: contrast *PP* 258c, and *BB* 9od: "Tables, ostensive definitions, and similar instruments I shall call rules, in accordance with ordinary usage." See §16b: "It is most natural, and causes least confusion, to reckon the samples among the instruments of the language."

very different roles: the table has various roles (§53ab) and there are different types of rules, different applications of the word *rule* (§54b), but this reference to the "roles" of rules seems somewhat odd, now that

W. no longer refers to the tables themselves as rules. Compare his talk about the "use" of concepts (§569, p. 209e).

§54 See *EPB* 139–42; *BB* 12b–13e; *PG* 85c–86b; cp. *PP* 264.

(a) As a reminder of what W. is about, see §81b ("according to definite rules"). On the parallel between language and games with respect to rules, see I, 8–9.

(b) Cp. *Z* 295; *BB* 11; *PB* 180f–181a; *Kreis*, 153–54; Frege, "Thought", 289, and *Basic Laws*, 12 ("In one sense a law asserts what is; in the other it prescribes what ought to be").

Or a rule is employed neither . . . : see §31; Man. 116, 34 (quoted for p. 185gh). Were there only this third sort of rule, suggests Man. 229, §1256, people would less readily suppose a *Vorbild* in the mind, guiding our moves.

because an observer can read . . . : W. does not here suggest, as he did in Man. 112, 160, then *PG* 86, that the player himself, "who plays without using a list of rules, who in fact has never seen one, could nevertheless give rules of his game if asked; and not because he ascertains through repeated observation what he does in this and that game situation, but because when confronted with a move he says 'In this case *one moves thus.*'"

like a natural law: see *BB* 98a.

But how does the observer . . . : as W. had said, "clearly the laws of logic cannot in their turn be subject to laws of logic" (6.123), and they are what is in question here. Thus §§241–42 are implicit in this number.

There are characteristic signs: symptoms or clues, not necessarily criteria; a criterion in this case is the natural law itself, the custom, the institution (§§145b, 199, 205). The hypothetical observer supposedly has not made a thorough survey of usage.

It would be possible: if not regularly, at least sometimes.

§55 After considering several aspects of the *Theaetetus* account (§46), W. now returns to the line of reasoning in §39, making explicit and discussing a premise implicit in that argument, namely, the indestructibility of 'simples'.

(a) Some readers, unfamiliar with W.'s dialectical style (GI 55), have taken these words as expressing his later doctrine, whereas they echo e.g. *NB* 116f; 2.0211–2.0212, 2.026–2.0271, 3.24; *Kreis*, 234, 251, 253; Russell, *Principles*, 44. Cp. *BB* 31d.

"everything destructible": I can think of no satisfactory interpretation for these words. If restricted to objects in the ordinary sense (houses, hats, and the like), the argument lacks the breadth of logical atomism, and the description (for instance, a speech act) would not need to be exempted from the destruction, as in (*b*). If the destruction is extended somewhat, but only to existing objects, actions, and events, the exemption still is not required. But if we suppose that all possible as well as actual complexes are meant, the hypothesis is no longer intelligible, nor does it correspond to the doctrine being criticized. The *Tractatus* recognized, for instance, that "a speck in the visual field, though it need not be red, must have some colour. . . . Tones must have *some* pitch, objects of the sense of touch *some* degree of hardness, and so on" (2.0131).

"otherwise the words would have no meaning": this phrasing suggests—though less clearly than the opening remark in (*b*)—that a present-tense description is envisaged. However, such a restriction is not mentioned, nor is it required by the atomist argument. Suitable referents would be equally lacking for prospective or retrospective description of the holocaust (see GI 35).

(b) See *PG* 130a. Though this paragraph has the external form typical of many dialogues between W. and his *alter ego* (GI 55), none of the remarks need be attributed to the "voice of temptation" or to the author of the *Tractatus*.

One might . . . object: true, the *Tractatus* had insisted that propositional signs are themselves facts, formed of objects in conjunction, which can therefore mirror other objects in conjunction (3.141–3.1431). But why suppose that the description is contemporary with the destruction? See above.

if it is true: from either the early or the late W. one would have expected "if it is meaningful": from the early W. because meaningful falsehoods were his problem (see §39; GI 35), and from the late W. because the early W. was his patient. The statement is accurate enough, but does not hit the nail on the head. Perhaps the appearance of tautology deterred W.

But he is destructible . . . : see §40.

is a paradigm: see §50bc.

used in connexion with: not merely in learning the language-game (§53a) but in its conduct (§53b).

§56 See Man. 110, 281; cp. §378; *Kreis,* 97.

we *bear in mind* **. . .** : a natural solution to W's earlier problem: "If I only see something black & say it is not red, how do I know that I am not talking nonsense, that is, that it can be red, that there is red?" (*PB* 75). "We can't say the meaning of the word 'red' depends on there being something red *somewhere,* even when I don't have it before me now. For if I have no evidence for the existence of such a red object, perhaps it does not in fact exist & in that case the word too has no meaning" (Man. 108, 247). However, " 'we could always call a color-impression "red" and stick to this appellation' " (NL 306). Such an impression, it seemed, might have the requisite simplicity. "There seem to be simple colors. Simple as psychological appearances" (Man. 105, 88).

the colour (for instance): Moore adduces another reason why a color might be taken as a simple object or 'individual': "We might say: 'There is a colour called "pure white"; and this one colour is in both these two different places at once—occupies the whole of both of them simultaneously.' . . . As against the objection that the view is paradoxical, it may be urged that it is merely treating space as if space were exactly analogous to *time*. We do all suppose, and it seems to be true, that one and the same thing may be at one and the same place at two different times. . . . But if a thing may be in the same place at two different times, why (it may be asked) should it not be at the same time in two different places?" (*Problems*, 341–42). See Russell, *Inquiry*, 97–100.

"And if we bear . . .": the quotation marks clearly pick out these words as the only ones which need to be attributed to an imaginary interlocutor.

"if it is always supposed to be possible . . .": see Man. 109, 52.

we do not always resort . . . : see *EPB* 130; *BB* 88d–89a; *PG* 95d; Man. 109, 300 (quoted for §604); Man. 108, 164; cp. *PB* 81b. Both rationalists like Descartes, when trying to work from immediate intuitions, and empiricists like Russell, when trying to reach beyond immediate acquaintance, do tend to take memory as an ultimate, though perhaps shaky, court of appeal. For W.'s similar tendency, see Man. 109, 300 (quoted for §604); *Kreis*, 48 (" 'I can *only* remember.' As though there were some other way and it were not rather the case that memory is the *unique* source from which we draw"); and *PB* 60 ("How do I know that the color of this paper, which I call 'white', is the same as I saw here yesterday? By recognizing it as the same; and this recognition is the only source of this knowledge"). To the objection in §56 he replied in *PB* 60: "The 'color' which I can recognize directly and the color which I determine through a chemical test are two distinct things. From the same source there comes just *one* thing." That is, if the method of verification is different, so is the sense, and we are not checking on the same thing in both cases. Thus "the question 'Have I seen this color before?' is senseless if I ask it in a primary sense, yet do not acknowledge memory as my *sole* arbiter" (Man. 109, 46). And if, as W. then held (X, 6–9), the primary sense is the basic one, alone direct and nonhypothetical, then memory really is the court of highest appeal. Cp. Ramsey, *Foundations*, 198: "It is only through memory that we can determine the degree of accuracy of memory; for if we make experiments to determine this effect, they will be useless unless we remember them."

The elimination of the primary-secondary distinction, already evident in the argumentation of §56, will be effected in Section X. On colors, see §§273–80.

§57 Cp. *BB* 31e. Again, the words in quotation marks are the only ones not expressing W.'s own thoughts.

"but red cannot . . .": on red itself as distinct from red here or there, see the quotation from Moore, above (§56). "We may recall by way of analogy the suggestion once made by Russell that genuine universals, such as must be admitted at least in the category of relation, were really identical in all their instances, and the way in which Whitehead speaks of the ingression of eternal objects into actual occasions" (Hawkins, *Cult,* 7–8). Thus Russell wrote, for instance, that " 'this is red' is not a subject-predicate proposition, but is of the form 'redness is here'; . . . 'red' is a name, not a predicate" (*Inquiry,* 97).

the colour red is torn up . . . : cp. *PG* 126.

don't clutch at the idea . . . : cp. the references for §449a, and e.g. Russell, "On Propositions", 21: "It is nevertheless the possibility of a memory-image in the child and an imagination-image in the hearer that makes the essence of the 'meaning' of the words."

suppose you cannot remember . . . : understood *ad hominem,* this might mean we can't summon the image before our minds; in the sense of *remember* indicated by p. 231, it means that regardless of what image we had before our minds, we still might not know what to call red. The eventuality dreaded by atomists would then be realized: The word *red* would lose its meaning. Language would turn out to be human.

§58 See §50.

(a) "I want to restrict . . .": the voice is that of the atomist (see §46 and commentary). " 'Romulus'," wrote Russell, "is not really a name [see III, 4]. . . . If it were really a name, the question of existence could not arise, because a name has got to name something or it is not a name, and if there is no such person as Romulus there cannot be a name for that person who is not there" (*Logic,* 243; see 241, 252). Such reasoning explains W.'s choice of "Red exists," rather than, e.g., "Healthiness exists" (Strawson, "Review", 30); if no one were healthy, the atomist would say, we could still talk about health. But simples are different. "What I formerly called 'objects', the simple, is simply what can be referred to without having to fear that it perhaps doesn't exist; that is, that for which there is neither existence nor non-existence, and that means: that of which we can speak *regardless of how things stand*" (*PB* 72; cp. Man. 108, 99).

Better: for "it should be asked what '*could*' means here" (§497; cp. §§359–60). "This proposition hides a grammatical rule" (*BB* 55c).

(b) 'in its own right': Plato's phrase (§46b).

metaphysical statement: "it obliterates the distinction between factual and conceptual" (Z 458; see *RFM* 40c; *PB* 86c; Man. 116, 256).

timeless: an allusion, no doubt, to Plato. By contrast, see e.g. Russell, *Logic*, 203–4.

(c) The first four sentences express the atomist attitude, particularly young W.'s: "Every *real* proposition *shews* something, besides what it says, about the Universe" (*NB* 107), and "what expresses *itself* in language, *we* cannot express by means of language" (4.121). We cannot, for instance, use a name both to pick out a referent and to assert that it has a referent. It cannot be both name and predicate. Thus, were we to say the words "red does not exist," we would not really succeed in contradicting ourselves (3.032); we cannot *think* illogically (3.03).

particularly where: the reference, it seems, is to red "in the mind" (§56), not to red in the sky or red lighting. For to imagine red is not to have a sample of red in the mind, to which one might attribute existence rather than to its color (cp. §§293c, 300–301, p. 196cd).

§59   For the quoted viewpoint, see e.g. Russell, *Principles*, 471b.

"only what is an *element*": see §§39, 55a.

"what remains the same": see *NB* 62ij and 2.024–2.2071 ("Objects are what is unalterable and subsistent; their configuration is what is changing and unstable").

experience does not shew us: this is truer of W.'s 'objects' than of Russell's 'individuals' (see §46c).

These are the materials . . . : a foundation of logical atomism, underlying young W.'s belief that linguistic analysis would lead to concatenations of names, was Russell's early viewpoint: "In every case of analysis, there is a whole consisting of parts with relations; it is only the nature of the parts and the relations which distinguishes different cases" (*Principles*, 466). Chairs, for example, are made of legs and bottoms and backs, related chairwise.

§60   See §§19, 179; *BB* 181c; cp. *PG* 269b; James, *Principles*, I, 278b; Ramsey, *Foundations*, 74, 154. The alternation between the later W. (W II) and earlier (W I), in the first third of this number, goes as follows: W II ("When I say"), W I ("Well, it could"), W II ("But why"), W I ("Well, if the"), W II ("Then does someone", to the end).

"A proposition," said the *Tractatus*, "must restrict reality to two alternatives: yes or no. In order to do that, it must describe reality completely" (4.023). Thus a statement about a complex (e.g. "The broom is in the corner") can be resolved into the product of a statement about the constituents (e.g. "The broomhandle is in the corner and the brush is in the corner") and into the propositions that describe the complex completely (e.g. "The broomhandle is screwed into the brush") (*NB* 99f; 2.0201).

why do I call it "further analysed"?: cp. *NB* 46: "The analysis makes the proposition more complicated than it was, but it cannot and must not make it more complicated than its reference was from the first. When the proposition is just as complex as its reference, then it is *completely* analysed." In that case, why not list all the atoms and molecules? Is it because the speaker doesn't mean all that (*NB* 68)? So does he "mean" just the bigger parts?

that would be the *right* answer: not because W. now confuses meaning *p* with thinking *p*, but because the view here criticized did. Young W., in particular, had precisely such details in mind when he wrote: "There is enormously much added in thought to each sentence and not said" (*NB* 70; translation slightly altered). See GI 37; *Z* 445, quoted for §63; cp. commentary on §20a ("rather tempts us"); *NB* 60j.

achieves the same: that is, the broom is brought. The cognitive effect might be quite different, whether for the order or for the statement. Compare the request to bring "a book" from the bookshelf with a similar request disjunctively listing the contents of the bookshelf. In shifting from statement to order and choosing an object of such simple, familiar structure, W. was kind to the opposition.

Does the former lie concealed: "My viewpoint in the *Tractatus Logico-Philosophicus* was mistaken: 1) because I was not clear about the sense of the words 'a logical product is *hidden* in a sentence' (and the like), 2) because I too thought that logical analysis had to bring hidden things to light (as chemical and physical analysis does)" (*PG* 210; see §91a and commentary; *PP* 323; *Kreis*, 182–83; cp. §102).

but does it follow: "By parity of reasoning, it ought to . . . but the temptation to say that the long rigmarole is an analysis of the shorter order is very much less than what you get with the indicative sentence—this is an excellent example of what Wittgenstein called reducing concealed nonsense to patent nonsense" (Geach, lecture notes).

§61   as I expressed it earlier: in §60 he said they achieve the same, in §20b that sense is equivalent to use. See 5.457321: "Signs that serve *one* purpose are logically equivalent." Cp. Ramsey, *Foundations*, 155c.

But that is not to say . . . : see §§62–64; cp. §§553, 556, 558. For instance, will an important change in circumstances change the meaning (*BB* 104b, 115b; *EPB* 150–51, 167)? And if saying "Milk me sugar" makes a person gape, do the words have the same meaning as an order to gape (§498)? The methodological implications of W.'s denial are important: "In any case the true state of affairs can only be seen when we look into the detail of the usage of our expressions" (*BB* 115). No general doctrine of meaning can save us the trouble.

§62   See *EPB* 134–35; cp. §§562–68; James, *Principles*, II, 333–35 (e.g.:

"The only meaning of essence is teleological, and . . . classification and conception are purely teleological weapons of the mind").

§63   See X, 6–8; *PB* 51a, 252d; *PP* 323 (quoted for §90b, which compare).

more fundamental form: "It immediately strikes one as probable that the introduction of elementary propositions provides the basis for understanding all other kinds of proposition. Indeed the understanding of general propositions *palpably* depends on the understanding of elementary propositions" (4.411). Test this against the suggestion in §62.

what is meant by the other . . . : "How can I understand a proposition *now*, if it is for analysis to shew *what* I really understand?—Here there sneaks in the idea of understanding as a special mental process" (*Z* 445). See *Kreis*, 129–30, quoted for §81a ("as if it took").

But can I not say . . . : §64 immediately illustrates this observation, similar to remarks of Russell (*Principles*, 51c; *Logic*, 178b); James (*Principles*, I, 278–79); Nicod (*Foundations*, 60–62, e.g.: "Common sense rebels at the disintegration resulting from the reduction of natural and vital terms into a mass of sensible minima"); Bradley (*Principles*, I, 95: "It is a very common and most ruinous superstition to suppose that analysis is no alteration"); and Gestalt psychologists such as Köhler (e.g. *Gestalten*, ix: "Following V. Ehrenfels we give the name *Gestalten* to psychical states and processes whose characteristic properties and effects cannot be achieved by combining similar properties and effects of their so-called parts"). A chord, for instance, is not equivalent to its component notes played individually. Likewise, the sketch of a face (like that on p. 194) "forms a unity, which is grasped only by someone who sees the whole thing. . . . If it has a sad expression, that is not composed of the *expression* of the nose, of the left eye, of the right, etc." (Man. 133, 39). Cp. *RFM* 192–93; *PB* 252b–253a; Man. 219, 15 ("Remember that the flower can be represented one time by means of a *single* painted picture, but also by means of pictures of the stem and the blossom, plus words which say the two are joined"); Man. 106, 59, 61.

§64   W. continues the theme opened at the end of §62, and illustrates the closing remark of §63.

(a)   See *RFM* 190–94; cp. Russell, *Logic*, 115a, 120a; and contrast with Russell's introduction to the *Tractatus*, xi: "It is impossible, for example, to make a statement about two men (assuming for the moment that the men may be treated as simples), without employing two names." The present number shows this to be either false or an empty tautology.

IV. Twin Myths: Essence and Precision
(§§65–78)

(1)   As has already been mentioned in III, 8 (relating Sections III, IV, and V), Wittgenstein listed "a false conception of 'logical exactness', ignorance of the notion of 'family' " as one of the chief sources of reasoning like that in §39, which led to logical atomism. The linking of these distinct themes—precision and uniformity—can be variously explained. If we consider Wittgenstein's principal target, we see that whereas the author of the *Tractatus* supposed precision (GI 37) but not uniformity (GI 23) in the everyday use of individual words, with regard to the key semantic terms which occurred in his own discussions (see §97b) he supposed both precision and uniformity. In particular, there was an essence of propositions and an essence of language, encapsulating timelessly and universally the sufficient and necessary conditions for anything's being a proposition or a language (GI 30–32). And if we consider the origins of such assumptions, we see that a single, unchanging word, such as *proposition* or *language,* possesses the power to suggest sameness, sharpness, and fixity of sense, all together (GI 22). So when Wittgenstein exorcises the myth of uniformity, in §§65–67, and thereby breaks the grip of the word (GI 58), he weakens as well the other two suppositions, of sharpness and fixity. And when he dwells in turn on the fluidity and freedom of language, in §§68–71, he of course reinforces the verdict against sameness. Here the connection is logical as well as psychological.

(2)   To the idea of constant essences Wittgenstein opposed the notion of 'family resemblance', in a way anticipated by James (*Varieties,* 26–28) and Ogden and Richards (*Meaning,* 128–29). I have already suggested several clarifications of his position, in answer to common objections and misunderstandings: (a) He did not deny merely that games, say, or statements, have something in common, but maintained besides that they reveal no common trait possessed by them alone (GI 59), which enters into the language-game and guides our use of the word *statement* or *game* (GI 60). For there to be an essence, these conditions too would have to be fulfilled. (b) He did not replace one generalization with another, but sought rather to eliminate *a priori* generalizations (GI 58).

"There are . . . countless different kinds of use of what we call 'symbols', 'words', 'sentences' " (§23). Thus notice for instance that the typical pattern of family resemblance (§67a) differs from that of a rope (§67b): In the first some traits are shared by any two members, in the second "there may be nothing in common between the two ends of the series" (*PP* 313). And obviously the hues designated by *red* and *blue* are not related in either of these ways (§72; *BB* 135). Nor are the primary and secondary senses of words like *meaning* and *understand;* Wittgenstein suggested a causal tie between them, not one of similarity (XXXVII, 17). Consider too the relation between father and son: "The father passes his name to his son, even when his son does not resemble him in the least" (Man. 229, §1590).

(3)   This rich diversity in pattern indicates the proper reply to a standard objection. "If there is no essence," many readers protest, "why do we use the same word for all these things? Why do we call all games by the same name if there isn't something common to them all?" Though Wittgenstein tended to avoid causal explanation (GI 49), he did offer this helpful hint: "It often happens that we only become aware of the important *facts,* if we suppress the question 'why?'; and then in the course of our investigations these facts lead us to an answer" (§471). Thus once we simply observe the structure of a concept like *language,* we see that "these phenomena have no one thing in common which makes us use the same word for all,—but that they are *related* to one another in many different ways. And it is because of this relationship, or these relationships, that we call them all 'language' " (§65). More generally, once we recognize how variously words are employed, the overall answer to the causal query becomes manifest: There is no one explanation of why we use the same word; doubtless the causes are as numerous as the ways in which words are used.

(4)   Less obvious, perhaps, is the solution to this further problem: "What is achieved and who is refuted by the denial of anything common in propositions or language? Isn't the correct answer, here as in §47e: 'That depends on what you understand by *common*'? Without further clarification the question is senseless." Wittgenstein was perfectly aware of this situation (§72); so it should not be cited against him, but should guide the interpretation of his meaning and intentions. His first answer to the objection might be: "Exactly! You have not yet said anything at all when you say that games have something in common, or when you insist on the essential 'sameness' of the reference. We are inclined to say, as Moore, for instance, so frequently did, that when we apply a predicate to several different things we indicate that they all have something in common, all share the same property, this latter fact being the reason for applying the common predicate. The true order,

though, is just the reverse: The main reason for saying, for instance, that two things are the 'same color' is that their color falls within the range of a single color predicate. The supposed explanation, therefore, is no explanation at all, but an unenlightening tautology" (see §350; *BB* 135f).

(5) A second reply opens wider vistas: "Say what you choose, so long as it does not prevent you from seeing the facts. (And when you see them there is a good deal that you will not say.)" (§79). The history of philosophy is full of things philosophers would not have said—for example about abstraction and about concepts as mental representations (Hallett, "Bottle", 97–98)—had they attended more closely to simple examples such as Wittgenstein here scrutinizes. His remarks acquire sharp meaning and evident relevance when contrasted with the dialogues of Plato (GI 23) or with the sayings of Frege, Russell, and Moore concerning the use of general terms. Wittgenstein did not offer exact definitions of *same, common,* or *essence* because his patients did not; he was not refuting precise theses (GI 68). However, texts like the following reveal clearly enough what illusions he sought to dispel.

(6) "Signs," wrote Frege, "would hardly be useful if they did not serve the purpose of signifying the same thing repeatedly and in different contexts, while making evident that the same thing was meant" (*Writings,* 194). "Thus when we use the same sign for diverse but similar things, we really no longer designate the individual things but what is common to them, the concept. And we acquire the concept only by designating it; for since in itself it is imperceptible it needs a perceptible representative in order to become known to us. Thus the sensible reveals to us the world of the non-sensible" (*Funktion,* 90). These, surely, are things Frege would not have said had he freed himself from *a priori* suppositions and demands. Nor would he have declared: "In order that a word like 'man' or 'planet' should have logical justification, it is necessary only that there should answer to it a sharply delimited concept" (*Writings,* 105); or have maintained that without "completely sharp boundaries", the concepts would, "strictly speaking, not be concepts at all, but inadmissible sham concepts" (ibid., 165; see §71).

(7) The effect of such views on young Wittgenstein was reinforced by Russell, who wrote for example: "A word is general when it is understood to be applicable to a number of different objects in virtue of some common property" (*Mind,* 184). Here he clearly puts the cart before the horse in the way already noted (IV, 4). A passage like the following suggests that his conception of proper names may also have played a part in generating this conception of general terms: "It is clear that all the propositions in which the word 'Socrates' occurs have something in common, and again all the propositions in which the word

'mortal' occurs have something in common, something which they do not have in common with all propositions, but only with those which are about Socrates or mortality" (*Logic*, 192).

(8) It is true that Russell stressed similarity more than essences as an explanation of general terms. However, for many people the two explanations are equivalent. They are inclined to suppose, for instance, that the similarity between white things "consists in the fact that there is *some pure white in,* or *present in,* all of them; that some amount of pure white is an *element* in all of them" (Moore, *Problems*, 340). Thus Moore remarked: "It was essential to my point that the patches of which I spoke should be of *exactly the same shade.* And if the purest white patches we can get are *not* all of exactly the same shade, that fact certainly introduces a new complication into the question: What is it that is common and peculiar to all white patches?" (ibid., 355). His preferred model appears, for instance, in the declaration: "This second constituent—the property of being near this left hand—is a *universal,* and one of the most indubitable instances of a universal. You see why it should be called a 'universal'. It is so called, because it is a property which can be (and is) *common* to this hand and to other things. . . . What I mean by being 'near' is something which is absolutely identical in all three cases" (ibid., 303–4; see the quotations for §72c).

(9) Such thinking had wide repercussions in the circles Wittgenstein knew best. Listen, for example, to the manner in which Russell defended his famous logistic thesis: "If there are still those who do not admit the identity of logic and mathematics, we may challenge them to indicate at what point, in the successive definitions and deductions of *Principia Mathematica,* they consider that logic ends and mathematics begins. It will then be obvious that any answer must be quite arbitrary" (*Introduction,* 194–95). As Wittgenstein's account makes clear, a similar situation arises in countless cases; but that does not mean that all chairs are really tables, or that chemistry is the same thing as physics, or any comparable absurdity. A kindred assertion of Schlick, related to Wittgenstein's abiding interest in logical versus empirical possibility, which is connected in turn with his distinction between philosophy and science, reveals further ramifications: "The dividing line between logical possibility and impossibility of verification is absolutely sharp and distinct; there is no gradual transition between meaning and nonsense. For either you have given the grammatical rules for verification, or you have not; *tertium non datur*" ("Meaning", 156; see idem, *Aufsätze,* 393; cp. Frege, *Writings,* 165). Wittgenstein's negative judgment on such declarations (§352) follows from his estimate of the terms used both in the utterances described and in the philosophical pronouncements themselves.

(10)   Still more pertinent to the rest of the *Investigations* are the implications of such thinking for the treatment of psychological concepts (GI
64). The unspoken essentialist supposition leads one to say: " 'But
surely designing a new shape isn't in itself changing one's taste,—and
saying a word isn't meaning it,—and saying that I believe isn't believing; there must be feelings, mental acts, going along with these lines
and these words.'—And the reason we give for saying this is that a
man certainly could design a new shape without having changed his
taste, say that he believes something without believing it, etc. And this
obviously is true. But it doesn't follow that what distinguishes a case of
having changed one's taste from a case of not having done so isn't
under certain circumstances just designing what one hasn't designed
before. Nor does it follow that in cases in which designing a new shape
is not the criterion for a change of taste, the criterion must be a change
in some particular region of our mind" (*BB* 143–44). Here, in synopsis,
is the line of criticism pursued in later sections of the *Investigations*.

(11)   This connection with psychological concepts exemplifies the universal relevance of the present section. An impressive number of major
philosophical problems are closely related to the essence issue: the
questions of abstraction, mental representation, verification, and logical
possibility already mentioned (IV, 5, 9); the criteria and methodology
of analysis; the possibility of definition, and of deductive or inductive
inference; truth conditions and the distinction between symptoms and
criteria; the neutrality of language and the historicity of truth; the distinctions between *a priori* and *a posteriori,* analytic and synthetic; the difference between sense and reference; questions of analogy and tran-
scendence; and so on. This wide relevance is predictable. For belief in
essences fixes the standard form of the all-encompassing scheme in
which "proposition, language, thought, world, stand in line one behind
the other, each equivalent to each" (§96). In the traditional version
which the *Tractatus* replaced (GI 31–38), each general term expresses a
concept in the mind, and the concept in turn pictures an essence. Beneath all the surface confusion, language is an exact, regular calculus,
thanks to the thought expressed and, ultimately, to abundant essences
in the world, without which the whole edifice would crumble to dust.
Here *world* means anything ever discussed, whether in philosophy, psychology, history, theology, or science. The implications of Wittgenstein's critique—including the methodological ones (GI 70)—are correspondingly comprehensive.

Relevant Reading: EPB 190; *BB* 17–19; *PG* 269–75; Pitcher, *Philosophy,*
chap. 9; Llewellyn, "Family Resemblance"; Lübbe, "zu Wittgenstein",
220–24; Hallett, *Darkness,* 22–52.

DETAILED COMMENTARY

§65(a) See §92; Mauthner, *Beiträge*, I, 3–5; contrast with *PB* 51bc; Schlick, "Form", 152. On W.'s former position, see GI 30–33, and e.g. 4.016, 5.47–5.472.

lies behind all these considerations: concerning the dogmatic insistence on analysis W. had observed: "Of course we have not reached a result, but we think we know the road to take" (*Kreis*, 182). For we know the essence of language and of propositions. On the other hand only faith in analysis made the essence seem plausible; for not even propositions all *look* like pictures (4.011).

Compare the connection between §91 and §92 ("This finds expression . . .").

gave you yourself most headache: see e.g. *NB* 33cd, 39fg, 41klm, 90g; Man. 106, 57, 59, 250, 252, 254; Man. 110, 65.

(b) no one thing in common: see §494. "The use of the words 'sentence', 'language', and so on has the vagueness of the ordinary use of concept terms in our language" (*PG* 120). "Consider the multifariousness of the things we call 'language'. Word language, picture language, gesture language, sound language" (*PG* 179; see Man. 110, 121). "Language is not defined for us as an arrangement fulfilling a definite purpose. Rather 'language' is for us a name for a collection, and I understand it as including German, English and so on, and further various systems of signs which have more or less affinity with these languages" (*Z* 322). See §§487ff; cp. §69. In the present section W. says no more about the concept *language,* the diversity of language having been stressed already in Section I. He says even less about the diversity of *Sätze*, a theme which is also emphasized in I and to which he returns in VIII, comparing the concepts *Satz* and *game* (§135) as he here compares *language* and *game.*

which makes us use . . . : see *BB* 17d; *PP* 313. On the importance of this restrictive modifier, frequently overlooked by readers and commentators, see GI 59. Without it, §207c might appear to create insuperable difficulties, since it seems to suggest that regularity, at least, is an essential trait of language. Many other activities are equally regular, and there is no essence of regularity, and §207c (as written, though not as translated) leaves open how much regularity is needed for application of the term *language.*

And it is because of . . . : as Llewellyn notes ("Family Resemblance", 345), this does not mean "that we consider various phenomena synoptically, see that they are related by family resemblance, and on the basis of this call them all languages."

§66 See GI 51–59, where this number is studied as a paradigm of W.'s later methodology; and *BB* 17–18; *PG* 68e, 75ab; *PP* 313; Man. 111, 79–80. Cp. *RFM* 99k–100g (on what constitutes a game) and Plato, *Sophist,* 218E (for a similar method: "Then what shall we select? It must be something unimportant and easy to identify, but no less capable of definition than an object of graver concern. Suppose we take the *angler;* he is something universally familiar and requires no very serious study. . . . And yet I fancy he will provide us with a line of enquiry and definitory formula serviceable enough for our purpose").

(a) ball-games: in *PG* 68b W. gives a similar treatment of just this one group of games.

"There *must* be something common": cp. Moore, *Studies,* 17–18: "We all know that the sensation of blue differs from that of green. But it is plain that if both are *sensations* they also have some point in common. . . . But another point is also plain, namely, that when the sensation exists, the consciousness, at least, certainly does exist; for when I say that the sensations of blue and of green both exist, I certainly mean that what is common to both and in virtue of which both are called sensations, exists in each case." For further quotations from Moore and similar thinking in Frege and Russell, see IV, 6–8; on the *Tractatus,* see GI 32. The power of the urge appears from the objections that have been made to the present account (see IV, 3).

common to *all*: W.'s first-level analysis easily leads to the impression that "games constitute a family; subclasses have something in common, but not the whole class" (Naess, *Philosophers,* 134). However, subsequent remarks, about multifarious relationships within the subclass board games and about differences in skill, indicate that second-level analysis might proceed in similar fashion; it does in *PG* 68b, on ball games. See GI 59; Z 646–47.

"The defining characteristic of a game has been suggested by Khatchadourian to be 'the capacity to serve a specific human need or needs, directly or indirectly, under what we shall call "standard" (causal) conditions or in "normal" contexts'; by Mandelbaum to be 'the potentiality . . . to be of absorbing non-practical interest to either participants or spectators'; and by Manser to be 'marked off from the normal area of human life, that of genuine "action" to which moral predicates apply'. But it can readily be seen that none of these proposals is really adequate. For the first two suggestions are so general as to apply to numerous non-games as well, such as singing, reading, and painting, and the latter runs afoul of the concept of game as employed by the discipline of Game Theory" (Simon, "When is", 408–9).

don't think, but look!: see GI 52; §§51b, 340; *PG* 212a; cp. Man. 111, 138, where after discussing Broad's contention that "Something *will* happen" is no proposition, W. remarked: "Here we come also to the

question: 'How far does thought help in finding the truth? (Johnson)."
The injunction's full purport appears from GI 8–25: Philosophy is a
battle against the bewitchment of our intelligence by language, whose
misleading influence can be counteracted only by close observation of
the way things actually are. Someone habituated to the traditional distinction between sensible and intellectual representations, images and
'concepts', may feel that the exhortation "look" prejudges the whole
question; however, W. does not mean simply "use your eyes." Contrary
to the idea that for W. thought is always verbal, he here enjoins a type
of reflection which as far as possible is to be nonverbal, and which will
succeed only to the extent that it is (cp. *BB* 23b). Language is to be its
object, not its medium. For W.'s general account of the concept *think*, as
opposed to the present idiosyncratic employment of the word, see XI,
1.

"*And now attend closely to what happens.* And pay no heed to what 'must
happen'. When we philosophize we are often tempted to represent
things as the painter Klecksel did when, as a child, he drew human
faces in profile" (*EPB* 226) and gave them all two eyes nonetheless
(Busch, *Gesamtwerk*, 249; *PG* 80). "The idea that in order to get clear
about the meaning of a general term one had to find the common element in all its applications has shackled philosophical investigation; for
it has not only led to no result, but also made the philosopher dismiss
as irrelevant the concrete cases, which alone could have helped him to
understand the usage of the general term" (*BB* 19–20). "Nothing is
harder than to treat concepts *without bias*. (That is the chief difficulty of
philosophy.)" (Man. 232, 622).
   Schopenhauer: "The author has *thought,* but not *perceived;* he has
written from reflection, not from intuition" (*World*, II, 72). Russell:
"Against such errors, the only safeguard is to be able, once in a way, to
discard words for a moment and contemplate facts more directly
through images. Most serious advances in philosophic thought result
from some such comparatively direct contemplation of facts" (*Mind*,
212).
(b) See *Z* 646–47; Ogden and Richards, *Meaning,* 128–29.
   similarities overlapping: W. seldom mentioned the similar overlapping of concepts, which Schopenhauer considered so important (*World*,
I, 49–50).
§67 See IV, 2; Bambrough, "Universals", 189–92. Cp. *BB* 145b–146a
and *EPB* 220–22 for a lengthy parallel discussion of what makes a face
"friendly". It is not clear whether W. would be ready to say that the
word *game* has a family of different meanings; cp. §§77b, 552–61; *EPB*
201; *PG* 474a.
(a) no better expression: family grouping is freer, more variable than

the overlapping pattern of artichoke leaves (§164) or of fibers in a rope (§67b). Furthermore, these latter comparisons do not so readily suggest the presence of multiple traits common to all members of the group. The members of any family group share a great many characteristics (they are all visible, speak, breathe, live on the Earth, and so on), but these common features tend to be so widely distributed that they are taken for granted in group characterizations. Only less-generalized traits, such as those W. mentions, are included in descriptions of the group. They are 'family likenesses'.

"family resemblances": Schopenhauer spoke of "that wonderful, unmistakable analogy of all nature's productions, of that family likeness which enables us to regard them as variations of the same ungiven theme" (*World,* I, 154). Family traits are "characteristic" in the sense explained in §35.

form a family: the same turn of expression occurs in *BB* 17d, 20d, 88c, 98c, 152c; *EPB* 127, 129. W. also referred to a "family of usages" (*EPB* 172), "family of meanings" (*EPB* 201; §77b), "family of cases" (*BB* 115a, 125a, 133e; *EPB* 166, 179), "family likenesses" (*BB* 17d, 20d, 33a, 117c; *EPB* 129, 170; §67), and so on. He used such terminology in discussing: ability (*BB* 117c; *EPB* 170), ability to continue (*BB* 114c–115a; *EPB* 166; §179), believing (*BB* 144d–145b, 152c), comparing (*EPB* 127), cultures (Man. 111, 119), deriving (*BB* 125a; *EPB* 179; §164), terms of ethics and aesthetics (§77), expectation (*BB* 20d), facial expressions (*BB* 145b; *EPB* 222), games (*BB* 17d; §67), general training (*BB* 98c; *EPB* 143), being guided (*BB* 119b; *EPB* 172), language (§108a), numbers (§67), observing attitudes (*BB* 152b), reading (§164), recognition (*BB* 88c; *EPB* 129), similarity (*BB* 133e; *EPB* 201), trying to copy (*BB* 33a), understanding and concepts in general (*PG* 75).

(b) See *EPB* 128; *PG* 113d–114a, 115a, 285de, 476, 481d; *Kreis,* 36, 102; Waismann, *Introduction,* 1–11, 235–37; cp. §135; *BB* 62c; *PB* 236; *Kreis,* 188; Man. 302, 27.

in the same way: see IV, 2.

Why do we call . . . : the illustration is not haphazard; W. passes from the concepts *proposition* and *language,* which he had considered basic for logic, to the concept *number,* which has similar importance in the philosophy of mathematics. "The question 'What is a number?'," said Russell, "is the pre-eminent philosophic question in this subject," but "is one which, until quite recent times, was never considered in the kind of way that is capable of yielding a precise answer" (*External World,* 191). "In the case of the small finite numbers, such as 2 and 3, it would be possible to frame definitions more nearly in accordance with our unanalysed feeling of what we mean; but the method of such definitions would lack uniformity" (ibid., 209). For Frege's similar attitude, see *Writings*, 159-66, for instance: "We may indeed specify that only numbers can stand in our relation, and infer from this that the Moon, not being a number, is also not greater than zero. But with that there would have to go a complete definition of the word 'number', and that is just what is most lacking" (p. 165). "If a concept fundamental to a mighty science gives rise to difficulties, then it is surely an imperative task to investigate it more closely until those difficulties are overcome; especially as we shall hardly succeed in finally clearing up negative numbers, or fractional or complex numbers, so long as our insight into the foundation of the whole structure of arithmetic is still defective" (*Foundations*, ii). Frege did not suggest a general definition of number, applicable to all the varieties W. mentions. Nor did Russell. Yet young W. was sure there must be something common to all numbers; as there is a general form of all propositions (4.5), so there is a general form of numbers (6.022).

Waismann's clear presentation mirrors W.'s later thought: "We must not forget that our idea of a number comes, in the first place, from the cardinal numbers. If we proceed from these to the integers, rational, and real numbers, and finally to the complex and hypercomplex, with each stage in this series we lose certain of the properties associated with 'number' as we first thought of it. The complex numbers, for instance, cease to be comparable as to magnitude, the hypercomplex numbers (such as the quaternions) cease to obey certain formal laws of calculation (such as the commutative law of multiplication), and the same applies to the transfinite cardinal numbers of Georg Cantor; in short, these which we call 'numbers' are progressively more unlike the cardinal numbers, which are, of course, our prototypes, till in the end this resemblance vanishes entirely" (*Principles*, 185).

fibre on fibre: see *BB* 87a; cp. Ogden and Richards, *Meaning*, 129-30. W. did not attend to the difference pointed out in IV, 2.

some one fibre: see *Z* 26c and comments above ("no better expression").

(c) Cp. §14, and Moore, *Problems*, 314-15: "Just as these three spaces form a group, so we may suppose *all* spaces form a group; and one property which certainly is common and peculiar to all members of this group, is simply that they *are* members of it. Why should it not be the case that, just as we are able to think of this group of three spaces, we are similarly able to think of the group of all spaces, and that the property which we mean to attribute to each of them when we say it is a space, is simply and solely that it is a member of this group? This property certainly is a universal or general idea, which does belong in common to all spaces."

§68 Cp. *PG* 236-40.

(a) See *PG* 76a, 204a, 261–64, 268b, 274cd, 300a; *PP* 261c; cp. *Z* 374, 683; *BB* 19c; *PG* 113b (on the concept *Satz*).

"**All right . . .**": this suggestion introduces a new theme; W. no longer insists merely on the multiplicity of use, but on the indefiniteness of our concepts. The prime target of this paragraph, his early dogmatism about precision, is especially evident in *NB*, e.g. 63: "If possibilities *are left open* in the proposition, *just this* must be *definite: what* is left open." If one of the concepts is disjunctive, the disjunction must at least be definite! See GI 37, and (b) below; cp. *PB* 137d–138.

"**set of sub-concepts**": a similar hypothesis would be to suppose a disjunction composed not of "individual interrelated concepts" but of possible combinations of family characteristics, some combinations exemplified by existing kinds of numbers (or games, languages, and so on), some not.

not **closed:** in terms of the hypothesis just mentioned, this could mean that there is no fixed list of family characteristics, nor fixed number required for admission, nor sharp border for the individual characteristics themselves.

(b) See *Z* 440; Man. 111, 83; Man. 106, 191; cp. *PB* 74ab; Mauthner, *Beiträge*, I, 95.

"**But then . . .**": "The requirement of determinateness could also be formulated in the following way: if a proposition is to have sense, the syntactical employment of each of its parts must have been established in advance" (*Prototractatus*, 3.20103). See *NB* 64, quoted in V, 3; cp. Man. 108, 153.

It is not everywhere . . . : "We are unable clearly to circumscribe the concepts we use; not because we don't know their real definition, but because there is no real 'definition' to them. To suppose there *must* be would be like supposing that whenever children play with a ball they play a game according to strict rules" (*BB* 25).

no more are there . . . : "We generally draw no boundaries where we need none (as in certain games we draw a line only in the center of the field, so as to separate the teams, but draw no borders elsewhere since they are not necessary)" (*PG* 117); or as "in listing the rules of chess it is not said with what sort of pieces the game is played" (Man. 108, 154).

§69 See §75; *PG* 76a, 119 cde, 270; cp. *PG* 351–52.

"***and similar things***": "If someone objects that the words 'and the like' do not define the concept, I can only reply that in most cases the use of a word is in fact not definite" (Man. 302, 14). See *PG* 116b–117a, e.g.: "Hence I call 'game' what is included in the list, as well as what resembles these games to a certain degree (which I have not more exactly determined). Moreover, I reserve the right to decide in each new case whether I shall count something as a game or not. And this is the way it is for the concepts 'rule', 'proposition', 'language', etc." Cp. §§186, 494; *Z* 322, quoted for §65b.

   Does it take . . . : see §88. "To think it is would be like saying that the light of my reading lamp is no real light at all because it has no sharp boundary" (*BB* 27). "The use of the words 'proposition', 'language', and so on has the vagueness of the ordinary use of concept-terms in our language. To suppose that this makes them unusable or not entirely suitable for their purpose would be like wanting to say: 'The heat of this stove is useless since we don't know where it starts and where it stops' " (*PG* 120).

   'one pace': see *PG* 113b.

§70   Developed from Man. 111, 82–83; see *PG* 117b; *PB* 260c; Man. 220, 55; Waismann, *Principles*, 207–11; contrast with e.g. *NB* 68f; 3.23; *PB* 145d; and *Kreis*, 51–52 (where W. still believed in at least the possibility of propositions which are 'complete pictures', leaving nothing indefinite).

(a)   "you don't really know . . .": Russell spoke in just this way, e.g.: "You can, for instance, say: 'There are a number of people in this room at this moment.' That is obviously in some sense undeniable. But when you come to try and define what this room is, and what it is for a person to be in a room, and how you are going to distinguish one person from another, and so forth, you find that what you have said is most fearfully vague and that you really do not know what you meant" (*Logic*, 179). On the general climate at Cambridge, Keynes remarked: "It was all under the influence of Moore's method, according to which you could hope to make essentially vague notions clear by using precise language about them and asking exact questions. It was a method of discovery by the instrument of impeccable grammar and an unambiguous dictionary. 'What *exactly* do you mean?' was the phrase most frequently on our lips. If it appeared under cross-examination that you did not mean *exactly* anything, you lay under a strong suspicion of meaning nothing whatever" (quoted by Levi, *Modern World*, 449). Imbued with this spirit, young W. declared: "It seems clear that what we MEAN must always be '*sharp*' " (*NB* 68), and, "It is clear that I *know what I mean* by the vague proposition" (*NB* 70). For a similar declaration by Waismann, see *Kreis*, 243b. On Frege, see IV, 6.

(b)   See §610; *PG* 270; Man. 229, §1747; Man. 111, 22; Man. 106, 181; contrast with Schlick, "Form", 160, and Russell, *Logic*, 338c.

   "The ground looked . . .": note the shift from object to appearance, similar to that in §47b, and similarly explained (see below). Though I may not be able to describe the grass completely, W. once thought, it is different for my sense-data (*Kreis*, 51–52), which give content to my statements about the grass (GI 37; X, 6–8).

I should not accept . . . : behind this verdict lies W.'s vain effort to conceive a phenomenological language (X, 8). If sense-data cannot be precisely described, what can be (Man. 107, 171)? Moore (*Papers*, 69) and Russell (*Mind*, 198a; *Inquiry*, 87) made much the same point.

in *this* sense: the *Tractatus* sense, of absolute precision (see GI 37, and e.g. 4.023, 4.04), most clearly revealed in *NB* 68c, 70d, and 61 (e.g.: "When I say this watch is shiny, and what I mean by 'this watch' alters its composition in the smallest particular, then this means not merely that the sense of the sentence alters its content, but also *what I am saying about this watch* straightway alters its sense. The whole form of the proposition alters").

Insert, p. 33   From *PG* 119. See also §125d; *EPB* 214–15; *BB* 142a; *PG* 273a; cp. §§19b, 185–87, 667, 693. To understand the connection between this insert, on what occurs in the mind, and the numbers on page 33, concerning precision of meaning, it is necessary to recall that W. saved his dogma of precision by recourse to a mental meaning act (GI 37). Here in Section IV, only this insert deals with that solution, hitting it squarely and fairly.

§71(a) blurred edges: see *PB* 263–64, e.g.: "And here I encounter the prime difficulty, for it seems as though the exact *delimitation* of the vagueness were also impossible" (cp. *NB* 63d).

"But is a blurred concept . . .": Frege thought not; see the long quotation below, and *Writings*, 165 (partially quoted in IV, 6). Cp. §99 ("An indefinite sense—that would really not be a sense *at all*"); Man. 105, 52 ("The apparatus of rules must be *complete* if we want to work with a concept at all").

Is an indistinct photograph . . . : cp. *NB* 67: "The difficulty is really this: even when we want to express a *completely definite* sense there is the possibility of failure. So it seems that we have, so to speak, no guarantee that our proposition is really a picture of reality." "If generalizations occur, then the forms of the particular cases must be manifest—and it is clear that this demand is justified, otherwise the proposition cannot be a picture at all, of *anything*" (*NB* 63). See GI 35.

exactly what we need: a misty, romantic blur characterizes many advertisements for jewelry or watches; the photographs from which background montages are formed often need to be vague. Cp. §63.

(b) See §88; Man. 111, 21–24; cp. §§208–11. Similar remarks on Frege occur already in Man. 302, 14. *Prototractatus* 3.20102–3.20103 reflect his influence.

Frege compares . . . : see *Writings*, 159: "A definition of a concept (of a possible predicate) must be complete: it must unambiguously determine, as regards any object, whether or not it falls under the concept (whether or not the predicate is truly assertible of it). Thus there must not be any object as regards which the definition leaves in doubt whether it falls under the concept; though for us men, with our defective knowledge, the question may not always be decidable. We may express this metaphorically as follows: the concept must have a sharp boundary. If we represent concepts in extension by areas on a plane, this is admittedly a picture that may be used only with caution, but here it can do us good service. To a concept without sharp boundary there would correspond an area that had not a sharp boundary-line all round, but in places just vaguely faded away into the background. This would not really be an area at all; and likewise a concept that is not sharply defined is wrongly termed a concept." See IV, 6; cp. Man. 111, 182.

    cannot be called an area: cp. §99 ("An indefinite boundary is not really a boundary at all").

    "Stand roughly there": cp. Man. 106, 191; *PG* 236 and 118: "The grammatical position of the word 'game', 'rule', and so on is given by examples somewhat as the place of a meeting is indicated by saying that it will take place *beside* such and such a tree."

    for some reason: see commentary on §72; Frege, *Funktion*, 90, quoted in IV, 6.

    indirect **means:** see §§182c, 210, 362; cp. Frege, *Writings*, 115b, and *Basic Laws*, 32b.

    "It was not the function of our examples to show us the essence of 'deriving', 'reading', and so forth through a veil of inessential features; the examples were not descriptions of an outside letting us guess at an inside which for some reason or other could not be shown in its nakedness. We are tempted to think that our examples are *indirect* means for producing a certain image or idea in a person's mind,—that they *hint* at something which they cannot show" (*BB* 125).

    For any general definition . . . : see p. 14n; *PG* 439d.

    The point is . . . : compare the German. W. states the positive point behind the negative assertion, "Here giving examples is not an indirect means"; having reached the concrete examples, we have reached bedrock: so *spielen wir eben das Spiel*.

    §72 See *EPB* 197; *BB* 130; *PG* 118ab; Man. 219, 9 (a note and its octave are the "same" note, but what do they have in common?); cp. *EPB* 205–7; Moore, *Problems*, 328c–330a. *BB* 134cd and *EPB* 201–2 suggest a parallel with §13 or §47; what meaning is left to the claim that something is 'common' if it can be made about concepts as diverse as *yellow ochre, blue, game,* and *good* (§77)? On the other hand, the quotations from Moore for (c) suggest a link with §71b ("which I—for some reason—was unable to express"). Moore's invisible blue, common to all blues, can be indicated neither in the manner of (a) nor in the manner of (b). So what happens in (c) when we use a formula like that in (a)? W. is employing the "method of §2" (see commentary on §48a): Even the simple paradigm does not work as supposed. And he focuses, as Moore did not, on learning, for reasons suggested in §77b and III, 1–2.

(ab) Far from dogmatically denying all essences, as so many suppose, W. here envisages precisely the sort of identity-in-diversity which is conceivable, does obtain, and hence may exercise the kind of baneful influence described in GI 11, inducing simplifications like those in GI 21–22 and IV, 6–8.

(c) See BB 130fg, 131abc, 133f, 134–35, the upshot of which is: "To say that we use the word 'blue' to mean 'what all these shades of colour have in common' by itself says nothing more than that we use the word 'blue' in all these cases" (BB 135). The clash with Moore is clear-cut: "This character wh. we express by 'is a shade of blue', is, of course, something which is common to all shades of blue—something which they have 'in common'. Some people seem loth to admit that they have anything 'in common'. And of course this character is not 'in common' to both of 2 blue shades, in the sense that it is a part or constituent of both. . . . Obviously this character also is not identical with any shade which possesses it, nor yet with any other shade of colour that we *see*. It is not similar in shade to any shade that we *see*. So that, if it is 'seen' at all, it is only in a completely different sense" (*Commonplace*, 19). "*All* the shades we *see* occupy some position in the colour octahedron; but 'blue', in the sense in which many of the shades in the octahedron are 'blue', occupies *no* position in it: therefore it is not seen" (ibid., 21). "When we see a white patch," explained Russell, "we are acquainted, in the first instance, with the particular patch; but by seeing many white patches, we easily learn to abstract the whiteness which they all have in common, and in learning to do this we are learning to be acquainted with whiteness. A similar process will make us acquainted with any other universal of the same sort" (*Problems*, 58). See IV, 8.

§73   See §139; Z 336; BB 36d–37c; PG 270–72; cp. Russell, *Logic*, 303.

This number brings out the pragmatic relevance of the question about something common, and the significance of the small step from *yellow ochre* to *blue*. When the difference between even these two simple concepts is pointed out, the defendant of traditional views about essences, concepts, and abstraction is wont to reply: "But who ever claimed that in all concepts there is the sort of perfect likeness found in samples of yellow ochre?" However, that is the sort required to make sense of most talk about 'abstraction' and to render at all plausible the representationalist account of concepts as mental representations accompanying speech. Even for a word like *blue* the model breaks down. As for images, once their merely symbolic function is recognized, they no longer appear indispensable (XII, 3; §§396, 449, 663), for words themselves are symbols.

(a) See *BB* 18a, 130f.

to putting a table in my hands: cp. §15; Man. 112, 130: "Here no concept lies before us, but a list."

may mislead: See Man. 112, 222–23; cp. p. 18n ("crucial superstition").

'what is common': see Man. 109, 50–51, quoted for §443 ("The red which").

(b) Cp. §251d.

to be understood: in the primary sense of *understand* (see XIX, 1–2).

resides in . . . : the contrast with Russell is clear: "What distinguishes a general idea from a vague idea is merely the presence of a certain accompanying belief" (*Mind*, 222); "a 'generic' image . . . is simply one intended to be generic" (*Logic*, 304); "the meaning of an image, according to this analysis, is constituted by a combination of likeness and associations" (*Mind*, 209). So is the contrast with James, e.g. *Principles*, I, 473b, 478n, 477b ("nor will swarms of copies of the same 'idea', recurring in stereotyped form, or 'by the irresistible laws of association formed into one idea', ever be the same thing as a thought of *'all the possible members'* of a class. We must mean *that* by an altogether special bit of consciousness *ad hoc*"). See XXXII, 1–3.

(c) See *EPB* 198; *BB* 131b; cp. *BB* 84; Man. 112, 167–68.

§74   For full development of these themes, see Section XXXVII.

it would only be to say . . . : if the hypothetical ("if you see this leaf . . .") is not an idle tautology, referring to the same experience in both clauses (cp. p. 186), it states an empirical connection between an experience and a practice. Such a connection is conceivable, but there is no good reason to suppose that every time we follow certain rules we have that specific experience (cp. XXXVII, 11). And even if we did, the experience would not encapsulate the rules (cp. §139); it would not "force a particular use on us" (see §140).

if you see the schematic drawing . . . : cp. p. 203b.

§75   See §89c; *BB* 25c; cp. §§208–11, 362; *PG* 51a, 112b (similar remarks on *Satz*).

This number restates points already made in §§69–71, but with an implicit comparison now between the mere examples of games and the mere samples of green or of the shape of a leaf. There is no definition of green or of the shape of a leaf, nor intuition of something common to all the samples.

an unformulated definition: see Russell, *Mind*, 146c–147a; Schlick, "Meaning", 154a ("these definitions have to be known to those who pronounce the sentence in question and to those who hear or read it. Otherwise they are not confronted with any proposition at all"); Man. 110, 111: "No proposition of language can come to us as a surprise (but a truth may). That is what I mean when I say: from one use of a word we can give the rules for the word. For that means describing its use in sentences. I.e. giving a general description of all possible sentences."

Isn't my knowledge . . . : see §§69–70 and commentary.

§76   See §69; *PG* 76a, 77a, 112c, 120b; Man. 115, 40–41 (the source of this number). Cp. Frege, *Foundations,* 100: "The more fruitful type of definition is a matter of drawing boundary lines that were not previously given at all."

§77(a) merge without a hint: the comparisons with light from a lamp and with the heat from a stove (see the commentary on §69) aptly suggest the difference between having no border and having no meaning. Anything—and nothing—is a good approximation of the border; but this does not mean that anything—and nothing—counts as good, beautiful, and the like. "There are words with several clearly defined meanings. It is easy to tabulate these meanings. And there are words of which one might say: They are used in a thousand different ways which gradually merge into one another. No wonder that we can't tabulate strict rules for their use" (*BB* 28). "There are," for instance, "an endless variety of actions and words, having a family likeness to each other, which we call 'trying to copy' " (*BB* 33). But this does not permit us to conclude that such an expression "has really no meaning, as by following up its meaning this seems to trail off into nothing" (*BB* 124). Fuzzy terms, too, have an established use, so do not resemble the sign in §258, with which we might be tempted to assimilate them, because of verbal similarities in W.'s treatment.

"Anything—and nothing . . .": notice, furthermore, that this is said of the conceptual border, not of an individual use, which may be sharper and either right or wrong. No *definition* would be right, any more than in the case of *game.*

in aesthetics or ethics: frequently assimilated by W. (e.g. *NB* 77, 83; *PP* 312–13). From Moore's account (ibid.) and from W.'s one example in (*b*), it is clear that the ethical and aesthetic terms he had principally in mind were vague ones such as *fine, good, lovely, beautiful,* rather than the more discriminating expressions he said were more frequently used in aesthetic evaluations (*LC* 3). On ethical terms, see LE 7, 9, and below. On both, see *LC* 2a.

(b) How did we *learn* . . . : see III, 1–3; §35b; *LC* 1–2; Gasking and Jackson, "Wittgenstein", 54a; cp. §179b.

"good" for instance: see the commentary on §182c. "I have maintained," wrote Moore in *Principia* (ix–x), "that very many different things are good and evil in themselves, and that neither class of things possesses any other property which is both common to all its members and peculiar to them." W., however, "seemed to hold definitely that there is nothing in common in our different uses of the word 'beautiful', saying that we use it 'in a hundred different games'—that, e.g., the beauty of a face is something different from the beauty of a chair or a flower or the binding of a book. And of the word 'good' he said similarly that each different way in which one person, A, can convince another, B, that so-and-so is 'good' fixes the meaning in which 'good' is used in that discussion—'fixes the grammar of that discussion'; but that there will be 'gradual transitions', from one of these meanings to another, 'which take the place of something in common' " (*PP* 313). By the time Moore took these notes, he agreed: "We all of us very often both use and understand sentences in which the adjective 'good' occurs. But it seems to me very certain that in different sentences we both use and understand this word in a considerable number of different senses" (*Papers*, 89). Even of just the ethical employment, W. wrote: "The use of the word 'good' . . . is composed of an enormous number of interrelated games. Facets of the use, as it were. But it is precisely the connection of these facets, their kinship, that here produces a *single* concept" (*PG* 77). On the spread of this viewpoint, see Ewing, *Second Thoughts,* 30. For a contrast with Russell, see *Essays,* 20.

must have a family . . . : not because all words must have a family of meanings (IV, 2), but because any words learned as these are must. See the references above, concerning the relation between learning and meaning. We should perhaps distinguish between a family of meanings and a family meaning (as in §67).

§78 A reworking of Man. 115, 41. The interest of this effective series centers on the middle member, the connection with the preceding numbers being most clearly revealed in §75. The same number fills out the comparison, suggesting that some account is possible in the second case, though nothing as simple and satisfactory as in the first (no single formula). On examples like the third, see §610.

If you are surprised: and perhaps tempted in the manner of §36 or §182c (see the commentaries on them). As usual the simpler case acts as paradigm (GI 12) and results in a crossing of pictures (cp. §191).

"Socrates: 'You know it & you know how to speak Greek, so you must be able to say it" (Man. 115, 40).

V. Critique of the "Calculus according to Definite Rules" (§§79–88)

GENERAL COMMENTARY

(1) For Frege, Russell, and others, a perfectly precise and regular linguistic calculus was a desirable possibility or goal; for young Wittgenstein it was a fact and had only to be revealed through an appropriate notation. The present section is directed against the supposed ideal which underlay both positions and against the pointless proposals and unrealistic analyses to which it gave rise. Ordinary language is no such calculus, nor need it be. In fact the ideal of absolute precision and regularity is ultimately unintelligible.

(2) All of this can only appear in the right light, said Wittgenstein, if we see what may lead us, and did lead him, to think that in ordinary speech we are operating a calculus according to definite rules (§81b). I have already discussed and documented the logical-atomist insistence on precision, and Wittgenstein's recourse to pinpoint mental projection to achieve it (GI 37; commentary on §70). But such momentary reference did not suffice. "One point on which he insisted several times," reports Moore, ". . . was that if a word which I use is to have meaning, I must 'commit myself' by its use. And he explained what he meant by this by saying 'If I commit myself, that means that if I use, e.g. "green" in this case, I have to use it in others,' adding 'If you commit yourself, there are consequences' " (PP 258). For a long time, the only consequences which interested Wittgenstein were logical, not pragmatic. "This is the point: Can we justly apply logic just as it stands, say in *Principia Mathematica,* straightaway to *ordinary propositions*?" (NB 66). His answer was, "Yes, we can" (NB 69), provided only that we properly analyze our statements. "For example, perhaps we assert of a patch in our visual field that it is to the right of a line, and we assume that every patch in our visual field is infinitely complex. Then if we say that a point in that patch is to the right of the line, this proposition follows from the previous one, and if there are infinitely many points in the patch *then infinitely many propositions of different content follow* LOGICALLY *from that first one.* And this of itself shews that the proposition itself was as a matter of fact infinitely complex. That is, not the propositional sign by itself, but it *together with its syntactical application*" (NB 64).

(3) Here "syntactical application" cannot be identified with the inferences people actually perform; the content is there from the start and only one precise set of propositions "follows logically" from it (*NB* 65c). The rules of this calculus are superrules, neither known by the speakers (4.002), nor invariably followed by them in their actual transactions, nor apparently affected by vagaries of practice (see *RFM* 6, quoted for §89a). "If a proposition is to make sense then the syntactical employment of each of its parts must be settled in advance.—It is, e.g., not possible *only subsequently to come upon* the fact that a proposition follows from it. But, e.g., what propositions follow from a proposition must be completely settled before that proposition can have a sense!" (*NB* 64; cp. *NB* 9i; 3.334, 3.42).

(4) For reasons considered in a later section (see IX, 2; cp. XXXVII, 2–6) but merely alluded to in this one (§81b), young Wittgenstein believed that these conditions are met in ordinary speech. "In fact, all the propositions of our everyday language, just as they stand, are in perfect logical order" (5.5563; see *NB* 2d; 5.4733; §98 and commentary). What they lack, above all, is perspicuity (3.323; *PB* 52c). As a consequence, philosophers frequently fail to understand the real logic of ordinary expressions (3.324) and construct nonsensical philosophical propositions without recognizing their lack of sense (6.53). Wittgenstein thought of perfecting a logical notation on their behalf which would render perspicuous both the real meaning of everyday propositions and the vacuity of metaphysical ones (3.325).

(5) In his introduction to the *Tractatus,* Russell read his own views into Wittgenstein's account, saying: "He is concerned with the conditions for *accurate* Symbolism, i.e. for Symbolism in which a sentence 'means' something quite definite. In practice, language is always more or less vague, so that what we assert is never quite precise. Thus, logic has two problems to deal with in regard to Symbolism: (1) the conditions for sense rather than nonsense in combinations of symbols; (2) the conditions for uniqueness of meaning or reference in symbols or combinations of symbols. A logically perfect language has rules of syntax which prevent nonsense, and has single symbols which always have a definite and unique meaning. Mr. Wittgenstein is concerned with the conditions for a logically perfect language—not that any language is logically perfect, or that we believe ourselves capable, here and now, of constructing a logically perfect language, but that the whole function of language is to have meaning, and it only fulfils this function in proportion as it approaches to the ideal language which we postulate" (x).

(6) Wittgenstein later agreed with Russell's factual judgment about existing languages, but rather than conclude that another would be better, he rejected even his own more modest proposal of a notation for

therapeutic purposes. The symbolism which he recommended in the *Tractatus* no longer seemed necessary, useful, or even possible. For the underlying idea of an ultimate, indubitable rendering of sense (§91)—one which would, as it were, wear its proper interpretation on its sleeve—is a mere "picture", not an intelligible hypothesis (§§84–87; cp. Brouwer, "Mathematik", 157–58). And the ideal exactness which was to characterize analytic translation is equally senseless, first because no statement we might analyze actually possesses such precision (§70), second because no conceivable purpose requires it (§88). Ordinary language, therefore, is in order as it is, not because wonderful precision and constancy lie beneath its surface, but because such 'ideal' qualities are irrelevant to the actual purposes of speech.

(7)   Wittgenstein's rejection of all three calculi—the one we supposedly use, the one proposed to replace it, and the one designed for therapeutic purposes—and his defense of ordinary language, with all its vagueness and ambiguity, could easily be misunderstood. "Apart from other things," writes Malcolm, "I think that there was indeed something in the content of his philosophy that, improperly assimilated, had and still has an unfortunate effect on those influenced by it. I refer to his conception that words are not used with 'fixed' meanings (*Investigations*, §79), that concepts do not have 'sharp boundaries' (ibid., §68, §76). This teaching, I believe, produced a tendency in his students to assume that precision and thoroughness were not required in their own thinking" (*Memoir*, 63). On others it has produced the impression that Wittgenstein himself preached and practiced slovenliness (Russell, *Development*, 216–17). For his actual attitude and practice, see GI 69.

(8)   Carnap's account of Wittgenstein's position is instructive even in its inaccuracies (indicated by my inserts) and opens broad perspectives: "In the Circle discussions we often made use of symbolic logic for the representation of analyses or examples. When we found in Wittgenstein's book statements about 'the language', we interpreted them as referring to an ideal language; and this meant for us a formalized symbolic language. Later [cp. V, 4] Wittgenstein explicitly rejected this view. He had a skeptical and sometimes even a negative view of the importance of a symbolic language for the clarification and correction of the confusions in ordinary language and also in the customary language of philosophers which, as he had shown himself, were often the cause of philosophical puzzles and pseudo-problems [cp. GI 24]. On this point, the majority of British analytic philosophers share Wittgenstein's view, in contrast to the Vienna Circle and to the majority of analytical philosophers in the United States" ("Autobiography", 38). The two tendencies may be characterized very roughly by saying that whereas the positivist looks to his logical computer for a solution, the

Wittgensteinian believes that a philosopher who has ascertained the adequacy of a given computer to deal with a given problem, and who knows what data to feed it in what form, already possesses sufficient clarity about the problems, prior to programming (cp. GI 68). For a fuller account of Wittgenstein's approach, and his reasons, see GI 46–62 and the next two sections.

DETAILED COMMENTARY

§79 Reworked from Man. 115, 43–45, which in turn grew from Man. 112, 185–86. See Waismann, *Principles*, 69–71; Bogen, *Philosophy*, 78–80; cp. *PB* 86d–87e; *NB* 68c; Man. 112, 193–95.

"Wittgenstein, as you will see, was a disguised-descriptionist about proper names, like Russell and Frege and himself in his youth—he remained an unreconstructed disguised-descriptionist about proper names to the day of his death. There is something to be said against disguised-descriptionism, I think; but I think it is a lot better theory than the no-connotation line of Locke and Mill—a view for which Wittgenstein several times expressed quite strong disapproval. What is new to the disguised-descriptionist view in these sections is something of general import; namely, he rejects the idea that there have to be rigid criteria for the use of a word if it is to be used at all" (Geach, lecture notes).

(a) following Russell: for instance in *Problems*, 29–31, and *Logic*, 242b–243b, 252a. See III, 4. Russell extended the account to names of living persons as well (*Mind*, 192b–192c).

   can be defined: see §28 and commentary ("define a proper name").

   And according as . . . : cp. Frege: "In the case of an actual proper name such as 'Aristotle' opinions as to the sense may differ. It might, for instance, be taken to be the following: the pupil of Plato and teacher of Alexander the Great. Anybody who does this will attach another sense to the sentence 'Aristotle was born in Stagira' than will a man who takes as the sense of the name: the teacher of Alexander the Great who was born in Stagira. So long as the reference remains the same, such variations of sense may be tolerated, although they are to be avoided in the theoretical structure of a demonstrative science and ought not to occur in a perfect language" (*Writings*, 58).

(b) Contrast this with *PB* 293d, or *NB* 61.

(c) Contrast this with Frege (*Writings*, 58): "To every expression belonging to a complete totality of signs, there should certainly correspond a definite sense; but natural languages often do not satisfy this condition, and one must be content if the same word has the same sense in the same context."

   on four legs . . . : the right way to put it, though the talk in (b) about removing props might suggest the reverse comparison. Cp. *RFM* 115f.

(d) Should it be said . . . : see §70a and commentary.

Say what you choose: see GI 68; §48b; NL 318a; cp. *LC* 55c; Augustine, *Confessions*, XI, 20, 26: "See, I do not object, or gainsay, or find fault, if only what is said be understood." Contrast this attitude with that in Man. 105,10 and 12.

"And all this about understanding is connected with his study of what it is to prove a thing, with the fact that people were often exasperated by his ending the discussion of a philosophical puzzle with 'Say what you like,' with his saying to me on one occasion when I spoke of an unsuccessful philosophical discussion, 'Perhaps you made the mistake of denying what he said,' with his saying, 'I hold no opinions in philosophy,' and with his saying that he didn't *solve* philosophical problems, but *dissolved* them" (Wisdom, "Wittgenstein", 47).

so long as it does not . . . : see §§38a, 81a, 149, 339b, 453, 482, 693.

there is a good deal . . . : "The cases in which particularly we wish to say that someone is misled by a form of expression are those in which we would say: 'he wouldn't talk as he does if he were aware of this difference in the grammar of such-and-such words, or if he were aware of this other possibility of expression' and so on" (*BB* 28).

(e) See §354 and commentary; cp. *NB* 68d.

§80 See *Z* 350; *PG* 117b; *BB* 62; cp. §183, p. 230a; *Z* 118, 393; *Kreis*, 259c; Britton, *Communication*, 187–88 (W.'s illustration there: "Was S. Dennis dead when he walked down the hill of martyrdom, carrying his head under his arm?"). W.'s effective use of these imaginary situations (see GI 62) does not depend at all on their being likely; rather, the less likely they are, the better his argument, for it is then less probable that we should have taken the possibilities into account and have made provision for them, sharpening the concept *chair* to meet such eventualities (cp. §84). By way of contrast:

"Indeed even our ordinary language must provide in advance for all cases of uncertainty" (*PB* 87).

"The terms we do not need to define are those which we know we could define if need arose, like 'chair' . . ." (Ramsey, *Foundations*, 264).

"This involves the requirement as regards concepts, that, for any argument, they shall have a truth-value as their value; that it shall be determinate, for any object, whether it falls under the concept or not. In other words: as regards concepts we have a requirement of sharp delimitation; if this were not satisfied it would be impossible to set forth logical laws about them" (Frege, *Writings*, 33).

Waismann, "Verifiability", 120–23, draws the important corollary of

W.'s remarks: "The fact that in many cases, there is no such thing as a conclusive verification is connected with the fact that most of our empirical concepts are not delimited in all possible directions" (122). "Open texture is a very fundamental characteristic of most, though not of all, empirical concepts, and it is this texture which prevents us from verifying conclusively most of our empirical statements" (123).

Moore draws W.'s apparent conclusion concerning the truth of the proposition "There's a chair" (*Commonplace*, 117f).

§81   Developed from Man. 112, 187. See Man. 111, 176–77.

(a) From Man. 115, 45. See *PG* 115cd; cp. *Kreis*, 45.

Ramsey once . . . : cp. *PB* 180ef.

'normative science': the English phrase used by W. in Man. 112, 187. The general idea is a traditional one; logic gives the "rules for right reasoning". Ogden and Richards (*Meaning*, 221) apply the same expression, *normative science,* to grammar.

only dawned on me . . . : notice that what dawned on W. was the realization of an error, not an interpretation of Ramsey's words. Since some have supposed that the notions here criticized were not W.'s own, this is part of the evidence to keep in mind.

we often *compare* **. . . :** this part is developed already in Man. 302, 14. See also *PG* 77b and compare *Z* 440–41. From *BB* 25: "For remember that in general we don't use language according to strict rules—it hasn't been taught us by means of strict rules, either. *We,* in our discussions on the other hand, constantly compare language with a calculus proceeding according to exact rules.

"This is a very one-sided way of looking at language. In practice we very rarely use language as such a calculus. For not only do we not think of the rules of usage—of definitions, etc.—while using language, but when we are asked to give such rules, in most cases we aren't able to do so."

but cannot say . . . : as W. still did in Man. 108, 153–54.

only *approximate:* see V, 5; cp. *NB* 67i.

ideal **language:** see §§98–105; cp. *Z* 440–41; *RFM* 190k. Russell spoke of "a logically perfect language" (V, 5); Frege of "a perfect language" (*Writings,* 58); young W. of "a perfect notation" (LF 37, below).

logic for a vacuum: in a vacuum there is no friction or air-resistance (§130); so a body falls, for instance, precisely as the laws of gravity prescribe. See §107; *PG* 77e; *PB* 52f.

logic does not treat of . . . : see GI 45; §§89b, 108c; *BB* 18c.

liable to mislead: see §§100, 105a.

as if these languages were better: see §§130, 132ab, 133a. Both Frege and Russell were very much of this opinion:

Russell: "The occurrence of tense in verbs is an exceedingly annoying vulgarity due to our preoccupation with practical affairs" (*Logic*, 248). "It is a disgrace to the human race that it has chosen to employ the same word 'is' for these two entirely different ideas—a disgrace which a symbolic logical language of course remedies" (*Introduction*, 172). "The only way you can really state it correctly is by inventing a new language *ad hoc*" (*Logic*, 234).

Frege: "This arises from an imperfection of language, from which even the symbolic language of mathematical analysis is not altogether free; even there combinations of symbols can occur that seem to stand for something but have (at least so far) no reference" (*Writings* 69–70). "In order to exploit the special advantages of visible signs, such a notation must be entirely different from all verbal languages. It goes without saying that these advantages are hardly realized in written words" (*Funktion*, 93; see the whole essay, "Über die wissenschaftliche Berechtigung einer Begriffsschrift"). "We have need of a system of symbols from which every ambiguity has been banned" ("Justification", 158).

As for the early W., though he held that everyday language is "in perfect logical order" (V, 4), he evidently thought that a language "governed by *logical* grammar" would be better (3.325). See, for instance, Man. 105, 88; Man. 106, 118; or LF 37: "It is, of course, a deficiency of our notation that it does not prevent the formation of such nonsensical constructions, and a perfect notation will have to exclude such structures by definite rules of syntax."

Not only did the later W. deny that such ideal languages would be better; he thought they would be worse. See Man. 138, 16A ("Philosophers figure out an *ideal* use for many words, which is then worthless").

as if it took . . . : see V, 5; cp. *PB* 326, 332; *Kreis*, 140.

"Whatever I discuss with Moore, the question is: Can logical analysis reveal for the first time what we mean by the sentences of ordinary language? Moore is inclined to say yes. Do people not know, then, what they mean when they say: 'The sky is clearer today than yesterday'? Must we wait for the logical analysis? What a hellish idea! Philosophy is to reveal to me for the first time what I mean by my statements and whether I mean anything by them" (*Kreis*, 129–30).

(b) See §102; *EPB* 178, 213, 215; *BB* 3e, 42a, 124c, 142a–143a; *PG* 53d–56a; Man. 302, 2; Man. 220, 81; cp. §449b; *PB* 63bc.

For the relation of this paragraph to the rest of Part One, see GI 64.

can lead us: e.g. Moore, *Commonplace*, 25–28; Stout, *Psychology*, II, 211; James, *Principles*, I, 270 ("Thought is in fact a kind of Algebra, as Berkeley long ago said").

and did lead me: see V, 2–3; IX, 2; XXXVII, 2–8; commentary on §292; *Kreis*, 168–70; Man. 112, 188 (quoted for §83a); Man. 111, 13; Man. 109, 104–5, and later pages, *passim;* Man. 108, 218–19; Man. 107,

38; cp. GI 37; *PP* 258–59. Man. 220, 60, here cites the *Tractatus*. Especially calculuslike is the *Tractatus* doctrine that "every proposition is a result of successive applications to elementary propositions of the operation $N(\bar{\xi})$" (6.001; see 5.234). On the incredible complexity of ordinary language so conceived, see Bogen, *Philosophy*, 49.

and *means:* see Man. 109, 281; "One would like to say: 'A person need only *mean* something by what he says, then everything essential is given.' So I take 'meaning something' & 'following a rule' as synonymous. . . . Can I say: . . . If I mean something, then I have made a portrait, that is, represented something according to a rule?" He had thought so (see comments on §292).

or *understands:* cp. §431b. "What I do with the words of language (when I *understand* them) is exactly the same as what I do with the signs in a calculus: I operate with them" (*Kreis,* 169–70).

according to definite rules: see §54; *LO* 50. "The words 'occur' [as in "*p* occurs in ~*p*"], etc. are indefinite, as is all such talk. Only the grammatical rules, which must finally show what is meant, are precise & unambiguous & incontestable" (Man. 109, 90). "Grammar consists of such universal rules" (ibid., 221).

§82 From Man. 112, 189, then Man. 115, 46–47, where it is preceded by the following: "Our investigation does not try to *discover* the proper, exact meaning of the words; rather in the course of our inquiries we often *give* the words exact meanings. For what do I call . . ."

What do I call: *PG* 119 brings out the fact that not merely are there different sorts of rules, but the concept *rule* fluctuates accordingly. On this point, alluded to at the end of §82, see also §§53–54 and commentary.

'by which he proceeds': in §79.

a definition: concerning this translation of *Erklärung,* see the commentary on §43a.

§83 Reworked from Man. 112, 189–90; Man. 115, 47. See *BB* 25c; cp. *PG* 68b.

(a) between language and games: see I, 1–10, and in particular I, 9.

now someone says . . . : "Wasn't it an error of mine (for now it so appears to me) to suppose that a person who uses language always plays a *definite game?* For wasn't that the sense of my remark that everything in a proposition—no matter how roughly expressed—'is in order'?" (Man. 112, 188; see §98).

(b) make up the rules as we . . . : in Man. 112, 187, W. used this expression for the situation described in §79.

§84 See §213ab, p. 224d; cp. *RFM* 45fg; 6.51.

(a) See *Z* 440; Man. 220, 92.

I said that . . . : in §68b.

Can't we imagine a rule . . . . : see §§86–87, 141a; *BB* 33–34, 97b.
§85 See *EPB* 142; *BB* 33b, 97bc; Man. 112, 176; cp. §§29b, 140–41, 433. *BB* 34 connects §84 and §85, and develops them, as follows: "Let us put it in this way:—What one wishes to say is: 'Every sign is capable of interpretation; but the *meaning* mustn't be capable of interpretation. It is the last interpretation.' Now I assume that you take the meaning to be a process accompanying the saying, and that it is translatable into, and so far equivalent to, a further sign. You have therefore further to tell me what you take to be the distinguishing mark between *a sign* and *the meaning*. If you do so, e.g., by saying that the meaning is the arrow which you *imagine* as opposed to any which you may draw or produce in any other way, you thereby say that you will call no further arrow an interpretation of the one which you have imagined." Cp. XXXVII, 6; §454.

Does the sign-post leave . . . : the answer is the same as for §84b: My eyes are closed to doubt (p. 224d).

sometimes leaves room: for instance, when a signpost is set aslant at a crossroads, and doesn't point squarely in one direction rather than the other.

no longer a philosophical proposition: being neither general nor necessary (cp. *BB* 17–19). Cp. *BB* 55, 97b, 98a.
§86 This number continues the theme of the previous two. See §163; *BB* 123d; *PG* 90d–91a, 93b–94b; cp. Man. 112, 154–58.
(a) See *EPB* 122–23, 131, 178; *BB* 82c, 89d–90a, 124c.
(b) See *EPB* 132, 178; *BB* 90e, 124c.
(c) See §§29a, 141a; *RFM* 34 ("However many rules you give me—I give a rule which justifies *my* employment of your rules"); *EPB* 133; *BB* 34ab, 91a, 97b, 124c.

"Every justification looks like this. In a certain sense it gets us no farther. Indeed, it cannot take us *farther*, that is, to the metalogical. (The difficulty here is: not to try to justify what admits of no justification.)" (*PG* 101).
§87 Reworked from Man. 112, 192–93. See §29a; *NB* 46def. Applying the preceding remarks to the example in §79, W. deals with a common reaction to the situation there described: "Granted, everyday speech vacillates in this way; but that is an undesirable situation and should be remedied" (see IV, 6; V, 3, 5). W.'s answer is: "Why?" Once we realize that absolute precision is an illusory ideal, the question becomes: Has this exactness still got a function here? (§88; see V, 6).
(a) Cp. GI 59.

to words like "red": that is, to the favorites of empiricists like Russell and positivists like Schlick, who hoped to escape from an endless regress of verbal definitions via mere pointing, once the meaning was simple and immediate enough to permit this expedient (II, 5–9).

"But then how does . . .": for illustrations of this attitude, see II, 8.

hung in the air: cp. *PG* 110, quoted for §485.

not every one that I can imagine: this helps to explain W.'s practice in the *Investigations* (GI 69–70), "his reluctance to make distinctions and classifications which are not of direct assistance to the fly in the fly-bottle" (Strawson, "Review", 27). Compare and contrast his viewpoint with Frege's: "We must not forget that not everything can be defined. If we insist at any price on defining what is essentially indefinable, we readily fasten upon inessential accessories" (*Writings*, 126). Though for W. explanations necessarily come to an end, they do not come to a necessary end (see §29a; §182c and commentary).

§88   See V, 6; §69; *PB* 259a, 260c, 263–64, 266d; cp. *RFM* 170lmn; *BB* 46a; *PB* 269.

This is pragmatism, but not in the form of a theory (say of meaning or of truth). Contrast W.'s discussion with Russell's in *Analysis of Mind*, 180–81 (e.g.: "All thinking is vague to some extent, and complete accuracy is a theoretical ideal not practically attainable"). "Through Russell, but especially through Whitehead, there entered philosophy a false exactitude which is the worst enemy of genuine exactitude" (*PG* 296; see GI 69–70). Its disastrous effects are evident in W.'s early thought (see GI 37; V, 3). The present number is his most explicit reply to the *a priori* requirement of precision which so clearly dominated his reasoning in *NB* 61–70.

(a) See §71.

(b) See §71; cp. *BB* 63, and Russell, *Mind*, 198 ("The meaning is an area, like a target: it may have a bull's eye, but the outlying parts of the target are still more or less within the meaning, in a gradually diminishing degree as we travel further from the bull's eye").

(c) This part comes from Man. 115, 51. See *BB* 81b; Man. 219, 9; cp. GI 37 for a prime target.

to set a pocket watch: W. enjoyed the joke about a computer which advised a Dutch scientist to buy a watch that didn't go at all rather than one that was slow by a second day, since the latter would be right only once every 120 years, whereas the former would be right twice a day. Cp. Man. 134, April 7.

VI. The Confessions of a Logical Atomist
(§§89–108)

(1)   "These considerations," writes Wittgenstein at the start of this section, "bring us up to the problem: In what sense is logic something sublime?" (§89). He then characterizes its sublimity in a manner which connects the section not just with the immediately preceding considerations but with the four preceding sections. The conception of language as a rigid, precise calculus (Section V), the conviction that language has an essence (Section IV), the belief in atomic names and objects (Sections II–III), did not result from empirical research but from an *a priori* ideal. So long as a person is dazzled by that ideal (§100), he will persist in his "pursuit of chimeras" (§94), ignoring the apparent trivialities which alone could resolve his problems (§§93a, 106–7). So Wittgenstein must now take countermeasures. For "greater clarity about the concepts of understanding, meaning and thinking" (§81), soon to be attempted (GI 64), will require close attention to empirical detail. And the philosopher who believes that "the essence is hidden from us" (§92), that thought is a quasi-supernatural process (§§93–95, 97) whose secrets, tucked away in the medium of the understanding (§102), must be divined, *a priori* (§§89, 97), by the understanding (*RFM* 6), will not give serious consideration to the mere "external" details (§120b) of which Wittgenstein would remind him (§89). The solution is to expose the ideal for what it is: a blind demand (§101), not based on facts of observation, but contradicting them (§§101, 105, 107). Describing and analyzing the syndrome vividly, from within, Wittgenstein builds to a climax, a breaking point (§107) corresponding perhaps to some moment in his own struggles when he realized that no halfway measures would do. "The *preconceived idea* of crystalline purity can only be removed by turning our whole examination round" (§108). "Back to the rough ground!" (§107). We must stop "thinking", and *look* (GI 50–52).

(2)   Such is the message of this section, such its function. It is the successor of *BB* 17–19, where Wittgenstein remarked, "I shall in the future again and again draw your attention to what I shall call language games" (*BB* 17), then noted and described "what makes it difficult for

us to take this line of investigation", namely, "our craving for general-ity" (ibid.; cp. §340). "Instead of 'craving for generality' I could also have said 'the contemptuous attitude towards the particular case' " (*BB* 18). "This tendency," as he knew from personal experience, "leads the philosopher into complete darkness" (ibid.). Section VI now documents this experience. Applying the method of models (GI 56, 71) to the study of philosophy itself, it replaces the general, explanatory analysis in the *Blue Book* with a detailed, realistic account of just how Wittgen-stein the atomist felt and thought within his bottle (§309), yet in terms which indicate affinity with many another thinker. It was not just young Wittgenstein who was led into darkness by a craving for general-ity or who approached philosophical problems in a dogmatic, *a priori* manner (§131; VII, 5). The 'scientific' ideal has dominated western thought (GI 70). Wittgenstein indicates this universal relevance at the start of this section as he does at the start of the book, by citing St. Augustine (§89) rather than his own *Tractatus*.

(3)   However, even a typical case reveals dissimilarities as well as simi-larities (§130). Somewhat idiosyncratic (though cp. VII, 2) was Wittgen-stein's view that "logical investigation explores the nature of all things" (§89). Whereas logicians have often been said to take no more interest in reality than do mathematicians, for Wittgenstein, young and old, logic was "interested only in reality" (*NB* 9; see GI 30–31); it was con-crete (§97), *sachlich* (Man. 108, 256). Similarly, whereas *grammar* has usually meant what is found in the books of grammarians, for Wittgen-stein it meant far more (see commentary on §29a; cp. I, 7–8). In fact the terms *grammar* and *logic* were for him roughly synonymous: "If it belongs to the description of a language-game, it belongs to logic" (*OC* 628; see *OC* 56, 82). However, *grammar* became his preferred term, at least for stating his later views, whereas *logic* is more likely to appear in an account of his former thought, as here. For, as the present section indicates, the early terminology was contaminated.

(4)   Thus the repeated occurrence of the word *logic,* in this sec-tion as in no other, is a warning to the reader. Here especially, where the style as well as the content suggests the title "Confessions", it should not be too readily supposed that any particular statement expresses Wittgenstein's viewpoint at the time of writing (see GI 55). Gross mis-understandings may otherwise result, and sometimes have.

DETAILED COMMENTARY

§89(a) These considerations bring us: *RFM* 6 makes the link with Sec-tion V thus: "But still, I must only infer what really *follows*!—Is this supposed to mean: only what follows, going by the rules of inference; or is it supposed to mean: only what follows, going by *such* rules of inference as somehow agree with some (sort of) reality? Here what is before our minds in a vague way is that this reality is something very abstract, very general, and very rigid. Logic is a kind of ultra-physics, the description of the 'logical structure' of the world, which we perceive through a kind of ultra-experience (with the understanding e.g.). . . ."

logic: on this term, see VI, 3–4.

something sublime: see §§38b, 94; *RFM* 6, above; *Z* 444, quoted for §104; 6.13 ("Logic is not a body of doctrine, but a mirror-image of the world. Logic is transcendental").

(b) Most of the points in this paragraph the later W. might accept, but the sense would need to be altered. Each reappears, reinterpreted, in subsequent paragraphs (especially of the next section), to which I shall refer. This double reference, both forward and backward to the *Tractatus*, confers a peculiar ambiguity on the whole paragraph.

peculiar depth: see *NB* 30hi; cp. §111.

universal significance: cp. §§118–19.

at the bottom: for it treats the possibilities of phenomena, underlying all physical laws and descriptions (§90a). Contrast this with §§124–25. Cp. 4.111 ("The word 'philosophy' must mean something whose place is above or below the natural sciences, not beside them").

the nature of all things: see GI 30; 2.022; cp. §§370–71. "Logic cannot treat a special set of things" (*NB* 99).

and is not meant to concern itself . . . : see GI 39; 6.1222, 6.1232–6.1233.

in the facts of nature: cp. §108c, p. 230a; Russell, *Logic*, 199 (quoted in III, 4).

to grasp causal connexions: cp. GI 49; 5.135–5.136.

the basis: see *PB* 51, quoted for §90a.

new facts: see *NB* 75lm, 89ghij; 4.112–4.1122; cp. §125.

in plain view: cp. §126.

in some sense: cp. §§122–23.

(c) In this third paragraph the ambiguity of the second disappears; no statement need be put into the mouth of the early W.

Augustine says . . . : in *Confessions*, XI, 14, 17; see the quotation in §436 (which is more appropriate here).

For W., this question about the nature of time was a paradigm philosophical problem (*PG* 193d; see *BB* 6, 26; Man. 219, 24; and below).

He recognized an analogy between his thought in this paragraph and Plato's doctrine of reminiscence (see commentary on §127). Cp. *Meno*, 80B (quoted by Pitcher, *Philosophy*, 190): "I have spoken about virtue hundreds of times, held forth often on the subject in front of large audiences, and very well too, or so I thought. Now I can't even say what it is." Similar remarks occur in Moore, e.g. *Problems,* 267b–268a, 309b, and in Russell and James: "When I say *every thought is part of a personal consciousness,* 'personal consciousness' is one of the terms in question. Its meaning we know so long as no one asks us to define it, but to give an accurate account of it is the most difficult of philosophic tasks" (James, *Principles,* I, 225; see 221b, 296–97). "That is a rather singular fact, that everything you are really sure of, right off is something that you do not know the meaning of, and the moment you get a precise statement you will not be sure whether it is true or false, at least right off. The process of sound philosophizing, to my mind, consists mainly in passing from those obvious, vague, ambiguous things, that we feel quite sure of, to something precise, clear, definite, which by reflection and analysis we find is involved in the vague thing that we start from, and is, so to speak, the real truth of which that vague thing is a sort of shadow" (Russell, *Logic,* 179–80).

For similar discussion of other examples, see §75 (*game*); *PG* 256a (symbolism and psychological processes); *BB* 121c and *EPB* 174–75 (reading). In such cases, where we can neither point to the thing nor encapsulate it in a definition, philosophers often say that the word or the thing is "indefinable", forgetting that there is another way to communicate the meaning of a word, namely the description of its use (*BB* 1; §182).

question of natural science: cp. *BB* 35 ("the characteristic of a metaphysical question being that we express an unclarity about the grammar of words in the *form* of a scientific question").

we need to *remind* ourselves: see §§109 (end), 127, 253c.

for some reason: W. stressed two main reasons:

(1)   the complexity of language, which makes it difficult to get a clear view of grammar (see §§122–23, 664; *Z* 121, quoted for §123; *BB* 119, quoted for §129).

"When we philosophize we are constantly bound to give an account of our technique of the usage of words and this technique we know in the sense that we master it & we don't know it in the sense that we have the very greatest difficulty in surveying & describing it" (Man. 166, W.'s English).

"What the person attempting a description lacks above all is any trace of a system. The systems he thinks of are unsatisfactory, and he seems suddenly to find himself in a wilderness instead of the well-laid-out garden he knew so well" (Man. 229, §1225).

(2)   misleading pictures, which arise "when we look at the facts through the medium of a misleading form of expression" (*BB* 31; see GI 9; §93a).

"The continuum seems puzzling, as time seemed puzzling to Augustine, because language misleads us into applying to it a picture which doesn't fit" (*PG* 471). "Comparing measuring time with measuring lengths. To get rid of the confusing picture remind yourself exactly *how* we measure time. The difficulty here is that those pictures are terribly insistent, forcing us to see everything in their likeness" (Man. 166, W.'s English). "Let us remember what difficulties the concept of temporal measurement caused St. Augustine and how they are removed when we perceive that temporal measurement and spatial measurement are not measurements in the same sense. [Later, W. was slower to label a different use a "different sense".] The word 'measurement' is used here only in analogous ways. We think of a certain use of a word (say 'try' or 'measure'), that is, of a use in combination with certain other words, and tell ourselves we now know the word's meaning and look for the same meaning, that is, the same grammar, when the context is different" (Man. 302, 24).

§90 See *EPB* 156 and *BB* 107e–108d for fuller development.

(a) We feel . . . : W. had. This first paragraph describes his former style of thought.

  not towards phenomena: contrast this attitude with §108c. See *NB* 3be; *PB* 51: "Physics differs from phenomenology in that it aims to establish laws. Phenomenology ascertains only possibilities. So phenomenology would be the grammar of the description of those facts on which physics builds its theories."

  towards the '*possibilities*' . . . : that is, logical possibilities. See §97a; *PB* 51d (above); 2.011–2.0141 (e.g.: "Logic deals with every possibility and all possibilities are its facts"), 2.19–2.203. Russell, "Method", 84: "We may sum up these two characteristics of philosophical propositions by saying that *philosophy is the science of the possible.* But this statement unexplained is liable to be misleading, since it may be thought that the possible is something other than the general, whereas in fact the two are indistinguishable." Schlick, "Form", 155: "The philosopher is concerned only with the essence or possibility of expression."

  We remind ourselves: despite the verbal similarity with §127 and the previous paragraph, W. is describing the mistaken approach of Augustine and the *Tractatus:* "Instead of looking at the *whole language game,* we only look at the contexts, the phrases of language in which the word is used" (*BB* 108; see Man. 302, 24, quoted for §89c). Thus immediately before the passage quoted for §436, Augustine wrote: "We talk of time . . . and times, 'how long a time is it since he said this,' 'how long a time since he did this,' and 'how long a time since I saw that'; and 'this syllable takes double the time of that single short syllable.' These words we speak, and these we hear, and are understood, and understand. They are perfectly obvious and ordinary. . . ."

that is to say: cp. Man. 108, 169: "Possibility always corresponds to a permission in grammar, concerning rules of the game." Augustine's observations about grammar occur in a logical, conceptual discussion (on whether present time can be long, whether there would be past time if time did not pass, and so on) not a scientific study of physical fact. For W. too the way to the world had been through language, the great mirror (GI 30, 50).

Thus Augustine recalls . . . : e.g. in *Confessions*, XI, 15, 18 ("And yet we say 'a long time' and 'a short time'; still, only of time past or to come. A long time past, for example, we call a hundred years ago, in like manner a long time to come we call a hundred years hence").

not *philosophical* statements: but "sentences containing such expressions as 'yesterday', 'a year ago', 'in five minutes', 'before I did this', etc." (*BB* 104). See the quotations above from Augustine.

(b) by clearing misunderstandings away: not misuses of language (GI 24).

concerning the use of words: see GI 9–10; *PG* 68c.

among other things: perhaps those mentioned in *BB* 18. See GI 9.

by certain analogies . . . : see GI 11–23. Further references: *BB* 49a, 55c, 108, 151a; *PG* 193e–194a; Pitcher, "Carroll", 330–34.

Some of them can be removed . . . : see *PG* 193d–194a. In the *Investigations* no entire proposition is analytically translated, in the manner of Russell or Moore. The formula W. substituted for *meaning* in §43a illustrates the present remark, but is rare; for definitions usually fail to resolve philosophical paradoxes (§182c).

may be called an "analysis": not in the sense of §383 (see above; GI 51–59), but in Moore's (see *Lectures*, 153–71). Previously W. had objected that "it was misleading to say that what we wanted was an 'analysis', since in science to 'analyse' water means to discover some new fact about it, e.g. that it is composed of oxygen and hydrogen, whereas in philosophy 'we know at the start all the facts we need to know' " (*PP* 323; see Man. 178e). He now notes a possible justification of the term, but immediately warns against the same illusion (§91).

§91(a) See *PP* 296; *LO* 49.

final analysis: "I myself spoke previously of 'complete analysis', with the idea that philosophy must definitively dissect all propositions, so as to lay bare all connections and eliminate any possibility of misunderstanding. As though there were a calculus in which this dissection were possible. What I had in mind was something like the definition Russell had given for the definite article. In like manner, I once thought that one might for instance define the concept of a sphere with the help of visual images, etc., and so reveal once for all the connection of concepts, the source of all misunderstandings, etc. At the bottom of all this there lay a false and idealized picture of the use of language. Of course in certain cases one can use definitions to clarify the relation between different kinds of use of expressions" (*PG* 211–12).

a *single* completely resolved form of every expression: as the preceding quotation indicates, analysis might thus articulate a concept (see also X, 8) or, should that prove impossible, at least the individual propositions in which the word occurs (GI 37). Thus despite the difficulties of *NB* 67–68, the *Tractatus* declared: "Nor does analysis resolve the sign for a complex in an arbitrary way: for instance, it would not have a different resolution every time that it was incorporated in a different proposition" (3.3442). And "a proposition has one and only one complete analysis" (3.25). For "I can devise different pictures of a fact. . . . But what is characteristic of the *fact* will be the same in all of these pictures and will not depend on me" (*NB* 46–47). "When the proposition is just as complex as its reference, then it is *completely* analysed" (*NB* 46). "A completely analysed proposition contains just as many names as there are things contained in its reference" (*NB* 11).

Such thinking was widespread; cp. e.g. Waismann's theses (*Kreis*, 234, 253); Britton, "Language", 29; Moore, *Commonplace*, 25, 207.

something hidden: see the commentary on §60 ("Does the former lie concealed") and on §102; *Z* 140 ("Ever and again comes the thought that what we see of a sign is only the outside of something within, in which the real operations of sense and meaning go on"), 445; *BB* 3e; 4.002 ("from the outward form of the clothing it is impossible to infer the form of the thought beneath it"), 4.011, 4.013.

completely clarified: cp. §133b; Russell, *Logic*, 179–80, quoted for §89c.

(b) Cp. §§81a, 88. Young W. equated the demand for a "*single* completely resolved form" with the requirement of "complete exactness": "If there is a final sense and a proposition expressing it completely then there are also names for simple objects" (*NB* 64); "The demand for simple things *is* the demand for definiteness of sense" (*NB* 63). For sharper insight into this connection, see GI 37.

§92 See *Z* 444; cp. §97; *NB* 7; *LC* 48b.

"The Atomists had been ostensibly concerned with such questions as 'What is a language? How do sentences *mean* something? What is a name, and what sort of things can be named?' The answers to these questions were not obvious; and here the first 'picture' began to operate. If the answers were not obvious, then obvious phenomena surely could not be relevant to the problem; the answer must surely be something quite different, something which the things we all see merely conceal" (Warnock, *English Philosophy*, 57).

(a) This finds expression: the *a priori* demand for precision passes from the interpretation of individual statements to the semantic concepts used in discussing them; they too must mean something clear-cut, for they show the way (cp. *Kreis*, 182).

as to the *essence* of language: see GI 32; §§65, 97b; 5.4711.

of propositions: see GI 30, 32; 3.143, 4.016, 4.027, 4.5, 5.471, 5.4711; *NB* 39gh.

of thought: see GI 36; §97a; Man. 108, 206.

already lies open to view: see §§126–29.

becomes surveyable: see GI 25, 52, 57–58. The italics of the German are explained by §122.

by a rearrangement: see commentary on §109 ("but by arranging"); *BB* 44c–45a (e.g.: "Some of the greatest achievements in philosophy could only be compared with taking up some books which seemed to belong together, and putting them on different shelves; nothing more being final about their positions than that they no longer lie side by side. The onlooker who doesn't know the difficulty of the task might well think in such a case that nothing at all had been achieved").

***beneath* the surface:** see §164a; *BB* 113, bottom; *NB* 7 ("This is still very much on the surface").

(b) Compare *BB* 1 (on such what-questions and their proper treatment); GI 20–22 (on the Essence Fallacy and its origin); and GI 30 (on this *a priori* approach to language, thought, and the world).

***The essence is hidden* . . .':** cp. *NB* 7 ("if I were not blind").

is to be given once for all: "In giving the general form of a proposition you are explaining what kind of ways of putting together the symbols of things and relations will correspond to (be analogous to) the things having those relations in reality. In doing thus you are saying what is meant by saying that a proposition is true; and you must do it once for all" (*NB* 112; see 5.47).

§93 See §110; *PG* 169d; cp. *BB* 6d.

(a) "very queer": see (*b*); cp. *NB* 39 ("The transition from the general consideration of the propositional form: *infinitely difficult, fantastic*"); Frege, *Writings*, 65 ("Judgments can be regarded as advances from a thought to a truth value. Naturally this cannot be a definition. Judgment is something quite peculiar and incomparable").

The forms that we use . . . : see GI 11ff; commentary on §94 ("all sorts of ways"); §§90, 94, 104, 110a, 115.

(b) the enormous importance: reflected in W.'s earlier identification of language with propositions (GI 32).

something extraordinary: see §95. In addition to the unfailing reference, both for the individual names (§§39, 57–59) and for the proposition as a whole (§95), there is the supposed exactness and regularity of this calculus (Section XV) operated by people who have no awareness of what they are doing (4.002). "These latter activities seem to take place in a queer kind of medium, the mind; and the mechanism of the mind, the nature of which, it seems, we don't quite understand, can bring about effects which no material mechanism could. Thus e.g. a thought (which is such a mental process) can agree or disagree with reality; I am able to think of a man who isn't present; I am able to imagine him, 'mean him' in a remark which I make about him, even if he is thousands of miles away or dead. 'What a queer mechanism,' one might say, 'the mechanism of wishing must be if I can wish that which will never happen' " (*BB* 3–4).

§94 See the parallel passage in *BB* 6.

pure intermediary: for Frege, "the realm of sense" ("Compound", 4), "the world of thoughts" (ibid., 5). As for W.: Since the sense of a proposition could not be the reported fact itself without making all propositions true (3.13), and yet had to be somehow identical with the reported fact if truth was to be possible (2.16–2.17, 2.2, 2.22), he had equated the sense of a proposition with a possible state of affairs, the one thought out and represented in the proposition. So the intermediate realm consisted of pure possibilities, logical shadows as it were of the states of affairs thought, wished, expected, hoped, feared, and so on (GI 35–36). These shadows seemed to be lodged neither in the objects named (for a different proposition might name the same objects) nor in the mere signs (for they could be differently meant), but in the understanding (§81b), which thereupon appeared a strange and marvelous medium (§102), since all sorts of things could take place in it without our being aware of their occurrence, and the pictures thus formed seemed to fix reference with a precision and certainty which no ordinary picture can match. On the other hand, one naturally thinks: "But can there be a possibility without some reality which corresponds to it?" (*PB* 164). So propositions, thoughts, must somehow penetrate to realities more basic than any of the contingent states of affairs mentioned in our propositions, that is, to the unalterable objects which constitute the substance of this or any world (2.014–2.0271). Though W. never managed to identify a single atomic object, supposedly our every statement makes unerring contact with myriads of them. Language did surely seem fantastic!

"Without changing anything in the least we could conceive the matter very simply. A command, expectation, etc. would always be that a thin line, drawn by the command, expectation, etc., be drawn thicker. The reality of the thin drawing is the possibility of the thick line" (Man. 108, 253).

"Being able to do something seems like a shadow of the actual doing, just as the sense of a proposition seems like the shadow of a fact, or the understanding of a command like the shadow of its execution. In the command the fact as it were 'casts its shadow before it'. But this shadow, whatever it may be, is not the event" (*PG* 159–60; see *GI* 36; *BB* 32). "Reality is not like the daylight that first gives color to things which are already there, colorless as it were, in the dark" (*PG* 136; cp. 2.0232).

"One chief view about propositions to which he was opposed was a view which he expressed as the view that a proposition is a sort of 'shadow' intermediate between the expression which we use in order to assert it and the fact (if any) which 'verifies' it. He attributed this view to W. E. Johnson, and he said of it that it was an attempt to make a distinction between a proposition and a sentence" (*PP* 265; see *BB* 36b, quoted for §36a).

"We are treating here of cases in which, as one might roughly put it, the grammar of a word seems to suggest the 'necessity' of a certain intermediary step, although in fact the word is used in cases in which there is no such intermediary step. Thus we are inclined to say: 'A man *must* understand an order before he obeys it,' 'He must know where his pain is before he can point to it,' 'He must know the tune before he can sing it,' and suchlike" (*BB* 130; *EPB* 196).

The viewpoint here criticized is, of course, traditional and widespread. In addition to Johnson and the logical atomists, see Moore and Frege, e.g.:

"First of all, then, I do *not* mean by a proposition any of those collections of *words,* which are one of the things that are commonly called propositions. What I mean by a proposition is rather the sort of thing which these collections of words *express.* No collection of words can possibly be a proposition, in the sense in which I intend to use the term. Whenever I speak of a proposition, I shall always be speaking, *not* of a mere sentence—a mere collection of words, but of what these words *mean*" (Moore, *Problems,* 57).

Frege's *Begriffsschrift* bore the title "a formalized language of pure thought". "Thought is in essentials the same everywhere. . . . Such differences as there are consist only in this, that the thought is more pure or less pure, less dependent or more upon psychological influences and on external aids such as words or numerals" (*Foundations,* iii). "The thought, in itself immaterial, clothes itself in the material garment of a sentence and thereby becomes comprehensible to us" ("Thought", 292). "A traveller who crosses a mountain-range does not thereby make the mountain-range; no more does the judging subject make a thought by acknowledging its truth. If he did, the same thought could not be acknowledged as true by one man yesterday and another man to-day; indeed, the same man could not recognize the same thought as true at different times—unless we supposed that the existence of the thought was an intermittent one" (*Writings*, 127). "We can generalize this still further: for me there is a domain of what is objective, which is distinct from that of what is actual. . . . The number one, for instance, is not easily taken to be actual, unless we are disciples of John Stuart Mill" (*Basic Laws*, 15–16).

to sublime . . . the signs themselves: see §39 ("the real names"); *PG* 265 ("Through a process of sublimation, so often employed"); cp. Frege on thought which "is more pure or less pure" (above) and *PG* 108 ("Is it, as it were, a contamination of the sense that we express it in a particular language, with its contingent features, and not as it were incorporeally and purely?").

"In reflecting on language and meaning, we can easily come to think that in philosophy we do not really speak of words and sentences in a quite plain, ordinary sense, but in a sublimated, abstract sense.—As though a given proposition were not precisely what some person utters, but an ideal entity (the 'class of all synonymous sentences', or the like)" (*PG* 121; cp. 3.31–3.313).

in all sorts of ways: see GI 12ff; *BB* 30–31. In the present instance: (a) when we say that we "mean" or "understand" a sentence, the surface parallel between these and other verbs suggests a mental process accompanying the words (GI 18); (b) the single word *proposition* suggests an essence, a single basic form (GI 20–22); (c) the distinction between a sentence and its sense, common to many different sentences, suggests an intermediate entity between words and things (3.34–3.341); (d) since the words in a proposition must have "meanings" and this substantive suggests referents, it seems these referents *must* exist at the moment of speech (III, 4–5); (e) the substantive *language* sends us in search of an essence which must then apply to all propositions; (f) since we use propositions to "talk about things", to "describe reality", the reality described must somehow exist even when the proposition is false; and so on. Though so diverse, these all illustrate the misleading influence of surface analogies (GI 11).

§95   See GI 34–35; XV, 1; §428; *BB* 5e, 31; *PG* 154–55; Man. 108, 206, 213, 218–19; cp. §§197, 461–63; *NB* 3c.

mean: in W.'s former view of things, it was intention, the act of meaning, which linked signs with reality (GI 37), sending forth projective rays, as it were, which stopped nowhere short of the things themselves. "*That* is how a picture is attached to reality; it reaches right out to it. It is laid against reality like a ruler. Only the end-points of the graduating lines actually *touch* the object that is to be measured" (2.1511–2.15121; see 3.11; cp. *LC* 67). In 1930 W. was still imprisoned in this view: "Someone says, 'I want to see a red piece of paper.' He is shown pieces of different colors, white, green, finally a red one; he says, '*That* is what I *meant*.' How could he *mean* the red without seeing it?—For even if he had an image, this was not what he then was shown (otherwise he would not have expected anything); so he first had somehow to *mean* this image too.—Isn't this how it is: he is able to compare this image with the present—not expected—visual impression & does compare it & thus as it were fixes the interpretation of the image" (Man. 108, 222). Man. 108, 265–66 shows him fighting free in that same year. By 1933 he merely described and analyzed the attitude: " 'But I meant *him*!' What a remarkable process, this meaning! Can you mean someone even when he is in America and you are in Europe? And even if he no longer exists?" (*PG* 103).

do not stop anywhere short: cp. *Kreis*, 249; see §§428, 455; *BB* 35f–36a, 38a–39a; and the quotations just given. A similar chronological series on this point:

"These correlations are, as it were, the feelers of the picture's elements, with which the picture touches reality" (2.1515).

"For me to be able to mean something, it must be there & if it is there, then it belongs to the thought (for it is a condition for the existence of this thought)" (Man. 109, 46). "So I still keep telling myself that the fact must already be there in the . . . sentence though I know that it isn't there" (Man. 108, 193). "The thought is distinct from *that* which verifies it, & yet it cannot be distinct in the sense of *not being the same*" (Man. 110, 30). "Everything essential about thought can be summed up thus: The thought that p is the case is not the fact that p is the case. The thought is *another* fact" (ibid., 37).

"A person can wish something were the case, although it isn't. And yet he wishes precisely that which is going to take place. It seems a marvel . . . I expect *him to come* and not just something similar" (Man. 302, 18).

"[Thought] strikes us as queer when we tell ourselves that it connects objects in the mind, since it is precisely the thought that *this* person is *doing that;* or that it isn't a sign or picture, as I would still have to know how this in its turn was meant; or that it isn't something dead, since *for me* what I think *really* happens. Whence this odd way of considering things?" (*PG* 154).

"If it weren't too absurd we should say that the fact which we wish for must be present in our wish" (*BB* 37).

this—is—so: likewise, "the wish, 'may he come,' is the wish that really *he* will really *come*" (*PG* 143; see 154, above). "I mean the fact itself and not another, third thing. . . . But that signifies merely that I mean what I mean" (Man. 108, 204–5). See GI 36–37; 4.5.

paradox: see the quotations above and the commentary on §94 (especially the quotation from Man. 302,16). The paradox can be stated in still other ways: according to the *Tractatus*, a thought or proposition presents a *possibility* yet affirms a *reality;* or, it pictures a *reality* which may *not exist* (*NB* 8a).

can also be expressed: each expression gives prominence to one side of the antinomy, the first to the infallible contact, the second to the undependable reality.

of what is *not* the case: see GI 34; §§518, 520; Man. 108, 265; cp. Moore, *Problems*, 250–51, 263.

"Here is a deep mystery.

"It is the mystery of negation: This is not how things are, and yet we can say *how* things are *not*" (*NB* 30).

"A person can imagine that something is the case when it is not the case: very odd! For it isn't remarkable that the image does not correspond with reality, but it is remarkable that it then represents" (Man. 108, 203).

"A great many philosophical difficulties are connected with that sense of the expressions 'to wish', 'to think', etc., which we are now considering. These can all be summed up in the question: 'How can one think what is not the case?' . . . If I think that King's College is on fire when it is not on fire, the fact of its being on fire does not exist. Then how can I think it? How can we hang a thief who doesn't exist?' " (*BB* 30–31).

"Is thinking of something like painting or shooting at something? It seems like a projection connection, which seems to make it indubitable, although there is not a projection relation at all. If I said 'My brother is in America'—I could imagine there being rays projecting from my words to my brother in America. But what if my brother isn't in America?—then the rays don't hit anything" (*LC* 67; paragraph divisions omitted).

§96   See GI 31; §97a.

unique correlate, picture: not that young W. contrasted thought and language with paintings and other modes of representation. "Every picture is *at the same time* a logical one" (2.182) and "a logical picture of facts is a thought" (3). It is in contrast with such activities as hanging and shooting (*BB* 31 and *LC* 67, above) that a thought, of whatever variety, appears unique (GI 34).

"The world of thoughts has a model in the world of sentences, expressions, words, signs. To the structure of the thought there corresponds the compounding of words into a sentence; and here the order is in general not indifferent" (Frege, *Writings,* 123).

stand in line: as they do in the very structure of the *Tractatus:* first the world (1.1, 2.04), then thought (3.01), then language and propositions (4.001, 4.26).

each equivalent to each: "There must be something identical in a picture and what it depicts, to enable the one to be a picture of the other at all" (2.161; see 2.17–2.171). "What any picture, of whatever form, must have in common with reality, in order to be able to depict it—correctly or incorrectly—in any way at all, is logical form, i.e. the form of reality" (2.18).

The language-game in which . . . : see §§38d, 116, 132b. In the ordinary employment of *proposition* we speak, for instance, of mathematical propositions, even though they do not mirror the world. Nor did young W. think that they do. But rather than take this as a disproof of his account, he concluded that they are not genuine propositions. The language-game was all his. Or rather, this picture of things was; he just kept staring through this window frame (§115).

§97 See §92 for similar remarks, and *PB* 85d for thoughts like those criticized.

(a) See Russell, *External World,* 190a; *Introduction,* 192b.

Its essence: "To give the essence of a proposition means to give the essence of all description, and thus the essence of the world" (5.4711).

logic: see 5.511 ("all-embracing logic, which mirrors the world"); Man. 108, 242 ("Logic is a geometry of thought"); cp. Russell, *External World,* 63 ("Pure logic and atomic facts are the two poles, the wholly *a priori* and the wholly empirical").

the a priori order of the world: see GI 30–31.

the order of *possibilities:* see §90a. "Logic deals with every possibility and all possibilities are its facts" (2.0121). "Logic must foresee all possibilities of whatever sort (that is, there must be no surprises in logic). And possibility in [logical] space does not consist of a number of discrete possibilities. Space is, so to speak, *one* possibility" (Man. 108, 137; see *PG* 261).

which must be common . . . : see 2.18, quoted for §96.

utterly simple: see *NB* 7 ("The solution to all my questions must be *extremely* simple"); *NB* 38d ("infinitely simple"); and especially 5.4541 ("The solutions of the problems of logic must be simple, since they set the standard of simplicity. . . ."). "You say this mostly because you wish it to be the case. If your explanation is complicated, it is disagreeable, especially if you don't have strong feelings about the thing itself" (*LC* 36).

***prior* to all experience:** see commentary on §108c; 6.1222; cp. Schlick, "Psychological", 399c; Russell, *Logic,* 199 (quoted in III, 4). "Logic is *prior* to every experience—that something *is so*" (5.552).

no empirical cloudiness . . . : "His reply was that at that time his thought had been that he was a *logician;* and that it was not his business, as a logician, to try to decide whether this thing or that was a simple thing or a complex thing, that being a purely *empirical* matter! It was clear that he regarded his former opinion as absurd" (Malcolm, *Memoir*, 86). Cp. 5.551; *NB* 62: "Or in other words, what vacillates is our determinations, not the world. It looks as if to deny things were as much as to say that the world can, as it were, be indefinite in some such sense as that in which our knowledge is uncertain and indefinite." See GI 39.

It must rather be . . . : see §108a ("the *preconceived idea* of crystalline purity"); cp. Frege, *Foundations*, 115: "In arithmetic we are not concerned with objects which we come to know as something alien from without through the medium of the senses, but with objects given directly to our reason and, as its nearest kin, utterly transparent to it."

the *hardest* thing: First, because definite: "Our problems are not abstract, but perhaps the most concrete that there are" (5.5563). "For if possibilities *are left open* in the proposition, *just this* must be *definite: what is left open.* The generalizations of the form—e.g.—must be definite. What I do not know I do not know, but the proposition must shew me WHAT I know. And in that case, is not this *definite* thing at which I *must* arrive precisely simple in that sense that I have always had in mind? It is, so to speak, what is hard" (*NB* 63). "My method is not to sunder the hard from the soft, but to see the hardness of the soft" (*NB* 44).

Second, because unalterable, indestructible: "The idea of a super-hardness. 'The geometrical lever is harder than any lever can be. It can't bend.' Here you have the case of logical necessity. 'Logic is a mechanism made of an infinitely hard material. Logic cannot bend' " (*LC* 16; see §§193–94). There is one thing—a form—which cannot change in any world, and logical "objects are just what constitute this unalterable form" (2.023). Rocks, diamonds, even atoms may be smashed, but not they.

Third, perhaps also because ultimate and indubitable. Cp. §217; Russell, *External World*, 77–78: "We are thus led to a somewhat vague distinction between what we may call 'hard' data and 'soft' data. This distinction is a matter of degree, and must not be pressed; but if not taken too seriously, it may help to make the situation clear. I mean by 'hard' data those which resist the solvent influence of critical reflection, and by 'soft' data those which, under the operation of this process, become to our minds more or less doubtful. The hardest of hard data are of two sorts: the particular facts of sense, and the general truths of logic."

(b) See *PG* 121c (quoted for §94); Man. 110, 189 (quoted for §121), 201–3.

super-**order:** cp. *NB* 39r, 40gi; 5.555. "Logic is not a field in which *we* express what we wish with the help of signs, but rather one in which the nature of the natural and inevitable signs speaks for itself" (6.124).

super-**concepts:** cp. 4.126; Man. 116, 16 ("I was long tempted to believe that 'understand' is a *metalogical* word").

"experience": see *NB* 89; cp. Russell, *Logic,* 127–28, 160, and *Mind,* 82–83.

"world": see W.'s dogmatic assertions in 1–1.2, 2.021–2.0231.

must be as humble . . . : though they may be important (§93b), "as a kind of construction block can be important, since it is used frequently & for important purposes" (Man. 110, 202). See §108; and §§65ff, in which 'super-concepts' such as *language, proposition,* and *number* are shown to be as vague and varied and unscientific as an everyday term like *game* (*PG* 120b). In the new, regular suburbs of language, some concepts are regular and precise; but the words here mentioned belong to the old town (§18). And for both new and old the same rule holds: Their meaning is determined by their use in the language (§§43, 116). Cp. *EPB* 138; *BB* 95a.

§98 Throughout this paragraph, W. expresses his earlier viewpoint. He later agreed that language "is in order as it is" (see §§81, 120; *BB* 28c), but in a different sense and for different reasons than those suggested here, continued in §99, and explained in GI 37. Only *a priori* certitude that language wasn't really as vague and fluid as it appeared permitted young W. to say: "In fact, all the propositions of our everyday language, just as they stand, are in perfect logical order" (5.5563; see *NB* 62b; *LO* 50; *Kreis,* 130a; *PB* 52f, 277c–278a; cp. *Kreis,* 240, 248–49). "Remember that even an unanalysed subject-predicate proposition is a clear statement of something *quite definite*" (*NB* 4). Only thus could it be 'justified' (*NB* 70b). This viewpoint lingers on in *PB* 87e and 188a, but is questioned already in Man. 112, 188 (quoted for §83a and §292). For a fuller account, and a comparison with Russell, see V, 1–6.

§99 See §§68–71, 84; *Z* 441; contrast with *PB* 188a; cp. §465.

may . . . leave this or that open: for instance: (a) young W. would have accepted a disjunction, provided it was definite; (b) a word's use in the language might be left indefinite provided its meaning in each proposition was precise (*NB* 70d).

a **definite sense:** see GI 37; the references and quotations under §98; *NB* 5a, 40e ("The proposition must describe its reference *completely*"), 61 ("Every proposition that has a sense has a COMPLETE sense, and it is a picture of reality in such a way that what is not yet said in it simply cannot belong to its sense"), 63 ("For if possibilities *are left open* in the proposition, *just this* must be *definite: what* is left open"), 67–70; 5.156 ("A proposition may well be an incomplete picture of a certain situation, but it is always a complete picture of *something*").

would really not be a sense: "The early Wittgenstein, in accepting the assumption, may also have had other reasons in mind. The sense of a proposition, he held, is the situation it describes; and a situation is something which either actually does, or at least might possibly, exist as part of the world. But nothing in the world can be vague or indefinite: everything is, after all, *precisely* as it is. So the sense of a proposition, being the situation it describes, must be perfectly definite" (Pitcher, *Philosophy*, 174; see *NB* 62j).

"Mathematics cannot be incomplete, as a *sense* cannot be incomplete. Whatever I can understand, I must understand completely" (*PB* 188).

"We might demand definiteness in this way too: if a proposition is to make sense then the syntactical employment of each of its parts must be settled in advance" (*NB* 64). This requirement is connected with the question of verification, which W. stressed—especially in his transitional period—as an indicator of sense. For every conceivable situation, "a proposition must restrict reality to two alternatives: yes or no. In order to do that, it must describe reality completely" (4.023). "I must, whatever *is the case,* be able to say whether the proposition is true or false" (*NB* 67; cp. §80). "If the question of the truth or falsity of a proposition is *a priori* undecidable, the proposition thereby loses its sense and consequently the principles of logic no longer hold for it" (*PB* 210d).

with a hole in it: cp. §84 ("whose rules never let a doubt creep in, but stop up all the cracks where it might"); §69 ("This *and similar things. . . .*").

But is that true?: not universally, for it will depend on the circumstances (e.g. a fire), who is locked in (e.g. a cripple, a blind man), how many doors there are, where the open one is (e.g. in the ceiling), and so on. Thus "a man is imprisoned in a room if the door, though unlocked, opens inward but he doesn't think to pull it" (Man. 125). Similarly, the fly-bottle referred to in §309 has a hole in it, which remains open all the time the fly buzzes around inside. See the passage from Gasking and Jackson, "Wittgenstein", quoted for §309. Cp. *Z* 441 ("that is not true"); Malcolm, *Memoir,* 51.

"An enclosure with a hole is as good as none only if the hole defeats our purposes in constructing the enclosure; it all depends upon what we are trying to enclose. A proposition which fails to meet the determinacy requirement is a sentence so used that border-line cases are possible. But the possibility of a border-line case is nothing more than the possibility of *a* border-line case. A sentence can be used in such a way as to allow an indeterminate truth value in some kinds of case without having an indeterminate truth value in the cases with which the speaker is concerned" (Bogen, *Philosophy*, 81). Cp. §499.

§100   See Man. 220, 71–72 (fuller); *Z* 441. For the link between this number and §98, see the quotation from Man. 112, 188, for §83.

"it isn't a game": "An amorphous thought is as inconceivable as an amorphous game of chess" (Man. 108, 217; see *PB* 131). In the original version of §83a, W. had someone suggest that such flexible proceedings were not really a game (Man. 115, 47).

"in the rules": as opposed, for instance, to our vague awareness of the game (see 4.002; *NB* 69; commentary on §89c) and fallible human conduct of it (*RFM* 6, quoted for §89a; commentary on p. 225h). Cp. commentary on §81b.

does this prevent . . . : see §§68, 83.

the role of the ideal in our language: the translation "our language" (for *unserer Ausdrucksweise*) fits two of the following lines of interpretation, but not the third: (1) that suggested by §88 (exactness is a relative ideal in everyday speech, not an absolute one); (2) that suggested (and more solidly supported) by §§110–15 and *BB* 43c ("certain pictures embedded in our language"); (3) that suggested by §81a ("here the word 'ideal' is liable to mislead") and by the next number ("nor do we understand the nature of this 'must' "). In this last, W. would be referring to the way philosophers, particularly logical atomists, expressed themselves (e.g. *NB* 66f). Cp. §§93a (*unserer Ausdrucksweise*), 94 (*unsere Ausdrucksformen*).

§101   can't be any vagueness: either in the formal system (5.451, 5.46; *PG* 115b) or in the propositions to which it is applied (above).

'must': see VI, 1; §131; cp. *BB* 43c.

we already see it: see §102; cp. *NB* 16c, 60d, 61c, 69e; 4.023.

"But it also seems certain that we do not infer the existence of simple objects from the existence of particular simple objects, but rather know them—by description, as it were—as the end-product of analysis, by means of a process that leads to them" (*NB* 50). "It seems that the idea of the SIMPLE is already to be found contained in that of the complex and in the idea of analysis, and in such a way that we come to this idea quite apart from any examples of simple objects, or of propositions which mention them, and we realize the existence of the simple object—*a priori*—as a logical necessity" (*NB* 60).

§102   See GI 37–41; IX, 2, 9; §81b; *RFM* 6b; *BB* 3e, 42a; *PG* 50bd; Man. 302, 2; cp. §229; *PG* 248d.

the background: "The understanding of language—of the game, as it were—seems like a background against which a particular sentence acquires meaning" (*PG* 50). "In our study of symbolism there is no foreground and background, not essentially a tangible sign and an intangible capacity or understanding which accompanies it" (*PG* 87; see *BB* 42a, quoted in IX, 2; *PG* 50b; Man. 110, 27).

a medium: "You do not understand your own transactions, that is to say you do not have a synoptic view of them, and you as it were project your lack of understanding into the idea of a medium in which the most astounding things are possible" (*Z* 273).

"It seems at first sight that that which gives to thinking its peculiar character is that it is a train of mental states, and it seems that what is queer and difficult to understand about thinking is the processes which happen in the medium of the mind, processes possible only in this medium. The comparison which forces itself upon us is that of the mental medium with the protoplasm of a cell, say, of an amoeba. We observe certain actions of the amoeba, its taking food by extending arms, its splitting up into similar cells, each of which grows and behaves like the original one. We say 'of what a queer nature the protoplasm must be to act in such a way,' and perhaps we say that no physical mechanism could behave in this way, and that the mechanism of the amoeba must be of a totally different kind. In the same way we are tempted to say 'the mechanism of the mind must be of a most peculiar kind to be able to do what the mind does' " (*BB* 5).

for I understand . . . : W. had written: "If understanding doesn't mean translating, then it means seeing the sign in the space of its grammatical rules" (Man. 110, 51).

§103 See Man. 229, §824; cp. §§112–15; *Z* 441. For an especially clear illustration, see GI 37 and *NB* 67–68 ("There does not seem to be any other possibility").

§104 The first sentence alone might apply to examples such as Russell's metaphysical dichotomy between substantives and verbs (*Logic*, 105–24; cp. Ramsey, *Foundations*, 117a); or it might suggest a parallel between Faraday's attitude in p. 46n and W.'s early viewpoint: As the single, unchanging word *water* suggested an immutable essence of water, so too W. saw language and propositions through the single terms *language* and *proposition* (Man. 220, 74). "We are under the illusion that what is sublime, what is essential, about our investigation consists in its grasping *one* comprehensive essence" (*Z* 444). However, neither of these illustrations fits the second sentence. The examples cited for §112 come closer. But the number as a whole alludes most clearly to cases like §§113–14 (with which it is linked explicitly in Man. 220, 88) and these:

(1)   "The *viewpoint* from which we study language is that of a game with strict rules. We compare it with such a game, measure it by it" (*PG* 77b). "That is, we continually *compare* language with such a procedure" (*PG* 63b; see §81a), so come to imagine that "if anyone utters a sen-

tence and *means* or *understands* it he is operating a calculus according to definite rules" (§81b; see §100). This illustration—this "ideal" (§81a)—is the one that fits best the preceding and following numbers.

(2) "When I compared the proposition with a ruler, what I did, strictly speaking, was to take a statement of length with the aid of a ruler as an example for all propositions" (*PG* 164; cp. §430; 2.1512).

(3) "It now occurred to Wittgenstein that one might reverse the analogy and say that a *proposition* serves as a *picture*" (von Wright, "Sketch", 7–8; see GI 32, 50; I, 1). "Here one seems *completely* justified in inferring: 'If *one* proposition is a picture, then any proposition must be a picture, for they must all be of the same nature' " (*Z* 444). "It must be possible to demonstrate everything essential by considering this case" (*NB* 7).

(4) Of attempts at phenomenological description (X, 8), W. wrote: "Why is it so difficult to describe these everyday appearances? Isn't it almost as though one wanted to describe a picture which one saw behind a fine & complicated wire netting, so that one always runs the risk of taking for a trait of the picture what is a feature of the netting? 'Description'. One thinks of a mental space whose contents one describes. As one describes the objects and events in a room" (Man. 130). See §§398–401, where the connection with this number is equally unmistakable.

We predicate of the thing . . . : cp. *NB* 16c, 19g; Man. 228, §493. If taken out of context, these words could be far more widely illustrated in W.'s philosophy, for instance by his remarks about misleading analogies, where similarity in form of expression suggests similarity in depth grammar (GI 11–13; cp. §§112–13). Russell spoke this way oftener than W. did; see *Mind*, 212b; *Matter*, 239b, 243b; *Logic*, 185 ("That is why the theory of symbolism has a certain importance, because otherwise you are so certain to mistake the properties of the symbolism for the properties of the thing").

§105 Revised from Man. 220, 74–75.

(a) "It is characteristic of the way we are accustomed to treat language that we believe there must in the long run be uniformity, symmetry; instead of holding, on the contrary, that there can be none" (Man. 229, §1575). See the commentary on §98; cp. *Kreis*, 250 ("The logical structure of elementary propositions need not have the slightest resemblance to the logical structure of the sentences in everyday speech"), 252 ("The categories of everyday language do not suffice to describe phenomena").

(b) See §39 on the "real names" revealed by analysis, and GI 37 on W.'s former recourse to mental meaning acts. If analysis reveals the preexisting sense of an ordinary proposition, then the atomic names and ele-

mentary propositions finally set down on paper must have been somehow present already in the unanalyzed proposition (X, 6–8), and if not
in the signs themselves, where else but in thought? "It must be possible
to distinguish just as much in the real propositional sign as can be distinguished in the situation" (*NB* 37). "The two must possess the same
logical (mathematical) multiplicity" (4.04). However, "if language is not
a picture & yet shows us how things stand in reality, it must (causally)
evoke pictures which it does not portray and therefore does not determine. Those pictures, then, I call the real language" (Man. 110, 168).
Cp. *Kreis*, 236; *PB* 184n.

Passages like *PG* 121c (quoted for §94) point back to a complementary feature of "the sign in the sign" (*NB* 18), of "the symbol" as opposed to the contingent mark or sound (3.326; see 6.124; *NB* 36).
"What is essential in a symbol is what all symbols that can serve the
same purpose have in common. So one could say that the real name of
an object was what all symbols that signified it had in common"
(3.341–3.3411; cp. 3.344). Similarly, "the sign 'not' is the class of all
negating signs" (*NB* 42); "the operation of negating does not consist in,
say, putting down a ~, but in the class of all negating operations" (*NB*
43). So too, "the class of all signs that assert both p and q is the sign for
p.q" (*NB* 44). See *NB* 55; cp. 5.46–5.461.

See also Russell, *Logic*, 201, and 238–39, e.g.: "Suppose I say: '*xRy*
implies that *x* belongs to the domain of *R*,' that would be a proposition
of logic and is one that contains only variables. You might think it contains such words as 'belong' and 'domain', but that is an error. It is only
the habit of using ordinary language that makes those words appear.
They are not really there." "In each case I can only utter an instance of
the word, not the word itself, which remains immovably in a Platonic
heaven" (*Inquiry*, 58).

§106   See commentary on §610; §120ab; *NB* 40 ("My difficulty is only
an—enormous—difficulty of expression"); Man. 107, 1–2 (quoted for
§436); cp. *BB* 46d; Russell, *Logic*, 336.

The commentary on the previous number suggests two main areas of
application for these remarks: first the alleged impossibility of expressing what is essential, necessary, logical—"what expresses *itself* in language, *we* cannot express by means of language" (4.12–4.1212; see
§§71b, 89–90, 97, 113, 120; 4.041–4.0411; *NB* 42, 107; Russell's introduction, x)—but especially the immense difficulty W. had experienced in "trying to produce ideal pictures of articulated propositions"
(*NB* 66). The precise rules in which he believed "cannot be laid down
until we have actually reached the ultimate analysis of the phenomena
in question" (LF 37; see *Kreis*, 42). But if we try to get an actual analy-

sis, "we meet with the forms of space and time with the whole manifold of spatial and temporal objects, as colours, sounds, etc., etc., with their gradations, continuous transitions, and combinations in various proportions, all of which we cannot seize by our ordinary means of expression" (LF 33). "Our mode of expression is *totally* inadequate" for this task (Man. 107, 165; see ibid., 1, 169; Man. 110, 258; PB 271b). Later W. viewed the impossible ideal (cp. NB 62aj) as an unintelligible one (X, 9–10, 20–21).

of our every-day thinking: cp. §§97b, 108bc, 116.

quite unable to describe: see commentary on §119 ("against the limits of language") and §120a.

spider's web: cp. 5.511 ("an infinitely fine network, the great mirror").

our fingers: even in BB 52 our gross physical terminology appeared "slightly cumbrous".

§107   crystalline purity: "What I am here understanding by thinking cannot be an essentially human process, for that does not interest me in logic" (Man. 109, 43; see commentary on §108, especially the quotes from Man. 108).

not a *result of investigation:* see §§101, 131; NB 65; cp. NB 50eh, 60de, 61ci, 62ij, 63cd, 64f, 67k, 89ghi, 117 ("It is true, in a sense, that logical propositions are 'postulates'—something which we 'demand'; for we *demand* a satisfactory notation"); Russell's introduction, xiii ("It is a logical necessity demanded by theory, like an electron").

The conflict becomes intolerable: see e.g. NB 41klm, 17 ("On the one hand my theory of logical portrayal seems to be the only possible one, on the other hand there seems to be an insoluble contradiction in it!"). "During our discussions Russell said to me, 'Logic's hell!' And this expressed perfectly what both of us, I as well as he, experienced in reflecting on logical problems; namely the awful difficulty, the hardness of these problems" (Man. 159).

in a certain sense . . . ideal: see §81a ("a logic for a vacuum").

Insert, p. 46   In Man. 228 this insert follows §223. See the comments on §104, and the quotation from Z 444. Compare what W. wrote himself in an early manuscript: "I believe that there cannot be instructions of different type. With all of them the point is just that they are instructions. And their results are always of the same type" (Man. 106, 88).

Faraday, whose book W. admired, said the same thing repeatedly: "Water is one simple thing—it goes through no change" (54); "Water is the same everywhere: the same when produced from the sea as when produced from a candle-flame" (61); "Now we men of science say that water is water, whatever form it is in,—solid, liquid or vapour; in the chemical sense it is water" (55). Cp. Schopenhauer, *World,* I, 139: "Water remains water . . . in every case it is true to its character, and always reveals that alone."

In his lectures, W. suggested that it is a good idea to ask: Could this nature change in time? A chair can change, but how about hydrogen? Is this an experiential matter? Cp. *PG* 339b.

§108   The last three paragraphs come from *PG* 121b and are developed further in *PG* 121c. Earlier, see *PB* 61bc.

(a) We see that . . . : see I, 10.

But what becomes of logic now?: "To what extent is logic rendered uncertain by uncertainty concerning the analysis of elementary propositions?" W. asked in 1930. "What stands fast?" (Man. 108, 30; cp. §§97a, 101). By 1933 he had concluded that " 'logic plays a part different from what I and Russell and Frege supposed it to play' " (*PP* 261).

preconceived idea **of crystalline purity:** see GI 45; §107; and the quotations below from Man. 108.

by turning our whole examination round: see the comments on (*bcd*); Man. 228, §44 (quoted for §255); cp. Waismann, "How I See", 361–62; Malcolm, *Memoir,* 51. This paragraph parallels *PG* 115c fairly closely, but omits a part that helps to clarify this statement and connects it with (*b*): "The task of philosophy is not to create a new, ideal language, but to clarify the use of our language—the existing one. Its aim is to remove particular misunderstandings; not, for instance, to produce a real understanding for the first time." Instead of deciding, then looking, we must look, then decide (GI 50–52; cp. §241). "This change of outlook is the most difficult thing" (Man. 112, 139; cp. §340b).

(bcd) See GI 39–40, 45, 50; Man. 110, 29, 221; Man. 109, 32; Waismann, "Relevance", 220, and *Introduction,* 238–39.

W. had written: "For us what makes a thought into a thought cannot be something *human,* something related to the nature and make-up of man; but something purely logical—something independent of the natural history of a living thing" (Man. 108, 217). "So the logician is not concerned with a specific human process. Logic is a geometry of thought" (ibid., 242). Thus W.'s remarks in *PG* 121, quoted for §94 ("to sublime"), were a self-critique, as are these in §108. For further light on this earlier, Fregean viewpoint, here alluded to, see the commentary on §105b; *NB* 65 ("For the question arises: If the individual forms are, so to speak, given me in experience, then I surely can't make use of them in logic"); *PB* 136 ("But here there appears the difference between pseudo-objects—color patches in the visual field, sounds, etc., etc.—and the elements of knowledge, the true objects"); Man. 161 ("I was about to say, 'This substitution could also be justified in the old viewpoint'!

But what is 'the old viewpoint'? I believe it is characterized by a *picture:* that of seeing, perceiving, an object which does not have its place among physical objects but someplace else").

"According to the customary view logic is an autonomous science, and a very high-class science at that, which deals only with forms and mustn't come too close to reality. But we shall see that all logical rules are only inflated concepts, and concepts are words, and that consequently the whole of logic is hidden in the words of language" (Mauthner, *Beiträge*, II, 14).

We are talking about . . . : see *OC* 306, 519; *PG* 52bc; Waismann, *Principles*, 82–83.

not about some non-spatial, non-temporal phantasm: see GI 45; the quotations above; the commentary on §120b; Frege, e.g.: "Whole", 482; "Compound", 2; "Justification", 156: "Since the concept is of itself imperceptible to the senses, it requires a perceptible representative in order to appear to us." "This divergence of expressive symbol and expressed thought is an inevitable consequence of the difference between spatio-temporal phenomena and the world of thoughts" ("Compound", 4–5).

in a variety of ways: for instance that of the linguist. "It would be misleading to say that we treat of what is essential in grammar (and he the accidental)." However, for various reasons, "we distinguish kinds of word where for him there is no distinction" (Man. 110, 194–95; Man. 213, 413). And "historical explanation, explanation as a hypothesis concerning development, is only *one* way of organizing the data—of synopsizing them. It is just as feasible to give the data in their relation to one another & to group them in a general picture without putting it in the form of a hypothesis regarding the signs' genesis" (Man. 110, 225; BUF 241; cp. §122). "The relation of the word to this sensation, whatever it may be, whether it is evoked by it, or is accompanied by it, or gives it outlet, does not interest us, any more than does any empirical fact about language, as such. We are concerned solely with the description of what happens, and it is not the truth of the description that interests us, but its form. What happens considered as a game" (*PG* 66; see *PG* 160d).

as we do about the pieces in chess: see GI 45; *BB* 7c; *PG* 60b, 63b, 121c (quoted for §94); *PP* 292; *Kreis*, 150; cp. Frege, *Writings*, 217d (quoted for §562); Ramsey, *Foundations*, 152 ("so that we need only consider the restrictions imposed by the rules of the game, and can disregard any others which might conceivably arise from the physical constitution of the men").

"We should attend to the *use* of the expression 'German language'! Otherwise we ask, for instance: 'What is the language—all the sentences ever spoken in it? the set of rules and words? etc. etc.' What is the system? Where is it? What is chess—all matches? the list of rules?" (*PG* 170).

Compare similar remarks on mathematics: "In Cambridge I was asked whether I believed, then, that mathematics deals with ink marks on paper. I reply: In exactly the same sense as chess has to do with wooden figures. For chess does not consist in my pushing wooden figures around a board. If I say, 'Now I shall make myself a queen with frightful eyes, which will clear the board,' you will laugh. It makes no difference what a pawn looks like. The truth is rather that the totality of the game's rules determine the logical place of the pawn. The pawn is a variable, like the 'x' in logic" (*Kreis,* 103–4). "*Frege* was right in opposing the idea that in arithmetic the numbers are the signs" (ibid., 105; see the rest of the page, and cp. *BB* 4d); however, he tended to overdo the point, in the way here criticized. See GI 45, and e.g. *Writings,* 134: "Of course we must never forget in this connexion that dressing up and putting things together are processes in time, whereas what corresponds to this in the realm of thoughts is timeless." The ancestry of W.'s former viewpoint is clear.

the rules of the game: that is, we talk in this abstract way, but not about abstractions (§§53–54). See GI 45; I, 8; *PG* 68c; Man. 112, 196; Man. 108, 178; cp. Man. 112, 292; *Kreis,* 184 ("so we can do nothing but *tabulate rules*"); Man. 109, 38 ("for they are the mirror—in whatever way—of the laws of the world").

not describing their physical properties: "any more than the laws of Euclidean geometry treat of pencil marks on paper" (Man. 110, 76). See *PB* 59g, 161a; *Kreis,* 163; Man. 108, 182; Waismann, "Relevance", 220.

"What is a piece in chess?": see §31; *RFM* 160hi; *PG* 59b, 67c; *PB* 61d.

VII. Philosophy as Therapy (§§109–133)

(1)   Having already treated the main themes of this section in the General Introduction, but separately, I shall here attempt to unite them in a synoptic view. One way is to consider the target of Wittgenstein's disparate remarks. In 1914 Russell delivered a paper "On Scientific Method in Philosophy". He was all for it. So was young Wittgenstein.

So were the logical positivists. "There was one common tenet: that philosophy ought to be scientific" (V. Kraft, *Circle*, 15). This viewpoint Wittgenstein now rejects. "Philosophers constantly see the method of science before their eyes, and are irresistibly tempted to ask and answer questions in the way science does. This tendency is the real source of metaphysics, and leads the philosopher into complete darkness" (*BB* 18; see GI 70).

(2) "If the notion of the universe and the notion of good and evil are extruded from scientific philosophy," wrote Russell, "it may be asked what specific problems remain for the philosopher as opposed to the man of science?" ("Method", 83). His answer: Whereas science deals with fact, "*philosophy is the science of the possible*" (ibid., 84). "It must not deal specially with things on the surface of the earth, or with the solar system, or with any other portion of space and time" (ibid., 83); its propositions "must be concerned with such properties of all things as do not depend upon the accidental nature of the things that there happen to be, but are true of any possible world, independently of such facts as can only be discovered by our senses." They are, therefore, *a priori*, and "philosophy, if what has been said is correct, becomes indistinguishable from logic as that word has now come to be used" (ibid., 84). "It is concerned with the analysis and enumeration of logical *forms*, i.e. with the kinds of propositions that may occur, with the various types of facts, and with the classification of the constituents of facts. In this way logic provides an inventory of possibilities, a repertory of abstractly tenable hypotheses" (ibid., 85).

(3) With much of this Wittgenstein continued to agree; the limits within which he restricted philosophical activity, narrow by traditional standards, were those prescribed by Russell. Philosophy was not in competition with science, offering a general view of reality or conduct in addition to science's partial views (GI 5), or adding a scientific account of its own special set of objects (GI 8). Philosophy concerns itself with logical forms, with the *a priori*. In this sense, philosophy and logic are one (see VI, 3), and neither is a science. But neither are they scientific, Wittgenstein would now add, at least not in the ways Russell and others suggested. Philosophy aims at no complete classification, no thorough coverage within the area of its competence, as science does (GI 29–30). Nor does it form hypotheses or theories (§109; GI 43–44, 70); for its goals are not positive but therapeutic (GI 8ff; §§109–19). It does not aim to explain anything but to straighten out our thinking. And to succeed in that it must resemble science in a way Russell did not mention. In its therapeutic attention to logical forms it must be factual, empirical (§§108–9, 116–17, 124–27; GI 51–52). Paradoxical as it may sound, the study of the *a priori* must be thoroughly *a posteriori*. "We

must do away with all *explanation,* and description alone must take its place" (§109; see §496).

(4)   Such prescriptions may sound as dogmatic as those of the *Tractatus,* but this time they were the fruit of experience. Wittgenstein was personally acquainted with the "complete darkness" into which the scientific viewpoint leads a philosopher. Section VI describes his futile struggles to 'explain', in the ways required for the superscience of logic (see VI, 1–2). It seemed he had to explain the nature of the proposition, of language, and of thought (GI 30), and thereby to explain their connection with the world (GI 31–36). For everything essential was hidden beneath the level of phenomena which might merely be described (§92). On the other hand, the ideal order thus arrived at, though not learned from all propositions or uses of words (ibid.), had nevertheless to be found in all (§101). But search as he might, he couldn't find it (§105). So the conflict became unbearable (§107). Such was the darkness in which Wittgenstein himself had groped.

(5)   And he was not alone. Though the prescriptions of the present section are based largely on his personal experience, Wittgenstein had reason to consider the experience typical. He encountered similar errors in theories of play (*LC* 49), Frazer's discussion of primitive rites (BUF), Frege's treatment of number (see commentary on §67b), Russell's explanations by means of feelings (see commentary on §598), James's account of thought (e.g. Section XXXII), Freud's uniform theory of dreams (*LC* 48), the logical-positivist approach to language: "Language is not studied from a psychological nor from a sociological point of view but solely with reference to the general conditions of a system of symbolization" (V. Kraft, *Circle,* 27). These and many other examples revealed a like craving for generality and consequent dogmatism and neglect of the individual case (*BB* 18).

(6)   It has appeared to some that Wittgenstein's later thought is vitiated by a methodological oversight analogous to the one he criticized. Logical atomists and logical positivists failed to grasp that even the *a priori* must be determined *a posteriori.* The later Wittgenstein, it has been objected, failed to note that *a posteriori* investigation is necessarily scientific. "Russellian logic," he complained, "says nothing about the kind and use of sentences . . . yet logic gets its whole sense (*only*) from its supposed application to sentences" (Man. 125). But to say how words and sentences are actually used calls for empirical research. Even if logic and philosophy do not merge with the science of language ("And why not?" the objector may ask), they have constant need of the linguistic facts which linguistic science, and it alone, can provide. This implication of his "linguistic turn", it is sometimes said, Wittgenstein appears to have overlooked (see Hallett, *Definition,* 148–56).

(7)   On the contrary, the present section is full of his reply. Philosophy, he maintained, is therapy, and the therapy has no need of science or scientific tools. All the facts we need are ready at hand (§§124–26). We need merely remind ourselves of things so obvious we fail to notice them or their importance (§§127–29). And the simple language-games which remind us of them (§§130–31), the perspicuous representations which evoke the forgotten landscape of language (§§122–23), require no technical refinements in language, but replace the scientific, 'ideal' languages proposed by atomists and logical positivists (§§132–33).

(8)   Told that philosophy is in no sense scientific, a person imbued with the scientific spirit is likely to lose all interest (see Russell, *Development*, 216–17). For him, to equate philosophy with therapy is to trivialize it, and to equate it with therapy for philosophical ills is to trivialize it still further. The tail it devours is its own. Wittgenstein's answer is to point out the importance of the problems resolved. Were the objector aware that his own scientific viewpoint and the puzzles it creates are among the ills in need of treatment, he might recognize the value of the therapy (§119). Section VII recommends linguistic therapy not only in place of, but for, "scientific" philosophy (see GI 70).

(9)   Besides, let us suppose that someone, on being told that medicine is primarily therapeutic, were to express amazement at the number of doctors, nurses, and other medical personnel, at the abundance of hospitals, clinics, pharmacies, and medical schools, at the sums spent on medical research and the generally high esteem in which the practice of medicine is held. We would be amazed at *him*. Yet a kindred reaction to Wittgenstein's description and practice of philosophy is common. For though people are well aware of the diseases which afflict their bodies, they are much less conscious, naturally, of the maladies of their minds, which are just as numerous and varied and perhaps still more disastrous. Few people are capable of noting the parallel: "If in the midst of life we are in death, so in sanity we are surrounded by madness" (*RFM* 157). Wittgenstein did, so willingly dedicated his life to the prevention and cure of intellectual ills. True, even after it is pointed out that the process by which one recovers from the sicknesses of the intellect is not purely therapeutic, that the medicine is also food (GI 28), it may be felt—rightly, I believe—that Wittgenstein's conception of philosophy is arbitrarily narrow. But this should not blind us to the value of Wittgensteinian therapy. The philosopher who agrees with Wittgenstein about the possibilities of philosophy has no reason to waver in his vocation. Man, *animal symbolicum*, will always need him; for language itself is an enduring, inevitable source of error (GI 9ff), and language pervades our whole life (*BB* 59). "Our language continually ties new knots in our thinking. And philosophy is never done with disentangling them"

(Man. 109, 238; see Man. 213, 422–24; Man. 111, 133–34, quoted for §109; Hallett, "Bottle").

(10)   "In answer to the question why this 'new subject' should be called 'philosophy' he said [in 1932–1933] that though what he was doing was certainly different from what, e.g., Plato or Berkeley had done, yet people might feel that it 'takes the place of' what they had done—might be inclined to say 'This is what I really wanted' and to identify it with what they had done, though it is really different. . . . But [in 1930–1931] he had also said that the 'new subject' did really resemble what had been traditionally called 'philosophy' in the three respects that (1) it was very general, (2) it was fundamental both to ordinary life and to the sciences, and (3) it was independent of any special results of science; that therefore the application to it of the word 'philosophy' was not purely arbitrary" (*PP* 322–23; see GI 71; *BB* 28d, 62c). The apparent tendency in the present section to appropriate the word *philosophy* for philosophy done in the way Wittgenstein approved (§§109, 119, 126–28; see §§254–55, 599) may be no more than a matter of style, but seems an unfortunate violation of his own injunction to return terms to their everyday use (§116). He himself reacted strongly against the equation of philosophy with what he was doing (Drury, "Symposium", 68, quoted re the title).

DETAILED COMMENTARY

§109   See *RFM* 157; *PG* 115c; cp. 4.112; James, *Principles*, I, vi–vii.

It is true to say . . . : as W. did in the *Notebooks* (e.g. 44j-m, 93b), in the *Tractatus* (e.g. 4.111, 5.551–5.5521, 5.557), and still in Man. 109, 258–59 (e.g.: "We are not interested in the nature of agreement, nor in its empirical consequences. We are interested in *nothing* which might be other than it is"). The preceding number indicates the sense such assertions would now have for W. "What interests *us* about a sign . . . is what is yielded by the grammar of the sign" (*PG* 87; see *PG* 45b, 160d).

'that, contrary to our preconceived ideas . . .': cp. §392. "Ramsey used to reply to such questions: 'But it *just is* possible to think of such a thing.' As, perhaps, one says: 'Technology achieves things nowadays which you can't imagine at all' " (*Z* 272). "We must avoid the severe mistake committed by some of the former Empiricists like Mill and Spencer, who regarded logical principles (e.g., the Law of Contradiction) as laws of nature governing the psychological process of thinking. The nonsensical statements attended to above do not correspond to thoughts which, by a sort of psychological experiment, we find ourselves unable to think" (Schlick, "Meaning", 154–55).

whatever that may mean: cp. §511; *PG* 39a, 44b. "When we hear the words, 'A tower which is both 100 feet and 150 feet high', the image of two towers of different heights may be in our mind, and we may find it psychologically (empirically) impossible to combine the two pictures into one image, but it is not this fact which is denoted by the words 'logical impossibility' " (Schlick, "Meaning", 155).

as a gaseous medium: see GI 19; commentary on §102 ("a medium"); §339; *BB* 47, quoted for §36a; *PG* 131b; *PB* 287e; Man. 108, 216–17. "We are accustomed to thinking of it as something ethereal, unexplored; as if we were dealing with something whose exterior alone is known to us but whose interior is as yet unknown, like our brain" (*PG* 108). "When we say that thought is a spiritual activity or an activity of the soul, we think of the mind as a cloudy, gaseous entity in which a great deal occurs which cannot occur elsewhere" (Man. 110, 26; *PG* 100).

And we may not advance . . . : see *PG* 120a, 283e; *PB* 327; *LC* 10cd; cp. Schlick, "Meaning", 148g. W. extends the preceding exclusion. In Man. 109, 121–22, after reaffirming his disinterest in scientific theories, he remarked nevertheless: "Can the essential difference between 'logical & phenomenological constants', too, be shown only in grammar? Isn't a theory necessary here? Say one which distinguishes between two kinds of grammar? . . . And consider: would the theory have to show something about negation & the color red that makes their difference clear?" Later he wrote: "We do not want to find any theory of color (neither a physiological one nor a psychological one) but the logic of color concepts. And this provides what has often been wrongly expected of a theory" (Man. 176, 7B). "It is a characteristic of such a theory that it looks at a particular, clearly illustrative case and says: '*This* shows the way it always is; this case is the prototype of *all* cases.'—'Of course, that's how it must be,' we say, and are satisfied. We have found a form of presentation which attracts us. But it is as though we now saw something which lies beneath the surface" (Man. 226, 71; cp. §§92, 104). "The difficulty in renouncing all theory: We must regard as complete something that seems so obviously incomplete" (Man. 229, §1391; see GI 29, 46–58; Man. 228, §§40, 434). W. included Carnap and the logical positivists in such criticism (*PG* 210c), and, by implication, those who still follow their example and that of Ramsey (e.g. *Foundations,* 212–36), Russell (e.g. *Logic,* 41–42; *Mind,* 101), young W. (GI 30–39), and countless others (GI 70).

There must not be anything hypothetical . . . : see GI 43; §156g; *BB* 40b; *PG* 82b; cp. Berkeley, *Dialogues,* III, 445–46. On W.'s resistance to this tendency in his own thinking, see the quotation from Man. 108, 160, in GI 43. On Russell, see e.g. "Scientific Method", 85: "A scientific philosophy such as I wish to recommend will be piecemeal and tentative like other sciences; above all, it will be able to invent hypotheses which, even if they are not wholly true, will yet remain fruitful after the necessary corrections have been made." If words' use in the language impedes progress (GI 70), one then 'corrects' usage (e.g. Russell, *Logic*, 44).

We must do away with all *explanation:* see §126; *Z* 309, 313–15; *BB* 18c; *PG* 66cd; Man. 117, 209 (quoted in the Appendix: Newman); Kenny, *Wittgenstein*, 146–47; cp. Moore, *Commonplace*, 16. To determine the intended sense and scope of this declaration and thereby obviate a standard difficulty, notice that W. not only tolerated but encouraged certain types of explanation. First, the sort of account to which he applies the term *erklären* in §43 and to which we might apply it in §66 is of course not excluded; to explain the use of a word in this way is to describe it. Furthermore, explanations of philosophical puzzlement are not only permitted but proposed (GI 9–24). The philosopher may profitably reflect, as W. did, on the origin of his own disquietude, of his questions and demands concerning language, thought, and the like, and of his subsequent lack of success (e.g. §§52b, 194b, 254, 308). "This is connected, I believe, with our wrongly expecting an explanation, whereas the solution of the difficulty is a description, if we give it the right place in our considerations" (*Z* 314). Our very insistence on explanation may manifest confusion (§435). "We need to know what explanation means. There is a constant danger of wanting to use this word in logic in a sense taken over from physics" (Man. 109, 108). Thus W. had viewed thought as a sort of supermechanism (see commentary on §§193–94) requiring a superexplanation uncontaminated by empirical detail (*PG* 99c; Man. 109, 121; for an illustration, see *NB* 5l–6a). Then too, when we ask the question "Why?" we frequently fail to determine whether we are requesting a motive or a cause (*BB* 15). And to solve our philosophical problems we seldom need a motive (I, 5), or cause (GI 49; §§496, 654–55, pp. 54n, 193fg, 201j, 203h, 212d, 216d, 230a; *Z* 220; *EPB* 129; *BB* 6a, 88b, 164b; *PG* 69a, 70b, 86b, 105a, 195a) or ground (I, 4; *Kreis*, 115–16) or essence (VII, 4–5, and above; *EPB* 179; *BB* 18c, 125bc; *LC* 48–50; *PG* 120). Thus the reason for W.'s sweeping rejection of such explanations (that is, the causal hypothesis on which it rests) is not merely that "the explanation is too uncertain, in comparison with the impression the description makes on us" (Man. 110, 180; *BUF* 236; cp. §§126–29), but that if a person is troubled by a philosophical problem, "a hypothetical explanation will help him little.—It will not quiet him" (Man. 110, 181; *BUF* 236; see §§122, 133; *Z* 313–15). "People who always keep asking 'Why?' resemble tourists who read Baedeker while they stand before a building and through reading about the building's history, origins, and so on are kept from *seeing* it"

(Man. 163). If they suppressed the question "Why?", they might find the facts they need (§471).

Already in the *Tractatus* (4.0031) W. rejected Mauthner's goal of genetic explanation: "Ultimately this critique too wishes to do just what all linguistic science has always aimed to do: explain the phenomenon of language. Explain language!" (*Beiträge*, I, 12). Man. 302, 8, also seems aimed at Mauthner.

description alone: see GI 43, 51–53; *OC* 189; *Z* 447b; *RFM* 101f; *EPB* 179; *BB* 125bc; *PG* 66c, 88e–89a; Man. 112, 144; Man. 110, 99, 235 (quoted for §466); Man. 109, 214. In 1913 young W., former disciple of Schopenhauer, declared: "In philosophy there are no deductions; it is purely descriptive" (*NB* 93). His philosophizing was then descriptive in a highly abstract, *a priori* fashion, though (GI 50–52), which ignored detail (GI 39). So he later insisted that "the true state of affairs can only be seen when we look into the detail of the usage of our expressions" (*BB* 115; see §340; *BB* 80a).

"Mere description is so difficult because we believe it necessary to fill out the facts in order to understand them. It is as though we saw a canvas covered with scattered patches of color, and said: as they stand, they are incomprehensible; they acquire a sense only when we complete them and form a figure.—Whereas what I want to say is: Here *is* the whole. (When you complete it, you falsify it.)" (Man. 229, §923; see §598 and commentary).

At an intermediate stage, W. wrote: "Physics strives for truth, i.e. correct predictions of events, whereas phenomenology does not do *that*. It strives after *sense* not *truth*" (Man. 105, 3). "Thus phenomenology would be the grammar of the description of the facts on which physics builds its theories. Explanation is more than description. But every explanation contains a description" (ibid., 5; see *PB* 51–53; cp. Nicod, *Foundations*, 14).

from the philosophical problems: see GI 8, 58. Thus (1) the descriptive method is used because the problems require such an approach, and (2) only those descriptions are to be given which the problems require. (1) "For what struck *us* as being queer about thought and thinking was not at all that it had curious effects which we were not yet able to explain (causally). Our problem, in other words, was not a scientific one; but a muddle felt as a problem" (*BB* 5–6). (2) "I ought, perhaps, finally to repeat what I said in the first part of this article (page 257), namely, that he held that though the 'new subject' must say a great deal about language, it was only necessary for it to deal with those points about language which have led, or are likely to lead, to definite philosophical puzzles or errors. I think he certainly thought that some philosophers nowadays have been misled into dealing with linguistic points which have no such bearing, and the discussion of which therefore, in his view, forms no part of the proper business of a philosopher" (*PP* 323–24). Herein lies the reply to W.'s early query: "Is grammar just the description of the actual application of language? So that its propositions can in fact be viewed as the propositions of a natural science?" (Man. 109, 281–82; see VII, 6–7).

not empirical problems: but "specific individual disquietudes which we call 'philosophical problems'" (*PG* 193; see §111a; GI 68). The facts we need are all familiar (§§126–29). Cp. the commentary on §97a (*"prior* to all experience").

into the workings of our language: this is not to say that "the Wittgensteinian method concerns itself strictly with description—a description of the sources of philosophical puzzles and disagreements" (Farrell, "Appraisal", 38). Relatively seldom, especially in the *Investigations,* does W. offer causal explanations. Such understanding may emerge from the therapy, and underly it, but is not its chief content.

in despite of **an urge . . . :** see Man. 229, §923, above; Man. 108, 160, quoted for GI 43; cp. §340; Man. 112, 221: "The difficulty to be overcome is not one of the understanding but of the will."

The problems are solved: Wisdom ("Wittgenstein", 47) mentions W.'s "saying that he didn't *solve* philosophical problems, but *dissolved* them." He did not provide the missing essence or definition, indicate the hidden referent, decide between realism and idealism, and so on. See commentary on §133b ("philosophical problems"); §§110a, 133c; *BB* 47b; Man. 219, 8; cp. 4.003, 6.5–6.53.

but by arranging: see GI 25, 44–47, 51, 57; §§92, 122, 132; *BB* 44d–45a, 46d, 125a (which connects this remark with §122a).

"The result of a philosophical investigation is sometimes a new 'filing-system'. . . . If we seek a deep understanding, we must treat what at first sight looks homologous as non-homologous. And we must be able to see homology where it escapes the superficial glance. (I believe this is also a method of mathematics.)" (Man. 130, 82–83). See, for example, XXVI, 2–3.

what we have always known: see §§89c, 127, 129, and commentaries.

Philosophy is a battle: see GI 8, 25, 28; VI, 1; VII, 3, 10; *PG* 193d.

"So a battle with language takes place and I am compelled to occupy myself with language although it is not my proper concern here" (Frege, "Thought", 298).

"Philosophy, as we use the word, is a fight against the fascination which forms of expression exert upon us" (*BB* 27).

the bewitchment of our intelligence: see commentary on §115; *OC*

435 (quoted for §30a); *EPB* 156; Man. 107, 1–2; Man. 105, 116; War-nock, *English Philosophy*, 54–55; cp. *RFM* 17cde.

Mauthner, *Beiträge*, I, 1: "He must free himself from words and from verbal superstition, he must try to liberate his world from the tyranny of language."

"Human beings are entangled in the net of language and do not know it" (*PG* 462).

"Our motto might be: 'Let us not be bewitched' " (*Z* 690).

by means of language: see GI 9–24 (especially the last); cp. *NB* 93 ("Distrust of grammar is the first requisite for philosophizing"); Russell, *Logic*, 330–33. Specht (*Foundations*, 19–20) sets this view in historical perspective, within "a long philosophical tradition" (Aristotle, Occam, Locke, Berkeley, Mill, Moore, Russell). Man. 111, 133–34, suggests another perspective: "One repeatedly hears it said that philosophy does not really make any progress, that the same philosophical problems as already occupied the Greeks occupy us still. But those who say this do not understand why it is [variant: has to be] so. The reason is that our language has remained the same & continually misleads us into asking the same questions. So long as there is a verb 'to be' that seems to function like 'eat' & 'drink', so long as there are the adjectives 'identical', 'true', 'false', 'possible', so long as people talk of the flow of time & the extension of space, etc., etc., they will keep on encountering the same puzzling difficulties" (cp. VII, 9; 3.323).

§110 See *PG* 108e–109a.

(a) See *PG* 155a.

"Language": "It is astonishing what language can do. With a few syl-lables it can express an incalculable number of thoughts" (Frege, "Com-pound", 1; cp. IX, 2).

"or thought": "The characteristic thing about thought," wrote W. in the days of his troubles, "which makes it so unique for us is that when we think we don't have the feeling of interpreting" (Man. 108, 224). See the quotation from *BB* 5–6, under §109.

"something unique": see §§93, 95.

a superstition: cp. Man. 138, 32B–33A, quoted re p. 178g.

not **a mistake:** see GI 68.

(b) retreats to these illusions: see §111.

§111 See GI 24; NL 309c (quoted for §255); Man. 109, 224; cp. Man. 213, 411–13, and Man. 110, 194 (a similar discussion, in terms of *fun-damental*); *PB* 63 ("Naturally a false conception of the functioning of language destroys the *whole* of logic and everything connected with it and does not create just a small disturbance at some one spot"). The part after the dash comes from Man. 110, 176–77.

the character of *depth*: see §§583, 594a; *RFM* 23 ("the depth of the essence"); BUF 247–50; Man. 302, 13, 29; Man. 228, §8; cp. *RFM* 148f; *EPB* 204; *BB* 137a; *NB* 40 ("The older a word, the deeper it reaches"); Schopenhauer, *World*, II, 135c–136a; Frege, *Writings*, 41; James, *Principles*, I, 296–97.

"Most of the propositions and questions of philosophers arise from our failure to understand the logic of our language. . . . And it is not surprising that the deepest problems are in fact *not* problems at all" (4.003).

They are deep disquietudes: see *PG* 193d.

their roots are as deep . . . : see §167a (the German); *Z* 58b.

"Error is never so difficult to be destroyed as when it has its root in language" (Bentham, quoted in Ogden and Richards, *Meaning*, xxiv).

"The idea that that which we wish to happen must be present as a shadow in our wish is deeply rooted in our forms of expression" (*BB* 37).

a grammatical joke: "Consider, for example, a cartoon by S. J. Perelman. It shows a distraught gentleman rushing into a doctor's office clutching a friend by the wrist and whimpering: 'I've got Bright's disease and he has mine' " (Cook, "Privacy", 309–10; cp. *BB* 21c). "It is worth noting that Wittgenstein once said that a serious and good philosophical work could be written that would consist entirely of *jokes* (without being facetious)" (Malcolm, *Memoir*, 29). For other examples, see the commentary on §88b, and the lengthy continuation of §111 in Man. 220, 77–79.

§112 See §308; *BB* 117d; Farrell, "Appraisal", 40.

A simile that has been absorbed . . . : "In such a case we can say the logs which *have passed* us are all down towards the left and the logs which *will pass* us are all up towards the right. We then use this situation as a simile for all happening in time and even embody the simile in our language, as when we say that 'the present event passes by' (a log passes by), 'the future event is to come' (a log is to come). We talk about the flow of events; but also about the flow of time—the river on which the logs travel" (*BB* 107–8; *EPB* 156). Distinguish such cases from those described in GI 11ff, where a natural form of expression suggests a comparison. In Man. 220, §112 was followed by examples of this latter type rather than by §113.

§113 **over and over again:** "There is always the danger of wanting to find an expression's meaning by contemplating the expression itself, and the frame of mind in which one uses it, instead of always thinking of the practice. That is why one repeats the expression to oneself so often, because it is as if one must see what one is looking for in the expression and in the feeling it gives one" (*OC* 601). See *EPB* 233; *BB* 150ab.

fix my gaze: cp. §413 and commentary. "This must yield the nature of truth straight away (if I were not blind)" (*NB* 7).

absolutely sharply: see 4.1121 and 4.5 ("It is clear that *only* what is essential to the most general propositional form may be included in its description—for otherwise it would not be the most general form").

§114 See Man. 228, §402 ("It is difficult to depart *even slightly* from a familiar path of thought"); Man. 220, 87–88 (earlier, fuller version); cp. Z 443.

§115 See §425; Man. 220, 87.

held us captive: see Man. 116, 220 (quoted for §48a). Consult Malcolm, *Memoir*, 69, on how the spell was broken in W.'s case. "Wittgenstein declared that this is the *kind* of mistake that occurs in philosophy. It consists in being *misled by a picture*" (ibid., 53) rather than in holding an erroneous but intelligible doctrine (GI 68). See Man. FW, 12 ("But it is one of the most important facts of human life that such impressions sometimes force themselves on you"); Man. 213, 422–23: "The reason why grammatical problems are so hard and apparently ineradicable is that they are linked with the oldest habits of thought, that is, with the oldest pictures, impressed in our language itself. (Lichtenberg)."

for it lay in our language: "If there is a temptation to conceive the differential calculus as a calculus with infinitely small quantities, it is understandable that elsewhere an analogous temptation can be much stronger—namely when it is fostered on every side by our forms of speech; one can then imagine its becoming irresistible" (Man, 130; Man. 229, §824). "Our ordinary language, which of all possible notations is the one which pervades all our life, holds our mind rigidly in one position" (*BB* 59; see GI 9).

Though many grammatical analogies helped to generate the *Tractatus* picture theory of propositions, the principal influence suggested here is that of the single word *language* or *proposition,* which sent W. in search of the essence or *"general form of propositions* and of language" (§65; see GI 22).

§116 Reworked from Man. 109, 246, and Man. 213, 430. See §108b; Z 455; *PB* 88; Man. 107, 177; cp. Z 391; *PG* 46a; *PB* 55f–56a.

(a) These sample words had all occupied W. himself.

"knowledge": see commentary on §30a. Contrast Russell, *Logic*, 134, with *OC* 260 or NL 278: "Or had we better cut these 'We never know' out of our language and consider how as a matter of fact we are wont to use the word 'to know'?"

"Many will say that my discussion of the concept of knowledge is irrelevant; for though this concept as understood by philosophers may not agree with that of everyday speech, it is in fact a more important, interesting concept, formed through a sort of sublimation from the common and rather uninteresting one. However, the philosophical conception results from all sorts of misunderstandings and strengthens the misunderstandings" (Man. 232, 679).

"being": see §50; Man. 111, 133, quoted for §109 ("by means of language"); cp. *NB* 39hij.

"object": see *EPB* 121; *BB* 81a, quoted for §2b.

"Frege would have said (I remember a conversation) that the coincidence of an eclipse of the moon with a court trial is an object. And what objection is there against that? Only that we then use the word 'object' in an ambiguous way, and so confuse the results of analysis" (*PB* 137).

"Red, left, many should not be objects; but only a red patch, a table, etc. Whoever is not content with these things would perhaps do better to stop using the word 'object' " (Man. 111, 112).

"I": see Section XIII; cp. Man. 110, 31: "Solipsism could be refuted by the fact that the word 'I' does not have a central place in grammar, but is a word like any other."

"proposition": "A thought too, is, of course, a logical picture of the proposition, and therefore it just is a kind of proposition" (*NB* 82). "In (II) he had said he was willing to admit that to call a proposition a 'picture' was misleading; that propositions are not pictures 'in any ordinary sense' " (*PP* 263; cp. 4.011).

"name": see §38 and commentary; *BB* 80–81: "It has been suggested that such words as 'there', 'here', 'now', 'this' are the *'real proper names'* as opposed to what in ordinary life we call proper names, and, in the view I am referring to, can only be called so crudely."

one must always ask: despite the accusation made in *LC* 2 (see GI 14), which doubtless points to a deeper failing, Moore did frequently ask this question and point out when terms were being used in a way discontinuous with ordinary usage (e.g. *Papers,* 141–42).

to grasp the *essence:* see GI 20–23; VII, 5; *BB* 17c–20a; cp. Man. 176, 2A: "Lichtenberg says that only a few people have ever seen pure white. So do people use the word incorrectly? And how did *he* learn the correct use?—He constructed an ideal use from the usual one. And that doesn't mean a better use but one refined in a certain direction."

(b) From Man. 110, 34, where the example is *"Alles fliesst,"* and Man. 220, 89, where W. adds examples, e.g.: "The man who said we can't enter the same stream twice said something false; we can enter the same stream twice."

In this statement two senses are fused, one suggested by the preceding paragraph and the other by the subsequent paragraph; the actual use of a word in the language guided both (1) the account W. gave of its meaning (§43a) or reference (§371) and (2) his employment of the term. These points are similarly joined in *BB* 56: "Our wavering between logical and physical impossibility makes us make such statements as this: 'If what I feel is always *my* pain only, what can the supposition mean that someone else has pain?' The thing to do in such cases is always to look how the words in question *are actually used in our language*. We are in all such cases thinking of a use different from that which our ordinary language makes of the words. Of a use, on the other hand, which just then for some reason strongly recommends itself to us." See also *BB* 61.

On (1) see e.g. *BB* 1e, 19c, and W.'s general practice. On (2) see §38d and commentary; commentary on §241 ("not agreement in opinions"); §§38–40, 79d, 132, 246, 280, 295, 398–403, pp. 216, 221; *BB* 46–50, 55, 66–74; *LC* 65 (e.g.: "If you now call him 'alive', you're using language in a queer way, because you're almost deliberately preparing misunderstandings. Why don't you use some other word, and let 'dead' have the meaning it already has?"); Man. 213, 420; Man. 127 (Feb. 27); Man. 116, 245; Cook, "Privacy", 311; Chihara and Fodor, "Operationalism", 402–3; cp. VII, 10; §§254, 339b, 393; *PP* 272; Berkeley, *Dialogues*, I, 380, 392; II, 429, 440.

A straitjacket interpretation of this remark, conflicting with W.'s stress on the flexibility of language (I, 9), might reasonably be argued from his blanket rejection of metaphysics (Z 55, 458), but is in fact more commonly connected with the misunderstanding discussed in GI 24. Had W. believed that most philosophical problems arise from the misuse of language, he would have been tempted to a corresponding, exaggerated stress on conformity with usage.

metaphysical: see §58b; *PG* 136de; NL 320b; Man. 110, 194; cp. Man. 168, 3. W.'s conversations (Drury, "Symposium", 68, quoted for §118; Carnap, "Autobiography", 36) contrasted with his writings, where he had no kind word for metaphysics and where the very terms *metaphysics* and *metaphysical* seem to acquire a pejorative sense (*BB* 35e, 46a, 55–56, 66a).

"Different philosophers have meant different things by 'metaphysical'. Kant also attacked metaphysics: but Kant would not have called 'Every rod has a length,' or 'Time is one-dimensional and has only one direction,' metaphysical in the sense in which he attacked metaphysics; whereas for Wittgenstein they are so" (Anscombe, *Introduction*, 151; cp. Z 458, quoted re the title).

their everyday use: which of course may be a technical one. However, philosophers do not generally take liberties with technical terms, nor do their perplexities generally arise from them, but from words like *meaning, I,* and *object* (cp. §18). Hence W.'s "ordinary-language philosophy" is such not only in the sense that it uses nontechnical terms but also in the sense that it is chiefly concerned with such.

§117 See §350a; *Z* 448; *BB* 65, 170c; *LC* 68fg.

(a) Worked up in Man. 127 (Feb. 27). See *OC* 601 (quoted for §113); *BB* 9e–10a; *PB* 307a; NL 305c; *PP* 258c, 304 (quoted for §334); Schlick, "Meaning", 147b; cp. 5.4733; *PP* 265a; Frege, *Foundations,* 71 ("We are indeed only imposed on by the opposite view because we will, when asking for the meaning of a word, consider it in isolation, which leads us to accept an idea as the meaning"). For W.'s account of meaning, see §43. Some background:

"Given the syntax of a language, the meaning of a sentence is determinate as soon as the meaning of the component words is known" (Russell, "Introduction", x).

"The meanings of simple signs (words) must be explained to us if we are to understand them. With propositions, however, we make ourselves understood" (4.026). "A proposition must use old expressions to communicate a new sense" (4.03).

"Propositions are the changeable, variable; words are the permanent, unchangeable. The meanings of words we must establish. But the sense of the proposition *follows* from the words" (*Kreis,* 237; compare with the preceding and following quotes).

"We constantly conceive things as though we need merely combine the words of ordinary language, and the combination thereupon has a sense, which we now have to inquire into—if the sense isn't completely clear right away. It is as though the words were the ingredients of a chemical compound, which we shake together and get to join, and we now have to investigate the properties of the compound in question" (*PG* 483).

"The meaning of a phrase for us is characterized by the use we make of it. The meaning is not a mental accompaniment to the expression. Therefore the phrase 'I think I mean something by it,' or 'I'm sure I mean something by it,' which we so often hear in philosophical discussions to justify the use of an expression is for us no justification at all. We ask: '*What* do you mean?', i.e., 'How do you use this expression?'" (*BB* 65).

As if the sense . . . . : see *PG* 481d, quoted for §352a. Section XXXVII investigates the truth behind this conception of meaning. Note that here as elsewhere in the *Investigations,* W. speaks of the *Bedeutung* of an individual word, and of the *Sinn* of a sentence, not vice versa; this terminology might have been mirrored in the translation by a corresponding distinction between *meaning* and *sense.*

(b) See XVII and references there; *OC* 433; Man. 111, 27–28; cp. §520; *OC* 412–13.

"This is here": "One sometimes hears that such a phrase as 'This is here,' when while I say it I point to a part of my visual field, has a kind of primitive meaning to me, although it can't impart information to anybody else" (*BB* 65). Cp. "I am here" (§514 and references).

does make sense: W. softens the categorical declaration in Man. 108, 147: " 'This is here' is nonsense."

§118 Revised from Man. 213, 411. See *PG* 115c; Man. 213, 413; cp. 4.003, 6.52, 6.53. Taken alone, this and the following number give a one-sidedly negative impression; for the other side, see GI 28. On W.'s therapeutic, antisystematic approach, see GI 8, 28–29, 58, 68; VI, 2; VII, 8–9. The first two sentences of the number come from Man. 112, 228, where W. asked: "Of what sort is my assertion about the table [*Tabelle*]: that it doesn't force me to use it thus & so? And: that the application is not anticipated by the rule (or table)?" (Cp. Section IX.)

Where does our investigation . . . : see VII, 8–10.

it seems only . . . : "But this is not all he does or thinks he does. For he says that he changes one's *way of looking at things* (§144)" (Malcolm, "Investigations", 190–91; see GI 28).

to destroy everything interesting . . . and important: including, in a sense, the problems themselves: "Roughly speaking, in the old conception—say that of the great western philosophers—there have been two sorts of problems in the scientific sense: essential, great, universal & unessential, quasi-accidental problems. On the contrary it is our view that there is no *great*, essential problem, in that sense" (Man. 110, 200; Man. 213, 407; cp. §§123–24). Yet there *are* problems: "Some philosophers (or whatever you like to call them) suffer from what may be called 'loss of problems'. Then everything seems quite simple to them, no deep problems seem to exist any more, the world becomes broad and flat and loses all depth, and what they write becomes immeasurably shallow and trivial. Russell and H. G. Wells suffer from this" (Z 456).

"Anyone who does not understand why we talk about these things must feel what we say to be mere trifling" (Z 197). Russell did: "I have not found in Wittgenstein's *Philosophical Investigations* anything that seemed to me interesting and I do not understand why a whole school finds important wisdom in its pages . . . if it is true, philosophy is, at best, a slight help to lexicographers, and at worst, an idle tea-table amusement" (*Development*, 216–17). The response of one who witnessed W.'s agonies: "It has always seemed to me very bizarre that his philosophy should be regarded by some as trivializing, or not taking philosophy seriously enough" (Britton, "Portrait", 57). W.'s explanation: "The thoughts are so trivial that it is difficult to take them seriously" (Man. 161, W.'s English). "We feel that there must be a big and essential difference somewhere. But if you look closely at what happens . . . you find that you can only detect a number of differences in details, each of which would seem inessential" (*BB* 92). Thus "when the philosopher draws a mathematician's attention to a distinction or to a misleading form of expression, the latter says: 'Yes, yes, we know all that already and it isn't very interesting.' But he does not realize that the philosophical questions which disquiet him are attributable precisely to unclear matters which he shrugged off earlier" (Man. 219, 10). "We fail to be struck by what, once seen, is most striking and most powerful" (§129). So we react similarly to W.'s philosophy (GI 69).

What we are destroying . . . : "That is, the difficulty & the conflict does not turn out to be something wonderful but an error" (Man. 110, 14). "In philosophical thought we see problems where there are none. And philosophy should show that there are none there" (*PG* 47b). Cp. Man. 112, 19.

"*Soc.* But if, Theaetetus, you chance to conceive again, you will be all the better for the present investigation, and if not, you will be soberer and humbler and gentler to other men, not fancying that you know what you do not know. These are the limits of my art; I can go no further, nor do I know aught of the things which great and famous men know or have known in this or former ages" (*Theaetetus*, final paragraph; cp. *Sophist*, 229C–230E).

houses of cards: see Britton, "Portrait", 62bc.

"Most quickly and quietly, like a house of cards, may that part collapse which we call logic and which we are accustomed to treat as the oldest, granite-like foundation of all knowledge" (Mauthner, *Beiträge*, I, 34).

"I find people writing and talking as if Wittgenstein knew little and cared less about the history of philosophy: as if he regarded his own work as abrogating all that had gone before him, and he confined all previous metaphysics to the limbo of the meaningless. This is a misunderstanding. In one of the earliest conversations I had with him he said: 'Don't think I despise metaphysics or ridicule it. On the contrary, I regard the great metaphysical writings of the past as among the noblest productions of the human mind'" (Drury, "Symposium", 68; cp. Carnap, "Autobiography", 36).

clearing up the ground of language: Drury ("Symposium", 70) quotes this passage from Kierkegaard: "It is true as the understanding says that there is nothing to wonder at, but precisely for this reason is wonder secure, because the understanding vouches for it. Let the understanding condemn what is transitory, let it clear the ground, then wonder comes in in the right place, in ground that is cleared in the changed man. Everything appertaining to that first wonder the understanding can consume; let it do so, in order that enigmatically it may help one to wonder." Cp. Man. 229, §1045, quoted for §524.

"For one thing, a philosophic question, if pursued far enough, may lead to something positive—for instance, to a more profound understanding of language. . . . For another thing, a question may decide to go in for another career than dissolving: it may pass into science" (Waismann, "How I See", 357–58).

§119   See GI 28–29; the references for §118; *PP* 323–24 (quoted for §109); cp. Man. 112, 224; Man. 109, 44, 99.

are the uncovering . . . : see §§464, 524c. "To untie knots, that is the philosopher's task" (Man. 138, 7B; see VII, 9). "The complexity of philosophy comes not from its matter but from our knotted understanding" (*PB* 52).

against the limits of language: the *Tractatus* aimed to set limits to language (GI 6), but W. later rejected its doctrine of limits (below); so what are these words doing here, in a later account of what went wrong? The present number originated in a discussion (Man. 108, 247) concerning the great problem of intentionality (GI 34). W. had just noted that any mental representation by which we sought to bridge the gap between sign and thing (for instance, between an expectation and its fulfillment) would be just another sign. We must know where to stop. Not (he would now add) that something inexpressible remains to be expressed—the sign within the sign (§105 and commentary) or something like that (§120b and commentary). No, the language-game we play must now be described, not justified, defined, or 'explained'. To clarify (GI 8) we pass from language to language, not from language to something transcendental; not to the metalogical (Man. 110, 160), the *a priori* essence of all language and thought (GI 30–31). No ladder can take us to those clouds (6.54).

"We have to do here with the Kantian solution of the problem of philosophy" (Man. 110, 61). Like Kant, young W. had drawn an *a priori* boundary to thought. Like Kant, he countenanced his own transgressions of that boundary (6.54) but not others'. Like Kant, while recognizing and respecting the human urge to "thrust against the limits" (NT 12–13; *Kreis*, 68–69), he wished to cure its metaphysical manifestations (6.53). Again like Kant, he sought to determine the limits of thought from within (*Tractatus*, Preface) by indicating the *a priori* structure of experience (X, 8). The rules of his 'primary language', underlying all meaningful speech, would have been analogous to Kant's categories. But W. looked closer than Kant did (see the transitional manuscripts, *passim*), so was never satisfied (as Kant was with his categories), and finally saw the error in his whole idea (GI 41, 43).

Logic was not transcendental (6.13). It was not a great mirror (5.511, 6.13) showing forth what it could not say: the essence of the world (6.13; PB 85). For there is no essence of language in which the world's essence is mirrored (PB 85), and therefore no *a priori* criterion with which to draw limits to sense (§499). Yet affinities with the former views remain, for instance with regard to: the propositions of ethics, religion, and aesthetics (GI 5–7); the status of sentences beyond the pale (3.03, 5.473, 5.61; Man. 110, 189; §500); the handling of metaphysical trespassers, and their initial reaction (6.53; PB 88a; §§116–18); the everyday things the therapist must tell them (6.53; Man. 109, 16; §120b); the peace which comes from accepting the limits and from the disappearance of questions (6.52–6.521; Man. 110, 99; §133). Some further references to the limits of language: PB 80bc; *Kreis,* 92–93; Man. 213, 411, 421, 425, 429; Man. 111, 134; Man. 109, 16, 79, 97, 212, 225; Man. 108, 260, 277. For buzzings of the fly as he knocked against the bottle's sides (§309), see: Man. 108, 192 ("I feel that here once again in replying I shall bump against the limits of language. But don't yet know how"), 269 ("I am always inquiring into the impossibility of expression, which is the real ground of the problem"), 265 ("This impossibility of expressing in language the conditions of agreement between a meaningful proposition—a thought—and reality is the solution of the puzzle"); Man. 109, 290 ("Whence the dissatisfaction? What is it that we would like to say that can't be said?"); Man. 110, 141 ("Isn't what I'm always attempting now, to replace the grammatical rules with something else?").

W. Kraft ("Wittgenstein", 834) quotes Karl Kraus's "Nachts": "When I can go no further, I have bumped into the wall of language. I then draw back with bloody head—and would like to go on." "Often I am near the wall of language and receive only an echo from it; often I bump my head against the wall."

These bumps: e.g. logical atomism, logical positivism, James's introspective psychology, solipsism, behaviorism, skepticism, and so on; that is, *big* bumps.

"Such a contradiction is of interest only because it has tormented people, and because this shews both how tormenting problems can grow out of language, and what kind of things can torment us" (RFM 52).

§120 This number, which comes from Man. 110, 230–31, via PG 121–22, connects with the remark in the preceding number about "the limits of language." W. too once strove to go beyond them, not in the direction of the "higher" but of that which can only be 'shown'. "My propositions serve as elucidations in the following way: anyone who understands me eventually recognizes them as nonsensical, when he has used them—as steps—to climb up beyond them. (He must, so to speak, throw away the ladder after he has climbed up it.) He must transcend these propositions, and then he will see the world aright" (6.54). *PG* 44d, 89d, and §402a also throw light on this number.

The final paragraph suggests an illuminating example which may be consulted throughout the number. In the *Tractatus'* ideal notation, ordinary words had to be replaced with genuine proper names and ordinary meanings with true *Bedeutungen*, that is, logically simple objects. So (following the paragraph order in §120): (a) how is the notation to be constructed, if we have only such crude words at our disposal for defining purposes? (b) how can we ever indicate the simple things themselves, the 'meanings', and not merely the game to be played, the moves to be made? (c) if we have in fact succeeded in talking about true *Gegenständen*, what is wrong with ordinary language, and if we haven't, then what is it that we can't express? (d) dissatisfaction with ordinary names arises from a misunderstanding about names, not a lack of suitable ones; (e) if the problem really has to do with *names*, then we must study actual names, not mythical ones; (f) and this we can do, for even though the referent may be 'indefinable', we can at least describe the word's use (p. 185h).

(a) See V, 1–6; X, 9–10; §§426b, 610; *PG* 100b, 108cd; *PB* 52f; *Kreis,* 57; Man. 109, 65; Man. 107, 176; Man. 105, 78; cp. §134a; *PB* 89a; *PP* 278; 5.452; Neurath, "Protokollsätze", 205–6.

When I talk about language . . . : notice, therefore, that the paragraph treats of dissatisfaction which W. once shared with others; for though he thought that everyday language does its own job well (4.002), for philosophical purposes he found it inadequate (V, 4; X, 8).

I must speak the language . . . : this is not a prohibition of technical terminology (§132a). It is worth noting, though, that technical terms, too, receive their meaning via nontechnical ones.

Is this language somehow too coarse . . . : see §§106, 426b, 436, 548–49 and commentaries; NL 283; cp. *PB* 103b, 104d, 266def, 270a; LE 7; Man. 110, 25–26; Man. 108, 290–91; Man. 105, 104; Russell, *Logic,* 198a.

Mauthner quotes Locke's *Essay* (3, 6, 19) at the start of *Beiträge:* "so hard is it to show the various meaning and imperfection of words, when we have nothing else but words to do it by."

"Of course this is no definition; but likewise none is here possible. I must confine myself to hinting at what I have in mind by means of a metaphorical expression, and here I rely on my reader's agreeing to meet me half-way" (Frege, *Writings,* 115; see his *Basic Laws,* 32b).

"These shortcomings are rooted in the imperfection of language, for the fact is that in order to think we must use sense symbols" (Frege, "Justification", 155). "Of course, this too must be taken with a grain of salt, for an operation in space and time is not intended" (Frege, "Compound", 10; cp. §108c).

"But with regard to unities, the question is more difficult. The topic is one with which language, by its very nature, is peculiarly unfitted to deal. I must beg the reader, therefore, ..." (Russell, *Logic*, 336).

"In speaking of a 'complex' we are, as will appear later, sinning against the rules of philosophical grammar, but this is unavoidable at the outset" (Russell, "Introduction", x).

"So we might say that the color too is completely described only when all its ingredients have been specified, of course with the addition that they are all of them. But how is this addition to be made?" (*PB* 109). (According to the picture theory it would be impossible; now in §120 W. says: *"What* is inexpressible? You have just said it!")

"All the logical forms of our everyday language—the subject-predicate structure, the relational structure—are connected most closely with objects and become unusable the moment we try to describe phenomena themselves" (*Kreis*, 258).

"It is simply ridiculous to believe we can succeed here with the ordinary forms of everyday language, with subject and predicate, binary relations, and so on" (*Kreis*, 42). "How can a physical language describe phenomena?" (*PB* 98).

"When we think in this way we seem to lose our firm hold on the objects surrounding us. And instead we are left with a lot of separate personal experiences of different individuals. These personal experiences again seem vague and seem to be in constant flux. Our language seems not to have been made to describe them. We are tempted to think that in order to clear up such matters philosophically our ordinary language is too coarse, that we need a more subtle one" (*BB* 45; see X, 8; §436).

Then how is another . . . : see X, 10, 20–21; §261; and (*b*); cp. *PG* 114 ("How did I come to the concept 'proposition' or to the concept 'language'? Just through the languages I've learned, of course"); *RFM* 155i; Ramsey, *Foundations*, 219ef.

And how strange . . . : if the words in question—*word, sentence, language*, and the like—are unfit for discussing words, sentences, language, and the like, what *are* they good for? They seem to have no function.

(b) See *PG* 283h; cp. §§503–4 and references; *PG* 156ab; *PB* 89a; 3.263; Man. 111, 49; Man. 110, 26; Man. 109, 282, 288, 293–94, 298; Man. 108, 194 (in GI 37), 277.

not some sort of preparatory, provisional one: see the quotes from Frege and Russell above; cp. §130; *PB* 54a; 6.54.

"It must be remembered that my sentences do not have the ambition to be propositions themselves, their purpose is to give a certain direction to the reader's attention" (Schlick, "Form", 206).

this by itself shews . . . : thus if to explain a color word I point and say "This color is called so-and-so" (§29), I do not indicate the color impression which belongs to me alone (§§277–80); and when I prick someone with a pin and say "What you feel is pain" (§288), I do not hook the word onto something he alone knows (§§272, 293). For I have used words of our common language—*color* and *feel* (§261). So too, if by word and gesture I explain a command, no logical shadow appears linking word and deed (§§431–35; cp. §452). For I had to use these "clumsy expedients" (see §549).

only exterior facts: see the preceding comments; GI 37; §§90a, 92, 454; *Z* 558; *PG* 112b, 133, 144a, 208abc; *PB* 122b; *NL* 297d, 301b, 304bc; Man. 116, 3; Man. 110, 123; Man. 109, 59; Man. 108, 186–88, 224, 260–61, 279, 290; Man. 105, 104, 106; cp. §§209–10; *EPB* 151–52; *BB* 105a; *PG* 108e; *PB* 66b, 150c, 170a; *PP* 278–79; *NB* 19f. Further indications of W.'s target: "Only that in thought which is expressed immediately by language"—that is, the primary (X, 6–8), the private (above), and especially intention itself (GI 37)—"can language not treat from without" (Man. 109, 53). "It seems somehow as though if we consider intention from without we never know it as *intention;* as though it were necessary to do the meaning oneself in order to grasp it as meaning" (Man. 108, 186). "But that would mean treating it not as a phenomenon, not as a fact, but as something intended—something to which a direction has been imparted. And what this direction is we do not know. It is something missing from the phenomenon as such" (*PG* 143; see *PG* 156; §§455–57). "Thought is constructing pictures of various kinds. However, grasping them as pictures, which is the essential thing, cannot be conceived as effecting an external connection, for that again would only provide connecting links; rather it must be something contained in the existence of the thought, like the description of hollow form and full form" (Man. 108, 217–18). "It is as though the thought were the shadow of the event, but in such a way that it is senseless to ask whether this event is really the one whose shadow we had before us. That is, the relation between shadow & fact cannot be external" (Man. 108, 230; cp. XXXVII, 3–6).

"Ever and again comes the thought that what we see of a sign is only the outside of something within, in which the real operations of sense and meaning go on" (*Z* 140; see *BB* 3e, quoted in XXXVII, 8). "One often encounters the view that a person can only imperfectly *show* his understanding. . . . It is said: 'Understanding is surely something *else* than the expression of understanding. *Understanding* can't be shown; it is something inner, spiritual' " (*PG* 44; see §153). For W., on the contrary: "If there has to be anything 'behind the utterance of the formula' it is *particular circumstances*" (§154); and: "Giving examples is not an *indirect* means of explaining" (§71b). Such are the "exterior facts" here alluded to.

(c) Cp. *PG* 104b.

Yes, but then how . . . : "Isn't understanding something different from its expression? Isn't it the case that the expression of understanding is an incomplete expression? But that means, of course, an expression that of its very nature omits something! The inexpressible. For otherwise I could of course find a better expression. Thus the expression would be a perfect *expression*" (Man. 109, 187; see *PG* 44d; Man. 116, 18; cp. §§433–34). "We can explain a language only through language, so we cannot explain *language*" (Man. 108, 277). "Language is unique, so cannot be explained. It must show itself" (Man. 110, 59).

(d) See §402; *PG* 121c; and the quotes under (*a*).

(e) **about words:** but not just about words (§370; I, 8–9).

(f) See *BB* 4–5; *PP* 260–61; cp. Man. 112, 201.

You say . . . : "The use of the substantives 'sense', 'meaning', 'notion' and other words leads us to believe that this sense etc. is correlated with the word as a word, a name, is correlated with its bearer" (Man. 112, 181; see GI 18; *BB* 1; *PP* 258c). Thus "for Frege the alternatives were these: Either we are dealing with ink marks on paper, or these ink marks are signs *of something,* and what they represent is their meaning" (*Kreis,* 105; see ibid., 150). W. "sometimes spoke of this . . . mistake as the view that words are 'representative' of their meanings, and he held that in no case is a word 'representative' of its meaning, although a proper name is 'representative' of its bearer (if it has one). He added in one place: 'The meaning of a word is no longer for us an object corresponding to it' " (*PP* 260–61; see §§40–43; *PG* 89d; cp. Man. 112, 206–11).

as a thing: see §§1bc, 264; *BB* 1d, 18a; Ryle, "Meaning", 242.

of the same kind: see X, 2; XXXVII, 15; Augustine, *De Trinitate,* XV, 19, quoted for §32b.

money, and its use: see *PG* 107a; Man. 107, 232–33; cp. *Kreis,* 105. *PG* 63 develops the comparison: "Money, and what you can buy with it. In some cases an object; but also permission to occupy a seat in a theatre, or a claim, or rapid transportation, or life, etc." In like vein, see Man. 228, §544.

§121 The technical terminology of the ramified theory of types does not clarify the opening remark or the subsequent comparison. However, W.'s frequent derogatory references to a "metagame" (*PB* 327; *Kreis,* 134), "metacalculus" (*PG* 296), "metalogic" (below), "metamathematics" (*PG* 290d, 297; *PB* 319; Man. 219, 1), and the like (see especially *Kreis*, 136; *PG* 116a, 296) suggest the general drift: What orthography says about the word *orthography* is not a theory, foundation, or justification of orthography, but standard orthography. Similarly, what philosophy says about the use of *philosophy* provides no theory of philosophy, but a verbal analysis like any other. Cp. Man. 110, 189: "As there is no metaphysics, so there is no metalogic. The word 'understand', the expression 'understand a sentence', is also not metalogical, but an expression like *any* other of the language." So too, *philosophy* is not a "super-concept" belonging to a "super-order" (§97b) which a superscience might explore so as to provide a justification or explanation of all philosophizing (cp. §124).

Links with the previous number are suggested by Man. 110, 214 ("The picture of the picture of the world must itself be a picture of the world") and by Russell's remark (concerning the *Tractatus*) "that every language has, as Mr Wittgenstein says, a structure concerning which, *in the language,* nothing can be said, but that there may be another language dealing with the structure of the first language, and having itself a new structure, and that to this hierarchy of languages there may be no limit. Mr Wittgenstein would of course reply that his whole theory is applicable unchanged to the totality of such languages" ("Introduction", xxii).

§122   From Man. 213, 417. See *EPB* 179; *BB* 26b, 125; *PB* 52bc; *PP* 256 ("he was really succeeding in giving what he called a 'synoptic' view of things which we all know"); Man. 110, 256–57.

(a) See BUF 241.

we do not *command a clear view:* see GI 9–10; in addition to the references there, see §§5a, 11–12, 156b, 182b, pp. 209c, 219c, 224i; *Z* 121, 273, 525; *RFM* 115ab; *BB* 6d; *PB* 304b; 4.002; Man. 213, 415–16. Not only is the structure of language extremely complex, but we seldom attend to it, success in communication requiring that we attend to the topic of discussion rather than to the system of communication, which must be second nature to us and is (Hallett, "Bottle").

perspicuous representation: see GI 25, 28–29, 47, 56–57; commentary on Preface (c); *Z* 273, 472, 474–75; cp. Frege, "Justification", 159–60.

"I imagine that it was in this respect of needing a 'synopsis' of trivialities that he thought that philosophy was similar to Ethics and Aesthetics" (*PP* 323).

Compare also his stress on the importance of perspicuity in mathematical proof (*RFM* 45b, 65, 66, 83ab) and on its being memorable (*RFM* 25–26, 69–70).

which consists in 'seeing connexions': rather than sharp borders, as in essence-mapping (*PG* 75a).

"It is not that a new building has to be erected, or that a new bridge has to be built, but that the geography, *as it now is,* has to be judged. We certainly see bits of the concepts, but don't clearly see the declivities by which one passes into others" (*RFM* 157; note the close affinity to Hardy, "Proof", 18).

inventing: see GI 62.

intermediate cases: see GI 57; *PG* 76, 212a; *PP* 313; cp. III, 9; *EPB* 190–91; *PG* 445b; Hallett, *Darkness,* chap. 2 (a series of thirteen, exemplifying the method).

"This kinship . . . may join the members as in a chain, so that one is linked to another *by intermediary links*; and two neighboring members may have common traits and may *resemble* each other, while distant ones no longer have anything in common and yet belong to the same family" (*PG* 75).

"The advantage of the language-game approach is that it permits us to examine *step-by-step* what we otherwise see only as a whole, and indeed in a confused tangle" (Man. 228, §660).

"The use of the word 'deriving' is indeed exhibited in 70), i.e., this example showed us one of the family of cases in which this word is used. And the explanation of the use of this word, as that of the use of the word 'reading' or 'being guided by symbols', essentially consists in describing a selection of examples exhibiting characteristic features, some examples showing these features in exaggeration, others showing transitions, certain series of examples showing the trailing off of such features" (*BB* 125; see §§162–64; *BB* 123c–124c).

Other illustrative examples, often with similar remarks: §72 and *BB* 130–31 (*common*); §78 (knowing and saying); §§159–61 and *BB* 122cde, *EPB* 176 (*reading*); §269 (*understanding*); §151 and *BB* 112c–113a, *EPB* 163–64 ("Now I understand"); *LC* 12b ("connection between these delights"); *Z* 484–85 ("the connecting link" between delight and a sensation); *BB* 129i–130a and *EPB* 195–96 (*looking*); *BB* 161c ("That's that"); *BB* 104d–106b and *EPB* 151–54 (talk about the past); *BB* 103a and *EPB* 149–50: "Now there is no sharp line between such 'artificial devices' and what one might call the natural expressions of emotion. Cf. in this respect: *a*) weeping, *b*) raising one's voice when one is angry, *c*) writing an angry letter, *d*) ringing the bell for a servant you wish to scold."

Contrast this approach with that of definition, both as a means of clarifying a concept and as a means of distinguishing one concept from another (§182c).

(b) Cp. *OC* 422; *PG* 40b; *PP* 316bc. This paragraph comes from BUF 241, save that the final parenthetical remark there (as in Man. 220, 81, and Man. 213, 417) is fuller: "A sort of 'Weltanschauung' such as is apparently typical of our time. Spengler."

It earmarks the form of account we give: the concept does. W. is not saying, notice, that the task of philosophy is to designate the way we look at things, our form of representation. In addition to the numbers from GI cited above, see GI 63, on W.'s original conception of the *Investigations;* and the third paragraph of the Preface, with commentary.

"Language is already in perfect order. The difficulty lies only in making the syntax simple and perspicuous" (*Kreis*, 46). "Once we achieve the perfectly clear formulation, once we reach that final clarity, there can be no more puzzling and struggling; for these always arise from the feeling: Now were something asserted, I don't know yet whether I should agree with it or not. If, instead, grammar is clarified, by taking tiny steps, with each individual step perfectly obvious, then there can be no more discussion. Disagreement always comes from our skipping certain steps or not stating them clearly" (ibid., 183).

"The pedigree of psychological concepts: I strive *not* after *exactness,* but after a synoptic view" (Z 464).

"Basically, I am a painter & often a very poor painter" (Man. 138, 31A).

Is this a 'Weltanschauung'?: see BUF 241; Bensch, *Wittgenstein,* 86–93; cp. Man. 105, 10, 12; Mauthner, *Beiträge,* I, 540; Ramsey, *Foundations,* 290–91; Spengler, *Untergang,* 138–40. Such is the approach W. recommended and practiced in all areas of philosophical inquiry, in discussing mathematics, psychological concepts, logic, colors, and so on; it was the manner he preferred in novelists, and a reason why he preferred nonphilosophical presentation of ethical, aesthetic, religious, and other important matters (GI 5–7). Thus the expression *Weltanschauung* clearly refers to a way of viewing things rather than to a view of things, to a manner rather than to a content. Already in *NB* W. spoke, for instance, of "the artistic way of looking at things, that it looks at the world with a happy eye" (*NB* 86), and of "the world seen *sub specie aeternitatis*" (*NB* 83). And the thought forced itself on him that to see things *sub specie aeternitatis* was to see them "together with the whole logical space" (ibid.). For the later W., logical space was grammar, and it could be seen only through "perspicuous representation".

"When Renan speaks of the precocious good sense of the semitic races . . . that means the *non-poetical,* direct, concrete. The characteristic of my philosophy. Things lie there directly before our eyes, no veil over them [cp. §5].—Here religion & art part company" (Man. 109, 202; see GI 6–7). "A work of art forces us, as it were, into the right perspective; without art the object is a bit of nature like any other. . . . Now it seems, though, that in addition to what the artist does there is still another way of grasping the world *sub specie aeterni.* It is—I believe—the form of thought which as it were soars above the world & leaves it as it is, viewing it from above in flight" (Man. 109, 28–30; cp.

Spengler, *Untergang*, 138). "This mentality differs from that of the great stream of European and American civilization in which we all stand. The latter expresses itself in a forward movement, in building ever larger and more complicated structures, whereas the former expresses itself in an effort to achieve clarity and perspicuity in any structures whatever" (*PB* 7).

§123   From Man. 112, 46, and Man. 213, 421. Man. 112, 211 is equivalent. See commentary on §122a; *RFM* 101, 104; *BB* 35e, 47b; Man. 229, §1217; Man. 213, 415; Warnock, *English Philosophy*, 58–59; Ambrose, "Universals", 336; cp. *PB* 176f. In his notebooks, W. frequently made such remarks as: "I am now frightfully confused" (Man. 109, 43). "The philosophical problem is: 'What is it that puzzles me in this matter?'" (NL 275). "It is already an advance to recognize the philosophical problem as logical" (Man. 167; cp. Z 458).

"It could very well be imagined that someone knows his way around a city perfectly, i.e. would confidently find the shortest way from any place in it to any other,—and yet would be quite incompetent to draw a map of the city" (Z 121). This is a closer comparison than that reported by Gasking and Jackson (GI 28)—"I'm like a guide showing you how to find your way round London"—for we do know our way around in language or mathematics in the instinctive way we know our way around a city. In philosophy we need the reflective knowledge of map makers. See Man. 166 and Man. 229, §1225, quoted for §89c.

§124   From Man. 110, 188–89, and Man. 213, 417–18. See I, 3–4; *PB* 52f, 319, 330; *Kreis*, 120–21, 136.

(a) See *BB* 18c.

Philosophy may . . . : the improvements "for practical purposes" mentioned in §§132b, 569, and 577 would not be suggested by philosophers for philosophical reasons. Quinton objects to W.'s view ("Excerpt," 16–17), Cavell defends it ("Availability", 166–72). The issue risks becoming purely verbal; though it may be true, as Quinton says, that the philosopher-scientists of the seventeenth century created the language of modern science, the question remains whether this was a philosophical achievement.

in no way interfere: re 'ideal languages', see V, 1–6.

actual use: this is not a general acceptance of what people say but of how they say it; thus W. is not bowing before the wisdom of the crowd, or subscribing indiscriminately to the views of common sense.

it can only . . . describe: see §109.

(b) See I, 3–4; p. 200b and commentary; *RFM* 171ef; cp. p. 232c; *NB* 89–90 ("infinitely fundamental", "it alone justifies us," etc.); Ramsey, *Foundations*, 81b; Waismann, *Introduction*, 121–22.

(c) See *PG* 121d. The quotes below suggest how W.'s claim should be taken.

"To be sure language is, by and large, left as it is. Nor does philosophy uncover new facts about the world. But those regions of our thought previously obscure to us and now perspicuously surveyed do not remain the same. Or, if one wishes, the fact that we now see them differently will lead to our treating them differently. For a mathematician like Hilbert who believed that Cantor had opened the gates to paradise the world will not remain the same after Wittgenstein has shown him that what he saw was nothing but a mirage in waterless desert. If something was thought to be good sense, and is revealed by a surview [*sic*] to be nonsense, it is at best misleading to claim that since it was nonsense before and is nonsense still therefore philosophy leaves everything as it is" (Hacker, *Insight*, 125). As W. himself remarked, "philosophical clarity will have the same influence on the growth of mathematics that sunlight has on the growth of potato sprouts. (In a dark cellar they grow yards long.)" (*PG* 381).

(d) See §125; *RFM* 157, 174ghi; *PG* 296abc; *PB* 334; *Kreis*, 143–44; cp. *PB* 176f, 180b, 319.

leaves mathematics as it is: see *RFM* 63g; *PG* 381, above. "Philosophy does not investigate mathematical calculations, but only what mathematicians say about them" (*PG* 396). "We do not interfere with what the mathematician does; only when he claims he is doing metamathematics do we check on him" (Man. 219, 1). "Indeed, what criticism makes disappear is the names, the insinuations, which occur in the calculus, so what I would like to call the *prose*. It is very important to distinguish most sharply between the calculus and this prose" (*Kreis*, 149).

no mathematical discovery . . . : for instance, "it might justly be asked what importance Gödel's proof has for our work. For a piece of mathematics cannot solve a problem of the sort that trouble *us*" (*RFM* 177). Besides, "the mathematician is an inventor, not a discoverer" (*RFM* 47; cp. p. 224j).

A "leading problem of mathematical logic": the expression is Ramsey's (Man. 110, 189; Man. 220, 81; Man. 213, 418; and below). See Man. 110, 12, e.g.: "Thus there can also be no 'leading problems' of mathematical logic, for those would be ones whose solution would finally give us the right to do arithmetic the way we do." "For instance, Ramsey wrote that there is a leading problem of mathematical logic, the decidability problem. This problem would have to be solved before we could know whether the calculus is in order. To that I would say: *There cannot be such 'leading problems'!* The question whether what I am doing is justified or not should not depend on what somebody will figure out in the calculus" (*Kreis*, 129; see Ramsey, *Foundations*, 82).

is for us a problem of mathematics: avoidance of contradiction, for instance, is a mathematical problem, whereas "the civil status of a contradiction . . . there is the philosophical problem" (§125).

"It is my task, not to attack Russell's logic from *within*, but from without" (*RFM* 174; W.'s italics restored).

"In mathematics there can only be mathematical troubles, not philosophical ones" (*PG* 369).

§125 See Man. 130, 83–88; Dilman, "Logic," 37–42. "What must strike the naive beholder above all," said W., "is that mathematicians are continually terrified of *one* thing, which is a sort of nightmare for them, namely contradiction" (*Kreis*, 131). The discovery of Russell's paradox and others brought on a crisis in which the avoidance of contradiction seemed the chief problem facing mathematicians, logicians, and philosophers of mathematics and logic. Their concern interested W. more than their solutions. What made the paradoxes so calamitous? Considered in purely formal terms, a calculus permitting such contradictions is as good as any other (*PB* 318). If it is the practical applications of mathematics which make contradiction undesirable, of what sort are they and where does the danger lie (*RFM* 111b)? How many bridges have collapsed because of Russell's paradox? How many people persist in uttering the grammatical sentence "I always lie" (*RFM* 183)? "I should like to ask something like: 'Is it usefulness you are out for in your calculus?—In that case you do not get any contradiction. And if you aren't out for usefulness—then it doesn't matter if you do get one' " (*RFM* 104).

Suppose it did seem necessary, for some reason, to take preventive measures. This might be done piecemeal, as in ordinary affairs. A woman leaves instructions to teach her children a game, then thinks of an undesirable value for the variable *game,* and adds: "But not gaming with dice" (cp. p. 33n). Likewise, "if contradictions crop up in the rules of the game in mathematics, it would be the easiest thing in the world to provide a remedy. We need only make a new stipulation covering the case in which the rules conflict, and the matter is settled" (*PB* 319). Why must logic and mathematics die the death if cures alone are possible and not total, once-for-all prophylaxis? "What I want to say is always the same: The proof of freedom from contradiction cannot be a *question of life and death for mathematics*" (*Kreis*, 141).

For thinkers such as Frege, Russell, and Hilbert, whom W. had chiefly in mind, it was just that. When Frege, for instance, learned from Russell of the cancerous growth (*RFM* 166) that *might* arise in his healthy-looking system, he replied: "Your discovery of the contradiction caused me the greatest surprise and, I would almost say, consternation, since it has shaken the basis on which I intended to build arithmetic. . . . It is all the more serious since, with the loss of my Rule V, not only the foundations of my arithmetic, but also the sole possible foundations of arithmetic, seem to vanish" (Heijenoort, *From Frege*, 127–28). W. asked: Why and in what sense does arithmetic need a foundation? Does language need a foundation? Does a game? (See I, 4.)

"In *Principia Mathematica* Russell had believed that his logical propositions said something, that they described something" (*Kreis*, 106). Within this perspective, it is understandable that contradiction should seem alarming. For there can be no contradiction in reality; our description—our ontology of the mathematical universe, as it were—must be wrong. But "mathematics is always a machine, a calculus. The calculus describes nothing. It can be applied to that to which it can be applied" (ibid.; see *RFM* 99e; Hallett, "Contrast", 695–97). On the Wittgensteinian middle road between formalism on the one hand and the objective viewpoint of Frege and Russell, on the other, see GI 45. For further background on the number, see *Z* 685–93; *RFM* 51–53, 101–11, 130–31, 166–71, 178–79; *PG* 189a. Cp. *PB* 214e–215a; Hertz, *Principles*, 7.

(a) See §124d, p. 232c; *Z* 463; *RFM* 104h; *PG* 369; *PB* 326–31; *Kreis*, 122, 124n, 133–34, 137–38; cp. *RFM* 181; *PB* 153d; 4.112; *NB* 93b.

And this does not mean . . . : "The philosopher must twist and turn about so as to pass by the mathematical problems, and not run up against one,—which would have to be solved before he could go further. His labour in philosophy is as it were an idleness in mathematics" (*RFM* 157). "Our motto might be: 'Let us not be bewitched!' " (Man. 228, p. 160, re this question). "The question itself keeps the mind pressing against a blank wall, thereby preventing it from ever finding the outlet" (*BB* 169).

(b) See *Z* 293; *RFM* 51d, 100–101, 178k–179a, 181c; *PB* 189cd, 318–19; *Kreis*, 119–20; Man. 228, 159–60 (fuller version); cp. §308; 3.03, 5.473–5.4732. In Man. 130, 11–12, this is a comment on Russell's Theory of Types (see *Z* 692).

"*Contradiction* . . . can *make its appearance* only in the *true-false game*, so only where we make assertions. That is: Contradiction can appear only in the *rules of the game*" (*Kreis*, 124; *PB* 321), and not, for instance, in some realm of mathematical objects explored by mathematicians. Thus W. saw much truth (see GI 45) in the view Frege criticized: "These rules are not established in the name of reason or nature; it is merely that through them some actions become legitimate in the calculating game. There is no question here of truth, as there is in meaningful arithmetic. . . . Only when such a prohibition is issued will there arise a contradiction, or, better, disagreement among the rules, some of which permit, and some of which prohibit" (*Writings*, 206, 213, discussed by W. in *PB* 325ff; *Kreis*, 130ff).

(d) Cp. p. 33n, §§187, 513b, 693.

(e) See *Z* 273 (used as motto for this commentary); *RFM* 101, 105–6, 109b, 166–68; *PG* 303–5; *PB* 318ff; *Kreis*, 119–20, 125, 132.

"The calculus *as* calculus is in order. It is senseless to speak of contradiction" (*PB* 319). However, "it is essential to mathematics that its signs are also employed in *mufti*. It is the use outside mathematics, and so the *meaning* of the signs, that makes the sign-game into mathematics" (*RFM* 133).

"We shall see contradiction in a quite different light if we look at its occurrence and its consequences as it were anthropologically—and when we look at it with a mathematician's exasperation. That is to say, we shall look at it differently, if we try merely to *describe* how the contradiction influences language-games, and if we look at it from the point of view of the mathematical law-giver" (*RFM* 110).

For example: "Can we say: 'Were this proposition usable in a language-game, it would lead to no contradiction'? Or rather: 'Were this proposition usable, people might perhaps have cause to become excited about it; yet since it is useless, the contradiction does no harm'? Or this: 'Since we don't know how this proposition, or what looks like a proposition, is to be verified, the contradiction needn't bother us'? But now what if we gave this structure a use? Well, *then* we would have to prevent the contradiction; & *how* we should have to prevent it would be shown by the sense" (Man. 130, 87–88).

§126   See GI 49; §§109, 127–28, 496, 598–99, 654–55, p. 230ab; *EPB* 179; *BB* 125bc; *PG* 283e; *PP* 323b.

(a) From Man. 213, 418. For explanation of these assertions, see GI 8–11, 47–52, 60; VII, 3–7.

Philosophy: on W.'s restrictive use of the term *philosophy*, see VII, 10.

neither explains: see references under §109 ("we must do away with all *explanation*").

what is hidden: for example:

(1)   Essences: " '*The essence is hidden from us*' . . . is the form our problem now assumes" (§92; see GI 20–23; §§153, 164; *EPB* 179; *BB* 125b).

(2)   Causes: "Now if it is not the causal connections which we are concerned with, then the activities of the mind lie open before us" (*BB* 6; see GI 49; §§109, 654–55, p. 220b; *Z* 220).

(3)   Mental phenomena: "One believes that the difficulty of the task consists in our having to describe phenomena that are hard to get hold of, the present experience that slips quickly by, or something of the kind" (§436; see §§153, 435).

(4)   The 'real signs' (§105), the real logic of our expressions (GI 10): "as if there were something hidden in them that had to be brought to light" (§91; see §60).

(5)   An underlying calculus: "The strict and clear rules of the logical structure of propositions appear to us as something in the background—hidden in the medium of the understanding" (§102).

(6)   Others' experiences: "The essential thing about private experience [in the view W. criticized] is . . . that nobody knows whether other people also have *this* or something else" (§272; X, 3–4, 9–10; cp. §293).

   is of no interest: see GI 60.

(b)   From Man. 108, 160 (then Man. 213, 419), where W. was criticizing his own tendency to "set up (construct) rules in philosophy, and to make assumptions (hypotheses) instead of simply seeing what is there". "In my earlier book the solution of the problems is still presented in too unprosaic a fashion; it gives too much the impression that discoveries are needed in order to solve our problems. The whole thing has too little the form of grammatical commonplaces conveyed in ordinary language" (Man. 109, 212–13).

   See *PG* 56b; Man. 105, 52 (quoted for p. 147n); cp. §125a; *PB* 182b; Chomsky, *Language*, 21 ("Wolfgang Köhler, for example, has suggested that psychologists do not open up 'entirely new territories' in the manner of the natural sciences, 'simply because man was acquainted with practically all territories of mental life a long time before the founding of scientific psychology . . . because at the very beginning of their work there were no entirely unknown mental facts left which they could have discovered' ").

   before **all new discoveries:** whether mathematical (§125), scientific (§109 and above; GI 49; cp. 5.551–5.552; Frege, *Basic Laws*, 18), or bogus, grammatical ones (§401, p. 224j). Cp. Hertz, *Principles*, 8 (quoted for §133b).

   "I once wrote in the manuscript of my book . . . . : The solutions of philosophical problems should never cause surprise [6.1251]. In philosophy there can be no discoveries. But I myself had not yet understood this clearly enough and offended against it" (*Kreis*, 182–83; see ibid., 63, 77).

   Theaetetus, when he simply noted cases known to everyone, was right and Socrates wrong. Thus "in a certain sense we keep making things ever easier for ourselves in philosophy" (*PG* 120–21).

§127   From Man. 213, 415. See §§89, 109, 126b, 129, 140b, 253c; Man. 220, 82; Man. 213, 419; cp. §593. Moore's notes already stress this line of thought: "He also said that he was not trying to teach us any new facts: that he would only tell us 'trivial' things—'things which we all know already'; but that the difficult thing was to get a 'synopsis' of these trivialities, and that our 'intellectual discomfort' can only be removed by a synopsis of *many* trivialities—that 'if we leave out any, we still have the feeling that something is wrong' " (*PP* 323; contrast with Man. 108, 215, below, suggested perhaps by different cases).

"In the end, what I always do is only draw attention to something" (Man. 111, 144; see GI 51–52)—"something that everyone knows, that is, immediately recognizes as true. (Socratic recollection of the truth.)" (Man. 110, 131–32; see Malcolm, *Memoir*, 51). "The answer to every philosophical question is a truism. It is just difficult to find *the* truism which disposes of the precise thing which troubles me now" (Man. 108, 215)—and to recognize it as the solution (Z 313–14; cp. Malcolm, *Memoir*, 66c).

for a particular purpose: see also the commentary on §109 ("from the philosophical problems").

§128   From Man. 110, 259, and Man. 213, 419, and explained in *Kreis*, 183, where W. told Waismann: "With regard to your theses [see *Kreis*, 233–61] I once wrote: Were there theses in philosophy, they should occasion no debate. That is, they would have to be so stated that everyone would say: Yes, yes, that is obvious." See the comments on §127; §§126, 415, 599; Z 211, 220; BB 70c; PG 56b; PB 65d; 4.112; Man. 159 (quoted in my preface); Man. 111, 48, 132 ("Nothing is accomplished in philosophy by 'sweeping statements' "); Man. 109, 16. The contrast is especially sharp with Russell, e.g. *Logic*, 193: "The point of philosophy is to start with something so simple as not to seem worth stating, and to end with something so paradoxical that no one will believe it." He and many other thinkers have alleged that the views they advocated "result inevitably from absolutely undeniable data" (ibid., 178–79; see 160). Schlick, for instance, made just such a claim for a crude form of the Verification Principle ("Form", 181–82). W., however, denied any intention to build up results, construct a system, prove a theory (GI 46). He would reverse the process and, starting with the philosopher's paradox, return to the simple observations which remove it. Difficulties for this number arise from the supposition that he did try to advance incontestable theses, for instance the thesis that the meaning of a word is its use in the language (§43). His practice might be more profitably compared with that of Socrates (see comments on §127), say in his interrogation of the slave boy. An analogous dialogue on the topic of §43 might proceed as follows: (1)   The therapist says (§§370–71): "Meaning is whatever we call meaning—it is not, for instance, a rosebud." People laugh. Yet philosophers have said that meaning is an object, a feeling, a mental representation, and so on; this was supposed to be debatable, but not whether a spoon is a spade or earthworms are comets. (2)   If the much-ignored connection with usage is acknowledged, the therapist then suggests: "In typical cases where, for instance, we speak of 'learning the meaning' of a word, what we learn is the word's use in the language" (see *BB* 1; §43). Who will deny that? (No general thesis about meaning, no debatable theory or essence, has been proposed.) (3) If nevertheless the other, still intent on definitions and 'scientific' precision, finds fault with even such an ordinarily acceptable use of words (objecting, for instance, that we do not learn the *whole* use of the word in the language, or do not learn to *report* it), the therapist, who is not interested in formulae but in facts, sidesteps the merely verbal issue and either asks the other to choose his own expression for the obvious facts (§79d), known to them both, or moves on to a different example (GI 68). " 'I shan't say anything that you won't all immediately agree with,' said Wittgenstein once, 'and if you do dispute something I'll drop it and go on to something else' " (Gasking and Jackson, "Wittgenstein", 51). In therapeutic philosophy nothing depends on the particular case (GI 58).

"A person with 'common sense' who reads one of the earlier philosophers, thinks (and not without justification): 'Sheer nonsense!' When he hears me, he thinks: 'Just insipid commonplaces!' Again, with justification. And thus the look of philosophy has changed" (Man. 219, 6).

§129   Revised from Man. 110, 259. See *PG* 256a; *Kreis,* 77d–78; Man. 110, 197 (full, concrete); Man. 108, 263; cp. Köhler, *Dynamics,* 5–7; Russell, *Logic,* 187: "It is very important to realize such things, for instance, as that *propositions are not names for facts.* It is quite obvious as soon as it is pointed out to you, but as a matter of fact I never had realized it until it was pointed out to me by a former pupil of mine, Wittgenstein."

that are most important: principally the use of words, their "depth grammar" (*BB* 4–5, 173a; §§90, 108–9, 432), but also general facts of nature which are the basis of grammar (p. 230a). The latter are "most important to us" as human beings, whereas W. considered the former more important for the solution of philosophical problems (ibid.).

because of their . . . : W. perhaps considered this observation unproblematic enough so as not to violate his ban on causal hypotheses in philosophy (§109). If, on the contrary, it sounds paradoxical, it is self-exemplifying; for there is nothing paradoxical about it. We sit up and take note when a horse talks, not when it walks, though walking horses, not talking ones, have been important in the history of mankind, to an extent not readily appreciated. Blindness to the ordinary has been remarked by numerous thinkers, including some W. knew:

Augustine: "These things I thus knew not, nor observed; they struck my sight on all sides, and I saw them not" (*Confessions,* III, 7, 14, and many other passages; see §436).

Schopenhauer: "It is an error as great as it is common that the most frequent, universal, and simple phenomena are those we best understand; on the contrary, they are just those phenomena which we are most accustomed to see, and about which we are most usually ignorant. . . . From the most powerful, most significant, and most distinct phenomenon we seek to learn to understand the weaker and less complete" (*World*, I, 124–25).

Moore: "It seems to me that, in philosophy, it is often a great achievement to notice something which is perfectly obvious as soon as it is noticed, but which had not been noticed before" (*Papers*, 166).

simplicity and familiarity: familiarity keeps us from taking note (see above, and §415), whereas simplicity (so failure to meet our preconceived notions and requirements) keeps us from paying further attention to such "trifling details" as we do note (*BB* 19, 172d–173a; *PG* 187c). P. 56n and p. 230a replace *familiarity* with *generality* (see *NB* 115f).

"The use of the word 'reading' is, of course, extremely familiar to us in the circumstances of our ordinary life (it would be extremely difficult to describe these circumstances even roughly)" (*BB* 119; *EPB* 172; see §156).

A parable, as it were, of the present point: In Man. 229, §2011, W. described as "*very* important" the fact that we take no notice of the indefinite periphery of our visual field. This and other examples are discussed in *PB* 80ab, 86b.

The real foundations of his enquiry: (1) facts of grammar, familiar but (reflectively) unknown (§122), which give rise to philosophical problems (GI 11ff); (2) the *a priori* requirements thus engendered in the searcher. Both the objective and the subjective components of the inquiry stare him in the face, too obvious to be seen. Could he, for instance, not only say but see: "I am looking for an essence, but cannot find one," he would know everything necessary about himself and about the troublesome topic, namely: (a) his *a priori* conviction, despite the contrary evidence; (b) mere examples and typical traits, rather than any essence. These, not the missing essence, are the truly important things. The "linguistic turn" in philosophy is incomplete as long as the philosopher merely studies language and does not reflect on the language-game he himself is playing when he asks his questions, makes his demands, proposes his arguments and solutions. Mere distinction of senses, in the manner of Moore, is not enough.

Reflecting now on this more immediate, evident content of the number, we can see that it is self-exemplifying. The blindness of which it speaks is itself a little-noticed fact of immense importance: the blindness of traditional philosophers to familiar facts of language; the blindness of even linguistic, analytic philosophers to evident facts of their own language-games. "We are doing prescriptive philosophy, not descriptive," they perhaps explain, "so can declare what number is or identity is, whereas the essentialist cannot." Yet the evident fact is that no agreement has been reached nor generally even been attempted with regard to the prescriptive criteria to be followed—completeness, force, facility, simplicity, common usage, and the like—and the relative weight to be accorded each of these often conflicting considerations. Cp. GI 70; §308.

do not strike a man at all: Man. 110, 259, and Man. 213, 419, here add: "(Frazer, etc. etc.)." With regard to this "etc. etc.", see *PB* 7 ("a different mentality from that of the mainstream of European and American civilization"), then look above.

§130 See GI 71; *BB* 28cd; *PG* 212a; *LC* 10b; cp. *RFM* 61e.

Links with §129: The simple language-games (§130) draw attention to the simple, familiar phenomena we tend to overlook (§129); and the refusal to sublimate (§130) is based on the judgment that these particulars are important as they stand (§129) without being either essences or clues to essences. The real problem of the one and the many in the history of thought consists in the fact that all progress in understanding comes through some sort of unification, starting from the disunified many, and that therefore people are tempted to unify beyond measure, to reduce, to simplify (*BB* 18). The danger is particularly great in philosophy, for philosophers have typically supposed that it is their task to achieve the broadest possible unification of reality, incorporating the largest number of particulars, and that the only way to grasp and express a comprehensive view of things is by means of general formulae—definitions, theories, principles, and so on. The later W. replaced this traditional approach, which he himself had once accepted unquestioningly (GI 50), with the method of models, and relegated the other to science (GI 70–71). Cp. Whewell versus Mill on types, in Coope et al., *Workbook*, 49–51; and Spengler, *Untergang*, 4–6.

language-games: see GI 56; §7.

of similarities: to reveal, for instance, a family likeness, so answer the question, "But why would we use the same term if there were nothing common to them all?" (§66; *BB* 17d).

but also of dissimilarities: especially these (§132a), since the errors treated were almost invariably false assimilations (GI 11–13). He would preclude any use of linguistic samples of the sort he formerly preached (3.3421) and practiced (GI 50), valuing the particular case only as a clue to the essential. As a motto for the *Investigations,* he once considered using the words from Lear: "I'll teach you differences" (Drury, "Symposium", 69).

§131   After the first sentence, Man. 220, 85, adds: "I am thinking of Spengler's method" (see above). On the use of such models, see the preceding remarks and references; GI 58, 71; and Man. 229, §1301. On the dogmatism of philosophers, see Man. 220, 85, and W.'s discussion in *Kreis*, 182–86. As a sample of his own former dogmatism, see the repeated *must*'s in *NB* 17b and 63. In Frege, see for instance *Writings*, 131: "If we *can* make do with one way of judging, then we *must*." On *must* (or *cannot*) as the sign of a philosophical problem, see Alice Ambrose's lecture notes, in "Universals", 340–41. For varied samples, and criticism of such dogmatism, see §§156g, 158; *Z* 299; *EPB* 203–4, 226; *BB* 42a, 43c, 130e, 136de, 137bc, 139c; Man. 111, 119; Man. 110, 216–17, 222. The dogmatic *must* should be distinguished from the logical (§437), that is, a blind requirement from one based on an actual rule. Thus the assertion that a person must know what he wishes (§437) differs from the claims that there *must* be something common to games (§66), language *must* be rigidly regular (§81a), thought *must* be precise (§101), and the like.

"One takes one's ideas, and one's language, about volition from this kind of example and thinks that they must apply—if not in such an obvious way—to all cases which one can properly call cases of willing.—It is the same case that we have met over and over again" (*BB* 150).

"The scrutiny of the grammar of a word weakens the position of certain fixed standards of our expression which had prevented us from seeing facts with unbiassed eyes. Our investigation tried to remove this bias, which forces us to think that the facts *must* conform to certain pictures embedded in our language" (*BB* 43).

ineptness or emptiness: for the reasons touched on in GI 70, a universal assertion in philosophy tends to be false or undecidable if we leave the words alone, and an empty tautology, true by definition, if we tinker with the meanings to make the thesis succeed.

§132(a)   See *BB* 28c; Man. 213, 415; cp. §17; *PP* 279.

We want to establish an order: see commentary on §109 ("but by arranging"); Man. 172, 3.

with a particular end in view: see GI 58; §109.

not *the* order: see GI 30; §105; Man. 220, 86.

giving prominence: italicized in the German.

distinctions which . . . : see GI 9ff.

ordinary forms: not philosophical misuses of language (GI 24).

This may make it look . . . : according to *BB* 59 similar motivation leads to reform proposals like those of solipsists: "We sometimes wish for a notation which stresses a difference more strongly, makes it more obvious, than ordinary language does, or one which in a particular case uses more closely similar forms of expression than our ordinary language. Our mental cramp is loosened when we are shown the notations which fulfil these needs." W. himself then said: "We shall also try to construct new notations, in order to break the spell of those which we are accustomed to" (*BB* 23). But he intended no reform of language.

With the present observation, he may wish to forestall repetition of a former misunderstanding: though the motivation for W.'s notational proposals in the *Tractatus* (GI 25; V, 4) and later (X, 8) resembled that just stated ("giving prominence to distinctions which . . ."), Russell (V, 5) and others (V, 8) supposed he meant to reform language.

(b) See V, 6; Z 467; cp. comments on §120a.

Such a reform . . . : see the comments above; §577; *Kreis,* 46; Frege, *Writings,* 125b; cp. 6.341.

in practice: as for instance in §577, but not in the phenomenological language W. once envisaged (X, 8), which would have been unusable (cp. §60) even if it had been comprehensible (X, 9–10). W. would no longer say as he did in Man. 105, 122: "The phenomenological language represents the same thing as our ordinary language and only has the advantage that we can express many things more briefly in it and with less danger of misunderstanding." His idea had been that with such a notation a person might, for instance, simply indicate a sense-datum without alluding to himself or any object of sense. But what function would such an utterance serve (§363c)? The engine was idling.

The confusions which occupy us . . . : besides the preceding, see §38d and commentary.

§133 See Man. 115, 50.

(a) **unheard-of-ways:** for instance, a phenomenological language (Man. 229, §1737; X, 8); or Russell's Theory of Types, then the Ramified Theory of Types, then still further refinements through the Principle of Reducibility. Cp. *PB* 79c; *Kreis,* 240.

(b) See §309; *NB* 55d; Man. 110, 98–99; Man. 109, 104; cp. §91a; *BB* 44c–45a; 6.521; *NB* 74ab; Man. 176, 13B ("There is no phenomenology, but there are phenomenological problems"); Man. 110, 17; Man. 109, 194.

the clarity that we are aiming at: see GI 8; commentary on §122b; *PB* 7; *LR* 45; Drury, *Danger,* ix–xii (e.g.: " 'For me on the other hand clarity, lucidity, is the goal sought' ").

philosophical problems: not as much mere unanswered questions as problems in the strong sense: paradoxes, puzzles, apparent contradictions, mental knots. "For philosophy consists in philosophical problems, that is, certain individual disquietudes that we call 'philosophical problems'. . . . So the characteristic thing . . . is that here a muddle gets expressed in the form of a question which does not acknowledge this confusion. That the questioner is *freed* from his problem through a certain alteration in his form of expression" (*PG* 193). "In philosophical thought we see problems where there are none. And philosophy should show that there are none there" (*PG* 47). "Philosophy unties knots in our thought, that we have foolishly tied there" (*PB* 52; see *Z* 452; §§109–12, 123, 309; *PP* 323).

W. was impressed (Man. 213, 421) by Hertz's similar views: "But we have accumulated around the terms 'force' and 'electricity' more relations than can be completely reconciled amongst themselves. We have an obscure feeling of this and want to have things cleared up. Our confused wish finds expression in the confused question as to the nature of force and electricity. But the answer which we want is not really an answer to this question. It is not by finding out more and fresh relations and connections that it can be answered; but by removing the contradictions existing between those already known, and thus perhaps by reducing their number. When these painful contradictions are removed, the question as to the nature of force will not have been answered; but our minds, no longer vexed, will cease to ask illegitimate questions" (*Principles,* 8).

should *completely* disappear: individually, not collectively (VII, 9).

"On several occasions Wittgenstein said to me: 'My father was a businessman and I am a businessman too; I want my philosophy to be businesslike, to get something done, to get something settled.' Kant said that a great deal of philosophy reminded him of one person holding a sieve while the other tried to milk the he-goat. Wittgenstein wanted above all things to make an end of sieve holding and he-goat milking" (Drury, "Symposium", 69; paragraph division omitted).

(c) From Man. 213, 431, and Man. 112, 93, with slight stylistic changes. Cp. Man. 213, 406, 409, 416; Man. 110, 189; Man. 109, 79–80.

The real discovery . . . : Rush Rhees writes, in a letter: "He had found some feature of what he had been saying unsatisfactory. This was typical: he would come back to the same questions again and again, often trying to see if they could not be done in another way. As he was leaving, this time, he said to me roughly this: 'In my book I say that I am able to leave off with a problem in philosophy when I want to. But that's a lie; I can't.'" Cp. *NB* 74ab.

On the one hand, the trouble often is that we are looking for an explanation (Man. 164, 92; *Z* 314–15) instead of simply saying "This language-game is played" (§§217, 654). Or we search for illusory "completeness" (Man. 138, 30B–31A). "The difficulty—I might say—is not that of finding the solution but rather that of recognizing as the solution something that looks as if it were only a preliminary to it. . . . The difficulty here is: to stop" (*Z* 314; see Man. 220, 93; Man. 164, 58).

On the other hand, W. mused, "Is it always and obviously desirable that philosophical problems be silenced?" (Man. 179). He viewed critically the "lack of deep puzzlement" in the work of a well-known philosophical movement, for one thing because he felt that philosophical questions are much harder than many philosophers suppose (Gasking and Jackson, "Wittgenstein", 54; see Z 456). "It is a *bodily* need of human beings to say in their work, 'Let's leave it for now' [see Malcolm, *Memoir*, 85–86]; and the fact that in philosophical thinking we must constantly go against this need is what makes the work such a strain. I have one of these talents which must constantly make a virtue of necessity" (Man. 168, 4).

"The intensity and the completeness with which Wittgenstein was occupied by the problems of the *Investigations* could hardly be exaggerated. I say 'occupied by the problems' advisedly, for they truly took possession of him. G. E. Moore was a deeply serious philosopher, but even he was not, I think, pursued and tormented by philosophical difficulties to the degree that Wittgenstein was. I imagine that after a few hours of work Moore could stop and turn his attention to other matters. Wittgenstein sometimes had to resort to a violent distraction, such as going to a 'flick', where he would sit in the front row with his field of vision filled up by the screen, so that the scenes and incidents of the film would hold off the thoughts that pressed upon him.

"In the *Investigations* he says, somewhat enigmatically: 'The real discovery is the one that makes me able to break off doing philosophy when I want to,' but I do not believe he ever made that discovery. I am inclined to say that philosophy was somehow *inside* Wittgenstein, giving him no rest" (Malcolm, "Symposium", 71).

To suppose, on the strength of the present remark and W.'s advice to certain of his students (Malcolm, *Memoir*, 30), that he regarded philosophy as a disease of which he had to rid himself and others, would be a mistake. "Wittgenstein never advised anyone to give up philosophy, if by that is meant thinking about first principles and ultimate problems. When I said goodby to him for the last time at Cambridge and we both knew he had not long to live, he said to me with great seriousness: 'Drury, whatever becomes of you, don't stop thinking'" (Drury, "Symposium", 69).

makes me: see Man. 112, 6: "Work in philosophy—as often in architecture—is in reality rather work on oneself. On one's own outlook. On one's way of seeing things. (And what one requires of them.)"

that gives philosophy peace: see above; §309; NL 300a; *RFM* 124b; Man. 220, 79–80; Man. 112, 44, 56; cp. *NB* 33c ("It is the *dualism*, positive and negative facts, that gives me no peace").

no longer tormented: "Philosophical unclarity is tormenting. It is felt to be shameful. We feel we don't know our way around where we *ought* to. And yet it *is* not so. We can live perfectly well without a doctrine concerning our concepts" (Man. 173, 10A).

which bring *itself* in question: as did the apparent impossibility of complete analysis when such analysis seemed the whole task of philosophy (*NB* 2e; §91). And this endeavor "finds expression in questions as to the *essence* of language, of propositions, of thought" (§92), so that doubts about essences would likewise entail doubts about philosophy. "These difficulties, as long as they are seen as problems, are tantalizing, and appear insoluble" (*BB* 46a).

"We are opposed above all to the idea that the question 'What is knowledge?'—for instance—is a burning issue. For *such* it appears to be, and it seems as though we didn't know anything at all until we can answer *it*. In our philosophical investigation we would like, as it were, to finish off something in the greatest haste, since everything else appears to hang in the air till it is completed" (Man. 219, 10). "One sometimes has described it by saying that no philosophical problem can be solved until all philosophical problems are solved; which means that as long as they aren't all solved every new difficulty renders all our previous results questionable" (*BB* 44; cp. Russell, "Method", 85c; *LR* 45; comments on §125, concerning Russell and Frege's similar attitude towards possible contradictions in logic and mathematics). Thus Russell wrote: "The question of relations is one of the most important that arise in philosophy, as most other issues turn on it . . . perhaps the very existence of philosophy as a subject distinct from science and possessing a method of its own" (*Logic*, 333). Cp. Ramsey, *Foundations*, 264: "If we regard philosophy as a system of definitions . . . how can philosophical inquiry be conducted without a perpetual *petitio principii?*"

we now demonstrate a method: therapeutic, *a posteriori*, nondogmatic (GI 50–52; VII, 1–9)—all of which might be said of various procedures (*d*).

Problems are solved . . . : "like a substance (a piece of sugar) in water," W. added in Man. 110, 99 (see Man. 213, 421). See §47f; NL 279a (quoted for p. 207e); commentary on §109 ("the problems are solved") and above ("philosophical problems").

not a *single* problem: as previously: "The problems of negation, of disjunction, of true and false, are only reflections of the one great problem in the variously placed great and small mirrors of philosophy" (*NB* 40; see *NB* 3c), that is, the problem of the nature of the proposition (*NB* 39), of the *a priori* order in the world (*NB* 53; see GI 30).

(d) not *a* philosophical method: for likely targets, see X, 13 ("the sole method of true philosophy"); 6.53 ("the correct method in philosophy"); *Kreis*, 183 ("I still hold to that"); *PP* 322 ("a 'new method' had been discovered"); Man. 105, 36 (to seek sense, not truth, "is the method of philosophy"); *BB* 12a ("the method of philosophy"); Farrell's article ("Appraisal") concerning "the Wittgensteinian method", which apparently infuriated W. (Malcolm, *Memoir,* 59). See comments on the motto; Pitcher, *Philosophy,* 315–19.

there are indeed methods: see GI 51–62. "The sorts of thing he means by 'methods' are, I take it, '[imagining or considering] a language-game for which [a given] account is really valid' (for example, §2, §48); 'finding and inventing intermediate cases' (§122); '[inventing] fictitious natural history', (II, p. 230); investigating one expression by investigating a grammatically related expression, for example, the grammar of 'meaning' by that of 'explanation of the meaning' (*BB,* pp. 1, 24); and so on" (Cavell, "Availability", 177). See also e.g. III, 1 (how learned, how verified); §464 (from disguised to patent nonsense); *BB* 4bc (sensible substitute); §156 (parallel case); discussion of §48 ("the method of §2").

like different therapies: see §255 and commentary.

VIII. The "General Form of Propositions" (§§134–137)

GENERAL COMMENTARY

(1)   After the long parenthesis of Sections VI and VII, Wittgenstein briefly reconnects with the *Tractatus* doctrines discussed in Sections IV and V, before starting to probe their unexamined foundations in Section IX (see GI 64). A notable idiosyncracy of the Tractarian treatment of propositions permits him to make the connection without repeating himself. Unlike the essence of language, on the one hand, or of names, on the other, the essence of propositions received double expression, first through general definitions (4.01, 4.021, 4.023, etc.), then through the "general form of propositions". In Section IV (§65a), after mentioning both ways of formulating what is common to all propositions, Wittgenstein focused on essences and definitions, leaving the more specialized type of generalization, specific to the *Tractatus,* for consideration here.

(2)   The formula Wittgenstein proposed in 4.5 was, as it were, a cancerous growth in the body of Russellian logic. Substitution of variables for words had yielded skeletal expressions such as "fx" and "xRy", revealing the logical form common to large and varied classes of prop-

ositions (see 3.311–3.315). But now, asked Wittgenstein, what is the structure shared by all these varied classes, making them all propositions? What is the logical skeleton of propositions as such, and how can it be expressed? On the one hand a variable like "p" (§134b) would not be a prototype (any more than a definition would be). On the other hand, any grouping of x's, f's, and R's would lack the requisite generality. So Wittgenstein fell back on words to construct the great *Ur-Urbild*. "The general form of a proposition," he wrote, "is: This is how things stand" (4.5). Every proposition, of whatever particular form or language, depicts reality (GI 32; see commentary on §136a).

DETAILED COMMENTARY

§134(a) How can I say . . . : see VIII, 1–2; cp. GI 32; *NB* 51g.

It is first and foremost . . . : this is not offered as a partial justification, but as a preparatory clarification. Not all propositions have the subject-predicate form.

how is this sentence applied: concerning this terminology, see the commentary on §20b.

For I got it from there . . . : cp. §120b. "From there" is italicized in the German.

(b) Revised from Man. 220, 94–95.

"said that this was how . . .": the translation, using *that,* obscures the apparent reason for W.'s differing verdict here and in §22a; the clause there begins with *dass,* so he denies that it is a *Satz.* Such an explanation may seem to accord exaggerated importance to surface grammar, but harmonizes with W.'s final judgment that the main reason for calling the present word-combination a *Satz* is that it sounds like one. With *dass* added, it would not.

as a propositional *schema:* each of the component words is indeterminate, like a variable waiting to be replaced by something more specific. See VIII, 2.

but *only* because: one would be less likely to say, "He explained his position to me, said that so and so, and that therefore he needed an advance."

it gets employed as . . . : rather, "only as". This lapse in translation obscures the train of thought. Since the start of the number, W. has distinguished between sound and use. Now, after noting similarity in sound, he denies similarity in use.

To say that this proposition agrees . . . : the author of the *Tractatus* concurred; had he supposed that the formula might itself picture reality, he would not have used it, for it would itself have been a *Satz,* not the general form of all *Sätze.*

would be obvious nonsense: to say the same of a longer sentence, in which these words occur (for instance the sample sentence at the start of the paragraph), would not be.

sounding like a proposition: the similarity deserves attention, for had the formula resembled ordinary propositions any more or any less ("It's raining" or "p"), W. would not have chosen it as the "general form of propositions".

"And what a proposition is is in one sense determined by the rules of sentence formation (in English for example)" (§136). However, "the mere *ring of a sentence* is not enough to give these connexions of signs any meaning" (*RFM* 54a). "So we speak of a meaningful or meaningless proposition" (*PG* 122).

"We are used to saying '2 times 2 is 4,' and the verb 'is' makes this into a proposition, and apparently establishes a close kinship with everything that we call a 'proposition'. Whereas it is a matter only of a very superficial relationship" (*RFM* 49). Cp. §21; *BB* 98e; *PG* 126b.

§135   See §65; *PG* 112a–113b; *PB* 190d; *PP* 261, 317a; cp. *PB* 150bc; Man. 110, 226.

"game": see §66.

we shall give examples: see §§71b, 75, 208–11.

inductively defined series [*induktive Reihen*]: one is given examples and proceeds from like to like (§§67b, 208–9), rather than detecting an essence in the first examples and proceeding deductively (§210). Compare mathematical induction, "that is to say, the argument in which we conclude that, because a property belongs to the number 0 and also to the successor of any number which has it, it must therefore belong to all natural numbers" (Kneale, *Development*, 467). As the status of each number in a series is guaranteed by its relation to the preceding number, so each sentence in the series would be called a proposition in virtue of its close similarity to the preceding sentence—*s* to *r*, and *r* to *q*, and *q* to *p*, the initial paradigm, though *p* and *s* may be so unlike that without the intermediate steps the term *proposition* would not be applied to *s*.

the concept of number: see §67b.

§136   See *RFM* 49; cp. 6.111; Man. 108, 178; Man. 106, 59.

(a) A reworking of *PG* 123bcd. See *RFM* 49cd; *PG* 124ef; *PB* 311a; *NB* 99gh; Man. 112, 25–27; Man. 109, 156; Ramsey, *Foundations*, 142–43.

is the same as: in the *Tractatus*, 4.5 does in fact follow immediately upon and from a discussion of truth and falsehood. The choice of this formula was clearly not motivated by basic similarity of verbal form, as on lower levels of generality, where, for instance, "F(x)" is used to suggest the duality of subject and predicate, or "xRy" substitutes for names and relational terms. It was meant rather to highlight the difference between propositions and names: "Every proposition is essentially true-false" (*NB* 93–94; see Russell, *Logic*, 187–88, 208; cp. 4.024). " 'True' and 'false' are not accidental properties of a proposition, such that, when it has meaning, we can say it is also true or false: on the contrary, to have meaning *means* to be true or false: the being true or false actually constitutes the relation of the proposition to reality, which we mean by saying that it has meaning. . . . In giving the general form of a proposition you are explaining what kind of ways of putting together the symbols of things and relations will correspond to (be analogous to) the things having those relations in reality. In doing thus you are saying what is meant by saying that a proposition is true; and you must do it once for all" (*NB* 112).

whatever can be true or false: the *Tractatus* treated tautologies, which can only be true, and contradictions, which can only be false, as pseudo-propositions (4.461, 4.466). As late as *PG* 376 W. wrote: "It belongs to the essence of what we call a proposition that it can be denied." And he continued to question the meaningfulness of statements which permit no contrast (§§253, 398; Hallett, "Contrast"). However, it does not follow that he still hesitated to apply the term *proposition*, for we do refer to "meaningless propositions" (*PG* 122). And the use of the word *sentence* (and therefore of the word *Satz* when it has the same sense) is of course still broader and looser (*RFM* 49cd). Already in 1930–1931 "he had said that the word 'proposition', 'as generally understood', includes both 'what I call propositions', also 'hypotheses', and also mathematical propositions; that the distinction between these three 'kinds' is a 'logical distinction', and that therefore there must be some grammatical rules, in the case of each kind, which apply to that kind and not to the other two; but that the 'truth-function' rules apply to all three, and that that is why they are all called 'propositions' " (*PP* 261). A proposition is simply what we apply the calculus of truth-functions to (*PB* 113a; Man. 109, 156). Number 134 suggests that the author of the *Investigations* would consider even this looser criterion, satisfied by tautologies and contradictions, to be at most a sufficient condition, not a necessary one, for applying the label *proposition*.

Or again: a literal translation ("but also") seems preferable, to make W.'s point. Why did he say in 4.5, "This is how things are," and not, "This is how things are not"? Perhaps because for him that would have been to confuse the psychological, the human, with the purely logical (GI 36). The *proposition*, whether positive or negative, says, "This is how things are"; *people* may affirm or deny it. W. would now reject such sublimations and adduce "only exterior facts about language" (§120). As something we *say* about propositions, "This is false" is on a par with "This is true." Cp. *NB* 51g, then §520.

'p' is true = p: this formula replaces the metaphysics of 4.5 with a mere equivalence, more readily recognized as grammatical. Therapy does not require that W. here raise the questions he did in Man. 116, 110: "The proposition 'It is raining' surely says something about the weather but nothing about the words I am speaking. But how can 'It is raining' say the same as: 'The proposition "It is raining" is true,' since *it* does say something about the words? Can the meaning be the same if I answer a question about the weather one time with 'It is raining' and another time: 'I tell you truly: "It is raining" '?"

'p' is false = not-p: though this equation parallels the first, 4.5 provides no metaphysical interpretation for it; and if it expresses a merely grammatical truth, then doubtless so does the first equation.

(b) See Man. 108, 178; cp. *OC* 200.

And to say: in the German text there is no new paragraph here.

in our language: italicized for reasons which appear in the next two paragraphs and are anticipated in 6.111: "One might think, for example, that the words 'true' and 'false' signified two properties among other properties, and then it would seem to be a remarkable fact that every proposition possessed one of these properties." The *can* in "whatever can be true or false" is neither empirical nor metaphysical, but logical, grammatical. "What we did in these discussions was what we always do when we meet the word 'can' in a metaphysical proposition. We show that this proposition hides a grammatical rule" (*BB* 55; see *BB* 16; Z 133–34; §§251, 360, p. 222bcd; Hallett, "Contrast", 692).

The existence of propositions in our language is equally contingent (§18).

we apply the calculus of truth functions: thus "negation and disjunction, we would like to say, concern the essence of a proposition, whereas tense does not, but only its content" (*PG* 215; see ibid., 217e; cp. *Kreis*, 80–81). The *Tractatus* asserted more specifically (see 5) that "the essence of a proposition—its 'most general form'—is the character of being a truth-function of elementary propositions" (Black, *Companion*, 236).

(c) See *PG* 124d; cp. §§90a, 97b; *PG* 186b–187a, 217e.

A transitional form of W.'s early metaphysics helps to explain the twist his critique now takes: See the commentary on §559, concerning meaning-bodies, and apply the idea to *true* and *proposition.* Positively, it is helpful to remember that for W. a word's meaning is its use in the language (§43); that the expressions it is customarily joined with are an important aspect of this use; and that therefore its combination with *true* belongs to the meaning of the word *proposition,* and vice versa. The concepts are not distinct or separable units which might be juxtaposed as the words are (§225).

fits: see §138; cp. *RFM* 15b, and Russell's way of speaking in *Mind,*

187, or *Logic*, 187: "A name would be a proper symbol to use for a person; a sentence (or a proposition) is the proper symbol for a fact."

(d) See *Z* 134; *RFM* 49d; cp. *NB* 53 ("My theory does not really bring it out that the proposition *must* have two poles"); *BB* 67a; §562 ("Is there some reality lying behind the notation, which shapes its grammar?"), p. 225a.

a bad picture: blurring the distinction between the factual and the conceptual (*Z* 458). Cp. §§247–48.

can say no more than: see §§370–71; cp. *Kreis*, 104.

we only predicate . . . : not, "Propositions are only what we predicate 'true' and 'false' of" (see the comments on the first paragraph).

And what a proposition is . . . : "Here, therefore, he seemed to be making a distinction between a proposition and a sentence [both covered by the German word *Satz*]. . . . He seemed to me sometimes so to use 'proposition' that every significant sentence *was* a proposition, although, of course, a significant sentence does not contain everything which is necessary to give it significance. . . . And very often he seemed to me to follow the example of Russell in the Introduction to *Principia Mathematica* in so using the word 'proposition' that 'propositions', and not merely sentences, could be without sense" (*PP* 262–63). See §134b and references, especially *PG* 122b, 126b.

in one sense: of the word *Satz*.

by the use of the sign: not of the word *Satz*, but of the candidate word-combination. See *PP* 262–63, above.

but does not 'fit' it: cp. W.'s slip in *BB* 151a, and Schlick, "Form", 180: "These rules must be taught by actually applying them in definite situations, that is to say, the circumstances to which they fit must actually be shown."

§137 Cp. Man. 106, 114. The shift in this number from propositions in general to the subject of a particular sentence and to a specific proposition to be tested makes talk of 'fitting' sound more acceptable, since the individual case can be distinguished from the language-game as a whole and can be tested by the criteria established in it. However, as the following section indicates, such talk, which makes rules and criteria sound as constant, substantial, and inflexible as rulers, is therefore misleading. "Why shouldn't both forms of expression enjoy similar freedom? And how can what one says limit what the other may say?" (*PG* 186–87).

"Who or what . . . ?": see *PG* 124d; Waismann, *Principles*, 333.

in what sense: conventional correctness (cp. §145b) and felt affinity (see p. 183d).

IX. Rules "in the Medium of the Understanding" (§§138–242)

GENERAL COMMENTARY

(1) Young Wittgenstein spoke for many a post-Humean philosopher when he wrote: "There is no compulsion making one thing happen because another has happened. The only necessity that exists is *logical* necessity" (6.37). Logic, as frequently conceived, provides the paradigm of true necessity and strict precontainment against which reality—or at least temporal reality (see the comments on §108c)—is measured and found wanting (cp. §§140a, 220; Z 296; RFM 36a; PP 293–94; NB 43, quoted for §437). Now it is conceivable that Wittgenstein's critique of this viewpoint, in the present section, should have an impact comparable to Hume's, shattering this remaining (if much diminished) bastion of rationalism. What Hume did for necessary connections in reality, Wittgenstein may do for necessary connections in "pure thought". Such, at any rate, was his intention. As he had insisted in the *Tractatus* that "belief in the causal nexus is *superstition*" (5.1361), so now he would dissect "this curious superstition . . . that the mental act is capable of crossing a bridge before we've got to it" (*BB* 143). For the notion belongs to the unexamined foundations of the picture theory, which he means finally to probe (GI 64); it characterizes his former conception of "strict and clear rules . . . hidden in the medium of the understanding" (§102) and his belief that "if anyone utters a sentence and *means* or *understands* it he is operating a calculus according to definite rules" (§81).

(2) The calculus chiefly in question, just alluded to in §136, is that of truth functions. Language, the *Tractatus* taught, consists of propositions (GI 32–33); and propositions, without exception, are truth-functions of elementary propositions (5). For "every proposition is the result of truth-operations on elementary propositions" (5.3), that is, "of operations with elementary propositions as bases" (5.234). These elementary propositions themselves contain all logical operations (5.47) as well as their results. Quite generally, "if we are given a proposition, then *with it* we are also given the results of all truth-operations that have it as their base" (5.442). Conversely, if we can infer an elementary proposition

239

from a general one, that must be because the elementary proposition is present in it, even if this requires that the general proposition be an infinite logical product (*PP* 298). For "if *p* follows from *q*, the sense of '*p*' is contained in the sense of '*q*' " (5.122). But where is this sense to be found? Where are all these operations present? "We are tempted to imagine this calculus, as it were, as a permanent background to every sentence which we say, and to think that, although the sentence as written on a piece of paper or spoken stands isolated, in the mental act of thinking the calculus is there—all in a lump. The mental act seems to perform in a miraculous way what could not be performed by any act of manipulating symbols" (*BB* 42). See GI 37; IX, 9; commentary on §229; 3.11, 3.42–3.5, 5.124; *NB* 64; *PP* 295; Man. 116, 105; Man. 112, 188 (quoted for §292); Man. 110, 51 (quoted for §549), 52, 294 (quoted for §20a); Man. 109, 35–36, 220 (quoted for §§20a, 192); Man. 107, 233 (quoted for §436).

(3)   This inner act differs from external calculations not only in the incredible richness of its contents, but in the necessity of the connections made, future steps being not merely predicted but somehow precontained (XXXVII, 3, 5; 5.122, 5.124, 5.514, 5.47; cp. §§190–95) and thereby predetermined with a sureness unequaled in nature (IX, 1). It is because all natural processes differ in this respect, one merely preceding another and not foreshadowing it (GI 34–36; §194), that belief in the causal nexus is superstition (5.1361). Only in logical inference is there true *inner* necessity (5.1362, 6.37). Thus "the exploration of logic means the exploration of *everything that is subject to law*. And outside logic everything is accidental" (6.3). Logic is not only precise (§101), but *hard* (§437)—harder than the hardest machine (§§193–94), in fact "the *hardest* thing there is" (§97; see *Z* 299; *RFM* 110, 121, 193j–194c; *LC* 16b).

(4)   As Wittgenstein was aware, many others had held similar views. Boole, for instance, described language "not as a mere collection of signs, but as a system of expressions, the elements of which are subject to the laws of the thought which they represent. That these laws are as rigorously mathematical as the laws which govern the purely quantitative conceptions of space and time, of number and magnitude, is a conclusion which I do not hesitate to submit to the exactest scrutiny" (see Kneale, *Development,* 405–6). As for the nature of "rigorously mathematical laws": "In his fundamental law Russell seems to be saying of a proposition: 'It already follows—all I still have to do is, to infer it.' Thus Frege somewhere says that the straight line which connects any two points is really already there before we draw it; and it is the same when we say that the transitions, say in the series +2, have really al-

ready been made before we make them orally or in writing—as it were tracing them" (*RFM* 9).

(5)   Such are the principal targets of this section, whose main thrust, like that of the *Investigations* as a whole, is therapeutic. Its message appears already in germ, and its connection with the past, in Man. 109, 179, where Wittgenstein was struggling to free himself from his former errors: "I always want to say: the application of a general rule is not enough, but the rule must be stressed somehow during its application.—But that is false" (see *Kreis*, 154–55, quoted for §153). Justification is provided, not in the moment, nor in the mind, but in the language-game (§197). For the criterion of correctness, whether in mathematics or in language, is the common practice of mankind (§§201–8, 241), which forms the background for our speech and calculations, and this criterion is not discernible in any momentary item, whether image (§239), picture (§§139–41), segment (§§143–45, 189, 213–14), formula (§§146, 151–54, 179), or any other expression of a rule (§§185–88, 198, 217–22, 230). As Augustine observed, however we conceive "this secret fore-perceiving of things to come, that only can be seen, which is. But what now is, is not future, but present. When then things to come are said to be seen, it is not themselves which as yet are not (that is, which are to be), but their causes perhaps or signs are seen, which already are" (*Confessions*, XI, 18, 24).

(6)   The overall tendency in Wittgenstein's later thought illustrated by this reply has been treated in the General Introduction (GI 43). So has the general viewpoint into which the earlier error fits (GI 36–42): "A wish," for instance, "seems already to know what will or would satisfy it; a proposition, a thought, what makes it true—even when that thing is not there at all! Whence this *determining* of what is not yet there? This despotic demand?" (§437). One might reply: "The only correlate in language to an intrinsic necessity is an arbitrary rule" (§372); the language-game is beholden to no one and nothing (I, 4). Yet to call its rules arbitrary might suggest that their adoption and retention are a matter of personal choice, and of little consequence, whereas language would not exist were it not for massive agreement which arises not through choice but through kindred reactions (§§143–45), and cannot continue to serve its function save as a shared form of life (§§241–42). One is inclined to say that our common nature explains this agreement, so is the ultimate basis of language and logic; but for Wittgenstein the bountiful reservoir of human nature, from which all our actions flow (*BB* 143–44), was as mythical as the ethereal logic machine grinding out inferences (*RFM* 36b). It may be true that a lion, if gifted with speech, would not understand us nor we him (p. 223), but for Wittgenstein that

was a matter of "our natural history" (§25), not of metaphysics. "The difficulty here is: to stop" (Z 314). We ought simply to say: "This language-game is played" (§654). There lies the true foundation of logic (OC 248, 401–2), the bedrock on which our spade is turned (§217).

(7) The language-games that Wittgenstein works with here are, as usual (GI 56), very simple ones. However, the transition from under-standing a word (§§138–41) to understanding arithmetical series (§§143ff) has perplexed some. "How odd," writes Mundle, "that Wittgenstein should try to convey what it is like to follow linguistic rules by discussing the rules of a calculus, though one of his main theses is now that linguistic rules are *not* like the rules of a calculus" (*Critique*, 197). The answer is that Wittgenstein is again employing "the method of §2" (see the commentary on §48a); that is, he is "attending to the source of our mode of representation" (Man. 116, 220) "in the sciences and in mathematics" (*BB* 25). He and others had conceived language on the model of a mathematical calculus (IX, 2–4), and mathematical calculi as mechanisms whose every movement is contained in advance (§§193–94). But even in mathematics, where exceptional agreement reigns (§240, pp. 225–27), so *a fortiori* in language (§142), this model is a myth. Wittgenstein's therapy is more effective than if he had consid-ered only words and had left the tempting paradigms intact.

(8) More specifically, the author of the *Tractatus* drew a parallel be-tween the truth-operations which generate propositions (5.234) and the internal relations by which series are ordered (5.232). Earlier he had cited the number-series as a paradigm of such ordering (4.1252). And still earlier he described propositions themselves as functions of the expressions contained in them (3.318). So he now reexamines these same examples, in the order of their *Tractatus* appearance—first a sin-gle word, *cube* (§139), then the series of natural numbers (§143), finally more complex series (§151)—and considers how the rules of each de-velopment might be "hidden in the medium of the understanding" (§102).

(9) It might be thought that no simpler, more perspicuous examples could be found than these. Already the fog lifts. However, mists of theory have so enwrapped the whole subject of understanding that vision may still be obscured, even in such samples. So Wittgenstein in-troduces a still simpler instance of rule-guided activity: reading, in the sense of "rendering out loud what is written or printed" (§156). To un-derstand the word *cube* is to understand a whole language (§199), to read the word *cube* is merely to react to a mark. In the direction of analytic simplicity such as the *Investigations* sought, this is rock bottom; it is, one might say, an elementary language-game, on a par with the elementary

propositions with which Wittgenstein once intended to serve the same clarificatory purpose (GI 25).

This very simplicity might seem to invalidate the comparison and to raise Mundle's difficulty all over again. But the answer is the same as before: Wittgenstein is moving into enemy territory. For just as he had compared language with a mathematical calculus, regular and sure, so he had compared it with reading, where agreement is equally rigid (see §292 and commentary). "There is a general rule," he had written, "by means of which the musician can obtain the symphony from the score" (4.0141), and if we penetrate to the essence of language (4.013) we find just the same thing there: "A gramophone record, the musical idea, the written notes, and the sound-waves, all stand to one another in the same internal relation of depicting that holds between language and the world" (4.014). Later "he explained this by saying that a 'picture' must have been given by an explanation of how '♯' and 'b' are used, and that an explanation is always of the same kind as a definition, viz. 'replacing one symbol by another'. He went on to say that when a man reads on a piano from a score, he is 'led' or 'guided' by the position of the crotchets, and that this means that he is 'following a general rule', and that this rule, though not 'contained' in the score, nor in the result, nor in both together, must be 'contained' in his intention" (PP 264). But how, and in what sense?

(10)   The parallelism in 4.0141, between score and gramophone record, suggests that the connections are causal; and in fact Wittgenstein's concern in this section about reading centers not on the idea that a reader notes a rule in the score (PP 264) but on the Russellian notion that the study of "causal processes is necessary for getting a clear understanding of the function of our language" (Waismann, "Relevance", 219). The drawback for this causal approach is that we know next to nothing about the physiological mechanisms involved in reading (§158), and pay little attention to past performance, yet know quite surely when we are reading and reading correctly (§159). It might seem, therefore, that in this case the words led, guided, follow "must be understood as expressing a more or less causal relation, and that this relation must be perceived, not merely inferred from frequent concomitance" (Russell, "Limits", 137). Reading, accordingly, will be the derivation of sounds from marks via an inner circuit in consciousness; it will be an essentially psychic occurrence (§§159, 165–71).

(11)   The corresponding notion of understanding is suggested most strongly by the occasions on which, after puzzling over some problem, we suddenly exclaim, "Now I understand!" or, "Now I know!" (§§151–55, 179, 183–84). The word now; the fact that a moment previously we did not understand nor think we understood, but now do;

the fact that we did not reason to this conviction or test it through successful performance; the fact, finally, that in the intervening instant an inner event may indeed have occurred of which we were aware (§151), and which established our right to the claim (§§155, 289)—all this suggests that understanding consists in a momentary, conscious occurrence reported by the words. Of course, similar observations might be made, for example, concerning spectators at a game who hear a whistle and exclaim, "We've won!": A moment previously they had not won and knew they hadn't, whereas now they have and know they have; they did not reason to their victory or put it to the test; an event did occur, of which they were aware, which warranted their shout. Yet no one would identify their victory with the shrilling of the whistle. Nor would anyone say that when a man steps out from prison and exclaims, "I'm free," his freedom consists in the step he just took. But in philosophy, when discussing knowledge, understanding, and the like, we are influenced by other paradigms (GI 18), so that " 'being able to go on' here seems to be something setting in suddenly in the form of a clearly outlined event" (*BB* 112).

(12)   Such, evidently, was Moore's conception of understanding: "Now, when I say these words, you not only hear *them*—the words—you *also* understand what they mean. That is to say, something happens in your minds—some act of consciousness—*over and above* the hearing of the words, some act of consciousness which may be called the understanding of their meaning" (*Problems*, 57). Like Russell (GI 38) he regarded such acts as essentially similar: "Each of them is an *apprehending* in exactly the same sense: they are obviously exactly alike in *this* respect. But no less obviously they differ in respect of the fact that *what* is apprehended in the one case, is different from what is apprehended in the other case" (*Problems*, 58; see 59c–60a).

(13)   In such passages, further targets of the section appear, closely related to the central theme of precontainment. If a series, when understood, must always be present in its entirety, the mental contents cannot vary. And if all steps are already infallibly taken by the mind, no further test is necessary; the mental act itself is a sufficient criterion of one's having understood and needs no corroboration through public repetition of its contents (§146). So Wittgenstein's comprehensive critique covered these points as well. No uniformity, he maintained, characterizes the psychic contents of one who understands (§151), nor are the contents the understanding (GI 19, 60; X, 22; §§151–54, 321; *Kreis*, 167–68; Man. 108, 261), not even when a person exclaims, "Now I understand!" For the exclamation is not a report (§179), based on introspective observation (Man. 108, 63), but a signal (§§180, 323), an avowal (GI 15). For others it serves as a criterion of my understanding;

for me there are no criteria (Z 472). And nonintrospective criteria might show I was wrong in my claim (IX, 5; p. 53n). Thus what was said of the steps in a series one understands applies to the word *understand* itself: This first-person, present-tense use of the verb is a reaction—a learned reaction (GI 16)—triggered, for instance, by remembering a formula. Here we touch on an important link with the next section (X, 22). Wittgenstein returns to the concept *understand* immediately afterward (§§318–25), and in Section XIX. Nowhere, naturally, does he attempt a definition of understanding (see §182c and GI 43–44; contrast with *Kreis*, 167).

DETAILED COMMENTARY

§138 This number serves to introduce the problem of understanding, not to indicate W.'s own views; only the central sentence ("Of course, if . . .") does that.

fit: see §136c; Man. 302, 5; Waismann, *Principles*, 234–37; cp. §559; *PG* 43b; *LC* 19e.

"And thus it is with vocal signs as with the things for which they stand; some can be fitted together and some cannot, and those which so fit together effect discourse" (Plato, *Sophist*, 261D–262E).

"It now follows from the fundamental difference of objects from concepts that an object can never occur as a predicate or unsaturated expression and that a concept can never logically take the place of an object. Figuratively, this point may be expressed in the following way: there are different logical places; some of them can be filled only by objects and not by concepts, and others only by concepts and not by objects" (Frege, "Geometry", 13).

"Here we think as though *this* comparison were before our minds: the words of a sentence fit together; that is, we can write down meaningless sequences of words, but the meaning of each word is an invisible body and these meaning-bodies do not fit together ('Meaning the sentence adds another dimension'). Hence the idea that we cannot think the sentence, since in thought I should have to *combine* the words' meanings so as to form a sense, and cannot" (Man. 229, §§710–11; see ibid., §912; *PG* 54d; Man. 110, 112–13).

If we recall that such failure to "fit together" or "cohere" is called incoherence, wide perspectives open for reflection. Cp. §125.

understand: italicized because it introduces a central theme of more than a hundred subsequent numbers.

when we hear or say it: see *PG* 55b. "So we should not think that in understanding or meaning a word there occurs an act of momentarily and, as it were, non-discursively grasping its grammar. As though one could, so to say, swallow it all in a single gulp" (*PG* 49). "As though understanding were the momentary grasp of something from which mere consequences followed later, consequences which in an ideal sense already exist before they are drawn" (*PG* 55).

Contrast James, *Principles*, I, 472 (quoted below, for p. 53n) and 256: "Again, when we use a common noun, such as *man*, in a universal sense, as signifying all possible men, we are fully aware of this intention on our part, and distinguish it carefully from our intention when we mean a certain group of men, or a solitary individual before us. In the chapter on Conception we shall see how important this difference of intention is. It casts its influence over the whole of the sentence, both before and after the spot in which the word *man* is used."

and what we grasp . . . : still the "voice of temptation" (GI 55). "If 'understanding the meaning of a word' means knowing the grammatical possibilities of its use, then I can ask: 'In that case how can I straightway know what I mean by a word when I speak it; surely I can't have the word's whole mode of application all at once in my head?' " (*PG* 49). For W.'s answer, see §197.

Insert, p. 53   See §§269, 323a, 517; *Z* 297; *PG* 81c–82a; cp. §513; *OC* 13–15, 442.

Must I *know* . . . : it would seem so, were James's account correct: "This added consciousness is an absolutely positive sort of feeling, transforming what would otherwise be mere noise or vision into something *understood*; and determining the sequel of my thinking, the later words and images, in a perfectly definite way" (*Principles*, I, 472). Concerning a feeling I cannot err. However (to paraphrase p. 18n), this shows clearly that the grammar of *to understand* is not like that of the expression *to feel* and the like. For understanding, "*bona fides* is not enough; if the man said that a word reminded him of something, or that he suddenly felt ill, or something like that, if he is an ordinary, sane and honest man you take his word for it; but you can't take his word for it that he understood. Understanding is a different sort of concept. . . . A man may assure you *bona fide* that he has understood you, have the look of understanding, etc., and when the examination time arrives it becomes deplorably obvious that he did not understand a word" (Geach, lecture notes; see his *God*, 5, 31; cp. Malcolm, *Memoir*, 87, quoted for §148). Generally speaking, understanding is not an act, feeling, or event about which one might be sure, but a capacity which is verified by performance (p. 181cd; *PG* 82a).

The same cannot be said of meaning. A person's assertions about what he means are self-authenticating in a way that claims of understanding are not. Hence in the *Investigations* no passage concerning meaning (*meinen*) parallels this insert on understanding. This difference may also help to explain why W. emphasizes understanding here, rather than meaning, which receives similar attention much later (Section XXVI). Section X relies heavily on the view developed in this section, that the criteria of correctness are public.

as I may . . . : this foreshadows the move from the present numbers, on understanding a word, to §§143ff, on understanding a mathematical series. See *RFM* 140hi; cp. *PG* 48a ("Similarly: 'I thought I could play chess, but I have already forgotten how' ").

§139 See XXXVII, 1–6; *PG* 54c–55b; Man. 110, 113–14.

"When Frege criticizes the formalist view of arithmetic, he says roughly this: these trifling explanations concerning the signs are superfluous if we *understand* the signs. And understanding them would be something like seeing a picture from which all the rules follow and which makes them intelligible. Frege seems not to notice, however, that this picture would itself be another sign or a calculus which explains the written one to us" (*PG* 40).

"It seems as though in a sentence containing for example the word 'sphere' the shadow of other uses of this word were already present" (*PG* 54; cp. §20, p. 181ab).

The choice of this example is appropriate in a way reference to, say, color samples (*PG* 90d–91a) would not be, since the *Tractatus* insisted on the preservation of "the same logical multiplicity" between a logical picture and what it projectively pictured (GI 32; see XXXVII, 5).

(a) Like p. 175a, on the same topic, these opening paragraphs indicate a puzzle which will then be treated; they are not a confused dialogue in which it is more than usually difficult to distinguish W. from his *alter ego*. Still less do they indicate an exception to §43a; W. would reject the first premise in a syllogism like the following: To understand a word's meaning is to have the meaning before one's mind; but when we understand a word the use does not come before our mind; therefore in this case (when we are speaking of "understanding the meaning") meaning is not use.

(b) also determined by this use: in addition to the supposed determination by the mental content. Even granted that this content determines the meaning, won't it have to agree with the use in the language? But if, as (*a*) suggests, it is not the use itself but something else, may they not conflict? So how can the content make me sure I know the meaning? (The answer: It doesn't.)

these ways of determining meaning: "We think of the meaning of signs sometimes as states of mind of the man using them, sometimes as the role which these signs are playing in a system of language" (*BB* 78). See XXXVII, 15; Hallett, *Definition*, 94–96; cp. §141b.

grasp *in a flash:* see §§191–92, 197, 318–19.

fit or fail to fit: cp. §138; *Z* 54.

(cde) See §§6b, 37, 73–74; *Z* 231 (quoted in XXXVII, 6); *PG* 81c–82a, 118a, 145b–146a; *BB* 36d–37c; *LC* 66c–68c; cp. *PG* 45e (similar remarks about propositions); *PB* 65c.

Isn't it something like a picture?: see (*a*) in the insert at the bottom of the page. For Russell and others images had been essential to thought (see commentary on §6b), but for the early W. logical pictures were (GI 32), and they might or might not use images (2.182; *NB* 130). See §389 and commentary.

Can't it *be* a picture?: not that there is an image before one's mind of something W. does not mention, but one imagines a picture, rather than a movement, speech act, or what have you. For W. denies that images are pictures (§301); and, as the next paragraph adds, the picture may be a sketch, and an image is certainly not a sketch. Cp. *BB* 36d.

"If we *see* such a cube, are the rules for possible combinations thereby already given, so the geometry of the cube? Can I read off the geometry of cubes from a cube?

"In that case the cube is a notation for the rule. And had we discovered such a rule, we could in fact find no better notation for it than the drawing of a cube" (*PG* 54).

In what sense can . . . : see §141c. Man. 110, 95–96, links this paragraph with (*a*) in the insert, thus: "If I can choose words according as they—in some sense—fit the facts, then I must already have had, beforehand, a concept of this fitting. And now the same question rises again, for how do I know that this state of affairs corresponds to the concept of fitting?"

method of projection: "The sense in which an image is an image is determined by the way in which it is compared with reality. This we might call the method of projection" (*BB* 53). W. often used the expression in this loose fashion, to indicate some kind of systematic correlation between one thing and another (*BB* 33b; *LF* 33; *LC* 66; *PP* 259, 265). Thus we might imagine something uncomplicated: Square surfaces of a prism and a square could, for example, fit together to form a rectangular surface; or, in another game, they might fit face to face (*PG* 54d).

did indeed *suggest* . . . : see (*b*) in the insert at the bottom of the page.

"Now there are pictures of which we should say that we interpret them, that is, translate them into a different kind of picture, in order to understand them; and pictures of which we should say that we understand them immediately, without any further interpretation" (*BB* 36).

Insert, p. 54

(a) This connects most directly with the question in §139c: "Isn't it something like a picture?" See also the quotation from Man. 110,

95–96, above; and pp. 218m, 219c; Man. 229, §§718, 742, 1029; cp.
§§527–31; *BB* 41c; *PP* 314a.

"I see that the word is appropriate before I know, and even when I
never know, *why* it is appropriate" (Man. 229, §743).

just because one can . . . : the familiar temptation "to make the
analogy hold throughout" (*BB* 7; cp. GI 11). Cp. *PP* 263b.

(b) This illustrates §139e. See Man. 232, 702–3.

I do not need to explain why . . . : see §109; cp. *BB* 87b and the
quotation above from Man. 229, §743. Causal explanation would not
help in dispelling the notion of a self-interpreting, intrinsically unambiguous representation (§140obc).

§140 See XXXVII, 5–6.

(a) See *PG* 55d–56a; cp. §§220, 388.

How could I think that?: see pp. 183def, 201; cp. §74; *EPB* 128; *BB*
87b. The hypothesis is meaningless, so how can I believe it? Can I, for
instance, believe that the picture twisted my arm?

What *did* I think?: in addition to XXXVII, 5–6, see GI 35–37; §426;
BB 36c; cp. §433. "It seems like a projection connection, which seems to
make it indubitable, although there is not a projection relation at all"
(*LC* 67; see §141a; 3.12–3.13). Thus in Man. 108, 238, W. had written:
"A geometrical figure together with its method of projection onto a
specific plane does not just *determine* a figure in this plane but already
contains this figure." Cp. Schlick (in *Kreis*, 79): "Shouldn't we construct
such a language that the rules of syntax reveal themselves immediately
in it?" Waismann agreed that this is possible, and W. (in 1930) raised
no difficulty (ibid., 79–80).

we might also be inclined . . . : see *PG* 145b and *Z* 231: "What we
have reached is a psychological, not a logical terminus."

as if we knew of two kinds: see IX, 1.

(b)   only the one case: see §593.

(c)   we shall say not: cp. §43a; 3.262.

§141 See *EPB* 129; *BB* 33–34, 88c–89a; *PG* 213–14; Man. 108, 243,
252–53; cp. §86; *EPB* 178; *BB* 124c.

(a) Suppose, however . . . : as W. once did: "The picture (in the narrow sense) does not suffice for there is not given with it the way in
which it is to be compared with reality. The method of projection must
be present. But then the picture reaches right into the place where its
object is" (Man. 108, 219; see ibid., 223; cp. *PP* 264). "This comparison
makes it look as if the picture *together with* the projective rays now no
longer permitted various modes of application, but that the pictured
reality, even when it does not in fact exist, is ethereally determined by
the picture and the projective rays as definitely as though it *did* exist"
(*PG* 213). Cp. XXXVII, 5–6.

How am I . . . : see *Z* 291.

the method of projection: see the commentary on §139d.

only we need to get clearer . . . : it might be a possible application, or a standard application not known as such, or one which causes me to apply the picture in such and such a manner, or one seen in a particular way (§74), and so on.

Suppose I explain . . . : compare this with showing a person sample leaves, from which he is to learn "what is common to all shapes of leaf" (§73a).

(b) two different kinds of criteria: see §139ab.

And can't it be clearly seen . . . : see XXXVII, 9; *BB* 3c, 4bc, 5a, 53d; *PG* 71b, 99c; cp. *PG* 49b, 83d–84a, 147d–148a, 182e. Despite the early psychologism revealed in the quotes above, this strand was continuous in W.'s thought; an outer picture would do as well as an inner— provided, young W. would add, that inner interpretation was supplied (GI 37).

(c) See *LC* 71; cp. *RFM* 34f; *PG* 55a.

There can . . . : contrast this with *PG* 184a.

§142 See §242.

It is only in . . . : see *NB* 67l and GI 37.

The more abnormal the case . . . : see §80.

no characteristic expression . . . : that is, Schlick's hypothesis (X, 14). Cp. §288c ("if we cut out human behaviour, which is the expression of sensation"); §207 ("there is no regular connexion between what they say, the sounds they make, and their actions").

if rule became exception: see p. 227b; NL 306d.

and exception rule: not some one exception, so that rule replaced rule, and the language-game shifted (p. 147n) rather than disappeared; for then there would be a characteristic expression, just a different one.

roughly equal frequency: when burned painfully, people would sometimes smile and laugh, sometimes grimace and cry out.

"If certain memory were not in general more reliable than uncertain memory, i.e., if it were not confirmed by further verification more often than uncertain memory was, then the expression of certainty and uncertainty would not have its present function in language" (*OC* 632; see *OC* 646).

lose their point: "This is how our children learn sums; for one makes them put down three beans and then another three beans and then count what is there. If the result at one time were 5, at another 7 (say because, *as we should now say,* one sometimes got added, and one sometimes vanished of itself), then the first thing we said would be that beans were no good for teaching sums. But if the same thing happened with sticks, fingers, lines and most other things, that would be the end of all sums. 'But shouldn't we then still have $2 + 2 = 4$?'—This sentence would have become unusable" (*RFM* 14).

Contrast all this (as W. perhaps did) with Schlick, "Meaning", 157: "No rule of expression presupposes any law or regularity in the world."

The procedure of putting . . . : see NL 287an; cp. *RFM* 159.

This remark will become clearer: in Section X.

§143 Cp. §185; *BB* 12–13.

(a) following kind of language-game: "And what is in question here is of course not merely the case of the expansion of a real number, or in general the production of mathematical signs, but every analogous process, whether it is a game, a dance, etc., etc." (*RFM* 139; see IX, 4).

when A gives an order . . . : this is as close as W. comes to suggesting that words might occur in the teaching or practice of the first game. Thus there is a close parallel between §§143–47 and §§2–7; there, too, the only words mentioned are those employed in the commands. Furthermore, of both games one might say: "We recognize in these simple processes forms of language not separated by a break from our more complicated ones. We see that we can build up the complicated forms from the primitive ones" (*BB* 17). And we have. That is, as our complex language contains words like *slab, beam, pillar,* and orders by means of them (as in the practice of waiters, calling out their orders), so mathematics contains natural numbers and the process of counting. Thus §§143–47 provide a direct insight, of the kind described by *BB* 17a, into the nature of mathematics (§240, pp. 225–26).

according to a certain formation rule: see §189. No formation rule appears here in §143, for it presents just "the first of these series" (*b*), and much as linguistic training must precede definitions (§6b), so in mathematics practice must precede formation rules (see below, on the "possibility of getting him to understand").

(b) it is not being used wrongly: an earlier version: "Do not balk at my saying 'series of numbers' instead of 'series of numerical signs' " (Man. 220, 102). "It is of course clear that in mathematics we do *not* use the word 'series of numbers' in the sense 'series of numerical signs', even though, of course, there is also a connexion between the use of the one expression and of the other. . . . A 'series' in the mathematical sense is a method of construction for series of linguistic expressions" (*RFM* 59). But it is not here.

a normal and an abnormal: cp. §§141–42.

the *possibility of getting him to understand:* at this basic level, where one cannot yet employ mathematical terminology or explanations, presupposing some familiarity with the game of arithmetic (Z 300–302), the teaching is training (cp. §5b), for instance by means of encouragement; and "these acts of encouragement will be of various kinds, and many such acts will only be possible if the pupil responds, and responds in a particular way" (*BB* 89–90). We cannot encourage him (react favorably to what he does) unless he continues correctly, on his own.

'mistakes': the quotation marks reflect the fact that our calling them such and correcting them is what makes them mistakes, there being no other, absolute criterion of correctness in this counting game (§145b). See *Z* 300.

(c) See *BB* 124–25 and §163, which suggest a corollary: The concept *understand*, like the concept *derive*, has no sharp boundary.

Insert, p. 56 See §§129, 415, p. 230. The remark is relevant to both §142 (the characteristic expression of pain and the like; the ordinary behavior of cheese) and §143 (the normal reactions of learners). Concerning both, see §242 (constancy in results of measurement depends both on the measured, e.g. cheese, and the measurer). In *BB*, at a point corresponding to the conclusion of §143, W. remarked: "I wish to say at this point that this form of training . . . is one of the big characteristic features in the use of language, or in thinking" (*BB* 105).

"It is a striking fact, although always under our noses, that from an instruction in the application of a word, employing only a few examples and fragmentary explanations, we go on to apply that word in new case after new case, the new cases differing in numerous ways from the examples we were originally given, yet we largely *agree!* It would seem that from the original instruction we could branch out in an indefinitely large number of paths, each of us going a different way. And it is true that we *could*. But we do not. The fact that we do not, the fact that almost everyone goes on in approximately the same way, is a feature of the natural history of human beings" (Malcolm, "Nature", 22–23). See *Z* 355.

§144 *PG* 94b is the forerunner of this number. See *Z* 461; cp. *Z* 355; *EPB* 131; *BB* 90a; Russell, *External World*, 78a.

For related remarks on method, see GI 58, 62; *BB* 12a; and *PP* 315: "*Reasons*, he said, in Aesthetics, are 'of the nature of further descriptions': e.g. you can make a person see what Brahms was driving at by showing him lots of different pieces by Brahms, or by comparing him with a contemporary author; and all that Aesthetics does is 'to draw your attention to a thing', to 'place things side by side'. He said that if, by giving 'reasons' of this sort, you make another person 'see what you see' but it still 'doesn't appeal to him', that is 'an end' of the discussion; and that what he, Wittgenstein, had 'at the back of his mind' was 'the idea that aesthetic discussions were like discussions in a court of law', where you try to 'clear up the circumstances' of the action which is being tried, hoping that in the end what you say will 'appeal to the judge'. And he said that the same sort of 'reasons' were given, not only in Ethics, but also in Philosophy."

"may **come to an end here":** as the parts of a machine may conceivably bend or break (§193b) and it would then be rejected, so "if a child does not respond to the suggestive gesture, it is separated from the others and treated as a lunatic" (*BB* 93; *EPB* 137). We tend to forget this possibility in both cases (§193), for "after all, man is a rational animal" (cp. §25). W. would have us be struck (§129) by this interesting (*RFM* 13f) and important (p. 225g) fact of nature underlying the game (p. 230a): our perfect agreement here (pp. 225–26), though not elsewhere.

what am I doing: for a close, clarifying parallel, see §140.

I wanted . . . : for a parable illustrating this method, see Man. 132, 15–16.

acceptance **of the picture:** as distinct from adoption of a theory in place of an equally intelligible but mistaken one (§140). W.'s therapy is not refutation nor his "picture" a theory (GI 68).

his *way of looking at things:* for instance: " 'But doesn't it follow with logical necessity that you get two when you add one to one, and three when you add one to two? and isn't this inexorability the same as that of logical inference?' " (*RFM* 4; see IX, 4). " 'Is it conceivable that these operations should give another result?'—One would like to say, no. For: in that case they wouldn't be these operations" (Man. 123, June 5). Or: "One thinks of the teaching as supplying a *reason* for doing what one did; as supplying the road one walks" (*BB* 14).

See §195; cp. §401b; *OC* 92.

Indian mathematicians: "I once read somewhere that a geometrical figure, with the words 'Look at this,' serves as a proof for certain Indian mathematicians. This looking too effects an alteration in one's way of seeing" (*Z* 461).

§145 (a) often: italicized in the German. Cp. §§142, 207, 284b.

Which only means . . . : with a pupil just learning to count I do not, for instance, use terminology like that in W.'s description. I do not say, "See, the same series occurs in the tens as in the units." Nor: "After ten I do the same thing all over again"—for I don't.

depends on his *reaction:* W. does not mean, of course, that it is the cause, but neither does he mean merely that it is a criterion of understanding. He is ruling out the supposed intermediary on which everything depends—"something drawn very fine . . . a characteristic design, which only needs the addition of 'and so on', in order to reach to infinity" (§229). See *BB* 14, above; cp. §245.

(b) correctly, that is, as we do it: see §§240–42, p. 147n (b). An individual may count wrong, but not everyone (§345; see *RFM* 4c; cp. 225h).

you cannot state a limit: the concept *understand* has no sharp border.

§146 See Man. 112, 145.

(a) if I should not speak . . . : cp. §§6c, 143b (*"getting him to understand"*), 148 (does one *understand* the multiplication tables or the ABC?).

our primitive language-game: presupposing neither acquaintance with arithmetic nor even with language (see the commentary on §143a).

which is the *source*: see *BB* 143f–144a.

(b) Isn't one thinking . . . : cp. *PG* 243: "If I say 'I know that (∃x).fx follows, since I understand it,' that would mean that when I understand it I see something *else* besides the given sign, as it were a definition of the sign, from which the entailment derives."

But this is where we were before: there is "something analogous" in §§139–41; or W. may mean that just as in supplying projective rays (§143) for the picture in §141, we return once again to a picture, so this substitution of an inner formula or the like simply provides another sign, as subject to interpretation as the first.

a criterion: not *the* criterion, as W. once said (Man. 109, 178–79). However, "an 'inner process' stands in need of outward criteria" (§580), and for understanding, application is at least the main outward criterion, especially at this early stage, where the learner cannot substitute mathematical explanations for performance, or cite past successes as proof of his understanding. Cp. *PG* 81c.

§147 See the commentary on §229, especially the quote from Man. 110, 113; cp. *PG* 243.

(a) See GI 15.

(b) The discussion shifts from understanding to knowing, a kindred concept (§150) which here overlaps; saying one understands a series may be equivalent to saying one knows how to continue it, whereas saying one knows the ABC (§149) is not equivalent to saying one understands it.

§148 See Man. 302, 1; and especially *BB* 117–18, for this and the subsequent number; cp. p. 59n; Moore, *Problems*, 77–79. Both numbers are aimed at a prime instance of the Reference Fallacy (GI 17–20), and consider both forms the fallacy typically takes for psychological verbs: conscious referent and physiological. "We easily overlook the distinction between stating a conscious mental event, and making a hypothesis about what one might call the mechanism of the mind" (*BB* 40, the forerunner of the present discussion).

When do you . . . : See *BB* 40c; on the inappropriateness of the question "When?" with regard to understanding, see *Kreis*, 167–68. For parallel questions on chess, see p. 59n (*b*).

do you know it: it is important that this sentence start with a capital, as in the German; otherwise "that is" seems to refer to just the previous question of the series, and so to suggest that one knows the alphabet and the multiplication table only when thinking of some rule, rather than day and night.

state of consciousness: see the notes in Malcolm, *Memoir*, 87, e.g.: "There is a tendency to think of knowledge as a *mental state*. Now I am supposed to know my own mental states. If I say I have a certain mental state and do not have it, then I have told a lie. But I can say that I know so & so, and it can turn out that so & so is false; but it doesn't follow that I lied. Therefore, knowing is not a mental state."

or a process: conscious or unconscious (*BB* 3e, 18b). For contrast, see for instance Schopenhauer and Moore:

"The *brain* alone, and with it knowledge, pause completely in deep sleep" (*World*, II, 241).

"When you are asked: How do you know that? it may be meant to ask: What sort of a thing *is* your knowledge of it? What sort of a process goes on in your mind, when you *know* it? In what does this event, which you call a *knowing*, consist?" (*Problems*, 25).

§149 See *Z* 408, 669; *EPB* 147, 170; *BB* 39e–40c, 117e; *Kreis*, 167; cp. §156g, p. 191k; *BB* 18b; Russell, *Mind*, 87bc.

If one says . . . : on the "various reasons which incline us to look at the fact of something being possible, someone being able to do something, etc., as the fact that he or it is in a particular state", see *BB* 117d–118a (quoted for §193).

knowing the ABC: see *RFM* 72gh.

state of a mental apparatus: see *PG* 49d ("Knowledge is the hypothetical reservoir from which the visible water flows"); *BB* 143 ("There is a kind of general disease of thinking which always looks for [and finds] what would be called a mental state from which all our acts spring as from a reservoir"); *BB* 40c ("aren't we assuming that whenever a tune passes through existence there must be some sort of a gramophone record of it from which it is played?"); cp. §§193–94; contrast with Schopenhauer, *World*, II, 191: "What is *knowledge*? It is above all else and essentially *representation*. What is *representation*? A very complicated *physiological* occurrence in an animal's brain, whose result is the consciousness of a *picture or image* at that very spot."

a disposition: "The general differentiation of all states of consciousness from dispositions seems to me to be that one cannot ascertain by spot-check whether they are still going on" (*Z* 72). On the dangers of this saying, accounting perhaps for its omission from the *Investigations*, see X, 20–22.

there ought to be two different criteria: if the disposition is not to be a mere logical construction, that is, if talk of the disposition is not to represent a purely grammatical shift (cp. §§104, 401)—which is what W. judged it to be (*BB* 117). Knowledge is *grammatically* a state (§572) and we reify the grammar.

If, as appears likely, W. is using the word *criteria* broadly, for "evidences" in general (*BB* 51b), his requirement may be reworded thus: If the phenomenal manifestations are mere symptoms or external signs of knowledge, criteria of knowledge itself must be supplied (cp. §354; Man. 109, 192). Otherwise the word *knowledge* would not yet have a sense, and talk about "signs of knowledge" would therefore be meaningless.

"Indeed the grammar of a mental state or process is in many respects *similar* to that of e.g. a brain process. The chief difference, perhaps, is that the possibility of a direct check is provided in the case of the brain process, say by opening the skull and seeing the process, whereas in the grammar of the mental process there is no question of such 'direct perception'. (This move does not exist in this game.)" (*PG* 82).

Nothing would be more confusing . . . : see §339b; *BB* 23b, 57–58; *PP* 310–11; Man. 116, 90–91; Man. 115, 31; cp. *BB* 55c; *PG* 106c.

"The expression 'conscious state' (in its earlier sense) does not have the same grammatical relationship to the expression 'unconscious state' as the expression 'a chair that I see' has to the expression 'a chair that I don't see, since it is behind me' " (*PG* 48–49).

§150   See §182; cp. Man. 108, 233 ("for what else does understanding the word 'twenty-three' mean besides understanding its syntax, being able to operate with it?").

With such capacity-words or verbs of potentiality, contrast verbs such as *mean, intend, think.*

closely related: not necessarily by similarity (cp. §225, p. 198d), though as the family traits of a single concept may overlap from case to case (§§66–67), so too not only may the family traits of kindred concepts overlap, but one expression may often replace the other (§§151b, 183), though in other contexts no such exchange is possible (see e.g. the commentary on §147b).

"can": see *BB* 100–104, 111–18.

"understands": " 'To understand a word' can mean to *know* how it is used; to *be able* to use it" (*PG* 47). "But this understanding, the knowledge of the language, is not a conscious state which accompanies the sentences of the language. . . . Rather it is of the same sort as the understanding or mastery of a calculus, so similar to: *being able* to multiply" (*PG* 50). See Man. 220, 106.

'Mastery': see §§20a, 145b, 199c; cp. p. 209a.

§151   This is the final version of material in *BB* 112–13 and *EPB* 163–64. Compare similar discussion of a game, in *BB* 96 and *EPB* 140–41, and of understanding a word, in *PG* 65a, and parallel treatment of recognition, in *BB* 85, 88; *EPB* 125–26, 129. See also *Z* 89; *RFM* 5c; Man. 109, 240–41, 266–68; cp. *BB* 11bcd, 13c.

(a) See IX, 11, 13; cp. *BB* 167a.

(b) the following example: cp. Man. 109, 223.

Various things may have happened: this much at least, personal experience (the reader's or W.'s) may establish, if not every variation mentioned. See the remarks on (d), below.

confirmed his hypothesis: in the sense that it satisfies the formula, not that it could satisfy no other. Absolute confirmation, excluding all possible doubt about the other's meaning, W. considered impossible in such cases. But doubt has an end (p. 224).

(d) See §§179c–180.

Or he says nothing at all: at this point two difficulties are likely to arise. Successful continuation without an inner clue may seem causally implausible, and such a performance may seem a dubious instance of understanding. In BB W. deals with both objections, the causal and the conceptual, when he reaches the final term of a similar series (BB 85; cp. BB 3c, 12a). In (14c), asked to bring a piece of cloth of the color of a sample, "B goes to the shelf without a memory image, looks at five bolts one after another, takes the fifth bolt from the shelf." In another case a helping image perhaps came to mind. "But was this *necessarily* what happened? If the training could bring it about that the idea or image—automatically—arose in B's mind, why shouldn't it bring about B's *actions* without the intervention of an image? This would only come to a slight variation of the associative mechanism" (BB 89). " 'But then B didn't really *recognize* the material as the right one.'—You needn't reckon 14c) among the cases of recognizing, but if you have become aware of the fact that the processes which we call processes of recognition form a vast family with overlapping similarities, you will probably feel not disinclined to include 14c) in this family" (BB 88). We shall be still readier to accept (14c) or its analogue in §151 if we recognize that performance is not merely on a par with other family traits in this concept, but is the dominant criterion (p. 181c).

Insert, p. 59   The themes are those of §149, but the focus—in (a)—is on understanding. See Man. 116, 88–90; cp. Z 672.

(a)   A reworking of PG 48b. See Z 71–86 (especially 85); Kreis, 167–68; Man. 228, §§79–80; cp. PG 73b, 106c, 141cd.

a state: unlike, e.g., thinking (PG 172h). See Z 675; EPB 146–47; cp. PG 84b: " 'Understanding' is not our name for the behavior—of whatever kind—which shows us the understanding, but for a state which the behavior indicates. And this is a remark about the grammar. . . ."

a *mental* state?: in Kreis, 167, and PG 71d, W. roundly denied that it is (cp. p. 181c; Z 26; BB 143f). However, "if someone asks: 'Is this a mental state?', we see that neither the answer 'Yes' nor the answer 'No' is any help. There are so many psychological categories all of which might be called 'mental states'. Classification no longer helps here. We must distinguish the concepts from each other one by one. . . . It is helpful to note both differences and similarities" (Man. 167; see §573; cp. GI 68; §182a; *LC* 54). First we should discriminate "between a mental state, meaning a state of a hypothetical mental mechanism, and a mental state meaning a state of consciousness (toothache, etc.)" (*BB* 18), then differentiate understanding from both. The mechanism model (*BB* 117–18) has been dealt with in §149; but the toothache comparison was the false analogy under which W. himself had labored (Man. 110, 236). So in *BB* 101 he drew a contrast between cases where "we use the expression 'state of an object' in such a way that there corresponds to it what one might call a stationary sense experience" and others where "to this 'state' there does not correspond a particular sense experience which lasts while the state lasts. Instead of that, the defining criterion for something being in this state consists in certain *tests*." Thus there are tests of one's understanding (IX, 5), but not of one's pain (cp. *Z* 72, quoted for §149), and accordingly the temporal physiognomy of understanding differs from that of a sensation: "What we call 'understanding' is connected with innumerable things which occur before and after the reading of *this* sentence" (*PG* 72; see GI 44–45). Closely related to these distinctive features of the concept *understand*—the tests, the temporal configuration—is this further characteristic: I can falsely say, without lying, that I understand something, but not that I am in pain (cp. Malcolm, *Memoir,* 87, quoted for §148).

"Continuously", though?: cp. *PG* 141d, quoted for §572; *Kreis,* 167.
interruption of understanding: cp. *BB* 157cd.
"When did you stop . . .": there are behavioral criteria here, but not for pain (see above). Cp. *PG* 43–44: "If we now ask: 'At what instant of translating into German does understanding begin?', we get a glimpse into the nature of what we call 'understanding'."
(b) From Man. 110, 235, via *PG* 50c. See §§138–39, 148, 191–97; *PG* 49cd; Man. 232, 613; Man. 109, 185; cp. *PG* 50ef. Notice the multiple differences between the italics in the original and those in the translation.
And the *whole* of chess . . . : see Man. 109, 182, where W. was still tempted by this view ("Can I say that I see the move in chess space?"). Cp. IX, 2.
How queer: wouldn't considerable time be required to mentally review "the list of rules of the game . . . the day-to-day practice of playing" (§197)?
§152 Here speaks the voice of one tempted to strip the artichoke of its leaves in search of the artichoke (§164). W. would agree with the first part—this one leaf is not the artichoke—but not with the final sentence (*BB* 125). See §179, p. 181cd; *Z* 162–63; *PG* 72b; and especially *BB* 113, *EPB* 164–65, e.g.: "Therefore we are inclined to say 'to be able

to . . .' must mean more than just uttering the formula—and in fact more than any one of the occurrences we have described. And this, we go on, shows that saying the formula was only a symptom of B's being able to go on, and that it was not the ability of going on itself. Now what is misleading in this is that we seem to intimate that there is one peculiar activity, process, or state called 'being able to go on' which somehow is hidden from our eyes but manifests itself in these occurrents which we call symptoms (as an inflammation of the mucous membranes of the nose produces the symptom of sneezing). This is the way talking of symptoms, in this case, misleads us. . . . The error we are in is analogous to this: Someone is told the word 'chair' does not mean this particular chair I am pointing to, upon which he looks round the room for the object which the word 'chair' does denote. (The case would be even more a striking illustration if he tried to look inside the chair in order to find the real meaning of the word 'chair')."

§153   See the references and quotation for §152. Cp. GI 60. If the solution of a problem is to be helpful, said W. (GI 54), a person must see the problem. So repeatedly in the *Investigations* he sought to evoke vividly and faithfully the muddles he and others had felt.

the mental process: W. himself was as reluctant to call understanding a mental process (§§36, 154c, p. 181c; *BB* 3e) as he was to call it a mental state (p. 59n).

visible accompaniments: cp. *Kreis*, 154: "The letters are not the expression of generality, for generality never gets expressed in symbols, but is revealed in induction. An algebraic formula corresponds to an induction, but does not express the induction, for it is inexpressible. . . . This generality must be *intuited* in the configuration."

why should *it* be the understanding?: see GI 20, 60; p. 181cd; cp. §§293, 413.

because **I understood:** for the puzzled inquirer, not for W. (GI 15–16; IX, 13), the words would supposedly be a report based on observation (§154a).

§154   See Man. 228, §194.

(a) See §179a; *EPB* 165; *BB* 113b. On this typical tendency (what I have called the Reference Fallacy), see GI 17–20; IX, 12–13.

(b) See §§179b, 182–83; *EPB* 165–66; *BB* 113b, 114b; *PG* 72b. Contrast with *BB* 115b.

If there has to be . . . : as a logical, *a priori* necessity, justifying the expression, not causing it (§155). Distinguish between justifying a language-game (I, 4) and justifying a move within the game, and between speaking without justification and speaking without right (§289).

(c) See §308; *Z* 446; *Kreis*, 167. In time, were the hypothesis of psychophysical parallelism (*Z* 611) established in this case and commonly accepted, a brain process causally connected with the present criteria of understanding might enter into the concept *understand*; but the present concept includes no such content.

when, that is . . . : W. is recommending the "method of §2" (see §48): If you consider more carefully you will find that even the case responsible for your notion (IX, 11) is not as you suppose (IX, 13).

(de) See §§151–52, 321; *Kreis*, 167; cp. p. 59n and commentary.

In the sense . . . : (*e*) indicates the general sense, and §152a makes clear that the phenomena of §151 (including thoughts) fall under it.

characteristic: see §35.

is not a mental process: W. is not simply denying, as in §152, that understanding can be identified with any of the processes which characterize it. To forestall the kind of move described in §36, he denies that it is any *such* process (momentary, introspectible, self-sufficient). A person cannot be mistaken about whether he has the thoughts described in §151b, but he can be about whether he understands the series.

§155 See *EPB* 165–67; *BB* 114–15.

justify him: these circumstances belong to the expression's meaning (*PG* 81c), to the word's use in the language (§43); and the present use is correct if it conforms with this established usage. The words "Now I understand" do not report these characteristic circumstances, nor do they require consultation of the verifying circumstances prior to utterance (cp. §179; *Z* 114–16).

§156 For the rationale of this excursus on reading (§§156–71), see IX, 8–11.

(a) See *EPB* 172; *BB* 119c.

"reading": italics in the German signal the start of a long discussion (cp. §§138, 416).

not counting the understanding: in either the primary, dispositional sense of the word *understand* or the secondary, experiential sense (§531). W. is not loading the dice in favor of a behaviorist analysis of *understand;* there is such a use of the verb *read,* and he had good reasons (IX, 8–9) for focusing on it.

playing from a score: besides IX, 9, see §22c.

(b) See *EPB* 172; *BB* 119; cp. GI 10; §182b; *Z* 111–16.

(cde) See *EPB* 172–73; *BB* 119c–120a. Re the method employed in (*c*), cp. §66 and GI 58.

we shall be inclined to say: not in the manner of §36, but of §593. See *BB* 99e.

(f) See *EPB* 173; *BB* 120a. Re (*e*) and (*f*) see §159.

We have yet to discuss: see X, 3–5, 9–10, 19, 24; §§246–47, 303, 409.

(g) See *EPB* 173; *BB* 120a.

But I want to say: to counteract the idea of introspective certainty (*f*) and still more the underlying notion that reading consists in "a special conscious activity of mind" (*e*).

we have to admit . . . : earlier W. concluded from this that "what in the one case we call an instance of reading we don't call an instance of reading in the other" (*BB* 120; see *EPB* 173). However, we don't call either experience an instance of reading.

who is 'pretending': note the scare quotes. In the sense indicated by (*a*) he does read; so he is the beginner discussed to the end of the paragraph. Since, however, he does not really 'read' (that is, in the manner of a practiced reader, which acts as paradigm), we are doubly inclined to say: "What goes on . . . *can't* be the same."

is applied *differently:* the omitted sentence just quoted from *BB* 120 stressed diversity of reference, and that is clear enough; but diversity of criteria or sense, on which the *Investigations* focuses, is less immediately evident.

only hypotheses: "not something which follows from the facts" (*EPB* 210) or which we know (§158) or which therefore figures in the concept *read* (GI 60–61).

models designed to explain, to sum up: two distinct functions. On the former, see *BB* 117e–118a, *EPB* 170 ("We regard these phenomena as manifestations of this mechanism, and their possibility is the particular construction of the mechanism itself"). On the latter, see *BB* 6b ("Its advantage may be that it can be taken in at a glance and easily held in the mind").

§157   As in the analysis of *game,* so in his study of automatic reading W. suggests first the inner heterogeneity of the concept (§156), then its vague boundary (here), pointing out, as in §68, that we could set a sharp limit, in terms of a mechanism or an experience or the number of words, but have not done so. Number 143 makes a similar point about understanding.

(ab) See *EPB* 173–74; *BB* 119c, 120b–121b.

(c) See *EPB* 171, 174; *BB* 118b, 121a.

(d) See *EPB* 174; *BB* 121b; Man. 116, 121.

§158   See p. 212d and commentary; *Z* 608–14; *EPB* 130, 170, 173; *BB* 89b, 118a, 120a; *LC* 42c ("Whereas to me the fact that there *aren't* actually any such laws seems important").

But isn't that . . . : on such confusions of the factual and the conceptual, and the reason for W.'s implicit denial, see GI 60–61.

it presumably *must* be . . . : cp. §131. The widespread attitude here questioned is evident for instance in Carnap's "Psychology in Physical Language": "A sentence about other minds states that the body of the person in question is in a physical state of a certain sort" (175). Thus

"Mr. A. is now excited" is equated with a proposition which "asserts the existence of that physical structure (microstructure) of Mr. A's body (especially of his central nervous system) that is characterized by a high pulse and rate of breathing, which, on the application of certain stimuli, may even be made higher, by vehement and factually unsatisfactory answers to questions . . . etc." (172). Jackson's version of W.'s postwar lectures contains this expansion of *Z* 608–14: "Russell said the other day 'A man who knew French and one who doesn't must be distinguished physiologically.' Why must? To say the opposite is almost to suggest a new principle, a solvent. It may sound obscurantist; it may suggest: (1) disregard the great success that men have had in this direction, (2) don't think you'll succeed in the future. This is unfortunate. All that you intend is: Don't say you must succeed!" (JN 90–91).

§159 Begun in *BB* 121, expanded to its present length in *EPB* 174–75.

when we think the matter over . . . : for "a man surely knows whether he is reading," yet he does not know "what goes on in the brain and the nervous system" (§158), or conjecture how he would justify his performance if asked (the criterion suggested in *PP* 264). W. recognizes some truth in this inference, but does not admit that a single experience characterizes reading as opposed, say, to reciting, much less that such an experience is the "one real criterion for anyone's reading". As for whether these experiences are criteria at all, see GI 60–61.

§160 Illustrating the method of "finding and inventing intermediate cases" (§122; GI 57), the number suggests three steps in the "continuous series of transitional cases" referred to in §161a, between repetition from memory (§159) and paradigm cases of reading. Since the first and third samples are instances of reading, the number contributes to the conclusion in §164b ("a family of cases").

(a) See *EPB* 175; *BB* 122a.

But imagine . . . : on the legitimacy of using one's imagination rather than factual findings in such a conceptual investigation, see GI 62, or consider this case: When only white swans were known, there was no need to actually discover black ones in order to dissolve the conviction that swans *must* be white; one might simply have asked, "What if we found a bird which resembled white swans in all respects save its color?"

Should we . . . : the expected answer to both questions is "No" (§165). W. continues his reply to the temptation at the start of §159 ("the one real criterion").

(b) See *EPB* 175–76; *BB* 122b.

words corresponding to the number: e.g. a five-letter English word when he sees a group of five letters.

In such a case: cp. §269.

a set of five marks: "which need not belong to any existing alphabet".

here we should certainly be inclined . . . : cp. the analogous observation about understanding in §143b.

§161   From *EPB* 176; *BB* 122cd.

(a) what he is supposed to be reading: as in §159.

(b) Cp. Man. 110, 119. The sample combines elements of the two extremes mentioned in (*a*); for a person knows this series by heart, as in sheer recital, and follows the figures one by one, correctly correlating each sound with a sign, as in spelling out words.

what did you do . . . : the answer suggested by Man. 110, 6 (quoted for §162b): You made what you did depend on what was there. But how did you do that? How could you?

Three interrelated questions may perplex the reader here: (1) Does W. think that the person would actually read the familiar numbers, in their familiar order, or that he would simply follow them round with his eyes while counting from one to twelve? (2) In the former supposition, what does he think would constitute the difference? (3) What, therefore, is the point of his suggestion and question? Doubtless he wishes to counteract the idea enunciated in §159 ("the conscious act of reading"). And this purpose would be achieved by the person's really reading (as the person in §621 really raises his arm) yet detecting nothing but the movements of his eyes (as the person in §621 detects nothing but the movement of his arm). The important circumstance that he, unlike the pretender in §159, has been trained to read numbers and can still do so (cp. §162b) would provide no introspectible difference. In a similar case (counting objects) W. remarked: "Couldn't we . . . have said 'Nothing else happens when we say the numerals than just saying them while looking at the objects'?" And he concluded: "It is in no way necessary that certain peculiar experiences more or less characteristic for counting take place while we are counting" (*BB* 149–50; *EPB* 232–33). Cp. §§164a, 166a, 170b.

§162   See *EPB* 176–77; *BB* 122e–123c.

In philosophical discussion people frequently pass from one unexamined term to another, in the conviction that the first is thereby clarified, when in fact the second expression is as vague as the first, and our ignorance of its analysis as complete. Thus after seeking to identify the specific essence of reading in the preceding ways (mechanism, performance, sensation, conscious act) someone may propose the act of *deriving* as the essence of reading (see below). After stating this suggestion in (*b*), W. starts in (*b*) to show the futility of the move. By §164 it is evident that the concept *derive* is as vague and varied as the one it was meant to clarify (cp. *BB* 41, quoted for §172).

(a) the following definition: see Man. 110, 6: "So far as he does not depend on what is there for what he does, he is not reading, even if what is there induces him to do what he does." Though no expression of a rule comes to mind, he as it were sees a rule in the marks themselves (*PP* 264).

(b) See Man. 110, 6: "When a person is reading he makes what he does depend on what is there. But the dependence can be expressed only through a rule." W. is working on this earlier suggestion, therapeutically (IX, 8–9). Cp. *PP* 264: "He is still 'guided by' the score, provided that he *would* use the general rule to judge whether he had made a mistake or not."

§163   See *BB* 123d–124c and *EPB* 177–78, where these remarks on deriving are intertwined with a parallel treatment of understanding. In the *Investigations* W. separates his treatment of the two concepts, making similar remarks on *understand* in §143. Cp. §86; Man. 228, §41; Man. 112, 154–58.

Again, W.'s target is clearly revealed by Man. 110, 6, which continues: "The intention must be such that its expression enables us to check whether it has been carried out. So from the model plus the expression of the intention it must be possible to derive (practically to calculate) the correct continuation." This demand for strict and clear rules hidden in the medium of the understanding (§102) leads to an infinite regress. No new expression satisfies the ideal.

(d) See §§70–71.

§164(a)   See GI 21–23; *RFM* 7a; *EPB* 179; *BB* 125a; cp. §65ab; Man. 220, 84. GI 59 supports van Buren's objection: "But an artichoke has a heart, whereas an onion is a flawless illustration of the point" (*Edges*, 54). For a similar illustration, which may have influenced W., see Harnack, *Wesen*, 9.

In the history of philosophy, such leaves or petals have been samples, as here and in Theaetetus's initial suggestions; or individual traits, as in §66; or definitions combining specific traits with more general ones, as in the proposal that knowledge is true opinion (see GI 71).

"Often it is only after immense intellectual effort, which may have continued over centuries, that humanity at last succeeds in achieving knowledge of a concept in its pure form, in stripping off the irrelevant accretions which veil it from the eyes of the mind" (Frege, *Foundations*, vii).

But we told ourselves . . . : cp. §§152–53.

family of cases: see §67a.

(b) And in different circumstances . . . : though circumstances figure among the varied criteria (cp. §162), there is nothing tautologous about this statement.

we apply different criteria: it might be objected: "No, we apply the same disjunctive set of criteria in each case, and they are satisfied differently." However, W.'s approach is more concrete; in given circumstances we do not run through the gamut of possible circumstances and corresponding criteria, but note whether the particular criteria relevant to that situation are verified, or simply that they are.

§165 The number, which derives practically unaltered from *EPB* 179–80, illustrates §164b, doing for *read* what W. has just done for *derive*, so that the remarks in §164a provide commentary on this number as well.

we should like to say: as often, the remark is autobiographical. Cp. Man. 110, 92: " 'I was guided by this rule' describes a particular (psychic, physical) process. A different one from the proposition: The results *follow* this rule." Here in §165 the print serves as rule of what to say.

a particular experience: see the insert at the bottom of the page. The treatment in *BB* 158–78, passing imperceptibly from *particular* to aspect-seeing, suggests a link with Section XXXVII. Cp. *EPB* 231–32; *BB* 149.

then it becomes quite unimportant . . . : W.'s interlocutor would of course not accept just any sequence of sounds as reading; yet he should, if reading is a particular experience. Cp. §232a.

Here I should like to say: that is, might be tempted to say.

"come in a special way": see §166, p. 219ab; cp. *BB* 149.

but the spoken words . . . : once again, an expression of the temptation, not W.'s present view.

Insert, p. 66 See §165, pp. 185–86; *BB* 158–60; cp. §§379, 412, 527, 610, pp. 182, 185h, 218m, 224j. The introduction to the long treatment of *particular* in *BB* suggests the general background of this cryptic note. "The troubles which we have been turning over since §7 were all closely connected with the use of the word 'particular'. We have been inclined to say that seeing familiar objects we have a particular feeling, that the word 'red' came in a particular way when we recognized the colour as red, that we had a particular experience when we acted voluntarily.

"Now the use of the word 'particular' is apt to produce a kind of delusion and roughly speaking this delusion is produced by the double usage of this word. On the one hand, we may say, it is used preliminary to a specification, description, comparison; on the other hand, as what one might describe as an emphasis" (*BB* 158).

"This face . . .": see §§536–39.

§166 This reworks *EPB* 180–81. For parallel remarks on reading, see *BB* 167e–168a. On the way words come in speech—W.'s implicit concern here (IX, 8–9)—see p. 219ab; *EPB* 231–32; *BB* 149a. Concerning such "fictions", see the commentary on §307.

(b) For remarks on this topic, see p. 231efg; *Z* 483, 654; *BB* 165d, 182c–184d; cp. p. 185d; *Kreis*, 54a. For the type of thinking questioned ("specific feeling", "superior force and vivacity", "feelings of pastness", and the like), see James, *Principles,* I, 223, 239a, 605a, 648–52; Russell, *Mind,* 161c, 175c, 176b, and *Logic,* 314a, and *Outline,* 196–97, 203d, 206c; Moore, *Problems,* 239b–240a; Ramsey, *Foundations,* 196c; Driesch, *Wissen,* 48–49.

§167   From *EPB* 181–82, with little change.

(a) enormously familiar: see *EPB* 191; typically, W. drops the debatable causal hypothesis advanced there, though it helps to explain his continued attention to the point: "And it is precisely this familiarity of the impression which seduces us into believing that we now have the essential thing."

   Think of the uneasiness . . . : see *Z* 184; cp. Augustine, *Confessions,* I, 18, 29.

(b) as its sound: and we do not *read* the sound, but just the printed word.

§168   From *EPB* 182, with minor changes. Cp. p. 212d; *BB* 180b.

§169   From *EPB* 182–83, with small changes.

(b) But why do you say . . . : see §§170c, 175b; Man. 110, 24 (I am sure of having read, in a way I couldn't be of the causes).

   felt a causal connexion: even Hume said that we "feel a determination of the mind to pass from one object to its usual attendant", and identified this feeling as the origin of our idea of causality (*Treatise,* 165). See IX, 10.

   So how could I say . . . : how could I feel the *regularity*?

   It is indeed true . . . : Russell was right in this, but wrong in his examples, for instance when he said that we feel the causal connection between seeing a cat and saying "I see a cat," and when he asserted generally: "We can say that the verbal premises of verbal empirical knowledge are sentences perceived to be caused by something perceived. If we refuse to admit 'cause' in this sense, it seems impossible to explain the connexion between what we perceive and the words in which we describe it" ("Limits", 137; see also the references under §170c).

   is not the only way: see Man. 232, 688; Man. 159; and *LC* 15–17, concerning e.g. "the cause of terror, pleasure, etc." and "the cause in a mechanism" (Man. 159): "The cause, in the sense of the object it is directed to, is also the cause in other senses. When you remove it, the discomfort ceases and what not" (*LC* 15; cp. §476); "(You can look on the mechanism as a set of concomitant causal phenomena. You don't, of course.) You say: 'Well, this moves this, this this, this this, and so on.' . . . Tracing a mechanism is one way of finding the cause; we speak of 'the cause' in this case" (*LC* 17). Cp. §§629–32; Bühler, *Development,* 151ff; Köhler, *Gestalt,* 360–64; Russell, "Method", 91–92: "It will be necessary to specify the causal law according to which the antecedents are to be considered. I received a letter the other day from a correspondent who had been puzzled by various philosophical questions. After enumerating them he says: 'These questions led me from Bonn to Strassburg, where I found Professor Simmel.' Now, it would be absurd to deny that these questions caused his body to move from Bonn to Strassburg, and yet it must be supposed that a set of purely mechanical antecedents could also be found which would account for this transfer of matter from one place to another. Owing to this plurality of causal series antecedent to a given event, the notion of *the* cause becomes indefinite. . . ."

are the *reason:* on cause versus reason, see *PG* 101cd, which suggests this line of reflection: Reasons, unlike causes, are not established by the observation of regularities, yet are frequently confused with causes, so that we suppose a hidden, more immediate connection which justifies our use of *because* and the like.

(c) was something that I said, or thought: not the letters, but my citing them.

I feel a kind of *influence:* cp. Schiller, "Value", 63: "Let us begin by recognising a psychological *feeling of necessity* or compulsion, a feeling of 'must'. This is the opposite of the feeling of 'freedom' or feeling of 'can'. It attaches itself to mental processes, acts, objects and situations and renders them 'necessary' in ways which vary with the minds that feel it."

when I make the *experiment:* "When you read, as it were attending closely to what happened in reading, you seemed to be observing reading as under a magnifying glass and to see the reading process. (But the case is more like that of observing something through a coloured glass.)" (*BB* 177). On the difference between experiment and ordinary occurrence, see §413 and commentary.

§170   From *EPB* 183–84. Cp. §175.

(a) Cp. §§20a, 607a; *EPB* 232–33; *BB* 149b–150a.

a *difference:* a complex and variable one, in general, so merely characteristic in a particular case (*EPB* 232–33; *BB* 149b–150a). See GI 19.

(b) appeals to us especially: no doubt because the experimental process differs more notably from the opposed paradigm. See §413 and commentary.

(c) See §§613 and 631a, directed at a view such as Russell's: "I think that the word 'because' in this sentence must be understood as expressing a more or less causal relation, and that this relation must be *perceived,* not merely inferred from frequent concomitance. 'Cause', accordingly, must mean something other than 'invariable antecedent', and the relation of causation, or some relation intimately connected with it, must be one which can sometimes be perceived" ("Limits", 137; see *Inquiry*, 60–61). See IX, 10; cp. *BB* 87b.

§171 A shortened version of *EPB* 184.

(a) *intimates:* see §§222–23, 232.

In the same way . . . : see the Appendix: Goethe; p. 215f; cp. p. 183def.

(b) See the commentary on §413.

Don't say . . . : see *BB* 23b; cp. §149.

§172 The connection of §172 with the preceding numbers is elucidated in *EPB* 185, the source of the materials reworked in this number. *Being guided* is third in W.'s list of expressions for the same basic notion—"I speak of the experiences of being influenced, of causal connexion, of being guided" (§170)—and the one to which in *BB* he related the whole section on reading: "Let us study the use of the expression 'to be guided' by studying the use of the word 'reading' " (*BB* 119).

"For when we recall what really happens in such cases we find a great variety of processes more or less akin to each other.—We might be inclined to say that in all such cases, at any rate, we are *guided* by something before our mind. But then the words 'guided' and 'thing before our mind' are used in as many senses as the words 'idea' and 'expression of an idea' " (*BB* 41). Such is the point of §§172 and 173.

§173 This is pieced together—(*a*) from *EPB* 185 and (*b*) from *EPB* 186–87. Cp. Man. 228, §§605–6.

(a) you are now *thinking:* see §593; *EPB* 233–34; *BB* 150b; cp. *BB* 100a, 159–61.

(b) Cp. Man. 112, 158, and similar treatments of comparing (*EPB* 127; *BB* 86b) and counting (*EPB* 232–33; *BB* 149–50), where W. is more direct and explicit, e.g.: "The more such cases we observe and the closer we look at them, the more doubtful we feel about finding one particular mental experience characteristic of comparing" (*BB* 86).

in one of the earlier examples: in §§162–63.

Here I should like to say . . . : see §§36, 598.

It is as if . . . : see §609; *BB* 86 (quoted for §645); cp. §607a; *BB* 177g–178d.

which dissipates: cp. §645. In behalf of a bad cause, the argument against introspection (see §171b) might here be turned around: "Of course, if I start introspecting, I cease doing whatever it is I want to observe, which can only be glimpsed from the corner of one's eye, as it were, while one is actually reading, being guided, doing something carefully, etc." It would then become evident, however, that the hypothesis of a constant, invariant experiment is the result not of reliable observation but of an *a priori* demand, begotten by the word *guidance, influence,* or the like (§175b).

§174   The most interesting difference between this and *EPB* 187 is the deletion of meaning and understanding from the list in (*b*).

(a) See Man. 109, 235–37.

   a particular look, a gesture: cp. *Z* 602.

   then you would like to say . . . : see *BB* 174b.

   to add nothing: "The word 'specific' (or the like), that we would like to use here, is no help. It is as uninformative as the word 'indefinable', when someone says the property 'good' is indefinable" (Man. 229, §826; cp. §182c). "We appear to ourselves to be on the verge of describing the way, whereas we aren't really opposing it to any other way" (*BB* 159). See *BB* 158–61, 170b, 175–77.

(b)   The connection is double: The problems (1) resemble one another, and (2) tend to merge. On their similarity, see *EPB* 233–34, *BB* 150 (quoted for §§622–23), and especially *BB* 158a: "The troubles which we have been turning over . . . were all closely connected with the use of the word 'particular'." As here we are tempted to say that deliberation "is a *particular* inner experience", so too "we have been inclined to say that . . . we had a particular experience when we acted voluntarily" (ibid.) or intended to do something (§§588, 591–93, 635–36). On (2), see Man. 108, 237 ("Must not willingness or reluctance make the execution or non-execution of the order into understanding it?"), and Man. 109, 260 ("To be guided by a pattern means nothing but to have the intention to copy the pattern this way"). "I give someone the order to draw a line from A parallel to *a*. He tries (intends) to do so, but with the outcome that the line is parallel to *b*. Now was the process of copying the same as if he had intended to draw parallel to *b* and had succeeded? I think obviously not. He let himself be led by *a*" (Man. 109, 238; see *PG* 98). "So it might be said: Even if the pencil doesn't conform to the pattern, intention always does" (Man. 109, 231; see *PG* 99). For *intend* W. sometimes substituted *will* (e.g. Man. 109, 237), much as in §197.

§175   Cp. §§607, 645. W. has in view musings like those in Man. 109, 230–31, where he made an arbitrary doodle, noted the diversity of "mental phenomena", attempted to characterize the essential element in copying, then remarked: "The rule followed in copying the pattern would in a certain sense be a description of the body of this copying. For it would describe *how* I let my pencil be guided by the pattern. It would be a subsequent description, as it were, of the mechanism set up between the pattern and the picture." See ibid., 238.

(b)   Cp. *BB* 167def, 177f.

no description satisfies me: for none lives up to expectations (§608) like these: "If the general rule of the copying is expressed in the activity of copying, it must consist in a trait of this activity, and the general rule must be a necessary part of the description of the process" (Man. 109, 238). W. had just tried this description: "If I intentionally copy a certain form, the process of copying—I mean the whole mental process—has the same form as the reality in some specific spot. The form is a facet of the process of copying; a facet that lies against the copied object and there coincides with it" (Man. 109, 229–30; see *PG* 98; cp. §605).

in particular when . . . : cp. §§177, 678; *Z* 602 ("Does he then have a sensation of such a 'drive'? Yes: when he thinks of the 'drive' "); *PG* 182d.

Only then . . . : see GI 19; §§36, 608–9; cp. §322; *Z* 89.

§176   Man. 220, 130, like *EPB* 188, adds comparisons. See §§36, 608; Man. 108, 264.

not a *phenomenon:* see §620; *BB* 151–52 ("there is not one common difference between so-called voluntary acts and involuntary ones, viz, the presence or absence of one element, the 'act of volition' ").

§177   Only slightly altered from *EPB* 188–89. See §175b and the references there.

through the medium of the concept: see GI 17–23; cp. §175b; *BB* 167def, 177f.

is not in general essential: for one thing, *guide* is not a success verb (cp. *PG* 98a and Man. 108, 237, both quoted for §174b). For another, one is also guided by a line when one intentionally draws another at an angle to it (§174).

§178   An abbreviated version of a passage in *EPB* 189.

(b) Cp. p. 219b; *Z* 602a; *EPB* 188.

a movement with my hand: cp. *BB* 78, bottom.

forces itself upon you: see p. 204k; cp. pp. 215a, 216.

a single form: this translation of *Erscheinungsform,* suggesting a particular instance or type of guiding rather than "a particular experience of being guided" (§173a), is therefore likely to cause difficulties.

§179   See GI 15–16; §323, pp. 175d, 181c.

(ab) See §324; *EPB* 165; *BB* 114a; cp. §325.

It is clear . . . : for a person might see a formula and later recall it without learning to do series.

just because: the addition of *just* in the translation renders the sentence incoherent; for the addition "unless experience shewed . . ." would negate the initial supposition thus worded. B would not be justified by just the occurrence of the formula; he would be justified by its occurrence, plus this other circumstance.

unless experience shewed: showed us, not necessarily B. "Wittgenstein's continual use of phrases like 'gave him the right to say', 'made it a correct use of', 'justified him in saying' in connexion with these first-person utterances might tend to obscure a little his own doctrine. The essential point is that a person does *not* have (or need) grounds or reasons (does not apply criteria) for saying correctly that he himself understands, in the sense in which others must have them to say it of him" (Strawson, "Review", 36).

But does B mean that . . . : cp. §197, p. 193j. The apparent supposition that a negative answer to this question entails a negative verdict on the preceding hypothesis may reflect a failure on W.'s part to notice how complex are the logical relations between the things we say about sentences and the things we say about speakers; he seems, for instance, to have paid little attention to the vagaries which prevent us from automatically equating the meaning of a sentence with what the speaker means. On the other hand, the fact that the meaning of a person's words does generally coincide with what he means seems sufficient justification for the present shift from sentence to speaker.

is only short for a description . . . : for one thing, we are incapable of giving an unabbreviated version (cp. §208f). To paraphrase §20: We say the words were correctly used because *our language* contains these patterns; the circumstances belong to the language-game played with *know.* See GI 61; cp. §244b.

Think how we learn . . . : see III, 1–2; §77b; *BB* 11. We are not, for instance, provided with a set of criteria to follow in using such expressions, criteria which then drop from view when their application becomes habitual.

(c) See §§181, 323a; *EPB* 164; *BB* 112e–113a; cp. Man. 109, 178–79. This repeats §151d, but indicates more explicitly the meager mental content.

§180   *This is how* . . . : the italics do not indicate the strength of W.'s conviction that "in this case too we should say . . . that he did know how to go on" (on which see §151d), but his insistence on accepting the language-game as it is and not sublimating it (§§120, 124).

a "description": see GI 15; p. 187i; cp. §24a. According to W.'s earlier doctrine, all statements, including those here discussed, are pictures, descriptions, of states of affairs (GI 35).

"of a mental state": see p. 59n (*a*) and the references there; and §§577, 585, 588.

a "signal": see GI 15–16; §323, p. 218hij. Of "I'm pulling as hard as I can," W. said: "The words are a signal, and they have a *function*" (Man. 229, §1520).

"Understanding is like knowing how to go on, so like a capacity: but

'I understand,' as 'I know how to go on,' is an *expression*, a *signal*" (Man. 229, §1543).

by what he goes on to do: see §146b; §181 suggests qualifications.
§181 Cp. Man. 109, 178–80.

Consider both kinds of case: this he does in §323; *EPB* 167–68; *BB* 115d–116b; *PG* 47f–48a.

"Suppose *a*) when he said he could continue he saw the formula before his mind, but when he was asked to continue he found he had forgotten it;—or, *b*) when he said he could continue he had said to himself the next five terms of the series, but now finds that they don't come into his mind;—or, *c*) before, he had continued the series calculating five more places, now he still remembers these five numbers but has forgotten how he had calculated them;—or, *d*) he says 'Then I felt I could continue, now I can't';—or, *e*) 'When I said I could lift the weight my arm didn't hurt, now it does'; etc.

"On the other hand we say 'I thought I could lift this weight, but I see I can't,' 'I thought I could say this piece by heart, but I see I was mistaken'" (*BB* 115–16).

§182(a) The point of similarity between these concepts, connecting them with the question just asked in §181, is indicated by W.'s queries. In each case there may be a gap between the statement and its typical test, so that in certain circumstances the assertion is justified even though the test result is negative (for instance, the cylinder fails to fit, the scales register a different weight, I fail to recite the poem or to lift the weight—because, for example, the cylinder has been heated, the object has absorbed moisture, I have taken a pill, and so on). However, the paragraph fans out from this starting point, suggesting (for the reason stated in the next paragraph) the great variety of tests and circumstances.

"to understand": see p. 59n. For the specially close relation in W.'s earlier thought, between *fit* and *understand,* see for instance §§137–39 and commentary, and Man. 109, 228–29, quoted for §175b.

In what kind of circumstances would it count . . . : for example, "Now I can't do it, since I am too tired" (*PG* 47). See also *BB* 115–16, quoted for §181.

(b) much more complicated . . . : see GI 10; cp. §§156b, 664; *Z* 111–13.

than we are tempted to think: W. himself had veered from one simplification to another—from "To understand a general rule means to *apply* it in some case (not, to be able to apply it)" (Man. 109, 178; see 179) to: "Being able & understanding are apparently to be described as states, like toothache, & this is the false analogy that I labor under" (Man. 110, 236). "To have an intention, to be able to do something, to wish something (to have an intention, an ability, a wish) is treated as a *tonus*, like rejoicing, being glad or sad" (ibid., 237).

(c) See *BB* 27b.

in order to resolve philosophical paradoxes: for the conflict usually consists in a clash between the observable facts and a model, theory, or supposition suggested to us by words whose use we have not examined (see GI 9–24 and e.g. §§105–7, 125, 201, 308). We tend "to represent the practice of our language in undue simplification. This, of course, is the way in which philosophical puzzles generally arise" (*BB* 144; *EPB* 217). "The man who is philosophically puzzled sees a law in the way a word is used, and, trying to apply this law consistently, comes up against cases where it leads to paradoxical results" (*BB* 27).

hence definitions usually fail: see GI 53; §239b. Several reasons may be distinguished: (1) a definition employs words about whose use we are often equally vague (*BB* 1f, 41b); (2) the definition is usually general, leaving out intricacies and variations which may be crucial for therapy (*PB* 206b); (3) it usually remains in the material mode, reflecting and perpetuating the confusion between fact and concept which W. considered the chief source and error of metaphysics (*Z* 458); (4) an accurate definition, respecting the word's actual use, is usually impossible (*BB* 19c; §77a; GI 70); so we discard one after another, in a fruitless, Socratic search (§164; *BB* 27b, 125a; Waismann, *Principles*, 84), or we "polish the word" "until it becomes suitable for technical purposes" (Russell, *Logic*, 129).

Frege felt that number "has to be either defined or recognized as indefinable" (*Foundations*, 5). Similarly, for Moore the definition of good was "the most fundamental question in all Ethics" (*Principia*, 5). Both he (*Problems*, 24) and Ramsey (*Foundations*, 264) stressed the general utility of definitions, to clarify and organize thought, but Ramsey noted: "That we so often seem to get no actual *definitions*, is because the solution of the problem is often that nominal definition is inappropriate, and that what is wanted is an explanation of the use of the symbol" (ibid., 265; see 267c). This was the method W. later preferred (GI 51–71); "The substitution of 'Ask for the use' for 'Ask for the meaning' is linked with the procedure of explaining meaning by presenting not a definition but cases, and not one case but cases and cases" (Wisdom, "Wittgenstein", 47; see *PG* 212a). However, earlier he too had been addicted to definitions (*PG* 211b; *Kreis*, 221).

'indefinable': see Man. 116, 34 (quoted for p. 185h). Thinkers like Frege, Moore, and young W. himself saw definition as feasible and necessary, but recognized that at some point it must come to an end (II, 6–8; *NB* 46f; Frege, *Writings*, 126b); the philosopher's job was either to give the definition or to declare that that point had been reached

(Frege, *Foundations*, 5). W. later felt not only that definition is much less feasible and useful than had been supposed, but that the philosopher who conceives his task in terms of definition is likely to leave off at the point where his work should begin. Thus Moore said: "My business is solely with that object or idea, which I hold, rightly or wrongly, that the word is generally used to stand for. What I want to discover is the nature of that object or idea, and about this I am extremely anxious to arrive at an agreement. But, if we understand the question in this sense, my answer to it may seem a very disappointing one. If I am asked 'What is good?' my answer is that good is good, and that is the end of the matter. Or if I am asked 'How is good to be defined?' my answer is that it cannot be defined, and that is all I have to say about it" (*Principia*, 6; paragraph division omitted). But, replied W. (§77b, p. 185), it must at least be possible to describe the use of the word. It is no help to say that "the property 'good' is indefinable. What we want to know and get a view of is the use of the word 'good' " (Man. 229, §826). It is equally unhelpful to be told: "It is probable that the content of the word 'true' is unique and indefinable" (Frege, "Thought", 291).

W. himself had once declared, "Indefinables are of two sorts: names and forms" (*NB* 98), so had left till later a genuinely attentive study of both (see, for instance, the investigation of names in Sections II and III, and the inquiry into the "general form" of propositions in Sections IV, VIII, XV, XVII, and XVIII). Indeed, he had judged logical forms (*PB* 208c) and the referents of names (§§46, 49; Man. 229, §§1295–98) to be not only indefinable but indescribable. Cp. GI 53.

Sensations, likewise, and other psychic experiences are frequently termed either "indescribable" or "indefinable" (§610 and references; *BB* 20f–21a; Man. 229, §§1295–98). For instance, "no connection which I imagine suffices & consequently it seems as though meaning were a specific connection, quite *incomparable* to all the others. (Thus, I believe, Moore found that the concept 'good' is indefinable.)" (Man. 116, 275).

§183   Parallel remarks in *BB* 114 and *EPB* 166 lead to the section of *BB* 115 and *EPB* 167 from which this number was mined.

in those circumstances: more precisely, in those described in the second paragraph of §151 and recalled in §179a.

have the same sense, achieve the same thing: if W. meant that the latter conveys what the former does, his expression is unfortunate; for §151 as a whole shows that saying "Now I can go on" would not "achieve the same thing" as saying "Now the formula has occurred to me," since it covers so many other possibilities as well.

The parentheses in the German original suggest more strongly (though compare §189bc) that W. is not making two assertions (identity of sense and identity of effect) but one, whose particular sense on this occasion (see §61; cp. §20b) is indicated by the parenthetical addition.

But here we must be on our guard . . . : a turning point, introducing the dominant theme of subsequent numbers. W. is not taking a diversionary swipe at physical or psychological determinism, such as Schopenhauer's (*World*, I, 124, 136, 139, 158; II, 319), but an opening blow at the logical analogue (IX, 1, 3; §220; *LC* 15–16), most fully characterized in §§193–95. Here as there, he uses patent nonsense (§524) to expose disguised nonsense about precontainment (IX, 2–4).

Man. 109, 192–93, explains the temptation. Since there are so many possible impediments of the sort just alluded to, it might seem "that I have only demonstrated my ability to do something if I actually do it" (see *BB* 116fg; *EPB* 168–69). W. himself momentarily drew this conclusion about understanding, a few pages earlier (Man. 109, 178, quoted for §182b). But of course the ability is not the deed. So "the ability to do something has just that shadow-like character" which seems to characterize propositions and commands (§§428, 431). "A command casts its shadow before it, as it were; or the deed casts its shadow before it in the command.—This shadow, though, *whatever* it may be, is what it is & not the deed."

Hence W.'s point is related to but distinct from that of *OC* 27 ("we recognize normal circumstances but cannot precisely describe them") or of §179b ("only short for a description of all the circumstances"). He is not denying, here, the possibility of completely listing the sufficient and necessary conditions of the ability, but the legitimacy of including the action (or its shadow) among them.

could not but **walk:** " 'All the steps are really already taken' " (§§188–90, 219).

§184 See *Z* 1–2; cp. §335, p. 219def; *Z* 669; James, *Principles*, I, 255b; Augustine, *Confessions*, XI, 28, 38.

is **it there?:** note the connection with the preceding number (here the singing, there the walking).

and this is a definition . . . : rather than a further description of something vaguely but unambiguously indicated by the expression, "is present to his mind". Cp. §§239b, 633, 665b, pp. 205i, 212d, 222j.

§185 A revised version of *BB* 141cd, *EPB* 213–14. Though reverting to §143, the number connects smoothly with the immediately preceding ones, since the central theme is still clearly the same: precontainment (IX, 2–5).

(c) See *RFM* 3d, 13e. Compare the readiness of some people to consider a shortened form of words the equivalent of a longer (§19b); thus we might say that when the numbers get long (four places) the pupil resorts to an "elliptical" series.

(d) See *PG* 94a.

§186 A tauter version of *BB* 141e–142, *EPB* 214–15. Implicit in the idea of a general or particular 'intuition' is the notion of intrinsic correctness; were it recognized that the 'correct' move is the one made and approved by the majority, such talk of 'insight' or 'intuition' would cease. "Suppose that one were to say 'guessing right' instead of 'intuition'? This would shew the value of an intuition in a quite different light. For the phenomenon of guessing is a psychological one, but not that of guessing right" (*RFM* 120). See *RFM* 33f.

"What you are saying, then . . .": the thinking in *PB* 171a and 198cd resembles this first quotation and helps to explain 6.233–6.2331 ("The process of *calculating* serves to bring about that intuition"). Cp. Weyl, "Die heutige", 23: "The intuition of essence, from which general propositions arise, is always based on complete induction, *the mathematical Ur-intuition.*"

"intuition": for further negative comments on intuition, see §§213–14.

the *mean*-ing: the supposed meaning act (*Meinung*), not the sense (*Sinn*).

almost be: a correction of the correction in *PB* 171 ("Act of *decision*, not of *insight*"), as already in *BB* 143, *EPB* 216: "It is no act of insight, intuition, which makes us use the rule as we do at the particular point of the series. It would be less confusing to call it an act of decision, though this too is misleading, for nothing like an act of decision must take place, but possibly just an act of writing or speaking." See §219c; cp. §634b.

a new decision: see §292; *RFM* 193d–g; *PG* 282g; cp. *RFM* 77gh; *BB* 2bc; *PG* 117a, 94b ("Each time I apply the table I make the transition anew. It is not, as it were, taken once for all in the table").

"What is general is the repetition of an operation. Each stage of the repetition has its own individuality" (*PG* 457; *PB* 147–48). "For actually the form to which the rule is applied is different at each step" (*PB* 171).

"I can understand intuitionism better now: each number has its individual properties. Now it is true that these are determined by the position in the series of operations 1 + 1 etc., but each such place is an individual place, that is, has the same individuality as the number itself which stands there. Thus we do not get away from the endlessly many individualities" (Man. 106, 282).

Cp. Ramsey, *Foundations,* 67, on Weyl (e.g.: "A real number is given by a sequence of integers, for instance as an infinite decimal; this sequence we can conceive as generated either by a law or by successive acts of choice"); and Weyl on Brouwer, in an article W. read, where he speaks of "the endless freedom which exists in the developing number series, always to make a new, unfettered act of choice, by which at each step the development of the series of natural numbers is forwarded anew and terminated at some arbitrary spot" ("Die heutige", 23).

§187   The *Investigations* continues to parallel the *Brown Book* and *Betrachtung*, this material being reworked from *BB* 142 and *EPB* 214–15. See Rhees, *Discussions*, 116.

"But I already knew . . .": "You might say 'Surely I knew when I gave him the rule that I meant him to follow up 100 by 101.' But here you are misled by the grammar of the word 'to know'. Was knowing this some mental act by which you at the time made the transition from 100 to 101, i.e., some act like saying to yourself 'I want him to write 101 after 100'? In this case ask yourself how many such acts you performed when you gave him the rule. Or do you mean by knowing some kind of disposition?—then only experience can teach us what it was a disposition for" (*BB* 142). See commentary on §30a ("to know").

and "mean": see XXVI, 1–7.

you don't want to say . . . : see §§692–93, pp. 33n, 217k; *BB* 142b; cp. §§19b, 667.

meant something like . . . : cp. *PP* 264.

"If he had fallen . . .": the patent nonsense of supposing that he has somehow fallen in advance into this and all possible bodies of water reveals the disguised nonsense of the corresponding supposition about series (§§188–89). Since the fall, too, is a determinant of the jump, and has not taken place, the jump is not predetermined or foreshadowed in the jumper (*RFM* 3gh).

Now, what was wrong . . . : §188 gives the answer.

§188   Cp. *PG* 249.

"The expression 'The rule meant him to follow up 100 by 101' makes it appear that this rule, as it was meant, *foreshadowed* all the transitions which were to be made according to it. But the assumption of a shadow of a transition does not get us any further, because it does not bridge the gulf between it and the real transition. If the mere words of the rule could not anticipate a future transition, no more could any mental act accompanying these words.

"We meet again and again with this curious superstition, as one might be inclined to call it, that the mental act is capable of crossing a bridge before we've got to it. This trouble crops up whenever we try to think about the ideas of thinking, wishing, expecting, believing, knowing, trying to solve a mathematical problem, mathematical induction, and so forth" (*BB* 142–43; see GI 36; *RFM* 9c; *EPB* 215–16; *BB* 4a, 142).

(a) act of meaning: W. rejected not only this account of the meaning act, but also the meaning *act* (GI 17–18; XXVI, 4–7; XXXVII, 11; *BB* 142a).

(b) See *RFM* 6–7.

you were inclined: as W. had been. He had said, for example: "A system is a formal series, and it is precisely in the rules that the iterations generating its successive members are described" (*PB* 182). And these rules were "hidden in the medium of the understanding" (§102; see IX, 2).

§189(a) a mistake: cp. §350; *RFM* 139ad. We might distinguish between the mistake "labelled by the word 'to make'" (*BB* 143), just touched on in §188, and the mistake of supposing that the word *determined*, by itself, has a clear sense (compare this entire number with §184). However, if we recognize that that notion of predetermination is not so much a false doctrine (GI 68) as a mere 'picture' which seems to fix the sense but doesn't (§426), then we see that the errors coalesce (cp. §191). "This is clear: that when a person says 'If you follow the rule it *must* be thus' . . . he has no clear idea of what it would look like to be *otherwise*. And this is very important" (Man. 125).

As the critique of essences can be carried to a second level, after the listing of family resemblances (§§66–67), by demonstrating that the family characteristics themselves are bundles and not essences, so too one may distinguish various senses for a vague general question such as that in (*a*), then demonstrate its ambiguity still more fully by subdistinguishing these alternative senses. Thus (*b*) and (*c*) as a whole indicate two different lines of interpretation ('subjective' and 'objective'), and these in turn are subdivided within the individual paragraphs.

(b) Identical with *RFM* 2a. See *RFM* 9d–10a.

(c) This is the same as *RFM* 2b, save that it substitutes simpler examples. See *RFM* 36a; Man. 221, 138.

now we must distinguish . . . : once the relevant conventions are established, the latter proposition is a timeless, grammatical truth, since it and it alone contains a verifying sample. The likeliest role for such sentences in actual discourse would be to teach the concept, and the corresponding question (at the end of the paragraph) would test knowledge of the concept (see Hallett, "Contrast", 692–93). In another mathematical system than the ordinary one, the double root, plus and minus, might not be a starting point, a simple rule of the game, but something to be proved; the statement, if true, would still be timelessly true, but not a mere grammatical truth, immediately known by anyone who had learned the calculus and the notion "determine y for a given value of x". Thus W.'s treatment of the final question parallels his usual manner of handling apparent necessary truths, for which, when possible, he was wont to suggest either a grammatical or a factual sense which would give them a function "in the stream of thought and life" (ibid., 687–88).

§190   Practically identical with *RFM* 2c–3c. See p. 33n; cp. §197.

(a) See §692.

(b) Cp. the earlier version in Man. 221, 139.

   how does one *mean*: "It is only in a language that I can mean something by something" (p. 18n); and " 'to mean it' did not mean: to think of it" (§692).

§191   This differs from *RFM* 38g only in the final expression (*pictures* instead of *similes*). See §139; Man. 119, 35; cp. *RFM* 37–40.

   "the whole use of the word": W. returns to the example of §§138–39.

   "in a flash": see *BB* 42a; cp. *PB* 146b.

   in a certain sense: see §§188b, 195, 197, 319. "It can seem to us as if the rules of grammar are in a certain sense the unpacking of something we experience all at once when we use a word" (*PG* 50).

   the crossing of different pictures: "We have got a picture in our heads which conflicts with the picture of our ordinary way of speaking" (§402). Thus we picture understanding as an act like seeing, with the total object before it, "and we say that there isn't any doubt that we understand the word, and on the other hand its meaning lies in its use" (§197); "we have this vivid picture—and that use, apparently contradicting the picture" (§427). See GI 9; cp. §195, pp. 175ab, 231d; *Z* 552; *BB* 37e–38c, 56a; Man. 302, 24 (quoted for §89c); Malcolm, *Memoir,* 54a.

§192   The first sentence occurs, alone, as *RFM* 38, §124. See *LC* 15d–16b.

   You have no model . . . : that is, neither an example in experience of something similar, nor an equally concrete idea of the way these words might be verified. "We make a picture . . . but on looking closer we find that we can't apply the picture which we have made" (*BB* 56). Thus in Man. 109, 220, W.'s thought can be seen moving from §191 to §193, as follows: (1) to form a proposition, words must be thought in a system, "in contrast with other propositions of the same system" (see §§19–20 and commentary); (2) "Can this have any other meaning than this, to see the position [here he sketched a piston attached to a wheel] of the mechanism as one of a system of positions? I think not." See IX, 2.

   superlative fact: "The mental act seems to perform in a miraculous way what could not be performed by any act of manipulating symbols" (*BB* 42).

   super-expression: the complete sentence at the start of §191, not merely "grasp in a flash". Cp. §97b.

"You say constantly in philosophy things like: 'People say there is a super-mechanism, but there isn't.' But no one knows what a super-mechanism is" (*LC* 15).

§193   Practically identical with *RFM* 37, §122, and Man. 119, 28–31. For the intended application, see especially §144.

In §192 W. has just said, "You have no model of this superlative fact." Seen in a certain way, a machine might appear to be one (see Man. 109, 220, above). But that, too, is merely an inapplicable picture, begotten in philosophy by the influence of words. As background to §§193–94, where this answer is developed, see *RFM* 30c, 36b–37d, 119g–120d; *EPB* 145; *BB* 100de; *PG* 69d–70a; *LC* 15–16; Man. 125; Man. 119, 26–33.

For futher light on the genesis of the model, see Man 123 (June 5): "*Must* I represent the rule as an impersonal mechanism which only works on me and through me? For the latter is what mathematicians would like to say. That the rule is an abstract mechanism. Now, whoever says this, is saying above all that mathematical propositions ought not to treat of a psychological or bodily mechanism. (For the person who says it is not uttering a mere stupidity, but something true hidden in a misunderstanding)." On this hidden truth, see GI 45 and the commentary on §108c.

W. had himself written: "The rule is a mechanism for generating numerals" (Man. 107, 48). Man. 109 (e.g. pp. 186, 226–27) is full of similar talk about language and thought. *BB* 117d–119b and *EPB* 170–72, too, suggest the wide relevance of the machine model: "This way of representation, or this metaphor, is embodied in the expressions 'He is capable of . . . ,' 'He is able to multiply large numbers in his head,' 'He can play chess': in these sentences the verb is used in the *present tense,* suggesting that the phrases are descriptions of states which exist at the moment when we speak. The same tendency shows itself in our calling the ability to solve a mathematical problem, the ability to enjoy a piece of music, etc., certain states of the mind; we don't mean by this expression 'conscious mental phenomena'. Rather, a state of the mind in this sense is the state of a hypothetical mechanism, a mind model meant to explain the conscious mental phenomena" (*BB* 117–18; *EPB* 170; paragraph division omitted). The immediate context here in the *Investigations*—both before (§188) and after (§197)—suggests greater interest in conscious foreshadowing, within the act of understanding, than in unconscious states (§§157–58). This emphasis corresponds to W.'s own former thinking (GI 37) and to the principal focus of the section (IX, 1–5).

(a)   See *RFM* 110g; *PG* 247b; cp. §426; Man. 109, 186, e.g.: "Should I now say that only in time can the mechanism's freedom of movement be revealed with certainty? But then how can I know that it can *not* make certain movements (and that it can make certain movements which it hasn't yet made)?"

The machine as . . . : Man. 109, 220, continues thus, connecting the comparison tightly with the discussion which starts at §151: "We could say that the mobility, the freedom of movement, of a mechanism . . . is expressed by a *general* equation $x = f(y)$, in which the values to be substituted are numbers (and it suffices to suppose that they are cardinal numbers) & these are given by their formation rule."

"We have a definite picture of what in a mechanism we should call certain parts being guided by others. In fact, the mechanism which immediately suggests itself when we wish to show what . . . we should call 'being guided by the signs' is a mechanism of the type of a pianola" (*BB* 118b).

For similar thinking, see Frege, *Foundations,* 24 and especially 93: "My definition lifts the matter onto a new plane; it is no longer a question of what is subjectively possible but of what is objectively definite. For in literal fact, that one proposition follows from certain others is something objective, something independent of the laws that govern the movements of our attention, and something to which it is immaterial whether we actually draw the conclusion or not. What I have provided is a criterion which decides in every case the question Does it follow after?, wherever it can be put; and however much in particular cases we may be prevented by extraneous difficulties from actually reaching a decision, that is irrelevant to the fact itself." For Frege, the logical mechanism was as objective as numbers, and numbers as objective as chairs.

(b) See *RFM* 30c, 119i–120d, 123j, 127h–128d; *LC* 16b; Man. 109, 255–56.

do we forget the possibility: W. did tend to forget it in Man. 109, till it occurred to him on page 240. Cp. *RFM* 107f.

(c) lying in a drawer: cp. *BB* 100e.

(d) "With this is connected the fact that we can say that proof must shew the existence of an internal relation. For the internal relation is the operation producing one structure from another, seen as equivalent to the picture of the transition itself—so that now the transition according to this series of configurations is *eo ipso* a transition according to those rules for operating" (*RFM* 196). "An operation is the transition from one term to the next one in a series of forms. Operation and form-series are equivalents" (*NB* 81). Cp. IX, 2; *RFM* 157a.

(e) Cp. *PG* 142c and *RFM* 37: "What if one were to say: the *must* of kinematics is much harder than the causal *must* compelling a machine part to move like *this* when another moves like *this*?" Cp. IX, 3.

The paragraph indicates with special clarity that W.'s contrast here (between applied physics and physics "for a vacuum") differs from Hume's (between physics and no physics, or an entirely different physics).

the machine-as-symbol: the intended parallel: "The rule, as it is actually meant, seems to be a driving power which reverses an ideal sequence like *this*,—whatever a human being may do with an actual sequence. This is the mechanism which is the yardstick, the ideal, for the actual mechanism" (*RFM* 129).

§194   *RFM* 38, §125, parallels this number, then adds an illustration of (*c*). See Man. 109, 269–70.

(a) See Man. 302, 5; cp. *PG* 355d–356a. For kindred discussions of the logical "shadow", cp. e.g. §102 (sense), §197 (intention), §442 (expectation), §443 (imagining), §§458–61 (orders).

when one is doing philosophy: or psychology; see Köhler, *Gestalt*, 112 ("in a steam-engine the piston can move only one definite way, determined by the rigid walls of the cylinder"). Cp. 2.012: "In logic nothing is accidental: if a thing *can* occur in a state of affairs, the possibility of the state of affairs must be written into the thing itself."

has: the possibility, therefore, is something actually present, though infallibly connected with acts of a specific sort in the past and future. On this influence of tense, see e.g. p. 175ab; *BB* 117d (quoted for §193); *RFM* 39d.

like a shadow of the movement: see *PG* 159b, 281de; *Z* 70: "Being able to do something seems like a shadow of the actual doing, just as the sense of a sentence seems like the shadow of a fact, or the understanding of an order the shadow of its execution. In the order the fact as it were 'casts its shadow before'. But this shadow, whatever it may be, is not the event." For such correlations in the *Investigations,* see above; on the historical background, see GI 35–37.

I do not mean some picture: "If someone asks: what makes the shadow of an event the shadow of just *this* event . . . we might for instance point out similarities connecting the shadow and the event. But in the case of thought & fact this does not work" (Man. 109, 194). Nor does it in the case of the possibility—for instance of walking (§183)—and actually walking.

would not have to be . . . : see §§139–41; *BB* 32–33; *PP* 265b.

of just *this* movement: cp. GI 34; §§99–102, 458–61; *PG* 160a, 143: "What I really want to say is that the wish, 'If only he would come,' is the wish that really *he* should really *come.*" Present state and future movement must fit unmistakably.

(b) as soon as we ask . . . : see §182.

for it can be doubted: see above ("would not have to be . . .").

'so it is not an empirical fact . . .': cp. 2.012–2.0121, 5.551.

(c) Cp. *PG* 75a; BUF 241a. *RFM* 39d adds an illustration.

we do not understand them: that is, have no reflective grasp of their depth grammar (cp. §196).

like savages, primitive people: see Pitcher, *Philosophy*, 211. "We find all infantile theories once again in contemporary philosophy, only they are no longer winning, as those of children are" (BUF 246).

§195 This differs only slightly from *RFM* 39, §126, the chief difference being the omission of a comparison. Cp. *BB* 6d.

"causally": "A mechanical, electrical, psychological connection can function or not function" (*PG* 97), but not the logical connection. " 'As a machine functioning causally, everything would depend on the thought; logically, it yields only what we meant by it' " (*PG* 247).

"in a *queer* way": see §196, p. 59n (*b*); *BB* 6, 73c–74a; *PG* 49c.

and the sentence: namely, "The use itself is in some sense present."

only seems queer when . . . : see §197.

in which we actually use it: see commentary on §20b ("But doesn't the fact . . ."); cp. §193bc.

Someone once told me . . . : the parallel is close enough for present purposes, but not complete, since the child did not understand the expression even in the ordinary, nonreflective sense of *understand;* he was not acquainted with this language-game.

§196 Condensed from *BB* 6d, e.g.: "When we are worried about the nature of thinking, the puzzlement which we wrongly interpret to be one about the nature of a medium is a puzzlement caused by the mystifying use of our language. This kind of mistake recurs again and again in philosophy; e.g. when we are puzzled about the nature of time, when time seems to us a *queer thing*." On the queerness of time, see also *BB* 26cd; on the queerness of thought and propositions, see §§93–95; *PG* 154b–155b.

a queer *process*: see §308; *PB* 67: "If I understand a demand and do not comply with it, the understanding can only consist in a process that *stands for* the execution, so in a *different* process than the execution" (yet one which stands for just *it*).

§197 This differs only slightly from *RFM* 40, §130. See §138; *BB* 42a; *PG* 49c, 50g–51a, 55d–56a; Man. 302, 2; Man. 109, 179; cp. §633. The paragraph continues discussion of the connection between understanding and future developments, but uses a new example—intending—to illustrate the problem of the connection and shifts for a stretch to the allied problem of how we can be sure of the connection. On intention, see §337, which indicates the main direction of the present paragraph. Neither there nor elsewhere in the *Investigations* does W. explain our sureness about what we intend (see *EPB* 230). Distinguish that question, in focus here, from the question whether we *intend* it.

It becomes queer when . . . : see §195; *PG* 50d.

in some way already be present: see §195 and commentary.

I now want to play: the similarity of the problem raised by both understanding and intention, and the close connection between them suggested by GI 37–38 and the commentary on §174b, justify their being lumped together in this therapeutic treatment, despite their differences.

chess: on intending to play chess or to make a move, and on the whole comparison implicit here between language and chess, see the commentary on §31a.

so is it impossible . . . : if the game is not foreshadowed in thought (I do not run through all the rules) nor actually played, it presumably must be ascertained causally; but if all I thus discover is a *usual* consequence, and if in sober fact I don't establish even that (cp. §147a), then how can I ever "be certain what I am intending to do?"

super-strong connexion . . . : cp. *RFM* 6d; *LC* 15–16, 67–68 (quoted for §457).

Well, in the list . . . : see GI 43; IX, 6; *BB* 183d–184a; *PG* 56a; *LC* 68 (quoted for §457).

§198 The answer to the initial question, in a nutshell: The rule can cause me to act in a given way, and the agreement of my reactions with those of others not only permits communication (§§240–42, p. 230a) but establishes the forms of life we call "following a rule", "going by a rule", "obeying a rule", and so on (see §199; cp. *RFM* 41a). Similarly, "rather than to say that we agree *because* we follow rules, it is more perceptive to say that our agreement fixes the meaning of the rules, defines their content" (Malcolm, "Wittgenstein", 338).

(a) The problem of the gap remains, as long as the rule (e.g. the formula) is considered in isolation from practice. See §§86, 141; cp. §380c.

(b) On the connection between 'history' (e.g. training) and use, see III, 1–2, and XXXVII, 17. On the relation between causal efficacy and meaning, see §§491–98.

(c) only to give a causal connexion: see §195 and commentary.

I have further indicated . . . : only implicitly, e.g. at the end of §197.

only in so far: this is the criterion of "going by" (see the initial comments above). The difference, on a given occasion, between a nonconventional reaction and a conventional one might consist only in the latter's being accompanied by the sort of characteristic experiences born of long practice (*Z* 277; cp. XXXVII, 17).

See XXXVII, 18.

§199 Cp. §§344–45; *RFM* 94efgh.

There would be no concept *red* if only one thing had ever been red, and probably no concept *bird* if only one bird had ever existed; but there might have been just one red thing (not so called) or just one bird (not so called), whereas "there cannot be a practice without cases falling under the practice any more than there can be cases falling under a practice without a practice" (Linsky, "Wittgenstein", 171). *Obey a rule* is this sort of concept (§202). For to obey a *rule* is, for instance, to act as one has been taught or in accordance with others' observed behavior (§54); "roughly speaking, it characterizes what we call a rule to be applied repeatedly, in an indefinite number of instances" (*BB* 96; *EPB* 140). And to *obey* a rule, whether formulated or not, is to do the "correct" thing, that is, what others do (§§145b, 258-59, 265).

(a) This paragraph connects with the preceding, showing that the words "in so far as" indicate a conceptual, not merely a causal or factual connection.

(b) See §345; Man. 180a, 2.

(c) See *PG* 131c, 133ab, 170d-171b, 172f; cp. §20a, p. 181cd; *BB* 5; *PG* 378b; *PB* 180e; 3.334, 3.42.

Since W. has been considering the grasp of a word's meaning, and this is the sort of rule one follows in making a report or giving an order, one might have expected him to say something like: "To understand a word is to understand, be master of (§§30-31), its use in the language (§43), so to understand a language." Such is the emphasis of *BB* 5, from which this paragraph derives.

§200 Cp. *BB* 92ab; *PG* 294ab. Man. 108, 157, indicates the general target of this paragraph: "I once said in discussion that two systems of signs are the same space if they are intertranslatable." Thus he had written in 3.1431: "The essence of a propositional sign is very clearly seen if we imagine one composed of spatial objects (such as tables, chairs, and books) instead of written signs." For "what constitutes a propositional sign is that in it its elements . . . stand in a determinate relation to one another" (3.14). It does not matter whether the signs are sounds or puppets in a courtroom (I, 1; 4.014); they still form propositions. Similarly, W. later compared "the rules of Arithmetic to the rules of chess, and used of chess the phrase, 'What is characteristic of chess is the logical multiplicity of its rules' " (*PP* 291-92). Moore took issue with this assertion, but not as radically as W. now does.

and if *we*: we, who know a game called chess, into which such moves might fit. Suppose, though, that this stamping were considered beneficial for the crops, or were inflicted as a punishment; suppose we saw a secretary recording it all, or the chief made a "reply".

What right would one have: paraphrasing §494, W. might say: "It is primarily the activities of our usual games that we call games, and then other things by analogy with these—for instance, games carried on by correspondence, without board or figures (Man. 108, 154). But such yelling and stamping we do not ordinarily associate with a game, still less with a game of chess."

§201(a) This was: in §§84–87; see §198.

our paradox: for what is a rule if not something which determines a line of action?

every course of action: "For describe whatever process (activity) of projection we may, there is a way of reinterpreting this projection. Therefore—one is tempted to say—such a process can never be the intention itself. For we could always have intended the opposite by reinterpreting the process of projection. Imagine this case: We give someone an order to walk in a certain direction by pointing or by drawing an arrow which points in the direction. Suppose drawing arrows is the language in which generally we give such an order. Couldn't such an order be interpreted to mean that the man who gets it is to walk in the direction opposite to that of the arrow? This could obviously be done by adding to our arrow some symbols which we might call 'an *interpretation*'. It is easy to imagine a case in which, say to deceive someone, we might make an arrangement that an order should be carried out in the sense opposite to its normal one. The symbol which adds the interpretation to our original arrow could, for instance, be another arrow. Whenever we interpret a symbol in one way or another, the interpretation is a new symbol added to the old one" (*BB* 33).

can be made out: if we abstract from common practice or conventions and seek an intrinsic or momentary norm.

(b) See *Z* 234–35; *EPB* 198; *BB* 131d–132a; *PG* 147bc; cp. *PP* 271.

a misunderstanding: concerning the nature of agreement with a rule: "The intention seems to interpret, to give the final interpretation; which is not a further sign or picture, but something else—the thing that cannot be further interpreted. But what we have reached is a psychological, not a logical terminus" (*Z* 231). "What happens is not that this symbol cannot be further interpreted, but: I do no interpreting. I do not interpret, because I feel at home in the present picture. When I interpret, I step from one level of thought to another" (*Z* 234; *PG* 147). See §§217, 506; *BB* 33 (above); *PG* 47d.

of our argument: an unfortunate translation, suggesting reference to the preceding polemic, where one explanation (not interpretation) follows another. A *Gedankengang* such as that in §433 is not an argument.

one interpretation after another: as in §§84–87 or §433.

(c) Hence there is . . . : *RFM* 34 makes just this transition, from: "However many rules you give me—I give a rule which justifies *my* employment of your rules," to: "We might also say: when we *follow* the laws of inference (inference-rules) then following always involves interpretation too."

But we ought to restrict . . . : see p. 212e; *PG* 147bc and *Z* 234 (above); and *BB* 36c and 33b (quoted for *a*) for other general remarks; and *Z* 208c for more detailed illustration.

"But an *interpretation* is something that is given in signs. It is this interpretation as opposed to a different one (running differently).—So when we wanted to say 'Any sentence still stands in need of an interpretation,' that meant: no sentence can be understood without a rider" (*Z* 229; *PG* 47c).

§202   And hence also . . . : were every action according to a rule an interpretation (§201c), a deviant action might be a personal interpretation, not disobedience. Just as, in W.'s earlier view, the strange words of a Helmholtz would be meaningful provided he 'projected' them specially (*PP* 265, 271; cp. §511), so a person might obey a rule by projecting it privately and acting accordingly, or by translating directly into unaccustomed actions (cp. §459). In that case too, "one would like to say: whatever is going to seem right to me is right" (§258). And the assertion "I *think* I am obeying this rule," like the declaration "I *believe* I mean something by these words" (NL 311), would hardly be open to doubt: It would be a report that the projecting had taken place. (For how can I think I am thinking of *x* without thinking of *x*—without performing the projective act—and how can I be mistaken about what I am thinking?) Cp. §§204, 243, 258–60, 269; *RFM* 34c.

§203   labyrinth: see GI 10; §18; *BB* 81e; *LC* 1c.

You approach from *one* side . . . : cp. the second and third paragraphs of the Preface, the commentary on them, and GI 28.

"If you see a thing from *one* side, you can't see it from the others. If you uncover one side, you cover up the others" (Man. 163).

Such references show that W. is not alluding to the puzzlement which arises (§§123, 664) when we start to reflect about the expressions we use with ease (cp. §89c), but to new problems which crop up when, for instance, we switch our consideration from obeying or following a rule to interpreting it, or to intention, as in the present numbers.

**§204   Having asked similar questions about obeying a rule (§199a), then compared obeying a rule to playing chess (§199b), then expanded the comparison to games in general (§200), W. now comes full cycle and develops the same point for games, in the same way. The answer in §199b to the question in §199a indicates how the present, parallel query should be answered. Cp. §345.

"Granted, I could invent a board game today which was *never* actually played. I would simply describe it. But that is possible only because similar games already exist, that is, because such games *are played*" (Man. 164, 93).

§205 The number connects the thought of §197 with §204. For W.'s own comment and answer, see §337.

(a) The quotation marks enclosing the whole paragraph indicate, as usual, that another speaks (for instance W.'s former self).

See Man. 138, 24B; cp. the start of §200.

"is not necessary to it": for illustrations of this attitude from W.'s earlier thought, see GI 37 and *PP* 270–71.

"and then be interrupted": without "finishing" the game. But by what standard would their play be "unfinished", "incomplete"? Cp. §§365, 633.

(b) Cp. *BB* 25c ("not only do we not think of the rules of usage—of definitions, etc.—while using language").

§206 See I, 6. The logic of this number resembles that of §200, suggesting that obeying an order, like playing a game, is essentially a practice (*a*), since we would apply behavioral criteria (*c*), in determining how to classify the imagined activity (*b*). "*Essence* is expressed by grammar" (§371).

Contrast this thinking with Man. 110, 16, and with Man. 108, 208–9 (quoted for §345c), where W. said it would be conceivable for no orders ever to be obeyed and for their meaning to be unaffected. The picture (GI 36) and the intention (GI 37) would still be there.

(a) is analogous to obeying an order: see §§199b, 345; *RFM* 184e; *BB* 98b. Compare §433 with §§84–87; *BB* 3b with §198a; *BB* 3c with §151; *BB* 3d and *BB* 14d with §201b.

We are trained: "One does not learn to obey a rule by first learning the use of the word 'agreement'. Rather, one learns the meaning of 'agreement' by learning to follow a rule. If you want to understand what it means 'to follow a rule', you have already to be able to follow a rule" (*RFM* 184; breaks suppressed).

"He must go on like this *without a reason*. . . . And the *like this* (in 'go on like this') is signified by a number, a value. For at *this* level the expression of the rule is explained by the value, not the value by the rule" (Z 301).

we react to an order: see §506.

Which one is right?: see §145b.

(bc) Cp. §§207, 494; *EPB* 137, 149; *BB* 94a, 103; Janik and Toulmin, *Vienna,* 228.

§207 See I, 8; Z 699; *RFM* 96ef, 103f–i, 180ef. Cp. *RFM* 34e for a similar treatment of thinking, and Man. 116, 117, for similar remarks about Robinson Crusoe, as he uses a personal language.

(a) apparently: the noises they utter vary greatly but certain sound units recur, in discernible patterns; perhaps also they face one another, gesticulate, make faces, and seldom utter these sounds when alone.

there is no regular connexion: *RFM* 103f suggests that a physiological connection might perhaps be discovered (cp. §493). But W. is not interested in explaining the phenomenon, scientific plausibility being irrelevant to his purposes (GI 62). Cp. *Z* 608–11.

as I feel like putting it: using shorthand for the complex effects adequately indicated by saying that the consequences would be the same as for us if we *all* were temporarily gagged (the reference to just one person seems a slip).

(bc) See §§206c, 494; *OC* 519c. Though not "one thing in common which makes us use the same word for all" (since many other activities are regular), W. does seem to be "producing something common to all that we call language" (§65b), namely regularity, and thereby apparently troubles his family-resemblance comparison (§§66–67). However, he immediately points out that regularity is not just one thing (§208; see GI 59). And see the comments on the opening words of §67.

There is not enough . . . : rather: "There is not the regularity of what we call 'language'." W. does not say whether "by analogy or comparability with this" (§494) we might extend the term to this imagined form of life. Perhaps "one will have to depict it as a limiting case" (§385), perhaps not, "because the phenomena gravitate towards another paradigm" (ibid.). Cp. §§233 (the extension of the terms *arithmetic* and *calculate* to irregular 'composing'), 234 (our actual calculation), 235 (the corresponding usage), 236, 528–29.

§208   The number counteracts the impression of an essence, whether of language or of obeying a rule (see §207), and continues the polemic against inner precontainment, returning to the examination of teaching as an indication of the language-game thus established.

(a) See §75; *RFM* 34d, 184 (quoted for §206a).

Then am I defining . . . : that is, am I working back through definitions to these basic 'indefinables', after the manner of Frege and Moore (§182c)? To learn the language-game is to acquire all these concepts, and without such acquaintance none of them is known (§199).

has not yet got the *concepts:* distinguish this case from ignorance of concepts in a known language-game. If, for instance, he lacked the concept *marsupial,* it might be verbally explained to him, whereas in the present case he needs to be acquainted with the larger language-game, so has to be trained in a way similar to that used for a child first learning to speak (§6). Cp. §75.

(c) Cp. *BB* 77c.

(e) comparable to that of pointing: when used in an order (cp. §71b) or in teaching somebody to do something (cp. §6), rather than in naming (§7).

(f) We should distinguish . . . : see *EPB* 137–39; *BB* 93f–95b, 99c; *PP* 298; cp. *EPB* 131; *BB* 89d–90a.

an abbreviated notation: say for a series with an upper limit, as when for example "the highest numeral observed in use is 159. . . . We could easily imagine the numeral 159 to be used on such occasions, in connection with such gestures and forms of behaviour as would make us say that this numeral plays the role of an unsurmountable limit" (*BB* 93–94).

not a human shortcoming: "as though we stopped writing numerals because after all we cannot write them all down, but they were there all right, as if in a box" (*PG* 285). "Isn't it like this? The concepts of infinite decimals in mathematical propositions are not concepts of series, but of the unlimited technique of expansion of series. We learn an endless technique: that is to say, something is done for us first, and then we do it; we are told rules and we do exercises in following them; perhaps some expression like 'and so on *ad inf.*' is also used, but what is in question here is not some gigantic extension" (*RFM* 144). "In the *Tractatus* he had made the mistake of supposing that an infinite series was a logical product—that it *could* be enumerated, though we were unable to enumerate it" (*PP* 298). Cp. *RFM* 141ijk; *PB* 167a; *PP* 302a; Ramsey, *Foundations*, 8.

(g) See *EPB* 143 and *BB* 98c ("the pupil is not just trained to use a single table; but the training aims at making the pupil use any table correlating letters with arrows").

§209 Cp. *BB* 92a.

(a) A very queer expression: suggesting that all the steps have somehow already been taken (§188).

a quite natural one: see §188b ("you were inclined to use such expressions"); *PP* 298 (why W. once was).

(b) See §§69, 75. Though not enclosed in quotation marks like the question which opens (*a*), these at the start of (*b*) also belong to the patient, not the therapist.

whence the feeling . . . : no doubt from "the mystifying use of our language" (*BB* 6); we say, for instance, that we "meant" him to do this or that, though neither we nor he did it (§§186–88); and he exclaims that he "sees" how to go on, beyond the examples (§§191–92).

(c) Is it like . . . : are we misled in the same way? Cp. *PG* 455f ("The endless road does not have an 'infinitely distant' end, but no end"); *PG* 464a ("And an 'infinite class' is not a class which has more members than a finite class, in the ordinary sense of 'more' "); *PB* 208e, 223 ("The infinity of a length is not the length's size").

§210   See §§73–75, 362, and references there; *Z* 302–7; *EPB* 151–52; *BB* 105a; *PG* 120a; Man. 116, 35; cp. *PG* 62a, 270–72.

"But do you really . . .": once again, the quotation marks make it doubly evident that the patient speaks, as also in *Z* 304: " 'Once he has seen the right thing, seen the one of infinitely many references which I am trying to push him towards—once he has got hold of it, he will continue the series right without further ado. I grant that he can only guess (intuitively guess) the reference that I mean—but once he has managed that the game is won.' But this 'right thing' that I mean does not exist. The comparison is wrong. There is no such thing here as, so to say, a wheel that he is to catch hold of, the right machine which, once chosen, will carry him on automatically. It could be that something of the sort happens in our brain but that is not our concern."

Cp. Waismann, writing under W.'s early influence: "The demonstration actually consists of two acts: an external action, that of pointing to different facts, and a mental operation, namely the inner grasp of what is common" (*Kreis,* 246). For W., this interiorization—the meaning or intention—had seemed inexpressible. See the commentary on §120; *Kreis,* 154 (quoted for §153), 157; cp. §§430–36; *BB* 5de.

§211   See I, 4–5; *Z* 300–304; *EPB* 216; *BB* 15, 143c; *PG* 96d–97a; cp. §505.

without reasons: reasons, that is for the last act in the chain. "A reason is a step preceding the step of the choice. But why should every step be preceded by another one?" (*BB* 88; *EPB* 129). "Giving a reason is like giving a calculation by which you have arrived at a certain result" (*BB* 15).

"Now there is the idea that if an order is understood and obeyed there must be a reason for our obeying it as we do; and, in fact, a chain of reasons reaching back to infinity" (*BB* 14). W. had declared several years earlier: "A foundation which stands on nothing is a bad foundation" (Man. 108, 166).

§212   See *BB* 14. The sequence §§211–12 parallels §§505–6.

lack of reasons: in the sense just indicated: a previous step (see §213a). If fear were suggested as the reason, one might cite *BB* 103 and 143f–144a: A person's fear consists largely in his reaction. However, there is no arguing with usage: people do use the word *reason* in this way too.

§213   Cp. 6.233–6.2331.

(a) See §84.

Not at all: for to say I *had* to would start an infinite regress; every interpretation which was not the action itself would leave a gap for further interpretations—interpretations of the interpretations (§141).

"This is as if one said: 'Wherever you are, you must have got there from somewhere else, and to that previous place from another place; and so on *ad infinitum*.' (If, on the other hand, you had said, 'wherever you are, you *could* have got there from another place ten yards away; and to that other place from a third, ten yards further away, and so on *ad infinitum*,' if you had said this you would have stressed the infinite *possibility* of making a step" (*BB* 14).

But that is not . . . : " 'But do you mean to say that the expression '+2' leaves you in doubt what you are to do e.g. after 2004?'—No; I answer '2006' without hesitation. But just for that reason it is superfluous to suppose that this was determined earlier on. My having no doubt in face of the question does *not* mean that it has been answered in advance" (*RFM* 3).

There is something to be said . . . : "It is as if at first all these more or less inessential processes were shrouded in a particular atmosphere, which dissipates when I look closely at them" (§173; see §§598, 607a, 609; *Z* 128). A kindred notion, in which W. recognized some truth, is that we see the samples in a special way and are thereby directed in our actions (§§74, 228). Thus concerning the impossibility of doubt in certain circumstances, cp. pp. 195d, 201cd, 206b.

(bc) See §186; Man. 164, 134; Rhees, *Discussions,* 117; cp. *PG* 96b; 5.1363; contrast with *PB* 212e.

So it must have been . . . : W. had said: "An inference can only be justified by what we see" (*PP* 295).

If intuition is an inner voice: see §232; cp. §223a and *BB* 5: "But one is tempted to imagine that which gives the sentence life as something in an occult sphere, accompanying the sentence. But whatever accompanied it would for us just be another sign," and once we take this supplementary sign to be a voice, which might just as well be vocal as silent, "it ceases to seem to impart any life to the sentence at all. (It was in fact just the occult character of the mental process which you needed for your purposes.)"

an unnecessary shuffle: see above; §659b and commentary; *PG* 271c; cp. *RFM* 71c.

"We are all too ready to invoke inner intuition, whenever we cannot produce any other ground of knowledge" (Frege, *Foundations,* 19).

§214 *RFM* 3ef, 116ef; *EPB* 128; and *BB* 87b suggest that W. is once again using "the method of §2", offering a sample which comes closest to the intuitionist account, then indicating that even in this case it is not appropriate. Such a series would seem the very paradigm of precontainment, with all future steps clearly foreshadowed in these few initial ones. But it is not so.

" 'But you surely know for example that you must always write the *same* sequence of numbers in the units: 2, 4, 6, 8, o, 2, 4, etc.'—Quite true: the problem must already appear in this sequence, and even in *this* one: 2, 2, 2, 2, etc.—For how do I know that I am to write '2' after the five hundredth '2'? i.e. that 'the same figure' in that place is '2'? And if I know it *in advance,* what use is this knowledge to me later on? I mean: how do I know what to do with this earlier knowledge when the step actually has to be taken? (If intuition is needed to continue the series +1, then it is also needed to continue the series +o.)" (*RFM* 3; cp. §185; Man. 106, 282, 284, 286).

"If a child writing down a row of 2's obtained '2, 2, 2', from the segment '2, 2' by adding '2' once, he might deny that he had gone on the *same* way. He might declare that it would be doing the same thing only if it went from '2, 2' to '2, 2, 2, 2' in *one* jump, i.e. only if he *doubled* the original segment (just as it doubled the original single '2')" (Malcolm, "Investigations", 187). If he does not, but obeys the order to "do the same" by adding another "2", that is not because he has figured out that this, among all possible interpretations, is the one required by the initial segment (§213).

the series 1 2 3 4: see 6.02, 6.03.

§215   The first two paragraphs express a common viewpoint (cp. §377), the third is W.'s questioning reply. Note the parallel with Waismann's early account of W.'s thought: "One imagines a gradual approximation, which is to *end* in identity, like this: first the two shapes draw nearer (the chairs grow more and more similar); then, when this process is complete, the final distinction, that of place, begins to disappear, and finally they coincide completely: they have become indistinguishable and consequently one. Thus we believe that in the course of this process they have become ever less distinguishable and we conceive identity as the limit of discernibility. But the situation is really this: If it makes sense to ask whether the chairs can be distinguished, then they are two chairs; if it makes no sense, then there is one chair" ("Identität", 60–61).

The *Tractatus* would have agreed with this much, and indeed helps to explain it. According to its author, identity is one of those things which cannot be said (5.5303), but shows itself, most perspicuously when the same name is used for the same thing and different names for different things (*NB* 130c; 5.53). Though the written sign may vary somewhat in size and shape, and the spoken sign in pronunciation, the identity 'shown' does not consist in being more or less similar, but simply in being the same (2.0233–2.02331). As Frege said, "identity is a relation given to us in so specific a form that it is inconceivable that various kinds of it should occur" (*Basic Laws,* 129). True, "in ordinary speech, and in that of science too, identity is not always taken in its strictest sense. Objects which are not identical in the strict logical sense people are also wont to treat verbally as identical" (Carnap, *Aufbau*, 217). "Identity," Russell agreed, "is a precise conception, and no word, in ordinary speech, stands for anything precise. Ordinary speech does not distinguish between identity and close similarity" (*Mind*, 180). Both for those who accepted Leibniz's principle of the identity of indiscernibles and for those who, like young W. (5.5302), did not, "the argument proceeds as though somewhere there exists in itself an exceptional sense of the word 'identical', in which things are really identical" (Waismann, "Identität", 59).

To all such thinking, with its disregard for ordinary language (§116) and its supposition of "a *super*-order between—so to speak—*super*-concepts" (§97), the later W. was opposed. "The point is that there is no such thing as being just *the same*—no such thing as identity pure and simple. It would be a mistake to think that the same is the same whether we are speaking of builds or coats or gaits or sensations. 'Same' must always be understood together with some general term, such as 'build' or 'coat', and the criterion of identity in any particular case is determined by the general term involved" (Cook "Privacy", 313).

For a development and defense of W.'s viewpoint, see Geach's "Identity" and "Reply".

(a) But isn't . . . : that is, "if we can't claim perfect identity for successive 2's in a series of 2's, at least the first is identical with itself. There is some intrinsic, unmistakable identity *somewhere!*"

(c) In addition to the comments above, see *RFM* 183i; cp. *PG* 351; Moore, *Problems*, 333–35; Waismann, "Identität", 62. This last suggests that the roots of (c) go back far, to W.'s early rejection (*NB* 4) of the treatment of identity in *Principia Mathematica*, where one and the same identity sign was used in affirming a thing's self-identity and in denying the identity of two things, as though it made sense to suggest that two things might be one: "Roughly speaking, to say of *two* things that they are identical is nonsense, and to say of *one* thing that it is identical with itself is to say nothing at all" (5.5303). W. renews this latter point in the next number. A variant formulation is suggested by §345: In keeping with Leibniz's law we are inclined to say, "If two things have *all* their properties in common then they are identical"; but mightn't we say instead: "then they are not two things"?

§216   See Man. 213, 412; cp. *EPB* 169. Worked up in Man. 119, 47–49.

(a) a useless proposition: though it has often been treated as a foundation of thought and knowledge, along with the principle of contradiction. For Frege, who was less concerned about utility (*Foundations*, 87), it was a "law of truth" (*Basic Laws*, 15). The reason for W.'s long-standing opposition, whether to the general formula "(x) x = x" (*NB* 116) or to the particular, "a = a" (*PB* 332; *Kreis,* 139a), is reflected in Waismann's *Thesen:* "It is meaningless to wish to formulate in a sentence *that* which is a condition for understanding it" (*Kreis,* 243). Only as indication of a linguistic convention might "A = A" serve a purpose (*PG* 195). Concerning identity statements such as "Edward VII is the King" there is of course no similar problem (Russell, *Principles,* 64).

"When I say 'Only this is seen,' I forget that a sentence may come ever so natural to us without having any use in our calculus of language. Think of the law of identity, 'a = a,' and of how we sometimes try hard to get hold of its sense, to visualize it, by looking at an object and repeating to ourselves such a sentence as 'This tree is the same thing as this tree.' The gestures and images by which I apparently give this sentence sense are very similar to those which I use in the case of 'Only *this* is really seen' " (*BB* 65–66).

"Frege calls it 'a law about what men take for true' that 'It is impossible for human beings . . . to recognize an object as different from itself.'—When I think of this as impossible for me, then I think of *trying* to do it. So I look at my lamp and say: 'This lamp is different from itself.' (But nothing stirs.) It is not that I see it is false, I can't do anything with it at all" (*RFM* 41).

(b) Cp. *BB* 163a; and Waismann on identity as the ideal terminus reached when two things finally coincide perfectly (see the first quote for §215).

"But now I wish to mention one other sense-datum, of a kind that we all saw, which might be thought to have more to do with the real envelope. Besides the patch of colour and its shape and size, we did, in a sense, all see the *space* which this patch of colour occupied. The patch of colour seemed to occupy a certain area; and we can by abstraction distinguish this area from the patch of colour occupying it" (Moore, *Problems,* 38).

(c) Revised from Man. 221,236–37, where it occasions a long digression.

***But that is just how . . .* :** a comparable case may clarify W.'s point and explain his emphasis: "He once greeted me with the question: 'Why do people say that it was natural to think that the sun went round the earth rather than that the earth turned on its axis?' I replied: 'I suppose, because it looked as if the sun went round the earth.' 'Well,' he asked, 'what would it have looked like if it had *looked* as if the earth turned on its axis?' This question brought it out that I had hitherto given no relevant meaning to 'it looks as if' in 'it looks as if the sun goes round the earth' " (Anscombe, *Introduction,* 151). Similarly, as far as appearances go, the contingent fact of fitting does not differ from the 'necessary truth'. Hence the principle of identity would need to be saying something else. But what? (Cp. §251de.)

§217(a) On the distinction between causes and reasons, motives, justifications, see *EPB* 129, 160–61; *BB* 14–15, 88, 110–11.

"And the mistake which we here and in a thousand similar cases are inclined to make is labelled by the word 'to make' as we have used it in the sentence 'It is no act of insight which makes us use the rule as we do,' because there is an idea that 'something must make us' do what we do. And this again joins on to the confusion between cause and reason. *We need have no reason to follow the rule as we do.* The chain of reasons has an end" (*BB* 143; *EPB* 216), whereas causes might be traced back *ad infinitum*. The common supposition that every act has a cause should not be confused with the thesis that every act has a motive or justification.

(b) See I, 4; *OC* 110, 204, 254; *Z* 391; cp. §§201b, 485; *PB* 194c; 6.123; *NB* 72j.

"At some point one has to pass from explanation to mere description" (*OC* 189; cp. §109).

"As if giving grounds did not come to an end sometime. But the end is not an ungrounded presupposition: it is an ungrounded way of acting" (*OC* 110). Compare this with Frege, *Foundations,* 2: "There may even be justification for a further hope: if, by examining the simplest cases, we can bring to light what mankind has there done by instinct, and can extract from such procedures what is universally valid in them, may we not thus arrive at general methods for forming concepts and establishing principles which will be applicable also in more complicated cases?" For Frege, people are instinctively right, whereas for W. their reactions establish what is right (§§241–42).

"For Wittgenstein, 'following a rule' is just as much a 'practice' as 'playing a game' is (§199). Now what are its rules? In the sense in which 'playing chess' has rules, 'obeying a rule' has none (except, perhaps, in a special code or calculus which sets up some order of precedence in the application of various rules); and yet it can be done correctly or incorrectly—which just means it can be done or not done. And whether or not it is done is not a matter of rules (or of opinion or feeling or wishes or intentions). It is a matter of what Wittgenstein, in the *Blue Book,* refers to as 'conventions' (p. 24), and in *Investigations* describes as 'forms of life' (e.g., §23)" (Cavell, "Availability", 158).

(c) Cp. §182c; *RFM* 47g, 59a, 171f; *PG* 294d, 399c; *PB* 131e, 193a–194b; *Kreis,* 221; Man. 302, 30; Man. 127, 33–35; Man. 108, 166.

"Were someone to come and give the definition $\sim p.\sim q = p|q$ he would, it is true, merely have introduced an inessential abbreviation; but it would be the expression of a discovery in the sense that it *emphasizes* a certain new aspect. (Russell rightly pointed out that the impor-

tance of definitions often comes from this emphasis.) (Somewhat as giving the name 'Mrs. John Robinson' stresses a certain relationship
between husband and wife.)" (Man. 108, 156). It does not establish the
relationship.

§218 See *RFM* 162h; cp. *PB* 224e–225b.

Whence comes . . . : "Here once again, as always in the realm of infinity, it is grammar which plays a trick on us" (*PB* 208). The present
number suggests that we are misled by the things we say about rules
(§147), for example: "The truths of arithmetic would then be related to
those of logic in much the same way as the theorems of geometry to the
axioms. Each one would contain concentrated within it a whole series
of deductions for future use, and the use of it would be that we need
no longer make the deductions one by one, but can express simultaneously the result of the whole series" (Frege, *Foundations*, 24; see ibid.,
99–103, and *PG* 281d).

we might imagine rails: cp. *RFM* 34e, 78m. "Only a path approaches
a goal, not places. And only a law approaches a value" (*PB* 228). "The
rule conducts you like a gangway with rigid walls" (*RFM* 184).

"Wittgenstein said you could explain the way people looked at natural laws by saying they regarded them as if they were rails, along which
things had to move" (Man. FW, 1).

correspond to . . . : see §209c; *PB* 208e ("*Possibility*, not reality!"),
223c, 228g, 313a.

"At least this much is clear—and it is the main thing—that there is no
duality: law & endless series that follows it; that is, in logic there is
nothing like description & reality" (Man. 106, 260; see *PB* 221).

"The rules for a number-system—for instance the decimal system—
contain whatever is infinite about the numbers" (*PB* 160–61).

§219(a) See *RFM* 9d–10a.

"All the steps . . .": see §188.

how would it help?: cp. §141.

(b) No; my description . . . : the talk of lines was not meant to explain understanding but to picture it. An analogous situation arises in
§339a. See Anscombe, *Introduction*, 163.

(c) Cp. §186.

(d) See §206a, p. 224d; *RFM* 101.

§220 See *RFM* 35cde; cp. §§140a, 198c, 437.

that symbolic proposition: namely, "All the steps are really already
taken."

a difference . . . : when an event conflicts with a causal law, the law
is wrong; when action conflicts with a logical law, the action is wrong.
The latter, as we say, holds *a priori*.

"How queer: It looks as if a physical (mechanical) form of guidance could misfire and let in something unforeseen, but not a rule! As if a rule were, so to speak, the only reliable form of guidance" (*Z* 296).

"And here it might occur to us to say: 'The law is *inexorable*—men can let the guilty go, the law executes him.' (And even: 'the law *always* executes him.')—What is the use of such a form of expression?—In the first instance, this proposition only says that such-and-such is to be found in the law, and human beings sometimes do not go by the law. Then, however, it does give us a picture of a single inexorable judge, and many lax judges. That is why it serves to express respect for the law" (*RFM* 35).

§221   a mythological description: suggesting not merely nonexistent but nonintelligible entities, as did Freud's "powerful mythology" (*LC* 51–52; *BB* 23). "So it really . . . says nothing at all, but gives us a picture" (§352). *"This is how it strikes me"* (§219). Cp. §339a.

§222 See §232; cp. §237.

irresponsibly: " 'It intimates this or that to me, irresponsibly' means: I cannot teach you *how* I follow the line. I do not presuppose that you will follow it as I do, even when you do follow it" (*Z* 282). See §213b and comment.

like a rule: nor that it was a rule (§237).

§223 Shortened form of Man. 228, §339. See ibid., §609.

(a) "I obey the rule *blindly*" (§219).

the whisper: see §§213b, 233.

(b) "I always do the same": the sentence serves as a connecting link between (a), which concludes a series of numbers on predetermination by a rule, and §224, which initiates a series on the related notion of sameness or agreement.

§224 Distinguish this general relationship, between the concept *agree* and the concept *rule,* from the parallel relationship for individual rules, for instance in §258, where critics are wont to suggest that the diarist might simply use the sign for the "same" sensation, not noting that there can be no agreement where there is no rule. Sameness is not an absolute notion (§§214–15).

Distinguish also (on the level of surface grammar) between the agreement of successive steps, stressed in the present and previous numbers, and agreement among those who play the game, prominent in numbers to come (§§240–42).

related **to one another:** "Which is *not* to say that they are alike" (p.198); they are 'cousins', not members of the same 'family' (§67a). Cp. §150.

he learns the use of the other: at least in a sense similar to that of §31a and §208a; he acquires the underlying practice if not yet the word itself. As "one learns the meaning of 'all' by learning that '*fa*' follows from '(*x*).*fx*' " (*RFM* 7), so "one learns the meaning of 'agreement' by learning to follow a rule" (*RFM* 184).

§225   The distinctions just suggested for §224 apply here as well.

interwoven: for instance in the way just mentioned for agreement and rule (*Z* 305). See *RFM* 121: "When I say: 'If these derivations are the same, then it *must* be that . . . ,' I am making something into a criterion of identity. So I am recasting my concept of identity."

As are the use . . . : a sample comparison: To follow a rule is to do the same, to state a proposition is to say something true or false (§136). Granted, the latter entailment is not rigorous (§352), but neither is the former (§226). Again, as the words *true* and *false* are among the "constituent parts" of the game played with *proposition* (§136), so the words *same* and *agree* are among the constituent parts of the game played with *rule* (and vice versa). (Consider the comparison with chess pieces.)

§226   The point of the number (cp. above) seems to be double: The criteria for sameness are variable; so the question needs to indicate them more precisely (cp. §§13, 47, 227). The two samples are basically similar, but the first is mathematical and the second linguistic, linking this discussion of rules and series with §§552–61, on meaning, which have a similar thrust. The present section as a whole (IX) divides its attention in like manner between the analogous cases of grasping a rule, for instance in a series, and grasping the meaning of a word.

§227   See the comments on §§13 and 226; cp. the remarks of §47f, applicable here.

§228   **"We see a series . . .":** see §229 and commentary; cp. §§74, 165, 167.

without appealing: see §§211–12, 217, 219, 230.

§229   The remark is developed in *Z* 276–77. Cp. §102; *NB* 89–90; *Kreis*, 107c; *PP* 295; Man. 110, 111 (quoted for §75).

"It is comparable to the idea that *properties* are *ingredients* of the things which have the properties; e.g. that beauty is an ingredient of all beautiful things as alcohol is of beer and wine, and that we therefore could have pure beauty, unadulterated by anything that is beautiful" (*BB* 17; cp. *RFM* 22e). As the general term is the expression for this essence, so the algebraic formula is the expression for the ethereal something present throughout the series (*Z* 276).

I believe that . . . : W. once had: "Mustn't I already see in it a very simply expressed rule?" (Man. 110, 113). "My idea is that it must be possible to read off the so-called general rule from the individual instance of guiding-oneself-by-something. Thus this general rule is not, for instance, a hypothesis which has to be determined more surely through further individual cases; on the contrary one must already be able to say of a second case that it is not formed according to the same rule as the first" (Man. 109, 251–52).

a characteristic design: namely, "the general form of the operation that produces the next term" (4.1273; see Man. 121, Jan. 4). For "the internal relation by which a series is ordered is equivalent to the operation that produces one term from another" (5.232). As an internal relation, it "cannot be expressed by the game's configuration" (*Kreis,* 157). " 'The examples are only there to explain the rule' " (*PP* 302).

"Much as I also used to say that when he understands variables as variables he sees something in them that he doesn't see in the sign for the individual case" (*PG* 270).

which only needs: to 5.232 (above) 5.2523 adds: "The concept of successive applications is equivalent to the concept 'and so on'."

"and so on": "The concept 'and so on' . . . is one of the most important of all and like all the others infinitely fundamental. For it alone justifies us in constructing logic and mathematics 'so on' from the fundamental laws and primitive signs" (*NB* 89).

§230   See *Z* 279.

my *last* arbiter: see §§211–12, 219, 228.

§231   See §101; *Z* 302; *RFM* 13e; cp. §§254, 386b.

the characteristic expression: cp. *PP* 295: " 'An inference can only be justified by what we see.' "

compulsion of a rule: see *RFM* 193jk.

§232(a)   See *Z* 282; cp. §§172, 222.

I cannot require him . . . : for the voice might tell him something different. The movement in §§228–33 parallels that within §165: Place the essence of reading or following a rule in a private experience and it becomes immaterial whether one's activity conforms to others'.

(b) not my experiences: neither purely factual (cp. §§198bc, 235) nor purely personal (cp. §§314, 316, pp. 206c, 219a). W. might have paraphrased §383: "We are not analyzing a phenomenon (e.g. inspiration, or following a rule) but a concept (e.g. that of being inspired or obeying a rule), and therefore the use of a word."

experiences of acting . . . : by "experiences of acting from inspiration" might be meant "the experiences which accompany acting from inspiration", as though it were already clear what acting from inspiration consists in, that is, how this expression is used (§371). W.'s interest centers rather on this latter question, antecedent to the empirical, scientific one.

§233   inner voice: see §§223, 232a.

like a sort of composing: both in its result, which is personal and creative, not necessarily conforming to any particular rule, and in its origin, since a composer, too, waits upon and follows his inspirations, with no preliminary knowledge of what may come into his head.

§234 The suggestion resembles somewhat that in §159, where the person's performance, indistinguishable from that of reading, is accompanied by sensations characteristic of cheating. And the "series of transitional cases" here in §§232–35 resembles that in §§159–60, both in structure and in purpose ("Should we here allow his sensations to count as the criterion?"). Cp. Z 280.

§235 That is, the preceding series (§§232–34) does not explain why we are not surprised by our agreement, or why we agree, but simply what things we are ready to call "obeying a rule" and what things we do so call (cp. *BB* 125a). W. is making no causal hypotheses when he writes "It would also be possible" (§233) and "Would it not be possible?" (§234). "The descriptions we give are not hints of explanations" (*BB* 125).

§236 See §364 for fuller remarks, and Z 699 for one or two members of the "family".

Are we to say . . . : W. would probably give a different verdict (cp. §§344, 364, 385) in these two cases:
(1) the person has never had any training in arithmetic or worked problems out on paper (cp. §344, p. 14n);
(2) the person started laboriously, as others do, but has now abbreviated the process, as practiced readers do, who can no longer give an account of the reading process (§156).

Cp. pp. 203ef, 209jkl.

§237 See Z 316.

apparently with great precision: cp. §§173–74, which make a similar point.

we see no kind of regularity: cp. §207.

one really would say: W. has imagined circumstances which might naturally elicit the expression criticized in §§222, 230, 232.

"not a rule": in accordance with "the method of §2" (see §48a), W. points out that even in this imagined game, where the expression *intimates* is more appropriate, it does not describe the use of a rule (§222).

§238 for me to call this colour "blue": see *RFM* 184j–185a.

Criteria . . . : e.g. absence of surprise (§524; cp. §234).

§239 A reworking of *PG* 70c, presenting another standard case of rule-following which is blind (*BB* 3c; *PG* 94c–95c). Man. 116, 37–38, where the number takes shape, adds in parentheses: "Related to what Frege and sometimes Ramsey said about recognition as a condition of symbolism. What then is the criterion for my having correctly recognized the color?" See §604 and commentary.

(a) Ultimately from Man. 110, 61–62. Cp. §§380–81.

But how is he to know . . . : see *BB* 87; *PG* 96b–97a. Giving the explanation, "he is to take . . . ," is like adding a scheme to the picture of a cube, as in §141, showing the method of projection. As one picture there supplements another, so here one expression helps another, and the same question arises for it. If anything, the second expression is more problematic than the first, for it introduces the mystifying relation between a visible color and its image (§§300–301; *PG* 74a). "The difficulty here is: to stop" (*Z* 314).

'whose image occurs to him': *PG* 95c suggests a difficulty with this part of the attempted solution: If the word *red* made him consistently imagine just scarlet—or even blue—and he chose accordingly, would he be correct? Only if the supposed explanation were no explanation but the statement of a rule. As a guide to accepted usage, the clue is both superfluous (§73; *PG* 96b) and dubious.

(b) See §182c (the point is not that this definition is inaccurate but that as a mere definition, and a skimpy one at that, it gives no idea how a word such as *red* is used). Cp. §§184, 633, 665b, pp. 205i, 212d, 222j.

§240 See I, 4–5.

among mathematicians, say: on §§239–42, see pp. 225f–227d, which use the same examples—colors and mathematics—to make similar points. See also *RFM* 164 and 173, e.g.: "The agreement of ratifications is the pre-condition of our language-game, it is not affirmed in it" (*RFM* 164). "Mathematics—I want to say—teaches you, not just the answer to a question, but a whole language-game with questions and answers" (*RFM* 173).

part of: the framework also includes "the *truth* of certain empirical propositions" (*OC* 83), in fact a "picture of the world" (*OC* 94), which is "the substratum of all my enquiring and asserting" (*OC* 162).

the framework: this is a major theme in *OC* (e.g. 88, 95, 105, 108, 124, 154, 156, 191, 599–600, 628), where the need of wider agreement for the conduct of the language-game is related to the need of agreement at the learning stage (*OC* 143–44, 170, 283, 310, 314–15, 329, 374, 450, 472–73; see also §§143–46, 185). "The child learns by believing the adult. Doubt comes *after* belief" (*OC* 160).

Cp. Schopenhauer, *World*, I, 47, e.g.: "It was soon observed that, even in the way in which the debaters went back to the jointly acknowledged truth, and sought to deduce their assertions from it, certain forms and laws were followed, about which, although without any previous agreement, there was never any dispute."

for example, in giving descriptions: "If a child has mastered language . . . it must, for example, be able to attach the name of its colour to a white, black, red or blue object without the occurrence of any doubt" (*OC* 522; see *OC* 429–32; cp. pp. 226ef, 227d). Notice the connection with the preceding number (§239).

§241   See I, 4, 6; commentary on §240 and p. 200b; Cavell, "Availability", 160–61; cp. p. 227b; Hempel, "Truth", 57–59; Brouwer, "Mathematik", 157.

"So you are saying . . .": Frege's likely reaction (see *Basic Laws*, 13). The connection with §240 becomes clear if we notice the concluding reference there to agreement in description, for instance of one thing as red and another as blue. The question of truth arises in such cases, not, for example, where agreement consists in continuing a series, "correctly" or "incorrectly".

what human beings *say:* compare similar italics in §23b and p. 227b. Here, however, W. wishes to emphasize the important difference between a conceptual system and its employment. The system—like methods of measurement (§242)—is theoretically neutral. For though it may reflect and result from theories, it endorses none of them (cp. below). In one and the same language—English, German, or French— any scientific, philosophical, or theological *theory* may be intelligibly asserted or denied (see Hallett, "Theoretical Content"). As for nontheoretical statements, employing such a system, they therefore require no theoretical justification (p. 200b). If *this* is what we *call* rain, then it is true to say "It is raining" (§§354, 429).

not agreement in opinions: see I, 4–5; *OC* 110 (quoted for §217b); *BB* 48 (quoted for p. 179c); cp. BUF 236. Even if taken as a comment on the concept *language* more than on the facts of language, W.'s denial may appear inconsistent with the later development of his thought in *On Certainty* (see the commentary on §240) or with the remark in §242 concerning agreement in judgments. As often in the *Investigations,* a therapeutic focus brings out the meaning.

Russell, for one, frequently equated acceptance of ordinary language with acceptance of common-sense views and therefore opposed W.'s suggestion in §116 that we bring words back to their everyday use. As this common confusion has caused much resistance to W.'s thought, it is worth illustrating. "The supposition of common sense and naive realism," wrote Russell (*Matter*, 155), "that we see the actual physical object, is very hard to reconcile with the scientific view. . . ." "To say that you see Jones is no more correct than it would be, if a ball bounced off a wall in your garden and hit you, to say that the wall had hit you. Indeed, the two cases are closely analogous. We do not, therefore, ever see what we think we see" (*Outlook,* 78). In such criticisms, "Russell failed to note sufficiently that what everybody says determines the sense of the expressions and that, most uses not being theoretical, neither are the senses" (Hallett, "Theoretical Content", 335; see 313–15). "'Naive language', that is to say our naive, normal way of expressing ourselves, does not contain any theory of seeing—does not show you a *theory* but only a *concept* of seeing" (Z 223).

but in form of life: see §§19a, 25, and commentaries; §146a; *OC* 196, 204, 212, 253–54, 344, 358–59, 373–75, 402, 426–28, 476–77, 534, 538; *RFM* 33–35; NL 286e.

Cp. Mauthner, *Beiträge*, I, 40: "The language of the masses is no more subject to criticism than is the chirping of birds. It stands beneath criticism. It does not unite people, but is a sign of their union."

§242 See references for §§240–41; Man. 164, 58; *PP* 312c (quoted for §373); Hacker, *Insight*, 162, 220–21; Nell, "Hardness", 68–69; cp. *RFM* 164e; Mauthner, *Beiträge*, I, 35–36; Schlick, "Foundation", 219cd; Quine, *Word*, 57.

If language is to be a means of communication: were it not, it would not be language (§491). Likewise, rather than say that without agreement there *could* be no language, as though the necessity were causal, we should say that there *would* be no language (Z 351).

not only in definitions: a definition, like the formula for a series, can be variously interpreted, variously applied (§§73, 143).

but also . . . in judgments: words get their meanings from their use, that is (in large part) from statements, that is from judgments. Reality does not dictate independently what people should say (p. 230b). See *OC* 206, 455; *RFM* 20g, 21fg, 196b; NL 287e. Concerning this agreement, note the following points:

(1)   There need not be agreement in every application of a term (§79). It is only necessary that "in a large number of judgments there be agreement" (Man. 164, 121; see 116–21). By a process analogous to that described in §164a, this admission can lead to a view like the following, which W. here opposed: "If being true is . . . independent of being acknowledged by somebody or other, then the laws of truth are not psychological laws: they are boundary stones set in an eternal foundation, which our thought can overflow, but never displace" (Frege, *Basic Laws*, 13).

(2)   Something similar holds for language as a whole: It is not characterized by equal agreement on all levels. Thus, "the statements in question are," for instance, "statements about material objects. And they do not serve as foundations in the same way as hypotheses which, if they turn out to be false, are replaced by others" (*OC* 402). And the words in question are, for instance, *hard, cold, ring.* "In the language-game with these words, one does not start by saying 'This *seems* red,' but 'This *is* red' (hard, etc.). Our agreement is essential for the language-game. But it is otherwise with 'pleasant', 'unpleasant', 'beautiful', 'ugly' " (Man.

229, §1564; see *RFM* 96d; cp. p. 227e). Thus it is true, as Frege said, that "there is no contradiction in something's being true which everybody takes to be false" (*Basic Laws*, 13), but there may be in *some* things' being true which everybody takes to be false.

(3)   Much of the agreement necessary for communication (for instance agreement concerning the range of a given term) is proper to a particular language; much is proper to a whole culture (*LC* 8d), for instance that of western or modern man; much extends beyond a given culture: Who, for instance, until very recently, would have made anything of another's claim to have been on the moon? "We should feel ourselves intellectually very distant from someone who said this" (*OC* 108). Still wider agreement in nature and form of life is evoked when W. remarks: "If a lion could talk, we could not understand him" (p. 223). No human being could.

(4)   "The philosopher," though, "is not a citizen of any community of ideas" (*Z* 455). Russell, for instance, when he raised his skeptical doubts about the existence of tables (*Problems*, 12–13), and argued that no one had ever seen the sun (*Matter*, 197) or heard a nightingale (*Mind*, 299), was not questioning or rejecting naive doctrines of "common sense", as he supposed (*Outline*, 48; *Logic*, 109), but was abandoning the language-game which gave his words sense (cp. the commentaries on §241 and §354). To get W.'s present remark in sharp focus, imagine that everyone were a Russell.

This seems to abolish logic: for it contradicts the words of Frege just cited (concerning "an eternal foundation"), so does abolish logic as he and many others conceived it (*RFM* 83g). For young W., too, "laws of truth" were eternal and universal, applicable to any world (§97a), any language (§97b), any thought (§96). For diverse worlds, languages, and thoughts, he then held, differ only in nonessentials; their basic structure is invariant (GI 30–33). Cp. §108a.

but does not do so: any more than the parallel denials about language, thought, and the world abolish language, thought, and the world. "The phenomenon of logic rests on agreement in men's lives no differently than language does" (Man. 164, 163–64). Thus though logic does not "take care of itself", as W. had insisted it must (*NB* 2; 5.473; Black, *Companion*, 273), it does not therefore collapse; for there is indeed "something still more fundamental than logic" (*NB* 4).

methods of measurement: "A *method* of measurement—for instance of a length—is related to the correctness of a statement of length in just the same way as the sense of a sentence is to its truth or falsehood" (*PG* 130). Each is dependent on the other: the measurements consistently gotten determine what measurements *should* be gotten and vice versa (see p. 225a). Herein lies the answer to misgivings one might feel about applying the word *judgments* to what seem like implicit definitions, since they establish the rule; no one statement sets the norm, as in the case of definition, and no one is more normative than another.

partly determined: cp. *RFM* 159d. On the one hand, if some technique, say a use of shock waves to determine the depth of water, gives somewhat unreliable results, we are likely to speak of an "estimate" rather than a "measurement". On the other hand, imagine that a water diviner (cp. *BB* 9–11), operating in the manner of §607, stated the depth with consistent accuracy: should we say that he *measured* it? (Cp. p. 14n, and commentary on §236.)

by a certain constancy: see *RFM* 14ab, 97f–98g, 159ab; cp. §§207–8, 344–45, pp. 225g, 226g, 227c.

X. The Problem of Privacy (§§243–315)

(1)   The basic but common error to avoid in interpreting this section is the supposition that, despite his disclaimers (§109), Wittgenstein intended to establish some thesis or theory, say concerning the impossibility of a private language or of names for sensations. Of course, the word *theory* is used widely, to cover just about any type of doctrine, but the nature of the error appears clearly when critics complain that the supposed thesis is not stated precisely enough—that the meaning of the word *private*, for instance, is left too vague—and that serious difficulties arise for any exact formulation one may propose. Wittgenstein knew they would (GI 70). Hence his interest in therapy, not theory (GI 68).

(2)   To sense the broad implications of the critique he here directs at private meanings and languages, consider for example the venerable doctrine of mentalese, that is, the idea that thoughts "are a special variety of linguistic expression, say the expression of a private language, which we now translate into the expression of a generally accessible language" (Man. 302, 25). Thinkers as varied and influential as Frege, Aquinas, Augustine, James, Russell, Moore, Plato—to mention only some of those whose views Wittgenstein knew (see XI, 4; §§32, 108c, 335, pp. 211k, 217d, and commentaries)—all espoused some version of the doctrine. So had Wittgenstein: "Thinking is a kind of language. For a thought too is, of course, a logical picture of the proposition, and therefore it just is a kind of proposition" (*NB* 82; see GI 40). However, his attention focuses here on sensible signs, in existing or conceivable

languages, and on their treatment by atomists and logical positivists. Particularly enlightening as background for this section are the writings of Russell, his precursor; Schlick, his follower; and Wittgenstein himself.

Russell: The Question of Knowledge

(3) "Within the empiricist tradition, prolonged by Russell, it was not to be doubted that a man has genuine knowledge of his own sentiments, passions, and feelings, which were conceived as kinds of transparent objects that we encounter in our experience. Such a knowledge of the so-called data of consciousness, or of experience, was taken to be the model of unquestionable knowledge of matters of fact. This kind of empirical knowledge was supposed to be unproblematical, while our claims to knowledge of the external world of physical objects was taken to be comparatively questionable and problematical" (Hampshire, *Mind*, 5; see Waismann, "Relevance", 211). Still more problematical, if anything, were the contents of other minds (Russell, *Problems*, 9–10). For "verification in the last resort would always reduce itself to the perception of facts" (*Logic*, 228), and "a man's percepts are private to himself: what I see, no one else sees; what I hear, no one else hears; what I touch, no one else touches; and so on" (*Outline*, 144).

(4)   The consequences for language are serious, for according to Russell *"every proposition which we can understand must be composed wholly of constituents with which we are acquainted"* (*Problems*, 32), and "every word that we now understand must have a meaning which falls within our present experience" (*Logic*, 134). Hence, "when one person uses a word, he does not mean by it the same thing as another person means by it. I have often heard it said that that is a misfortune. That is a mistake. It would be absolutely fatal if people meant the same things by their words. It would make all intercourse impossible, and language the most hopeless and useless thing imaginable, because the meaning you attach to your words must depend on the nature of the objects you are acquainted with, and since different people are acquainted with different objects, they would not be able to talk to each other unless they attached quite different meanings to their words" (*Logic*, 195). Since each one's experiences are not only different but private, so are the meanings: "Broad says, & Russell commends his opinion, that I can never tell (even with the smallest probability?) that when I judge with certainty that a particular colour is a shade of blue, what I mean by using the words 'is a shade of blue' is the same as what anyone else means" (Moore, *Commonplace*, 18).

(5)   Only by means of such private meanings, thought Russell, is it possible to make assertions which are incorrigible yet empirical: "At

any given moment, there are certain things of which a man is 'aware', certain things which are 'before his mind'. Now although it is very difficult to define 'awareness', it is not at all difficult to say that I am aware of such and such things. If I am asked, I can reply that I am aware of this, and that, and the other, and so on through a heterogeneous collection of objects. If I describe these objects, I may of course describe them wrongly; hence I cannot with certainty communicate to another what are the things of which I am aware. But if I speak to myself, and denote them by what may be called 'proper names', rather than by descriptive words, I cannot be in error. So long as the names which I use really are names at the moment, i.e., are naming things to me, so long the things must be objects of which I am aware, since otherwise the words would be meaningless sounds, not names of things" (*Logic,* 130). I may err in my use of terms like *table,* but not in the private language of which I alone am master.

Wittgenstein: The Question of Meaning

(6)   Foolproof particulars interested Wittgenstein the atomist because they assured meaning. "What I formerly called 'objects'," he later explained, "amount merely to what I can refer to without having to fear that perhaps they don't exist" (*PB* 72; see GI 35). For "the analysis of propositions," he had held, "must bring us to elementary propositions which consist of names in immediate combination" (4.221), and names without referents are not names at all. Thus "when I say, e.g., that the table is a yard long . . . I presumably mean that the distance between THESE two points is a yard, and that the points belong to the table" (*NB* 68). However, what about the other points, the ones I don't see (Man. 105, 86)? And what about the table's past and future? It would seem that every statement in ordinary speech reveals a basic dichotomy, between the hypothetical and the assured (Man. 107, 249; see *PG* 220–21; *PP* 261, 266; *Kreis,* 210; Man. 109, 32, quoted for p. 180d; Kenny, *Wittgenstein,* 130–33; cp. Russell, *Logic,* 253; Helmholtz, *Schriften,* 129–31).

(7)   Wittgenstein therefore concluded "that there is ordinary language in which we all customarily speak, and a pimary language which expresses what we really know, so phenomena" (*Kreis,* 45). This conception—Tractarian yet empiricist—is not spelled out, so clarified, in any surviving manuscript; but the use of the term *primary* resembles Ramsey's (*Foundations,* 212–14, 260–61) and Russell's (*Logic,* 250–51), and Waismann indicates the general line of thought in his *Thesen:* "What elementary propositions describe are phenomena (experiences)" (*Kreis,* 249). "The primitive signs are the ones that describe directly; all other signs describe indirectly, via the primitive signs" (ibid., 250; cp. *NB*

22h). "They, then," wrote Wittgenstein, "are the kernels of every proposition, *they* contain the material, and all the rest is only a development of this material" (LF 32).

(8)   The effort to specify the supposed material of this supposed development led to such insuperable difficulties (Man. 105, 116; LF 33, quoted for §106; cp. §354; BB 45) that Wittgenstein soon declared: "We have only one language and that is ordinary language" (*Kreis*, 45; see *PB* 84c, 271a). It is a mistake to think we can discover primary propositions hidden in our ordinary ones (*Kreis*, 183). Yet he still dreamed of constructing a phenomenological language for therapeutic purposes (see GI 25; commentary on §106). It seemed clear "that we need a form of expression in which we can, for instance, represent the phenomena of visual space, as such, in isolation" (Man. 105, 118; *PB* 98; see XXXIV, 1–2). "I once thought," he later remarked, "that it would be possible, for instance, to define the concept of a sphere by means of visual images, etc. and so reveal once for all the connection of concepts, the source of all misunderstandings, etc." (*PG* 211). "It is the same when one tries to define the concept of a material object in terms of 'what is really seen' " (p. 200); one supposes that "visual space as it is has its own independent reality. It contains no subject. It is autonomous. It can be directly described (but we are far from knowing a form of expression which describes it). Ordinary physical language is related to it in an *extremely* complicated way, which we know instinctively" (Man. 107, 1). A phenomenological language would have the advantage of presenting such data more simply and directly, so with less danger of misunderstanding (Man. 105, 122; Man. 110, 98; Man. 213, 491–92; *BB* 51–52).

(9)   "However, could such propositions be used for communication? Wouldn't they be primary for the speaker but hypotheses for the one spoken to?" (Man. 109, 20). Russell had already noted the difficulty: "A logically perfect language, if it could be constructed, would not only be intolerably prolix, but, as regards its vocabulary, would be very largely private to one speaker. That is to say, all the names that it would use would be private to that speaker and could not enter into the language of another speaker" (*Logic*, 198). For Wittgenstein there was this further difficulty: He still felt the solipsistic temptation to say, "The only reality is *my* present experience" (*PP* 311).

(10)   "What the solipsist *means* is quite correct," he had written in the *Tractatus;* "only it cannot be *said,* but makes itself manifest" (5.62). How, though, does it manifest itself to others? How can it be rendered perspicuous to them and not just to myself that the pain I speak of when I say "I have a pain" is a real pain and not a mere hypothesis—a mere logical construction—like theirs? In *PB* 89 Wittgenstein en-

visaged various languages "which have different people as their center and all of which I understand". They are readily interchangeable and can take anyone as center, so in a sense are all on a par. However, "the one of which I am the center has a special status. It is specially adequate" (ibid.; cp. *PB* 102c; NL 299, 308–10). It is "the one in which, so to speak, I can say that I feel *real* pain" (*Kreis*, 50; cp. *BB* 72c; NL 277). But "how can I express this? That is, how can I correctly describe its advantage in words? This is not possible. For if I do so in the language which has me as center, it is no wonder if in a description of this language in its own terms it turns out to have an exceptional status; and when I use the form of expression of another language, my language assumes no privileged status whatever" (*PB* 89; cp. 5.62). "I could also express my claim," Wittgenstein later commented, "by saying: 'I am the vessel of life' [cp. Schopenhauer, *World*, II, 332; 5.621–5.63; *NB* 79]; but mark, it is essential that everyone to whom I say this should be unable to understand 'what I really *mean*', though in practice he might do what I wish by conceding to me an exceptional position in his notation. But I wish it to be *logically* impossible that he should understand me, that is to say, it should be meaningless, not false, to say that he understands me. Thus my expression is one of the many which is used on various occasions by philosophers and supposed to convey something to the person who says it, though essentially incapable of conveying anything to anyone else" (*BB* 64–65).

Schlick and the Vienna Circle

(11) "The genuine positivist," wrote Schlick, ". . . cannot possibly take the 'egocentric predicament' seriously" ("Meaning", 162). As we shall see, this declaration needs to be taken with a sizable grain of salt, especially in the case of Schlick himself. It does appear, however, that other aspects of Wittgenstein's transitional thought—for example his stress on verification as the criterion of sense (see the commentary on §353) and his search for a phenomenological language revealing expressions' sense—found a wider echo in the Vienna Circle. Carnap, for one, set out "to show that all meaningful statements (*Aussage*) could be reduced to primary statements. He chose as his base what he called 'the autopsychological', and endeavored to show how statements about physical objects, 'the heteropsychological' or other minds, and cultural objects are reducible to statements about bare unowned experiences. Accordingly he named the constructional programme 'methodological solipsism'. Other members of the Vienna Circle, e.g. Schlick and Feigl, though they disagreed with Carnap on some matters of detail, adopted a similar position" (Hacker, *Insight*, 187).

(12) Some put more stress on privacy: "The elements of a sentence,

words, designate in the ultimate analysis nothing but what can be pointed to, data of experience, that is. Such data are qualitative, like sensory qualities, qualities of feelings or other psychical qualities. But this qualitative content does not admit of linguistic communication. You cannot communicate qualitative content to somebody by means of words and sentences" (V. Kraft, *Circle*, 41–42; see Carnap, "Psychology", 192). "Thus words (signs) acquire on the one hand a *subjective* meaning, designating a qualitative content, on the other hand an *intersubjective* meaning capable of being communicated in that they designate but the structure of the given" (V. Kraft, *Circle*, 84; cp. Frege, *Writings*, 59–60).

(13)   This notion of a double meaning—private content and public form (Z 87)—is suggested already by 3.221; but Schlick, in whom the conception appears most clearly, followed a different lead: "Here we shall apply the method which seems to me the sole method of true philosophy: We shall turn our attention to the way in which propositions about physical objects are *verified*. . . . All propositions are tested with respect to their truth or falsity by the performance of certain operations, and to give an account of the meaning of the propositions consists in specifying these operations" ("Psychological", 396). But no operations can be specified by which quality is checked, whereas structure is publicly verifiable. When, for instance, I look at an object, my conscious content may differ systematically from others', but if I call the thing red so do they, and our spectral readings agree. On such happy coincidences is the possibility of physical language based (cp. *BB* 52a). "The meaning of all physical propositions thus consists in the fact that they formulate either coincidences or laws relating to coincidences; and these are spatio-temporal determinations" (Schlick, "Psychological", 398; cp. XXXIV, 1–2).

(14)   Since "the circumstances on which rests the universality of the physical language . . . are of an empirical rather than a logical character", it is possible, though difficult, to conceive a world in which "there would be no uniform one-to-one correspondence between coincidences and qualities [cp. XXXIV, 2, for Wittgenstein's similar suggestion]. Perhaps we can imagine this most easily if we consider *feelings*. I can, for example, imagine that my feeling of grief corresponded in no way to any bodily condition. If, for example, I laughed, skipped around, sang and told witty stories, no one would be able to conclude from this that I was gay, rather this behavior would be as compatible with a sorrowful as with a cheerful mood. Above all, and this is a significant point, it would have to be impossible for me to communicate my state of feeling under interrogation. I must not be able, even if I desired, to give information concerning my feelings. . . . For if I could say some-

thing concerning my feelings, then there would be spatially describable processes, namely, speech movements and speech sounds—by reference to which the feeling qualities could be unambiguously described, and that would contradict our hypothesis." In this situation our ordinary, 'physical' language "would no longer be universal, for in addition to it there would be a private language in which I could reflect about the world of feeling" (Schlick, "Psychological", 404–5).

(15)   Schlick proposed a kindred hypothesis concerning "a universe which contains no living being beside myself. . . . I can express facts to myself and communicate with myself—in fact, I do so every time when I take down something in my notebook or commit something to my memory. . . . You observe that for the essence of communication it makes no difference whether the notebook is what the metaphysician would call 'a mere dream' or possesses what he might call 'objective reality'. The marks in it, whether 'real' or 'imagined' (whatever that may mean) do express something, either correctly or incorrectly" ("Form", 178). On my own, without any linguistic experience or training, I could simply make up a language game and play it—by myself (cp. §§204–5).

(16)   It is significant that Waismann, too, advanced a hypothesis like Schlick's first: "If there were no such parallelism, if sensations of cold came and went without being associated in any way with bodily phenomena, so that no physical investigation, however careful, could disclose the conditions under which the sensation arose, I could still invent a word to designate this peculiar experience in a 'monologous' language, but I should get into difficulties as soon as I tried to explain its meaning to anyone else" (*Principles*, 258–59). It would be as in Wittgenstein's hypothesis of a blind man endowed with red phantasms: "*I* could not give the blind man an ostensive definition 'This is red.' But he could give himself one in his imagination" (Man. 110, 170). Such a quotation; the preceding numbers on Wittgenstein's views; the parallel between this thinking of Schlick and Waismann and that in XXIV, 2; the agreement between precisely those two members of the Vienna Circle who were most strongly influenced by Wittgenstein—all this evidence leaves little doubt about the paternity of the doctrine. And passages like *BB* 52 and Man. 116, 116–17 (quoted for §280) show how long such notions lingered. Only in the *Investigations* are they finally subjected to a thorough critique.

Wittgenstein's Critique

(17)   I shall suggest a fairly simple scheme which groups many of the points just made, indicates connections between them, and serves as a unified target of the main criticisms in this section; and I shall tie section and background still more tightly together by citing numbers in

the section and paragraphs in this introduction where each point comes most clearly to the surface. The scheme takes the form of a polysyllogism:

$$PE, K \rightarrow OM$$
$$OM, EM \rightarrow PM$$

where the abbreviations have the following general significance:

PE (Private Experience): Each person has only his own experience. For instance, he cannot feel another's pain, nor have the self-same visual impression of a color (§253; X, 3, 18).

K (Knowledge): We truly know only what we directly experience or deductively infer from experience (X, 3–5, 7, 13).

OM (Other Minds): So we cannot know others' experiences—whether, for instance, they feel pain when cut or have the same experience as we when they look at a red object (§§243, 246–50, 272, 303; X, 3–4).

EM (Experiential Meaning): Through private definition, names may be given to personal experiences (pains, visual sense-data, and the like), which then serve as criteria for the proper application of the terms (§§243–44, 256–58, 263–64; X, 4–6, 14–16).

PM (Private Meaning): Private meanings are therefore possible; that is, the meaning of terms employed by one person may be incommunicable to others, in whole (§§243, 256–61, 269; X, 4–5, 9, 14–16) or in part (§§275–80, 293; X, 10, 12–13). Private systems of signs such as mentalese, for ordinary objects (X, 2), or notations invented for the analytic translation of ordinary statements into descriptions of sense-data (X, 9, 11) are a fortiori conceivable, in virtue of similar projective hookups in the mind.

Most of these points are indicated in rapid succession in NL 276–78, and most appear in Frege (*Writings*, 60a, 79; *Foundations*, 36; "Thought", 299–302). See Hacker, "Frege".

(18) (*Private Experience*) Wittgenstein said early in his discussion of these matters "that the whole subject is 'extraordinarily difficult' because 'the whole field is full of misleading notations'; and that its difficulty was shown by the fact that the question at issue is the question between Realists, Idealists and Solipsists. And he also said, more than once, that many of the difficulties are due to the fact that there is a great temptation to confuse what are merely experiential propositions, which might, therefore, not have been true, with propositions which are necessarily true or are, as he once said, 'tautological or grammatical statements'. He gave, as an instance of a proposition of the latter sort, 'I can't feel your toothache,' saying that 'If you feel it, it isn't mine' is a 'matter of grammar', and also that 'I can't feel your toothache' means the same as ' "I feel your toothache" has no sense'; and he contrasted this with 'I hear my voice coming from somewhere near my eyes,'

which he said we think to be necessary, but which in fact is not necessary 'though it always happens' " (*PP* 306; see *BB* 54–55; cp. §§247,
251; Man. 229, §1249). Likewise, "in so far as it makes *sense* to say that
my pain is the same as his, it is also possible for us both to have the
same pain" (§253). No absolute, metaphysical barrier (*Z* 458) separates
mind from mind. (See Hacker, "Frege", 275.)

(19) (*Knowledge, Other Minds*) However, "the essential thing about private experience," in the sense that interested Wittgenstein, "is really not
that each person possesses his own exemplar, but that nobody knows
whether other people also have *this* or something else" (§272). "Only I
can know whether I am in pain," says the philosopher; "another person
can only surmise it" (§246). Yet in the ordinary sense of the word *know*,
"other people very often know when I am in pain" (§246; see §303). So
whence the impression that they never can? We notice, perhaps, that a
person may err in asserting "He is in pain" but not in asserting "I am in
pain," and we conclude that the evidence available in the first case—
wounds, words, grimaces, and groans—is inadequate and that only in
the second case does he have access to truly decisive evidence (the pain
itself). But in drawing this conclusion we overlook the possibility that
error and doubt are excluded by the language-game and not by the nature or immediacy of the evidence. The contrast is not between two
reports, one based on fallible, external clues and the other on fool-
proof, inner evidence, but between a report and an avowal, one following public criteria and the other following none (GI 15–16; X, 25;
§§246–48; NL 277–78; Man. 138, 28B, 30A). Thus Moore reports that
whereas in 1930–1931 Wittgenstein had proposed "I have a toothache"
as the paradigm of a proposition which has a "definite verification" (see
Man. 105, 108), by 1932–1933 he had decided that it cannot be verified
at all. If someone says "I have a toothache," it makes no sense to ask,
"How do you know you have?" (*PP* 266).

(20) (*Experiential Meaning*) For has he learned to identify pain as pain?
Does he possess an inner chart as it were, listing all the positions, degrees, and varieties of sensation which qualify as pain and all the
kindred feelings which fail to qualify? For words like *car* and *canary*
something analogous exists, in the form of familiar usage (§241), but
what about *pain*? The common, simplistic notion is that once a person
has somehow spotted the inner reference of the word, he has understood it fully (§264). Thereafter, whenever the same inner object appears directly in consciousness, he cannot err in his identification.
Memory is somehow rendered infallible. Thus once again (X, 18) a fact
of nature (standard human reactions) and a fact of grammar (the elimination of doubt and error) are conflated into a metaphysical theory.
Wittgenstein's answer is evident from the preceding section (IX): Un-

derstanding the meaning of the word does not consist in an atomic intuition of the whole future development, but principally in the development itself, this form of life (§241), all of us agreeing sufficiently (§242), especially in our behavior (§§288–90; cp. §§185–86). "What I do is not . . . to identify my sensation by criteria: but to repeat an expression" (§290). For even were pains as uniform a series as 2, 2, 2, nothing in the series would tell us how to continue (§214). And how does this inner series get started? Behind the idea of an infallible ascription lies the notion of a private ostensive definition: If I am to apply the word correctly to my experiences, somebody must show me the correct way. But they can't; so I do (§362). There is the pernicious notion (§380). (On this paragraph, see Hunter, *Essays*, 134–43.)

(21) *(Private Meaning)* The assignment of new meanings to personal signs is problematic enough when the person fixing the meanings already knows a language, which he can utilize in the process ("In the future I shall do so-and-so") and from which he can derive ready-made semantic categories and concepts ("I shall use this sign as a substantive designating sensations of this quality and intensity"). But the notion of private definition becomes especially problematic and perilous when the performance is attributed to someone who is acquiring language for the first time (§§257, 262), for instance a child (cp. §32), or Schlick's solitary speaker in X, 16. It is problematic because, as we have seen (II, 3–12), the means available to such a person are inadequate for the task; attending to the present experience, addressing it, imagining future experiences—none of this establishes a rule or a technique (see commentary on §258). The notion is dangerous because a sign thus independently introduced might be used with equal independence. Doing the "same" would no longer be a custom, a practice (§208), and correctness would no longer be agreement with others (§§241–42), but obedience to a mystic mental hookup between sign and thing (§38). The terrain thus would be prepared for private meanings and languages (X, 17), for instance mentalese (X, 2); for falsified schemes of our mental life, such as the picture theory, with its pinpoint names (GI 37–38); for the problem of other minds (X, 17, 24); and, at the extreme, for idealism or solipsism (§§402–3).

(22) *(Introspective Method)* The methodological implications deserve special attention. As a child learning the use of a word like *pain* is not led to pick out the inner referent by himself, so the philosopher in search of the referent cannot spot it on his own, through introspective examination. How would he know what to look for, there in the inner stream (p. 231)? And even if the child and the philosopher did somehow identify a referent, that would not give them the use of the word (§264; see §370). They would understand it no better than a person

who sees an object pointed at (say a pencil) and hears the words "This is tove," but has no idea as yet whether *tove* designates the color, hardness, size, cost, use, shape, or what-have-you (*BB* 2). For the inner referent too is not just painful, but mine, momentary, sharp, unpleasant, worrisome, unexpected, recurring, localized, and so on. And the fact that it is personal whereas the pencil is public does not mar this parallel (*BB* 4). Thus "it shews a fundamental misunderstanding, if I am inclined to study the headache I have now in order to get clear about the philosophical problem of sensation" (§314; cp. §182c) or if I watch myself thinking in order to get clear about the meaning of *think* (§316). As a mere gaze did not establish the meaning, so a mere gaze cannot now reveal it.

(23)   (*Private Language*) Or rather, the hypothesis is not intelligible; nor, therefore, are the varied views which rest on it (GI 68). A private language like Schlick's, we might take Wittgenstein to be saying, is not a language at all: Here, finally (§243), the frontier is crossed; there comes a transition "from quantity to quality" (§284; see §§200, 385). But *what* quality? To the philosophical query "Is a private language possible?" the correct answer is: "That depends on what you mean by 'private' " (cp. §47f). And for all the theories here reviewed, that is not an answer but a rejection of the question (ibid.). For what is Schlick's solitary speaker (X, 15) supposed to do with his words (cp. §260)? What is their relation to ours (cp. §§261, 342)? And when it is said (X, 10, 12–13) that all our sensation words have a double sense, does this mean that we constantly inform ourselves of just how it is within (§280; NL 276mn)? Is the one meaning just like the other, only privately established?

(24)   (*Other Minds*) If no one else ever learns the secret content and neither do I, it is not a content; it drops out of the game entirely (§293). It comes back in only if we recognize another sort of game, in which we express our feelings but do not identify them and in which this and other expressions permit other people to know our inner experience. Schlick cannot have it both ways: the model of "object and designation" *and* a private designatum (ibid.). Nor can the skeptic: If his words of doubt designate anything at all, it must be in virtue of a regular connection with the very thing he claims to doubt. If, for instance, there were no pain but his, the word *pain* would not be a name for it, and he could not put his doubt into words (NL 316). "Scepticism is *not* irrefutable, but *obvious nonsense* if it tries to doubt where no question can be asked" (*NB* 44; see *NB* 51k; 6.51). "If you are not certain of any fact, you cannot be certain of the meaning of your words either" (OC 114; see OC 24, 369–70, 383, 456; PB 203c; Man. 109, 299;

Hacker, *Insight*, 278–79; concerning more complex cases, starting with rain, see the commentary on §354).

(25) (*Knowledge*) Wittgenstein did not simply suggest an alternative reply to skepticism; he rejected the classic one, common to varied traditions. When Descartes cited "I think" as an irrefutable truth, he spoke for generations of rationalist disciples, for Augustine before him, and for empiricists like Russell after him (X, 3). All viewed immediate, personal experience as immune to doubt. And so it is, said Wittgenstein; but not because our knowledge is so sure. In most cases it does not make sense to say we do or do not know our own present pains, doubts, wishes, intentions, and the like (§246, p. 221). And when it does make sense, the knowledge is not assured *a priori* (p. 221); we can then say, for instance, "I don't know myself what I wish for" (§441). Since even benevolent readers may feel skeptical about this position, I shall suggest in brief, dialogue form the reasonable defense that Wittgenstein might present (see also the detailed commentaries on §§246, 441b, and p. 221):

Wittgenstein: "I would like to reserve the expression *know* for the cases in which it is used in normal linguistic exchange (*OC* 260; §116). And no one save a philosopher ever says 'I *know* I have a pain.'"

Objection: "Neither does anyone who is standing in a downpour say, 'I know it is raining.' The assertion may be futile, since its truth is so obvious, but it is meaningful and true nonetheless; he does know it is raining (cp. p. 180b; *OC* 431, 460–61, 464; Man. 232, 676, 678; Man. 138, 16A; Searle, *Speech Acts*, 141–42)."

Wittgenstein: "Yes, because there are criteria (*OC* 540) which he sees satisfied: drops of water, from clouds, at the moment of speech, nearby (§354). But statements about one's own pains have no such basis (§290). Much less are they based on reasoning. So your claim of knowledge suggests a nonexistent parallel (p. 221)."

Objection: "The difference is merely one of complexity versus simplicity. The criteria for rain are complex, those for pain are simple—as simple as the color red."

Wittgenstein: "Even were that so (see X, 19–21), what about the criteria for *having* pain? The person who has pain is the one who gives it expression, for instance the one who says he is in pain (§302 and commentary). But does he observe himself saying he has pain and thereby learn the truth of his own statement (*BB* 68a; NL 310–11; §404)? Our relation to our own words is entirely different from other people's (p. 192b)."

Objection: "Maybe so. But knowledge is also a disposition, an ability, revealed in word and act. And a person who has a pain reveals typical characteristics of knowledge when he tells his doctor about it, takes an aspirin, and so on. So he does know he is in pain (see *OC* 397, 431; cp. NL 314bc)."

Wittgenstein: "This answer suffers from several difficulties. First, it supposes the thing to be proved. For why take these subsequent words and actions as signs of knowledge? Why not, say, of fear (§§472–74)? Second, it is difficult to imagine circumstances in which a person would use the words 'I know I am in pain' to predict his own ability to take an aspirin, inform the doctor, and so on (*OC* 588–90). Third, if that were the sense of the sentence, it would no longer state the kind of infallible truth philosophers are interested in (*OC* 409, 520–21, 580; Malcolm, *Memoir*, 91). And it is their claims, the only ones in which this use of *know* occurs, which I am answering (*OC* 406–8, 481–83, 553–54). They have viewed all inferential knowledge of fact as approaching this ideal terminus: immediate awareness (X, 3). But awareness of a sensation is not knowledge that I am in pain. The proposition is not a sensation, and does not logically follow from a sensation (§486 and commentary). That step is taken when I learn the language (X, 20; cp. §381). Thus the terminus at which all sane doubt ends is not the indubitable but the undoubted (*OC* 143–44, 160, 165–66, 374–75, 450, 472). We simply agree in what we say (§241). Concerning this ungrounded agreement in judgments (§242), we should say, 'This language-game is played,' and not (unless we wish to perpetuate the misconceptions of millennia): 'These things are known for sure' (I, 5; *OC* 204; Man. 232, 679, quoted for §116a; Man. 159, quoted for p. 221a)."

DETAILED COMMENTARY

§243   See Hacker, *Insight*, 221–22; Cooke, "Private", 29–30.

(a) Here two quick intermediate cases (§122a) connect the previous section with the new one; W. proceeds from the agreed and common games of the preceding numbers to the supposed private game of (*b*), via one-man but derived and intelligible language-games, then one-man and nonderived but still intelligible language-games, thus delimiting the sort of hypotheses to be considered in Section X. The orders, obeying, and so on, here at the start of (*a*) would not be such in the primary sense of these terms, but would be in a common, perfectly respectable sense (cp. §§282c, 364, 385–86, 531–32, pp. 216, 220). The second supposition, however, is more difficult to work out (besides the preceding, see §§344–45; Teichman, "Persons", 146–48). "It seems possible, and indeed probable, that . . . Wittgenstein was as it were making a *maximum concession* to any readers who might be attracted to the idea of a 'private language theory' of the origins of language and meaning. This maximum concession, however, consists of an atypical and under-described example" (Teichman, ibid.).

(b) See X, 15; cp. Man. 110, 20–21, 62.

But could we also . . . : "He would have to play language-games with himself—and that he can do *for sure:* think of a Robinson Crusoe, who employs a language for his own private use; imagine that you watched him do it," as in §207, but discovered regularities (Man. 116, 117).

Well, can't we do so . . . : cp. X, 15. "The private language. The game someone plays with himself. When do we call it a *game*? If it resembles a public game. The diary of Robinson Cr." (Man. 166; W.'s English). "Signs linked with the natural expression of the sensation. Then the diary is intelligible to all. But what if there is no natural expression of the sensation?" (Man. 179).

that is not what I mean: it would be a private use of a public language, not a private language (§256).

what can only be known . . . : see X, 3–4, 13; §§246–49; NL 276 (" 'I know what I mean by "toothache", but the other person can't *know* it' ").

his immediate private sensations: in the philosophical sense of *private* (X, 19). "Of course Wittgenstein did not want to deny the obvious truth that people have a 'private' mental life, in the sense that they have for example thoughts they do not utter and pains they do not show; nor did he try to analyse away this truth in a neo-behaviouristic fashion. In one of his lectures he mentioned Lytton Strachey's imaginative description of Queen Victoria's dying thoughts. He expressly repudiated the view that such a description is meaningless because 'unverifiable'; it has meaning, he said, but only through its connexion with a wider, public, 'language-game' of describing people's thoughts; he used the simile that a chess-move worked out in a sketch of a few squares on a scrap of paper has significance through its connexion with the whole practice of playing chess" (Geach, *Mental Acts,* 3).

So another person cannot . . . : see X, 4–5, 9–10, 12–17; Hacker, *Insight,* 233. After an interlude explained by X, 17, and the opening remarks of §256, this suggestion is taken up again in §256.

"One sometimes hears that such a phrase as 'This is here,' when while I say it I point to a part of my visual field, has a kind of primitive meaning to me, although it can't impart information to anybody else" (*BB* 65).

§244   See p. 218bc; Z 545; NL 293, 301d, 302d; Moore, *Commonplace,* 44; cp. Mauthner, *Beiträge,* I, 17.

A basic, underlying concern of this number is the idea of private ostensive definition, with all its consequences (II, 9; X, 17, 21). This concern is not confined to *pain* or even to psychological expressions. The main point of the number applies to *red* as much as it does to *pain:* The language-game starts with reactions, not with translations from menta-lese, or ingenious calculations concerning the grammar of this new lan-guage (as though the child already knew all about the parts and pat-terns of speech). The movement of the number as a whole illustrates W.'s opposition to simplistic alternatives, whether introspectionism and dualism on the one hand (*a*) or behaviorism and physicalism on the other (*b*). (See GI 45; *RFM* 63f, 99i.)

On private ostensive definition, see X, 20–22; Z 545; Man. 229, §§971, 975–76; cp. §417a; *LC* 2a. "We would like to say: 'If a person is not acquainted with sweet, bitter, red, green, tones, and pains, we can-not get him to understand what these words mean,' whereas if he hasn't yet eaten a sour apple, we can explain to him what that means. Red is just *this*, and *this*, and *this*. But when we say this, we must really point out what these words mean; that is, we must show something red, taste something bitter, or have it tasted, cause oneself or the other pain, etc. *And not think that it is possible to point privately to one's pain*" (Man. 229, §866). At this point, apply §362 to the present case.

On reactions at the start, before reasoning, see I, 5; p. 218bc; *LC* 2a.

On the basic similarity of *pain* to other terms, in addition to the quo-tation above from Man. 229 see §§379–81, 601, and the quotations for them. Note, for instance, the parallel between §381 (*red*) and §384 (*pain*).

(a) See NL 312e; Pitcher, *Philosophy*, 301; contrast with Russell, *Inquiry*, 126–27.

How do words *refer* . . . : see NL 315def.

There doesn't seem to be any problem: "The idea is here that there is an 'expression' for everything, that we know what it means 'to express something', 'to describe something'. Here is a feeling, an expe-rience, and now I could say to someone 'express it!' " (NL 312; cp. §304). See §27a; NL 309hi; cp. Russell in X, 4, and Schlick in X, 15.

But how is the connexion . . . : "One is inclined to say 'we *mean* this feeling by its expression,' but what is meaning a feeling by a word like? Is this quite clear if, e.g., I have explained what 'meaning this person by the name "N" ' is like?" (NL 312; see Z 434). "It seems to us as if one spoke *of* a sensation by directing one's attention to it" (§669).

how does a human being learn the meaning: see §5b; *BB* 17a; and especially *LC* 1–2, quoted for §5a. The misconception to be dissipated here is that of our being shown a pain, or pointing it out to ourselves, and thereby learning when to say "I have a pain." This picture is re-placed by another (§144), not by a causal hypothesis (seen from that perspective, W.'s account would appear unsatisfactory). Notice, too, how this move corrects W.'s former one-sided stress on mode of verification as *the* determinant of meaning, so avoids the behavioristic conclusion to which it leads (*PB* 94g–95a; *Kreis*, 244).

As III, 1–2, point out, between learning and use there is discontinuity as well as continuity. Thus no automatic connection can be made between §244, which stresses the absence of criteria and replaces crying with "I have a pain," and §281, which asserts the need of outer criteria in third-person predications. A more likely point of continuity is suggested by p. 174g–j and p. 189: What starts as a verbal reaction may continue as such. And when no private definition occurs at the start no private meaning follows. Concerning the continuity and discontinuity between crying and verbal pain-behavior, see the commentary on (*b*).

of the word "pain" for example: given the broad scope of this section, one perhaps wonders why W. concentrated on sensation expressions and in particular on *pain*. Many reasons suggest themselves. For one thing, this concept is simpler than those that follow, so therapeutically preferable (§5). Pain has no object, for instance, and no target; so problems of intentionality and correspondence (GI 34–35) do not arise to complicate the discussion. For another thing, no fluctuation of sense occurs similar to that for *wish* (§441). W., the one-time atomist, may also have preferred this example "because there is little inclination to regard it as analyzable into other concepts, and also because pains are genuinely objects of attention, not 'dissolving' when Wittgenstein's technique of description is brought to bear. It would seem that there could not be a more perfect example of a simple concept obtained from introspection" (Malcolm, *Problems*, 55; see *PG* 80a). This last remark alerts us to the possibility that here too W. employed "the method of §2" (see the commentary on §48a), picking the sample which appeared most favorable to the views he opposed, and showing their inadequacy even there. Russell's remarks tend to confirm this hypothesis: "Sight and hearing are the most public of the senses; smell only a trifle less so; touch, again, a trifle less, since two people can only touch the same spot successively, not simultaneously. Taste has a sort of semi-publicity, since people seem to experience similar taste-sensations when they eat similar foods; but the publicity is incomplete, since two people cannot eat actually the same piece of food. But when we pass on to bodily sensations—headache, toothache, hunger, thirst, the feeling of fatigue, and so on—we get quite away from publicity, into a region where other people can tell us what they feel, but cannot directly observe their feeling" (*Mind*, 118; paragraph division omitted; see *Logic*, 295). Here, if anywhere, is a realm of "private meanings", introspectible, designatable, simple. They approach closest to the referents W. envisaged for his phenomenological language (X, 8), for example "colors of spots in a visual image, which would now be independent of any spatial or physical interpretation, since here there is neither illumination, nor shadow, nor brightness, etc. etc." (Man. 176, 16A, in another connection; see *BB* 47a).

These remarks indicate how mistaken it would be to object that the single sample chosen differs importantly even from other sensations (Man. 229, §1564) and still more from the concepts W. goes on to consider in later sections. That is why he chose this sample. For he had therapy, not theory, in view (GI 8, 28–29, 70; X, 1). And his therapy was really that, not formal refutation; so it rests on no implicit "premises" (GI 68). W. noted what many critics apparently have not, that the very multiplicity of importantly different cases shows how misleading it would be to claim, for instance, that *pain* names a sensation (as though it too were a name just like any other) and how futile it would be, on the other hand, to claim that it does not name a sensation (as though a clear distinction were thereby drawn and the logic of sensation-words laid bare) (Z 434; Man. 229, §972). Blanket terms like *refer* (§§244, 274), *describe* (§§290–91, p. 189), and *name* (§§37–38) clarify nothing, but the differences they paper over do. The question, therefore, is not *whether* the word *pain* is connected with the feeling, but *how*. Calling it the "reference" settles nothing. See GI 70; Malcolm, "Investigations", 206.

Here is one possibility: for another, see §288a. In choosing this one, W. does not load the dice. For therapeutic purposes and against *a priori* pictures and necessities, one counterexample suffices (GI 58). Schlick's general requirement of ostensive definition, for instance (see II, 8), which suggests inner pointing in the case of pain, is eliminated (see II, 10–11).

expressions of the sensation: for highly relevant remarks, see §142.

new pain-behaviour: see Man. 229, §979; Man. 138, 20A; cp. p. 190; Man. 228, §288.

"We have already seen reasons to reject the idea that Wittgenstein meant to answer the sceptic on his own terms and so thought of behaviour as 'bodily movements'. Indeed, it is by rejecting this very notion of 'body' and 'bodily movement' that Wittgenstein undercuts the whole problem" (Cook, "Human Beings", 131–32). Thus the child's cries are not mere noises; he has *hurt* himself. Even were there equivalence between the new behavior and the old (see below), it would be an equivalence between the forms of *pain* behavior.

"Wittgenstein presents us with the suggestion that the first-person sentences are to be thought of as similar to the natural nonverbal, behavioral expressions of psychological states. 'My leg hurts,' for example, is to be assimilated to crying, limping, holding one's leg. This is a bewildering comparison and one's first thought is that two sorts of things could not be more unlike. By saying the sentence one can make a *statement;* it has a *contradictory;* it is *true* or *false;* in saying it one *lies* or *tells the truth;* and so on. None of these things, exactly, can be said of crying, limping, holding one's leg. So how can there be any resemblance? But Wittgenstein knew this when he deliberately likened such a sentence to 'the primitive, the natural, expressions' of pain, and said that it is 'new pain-behavior'. . . . This analogy has at least two important merits: first, it breaks the hold on us of the question 'How does one *know when to say* "My leg hurts"?', for in the light of the analogy this will be as nonsensical as the question 'How does one know when to cry, limp, or hold one's leg?'; second, it explains how the utterance of a first-person psychological sentence by another person can have *importance* for us, although not as an identification—for in the light of the analogy it will have the same importance as the natural behavior which serves as our preverbal criterion of the psychological states of others" (Malcolm, "Knowledge", 383; see GI 16).

(b) See GI 16; NL 295–97, 301cdn, 302g; cp. §179bc, p. 209; *RFM* 159bcd; Man. 138, 5–6, 31B.

"The first point is this that this verbal expression is in the first person used to replace an *expression* of pain. So that if some people say that 'having pain' in the end refers to pain behaviour we can answer them that 'I have pain' does not refer to pain behavior but *is* a pain behaviour. It corresponds to a cry of pain not to the statement I am crying" (Man. 166; W.'s English).

"So you are saying . . .": members of the Vienna Circle spoke in this way, for instance Carnap: "In what follows, we intend to explain and to establish the thesis that *every sentence of psychology may be formulated in physical language.* To express this in the material mode of speech: *all sentences of psychology describe physical occurrences, namely the physical behavior of humans and other animals.* This is a sub-thesis of the general thesis of *physicalism* to the effect that *physical language is a universal language,* that is, a language into which every sentence may be translated" ("Psychology", 165). "So statements which seemed to report the individual's private experience had to be reconstrued as referring to the state of his body, or to his behaviour, in which his use of language was included" (Ayer, "Circle", 82). See V. Kraft, *Circle,* 163–64; Malcolm, *Problems,* 80–84; Waismann, in *Kreis,* 244; Schlick, *Aufsätze,* 175; cp. NL 293i.

replaces crying: an echo of W.'s earlier view that verbal signs translate primitive ones (see the commentary on §32b). Now, however, the remark does not indicate equivalence. Words of praise are not equivalent to a smile, nor are words of blame equivalent to a frown; they are different expressions, though still of approval or disapproval (*LC* 2a). Consider too the case of proper names, introduced by pointing, which then drops out of the game; W. stressed the difference between the pointing, which requires a referent, and the name, which does not (III, 2; cp. *PG* 89b, 90c). "Our language-game is an *extension* of primitive behaviour" (*Z* 545; my italics; see NL 293i). Hence it should not be supposed that "I am in pain" is always forced from us, like a shriek (*BB* 155b) or a cry (pp. 189, 197d). Nor, in particular, may inferences be drawn concerning the referring or nonreferring use of the expression. "When we feel that we wish to abolish the 'I' in 'I have pain,' one may say that we tend to make the verbal expression of pain similar to the expression by moaning.—We are inclined to forget that it is the particular use of a word only which gives the word its meaning" (*BB* 69; see Malcolm, above). And even with respect to the learning of the word, "he emphasized the fact that in teaching the child the use of 'in pain' we not only point to others who are moaning, perhaps, but also pinch the child until it hurts, and say, 'That's pain'" (Wisdom, "Wittgenstein", 48; see §288a, and Man. 229, §866, above).

"In what sense does the verbal expression 'replace' the non-verbal expression? In the sense, I think, that other persons will react to the child's mere words in the same way that they previously reacted to his nonverbal sensation-behavior; they will let the mere words serve as a *new* criterion of his feelings" (Malcolm, "Investigations", 192).

does not describe it: cp. *Z* 471.

§245 See *OC* 359; NL 301f, 310–13; *PB* 54c; Man. 228, §4; Man. 116, 243; Man. 107, 157; Kenny, "Privacy", 367–68; cp. GI 15–16; *Z* 541; *EPB* 204; *BB* 137bcd; *PG* 164d; *PB* 87d, 282b; Man. 302, 22. The word *denn,* so placed, suggests a certain surprise, not a logical connection; thus the question stands on its own, as a separate *Bemerkung.* To indicate its purpose and its connection with §244, we may add *for* (as in the translation) or *then,* depending on which of the following interpretations we choose:

(1) "For how can I be so wrong-headed as to interpose another linguistic step—the descriptive one (§244b)—between pain and its linguistic expression. *Expression* of *pain* is not mediated by a *description* of *behavior.*" In this interpretation, the query would be aimed still at Carnap's physicalese (see above).

(2) "How, then, if a linguistic expression like pain signifies via nonlinguistic ones, can I wish to step between pain and its expression, with a private language of pain, and apply names to the bare sensations themselves" (see Malcolm, "Investigations", 206; Cook, "Solipsism", 44–45). In this interpretation, the movement from §244b to §245 paral-

lels that from (*c*) to (*d*) on p. 179. From his vain efforts to construct a phenomenological language (X, 8) W. came to recognize both that ordinary sensation expressions signify via outer connections such as that just indicated, and that the contrary is not conceivable; it is not possible simply to pick out an inner referent and label it (X, 20). This reading has the advantage of indicating the relevance of §244 for the question of privacy raised in §243 and resumed in §256. However, so does the following interpretation.

(3) "How, then, if the verbal expression is similar to a cry, can I wish to interpose rules, criteria, recognition and the like, between it and the pain?" Numerous passages back this reading. See e.g. §§379–80, 597; *EPB* 193, 196; *BB* 128g, 130e; NL 312h, 315j; cp. §§239, 290, 362, 404; commentary on §32b; *EPB* 204; *BB* 68a, 137b; Russell, *Outline*, 77 ("The association seems to go, not direct from stimulus to words, but from stimulus to 'meaning' and thence to words expressing the 'meaning' "); *Inquiry*, 204 ("I call language 'spontaneous' when there is no verbal intermediary between the external stimulus and the word or words"). Texts like the following suggest more specifically that W. is criticizing his own former conception of language as a calculus (§81), whose rules, hidden in the medium of the understanding (§102), dictate one's every word: "One would like to say that one correlates the words with reality according to a rule. But that is false, for the rule would run: 'Say "p" if p is the case' " (Man. 108, 205; see 216c; cp. Sellars, *Science*, 333). However, "in order to describe a reality I must see it already articulated.—I have *already, in a certain way,* translated the reality into the proposition & have thus already fixed the use of language" (Man. 109, 228). For more in the same vein, see the commentary on §292. Such self-sufficient operations of the mind would lend ready support to private meanings and languages (see §§258, 262–64).

For still another interpretation, see Hintikka, "Private Language", 423–24.

§246 See §303; *PG* 44d; NL 278–79, 283–84, 289, 304–5, 309–10, 314–15, 319; cp. *PG* 83b.

(a) See commentary on §681; *Z* 538; *BB* 46, 48d, 53e–54a; Man. 232, 753, 756–58; Man. 229, §1677; Malcolm, "Philosophy", 329–36; cp. *BB* 60b; *PG* 82a; Man. 229, §§1232–34, 1241; Moore, *Problems*, 77c.

In what sense . . . : two main senses are considered: (1) only I can know them (here); (2) only I can have them (§§253–54). See X, 17–18.

only I can know . . . : see X, 3, 5, 7, 9, 13, 19; Moore, *Papers*, 42c, and *Commonplace*, 173–74; Russell, *Outline*, 224–25, and *Mind*, 132; cp. §156f; Augustine, *Confessions*, I, 6, 8.

"That it is felt in the same way, that my feelings of it resemble yours, is something of which we never can be sure, but which we assume as the simplest hypothesis that meets the case. As a matter of fact, we never *are* sure of it" (James, *Meaning*, 37; see 39).

"One wants to say," therefore—as W. momentarily did (X, 7)—"that nothing that goes on in the outer world is really known, but only what happens in the domain of what are called sense-data" (*OC* 90).

In one way this . . . : the first part is nonsense (knowing my own pain), the second is wrong (not knowing another's pain). For a parallel case, see p. 223j.

and how else are we . . . : see §116.

other people very often know: see X, 19; §303; Black, "Relations", 27; Malcolm, "Certainty", 24–25; cp. *EPB* 229. To appreciate W.'s approach, consider *what* supposedly renders knowledge impossible: not feeling pain, nor even feeling pain in his body, but feeling *his* pain. Only that would satisfy the skeptic. But the hypothesis does not make sense; it is ruled out by grammar. Nor therefore does the denial make sense (Man. 176, 48). So we need some other criterion for knowing his pain. But what criterion? Well, the ordinary one—the one that permits us to say we know he is in pain.

not with the certainty . . . : see XXXVIII, 2.

It can't be said of me . . . : for a long treatment, see X, 25. See also Cook, "Privacy", 290–94; Coope, "Knowledge", 246–48; Malcolm, "Defending"; cp. §679; Schlick, *Aufsätze*, 190. Various strands can be distinguished in W.'s critique:

(1) *Contrast:* "I can't be said to know that I have toothache if I can't be said not to know that I have toothache. I can't be said to know indirectly what the other has if I can't be said to know it directly. The misleading picture is this: I see my own matchbox but I know only from hearsay what his looks like. We can't say: 'I say he has toothache because I observe his behavior, but I say that I have because I *feel* it' " (NL 319). "Here is the picture: he sees it directly, I only indirectly. But such is not the case. He doesn't see something & describe it for us" (Man. 176, 48A). See §251; *OC* 58 (quoted for §247a); *PB* 98f.

(2) *Verification:* "One says 'I know' where one can also say 'I believe' or 'I suspect'; where one can find out" (p. 221). (For exceptions, see Malcolm, *Memoir*, 89–90.) And I do not *learn* about my sensations (§246b). "In this connection he said later, first, that the meaning of 'verification' is different, when we speak of verifying 'I have' from what it is when we speak of verifying 'He has', and then, later still, that there is no such thing as a verification for 'I have', since the question 'How do you know that you have toothache?' is nonsensical" (*PP* 307).

(3) *Falsification:* "These philosophers want to make a *logical* point. They want to say we don't know something to be true if future experi-

ence can disprove it. There are kinds of statements that future experience cannot refute, e.g. sense-datum statements, and mathematical or
logical statements. To use 'I know' with sense-datum statements is silly.
It adds nothing. In mathematics it isn't silly. And there is a close resemblance between some experiential statements and mathematical ones—
namely, future experience won't provide reasons for rejecting them"
(Malcolm's notes, *Memoir*, 91; see also 90).

(4) *Doubt:* "One thinks that the words 'I know that . . .' are always in
place where there is no doubt, and hence even where the expression of
doubt would be unintelligible" (*OC* 10). But this is wrong (p. 221).
Hence the words are out of place in talk of one's own present sensations, for in this game doubt is ruled out (§§246c, 288; *OC* 58, quoted
for §247a). To object that doubt might arise in borderline cases of pain
supposes a false parallel with words like *table* and *red* (§304).

(5) *Utility:* "When in a metaphysical sense I say 'I *must* always know
when I have pain,' this simply makes the word 'know' redundant; and
instead of 'I know that I have pain,' I can simply say, 'I have pain' " (*BB*
55; see §520; cp. *OC* 460; 3.328).

(6) *Setting:* see GI 14. Such a statement as "I know I am in pain,"
"used in an *unsuitable* situation, seems not to be nonsense but rather
seems matter-of-course, only because one can fairly easily imagine a
situation to fit it" (*OC* 10; see *OC* 622). Thus Moore suggested this
sample sentence: "I know it's an important meeting and I'm expected, but I also know I have a headache." The context of such a
statement differs from that of the philosopher (§§514, 520), and he is
W.'s concern.

except perhaps that . . . : see *OC* 585–89; *BB* 55 (above, re Utility);
Locke, "Pains", 149–50; Kenny, "Privacy", 363–64; cp. §417a; *OC* 424;
5.47321; Moore, *Commonplace*, 174 ("that I have a pain is something
which *couldn't be the case without my knowing it*"); Russell, "Relevance", 50
("There is a sense in which I know an experience merely because I
have it").

(b) It has been suggested that these words be attributed to a Cartesian
adversary (Gustafson, "A Note", 143–44; cp. Man. 108, 241). But see,
for instance, p. 221e, and Murphy, "Another Note".

Other people cannot: this can be read two ways: (1) it would be an
error to say so, since the supposed contrast between learning directly,
through observation of behavior, is nonexistent; (2) it would be meaningless to say so, since the supposed alternative, and therefore the
whole contrast, is senseless. (See the quotation and reference above, re
Contrast.)

(c) For explanation, see §288 and *BB* 30c. See also §441a and this addition to it in Man. 228, §245: "We interpret the lack of doubt as a *knowl-*

edge." See *BB* 67a; *PP* 307b; cp. §679, pp. 184ab, 190i–192f, 221a, 222bcd; *BB* 21d, 71d; *PB* 258b; Man. 302, 10.

Many philosophers have said it is impossible to be mistaken about one's own feelings, or to doubt them. For W., all *a priori,* noncausal impossibilities were grammatical. If you can conceive something, it could happen; if you can't conceive it, that is because of the terms used in stating it. It is eliminated by the rules of the game. The only alternative here is a classical synthetic *a priori* intuition, joining knowledge and pain. But this requires that language provide an invariant sense of *know* which applies automatically in the case of sensations; for usage gives no more specific indication of what it might mean to say "I know I am in pain" (X, 25). This notion of a meaning accompanying a word into every context has been criticized in §117, which is basic for understanding §246.

§247 Again, W. suggests a grammatical interpretation of the apparently metaphysical *can* (*BB* 55). "Both about Solipsism and about Idealism he had insisted earlier that neither of them pretends that what it says is learnt by experience—that the arguments for both are of the form 'you can't' or 'you must', and that both these expressions 'cut (the statement in question) out of our language' " (*PP* 311; see X, 18).

(a) Cp. *OC* 36; *PP* 274c–275.

One might: see the commentary on p. 221c. P. 192 suggests how difficult it would be to find an alternative interpretation, factual and contingent. Without this saving context of explaining the meaning of the word, W.'s verdict would doubtless be the same for this statement as for the one in §246a: in one sense wrong, and in another nonsense. For we sometimes do know others' intentions (cp. *EPB* 229). And "if 'I know etc.' is conceived as a grammatical proposition, of course the 'I' cannot be important. And it properly means 'There is no such thing as a doubt in this case' or 'The expression "I do not know" makes no sense in this case.' And of course it follows from this that 'I *know*' makes no sense either" (*OC* 58).

(b) See p. 224g; cp. *OC* 24, 32, 57–59; *BB* 54a. This remark might be more helpful if placed at the end of (*a*), which is hardly intelligible without it. Told that "Only you can know if you had that intention" indicates how the word *intention* is used, we would naturally infer that only a person himself speaks of knowing his intention, whereas W. held just the opposite view. He is thinking rather of the limited analogy between lack of doubt where we know and lack of doubt where doubt is senseless. Cp. *BB* 30, quoted for p. 221e.

§248 See *PG* 82c; Man. 302, 11; Cook, "Privacy", 297.

"Do not say 'one cannot', but say instead: 'it doesn't exist in this game.' Not: 'one can't castle in draughts' but—'there is no castling in draughts'; and instead of 'I can't exhibit my sensation'—'in the use of the word "sensation", there is no such thing as exhibiting what one has got' " (Z 134).

"That is, you did not state that knowing was a goal which you could not reach, and that you have to be contented with conjecturing; rather, there is no goal in this game. Just as when one says 'You can't count through the whole series of cardinal numbers,' one doesn't state a fact about human frailty but about a convention which we have made. Our statement is not comparable, though always falsely compared, with such a one as 'it is impossible for a human being to swim across the Atlantic'; but it *is* analogous to a statement like 'there is no goal in an endurance race' " (BB 54).

Thus the parallel temptation would be to say: "I can't play your game of patience" (whereas I can play your game of football).

§249 See p. 229b and commentary; NL 295c, 296b; Man. 138, 27B, 28B.

Are we perhaps . . . : still on the theme of private sensations, W. is asking in effect: "What of an infant's happiness or pleasure? Is it private, unknowable?" Cartesian doubt might permit us to suppose that adults only pretend to be glad, but what of infants who have not learned the game of pretense? Do the clever little devils know what feelings we expect to go with smiles, and mix the signals (cp. Anscombe, "Pretending", 306–7)? "Not every being which can express fear, joy, pain can feign it. . . . Only in a quite precise setting can something be an expression of pain, but only in a much more extensively determined setting can there be simulation of pain" (Man. 138, 19A). "What must a child learn, before it can pretend? For instance, the use of words like: 'He believes I am in pain, but I'm not.' A child experiences that it is treated kindly when for instance it cries in pain; now it cries so as to be treated that way. This would be no pretense, but only a root of pretense" (ibid., 19B; divisions omitted; see 20A).

And on what experience . . . : the argument from analogy would say we conclude from similarity in behavior to similarity of sensations, feelings, and so on. And we adults still do smile with pleasure, though we don't generally wail when distressed. But this similarity would not help us with the question whether the child is pretending. For the child is doing just what a child should do if it wanted to simulate pleasure. What is lacking is not just a plausible motive, but a whole background and setting. See above, and Z 570–71.

A skeptic who suggested that even infant smiles might be pretense would be supposing that all behavior might always be pretense. "But then this concept would be unusable, for pretending would have no criteria in behaviour" (Z 571; cp. §§344–45). So W.'s question might be reworded thus: "What conclusive evidence could there be if even this doesn't settle the matter? What would be better evidence than the baby's smile?"

§250   See the references and comments for §249. Cp. §357, pp. 174bc, 228j–229b; Z 389.

Why can't a dog simulate pain?: in Man. 179, W. used joy rather than pain, making the connection with §249 still closer. Manser, quoting Konrad Lorenz, contests the supposed inability of a dog to pretend: "When he rode his bicycle in the direction of the barracks, where the dog would have to remain all day, the dog limped, but if Lorenz turned round towards the country the limp was forgotten and the dog ran normally" ("Pain", 178–79). The passage from Man. 138, 19B, quoted for §249 indicates W.'s answer still more appositely than the remarks here. We should ask: What makes it, e.g., *pain* that the dog is simulating? And what is the difference between acting in a way that has brought certain results and pretending that one is in pain? Doesn't the latter require the intention that the affected person not merely act in a certain way, but believe I am in pain? But a person cannot believe another is in pain unless he possesses the concept *pain*. And what does the dog know about concepts, or believing? "A dog cannot simulate pain because his life is too simple. It doesn't have the necessary links with these movements" (Man. 138, 19B).

Is he too honest?: Schopenhauer thought so: "Incidentally, his sole friend, the dog, also has an analogous and characteristic action peculiar to him alone, and as an advantage over all other animals, namely fawning and tail-wagging, which are so expressive, so kindly disposed, and thoroughly honest. Yet how favourably does this salutation, given to him by nature, contrast with the bows and simpering civilities of men! At any rate for the present, it is a thousand times more reliable than their assurance of close friendship and devotion" (*World*, II, 98–99).

"Nothing stands between the animal and the external world; but between us and that world there are always our thoughts and ideas about it, and these often make us inaccessible to it, and it to us. . . . Therefore animals are not capable either of purpose or of dissimulation; they have nothing in reserve. In this respect, the dog is related to the man as a glass tumbler is to a metal one, and this greatly helps to endear the dog so much to us. It affords us great pleasure to see simply and openly displayed in him all those inclinations and emotions that in ourselves we so often conceal. In general, animals play always with their cards on the table, so to speak" (ibid., 61).

§251   A precipitate from Man. 110, 291, then *PG* 129b and Man. 116, 75–76. See *RFM* 41b, 183i; *PG* 130a; *BB* 30cd; NL 320b; *PP* 267bc; Man. 109, 296; cp. Z 401–2; *PB* 86b, 109b; *PP* 311b.

PP 306 (quoted in X, 18) and *PP* 311 (quoted for §247) indicate the number's drift. In his *Tractatus* days, W. restricted the word *sense* to propositions which "picture reality" (4.462), so concluded that tautologies lack sense (4.461); they "are not, however, nonsensical" (4.4611), as are metaphysical sayings (6.53). Here, too, in §251, he stresses the difference between tautological, 'grammatical' propositions and empirical ones, but does not question their meaningfulness, as he does that of the propositions in §246a and §252. Thus the number looks like an updated version of 6.111–6.112: "The logical proposition acquires all the characteristics of a proposition of natural science and this is the sure sign that it has been construed wrongly. The correct explanation of the propositions of logic must assign to them a unique status among all propositions."

(abc) See *Z* 134, 442, 717; *RFM* 121hi; *BB* 16b; Ambrose, "Metamorphoses", 70–75; cp. *RFM* 34e; 5.61; *PP* 306; Schlick, "Meaning", 163–66.

What does it mean . . . : "When the question is one of logic, 'It is impossible to imagine that' means: we don't know what we are supposed to imagine" (Man. 176, 9A).

when we say: "Elsewhere he said that both Solipsists and Idealists would say they 'couldn't imagine it otherwise' " (*PP* 311).

or that only I myself can know . . . : see §§243, 246–47.

and similar things: which *PG* 129 termed "senseless metaphysical ways of speaking."

really a grammatical one: see §§360, 458, 574; *BB* 55c (quoted for §136b); Bensch, *Wittgenstein*, 44–55; Hacker, *Insight*, 153–54; Hallett, "Contrast", 692–95; cp. *PP* 267–68. One main test of a proposition's sense, its mode of verification (§353), leads to this conclusion; so does the correlative consideration of informative power. The proposition communicates information about contingent grammar, not a necessary truth about the world; and in establishing its truth, one can invoke only grammar, not grammar plus fact, as in establishing the truth of "It's raining" (§§354–56). This demonstration also suggests the general sense of W.'s assertion (cp. p. 220e).

Why not . . . : "If it is unthinkable, so is the contrary unthinkable" (*PG* 207). For a full illustration, see §216.

(d) Cp. §73b; *PG* 351–352a.

Example: akin to "the Kantian example: 'all bodies are extended' " (V. Kraft, *Circle*, 37). Cp. Man. 125: " 'Every body has a definite size and shape.' I.e., for example, we can always ask 'What shape does this body have?' We can always play this language-game. The sentence as it were stands for the description of a language game."

has a quite different role: "A proposition which it is supposed to be impossible to imagine as other than true has a different *function* from one for which this does not hold" (*RFM* 114).

For here I understand . . . : cp. §398a; *PB* 90e. "To say of a proposition 'This could be imagined otherwise' or 'We can imagine the opposite too,' ascribes the role of an empirical proposition to it" (*RFM* 114).

mental picture: see the commentary on §301, where W. denies that images are pictures.

(e) Cp. *RFM* 143l; 4.462.

what should the opposite picture be?: to undermine the idea that the stated impossibility can be "conceived", and is therefore not merely a matter of grammar, W. asks how a rod without length is to be mentally represented. Or how will the image of the length denied differ from that of the length affirmed? "So we cannot say in logic, 'The world has this in it, and this, but not that' " (5.61); rather, we exclude an *expression* from *language* (cp. §500). See §520 and commentary.

(f) "Its opposite really becomes unthinkable, as a form of thought, form of expression, corresponds to it, which we have excluded" (Man. 226, 70, earlier version of the *Investigations*). Cp. *PB* 247d, 249d, 250e; Hallett, "Contrast".

"It is logically impossible that the negation of a tautology should be true, and hence, if it is true that 'It is logically impossible that *p*' means the same as 'The sentence "*p*" has no sense,' then it will follow from the conjunction of this proposition with his principle, that a 'tautology' . . . also has none" (*PP* 275–76).

"Let us suppose now that the statement 'An object cannot be both red and green' were a synthetic judgment and that the words 'can not' indicate a logical impossibility. Since a proposition is the negation of its negation, there must also be the proposition: 'An object can be both red and green.' This proposition would likewise be synthetic. As a synthetic proposition it has sense, and that means that what it represents *can be the case*. Thus if 'cannot' indicates a *logical* impossibility, we reach the conclusion that the impossible is in fact possible. To this I would reply: Words can no doubt be thought up; but I can find no sense for them" (*Kreis*, 67–68).

"We make a picture like that of the two colours being in each other's way, or that of a barrier which doesn't allow one person to come closer to another's experience than to the point of observing his behaviour; but on looking closer we find that we can't apply the picture which we have made" (*BB* 56).

§252 Reworked from Man. 110, 291, then *PG* 129.

we might reply: "Nonsense!": as W. did in *PG* 129, in accordance with his declaration, "Only when I know what is the case if a proposition is false does the proposition make sense" (*PB* 181; see Hallett, "Contrast"). The sample statements in §251, being general, can at least serve as guides to contingent grammar, whereas this sample, being particular, cannot readily serve even that function.

Why is this?: in *PG* 129, W. suggested that we see the proposition verified by "It is four meters long" and "Four meters is a length," and forget that the latter proposition is grammatical. So when we imagine a body that long, we suppose that we are imagining a body's having an extension; and whatever we can imagine makes sense (§512; *PG* 128–29).

§253 For an illuminating parallel with §253, see pp. 221h–222a. See also Man. 110, 7; *Kreis,* 49.

(a) "Another person can't have . . .": see X, 3, 18; *BB* 49–55; *PP* 306.

"No other person has my pain. Someone can have sympathy for me but still my pain always belongs to me and his sympathy to him. He does not have my pain and I do not have his sympathy" (Frege, "Thought", 300).

Which are *my* pains?: see §411. This question is distinct from the next. "The subject of pain is the person who gives it expression" (§302). Thus if two people truthfully say "I am in pain," these two people are in pain. But how many pains are there? Can they both feel the *same* pain? This is the focus of §253.

Consider what makes it possible . . . : it will then appear that any absolute, *a priori* barrier separating mind from mind is erected by language, not by nature (X, 18). "We use the phrase 'two books have the same colour,' but we could perfectly well say: 'They can't have the *same* colour, because, after all, this book has its own colour, and the other book has its own colour too.' This also would be stating a grammatical rule—a rule, incidentally, not in accordance with our ordinary usage. The reason why one should think of these two different usages at all is this: We compare the case of sense data with that of physical bodies, in which case we make a distinction between: 'this is the same chair that I saw an hour ago' and 'this is not the same chair, but one exactly like the other.' Here it makes sense to say, and it is an experiential proposition: 'A and B couldn't have seen the same chair, for A was in London and B in Cambridge; they saw two chairs exactly alike.' (Here it will be useful if you consider the different criteria for what we call the 'identity of these objects'. How do we apply the statements: 'This is the same day . . . ,' 'This is the same word . . . ,' 'This is the same occasion . . . ,' etc.?)" (*BB* 55). Cp. Russell, *Logic,* 272–73.

(b) See §398a; *BB* 54b; *PB* 92c; Man. 176, 48; Morick, *Other Minds,* xvii–xviii; Schlick, "Meaning", 163–67; cp. *PB* 94b; Russell, *Logic,* 162a.

In so far as it makes *sense* . . . : the repeated declarations of philosophers suggest that were people presented with the strange cases envisioned, they would still refuse to acknowledge the identity of two people's pains. And W. tended to accept this exclusion as a fact of language (*BB* 53b, 55b; *Kreis*, 49). He never said, for instance, that it would be imaginable for two people to have the same pain, as he said they might feel pain in the same (not just the corresponding) spot. Thus the strategy of §253 resembles somewhat that of §293: *If* you make the supposition required by your statement, then it turns out to be wrong. Make the privacy thesis into a factual, non-grammatical proposition and it ceases to be a necessary truth.

it is also possible: logically possible.

it would also be imaginable: "If we imagine such a case, this simply means that we imagine a correlation between visual, tactual, kinaesthetic, etc., experiences different from the ordinary correlation. Thus we can imagine a person having the sensation of toothache plus those tactual and kinaesthetic experiences which are normally bound up with seeing his hand travelling from his tooth to his nose, to his eyes, etc., but correlated to the visual experience of his hand moving to those places in another person's face. . . . If we had a sensation of toothache plus certain tactual and kinaesthetic sensations usually characteristic of touching the painful tooth and neighbouring parts of our face, and if these sensations were accompanied by seeing my hand touch, and move about on, the edge of my table, we should feel doubtful whether to call this experience an experience of toothache in the table or not. If, on the other hand, the tactual and kinaesthetic sensations described were correlated to the visual experience of seeing my hand touch a tooth and other parts of the face of another person, there is no doubt that I would call this experience 'toothache in another person's tooth' " (*BB* 52–53; for modifications, see XXXIV, 2–5).

(c) See NL 310g–311b.

is to suggest: *vorspiegeln* requires "wrongly suggest". These words and this chest-thumping are *not* comparable to the case in which we call attention to a familiar criterion of identity, saying, for instance, "You can't have seen the same automobile as he did if he was in London and you were *here!*" Nor is W. suggesting that they are an embryonic but relevant response, revealing a criterion of which we still need to be reminded (cp. §§89–90, 127, 129). Only had he used a word like *wiederspiegeln* might we say: "The blow on the chest and emphasis upon 'this' is merely a reminder that persons are the individuators, the identificatory matrix of pains (or experiences in general)" (Hacker, *Insight*, 247; cp. §§281, 302). In confirmation, note his attitude towards "another typical expedient" in §254, and compare *PP* 311: "The Solipsist sees that a person who says 'No: my experience is real too' has not really refuted him, just as Dr. Johnson did not refute Berkeley by kicking a stone." Nor does the chest-thumper refute anyone, whereas the person above, who observes "and you were *here*," does.

Note also that the German has *nur* ("only").

§254   Cf. §274.

The substitution . . . : see Morick, *Other Minds*, xviii.

for "the same": cp. Berkeley, *Dialogues*, III, 467: "If the term *same* be used in the acceptation of philosophers, who pretend to an abstracted notion of identity, then, according to their sundry definitions of this notion (for it is not yet agreed wherein that philosophic identity consists), it may or may not be possible for divers persons to perceive the same thing."

for instance: more common is stress on the difference between identity and close similarity, as in Moore, *Problems*, 146–47; Russell, *Mind*, 180; James, *Principles*, I, 533. Jackson's notes cite Stout to the same effect, and add this example: "We do not deal in nuances; e.g. we don't say 'things exist, relations subsist,' as though existing and subsisting differed by a degree, a nuance" (JN 62). See also the discrimination between *have* and *possess* in *Theaetetus*, 197, or Moore's fine distinction between *communicate* and *convey,* in *Commonplace*, 180e.

a particular kind of expression: for instance, solipsistic expressions like "Only this is really seen" (*BB* 58–59, 63–66, 71), or the uses of *peculiar* and *particular* to which W. gave so much attention in *BB* 149–50, 158–62, 165–66, 174–77. These pages contain many attempts to "give a psychologically exact account" in words which "hit on the correct nuance". Cp. *BB* 30b, 55b. In the *Investigations,* see for instance §§38d, 58c, 89–105, 113–15, 170–71, 175, 274, 277, 295c, 398.

is . . . not philosophy: re W.'s apparent appropriation of the word *philosophy* for philosophy done his way, see VII, 10. A paraphrase of §386b may suggest his attitude: "What a philosopher says in such a case is not *testimony* of how things are, which I must accept or reject, but rather an indication of what he is *inclined* to say." So he must be treated, not refuted (GI 68). "All that I can do, is to shew an easy escape from this obscurity and this glitter of the concepts" (*RFM* 142). "My method is in a certain sense a psychological one" (Man. 109, 279).

what a mathematician is inclined to say . . . : see e.g. commentary on §10 and p. 225h; *RFM* 60, 77bcd, 142; *BB* 28d–29a; Man. 302, 28–29; Frege, *Foundations*, i–ii.

§255   In Man. 228 this number followed §370 of the *Investigations*. See GI 68; commentary on §254 ("is not philosophy"); §133cd; *RFM* 57cd, 157hi; NL 309c; Man. 213, 410; Man. 168, 3; Rhees, "Symposium", 77–78; Waismann, "How I See", 357–64; cp. §§109, 309; BUF 235–36; Man. 229, §1217; Man. 220, 83, and Man. 110, 230, and Man. 109, 174 (comparisons with psychoanalysis); Weiler, *Critique*, 304–5. On philosophy as therapy, see GI 8–24, 28. On the importance of such therapy, see VII, 8–9. On W.'s methods, see GI 29, 46–62, and especially 68.

The omission of the semicolon in the translation hurts both the style and the sense (Wiedmann, *Strömungen*, 66). The German is terse, epigrammatic. And W. does not say, here, that the treatment of a philosophical question resembles the treatment of an illness, but that, as in the case of an illness, one treats a philosophical question, one does not answer it (GI 68). Thus read, the number connects more directly with §254, simply repeating the final point in general form, then adding a comparison.

Yet W. did in fact suggest that "a philosophical problem is like a serious illness from which I must free myself and others" (Man. 163; see Man. 138, 4B; VII, 8–9). "It is a misunderstanding & can only be removed as such. That is, without force" (Man. 109, 298). Concerning his own former condition, he wrote in the flyleaf of Schlick's copy of the *Tractatus:* "Every one of these sentences is the expression of an illness" (Maslow, *Study*, x; see Hallett, *Definition*, 33–34). "We are misled by false analogies & cannot extricate ourselves. This is the *morbus philosophicus*" (Man. 110, 86–87; see GI 9–11).

As appears already from these passages, W. also suggested that philosophical troubles be treated like illnesses. "One must put up with them: the worst thing a person can do is to rebel against them. They too come in attacks, brought on by inner or outer causes. One must then say: 'Still another attack' " (Man. 138, 4B). "*Slow* cure is all-important" (Z 382). You do not answer the patient's "theories" and "proofs" with countertheories and counterproofs (waging germ warfare, as it were on his germs), but for instance you alter or enrich his diet of examples (§593). "Bring a person into the wrong atmosphere & nothing will work as it ought. He will appear unwell in every part. Bring him back into his right element & everything will unfold & assume a healthy appearance" (Man. 125). "The matter cannot be clarified by raging against your words [see §79d], but by trying to turn your attention away from certain expressions, illustrations, images and towards the use of the words" (Man. 228, §44; cp. §§120, 144). "It is never right to say simply: 'no, that is false, it must be abandoned' " (Man. 112, 197; cp. §§423–24; Z 460).

For strikingly similar suggestions, see Berkeley, *Dialogues*, II, 438.

§256   His preparations completed, W. returns to the theme of §243b, that is, to the kind of private language that Schlick envisaged (X, 14–15) and that W. describes more fully in §257.

natural expressions of sensation: for pain, see §§244, 257, 288c, etc. Some sensations, however, have no natural expression, but have natural causes and are verbally expressed. Schlick envisioned the elimination of *all* regular connections.

I simply *associate*: see II, 4–8.

names with sensations: W. shifts momentarily from the singular to the plural; in §§257–58 he returns to the more manageable hypothesis of a single private sensation.

§257 "What would it be like . . .": in this restricted hypothesis, limited to pain, they would still be human beings; and this is the supposition W. retains in this number and the next.

"Then it would be impossible . . .": note that these words, too, are enclosed within the quotation marks; they are not W.'s reply. Connection with the cause of pain (§288) as well as with its natural expression (§244) may be used in teaching the word *pain*. W. abbreviates the type of hypothesis proposed by Schlick (X, 14–15) and others.

without being able to explain its meaning: concerning his imagined language (X, 14) Schlick concluded: "It would be impossible to give a definition for such a word" ("Psychological", 405).

How has he done this naming: for the type of view being criticized, see II, 3–8, and §33a.

"But what is it like to give a sensation a name? Say it is pronouncing the name while one has the sensation and possibly concentrating on the sensation,—but what of it? Does this name thereby get magic powers? And why on earth do I call these sounds the 'name' of the sensation? I know what I do with the name of a man or of a number, but have I by this act of 'definition' given the name a use?

" 'To give a sensation a name' means nothing unless I know already in what sort of a game this name is to be used" (NL 290–91).

one forgets: "When we envisaged the possibility of that private language, intelligible to the speaker alone, its use was immaterial to us; foremost was the idea that we can *name* our sensations. The use will take care of itself" (Man. 180a). "In this way we sometimes believe that we have named something when we make the gesture of pointing and utter words like 'This is . . .' (the formula of the ostensive definition). We say we call something 'toothache', and think that the word has received a definite function in the dealings we carry out with language when, under certain circumstances, we have pointed to our cheek and said: 'This is toothache' " (*BB* 69; see the rest of the page). See §§33a, 38d; *BB* 172a.

a great deal of stage-setting: see Section II in general and §§28–31 in particular; and Cook, "Solipsism", 54–63.

what is presupposed . . . : see §384.

it shews the post . . . : see §§30a, 31a.

§258 See X, 20–21; the references and quotations for §257; §§142,

380; NL 276, 315g; Man. 229, §930; Man. 180a; Malcolm, *Memoir,* 47; Cook, "Solipsism", 70–71; Mounce, Review, 619–20; cp. *BB* 159b; Man. 112, 154–55; Man. 110, 72–73.

This is perhaps the most misunderstood number in the *Investigations.* One main error is to suppose that W. intended to establish some general thesis, whether positive (concerning sensation words) or negative (concerning the impossibility of any private language, or of a particular sort). As in §§256–57, his target is still a Schlickian private language (X, 14–15), which is a mere picture (cp. p. 223g) and ultimately unintelligible, not a coherent hypothesis which might be systematically refuted (see GI 68). It is this realization which the number aims to convey. (See e.g. Garver, "Private Language", 393–94.)

Another mistake is to look to the use of "S" rather than to the learning. It is clear that in the present number W. is having recourse to his other favorite approach, observing the learning rather than the use (III, 1–2), and that his objection is not that this private sign won't work once it is given a meaning, but that the staring ceremony (his attempt to fill out the Schlickian hypothesis) does not give it a meaning. No criterion is thus established which might then be followed, publicly or privately, or used as an ultimate check in verifying the supposed report (X, 20–21). W. is not himself succumbing to the illusion that all evidence is fallible or subject to Cartesian doubt (§354; X, 24–25), but is pointing out that no ultimate evidence has been established, none whose rejection would amount to rejection of the very concept rather than of the thing supposedly doubted (§354). Here there is no "bedrock" (§217).

Thus his target exemplifies the more general error treated in Section II, and his critique parallels his earlier, more general response to that error. Just as "when one shews someone the king in chess and says: 'This is the king,' this does not tell him the use of this piece—unless he already knows the rules of the game up to this last point" (§31), so too, " 'to give a sensation a name' means nothing unless I know already in what sort of a game this name is to be used" (NL 291). To make his point, W. uses "the method of §2" (see commentary on §48): a simple language-game, stripped to the essentials, in which all ties with ordinary language are cut, so that the proponent of private meanings can see just what his supposition looks like when worked out in detail.

Let us imagine . . . : since W. is still working on the limited supposition of a single private sensation, as in §257, he can still imagine a human being and typical human activities. In a general hypothesis like that in X, 14, it is not clear what might be imagined. Certainly not human beings (see Cook, "Solipsism", 40–42).

a diary: see X, 15; *PG* 195; Man. 166 and Man. 179, both quoted for §243b ("Well, can't we do so . . .").

a certain sensation: W. goes along with the patient's way of talking, stating the hypothesis as he would. But this part has already been eliminated by the supposition of absolute privacy (§261); something un-connected with either characteristic causes or characteristic natural ex-pressions is nothing like what we call a sensation, for instance pain (Man. 180a, below).

associate it with . . . : see *BB* 171b–172a and references for §§38d, 257.

a definition . . . cannot be formulated: for §258, continuing §257, still makes the Schlickian supposition that this sensation is not regularly connected with any public phenomena. And in this supposition we can-not say, for instance, "What you feel when I stick this pin in you is S" (§288). For one thing, the expression *feel* derives its meaning from an entirely different situation; for another, we have no idea now what ef-fect the pin may have. This indefinability Schlick ("Psychological", 405, quoted for §257) and Waismann (X, 16) already recognized, as W. him-self doubtless had (X, 16). W. is presenting the position, not yet criticiz-ing it.

Not in the ordinary sense: see §§33–36.

concentrate my attention: see §§33a, 34, 268. An act of intention, if invoked, would be no more effective (cp. §§205, 337), and in fact was often not envisioned (II, 5).

But what is this ceremony for?: see NL 312, quoted for §244a.

serves to establish the meaning: that is, the use in the language (§43); even to establish the bearer or referent would be to establish the linguistic relationship which made it the referent, and a referent of this or that sort, in a given sense of the word *referent* (Z 434; NL 312).

can only mean: "If for instance I am learning Russian, I can let my gaze wander around the room and, for practice, name every object I see; and I could even direct my attention to my stomachache and say the corresponding word. And experience perhaps teaches me that this is a good way of impressing the word and its meaning on my mind. But here the criterion that I am using the word correctly is not that I believe I am using it correctly" (Man. 180a).

If it be asked why there need be any question of correctness, the an-swer is that the hypothesis of a diary, like the hypotheses of logical atomists, logical positivists, and many others, suggests such a game, and not mere effectiveness in achieving some personal purpose. A hunter's private notches to keep track of his kills are neither correct nor incor-rect; he might, for instance, make a double notch any time he pleased to indicate an extra-large animal, and if this confused him later in his counting, or hindered whatever purpose the notches were to serve, the double notch would be unfortunate, not wrong. But the philosophers whom W. had in mind (X, 3–16) conceived private uses of signs "on the model of 'object and designation' " (§293), that is, as basically similar to public uses, and specifically to reports and identifications.

I have no criterion of correctness: see NL 293; Man. 109, 22 (quoted for §379); cp. §§145b, 241–42, p. 147n (b); Moore, *Ethics*, 100–103. "The point of this sentence is not to cast doubt on the accuracy or reliability of the diarist's memory. Wittgenstein is claiming not that he might misremember the criterion that he has, just for this instant, fixed; but that he has not by this ceremony fixed any criterion at all" (Holborow, "Kind", 347; see Man. 116, 135). Suppose that a copy of the original sensation comes to his mind, one which he somehow knows to be a perfect replica, at the same moment that he experiences a similar sensation. Now what is he to do? "It is no explanation . . . to say: simple enough, we compare it with our memory image. For how are we given the method of comparison we're to use in making the comparison; that is, how do we know what we're to do when we are told 'to compare'?" (*PG* 70–71; see X, 20).

"In fundamental discussions of language," wrote Russell, "its social aspect should be ignored, and a man should always be supposed to be speaking to himself—or, what comes to the same thing, to a man whose language is precisely identical with his own. This eliminates the concept of 'correctness'. What remains—if a man is to be able to interpret notes written by himself on previous occasions—is constancy in his own use of words: we must suppose that he uses the same language today as he used yesterday" (*Inquiry*, 186–87). Or, as W. had put it: " 'If a word is to have significance, we must commit ourselves'. . . . 'There is no use in correlating noises to facts, unless we commit ourselves to using the noise in a particular way again' " (*PP* 259). With the rules thus established in intention (*PP* 264), he would have added, we can proceed to play the true-false game (IX, 2).

Now he would reply that the mental act establishes no criterion either of sameness or of truth. "Sameness" is a relative notion (§215), the sameness of a sensation, for example, being determined by the concept *sensation*. "And for the recognition, the presence, of a sensation there are characteristic *expressions* & *criteria*. One who gives expression to a sensation does not go by any criterion that he has the sensation. But his expression is *used* along with the rest of language in his life. It is not an occult relation of meaning which makes a word into the name of a sensation and propositions into propositions about sensations" (Man. 180a; see NL 288e; Pitcher, "Same", especially 134–36).

"The private object does not only not enter the public game but it can't enter a private *game* either. You can see this if you replace the one private object which is to justify his use of a pain expression by a series of different objects which he *has* at different times when he says he has pain. 'But surely the use of the word pain is based on the fact that he "recognizes" his private object as always being the same on those occasions!' What is the meaning in this case of being the 'same', or 'recognizing'? Neither he nor we have ever learnt to apply these words to his private object" (Man. 166; W.'s English).

One would like to say . . . : cp. Man. 110, 21 ("Things are called whatever I conceive they are called"); *PP* 258–59.

whatever is going to seem . . . : see the initial comments and above; cp. §202, p. 207e; *OC* 368; *BB* 171a; *PB* 60a, 104b, 282e.

we can't talk about 'right': note the contrast with Schlick (X, 15). Cp. *RFM* 6: "But what is the reality that 'right' accords with here? Presumably a *convention*, or a *use*, and perhaps our practical requirements." Nothing of the sort has been specified here.

"In our private language game we had, it seemed, given a name to an impression—in order, of course, to use the name for this impression in the future. The definition, that is, should have determined on future occasions for what impression to use the name and for which not to use it. Now we said that on certain occasions after having given the definition we did use the word and on others we didn't; but we described these occasions only by saying that we had 'a certain impression'—that is, we didn't describe them at all. The only thing that characterized them was that we used such and such words. What seemed to be a definition didn't play the rôle of a definition at all. It did not justify one subsequent use of the word; and all that remains of our private language game is therefore that I sometimes without any particular reason write the word 'red' in my diary" (NL 291).

§259 See §§202, 265–69. A helpful parallel is with §§139–41, where, after the picture before one's mind fails to fix the right use of *cube*, recourse is had to a pictured method of projection. As there the move is from picture to auxiliary picture, which therefore succeeds no better, so here in §§258–59 the natural move is from experience to auxiliary experience, which consistency requires to be equally private. The sensation, like an arrow which points, now seems to "carry in it something besides itself" (§454). W.'s question, once again, is: "Does this really get me any further?" (§141).

§260(a) Cp. *OC* 486–90; NL 311c; Man. 110, 21 (quoted for §258).

Perhaps you *believe* **. . . :** "His meaning is that on this sort of view, 'believing' is also only the name of a private experience, and is conferred in the same way as the name 'pain' or 'seeing' or the like. And how do you know, therefore, that you are even right in saying, 'At least, I believe I have the same sensation over again'? for you may be giving the wrong name, namely 'believing', to what you are doing" (Geach, lecture notes). There are criteria for believing p, and if p is strictly private, so are the criteria for p and for believing p (§§261, 269). For a position like the one Geach describes, see Ogden and Richards, *Meaning*, 62–63.

(b) For clear insight into the mentality being treated and the nature and need of the treatment, see for instance Russell in X, 5; e.g.: "If I describe these objects, I may of course describe them wrongly; hence I cannot with certainty communicate to another what are the things of which I am aware. But if I speak to myself"—do I communicate them to myself? (§268)

   so far: see §270.

(c) To the simplistic notion that ordinary language always serves the same purpose, namely the transfer of thoughts from one mind to another (§363b), would correspond the simplistic supposition that in a private language a person would communicate thoughts to himself, or that whereas in ordinary language we talk to others, in private language we talk to ourselves. What else? We are alone in this inner world of discourse. Yes, W. typically replies (see §3), that is one possibility: When we speak alone, we sometimes speak to ourselves. But other times we pray, or recite, or practice pronunciation, or curse our employer at a discreet distance. The mere supposition of privacy settles nothing about the use of a sign.

§261   See §398a; *BB* 52; *PB* 58a; NL 283e, 288; Man. 302, 30; Cook, "Solipsism", 51–54; cp. §§270, 280; *Theaetetus*, 183.

   What reason have we . . . : Schlick wrote for instance: "I can, for example, imagine that my feeling of grief corresponded in no way to any bodily condition" ("Psychological", 405). Why, then, call it a feeling, or a feeling of grief (p. 174)? "Well, the word's *reference* is similar to that of sensation words, though its sense is not." Very well, but does it have nothing but a reference? Then it has no reference either; for being a referent means being related to a word in a specific manner. And if there is some new relation here between reference and word, what is it? The situation is as follows: Either the word *sensation* retains its ordinary (elastic) meaning in the description of the private language, in which case the hypothesis is rendered incoherent (since the language is not private), or it does not, and the hypothesis becomes vacuous, since the terms no longer have any meaning. Grunts and gesticulations are no solution to this dilemma.

   Passages like this one have created in some readers the impression of being enclosed in a linguistic prison—a new, linguistic principle of immanence—from which it is impossible to break out and make transcendent use of words. But the paragraph carries no such implications. The proponent of private meanings is caught in the dilemma because of his skepticism, not because he would spin fiber on fiber (§67). In terms of this comparison, applicable to a variety of counterproposals: If there is no continuity, no overlapping, meaning is broken off; if there is overlapping, privacy ceases. See XXXVII, 16–18; cp. X, 24; §120.

intelligible to me alone: the same stipulated conditions which supposedly lead to the private meaning of "S" would require that the word *sensation* also have a private meaning, when used to designate S. It could not indicate either outer connections or inner similarities ordinarily found in sensations.

has *something*: see Man. 213, 489; quotation for §304 from Man. 166; cp. Berkeley, below, or especially Driesch, who focuses on "everything that is *something*, an 'object', that is, consciously had, in an immediate sense" (*Wirklichkeitslehre*, 3).

"Has": again, reminiscent of Driesch, whose relevance for this number appears still more clearly in the quotation from Man. 229, below. "*Oject*," he wrote, "I call with Meinong, Husserl and others every specific Something which I have, as such—(I could say, 'have in the *now*' . . .)" (*Wissen*, 15). Universal logic concerns itself with this "something as something had *immediately*" (ibid., 14). "An object is *immediate* in so far as it is merely had" (ibid., 15).

See §§302, 398a and commentaries.

So in the end . . . : cp. §§379–80; *NB* 40k; *BB* 177; Man. 213, 491–92; or Hylas' plight in Berkeley's second *Dialogue*: "To prevent any further questions, let me tell you I at present understand by *Matter* neither substance nor accident, thinking nor extended being, neither cause, instrument, nor occasion, but Something entirely unknown, distinct from all these." Philonous then takes even the word *something* from him, much as here.

"This is related to the primal expression which is just an inarticulate sound. (Driesch)" (Man. 229, §1389; Man. 113, 247). "Everything that I *have*," wrote Driesch (*Wissen*, 17), "should be *one*, and, to be sure, in the (nontemporal, so-called) Now; everything, including the whole past and future. Were the primal wish of logic realizable, the distinction of *here and now* and of *nature*, which is practically so important, would not exist, nor the distinction of *essence* and *existence*. Everything would be one *essence*, which would also be existence, the object. . . . But this ideal of monistic order is unrealizable. . . . And the I does . . . what it can."

The best Driesch could do was the utterance W. adds to his name in Man. 213, 492: "Ich habe, um mein Wissen wissend, bewusst etwas."

"This," wrote Driesch, "is our first philosophical sentence, the primal philosophical proposition" (*Ordnungslehre*, 19; see idem, *Wirklichkeitslehre*, 8).

§262   See §§379–80; cp. §§205, 337–38.

then you must inwardly *undertake* . . . : or, as W. once put it: "We must commit ourselves" (see *PP* 258–59). "Each thought decides, by its own authority," wrote James (*Principles*, I, 468), "which, out of all the conceptive functions open to it, it shall now renew." However, if we suppose it can simply make up a function, on the spot, and intend it, "we are constructing a misleading picture of 'intending', that is, of the use of this word. An intention is embedded in its situation, in human customs and institutions" (§337).

Is it to be assumed . . . : against this solution, see §§204–5.

or that you found it ready-made?: in that case, the difficulties of §261 return.

§263   See §§34, 268, 379–80; NL 296fg.

"Any fact, be it thing, event, or quality, may be conceived sufficiently for purposes of identification, if only it be singled out and marked so as to separate it from other things. Simply calling it 'this' or 'that' will suffice" (James, *Principles*, I, 462).

A queer question: as p. 184 suggests, it is somewhat as though one were to ask: "Are you quite certain that the carbon atoms in benzene lie at the corners of a hexagon?" This is not a questionable hypothesis; it is a picture. Cp. §§222, 398b, 219 ("my description only made sense if it was to be understood symbolically.—I should have said: *This is how it strikes me*").

§264   See II, 4; §§27, 33a (and commentary), 120f, 379–80; *BB* 69a, 172a (quoted in II, 2); Man. 116, 144–45; cp. NL 312e; James, *Principles*, I, 463.

"stands for": as this notion is generally expressed by *vertreten* or *stehen für* (see, for instance, a lengthy discussion in Man. 130), "designate" might be a preferable translation.

§265   Worked over in Man. 116, 249–50. See Man. 229, §1076; Schlick, "Form", 178–79; Morick, *Other Minds*, xvi–xvii; cp. *BB* 171a.

As §261 is to §258, so §265 is to §259: §258 spoke of a "sensation", and §261 asked "With what right?"; §259 introduced the idea of a private rule to check by, and now §265 asks: "Would this still be justification?" This *completely* private operation is as remote from our concept *justification* as is the completely private reference from our concept *sensation*. For notice that both the table and the consultation are hidden in the mind, whereas even if a person recalls a timetable to check another recollection, at least the table he recalls is public. Consequently, as §259 has already hinted, there can be no question yet of correctness, nor therefore of memory or its failure. No criterion of correctness is reached as long as the whole game remains private. See the commentary on §259.

Again: Here, as in §258, the main question is not the reliability of memory, or the criteria of a reliable memory as opposed to an unreliable one, but *what* is to be remembered. To *rightly* remember a pain is to rightly remember a *pain;* the criteria of pain enter into the criteria for remembering pain, and here there are no criteria for the thing to be remembered. Only a public table could provide genuine criteria, not just impressions of criteria (§259). Thus in reading this number, one should avoid a simplistic notion of memory (§305) analogous to the simplistic notion of naming or defining just alluded to in §264. In Man. 228, §177, W. used §265 (slightly altered) to make this point, placing it after §306. See Chappell, "Dreaming", 204–5; Holborow, "Kind", 347–48 ("The point is not that this procedure is of no use unless one has an infallible memory, but that the possibility of testing it makes it possible to speak of its being correct or mistaken").

(a) As if someone . . . . : recourse within memory to a different memory, one perhaps thinks, is comparable to recourse within the press to a different newspaper, not to a different copy of the same paper. And consulting a different paper *is* something of a check (unless the second paper has relied on the same dispatch). Similarly, isn't a second memory a partial justification? In ordinary circumstances, yes. But W. has not imagined ordinary circumstances. So we should ask instead: What checking of a public sort, usable as a parable, would be as completely ineffectual as W. held this internal checking to be, for the reasons mentioned above? The answer: only the comparison he used, not the alternative just suggested. Think of the person who imagines a cube, then imagines rays projecting from the imagined cube, in §141, and consider how far that gets him. Nowhere.

(b) Cp. §§202, 259; *EPB* 194; *PG* 155d.

§266   Cp. §§141b, 305, 607; *BB* 171a.

W. introduces an external illustration to make the same point as in the previous number: Mere fixing of attention does not constitute checking, reading, verifying, and so on; circumstances make it such. Thus: "Suppose I am asked what time it is and I say 'It's 6:23—by the imagined clock that is before me.' Have I looked at a clock? And have I *read* the time?" (JN 27).

in order to *guess:* one may look, then guess; but that is not looking in order to guess. Number 607 fills out the suggestion slightly.

in imagination: this suggests both a related case (§607) and a connection with §265, via this intermediary step. See above.

§267   The application is still the same: A private consultation of a private table to justify a private appellation may be an inner representation of what is ordinarily called consulting a table, but is not a consultation; it is mere play-acting, comparable to what children do when they play trains (§282).

§268 In Man. 228, §181, this follows (and appropriately comments on) §263. In Man. 116, 251–52, where it is worked over, it is preceded by the parenthetical phrase: "The point of the concept is lost."

"If I look at something red and say to myself, this is red, am I giving myself information? Am I communicating a personal experience to myself? Some people philosophizing might be inclined to say that this is the only real case of communication of personal experience because only I know what I really mean by 'red'" (NL 276–77).

"Compare: playing a game of chess in one's head—playing a football game in one's head—giving oneself a birthday gift—buying a house from oneself" (Man. 228, §169).

Pitcher ("Carroll", 319) compares W.'s example with Alice's idea of sending gifts by mail to her distant feet, and her alarmed realization, "Oh dear, what nonsense I'm talking" (*Alice,* chapter 2).

would not be those of a gift: see Malcolm, *Memoir,* 31–32.

had given himself a private definition: see §§257–58.

has directed his attention: see II, 5; §§33, 258.

§269 Cp. §§513, 540–42; Man. 228, §349.

The notion of an inner, subjective rule (§§259–60, 265–67) regulating the use of "S" is here filled out through comparison with an actual experience, where we seem to be guided, seem to know what to do, yet neither conform in our actions to any existing rule nor act under its influence, immediate or remote. For a slightly fuller description of the experience alluded to, see p. 53n. Of course the situation there differs in that a word like *relative* or *absolute* does have a use in the language, though unknown to us; but that might have been the case in §258 as well. As far as the single individual is concerned, the parallel holds, though not in complete detail.

§270 See Man. 229, §§1067–76; Schlick, "Positivism", 93.

Let us now imagine a use . . . : let us fill in the vacuous hypothesis of §258 just enough perhaps to provide meaning for "S"; then we see that even so no inner criterion of correctness is established, any more than in §258, permitting the person himself to know for sure what others can merely surmise (see the next numbers, and X, 19). Claims of impenetrable privacy are still not justified.

in my diary: see §258.

it seems quite indifferent . . . : as in p. 222i, we might say: "The importance of the expression here does not reside in its being a correct and certain report of an experience."

Let us suppose . . . : see p. 207e.

it does not matter in the least: since this game is one invented for a practical purpose (§492), this is the relevant way to judge it, by its success in achieving the purpose. In another language-game, pragmatic considerations might be irrelevant.

is mere show: see Kenny, *Wittgenstein,* 195. In this number, too, §245 applies: Language cannot get between this sensation and its expression. There is not some independent criterion which establishes this expression as a correct or incorrect report. Nor is there any agreement with others, establishing what is right (§§241–42). So the conclusion of §258 still holds, not because the language is private, but because it is of a different kind. Its utility resembles that of a natural expression which is neither right nor wrong, yet allows us to draw conclusions (GI 15–16).

it was a mere ornament: we do not infer the physiological fact from the inner something but from its expression (p. 220h); it is the inner criterion which is mere ornament, not the sensation whose expression "S" is. The sensation enters into the description of the game, much as being hurt entered into the description of "I have a pain" (§244).

(b) And what is our reason . . . : a crucial question. It means: Is the hypothesis we have made really intelligible? Is it possible, for instance, to indicate just a practical purpose, using concepts which are not purely pragmatic, since they belong to a different sort of language, one not invented for a purpose (§§492–98)?

the name of a sensation: why a name (§293; *Z* 434; *PG* 67c–68a) and why a sensation (§261)?

Perhaps the kind . . . : "He means that the man will now say from time to time, either aloud or to himself, 'There's E again; I'd better take my pill,' that he might also say or write in his diary, 'Haven't had E all week; those pills must be working' or perhaps 'Have had E every day this week; it's time to see the doctor again,' and so on, and given this use of 'E' what *should* we call E if not a sensation?" (Cook, "Solipsism", 46).

Well, aren't we supposing . . . : cp. *BB* 130de; and see §350, which explains this fully. Sameness is not absolute, but is determined by the use of the term which *same* modifies, for instance "S". The *same* S is the same *S*.

"What is the criterion for his connecting the word always to the same experience? Is it not often just that he calls it red?" (NL 287).

§271   See §290; NL 279a; Cook, "Solipsism", 71; cp. pp. 181c, 222h; NL 284. Most revealing is *BB* 72–73, quoted for §273. To get rid of the "particular impression" which serves as justification, W. follows the advice of p. 207e.

By way of comparison, think of the familiar hypothesis that the universe (and everything in it) suddenly doubles or triples in size. That's the way it would be here. Neither the "forgetful" person nor anyone else would notice a thing. By way of contrast, imagine instead a person whose memory could not retain what the word *red* meant. Notice, though, that when applied to *red* this question about memory, distinguishing word from datum, would be equally ruinous for the empiricist supposition of experiential infallibility. And since absolute privacy (see the next number) is the correlate of such absolute certainty (§246a), it too is eliminated (X, 19).

not part of the mechanism: that is, of the language-game, whose rules W. is examining rather than its causes (§108c). "The piece of redundant mechanism here is the exemplar, the private object which the private linguist alleges gives meaning to his words" (Hacker, *Insight,* 237; cp. §272).

§272 See X, 3, 12–13, 17; *BB* 60–61, 72c; first pages of Man. 166; Schlick, "Positivism", 93; start of Broad's *Examination;* cp. X, 4. W. leaves pain and turns to color sensations (§§272–80), which have likewise been considered private in the sense here described. The transition is smooth: He makes a remark applicable to the foregoing example, then illustrates it with the new.

The essential thing: the specifically philosophical note (see the commentary on §243b), responsible for a variety of philosophical problems (X, 17).

nobody knows . . . : "Qualitative content as such cannot be controlled, it belongs to the private sphere of each person and is inaccessible to anyone else" (V. Kraft, *Circle,* 43).

also have *this*: cp. §§379–80.

though unverifiable: unlike color blindness. W.'s later line of reply is foreshadowed in *PB* 66: "The sense of a question is the method of answering it: What therefore is the sense of the question 'do two men mean the same thing by the word "white"?' " For a treatment similar to that in §293, see Man. 109, 299.

§273 See §277; NL 279; Moore, *Papers,* 21–22; Hacker, "Frege", 276–77; cp. Man. 108, 228. For such double-meaning theories, see X, 10, 12–13; cp. Russell in X, 4, and Frege, *Writings,* 79.

'confronting us all': "a quotation from Frege's *Grundgesetze der Arithmetik*, p. xviii, '*etwas Allen gleicherweise Gegenüberstehendes*'. It is clear from much of the argument that Wittgenstein has Frege in mind at a number of points in the dialectical debate" (Hacker, *Insight,* 217).

should really have another . . . : this is reminiscent of W.'s former project of a phenomenological language, which would clearly distinguish between the directly given sense-datum and the hypothetical redness of things, expressed in our physical, ordinary language (X,

7–8). "Here, I believe, is a chief source of the misunderstanding that the occurrence of 'red' in two situations has a double sense. In one case it means that here as there something *is red*—that is, has the property of redness. In the other there is no question of sameness of color (which might be expressed by a color designation). This sameness of color is precisely the agreement between thought & reality which must still be described" (Man. 109, 226; cp. *PG* 135).

"What we are talking about is connected with that peculiar temptation to say: 'I never know what the other really means by "brown", or what he really sees when he (truthfully) says that he sees a brown object.'—We could propose to one who says this to use two different words instead of the one word 'brown'; one word *for his particular impression*, the other word with that meaning which other people besides himself can understand as well. If he thinks about this proposal he will see that there is something wrong in his conception of the meaning, function, of the word 'brown' and others. He looks for a justification of his description where there is none" (*BB* 72–73).

Or perhaps rather . . . : cp. Moore, *Commonplace*, 119 (quoted for §275); and Russell, *Logic*, 315: "I shall say that a proposition 'refers to' its objective. Thus, when we are concerned with image-propositions, 'referring to' takes the place of 'meaning'."

§274   Cp. NL 284g.

does not help us: see the commentary on §244 (the second paragraph of comments on "of the word 'pain' for example").

more psychologically apt: see §254.

§275   For the kind of view here criticized, see X, 4–5, 10, 12–13. See the quotations for §277; §398; *PG* 220def; cp. Köhler, *Gestalt*, 21–23; Russell, *Mind*, 111–12, and *Logic*, 147, and *Inquiry*, 15, 191; Frege, "Thought", 299 (quoted for §398a), and *Writings*, 79; Schlick, "Meaning", 163a.

"The difficulty which we express by saying 'I can't know what he sees when he (truthfully) says that he sees a blue patch' arises from the idea that 'knowing what he sees' means: 'seeing that which he also sees'; not, however, in the sense in which we do so when we both have the same object before our eyes: but in the sense in which the object seen would be an object, say, in his head, or in *him*. The idea is that the same object may be before his eyes and mine, but that I can't stick my head into his (or my mind into his, which comes to the same) so that the *real* and *immediate* object of his vision becomes the real and immediate object of my vision too. By 'I don't know what he sees' we really mean 'I don't know what he looks at,' where 'what he looks at' is hidden and he can't show it to me: it is *before his mind's eye*. Therefore, in order to get rid of this puzzle, examine the grammatical difference between the statements 'I don't know what he sees' and 'I don't know what he looks at,' as they are actually used in our language" (*BB* 61).

Look at the blue of the sky . . . : see the quotation from Schlick, under §277.

When you do it spontaneously: Russell might reply: "Our spontaneous, unsophisticated beliefs, whether as to ourselves or as to the outer world, are always extremely rash and very liable to error" (*Mind*, 122). However, this he said because he supposed theoretical content in concepts which, by his own account, are formed unreflectively (see the comments on §§241–42).

the idea never crosses your mind: for justification of this apparently irrelevant evidence, see the commentary on §60. The therapeutic context must be kept in mind: The patient supposes that the inner meaning is attached in thought; so W. points out that in the ordinary use of *blue* no such thinking takes place.

belongs only to *you*: see §§253, 398.

pointing-into-yourself: "It is certain that, when I point at an object I am seeing & say 'That's a match-box' or 'There's a match-box,' I am *referring* to some object or set of objects which I am seeing (= 'directly' seeing = in same sense as after-image with closed eyes)" (Moore, *Commonplace,* 119).

with your attention: see §411.

Consider what it means . . . : see §§33–35.

§276 "It seems that the visual image which I'm having is something which I can point to and talk about; that I can say of it, it is unique. That I am pointing to the physical objects in my field of vision, but not meaning them by the *appearance*. This object I am talking about, if not to others then to myself. (It is almost like something painted on a screen which surrounds me.)" (NL 311).

at least: the manner of the attending may be varied (§§33–35) and the use of the word complex and vague (*NB* 67–68), but at least what we *mean* is sharp (*NB* 68).

It is as if . . . : see passages in Moore such as *Commonplace,* 20, where he considers whether sense-data are identical with the surface of the thing we see, and says: "Whenever a sense-datum *looks* blue, the s.-d. either *is* (= is identical with) some particular shade of blue (which is the view implied by those who say that some sense-data *are* colours) or looks to be *of* some particular shade of blue. This particular shade of colour is the colour which is *seen* when it looks blue; & the colour blue itself is *never* seen in the sense in which this shade is." Cp. ibid., 270; *PB* 254a.

§277 See especially *BB* 175–77; cp. *BB* 72–73.

But how is [it] even possible . . . : "To get clear about philosophical problems, it is useful to become conscious of the apparently unimportant details of the particular situation in which we are inclined to make a certain metaphysical assertion" (*BB* 66; cp. §413).

that we use a word . . . : see §273. W. was familiar with a number of double-meaning views. In addition to X, 10, 12–13, see for instance:

"The word 'white' ordinarily makes us think of a certain sensation, which is, of course, entirely subjective; but even in ordinary everyday speech, it often bears, I think, an objective sense. When we call snow white, we mean to refer to an objective quality which we recognize, in ordinary daylight, by a certain sensation. If the snow is being seen in a coloured light, we take that into account in our judgment and say, for instance, 'It *appears* red at present, but it *is* white'. . . . Often, therefore, a colour word does not signify our subjective sensation, which we cannot know to agree with anyone else's (for obviously our calling things by the same name does not guarantee as much), but rather an objective quality" (Frege, *Foundations*, 36; contrast this with "Thought", 299).

"When we say a lily is white, what we might mean is that, in a normal light, when we are looking at the lily, it *causes* us to perceive a sense-datum of the kind which we call a patch of white. This or something similar is the only sense in which, on the ordinary philosophical view about sense-data, a lily or snow or any other material object *can* really be white at all: it can only be white, in the sense that under certain normal circumstances, it *causes us* to perceive one of the sense-data which I call 'a patch of white' " (Moore, *Problems*, 327). "The sense, therefore, in which lilies and snow may be white, must be strictly distinguished from the sense in which those sense-data or sensations which may be called patches of white, are white. The property called 'whiteness', which belongs to lilies and snow, does *not* belong to these sense-data; and any property called 'whiteness', which does belong to these sense-data, does *not* belong to lilies and snow" (ibid., 354–55; see *Commonplace*, 146, 225a, 328).

"But what occurs in the process of understanding the designation is that each one of us substitutes for these variables qualitative contents from his own experience which are determined by these relationships. The designation is thus connected for each person individually with a subjective qualitative content, not just with a structure. The designation, then, has an individual-subjective meaning over and above its intersubjective meaning; for each individual it also designates a qualitative content known to him from his own experience. And each individual interprets the quality-designations contained in a given communication as referring to the qualities he has experienced himself. Everybody has his own interpretation for them" (V. Kraft, *Circle*, 44–45).

"This difference is shown in ordinary language in a difference of usage. Thus we can say of a physical object but not of a sense-datum that though it looks red in this light it is really brown. As applied to physical objects 'red' stands for a lasting quality of the object, a disposition; as applied to sense-data it describes a momentary colour-sensation" (Waismann, *Principles,* 230).

See also Russell, *Logic,* 140 (Mach) and 146 (Stout).

W.'s paraphrase: " 'Toothache' is a word which I use in a game which I play with other people, but it has a private meaning to me' " (NL 289).

   I don't turn the same kind . . . : cp. §398b; *BB* 158–60, 162, 165, 167–68. Given the abundance of more theoretical considerations just cited, and W.'s own former addiction to just such reasoning, this answer appears puzzling if we suppose that he could think of no other explanation or that he proposed this account as the only genuine explanation of the temptation. As an antidote for such puzzlement, compare for instance the psychologistic explanation of another temptation, in §§113–14, with the more theoretical explanation of the same temptation, in §136. Closer to the present case is *BB* 66: "Thus we may be tempted to say 'Only this is really seen' when we stare at unchanging surroundings, whereas we may not at all be tempted to say this when we look about us while walking." Passages like these reflect W.'s belief that much can be learned from noting "the state of a philosopher's attention" when he says the strange things he does (§413). In a complete account, such etiology would have to be added to that in GI 9–24.

   belongs to me alone: cp. §398a.

   I immerse myself . . . : see *BB* 175i–177. Concerning the inexpressible blueness of blue which only intuition can furnish, Schlick wrote: "When I look at the blue sky and lose myself in the contemplation of it without thinking that I am enjoying the blue, I am in a state of pure intuition, the blue fills my mind completely, they have become one, it is the kind of union of which the mystic dreams" ("Form", 194). Cp. §§38d, 113–14, 413–14; *BB* 150b.

§278   Cp. §§379–80.

   "looks to *me*": see e.g. X, 3–4. " 'Surely I know what it is like to have the impression I call "green"!' But what is it like? You are inclined to look at a green object and to say 'it's like *this!*' And these words, though they don't explain anything to anybody else, seem to be at any rate an explanation you give yourself. But are they?!" (NL 317). The next two numbers develop this query. The connection with the preceding numbers appears when W. adds: "Will this explanation justify your future use of the word 'green'?" Will it establish a private meaning, distinct from the public one? Cp. §380.

Certainly: if you provide a sense (GI 14). Cp. §117b.

§279 Though similar, this is not a repetition of §268, but a comment on §278. My acquaintance is equally certain in both cases—color and height—and the point of the quoted remark equally dubious. The equivalent of hand on head would be the sidelong glance in §274 ("See, *that's* how it looks"). Both are equally futile, whether as personal confirmation, proof to others, or ostensive gesture. "When I said 'I am mistaking the function of a sentence' it was because by its help I seemed to be pointing out to myself which colour it is I see, whereas I was just contemplating a sample of a colour" (*BB* 175).

"(Compare: 'I am here.') Or also: 'Everyone knows how tall he is.' (Example of the steamroller)" (Man. 228, §695; see Man. 116, 339, which adds further comparisons; on the nonfunctional steamroller seen by W.'s father, see e.g. Z 248).

Pitcher ("Carroll", 319) notes the similarity with a passage in *Alice in Wonderland,* chap. 1: "She ate a little bit, and said anxiously to herself 'Which way? Which way?', holding her hand on the top of her head to feel which way it was growing; and she was quite surprised to find that she remained the same size."

BB 177 makes the connection with §280: "You are under an impression. This makes you say 'I am under a *particular* impression,' and this sentence seems to say, to yourself at least, under what impression you are. As though you were referring to a picture ready in your mind, and said 'This is what my impression is like.' "

§280 See commentary on §279; p. 196de; *BB* 175; *PG* 44d; NL 280, 310–12; Man. 232, 612; Man. 159; Man. 138, 2; cp. p. 199hij; Z 341, 482, 536; *BB* 65c; *PB* 74a, 260bc; NL 288b, 294d, 299; Russell: *Outline,* 160–61; *Mind,* 202; *Logic,* 130 (quoted in X, 5).

The intended analogy (not a perfect parallel) is between this picture and a word like *green* (§278) or *blue* (§275) which supposedly has an incommunicable, private meaning for each speaker in addition to its public meaning (see the quotations and references under §277). The point of the comparison is to extend §261 to pragmatic terms such as *represent* and *inform.* If a double-meaning theorist (X, 10, 12–13; quotes for §277) attempted to enunciate the implicit parallel between public and private meanings, he could not use such terms in their customary senses. In what senses, then? Once again, the hypothesis evaporates.

"This is likely to be the point at which it is said that only form, not content, can be communicated to *others.*—So one talks to oneself *about the content.*—But how do my words 'relate' to the content I know? And to what purpose?" (Z 87).

"It is as though the sentence was singling out the particular colour I saw; as if it presented it to me. It seems as though the colour which I

see was its own description. For the pointing with my finger was ineffectual. (And the looking is no pointing, it does not, for me, indicate a
direction, which would mean contrasting a direction with other directions.) What I see, or feel, enters my sentence as a sample does; but no
use is made of this sample; the words of my sentence don't seem to
matter, they only serve to present the sample to me. I don't really speak
about what I see, but *to* it. I am in fact going through the acts of attending which could accompany the use of a sample. And this is what makes
it seem as though I was making use of a sample. This error is akin to
that of believing that an ostensive definition says something about the
object to which it directs our attention" (*BB* 175; paragraph divisions
suppressed).

Someone paints a picture: Man. 110, 8, reveals W.'s target: "There
seems to be an objection against the description of immediate experience: 'For whom do I describe it?' But what if I draw it? [Haven't I
done a drawing for myself too?] And description must always be copying" (cp. §292 and commentary). Cp. JN 79: "(1) Suppose a child were
taught 'table'. (2) Then suppose we were taught A, B, C, D, for the
'view of the table'. . . . . Now after he'd been taught (1) he could then
go on to say 'The table looks C.' In this way we see that the view-
language has an appeal when we talk of visual-sense-data; you seem to
be able to do with it what you can with ordinary language; you tend to
say 'Well, I'll draw a picture' to the question 'How does it look to you?' "

how he imagines: so the picture is not of a theater scene, but of the
imagining, as in the quotation just given the picture was to be of the
sense impression, not of the table. Thus the passage resembles the following ones on believing and thinking, which in turn connect it with
W.'s earlier conception of thought (GI 36):

"We are now tempted to think that a double description must be possible for the process of believing that p is the case. One, we might suppose, would treat of psychic elements and their relationships [see *NB*
129–30], and thus if I believe, for example, that yonder house will
collapse in half an hour, then in this (direct) description of the believing process there would be no mention either of a house or of a collapse. This description would be contrasted with the one which runs: 'I
believe that the house will collapse' " (Man. 302, 31).

"If someone *tells* me what he has thought—has he really told me:
what he *thought*? Wouldn't the actual spiritual occurrence have to remain undescribed? . . . Wasn't *that* the hidden thing, of which in
speaking I gave the other person only a picture?" (Man. 229, §1243;
see ibid., §1244).

a theatre scene: "But that is only a picture: I don't really want to say
that the directly perceived has a foreground and a body behind that. It

is true, to be sure, that we sometimes represent a sense-datum to ourselves as a sort of theatrical prop, say something which looks like a bed
& in front there is painted paper which simulates a bed" (Man. 150; see
NL 311, quoted for §276).

"has a double function": cp. Man. 109, 20–21 (divisions omitted):
"Wouldn't these propositions be primary for the speaker but hypotheses for the one spoken to? At any rate there can be no difference between a hypothesis used as the expression of immediate experience & a
proposition in the stricter sense. But the meaning of the truth functions applied to hypotheses rather than to primary propositions is then
peculiar. The difference would of course correspond to that of the
meanings of the word true (& false) in both those cases."

"it informs others": see NL 308l.

"for him it is the picture . . .": cp. "looks to *me*" in §278, which this
number follows directly in Man. 163.

"as it can't be for anyone else": see Frege, *Writings,* 60 (quoted for
§374). "Some people philosophizing might be inclined to say that this is
the only real case of communication of personal experience because
only I know what I really mean by 'red' " (NL 276–77; see *BB* 65c).
And for the solipsist W. once was (X, 10): " 'This picture is unique, for
it represents what is really seen' " (NL 306). Even in Man. 116, 116–17,
he had distinguished between subjective and objective understanding,
and concluded: "Thus we could also say that in so far as a person understands language only subjectively it is not a means of communication with others, but an instrument for the *private* use of each
individual. But the question is whether this uttering of sound combinations, writing of marks, and the like would still be called 'language' or
an 'instrument'."

"Imagine a game: One person tells the other what he (the other)
sees; if he has guessed it rightly he is rewarded. If *A* hasn't guessed correctly what *B* sees, *B* corrects him and says what it is he sees. This game
is more instructive if we imagine the persons not to say what is seen but
to paint or make models of it. Now let me imagine that I am one of the
players. Wouldn't I be tempted to say: 'The game is asymmetrical, for
only what I say I see corresponds to a visual image' " (NL 307; see X,
10).

"means what he has imagined": better, tells him (*sagt ihm*) what the
original image was like. Cp. *BB* 175, quoted in part for §279.

what right have I . . . : see the initial comments; §273; the commentary on §244a (the second paragraph on "of the word 'pain' for example"); Man. 116, 117 (above), 136–39; cp. §§402, 426b, 610; *BB* 185.
Schlick had acknowledged without qualms that, unlike the physical
world, the private world he envisaged would be "suited only to mono-

logue. The latter would be to such an extent mine alone, that I couldn't even arrive at the thought of communicating facts concerning it to others" ("Psychological", 406). And the same would hold, for the same reasons, of the private meanings of actual language (X, 13).

§281 See §571b; *PG* 105bc; Man. 229, §1229; Man. 108, 208; cp. §§360, 573a; *Z* 129; Moore, *Problems*, 8–9.

The number introduces a series (§§281–86) in which the same point, the use of public criteria, is made by considering how the subject of pain is determined: living versus nonliving (§§282–85), a person versus his body (§286). W. was once more favorable to the idea that a machine too might feel pain (*PG* 105), and went so far as to assert: "The phenomenon of pain, which I describe when I say for instance 'I have toothache,' does not presuppose a physical body. (I can have toothache without teeth.)" (*PG* 105). "Our body is not at all essential for the occurrence of our experience. (Cf. eye and visual field.)" (*PG* 146–47). See below, under "it sees". Cp. GI 27; Man. 109, 271.

"what you say": in the whole preceding criticism of private meanings, centering on this example (pain), to which W. now returns after the interlude on colors (§§272–80); but also in the rejection of private pain-identification implicit in the previous number.

It comes to this: for the reason indicated in X, 18, W. switches from the material into the formal mode of speech, that is, from talk about pain to talk abot pain-talk. The material mode sentence at the start could be taken as stating either a contingent fact or a metaphysical truth; the translation into the formal mode indicates that the link is logical, grammatical. For a similar translation with regard to pain alone, see *Z* 533.

living: as opposed to a corpse (§284b). But the word also suggests the breadth of the resemblance, as just "human being" would not, so prepares for §§282–84, before the focus on human pain in §§286ff.

resembles: within broad limits, whether with respect to sense organs (Man. 229, §925) or behavior (§284a).

behaves like: see §283e. "There is, then, an essential connexion of sensations with living organisms. But to admit this is not to accept some form of behaviourism. We can avoid behaviourism while acknowledging the essential connexion if we also acknowledge a certain complexity in the creatures to which sensation words and other psychological concepts apply" (Cook, "Human Beings", 147; see GI 44–45).

can one say: contrary sayings have "no place in the language-game" (§288c).

it has sensations: cp. *PG* 105: "To be sure, it makes no sense to speak of artificial seeing or hearing. We do speak of artificial feet, but not of artificial pains in the foot."

it sees: for the contrary view, see *PG* 146–47, above, and *PP* 306: "He seemed to be quite definite on a point which seems to me certainly true, viz. that I might see without physical eyes, and even without having a body at all; that the connection between seeing and physical eyes is merely a fact learnt by experience, not a necessity at all." Russell concurred: "It seems to me possible to imagine a mind existing for only a fraction of a second, seeing the red, and ceasing to exist before having any other experience" (*Logic*, 148).

is blind: see *Z* 251, 619.

is conscious: for a contrasting Cartesian viewpoint, see for instance Berkeley, *Dialogues*, III, 448 ("The Mind, Spirit, or Soul is that indivisible unextended thing which thinks, acts, and perceives") or James: "Whether anywhere in the room there be a mere thought, which is nobody's thought, we have no means of ascertaining, for we have no experience of its like. The only states of consciousness that we naturally deal with are found in personal consciousnesses, minds, selves, concrete particular I's and you's" (*Principles*, I, 226). "Even the spinal cord may possibly have some little power of will in this sense, and of effort towards modified behavior in consequence of new experiences of sensibility" (ibid., 78).

§282 The number opens with an objection to the preceding sentence, then considers the objection in detail. In general, the objection would assimilate an aching stone (§§283–84) to a blue moon: rare, but conceivable. Compare James's free-floating thought, above, which might lodge in a chair or an ashtray, without giving any sign of its presence.

(a) it *can* also talk: this might be read in two ways: (a) as an *ad hominem* reply ("You see, the pot is no exception to the rule; it does behave in the way required"); (b) as an indication of what importance should be attached to the pot's seeing and hearing. By citing an act which clearly requires perceptible behavior, W. effectively destroys the impression that such talk about pots leaves the concept intact. This second line of thought is the one then developed.

(b) Cp. *RFM* 137d. In answer to the objection, two points are made: (1) When and if we apply such terms to things which do not resemble human beings, we are no longer using them in the same sense; thus the "exceptions" do not pove that "these things too can hear and see and think", since such a claim would suggest that they do the same things we do—that they hear, see, and think in the same sense as we do. W.'s admission does, however, amount to a modification of his original assertion; it should now read: "Only of a human being . . . can one say these things in the same sense as one says them of human beings." (2) Even in these extended uses, the (indirect) connection with behavior is essential.

(c) when playing with dolls: cp. p. 194e.

use of the concept: since a concept is often equated with the meaning of a word, and for W. the meaning is the use, his repeated references to the use of concepts (§§316, 569, p. 209e) might appear unfortunate. See the discussion under §569.

is a secondary one: for other examples of secondary senses or uses, see p. 216 and §§531–36. For a fuller analysis, see XXXVII, 14–18. For an extended presentation of the main instance (*meaning*), see Hallett, *Definition*, 94–98.

Imagine a case . . . : cp. the analogous suggestions in §§344–45 and 385, where W.'s comments seem to confirm Malcolm's judgment: "Wittgenstein means, I think, that this is an impossible supposition because we should not want to say that those people *understood* ascriptions of pain. If they did not ever show pity for human beings or animals or expect it for themselves, then their treatment of dolls would not be *pity*" ("Investigations", 201).

play at trains: see Man. 132, 11–12.

One might say: W. was hesitant in the *Investigations* to make categorical declarations about sameness or difference of sense (§§61, 140c, 552–53, 556).

did not make the same *sense*: "Only of children who know about real trains do we say that they play at trains" (Man. 138, 13A).

§283   See Cook, "Human Beings", 126.

(b) See §302; *BB* 24bc; cp. Schlick "Form", 243–44. Earlier W. had "said that we *conclude* that another person has toothache from his behaviour, and that it is legitimate to conclude this on the analogy of the resemblance of his behaviour to the way in which we behave when we have toothache" (*PP* 308; cp. *NB* 85). Familiar difficulties arise from the fact that the sampling is limited to one's own sensations. Less obvious is W.'s later point that we neither do nor could take the initial step of observing constant correlations between our sensations and our own spontaneous reactions (gestures, grimaces, groans, words, smiles, and the rest) (see commentary on p. 187abc).

I do not transfer . . . : such cryptic remarks often have the force of veiled refutations; even in a simple form the argument from analogy looks rather complicated for a three-year-old learning the word *pain,* and if we turn all these moves into denials based on arguments from analogy, the hypothesis looks still more implausible. "As you don't in fact make any such inference, we can abandon the justification by analogy" (Z 537; see Z 541–42, 565; p. 179ef). What seemed mere symptoms of pain then emerge as criteria (§354), and the argument from analogy becomes superfluous and inappropriate (cp. X, 24).

(c) Were views like those quoted for §281, which underly the argument from analogy, really correct, there should be no logical difficulty in a stone's feeling pain. But the hypothesis is unintelligible.

turning to stone: as Lot's wife turned into a pillar of salt.

And why need the pain . . . : see James, *Principles*, I, 226 (quoted for §281).

(d) Cp. BUF 252–53; *NB* 85.

and *that* is what has . . . : see §573a; *BB* 73b (quoted in XIII, 4).

(e) See §§281, 302b; cp. Man. 110, 35–36.

(f) of a body: see §286; cp. Man. 228, §117. In the light of §286 and §302b, this may seem a strange way to make the point; but here the statement remains general, applying to snakes and flies as well as humans, and the main aim is to break away from the notion of atomic pain, pleasure, and the like. Were the notion of the hidden, inner referent correct, pain might conceivably float in mid-air, like thought in the quotation from James (§281).

or, if you like . . . : a concession (cp. §79d) to a natural reaction (see below, and *BB* 73b, quoted in XIII, 4). Cp. Berkeley, *Dialogues*, I, 408 ("all equally passions or sensations in the soul").

how can a body *have* a soul?: we generally say that a person, not a body, has a good mind, kind heart, pure soul, and so on (cp. §422, p. 178f). "Whoever has a soul must be capable of pain, joy, worry, etc." (Man. 173, 42). And can a *body* have pain (§286) or joy?

Difficulties would also arise if one conceived the soul as a "gaseous human being" (*PP* 312), that is, as "the transcendent hypostasis" of the self, the I (Schopenhauer, *World*, II, 198). How would it sound to say that my body *has* me?

§284 Cp. *Z* 129. The number's therapeutic aim and its continuity with the preceding paragraph (see the commentary) appear more clearly in *BB* 73, quoted in XIII, 4.

(a) See Man. 232, 761; cp. *Z* 531; *PB* 94f.

to a *thing*: for instance, "Can a machine have toothache?" (*BB* 16; see *PG* 105).

(b) Our attitude: cp. p. 178f.

All our reactions . . . : cp. p. 179e.

If anyone says . . . : "You want to say that a break occurs, a brand new experience happens, that such a series would be non-continuous. (Compare the slogan 'Quantity into quality')" (JN 19; cp. pp. 184ef, 224j). "The concept of a living thing has the same indefiniteness as the concept of language" (Man. 228, §111).

'from quantity to quality': "In his *Dialectics of Nature* Engels speaks of the law of the transformation of quantity into quality, and *vice versa*, as the law by which changes in Nature take place. A transformation of this kind occurs when a series of quantitative changes is succeeded by an abrupt qualitative change. Thus when matter has reached a certain pattern of complicated organization mind emerges as a new qualitative factor" (Copleston, *History*, VII, 314). The transition W. has in mind is conceptual (cp. p. 224j). And the quantity in question is the amount of overall resemblance, especially in behavior (§281), not, for instance, of mere physiological complexity. It is as when a slight deviation of the eyebrow or puckering of the lips makes a face friendly or unfriendly (*EPB* 221; Man. 229, §1622), the mouth, for instance, not being friendly or unfriendly by itself (*BB* 145). "The most important thing here is this: there is a difference; one notices the difference which is 'a category-difference'—without being able to say what it consists in" (*Z* 86). On all this, see §285.

§285   See preceding commentary; §393b; Man. 229, §§1621–22, 1657; cp. Man. 229, §1611.

The best commentary on §§284–85 is *LC* 31. For example, the sense of the final words of §284, and their connection with §285, is clarified by this exchange: "I say, e.g. of a smile: 'It wasn't quite genuine.' 'Oh bosh, the lips were parted only 1/1000th of an inch too much. Does it matter?' 'Yes.' 'Then it is because of certain consequences.' But not only that: the reaction is different." W. considered facts like the following "enormously important for all philosophy": "I may draw you a face. Then at another time I draw another face. You say: 'That's not the same face.'—but you can't say whether the eyes are closer together, or mouth longer . . . or anything of this sort. 'It looks different, somehow.' " Such is our use of words, such our perception of reality: complex, indefinite, nonanalytic.

The continuity between §284 and §285 might be further indicated in this way. Friendliness, fear, hope, courage, and the like we might consider 'inner', too, like pain, with the facial expressions mere clues, as behavior supposedly is for pain. But when we follow this up and try to think of a fearful face as that of a brave, resolute man, we do not succeed (§537; cp. §§391–93), any more than we could imagine pain in a stone (§284). Our concepts are not as imagined. Yet no one of these externals is decisive by itself. Hence our inability to describe the difference (Man. 229, §1461). This should not lead us to suppose, though, that the distinction is of another order (§36; *BB* 73b, quoted in XIII, 4). Our discriminations are indeed based on externals, but on an overall impression, to some extent subjective (Man. 229, §1660; *LC* 39–40), as is our mimicry. Thus W. steers a middle course between dualism on the one hand and physicalism on the other, while avoiding his own earlier tendency to analyze all expressions as precise reports (GI 37).

   Think of the recognition . . . : see Man. 229, §933.
   which does not consist . . . : cp. p. 200d; Man. 229, §1586.

Think, too, how . . . : see §450; *LC* 39bcd, 40bc; Man. 229, §§1660, 1733, 1739; cp. p. 188m; *EPB* 201; Russell, *Mind*, 201.

without seeing one's own: and checking precise details. See the commentary above.

§286 Cp. §573; Man. 229. §1591.

(a) But isn't it absurd to say . . . : as in §283f. Cp. Berkeley, *Dialogues*, I, 385–86, 402: "it being too visibly absurd to hold that pain or pleasure can be in an unperceiving Substance". Many, like Berkeley, have attributed sensations, emotions, and the rest to a spiritual, Cartesian self (*BB* 73b). W. here indicates the element of truth in such ascriptions, but counteracts the idea "that what has pain . . . must be of a mental nature" (ibid.). In its concession and correction (citing patterns of behavior) the number thus parallels the implicit movement of §283f. Cp. Schlick, "Meaning", 163.

(b) something like this . . . : mere grammar does not decide the issue. For we do in fact say, "My hand hurts," or, "His whole body was wracked with pain." Cp. §302.

§287 Continuing the final point of the previous number, W. raises the problem of intentionality, which had so exercised him (GI 34–43). In partial answer to the question whether we should say that a person or his body has a pain, we might point out that we pity the person, not his body. But how does that come out? Note that the answer suggested in §286 does not have recourse to words ("I pity you" rather than "I pity your body"). For the interest of this point, see GI 43.

§288 See Malcolm, "Investigations", 209; cp. §272, p. 184ab.

The number introduces a series (§§288–92) on identifying pain (and sensations in general), after the series (§§281–87) on the subject of pain. An appropriate context within which to set the new series is this account of Schlick's view regarding the "privileged sentences . . . that constitute the *end-point of knowledge*": "The meaning of such a sentence can be understood only by following this reference and attending to what is referred to. Consequently, to understand such a sentence and to verify it is all one, for that which constitutes its meaning is, after all, immediately given. While normally understanding the meaning of a sentence and ascertaining its truth are two totally distinct phases of the process of verification, they here coincide" (V. Kraft, *Circle*, 120–21). W.'s verdict, roughly: At the limit where the two values meet they do not coincide, but disappear. Here there is neither understanding nor verification in the ordinary sense, nor knowledge, but that agreement in expression on which language is based (§§290, 292; X, 19–20, 25). Schlick's error: He looks for justification where there is none (*BB* 73; §289). Here the word *description*, too, if applicable at all, changes its sense (§§290–91).

(a) I turn to stone . . . : W. returns to the hypothesis of §283c, but not to make a point parallel to that developed in the intervening numbers; he does not now say, as he might, that human behavior provides the criteria of pain as well as of the subject of pain. Instead, he switches to the first-person perspective, where there are no criteria (GI 15–16).

But I can't be in error . . . : the typical declaration of one who views statements like "I am in pain" as the epistemological ultimates on which all other knowledge rests (e.g. X, 3). "In all previous theories of knowledge," wrote Carnap, "there appears a certain *absolutism:* in realism an absolutism of the object, in idealism (including phenomenology) an absolutism of the 'given', 'experience', the 'immediate phenomenon'. In positivism too one discovers a trace of this idealistic absolutism; in the logical positivism of our Circle—in the works on scientific logic (theory of knowledge) by Wittgenstein, Schlick, and Carnap which have appeared till now—it takes the refined form of an absolutism of the primitive propositions ('elementary propositions', 'atomic propositions'). *Neurath* was the first to react decisively against this absolutism, when he denied the incorrigibility of protocol statements. Popper, from different starting points, went a step farther: in his verifying procedure there are no ultimate statements; thus his system represents the most radical elimination of that absolutism" ("Über Protokollsätze", 228). The later W., too, opposed such absolutism, but countered it in his own way, one which appears already in the next sentence of this paragraph, and in §§288–92 as a whole, and is summed up neatly in §355. See also I, 3–5, and below ("I do not know").

Concerning dubious borderline cases of pain, see the commentary on §246a ("It can't be said of me").

That means: as usual (*BB* 55c) the metaphysical-sounding *can* receives a grammatical interpretation. This is W.'s answer to absolutism: contingent agreement in forms of life. Cp. §251b.

"I do not know": on the senselessness of such declarations, by anyone who does know the meaning, see §§246–47, pp. 211a, 222bcd. "You learned the *concept* 'pain' when you learned language" (§384), and neither then nor thereafter did you learn that *this* (inner referent) really is pain (§§379–81). Change the example from red to pain, and §381 encapsulates the message of §288.

pricking him with a pin: cp. Man. 176, 14B.

like any other: cp. similar remarks in §§143–44.

as in other cases: e.g. §§145–46.

(b) Cp. *OC* 446, 526. A difficulty: "The same could be said of the word *red*. But red is publicly verifiable. So what is W.'s point?" The one in (*c*): the grammatical nature of the supposed infallibility. What would it *mean* to doubt whether it is pain you feel (X, 20, 24)?

(c) Cp. *OC* 481–82. A restatement: In this language-game with *pain,* I do not identify the sensation by criteria, but express it; and the expression—together with the criteria of truthfulness (p. 222)—serves as criterion (§290) for others (GI 61). Were my expression a report, I would need some criterion and naturally one distinct from the expression itself. In that case error would become possible, and where error is possible doubt may be legitimate.

That expression of doubt . . . : see the commentary above, for "I do not know".

My temptation . . . : to grasp the nature and possible origin of the temptation, note that *red* is a quite similar concept (*RFM* 184), for which, however, human behavior is not decisive, a slip in memory being conceivable. To see that it is a temptation, consider why we never talk of feeling-blind people, as we do of color-blind people.

if I assume the abrogation . . . : "That is, we are to contrast that 'form of life' in which there is a place for exclaiming ('Ouch, that hurt!'), reproaching ('Be careful, that hurt!'), asking apprehensive questions ('Will it hurt?'), complaining, comforting, diagnosing, and so on, with the supposed use of words by a being of some sort who, although 'endowed with no natural expression of sensation', nevertheless 'associate[s] names with sensations and use[s] these names in descriptions' (256)" (Cook, "Solipsism", 63).

§289   See §378; cp. *PG* 85a. For the general context, see the initial comments on §288.

(a)   The next number suggests W.'s answer, which is summed up in the words of *Z* 659: "I do *not have grounds* for my judgment or my exclamation," either in the sense that I consult a criterion or that there is one.

"before myself": see NL 293j (e.g.: "You didn't mean this by justification, but one which justifies me privately, whatever the others may say").

Does it mean . . . : cp. *RFM* 184: "And does this mean e.g. that the definition of 'same' would be this: same is what all or most human beings with one voice take for the same?—Of course not.

"For of course I don't make use of the agreement of human beings to affirm identity. What criterion do you use, then? None at all.

"To use the word without a justification does not mean to use it wrongfully."

(b)   See I, 3–5; p. 200b; *BB* 73a; cp. Man. 176, 58.

§290   Again, for the context see the general remarks on §288. See Man. 116, 170, 243, 246–47 (connecting with p. 184b).

(a)   See GI 15–16; X, 19; the references for §289b; *RFM* 184 (quoted for §289a).

"The problem of the preceding language-game exists also here: Bring me something red. For what shews me that something is red?

The agreement of the colour with a sample?—What right have I to say: 'Yes, that's red'? Well, I say it; and it cannot be justified. And it is characteristic of this language-game as of the other that all men consent in it without question" (*RFM* 184–85).

"It does not follow nor, I think, does Wittgenstein mean to assert that there is *no* proper use of 'identify' or 'recognize' with sensations. He acknowledges a use of 'recognize' with mental images, as previously noted. It would be a natural use of language, I believe, if someone who upon arising complained of an unusual sensation were to say, 'Now I can identify it! It is the same sensation that I have when I go down in an elevator.' Wittgenstein, who has no interest in reforming language, would not dream of calling this an incorrect use of 'identify' " (Malcolm, "Investigations", 210). Notice, however, that the appropriateness of the expression *identify* in the case Malcolm imagines does not show its appropriateness in the cases W. had in mind (cp. §§602–3) or that identification in either case would resemble that of physical objects. "The philosophical use of 'identify' seems to make possible the committing of *errors* of identification of sensations and inner experiences" (Malcolm, "Investigations", 211).

by criteria: the decisive phrase, explaining the "of course". It is obvious that we perform no act such as that described in §604. It is not equally obvious that we should not speak of recognizing or identifying the familiar things we encounter and name (§§601–3), including pain, though as a matter of fact we don't so speak, and it would be misleading to do so, since it would suggest an act of identification or recognition, or the kind of situation in which we do speak of identifying or recognizing something (see Malcolm's example, above).

it is the beginning: see I, 4–5; Z 532–34; cp. §244, pp. 179e, 218bc, 222i.

(b) But isn't the beginning . . . : for W. such data once constituted the "primary experiences" (*PP* 308) of a "primary world" (Man. 105, 114) portrayed in a primary system of immediate representation (Man. 105, 84, 86). See X, 7–8.

which I describe: cp. *BB* 73a and *PG* 105c ("On the contrary, the phenomenon of pain, which I describe when for instance I say 'I have toothache' . . .").

tricks us here: as Malcolm points out ("Investigations", 205–6), "he does not mean it is a mistake to speak of 'describing' a sensation." For W. himself adopts that mode of expression in §24, where his point is the same as here and in §291 ("how many different kinds of thing are called 'description' "). However, with regard to a mere "I am in pain," see p. 187i and commentary; p. 189; NL 302b.

§291 See I, 10; §§23, 24b, 363; *Z* 311b, 347; *PB* 57a, 63a; cp. pp.
179e, 187–89; *PB* 97; Man. 108, 237.

Think of a . . . : "If we consider instead an engineer's machine
drawing or an elevation with measurements, then the *activity* of using
the picture will be seen to be the important thing" (Malcolm, "Wittgenstein", 337).

as a word-picture: as in the *Tractatus* account. See GI 32; 3.1431,
4.016; *NB* 7.

how a thing looks: cp. 4.5: "The general form of a proposition is:
This is how things stand."

are as it were idle: notice how clearly such an attitude is revealed in
W.'s earlier view (*NB* 130) that words have the same relation to reality
as our inner thoughts, which have no direct effect on others or their actions. "Describing is copying," he wrote in Man. 110, 8, "and I needn't
necessarily copy *for* anyone."

§292 From Man. 180b, 47–48, where it follows an early version of
§648. See §186 (end); *Z* 306; *BB* 73a; NL 319–20; Man. 112, 188; Man.
109, 227; Man. 108, 205 (quoted for §245); cp. Hunter, *Essays*, 147–69.

The connection with §291 appears clearly in Waismann's *Thesen:*
"The proposition *describes* the state of affairs, and the description consists in this, that in the propositional sign we trace the form of reality"
(*Kreis*, 236). "The form of elementary propositions must conform to
the form of phenomena, and we cannot foresee what that will be" (ibid.,
249).

W. himself wrote in Man. 110, 6–7 (after passages quoted for
§§162–63, which see): "If I describe something, I must read off the
description from the thing to be described (if I describe something &
don't read off the description from the thing to be described, it isn't a
description)."

From such passages it is doubly evident that W. is not denying
merely that in avowals, say (for instance of intention or of pain), we
resemble an on-the-spot reporter who constructs a running verbal account of what he sees happening. His denial takes in such reporters
too.

that you read off: in addition to the quotes above and below, see *BB*
118b; *PG* 164a (quoted for §104), 181b; *Kreis*, 50b; Man. 109, 145.

that you portray . . . : "That is, I do a portrait of the facts" (Man.
109, 63–64; see ibid., 231).

according to rules: "How do I know that this proposition describes
this fact? And I always want to reply: 'Because I read it off from this
fact.' And: 'I must know how I came to give it' " (Man. 110, 95). "If I
don't read off the description from the fact, it is a collection of sounds

arbitrarily related to the fact" (Man. 110, 7). "And doesn't that presuppose in turn that this whole list of rules is somehow already present in each individual move of the game?" (Man. 112, 188; see IX, 2).

without guidance: "Think of the justification by a general formula for performing mathematical operations; and of the question: Does this formula compel us to make use of it in this particular case as we do?" (*BB* 73). See I, 4; IX, 5–6; §§139–41, 186, 198, 201, 211–13.

§293 See GI 60–61; X, 24; p. 181abcd; NL 281cd, 290fg, 297g, 316a–317b, 320fg; cp. p. 227b; Z 649; 3.328; LC 69; NL 286e, 287e; Carnap, "Psychology", 176; Schlick, "Psychological", 405–6 (quoted in X, 14). In Frege, cp. *Foundations*, 35b–36a; *Writings*, 120c–121a; "Thought", 299 ("Now does my companion see the green leaf as red, or does he see the red berry as green, or does he see both as of one colour with which I am not acquainted at all? These are unanswerable, indeed really nonsensical, questions. For when the word 'red' does not state a property of things but is supposed to characterize sense-impressions belonging to my consciousness, it is only applicable within the sphere of my consciousness").

(a) If I say of myself . . . : see *BB* 60b; Man. 229, §866 (quoted for §244); and the quotation from Schlick for §295a. On typical reasons for this move, see X, 17 (I know what pain is from pains; but pains are private; therefore . . .).

so irresponsibly: the skeptical view which leads to the assertion that I know only from my own case (see X, 17), *ipso facto* raises doubts about what others feel and how they learn and therefore whether what I have discovered is really the meaning of the word. (Cp. *LC* 69: "If you treat this [your idea] as something private, with what right are you calling it an idea of death? . . . If what he calls his 'idea of death' is to become relevant, it must become part of our game.") Thus this sentence anticipates the movement of the number as a whole, using the skeptic's skepticism against him.

(b) Cp. §§270–71; *PB* 94g–95a, 282e.

had a box: both Schlick (*Aufsätze*, 239; see ibid., 199) and Carnap ("Psychology", 176) used a similar illustration, similarly.

No one can look . . . : cp. §272: "The essential thing about private experience is really not that each person possesses his own exemplar [his own beetle], but that nobody knows whether other people also have *this* or something else." The present paragraph concretizes this view, employing once again "the method of §2" (§48).

One might even imagine . . . : see §§142, 258, p. 207e. Think, for instance, how various are the things we call "flowers", or "insects"; or the object might alter as profoundly as does a single individual, called by a single name, from birth to old age.

it would not be used as the name . . . : see *BB* 171a; cp. *BB* 173d.

no place in the language-game: cp. *NB* 61: "What is not yet said in it simply cannot belong to its sense."

not even as a *something:* see §304; cp. Frege's critique of Husserlian abstraction (*Writings*, 85), which concludes: "Finally we thus obtain from each object a *something* wholly deprived of content; but the *something* obtained from one object is different from the *something* obtained from another object—though it is not easy to say how."

might even be empty: "How can someone retort 'But there isn't anything in my box,' if he's been taught that a beetle is '*whatever* is in the box'? If this is what 'beetle' is taken to mean, there can never fail to be a 'beetle' in the box" (Thornton, "Criticism", 268).

'divide through': as in algebra.

it cancels out: cp. NL 293: "It is senseless to say: the expression may always lie."

(c) See X, 24; XXXI, 4–5; NL 281cd, 297g; Cook, "Privacy", 320–22.

if we construe . . . : but W. doesn't; so he doesn't draw these conclusions. Thus the number is not behavioristic, but "is intended as a *reductio ad absurdum* of the form: if *this* is how you think of sensations, certain consequences follow, in particular that it is impossible to communicate meaningfully about them" (Holborow, "Kind", 356). "This passage has been misunderstood by people who have failed to appreciate Wittgenstein's insistence that sensations are states of living organisms; they have taken him to be saying that sensations do drop out of the language-game as irrelevant. Yet Wittgenstein explains his meaning when he says that a sensation 'is not a *something* but not a nothing either' and explains that in saying this he has 'only rejected the grammar which tries to force itself on us here' (304)" (Cook, "Human Beings", 145). On the genuine grammar of such expressions, see GI 15–16.

"To understand this sentence, you must remember that the grammar of words of which we say that they stand for physical objects is characterized by the way in which we use the phrase 'the *same* so-and-so', or 'the *identical* so-and-so', where 'so-and-so' designates the physical object" (*BB* 63). "And now don't think that the expression 'physical objects' is meant to distinguish one kind of object from another" (*BB* 51). For I don't identify my pain by private criteria (§290), learned by observing the thing within (X, 20).

on the model of 'object and designation': as Hacker points out (*Insight*, 237), since "*Bezeichnung eines Dings*", in the previous paragraph, is translated as "name of a thing", it might be better to translate "*Gegenstand und Bezeichnung*" similarly, as "object and name", so as to bring out the connection. For more on this model, see Z 487 and the commentary on §304a. Cp. Russell, in X, 3–4.

§294 If you say . . . : for the connection with pain and the preceding number, see the quotations for §280; and compare §§300, 373, p. 196e.

"money, or debts": cp. "it would be quite possible for everyone to have something different in his box" (§293).

"or an empty till": cp. "the box might even be empty" (§293).
§295(a) Cp. §315.

"I know . . .": the full proposition is in §293a. Cp. Schlick, "Form", 194: "A definition gives the meaning of a term by means of other words, these can again be defined by means of still other words, and so on, until we arrive at terms that no longer admit of a verbal definition—the meaning of these must be given by direct acquaintance: one can learn the meaning of the words 'joy' or 'green' only by being joyful or by seeing green."

No: for the suggestion does not mean that I, unlike others, so learn it, but that everyone does; and experience does not teach me that (§293a). I am sure of it *a priori*. Compare this other conviction, which might also be *a priori:* "Only by tasting cheese myself can I know what cheese tastes like." Here one's assurance might be upset by artificial cheese flavoring. But no such discovery is conceivable in the case of pain. An "artificial pain" would be painful—that is, would be a pain like any other. So I must feel a real pain, concludes the philosopher, if I am to know the meaning of *pain*.

A grammatical one?: suppose it were said that if a person has never tasted the flavor of cheese he cannot understand the expression "taste of cheese", or know its meaning. That would amount to an arbitrary terminological decision, not a verdict based on established usage. And according to (*b*), the same holds for *pain*.
(b) Cp. §§299, 386b.

it gives no information: cp. §298 and §352: "So it really . . . says nothing at all, but gives us a picture."

still it is a picture: see (*c*); cp. §§222, 352. The picture might show, for example, a person concentrating on a pain, telling himself it is pain, impressing on himself the connection between the sign and the sensation (§258); or perhaps it adds inferential reasoning, in the manner of St. Augustine (§§1, 32).

why should we not want . . . : cp. §§374, 423–24; *BB* 7.
taking the place of those words: cp. p. 178g.
(c) Besides the passages cited for (*b*), see *LC* 71–72f; cp. §413.

our grammar: not just familiar forms of speech, but also "the kind of way in which we talk" (§194) when we philosophize. This broader interpretation, warranted by the present example, is illustrated by many others, for instance §§193–94, 218–19, 222, 274, 352, 426–27, 431, 435–36, 439, 455–56, 507, 549–50, 559, 592, 594, 604–5, 618, 620. A passage like §305 reveals clearly both that and why a representation (e.g. "the picture of the inner process") which illustrates or prompts philosophical sayings (e.g. "Still, an inner process does take place here"—"After all, you *see* it") often also portrays popular usage as we conceive it (e.g. of *remember,* or *understand*).

Typically, W. does not mention the kind of causal connection which might bring out the significance of his remarks, for example the importance of such pictorial representations in fostering philosophers' sureness that they know what they are talking about and that their statements all make sense (GI 14).

§296   The number aims to counteract the idea that "language always functions in one way" (§304), for instance that described by §292, and the "particular way of looking at the matter" (§308) which results from that idea. See §297 and commentary; p. 189.

"there is *something* there": see NL 283e; cp. *BB* 7: "We say, 'surely the thought is *something;* it is not nothing'; and all one can answer to this is, that the word 'thought' has its *use,* which is of a totally different kind from the use of the word 'sentence'."

Only whom are we informing: not the doctor and nurse in p. 179e (cp. *Z* 544), but perhaps "a behaviourist, who holds that there is no more to pain than dispositions to such behaviour as writhing and crying out" (Donagan, "Sensation", 336).

§297   The sense: Of course, if a person is in pain, his behavior shows it. But if we observe his behavior and talk about his pain, must we supply a substitute for the missing pain—that is, the one he feels, but we neither feel nor observe? "It is—we should like to say—not merely the picture of the behaviour that plays a part in the language-game with the words 'he is in pain,' but also the picture of the pain" (§300; see §448b). See Kenny, *Wittgenstein,* 198; cp. *PB* 66d.

§298   is enough to shew: more evidently than in §296, now that private pointing replaces the words "there is *something.* . . ."

how much we are inclined: "because we have not considered its application sufficiently" (§520).

which gives no information: cp. §§280, 295, 352, 520.

§299   See *BB* 57a; cp. §§178, 254, 303a, 306, 386, 594.

"The solipsist who says 'only I feel real pain,' 'only I really see (or hear)' is not stating an opinion; and that's why he is so sure of what he says. He is irresistibly tempted to use a certain form of expression; but we must yet find *why* he is" (*BB* 59–60)

into an *assumption:* cp. NL 290bcd. The italics may be partly motivated by a desire to rectify the assimilation in *BB* 40b, of language-generated pictures (GI 9), expressed by such noninformative declarations (§§422–26), with hypotheses.

§300 A combination of Man. 228, §§650 and 651. See pp. 196e, 207b, 213c; *Z* 552, 621, 637–38, 642; NL 313hij; *PB* 93; Man. 229, §§827–28; Köhler, *Gestalt,* 260–61; cp. p. 202cde; Man. 108, 227; contrast with *PB* 73d.

we should like to say: as an illustration of this tendency, see the passage in the *Confessions* (X, 15, 23) where Augustine says that when I speak of pain, I may not be in pain, yet the image of pain is in my memory; were it not, I wouldn't know what I was saying. See §449; cp. *PB* 66d.

The image of pain is not a picture: not because it is an image of pain, but because it is an image (§301).

" 'I had a toothache'—when I say that, I do not recall my behavior, but my pain. And how does that take place? Does a dim picture of pain pass through my mind?—So is it as if one had a *very* weak pain? 'No; it is another sort of picture; something specific.' Then is it as though a person had never seen a painted picture but only busts, and someone told him 'No, a painting is entirely different from a bust; it is an entirely different sort of picture'?" (Man. 229, §825).

"The sense in which an image is an image is determined by the way in which it is compared with reality. This we might call the method of projection. Now think of comparing an image of A's toothache with his toothache. How would you compare them? If you say, you compare them 'indirectly' via his bodily behaviour, I answer that this means you *don't* compare them as you compare the picture of his behaviour with his behaviour" (*BB* 53).

and *this* image is not replaceable: "As to the use of the word 'imagine'—one might say: 'Surely there is quite a definite act of imagining the other person to have pain.' Of course we don't deny this, or any other statement about facts. But let us see: If we make an image of the other person's pain, do we apply it in the same way in which we apply the image, say, of a black eye, when we imagine the other person having one? Let us again replace imagining, in the ordinary sense, by making a painted image. (This could quite well be *the* way certain beings did their imagining.) Then let a man imagine in this way that A has a black eye. A very important application of this picture will be comparing it with the real eye to see if the picture is correct" (*BB* 53). But how could one make a picture of a pain, and how compare it with a past pain? In this instance the advice of *BB* 4 is not applicable (see XXXVII, 9).

certainly enters into the language game: cp. *Z* 636; *BB* 53; NL 313j. "Naturally I do not mean that it is not essential in some language-games to make a transition at certain points from the words to an image.—When we tell a doctor that we have been having pains—in what cases is it useful for him to imagine pain?—And doesn't this happen in a variety of ways? (As great a variety as: recalling pain)" (Man. 116, 84, which follows §449; see Z 544).

This is perhaps the clearest acknowledgment in the *Investigations* (as explicit as *BB* 103a) that the mental not only cannot be reduced to behavior, but cannot be eliminated from our accounts of language-games (see GI 44–45).

in a sense: " 'But surely I know what "He has a pain" means.' Does that mean I can *imagine* it? And what importance does the imagining have? That I can explain this statement at any time by recalling my own pains or can make the transition—can now give myself pains, etc.—is doubtless important" (Man. 130).

only not as a picture: cp. Z 655. Even were it possible to compare an image of a black eye with the black eye, to see if it really is that black, how could one check a faint image of pain for proper intensity, or compare one's present image with the past pain one describes? (Should anyone be inclined to say, "Well, the faint image shows a sharp pain or a weak one, just as the dim image shows a dark shiner or a light one," let him try imagining a sharp pain; he will then see what W. is talking about.) Besides, even the image of a black eye could not be compared with a black eye in just the same way or in the same sense as a picture is.

Again, a mental representation might picture one person rather than another with a black eye, or the right eye blackened rather than the left. But how might an image show pain in one person rather than another, or in the big toe rather than the little one (§§302, 448b)? We cannot mentally picture pain as we can a black eye, and even the latter image is no picture (§301).

"When I say 'A has toothache,' I use the image of pain in the same way as, for instance, I use the concept of flowing when I talk about the flow of an electric current" (PB 93).

§301 This follows on much discussion in *PB;* see especially *PB* 260c and 263b. See also the commentary on §300; §386a; Z 638, 652; Man. 232, 628–29; Man. 179, 72; Man. 116, 206–7; cp. *Kreis,* 55b, 97; Man. 108, 253–54; Hunter, *Essays,* 45–46, 65–66.

is not a picture: "Note how the terminology of psychology derives almost exclusively from visual perceptions, since sight provides us with the richest data for knowing the world. Thus for two thousand years our memories of perceptions, or rather the events of our inner life, have been termed 'pictures'. From Plato to Taine, the whole of psychology treats of these pictures" (Mauthner, *Beiträge,* I, 236). Stout, for instance, spoke of images as pictures ("Thought and Language", in *Analytic Psychology*). So did Russell (e.g. *Outline*, 184c, 186b), and described them just as one might a picture (*Mind*, 80b, 274; *Outline*, 189b–190). Though W. himself employed a similar terminology (e.g. Man. 302, 12; Man. 116, 116–17; Man. 108, 218) as late as *PG* 102c and 147d, already in Man. 110, 241, he wrote: "If realism says that images are 'just subjective copies of things', it must be pointed out that this rests on a false comparison between the image of a thing and the picture of a thing."

Even outside philosophy people sometimes say, for instance: "A picture of him swam before my mind" (§663; cp. §37). But from such usage we should be slow to infer either that pictures can swim or that images are pictures. "In part of their uses the expression [*sic*] 'visual image' and 'picture' run parallel; but where they don't, the analogy which does exist tends to delude us" (NL 285; see *BB* 171a; *PB* 82a; Man. 164, 167–68). Perhaps it would be better to say that though the two concepts are intimately related (see the commentary on "can correspond to it", below), they are not very similar (cp. p. 198d). For: (1) When a portraitist blurs the rest of the picture to highlight the face, he does so with definite dabs of gray and brown and green, at precise spots on the canvas, whereas nothing similar occurs in a memory where the face stands out (*PB* 260). (2) "Just as the memory of a picture cannot be represented by painting the picture in faint colors. The faintness of memory is something entirely different from the faintness of a seen hue, and the unclarity of vision different *in kind* from the vagueness of an imprecise drawing" (*PB* 271). (3) Whereas a picture can be measured and described ever more precisely, "if I say, for instance, 'I now see a red circle on a blue ground and I remember seeing one a minute ago which was the same size or perhaps a little smaller and a little lighter,' then *this* experience cannot be more exactly described" (*PB* 263; see Man. 110, 259). (4) An image has no location, whereas a picture does (*BB* 7). (5) Images are under our control in a way pictures are not (p. 213f; Z 640–43); we can terminate them at will. (6) The criteria by which we determine who has an image differ entirely from those for the ownership of a picture (cp. §302). (7) "You can't make a visible picture of the visual image" (*PB* 267) as you can of a physical picture. (8) The picture of a red thing may itself be red, whereas an image of a red thing, if red, is so in a different sense. (9) For a picture can be seen, but not an image (Man. 110, 241). (10) So an image cannot be compared with its object as a picture can (*BB* 53, quoted for §300; *Kreis*, 53–54; Man. 110, 38)—and not merely in the sense that we cannot place them side by side (Man. 110, 241). (11) Images are not durable objects, like paintings and chairs. "It is, e.g., one of the essential points about the use of a 'material' picture that we say that it remains the same not only on the ground that it seems to us to be the same, that we remember that it looked before as it looks now. In fact we shall say under certain circumstances that the picture hasn't changed although it seems to have changed; and we say it hasn't changed because it has been kept in a certain way, certain influences have been kept out. Therefore the expression 'The picture hasn't changed' is used in a different way when we talk of a material picture on the one hand, and of a mental one on the other" (*BB* 171). (12) "With this is connected: could I recognize the visual image, then, with all its details? Or rather, does this question make any sense?" (Man. 110, 261). (13) "Still another question: Can we speak of different interpretations of a memory image?" (Man. 110, 263).

The connection between this number and W.'s early conception of propositions and thoughts as pictures (GI 36) is close but complex; for on the one hand he did not identify thoughts with images, and on the other hand he did conceive of thoughts as inner pictures (*NB* 82) composed of various psychic components (*NB* 130; cp. Man. 228, §54), doubtless including images; and such inner representations, like images, would differ from physical pictures in the ways just enumerated. "The shadow, as we think of it, is some sort of a picture; in fact, something very much like an image which comes before our mind's eye; and this again is something not unlike a painted representation in the ordinary sense" (*BB* 36).

can correspond to it: cp. §§364b, 366–67, p. 212a; *BB* 36d; Man. 229, §838. Image and picture may be sharp or vague, detailed or general, highlight this or that, each in its own fashion (*PB* 260, 271, above). They may be of the same thing, again in diverse ways (§367). And a person may picture what he has imagined (cp. p. 220c), or describe the image much as he describes the picture, simply declaring what it represents (p. 177; cp. §389); "and such a description can also simply take the *place* of the image" (p. 177), as it can of the picture (§449). The image gets translated, as it were, into these words (*BB* 36d; §386).

§302   See *BB* 56b. For the connection with the previous two numbers, see §449 and NL 317. Imagining his pain is not forming a picture of it.

Philosophers have tended to overlook this question of individuation when treating the problem of other minds. "It seems a direct and simple thing to understand 'thinking that he has what I have' " (NL 319). "But is it an hypothesis at all? For how can I even make the hypothesis if it transcends all possible experience? . . . The solipsist asks: 'How *can* we believe that the other has pain; what does it mean to believe this? How can the expression of such a supposition make sense?' Now the answer of the common-sense philosopher . . . is that surely there is no difficulty in the idea of supposing, thinking, imagining that someone else has what I have" (*BB* 48; paragraph division omitted). And this is true—provided that what I have is not that private, atomic something (X, 24; Malcolm, "Investigations", 189–90) and that imagining he has pain differs radically from imagining he has a gold tooth (*BB* 49; commentary on §300) or seeing a pen in one man's hand rather than another's (NL 318). "How does *he* 'have' it?" (Z 433).

"In explanation of the statement 'He has toothache,' people say for instance: 'It's quite simple; I know what it means for *me* to have toothache, and when I say that he has toothache, I mean that he now has what I had previously.' But what does 'he' refer to, and what does it mean to '*have* toothache'? Is it a relation which the toothache once had to me and now has to him? Then I would also be conscious of the toothache now and of the fact that he now has it, as I can see a wallet now in his hand which I previously saw in mine" (*PB* 91; cp. Man. 116, 160).

(a) See §386a; Z 547; *PB* 91b, 94e; cp. §§391–94, 442; *BB* 61b; *PG* 134–35; *PB* 91a, 92d, 93d, 94a; Stout, "Phenomenalism", 3.

this is none too easy: like Augustine, Russell, and so many others, W. had thought: "Doubtless the proposition 'A has toothache' relates to my experience of toothache" (Man. 107, 271). "When I say of someone that he has toothache, by 'toothache' I mean something like an abstract of what I usually call '*my* toothache' " (ibid., 199). So when he noted the present difficulty, he concluded: "I can imagine a match-box the other has, but not the pain he has" (ibid., 286–87). The correct conclusion is that one does not "imagine someone else's pain on the model of one's own". Much as imagining something red does not entail the presence of something red in the mind (§443), and imagining someone's coming in five minutes does not require a future image (cp. Man. 108, 233), and imagining that someone sees a chair is done without seeing a chair (Z 264), so in imagining pain we do not feel pain—pricking ourselves with a needle, say, so as to have a paradigm at hand (Man. 229, §818).

In terms of the preceding numbers: I can make a picture of the steaming pot *or* of the boiling water (§297), but how can I picture the water boiling in the pot? That is: I can conjure up pain in myself (perhaps with the aid of a pin) *or* picture the other person writhing and groaning, but how can I picture the pain within his writhing body?

The parallel with §515 is equally close.

For I am not to imagine . . . : "I said that the man who contended that it was impossible to feel the other person's pain did not thereby wish to deny that one person could feel pain in another person's body. In fact, he would have said: 'I may have toothache in another man's tooth, but not *his* toothache' " (*BB* 53).

Which would also be possible: See §253b; *BB* 49–54.

(b) Reworked from Man. 179. See §§283, 286b; *BB* 68ab; Man. 116, 179–80 ("The person who is said to *have* a memory, a pain, a visual impression, is the one whose mouth gives it expression"); cp. *BB* 69b; *PB* 93b; *NL* 298a; *PP* 308b.

"The mouth which says 'I' or the hand which is raised to indicate that it is I who wish to speak, or I who have toothache, does not thereby point to anything. If, on the other hand, I wish to indicate the *place* of my pain, I point. And here again remember the difference between pointing to the painful spot without being led by the eye and on the other hand pointing to a scar on my body after looking for it. ('That's where I was vaccinated.')—The man who cries out with pain, or says that he has pain, *doesn't choose the mouth which says it.*

"All this comes to saying that the person of whom we say 'he has pain' is, by the rules of the game, the person who cries, contorts his face, etc. The place of the pain—as we have said—may be in another person's body" (*BB* 68).

This little-noticed grammatical fact underlies the "absolute breaches" between mind and mind of which James and others have spoken, so accounts in large part for the other-minds problem, belief in private meanings and languages, mind-body dualism, introspective psychology, and so on (X, 17). Such problems, beliefs, and methods tend to disappear once this origin is recognized (X, 18).

"One of the roots of the confusion, Wittgenstein argued in the *Blue Book,* lies in the grammar of the word 'I' (*BB*, p. 66). He distinguished between the use of 'I' as object (e.g. I have broken my arm, I have grown six inches, I have a bump on my forehead) and the use of 'I' as subject (e.g. I see so and so, I hear so and so, I try to lift my arm, I think it will rain, I have toothache). The salient feature of the use of 'I' as subject is that it is immune to error through misidentification of the subject. When I say sincerely that I see or hear, think or have toothache, it is not possible that I should have correctly identified (or have a title to predicate) the seeing, hearing, thinking, or toothache, but be mistaken in thinking that it is I who see, hear, think, or have toothache" (Hacker, *Insight*, 204–5).

the subject: a more literal translation of the German *Person* might be preferable, since the more philosophical term, *subject,* has often been employed to express the kind of view here criticized. See §398a, or Russell, *Logic*, 162: "We will define a 'subject' as any entity which is acquainted with something, i.e., 'subjects' are the domain of the relation 'acquaintance'." "When we have recognized that an experience is constituted by the relation of acquaintance, we may define 'I' as the subject of the present experience" (ibid., 165).

§303 See pp. 223e, 224c; cp. *OC* 563. For a much fuller development, stressing the need for contrast (cp. §251), see *BB* 53–54. For argumentation which is lacking here, see §246. The connection with the preceding number is suggested for instance by Schopenhauer's contention that "all knowing is essentially a making of representations" (*World*, II, 194). Add the premises that "on the path of *objective knowledge*, thus starting from the *representation*, we shall never get beyond the representation" (ibid., 195) and that "my making of representations, just because it is mine, can never be identical with the being-in-itself of the thing outside me" (ibid., 194), and it will appear that others' pains cannot be objectively known.

(a) On the contrast between knowing and believing, see *BB* 48d, 54a; *OC* 364–68; Man. 229, §804. Cp. §274.

"I can only *believe* . . .": see e.g. James, *Meaning*, 37 (quoted for §246a). Cp. NL 314: "We say 'only he knows whether he says the truth or lies.' 'Only you can know if what you say is true.' " The nonsense rises closer to the surface if we say: " 'So-and-so has excellent health, he never had to go to the dentist, never complained about toothache; but as toothache is a private experience, we can't know whether he hasn't had terrible toothache all his life' " (NL 289–90).

"but I *know* . . .": " 'I can persuade myself that nobody else has pains even if they say they have, but not that I haven't' " (NL 310).

is in truth . . . : cp. §§254, 299.

(b) See *Z* 554–57; NL 293f, 313f; Man. 138, 30A–31B.

in a real case: §246, §310a, and p. 221a indicate W.'s meaning more clearly. Doubt is possible in some cases, "but naturally it is not true that we are never sure of the mental processes of others. We are sure in countless cases" (Man. 176, 51B). "I can be as *certain* of someone else's sensations as of any fact" (p. 224). "In *certain* cases I am uncertain whether or not the other person is in pain" (Man. 229, §803), but "if I see someone writhing in pain with evident cause I do not think: all the same, his feelings are hidden from me" (p. 223; see NL 318).

"The uncertainty is not founded on the fact that he does not wear his pain on his sleeve. And there is not an uncertainty *in each particular case*. If the frontier between two counties were in dispute, would it follow that the county to which any individual resident belonged was dubious?" (*Z* 556).

§304   See X, 24–25; *RFM* 63f; NL 297gh, 314f (quoted for §308).

(a) See NL 304c, 313f, 319b–320a; *PP* 308a; Hacker, *Insight*, 239.

"And yet you again and again . . .": §293 has frequently been read in this way.

" 'Doesn't what you say come to this: that it doesn't matter what the persons feel as long as only they behave in a particular way?' " (NL 296).

" 'You talk as though the case of having pain and that of not having pain were only distinguished by the way in which I expressed myself!' " (NL 318; cp. §302b).

It is not a *something*: cp. §261 and commentary. The denial can be understood from both parts of the italicized word: (1) *some:* "But I wish to say that you can't explain that difference by saying that if he has pain there is behind his behaviour a certain something present which he expresses by his behaviour. If instead of 'a certain something' or some such phrase you're bold enough to say 'pain' then the statement becomes tautologous. If we want to avoid the mention of pain because this already presupposes that we know what is behind his expression then it doesn't help you to say 'a certain feeling' or 'a certain something' for how do you know that you are allowed to call it a feeling or even a something. For the word something has a public meaning if it means anything at all. And then if you risk saying that he *has something* you might as well say all you know & say that he has pain. The point is that an essentially private object can't *justify* the use of a word—neither for the others *nor* for him" (Man. 166; W.'s English; cp. §261). (2) *thing:* "It is obvious . . . that we invariably use this term *something* of a *being* of some sort" (*Sophist,* 237D). "If we ourselves try to define *something,* we can hardly say anything better than that *something* is everything that can receive a name" (Bühler, *Development,* 151). But W. rejected the model of "object and name" for pains (§293), as he did for other psychic entities. "The same holds for the psychic process of understanding as for the mathematical object Three. The word 'process' in the one case and the word 'object' in the other give us a false grammatical *attitude* toward the word" (*PG* 85). So does talk about pain as an inner object which we observe, name, identify, remember, report, and so on. "Here too . . . the expressions 'directly aware'—'indirectly aware' are *extremely* misleading. What gives us the idea that the person who feels pain is aware of an object, as it were sees it, whereas we are only told that it's there but cannot see it? It is the peculiar function of the verbs like feeling, seeing, etc." (Man. 166; W.'s English). Consider how our conception of heat might change if we customarily said, "I feel a hot," or, "I had intermittent hots all night," and on the other hand how our notion of pain would be affected were the surface grammar of *pain* similar to that of *hot.* Substantives tend to make us conceive discrete items which correspond to them (*BB* 1; GI 17–19). To break their grip, we might ask ourselves why such inner objects—pains or hopes or thoughts—cannot be situated in bottles or in stones (§283). "But 'joy' surely designates an inward thing.' No. 'Joy' designates nothing at all. Neither any inward nor any outward thing" (Z 487). "We say, 'surely the thought is *something,* it is not nothing'; and all one can answer to this is, that the word 'thought' has its *use*, which is of a totally different kind from the use of the word 'sentence' " (*BB* 7). "The chief difficulty comes from our conceiving the experience (pain, for example) as a thing, for which of course we have a name & whose concept is therefore very easy to grasp. So we always want to say: We know what 'pain' means (namely this) & the only difficulty is that we can't tell for sure whether there is the same thing in others" (Man. 169). See also Man. 229, §1777; *PG* 374bc; and subsequent comment on this paragraph.

   but not a *nothing* either: see *PG* 80a; *PP* 308a; cp. *RFM* 193g. Paraphrasing p. 179d, we might ask: "Is 'I saw he was in pain' a report about his behavior or about his feelings?", and answer: "Both; not side-by-side, however, but about the one *via* the other." Or, paralleling *Z* 487, we might see W. as denying both that the sensation is "some *one* thing" and that it is "not *any* thing"; a person's being in pain is not just his behavior nor just an inner feeling nor just a neural impulse nor just a wound, etc., but all these things; not side-by-side, however, nor as a collection or even a pattern which the expression "refers to". Rather, such items belong to the *concept pain,* that is, to the use of this word in the English language. "*Essence* is expressed by grammar" (§371). W.'s double negation can also be understood by transposing §370 and applying it to sensations.

   about which nothing could be said: as in the hypothesis of §293 (not W.'s), where the conclusion is that nothing would serve just as well as the skeptic's 'beetle'. See X, 3–4, 9–10, 12–13; Schlick, *Aufsätze,* 164; cp. §271.

   We have only rejected the grammar . . . : viz. "the model of 'object and designation' " (§293). See the preceding quotations and citations, especially §370; *Z* 487; *BB* 7; *PG* 85; Man. 166; also §1b; *NL* 302b.

   " 'But aren't you saying that all that happens is that he moans, and that there is nothing behind it?' I am saying that there is nothing *behind* the moaning" (*NL* 320). It is not used to convey from one person to another how things stand (4.5) in his stomach (§317).

(b)   Concerning W.'s stress on the diversity of language, see I, 9–10. "There is no one reason why people talk. A small child babbles often just for the pleasure of making noises. This is also one reason why adults talk. And there are countless others" (*LC* 50). As for the transfer of mental representations, language might conceivably function that way (§6) but doesn't (I, 6–7).

   Said Russell: "The use of words is, of course, primarily social, for the purpose of suggesting to others ideas which we entertain or at least wish them to entertain" (*Mind,* 211). And Frege: "I call any sentence 'genuine' if it expresses a thought" ("Compound", 3). For other examples of such thinking, see the quotations for §25. "Here the sign is treated as a sort of medicine which is supposed to elicit in the other person a stomachache like the one I have" (Man. 110, 238–39).

convey thoughts: see Moore, *Commonplace,* 180e.

which may be . . . . : "Whatever may be an object of thought, or may occur in any true or false proposition, or can be counted as *one,* I call a *term.* . . . A man, a moment, a number, a class, a relation, a chimaera, or anything else that can be mentioned, is sure to be a term; and to deny that such and such a thing [e.g. a pain] is a term must always be false" (Russell, *Principles,* 43).

§305 See GI 17; §§306, 308, p. 231; Z 51, 211, 662; *BB* 183bc; Man. 116, 252–54; cp. §§314, 316, 370; Z 605–6; *PG* 80a; NL 314fg. For similar remarks on pain rather than remembering, see Man. 166, e.g.: "What could it mean to deny pain except to deny that people have ever felt pain or to deny that it makes sense to say that someone has pain. What I do deny is that we can construe the grammar of 'having pain' by hypostatizing a private object" (W.'s English).

the picture of the 'inner process': see *PG* 85, just quoted for §304, and p. 231ab. The view criticized appears clearly in James, *Principles,* I, 648–52 ("the whole forming one 'object' . . . known in one integral pulse of consciousness").

§306 See §307 and commentary; cp. GI 68; NL 314fg.

"To every truth someone brings against me I always have to reply: 'I have nothing against it! just analyse it thoroughly, then I'll have to agree with you' " (Man. 108, 136). But not necessarily with the expression chosen (§79d), for instance "inner process".

§307 See GI 44–45; NL 314fg; Man. 130, 3; Man. 119, 79; cp. *BB* 157b; Man. 302, 11.

In allegorical form: A person denies neither paper money nor its value nor the gold in Fort Knox if he refuses to equate the value of the money with the ingots; but he does deny the mythical entity "value stored in Fort Knox".

"He said, that when he said this, people supposed him to be saying that other people never really have what he has, but that, if he did say so, he would be talking nonsense; and he seemed quite definitely to reject the behaviourist view that 'he has toothache' means only that 'he' is behaving in a particular manner; for he said that 'toothache' doesn't in fact only mean a particular kind of behaviour, and implied that when we pity a man for having a toothache, we are not pitying him for putting his hand to his cheek" (*PP* 307–8).

grammatical **fiction:** that is, a false picture of how words function, and therefore of reality, the imaginary use of the word often entailing an imaginary entity (e.g. §§166, 177), whether essence or reference (§36; GI 17–23); "the means of representation produces something *imaginary*. So let us not think we *must* find a specific mental process, because the verb 'to understand' is there and because one says: Understanding is an activity of mind" (Z 446). "In philosophy one is in constant danger of producing a myth of symbolism, or a myth of mental processes. Instead of simply saying what anyone knows and must admit" (Z 211).

In an earlier version, W. replied: "But the object behind the expression *is* a fiction. It is a fiction that if our words are to have meaning they must designate a something which I can show myself even if I can't show it to others" (Man. 161).

Though the inner process does not dissolve completely upon analysis, it shows considerable analogy with that mysterious mathematical object, the number one (*PG* 108e–109a), and with other instances of what Russell called "logical fictions". "If you think that 1, 2, 3, and 4, and the rest of the numbers, are in any sense entities, if you think that there are objects, having those names, in the realm of being, you have at once a very considerable apparatus for your metaphysics to deal with" (Russell, *Logic,* 269). "Persons are fictions and so are propositions, except in the sense in which they are facts on their own account" (Russell, "Introduction", xix). "The subject . . . appears to be a logical fiction, like mathematical points and instants. It is introduced, not because observation reveals it, but because it is linguistically convenient and apparently demanded by grammar" (Russell, *Mind,* 141).

§308   Worked up in Man. 116, 331–32, 335. See GI 17–18; §§196, 370 (the point overlooked); Z 446; PG 74b–75a; NL 314; Man. 302, 14–15; Man. 229, §1760; Man. 123 (May 23); Man. 109, 43 (quoted for §428), 261–62; cp. *Kreis,* 182.

The first step . . . : watch Moore take it: "*If* some person were believing now that we are hearing the noise of a brass-band, in what would this belief of his consist? What is the correct analysis of the event that would be happening in his mind?" (*Problems,* 258). Or W. himself: "The process of meaning that the door will open can amount to no more than is experienced by the one who means it" (Man. 108, 205).

We talk of processes and states . . . : see quotes from Russell and young W., above and below, and e.g. Moore, *Problems,* 25 (quoted for §148); Köhler, *Gestalt,* 54–55; Helmholtz, *Optik,* 580b; James, *Principles,* I, 304–5, e.g.: "I will therefore . . . continue to assume (as I have assumed all along, especially in the last chapter) a direct awareness of the process of our thinking as such, simply insisting on the fact that it is an even more inward and subtle phenomenon than most of us suppose." Cp. Moore, "Cognitive Acts", 132: "It seems to me that there can be no doubt at all as to their *existence;* the only possible doubt is as to their nature."

and leave their nature undecided: see §363c; *PG* 143e; James, *Principles*, I, 186ab; cp. §383.

" 'But a Gedanke is a Tatsache: what are its constituents and components, and what is their relation to those of the pictured Tatsache?' I don't know *what* the constituents of a thought are but I know *that* it must have such constituents which correspond to the words of Language. Again the kind of relation of the constituents of the thought and of the pictured fact is irrelevant. It would be a matter of psychology to find out" (*NB* 129).

"Understanding (whatever that is) must find its expression in the fact of understanding. The understanding must be *expressed* in the process of understanding (whatever it may be)" (Man. 109, 173).

"The mental factors of such a belief I take to be words, spoken aloud or to oneself or merely imagined, connected together and accompanied by a feeling or feelings of belief or disbelief, related to them in a way I do not propose to discuss" (Ramsey, *Foundations*, 144; see §594 and commentary).

Sometime perhaps . . . : see *BB* 39c; Man. 108, 217; Waismann, "How I See", 380 (quoted in XXVII, 1). "It is as though we supposed there must be east and west poles, since in certain cases the directions north, south, east and west seem to be on a par. We are then often inclined to say in philosophy that the east and west poles have not yet been found" (Man. 302, 24). "Thus if, in accordance with the wishes of cerebral anatomists, we could inspect the molecular changes whose effects or conscious appearances are memory images, we would know what memory acts are. . . . Then too we would really possess a physiological psychology which would have to answer our questions. Such a science, however, we do not possess" (Mauthner, *Beiträge*, I, 221). For James, introspection might provide the missing answers: "The whole mind-stuff controversy would stop if we could decide conclusively by introspection that what seem to us elementary feelings are really elementary and not compound" (*Principles*, I, 191). Russell provides a still more perfect example of the attitude described: "I, personally, do not profess to be able to analyse the sensations constituting respectively memory, expectation and assent; but I am not prepared to say that they cannot be analysed" (*Mind*, 250). See also Köhler, *Gestalt*, 203.

a particular way of looking: "We imagine something similar or analogous to what we imagine for the word chemical process or physiological process" (Man. 109, 261).

For we have a definite . . . : cp. *BB* 118b ("we have a definite picture"). "I am talking of the actual occurrence of a belief in a particular person's mind at a particular moment, and discussing what sort of fact that is" (Russell, *Logic*, 217). So of course the thing to do is to take a sharp look inside ourselves as we perform this act of believing (or thinking, remembering, hoping, and so on) (§§314, 316). See Kenny, *Wittgenstein,* 141; Zemach, "Nature", 47–49 (Reference Fallacy more than Essence Fallacy).

The decisive movement . . . : "The first error we make in a philosophical inquiry is the *question* we ask" (Man. 179). "We start off by saying to ourselves: 'What is remembering? What is the process of remembering? What takes place when one remembers?' And already we have gone wrong!" (Malcolm, "Nature", 29; see §§321, 370; Man. 229, §1268). "The question itself keeps the mind pressing against a blank wall, thereby preventing it from ever finding the outlet. To show a man how to get out you have first of all to free him from the misleading influence of the question" (*BB* 169; see Man. 228, §324). For a perfect illustration, see the quotation from Moore, *Problems,* 25, in the commentary on §148. Cp. *BB* 1d.

And now the analogy . . . : see GI 11ff; *Z* 236; *PG* 148b; Man. 302, 24; cp. §§112, 125b; *BB* 7c, 27b. For a clear illustration, see §153, then the remarks in §154.

So we have to deny . . . : see §§305–7 and comments; p. 218h; *PG* 80 ("Were people to then ask me whether I mean that there is no such thing as understanding, but just expressions of understanding, I would have to reply that this question is as meaningless as the question whether there is a number three"). "The 'private experience' is a degenerate construction of our grammar (comparable in a sense to tautology and contradiction). And this grammatical monster now fools us; when we wish to do away with it, it seems as though we denied the existence of an experience, say, toothache" (NL 314).

the yet uncomprehended process: "Indeed the expression 'mental process' suggests that there is question here of uncomprehended processes in an inaccessible realm" (*PG* 106; cp. §36).

And now it looks . . . : Man. 116, 332 adds: "So no imagining, no thinking, no feeling, etc."

naturally we don't want to: see GI 17, 44–45.

§309   See GI 8ff, 28, 68; §133bc; *RFM* 17cde; *PG* 193d; Man. 117, 92 (longer); cp. *RFM* 125d; Man. 169 (Moore stuck in a "philosophical wasps' nest"). The preceding number is a full illustration of this remark; the connection is indicated clearly by *BB* 169, just quoted re "The decisive movement" (the fly flies in, unsuspecting).

"The solipsist flutters and flutters in the flyglass, strikes against the walls, flutters further. How can he be brought to rest?" (NL 300; cp. §119 and commentary).

"Philosophy is an instrument whose only use is against philosophers and against the philosophers in us" (Man. 219, 11; but see GI 28).

"The philosopher exaggerates, almost cries out, in his helplessness, as long as he hasn't yet discovered the kernel of his confusion" (Man. 112, 106). Cried one such philosopher: "I can't discover the central grammatical error on which all these problems rest" (Man. 110, 95).

"Philosophical problems are like safe locks which are opened by a certain word or a certain number, so that no force can open the door until just that word is hit on, & once it is found, any child can open it" (Man. 109, 191; see ibid., 214–15). Thus the magic word for §308 is that of §370.

"Cf. Ryle's pertinent question: 'But what has the fly missed, that has never got into the bottle and therefore never looked for or found the way out of it?' . . . The simple answer seems to be that such a fly has missed philosophical insight" (Hartnack, "Kant", 132; see GI 28).

"The similarity between Kant and Wittgenstein is striking. For Kant the aim of the *Critique* is therapeutic. Its aim is to cure us from the dialectics of reason" (Hartnack, ibid.).

the fly-bottle: the fly enters through a hole in the bottom, drawn by the fumes of beer in a trough surrounding the hole; since it then flies only upward or sideways in its efforts to escape, never downward, it is effectively trapped, for there is a stopper in the top. Hence the similarity with another description W. once gave of the situation in philosophy: " 'It is as if a man is standing in a room facing a wall on which are painted a number of dummy doors. Wanting to get out, he fumblingly tries to open them, vainly trying them all, one after the other, over and over again. But, of course, it is quite useless. And all the time, although he doesn't realize it, there is a real door in the wall behind his back, and all he has to do is to turn around and open it. To help him get out of the room all we have to do is to get him to look in a different direction. But it's hard to do this, since, wanting to get out, he resists our attempts to turn him away from where he thinks the exit must be' " (Gasking and Jackson, "Wittgenstein", 52; see Man. 109, 298; Malcolm, *Memoir*, 51).

§310   Cp. p. 179ef.

(b) Doesn't that prove . . . : for "surely he is not saying that the *words* are not so bad, but something that the words report."

His attitude is a proof of his attitude: a disbelieving utterance, for example, is a proof of disbelief. "But disbelief in *what*?" In pain. So we are back where we started. It has not been shown that the belief or the words have what might be called purely inner reference.

Imagine . . . : the aim, once more, is to make a "break with the idea that language always functions in one way" (§304), to report facts. As "I am in pain," for instance, may be a complaint (p. 189d), so "It's not so bad" may be a reproach for complaining. Or it may resemble a mother's cooing when her baby cries (cp. §244).

not merely the words: cp. §244, or p. 179e.

§311 Cp. §300.

"What difference . . .": see §304.

for instance, you screw up . . . : cp. §302b, p. 219b. "But no! You produce an inner replica of *pain!*" Really? Is it just like imagining a tree without becoming one? Is the pain somehow there, but not a real one? (§§448, 300–302). Is all imagining just alike? And isn't acting pain just as good as imagining it (§450)? Short of actually giving yourself pain, can you hope for anything better than an *expression* of pain (§452; NL 313j)?

Cp. James, *Principles*, I, 497, e.g.: "We are constantly busy comparing feelings with whose quality our imagination has no sort of *acquaintance* at the time—pleasures, or pains, for example. It is notoriously hard to conjure up in imagination a lively image of either of these classes of feeling. The associationists may prate of an idea of pleasure being a pleasant idea, of an idea of pain being a painful one, but the unsophisticated sense of mankind is against them, agreeing with Homer that the memory of griefs when past may be a joy, and with Dante that there is no greater sorrow than, in misery, to recollect one's happier time."

And do you know that . . . : cp. §73c.

And how do you know . . . : cp. p. 219b; Z 535; and the case of obeying the order "Imagine a red patch!" (*BB* 3; §451). Must you first imagine a red patch so as to know what color to imagine? Likewise, must you first imagine a pain to guide you in your imagining, and so on *ad infinitum*? If not, why do you need the image at all?

is an illusion: if you need the demonstration, how are you competent to give it; and if you are competent to give it, how can it help you (§268)?

§312(a) See the comparison with *BB* 3 and §451, just given.

as little: since I must be able to recognize the one as pain and the other as a broken tooth, so already know what it is the exhibition would supposedly show me; and the same holds for imagined pains or teeth.

or as well: since I can either cause a pain or break a tooth, and know what a pain is as well as I know what a broken tooth is. And I can demonstrate both to others (§§288, 313), though not to myself (§268), at least in private fashion (Z 665).

(b) See NL 298d. "I want to describe a situation in which I should not be tempted to say that I assumed or believed that the other had what I have" (NL 282). "The pain begins and ends with the contact. Then our pain-language might have a logic wholly different from that which it does have. Instead of ascribing pains to sufferers, we might ascribe painfulness to surfaces, much as we at present call them rough, smooth, hard, soft, etc. Another possibility is this. We say things like 'It's hot in here,' 'It's cold out there,' and so on, ascribing temperatures

(I do not mean in degrees Fahrenheit or Centigrade) to regions. Let us suppose that any person felt pain if and only if every other normal person in the same region (which could be the size of a room or a continent) at the same time also felt pain. Then we might ascribe painfulness to regions instead of pain to persons; saying, *e.g.* 'It's painful today,' or 'It's painful in here.' The point of both examples is that in each case we should have as *impersonal* a way of describing pain-phenomena as we have of describing colour-phenomena. But of course the incidence of physical pain is not like this. The causes of pain are often internal and organic. Even when pain is caused by contact, it generally requires a special kind of contact rather than contact with any special kind of thing; and it generally does not cease when contact ceases" (Strawson, "Review", 47–48).

I am supposing . . . : cp. §§569–70.

§313   "I give myself an exhibition of something only *in the same way* as I give one to other people" (Z 665; cp. Z 667), so not privately (§311). If, for instance, I want to recall just how a pinprick feels, I do to myself what I would do to another (cp. §288), and the demonstration is just as effective in one case as the other. Were mine alone reliable—that is, the inner glance, not the mere jab (cp. §274)—it would neither exhibit *pain* (X, 24) nor *exhibit* pain (cp. §288).

§314   See GI 48; X, 22; cp. §316, pp. 174ef, 219a, 231c; Z 567.

a fundamental misunderstanding: "For one's headache or one's thought are phenomena, and what we are studying in philosophy are concepts rather than objects, and hence the use of a word rather than the object to which the word refers (PI, §383)" (Hacker, *Insight*, 238). "This role is what we need to understand in order to resolve philosophical paradoxes" (§182; see §122). And, "as Wittgenstein said, to think you get the concept of pain by having a pain is like thinking you get the concept of a minus quantity by running up an overdraft" (Geach, *God*, 19). "Do you note the essence of one when you eat *one* apple and the essence of nil when you eat none?" (Man. 229, §1472).

the philosophical problem of sensation: not one specific problem— "What is sensation?", "Do others feel what I do?", "How can I know that they do?", etc.—but the general unclarity from which such queries arise. "A philosophical problem has the form: 'I don't know my way about'" (§123).

§315   See §295a and commentary; Augustine, *Confessions*, X, 15, 23; cp. §295; NL 285d.

The general drift of the number is suggested by the numbers which bracket it: These questions, too, require that we consult the use of the words—not only *pain*, but also *understand* and *imagine*. Experience can provide no answer as long as the conceptual requirements to be satisfied are unclear—not just what will count as pain, but what will count as imagining pain. Thus the number serves as a transition from the discussion of sensations like pain, now terminating, to the discussion of "mental acts", and in general, thinking, in Section XI.

The intended connection with §313 and §316 may be more specific: The imagined speaker would no doubt conceive imagining pain, or understanding the word *pain,* as a strictly private event, in particular the occurrence of a Humean copy in the mind. In that case how could the question possibly be decided by experience? The person who had never felt pain could not compare his image with the pain he had never felt, nor could those who had felt pain compare their pains with his image, so as to determine whether he had succeeded.

XI. Thinking (§§316–362)

GENERAL COMMENTARY

(1) "Remember," wrote Wittgenstein, "that our language might possess a variety of different words: one for 'thinking out loud'; one for thinking as one talks to oneself in the imagination; one for a pause during which something or other floats before the mind, after which, however, we are able to give a confident answer. One word for a thought expressed in a sentence; one for the lightning thought which I may later 'clothe in words'; one for wordless thinking as one works" (Z 122). Thus the aim of this section is not to deny that thinking is ever an act, even a mental one (Z 123; Geach, *God,* 32). Nor is it Wittgenstein's purpose to show that nonverbal thought is impossible (see also Z 109–10; cp. *PB* 54b). After all, his injunction in §66 to look and not think is an invitation precisely to nonverbal thinking; such looking is not done with the eyes.

(2)   The true focus of the present section appears, and its relation to the preceding two sections, if we read on in *BB* 42 after the words quoted for IX, 2. "When the temptation to think that in some sense the whole calculus must be present at the same time vanishes, there is no more point in *postulating* the existence of a peculiar kind of mental act alongside of our expression." The preceding sections have dealt with this temptation, Section IX by contesting the presence of the whole calculus in the mind, Section X by questioning whether a set of private signs, even if present, would be equivalent to the public expressions. That is, Wittgenstein has just rejected this combined picture, that

"there is enormously much added in thought to each sentence and not said" (*NB* 70; translation slightly altered), and that "thinking is a kind of language. For a thought too is, of course, a logical picture of the proposition, and therefore it just is a kind of proposition" (*NB* 82). So he is now in a position to criticize the related notion that in a spoken or written proposition such an inner proposition, or "thought", "finds an expression that can be perceived by the senses" (3.1; see §§317–30). "Thinking is not an incorporeal process which lends life and sense to speaking, and which it would be possible to detach from speaking" (§339), as his earlier account had implied.

(3)   Treating this same theme, the *Brown Book* ties a string of numbers together (§§330–41), and adds more causal explanation than is typical of the *Investigations*, when it says: "We very often find it impossible to think without speaking to ourselves half aloud [§331],—and nobody asked to describe what happened in this case would ever say that something—the thinking—accompanied the speaking, were he not led into doing so by the pair of verbs 'speaking'/'thinking', and by many of our common phrases in which their uses run parallel. Consider these examples: 'Think before you speak!' [§§334, 337–38], 'He speaks without thinking' [§§330, 341], 'What I said didn't quite express my thought' [§335], 'He says one thing and thinks just the opposite,' 'I didn't mean a word of what I said' [§332], 'The French language uses its words in that order in which we think them' [§336]" (*BB* 148; see GI 17–19).

(4)   The case cited by James (§342) not only suggests but seems to prove that thinking is a detachable inner process, equivalent to speech. "I remember at one time," wrote Ballard of his deaf-mute childhood, "when my eye fell upon a very large old stump which we happened to pass in one of our rides, I asked myself, 'Is it possible that the first man that ever came into the world rose out of that stump? But that stump is only a remnant of a once noble magnificent tree, and how came that tree? Why, it came only by beginning to grow out of the ground just like those little trees now coming up" (James, *Principles*, I, 267). It is clear why Wittgenstein needed to treat the notion of private language before discussing this conception of thought: All this questioning and replying supposedly went on in the mind of a boy who had never heard, read, or spoken a word. It was conducted in his own private system of signs.

(5)   For Wittgenstein, Ballard's recollections were merely "a queer memory phenomenon" (§342), not significant testimony (§386), as they were for James. Subsequent numbers indicate why. First, the implication that people might never get beyond that initial stage and just say things to themselves in the imagination is not an intelligible hypothesis

(§§344–45, 348), nor therefore is the supposition of such an initial stage (cp. §32). Second, if Ballard identified his activity from his own case—as talking, asking, replying—there is no telling what he did (§347). In general, we cannot assume uncritically that such familiar-sounding words (*talk, ask, reply*) make good sense regardless of the circumstances (§§349–50). Mere images (§351) or pictures (§352) do not establish or determine a sense, but a mode of verification (§353) and criteria (§§354–57) do, and the criteria for thinking are not unobservable items (§358) which might conceivably be present in a machine (§§359–60) or a chair (§361). Wittgenstein thus returns to the point from which he started: the myth of the inner referent, privately identified (§316) and privately defined (§362).

(6)   "At section 316 the discussion [of private meanings] does not end but is given a new turn; the investigation of the concept *thinking* and others in sections 316–76 should be seen as containing a further account of the way in which Wittgenstein means to oppose the idea of an inward or private identification of a mental state or process. He makes this connexion explicit in the next group of passages, 377–97, and then in section 398 the discussion returns to the question raised in 281–7 about the nature of the *subject* of pain or thought. Here he first discusses (398–413) puzzles about the first person pronoun and the idea that the 'self' is discerned by an inward gaze, and he then concludes the discussion of the whole topic by taking up questions about human beings, souls, and automata (414–27)" (Cook, "Human Beings," 121). A dominant concern thereafter till the end of Part I, but especially in §§428–65 and §§629–93, and one which does not appear at all in the present discussion of thought, "could be put this way: We think about things,—but how do these things enter into our thoughts? We think about Mr. Smith; but Mr. Smith need not be present" (*BB* 38).

DETAILED COMMENTARY

§316   See GI 48; X, 22; commentary on §314; p. 188l; Man. 110, 3–4.

we watch ourselves: W. himself had written: "We do not want to describe what happens during thought, but what happens *in* thought" (Man. 108, 205–6). "Thinking interests us only in so far as it is directly present in consciousness. It is a process only in what is immediately given" (Man. 110, 3).

is not used like that: even were it safe to call it the name of an inner process, which we identify and report when we say, for instance, "I was thinking about the same thing," or, "I'm thinking it over" (see *BB* 147, below), the meaning of a word is not its reference (§43).

"One of the most dangerous ideas for a philosopher is, oddly enough, that we think with our heads, or in our heads. The idea of thinking as a process in the head, in a completely enclosed space, makes it something occult" (Z 605–6, translation altered; cp. §293).

Concerning such references to "using" concepts, see the commentary on §569.

It would be as if . . . : cp. Man. 179: "It would be as if someone were to observe a piece of cheese to see how the price of cheese rises."

observation of the last move . . . : "By the expression 'checkmating somebody' we refer to the act of taking his king. If on the other hand, someone, say a child, playing about with chessmen, placed a few of them on a chess board and went through the motions of taking a king, we should not say the child had checkmated anyone" (BB 147; see EPB 229).

§317 Cp. I, 6; the passages from Schopenhauer quoted for §25; p. 197de; BB 185; PG 107b; 3.1 ("In a proposition a thought finds an expression that can be perceived by the senses").

The parallel is mistaken at both ends, joining a misconception treated in the last section with a similar one treated in this section: As the expression of pain "brings it about that he *knows* that I am in pain" (§363; cp. p. 179ef), so the proposition brings it about that he knows that I think such-and-such (§24d). In this view, both expressions are, as it were, "descriptions of *my* inner life" (ibid.).

Cp. Moore, *Commonplace*, 45: "The *name* is related to the *content* of the judgment, in the same way as the cry to the *nature* of the feeling. . . . In order that a child may intend to convey its anger, it must not only be angry, but *know* that it is: & it is this knowledge, wh., in one sense, the expression then *expresses*."

"So every judgment is about the person judging? No, inasmuch as I don't want the main conclusions to be drawn concerning *me*, but about the object of the judgment. If I say, 'It's raining,' I don't generally want the other person to reply, 'So *that*'s how it seems to *you*.' 'We're talking about the weather,' I could say, 'not about me'" (Man. 229, §1418). See §501.

(b) See BB 3e (quoted for §6b); Man. 110, 238–39 (quoted for §304b).

in his thinking part: "So we no longer think of the mind as though it were some sort of protoplasm in which things seem to happen which are unknown either to physics or to chemistry. For the sense does not stand behind the sentence in the sphere of the mind" (Man. 302, 19; see GI 37; IX, 2). In Man. 110, 1–2, W. had compared thought with digestion.

§318 See §§334–35; cp. p. 59n (b). BB 43 makes the same point in a way that connects still more clearly with the closing words of §317: "Now ask yourself: Does thinking the sentence without speaking it consist in turning over the switch (switching on what we previously switched off and vice versa); that is: does thinking the sentence without speaking it now simply consist in keeping on what accompanied the words but leaving out the words? Try to think the thoughts of a sentence without the sentence and see whether this is what happens.

"Let us sum up: If we scrutinize the usages which we make of such words as 'thinking', 'meaning', 'wishing', etc., going through this process rids us of the temptation to look for a peculiar act of thinking, independent of the act of expressing our thoughts, and stowed away in some peculiar medium. We are no longer prevented by the established forms of expression from recognizing that the experience of thinking *may* be just the experience of saying, or may consist of this experience plus others which accompany it."

while we talk or write: that is, as we actually utter or write the words, not in the pauses for reflection, when we sometimes see far ahead, in the way described by James and discussed here (§§318–20).

and so on: "How could Mozart, as he recounts, all at once see a whole piece of music before him? How did he know it was a piece of music, since he certainly could not hear it all at once?" (Man. 180a, where W. was working up these numbers).

lightning-like thought: see Man. 130 (quoted for §337).

§319   See e.g. §§184, 197, 633–36.

in exactly the sense: "If you are puzzled about the nature of thought, belief, knowledge, and the like, substitute for the thought the expression of the thought, etc. The difficulty which lies in this substitution, and at the same time the whole point of it, is this: the expression of belief, thought, etc., is just a sentence;—and the sentence has sense only as a member of a system of language; as one expression within a calculus" (*BB* 42).

"(Thoughts, as it were only hints.) Isn't it the same here as with a calculating prodigy?—He has calculated right if he has got the right answer. Perhaps he himself cannot say what went on in him. And if we were to hear it, it would perhaps seem like a queer caricature of calculation" (*Z* 89).

§320   See §§179, 186–90. This number indicates the connection of the following numbers (§§321–26), on sudden understanding, with the preceding (§§318–19), on lightninglike thought. The general perspective for both is indicated by *BB* 42a.

§321(a)   See §154; cp. *Kreis*, 167.

The question is badly framed: see §308, especially the commentary on "the decisive movement". This question, perhaps still more than "What is understanding?", tends to blur the distinction between a conceptual inquiry into meaning and an empirical inquiry into characteristic accompaniments. See §354, and compare: "What happens when it rains?" Should the answer be: "It often thunders" (token, symptom), or "Water falls from clouds" (criterion)?

the answer is not to point . . . : both because understanding is not a process (*BB* 41–43; §§152–55, 183, p. 181cd) and because, even if it were, the process would not be the meaning of the word *understand* (§43).
(b) The point of this parenthetical remark: There is no reason to suppose that the person who says "Now I understand" has noticed the psychic accompaniments of the expression (he is usually intent on solving a problem, not on introspecting the solving process); so when he says these words he is not reporting his inner experience (GI 15–16), nor, therefore, do such experiences constitute the criteria of understanding, or the meaning of the word *understand* (§322; see GI 60–61). Cp. §171b.

There is no ground . . . : "If someone acts grief in the study, he will indeed readily become aware of the tensions in his face. But be really sad, or follow a sorrowful action in a film, and ask yourself if you were aware of your face" (*Z* 503).

Posture: this insert is explained by Malcolm's notes, *Memoir*, 48–49: As I usually do not know the position of my limbs by means of accompanying sensations (Section XXXIV), so I do not learn my understanding from inner experience, then report it. To grasp W.'s point, paraphrase the whole of §625, applying it to this case. Cp. *RFM* 25efg; *BB* 158c–159; James, *Principles*, I, 241–42 ("Our own bodily position, attitude, condition, is one of the things of which *some* awareness, however inattentive, invariably accompanies the knowledge of whatever else we know. We think; and as we think we feel our bodily selves as the seat of the thinking").

§322 by such a description: of "characteristic psychical accompaniments" (§321). See §154c.

and this misleads us . . . : cp. §§36, 153–54a, 175, 608, 610; *BB* 31a.

specific: cp. p. 66n and commentary; §§165, 167, 174, 542.

indefinable: cp. §182c, p. 185h.

how do we *compare* . . . : cp. §§75, 376–78.

what criterion of identity: establishing that this, and not that, is a case of understanding.

do we fix: the meaning of a word is its use "in the language" (§43), not one we might guess *a priori* (§340), then fill in the missing details (§308). Cp. the italics in §313.

"But let's not forget that a word hasn't got a meaning given to it, as it were, by a power independent of us, so that there could be a kind of scientific investigation into what the word *really* means. A word has the meaning someone has given to it" (*BB* 28).

"We are inclined to forget that it is the particular use of a word only which gives the word its meaning" (*BB* 69). See *BB* 27e.

§323 In answer to the question in §322, the first paragraph suggests two reasons for rejecting the idea that some inner experience is an adequate criterion of understanding: First, when we say we understand, we do not consult such a criterion (see GI 15–16); second, failure in performance may show that one did not understand (p. 53n). This is the point of the remark, "what is unforeseen must not simply be that I get stuck"; there *are* cases in which, despite my awareness of my inner feelings, my declaration proves mistaken. The second paragraph suggests that for a given individual this might always be the case; he might always be mistaken in this way. Were understanding an immediate datum of consciousness, like the color red, this would not be conceivable, not if the person knew the meaning of the word (cp. §288).

(a) See §179.

(b) Cp. §269, pp. 207e, 219f. W. might be imagined to say: "Once you see that this is a possibility, you will be less impressed by a person's exclamation, less inclined to suppose that he has read off what he says from his inner experience" (cp. §292).

§324 Recognizing that inner experience is not an infallible criterion of understanding (§323), the advocate of a mental-calculus view of language (§81b) might propose that it is at least a reliable clue which we consult before declaring "Now I know how to go on." "For after all," he might urge, "we must have some reason for the assertion." W. has already questioned the accuracy of such an account (§179; cp. pp. 193j–194a). Here he attempts to exorcise the impression that it *must* be so (see commentary on §326). Reasons come to an end (I, 4).

better **than success:** to go by the experience, one would have to recognize it as characteristic of knowing-how; but the surest sign of that is precisely success in going on. Cp. §625.

§325 Cp. *Z* 309; Russell, *Inquiry*, 314c.

(a) Cp. p. 215d; *PG* 101c.

Does that mean . . . : see §§179a, 477–80.

the *cause* of my certainty: "At this point . . . another confusion sets in, that between reason and cause. One is led into this confusion by the ambiguous use of the word 'why'. Thus when the chain of reasons has come to an end and still the question 'why?' is asked, one is inclined to give a cause instead of a reason. If, e.g., to the question, 'why did you paint just this colour when I told you to paint a red patch?' you give the answer: 'I have been shown a sample of this colour and the word "red" was pronounced to me at the same time; and therefore this colour now always comes to my mind when I hear the word "red",' then you have given a cause for your action and not a reason" (*BB* 15).

Whether the earlier experience . . . : the point of this remark, which appears so obvious as to be trite, is revealed clearly by the foregoing quotation. To get clear about the difference between ground and cause, ask: How is the ground *discovered,* and how the cause (p. 224k; see §475)? "That previous experience may very well be the *cause* of my present certitude; but is it its ground?" (*OC* 429). "A *ground* [*reason*] can be given only *within* a game. The chain of reasons comes to an end, at the boundary of the game. (Ground and cause.)" (*PG* 97).

W.'s stress on this distinction may have roots directly in Schopenhauer's fundamental idea that we have twofold knowledge of ourselves, so indirectly in Kant's discussion of free will. "According to Kant, we can regard ourselves as on one side belonging to the 'world of sense' and as such subject to universal laws of nature, and on the other side as belonging to the 'intelligible world' where the only laws to which we are subject are those founded on and prescribed by 'reason' " (Gardiner, *Schopenhauer,* 57).

the system of hypotheses . . . : and this will differ not only because opinions differ but because " 'Cause' is used in very many different ways" (*LC* 13).

(b) is shewn by . . . : rather: "shows how they think and live" (and not, for the most part or ultimately, their epistemological views). Cp. §§241–42, 472–80.

§326 See I, 3–4; *Z* 301; *EPB* 216 and *BB* 143c (quoted for §217a).

I would be very surprised to look and see that I have only four toes on each foot; yet this certitude is not based on anything past or present of which I am more certain than that I have five toes on each foot (*OC* 429). The point of such remarks here: to destroy the sort of prejudice which demands an observed basis for the utterance, "I understand," so turns it into a report. "I have been trying in all this to remove the temptation to think that there '*must* be' what is called a mental process of thinking, hoping, wishing, believing, etc., independent of the process of expressing a thought, a hope, a wish, etc." (*BB* 41).

§327 Cp. *PB* 61a.

"Wittgenstein held that no answer to a philosophical question was any good unless it came to a man when he needed it. This involved an attempt to make you see that you really did need such an answer. Add to this that he 'hoped to show that you had confusions you never thought you could have had' " (Gasking and Jackson, "Wittgenstein", 52–53).

"without speaking?": see X, 2; XI, 1.

what is *thinking*?: see GI 18.

in a hurry: cp. §§436, 456.

§328 See the comments on §327.

need I always be right?: is this concept like *understand* (§§179c, 323, p. 53n) or like *pain* (§288)? For a discussion and answer, see p. 222hi.

What *kind* of mistake: may I, for instance, be mistaken about the occurrence, or in my identification of it as thinking?

Are there circumstances . . . : see p. 222hi.

has he interrupted . . . : p. 223b suggests a negative verdict. Here W. is not interested in answers, but in a lesson like this: "We are not at all *prepared* for the task of describing the use of e.g. the word 'to think' " (Z 111). Thus "if a normal human is holding a normal conversation under normal circumstances, and I were to be asked what distinguishes thinking from not-thinking in such a case,—I should not know what answer to give" (Z 93).

§329   A retouched version of *PG* 161b. See XI, 2–3; *Z* 123; *BB* 41, quoted for §326; cp. *BB* 6–7; *PB* 69c; Man. 109, 177; Man. 108, 273.

When I think in language: I don't always (XI, 1). Thus §329 does not echo *PG* 106b ("I could also say: thinking is operating with language") but (distantly) *PG* 51c ("By 'thought' one means a particular mental process, say one which accompanies the uttering of a sentence; but also: the sentence itself in the system of language").

"The sense—the thought 'It's raining'—is not even the words *with* the accompaniment of some sort of imagery. It *is* the thought 'It's raining' only within the English language" (*LC* 30).

"If anything in such a case can be said to go with the speaking, it would be something like the modulation of voice, the changes in timbre, accentuation, and the like, all of which one might call means of expressiveness. Some of these, like the tone of voice and the accent, nobody for obvious reasons would call the accompaniments of the speech; and such means of expressiveness as the play of facial expression or gestures which can be said to accompany speech, nobody would dream of calling thinking" (*BB* 148).

there aren't 'meanings' . . . : see pp. 176gh, 181e, 218e; *PG* 130d. Even in the secondary sense of *meaning* (XXXVII, 15) it would be misleading to speak of meanings "accompanying" the words (pp. 182–83; Hallett, *Definition*, 61–63).

the language is itself . . . : that is, we think in words and not merely by means of them, much as we play chess with chess pieces and not merely by means of them (*BB* 147c). Cp. Lichtenberg, "Sprachbemerkungen", 276 ("since we think in words"); Frege, "Justification", 156 ("we think in words or, when not in words, then in mathematical or other symbols"); James, *Meaning*, 31 ("I am sure that my own current thinking has *words* for its almost exclusive subjective material"), 33–34.

the vehicle of thought: the metaphor, which is not very happy as an expression of W.'s view (cp. *Kreis*, 109: "The proof is not merely the vehicle by which one gets some place, but the thing itself"), may have been suggested to him, at least indirectly, by T. Vischer's talk of language as the "vehicle of meaning" (Fischer, "Nachwort", 442).

§330 See §§501–2; *BB* 43c; cp. §§507–11, p. 18n. On the topic introduced in this number, see *Z* 92–107. For background in W.'s thought, see XI, 2.

(a) Is thinking a kind of speaking?: that is, mentalese (X, 2).

One would like to say . . . : much as Russell did: "The association seems to go, not direct from stimulus to words, but from stimulus to 'meaning' and thence to words expressing the meaning' " (*Outline*, 77). "One imagines thinking as the stream which must be flowing under the surface" (*Z* 107)—as Frege did when he spoke of "that train of thought which accompanied the affair for us and actually made it interesting" (*Writings*, 186; see *BB* 3e); or James, in his chapter on "The Stream of Thought", in *Principles*, I, or e.g. p. 297: "whilst in the thoughts that do resemble the things they are 'of' (percepts, sensations), we can feel, alongside of the thing known, the thought of it going on as an altogether separate act and operation in the mind". See §507.

an accompaniment of speech: as in Man. 107, 267–68 (like a tune one whistles from, there in the mind).

may accompany something else: for instance different words (§510).

or can go on by itself: "If thinking and speaking stood in the relation of the words and the melody of a song, we could leave out the speaking and do the thinking just as we can sing the tune without the words" (*BB* 42).

"In this case, it is not the actual words that we repeat, but only their meaning" (Russell, *Outline*, 77).

" 'Les paroles ne sont que des sons dont on fait arbitrairement les signes de nos pensées. Ces sons n'ont en eux-mêmes aucun prix.' (Fénelon)" (Man. 133, Nov. 19).

To see the difference between W.'s second formulation here and the first, compare the following two passages from James: (1) "Such a vague sense as this of the words belonging together is the very minimum of fringe that can accompany them, if 'thought' at all" (*Principles*, I, 262); (2) "A good way to get the words and the sense separately is to inwardly articulate word for word the discourse of another. One then finds that the meaning will often come to the mind in pulses, after clauses or sentences are finished" (ibid., 281). This latter accompaniment is supposedly separable from the words, the former evidently not.

(b) See p. 223b; *Z* 100–101; Man. 232, 601–2.

then without thought: see *BB* 43b on how this might be attempted.

then just think the thought: see §§339, 501–2.

is not some process which . . . : "For the thinking is not an accompaniment of the work, any more than of thoughtful speech" (Z 101). "I need not be talking to myself either out loud or silently at the time" (p. 223).

§331   On the point of this remark, see *BB* 42a, quoted for §319.

who could only think aloud: cp. *BB* 42c, 148a (quoted in XI, 3).

who can only read aloud: a condition resulting from a psychological block, not from a physical defeat (as in cases of aphasia, for example, which prevent a person from speaking, but not from reading aloud).

§332   Moore typifies the viewpoint here criticized: "Our second point, then, with regard to propositions and our apprehension of them is this: namely, that in exactly the same sense in which we apprehend them, when we hear certain words spoken of which we understand the meaning, we also often apprehend them, when we neither see nor hear any words which express them, and probably often without even having before our minds any *images* of words which would express them" (*Problems*, 61).

to accompany a sentence . . . : as the next sentence makes clear, W. is not adding to the list in *Z* 122 (see XI, 1) and conceding that thinking sometimes does consist in a process which accompanies speech (XI, 2–3); he is repeating the point of *BB* 43: "The experience of thinking *may* be just the experience of saying, or may consist of this experience plus others which accompany it."

that accompaniment: to be distinguished from, for instance, "the lightning thought which I may later 'clothe in words' " (Z 122).

a "thought": this switch to the substantive might by itself explain the negation; for a process is not a proposition. But even were the verb retained and just the process meant, the negation might still be justified. For compare: "While we sometimes call it 'forgetting' when we do not think of a thing, failing to think of a thing is not what we mean by forgetting."

with understanding: said W. earlier: "Language is *understood*, thought not. (Understanding language is thinking, but the understanding of language is not in turn understood)" (Man. 108, 188).

And now do not say it . . . : see *BB* 43b; *PG* 155 ("Try the following: Say a sentence, for instance, 'The weather is very fine today.' Good, and now think the thought of this sentence, but without the sentence, pure").

Sing this tune . . . : see *LC* 29e.

And here one . . . : cp. p. 219b.

§333   From *PG* 155f. Cp. §§540–45, 578. Conviction appears here, in the treatment of thought, not because W. confused the two, or because others have (§574), but for the reason indicated by XI, 3: Expressions like the one cited also suggest a thought process accompanying speech (§§330, 339). They puzzle us in similar fashion (*BB* 42a).

What if someone were to say . . . : see *BB* 40bc, e.g.: "Aren't we making a mistake like mixing up the existence of a gramophone record of a tune with the existence of the tune? And aren't we assuming that whenever a tune passes through existence there must be some sort of a gramophone record of it from which it is played?" For such thinking, see Augustine, *Confessions*, XI, 28, 38 ("I am about to repeat a psalm that I know. Before I begin, my expectation is directed to the whole; but when I have begun, as much of it as becomes past by my saying it is extended in my memory; and the life of this action of mine is extended both ways between my memory, on account of what I have recited, and my expectation, on account of what I am about to recite. . . . And what takes place in the entire psalm, takes place also in each individual part of it, and in each individual syllable") and 31, 41.

§334   For the general context, and the connection with the preceding and following numbers, see X, 3. As indicated there, §§337–38 return to the same item in the list. Cp. the end of §19b; *BB* 29a.

solutions of mathematical problems: see *RFM* 54–55; *PB* 170c; Man. 123 (June 4), re Goldbach's theorem: "Suppose it had been proved— would we then know better than we do now what is meant by the words 'proof of Goldbach's theorem'? Or would we rather know it *differently*? Do the words then have a different meaning? Or is it as when I wish an apple and know what the object of the wish is just as well before I get it as afterwards?"

'trisection of the angle': see *Kreis*, 36–37; Goodstein, "Mathematics", 277–78; cp. *Kreis*, 135–36.

"He said that a man who had spent his life in trying to trisect an angle by rule and compasses would be inclined to say 'If you understand both what is meant by "trisection" and what is meant by "bisection by rule and compasses", you must understand what is meant by "trisection by rule and compasses" ' but that this was a mistake; that we can't imagine trisecting an angle by rule and compasses, whereas we can imagine dividing an angle into eight equal parts by rule and compasses; that 'looking for' a trisection by rule and compasses is not like 'looking for' a unicorn, since 'There are unicorns' has sense, although in fact there are no unicorns, whereas 'There are animals which show on their foreheads a construction by rule and compasses of the trisection of an angle' is just nonsense like 'There are animals with three horns, but also with only one horn': it does not give a description of any possible animal. And Wittgenstein's answer to the original question was that by proving that it is impossible to trisect an angle by rule and compasses 'we change a man's idea of trisection of an angle' but that we should say that what has been proved impossible is the very thing which he had been trying to do, because 'we are willingly led in this case to identify two different things' " (*PP* 304–5).

"We should be inclined to say that the proof of the impossibility of trisecting the angle with ruler and compasses analyses our idea of the trisection of an angle. But the proof gives us a new idea of trisection, one which we didn't have before the proof constructed it. The proof led us a road *which we were inclined to go;* but it led us away from where we were, and didn't just show us clearly the place where we had been all the time" (*BB* 41).

§335 For the general point and context, see XI, 3. See also §597, p. 54n; Man. 115, 48–49 (source of the number); Man. 302, 25–26 (full discussion); Man. 228, 120–21 (another version).

Moore wrote: "But it is, I think, obviously possible that we should apprehend propositions, in exactly the same sense, without even having before our minds *any images* of words which would express them. We may thus apprehend a proposition, which we desire to express, before we are able to think of any sentence which would express it. We apprehend the proposition, and desire to express it, but none of the words we can think of will express exactly *the* proposition we are apprehending and desiring to convey" (*Problems,* 60–61).

W.'s comment: "The phrase 'to express an idea which is before our mind' suggests that what we are trying to express in words is already expressed, only in a different language; that this expression is before our mind's eye; and that what we do is to translate from the mental into the verbal language. In most cases which we call 'expressing an idea, etc.' something very different happens. Imagine what it is that happens in cases such as this: I am groping for a word. Several words are suggested and I reject them. Finally one is proposed and I say: 'That is what I meant!' " (*BB* 41).

(a) This phrase compares . . . : that is, it suggests such a view (XI, 3) and may be what the speaker supposes.

are already there: see §184. "The thoughts are already there, and I want to find the verbal expression for them. Here the idea might occur to us that the thoughts are feelings and that their adequate expression would be words or sounds which vent these feelings as a sigh does sorrow; or that the thoughts are pictures and their expression is the description of these pictures; or that they are a peculiar kind of linguistic expression, say the expression of a private language, which we now translate into the expression of a generally accessible language" (Man. 302, 25).

more or less appropriate: "There really are cases in which the sense of what a person wants to say comes before him more clearly than he can express it in words. (This happens to me very often.) It is then as if one saw clearly a dream image before one but could not describe it so that the other also sees it" (Man. 138, 2A).

But can't all sorts . . . : this is not a question in the German. One may feel that some of these are not very good descriptions of what happens on the occasions when we might say we had made an effort to find the right expression for our thoughts; but is that because we have been introspectively attentive to what occurs on such occasions or because the details we actually find do not conform to the picture we had formed, that is, seem hardly to constitute a thought? "It is as if at first all these more or less inessential processes were shrouded in a particular atmosphere, which dissipates when I look closely at them" (§173). See §§608, 635, 645–46, 678; *BB* 86.

(b) See the numbers just cited.

§336   See Man. 302, 12.

This case is similar: see XI, 3.

in which someone imagines that . . . : cp. Pedersen, *Israel,* 112: "Hebrew, like other Semitic languages, has preserved its primitive character and gives an immediate expression of the processes of thought."

A French politician: "I believe M. Briand" (Man. 109, 177).

once wrote: "a few years ago" (Man. 228, §240).

"The idea that one language, in contrast to others, can have a word order which corresponds to the order of thought arises from the notion that thinking goes on separately from its expression, and is an essentially different process. (No one would ask whether the written multiplication of two numbers in the decimal system runs parallel with the thought of the multiplication.)" (*PG* 107).

Cp. Frege, "Compound", 1: "The structure of the sentence serves as an image of the structure of the thought."

§337   See XI, 3; §§633–37, 656–60.

But didn't I already . . . : "Compare James's idea that the thought is already complete at the start of the sentence with the lightning-like speed of thought [§318] and the concept of intending to say this and that [e.g. §§334, 633]" (Man. 130). See James's *Principles,* I, 278 ("*Whatever things are thought in relation are thought from the outset in a unity, in a single pulse of subjectivity, a single psychosis, feeling, or state of mind*") and 280 ("Even before we have opened our mouths to speak, the entire thought is present to our mind in the form of an intention to utter that sentence").

for example: see §333, and the quotation from Augustine in the commentary on it.

in some different word order: see §336.

a misleading picture: see §205.

embedded in its situation: cp. §581 and commentary.

If the technique of . . . : see §§197, 205; *EPB* 225, 229–30; *BB* 147cd; cp. p. 181ab. The remark may seem banal, but its point (§205) is not. And just how, for example, does this case differ from the possibility of intending to jump over a fence but impossibility of intending to jump over the moon?

is made possible: logically possible; see §338.

§338(a) Therefore: for such is the concept *want* or *intend*. We do not say we want to do something unless there is some possibility, not only logical but physical, of our doing it. A person with no limbs does not say "I want to play the piano" or "I intend to play the piano," but "I wish I could."

and yet it is clear . . . : the need to know a language in order to speak is not due to the necessity of speaking silently before speaking out loud.

(b) And when we think about this: (1) about the lack of an object (here, actual speech) for the act of intention; "the next step we are inclined to take is to think that as the object of our thought isn't the fact it is a shadow of the fact" (*BB* 32); (2) about the absence of inner speech when we want to speak; "we imagine something like *imagery,* which is the international language" (*LC* 30).

§339(a) Thinking is not . . . : characteristically, and in keeping with his therapeutic intent, W. makes a negative generalization, but does not attempt, here or elsewhere, to capture the concept *think* in a single formula and say what thinking is.

an incorporeal process: see *BB* 47, e.g. the portion quoted for §36 (which see); *PG* 100d, 108e; cp. *EPB* 130.

which lends life and sense . . . : see XI, 2; §§430–33.

"Frege ridiculed the formalist conception of mathematics by saying that the formalists confused the unimportant thing, the sign, with the important, the meaning. Surely, one wishes to say, mathematics does not treat of dashes on a bit of paper. Frege's idea could be expressed thus: the propositions of mathematics, if they were just complexes of dashes, would be dead and utterly uninteresting, whereas they obviously have a kind of life. And the same, of course, could be said of any proposition: Without a sense, or without the thought, a proposition would be an utterly dead and trivial thing. And further it seems clear that no adding of inorganic signs can make the proposition live. And the conclusion which one draws from this is that what must be added to the dead signs in order to make a live proposition is something immaterial, with properties different from all mere signs" (*BB* 4).

which it would be possible to detach . . . : see the quotes for §330a.

rather as the Devil . . . : in Adelbert von Chamisso's tales of "Peter Schlemihl" (1814). For comments on the story, see Man. 111, 77.

But how . . . : see GI 68. Already in the *Tractatus* "what a philosopher declares to be philosophically false is supposed not to be possible or even really conceivable; the false ideas which he conceives himself to be attacking must be presented as chimaeras, as not really thinkable thoughts at all. Or, as Wittgenstein put it: An *impossible* thought is an impossible *thought* (5.61)—and that is why it is not possible to say what it is that cannot be thought; it can only be forms of words or suggestions of the imagination that are attacked. Aristotle rejecting separate forms, Hume rejecting substance, exemplify the difficulty: if you want to argue that something is a philosophical illusion, you cannot treat it as a false hypothesis" (Anscombe, *Introduction*, 163; cp. §§219–21, 398b).

in a primitive way . . . : see *BB* 173, quoted for §35c; cp. §194c.

(b) Only that makes . . . : that is, that manner of stating the difference.

It is like saying . . . : cp. p. 196e. "When I say that thought is something quite ordinary, I mean that the same thing holds for this concept as for a concept like that of the number one. There seems to be something mysterious about it, because we misunderstand its grammar and feel the lack of a tangible thing corresponding to the substantive" (*PG* 108–9; see *BB* 1d).

An unsuitable type . . . : cp. commentary on §308 ("the decisive movement"); §§79d, 149, 352; 3.325.

§340   For the link with the preceding numbers, see XI, 3.

(a) See I, 10; §182b; *Z* 110–13, 121; *PG* 212a; *PB* 307a.

"But the use of this word [*think*] is confused. Nor can we expect anything else. And that can of course be said of all psychological verbs. Their employment is not so clear or so easy to get a synoptic view of, as that of terms in mechanics, for example" (*Z* 113).

One has to *look at*: see GI 52; commentary on §66a ("and now attend closely").

(b) to remove the prejudice: "Now what makes it difficult for us to take this line of investigation is our craving for generality" (*BB* 17) and the supposition that one case can reveal the essence of all (GI 50). See *BB* 19–20, quoted for §66a.

not a *stupid* prejudice: an important remark. People unacquainted with the explanation W. actually gave of philosophical ills (GI 9–23)—and such ignorance is widespread, even among those who write about him (GI 24)—will tend to wonder how intelligent men could be as mistaken as he supposed them to be; and they are likely to conclude that any account which impugns the intelligence of a Plato, an Augustine, or a Kant is doubtless itself in error. The answer is that muddles arise from our ignorance of language—how it works and how it tricks us—and that such ignorance is natural, given the complexity of the instrument and the unreflective ease with which we use it, directing our attention far more to the message than to the medium of discourse (see Hallett, *Darkness*, 109–11).

Cp. W.'s remark about St. Augustine (Malcolm, *Memoir*, quoted for §1), and *RFM* 55: "A clever man got caught in this net of language! So it must be an interesting net." "A philosopher is not a man out of his senses, a man who doesn't see what everybody sees" (*BB* 59).

§341   See §§330, 527–29. In neither case is there a stream of meanings in the mind, accompanying the sounds (§329) and accounting for their interest (§339a; I, 3).

without thought: cp. Mauthner's reaction to the very idea: "Of course there can be no speech without thought; for a word or a sentence without meaning and sense we do not count as speech" (*Beiträge*, I, 223).

§342   For a fuller account of this case, and further explanation of W.'s misgivings, see XI, 4–5. See also the commentary on §32 for pertinent quotes and references. Cp. Man. 116, 203.

thought is possible without speech: W. would agree with this much (XI, 1). His target is still that indicated in XI, 2–3.

What can he . . . : literally: "Whatever that may mean!"

And why does this question . . . : contrast this case with that in *Z* 100, where W. concludes: "May he not later give his wordless thoughts in words? And in such a fashion that we, who might see the work in progress, could accept this account?" Ballard did nothing we might see in progress; nor did he himself verbalize his thoughts soon afterwards, reacting with words to the nonverbal antecedents (§343); nor did natural equivalents of his later terms (*God, world,* and so on) pass through his mind (Section X). It is somewhat as though a person were finally to become acquainted with chess and learn its rules, without so much as having heard it referred to, and were then to declare that it was the game he had always desired to play (cp. §197). Thus the appropriate parallel is not with §386 (despite the similar sound) but with §288c ("I might *legitimately* begin to doubt . . . if I assume the abrogation of the normal language-game").

Another contrast: When a person tells us what he was about to say, though he did not say those or any other words (§635; see *Z* 137), we do not learn what went on inside him (§636); we might, however, "fill out the picture" with *typical* details (ibid.). But what details are typical of a deaf-mute who is inclined, many years later, to give a report like Ballard's? Here, too, W. might say: "I haven't got these thoughts or anything that hangs together with them" (*LC* 55).

a queer memory phenomenon: cp. §288b.

§343   See p. 231; *Z* 659; *PG* 181b; cp. §386; *PG* 152ab; *PB* 60a.

"They themselves are the remembering" (Man. 116, 181).

"Why do people tend much more to consider a visual image, rather than 'talk', characteristic of memory? We are inclined to speak of 'mere words', but not of a 'mere visual image'. The way a picture is to be applied seems to be much more obvious than the way sentences are to be applied" (Man. 125, 2).

"My memory-image is not evidence for that past situation, like a photograph which was taken then and convinces me now that this was how things were then. The memory-image and the memory-words stand on the *same* level" (Z 650).

"Thus remembering is not at all the psychic process one would take it for at first glance. If I say, rightly, 'I remember it,' the most *varied* things may happen; perhaps even just that I say it" (*PG* 85).

JN 49 spells out the connection with §342: "James reports about a deaf and dumb man who went for long car rides and much later learnt to speak. Then he said he had previously asked the question 'How did the world arise?' James trusts him and says 'we can think without words.' Now is there a complete misunderstanding? W. would say this is correctly described as 'it seemed to him later that at 9 he had asked the question.' And this says only what it does say; it is not an *example* of thinking without speaking." Cp. §§299, 310 ("His attitude is a proof of his attitude"), 386b.

§344   See XI, 5, for the context and role of the number.

(a) Were we all like Ballard and Augustine (§32), as viewed retrospectively by themselves, and did we then encounter no one to teach us an audible language, the hypothesis would be fulfilled. For analogous questions and hypotheses, see §§205, 282c, 385.

(b) "only to themselves": the German adds *in ihrem Innern* ("interiorly").

So it is quite easy . . . : the remark is, of course, ironic.

the easy transition from some to all: for examples in Lewis Carroll, see Pitcher, "Carroll", 323. Such moves are common in Russell, for instance: "There is no logical impossibility in the supposition that the whole of life is a dream, in which we ourselves create all the objects that come before us" (*Problems*, 10).

"An infinitely long row . . .": see *PB* 306b–307a.

Our criterion: not merely exterior symptoms (§354) for something we have privately and individually identified as genuine, though inaudible, speech (X, 21–22).

in the ordinary sense . . . : as opposed to (1) silent speech (cp. §282c); (2) parrot talk (cp. Z 396e). "A parrot utters significant sentences, but it does not really 'speak' in the proper sense of the word" (Schlick, "Form", 155; see Mauthner, *Beiträge,* I, 223, quoted for §341).

And we do not say it . . . : though they make similar sounds; thus talking to oneself may be added to the list in §281: Only of what resembles (behaves like) a human being can we say that it speaks; and the mere utterance of like-sounding noises is a very slight similarity with human speech.

§345 See *OC* 627; *Z* 571; NL 316b; Man. 172, 21; Ambrose, "Metamorphoses", 74–75; cp. X, 16; *OC* 55, 115, 496; *NB* 12g, 13f. W. passes from the particular (§344) to the general.

(a) It is like . . . : if "F" stands for one specific predicate—for example, "say things only to themselves" (§344b) or "make a false move" (§345b)—the new formulation is not equivalent to the former; however, it should probably be read: "If a predicate can be meaningfully applied to one thing it can be meaningfully applied to all things." A more accurate formulation of the error implicit in the cases cited would be: "If a particular predication about a single member of a class (e.g. persons) makes sense, so does the same predication about all members of that class"—or: "If 'Fa.Ga' makes sense, then so does '(x)(Fx ⊃ Gx)' make sense." The fact that the conditional does make sense for so many F–G combinations is doubtless what throws us off.

Two varieties of universal statement drew W.'s fire: those which pose as statements of necessarily universal fact (see §251, and commentary) and those which pose as statements of possibly universal fact (here). Neither are statements of fact, for the former are at best veiled tautologies, expressing grammar (e.g. "All rods have length"), and at worst serve no function at all (e.g. "Everything is identical with itself"); whereas the latter do not express but contravene the grammar of the terms they use, so are veiled contradictions. Cp. 4.461: "A tautology has no truth-conditions, since it is unconditionally true: and a contradiction is true on no condition. Tautologies and contradictions lack sense."

(b) "a false move": for the same point on false moves in general, see *Z* 133; on false moves in mathematics, see p. 227b and cp. *OC* 303.

(c) Cp. similar remarks on pretense (*Z* 571); lying (NL 295); deception (NL 293; §354); winning (*RFM* 109e); obeying rules (§199b); doubts (*OC* 450, 625); sad expressions (Man. 138, 8B). "It could happen sometimes that my senses deceived me, but not all the time. Hallucinations must be the exception. Mistakes in mathematics must be the exception. A physical-object judgment turning out to be false must be the exception" (Malcolm's notes, *Memoir,* 92).

what would it be like . . . : "It would also be conceivable," W. had once written, "that no orders were ever obeyed, and they would still keep their sense" (Man. 108, 208–9). After all, the unmistakable picture would still be there in the mind of the speaker (GI 33); he would still *mean* what he said (GI 37).

§346.   Cp. Man. 164, 99ff. This is continuous with the last remark in §344, after the aside in §345, occasioned by §344. The question contests the *logical* exclusion of parrots. "We do not say they speak," the objector says, "but we would if they did; their exclusion is a merely contingent fact."

here it is an important fact: either: (a) because it shows how remote the hypothesis is from our ordinary concept, whether of parrots or of speech (it is not as though we imagined an explorer who had come across talking parrots, just as others encountered black swans); or (b) because the change in the parrot, if complete enough to make the hypothesis acceptable, would have to be so far-reaching (think of the resistance to the idea that machines can think, even when they are the most complex modern computers). To turn mice into Cinderella's horses, a fairy godmother was required.

"This theory imagines that all we need do is make postulates; that these are satisfied then goes without saying. It conducts itself like a god, who can create by his mere word whatever he wants" (Frege, *Foundations,* 119).

" 'Aren't you making the child into a mere parrot that is trained to talk?'—But *can* you train a parrot (or an ape, say) to use tables, name things, count, etc.?—'But isn't thinking a *spiritual* activity?' " (*EPB* 152; cp. *EPB* 164–65; *BB* 113b).

§347   Cp. §293a.

(a) **"to myself":** the German adds *in mir* ("interiorly"). This imagined reply is an attempt to eliminate outer, public criteria, and thereby to salvage the hypothesis of §344a. If I know from introspection of my own inner speech what talking to oneself is, then the conceptual ties with audible, interpersonal speech are cut, and it becomes conceivable "that people should never speak an audible language, but should still say things to themselves in the imagination."

(b) Cp. §§272, 376, pp. 181b, 219a; *BB* 79a. On the connection between knowledge and concept, see GI 60–61.

§348   See GI 14; Man. 119, Nov. 15.

"have learned only a gesture-language": thus were there some connection between this public language and the inner one, the difficulties of Section X against private language might be avoided. However, no connection is indicated or readily conceivable.

"in a vocal language": this renders the hypothesis causally improbable (in the case of deaf-mutes) as well as conceptually problematic.

don't you understand that?: see §344b.

"It's an English . . .": "(*a*) it sounds English, or German, etc., all
right, and (*b*) there are closely similar forms of expression used in other
departments of our language" (*BB* 56).

"calloused by doing philosophy": see e.g. §§38d, 413, 514, 520.

§349 See *BB* 72ab (e.g.: "We are like people who think that pieces of
wood shaped more or less like chess or draught pieces and standing on
a chess board make a game, even if nothing has been said as to how
they are to be used").

"But this supposition . . .": since the supposition of §348 concerning deaf-mutes, if taken as a whole, is not a picture with any familiar
application, it might be thought that W. is now thinking of statements
such as "I am here" (§514; *BB* 72). However, the familiar supposition
he has in mind is that of someone's talking to himself inwardly in a
vocal language, which makes perfectly good sense in ordinary circumstances, but not in those of §348.

But if we suppose . . . : cp. §288c.

§350 See X, 20, 22; *EPB* 213; *BB* 140c–141b; Man. 229, §1478; Man.
116, 158–61; Pitcher, "Same" (whole article); Geach, *God,* 20; Vesey,
"Other Minds" (whole); cp. p. 224l and commentary.

W. is not questioning the supposition that someone has pain, as he
questioned the supposition about deaf-mutes in §348, but is probing
the simplistic notions concerning pain, inner talk, and other "inner occurrences" which underlie such hypotheses. Thus the present inquiry
into criteria of identity for the sensation resembles that into criteria of
identity for the subject, in §302. Both numbers may strike the reader as
skeptical in tendency, yet they tend to undercut all skepticism (X, 24),
since their true purpose is to indicate the outer, public criteria, both for
having pain (§302) and for having *pain* (e.g. it is *he* who *cries out*). Such
criteria seem unnecessary as long as one supposes an introspective recognition that one's sensation is "the same" (see commentary on §258)
and assumes that other people's sensations are related to one's own by
the same absolute relation of sameness. On the relativity of *same,* see
for instance *EPB* 201; *BB* 134c, 140c–141b; *PG* 353b; *PB* 68c; *LC* 32.

(a) "that someone has a pain . . ." : "The trouble with the realist is
always that he does not solve but skip the difficulties which his adversaries see, though they too don't succeed in solving them. The realist
answer, for us, just brings out the difficulty; for who argues like this
overlooks the difference between different usages of the words 'to
have', 'to imagine' " (*BB* 48–49).

'5 o'clock': see *EPB* 154; *BB* 106b. "You are forgetting what Einstein
taught the world: that the method of measuring time belongs to the
grammar of the time-expression" (Man. 119, Nov. 15).

(b) For *that* part of the grammar . . . : see §270b.

"When we hear the diatonic scale we are inclined to say that after every seven notes the same note recurs, and, asked why we call it the same note again one might answer 'Well, it's a c again.' But this isn't the explanation I want, for I should ask 'What made one call it a c again?' And the answer to this would seem to be 'Well, don't you hear that it's the same note only an octave higher?'—Here, too, we could imagine that a man had been taught our use of the word 'the same' when applied to colours, lengths, directions, etc., and that we now played the diatonic scale for him and asked him whether he'd say that he heard the same notes again and again at certain intervals, and we could easily imagine several answers, in particular for instance, this, that he heard the same note alternately after every four or three notes (he calls the tonic, the dominant, and the octave the same note)" (*BB* 140–41; cp. *PG* 186a).

"To say that we use the word 'blue' to mean 'what all these shades of colour have in common' by itself says nothing more than that we use the word 'blue' in all these cases" (*BB* 135).

§351   Revised from Man. 116, 142–43.

I might agree: previously, W. had argued that things differently established are different things (*PB* 60bc), and that since "what verifies or is a criterion for 'I have toothache' is quite different from what verifies or is a criterion for 'He has toothache' . . . the *meanings* of 'I have toothache' and 'he has toothache' must be different" (*PP* 307). Now he recognized the arbitrariness of thus applying *different* and *same* without guidance from usage (§§61, 350, 551–61) and no longer equated sense with mode of verification (see commentary on §353) or held that we verify our own sensations (X, 19) and thereby come to know them (X, 25).

"Don't you know, then . . .": as an illustration of this attitude, see James, *Principles*, I, 463c.

"the stove is in pain": see §§283–88.

These words may lead me . . . : see §390.

a still better example: this one is not only natural, clear, and familiar, but a sort of allegory, suggesting the bipolarity of psychological expressions (GI 15–16; *PP* 307) and the problems to which their asymmetry gives rise (X, 10, 19). Compare, for example, the declaration "I see well enough that I am on top" with the solipsist's tendency to say "Only my experience is real" (*PP* 311). We must recognize others' right to use the same expression.

much easier to bury . . . : see Moore, *Commonplace*, 241–42.

cannot be used in the ordinary way: if, for example, an apartment floor is beneath me and someone is on the other side of it, then he too is beneath me, and I am not beneath him. But substitute the Earth for the floor and the entailment no longer holds.

§352   Gleaned from Man. 116, 148–51. See GI 14; Man. 228, §170;

Moore, *Commonplace*, 117f; cp. *Kreis*, 82. For the overall setting and direction of the number, see XI, 6. On the connection with the *Tractatus* and with §353, see Hacker, *Insight*, 44, e.g.: "The starkly realist features of the *Tractatus* semantics, inherited from Frege, help to explain its indifference to epistemology. . . . The commitment to the Excluded Middle is merely another form of the requirement of determinate sense. But again, whether a proposition is true or false is independent of whether it is possible to tell which it is. All necessary truth is a matter of logical necessity, and logical necessity is independent of how things happen to be in the world. *A fortiori* it is independent of our knowings and ways of knowing, and indeed independent of natural languages" (cp. GI 30, 39).

"Thus there must not be any object as regards which the definition leaves in doubt whether it falls under the concept; though for us men, with our defective knowledge, the question may not always be decidable. . . . The law of excluded middle is really just another form of the requirement that the concept should have a sharp boundary. Any object Δ that you choose to take either falls under the concept Φ or does not fall under it; *tertium non datur*. E.g. would the sentence 'any square root of 9 is odd' have a comprehensible sense at all if *square root of 9* were not a concept with a sharp boundary?" (Frege, *Writings*, 159).

A similar dissociation of sense from use in the language (in particular from mode of verification, setting truth conditions) appears in Ramsey (*Foundations*, 66–67); Schlick (IV, 9); James (below).

(a) See GI 9; *Z* 677; *RFM* 138–44; *PP* 302–4; Bogen, *Philosophy*, 81–82; cp. *PB* 212, 272b.

We want, that is . . . : "In the law of excluded middle we think that we have already got something solid, something that at any rate cannot be called in doubt. Whereas in truth this tautology has just as shaky a sense (if I may put it like that), as the question whether p or $\sim p$ is the case" (*RFM* 140).

law of excluded middle: see *RFM* 139–40; *PB* 193a; Man. 131, 72–76; and below.

"no third possibility": cp. Frege (above) and Schlick (IV, 9). After a similar discussion in Man. 228, §121, W. adds: "See Weyl." See also W.'s earlier views and later comments:

"Our expression of what we mean can in its turn only be right or wrong. . . . There does not seem to be any other possibility" (*NB* 68; see *NB* 22a; cp. *NB* 57k).

"A proposition must restrict reality to two alternatives: yes or no" (4.023).

"A picture agrees with reality or fails to agree, it is correct or incorrect, true or false" (2.21; see 2.201).

"The 'law of excluded middle' is valid" (Man. 106, 229, concerning the expansion of π).

"The proposition . . . seems to require that reality be compared with it" (*PG* 132).

"The reason why the use of the expression 'true or false' has something misleading about it is that it is like saying 'it tallies with the facts or it doesn't,' and the very thing that is in question is what 'tallying' is here" (*OC* 199; see *OC* 200).

in other regions of philosophy: see *PB* 151b; Waismann, "Analyse", 229. Geach reports the following exchange. Broad: "Either God exists or God does not exist." Wittgenstein: "Couldn't he half exist?" Broad walked out.

"in the decimal expansion of π": the German has "infinite expansion". See §516 and commentary; *RFM* 138, 147g; *PP* 302–3; Man. 106, 229 (above); cp. Russell, *Development*, 110–11, and *Inquiry*, chaps. 20–21.

"In his original discussion of this problem [infinity] Brouwer chose to search for three consecutive sevens in the expansion, presumably because the digit seven occurred with less than average frequency in Shanks' famous nineteenth-century expansion of π. In fact Shanks' calculation was erroneous and recent determinations of π to several thousand decimal figures show that the digit four rather than seven occurs relatively infrequently, but this is of only indirect significance" (Goodstein, "Mathematics", 273).

"God sees": see p. 226a; cp. *PG* 484a; *PB* 212a.

"The hundredth decimal of π, the ratio of the circumference to its diameter, is predetermined ideally now, tho no one may have computed it" (James, *Pragmatism*, 211).

"An omniscient being, indeed, would at once know everything that is implicitly contained in the assertion of a few propositions. It would know immediately that on the basis of the conventions concerning the use of the numerals and the multiplication sign, '24×31' is synonymous with '744'. An omniscient being has no need for logic and mathematics" (Hahn, "Logic", 159).

"A good question for the schoolmen to ask would have been: 'Can God know all the places of π?' " (*PG* 479).

"I want to say: Even God can determine something mathematical only by mathematics. Even for him the mere rule of expansion cannot decide anything that it does not decide for us" (*RFM* 185; cp. with Hahn, above).

" 'Surely the position of all the prime numbers must be somehow predetermined. We work them out only successively, but they are all already determined. God, as it were, knows them all. And yet for all that it seems possible that they are not determined by a law.'—Always the picture of the meaning of a word as a full box, with its contents packed into it, and needing only to be investigated" (*PG* 481).

We use a picture: for an illustration, from W.'s lectures, see Goodstein, "Mathematics", 272–73.

which one person sees: cp. Man. 106, 245, e.g.: "When Brouwer attacks the use of the law of excluded middle, he is right, so long as there is question of seeing ahead." Not even God does.

and another not: cp. Man. 106, 84.

says nothing: as "I know nothing about the weather when I know that it is either raining or not raining" (4.461), so too I know nothing about the series if I know that it looks like this or doesn't. It is not like saying, "It looks either this way or that"; for *not* covers all possibilities not covered by *this*. Furthermore, what possibilities they are is not revealed by the disjunction "like this or not", any more than the number of drops which verifies "It's raining" is settled by saying "It's raining or it isn't."

this picture *seems* **to determine . . . :** cp. §§389, 426a; LF 36.

how it is to be applied: see *LC* 71–72.

"The question—I want to say—changes its status, when it becomes decidable. For a connexion is made then, which formerly *was not there*" (*RFM* 138).

"He said that if anyone actually found three consecutive 7's this would prove that there are, but that if no one found them that wouldn't prove that there are not; that, therefore, it is something for the truth of which we have provided a test, but for the falsehood of which we have provided none; and that therefore it must be a quite different sort of thing from cases in which a test for both truth and falsehood is provided" (*PP* 303).

our inability to turn our eyes away: cp. §115.

(b) See NL 285n.

when it is said: for instance in making the distinction between knowledge by acquaintance and knowledge by description (cp. Russell, *Logic*, 161) or in discussing the perception of parallel lines: "It cannot be said: There are three classes: parallel, non-parallel, and doubtful. For we see no lines of this third class. . . . And the essential thing in all these cases is this: If the description is to have the proper multiplicity of the phenomenon, only *one boundary* should occur in it" (*Kreis*, 61).

"Either he has . . .": cp. Man. 108, 251.

which by itself seems . . . : see §§73, 193, 426, p. 184de.

§353 The first sentence is from Man. 112, 97, the second from Man. 110, 238. See commentary on §20b; §§475, 572, pp. 220e, 221g, 224k, 225a; Z 437; PG 48a, 88c, 127b, 130c, 219c–220a, 227b, 413g, 459; *PB*

87, 134ef, 289b; *PP* 266, 298–99, 307; *Kreis,* 161, 186, 243–45; Man. 112, 202; Man. 110, 240; Man. 108, 69; Ambrose, "Metamorphoses", 68; Cavell, "Availability", 164–65; Lazerowitz, "Necessity", 237; cp. 4.024; *NB* 23fgh.

Here is the place to comment on W.'s relation to the Verification Principle, or rather to the various formulae which went by that name. None is found in the *Tractatus,* though some have been read into it. If W. did then believe that "the meaning of a proposition is determined by its method of verification" (V. Kraft, *Circle,* 31), that would not rule out other, complementary determinants of meaning or require that the verification be empirical (in any of the senses proposed by logical positivists). It might suggest, however, that only sentences for which some method of verification has been provided are meaningful. And despite W.'s later disclaimers of having intended any theory (Gasking and Jackson, "Wittgenstein", 54; cp. *Kreis,* 186; *PP* 266), his earlier writings repeatedly suggest at least this restriction, sometimes quite dogmatically (*NB* 95b; 4.063, 4.431; *PB* 77e, 174c, 210d; *PG* 452). In the transitional years he went farther and identified the sense of a proposition with its method of verification (*Kreis,* 79d, 227a; *PB* 200f; *PG* 81c; *PP* 266; cp. *Kreis,* 47), in the very formulae adopted by Waismann (*Kreis,* 244; "Analyse", 229) and Schlick ("Meaning", 148). As Miss Anscombe notes, at this time his ideas "were more closely akin to those of the logical positivists than before or after" (*Introduction,* 152; see X, 6–16; Hacker, *Insight,* 105–7; Malcolm's review of *PB,* 224–25).

The bottom of *PP* 303 reveals the rapid metamorphosis that led to his later viewpoint, expressed in the parable he recounted to Stout (see Malcolm, *Memoir,* 65–66; cp. Man. 138, 30B, quoted for §373): "Imagine that there is a town in which the policemen are required to obtain information from each inhabitant, e.g. his age, where he came from, and what work he does. A record is kept of this information and some use is made of it. Occasionally when a policeman questions an inhabitant he discovers that the latter does not do *any* work. The policeman enters this fact on the record, because *this too* is a useful piece of information about the man!" "The application of the parable," writes Malcolm, "is, I think, that if you do not understand a statement, then to discover that it has no verification is an important piece of information about it and makes you understand it better. That is to say, you understand it *better;* you do not find out that there is nothing to understand." Thus in mathematics "there can be a proof of a proposition even when there is nothing that could be called a 'method of verification' " (Man. 123, June 4). And "experiential propositions do not all have the same logical status. With regard to some, of which we say that we *know* them to be true, we can imagine circumstances on the basis of which we should say that the statement had turned out to be false. But with others there are no circumstances in which we should say 'it turned out to be false' " (Malcolm's notes, *Memoir*, 90). Already in 1933 W. had concluded that " 'in some cases the question "How is that verified?" makes no sense.' He gave as an example of a case in which that question 'makes no sense' the proposition 'I've got toothache,' of which he had already said that it makes no sense to ask for a verification of it—to ask 'How do you know that you have?' " (*PP* 266). For his mature treatment of this theme and for further examples, see especially Sections X and XXXVII, and GI 15–16. Rather than stress verification alone he would now say more generally: "To understand a sentence is to be prepared for one of its uses. If we can't think of any use for it at all, then we don't understand it at all" (Malcolm's notes, *Memoir*, 90; cp. *LC* 70–72). "The whole point of investigating the 'verification' e.g. is to stress the importance of use as opposed to that of the picture" (Man. 166; W.'s English; cp. §§363, 511–12).

For connections with the previous number, see the preceding quotation; *PB* 176e; the quotation from Hacker for §352; or *PP* 303 (above). *PP* 266–67 lead into the next number: "He went on to say 'Verification determines the meaning of a proposition only where it gives the grammar of the proposition in question'; and in answer to the qustion 'How far is giving a verification of a proposition a grammatical statement about it?' he said that, whereas 'When it rains the pavement gets wet' is not a grammatical statement at all, if we say 'The fact that the pavement is wet is a *symptom* that it has been raining' this statement is 'a matter of grammar' " (see *BB* 24a).

only a particular way: not always applicable (above), nor the only way even when it is (see III, 1; cp. Man. 108, 69). This is one reason why the later W. would not maintain that if *p* can be verified in two different ways, it must have two different meanings (cp. §§61, 444, 551–56). "The grammar of propositions which we call propositions about physical objects admits of a variety of evidences for every such proposition" (*BB* 51).

§354   See §§79, 392; *RFM* 26h, 121; *PG* 452; *Kreis*, 47–48; Man. 178e; cp. *OC* 519; *RFM* 25c, 120cd; *PP* 305b.

fluctuation: see *OC* 96–99, 167–68; *Z* 438, 466; *BB* 25b; cp. *OC* 319; *Z* 526; *BB* 51–52; *Kreis*, 54–55; 4.123. Concerning the importance of this fact for philosophy, see for instance GI 70 and Hacker, *Insight*, 150.

"But wouldn't one have to say then, that there is no sharp boundary between propositions of logic and empirical propositions? The lack of sharpness *is* that of the boundary between rule and empirical proposition" (*OC* 319). Such fluctuations account for "our wavering between logical and physical impossibility" (*BB* 56). "The analysis oscillates between natural science and grammar" (§392).

grammar: both the study and the studied; see the preceding quotes.

criteria and symptoms: see GI 60–61; §573; *PB* 208d, 283b; *PP* 266, 313b; *Kreis,* 158–59; Kenny, "Criterion"; cp. *Z* 526; *PG* 370d–371a; *PB* 179g, 204d; Man. 108, 282 ("in mathematics there are no symptoms"). As in the *Tractatus* (see Black, *Companion,* 238), so in the later writings, W. more frequently introduced a 'technical' term to mark a distinction in grammar; see also "secondary sense" (§282, p. 216) and *Äusserung* (GI 15). However, nothing precise is intended (GI 70), or needed (cp. §71).

Telling how a proposition can be verified, W. has just said, "is a contribution to the grammar of the proposition". It is a further contribution if one distinguishes between inferential evidence and ultimate evidence, that is, between what W. called "symptoms" and "criteria". As has been pointed out, the question "How do you know?" is not appropriate for all statements, but when it is, we cannot extend our questioning to "the primal thing which alone makes questions possible at all. Not to that which first gives the system a foundation. It is clear that there must be something of the kind" (*PB* 203; see X, 24–25; commentary on §258; §356; *PG* 97a; *PB* 171c; *Kreis,* 97; Man. 108, 163–64; cp. *Prototractatus,* 3.20101). If, for instance, one person hears thunder and says it is raining nearby, another person may question his inference. Thunder is a mere symptom of rain, a helpful bit of evidence that might conceivably be wrong. But if one person sees plentiful drops falling from clouds and another accepts these facts but questions whether it is raining, he is no longer speaking the English language. This is simply what people call rain, and there's an end on it. It is what thunder is evidence for (see §§241–42; *PP* 266–67).

Though given phenomena in given circumstances may be adequate evidence (*OC* 82), for instance of whether it is raining, they do not constitute necessary conditions. How many drops are required to verify "It's raining"? How many words are required to verify "He's reading" (§157)? Generally no border has been drawn (§69), determining in advance and for all conceivable circumstances whether a term is to be applied (§§79–80, 138–40). Even in science, where explicit conventions might warrant our speaking of a "defining criterion" (*BB* 25a), borders often fluctuate (*BB* 25b).

W. was more interested in individual fluctuations from occasion to occasion than in the sort of gradual, overall shifts which interested Carnap (e.g. in "Meaning and Synonymy"). Such waverings in the criteria and therefore in the concept (cp. §79) should be distinguished from mere multiplicity in the criteria employed, now these being *satisfied,* now those (§66). Both types of variation account for the delusion here warned against (that there are only symptoms), but only in the former case does criterion become symptom and *vice versa* (*BB* 24–25); when, for instance, we call football, then solitaire, a game, the game characteristics of the first do not cease to be a criterion and become a symptom, or *vice versa*. The flexibility of conceptual borders (Section V) is W.'s present concern, not the heterogeneity of conceptual contents (Section IV). For opposed views, see e.g. Frege (under §352); Schlick (IV, 9); or Waismann: "What is logically possible results from the rules of grammar, quite independently of experience; what is causally possible experience alone can show. The two are fundamentally different, and the line between them is absolutely sharp" (*Principles,* 340). W.'s answer: "Propositions are often used on the borders of logic and experience [*Empire*], so that their sense fluctuates back and forth across the borders, and they are half expression of a norm, half expression of experience. (For it is no psychic accompaniment—as people represent thought—but use which distinguishes a logical proposition from one of experience.)" (Man. 176, 10A).

makes it look as if . . . : the description fits, for instance, Russell's treatment of tables in *Problems,* 13 (see commentary on §242), or a futile search for essences (*BB* 145; §§36, 164, 608). However, W. is reporting and correcting his own former thought, strong traces of which can still be discerned in *BB* 51–52: "If I regard the proposition 'I see my hand move' as one of the evidences for the proposition 'my hand moves,' the truth of the latter is, of course, not presupposed in the truth of the former. One might therefore suggest the expression 'It looks as though my hand were moving' instead of 'I see my hand moving.' But this expression, although it indicates that my hand may appear to be moving without really moving, might still suggest that after all there must be a hand in order that it should appear to be moving; whereas we could easily imagine cases in which the proposition describing the visual evidence is true and at the same time other evidences make us say that I have no hand." And the same holds for tactual, auditory, kinesthetic and other evidences (ibid.). It seemed, therefore, that only the appearances are certain (X, 5–7; *PG* 222e) and that they need not be appearances *of* anything. Doubtless this is one main reason why when W. attempted to construct a phenomenological language, everything seemed to disappear (Man. 105, 116); he found only symptoms and nothing they were symptoms of—no hands or tables. To surmount these difficulties, said W., and "to determine the sense of a proposition, I would have to know a quite definite procedure which would count as verifying the proposition. In this respect ordinary language fluctuates widely, much more than scientific language" (*Kreis,* 47; see 48).

sense-impressions can deceive us: note the parallel with pretense, brought out in Man. 130.

But here one fails . . . : see *Z* 415–20; Man. 116, 56; cp. *Z* 411.

" 'It looks red to me.'—'And what is red like?'—'Like *this.*' Here the right paradigm must be pointed to" (*Z* 420). In other circumstances I might doubt; in these I don't—nor do others. Here is how the language-game gets started (§§241–42). "To begin by teaching someone 'That looks red' makes no sense" (*Z* 418). Thus "whether a proposition is true or false is determined by experience, but not its sense" (*PB* 65). As for more complex concepts, it might be observed that antiskeptical arguments like those in X, 24, "have some force when applied to simple ostensive terms, such as colour words, but the sceptic's attacks are generally directed at highly complex terms such as 'temperature', 'external object', or 'identity'. It is generally a mistake to infer directly from the existence of a term in a language to that of some corresponding item in the world" (Bird, *Tasks,* 105). Thus all men might err factually in asserting the existence of ether. However, the skeptic who could call *ether* in question cannot treat the criteria as mere symptoms and, acknowledging their fulfillment, still doubt or deny the ether. The fate of §261 awaits him if he continues to doubt even at that level (see *OC* 114). These brief remarks aim to suggest that the ordinary-language treatment of skepticism favored by W. does not require illegitimate extensions of the paradigm-case argument.

§355 "Our sensations can always deceive us," the philosopher says. "No, not always," replies W. (adopting the same figurative mode of speech), "for then we wouldn't understand them" (§§242, 345). What holds for us holds (figuratively) for them too: "The word 'lying' was taught us in a particular way in which it was fastened to a certain behavior, to the use of certain expressions under certain circumstances. Then we use it, saying that we have been lying, when our behavior was not like the one which first constituted the meaning" (NL 295). Thus when W. envisaged unusual behavior on the part of our sensations— "cases in which the proposition describing the visual evidence is true and at the same time other evidences make us say that I have no hand" (see commentary on §354)—he showed he understood their language: He knew when there would be a hand, when not. He knew when they were "lying" (see *Z* 118).

their language: not the language-game in which we speak about sense-impressions (p. 180d), but the one in which they "tell us" about tables and rain.

founded on convention: see I, 4–5.

§356   See §§353–54, 485–86; Man. 228, §§455–57.

A Russell, for instance, would not readily accept as final evidence for rain the report: "I see water falling from clouds." Doubt can still find an opening: "It is conceivable that your senses have deceived you; to get from the sense-impression of rain to rain you must suppose that the sensation correctly informs you of the external state of affairs." So now W. switches his attention from the concept *rain* to this quixotic notion of "information". Sense-impressions do not inform as words or pictures inform; so "what right have I to speak in this second case of a representation or piece of information—if these words were rightly used in the *first* case?" (§280). Tamper with one set of concepts and all are distorted (§398).

"is another matter": "Thus the difference between an *a priori* general proposition and an empirical generalization does not come in the *meaning* of the proposition; it comes in the nature of the *evidence* for it" (Russell, *Problems,* 61).

Or have I only . . . : sooner or later—and better sooner—we must simply accept the criteria others accept, so as to be able to speak with them (§§241–42, 654–55). "That is not agreement in opinions ["naive common-sense"] but in forms of life" (§241). Cp. the similar regress in §260.

misleading metaphor: cp. §398a. For instance, are my eyes not *me*? So doesn't this supposed report resemble the supposed gift in §268? Isn't it as though a person took money from another, put it in his pocket, and said: "He gave my hand the money and my hand gave it to me"?

§357   Cp. §250, p. 174bc. The transition back to the topic of §§344–48, which occasioned the digression in §§349–56, is smooth. As Russell (e.g. *Problems*) tended to regard sense-data as fallible clues to the existence of objects which we never see, hear, or touch (namely the unperceived chairs, rain drops, etc. which supposedly cause our sense-data) so many philosophers have looked on human behavior as a mere concomitant of thought, inner speech, and the like, permitting us to infer the unperceived process (the actual thinking, calculating, inner speech, etc.) in the case of other people but not in the case of dogs, cats, stones, etc. But if the inference is based on induction—and on in-duction from a single person's experience, at that—shouldn't it be readily conceivable, even if unlikely, that dogs do calculate roots in their heads, stones do have aches and pains, and so on? So W. asks, "Why do we rule out the very *possibility* of a dog's talking to itself?" The answer, of course, is that the ultimate criteria applied (§354) in verification (§353)—the human behavior in this case as the sensations of wet and cold in §354—belong to the sense of the statement (§360).

We do not say . . . : cp. Frege, *Foundations*, 41–42.

Is that because . . . : cp. the quotations from Schopenhauer for §250, suggesting that a dog's soul was in fact an open book to him.

Well, one might say . . . : see §391, p. 178hi.

But do I also . . . : see GI 15–16.

I do *not* say it . . . : cp. §§288–89, 404.

But it only makes sense . . . : even first-person avowals have meaning only insofar as they belong to a public language-game. Cp. GI 60–61.

Then it is not . . . : for young W., it would have sufficed that the speaker projectively relate his words to the inner process; he could bypass the outer criteria (GI 35–37).

§358(a) But isn't it . . . : see GI 35–37.

here, of course, belongs . . . : were we able to mean meaningless words, it would be clear that their meaning does not come simply from our meaning them. But as it is, one is tempted to say that they are meaningless *because* we cannot mean them (as objects are invisible because we cannot see them).

one cannot mean . . . : see p. 18n.

But it is also something . . . : see commentary on §120b ("only exterior facts"); Z 605–6, quoted for §316.

(b) How could this . . . : the German has an exclamation: "How ludicrous this could seem!" (Cp. *BB* 6: "If we look into the grammar of that word, we shall feel that it is no less astounding that man should have conceived of a deity of time than it would be to conceive of a deity of negation or disjunction.")

a dream of our language: see §§194, 295, 307.

§359 Condensed from Man. 110, 35–36. Earlier W. had said: "We shall investigate thought from the point of view that it could also be performed by a machine" (ibid., 2).

The connection with §358 is indicated thus in *BB* 16: "Thinking, one wants to say, is part of our 'private experience'. It is not material, but an event in private consciousness. This objection is expressed in the question: 'Could a machine think?' "

"And the trouble which is expressed in this question is not really that we don't yet know a machine which could do the job. The question is not analogous to that which someone might have asked a hundred years ago: 'Can a machine liquefy a gas?' The trouble is rather that the sentence, 'A machine thinks (perceives, wishes)': seems somehow nonsensical. It is as though we had asked 'Has the number 3 a colour?'

('What colour could it be, as it obviously has none of the colours known to us?')" (*BB* 47–48).

"Is thinking a specific *organic* process of the mind, so to speak—as it were chewing and digesting in the mind? Can we replace it by an inorganic process that fulfils the same end, as it were use a prosthetic apparatus for thinking? How should we have to imagine a prosthetic organ of thought?" (*Z* 607).

Could it be in pain?: see the parallel between §281 and §360.

It surely comes as close . . . : see §§283, 493–95; *PG* 105c.

"Turing's 'machines'. These machines are in fact human beings who calculate" (Man. 229, §1763; cp. §157).

§360   See *BB* 105b; *PG* 105; Man. 220, 605–6; Malcolm, "Knowledge", 375–78; cp. §§284, 573a. The number parallels §§281–82, noting the primary sense ("We only say . . ."), as in §281, then the secondary sense ("We also say . . ."), as in §282. It contains W.'s synthetic resolution of the antithesis stated by Schlick: "Lichtenberg, the wonderful eighteenth-century physicist and philosopher, declared that Descartes had no right to start his philosophy with the proposition 'I think,' instead of saying 'it thinks' " ("Meaning", 166). Both Descartes and Lichtenberg ignored the fact that "we only say of a human being and what is like one that it thinks." So had W.: "The objection occurs to us: A machine surely cannot think. But thought in the primary sense contains no subject. ('It thinks')" (Man. 110, 58). "What I always want to say is that thought is nothing human" (Man. 108, 241). See *BB* 6e, 16a (an intermediate position); Man. 109, 43 (quoted for §107); Man. 108, 217 (quoted for §108); 5.631.

Is that an empirical statement?: is it verifiable or falsifiable by experience? See §251b; *BB* 55 (quoted for §136b); cp. §286b.

No. We only say . . . : and this agreement indicates the criteria of thinking—the meaning of the word *think* (§§353–54)—and therefore the range of possibilities (§90; cp. §§370–73). For contrary viewpoints, see the quotes from Berkeley and James, under §281 ("is conscious").

and what is like one: see *Z* 102–5, 129; cp. §§281, 283e; *Z* 109–10. "And there is no deciding *how* close the correspondence must be" (*Z* 102).

as a tool: see §23c, and references there, on the multiplicity of ways such tools are used (§11).

§361(b)   Note the parallel with §284, on pain; cp. pp. 221h–222a.

how is it with man: on the location of thought, and in particular the idea "of the head or the brain as the locality of thought", see *BB* 7–9.

like a human being . . . : for the reason indicated in §360.

(c)   See XXXVII, 16; *Z* 114–19; cp. §§344, 385–86.

to oneself: again, the German adds *im Innern* ("interiorly").

no one is going to say . . . : see I, 5.
§362   See X, 20–21;§§32, 210, 262–64, 380; Z 545; NL 285e–286a; cp.
§75; *BB* 125b, 130f; *PG*̇a.
   without telling him it directly: cp. p. 194a; *BB* 185.

XII. "Each Equivalent to Each" (§§363–397)

GENERAL COMMENTARY

(1) "Thinking," wrote Wittgenstein in 1930–1931, "is forming pictures of various kinds and in various ways" (Man. 108, 217). After discussing thought in general, he now turns to such varied kinds and
ways, especially these two: imagining things (§§363, 370, 390–97), by
means of images (§§377–83, 388–89) or mental pictures (§§367–68);
and calculating, doing sums in one's head (§§369, 385–86). The former
samples are accounted for by the fact that "the play of images is admittedly the model according to which one would like to think of thinking"
(Z 94); "we imagine something like *imagery*, which is the international
language" (*LC* 30; see commentary on §443). The latter are relevant to
Wittgenstein's earlier view that, regardless of what psychic materials we
employ (GI 39), in speaking thoughtfully we operate a calculus (IX, 2).
These perspectives are not as disparate as they may seem, nor the
samples as diverse; for "calculating in the head may be the only case in
everyday life where we make orderly use of the imagination. Hence its
special interest" (Man. 229, §1317).
(2) About these new samples, Wittgenstein asks new questions:
Whereas his interest in Section XI centered on the meaning of *think*
(§316) and consequently on the criteria of thinking, it now shifts to
"what happens" (§§363, 370, 394); for whereas his concern there was
chiefly with thought as "an incorporeal process", it turns now to
thought as "the unique correlate" of language and the world (§96). He
repeatedly questions the supposed correspondence or projective relationship between thought and sensible signs (§§364–66, 369, 374–75,
385–86), thought and thought (§§376–78, 382), thought and the world
(§§367–68, 382, 388–93), world and words via thought (§§379–81). The
upshot is that mental pictures are no more essential to speech than are
visible ones (§§396–97).
(3) Somewhat similar reflections led to a similar conclusion in the *Blue
Book:* "If we keep in mind the possibility of a picture which, though
correct, has no similarity with its object, the interpolation of a shadow

between the sentence and reality loses all point. For now the sentence itself can serve as such a shadow" (*BB* 37). Still earlier Wittgenstein had written: "All my reflections tend always to show that it is no *use* representing thought as hallucinating. That is, it is *superfluous*, the difficulty remains. For the hallucination, too, *no* picture, can bridge the gulf between picture and reality, and the one no more readily than the other" (Man. 108, 268). However, he believed then that *intention* bridges the gap (GI 37). This view will be dealt with in Sections XV and XXVI. Later he will return to imaging and ask of it too: "What makes my image of him into an image of *him?*" (Section XXIX).

DETAILED COMMENTARY

§363 See I, 6–7, 9–10; §§290–91; Man. 229, §1243 (quoted for §280); Hunter, *Essays*, 91–114; cp. *BB* 185.

(a) "But when I imagine . . .": the objection parallels those in §§304–5, where the supposition of a unique inner criterion had been similarly questioned. Here W. has just denied that a pupil learning an expression like *imagine* or "say something to oneself" has made an inference from what the instructor tells him and thus identified the inner referent. "But surely there is something there, besides the words and the behavior," the objection wants to say, "and that is what we report when we say we imagine something." W. now examines the supposition which underlies such claims, namely the assumption that language operates uniformly, simply describing "how things stand" (4.5).

(b) See GI 14; commentary on §§216, 304b, 520; *BB* 3e; *PG* 107b; cp. *PB* 64a.

For viewpoints like that criticized, see Frege, *Writings*, 120–21; Ogden and Richards, *Meaning*, 205–6; Schlick, *Aufsätze*, 152; Moore, *Problems*, 57c; Kretzmann, "Semantics", 391; James, *Principles*, I, 29a; Russell: *Philosophy*, 11–12; *Essays*, 97b; *Logic*, 302d. James quotes with approval: "By an entirely mysterious world-order, the speaker is enabled to produce a series of signs which are totally unlike [the] thought, but which, by virtue of the same mysterious order, act as a series of incitements upon the hearer, so that he constructs within himself the corresponding mental state" (*Principles*, I, 219).

(c) See *PG* 39e; *Kreis*, 167; Man 138, 28B; Cook, "Solipsism", 54–55; cp. §505; *OC* 89–90; *PB* 131d.

that he *knows* . . . : this is not a different viewpoint from that mentioned in §304b; not only are knowledge and thought both "something mental", but knowing is frequently conceived as similar to thinking, that is, as a "mental process". For criticism of this assimilation, see e.g. §§184 and 187.

everything else is inessential: both (1) intended consequences: "Whatever may be the speaker's intentions and motives for saying just this and not that, our concern is not with these at all, but solely with what he says" (Frege, "Compound", 8); (2) the words themselves: "Kleist once wrote that the poet would be happiest if he could transmit the thoughts by themselves, without words" (Man. 111, 173). See quotation from Man. 133 for §330a.

As for what . . . : see §308.

just are queer: see *BB* 5e–6a.

It is as if . . . : see *EPB* 154; *BB* 106ab.

§364 See p. 220f; cp. p. 224l and commentary; NL 292c.

(a) does a sum: on the interest of calculating in the head, and its connection with the previous number, see XII, 1.

Are you trying to say . . . : the objection, which continues to the next dash, does not refer to a view implicit in the opening words, but to the insistence in previous numbers on external criteria; that is, it reiterates the reaction expressed in the first sentence of §363. Again, cp. §§304–5, and the overall sequence into which they fit.

For he *knows* . . . : but would it make any more sense in this case than in that of pain (§§246, 288) for him to wonder whether he really had calculated. Mightn't we say again: "And here 'know' means that the expression of uncertainty is senseless" (§247)?

But what if I said . . . : "Always get rid of the idea of the private object [the one only I know, so must name for myself, etc.] in this way: assume that it constantly changes, but that you do not notice the change because your memory constantly deceives you" (p. 207). Then you will realize that the supposed inner criterion, the justification to oneself (cp. §289), "is not part of the mechanism" (§271; see §270). What we do is not to identify the inner process by criteria, but to repeat an expression (*calculation*). "But this is not the *end* of the language-game: it is the beginning" (§290).

"he was able to CALCULATE": that is, to do something so different from his training, yet reach the same result; and to do something so different, yet have it count as the same operation: calculating. Thus the lesson is double: hesitation to establish *a priori* laws for thought (cp. *Z* 624); readiness to recognize the conceptual point just made above: When we say we have calculated in our head, we do not identify the activity as being identical with what we did with pencil and paper; rather we judge it to be the "same" act because, without any 'justification', we extend the word *calculate* to it too.

(b) See §319; *Z* 89 (quoted for §319); Man. 229, §1729; cp. §301.

a bit of white paper with . . . : such as the sketches of figures W. used to make to illustrate his picture theory (*NB* 7; cp. p. 11n).

§365 Adelheid and the Bishop: in Goethe's *Götz von Berlichingen.* Scene 1 of Act 2 opens with the game almost over.

Of course it has: see *PP* 292. Compare: "Does the pot in a picture of a boiling pot (§297) have anything in it?" "Of course it does, or it wouldn't be boiling." Yet the picture does not picture the contents of the pot, nor does Goethe recount the start of the game, nor does inner calculation duplicate every feature of outer (see XII, 2). For example, the mental addition of 17 and 18 may contain no plus sign, or figure 17. Yet we rightly say we added 17 and 18 (§§367–69). Cp. the comments on §297 and on p. 216c. For a full illustration of such secondary uses of terms (§282), see the treatment of *see* in Section XXXVII, e.g. pp. 196e, 199hi, 203ef ("But this is seeing! *In what sense* is it seeing?").

§366(a) are only logical constructions: as in logical atomism, or James's radical empiricism (*Essays,* 4). "A thing, of the everyday sort," wrote Russell (*Logic,* 109), "is constituted by a bundle of sensible qualities belonging to various senses, but supposed all to coexist in one continuous portion of space." Jones, for instance, is merely "a convenient hypothesis by means of which certain of your own sensations can be collected into a bundle" (idem, *Scientific Outlook,* 78). For W.'s early agreement, see especially *Kreis,* 258. "Personal experience," he commented later, "far from being the *product* of physical, chemical, physiological processes, seems to be the very *basis* of all that we say with any sense about such processes" (*BB* 48; see X, 7–8; *BB* 45b; cp. *PB* 51d, 100c).

(b) do I perhaps not *believe* . . . . : §386 indicates the sense of the question. W. is not defending himself against charges of behaviorism, as in §364a, but citing supposedly sure testimony and its treatment as such. Cp. analogous italics in §260 and §276.

but *this* one: identified by the missing phrase (e.g. "13 by 19") in the quoted statement.

at which I go wrong: cp. §350, p. 220c.

For I now want to say . . . : according to Moore, W. once maintained that the essential thing about chess is the logical multiplicity of the moves, as distinct, for instance, from the pieces used (*PP* 292). One could thus detect a game of chess even in the guise of stamping and yelling (§200). Likewise, inner thoughts would have just the same logical multiplicity as outer (*NB* 130), so that an inner process could be recognized as essentially, logically identical (3.1431, 3.3312, 4.016) with an outer process, and so be unmistakably identified as an instance of doing this sum rather than that.

corresponding: see *NB* 129: "I don't know *what* the constituents of a thought are but I know *that* it must have such constituents which correspond to the words of Language." Cp. §§51, 53a, 301.

method of projection: see especially 4.0141; cp. *BB* 53d.

§367 The remark sounds banal if taken factually, but not when understood grammatically. It switches the criteria from within to without, thereby indicating that the mental picture is not a picture, at least in the primary sense of the word (§301 and commentary). The criteria for the truth of the report that I am imagining such-and-such are not the criteria for a true description of a process (cp. §386). And the importance of the true confession does not reside in its being a correct and certain report of a process (cp. p. 222). "If someone says he's imagining Smith he will usually stare if he's asked 'are you getting all of him?' " (JN 86). See p. 202b; cp. §§297, 631, 633–37; Z 637, 641.

§368   Though the example leaves intact the sort of "formal identity" the *Tractatus* demanded (see commentary on §366b), it undermines the unthinking supposition on which such views rest (§363). Nothing can be concluded *a priori* about a person's psychic contents from the mere report "I added 17 and 18" (§§366b, 369). We need to know his "style" of speech (GI 15–16). See commentary on §369; cp. *BB* 36–37.

§369   Cp. §§350b, 386.

One would like to ask . . . : as Russell was wont to (GI 27). James's approach was similar (GI 48).

by *such* an answer: for it doesn't say what happens when one *thus* adds 17 and 18 (see commentary on §366b); it is a typical instance of "passing the buck" (cp. e.g. §350).

§370   **One ought to ask . . .** : see §308 and commentary (especially on "the decisive movement").

not what images are: cp. Russell, *Mind,* 144: "What images are, and how they are to be defined, we have now to inquire." (Ignoring the use of the word, he considers various theories.) See GI 27, 70.

or what happens: on the difference, cp. p. 211i.

But that does not mean . . . : "We seem to be on a side-track when we ask the question 'What is it like in this case "to get to know"?' But this question really is a question concerning the grammar of the word 'to know', and this becomes clearer if we put it in the form: 'What do we *call* "getting to know"?' It is part of the grammar of the word 'chair' that *this* is what we call 'to sit on a chair', and it is part of the grammar of the word 'meaning' that *this* is what we call 'explanation of a meaning' " (*BB* 24). See I, 7.

"He said, more than once, that he did not discuss these questions because he thought that language was the subject-matter of philosophy. . . . He discussed it only because he thought that particular philosophical errors or 'troubles in our thought' were due to false analogies suggested by our actual use of expressions" (*PP* 257).

And I am only saying . . . : see X, 22.

The first question . . . : concerning "what images are or what happens".

§371   See GI 27, 30–31; §58bc; *BB* 57a; NL 277cde; Man. 176, 11A;

Man. 116, 340–41; cp. Z 55; PB 85d; 5.552; Schlick, *Aufsätze,* 195. Chihara and Fodor term this a dramatic style of speaking. The attitude of W., an admirer of Lichtenberg, was rather: "A few good epigrams . . . are better than my longwinded explanations" (Man. 302, quoted more fully in the commentary on W.'s preface (*c*)). Sample quotations suggest the genesis of this epigram, then its meaning:

"The whole world of objects is and remains representation, and is for this reason wholly and for ever conditioned by the subject" (Schopenhauer, *World,* I, 15).

"A particular mode of signifying may be unimportant . . . but the possibility of each individual case discloses something about the essence of the world" (3.3421; see *PB* 51b; GI 30).

"The fact that the propositions of logic are tautologies *shows* the formal—logical—properties of language and the world" (6.12; see VI, 3).

"For logical investigation explores the nature of all things" (§89).

"The propositions of logic are 'laws of thought', 'because they bring out the essence of human thinking'—to put it more correctly: because they bring out, or shew, the essence, the technique, of thinking. They shew what thinking is and also shew kinds of thinking" (*RFM* 41).

"The rules do not *follow* from the nature of negation, but express it" (Man. 110, 107; cp. p. 147n).

"Whoever agrees with Goethe feels that Goethe has seen the *nature* of color. And nature here is not what experiments show, but lies in the concept of color" (Man. 176, 18B; see also 19A).

Essence: not, of course, "what is common" (§65), though if there were something common it would be expressed by grammar (GI 59). The word is a connecting link between §370 and §372, for, as the quotations just given indicate, *essence* here means what a thing is, its nature (see also §373; *RFM* 125f), and what it is necessarily, in virtue of the concept (see *RFM* 23, quoted in XXXIX, 5).

grammar: the word *grammar,* like the word *history,* has two senses: the study and the object. Switching to the latter, we might say: "Essence is *determined* by grammar."

Concerning W.'s broad use of the term, see the commentary on §29a, and VI, 3. A pertinent illustration here: "The inquiry whether the meaning of a word is its effect or its purpose, etc., is a grammatical inquiry" (*PG* 71).

Since in the *Investigations* W. often adopts the material mode of speech (e.g. §§301, 574, 615), it is necessary to keep §371 in mind.

§372 Slightly revised from Man. 110, 114–15. See IX, 1, 5–6; §50c; §251 and commentary; *RFM* 23 (quoted in XXXIX, 5), 73b ("Logic compels me only so far as the logical calculus compels me"), 81d ("To accept a proposition as unshakably certain—I want to say—means to use it as a grammatical rule"), 128; *PG* 45g; *PB* 107d; *LE* 7; *PP* 295, 318a. A penciled addition to this, in *PG* 184d: "Perhaps relate to the paradox that mathematics consists of rules." *RFM* 125–26 show W. ready to recognize that mathematics is in a sense "synthetic *a priori*", as "appears most obviously in the unpredictable occurrence of the prime numbers". See Hallett, "Contrast", 697–705; cp. *RFM* 193–94. On *a priori* and *a posteriori* in geometry, see *PB* 217–18.

"an intrinsic necessity": "The connexion which is supposed to be a causal, experiential one, but much stricter and harder, so rigid even, that the one thing somehow already *is* the other, is always a connexion in grammar" (*RFM* 40).

In the *Tractatus* W. had written: "The only necessity that exists is *logical* necessity" (6.37; see 6.3, 6.3211). But he did not consider logic reducible to 'grammar': "It is clear that something about the world must be indicated by the fact that certain combinations of symbols—whose essence involves the possession of a determinate character—are tautologies. This contains the decisive point. We have said that some things are arbitrary in the symbols that we use and that some things are not. In logic it is only the latter that express: but that means that logic is not a field in which *we* express what we wish with the help of signs, but rather one in which the nature of the natural and inevitable signs speaks for itself. If we know the logical syntax of any sign-language, then we have already been given all the propositions of logic" (6.124). Already in 1930 W. was saying: "The fact that the conclusion is *a priori* means only that syntax decides whether the conclusion is right or not. Tautology is only a way to reveal syntax" (*Kreis*, 92; see 91). "What looks as if it *had* to exist, is part of the language" (§50).

"arbitrary": see *Kreis*, 103; cp. 3.342; *NB* 113. W. once believed in an *a priori* order of language, thought, and world (GI 30–31), so that the rules of any language might be replaced by others, yet the rules themselves had to obey deeper, "inexpressible" rules (see 6.124, above). Later he recognized only an *a posteriori* world-order underlying language (p. 230), so that in contrast to his former viewpoint he would call the rules arbitrary (see *Z* 331), but in contrast to sheer conventionalism would deny that they are purely arbitrary (see IX, 6; *RFM* 23, quoted in XXXIX, 5). "What Wittgenstein is saying is that logical necessity arises out of language rather than the reverse, and that explicit logical rules are conventionalized transcriptions of standardized behavioral forms which have arisen naturally and 'unconsciously' from the kind of world in which we find ourselves" (Levison, "Laws", 311).

§373 Grammar tells: see commentary on §371; cp. *PB* 54 ("Grammar is a 'theory of logical types' ").

what kind of object: cp. *BB* 19b; *PG* 463c–464a; *NB* 70i.

Theology as grammar: see GI 7; *Z* 717; Man. 173, 92–93; Man. 130, 6–11; last pages of Man. 128 (the most important manuscript on religion); cp. *Kreis,* 115; Vesey, "Locke", 267 (quoted for §664); Ogden and Richards, *Meaning,* 132 ("closer scrutiny suggests that these subjects, of which Theology appears to be a good example, are themselves merely word systems"). Miss Anscombe has said that nobody understood W.'s views on religion. Similar obscurity surrounds this number. To avoid elemental confusions, we should distinguish theology from religious discourse, and consider whether the remark is an assessment of what theology has been or of what it should be (cp. a similar duality in W.'s use of *philosophy*), and especially whether the identification is meant to be complete, that is, whether theology is reduced to grammar. The passages quoted below suggest an attitude similar to James's, in a work W. admired: "What is their deduction of metaphysical attributes but a shuffling and matching of pedantic dictionary-adjectives, aloof from morals, aloof from human needs, something that might be worked out from the mere word 'God' by one of those logical machines of wood and brass which recent ingenuity has contrived as well as by a man of flesh and blood" (*Varieties,* 446). "We must therefore, I think, bid a definitive good-by to dogmatic theology" (ibid., 448). Kierkegaard's writings, Augustine's *Confessions,* Dostoievski's novels, Tolstoi's account of the gospels, W. esteemed; but Newman's theological works he did not. (See the appendix.)

"How words are understood is not told by words alone. (Theology)" (*Z* 144; cp. *Z* 273–74).

"About 'God' his main point seemed to be that this word is used in many *grammatically* different senses. He said, for instance, that many controversies about God could be settled by saying 'I'm not using the word in such a sense that you can say . . . ,' and that different religions 'treat things as making sense which others treat as nonsense, and don't merely deny some proposition which another religion affirms' " (*PP* 312).

"How you use the word 'God' does not show *whom* you mean but what you mean" (Man. 229, §1143).

"Religious belief & superstition are completely different. One comes from *fear* & is a sort of false science. The other is a trust" (Man. 168, 2).

"Once when Wittgenstein talked about religion, the contrast between his and Schlick's position became strikingly apparent. Both agreed of course in the view that the doctrines of religion in their various forms had no theoretical content" (Carnap, "Autobiography", 35).

"*Religion.* Is speech essential for religion? I can quite well imagine a religion in which there are no doctrines, and hence nothing is said. Obviously the essence of religion can have nothing to do with the fact that

speech occurs—or rather: if speech does occur, this itself is a component of religious behavior and not a theory. Therefore nothing turns
on whether the words are true, false, or nonsensical" (NT 16; *Kreis,*
117).

"That the essence of God guarantees his existence—that really means
that here there is no question of existence. Couldn't we say then that
the essence of a color guarantees its existence? In contrast for instance
to the white elephant. For that means only: I can't explain what 'color'
is, what the word 'color' means, except by means of a color sample. So
there is no explanation here of 'what it *would* be like if there *were* colors'. And now it might be said: we can describe how it would be if there
were gods on Olympus—but not: how it would be if God existed?
And thereby the concept 'God' gets more precisely determined. How
are we taught the word 'God' (that is, its use)? I can give no exhaustive, systematic description of it. But I can give leads as it were for
such a description; I can say much on the topic & perhaps eventually
provide a sort of collection of examples" (Man. 138, 30B; paragraph
divisions suppressed).

"A man says 'O God' and looks up to heaven. Now, it is this which
can teach us the sense of the proposition that 'God lives on high.' We
might say, very roughly, of people whose nature it is to kneel down on
certain occasions and fold their hands, that in their language they have
a personal God. . . . Keller writes (in *Der grüne Heinrich*) about a man
who said indeed that he did not believe in God, yet used all the usual
expressions which contain the word 'God' ('Thanks be to God,' 'God
willing,' etc.). And Keller thinks that he thereby contradicts himself.
But there *need* not be any contradiction in that, and we could say: what
you mean by the word 'God' I shall learn from what sentences you use
this word in and which ones are meaningless for you. For I too use the
expressions 'sense of a sentence' and 'meaning of a word' in certain
contexts, yet am acquainted with no object 'the meaning of a word'
and no shadow of an event [called] 'the sense of a sentence' " (Man.
219, 6).

§374   See Man. 229, §1243 (quoted for §280); cp. Russell, *Problems,*
15–16.

In Man. 228 (§175) these remarks follow §376, a connection which is
made clear by views like Frege's: "If two persons picture the same
thing, each still has his own idea. It is indeed sometimes possible to establish differences in the ideas, or even in the sensations, of different
men; but an exact comparison is not possible, because we cannot have
both ideas together in the same consciousness" (*Writings,* 60). This is
the sort of view W. here has in mind. See also Russell, *Logic,* 201
(quoted for §380a).

The great difficulty: one which illustrates the error combated in the previous numbers; a grammatical impossibility is taken for a metaphysical one (see *BB* 55c, quoted for §136b, and *Z* 458).

As if there really were . . . : "We make a picture like that of the two colours being in each other's way, or that of a barrier which doesn't allow one person to come closer to another's experience than to the point of observing his behaviour; but on looking closer we find that we can't apply the picture which we have made" (*BB* 56).

from which I derive . . . : see §§280, 378–80, pp. 185j–186c, 221–223a; Russell, *Logic*, 302 ("his words are chosen so as to describe the picture"); cp. §291.

And the best that I can propose . . . : cp. §§352, 422–27.

§375 See XXXVII, 15–18. The questions are an implicit warning against the idea of private ostensive definition (§§258, 262–64, 380), private criteria (§§314, 316), and recognition on the basis of the inner object alone (§§377–81).

§376 For the general context, see XII, 2. See Chihara and Fodor, "Operationalism", 394; cp. §350. In Man. 228, §174, the number is followed by §374.

To distinguish between physical objects, events, etc., and psychological processes, experiences, etc., we need to see what makes them the "same" so-and-so; for obviously there is a difference (*BB* 63). Cp. the quote from Frege under §374.

to myself: again, the German adds "inwardly".

what is the criterion: see X, 22; §§354, 377b, 580.

It might be found . . . : on the irrelevance of such physiological tests, see GI 60; pp. 212d, 220gh; *BB* 7d–8b; cp. p. 222f.

did we learn . . . : see III, 1–2; X, 20.

"to oneself": the German adds "silently". (Cp. p. 211k.)

The question is: the relevance of the question appears from, e.g., Russell, *Mind*, 155: "It is this fact, that images resemble antecedent sensations, which enables us to call them images 'of' this or that. For the understanding of memory, and of knowledge generally, the recognizable resemblance of images and sensations is of fundamental importance." However, "it is certainly also true," wrote James, "that no two 'ideas' are ever exactly the same." This assertion, he observed, "is more important theoretically than it at first sight seems. For it makes it already impossible for us to follow obediently in the footprints of either the Lockian or the Herbartian school, schools which have had almost unlimited influence in Germany and among ourselves" (*Principles*, I, 235–36).

§377 The number is guided by §§353–54: If you want to know the meaning of assertions about sameness, see how they are verified and whether they are. The word *same* does not carry its meaning with it, unaltered, into every context (§117). For the target and implications of the inquiry, see the quote just given from Russell, or James, *Principles*, I, 459 (e.g. "One might put it otherwise by saying that *'the mind can always intend, and know when it intends, to think of the Same.'* This *sense of sameness* is the very keel and backbone of our thinking").

(a) See §§215–16 and commentary; *BB* 140–41, 171 (quoted for §301); Man. 112, 217.

(b) See Moore, *Commonplace*, 144; cp. §404; *Z* 657–60, 472 ("Psychological verbs characterized by the fact that the third person of the present is to be verified by observation, the first person not").

What is the criterion . . . : the emphasis is not on ultimate evidence versus mere clues—criteria versus symptoms (§354)—but on the distinction between evidence and no evidence, observation and no observation (GI 15–16; see the quotation just given). W. had once held that redness, as well as pain, is both privately and publicly ascertained. See the comments on §56 ("we do not always resort"), and, more generally, X, 6–8.

The connection between the question of sameness and the question of redness comes out also in *RFM* 184–85 (quoted for §290); Russell, *Logic*, 206 (quoted for §50b) and 202–3: "*Mr. Neville:* I do not feel clear that the proposition 'This is white' is in any case a simpler proposition than the proposition 'This and that have the same colour.' *Mr. Russell:* That is one of the things I have not had time for. It may be the same as the proposition 'This and that have the same colour.' It may be that white is defined as the colour of 'this', or rather that the proposition 'This is white' means 'This is identical in colour with that,' the colour of 'that' being, so to speak, the definition of white." Russell's thinking took this direction in *Inquiry*, 35, quoted for §32b.

what he says and does: cp. §367; Man. 176, 48B.

nothing: see §378; cp. §§289–90. "What do I call comparing my own images? Well, I say for instance that I now see the same red before me as previously. Fine. How do I compare them both? How?—Well, I directed my attention to whether they were the same or different. But how do I do that?! Isn't this mere prattle? Under certain circumstances, asked if it was the same red both times, I react, with words" (Man. 180a; see discussion near the end; cp. §441). "For of course I don't make use of the agreement of human beings to affirm identity. What criterion do you use, then? None at all" (*RFM* 184).

§378 See §289; NL 288–89, 291f–292a, 293j; Man. 109, 197; cp. §§56, 292–95; *Z* 630–31, 659; *EPB* 232; *PB* 263b, 267a.

(a) **"I must recognize them . . .":** see the quotation from Russell for §376.

how am I to know . . . : once again, no connection has been made with the word. As the color does not dictate that it be called "red", so the colors' kinship does not dictate, prior to all praxis, that they be called "the same". After all, grammar decrees that no one be said to have the *same* pain as another, no matter how similar the sensations. And how alike should these images be? This verbal matter is not decided by attention to the mere images; they carry no labels. See NL 292c.

Only if I can . . . : see p. 186abc; cp. pp. 222i–223a ("The criteria for the truth of the *confession* that I thought such-and-such [e.g. had the same image] are not the criteria for a true *description* of a process"); *EPB* 193; *BB* 129. The remarks in §§290–91 on descriptions are applicable here.

in some other way . . . : the inner beetle (§293)—that is, the image—is not enough by itself to establish a language-game "on the model of 'object and designation' " (ibid.).

for someone else to . . . is the correct word: cp. §258 and commentary.

"A language-game: to bring something *else;* to bring the *same.* Now, we can imagine how it is played.—But how can I explain it to anyone? I can give him this training.—But then how does he know what he is to bring the next time as 'the same'—with what justice can I say that he has brought the right thing or the wrong?—Of course I know very well that in certain cases people would turn on me with signs of opposition. And does this mean e.g. that the definition of 'same' would be this: same is what all or most human beings with one voice take for the same?—Of course not" (*RFM* 184).

(b) See §380c; NL 28gj, 293bc. Cp. §293, especially (*c*); in neither case does W. accept the hypothesis, that we need a justification or that the first-person expression is modeled on the language-game of "object and name".

§379 See NL 311; Man. 180a: "Should I say: 'But first I *see* it is blue, then I *say* it'? What does it mean to just see that it is blue? Ask yourself: In what circumstances does a normal person say that?"

In *PG* 187, after noting difficulties like those in the previous number, W. raises and discusses the question: "But can't the justification simply *point* to the reality?" Granted, I cannot justify my use of words by saying, "I call this patch red because it is red"; but can't I say, at least to myself, "I call it red because it is *this*"? "We would also like to say, for example: 'I already know *something*, namely what I *see*; I just don't know whether it is a ball.' But in that case does it make sense to say, 'I know what I see'?" (Man. 109, 21–22). "This much is clear: I must be able to spot 'This', the thing that is yellow, again even if it is red. (If 'this' and 'yellow' formed a unity, they could be represented by a *single* symbol, and we would have no proposition.)" (*Kreis,* 97; see p. 186c).

First I am aware . . . : the kind of thinking W. has in mind and its importance are illustrated by Moore, *Papers,* 53–55, quoted for §380.

in what cases . . . : "In order for there to be a proposition, circle, yellow, etc., would have to be concepts that are already understood" (Man. 109, 22).

§380 See NL 287–88; Man. 232, 681–82; Man. 109, 183 ("Every distinction must be expressed as a distinction in *some* language"); cp. §245 and commentary; §38d; *BB* 64b; Man. 116, 120; Man. 109, 22. "We are treating . . . of cases in which, as one might roughly put it, the grammar of a word seems to suggest the 'necessity' of a certain intermediary step, although in fact the word is used in cases in which there is no such intermediary step" (*BB* 130; *EPB* 196). Here the troublesome word is *recognize* (see §604).

(a) See II, 5; §239; *EPB* 192; *BB* 128–29; *PG* 74a; Man. 228, §262; Man. 115, 3; Russell, *Logic,* 202–3 (quoted above for §377); cp. *Kreis,* 97; Man. 109, 245.

"The simplest imaginable facts are those which consist in the possession of a quality by some particular thing. Such facts, say, as 'This is white.' They have to be taken in a very sophisticated sense. I do not want you to think about the piece of chalk I am holding, but of what you see when you look at the chalk" (Russell, *Logic,* 198).

"that it is *this*": "I say this because I don't want to name what I see. I don't want to say, 'I see a flower,' for that presupposes a linguistic convention, and I want a form of expression that makes no reference to the history of the impression" (*PG* 165–66).

"What distinguishes the objects to which I can give names from other things is the fact that these objects are within my experience, that I am acquainted with them, but it is only subsequent reflection that proves that they all have this distinguishing characteristic; during the process of naming they appear merely as this, that, and the other" (Russell, *Logic,* 167; see II, 5).

"It seems to me quite evident that my knowledge that I am now perceiving a human hand is a deduction from a pair of propositions simpler still—propositions which I can only express in the form 'I am perceiving *this*' and '*This* is a human hand' " (Moore, *Papers,* 53).

"When I stare at a colored object and say 'this is red,' I seem to know exactly to what I give the name red. As it were, to that which I am drinking in. It is as though there was a magic power in the words *'this is . . .'* " (NL 308).

"It seems that you wish to specify the colour you see, but not by saying anything about it, nor by comparing it with a sample,—but by pointing to it; using it at the same time as the sample and that which the sample is compared with" (*BB* 174).

This?—What?!: Russell, for one, was untroubled by problems of communication: "If you agree that 'This is white,' meaning the 'this' that you see, you are using 'this' as a proper name. But if you try to apprehend the proposition that I am expressing when I say 'This is white,' you cannot do it. . . . It is only when you use 'this' quite strictly, to stand for an actual object of sense, that it is really a proper name. And in that it has a very odd property for a proper name, namely that it seldom means the same thing two moments running and does not mean the same thing to the speaker and to the hearer" (*Logic*, 201; cp. §293). As for Moore's sense-data, he could not make up his mind what they were (see e.g. *Papers*, 54–58).

What kind of answer . . . : not: "I should know what it is I mean. I mean just these shades of color and shapes, the *appearance*" (see NL 311b). Cp. *BB* 174d.

(b) See X, 17, 20–21; Man. 229, §866; Schlick, "Form", 194 (quoted for §295a).

(c) See §§202, 258, 288c, 362, 486. "I wish to say that we can't adduce the 'private experience' as a justification for expressing it" (NL 312).

§381   See II, 10–11; X, 20; §384; *RFM* 184j; Man. 180b, 1–2; Man. 109, 196, 300; Malcolm, "Investigations", 212.

W. now suggests a correct answer to the question of §380. To know whether a color is red I must know what colors are called red (§371). And I generally do not acquire that knowledge through a definition, employing other terms, but in the process of learning English. "Unless words like 'red' and 'chair' are learned there isn't any language" (Malcolm, *Memoir*, 92).

However, the main thrust is negative. W. is rejecting his earlier answer: "The word 'red' is used via a memory image" (Man. 109, 248; see §604); "I remember having seen this color before & having always called it so" (Man. 107, 245). (Is another criterion needed for that?) (Cp. Man. 228, §38; Man. 110, 61–62.)

"What was thought of as a paradigm of a verifiable proposition becomes a paradigm of a proposition concerning which it makes no sense to speak of verifying it. The underlying thought is the insistence that what makes a proposition true cannot be identical with what gives it sense. Wittgenstein embraced this principle in his earliest writings and adhered (*PB*, §23) to it, though with a special qualification, throughout his life. For only, it seems, by adopting this principle, is the possibility of expressing false yet meaningful propositions adequately secured" (Hacker, *Insight*, 161; see X, 25).

§382 See I, 4–5; X, 20.

(a) At these words . . . : "If I give someone the order 'fetch me a red flower from that meadow,' how is he to know what sort of flower to bring, as I have only given him a *word*?

"Now the answer one might suggest first is that he went to look for a red flower carrying a red image in his mind, and comparing it with the flowers to see which of them had the colour of the image. . . . Thus, if you are asked what is the relation between a name and the thing it names, you will be inclined to answer that the relation is a psychological one, and perhaps when you say this you think in particular of the mechanism of association" (*BB* 3).

"The essence of language," wrote Russell (*Mind*, 191), "lies, not in the use of this or that special means of communication, but in the employment of fixed associations (however these may have originated) in order that something now sensible—a spoken word, a picture, a gesture, or what not—may call up the 'idea' of something else."

How can I *justify* this?: if I need a justification for the choice of flower (see above), I need one for the choice of image—which shows that I don't need a justification (§289); for of course the image would be no redder than the flower, nor would it be labeled "certified red".

(b) From Man. 109, 199.

(c) See pp. 185g–186c. W. is doing for *red* what §§300–301 do for *pain*. After training by means of a color chart, a person might justify his execution of an order by pointing to a color sample, the same one his teacher pointed to, and say: "*This* sample you called red" (see *BB* 14). Now is something similar possible for images? No, an inner color chart is not a color chart (cp. §§259–60).

§383 Contrasting "the theory of Mr Russell that . . . in every atomic fact there must be one constituent which is in its own nature incomplete or connective" with "Mr Wittgenstein's theory that neither is there a copula, nor one specially connected constituent", Ramsey had Russell urge against this more radical atomism that his "was the only account of the difference between particulars and universals which made them really different kinds of objects, as they evidently were, and not merely differently related to us or to our language" (*Foundations*, 121–22). It might seem that W.'s later position too, with its rejection of essences (now genuine) and its similarity to radical empiricism (GI 44), fits into this second category. However, he has broken out of the framework within which the debate was conducted. If "*essence* is expressed by grammar" (§371) and the grammar of words varies so, not only from name to name but from name to nonname (I, 10), it makes little sense to argue "whether there is a fundamental division of objects into two classes, particulars and universals" (Ramsey, *Foundations*, 112).

In logic, "different kinds are different grammatical structures" (*BB* 19), and these often diverge, in different ways and to different degrees, from the structure "object and designation" (§293). In particular, "the psychological verbs to see, to believe, to think, to wish [here being considered], do not signify phenomena [appearances]. But psychology observes the phenomena *of* seeing, believing, thinking, wishing" (*Z* 471; see §571), and philosophy studies the concepts, that is, the uses of these verbs.

§384   See §381 and commentary; cp. §288.

the *concept:* italicized because here, as in the preceding number, W. would stress the difference between concept ("the use of a word") and object. "One wants to exclaim: 'You have not learned the *concept* until you have learned *what* pain is, and this requires the experience of pain. In learning language you might come to know a lot about how to *use* the *word:* but this will not give you the essential thing'" (Malcolm, *Problems,* 56; see 57). For W.'s reply, see X, 20.

§385   Compare: Might children play at trains without ever seeing or hearing about trains? What would that be like? And would there be enough connection with trains for us still to call what they did playing at trains (§282)?

Would it be imaginable . . . : p. 220 gives a negative answer: "You can only learn to calculate in your head by learning to calculate" (see the commentary on this).

Only the question arises: for sheer results do not show that a person has calculated (cp. p. 14n); and results are all the rest of us have to go by here, and he is supposedly calculating, not attending to the inner process and comparing it with the public procedures of others to determine whether it is really calculating. And what would the inner activity have to be like to qualify as calculating (§366)? How is he to judge? "Only if you have learned to calculate—on paper or out loud—can you be made to grasp, by means of this concept, what calculating in the head is" (p. 216). See XXXVII, 16.

is it also possible for some tribes . . . : see §344.

a limiting case: that is, a borderline case, as in §200. Cp. §284b.

gravitate towards another paradigm: as the yelling and stamping in §200 gravitate toward dancing. Cp. p. 219 ("it is the field of force of a word that is decisive").

§386   The connection with the previous two numbers: Were learning a word's meaning merely learning what it stands for (see §264; cp. §384), so that it could then be applied without regard to circumstances (see §116), there would be no problem with the hypothesis of §385. We would simply be supposing that members of the tribe do always inwardly what we do sometimes inwardly and sometimes outwardly (see

§§344–45). W. continues to question this supposition of invariance. Here, too, "what I have to do is not simply to make a transition in imagination from one place . . . to another" (§302), from calculating on paper to calculating in the head. "It is not our intention to criticize this form of expression ["in the head"], or to show that it is not appropriate. What we must do is: understand its working, its grammar" (*BB* 7).

(a) See §342, p. 196de.

    The difficulty is not . . . : cp. §350.

    But it is *this*: cp. §342.

    Are they then so alike . . . : see §§366–68.

(b) See §§254, 299, 343, 594c, p. 222hi; cp. pp. 211b, 215d, 216d; *OC* 360, 363–65; Man. 229, §1775.

    his testimony: for instance Ballard's (§342).

§387 Cp. §573b. We are so busy 'thinking' (§66), in the manner illustrated by the opening remarks of §386, that we skate without problems over the surface of language, neither realizing our ignorance of depth grammar (§664) nor how difficult it is to discern, nor all the problems such ignorance causes, nor the significance of what we might find (§111).

"He spoke about the 'lack of deep puzzlement' in the work of a well-known philosophical movement. Some other philosophers whose work was plainly influenced by some of his teaching he was heard to describe (on slight evidence) as 'more linguists than philosophers': in his view they did not come at problems in a natural way but rather fitted situations into prepared linguistic boxes" (Gasking and Jackson, "Wittgenstein," 54).

"Wittgenstein liked to draw an analogy between philosophical thinking and swimming: just as one's body has a natural tendency towards the surface and one has to make an *exertion* to get to the *bottom*—so it is with thinking" (Malcolm, *Memoir*, 55).

"To go deep you needn't go far; you can do it in your own back-garden" (Man. 131, 182; W.'s English at the end).

§388 See Man. 110, 70. Cp. §197, and especially §§139–40, e.g.: "What was the effect of my argument? It called our attention to (reminded us of) the fact that there are other processes, besides the one we originally thought of." W. had thought of this one: "The word 'red' is used via a memory image" (Man. 109, 248).

(a) Cp. *BB* 3 (quoted for §382a) and the further development in *PB* 57 ("Two sorts of thing might be meant here . . .").

(b) **How do I know . . . :** cp. §148. For one thing, "are they then so alike that one might mix them up?" (§386). For another, even if they were, the image does not bear a name tag.

(c) Is there some present criterion which I can observe (*PB* 57), or do I base myself on past successes and reason inductively (§147)? Is this the evidence I go on when I say "I can" and therefore the criterion of the ability? W.'s answer is clear from previous sections, especially IX (see IX, 5–6; GI 15–16; §§154–55). Cp. p. 181d.

§389 Worked up in Man. 116, 28. For a full explanation, see GI 34–37 and *BB* 36cd (e.g.: "Another source of the idea of a shadow being the object of our thought is this: We imagine the shadow to be a picture the intention of which *cannot be questioned,* that is, a picture which we don't interpret in order to understand it, but which we understand without interpreting it"). See also §§139, 352, 426, 512; Man. 109, 57–58, 300 (quoted for §604); cp. XXXVII, 6.

"The first idea [you have] is that you are looking at your own thought, and are absolutely sure that it is a thought that so and so. You are looking at some mental phenomenon, and you say to yourself 'obviously this is a thought of my brother being in America.' It seems to be a super-picture. It seems, with thought, that there is no doubt whatever. With a picture, it still depends on the method of projection, whereas here it seems that you get rid of the projecting relation, and are absolutely certain that this is the thought of that" (*LC* 67).

§390 In these final numbers of the section, W. examines the assumption that "the language of imagining does not allow us to imagine anything senseless" (§512) and concludes that there is no such guarantee (§397). Sometimes the imagining makes sense, sometimes not (§390). Imagining varies so, especially in philosophy, both in its manner and in its content (§394 and commentary on §391).

why should that not . . . : that is, rather than conclude that the hypothesis makes sense since he can imagine it, why not conclude that since the hypothesis is senseless (§§281–84) images are no guarantee of sense (§§395–96)?

§391 W. continues to investigate the extent to which imaginability ensures that a proposition makes sense (§395), in basically the same manner as in the preceding number. In both instances he suggests that we imagine a member of the list in §281 to be dissociated from its ordinary criteria and asks whether the hypothesis will be merely contrary to fact.

it is important: if the imagining is to make sense, we must imagine an exceptional case (§§344, 580), not disregard completely the usual criteria (cp. §354).

"Well, his soul . . .": see §357, p. 178i.

what do I do: to determine to what extent imaginability assures sense, it is necessary to consider what the imagining consists in, in this case or that: an uncanny feeling (§420a)? a mental twiddle (§420b)? working in a piece of fancy (p. 206e)? supplying a context (§539)?

play a part: cp. pp. 188mn, 219b.

§392 The variability of imagining, which casts doubt on the assurance expressed in §389 and §512, is conceptual as well as factual. What is to count as having imagined *p*? Here too the fluctuation between criteria and symptoms may make it look as if there were nothing but symptoms (§354). Hearing the account in §391, someone might reply that none of that is necessary; there is no need, for instance, to say those words, or any words. And if *imagine* is, for example, a family-resemblance word (§67), the claim may be true (GI 43). All of this contributes to the "lack of clarity about the role of *imaginability* in our investigation" (§395).

§393 Cp. p. 188j-m. In the typical situation described by §392, the only remedy is to "bring words back from their metaphysical to their everyday use" (§116). Number 392 prepares this step and §393 takes it. It then appears that what "goes on in me" (§§392, 394) is not to the point at all. It does not serve as criterion in the actual use of the term *imagine* (cp. GI 60–61).

(a) And I do not necessarily . . . : see §302 and commentary.

(b) the suggested analysis: in terms of "What goes on in me" (§§392, 393a, 394).

We now watch the actor . . . : we are interested in his outer, not his inner acts. Cp. §§281, 285–87, 450.

§394 In §393 W. casts doubt on the equation "imagining = what happens inside," by considering how the expression "imagine he is in pain" might normally be used. In a situation like the one he suggests, the inner process is of no more interest than in a game of chess (p. 181c). Now, working on the other side of the equation, he asks in what circumstances the inner happening would be of interest, no doubt expecting us to recognize that the point of such an inquiry would not be to determine whether the person really imagined, or what imagining consists in, but for instance (in a psychological investigation) whether the imagery was purely visual or largely verbal, which details were prominent and which omitted, and so on. "The psychological concept hangs out of reach of this explanation. And this makes the nature of the problem clearer" (p. 212).

§395 See §§511–12; *OC* 35; *Z* 247, 262–63; *BB* 53e–54a; *PG* 128ab; NL 316b; Man. 110, 194; Man. 109, 42; Man. 106, 61; cp. XXXVII, 3; 3.001; *NB* 24a; *LO* 24; Schlick, "Meaning", 158c. Earlier W. tended to look on imaginability as a necessary and sufficient condition of sense. Necessary condition: "It is nonsense to say that I wonder at the existence of the world, because I cannot imagine it not existing" (LE 9). Sufficient condition: "I have never actually seen a black speck grow gradually lighter till it was white, then redder and redder till it was red; but I know it is possible, since I can imagine it. That is, I operate with my images in color space and do with them what would be possible with the colors. And my words take their sense from the fact that they mirror more or less completely the operations of the images. Somewhat like musical notation, say, which can be used to describe a piece that is played, but does *not* for instance reproduce the strength of each individual note" (*PB* 73–74; cp. 4.014 before and *BB* 36d after; see also XXXVII, 3; *PB* 84d, 247d). As this example suggests, "the naive theory of *imagining to oneself* can't be completely wrong" (*PB* 58; see Man. 110, 193–94). Such is still W.'s attitude here (see §397).

§396   See §449; *Z* 25, 239–40, 544, 546, 548; *EPB* 130; *BB* 36–37, 53d, 88–89; *PG* 73b, 74ab, 182e; Man. 229, §1344; Man. 179; Man. 109, 45–46, 188–89, 275; cp. §663; Frege, *Foundations*, 70–71; Russell, *Logic*, 300; James, *Principles*, I, 265–66; Hertz, *Principles*, 2–3. Here and in §397 W. suggests partial answers to the question raised in §395. The present remark does not deny the relevance of imaginability for sense (see §§397, 517, and the quotations above); for the need to actually imagine something differs from the ability. It might be that any proposition makes sense if one *could* imagine the state of affairs described, or that no statement makes sense unless one *could* imagine the state of affairs it purportedly describes. "One is inclined to think that understanding a sentence must consist in something at least *similar* to having a picture of the 'fact the sentence refers to' before one's mind. What is true in this is that there is a connection between the capability to produce such a picture & understanding" (Man. 166; W.'s English; see Man. 110, 194; commentary on §395).

Among those so inclined were Augustine (below), James (*Principles*, I, 28–29, 271), and young W. himself. See XII, 1; XXXVII, 2–8; commentary on §6b ("one very likely thinks"); 3.001; *NB* 24a; Man. 108, 248–49.

"When I speak, the images of all I speak about are present, from the same treasury of memory; nor would I be speaking thereof were the images missing" (*Confessions*, X, 8, 14; see ibid., 15, 23).

make a sketch: "Mental images of colours, shapes, sounds, etc., etc., which play a role in communication by means of language we put in the same category with patches of colour actually seen, sounds heard" (*BB* 89). "We could perfectly well, for our purposes, replace every process of imagining by a process of looking at an object or by painting, drawing or modelling" (*BB* 4; see *BB* 5a). "No psychological process can symbolize any better than signs put on paper" (Man. 110, 18). "It can never be essential for us that a phenomenon takes place in the mind & not on paper, visible to others" (Man. 110, 24). "This, of course, doesn't mean that we have shown that peculiar acts of consciousness do not accompany the expressions of our thoughts! Only we no longer say that they *must* accompany them" (*BB* 42).

from it: thus we should not think of a person who understands a description by means of a sketch, but of a person who, having understood a statement, proceeds to illustrate it. Cp. §663.

§397 The number indicates a limited connection between imaginability and sense (§395). Cp. W.'s earlier views, under §395.

by a particular method: "in a particular medium" (words, pictures, mental images, and the like) seems a preferable translation. Cp. *BB* 16.

may **indeed safely point . . . :** see p. 178g; Man. 228, §49.

On the other hand . . . : see for example §§59, 216, 295, 352; *RFM* 137cd; Man. 228, §170; cp. §512; *PB* 97.

XIII. The I (§§398–411)

GENERAL COMMENTARY

(1) "The I, the I," wrote young Wittgenstein—"that centre of the world, which we call the I, and which is the bearer of ethics"—"is what is deeply mysterious" (*NB* 80). But is such a "centre" what we call the "I"? Do we call anything the "I"? How is the word used? In particular how is it employed in the first-person, present-tense psychological utterances ("I know," "I understand," "I am in pain," "I think," etc.) which Wittgenstein has been discussing since Section IX? In the two sections prior to this one he focused on act and content; now, returning to the simpler example of Section X, he focuses on the subject. That is, considering once again an utterance such as "I have a pain," he studies the word *I*, as he previously studied *pain*, and reaches the same conclusion: The utterance is not based on observation or criteria, but is the kind of primitive verbal reaction which establishes criteria (see X, 20–21). In this game, the person in pain is the person who gives it (sincere) expression (see §302 and commentary); the cry or the verbal substitute is not a mere clue to genuine possession. For what would that be, and how established? Is it written in some Platonic heaven that the possessor of pain is a Cartesian self who contemplates it, or a body in whose nervous system certain changes take place?

(2) The main question in many readers' minds may be formulated thus: "In adopting this grammatical approach, did Wittgenstein simply bypass the transempirical self in which he once believed, or did he re-

pudiate it as a grammatical fiction, on a par with the acts of intending, understanding, and meaning as he once conceived them?" To answer this question, it will be necessary to add further historical background to that already supplied in X, 10. Schopenhauer, Wittgenstein's first master, rejected the Kantian subject-object dichotomy. "Our method of procedure," he wrote, "is *toto genere* different from these two opposite misconceptions, since we start neither from the object nor from the subject, but from the *representation*, as the first fact of consciousness" (*World*, I, 34). The *Tractatus* reveals a basically similar viewpoint: "These concepts: proposition, language, thought, world, stand in line one behind the other, each equivalent to each" (§96; see GI 31–41). The self does not intrude into this scheme, even when the proposition is psychological (5.542). For propositions are pictures of possible states of affairs in the world, and "the subject does not belong to the world: rather, it is a limit of the world" (5.632). Thus the self is not even "shown", in the way that logical form was said to be shown by propositions. As "nothing *in the visual field* allows you to infer that it is seen by an eye" (5.633), so nothing in the world pictured by propositions or in the propositions picturing the world reveals the presence of a self which observes the world or "means" the signs (5.633, 5.641; *PB* 100c; NL 282g). Thus, if in the *Investigations* the metaphysical self drops out of grammar, that is nothing new.

(3)   "What brings the self into philosophy," Wittgenstein had written, "is the fact that 'the world is my world'" (5.641; *NB* 80; see Hacker, "Soul", 170–71). "It seems absurd to us that a pain, a mood, a wish should rove about the world without a bearer, independently. . . . The inner world presupposes the person whose inner world it is . . . ideas need a bearer" (Frege, "Thought", 299; see 299–301). So too, "the act of judging is a psychical process, and as such it needs a judging subject as its owner" (idem, *Writings*, 128). "It seems as if the elementary psychic fact were not *thought* or *this thought* or *that thought*, but *my thought*, every thought being *owned*" (James, *Principles*, I, 226). And of course the owner of thought is not the body (*BB* 69b). "These things did my inner man know by the ministry of the outer. I, the inner, knew them; I, the mind, through the senses of my body" (Augustine, *Confessions*, X, 6, 9; see ibid., 7, 11). This inner self is the one of which a latter-day Augustinian wrote, "I think, therefore I am" (see *BB* 69b). In reply to this particular version of the syndrome, the later Wittgenstein observed: "If a man says to me, looking at the sky, 'I think it will rain, therefore I exist,' I do not understand him" (Coope et al., *Workbook*, 21). "One must always ask oneself: is the word ever actually used in this way in the language-game which is its original home?" (§116).

(4)   In everyday use "'I' is not the name of a person," Cartesian or

other (§410), much as *pain* is not the name of an inner object. Nor therefore does it designate the inner owner of inner objects. But we need not conclude that the self, any more than thought or pain, "cancels out" (§293). "It is not a *something*, but not a *nothing* either! The conclusion was only that a nothing would serve just as well as a something about which nothing could be said [see XIII, 2; *BB* 64–65, quoted in X, 10]. We have only rejected the grammar which tries to force itself on us here" (§304; see GI 17; *BB* 69b). "One is inclined to say: 'How can the body have pain? The body in itself is something dead; a body isn't conscious!' And here again it is as though we looked into the nature of pain and saw that it lies in its nature that a material object can't have it. And it is as though we saw that what has pain must be an entity of a different nature from that of a material object; that, in fact, it must be of a mental nature. But to say that the ego is mental is like saying that the number 3 is of a mental or an immaterial nature, when we recognize that the numeral '3' isn't used as a sign for a physical object" (*BB* 73; see *BB* 74b; NL 282b).

(5) *NB* 80 was right when it declared: "The I is not an object." And even when it added: "I objectively confront every object. But not the I." Straightened out, this might now be taken to mean: "My own relation to my words"—in particular my avowals (GI 15–16; *Z* 539–40)—"is wholly different from other people's" (p. 192). For instance, "the man who cries out with pain, or says that he has pain, *doesn't choose the mouth which says it*" (*BB* 68) and thereby designate the person in pain, pointing to his mind via his body (*BB* 66). "Someone else sees who is in pain from the groaning," but the one who groans follows no criteria (§404). And "to say, 'I have pain' is no more a statement *about* a particular person than moaning is" (*BB* 67).

(6) *NB* 80 was also correct, if still for the wrong reasons, when it continued: "So there really is a way in which there can and must be mention of the I in a *non-psychological sense* in philosophy," that is, of a self which "is not the human being, not the human body, or the human soul, with which psychology deals" (5.641). For "the word 'I' does not mean the same as 'L. W.' even if I am L. W., nor does it mean the same as the expression 'the person who is now speaking'. But that doesn't mean: that 'L. W.' and 'I' mean different things [a human being and a metaphysical subject]. All it means is that these words are different instruments in our language" (*BB* 67; see *OC* 42). And the non-psychological way the I must enter into philosophy, and does in this section, is through the study of such differences. This "essence" too must be expressed by grammar (§§116, 371), if clarity is to be reached concerning the deeply mysterious I.

DETAILED COMMENTARY

§398 See §§273–78; *PB* 99b–100e, 102–3, 254–81; *NL* 298d–300c; Man. 213, 463–64; Man. 105, 122–26; Russell, *Development*, 24–25; cp. von Wright, "Lichtenberg", 210–13. W.'s fuller remarks in the early thirties reveal both continuity (XIII, 2) and discontinuity (XIII, 4–6) between this number and his earliest thought: "One of the most misleading modes of representation in our language is the use of the word 'I', especially where it is used to describe our immediate experience, as in 'I see a red patch' " (Man. 108, 8; *PB* 88). "He was quite definite that the word 'I' . . . is used in 'two utterly different ways', one in which it is 'on a level with other people', and one in which it is not. . . . As an instance of one of these two uses, he gave 'I've got a match-box' and 'I've got a bad tooth,' which he said were 'on a level' with 'Skinner has a match-box' and 'Skinner has a bad tooth.' He said that in these two cases 'I have . . .' and 'Skinner has . . .' really were values of the same propositional function, and that 'I' and 'Skinner' were both 'possessors'. But in the case of 'I have toothache' or 'I see a red patch' he held that the use of 'I' is utterly different" (*PP* 310). "He said that 'what characterizes "primary experience" ' is that in its case ' "I" does not denote a possessor.' In order to make clear what he meant by this he compared 'I have toothache' with 'I see a red patch'; and said of what he called 'visual sensations' generally, and in particular of what he called 'the visual field', that 'the idea of a person doesn't enter into the description of it, just as a (physical) eye doesn't enter into the description of what is seen' " (*PP* 308–9). "Visual space is essentially ownerless. Let us suppose I always see a certain object along with the rest in my visual field— namely my nose. Naturally someone else does not see this object in the same way. Doesn't this mean that the visual field of which I speak *belongs to me*? That it is therefore subjective? No. It is just subjectively conceived here and contrasted with an objective space, which however is only a construction, with visual space as its basis [see X, 7–8, on this transitional viewpoint]" (*PB* 100; Man. 105, 124). "Now the danger we are in when we adopt the sense datum notation," W. noted a year or two later (*BB* 70), "is to forget the difference between the grammar of a statement about sense data and the grammar of an outwardly similar statement about physical objects." It may seem that objects in visual space are ones which I alone see, in a sense of *see* which requires a spiritual subject, and which I point to, not with my finger but with my mind (*BB* 71). "We feel then that in the cases in which 'I' is used as subject, we don't use it because we recognize a particular person by his bodily characteristics; and this creates the illusion that we use this word to refer to something bodiless, which, however, has its seat in our body. In fact *this* seems to be the real ego, the one of which it was said 'Cogito, ergo sum' " (*BB* 69; see XIII, 3).

(a) See XIII, 3; §§273, 275; Man. 302, 11; Cook, "Privacy", 301–3; Schlick, "Meaning", 163.

"or even actually *see* objects": cp. Frege, "Thought", 299: "I go for a walk with a companion. I see a green field, I have a visual impression of the green as well. I have it but I do not see it.

"Secondly: ideas are had. One has sensations, feelings, moods, inclinations, wishes. An idea which someone has belongs to the content of his consciousness."

"I have *got* something . . .": see *BB* 49a; cp. §261 and commentary.

"I have got THIS": see *BB* 71 re "the solipsistic way I say '*This* is what's really seen.' " "We say: 'When I say that I see a chair there, I say more than I know for certain.' And generally this means: 'But there is *one* thing I know for sure.' However, if we want to say what it is, we are somehow at a loss" (*PG* 220; see X, 6–10). So we perhaps fall back on the noncommittal *this*, and use it to simply "refer" (§38; III, 5).

What are these words for?: see *BB* 174–75.

"no question of a 'seeing' ": see (*b*); §401; *BB* 60–61. To say that I see my sense-data would involve a radical revision of the concept *see*, not a mere switch from many viewers to one (*PB* 88c; cp. p. 180d). And since this limitation to one is logical, we can say of this verb too: "If as a matter of logic you exclude other people's seeing something (viz. your sense-datum), it loses its sense to say that you see it."

Russell was aware how greatly seeing a sense-datum would differ from seeing a physical object, but decided that the sense-datum is the only thing we really see (*Mind*, 299; cp. *BB* 60–61, quoted for §275).

"therefore none of a 'having' ": see (*b*) ("I can as little own it . . ."). W. does not mean to imply that nonvisible things (e.g. pains or dreams) cannot be had. He is characterizing his former viewpoint: " 'If anybody asks me to describe *what I see*, I describe *what's seen*' " (NL 308). "Visual space . . . is autonomous" (Man. 107, 1).

"nor of a subject": on this "subject", see the quotation from Russell for §302b ("the subject").

if as a matter of logic . . . : see §251 and commentary; §253b; *PP* 275, 306b; Schlick, "Meaning", 166–67; Malcolm, *Problems*, 20–21. The idea of possession arises from such statements as "He can't have my toothache, my sensations," which sound factual, but are actually grammatical (X, 18). The impossibility of another's sticking his head or mind into mine (*BB* 60–61) and observing my sensations is not a metaphysical truth or fact of nature which I intuit, thereby establishing my unique ownership, in contrast to some intelligible alternative (Man. 228, §171;

BB 55a), but a reflection of grammar. " 'I can't feel your toothache' means the same as ' "I feel your toothache" has no sense' " (*PP* 306).

"When the sense of the word 'sense-data' makes it unthinkable for another person to have them, we are prevented for this very reason from saying he doesn't have them. And it is therefore meaningless to say that *I*, in contrast to the other person *have* them" (*PB* 90).

(b) See NL 284g, 298, 308k–309b, 315g; Man. 110, 7–8; Man. 109, 270–71.

  this object: not the self, but the sense-datum. See X, 3–4.

  one's looking and pointing: see §§274–77; *BB* 64b, 71bc; cp. §38d.

  I know how one stares: see §413 and commentary ("And a good deal . . ."); Man. 116, 224–25.

  has no owner: see XIII, 2; Man. 116, 224, 235–36 (quoted for §414).

  or point to it: see *BB* 71cd.

  Inasmuch as it cannot . . . : see comments on (*a*) ("if as a matter of logic"); Man. 110, 7; cp. §253b; *BB* 55: "Of course, if we exclude the phrase 'I have his toothache' from our language, we thereby also exclude 'I have (or feel) *my* toothache.' "

(c) Cp. Man. 116, 185.

  The answer . . . might be: the caption might be "Farmer Brown in front of his house". Cp. §365.

  But then he cannot . . . : so he owns it in a secondary (§282), very different sense (cp. Malcolm, *Memoir*, 31c).

§399   See the commentary on §398 and, for background, XIII, 3. Cp. §297.

  would have to be the same kind: would have to be phenomenal, "immediately given", along with the other phenomena, just as physical objects are owned by physical people.

  but he is not to be found in it: the "metaphysical subject", introduced into philosophy through "my world", is nevertheless absent from that world (5.641). "If I wrote a book called *The World as I found it* . . . it alone could *not* be mentioned in that book" (5.631). See *PB* 100be.

  there is no outside: "since the visual image borders on nothing" (Man. 116, 220). "I can say: 'in my visual field I see the image of the tree to the right of the image of the tower' or 'I see the image of the tree in the middle of the visual field.' And now we are inclined to ask 'and where do you see the visual field?' Now if the 'where' is meant to ask for a locality in the sense in which we have specified the locality of the image of the tree, then I would draw your attention to the fact that you have not yet given this question sense" (*BB* 8).

§400   See §401; *PB* 100c; cp. *Z* 423.

  a discovery: "At first sight it may appear . . . that here we have two kinds of worlds, worlds built of different materials; a mental world and a physical world" (*BB* 47). See Man. 107, 1, quoted in X, 8.

   a new way of speaking: see p. 224j and commentary.

   a new comparison: see §104.

   a new sensation: "one you can have only if you are capable of applying certain words in the ordinary ways" (Diamond, "Secondary", 199); "what we have here is a modified concept of *sensation*" (p. 209).

§401 Worked over in Man. 116, 222–23; see §400 and references; *BB* 59a, 70c (e.g.: "Queerly enough, the introduction of this new phraseology has deluded people into thinking that they had discovered new entities, new elements of the structure of the world, as though to say 'I believe that there are sense data' were similar to saying 'I believe that matter consists of electrons' "); *Z* 458 ("The essential thing about metaphysics: it obliterates the distinction between factual and conceptual investigations").

(a) "the material of which . . .": see §366a and commentary.

(b) Cp. p. 230c; *Z* 455.

§402(a) See X, 10; §280, p. 200b; Man. 116, 215–19; cp. *BB* 175ab; *PB* 88a.

   "to someone *else*": "and that should mean: I don't need this indication—so perhaps: I know that it is *my* image" (Man. 116, 218). See X, 10; commentary on §404; cp. *PB* 93b; *BB* 66: "When I said, from my heart, that only I see, I was also inclined to say that by 'I' I didn't really mean L. W., although for the benefit of my fellow men I might say 'It is now L. W. who really sees' though this is not what I really mean. . . . (I meant my mind, but could only point to it via my body.)"

   "a *complete* account . . .": see XIII, 2; Man. 116, 215 (below).

   You are inclined to say . . . : earlier "he quoted, with apparent approval, Lichtenberg's saying 'Instead of "I think" we ought to say "It thinks" ' ('it' being used, as he said, as 'Es' is used in 'Es blitzet')" (*PP* 309). The *Tractatus*, too, would have done away with the personal pronoun (5.542), thereby revealing "that there is no such thing as the soul—the subject, etc.—as it is conceived in the superficial psychology of the present day" (5.5421).

   " 'When I have pains they are simply pains & nothing is said about a person.'—You would like to say merely: 'Pain!'—This describes—you would say—the whole fact. However, for one thing, is it a description? For another, what good is it?" (Man. 116, 215).

   See Man. 116, 237; cp. *BB* 60; Russell, *Mind*, 18a (same view).

   Perhaps simply by . . . : for "the hand which is raised to indicate that it is I who wish to speak, or I who have toothache, does not thereby point to anything" (*BB* 68). "When we feel that we wish to abolish the 'I' in 'I have pain,' one may say that we tend to make the verbal expression of pain similar to the expression by moaning" (*BB* 69).

When as in this case . . . : see §426 and commentary; cp. Russell, *Outline*, 172.

which are after all . . . : some commentators have supposed that the present section of the *Investigations* shows the pronoun *I* to be superfluous, whereas the truth is that *I* or any other pronoun could be dispensed with were it agreed, for instance, that "There is pain" would be equivalent to "I am in pain," or "You are in pain," or "He is in pain" (cp. *BB* 57a, 59b, 66b). But no such convention exists in the English language; so the pronoun is not superfluous, even in the sense that a variant form of expression is available in which the pronoun does not appear (cp. §410). As W. says here, the ordinary expression "performs its office".

we have got a picture . . . : see GI 9; X, 10; *BB* 56b–57; 5.62; Man. 116, 235–36 (quoted for §414). In Man. 116, 215–16, W. characterizes the picture thus: "You evidently *compare* the situation with that in which you have to give a description. The image is a world which is to be described, say as America is described in a geography book. The description could be spoken by a phonograph."

could be false in some other way . . . : by his not having *real* pain, the pain I have (X, 10). Cp. §427. On such double content in W.'s earlier thought, see X, 6–10, and §§275–77, 280. Russell, too, had a way of attributing both a naive, common-sense meaning and a correct, "scientific" meaning to a proposition "reporting direct experience", his general idea being that we don't directly experience what we think we do, but something else, and that this latter perception is what the proposition really states. See below.

As if the form of expression . . . : see §280 and commentary; NL 308c; cp. 6.54 and numerous illustrations in Russell, e.g.: "Science holds that, when we 'see the sun', there is a process, starting from the sun, traversing the space between the sun and the eye, changing its character when it reaches the eye, changing its character again in the optic nerve and the brain, and finally producing the event which we call 'seeing the sun' " (*Matter*, 197). So "the supposition of common sense and naive realism, that we see the actual physical object, is very hard to reconcile with the scientific view" (ibid., 155). We are wrong when we assert that we see the sun, yet somehow right as well, since the visual sensation, which actually does occur, "is popularly called seeing the object from which the light-waves started" (*Philosophy*, 148–49). If W.'s account here sounds confused, that is because the views he had in mind were so confused.

faute de mieux: "we are far from knowing a form of expression which describes" our direct experience (Man. 107, 1; see X, 8; commentary on §106). Cp. §426b and commentary; *PG* 456a; Man. 112, 181–82; *NL* 311: "This object is inadequately described as 'that which I see', 'my visual image', since it has nothing to do with any particular human being. Rather I should like to call it 'what's seen'."

(b) There is full discussion of this in *BB* 48; *PP* 311; Man. 178e. See also XXXI, 6; *Z* 413–14; *BB* 57b–58a; *PB* 86c; Man. 229, §1736; Man. 178(b), 6–8; Man. 110, 241; cp. *BB* 23b; Man. 112, 29; von Wright, "Lichtenberg", 214–15.

"We are up against trouble caused by our way of expression" (*BB* 48). One verbal analogy suggests a false notion of knowledge; so assertions about others' experiences seem dubious hypotheses (ibid.; cp. §246). Another suggests a false conception of meaning; so the assertions appear meaningless (*BB* 48). The common-sense philosopher, who shares many of the same primitive notions but has not noticed where they lead, replies "that surely there is no difficulty in the idea of supposing, thinking, imagining that someone else has what I have. But the trouble with the realist is always that he does not solve but skip the difficulties which his adversaries see, though they too don't succeed in solving them" (ibid.).

"In this connection he said that he thought that both the Realist and the Idealist were 'talking nonsense' in the particular sense in which 'nonsense is produced by trying to express by the use of language what ought to be embodied in the grammar'; and he illustrated this sense by saying that 'I can't feel his toothache' means ' "I feel his toothache" has no sense' and therefore does not 'express a fact' as 'I can't play chess' may do" (*PP* 311–12).

attack the normal form of expression: "When idealism says the tree is only my image, it must be objected that the expression 'this tree' does not have the same meaning as 'my image of this tree'. If idealism says that only my image exists (is real), not the tree, it misuses the expression 'exist' or 'be real' " (Man. 110, 240).

the others defend it: "Realism says that what we say in ordinary speech is rightly expressed" (Man. 178(b), 6).

§403 See *BB* 59–60, 66b; *Kreis,* 49.

The solipsist, said W., "is not aware that he is objecting to a convention. He sees a way of dividing the country different from the one used on the ordinary map" (*BB* 57). "We could answer [as the present paragraph does, in effect]: 'What you want is only a new notation, and by a new notation no facts of geography are changed' " (ibid.). As the preceding number denied that our existing notation is inadequate, so the present number denies that this other notation would be more adequate.

In the *Tractatus*, W. held that "what the solipsist *means* is quite correct; only it cannot be *said,* but makes itself manifest"—"manifest in the fact that the limits of *language* (of that language which alone I understand) mean the limits of *my* world" (5.62). Now the language which alone I understand consists of the signs with the meanings *I* give them, by thinking them out and projectively relating them to the objects of *my* world (X, 10; GI 37). If, for instance, I say "I am in pain," I alone can make the connection between sign and referent. Others may say, "He is in pain," but (thought W.) their statement is a mere hypothesis, not a true proposition equivalent to mine (X, 6–7). Existing language, with its parallel between *he* and *I,* veils this radical diversity (cp. *PP* 307–8; *PB* 93b). In line, therefore, with his former hope of clarification through perspicuous syntax (GI 8, 25), W. envisaged a notation which would not use "in a superficially similar way signs that have different modes of signification: that is to say, a sign-language that is governed by *logical* grammar—by logical syntax" (3.325). As late as *PB* 89, he felt that no notation permits us to actually state the difference, but that "the one which has me as center has a special status. It is specially adequate" (see X, 10).

The solipsistic temptation which W. had felt to say that "only my pain is real" (*PP* 311; cp. *BB* 56–57) would make the self-centered syntax seem still more appropriate as a reflection of reality. A thoroughgoing solipsist "would say that it was *inconceivable* that experiences other than his own were real. He ought therefore to use a notation in which such a phrase as 'A has real toothache' (where A is not he) is meaningless, a notation whose rules exclude this phrase as the rules of chess exclude a pawn's making a knight's move. The solipsist's suggestion comes to using such a phrase as 'there is real toothache' instead of 'Smith (the solipsist) has toothache' " (*BB* 59; see *BB* 48d).

Notice also that the arrangement would have this further advantage, in W.'s former view, that no personal pronoun would be necessary, and therefore no deceptive use of *I,* suggesting a nonexistent object within the world (*PP* 309).

(a) Other people would still be . . . . : "Certainly we shouldn't pity him if we didn't believe that he had pains; but is this a philosophical, a metaphysical belief? Does a realist pity me more than an idealist or a solipsist?" (*BB* 48). See *BB* 59b.

be *no* objection . . . : for concepts are not theories (*BB* 57a; p. 230b), and "the man whom we call a solipsist and who says that only his own experiences are real, does not thereby disagree with us about any practical question of fact" (*BB* 59; see the rest).

(b) See *BB* 59a (e.g. the quotation for §132a).

§404 See XIII, 2, 4; §302 and commentary; *PB* 94c; *PP* 308–10; Man.

228, §128; Zemach, "Reference"; cp. *PB* 93, 95cd; *NB* 80, 82; Russell, *Logic,* 276b, 306b.

The troubles treated in §403 are "connected with the peculiar grammar of the word 'I', and the misunderstandings this grammar is liable to give rise to" (*BB* 66; see *BB* 49a). "The thing to do in such cases is always to look how the words in question *are actually used in our language*" (*BB* 56). The logical atomist asked: "What is the logical multiplicity proper to the statement that I am in pain?" And the logical positivist: "How do you verify it?" (*PB* 93a). And the general answer is: It would be better not to call the utterance a statement at all (*Z* 549), but an *Äusserung,* an avowal (GI 15–16). Neither for the subject nor for the predicate do we apply criteria (XIII, 1; §290a; *PP* 307).

(a) See XIII, 4; NL 307k; *BB* 66–69.

"in a certain sense I have no idea . . ." : "For, queer enough, I don't mean: 'always L. W.' " (*BB* 61). "The philosophical self is not the human being . . . but rather the metaphysical subject, the limit of the world—not a part of it" (5.641; see 5.633). See *BB* 66b, quoted for §402a; and *BB* 64–65, quoted in X, 10.

but "I am . . .": and *I* is not a name (§410).

I don't name: "There is no question of recognizing a person when I say I have toothache. To ask 'are you sure that it's *you* who have pains?' would be nonsensical. Now, when in this case no error is possible, it is because the move which we might be inclined to think of as an error, a 'bad move', is no move of the game at all. (We distinguish in chess between good and bad moves, and we call it a mistake if we expose the queen to a bishop. But it is no mistake to promote a pawn to a king.) And now this way of stating our idea suggests itself: that it is as impossible that in making the statement 'I have toothache' I should have mistaken another person for myself, as it is to moan with pain by mistake, having mistaken someone else for me. To say, 'I have pain' is no more a statement *about* a particular person than moaning is" (*BB* 67). "The difference between the propositions 'I have pain' and 'he has pain' . . . corresponds to the difference between moaning and saying that someone moans" (*BB* 68).

Though someone else . . . : see §302b.

(b) **a great variety of criteria for personal '*identity*':** for a long and interesting treatment which has stimulated much discussion, see *BB* 61d–64a. See also *PG* 203.

(c) See commentary on (*a*); NL 309ab; Man. 116, 156–57; cp. §377b; NL 308; Russell, *Logic,* 276b. I do not, for instance, look in a mirror to make sure the words are coming from the right mouth (*BB* 68). But "it seems that I can *trace* my identity, quite independent of the identity of my body. And the idea is suggested that I trace the identity of something dwelling in a body, the identity of my mind" (NL 308).

§405   No, I want . . . : the omission of *only* (*nur*) seems unfortunate.

The "particular person" in question would be Ludwig Wittgenstein, and how would it sound for him to say, "I want to draw their attention to Ludwig Wittgenstein"? *I* and *Ludwig* are different concepts (*OC* 42; *BB* 67, quoted in XIII, 6). Cp. NL 298 (" 'I see so-and-so' does not mean 'the person so-and-so, e.g. L. W., sees so-and-so' "), 307; Man. 116, 175 ("A cry does not name the one who cries, although it draws attention to him").

§406   Revised from Man. 116, 155–56. See GI 15–16; NL 298fgh; Man. 116, 164–68; cp. ibid., 171–72 ("I thank you," etc.).

"But surely . . .": as in §405, the voice is that of a person who believes that the depth grammar (GI 10) of "I am in pain" and "He is in pain" is as similar as the surface grammar.

Can this be said . . . : cp. p. 189.

I merely groan: see Man. 116, 175 (quoted for §405); cp. §404a and commentary.

do I want to distinguish . . . : is that how I would express my wish (see §405 and comments)? But what better indication is there of what I wish (§§452–53)?

§407   "The cry does not say *who* cries" (Man. 228, §130). Yet we see who is in pain from the cry or groan (§404a). Now, "the verbal expression of pain replaces crying" (§244) and retains much the same character (GI 16).

§408   "But you aren't . . .": the idea is: "I know who is in pain and express this knowledge in my words" (see §363). And this knowledge is supposedly indicated by the absence of doubt. But that might be the case only if doubt and finding out were conceivable (§246, p. 221).

a logical product: of "I don't know whether I have the pain" and "I don't know whether someone else has the pain."

and that is not . . . : see §§246–47, p. 221; cp. X, 25.

§409   Revised from Man. 116, 169–70. Cp. §117; *PB* 92e; Man. 116, 151–52; *OC* 622, e.g.: "(Indeed, I do not know what 'I know that I am a human being' means. But even that might be given a sense.) For each one of these sentences I can imagine circumstances that turn it into a move in one of our language-games."

This would be a rather queer . . . : for why use this terminology to express the difference between my feeling a shock and someone else's feeling it (cp. §246a), or between feeling a shock and judging from his expression that someone else has? And if these are not the contrasts intended, what is? I do not perform an inner identification in one case (X, 20) and a causal inference in the other. Still, in these circumstances, philosophical mystification would apparently not account for the mode of expression (cp. §411a), nor result from it; so W. is less severe than in §246 (see X, 25).

if I make the supposition . . . : cp. §253.

becomes quite unsuitable: the contrasts mentioned above disappear, leaving no "application in our life" (§520). And though the supposition of shared shocks simply alters the game and does not mark a return to everyday circumstances, the implicit question is whether in our ordinary language-games there is any more application than here for a statement like: "Now I know who is in pain, for I am."

§410   See *EPB* 121; *BB* 80–81 (quoted for §116a); Man. 130, 33; Zemach, "Reference", 75; cp. Berkeley, *Dialogues*, III, 447–48.

"One has been tempted to say that 'now' is the name of an instant of time, and this, of course, would be like saying that 'here' is the name of a place, 'this' the name of a thing, and 'I' the name of a man. (One could, of course, also have said 'a year ago' was the name of a time, 'over there' the name of a place, and 'you' the name of a person.) But nothing is more unlike than the use of the word 'this' and the use of a proper name—I mean *the games* played with these words, not the phrases in which they are used" (*BB* 108–9).

The general viewpoint criticized is Russell's: "The word 'this' is always a proper name, in the sense that it applies directly to just one object, and does not in any way *describe* the object to which it applies. But on different occasions it applies to different objects. For the purposes of our present problem, we may say that 'this' is the name of the object attended to at the moment by the person using the word" (*Logic,* 167–68). "Such 'emphatic particulars' as 'this' and 'I' and 'now' would be impossible without the selectiveness of mind" (ibid., 169). "The subject attending to 'this' is called 'I', and the time of the things which have to 'I' the relation of presence is called the present time" (ibid., 168). Later Russell recalled with approval "the argument about 'emphatic particulars', 'this', 'I', all that class of words, that pick out certain particulars from the universe by their relation to oneself, and I think by the fact that they, or particulars related to them, are present to you at the moment of speaking" (ibid., 222). See II, 5.

"I": see XIII, 4–6. For contrasting views, see Russell, *Logic,* 163–64; James, *Principles,* I, 238b.

not the name: furthermore, "In 'I have pain,' 'I' is not a demonstrative pronoun" (*BB* 68). See Man. 228, §128.

of a person: nor of a body, as W. supposed in *PB* 86b. Cp. Schlick, "Psychological", 404.

nor "here": cp. W.'s remarks on "I am here" (§514) and "This is here" (§117).

and "this": see §§38, 45 and commentary. Moore makes the same point in *Papers,* 126b. Contrast with Russell, above.

But they are connected . . . : cp. *BB* 108: "The word 'today' is not a date, but it isn't anything like it either. It doesn't differ from a date as a hammer differs from a mallet, but as a hammer differs from a nail; and surely we may say there is both a connection between a hammer and a mallet and between a hammer and a nail."

Names are explained . . . : see §§28–31, 38c, 45, 288a, 429.

not to use these words: just as it doesn't use proper names.

§411 Worked over in Man. 116, 183–84. Cp. §253a; *BB* 66–67. For contrast, and a connection with the preceding number and the theme of this section, see James, *Principles,* I, 291: "*In its widest possible sense,* however, *a man's Self is the sum total of all that he* CAN *call his,* not only his body and his psychic powers, but his clothes and his house, his wife and children, his ancestors and friends, his reputation and works, his lands and horses, and yacht and bank-account." James relates them all uniformly to the "self": "All these things give him the same emotions. If they wax and prosper, he feels triumphant; if they dwindle and die away, he feels cast down,—not necessarily in the same degree for each thing, but in much the same way for all" (ibid.; see also pp. 239a, 242a, 319a).

"*my* foot": see Man. 116, 182–83 (one criterion is connection with my body, but which body is that?).

"*my* body": see Man. 116, 184–85. "In this connection, that in 'I have toothache' 'I' does not 'denote a possessor', he pointed out that, when I talk of '*my* body', the fact that the body in question is 'mine' or 'belongs to me', cannot be verified by reference to that body itself, thus seeming to imply that when I say 'This body belongs to me,' 'me' is used in the second of the senses which he distinguished for 'I', viz. that in which, according to him, it does not 'denote a possessor' " (*PP* 309).

Cp. Schlick, "Meaning", 162: "This body is distinguished from the 'bodies of other beings' by the fact that it always appears in a peculiar perspective (its back or its eyes, for instance, never appear except in a looking glass); but this is not nearly so significant as the other fact that the quality of *all* data is conditioned by the state of the organs of this particular body. Obviously these two facts—and perhaps originally the first one—form the only reason why this body is called 'my' body. The posseesive pronoun singles it out from among other bodies; it is an adjective which denotes the uniqueness described."

"*my* sensation": see §§302, 402 and commentary.

Which sensation does one mean . . . : here W. suggests no practical application, as for the others, but only raises difficulties, in a way that suggests the reason: It is with regard to sensations, thoughts, and the like that the specter of private ostensive definition arises (§380). And the quotations from Russell just given under §410 show that an inner self, called the "I", tends to be invoked for such inner naming-by-attending.

Certainly otherwise . . . : see §§398–99.

one imagines that by directing . . . : see §§33a, 275, 666–69 (with which this remark is tied in Man. 228); Z 426; cp. Man. 116, 120. W.'s point in this number: "We have got a picture in our heads which conflicts with the picture of our ordinary way of speaking" (§402).

XIV. Consciousness (§§412–427)

GENERAL COMMENTARY

(1) "At the basis of our knowledge of our selves," James reports Kant as saying, "there lies only 'the simple and utterly empty idea: *I;* of which we cannot even say we have a notion, but only a consciousness which accompanies all notions' " (*Principles,* I, 362). Many philosophers have held similar views (Schopenhauer, *Freiheit,* 482; Moore, *Papers,* 48), among them young Wittgenstein (XIII, 3). The "metaphysical subject", of which the preceding numbers treat, was hardly distinguishable from consciousness, theme of the present section. Thus at the time of *PP* 310 he still asserted, as "a final thing", that " 'in one sense "I" and "conscious" are equivalent, but not in another,' and he compared this difference to the difference between what can be said of the pictures on a film in a magic lantern and of the picture on the screen; saying that the pictures in the lantern are all 'on the same level' but that the picture which is at any given time on the screen is not 'on the same level' with any of them."

(2) Philosophers have debated endlessly about what consciousness is and whether it is. "Properly speaking," wrote Stout, "definition is impossible. Everybody knows what consciousness is because everybody is conscious" (*Manual,* 7). James, inspecting his own consciousness, decided first that "in one person at least, *the 'self of selves', when carefully examined, is found to consist mainly of the collection of . . . peculiar motions in the head or between the head and throat*" (*Principles,* I, 301). Later he declared: "The 'I think' which Kant said must be able to accompany all my objects, is the 'I breathe' which actually does accompany them" (*Essays,* 37). "I believe that 'consciousness' . . . is the name of a nonentity, and has no right to a place among first principles. Those who still cling

to it are clinging to a mere echo, the faint rumor left behind by the disappearing 'soul' upon the air of philosophy" (ibid., 2). "My own belief," wrote Russell in *Analysis of Mind* (25), ". . . is that James is right in rejecting consciousness as an entity." "I think the person is not an ingredient in the single thought: he is rather constituted by relations of the thoughts to each other and to the body" (ibid., 18).

(3)   Breathing, feelings in the head, "relations of the thoughts to each other and to the body", an indefinable something present in all our thoughts and experiences, a nonentity—obviously the discussion had to be brought down to earth. W.'s standard procedure in such a situation was to "bring words back from their metaphysical to their everyday use" (§116). But the everyday use of the substantive *consciousness,* unlike that of *conscious* or *I,* is principally speculative (cp. §416). So Wittgenstein examines this stream of thought and life—the feelings (§412), the statements (§§412, 416–18) and surroundings (§412), the reactions (§421), beliefs (§422), and pictures (§§422–27)—in which the expression *consciousness* (or *Bewusstsein*) has whatever meaning it possesses (Z 173). As in the discussion of the soul on page 178, he "looks for *sense* not *truth*" (Man. 105, 2). And he has a hard time finding it.

(4)   His strategy is suggested in greater detail by Man. 229, §1774. Concerning remarks like Moore's: "The fact that I am conscious now is obviously, in a certain sense, a fact" (*Papers,* 46), he observed: " 'Obviously' for this reason, that everyone admits it [§416]; and we are brought to admit it through grammar [§281]. Thus we here ground a sentence through a *picture,*" the picture of consciousness, over and above the acts of seeing, hearing, feeling, thinking, and the like. "Where our language suggests a body and there is none: there, we should like to say, is a *spirit*" (§36; see Moore, *Studies,* 17, 20). After this logical sleight of hand (§412) we find it inconceivable—as in a sense it is (cp. §307)—that consciousness or its contents should result from physical processes (ibid.; see §§421, 427). So Wittgenstein elicits reflection on the origin (§§417–20) and contents (§§422–27) of this puzzling picture, with queries that suggest its poverty and nonempirical source.

DETAILED COMMENTARY

§412   The two paragraphs of §417 parallel these two.

(a) Cp. Man. 116, 325.

The feeling of an unbridgeable gulf . . . : W. was acquainted with such thinking especially through James's *Principles.* Some samples: "The ultimate of ultimate problems, of course, in the study of the relations of thought and brain, is to understand why and how such disparate things are connected at all" (I, 177). "The relations of a mind to its own brain are of a unique and utterly mysterious sort" (I, 216).

"Mental and physical events are, on all hands, admitted to present the strongest contrast in the entire field of being. The chasm which yawns between them is less easily bridged over by the mind than any interval we know" (I, 134). Tyndall's statements on I, 147, declare the chasm unbridgeable (e.g.: "We do not possess the intellectual organ, nor apparently any rudiment of the organ, which would enable us to pass, by a process of reasoning, from one to the other"). See also I, 135–36, 182; and Russell, *Mind*, 10. Cp. Berkeley, *Dialogues*, III, 461.

   giddiness: cp. §§195, 420; *RFM* 20ab, 60f, 63a, 136g, 148d.

   sleight-of-hand: see XIV, 4; §308; cp. §52a; *RFM* 53e.

   in set theory: see §426, p. 232a and commentary.

   But what can it mean . . . : "But also *self-consciousness*, as already mentioned, contains a knower and a known, otherwise it would not be a *consciousness*" (Schopenhauer, *World*, II, 202). See Moore in XIV, 1.

   a particular act of gazing . . . : cp. *BB* 176–77; James, *Principles*, I, 404–5.

   that I called: here the translation omits a parenthetical remark: "for of course these words are not used in everyday life."
(b) See *OC* 622.

   has nothing paradoxical about it: see Man. 229, §735 ("Only when we disregard its use is a proposition paradoxical").
§413 Cp. §295.

   William James: see fuller quote in XIV, 2; *Principles*, I, 299–302; *Essays*, 36–37.

   in the head and between . . . : James wrote "or", not "and".

   not the meaning . . . : see §43; cp. §§299, 386b, 594; Russell, *Logic*, 164. Empiricists have been wont to suppose that the meaning of a word is an experience which causes or accompanies it, for they have paid little attention to the grammar of the word *meaning*.

   but the state of . . . : see §§38d, 113–14, 277, 412; NL 284g; *BB* 159c, 160, 167d–168a, 174–77; Man. 116, 225; and the references below (for "a good deal . . .").

   "This attention to thought as such, and the identification of ourselves with it rather than with any of the objects which it reveals, is a momentous and in some respects a rather mysterious operation, of which we need here only say that as a matter of fact it exists" (James, *Principles*, I, 296; cp. §381).

   W.'s description may sound odd, but is exact. Ask: Why did James connect the word *self* with these motions? Because, he said, "I feel quite sure that these cephalic motions are the portions of my innermost activity of which I am *most distinctly aware*" (*Principles*, I, 301). But when? Always? Or whenever he thought? No, when he play-acted thought, *attending to what he felt.*

And a good deal could be learned: "it shews a fundamental misunderstanding" (§314; see §316); "we look at the facts through the medium of a misleading form of expression" (*BB* 31); "the decisive movement in the conjuring trick has been made" (§308); "philosophical problems arise when language *goes on holiday*" (§38; see §412b). "The phenomenon of *staring* is closely bound up with the whole puzzle of solipsism" (NL 309; see *BB* 65a, 66a, 71c; §398). It begets "the idea of the *'realm of consciousness'* " (NL 320). For other instances of creative gazing and play-acting, and comments on them, see §§170–71, 174a, 175a, 178, 321b (and commentary), 420, pp. 187c, 215g–216a, 219b; Z 251, 446, 602; *RFM* 23b, 41b; *EPB* 188, 190–91, 194, 218–19, 232–33; *BB* 149b–150b, 156b, 159c, 165c, 167–68, 177fg; *PG* 182d.

§414   In addition to §§412–13, on which this is a comment, see §§38d, 132b, 520; *BB* 150b, 175h (quoted for §280). Wrote James: "But whether we take it abstractly or concretely, our considering the spiritual self at all is a reflective process, is the result of our abandoning the outward-looking point of view, and of our having become able to think of subjectivity as such, *to think ourselves as thinkers*" (*Principles*, I, 296). Our task is set: We shall observe and describe the self—whatever that is.

Man. 116, 215–16 (quoted for §402) and 221, connect this number with the supposed description of the inner world, commented on in §398 and §402; and Man. 116, 235–36, while relating the number to the preceding one, indicate still more clearly that W. himself is a target: " 'Nothing in the visual field indicates that, etc.' (*Tract. Log. Phil.*). This means as it were: You will look in vain in visual space for the *seer*. He is nowhere to be found in visual space.—But the truth is: You merely *act* as though you were looking for something, for a person who isn't there in visual space."

§415   See p. 56n; *RFM* 43b.

the natural history of human beings: see §25, p. 230; Ogden and Richards, *Meaning*, 221 ("what is usually called grammar, which may be regarded as the Natural History of symbol systems").

"Wittgenstein says that his philosophical observations are 'remarks on the natural history of human beings'. It would be difficult to exaggerate the significance of that comment. It is often said that Wittgenstein's work belongs to 'linguistic philosophy'—that he 'talks about words'. True enough. But he is trying to get his reader to think of how the words are tied up with human life, with patterns of response, in thought and action. His conceptual studies are a kind of anthropology. His descriptions of the human forms of life on which our concepts are based make us aware of the kind of creature we are" (Malcolm, "Nature", 22).

The present setting suggests reference to philosophers' mode of life (XIV, 3).

only because they . . . : see §129.

§416 See XIV, 2–4; Z 401–2; Man. 229, §1774; cp. Russell, *Problems,* 27b.

"Human beings agree . . .": see XIV, 4; Moore, *Problems,* 4; Russell, *Problems,* 28.

"The word introspection need hardly be defined—it means, of course, the looking into our own minds and reporting what we there discover. *Every one agrees that we there discover states of consciousness.* So far as I know, the existence of such states has never been doubted by any critic, however sceptical in other respects he may have been" (James, *Principles,* I, 185).

"So they are . . .": the entailment is explained by a theory which, as Russell noted (*Mind,* 9), "is widely held, and which I formerly held myself: the theory that the essence of everything mental is a certain quite peculiar something called 'consciousness', conceived either as a relation to objects, or as a pervading quality of psychical phenomena." See Moore in GI 17; cp. Russell, *Problems,* 28b.

"their own witnesses . . .": cp. §§386b, 594.

how strange this is!: "It is strange that I know it is called 'consciousness' " (Man. 179).

Whom do I really inform . . . : cp. p. 178d.

What is the purpose . . . : if anyone who is awake and speaking is conscious, isn't the declaration similar to "I am here"? (§514; see §117).

§417 For W.'s aim in this series of numbers, consult XIV, 4. Not observation, but language founds our conviction; that is the source of our picture of consciousness.

(a) Do I observe myself, then . . . : see Russell, *Problems,* 27–28; Moore, *Problems,* 110–11 and 49: "And, in fact, it seems to me quite certain that sense-data and images are not the only kinds of things which we directly apprehend. For instance, suppose I look at this envelope again, and directly apprehend the whitish colour; it seems to me that if I try to observe what is happening in my mind, I can *also* directly apprehend not only the whitish colour but *also* my own direct apprehension of it: that is to say, that just as my seeing of the colour consists in my direct apprehension of *it,* the colour, so, if I happen to observe *my seeing* of it, this observation consists in the direct apprehension of my seeing of it—of something, that is to say, which is neither a sense-datum, nor an image, but the direct apprehension of a sense-datum. I think, therefore, we certainly sometimes directly apprehend not only sense-data and images, but also our own acts of consciousness."

And why talk . . . : cp. §316.

But what are the words . . . : cp. §§246a, 453.

which is ordinarily not the case: we are not going through the performance described in §412.

(b) a particular experience: see *BB* 149–50, 158–60.

In what situations . . . : see §416.

§418   Cp. Russell, *Mind*, 11b.

(b) But doesn't one say . . . : it is not a matter of experience that a tree or stone is not conscious. The true reason is grammatical (§281). Cp. the argumentation in §283 ("I do not transfer my idea to stones, plants, etc.") and §284.

a tree: "Consciousness is known to us positively only as a property of animal nature; consequently we may not, indeed we cannot, think of it otherwise than as *animal consciousness,* so that this expression is in fact tautological" (Schopenhauer, *World,* II, 203).

or a stone: see §390.

What would it be like . . . : the question is meant to show that the attribution to humans as well as the denial to stones is a matter of logic (§281), not the result of introspection. Were consciousness a matter of experience, its absence might be a matter of experience. And in a sense it is: We go to sleep, are anesthetized, and so on. And when that happens, our thoughts and feelings stop; they do not continue minus an introspectable accompaniment.

No; not in the ordinary . . . : I take this to be a reply of the type W. might get. "No, I don't mean that everyone would be anesthetized or asleep, but that, though continuing to behave in the same way as usual (§420), they would lack that introspectable something which we call consciousness."

§419   *Z* 394 looks like a comment on this.

In what circumstances . . . : not on the basis of inductive inferences about his inner state; yet it seems evident that where there is a chief there must be consciousness. "To a certain extent we know this *a priori.* For amazingly varied as the innumerable species of animals may be, and strange as some new form of them, never previously seen, may appear to us, we nevertheless assume beforehand with certainty its innermost nature as something well known, and indeed wholly familiar to us" (Schopenhauer, *World,* II, 204).

a *chief:* the quotation from Schopenhauer (above) indicates the true connection with Frege's remark: "It is surely clear that when anyone uses the sentence 'all men are mortal' he does not want to assert something about some Chief Akpanya, of whom perhaps he has never heard" (*Writings,* 83). The oddity of W.'s borrowed example, which has irritated some readers, is the very point of it: Strange as some man may be, never previously seen or heard about, we are sure he "must surely have *consciousness*". Yet were consciousness something inner, inferred from external symptoms, wouldn't this conclusion be somewhat hasty? Shouldn't we learn more about the chief's behavior? And isn't it even conceivable, on this supposition, that he behaves in the usual way but is really an automaton, without consciousness (§420)?

§420   For the connection with §419, see the preceding remarks. Cp. §§157–58, 493; Z 251; NL 320b; Man. 228, §170. See p. 178abcd; Z 528–30; Cook, "Human Beings", especially 140–44; and James's chapter on "The Automaton-Theory", which starts with the question: "Suppose we restrict our view to facts of one and the same plane, and let that be the bodily plane: cannot all the outward phenomena of intelligence still be exhaustively described?" (*Principles*, I, 128). "To Descartes," James notes, "belongs the credit of having first been bold enough to conceive of a completely self-sufficing nervous mechanism which should be able to perform complicated and apparently intelligent acts" (ibid., 130).

"When we talked of: 'So and so is an automaton,' the strong hold of that view was [due to the idea] that you could say: 'Well, I know what I mean' . . . , as though you were looking at something happening while you said the thing, entirely independent of what came before and after, the application [of the phrase]. It looked as though you could talk of understanding a word, without any reference to the technique of its usage" (*LC* 68; see GI 14; §117; Z 530).

(b) as a swastika: see *BB* 164ab.

§421   For the setting, see XIV, 4. Cp. Man. 116, 325.

make such a medley: see James, *Principles*, I, 24 ("I hope that the reader will take no umbrage at my so mixing the physical and mental, and talking of reflex acts and hemispheres and reminiscences in the same breath"); Schlick, "Psychological", 403 ("The so-called 'psycho-physical problem' arises from the mixed employment of both modes of representation in one and the same sentence. Words are put side by side which, when correctly used, really belong to different languages"); cp. X, 6–8.

tangibles and intangibles: see §608.

as an instrument: not as a picture, for instance. To represent the mysterious constituents of thought (*NB* 130) together with beds and bodily movements, in one and the same picture, might indeed have seemed odd to young W.

as its employment: see commentary on §20b.

§§422–24   See §425, pp. 178fg, 184e; Z 127, 273–74; *RFM* 30f; *LC* 71–72; Man. 131, 68–69; Man. 116, 282–84 (for §422), 323–24 (for §423). In Man. 228 (§205) §422 is wedged between paragraphs on the verb *mean*. The connection is indicated by Z 272, e.g.: "*What* you mean—how is that to be discovered? We must patiently examine how this sentence is supposed to be applied. What things look like *round about it*. Then its sense will come to light" (cp. §421).

Think of the picture of blindness . . . : this picture recurs, with illustrations, in Man. 123; Man. 130; Man. 116, 232. On the last page of Man. 123 W. wrote: "The picture of blindness [here a face is sketched with a darkened oval area above the eyes] can naturally be so employed that the characteristic behavior of the blind counts as the criterion of another's blindness. But we can easily let this criterion be vaguely defined and explain this by saying that by 'blindness' we really mean the inner [same sketch] and not the behavior. . . . Imagine though that instead of 'blindness' we spoke of 'inner darkness'." Earlier, on May 23: "Imagine that I explained to someone what sight and blindness are, by means of pictures like these [here two faces are sketched, one with a darkened oval, the other with representations in it]. (Who can say that he wouldn't understand me?) What if someone said now: 'the use of these two pictures is not the *same* as that of a description of the behavior, though it *partially* overlaps it'?"

§425   Man. 116, 158–61, connect this with §350.

(a) we exert ourselves . . . : as when W. sought to find the essence of the proposition and of language, then hit on a picture which supposedly solved everything (I, 1). "It does not go against our feeling, that *we* cannot analyse PROPOSITIONS so far as to mention the elements by name; no, we feel that the WORLD must consist of elements . . . what vacillates is our determinations" (*NB* 62).

comes about of itself: "The way a picture is to be applied seems to be much more obvious than the way sentences are to be applied" (Man. 125, 2; see *Z* 231).

In this case . . . : with respect to the spiritual self, the soul, there is seldom such searching. Young W., for example, took for granted that there was some such thing, and simply refined the notion (XIII, 1–3).

which forces itself on us: cp. §115.

out of the difficulty: see *NB* 80, quoted in XIII, 1.

(b) The paragraph illustrates the way a picture can solve our problems or end our doubts even though it does not indicate unambiguously how it is to be applied. See §§139–40, 144; *Z* 231; *RFM* 20; Man. 125, 2 (above).

§426(a) which seems to fix . . . : see §§139–41, 352b, 389, 433a, p. 184ef; *PG* 40a (quoted for §139); *NB* 62 (quoted for §425); cp. *PG* 145b (=*Z* 231, quoted in XXXVII, 6); Man. 108, 230 (quoted for §120b).

in set theory: "When set theory appeals to the human impossibility of directly symbolizing the infinite, it begets the crudest imaginable misinterpretation of its own calculus. Doubtless it is this very misconception that is responsible for the invention of the calculus" (*PG* 469). "It says that the actual infinite cannot be grasped at all by means of mathematical symbolism, and that therefore it can be only described, not represented. The description would encompass it somewhat as when we pack a large number of things in a box and carry them that way, since we can't carry them all in our hands. They are then invisible, but we know we are carrying them (indirectly, as it were)" (*PG* 468). See commentary on p. 232a; *BB* 91b; *PG* 452, 455g–456a; *Kreis*, 103, 112n; cp. Ramsey, *Foundations*, 8.

for a god: see §352a; *PG* 452, 463b; cp. Frege, *Writings*, 159 (quoted for §§71b, 352); Wisdom, "Constructions", 474.

knows what we cannot: see Man. 106, 262, quoted for p. 226a; cp. pp. 225h–226a; *Z* 273 ("the 'finite' that can't conceive the infinite is not 'man' or 'our understanding', but the calculus").

he sees the whole: "A good question for the schoolmen to ask would have been: 'Can God know all the places of π?' " (*PG* 479).

he sees into human consciousness: as we should like to, but cannot (§427). Compare Russell's assertion that we seem to know the sun immediately when we "see" it, but of course do not and cannot have such knowledge (*Matter*, 133). *What* sort? "A picture is conjured up which seems to fix the sense unambiguously."

like pontificals: see Man. 138, 16A (quoted for §81a); Russell, *Logic*, 198: "I shall, however, assume that we have constructed a logically perfect language, and that we are going on State occasions to use it." It "would of course be wholly useless for daily life" (ibid., 338).

(b) See §§120, 402a; *PG* 44d, 114d; cp. §610; Köhler, *Mentality*, 17; Ramsey, *Foundations*, 70c. Some illustrations (in addition to those for §120a):

Augustine: "For there are only a few things that we say properly, most we say improperly; nonetheless, the things intended are understood" (*Confessions*, XI, 20, 26).

Frege: "By a kind of necessity of language, my expressions, taken literally, sometimes miss my thought; I mention an object, when what I intend is a concept" (*Writings*, 54). " 'Complete' and 'unsaturated' are of course only figures of speech; but all that I wish or am able to do here is to give hints" (ibid., 55). "For over the question what it is that is called a function in Analysis, we come up against the same obstacle; and on thorough investigation it will be found that the obstacle is essential, and founded on the nature of our language; that we cannot avoid a certain inappropriateness of linguistic expression; and that there is nothing for it but to realize this and always take it into account" (ibid.). See also *Writings*, 46b, 115b; "Foundations of Geometry", 13; "Justification", 157.

Jeans: "A scientific study of the action of the universe has suggested a conclusion which may be summed up, though very crudely and quite inadequately, because we have no language at our command except that derived from our terrestrial concepts and experiences, in the statement that the universe appears to have been designed by a pure mathematician" (*Universe*, 132).

Russell: "What pass for names in language, like 'Socrates', 'Plato', and so forth, were originally intended to fulfil this function of standing for particulars, and we do accept, in ordinary daily life, as particulars all sorts of things that really are not so . . . but we certainly do not use the name as a name in the proper sense of the word. That makes it very difficult to get any instance of a name at all in the proper strict logical sense of the word" (*Logic*, 200–201; see ibid., 198). "Strictly speaking, we are still simplifying. True adjectives and relations will require particulars for their terms; the sort of adjectives we can know, such as 'blue' and 'round', will not be applicable to particulars. . . . That is to say, no word that we can understand would occur in a grammatically correct account of the universe" (*Outline*, 268; see 267). See also *Inquiry*, 255; *Problems*, 31–32; quotes for §120a.

Early Wittgenstein: "My difficulty surely consists in this: In all the propositions that occur to me there occur names, which, however, must disappear on further analysis. I know that such a further analysis is possible, but am unable to carry it out completely" (*NB* 61; see Man. 116, 245–46). "The description of phenomena by means of the hypothesis of a physical world is indispensable because of its simplicity in comparison with phenomenological description, which is inconceivably complicated" (*PB* 286; see X, 9). " 'But somehow our language doesn't bring it out that there is something unique, namely real present experience, and do you just wish me to resign myself to that?' " (NL 283; see X, 10; commentary on §§106, 120).

§427 See *BB* 6–7; *PG* 106a.

"in his head": see also *Z* 605–7; cp. Russell, *Outline*, 296c.

should be taken seriously: cp. §589 and Man. 229, §§943–45, 1012–19 (where head and heart are discussed together).

apparently contradicting the picture: "Perhaps the main reason why we are so strongly inclined to talk of the head as the locality of our thoughts is this: the existence of the words 'thinking' and 'thought' alongside of the words denoting (bodily) activities, such as writing, speaking, etc., makes us look for an activity, different from these but analogous to them, corresponding to the word 'thinking' " (*BB* 7). Yet if we ask a person what he is thinking and he answers us in the ordinary manner, we never say: "This is only words, and I have got to get behind the words" (§503).

XV. The Agreement of Thought with Reality (§§428–465)

GENERAL COMMENTARY

(1)   Repeated remarks of Russell, suggesting the connection between the preceding section, on consciousness, and this one, on intentionality or the agreement of thought with reality, may therefore also indicate Wittgenstein's reason for treating the topic at this point in the *Investigations*. "There is one element which *seems* obviously in common among the different ways of being conscious, and that is, that they are all directed to *objects*. We are conscious 'of' something. The consciousness, it seems, is one thing, and that of which we are conscious is another thing" (*Mind*, 13–14; see Schopenhauer, *Freiheit*, 482). So a problem arises (see GI 34): "We think about things,—but how do these things enter into our thoughts? We think about Mr. Smith; but Mr. Smith need not be present. A picture of him won't do; for how are we to know whom it represents? In fact no substitute for him will do. Then how can he himself be an object of our thoughts?" (*BB* 38; see §§431–34; *BB* 36–39; *LC* 66–68). We have seen young Wittgenstein's typical answer (GI 36–37). "The mental act seems to perform in a miraculous way what could not be performed by any act of manipulating symbols" (*BB* 42; see §95 and commentary). *Intention* bridges the chasm, by means of a logical picture as unmistakably related to a specific reality as is a shadow to the figure which casts it (see XXXVII, 3).

(2)   Through comparisons and applications which are often patent nonsense W. attempts here to lay bare the hidden nonsense in his former viewpoint. Just as no mental equivalent of the whole series exists in the mind of one who understands a series (Section IX), and no inner surrogate of the person meant occurs in the mind of one who means him (Section XXVI), so no logical shadow assures a target for the thought of one who asserts, commands, negates, hopes, expects, and so on (*BB* 143b). The connection, W. repeatedly suggested, is made in and by language (GI 43; XII, 3), not by a mere act of the mind (GI 44).

(3) The linguistic connection may be made in various ways. Least problematic, it would seem (*PG* 140c), are the cases in which a person actually names the object he fears, wishes, expects, regrets, and so on. He says for instance, "I hope N. comes," or "N. should be here any minute." Or perhaps two weeks ago he said "N. would be a big help," and now someone who heard him says, "He wishes N. were here." It would seem that in most cases of a person's wishing N., expecting N., and so on, he makes some such explicit verbal connection. But not always (*PG* 142a). The naming may be done afterwards or by others. Thus though the person himself may make no mention of N., the circumstances and the person's verbal and other behavior may be such that we say, "He's expecting N." (Man. 302, 15). This is how the expression *expect* is used and this is how we assign an object. We do not infer an inner act which is the real expecting and therefore apply the expression; and even if we did, it would be in virtue of this connection in language—this use of the word *expect*—that the inner act would be an expectation and an expectation of N. (§371). Such matters are not Platonically determined prior to all praxis.

(4) The objects of linguistic acts—of descriptions, negations, commands, and the like—are more readily accounted for, it would seem, than those of "psychological acts" (hoping, expecting, wishing, and so on). For in the former the object is regularly named; even if a person says merely "Bring me that one," the generic term for the sort of thing desired probably preceded the request. However, the name itself, or other connecting expression, is quite variously related to the object (§53; Man. 302, 15). It may be that the word we now use, without pointing, in describing something as red was used on previous occasions by people who pointed to red objects; or perhaps they made use of red samples in explaining the word (see III, 8; §§43, 429). These are two possibilities. But how can one *point* to a bang, like the one announced in §442, or to an action like that ordered in §451 ("Imagine a red circle here")? Cases vary endlessly. So W. makes no attempt to catalog or order them (Man. 302, 15). His purpose is therapeutic, and his chief target is the simple projective connection, in the moment, in the mind, by means of the logical shadow (*BB* 38c).

(5) Doubtless this therapeutic purpose explains the section's emphasis on forward-looking examples, such as orders (§§431–34, 451, 458–61), wishes (§§437–41), and expectations (§§438–39, 442, 444–45, 452–53, 465), rather than on truth and statements of fact (§§429–30, 437), or "acts" with past or present targets, such as love, regret, hatred, remembrance, and so on. How can the mind "reach right out" (2.1511; §§431, 455–57) to something which doesn't yet exist and perhaps never will (*PG* 137a)? Negation (§§446–48) is similarly troublesome for the projec-

tive viewpoint: Something commanded, wished, expected, and so on, may eventually occur, but the truth of a negation depends on the non-existence or nonoccurrence of what is negated. How, then, is the mind to make contact (§95)? W. once replied that it intends indestructible, logical atoms (GI 35); but that solution has already been eliminated (Sections III, X; see GI 41).

DETAILED COMMENTARY

§428 A reworking of *PG* 154cd. See GI 34; XV, 1; §95; *PG* 99c, 103d–104a, 105a, 114d, 136f–137a, 155b; cp. §435.

"This queer thing": " 'What a queer mechanism,' one might say, 'the mechanism of wishing must be if I can wish that which will never happen' " (*BB* 4).

the very object *itself:* see §§518, 681; *BB* 4a, 35e–38; *PG* 213a.

"If it weren't too absurd we should say that the fact which we wish for must be present in our wish. For how can we wish *just this* to happen if just this isn't present in our wish? It is quite true to say: The mere shadow won't do; for it stops short before the object; and we want the wish to contain the object itself.—We want that the wish that Mr. Smith should come into this room should wish that just *Mr. Smith*, and no substitute, should do the *coming*, and no substitute for that, *into my room*, and no substitute for that. But this is exactly what we said" (*BB* 37).

"*That* is how a picture is attached to reality; it reaches right out to it. It is laid against reality like a ruler. Only the end-points of the graduating lines actually *touch* the object that is to be measured" (2.1511–2.15121; see 2.1515; *NB* 13d; *PG* 213–14). "And yet the thought process must be autonomous, for it must *contain in itself* everything that makes the thought meaningful. Everything *relevant* to the sentence's having a sense . . . must lie within the thought. When I say 'I would like to see a red circle here,' the statement's making sense cannot depend on whether a red circle actually exists somewhere" (Man. 109, 43).

§429 From *PG* 163. Cp. NL 301f; *PG* 183c; *PB* 61e; 4.06; *NB* 4ab, 8f, 15, 25cdef, 26f; Man. 229, §1167; Man. 110, 60; Man. 109, 22–23, 31; Man. 108, 185, 196, 204–7.

"And here we have the old problem, which we would like to express as follows: 'the thought that p is the case does not presuppose that it is the case; but on the other hand something in the fact must be a presupposition for even having the thought (I cannot think that something is red if the color red doesn't exist).' It is the problem of the harmony between world and thought" (*PG* 142). W.'s answer now: "Like everything metaphysical the harmony between thought and reality is to be found in the grammar of the language" (Z 55; PG 162). Thus, "if we were doubtful about how the sentence 'King's College is on fire' can be a picture of King's College on fire, we need only ask ourselves: 'How should we explain what the sentence means?' Such an explanation might consist of ostensive definitions. We should say, e.g., 'this is King's College' (pointing to the building), 'this is a fire' (pointing to a fire). This shews you the way in which words and things may be connected" (BB 37; cp. §197).

W.'s earlier correspondence account required existing objects, to be named (GI 35; III, 5–6), and an act of the mind which named them (GI 37). Then if the form of the resulting picture matched that of the reality pictured, the proposition was true (GI 36; 2.222; PG 212; cp. Russell, *Logic*, 319). The apparently banal remark in the second sentence of §429 repudiates all three claims—the need of an existing referent, the mental pointing, the similarity of form—and in fact all traditional correspondence accounts of truth.

The result is not necessarily a no-truth account such as Ramsey defended, namely "that 'it is true that p' means no more than 'p' " (Moore, *Papers*, 82). W. himself had said the same thing, but for his own Tractarian reasons: " ' "p" is true' is . . . only a pseudo-proposition like all those connexions of signs which apparently say something that can only be shewn" (NB 9). Such an account, already termed "nonsensical" by the *Tractatus* (6.54), W. later rejected. However, if §136a represents W.'s later view, and he still agreed with 5.141, a Ramseyan view of truth does result. See Man. 108, 194; Moore, *Lectures*, 143–44; PG 124b; cp. §22a.

if I say falsely . . . : see 4.25. Falsehood had been the great problem for W.'s picture theory (GI 34; XV, 5); hence the reference to it rather than to truth. The switch from "thought" to "say" has various possible explanations: Most thought is verbal (cp. XI, 5); nonverbal thought is not called true until verbalized; the view W. has in mind turned thought into inner speech (X, 2).

it isn't *red*: this sounds like a traditional correspondence account (see e.g. Prior, "Correspondence", 224; Moore, *Papers*, 83); but the italics make the difference. The absence of *red* is what makes the proposition false, not the absence of the satisfaction I might feel were my proposition verified, or the failure of fact to match my mental representation, or any of the other supplementary items with which philosophers have traditionally filled out their correspondence accounts. In PG 163, before making the remarks here in §429, W. said of the agreement between thought and reality: "In the *Tractatus* I had said something like: it is an agreement of form." "It is only possible by means of the correlation of the components; the correlation between names and things named gives an example. (And it is clear that a correlation of relations too takes place somehow.)" (*NB* 6; see *NB* 112b; 2.222; GI 36–37). "That is, for me only two things are involved in the fact that a thought is true, namely the thought and the fact; whereas for Russell there are three, namely the thought, the fact and a third occurrence. . . . It makes little difference here how this third event is described" (*PB* 63; see Russell, *Outline*, 273b). Now W. himself adds a "third event": learning the word. There red itself is found, and no mere shadow (III, 7). The connecting link between statement and reality is the *word* (same in learning and in later speech), not the thing (present still in the mind, or as an indestructible logical atom). (See *PG* 135c; *Z* 54; cp. *PG* 123e; Man. 108, 265.)

And when I want . . . : "*The* property which a belief has, when it is true," wrote Moore (*Problems*, 267; see 255–56, 263, 276b), ". . . is the property which can be expressed by saying that *the* fact to which it refers *is*. This is precisely what I propose to submit as the fundamental definition of truth. And the difficulty we found about it was that of defining exactly what is meant by '*referring to*', by talking of *the* fact to which a belief refers." W. here suggests an answer. "The connection between 'language and reality' is made by explanations of words" (*PG* 97), still more than by "the day-to-day practice of playing" (§197). In the ordinary use of *red*, nothing red need be present or be pointed out, whereas in one way or another red objects do generally enter into the learning of the word *red*, for instance through someone's pointing to a red object and saying "This is red." Though we often say that something is not red, we do not define *red* by pointing to something which is not red (p. 14n).

"We said the connection between our thinking, or speaking, about a man and the man himself was made when, in order to explain the meaning of the word 'Mr. Smith' we pointed to him, saying 'this is Mr. Smith.' And there is nothing mysterious about this connection. I mean, there is no queer mental act which somehow conjures up Mr. Smith in our minds when he really isn't here. What makes it difficult to see that this is the connection is a peculiar form of expression of ordinary language, which makes it appear that the connection between our thought (or the expression of our thought) and the thing we think about must have subsisted *during* the act of thinking" (*BB* 38).

§430 See *Z* 233; cp. commentary on §§433, 519; *Z* 128; *BB* 5a; *NB* 19k; Man. 110, 75–76. Man. 107, 241, reveals the link between this number and the preceding: "Checking the truth of a proposition always means holding it alongside reality."

The ruler which failed W., since it did not fix a sense unambiguously (§§139–41, 426), being itself at best just another sign (*PG* 40a), was the logical picture (*PG* 148b; *Z* 236) in which he formerly believed (GI 32–36). "I said the proposition was like a ruler laid against reality. And, like all logical models of the proposition, the ruler is itself in a particular case a propositional sign. And one would like now to say [the present number follows]" (*PG* 132; Man. 109, 272). The transition from picture to use here in §§430–32 parallels that in §§139–41, and both mirror the overall movement in W.'s thought, from *Tractatus* to *Investigations* (I, 1).

   "Put a ruler . . .": W. is citing an early difficulty, not one which arose in the transition years. In *NB* 32 he had written: "Proposition and situation are related to one another like the yard-stick and the length to be measured. . . . In the proposition we hold a proto-picture up against reality." Then it occurred to him, some weeks later, that "a yardstick does not say that an object that is to be measured is one yard long. Not even when we know that it is supposed to serve for the measurement of this *particular* object" (*NB* 37–38). "It is clear that the closest examination of the propositional sign cannot yield what it asserts—what it can yield is what it is *capable* of asserting" (*NB* 40). Meaning, understanding, does the rest (see §431).

   On this model of the ruler, see also 2.1511–2.15121 (quoted for §428); Man. 109, 52, 61; *Kreis*, 185; *PB* 75, 77i, 78def, 85b, 110a; *PG* 123e–124a, 164a (quoted for §104).

§431   In Man. 116, 22–23, this is followed by comments. See *BB* 42a; *PG* 50b; Man. 112, 181–83; Man. 110, 26–27, 117–18, 238; Man. 109, 181, 278; Man. 108, 192–93, 202, 233–34, 256; cp. §§503–5. As usual, note the quotation marks. W. is not expressing his view at the time of writing.

   (a) "There is a gulf . . .": see §430 and commentary; *EPB* 141–42; *BB* 38, 97bc; *PP* 265b–266a.

   "It has to be filled . . .": see *Z* 285; *BB* 142–43 (quoted for §188); *PG* 45g, 46c–47a.

   (b) "Only in the act . . .": see *PG* 40a (quoted for §139), 99c, 100d.

   "is it meant": see GI 37; §81b.

§432   See §454; *Z* 173, 235–38; *BB* 4d–5a; *PG* 107a, 144c, 147c, 149, 150a, 153c; Man. 110, 27; Man. 108, 278. Note how appropriate in W.'s perspective is the parallel: Mark or sound is to meaningful word as body is to living human being.

   Every sign *by itself* . . . : see commentary on §§430–31. "The signs of our language seem dead without these mental processes; and it might seem that the only function of the signs is to induce such processes" (*BB* 3e).

   In use it is *alive*: cp. p. 210e. "If I say, 'I'm going there now,' there is much more in the symbol than in the sign alone. If I come across the sentence somewhere written by an unknown hand on a slip of paper, it says nothing; the word 'I', the words 'now' and 'there' are meaningless without the presence of the speaker, the present situation & a spatial indication of direction" (Man. 109, 134)—as in the next number.

is the *use* its life?: Man. 109, 40; *BB* 4d; and p. 209c favor an affirmative answer; but see pp. 205jk, 214f; *PG* 172bc.

§433 See *PG* 90b, 145b (=*Z* 231, quoted in XXXVII, 6), 149b (=*Z* 237); *PB* 66d; Man. 302, 7; Man. 228, §55; Man. 110, 63, 71–72, 74–75, 122; Man. 109, 135–36, 277; Man. 108, 188–89, 228, 231–32, 234, 237; cp. §§85, 140–41. The number illustrates Man. 108, 224, quoted for §110. It comes (with the omission of an illustration) from *PG* 133, which adds: "The appearance of awkwardness, when a sign tries, like a dumb person, to make itself understood through all sorts of suggestive gestures—this disappears when we reflect that only in a grammatical system does the sign do its job."

(a) When we give an order . . . : in Man. 110, there are many passages like the following: "Understanding becomes important when we regard it as the condition for—e.g.—executing an order. The order may be given by means of a picture of the action ordered. 'Yes, but I must also understand the picture.'—What does this mean?—'I must know that I am to do *this*.' However, since the order is not yet carried out through understanding it, this knowledge can only consist in my possessing some *other* fact than the execution" (190). Cp. GI 33.

it can look as if . . . : see Man. 108, 200; Man. 109, 195: "If a person translates the thought or rather the expression of the thought into the deed, then to be sure the expression plus the method of projection, that is, the thought, reaches right out to the fact and touches it as a ruler touches an object." Cp. §141.

there is always a gulf: see §431 and commentary.

to raise his arm: cp. Man. 108, 250.

To make it quite clear . . . : "If it is said that the person who receives the order forms images from the words, images which resemble the execution of the order (whereas the words do not), then I go farther still and suppose that the order is given by mechanically causing the person (by leading his hand, etc.) to perform the movements he is to carry out say in five minutes; and I cannot approximate any closer to the execution of the order in the expression of the order. We have then replaced the similarity of the image with a far greater similarity" (Man. 109, 274–75; see Man. 116, 22; cp. *BB* 4). However, my making the movement *voluntarily*, by myself, comes just as close as *his* making it in this involuntary fashion.

This picture seems unambiguous: cp. §426a and commentary.

that *he is to make that movement*: cp. Man. 108, 191, on two unequal lines: "Everyone sees that the upper line is longer & the lower is shorter; but he doesn't see there that the lower line is *supposed to be* or *will be* as long as the upper. And how can a picture, of whatever kind, show that?" Likewise, "in a ruler set beside the growing object, the height is foreshadowed but not that this object will reach it" (Man. 108, 230). Or "suppose we say the wish that this table were a bit higher consists in the act of holding my hand over the table at the desired height. Now the objection is: 'The hand over the table cannot be the wish: it doesn't indicate that the table should be higher; it is where it is and the table is where it is. And *whatever other* gesture I made, it would make no difference'" (PG 148–49). "We do not perceive in the gesture the actual shadow of the fulfilment, unmistakable, or no longer interpretable" (PG 150). See also PG 151–52. Cp. PG 42c.

(b) **by what token:** rather: "in what signs" (cp. §201c). Ultimate, uninterpretable ones (XXXVII 6–7)? W. once said: "I must have become conscious at some moment of the agreement or disagreement between my action and the command. If (i.e. only if) that happens do I understand the command" (Man. 110, 16). "To understand must be to grasp the order as such, to experience the order as an order" (Man. 110, 17). "But this is where we were before," W. now replies. "The application is still a criterion of understanding" (§146). For "no matter how many intermediary steps I insert between the thought and its application, each intermediate step follows the former—and the application follows the last—without any intermediary. It is the same here as when we wish to mediate between decision and act by means of intermediate steps" (PG 160; Man. 109, 223–24; see PG 101ab). "Now you might ask: do we *interpret* the words before we obey the order? And in some cases you will find that you do something which might be called interpreting before obeying, in some cases not" (BB 3).

§434 From PG 150. The quotation marks there show still more clearly that the words do not express W.'s view at the time of writing. See the commentary on §§120c, 339a, 433.

§435 A reworking of PG 104cd, derived from Man. 110, 33–34. See §102; PG 149f; Man. 109, 173–74, 213–15; cp. BB 30f–31a.

(a) **"How do sentences . . .":** see GI 34; commentary on §95 (e.g. Man. 110, 30). "It might be said: How can I expect an event, since it isn't yet there?" (Man. 108, 265). For a glimpse of W. in this morass, see Man. 107, 243.

nothing is concealed: see §126. The important thing (sense, thought, understanding, and the like) seems hidden and hard to grasp because we suppose it to be something relatively simple (§§36, 308), in the moment, in the mind (§102), whereas it is coextensive with the language-game, whose details are so trifling we ignore them (e.g. §608), so familiar we overlook them (§129), and so complex that they are hard to trace even when we are attentive (§664).

(c) "it all goes by so quick . . .": see §197; *BB* 42; Man. 110, 141; and the final paragraph of Man. 228, §369, following these three in §435. "Thought can as it were *fly*, it doesn't have to walk" (*Z* 273).

"It somehow worries us that the thought in a sentence is not wholly present at any one moment. We regard it as an object which we are making and have never got all there, for no sooner does one part appear than another vanishes" (*Z* 153; *PG* 108a; Man. 228, §88; Man. 111, 7). James, for one, was so troubled (see §436a and commentary).

§436   From *PG* 169 (save for the final sentence). See *PG* 87de, 175c; Moore, *Studies*, 25; Russell, *Mind*, 250, and *Logic*, 128–32; James, *Principles*, I, 472: *"The sense of our meaning is an entirely peculiar element of the thought. It is one of those evanescent and 'transitive' facts of mind which introspection cannot turn round upon, and isolate and hold up for examination, as an entomologist passes round an insect on a pin. In the (somewhat clumsy) terminology I have used, it pertains to the 'fringe' of the subjective state, and is a 'feeling of tendency', whose neural counterpart is undoubtedly a lot of dawning and dying processes too faint and complex to be traced."*

W. himself once experienced similar difficulties. "The approach which leads us into an enclosed valley, as it were, from which there is no escape into the open countryside is taking the present as the only reality. This present, constantly flowing or rather constantly changing, cannot be arrested or caught hold of. It disappears before we can think of grasping it. We stick in this valley, as though bewitched, in a whirl of thoughts. The error must be that we try to grasp the fleeting present by scientific methods. It must be as though we wanted to determine the strength of a beam in abstraction from it. . . . And nevertheless there can be a phenomenological language (where must it stop?)" (Man. 107, 1–2). "It's as if the phenomenological language led us into a bewitched morass in which everything tangible disappears" (Man. 105, 116; see X, 8; Man. 108, 26–27; quotations below; cp. *PB* 98).

BB 30f–31a connects §436 with §435, thus: "This is a beautiful example of a philosophical question. It asks 'How can one . . . ?' and while this puzzles us we must admit that nothing is easier than to think what is not the case. I mean, this shows us again that the difficulty which we are in does not arise through our inability to imagine how thinking something is done. . . . I say this because sometimes it almost seems as though our difficulty were one of remembering exactly what happened when we thought something, a difficulty of introspection, or something of the sort; whereas in fact it arises when we look at the facts through the medium of a misleading form of expression." See *PB* 83d; cp. *PG* 169d.

that dead-end: "the difficulty of the: *Alles fliesst*", which W. discussed so frequently and thought of putting at the start of his book (Man. 110, 10). "The stream of life, or the stream of the world, flows on and our propositions are as it were only verified in instants. Only the present verifies our propositions" (Man. 107, 222; *PB* 81). "It is easy to understand the use of words as extended in time, but I find it infinitely difficult to grasp the sense in the moment of use. What does it mean e.g. to understand a sentence as member of a system of sentences?" (Man. 107, 233; see IX, 2, 3, 5).

hard to get hold of: see above, and §608; XXXII, 2; *PG* 75a; James, *Principles*, I, 191, 244, 300a, 480b ("Introspective psychology must here throw up the sponge; the fluctuations of subjective life are too exquisite to be arrested by its coarse means"). "We feel that thought is like a landscape which we have seen and have to describe, but that we don't remember it exactly enough to be able to describe it with all its connections. Similarly, we believe, we cannot describe thought subsequently because the many detailed processes are then lost sight of. We would like, as it were, to see all these fine hook-ups under a magnifying glass" (Man. 110, 36; *PG* 104; cp. §§645–46; James, *Principles*, I, 276c).

the present experience: "in the world of data" (Man. 105, 86). "The immediate is grasped in constant flux. (Indeed it has the form of a stream)" (Man. 107, 159).

slips quickly by: see §456; *Z* 153 (quoted for §435); James, *Principles*, I, 90b, 191b, 253a, 341.

ordinary language too crude: see §§120, 610; *BB* 45bcd; Russell, *Essays*, 275–76.

with ones that . . . : cp. e.g. James, *Principles*, I, 258b.

Augustine . . . : the arrangement in the German text seems preferable; the quotation, like *PG* 169d which it replaces, is related to the whole preceding paragraph, not just to the preceding sentence, as its inclusion in the paragraph might suggest. Compare the use of the same quotation (from *Confessions*, XI, 22, 28) in Man. 228, 179.

Manifestissima et . . . : "They are perfectly obvious and ordinary, and yet the same things are too well hidden, and their discovery comes as something new."

rusus: one might expect *rursus* or *rusum*. Geach replies: " 'Rusus' is W.'s own spelling . . . it seems to be a correct spelling for Latin of Augustine's time."

§437 See GI 32–36; XV, 1; *Z* 70; *EPB* 216; *BB* 37e–38, 143b (quoted for §188); Man. 110, 17, 69; Plato, *Philebus*, 35.

A wish: see *PG* 150d, 150g–151a. After several numbers on orders (§§431–34), a series now starts on wishes. For the picture theory had assimilated command and wish: "To understand a command before one executes it is akin to wishing an action before one performs it" (*PB* 58). "If I wish that p were the case, p is not the case; and in the fact of wishing, something must deputize for p, as also of course in the expression of the wish" (*PB* 66). "Here it is always as though something were already done before it is done" (Man. 108, 253). See GI 36.

seems already to know: see §458; *PG* 103a. "I have said elsewhere that a proposition 'reaches up to reality', and by this I meant that the forms of the entities are contained in the form of the proposition which is about these entities. For the sentence, together with the mode of projection which projects reality into the sentence, determines the logical form of the entities" (LF 36). "When I say, Draw a line somewhere between these two | |, I do not thereby give an infinitely complicated command. On the other hand, the command must foresee what will be allowed to count as its fulfilment" (Man. 108, 183).

Whence this *determining*: see §§193–94; *Z* 288 ("because the form: 'He ordered *such-and-such*' swam before your mind"); *RFM* 3i, 4b, 7f. "The proposition . . . seems to require that reality be compared with it" (*PG* 132). "Here we are misled by our language's form of expression, by its saying 'knowledge of *what* you have to do' or 'knowledge of the action'. For it thus looks as if this something, the action, were a thing that is to come into existence when the order is obeyed, and as if the order acquainted us with this very thing, hence showed it to us; so that in a certain sense it already brought it into existence" (*PG* 159). "The shadowy anticipation of the fact consists in our being able to think now that *that very thing* will occur which only later *will* occur" (*PG* 160). "It is difficult for us to shake free from this comparison: a man makes his appearance—an event makes its appearance. As if the event already stood, in figure, before the door of reality and now entered it (like a room)" (*PG* 137).

This despotic demand: "The proposition must *contain* (and in this way shew) the *possibility of its truth*" (*NB* 16; see XXXVII, 3; Man. 109, 83, quoted for §438).

"The hardness of the logical must": see IX, 1–3.

"If it is a logical must, then the sentence is a grammatical remark" (*PG* 45; see §372).

An expression of W.'s former outlook: "The freedom of the will consists in the fact that future events *cannot* be KNOWN now. It would only be possible for us to know them, if causality were an INNER necessity—like, say, that of logical inference.—The connexion between knowledge and thing known is *the* connexion of logical necessity" (*NB* 43).

§438   A reworking of *PG* 132a (see also 132b). It refers to thinking like that in 3.13 (e.g.: "A proposition contains the form, but not the content, of its sense") and Man. 109, 83–84, which connect it with the preceding number: "Thus the plan can only reach its feelers to where the event occurs or does not occur. And the *demanding* reach is what we understand in the plan as plan.

"The demand consists in the plan's being incomplete (not a fact); for were it a complete complex it would cease to refer beyond itself."

(a) From Man. 109, 84, *verbatim*, except that W. now encloses his former view in quotation marks. On page 77 he had written: "Thinking means making a plan."

(b) Or put it this way: According to the picture theory the proposition present in every such act (GI 36) contains and thus shows the possibility of its truth. "But not more than the *possibility*" (*NB* 16). And a possibility is essentially, as such, unsatisfied.

§439   From *PG* 133–34, which reworks Man. 110, 63. See ibid., 71. W. does not reject the expression *unsatisfied*, but seeks to demythologize it.

(a) This is strongly reminiscent of Plato's *Philebus*, 35–36. Concerning such strings of questions, see GI 54.

Is it a hollow space?: it had been for W. "The expectation of p and the occurrence of p correspond, say, to the hollow figure and the full figure of a body: p corresponds to the shape of the volume, and the different ways in which the shape is given correspond to the difference between expectation and occurrence" (*PB* 71; see Man. 108, 212 [quoted for §444b], 213–14, 218). "It seems as though in a certain sense the two must fit. The picture of a hollow and a solid immediately comes to mind. How must the solid be made so as to fit into the hollow? *One* description must do for both (this is the answer)" (Man. 302, 12; see Man. 108, 217–18, quoted for §120b; cp. Z 54). In a sense, it is the answer (§458), but not because the shape is there in the wish (XV, 3; GI 43); the words used to express the wish are the ones used in describing its fulfillment.

say hunger?: "One may characterize the meaning which Russell gives to the word 'wishing' by saying that it means to him a kind of hunger" (*BB* 21–22). Earlier W. had objected that "hunger and the apple which satisfies it do not have the same multiplicity" (Man. 108, 236), so had rejected this model of intentionality (*PB* 63–65).

(b) In a particular system: granted, such a sample and such a use are conceivable (if I show someone a hollow cylinder, he learns the size and shape of the solid cylinder which 'satisfies' it). "On the other hand compare the meaning of: 'These trousers don't go with this jacket' " (Z 54). Thus we should not too readily suppose that in thought satisfaction or fitting is some sort of repetition or duplication of an identical form (the *Tractatus*'s "logical form").

§440 See GI 15–16; Man. 179 (quoted for §441c); cp. §460; Z 68; *PG* 138e, 140e, 157e–158b; Malcolm, Review of *PB*, 223–24. Russell had written: "A desire is called 'conscious' when it is accompanied by a true belief as to the state of affairs that will bring quiescence" (*Mind*, 76; see also 32). Against this linking of object and quiescence "the only objection is that in a large group of cases the word isn't used that way. The use of the words 'believe', 'wish', etc. which we want to discuss here is rather that in which it is *tautologous* to say: the belief that p is the case is verified by the occurrence of p" (Man. 302, 31).

   does not mean . . . : for one thing, the expression does not report that my feeling is "accompanied by a true belief", as Russell put it (above); for another thing, even in the cases alluded to in §441b, "it isn't like this: I wish for an apple; so whatever quenches the wish I'll call an 'apple' " (*PG* 134). In that hypothesis, "if I wanted to eat an apple and someone punches me in the stomach so that I lose my appetite, then the punch was the thing I originally wanted" (*PB* 64).

   but of nonsatisfaction: here the word *Äusserung* would not have its frequent sense of "spontaneous expression" (§441) or "word-reaction" (Man. 228, 71). "I'm dissatisfied" might, but not "I believe an apple will quell my feeling of nonsatisfaction." In that case I would be stating a hypothesis (*PG* 141b).

§441 Russell's views are still the main target; see his *Mind*, 30–32 (quoted below), 58–66, 76 (quoted for §440).

(a) See *PG* 138e; cp. Man. 116, 286.

   By nature and . . . : see GI 16.

   in certain circumstances: "which, however, one does not learn to describe" (Z 114–16).

   A *wish* is . . . : the expression is not a mere symptom, indicating how it is within (GI 15), but a principal component of the variable weave called wishing (GI 45), serving as chief criterion of subject, "act", and object (GI 60–61; X, 22).

   cannot arise at all: see p. 221cde; Z 53; cp. §§246–47; *BB* 21d.

   And the fact that . . . : see *PB* 64, quoted for §440; cp. §460; Russell, *Mind*, 32: "The thing which will bring a restless condition to an end is said to be what is desired. But only experience can show what will have this sedative effect, and it is easy to make mistakes."

(b) An important observation, indicating a reason why §246, on *pain* (which has no such alternative use), excludes first-person knowledge more categorically than does p. 221c, which allows for the present variation. Here the first-person use resembles the third-person. Yet Russell's account is still inaccurate, even here (see the commentary on §440). And his fundamental mistake was to suppose that wishing is uniform. See e.g. *Mind*, 30: "When we think of our own desires, most people believe that we can know them by an immediate self-knowledge which does not depend upon observation of our actions. Yet if this were the case, it would be odd that people are so often mistaken as to what they desire. It is a matter of observation that 'so-and-so does not know his own motives.' " W. rejects the supposition of uniformity and Russell's description of both alternatives. See *BB* 22b (quoted for p. 189c); Man. 232, 600; cp. §586, p. 192e; *BB* 21d.

(c) Cp. §384. Returning to the commoner use, W. answers Russell's claim (above) that "only experience can show" what I really want. Man. 179 is fuller: "Does a person know what he wishes before he gets it? If that means 'Can he say it?' the answer is generally 'Yes.' Now is 'I would like to drink a glass of wine' the expression of an *opinion*? In general *no*. As little as the words 'Wine, please!' or the cry 'Help!' when I fall into the water. (Granted, there are cases when the word 'wish' or 'want' is used differently.)"

then I do know: in the sense, for instance, that there is no room for doubt (§247) or that I can say it (Man. 179, above). Cp. X, 25; *Z* 53: "The statement 'I am expecting a bang at any moment' is an *expression* of expectation. This verbal reaction is the movement of the pointer, which shows the object of expectation."

§442 See GI 54 (on the technique here employed); *Z* 53, 68; *BB* 38, 40d. The number comes from *PG* 134–35 (earlier, Man. 109, 60–61, and Man. 302, 18). Its target is thinking like the following:

"A 'long future' is 'a long expectation of the future' " (Augustine, *Confessions*, XI, 28, 37).

"When I have seen a flash of lightning and am waiting for the thunder, I have a belief-feeling analogous to memory, except that it refers to the future: I have an image of thunder, combined with a feeling which may be expressed in the words: 'this will happen' " (Russell, *Mind*, 176).

"Expectation and fulfillment are related as hollow and solid" (Man. 108, 214). "The difficulty is to understand that the fact is *entirely* prefigured in expectation" (Man. 108, 230). "We say, 'I thought the pointer would already be there, and now it isn't yet there.' We made a picture, that is clear. But to what extent is this picture a picture of *this* pointer? . . . Here it is always as though something had already been done even before it has been done" (Man. 108, 251–53). See GI 35–36.

"I expect": as background for this and subsequent numbers on expectation, see Man. 108, 210–14, 221, 225–28, 248–50, 265–74.

somehow already exist: "Many will perhaps want to say, 'The expectation is a thought' " (Man. 228, §547).

it was not an accompaniment: as in Russell's view: "Does the image persist in presence of the sensation, so that we can compare the two? And even if *some* image does persist, how do we know that it is the previous image unchanged? . . . It is better, I think, to take a more external and causal view of the relation of expectation to expected occurrence. If the occurrence, when it comes, gives us the feeling of expectedness, and if the expectation, beforehand, enabled us to act in a way which proves appropriate to the occurrence, that must be held to constitute the maximum of verification" (*Mind*, 270).

"Fulfilment of expectation doesn't consist in this: a third thing happens which can be described otherwise than *as* 'the fulfilment of this expectation', i.e. as a feeling of satisfaction or joy or whatever it may be" (*Z* 68). And "it isn't as though the event somehow consisted of qualities which the expectation of the event already possesses in part, in part not" (Man. 108, 213).

what *was* extra: "Does an imagined note differ in timbre from the same note actually heard?" (Man. 108, 230).

§443   From *PG* 135b. See XV, 5; *BB* 60; *PB* 271 (quoted for §301); Man. 110, 87; cp. §§194, 197, 302, 458–61; *PB* 75 (quoted for §56); *PP* 266a; Man. 109, 53–54, 233.

" 'Yes, *that* is what I expected.' How could you expect it, since it wasn't yet there. (This misunderstanding contains the whole difficulty of our discussion but also its solution.)" (Man. 108, 265–66).

Imagining is not simply a comparable case, but the medium in which W., like Russell and others, had supposed that expectation is frequently effected (see XII, 1). If the yellow I finally see "can be the same yellow as I imagined (so that there is not some further criterion of that, say a reaction) then the expectation had to refer to what is common to the image and the reality, for the image as image is distinct from the reality" (Man. 108, 225). "However, if I wish to replace the image which occurs in expectation etc. with a picture which is actually seen, something like the following happens: I am supposed to draw a thick, black line & have drawn a thinner one as a picture. But the image goes farther & says it already knows that the line is supposed to be thick. So I draw a thick one, but somewhat paler. But the image says it also knows that the proper color is black, not gray. (But if I draw the thick, black line, that is no longer a picture.)" (Man. 108, 253). "So first of all he had to somehow *mean* this image.—Now isn't this the way it is: that he can compare this image with the present—not the awaited—visual impression & does compare it & thereby fixes this image's interpretation, as it were" (Man. 108, 222). W.'s answer now: No, that is not the way it is. No red need be on hand anywhere, whether in his mind or in his surroundings (cp. §396). For "consider this argument: 'How can we wish that this paper were red if it isn't red? . . . The imagery of the wish surely shows us something less definite, something hazier, than the reality of the paper being red. I should therefore say [if I insist on something present and common], instead of "I wish this paper were red," something like "I wish a pale red for this paper." ' But if in the usual way of speaking he had said, 'I wish a pale red for this paper,' we should, in order to fulfil his wish, have painted it a pale red—and this wasn't what he wished" (*BB* 60).

"The red which . . .": in Man. 109, 50–51, W. asked the same question (the words within quotation marks) but answered (cp. §73): "Doesn't this show merely that what I call 'this red' is what is common to my image and reality? For imagining red of course differs from seeing red. . . . However, in both expressions the same word 'red' occurs & it must therefore designate just what is common to *both* processes.

"Isn't it the same in the propositions 'Here is a red patch' and 'Here there isn't a red patch'? The word 'red' occurs in both; so this word cannot indicate the presence of something red." W. still accepts the parallel, but for a very different reason. The conclusion to be drawn from the analogous case is purely negative (cp. §545 and commentary).

§444 See GI 43; *PB* 66a, 69bc, 286c; *PP* 265b–266a; Man. 228, §242; Man. 109, 48–50, 60, 62; Prior, "Correspondence", 227, col. 1. The number as a whole (a shortened version of *PG* 139a, derived from Man. 109, 216–17) leads to §445, and illustrates W.'s rejection of the connection of thought with its object via a logical shadow (GI 36) and his suggestion that the connection is made via language (GI 43; XV, 3–4).

(a) Cp. §458; *PG* 134b; *PB* 68b; Man. 110, 172; Man. 108, 222–23, 272.

One may have the feeling . . . : for one thing, the mode of verification differs (*PG* 62b), and the method of verification determines the sense (§353 and commentary). For another thing, *red* may seem in one case a name and in the other what Russell called an "incomplete symbol". This second line more fully: (a) "I believe that the signs A & B have a different meaning when the circles to which they belong no longer exist" (Man. 109, 144). (b) However, "could it perhaps be said that 'red' has two different meanings when someone calls an actual patch of color red & on the other hand an imagined patch? No. Red is what is common to both" (Man. 108, 228; cp. §277). (c) But once call this common something in question, or the need for an image in so-called psychological acts (see commentary on §443), and they might seem to require the same verdict as the circles A and B. It could appear that when *red* occurs in expressions of seeing, then in expressions of expecting, believing, and the like, "the former was indeed the name of a reality whereas the latter is only a tentative combination of concepts" (Man. 108, 215). "It is clear," W. then felt, "that the two propositions describe entirely different facts. The question is whether in the two cases the words are differently used. Whether, as it were, in the second case there were question only of words & the proposition p belonged in quotation marks. But that is obviously not the case.

"The feeling is that the proposition 'I believe that p is the case' does not describe the process of belief (that only the cards of the loom are given & all the rest is merely hinted at)" (Man. 109, 215–16; cp. X, 6–7; *PG* 104b; 5.542).

how could I say that . . . : cp. *PB* 60: "It is clear that the *sole* source of my knowledge here [whether what happens is what I expected] is the comparison of the *expression* of my expectation with the event that has occurred."

If I wanted to explain . . . : for similar moves, see §43b and §429 and commentary there.

(b) See *BB* 20d (fuller); *PG* 141e–142a; Man. 219, 6–7; Man. 109, 70; Man. 108, 267; cp. *BB* 39d; Man. 108, 255. The conflict with 5.542, veiled in the first paragraph, now becomes apparent. Man. 108, 215–17, might be taken as an expression of either view: "A person cannot *amorphously* see that something is so, believe it is so, wish, fear, think, etc." "An amorphous thought is as unthinkable as an amorphous chess game" (ibid.). But *PB* 71 still said: "Our expectation anticipates the event. In this sense it makes a model of the event" (see also below, and quotations for §439a).

what's it like . . . : contrast the following descriptions (a door in one, not in the other, and so on) with Man. 108, 224: "Indeed it is evident that the expectation has to do with the same thing, the same reality, as does the fact that fulfils it. . . . We look in expectation at the same, real door as the expected person is to walk through."

So how can one use . . . : difficulty would arise from W.'s earlier view: "The expectation & the fact which fulfils it somehow fit together. . . . One thinks straight off of a full form and a corresponding hollow form. But now if we wish to describe both, we see that in so far as they fit together, one description holds for both. . . . The full form differs from the hollow merely through an index, something amorphous" (Man. 108, 212–13; cp. *Z* 54).

But of what kind?!: the kind already indicated at the end of (*a*) and immediately in §445.

§445 From Man. 109, 60, then *PG* 140, slightly changed. See GI 43; XV, 3–4; §452; *Z* 54–55, 68; *BB* 38c; *PG* 88d, 141e–142a, 143c, 151a; *PB* 60a (quoted for §444); *PP* 265–66; Man. 302, 15; Man. 109, 172, 217, 225; Man. 108, 276; cp. p. 217f; *Z* 290; *PG* 154b. As a warning against overstressing the verbal connection, as though it were decisive by itself, see §641. On the "fascinating mixture of ideas from the *Tractatus* and the *Investigations*" in *PB* on this topic, see Malcolm, Review of *PB*, 223–24.

W. might have accepted this dictum even in his *Tractatus* days, but then the words "in language" would have had a different sense; the all-important act of meaning or intending which then made the connection (GI 36–37) is what W. now denies (XV, 5). Also denied is Russell's view: "One might apply the words 'true' and 'false' to such expectations quite as legitimately as to verbal statements: they are false if they end in surprise, and true if they end in an emotion which might be described as 'quite so'. . . . Surprise proves the expectation to have been false, and its converse proves the expectation to have been true" ("Verification", 16).

On the contrary, "we could say that it is thus that we check whether an expectation has been fulfilled: if the expectation was expressed by the statement that *p* would be the case, and the state of affairs which comes about is described by the sentence 'p', then the expectation has been fulfilled" (Man. 108, 271; see 272). Compare this case: "How does the intention to play chess in half an hour differ from the intention to play chess in 28 minutes?—Not at all, unless it is articulated. To simplify, we can look on what he *says* as the criterion of the intention" (Man. 219, 3). Similarly (Z 53), "the simplest typical example of the use of the word 'expect' . . . is the case where the expectation that p will occur consists in the expectant person's *saying:* 'I expect p to happen'" (*PG* 140).

But suppose a person merely set table for two persons instead of for just himself, without uttering the name of Mr. N.; "even so, were it always the case that Mr. N. dines with him on this day of the week, we would here call his expectation the expectation of Mr. N., provided special circumstances did not point in another direction" (Man. 302, 15). "What characterizes all these cases is that the object of the expectation can be read off from the expectant behavior" (*PG* 140; see XV, 3). No later experience, no isolated act of mind, determines what is expected. Thus, giving the number a second twist, we might say that it is the concept *expect*, as actually operative—accepting behavioral determinants as well as mental, and nonlinguistic behavior as well as linguistic—which makes the supposedly mysterious connection. See commentary on §457.

§446 From Man. 109, 53, then *PG* 136b. Cp. *Z* 59–60. On the therapeutic affinity of this example (negation) with the former (expectation and wishes), see XV, 5, and *BB* 60b–61a, e.g.: "Consider this argument: 'How can we wish that this paper were red if it isn't red? Doesn't this mean that I wish that which doesn't exist at all? Therefore my wish can only contain something *similar* to the paper's being red. Oughtn't we therefore to use a different word instead of "red" when we talk of wishing that something were red? . . .' (All this connects our present problem with the problem of negation. I will only give you a hint, by saying that a notation would be possible in which, to put it roughly, a quality had always two names, one for the case when something is said to have it, the other for the case when something is said not to have it. The negation of 'This paper is red' could then be, say, 'This paper is not rode.' Such a notation would actually fulfil some of the wishes which are denied us by our ordinary language and which sometimes produce a cramp of philosophical puzzlement about the idea of negation.)" For the connection between negation and expectation, see e.g. Man. 228, §494 (quoted for §447a) and *Z* 68 ("Expectation of what is not").

§447 See *PG* 151b; *PB* 57a, 76b; Man. 109, 87, 103; Man. 108, 231; Moore, *Papers*, 77–78; cp. §548; Man. 108, 268. W. had insisted that "only a *proposition* can be negated" (Man. 108, 279); and every proposition said: "This is how things stand" (GI 33).

An earlier version: "The feeling is as if '~p' had to make 'p' true in a certain sense, in order to negate it. We ask, '*What* is not the case?' This must be represented.—But it *is* in fact represented by p. We fail to get away from the idea that the sense of a sentence accompanies the sentence" (Man. 116, 85; cp. §449a).

Man. 109, 213, connects §447 with §446, then with §448, thus: "We confuse the word 'green' with the proposition 'a is green.' (Hence too our difficulty in explaining it in the proposition 'a is not green.') . . . As in the difficulty concerning 'toothache' we confuse the word 'toothache' with the proposition 'I have a toothache.' That means we believe that what is expressed in this proposition already lies in the *word*." The atomist, needing something to name, required green or pain somewhere, if only in the imagination (§§56, 297, 300). Thus the whole series leads to §449a.

(a) See *NB* 33k ("Can one negate a *picture*? No"), 39 ("The negative proposition excludes reality"), 115 ("p is false = ~[p is true] Def."); *Kreis*, 85 (quoted for §448b); Man. 108, 250–51 (" 'I know how this is when it happens & now that is to be *not* the case, it is to be eliminated, as it were' "); cp. §448; Man. 108, 58, 259, 262; Russell, *Inquiry*, 71c. In Man. 228, §494, after this remark, W. added: "Compare: expectation and fulfillment." Man. 108, 250, reveals the connection in his earlier thought: "We might say that the proposition lies in wait & now the event either occurs or does not occur.—But how about the non-occurrence? Doesn't it presuppose the occurrence in some sense or other?"

Suppose that we negate *p*, then somebody says, "You're wrong, for here is the very thing you negated." What he points to is not merely the logical atoms of *p*, which might be otherwise conjoined (GI 35), but *p* itself. So it would seem that somehow, even in negation, we had caught a reality in our net (§428). The model we form of reality (4.01), whether in assertion or negation, seems to conjure up "a pure intermediary between the propositional *signs* and the facts" (§94; see §95).

(b) "The negated proposition can be negated again, and this in itself shows that what is negated is already a proposition, and not merely something that is preliminary to a proposition" (4.0641; see *NB* 27h). See *NB* 21c, 24j, 25–26, 28fg, 30c, 32fgh, 33, 96b, 97 ("In not-p, p is exactly the same as if it stands alone"); *PB* 250f; Man. 108, 182–83: "What does it mean: He is not bigger than I? Obviously the proposition does not deny all sizes larger than mine. I believe we can understand it only through the proposition 'He is larger than I' "—and that (according to W.'s early view) specifies his size, not indefinitely many different sizes (GI 37).

"It must be possible to negate a false thought, and for this I need the thought; I cannot negate what is not there" (Frege, *Writings*, 122).

§448   See §§446–47; *PB* 113c–114a; Man. 108, 56–57; cp. *PB* 72b, 73a, 110c–111c, 164n, 286c; *NB* 16i. For the connection with §447, see the parallel sequence in *NB* 24jk. A sentence from §604 suggests the proper therapeutic perspective, tying together these apparently disparate parts: "It is as if I carried a picture of an object with me [GI 32–36] and used it to perform an identification of an object as the one represented by the picture." And the picture cannot be of just the dream, pain, or the like: "Each thing is, as it were, in a space of possible states of affairs. This space I can imagine empty, but I cannot imagine the thing without the space" (2.013). Thus a logical picture, a proposition, "represents a possible situation in logical space. A picture contains the possibility of the situation that it represents" (2.202–2.203; see Man. 108, 251). Thus "it is all simply a matter of the existence of the logical place. But what the devil is this 'logical place'?!" (*NB* 31).

(a) Cp. *PB* 65 ("for the intention is already expressed in the way I *now* compare the picture with reality"), 75d, 77di; Man. 107, 256.

"**I did *not* dream**": "The negated proposition not only draws the boundary between the negated domain and the rest; it actually points to the negated domain" (*NB* 26). "The negation is a *description* in the same sense as the elementary proposition itself" (*NB* 29).

"**I must know where to look**": cp. *NB* 27 and 3.411: "In geometry and logic alike a place is a possibility: something can exist in it." "The existence of this logical place is guaranteed by the existence of the component parts alone, by the existence of the significant proposition" (*NB* 24). Thus, for the possibility of stomachache "it is only essential that I have the space before me in which the stomach is situated and that in which pains are situated" (Man. 107, 157–58). "The knowledge of the representing relation *must* be founded only on the knowledge of the component parts of the situation!" (*NB* 24). See Man. 108, 96; cp. *PB* 70bc, 79d.

"**but mustn't be senseless**": Frege and also Russell (till W. influenced him) had regarded propositions as complex names; but a name must have reference, or else it is a meaningless mark or sound. How, then, could propositions be false yet meaningful? To allow the distinctive trait of truth and falsehood in propositions, W. had replied that the sense of a proposition is a *possible* state of affairs. "A proposition includes all that the projection includes, but not what is projected. Therefore, though what is projected is not itself included, its possibility is" (3.13). "What a picture represents it represents independently of its truth or falsity, by means of its pictorial form" (2.22). It shows just where the possible dream, pain, and so on would be (GI 36).

(b) See *BB* 49b–50a, 53d, 130e (quoted for §94); *PG* 159b (quoted for §94a); Man. 219, 4; Man. 107, 157, 203–4; cp. *Z* 498; *PB* 75d; Man. 123, June 3; Man. 109, 232; Russell, *Logic*, 295b. W.'s own former views are the main target, but others have thought somewhat similarly, for instance Augustine: "I name a bodily pain, yet it is not present within me, when nothing aches: yet unless its image were present in my memory, I would not know what to say about it, nor in conversation discern pain from pleasure" (*Confessions*, X, 15, 23).

"My chief point is that the proposition is compared with reality" (Man. 107, 155). "If the knife doesn't lie on the book, neither does any shadow of the knife lie on the book, but the multiplicity is present which provides the possibility & it is used in the proposition & is represented as real. And it must be just the same for stomachaches and dreams etc. as for the position of objects in space" (Man. 108, 57–58). "For if I say: 'I have no stomachache,' in this proposition I already presuppose the existence of the positive proposition, I presuppose the possibility of stomachache, and my proposition specifies the place in stomachache space. . . . When I say: 'I have no stomachache,' I say, as it were: 'I am at the zero point of stomachache space' " (*Kreis,* 85–86; cp. XXXIV, 1).

(c) See the quotations above from the *Tractatus,* and 3.02: "A thought contains the possibility of the situation of which it is the thought." For though the sense of a thought or proposition is not the actual state of affairs it describes, the meanings of the component names are the actual objects named (GI 35). And "objects contain the possibility of all situations" (2.014). It is this viewpoint that W. is here probing in specific, problematic cases. The simple *Tractatus* paradigm was a spot in the visual field which, "though it need not be red, must have some colour" (2.0131). Now is this the way it is with pain? Is there a pain spot which can be occupied or empty? What sense does talk about "possibility" have here? "We seem to be saying something about the state of painlessness when we say that it must contain the possibility of pain. But we are only speaking of the system of pictures that we use" (Man. 228, §493).

(d) W. is answering his former view: "If I say 'I have no toothache now, but will have one soon,' that presupposes that I recognize the feel of the toothache as such if it occurs. . . . 'I have no pain' means: If I compare the proposition 'I have a pain' with reality, it proves to be false.—So I must be able to compare it with what is actually the case. And this possibility of comparing—even if there is no correspondence—is what we mean by the expression" (Man. 107, 203–4; see *PB* 63e, 65a; cp. §388a; *PB* 92b). The paragraph is also "related to what Frege and sometimes Ramsey said about recognition as a condition of symbolizing" (Man. 228, §38; Man. 116, 37).

"One would then suppose that if someone says, 'I didn't feel any pain in my knee that time,' he is reporting an observation: I felt around in my knee for a pain and found none" (Cook, "Privacy", 298). But this is obviously not what happens. Thus W.'s tactic here resembles that in §443 and §545a.

§449 Worked up in Man. 116, 83–84. See I, 6; *PG* 73b, 74, 152c, 182e; *PB* 58b.

(a) See §§297, 300; Man. 116, 85 (quoted for §447); Ambrose, "Universals", 341a; Moore, *Problems,* 271b. "We don't get free of the idea that the sense of a sentence accompanies the sentence: is there alongside of it" (Z 139). We conceive the sense as "concentrated in a mental state of the speaker or hearer", especially his images (Man. 228, §71; see XII,1). The tendency is clear in Augustine, e.g.: "That which I behold is present; what I foretell is future—not that the sun is future, which already is; but its rising, which is not yet. Yet even its rising I could not predict unless I had an image of it in my mind (as I now have while I speak of it)" (*Confessions*, XI, 18, 24; see ibid., X, 8, 15; and 14–15, 21–23, e.g. the quote for §448b, above). W. himself had written: "Isn't it clear that the only condition for a sentence's having a sense is that its words have meaning, & this in turn means nothing else than that the external signs are connected with specific images or other processes . . . ?" (Man. 108, 290; see Man. 110, 168, 220). Soon afterwards he observed: "It would be important to give a general account of the error I am inclined to make in all these considerations. The false analogy from which it springs. . . . I believe that that error lies in the idea that the meaning of a word is an image which accompanies the word" (Man. 110, 229–30).

(b) See §§396, 459 (and commentary); *RFM* 6e–7a; cp. §120f; *BB* 153–157a.

   we *calculate* . . . : see *PG* 51b, 160de. Distinguish between the notion that a "sentence has sense only as a member of a system of language" (*BB* 42), which W. accepts, and the idea alluded to in §81b, that "in the mental act of thinking the calculus is there—all in a lump" (*BB* 42; see IX, 2).

§450   See *Z* 34; *EPB* 194; cp. *Z* 97. We not only translate words into pictures and vice versa (§449b), but we sometimes replace both with gestures (*PG* 42) or other actions (here). Cp. §459.

   but also . . . : W. applies a technique like that of *BB* 4, so as to avoid "at least partly the occult appearance of the processes of thinking".

   Need one imagine it . . . : see §285 and commentary.

   And isn't mimicking it just as good: for purposes of communication it might be far more effective (cp. p. 178g).

§451   Revised from Man. 116, 28. See GI 62; *BB* 3c, 12a, 50a; *PG* 90a; Man. 302, 26 (especially full); Man. 112, 172. "Only in the act of understanding," W., like others, had thought, "is it meant that we are to do THIS" (§431). Do we imagine the red circle twice, then, once to understand the order and the second time to obey it? If such representation is not necessary here, why suppose it is elsewhere? W. is still attacking the notion "that using a sentence involves imagining something for every word" (§449a).

§452   See GI 37; §430 (with which this number is connected in *PG* 132); *Z* 36, 56; cp. p. 217f.

   I want to say: not at the time of writing, but earlier: "My whole thought is always that if someone could see the expectation he would necessarily see what was being expected" (Man. 108, 271; cp. *PG* 132e). "(But in such a way that it doesn't further require a method of projection, a method of comparison, in order to pass from what he sees to the fact that is expected)" (*Z* 56).

   But that is the case: not because expectation contains such a super-picture (*LC* 67), but because "if the expectation was expressed by the statement that *p* would be the case, and the state of affairs which comes about is described by the sentence 'p', then the expectation has been fulfilled" (Man. 108, 271; see XV, 3–4; §§444–45 and commentary). However, even the most explicit verbal expression of what one expects is by itself insufficient evidence of expectation (cp. §641).

the expression: not just verbal expression (see the commentary on §445; cp. §§581–82), though that is the clearest clue: "Suppose I had written my intention down on a slip of paper, then someone else could have read it there. And can I imagine that he might in some way have found it out *more surely* than that? Certainly not" (*Z* 36).

in what other way . . . : not by observing the expected fact itself (*BB* 38) nor by looking into the other's mind (*Z* 36; §453). See *BB* 38a; cp. Man. 109, 203–4.

§453 See Man. 228, §203; cp. *PB* 72ab. As in the preceding number, the "voice of temptation" comes first, then the "voice of correctness" (GI 55).

who perceived my expectation: see GI 37, and Man. 108, 271 (first quotation for §452). Cp. Russell, *Mind,* 44: "Such things as desires and beliefs, which seem obvious to introspection, are not visible directly to external observation."

would not have to infer: he would see the form into which the fact fitted (*PB* 71), the model to which it conformed (ibid.); nothing extra would be required (see GI 37; IX, 2–3; commentary on §442; Man. 228, §53, quoted for §452). For the truth in all this, see *Z* 57.

makes no sense: cp. §246. One might fear a category mistake even in talk about perceiving someone's promise. But that is at least an act, whereas expectation is no such thing. "Some will perhaps want to say 'An expectation is a thought.' And we need to remember that the process of thinking may be *very various*" (*Z* 63; see 64–65).

Unless indeed it means . . . : see §§444–45, 452; cp. Man. 108, 215–16 (quoted for §444).

instead of saying: W. is contrasting two accounts of first-person psychological expressions, one treating them as reports of introspected processes or events, the other as avowals, that is, acts of expectation, hope, belief, and the like (see GI 15–16), forming an integral part of the expectation, hope, and so on (GI 45).

§454 See Man. 110, 76, 127–36.

(a) "Everything is already there . . .": see *PG* 93b–94a.

this arrow: cp. 3.144: "Propositions are like arrows—they have sense." "But as something intended—something to which a direction has been imparted" (*PG* 143; see commentary on §120b).

"not the dead line": cp. §432; *BB* 4d; *PG* 107a.

"only the psychical thing, the meaning . . .": see GI 37; §§102, 431; *BB* 4d (quoted for §339a), 34bc.

only in the application: there is no conflict with the bottom of p. 205; the word *points* as here used refers to more than the kind of psychic phenomena there described. Contrast "Go where the arrow points" with "Now I see it pointing" (cp. p. 205l). "Only dynamically is something a sign, not statically" (*PG* 55; cp. Z 173).
(b) See above ("only the psychical thing . . .").
§455   See Z 236; *PG* 148b.

We want to say . . . : to express "the concept of living activity as opposed to dead phenomena" (*PG* 156). "And if we say 'considered from without intention cannot be recognized as intention, etc.,' we wouldn't by any means wish to say that meaning is a special experience, but rather that it is not anything that happens, or happens to us, (for then it would be dead) but something we do" (ibid.). "But here we construct a false contrast between experience and something else, as though experience were a matter of sitting still and letting pictures pass before us" (*PG* 157). "If we had to name anything which is the life of the sign, we should have to say that it was its *use*" (*BB* 4).

We go up to . . . : see GI 37; §457; 2.1511–2.15121.
§456   See XXIV, 4; §§327, 436; Z 237; cp. p. 183b; *NB* 88jk. W. once thought this way himself (Man. 108, 186–87). So did James. The phrase about "rushing ahead" recalls *Principles*, I, 244: "The rush of thought is so headlong that it almost always brings us up at the conclusion before we can arrest it. Or if our purpose is nimble enough and we do arrest it, it ceases forthwith to be itself. . . . The attempt at introspective analysis in these cases is in fact like seizing a spinning top to catch its motion, or trying to turn up the gas quickly enough to see how the darkness looks." " 'The thinker cannot divide himself into two, of whom one reasons whilst the other observes him reason' " (ibid., 188). See also ibid., 300a; Stout, *Manual,* 18–19; Russell, *Mind,* 113b.

"(The subject—we want to say—does not here drop out of the experience, but is so much involved in it that the experience cannot be described.)

"It is almost as if one said: we can't see ourselves going hither and yon, since it is we who are doing the going (so we can't stand still and watch)" (*PG* 156). See the commentary on §120b ("only exterior facts").
§457   Yes: but not with the mind; thus the comparison is better than intended. The connection is made by means of bodily acts, such as pointing to the person, or having him pointed out on another occasion, or meeting him and shaking his hand. That is the type of varied background which makes the connection between one's words and their object (XV, 3–4).

"How is the connection made?—We imagine first a connection like strings. . . . It seems like a projection connection, which seems to make it indubitable, although there is not a projection relation at all. . . . The most important thing is this—if you talk of painting, etc. your idea is that the connection exists *now,* so that it seems as though as long as I do this thinking, this connection exists. Whereas, if we said it is a connection of convention, there would be no point in saying it exists while we think. There is a connection by convention—What do we mean?—This connection refers to events happening at various times. Most of all, it refers to a technique" (*LC* 67–68; paragraph division omitted; see *BB* 5; cp. §197). "The *calculus* of thought connects with reality outside of thought" (*PG* 160).

§458   See §437; *PG* 161e–162a; cp. §§194ab, 197, 444a; *PB* 66a; Man. 116, 74.

So it knows its execution . . . : the target is W.'s former viewpoint (see GI 36). "We suffer from a strange delusion that in the proposition, the thought, objects do what the proposition asserts of them. It's as if an order contained a shadow of its execution. But a shadow of just *this* execution. In the order it is *you* who go to such and such a place.—Otherwise it would just be a *different* order" (*PG* 103; see *PG* 159a). It is not enough for a mere image of you to go throught the ordered motions (cp. §§442–43).

that was a grammatical proposition: as W. judged all such necessary truths to be (§§371–73), and metaphysical truths like the agreement between thought and reality (Z 55, quoted for §429). Cp. *PG* 159a.

If an order runs . . . : see XV, 4; cp. commentary on §445. This simple, familiar fact (§129) W. finally took due note of in Man. 108, 240: "The solution to the puzzle must lie in the way the phenomenon is described when it occurs."

then executing . . . : rather: "then 'doing such-and-such' is called executing the order."

§459   This number is related to §458 as §449b is to §449a, and makes the same point: "We *calculate,* we operate with words." See Z 290–92 (e.g.: "Why should one not say here: There is an identity between the action and the *words*?! Why should I interpose a shadow between the two?"); *PG* 159b ("even this further description isn't there until I have derived it, and doesn't have a shadowy existence in the order itself"); cp. Z 227; *PG* 42c; *PB* 63a.

into action: "when he finally carries out the order to show he has understood it" (Man. 108, 189–90).

§460   For this new example (command rather than wish) W. momentarily attends again to the Russellian, extrinsic explanation (cp. commentary on §§440–41), which he long opposed with his picture theory

(GI 36), insisting on an "inner" connection between wish and fulfillment, command and execution, and so on. His final position synthetic-
ally joins the truth in both answers: As in Russell's account, the command does not precontain its execution (§§458, 461); as in the picture
theory, there is nonetheless a logical (linguistic) link between them
(§458).

The number is from *PG* 157e, a revision of Man. 110, 264. See *PB*
63e, 64b; cp. *Z* 68; *PG* 158b; *PB* 66a; Schlick, "Foundation", 222a,
223a.

§461   From *PG* 161c. See GI 36; *Z* 59, 60; *PG* 159–60 (quoted in part
for §437, which see); cp. §95 and quotations there.

(a) See *Z* 288–90.

By ordering *just that* . . . : such (practically *verbatim*) was W.'s initial
answer in Man. 110, 69–70.

But one would have to . . . : see GI 34; XV, 5.

is to say nothing: see §352a; 4.461 ("For example, I know nothing
about the weather when I know that it is either raining or not raining"); cp. §13.

(b) See GI 34; XV, 1; cp. *Z* 62; Man. 108, 203 (quoted for §95).

"still it does . . .": again, W. is quoting his own words, in Man. 110,
70–71. The rest of §461 follows shortly thereafter.

surprised: "If it strikes you as strange, compare it with something
with which it is not comparable.—For instance this: How can I now
shake the hand of a man who will arrive in five minutes? Or: How can I
shake the hand of a man who perhaps doesn't exist?" (Man. 110, 69;
see quotes for §462a).

but at his being able . . . : see Man. 302, 19, quoted for §518b; cp.
Man. 108, 229: "For insofar as reality is describable, expectation describes it & insofar as reality is foreseeable, expectation foresees it."

(c) foreshadowed the future: see e.g. GI 36; §§94, 437; *PG* 136c; 3.02.

cannot know less than nothing: for want of even the "pure intermediary" (§94), the logical shadow. It isn't as though we saw no man
ahead of us, but at least heard his voice (*PG* 109). Cp. §521 ("cannot
have less than no combination").

§462   From *PG* 138a. See GI 34; quotes for §95 (especially Man. 109,
46); *EPB* 195; *BB* 129h–130d; *PB* 67e; Man. 110, 274–76; cp. §§518,
689d; *Z* 69.

(a) "Compare 'I expect him' and 'I shoot him.' We can't shoot him if he
isn't there. This is how the question arises: 'How can we expect something that is not the case?', 'How can we expect a fact which does not
exist?' " (*BB* 35–36). "The feeling expressed in the sentences above is: I
can't catch a thief who doesn't yet exist; how can I sit on a chair which
doesn't exist? And that only shows, of course, that we see a false anal-

ogy here; i.e. think we see an analogy where there is none" (Man. 108, 266). See Man. 110, 69, quoted for §461b.

(b) Ultimately from Man. 110, 274. See *PG* 137b.

One might want to say . . . : perhaps emphasizing the "him" ("After all, we are not looking for anyone or anything else, but just *him*").

§463   Polished form of *PG* 138c and Man. 110, 275–76. See §462 and references; *PG* 359–65; *PB* 175–77, 334; *Kreis,* 143; Man. 159 (e.g.: " 'He not only cannot do it, he cannot even try,' means: I will recognize no process as success in the attempt & accordingly none as the attempt"); Waismann, *Principles,* 391–96; cp. *PB* 178f, 190a.

in mathematics: see *PB* 184–85, 227h–228a; cp. *RFM* 147i; *PB* 170a. In Man. 108, 158, and *PG* 363–64 W. wrote: "We might put it this way: If I am looking for something—I mean, the north pole, or a house in London—I can *fully* describe what I am looking for before I have found it (or have found that it isn't there), and this description will be logically unobjectionable in either case. Whereas when I 'look for' something in mathematics, yet not *within* a system, what I am looking for cannot be described, or can only apparently be described; for if I could describe it in every particular, I would already actually *have* it, and before it is *fully* described I cannot be sure whether *what* I am looking for is logically unobjectionable, so can be described at all. That is, this incomplete description leaves out just what would be necessary in order for something to be capable of being looked for at all." "What we did bore an external resemblance to seeking, no doubt, but was an entirely different sort of thing. . . . It wasn't seeking at all, any more than I can seek to wiggle my ears. The only thing I can do is to move my eyebrows, brow, and neighboring parts, in the hope that my ears too will move" (*PB* 329; *Kreis,* 136; cp. *BB* 129–30).

how was it possible . . . : W. himself had declared it impossible (*Kreis,* 36–37).

the trisection of the angle: here too there is no such thing, yet people have looked for it (§334). See Man. 219, 10; *Kreis,* 204–5 (where W. attacked the idea that something "analogous" is sought); *PP* 304–5 (where he contrasted looking for the method of trisecting the angle, which cannot exist, with looking for a unicorn, which does not exist); cp. Man. 112, 57–62.

§464   The movement is illustrated in §462b. "Disguised nonsense has a surface air of plausibility and naturalness about it, so that it can take in even a sensible man. It has the semblance of sense. But when one examines it carefully and follows out its consequences, its inherent absurdity becomes manifest" (Pitcher, "Carroll", 316). Cp. Anscombe, *Introduction,* 151, quoted for §216c.

Concerning the apparent contrast with §524c, see the commentary on that number.

nonsense: cp. §119.

§465   A reworking of *PG* 161d, and ultimately of Man. 109, 170–72. See *PG* 214; Man. 108, 159, 266; cp. §352; *NB* 22e; Man. 138, 29A; Man. 108, 219–20, 229, 241; Russell, *Inquiry*, 83.

(a) See §437 and references there; *PG* 132b; *PB* 70g–71a; Man. 108, 250–51.

(b) is it defined . . . : rather: "Is it determined which answer [yes or no] an expectation receives from whatever event may occur?" The expectation of a red circle (Man. 109, 170) is answered negatively by a green circle, affirmatively by a red one. But what verdict does the same green circle give if I expect a red circle *or* a thundershower? "Undecided."

"for example": some other varieties and examples of indefiniteness:
(1)   "If I say, 'that will probably happen,' is this proposition verified by its happening or falsified by its not happening? Obviously not, I believe" (*PB* 289).
(2)   " 'Yes' and 'No' divide the field of possibilities in two parts.—And naturally that need not be the case. ('Have you stopped beating your wife?')" (Man. 229, §940).
(3)   "I assert: 'If *this* happens, *that* will happen. If I am right, you pay me a shilling, if I am wrong, I pay you one, if it remains undecided, neither pays.' This might also be expressed like this: The case in which the antecedent does *not* come true does not interest us, we aren't talking about it" (Z 677).
(4)   "Many sentences express cognitive attitudes without being propositions; and the difference between saying yes or no to them is not the difference between saying yes or no to a proposition. This is even true of the ordinary hypothetical . . . and much more of the variable hypothetical" (Ramsey, *Foundations*, 239–40; see 246–47).
(5)   "Some day, man will certainly go to Mars" (cp. Man. 108, 138; *PB* 294).
    See Man. 229, §§935–39; cp. *Kreis*, 40.

"a disjunction": as W. was aware (*NB* 38d; Man. 111, 97), facts are defined one way or the other by (definite) disjunction, in the sense that it is determined for whatever event may occur whether it fulfills the disjunction. Hence the importance of the rewording above.

It may be noted that though the author of the *Tractatus* made allowance for disjunction, he tended to take the simple, atomic proposition as his paradigm, so continued to make assertions which a disjunction or hypothetical would hardly have suggested to him. For instance: "It is here always as though something were already done before it is done"

(Man. 108, 252; see Z 58; GI 36). Clearly he did not suppose that a *disjunction* was performed in advance. And as for picture-thinking (XII, 1) "how can we hallucinate a person taking one road *or* another?" (Man. 108, 258; my italics).

"of different possibilities": different in a strong sense. If the disjunction were "red or blue circle", any color (for instance green) would yield a decisive verdict, yes or no, but not if the disjunction were "red circle or *earthquake*".

XVI. Bedrock: "This Game Is Played" (§§466–497)

GENERAL COMMENTARY

(1)   Russell and Moore defined the mental in terms of intentionality, the topic of the preceding section (XV, 1). James took a different view: *"The pursuance of future ends and the choice of means for their attainment are . . . the mark and criterion of the presence of mentality* in a phenomenon" (*Principles*, I, 8). This would seem to imply that our thinking, beliefs, and uses of words are all pragmatically motivated. It suggests furthermore that *"our fundamental ways of thinking about things are discoveries of exceedingly remote ancestors, which have been able to preserve themselves throughout the experience of all subsequent time"* (*Pragmatism*, 170). They are among the great inventions of mankind.

(2)   Wittgenstein's standard objection to such accounts is that they are unilateral, simplistic; we nourish our thinking with only one kind of example (§593 and commentary). The institution of royalty provides a helpful comparison. Kings are often useful, and royal lines have sometimes been initiated for that reason, as in the Old Testament account; but others have started otherwise, and in any case kingship cannot be defined in terms of its utility. So it is with thinking, language, beliefs, concepts. Thus "what I have to do," wrote Wittgenstein, "is something like: to describe the office of a king;—in doing which I must never fall into the error of explaining the kingly dignity by the king's usefulness, but I must leave neither his usefulness nor his dignity out of account" (*RFM* 160; translation slightly altered). It is in this spirit that he considers first thinking, then beliefs, and finally language. I shall follow the same order.

(3)   "The ultimate purpose of thought," wrote Ramsey, "is to guide our

action" (*Foundations*, 245). But isn't thought itself an activity? "And this too is important: if I get the number 15 as answer, so make the boiler 15 mm. thick, the construction of the boiler *is another step in this calculus* and not something entirely different" (*Kreis*, 172). The thinking, the speaking, the making are all parts of the language-game, all forms of life (§23b). And "do we live because it is practical to live? Do we think because thinking is practical?" (*RFM* 171; see §467). Sometimes, yes, but it would be absurd to say we always do (§470).

(4)   Furthermore, we should not suppose that the whole broad practice of calculating pragmatically in accordance with the laws of nature is a form of life we have reflectively adopted (*OC* 317; *RFM* 6c; §466). Wittgenstein would have subscribed in general to Ramsey's remarks: "Among the habits of the human mind a position of peculiar importance is occupied by induction. Since the time of Hume a great deal has been written about the justification for inductive inference. Hume showed that it could not be reduced to deductive inference or justified by formal logic. So far as it goes his demonstration seems to me final; and the suggestion of Mr Keynes that it can be got round by regarding induction as a form of probable inference cannot in my view be maintained. But to suppose that the situation which results from this is a scandal to philosophy is, I think, a mistake" (*Foundations*, 196–97). To these observations Wittgenstein might want merely to add a warning about the expression "inductive inference": We should not imagine that beliefs for which inductive reasons could be given typically result from such reasoning (§§472–73, 477–79).

(5)   While recognizing how unreflective our beliefs generally are, Russell felt that they should at least run parallel to some discoverable logical inference (*Problems*, 78). "If we are to be able to draw inferences from these data—if we are to know of the existence of matter, of other people, of the past before our individual memory begins, or of the future, we must know general principles of some kind by means of which such inferences can be drawn. It must be known to us that the existence of some one one sort of thing, A, is a sign of the existence of some other sort of thing, B, either at the same time as A or at some earlier or later time, as, for example, thunder is a sign of the earlier existence of lightning. If this were not known to us, we could never extend our knowledge beyond the sphere of our private experience; and this sphere, as we have seen, is exceedingly limited. The question we have now to consider is whether such an extension is possible, and if so, how it is effected" (ibid., 33). How can we turn mere animal assurance into *knowledge*?

(6)   Wittgenstein himself had once spoken this way. "The procedure of induction . . . has no logical justification, but only a psychological

one. It is clear that there are no grounds for believing that the simplest eventually will in fact be realized" (6.363–6.3631). Hence "it is an hypothesis that the sun will rise tomorrow: and this means that we do not *know* whether it will rise" (6.36311). In the *Investigations* he brought the word *know* back to its everyday use (§§116, 246, 481c) and thereby resolved the purely verbal problem. More basic was the need Russell and others felt to somehow 'justify' induction. As usual, Wittgenstein's response was not simply to deny that justification is necessary, but to probe the meaning of the demand. "If *these* are not grounds, then what are grounds?" (§481). Russell had a picture which seemed to make the sense of his search unmistakable (cp. §352): The problem of induction was "to see why we should believe it to be a valid logical process" (*Outline*, 14). Yet he was unable to fill out the picture and "state what must be the case for us to have the right to say that there are grounds for our assumption" (§481). We cannot give a ground for every ground (§§483–85; I, 4), nor finally intuit a *logical* connection between *events* (6.37; §372). "The limits of empiricism," Wittgenstein therefore concluded (in reference to Russell's article of that title), "are not assumptions unguaranteed, or intuitively known to be correct: they are ways in which we make comparisons and in which we act" (*RFM* 176).

(7) Wittgenstein's comparison of language with games (I, 2–7) reflects similar thinking. Against this assimilation it is frequently objected that "games, in contrast to language, have no function whatever important for life. They serve no serious end; nor do they belong to the 'form of life' of a society. Games are thus in no way an 'instrument', whereas language is essentially an instrument" (Specht, on H. Smart, in *Foundations*, 47). Wittgenstein was familiar with this point of view (*Kreis*, 170), for instance in Frege (*Writings*, 185b), and in Ogden and Richards, who wrote: "Language, though often spoken of as a medium of communication, is best regarded as an instrument" (*Meaning*, 98). So he briefly assesses it in the final numbers of this section.

(8) What does it mean to say that language is "essentially an instrument"? Was it invented, the way an instrument is, for a particular purpose (§492)? And is it now reflectively employed for just that purpose? So do people talk because it is useful to talk? And are jokes, cheers, poetry, gossip, storytelling, and the rest "nonessential" uses of speech? Wittgenstein's reaction to such simplifications resembled Mauthner's: "What nearly all investigators of language, one after another, subscribe to, namely that language is an instrument of our thinking (and a remarkable instrument at that), strikes me as mythology. In this view, which populates all heads these days, somewhere beneath the stream of language there sits a godhead . . . , so-called thought, which, guided by the promptings of a similar godhead, logic, rules over

human speech with the help of a third godhead, grammar" (*Beiträge*, I, 11; see 15–16). "A language-game," Wittgenstein agreed, "does not have its origin in *consideration*. Consideration is part of a language-game" (Z 391). Thus it cannot be maintained in general that we have the concepts we have, for instance psychological concepts like *pain* (Man. 229, §1335), because it has proved advantageous to have them (Z 700). "And yet we do have *certain* concepts on that account, we have introduced them on that account" (ibid.; cp. Man. 138, 20B; §132).

(9) Wittgenstein took interest in such facts of language because they affect the concept *language;* that was his chief concern (p. 230a; GI 49). Like Schlick, who equated the nature of language with the set of properties which permitted it to "serve a common purpose" ("Form", 152), he had been inclined to define language in terms of its purpose (*PB* 51; Man. 108, 97). But he later declared: "Language is not defined for us as an arrangement fulfilling a definite purpose" (Z 322). More crucial is regularity (I, 8). Thus "a language-game can lose its sense through a contradiction, can lose the character of a language-game. And here it is important to say that this character is not described by saying that the sounds must have a certain *effect*. For our language-game (2) would lose the character of a language-game if the builders kept on uttering different sounds instead of the 4 orders; even if it could be shewn, say physiologically, that it was always these noises that moved the assistant to bring the stones that he did bring" (RFM 103). "It is *primarily* the apparatus of our ordinary language . . . that we call language; and then other things by analogy or comparability with this" (§494). And in a jumble of sounds and actions like that described there is not the regularity of what we call language (§207).

(10) "Even here it could be said that of course the examination of language-games gets its importance from the fact that language-games continue to function. And so that it gets its importance from the fact that human beings can be trained to such a reaction to sounds" (RFM 103; cp. §495). In the *Investigations* Wittgenstein stressed the workings of language (§§363, 491, 520); compared words with tools (§§11, 23, 421, 569); and was inclined to say: "The game has not only rules but also a point" (§564). But "*essence* is expressed by grammar" (§371), and the grammar of the word *language* does not emphasize utility in the way the remarks of Smart and Schlick suggest. When philosophers use a word like *language* "and try to grasp the *essence* of the thing, one must always ask oneself: is the word ever actually used in this way in the language-game which is its original home?" (§116). His answer here is that it could be but isn't (§492). Thus when he remarked that "for us" language is not an arrangement fulfilling a definite purpose (Z 322) he was not expressing a mere personal choice of perspective but was re-

turning another key word to its home. "Why don't I call cookery rules arbitrary, and why am I tempted to call the rules of grammar arbitrary? Because 'cookery' is defined by its end, whereas 'speaking' is not. That is why the use of language is in a certain sense autonomous, as cooking and washing are not" (Z 320; see I, 3–4).

DETAILED COMMENTARY

§466 See XVI, 2–4; *PG* 109b; *Kreis,* 171–72; Man. 302, 22. As in the preceding number, W.'s critique is aimed at a passage in Man. 109, this time pp. 72–73: "What do we think for, for that will show whether thinking is an important affair. It is perfectly clear that we think for a purpose. The purpose of thinking evidently consists in directing my actions by it & indeed just as I guide them by the calculation for a boiler. This calculation, too, is a thought act." "Thinking means making a plan & working with it" (ibid., 77).

not interested in causes: cp. *PG* 105a. On the difference between cause and ground, see §325 and references.

Oh, yes: boilers so made do sometimes explode; and the regularities of nature are not logical necessities (XVI, 4–6). "So do we adopt the calculus arbitrarily? No more than our fear of fire" (*PG* 110). " 'But surely you believe, all the same, that there would be more boiler explosions if people didn't calculate when they made them!'—Yes, I believe it;—but what does that signify? Does it follow that there will in fact be fewer explosions?—And what then is the basis of this belief?" (ibid.). "We can base one thought on others, but not thinking. It is this fact, I believe, which makes our inquiry purely descriptive" (Man. 110, 235).

§467 See XVI, 3; the preceding quotations; James, *Principles,* II, 386c–387a; cp. p. 188q; *OC* 170; *RFM* 44h–45a; *PG* 109c. Note the connection with Schopenhauer's "conception of the intellect . . . as being 'exclusively intended for practical ends' " (Gardiner, *Schopenhauer,* 141). "What puts into activity the association of ideas itself . . . is the *will.* This drives its servant, the intellect, according to its powers to link one idea on to another, to recall the similar and the simultaneous, and to recognize grounds and consequents. For it is in the interest of the will that we should generally think, so that we may be in the best possible situation for all the cases that arise" (Schopenhauer, *World,* II, 136).

Sir Frederic Bartlett, a Cambridge professor, wrote: "I propose to adopt here the view that thinking is a high-level cognitive form of behavior, and an achievement effected only at a relatively advanced stage of development when, and because, simpler and more direct methods of dealing with environmental demands have broken down. This is a position, foreseen long ago by a few people, that is now coming to be widely accepted in professional psychological circles" (Whittaker, *Introduction*, 320).

§468 "Naturally the question is about grounds, not about causes" (*PG* 110). And the grounds would belong to an ungrounded system of grounds (I, 5). Thus the implicit lesson is that of §654. Hence the adversative opening of §469 ("And yet . . .").

§469 See XVI, 2–3; *OC* 603.

§470 *sometimes:* universalization is the disease to avoid (GI 43).

"As regards Frazer's *Golden Bough*, the chief points on which he seemed to wish to insist were, I think, the three following: (1) That it was a mistake to suppose that there was *only one* 'reason', in the sense of 'motive', which led people to perform a particular action—to suppose that there was 'one motive, which was *the* motive'. . . . But he said that the tendency to suppose that there is 'one motive which is *the* motive' was 'enormously strong', giving as an instance that there are theories of play each of which gives *only one* answer to the question 'Why do children play?' (2) That it was a mistake to suppose that *the* motive is always 'to get something useful'. He gave as an instance of this mistake Frazer's supposition that 'people at a certain stage thought it useful to kill a person, in order to get a good crop'. . . ." (*PP* 315).

because: for further indication of the sense, cp. *OC* 474: "This game proves its worth. That may be the cause of its being played, but it is not the ground."

§471 See IV, 3; commentary on §109 ("we must do away with all explanation"); *Z* 671; *EPB* 129; *BB* 88b; *PP* 314a; cp. §§480, 486b; *RFM* 170g; *BB* 169d; *PP* 323b; James, *Principles*, I, 2–3 (nearly a full page of *why*'s); Schopenhauer, *World*, I, 82 (the what of the world versus its purpose). *PG* 110c throws much light on this observation, as a link between the preceding numbers, on reasons for thought, and the following ones, on the grounds of belief. The remark is relevant to both.

"This question is an utterance of unclarity, of mental discomfort, and it is comparable with the question 'Why?' as children so often ask it. This too is an expression of a mental discomfort, and doesn't necessarily ask for either a cause or a reason" (*BB* 26).

"He said that our puzzlement as to why it impresses us is not diminished by giving the *causes* from which the festival arose, but is diminished by finding other similar festivals: to find these may make it seem 'natural', whereas to give the causes from which it arose cannot do this" (*PP* 315–16; cp. §524).

"Not that it is useless to ask 'Why?' But this question creates the false impression that we have a method for replying where as yet we have none. We do not yet know what could be called an explanation of this fact. The question tells us: 'Don't stop, go on (in this direction)!' " (Man. 130, 59).

"I believe that the attempt to explain is already wrong, since we need only put together what we *know* and add nothing to it, and the satisfaction which we seek through an explanation will come of its own accord" (BUF 235; cp. §§122–23).

"Thus we see the problem in the *how*" (Man. 229, §1034; see Man. 228, 102–3; contrast with 5.552). A classic illustration: "But why would we use the same word if there weren't something common?" (see *PG* 75a; *EPB* 220). The reply: "See how we do use the word, and you will find the answer." In this sense, "we are interested in the that, not the why" (Man. 116, 344).

§472   See XVI, 4; *LC* 56i (quoted for §473); cp. Russell, *Mind,* 77. Numbers 472–74 come from *PG* 109d, slightly altered; §472 appears already in *PB* 285.

belief in the uniformity of nature: "The problem we have to discuss is whether there is any reason for believing in what is called 'the uniformity of nature'. The belief in the uniformity of nature is the belief that everything that has happened or will happen is an instance of some general law to which there are *no* exceptions" (Russell, *Problems,* 35).

"What does it mean to follow this principle? Do we really introduce it into our reasoning? Or is it merely the *natural law* which our inferring apparently follows? This latter it may be. It is not an item in our considerations" (OC 135).

"The squirrel does not infer by induction that it is going to need stores next winter as well. And no more do we need a law of induction to justify our actions or our predictions" (*OC* 287).

in which we fear: see §473.

only in the past: which does not precontain or logically entail the future (IX, 1). "There is no compulsion making one thing happen because another has happened" (6.37).

§473   They are not based on observation, reflection, or intuition of the causal nexus. See XVI, 4; Man. 302, 21. The line of thought, and the example, are Russell's: "Scientific theories of induction generally try to substitute well-chosen instances for numerous instances, and represent number of instances as belonging to crude popular induction. But in fact popular induction depends upon the emotional interest of the instances, not upon their number. A child who has burnt its hand *once* in a candle-flame establishes an induction" (*Philosophy,* 269; see 80–84). Doubtless Russell had read James (*Principles,* I, 25).

"A man would fight for his life not to be dragged into the fire. No induction. Terror. That is, as it were, part of the substance of the belief" (*LC* 56).

§474   Ultimately from Man. 111, 121. See the paragraph which follows this on *PG* 109.

(a) If certainty is psychological, how is it that kinds of certainty differ logically? See the commentary on p. 224c.

(b) Concerning the parenthetical remark, which in view of §371 may seem problematical: If someone is unsure about the meaning of *X* and you use a sample to give him an ostensive definition, he thereby learns the meaning of *X*; but if he then examines the sample, he is not examining the meaning, nor learning merely how the word is used. Compare: "Only someone who has been in combat knows what war really means"—though others know the meaning of the word. See *LC* 56 (quoted for §473); cp. §578, p. 209m; *OC* 45 ("We got to know the *nature* of calculating by learning to calculate"); *PB* 236d; Man. 138, 3A, 6B.

§475   See §325, p. 215d; *OC* 429; *EPB* 161–62; *BB* 110–11; *PP* 317; cp. p. 224k (motive and cause); *Z* 437. This distinction, often noted by W., was strongly stressed by Schopenhauer (Gardiner, *Schopenhauer*, 70–74).

Both answers require reflection, and the facts one cites as grounds may have preceded the reflection, as did the causes; but see the distinction in §479. Furthermore, even when the grounds are a path actually followed in reaching the supposition, one need not consult empirical regularities and coincidences, as in the case of causes, to determine whether the antecedents were grounds (Man. 302, 20). Yet does simple observation of the one-time process show me that those thoughts were the grounds of my conclusion? (Cp. §490, which precedes §475 in Man. 228.)

§476   See *Z* 488–89, 492c; *LC* 14g; Man. 108, 184–86; Anscombe, "Intention", 323; Gosling, "Causes"; cp. *LC* 14–15; Man. 110, 21–22 (similar remarks about worry, hate), 23 (one may be unsure about the cause of one's hate, but not about its object); Man. 108, 275–76; Russell, *Outline*, 210d–211a, 226–27; Moore, *Principia*, 69–70; Köhler, *Gestalt*, 353, 360, and *Mentality*, 244–45 ("It is commonly said that all emotional behaviour is 'directed towards an object', meaning that it is that object that calls forth the feeling").

JN 76 makes the connection with §475: "Giving a motive is like naming the object of a fear." There too no causal calculation is required, and no doubt or error is possible (Man. 108, 184–85, below). And though the cause may be the target, it need not be and often is not. As for §477: A belief, like fear, may have no reasons.

(a) the object: "Among emotions the directed might be distinguished from the undirected. Fear *at* something, joy *over* something" (Z 488). W. felt that James's anlaysis in terms of bodily feelings left out the objective aspect of emotions (Man. 229, §§1395–98). "If anyone asks whether pleasure is a sensation, he probably does not distinguish between reason and cause, for otherwise it would occur to him that one takes pleasure *in something,* which does not mean that this something produces a sensation in us" (Z 507). So too, " 'I am glad that you are coming' does not mean I am glad because you are coming" (Man. 108, 200).

(b) not on that account: though cause and object might be identical in this case, and often are in others (Z 492), we may not generalize. "The language-game 'I am afraid' already contains the object" (Z 489; cp. XV, 3–4; §§166b, 490, p. 177), but not the cause (cp. Man. 108, 200, above). And on the other hand "we could describe all that happens when we cry [including the immediate causes] without mentioning what we are crying about" (*BB* 22). Thus " 'to be angry about something' is not related to the object of anger as an effect is to its cause, so not as an upset stomach is related to the food that upset it. A person can be uncertain about the cause of his upset stomach & the food that caused it does not enter the stomachache as a constituent of the stomachache, whereas in a certain sense a person cannot doubt about the object of his anger, fear, or belief. (One doesn't say, 'I don't know'—'Today I believe, but I don't know what'!)—And here of course we have the old problem, namely that the thought that such & such is the case does not presuppose that it is the case" (Man. 108, 184–85; cp. p. 221c). (Thus I can fear something that perhaps will never occur—but not as a result of something that never happened.)

§477   Have you reasons . . . . : see XVI, 4; cp. §607, p. 215d.

   do you need reasons?: see §§325b, 485; cp. XVI, 6.

§478   With §477, this prepares the distinction in §479. One "produces" these hundred reasons, "bethinks oneself of them" (§475); they are not premises in a deduction. See §325.

§479   See §480; OC 135 (quoted for §472); Z 659; LC 22c; BB 14c (e.g.: "Giving a reason for something one did or said means showing a *way* which leads to this action. In some cases it means telling the way which one has gone oneself; in others it means describing a way which leads there and is in accordance with certain accepted rules"); PP 317; Frege, *Foundations,* 3b; Russell, *Outline,* 83–84; cp. Russell, *Problems,* 35.

§480   But how *can* . . . : "If inferences as to the future *are* valid, what principle must be invoked in making them?" (Russell, *External World,* 225). See XVI, 5.

   I refer you to the *effect:* see Russell, *Outline,* 83–84; cp. Frege, *Foun-*

dations, 16 ("whereas our habits are determined by the number and strength of the impressions we receive and by subjective circumstances, which have no sort of right at all to influence our judgement").

§481   See XVI, 6; *RFM* 179; Strawson, *Introduction,* 248–63; Ramsey, *Foundations,* 191–94.

Within the general Humean perspective which was W.'s, it is not merely that we fail to find a necessary connection in reality; rather, it is not conceivable that we should, that is, that temporal sequences should be logical sequences. The rationalist "ideal" is not even that (Man. 228, 131, quoted for §485). Various things might be said for the inductive approach—that it works (§466), that only past regularity *could* serve us as guide, and so on—but nothing for the sort of ultimate, unquestionable foundation which philosophers like Frege and Russell have vaguely envisaged and postulated.

(a) If anyone said . . . : as Russell did: "All scientific laws rest upon induction, which, considered as a logical process, is open to doubt, and not capable of giving certainty" (*Outlook,* 67).

could not convince him: or provides no basis for conviction, though, willy-nilly, he believes nonetheless.

I should not understand him: cp. §398b.

One might ask him . . . : "A more reasonable approach would consist in investigating instead the nature of the principle, and in trying to exhibit as accurately as possible its functions in guiding and structuring our thinking and experience. Such is the course Schopenhauer himself undertakes to pursue" (Gardiner, *Schopenhauer,* 75).

What do you call "conviction"?: in such discussions, the term *conviction,* like *certain* and *certainty,* tends to take on a logical sense rather than the more familiar psychological one. But a logical sense is determined by rules of evidence, and none are provided by the person who demands better evidence than phenomenal correlations.

then you must surely be able . . . : Russell, for example, did suggest principles which would justify induction—provided the principles themselves could be justified. The attempt to discover the foundation of induction is comparable to the primitive supposition that the Earth must rest on something, though of course no support proves satisfactory, since each would have to rest on something else (*PG* 110).

(b) See XVI, 4; §183; cp. pp. 224cdef, 225e; *OC* 27; *RFM* 193h; *PB* 289–90; 5.135–5.1361, 6.3631; *PP* 293b–294a; Russell, *External World,* 43; Schlick, "Causality", 521.

"There are in fact many ways," wrote Russell, "besides logical inference, by which we pass from one belief to another: the passage from the print to its meaning illustrates these ways. These ways may be called 'psychological inference'. We shall, then, admit such psychological inference as a means of obtaining derivative knowledge, provided there is a discoverable logical inference which runs parallel to the psychological inference" (*Problems,* 78). That is, writes W., "I must only infer what really *follows*!—Is this supposed to mean: only what follows, going by rules of inference; or is it supposed to mean: only what follows, going by *such* rules of inference as somehow agree with some (sort of) reality? Here what is before our minds in a vague way is that this reality is something very abstract, very general, and very rigid. Logic is a kind of ultra-physics, the description of the 'logical structure' of the world, which we perceive through a kind of ultra-experience (with the understanding e.g.). Here perhaps inferences like the following come to mind: 'The stove is smoking, so the chimney is out of order again.' (And *that* is how this conclusion is drawn! Not like this: 'The stove is smoking, and whenever the stove smokes the chimney is out of order; and so. . . .')" (*RFM* 6).

(c) See Malcolm, *Memoir,* 88a; cp. *OC* 338; *PB* 285b; *NB* 43 (quoted for §437); Malcolm, "Certainty", 22; Nicod, *Foundations,* 214; Jeans, *Universe,* 123–24.

"Or are we to say that *certainty* is merely a constructed point to which some things approximate more, some less closely? No. Doubt gradually loses its sense. This language-game just *is* like that. And everything descriptive of a language-game is part of logic" (*OC* 56).

"For it is not a question of support falling generally short of entailment; of entailment being the perfection of support. They are not related as the winner to the runner-up and the rest in the same race. The perfection of support is proof, but not deductive proof; it is conclusive evidence" (Strawson, *Introduction,* 238).

"In spite of this nearly all philosophical thought about human logic and especially induction has tried to reduce it in some way to formal logic. Not that it is supposed, except by a very few, that consistency will of itself lead to truth; but consistency combined with observations and memory is frequently credited with this power" (Ramsey, *Foundations,* 191–92).

"According to Mr. Keynes valid deductive and inductive arguments are fundamentally alike; both are justified by logical relations between premiss and conclusion which differ only in degree. This position, as I have already explained, I cannot accept" (ibid., 185; cp. *LR* 112).

The type of viewpoint criticized appears also in Broad ("Two Lectures", 71) and in Russell: "The most we can hope is that the oftener things are found together, the more probable it becomes that they will be found together another time, and that, if they have been found together often enough, the probability will amount *almost* to certainty. It can never quite reach certainty, because we know that in spite of frequent repetitions there sometimes is a failure at the last. . . . Under the same circumstances, a sufficient number of cases of association will make the probability of a fresh association nearly a certainty, and will make it approach certainty without limit" (*Problems*, 36–37; see *External World*, 225–26; *Philosophy*, 269).

See also the *Tractatus:* "Certain, possible, impossible: here we have the first indication of the scale that we need in the theory of probability" (4.464). "We use probability only in default of certainty—if our knowledge of a fact is not indeed complete, but we do know *something* about its form" (5.156). Thus "it is an hypothesis that the sun will rise tomorrow: and this means we do not *know* whether it will rise" (6.36311). "The connexion between knowledge and thing known is *the* connexion of logical necessity" (*NB* 43). See Black, *Companion*, 251–58.

Waismann's treatment echoed and developed these suggestions. "Three cases must be distinguished. Either P is so constituted that we can infer *q* in a purely logical fashion. This happens when we predict an event from known data on the basis of specific natural laws. Or P contradicts *q;* we then say that such an occurrence is excluded by the laws of nature. In neither of these two cases do we speak of probability. Probability makes its appearance only where we know something about the circumstances in which the event occurs but where this knowledge does not suffice to make certain assertions" ("Analyse", 237).

§482   See the preceding quotations; *PB* 289–90; Russell, *Mind,* 89.

this way of putting it: or the reverse: "Provided that the proposition in question does render it *positively probable* that they exist, then, if it also conforms to the conditions which I am about to mention, I shall call it a 'good reason' " (Moore, *Studies,* 41).

"makes the occurrence of the event probable": see Russell, *Outline,* 282–86, and *External World,* 45–46. "As Imre Lakatos has pointed out, the Cambridge School of Inductive Logicians, of which Broad, Keynes, and Johnson are the best known members, triumphantly stated (almost without argument) that a valid inductive inference is one in which the evidence makes probable the hypothesis to a certain degree" (Smokler, Review, 47, citing Lakatos, "Changes", 323; cp. *LR* 112). Moore (*Lectures,* 51) debated Broad's claim that "*unless* inductive conclusions be expressed in terms of probability all inductive inference involves a formal fallacy" (Broad, *Induction,* 1). W.'s verdict: "The calculation of the probability can only cast the natural law in a different form. It transforms the natural law" (*PB* 290).

is to say nothing except . . . : "We can state it this way: statistical causal analysis presupposes a fundamental system within which it moves and which it leaves unchanged; this neither is nor appears to be treated like a proposition. What appears to be so treated is a narrower system derived or derivable from the fundamental system by the addition of an empirical premiss, and what is really treated as a proposition and modified or rejected is not the narrower system but the empirical premiss on which it is based" (Ramsey, *Foundations*, 210). Cp. *RFM* 193h.

but the standard has no grounds: this is a main theme of *OC;* see the quotations and citations under §485. "People today stop at the laws of nature, treating them as something inviolable, just as God and Fate were treated in past ages. And in fact both are right and both wrong: though the view of the ancients is clearer in so far as they have a clear and acknowledged terminus, while the modern system tries to make it look as if *everything* were explained" (6.372, continuing 6.371; see *NB* 72hij). Russell, recognizing that "the inductive principle . . . . is equally incapable of being *proved* by an appeal to experience" (*Problems*, 38), sought in vain some other way "to justify inferences from experience" (*External World*, 46), deductively, by means of general principles (ibid., 43).

§483 See Ramsey, *Foundations*, 197b. Russell is still the paradigm target: "Unfortunately, no one has hitherto shown any good reason for supposing that this sort of inference is sound" (*Outlook*, 75–76). Indeed, "we have no very good reason to feel sure that there will be a future" (*Logic*, 134).

"Is it wrong for me to be guided in my actions by the propositions of physics? Am I to say I have no good ground for doing so? Isn't precisely this what we call a 'good ground'?" (*OC* 608). "Sure evidence is what we *accept* as sure, it is evidence that we go by in *acting* surely, acting without any doubt" (*OC* 196). Not that some reasoning is not better, more reliable; "but the standard has no grounds" (§482). "The difficulty is to realize the groundlessness of our believing" (*OC* 166). "The reasonable man does *not have* certain doubts" (*OC* 220; see 294–98).

Such observations may sound like an apologia for popular indolence and naiveté, and may seem "to represent inductive, as well as deductive, inference as a matter of linguistics, and the sceptic about induction . . . either as contradicting himself or as proposing a revision of language" (Ewing, "Pseudo-Solutions", 43). However, such an assessment would miss W.'s main points: (1) the demand for further justification is a blind demand, which cannot possibly be satisfied (XVI, 6); (2) for it is not intelligible (§§481, 485, and comments).

like this: like the ground in question, a sample of good grounds.
§484 Cp. *PG* 227d; *PB* 290ab, 291b; 5.153; Waismann, "Analyse", 239–40; Russell, *Outlook*, 74: "The plain man thinks that matter is solid, but the physicist thinks that it is a wave of probability undulating in nothingness" (cp. Jeans, *Universe*, 122–23). W.'s objections are already

indicated in §482. See also *PB* 286: "The probability of a hypothesis is measured by the amount of evidence required to make it advantageous to abandon it. Only in this sense can we say that repeated uniform experience in the past makes probable the continuation of this uniformity in the future." (Cp. Waismann, "Analyse", 228.)

§485 See §326; *Kreis*, 247; Carnap, "Protokollsätze", 224–26; cp. I, 4.

"Now someone says: But you must have a reason to suppose that, or else the assumption is unsupported and worthless.— (Recall that we do indeed stand on the Earth, but the Earth doesn't stand on something else; children think it must fall if it isn't supported.)" (*PG* 110; see 111).

"At the foundation of well-founded belief lies belief that is not founded" (*OC* 253; see ibid., 130–31, 163–64, 172, 191–92, 204).

"I might also put it like this: the 'law of induction' can no more be *grounded* than certain particular propositions concerning the material of experience" (*OC* 499).

"The reasoning that leads to an infinite regress is to be given up not 'because in this way we can never reach the goal', but because here there is no goal; so it makes no sense to say 'we can never reach it' " (*Z* 693).

"It is true that if any one has not the habit of induction, we cannot prove to him that he is wrong; but there is nothing peculiar in that. If a man doubts his memory or his perception we cannot prove to him that they are trustworthy; to ask for such a thing is to cry for the moon, and the same is true of induction" (Ramsey, *Foundations*, 197; see 198).

Contrast this viewpoint with the following: "The foundation or basic content of every science does not consist in proofs or in what is proved, but in the unproved foundation of the proofs; and this is ultimately apprehended only through perception" (Schopenhauer, *World*, II, 77). "Thus we must either accept the inductive principle on the ground of its intrinsic evidence, or forgo all justification of our expectations about the future" (Russell, *Problems*, 38). A terminus is envisaged, but in intuition. Here, too, W. considered intuition "an unnecessary shuffle" (§213), for reasons basically similar to those in Section IX (see IX, 5).

§486 See *Z* 477; *RFM* 5c, 8; *PB* 287d; Moore, *Studies*, 234, and *Commonplace*, 8; cp. *PG* 219–23; *PB* 287f–288a; Man. 178b, 7–9; Man. 110, 240–41 (related dialogue with an idealist); Ambrose, "Metamorphoses", 63; Russell, *Matter*, 146–47, 181b; Schlick, "Positivism", 90.

(a) See X, 6–8; *PG* 211–12; *PB* 282–84; *Kreis*, 158–61; 257–60; Ogden and Richards, *Meaning*, 79–81; Russell, *Matter*, 218, and "Limits", 132.

Does it *follow* . . . : cp. *Z* 547–48; Russell, *Problems*, 3–4 ("The real table, if there is one, is not *immediately* known to us at all, but must be an inference from what is immediately known"); Moore, *Papers*, 53–55, e.g.: "It seems to me quite evident that my knowledge that I am now perceiving a human hand is a deduction from a pair of propositions simpler still—propositions which I can only express in the form 'I am perceiving *this*' and '*This* is a human hand.' . . . . Two things only seem to me to be quite certain about the analysis of such propositions . . . namely that whenever I know, or judge, such a proposition to be true, (1) there is always some *sense-datum* about which the proposition in question is a proposition—some sense-datum which is *a* subject (and, in a certain sense, the principal or ultimate subject) of the proposition in question, and (2) that, nevertheless, *what* I am knowing or judging to be true about this sense-datum is not (in general) that it is *itself* a hand, or a dog, or the sun, etc. etc."

that there is a chair: W. had written: "If I say 'There is a chair over there,' this proposition points to a series of expectations. . . . If certain of these expectations are verified, I shall take this as a proof that there was a chair there" (Man. 107, 248; see Russell, *Logic,* 275). "That is, immediate experience need only . . . verify some *one* facet" (*PB* 282). "To say, for instance, that I see a sphere, means only that I have a view of the sort a sphere gives, but this means only that I can construe views according to a certain law, that of spheres, and that this is such a view" (*PB* 286).

Thus to pinpoint W.'s main target in this paragraph, read §292 concerning "reading off what you say from the facts" (his former view), and add the particular case: "We say 'Here is a chair' when we see only a *single* side" (*PB* 282). The phenomenological language W. had envisaged (X, 8) was to lay bare all these hidden laws—the logic of the calculus we supposedly operate (IX, 2–3).

How can a *proposition* . . . : see NL 319b; Man. 110, 54 ("Can I say: When I perceive a body in visual space, it gives me rules for the word that designates it?"); cp. X, 25; §380c; *Z* 547; *BB* 73a; *PB* 200c.

"If we want to find a basis for empirical science, we cannot be content with an unverbalized awareness, but must demand sentences in which what we know is asserted. We cannot consider the epistemological problem solved if we stop short of the verbal expression of what we know. We are thus involved in the problem of meaning. . . . On such grounds, by merely common-sense arguments, we are led to the sense-datum as the only thing that is indubitable. The sense-datum, however, is not a proposition, and what we are in search of is an indubitable proposition. To make a proposition out of a sense-datum, we must analyse or classify it" (Russell, "Relevance", 50).

"That is, the hypothesis is a system of signs & stands completely and entirely outside experience. It is like a many-faced body whose every face *can* correspond to an experience" (Man. 109, 123–24).

does it follow from the propositions . . . : see *RFM* 103abc; cp.

Russell, *Mind*, 98: "Instead of supposing that there is some unknown cause, the 'real' table, behind the different sensations of those who are said to be looking at the table, we may take the whole set of these sensations (together possibly with certain other particulars) as actually *being* the table."

No: see Carnap, "Protokollsätze", 219; Moore, *Papers*, 54 (quoted above); Waismann, "Verifiability", 119–31; Schopenhauer, *World*, II, 37; cp. §§183, 354, 481b, p. 180d.

"Our perception is made up of sensations, images and beliefs, but the supposed 'object' is something inferential, externally related, not logically bound up with what is occurring in us" (Russell, *Mind*, 112; cp. idem, *Outline*, 140).

"The seeing of sense-data consists in directly apprehending them. But the seeing of a material object does *not* consist in directly apprehending *it*. It consists, *partly* in directly apprehending certain sense-data, but partly also in *knowing, besides and at the same time*, that there exists *something* other than these sense-data. And so, too, if we ever *see* that a material object is round or square, or in a particular position in space; this also would consist, *not* in directly apprehending these things, but in knowing, when we do directly apprehend certain sense-data, certain things about something quite other than these sense-data" (Moore, *Problems*, 51).

"If I had to describe the grammar of the hypothesis [cp. X, 6–7], I would say: it follows from no single proposition and from no collection of singular propositions. It is—in this sense—never verified" (*Kreis*, 211).

"*Why* doesn't it follow? Wittgenstein does not say, but the reason would appear to be of the same sort as in the example 'He is in pain.' The propositions describing my sense impressions would have to be conjoined with the proposition that I am not looking in a mirror, or at a painted scenery, or at a movie film, or . . . , etc. Here too there cannot be an exhaustive enumeration of the negative conditions that would have to be added to the description of sense impressions *if* 'There's a chair over there' *were* to be logically implied" (Malcolm, "Investigations", 199; cp. §80).

don't I infer . . . : see James, *Principles*, II, 326–27; Ogden and Richards, *Meaning*, 245; and especially Russell: "When you translate the occurrence into words, you are making generalizations and inferences, just as you are when you say 'there is a chair' " (*Outline*, 12; see ibid., 3–5, 8–9, 10c, 13). "But the 'real' shape is not what we see; it is something inferred from what we see" (*Problems*, 3; see *Mind*, 98). "Thus it becomes evident that the real table, if there is one, is not the same as what we immediately experience by sight or touch or hearing.

The real table, if there is one, is not *immediately* known to us at all, but must be an inference from what is immediately known" (*Problems*, 3–4). "It is generally agreed that the public physical world is an inference, and that basic propositions are not directly concerned with it" ("Verification", 6).

I make no inference!: see James, *Principles*, II, 112–13; cp. §§475, 479; *Kreis*, 87ab.

> **but not one . . . :** see *RFM* 6 (quoted for §481b).

> **is a transition to an assertion:** see *RFM* 5c, 8e.

> **but also in action:** see *RFM* 179de; Russell, *Outline*, 85bc, 87a.

(b) Cp. §471. Contrast this *a posteriori* approach with Russell's: "The reason is not to be any other proposition; it must, therefore, be an 'experience'. And this brings us, at last, to the fundamental question: How can 'experience' afford a ground for a verbal proposition? And how can it be *known* to afford such a ground?" ("Verification", 7). "In what follows . . . it is argued that, on the basis of a single experience, a number of verbal statements are justified. The character of such statements is investigated, and it is contended that they must always be confined to matters belonging to the biography of the observer; they can be such as 'I see a canoid patch of color,' but not such as 'there is a dog.' Statements of this latter kind always involve, in their justification, some element of inference" (*Inquiry*, 21–22).

§§487–89 Cp. GI 15–16; §§475, 479; *PG* 101e. Between §487 and §486 there is the same apparent break as between §472 and §471, for the same reason; after the injunction "Describe language-games," W. proceeds to do so, or rather to draw attention to them by means of questions.

The demand for justification often reflects the notion that each meaningful statement is a report, understood in terms of its truth-conditions and justified or not by their satisfaction. W.'s answer to this attitude, and to the question in §486b, remains implicit in §§487–89 but is stated explicitly in p. 200b.

> **is the answer perhaps . . . :** "the confusion that a motive is a cause of which we are immediately aware, a cause 'seen from the inside', or a cause experienced" (*BB* 15).

> **Think of a greeting:** is it justified? is it a report?

> **will they be used:** rather: "are they used".

§490 Cp. *BB* 15d. This kindred example reinforces the implicit verdict in §487. As obeying a command consists in something more than hearing it and performing the action, and as no observation shows me I am obeying (and not merely performing the action), so doing an action for a given reason consists in more than doing the action after thinking of that motive, and no observation of the antecedent thought reveals it as my reason for acting. Thus, when asked how I know the connection, I do not attempt to recall the qualities of the thought quite precisely, and the exact sequence, but fall back on a picture of the way I suppose these things transpire.

§491   Worked over in Man. 116, 133, after §501, where an analogous assertion occurs. On the series of numbers here begun, see XVI, 7–10. Cp. §363; *PG* 191d–192a; *Kreis*, 172, 235; Man. 112, 166.

Not: W.'s main objection to this factual-sounding assertion appears in *PG* 193: "Whence does language get its significance? Can we say: 'Without language we could not communicate with one another?' No. The case is not analogous to this one: without the telephone we could not speak from Europe to America. But we can indeed say: 'without a mouth people could not communicate with one another'; whereas the concept of language *is contained* in the concept of communication." For a similar critique of a similar tautology, see *Z* 477. See Man. 110, 165 (the original seed of this number), 201; *EPB* 121 and *BB* 81 ("Systems of communication . . . we shall call 'language-games' "); Waismann, *Principles*, 93; cp. §13; *OC* 534.

"we could not": no, we would not (*Z* 351; cp. §497; *BB* 55c).

but for sure: the tautology disappears. For language has other functions than these (cp. §§23, 65b).

And also: for language need not be verbal (Man. 112, 183). It is a contingent fact that if a person loses his voice and the use of his hands, he has a hard time communicating. (He has not learned, for instance, to wink or stamp in Morse code.)

§492   From *PG* 192. See XVI, 2, 9–10; *PG* 68e–69a, 187e–188a; Man. 232, 715 ("So did we *invent* human language? No more than walking on two legs"); Man. 116, 49; Man. 115, 34; cp. Man. 108, 102; Rhees, *Discussions*, 132 (an analogous distinction for mathematics).

(a) To invent a language: cp. Mauthner, *Beiträge*, I, 78. This paragraph might be seen as indicating how to handle W.'s early question: "If I were to try to invent *language* for the purpose of making myself understood to some one else, what sort of rules should I have to agree on with him about our expression?" (*NB* 37). The answer is: It will depend on what sort of language you are inventing; language is no one thing (§65). If you are simply inventing a language-*game,* you may ignore laws of association and the like and choose the rules as you please; in the other hypothesis, scientific calculations may be required.

could mean . . . : it is thus that "we twist fibre on fibre" (§67; see §494; *PG* 115a; commentary on §2b). W. is correcting Man. 110, 199–200, from which this number derives.

for a particular purpose: for instance, to evoke images (§6b) or cause pleasant experiences (Man. 110, 122).

or consistently with them: as in a complete language (§18) like that in §2. See *PG* 187, quoted for §493a.

invention of a game: see §204 and commentary.

(b) "An explanation of the working of language as a psychophysical mechanism does not interest us. Such an explanation itself uses language to describe phenomena (of association, memory, etc.); it is itself a speech act and stands outside the calculus [the one to be explained]; whereas we need an explanation that is *part of the calculus*" (*PG* 70), as "invent a language" is part of the language-game played with *language*, and "explain the meaning" is part of the game played with *meaning* (*BB* 1; §560), and "measure a length" is part of the game played with *length* (*BB* 1). If "*essence* is expressed by grammar" (§371), then we should look to such composite expressions in order to answer the question "What is length?" or "What is meaning?" or "What is language?" (*BB* 1).

§493   From Man. 115, 37. See *RFM* 103; *PG* 68–70; Man. 115, 103; Waismann, *Principles*, 124; cp. *Z* 521–22; *LC* 20b.

The logic of this and the following two numbers resembles that of §§359–60, which we might paraphrase thus: "Is language to be called an invention based on (or in conformity with) the laws of nature (§492)? It certainly comes close to being such a mechanism (§495). But surely language is not a mere piece of machinery, setting people in motion (§493)! No, we only say of our ordinary word-language and what is like it that it is language (§494). We say it also of the pragmatic game of orders in §2."

(a) "The cock . . .": K. Bühler often treated a like example, hens' clucking to chicks, as a sort of language. See e.g. *Development*, 51, 56; cp. *PG* 69a.

"calls": *PG* 187 reveals the rationale behind the choice of this example: "Naturally we can treat language as part of a psychological mechanism. It is simplest if we narrow the concept of language so that language consists only of commands. We can then consider how a foreman directs the labors of a group of people by means of shouts." Cp. §506.

Isn't the aspect . . . : cp. *PG* 69a; Man. 110, 131; Russell, *Mind*, 64 ("if we knew more about animals, we might equally cease to attribute desires to them, since we might find physical and chemical reactions sufficient to account for their behaviour").

(b) For the comparison of speech with a mechanism, see *PG* 187–92.

§494   Revised from Man. 115, 37. See initial comments on §493; *Z* 322, 325; *RFM* 103i; *PG* 170e, 191 (quoted for §496); cp. §206b; Man. 110, 186. By way of contrast, and as an indication of the number's implications, compare Chomsky, *Language*, 24: "The study of universal grammar, so understood, is a study of the nature of human intellectual capacities. It tries to formulate the necessary and sufficient conditions that a system must meet to qualify as a potential human language, conditions that are not accidentally true of the existing human languages, but that are rather rooted in the human 'language capacity', and thus constitute the innate organization that determines what counts as linguistic experience and what knowledge of language arises on the basis of this experience." Chomsky overlooked §371. See GI 70.

§495 See *BB* 157de; *PG* 187–92; cp. Russell, *Mind*, 87a. For the point of this number, and its connection with preceding ones, see the commentary on §493. For its connection with the next number, see *PG* 187–88: "Can we say that grammar describes language: language, that part of the psychophysical mechanism which we use when we utter words—like pressing keys on a key board—to make a human machine work for us?"

(a) Cp. *BB* 157b: "That seems to be saying that part of the time we act as mere automatons. And the answer is that in a sense we do and in a sense we don't."

(b) adjusting a mechanism to respond: see §§6, 198; *BB* 12c.

  and it may be all one to us . . . : see the quotation from *PG* 191, under §496. W. was interested in the origins of speech only insofar as they reveal characteristics of the language-game actually played, those which determine the concept (e.g. *language*). After describing training for a mechanical type of language-game, in which moves are made according to letters, W. suggested: "We could also imagine a case: 40). where even this training is not necessary, where, as we should say, the look of the letters abcd naturally produced an urge to move in the way described. This case at first sight looks puzzling. We seem to be assuming a most unusual working of the mind. Or we may ask, 'How on earth is he to know which way to move if the letter a is shown him?'. But isn't B's reaction in this case the very reaction described in 37) and 38), and in fact our usual reaction when for instance we hear and obey an order? For, the fact that the training in 38) and 39) *preceded* the carrying out of the order does not change the process of carrying out. In other words the 'curious mental mechanism' assumed in 40) is no other than that which we assumed to be created by the training in 37) and 38). 'But *could* such a mechanism be born with you?' But did you find any difficulty in assuming that *that* mechanism was born with B, which enabled him to respond to the training in the way he did? And remember that the rule or explanation given in table 33) of the signs abcd was not essentially the last one, and that we might have given a table for the use of such tables, and so on" (*BB* 97).

§496 See §§108–9, 124a, p. 230a; *PG* 188 (quoted for §495), 190c,

195a; *PB* 59fg; Man. 116, 134–35 (quoted for §497). W.'s therapeutic perspective (GI 49–52; VII, 1–7) need not be invoked to justify these statements (XVI, 9–10); it indicates rather why he was interested just in grammar—that is, in the rules of language (§108c) and not in its causes (GI 49; see *BB* 97, above).

"When I said that for us language is not something which fulfills a specific purpose, but that the concept is determined by certain systems which we call 'language', and such systems as are constructed by analogy with them—I could also have expressed the same thing this way: I feel free to *think up* causal connections for the operation of language" (*PG* 191).

§497   See I, 3–4; p. 230; *PG* 246; *PP* 277–79; Man. 110, 142–43, 176. **(a)** For senses in which they cannot be called arbitrary, see §520, p. 230. These reveal why W. abandoned this earlier formulation: "When I say that the rules are arbitrary I mean that they are not determined by reality" (*PG* 246). "Are the rules of chess arbitrary? Let us imagine it were found that only chess entertained and satisfied people. In that case these rules are not arbitrary, not if the purpose of the game is to be achieved" (*PG* 192; see Man. 116, 134). Likewise, concerning language we might ask: "Do we adopt this calculus arbitrarily? No more than our fear of fire or of a raging man coming at us" (*PG* 110; cp. §480). " 'The rules of a game are arbitrary' means: the concept 'game' is not defined by the effects the game is supposed to have on us" (*PG* 192). And the same is true of language (*PG* 184; XVI, 9–10).

the *aim*: language, like games, has a point (§§564–69).

(b) This parallels the warning in §491. See the commentary on that number, and *Z* 320, 356; *PG* 126, 184e; *PB* 53d; cp. Russell, "Introduction", ix; Schlick, "Psychological", 399b.

The former sequel to (*a*) in Man. 116, 134: "and it is senseless to say: language must have nouns, adjectives, verbs, and numerals since there are things, properties, acts, and numbers, or the like."

The connection with the next section (on sense) appears from 3.34: "A proposition possesses essential and accidental features. . . . Essential features are those without which the proposition could not express its sense."

If someone says: as so often, the someone is W. himself. He had written for instance: "Could one then manage without names? Surely not. Names are necessary for an assertion that *this* thing possesses *that* property and so on" (*NB* 53).

what *"could"* means here: whether physical possibility or logical (*PB* 311d–312). In the Kantian tradition in which W. grew up, this basic distinction is frequently ignored. Thus Kant himself did not clarify whether his "conditions of possibility" were causal or logical—mental mechanisms or defining properties. And W. was equally ambiguous in *PB* 51 (the chief passage probed here and in the preceding number), for example when he referred to "a grasp of what is essential to our language, for representation, and what is inessential; a grasp of what parts of our language are idly-spinning wheels".

XVII. The Sense of a Sentence (§§498–517)

GENERAL COMMENTARY

(1)   The preceding treatments of understanding (Section IX), thought (Section XI), and the agreement of thought with reality (Section XV) have prepared the conclusion of this section, that the sense of a sentence is not guaranteed by or dependent upon an accompanying mental act, as Wittgenstein had once supposed (GI 37). "He said . . . that he had himself been 'misled' by the expression 'sense', and . . . implied that where we say 'This makes no sense' we always mean 'This makes nonsense *in this particular game*'. . . . He concluded finally that ' "makes sense" is vague, and will have different senses in different cases' " (*PP* 273–74). He thus abandoned the *Tractatus* aim of setting a limit to thought (Preface); but his later therapeutic purpose, too, required that he investigate the limits of sense, as here (§§499–500, 511–17). How dominant the therapeutic intention was (see GI 8, 28) appears from the fact that in this, the major treatment of sense in the *Investigations,* he made no attempt to develop his positive suggestion that the sense of a proposition is its use (see the commentary on §20b).

(2)   "Just as 'sense' is vague, so must be 'grammar', 'grammatical rule' and 'syntax' " (*PP* 274)—and *language* (§499). Here is one connection with the immediately preceding numbers of Section XVI, on the concept *language* (XVI, 9–10). The tie-in is closest in §498, which points out that sense, like language, is not defined in terms of intention or effect. The section is similarly related to the next one, on the *Tractatus* conception that all propositions are logical pictures. "He went on to say," reports Moore in *PP* 273, "that his present view was that ' "sense" was correlative to "proposition" ' . . . and that hence, if 'proposition' was not 'sharply bounded', 'sense' was not 'sharply bounded' either."

DETAILED COMMENTARY

§498   See *PG* 188–90; Man. 108, 288; cp. p. 14n; *PG* 185b; *LC* 29d (quoted for §523); Man. 109, 258.

The example illustrates two points: " 'This word-combination has no sense' does not mean it has no effect. Nor 'it does not have the desired effect' " (*PG* 189, where these words link §498 and §499).

§499 See commentary on §520 ("So does it depend"); *PG* 125d; Man. 226, 70 (quoted for §251f); Man. 116, 64–65; cp. §68; *PB* 85d, 135c; *PP* 275–76, 311 (quoted for §247). Of his *Tractatus* W. wrote in the Preface: "The aim of the book is to set a limit to thought, or rather—not to thought, but to the expression of thoughts" (cp. 4.113–4.115). By the end he arrived at the conclusion that all his own propositions lacked sense (6.54), for they did not picture possible states of affairs (3.11). Logical positivists like Schlick drew the line elsewhere or at least otherwise: "Verifiability . . . is the sufficient and necessary condition of meaning" ("Meaning", 155). These fences were built to keep metaphysicians out (see e.g. 6.53), but the builders themselves jumped over them. There was in fact general unclarity about the function of the boundaries. (If the *Tractatus* as a whole, and the Verification Principle itself, were such helpful nonsense, why not talk nonsense?)

W. had also declared that "tautologies and contradictions lack sense" (4.461); and to avoid contradictions Russell declared certain combinations of signs to be meaningless (Theory of Types). Yet "tautologies and contradictions are common in ordinary speech" (*JN* 107; see *BB* 161; §125 and commentary).

it may be for various kinds of reason: cp. §§17, 108c, 334, 517, p. 184c; Schlick, "Meaning", 155a. For instance, "misunderstandings can be avoided" (*RFM* 31). However, that is not the only possible motive. W. is correcting his assertion in *PG* 130 and *PP* 273–74 that the reason for expressly excluding certain word-combinations "can only consist in this that *we are tempted* to mistake them for a sentence of our language." More generally, he is reacting against the simplistic attitude revealed in Man. 110, 145: "One thing can be said for sure, that in this language this combination of signs is no proposition. And that thereby no sense is lost. And that should already be enough."

§500 See commentary on §520 ("So does it depend"); *PG* 126a; *PP* 273; Man. 232, 679; Cook "Privacy", 308–11; Waismann, *Principles*, 37–39; Kenny, *Wittgenstein*, 43–44; cp. *Z* 259; *BB* 56a; *PG* 39a; 5.473, 5.5422; *NB* 2b (e.g.: "NOT because a sign is, shall we say, illegitimate in itself"); *Kreis*, 239–40; *PP* 262c; Man. 110, 145 (just quoted for §499); Schlick, "Meaning", 154–55.

not as it were its sense that is senseless: in view of the equivalence between sense and use (§§20b, 421), we might paraphrase thus: "It isn't its use that is useless"; or, following *PG* 125d, we might say: "It isn't a chess move that is no move at all; but a move is excluded from the game of chess."

"In order to be able to set a limit to thought, we should have to find both sides of the limit thinkable (i.e. we should have to be able to think what cannot be thought)" (*Tractatus*, Preface; cp. 4.114–4.115).

"Thought can never be of anything illogical, since, if it were, we should have to think illogically" (3.03).

"The nonsensical statements alluded to above do not correspond to thoughts which, by a sort of psychological experiment, we find ourselves unable to think; they do not correspond to any thoughts at all" (Schlick, "Meaning", 155).

"When we say 'I can't feel his pain,' the idea of an insurmountable barrier suggests itself to us" (*BB* 55–56), rendering *a priori* impossible what is somehow conceivable. Compare statements like Ayer's, that "it is logically impossible that one person should literally feel another's pain" (*Problem*, 229), and Pole's, that "one person cannot be said literally to feel another's feelings" (*Later Philosophy*, 68), suggesting in each case that there is a literal sense which does not make sense. Cook comments: "In order to specify what it is that one is condemning as nonsense, one must repeat that nonsense in *some* form, and if a reader insists on taking one's words 'straight' at this point and thus looks for or imagines a sense where none was intended, then one's argument will have the paradoxical air of trying to prove that the sense of something is senseless" ("Privacy", 308). Thus Bridgman wrote: "A somewhat similar paradoxical and embarrassing situation arises whenever we make a statement of the form 'The statement A has no meaning.' For if the statement A did not have a meaning of sorts, we would not be able to assent to the statement that it has no meaning. We may recognize this 'meaning of sorts' as a second kind of meaning, which may be defined in terms of the response elicited when the statement is made" (*Way*, 34).

§501   See §317 and commentary; *PG* 107b; cp. Russell, *Logic*, 309b, and *Mind*, 250. The sequence *PG* 51d–51e parallels §§501–2, but is more explicit. *PG* 51c ties both with §500. Man. 110, 209, makes the connection with §502: " 'I always mean the same thing when I write "It's raining" in my diary.'—'And what is that?' To this the only answer would be 'Just that it is raining,' or another picture would have to be used. Real rain would be indicated, or a painting of rain, or a 'more precise' description," not that inner something which for some reason I cannot express (see §§503–4 and commentary on §120b).

"is to express thoughts": see 3.1 ("In a proposition a thought finds an expression that can be perceived by the senses"); §§304b, 363b.

Then what thought is expressed . . . : "It says that it is raining" (Man. 302, 11; see *PG* 51d; §429 and commentary). " 'We are talking about the weather,' I could say, 'not about me' " (Man. 229, §1418; see §317 and Man. 229, §§1487–89). "Aim? to remove the point by point correspondence of thought to words" (JN 89; see §96). "Make the following experiment: say and mean a sentence, e.g.: 'It will probably rain tomorrow.' Now think the same thought again, mean what you just meant, but without saying anything (either aloud or to yourself). If thinking that it will rain tomorrow accompanied saying that it will rain tomorrow, then just do the first activity and leave out the second" (BB 42; see p. 18n; cp. p. 223b). "The sense—the thought 'It's raining'—is not even the words *with* the accompaniment of some sort of imagery. It *is* the thought 'It's raining' only within the English language" (LC 30; see §499).

by the sentence "It's raining": it is sometimes suggested that the classical subject-predicate view has a good point in maintaining that every statement must have both a referential and a descriptive aspect. But where are they here? W.'s refined account succeeded no better. "He said that both he and Russell had the idea that non-atomic propositions could be 'analysed' into atomic ones, but that we did not yet know what the analysis was: that, e.g., such a proposition as 'It is raining' might, if we knew its analysis, turn out to be molecular, consisting, e.g., of a conjunction of 'atomic' propositions" (PP 296). But as a start in this direction, one would need to designate the raindrops, and "consider this: 'How many drops do you see when you look at the rain?' " (PG 175; see X, 6).

§502   See Z 691; BB 38a, 161ab; PG 289c; LC 30 ("Well, give us the expression without the face"); Man. 112, 2; Man. 108, 247; Schlick, *Aufsätze*, 180; cp. §527 ("I should not be able to say"); Z 30; PG 41ab; Man. 116, 16; Man. 109, 279; Man. 108, 194–95, 277, 279, 288–89. In Man. 228 (§91) the number follows §332 of the *Investigations*. Its point also appears from antecedent passages like the following:

" 'This sentence has a sense' is an unfortunate turn of speech. 'This sentence has a sense' sounds like 'This man has a hat' " (*Kreis,* 108).

"The sense is not something someone can point to as for instance he can point to me as the referent of my name, but a property of the sentence which has it. The sentence has it in itself" (Man. 108, 237).

"Just as in a certain sense we cannot speak of the sense of a sentence, so too we cannot speak of the expression of a thought, wish, command, etc.; for to the query 'What wish is expressed by this sentence?' an expression of the wish must be given in reply" (Man. 108, 289; see BB 38a).

"On hearing the assertion 'this sentence has a sense' we cannot really ask 'What sense?' Just as on hearing the assertion 'this combination of words is a sentence' we cannot ask 'What sentence?' " (*PG* 51; Man. 108, 88; see Man. 302, 7).

"The question 'What does this sentence *p* mean?', if it doesn't ask for a translation of *p* into other symbols, has no more sense than 'What sentence is formed by this sequence of words?' Suppose to the question, 'What's a kilogram?' I answered, 'It is what a litre of water weighs,' and someone asked, 'Well, what does a litre of water weigh?' " (*BB* 161).

"Yet it is possible to answer the question, 'What does a chair in the style of Louis XIV look like?'—or, 'What does a plaintive melody sound like?'—Show me such chairs, sing me such melodies!" (Man. 138, 7A).

Cp. Schlick, "Future", 49–50, or "Meaning", 146: "Is it not the very nature and purpose of every proposition to express its own meaning? In fact, when we are confronted with a proposition (in a language familiar to us) we usually know its meaning immediately. If we do not, we can have it explained to us, but the explanation will consist of a new proposition; and if the new one is capable of expressing the meaning, why should not the original one be capable of it? So that a snippy person when asked what he meant by a certain statement might be perfectly justified in saying, 'I meant exactly what I said!' "

§§503–4 See §§431–33; *Z* 276–77; *BB* 3e (quoted for §432); *PG* 44d; *PP* 265b–266a; Man. 116, 18–19; Man. 108, 216–17, 224. For earlier settings of these numbers, see *PG* 40 and Man. 228, 1, and ultimately Man. 109, 200 (for §503) and Man. 108, 277 (for §504). For their connection with §502, see *BB* 38, which states the apparent difficulty in terms of the object, "*the actual fact*—which, we are afraid, can't yet be shown as it has not yet entered." Nor, it seems, can the speaker's intention, which bridges the gap, be conveyed by mere words (see the commentaries on §§120b, 501–2).

According to the *Tractatus*, "a proposition states something only in so far as it is a picture" (4.03) and it is a picture only insofar as the propositional sign is "thought out" (3.11). But each person has to do that on his own; the sign does not do it for him. At the moment of conversion from his old way of thinking, W. stated the problem in these terms: "If I say: I derive my action from the order with the help of a rule, this makes sense only if I can say: with the help of *what* rule? And the answer to this question must consist in an expression of the rule" (Man. 109, 279–80). But what better expression is there of *this* rule than the order itself? And wouldn't any other have to be synonymous with it? And wouldn't it too consist of mere signs? (Should such queries strike anyone as odd, let him reflect on the long tradition to which young W. belonged, and seriously attempt to render it intelligible.)

"How is *he* to know . . .": "We say: 'Understanding is something *different* from the expression of understanding. *Understanding* cannot be exhibited; it is something inner, spiritual' " (*PG* 44). So it is private, and the other has only sensible clues. W. has argued in the previous section that the connection between signs and reality is made in language, not in the mind; and in Section XI that "thinking is not an incorporeal process which lends life and sense to speaking" (§339). Section XXVI treats meaning similarly. See also §§652–53. Cp. p. 192.

"when he has nothing but the signs": W.'s answer is *ad hominem*. As a matter of fact, both of them have the context (§§349, 686) and their mastery of the language—"the institution of language and all its surroundings" (§540)—and that suffices. Cp. p. 181c.

§505   From Man. 116, 20–21. See *Z* 284–86; cp. §211.

Must I understand . . . : see §451; *BB* 3e, 12a. "Naturally the statement 'I must understand the order before I can act on it' has an acceptable sense" (*PG* 46). W. is questioning the necessary presence of an *act* of understanding (§431) which would fill the gap between the words of the command and its fulfillment—would as it were perform the act in advance (GI 36).

"Here the 'must' is fishy. If it is a logical must, then the statement is a grammatical remark. . . . If 'understanding a sentence' means acting on it in some manner, then understanding cannot be a precondition for our acting on it" (*PG* 45–46).

isn't there in turn a jump . . . : in the German this is an exclamation, not a question.

See §§433–34; Man. 109, 273: "If understanding was a necessary preparation for acting, something must have been added to the sign, but something that in any case was not the execution.

"Is it possible, then, and in what sense is it possible, to derive the execution from the sign plus the understanding (so the interpretation), before it occurs? Whatever one derives is, to be sure, just another description of the execution & this description too was not present till it had been derived.

"We derive the *execution* of the order from the order only when we carry it out."

from *knowing:* cp. §363c (" 'Telling brings it about that he *knows* . . . everything else is inessential to the telling' ").

§506   The example is from Man. 110, 158; the number from Man. 116, 25. See *BB* 97b; cp. *Z* 287. Note the close parallel between §§505–6 and §§211–12.

The absent-minded man: "Let us suppose that you are walking in London with an absent-minded friend. You say 'look out, there's a motor coming.' He will glance round and jump aside without the need of any 'mental' intermediary" (Russell, *Logic*, 300).

at the order **"Right turn!":** "to soldiers in drilling, for example. In such a case there need not be anything mental, but merely a habit of the body" (Russell, *Mind*, 80–81).

An interpretation?: (a) "I mean: I would not first have to grasp an abstract sense" (*PG* 46). (b) Nor do I imagine a different setting for the order, as may happen when an order at first seems absurd and then an explanation occurs to me (ibid.). (c) Nor does the order get translated into some other form (*PG* 47c; §201c), as for instance "if you say the same thing to a Frenchman with a slight knowledge of English" (Russell, *Logic*, 301). Thus with regard to orders in general: "In some cases you will find that you do something which might be called interpreting before obeying, in some cases not" (*BB* 3)—as here. Earlier, nurtured on a more limited diet of examples (§593), W. had declared: "An unarticulated understanding is for us no understanding" (Man. 110, 54).

§507 Reworked from Man. 110, 98, and Man. 116, 16–17. The statement is handled quite differently in Man. 110, 115. See GI 37; *PG* 41; James, *Principles*, I, 280–81.

"This view of meaning (or something like it) is in Frege. He said Mathematical Propositions are not spoken like a parrot; we mean something by them" (JN 108). W. too had written: "The meaning [*Meinung*] is the sense of the proposition" (Man. 108, 247).

§508 From Man. 110, 202, with the sample sentence changed. See p. 18n; *Z* 5–6; Man. 228, §§6, 105–7; cp. *PG* 122c–123a.

(a) But I don't mean . . . : just as understanding and feeling at home in a foreign language do not consist in connecting each of the words with a word of one's mother tongue.

in the place **. . . :** see §29a and the quote there from *PP* 257.

"So if I learnt the language in which '*abcd*' meant that—should I come bit by bit to have the familiar experience when I pronounced the letters? Yes and no.—A major difference between the two cases is that in the first one I *can't move*. It is as if one of my joints were in splints, and I not yet familiar with the possible movements, so that I as it were keep on stumbling" (*Z* 6). Thus W. is not making the point of p. 214h, to explain the impression that something "in us" is coupled with the words (§507). See also the following quotation.

(b) "And there is even something in saying: he can't *think* it. One is trying e.g. to say: he can't fill it with personal content; he can't really *go along with it*—personally, with his intelligence. It is like when one says: this sequence of notes makes no sense, I can't sing it with expression. I cannot *respond* to it. Or, what comes to the same thing here: I don't respond to it" (*RFM* 34).

§509 See §665.

(a) Why is this answer . . . : only in a language (§508) is it possible either to describe (§§24, 291) or to "mean something by something" (p. 18n). No act of meaning determines the sentence's place in the language-game.

(b) Cp. GI 37.

(d) "How is the 'undertone' to be separated from the rest of the experience of speaking?"—e.g. of saying "The weather is fine" (§592). "Can this feeling be separated from the phrase?" (p. 182). See pp. 175h–176b; cp. pp. 185j–186d.

§510 See p. 176gh. The original setting is Man. 115, 39. The point of this and §509 is stated in §329. Cp. §330 ("a process, which may accompany something else"—e.g. another set of words—"or can go on by itself").

Make the following experiment: cp. p. 18n.

is there only one way: if there are many, yet the sense is the same, then the inner imaginings, feelings, translations, and so on, are not what determine the meaning (cp. p. 182).

§511 Passages from which this and the following number grew: Man. 110, 292; Man. 302, 16–17; PG 128b–129a, 130d; Man. 228, §506. See also §§395–97 and commentary; RFM 145hi; Man. 228, §49; Man. 109, 42; PG 126a, e.g.: " 'How then do I manage to always use a word meaningfully? Do I always consult grammar? No, the fact that I mean something—what I mean keeps me from talking nonsense.'—But what do I mean?—I would like to say: I talk about parts of an apple but not about parts of the color red, since for the words 'parts of an apple' I can think something, imagine something, wish something—but not for the expression 'parts of the color red'."

Cp. §109 ("whatever that may mean"); Z 251, 297; PG 39a, 44b; PB 304c–305a; Ramsey, *Foundations,* 269b.

In Z 247, after asking the same two questions as here in §511, W. answers: "The first presumably means: not to be misled by the appearance of a sentence and to investigate its application in the language-game. And 'if I mean something by it'—does that mean something *like:* 'if I can imagine something in connexion with it'?—An image often leads on to a further application."

"discovering that an . . .": see §§513, 517; cp. p. 53n, §§334, 463.

"If I mean something by it . . . ": as late as PB 55f–56a and PP 270–71, W. still thought this way. E.g.: "He seemed to be saying that if Helmholtz was 'projecting' the sentence 'I can imagine a piece of chalk being thrown into the fourth dimension' 'with the common method of projection', then he was talking nonsense, but that if he had been 'projecting' that sentence in an unusual way, so that it meant the same as 'I can imagine a piece of chalk first disappearing and then appearing again,' then he would have been talking sense" (PP 270). See GI 37;

Man. 109, 281 (quoted for §81b, which see); Man. 108, 247 (quoted for §507); cp. §125d.

If I mean *what* by it?!: the answer would have to be in words—the same or synonymous ones (§502). Thus "I mean something by it" is no answer at all (cp. §509a).

but also think: see the quotations above; those for §512, below; Man. 229, §§710–11, quoted for §138; 3.11 and 4.01 (my translation: "A proposition is a model of reality as we think it").

§512 Reworked from Man. 109, 45. Man. 116, 77 (where this number appears in the midst of §251) provides illustrations. See §389; *PG* 127d–128a; Man. 110, 230; Baker and Hacker, Notice, 277e; cp. Z 253. See also the initial comments on §511, where the quotation from *PG* 125 indicates the link with this number. So does *NB* 24: " 'A situation is thinkable' ('imaginable') means: We can make ourselves a picture of it." See XII, 1; 3.001, 4.01; *LO* 24.

It looks as if we could say: cp. XXXVII, 3; *NB* 13b; 3.02–3.032 (in the light of the preceding quotation from *NB* 24).

"the language of imagining": see X, 2, and Russell, e.g. the quote from *Mind*, 250, for §501.

doesn't allow of senseless drawings?: see Man. 110, 41; cp. §526.

"Such is not the case: for a drawing may be senseless in the same way a sentence is. Think of a mechanical drawing from which a turner is to work; here it is very easy to imagine an exact analogy with a senseless pseudo-proposition. Remember too the example of drawing a route on a projection of the globe" (*PG* 129). This second illustration may have been suggested by Waismann's assertions: "A map can represent reality truly or falsely, but never senselessly. Everything the map shows is possible. On the contrary, verbal description can be meaningless. I can say for instance: 'A lies to the north of B and B lies to the north of A' " (*Kreis*, 239). "But a map cannot represent this nonsense, since it has the right multiplicity" (ibid., 79).

Suppose they were . . . : W.'s earlier comment on the last sentence of §511: "That would be like saying: a meaningful picture is one which can not only be drawn but also be modelled. And that would make sense" (*PG* 130). In the *Investigations*, on the contrary, he stresses that there are many kinds of pictures (§§291, 552), so straightens out the remark. (How would one "model" the route mentioned in *PG* 129, above?)

some not: cp. §397.

What if I imagine . . . : wouldn't that be an instance of imagining something senseless?

§513 See §269; Z 246, 248; *RFM* 146g; *PG* 194b; *PB* 213cdef; Man. 106, 270; cp. p. 53n; Z 74; *Kreis*, 249; Frege, *Writings*, 118a.

This is reworked from Man. 228, §506; Man. 116, 60–61; and *PG* 130d–131, where the first example is preceded by the following introduction, suggesting what sort of light the number throws on the concepts *understanding* and *meaning*, and its relation to the preceding and subsequent numbers: "But thinking a sentence is not an activity which we perform in accordance with words (somewhat like singing from notes). The following example shows this."

An earlier example: "Euclid's axiom and the axiom: the sum of the angles in a triangle = 181°. Here I don't see the contradiction right off; for I don't see straightway that the sum 180° follows from the axioms" (*Kreis*, 126; *PB* 323).

(a) yield no sense: "The sense of a sentence isn't spiritual (as thinking isn't), but is what we give in answer to a request for an explanation of the sense" (*PG* 131; cp. §560), and no explanation can be given in these cases. For the roots of the first equation are two imaginary numbers and the number one, and those of the second equation are just two imaginary numbers.

(b) "How odd, if a person means something for every word, that a combination of such words can still be nonsense!" (*PG* 108). See §125cd, and comments above.

If meaning or understanding a sentence were a mental act accompanying it, for instance one's imaginings in connection with it (p. 18n), or a parade of word meanings through the mind (p. 176), we might mean or understand even sentences like these (§117) and, given the connection between understanding and sense, they would have a sense. But "nothing is more wrong-headed than calling meaning [or understanding] a mental activity!" (§693; see *PG* 131, above).

§514   "I am here": see §117; *OC* 10; *BB* 72ab; cp. Moore, *Commonplace*, 240d.

"Just as the words 'I am here' have a meaning only in certain contexts, and not when I say them to someone who is sitting in front of me and sees me clearly,—and not because they are superfluous, but because their meaning is not *determined* by the situation, yet stands in need of such determination" (*OC* 348). "Only the accustomed context allows what is meant to come through clearly" (*OC* 237).

he doesn't think at all . . . : see §520.

"A rose is red . . .": the example suggests how irrelevant to meaning are acts of imagining; for of course saying the rose is red in the dark doesn't mean it appears red in the dark (§515).

**§515   Cp. §302b; *PB* 106d; Russell, *Problems*, 5, and *Logic*, 195b. It is easy to miss the beauty of this example as therapy for representationalism. We talk about a red rose in the dark; but how are we to represent it to ourselves? It appears we must eliminate either the rose or the darkness in our accompanying illustration; so any mental picture seems grossly inaccurate. Only conventions might be cited in its favor, not similarity, and the same might be said for words. (See *BB* 37, quoted in XII, 3.)

§516 See GI 14; §352, p. 224l, and comments; *RFM* 138c–139c, 140i, 155h, 185; *PG* 480a; *PP* 302–4 (especially the quotation for §334); Man. 228, §§665–69 (where §§516–17 are connected with *Z* 695–97, which see); Goodstein, "Mathematics", 272–73 (for an interesting and relevant comparison from one of W.'s lectures) and 274–77; cp. §§426, 463; *Z* 258; *RFM* 116d, 150gh; *BB* 37c; *PG* 483a, 372 ("What can you do with this knowledge? for that will show you in what the knowledge consists"); *PB* 155c, 167cd, 175–77, 185d, 189a, 234cd, 235a, 236f, 334; *Kreis*, 82n, 102, 143–44, 202a; Waismann, *Principles*, 395–96; Man. 110, 114: "This brings me back to the fact that every explanation of a sign should be able to serve in place of the sign. That is, if I as it were construct a sign by means of an explanation, the construction must be equivalent to the result of the construction."

reaches just so far . . . : once again, imagination leaves us in the lurch (see §517). Cp. p. 220de and commentary; Baker and Hacker, Notice, 282a.

"Not that a mathematical proposition is assured a sense only when it (or the opposite) is proved" (*PB* 170; cp. 172bc). But "the question—I want to say—changes its status, when it becomes decidable. For a connexion is made then, which formerly *was not there*" (*RFM* 138). Thus we should not too readily assimilate *occurs* to *gives*, say in "25 × 25 gives 625" (*PB* 175). And the complete phrase differs still more from Russell's example: "The word 'red' can only be understood through acquaintance with the object, whereas the phrase 'Roses are red' can be understood if you know what 'red' is and what 'roses' are, without ever having heard the phrase before" (*Logic*, 195). I can picture the red roses, even if I have never seen them, but not the occurrence of the sevens.

§517 See Waismann, *Principles*, 391–96.

(a) Cp. p. 53n.

(b) See §§334, 463, and commentaries; Man. 125.

cannot **imagine:** as "we can't imagine trisecting an angle by rule and compasses, whereas we can imagine dividing an angle into eight equal parts by rule and compasses" (*PP* 304). "And here imagining is not a particular mental process during which one usually shuts one's eyes or covers them with one's hands" (*RFM* 113; see commentary on §515).

construction of the heptagon: cp. this similar case: "a schoolboy trying to find the geometrical construction of a regular pentagon. The goal towards which he is struggling seems at first perfectly evident: he is trying, by means of ruler and compasses, to inscribe in a circle a pentagon with sides of equal length" (Waismann, *Principles*, 391).

XVIII. Propositions and Pictures (§§518–524)

(1)   Moore reports that "in connection with the *Tractatus* statement that propositions . . . are 'pictures', [Wittgenstein] said he had not at that time noticed that the word 'picture' was vague; but he still, even towards the end of (III), said that he thought it 'useful to say "A proposition is a picture *or something like one*" ' although in (II) he had said he was willing to admit that to call a proposition a 'picture' was misleading; that propositions are not pictures 'in any ordinary sense' " (*PP* 263). In the present numbers a genuine analogy between pictures and propositions proves useful precisely as a corrective to the Tractarian doctrine. Nourishing his thinking with a limited diet of examples—the scheme of an automobile accident (I, 1), hieroglyphs (4.016), a *tableau vivant* (4.0311)—that is, with "likenesses of what is signified" (4.012) by means of which "we picture facts to ourselves" (2.1), he had declared quite generally: "A picture presents a situation in logical space, the existence and non-existence of states of affairs" (2.11). Hence if a proposition is a logical picture of reality, it too proclaims "This is how things stand" (4.5; see GI 32–35). However, this is a very narrow view not only of propositions but also of pictures (§522 and commentary). In particular, pictures, like propositions, often have no "reference".

(2)   Wittgenstein introduces this theme in §518, then begins to focus on his own early version of the general error. According to the *Tractatus* a proposition did indeed picture something even if the something did not exist and never would (GI 34–36). For it represented a possible state of affairs, which (since merely a possibility) might not be realized and (since a state of affairs) was something more than a thought in the mind or a *flatus vocis* (§519). A proposition reached right out to reality by means of its names, touching real objects (2.15121), which "contain the possibility of all situations" (2.014). Furthermore, the components of a proposition are themselves objects, possessing the same logical properties as their referents; and through their actual combination in the proposition they realize vicariously the possible configuration they represent (*NB* 26–27). Thus the picture itself "contains the possibility of the situation that it represents" (2.203). As for tautologies and contradictions, though they do not portray any specific state of affairs, they

do show "the formal—logical—properties of language and the world" (6.12, 6.1202). They have at least this minimal relation to reality, so are not nonsense as are metaphysical assertions (see commentary on §521). Wittgenstein first deals with these refinements (§§520–21), then attacks the whole conception of propositions and language as necessarily referential (see I, 3). The very comparison with pictures teaches the lesson (§§522–24).

DETAILED COMMENTARY

§518 On this and the following two numbers, see *BB* 37d–39a. On §518, see also Meinong's views as recounted by Russell (*Logic*, 169–70; *Mind*, 16–17); *BB* 35d–36a; *PG* 137; Man. 111, 14, 20; and especially *Z* 69. Cp. §§462–63; *NB* 870pq.

"Our first instinct is to suppose that a judgment, whether true or false, must be analysable into a mind and an object in relation. In a sense this is admitted to be true by everybody; it is undisputed that there is something objective, what Russell and Wittgenstein call the 'proposition as fact', which enters into any judgement. When we judge, we form a picture of the reality about which we are judging, a form of words, a set of marks or noises, which we suppose, rightly or wrongly, to afford an image of the facts. This is the 'proposition as fact'; the question is, what, if anything, is there more?" (Hardy, "Proof", 22).

Russell argued that when, for instance, we believe that Caesar crossed the Rubicon, what we are really believing is something in our mind, since the crossing has passed out of existence (*Mind*, 233–34). "Every presentation and every belief must have an object other than itself and, except in certain cases where mental existents happen to be concerned, [the object is] extramental" ("Meinong's Theory", 204).

"We are here misled by the substantives 'object of thought' and 'fact', and by the different meanings of the word 'exist'.

"Talking of the fact as a 'complex of objects' springs from this confusion (cf. *Tractatus Logico-Philosophicus*). Supposing we asked: 'How can one *imagine* what does not exist?' The answer seems to be: 'If we do, we imagine non-existent combinations of existing elements.' A centaur doesn't exist, but a man's head and torso and arms and a horse's legs do exist. 'But can't we imagine an object utterly different from any one which exists?'—We should be inclined to answer: 'No; the elements, individuals, must exist. If redness, roundness and sweetness did not exist, we could not imagine them'" (*BB* 31; notice that the German verb in §518a is *vorstellen*, not *denken*).

(a) The quotation is from *Theaetetus*, 189A; see also 188, and *Sophist*, 262E, 263CE. Cp. Frege, *Writings*, 127; Moore, *Problems*, 213–14, 289b, and 62: "If we take some one of the words of which it is composed, for instance the word 'two', this word by itself does not make a complete sentence and does not express a proposition. But it *does* express *something*. What we mean by the word 'two' is certainly something. This something, therefore, *is*—is something, and yet is not a proposition." *PG* 137 discusses the subsequent lines in *Theaetetus*, 189A, viz.: "*Soc.*: Then he who thinks of that which is not, thinks of nothing?—*Theaet.*: Clearly.—*Soc.*: And he who thinks of nothing does not think at all?— *Theaet.*: Obviously.—*Soc.*: Then no one can think that which is not, either as a self-existent substance or a predicate of another?—*Theaet.*: Clearly not."

"if someone thinks": this translation of *vorstellt* obscures the connection with §517.

(b) And mustn't someone . . . : "We would like to object that the drawing is not the fact that will later occur, so cannot portray what will then happen, but only something similar [see Russell, above]. Much less therefore can I *say* that something will happen. To explain this paradox let us imagine that someone were to say that this portrait cannot represent Mr. N. but only something like him" (Man. 302, 19). After all, Mr. N. may cease to exist, but "the portrait of a person who doesn't exist is an absurdity. The person it represents *belongs* to the portrait" (Man. 108, 251).

Well, tell me . . . : cp. §519; *Z* 29b ("When he used an expression, did he mean something other than the expression or did he simply *mean* the expression?"); *PG* 169–70; *BB* 38 ("I am here using the expression 'object of our thought' in a way different from that in which I have used it before. I mean now a thing I am thinking *about,* not 'that which I am thinking' ").

§519 From *PG* 212, where the connection with §518 is made evident by the introductory sentence: "Above all, 'picture' is ambiguous here." A portrait of the way we would like someone to look would not be a portrait; but we use the word *picture* both ways.

One wants to say: W. had (GI 36), but later he "pointed out that it is paradoxical to say that the words 'Leave the room' is a 'picture' of what a boy does if he obeys the order, and . . . asserted that it is, in fact, *not* a 'picture' of the boy's action 'in any ordinary sense' " (*PP* 263–64).

§520 A revision of Man. 116, 79–80 (which adds an illustration of the final remark) and of *PG* 127c (from which the quoted words are taken, somewhat altered). These represent the antithetical moment in W.'s thought, whereas the present number suggests a synthetic solution (see XXXIX, 1–5). At the start W. had written: "We can indeed say: everything that is (or is not) the case can be pictured by means of a proposition" (*NB* 51). But here an ambiguity lurks. It is one thing to mistakenly picture as fact a positive but nonexistent state of affairs, and quite another to represent the same state of affairs and negate it. In the latter case we do not picture or portray reality, not in any ordinary sense of these terms. (Who ever heard of a negative portrait?) So neither do we read off the statement from reality (§292). Nor, therefore, are the rules we follow in the least "natural and inevitable" (6.124)—save perhaps in another sense than that intended by the author of the *Tractatus* (XXXIX, 5).

"If a proposition too is conceived . . .": as in W.'s former view (GI 32, 35; 4.01–4.024).

"is what a painting . . .": " 'I can't show him to you now, as he isn't here. All I can show you is a picture of him' " (*BB* 38). And "only the contrary negative, not the contradictory, can be drawn (that is, positively represented)" (Man. 109, 103).

"not set forth . . .": "If a picture presents what-is-not-the-case in the forementioned way, this only happens through its presenting *that* which *is* not the case. For the picture says, as it were: '*This* is how it is *not*,' and to the question '*How* is it not?' just the positive proposition is the answer" (*NB* 25). Thus "the proposition must *contain* (and in this way shew) the *possibility of its truth*. But not more than the *possibility*" (*NB* 16; see 2.173, 3.13; Man. 213, 109–10).

"So does it depend . . .": this has the form of a statement in *PG* 127. Thoughts like the following explain it: "Then—picture *and way of representing* are completely outside what is represented!" (*NB* 21). So "for any sign whatever there *could* be a method of projection such that it made sense" (*PP* 265; see LF 33a); and "the projective properties of the original figure remain unchanged whichever of these ways may be adopted" (Russell, "Introduction", xi). "In trying to explain why we can't give reasons for following any particular rule, he laid very great stress on an argument, which he put differently in different places, and which I must confess I do not clearly understand. Two of the premises of this argument are, I think, clear enough. One was (1) that any reason 'would have to be a description of reality' . . . . And the second was (2) that 'any description of reality must be capable of truth and falsehood.' . . . He gave as an illustration of his meaning that it cannot be because of a 'quality in reality' that 'I use sweet' in such a way that 'sweeter' has meaning, but 'identical' in such a way that 'more identical' has none; giving as a reason 'If it were because of a "quality" in reality, it must be possible to say that reality hasn't got this quality, which grammar forbids' " (*PP* 277–78).

But surely . . . : for W.'s early opposition to this conclusion, see the commentary on p. 230b, and XXXIX, 1–3.

Is it arbitrary?: see XVI, 10; XXXIX, 4–6; §497 and commentary; *PG* 92c, 126b; *PP* 279: "He seemed, therefore, here to be admitting that reasons *of a sort* can sometimes be given for following a particular 'grammatical rule'."

and when we are tempted in philosophy . . . : see GI 14; §414;

RFM 3of, 31d, 54a, 146; *BB* 72ab, 170c, 174cd; *PG* 194b; 3.328; *PP* 319a.

some quite useless thing: for instance the principle of identity, "A thing is identical with itself" (§216); the solipsist's assertion, "Only this is *really* seen" (*BB* 65–66); Russell's Paradox (*RFM* 166); Descartes' *Cogito* (Coope et al., *Workbook*, 21); Moore's declarations, "I know that this is a hand" (*OC* 371–72) and "I know that I have two hands" (*OC* 245, 247). Cp. Berkeley, *Dialogues*, II, 437 ("you employ words to no manner of purpose").

we have not considered its application sufficiently: see e.g. §514; *OC* 622; *LC* 2. Cp. Frege, "Compound", 15–16: "In such a case the questions arise: 'Does this sentence express a thought? Doesn't it lack content? Do we learn anything new upon hearing it?' . . . It is surely an undeniable fact that the Schneekoppe is higher than the Brocken if the Schneekoppe is higher than the Brocken. Since only thoughts can be true, this compound sentence must express a thought; and, despite its apparent senselessness, the negation of this thought is also a thought."

§521   See *PG* 128a; Man. 302, 17–18; cp. Russell, *Logic*, 150.

"We are constantly confused by the thought, 'But can there be a possibility, without there being a reality that corresponds to it?" (*PB* 164). Thus it seems that chemistry treats of the fact, logic of the possibility (§97). "It is as though something were not real but more real than if it were impossible" (Man. 302, 16; see §462b; *PG* 138d).

'chemically possible': cp. *PG* 483a, quoted for §117a.

cannot have less than no . . . : "That is, the possibility is not a sort of half reality" (Man. 107, 258; see §94). Cp. §461c; *PG* 137b; 4.063. W.'s target appears in Man. 106, 167: "The proposition which according to Dedekind says that the class F is infinite, is at any rate only false—not nonsensical—if only a finite number of things satisfy the function F; but it is nonsensical if only a finite number of things exist." Such thinking reflects the *Tractatus* distinction between meaningful, meaningless, and nonsensical statements (XVIII, 2), for instance with regard to colors: (1) Analysis reveals that "the statement that a point in the visual field has two different colours at the same time is a contradiction" (6.3751), as are other such "logical impossibilities". (2) Contradictions do not have sense, but neither are they nonsense (4.461–4.4611), like the sayings of metaphysicians (6.53). (3) For a proposition such as that just cited does at least name things (the colors, the point), whereas the metaphysician has generally "failed to give a meaning to certain signs in his propositions" (ibid.). (4) His failure is purely grammatical, whereas "the simultaneous presence of two colours at the same place in the visual field is impossible, in fact logically impossible, since it is ruled out by the logical structure of colour" (6.3751). But what is this *logical* structure of colors? It too, W. now replies, is a matter of grammar (§372): As the metaphysician failed to provide a meaning for certain signs, so we have failed to give any meaning to certain *combinations* of signs, e.g. "This point is now both green and blue" (cp. §138a).

§522   See *PG* 42a; Man. 302, 8–9; Man. 115, 11–13; Man. 111, 9–11; Man. 107, 155; cp. §§518b, 519; Man. 109, 233. *PG* 164b adds, "Sentences in fiction correspond to genre-pictures," and thereby indicates the intended application of these remarks: the contrast between language-games such as poetry (§531) or fictitious narratives (§§524–25), on the one hand, and descriptions declaring "This is how things stand" (the general form of all propositions, according to 4.5), on the other. Thus W. is again stressing the diversity of language (I, 10). "We think: 'Propositions serve to describe how things stand.' The proposition as *picture*. And that is all right, but there are still lifes, portraits, landscapes, mythological representations, ornaments, maps, diagrams, etc. etc." (Man. 228, §168). So W. had erred about pictures too (2.182).

(a) a portrait: of an actual person. Thus "propositions in poems . . . are related to verifiable propositions as a genre-picture is to a portrait" (Man. 109, 26). Cp. Man. 108, 251, quoted for §518b.

   a genre-picture: the comparison is apt, for just as fictitious narratives describe people, actions, surroundings, and the like, after the manner of factual reports, so genre-pictures depict people, objects, buildings, and so on much as do representations of actual scenes (cp. Man. 109, 26).

(b) Considerably revised from Man. 109, 26–27, and *PG* 164. See *PG* 77f–78.

   or that there have . . . : it isn't just that in such pictures (and narratives) "the connection with here and now is missing" (Man. 109, 26), for that would hold equally were the world "completely described by completely general propositions, and hence without using any sort of names or other denoting signs" (*NB* 14; see 5.526).

   But suppose . . . : better: "For suppose . . ." (*Denn*).

   "What does it tell me, then?": "What's understood is as it were autonomous, and understanding it is comparable to understanding a melody" (*PG* 79). See I, 3; commentary on §523; cp. §526.

§523   See I, 3–4; *Z* 195; *PG* 79 (above), 169, 172i–173a; *LC* 29–30, 34; *PP* 314–15; Man. 115, 1.

   I should like to say: W. did in *PG* 165, then explained: "Its telling me something will consist in my recognizing in it objects arranged in some characteristic manner. (If I say: 'I see a table in this picture,' then this characterizes the picture—as I said—in a way that has nothing to do with the existence of a 'real' table. . .)."

What would it mean to say . . . : see the commentary on §527, especially the quotation from *BB* 166.

"It has sometimes been said that what music conveys to us are feelings of joyfulness, melancholy, triumph, etc., etc. and what repels us in this account is that it seems to say that music is an instrument for producing in us sequences of feelings. And from this one might gather that any other means of producing such feelings would do for us instead of music.—To such an account we are tempted to reply 'Music conveys to us *itself*!'" (*BB* 178).

"You could play a minuet once and get a lot out of it, and play the same minuet another time and get nothing out of it. But it doesn't follow that what you get out of it is then independent of the minuet. Cf. the mistake of thinking that the meaning or thought is just an accompaniment of the word, and the word doesn't matter. 'The sense of a proposition' is very similar to the business of 'an appreciation of art'. The idea that a sentence has a relation to an object, such that, whatever has this effect is the *sense* of the sentence" (*LC* 29).

§524(a) See *Z* 652; BUF 240b; *PG* 182e; cp. p. 205g; Man. 229, §1741.

Don't take it . . . : cp. §363b.

but as a remarkable fact: "Consider: What an odd thing is reading a story. He talks about men who never lived and tells the thoughts of men who never lived" (JN 38).

that pictures and fictitious narratives . . . : "A sentence in a story gives us the same satisfaction as a picture does" (*PG* 171). "A picture can be fascinating *in itself* and compel us to use it without any regard to whether it is right or wrong" (Man. 163).

(bc) See pp. 190k, 191g, 212g, 220g; *RFM* 186g; Man. 229, §§1289, 1633–35, 1682; cp. *RFM* 178ab; *PB* 80b; Man. 130, 20–21.

"Often philosophy resolves a problem only by saying: *Here* there is no more difficulty than *there*.

"So only by making a difficulty where there previously was none.

"It says: 'Isn't it equally odd that . . . ,' then lets the matter rest" (Man. 229, §1667).

The present context suggests this illustration: "How strange," one says, "that we should think and talk of someone who is not present—in fact who may not even now exist!" (see §95). "Well, how strange then," W. now replies, "that we should speak of people who never have existed!" Thus the requirement of mental projection (GI 37) finally snaps. For it would be evident nonsense to suppose that in recounting the life of some fictitious hero we have to pick out a nonexistent referent. So we come to recognize the veiled nonsense in requiring such projection elsewhere, and finally accept the language-game as it is actually played (see GI 58, 62).

" 'When you speak of dreaming, thinking, and experiencing—don't all these things seem to lose the mysteriousness which appears their essential characteristic?' Why should a dream be more mysterious than a table? Why shouldn't they both be equally mysterious?" (Man. 229, §1045). "Yes, every such use of language is remarkable, peculiar, if one is adjusted only to consider the description of physical objects" (Z 40).

from patent nonsense to . . . : this remark appears to reverse §464, but does not. Two steps may be distinguished in the same therapeutic process: one from confusing cases to a clear case, where the view to be exorcised is patent nonsense; the other from recognition of the nonsense in this evident case to like recognition in the other cases. For example: If someone supposes that obedience to an order requires a preliminary act of understanding, picturing the act to be performed, W. asks him to consider the command "Imagine a yellow patch." Seeing the absurdity of requiring two acts in this case, he will then recognize the absurdity of requiring two elsewhere (GI 62). Or, in the present instance: The logical atomist supposes that pictures, whether logical or other, must have reference; so W. suggests that he consider genre-pictures and fictitious narratives, view them the same way, and so be surprised at their lack of reference. This patent nonsense will open his eyes to the other. The same double movement occurs in the numbers that precede §464.

XIX. Different Uses of *Understand* and *Meaning* (§§525–546)

GENERAL COMMENTARY

(1)   Already in Man. 302, 8–11, Wittgenstein had thoughts like those which turn up later in Waismann's *Principles*, 360: "We have so far laid great emphasis on the fact that understanding is a disposition. It is now time to rectify this conception a little. There are also *experiences* which can be described as understanding. Such an experience, for example, is seeing a sign in a certain way." This quotation indicates the general thrust of the present numbers. It also suggests their main connections in the *Investigations,* with antecedent numbers on understanding as a disposition (Section IX) and with subsequent pages on seeing signs in a

certain way (Section XXXVII). In Sections XXXII and XXXVII, understanding and meaning are treated together as they are here, and in similar fashion, though in those later sections the concept *meaning* (*Bedeutung*) is far more prominent than *understand*.

(2)   Wittgenstein judged that, as a matter of grammatical fact, both *understand* (§§526, 531–33) and *meaning* (§§529, 540–45) are sometimes extended, in a similar way (XXXVII, 15), to designate experiences, and that the experiences they then designate are similar. This does not mean that some words have use-meanings and others have experience-meanings, or that when we understand we sometimes have a certain experience and other times a capacity. Roughly, the distinction is one of intension, not extension. Of understanding we might say, somewhat as of meaning (§43), that for a large class of cases in which we use the word *understand* it indicates an ability, whereas on other occasions it designates an experience. However, the division is not clear-cut (§§526–27).

(3)   A somewhat similar duality characterizes certain nonsemantic terms, for instance *hear* (§534), *feel* (§535), and *see* (XXXVII, 13–19), which not only have secondary, more "subjective" uses, as do *meaning* and *understand,* but are applied in these senses to much the same linguistic, musical, and artistic samples.

DETAILED COMMENTARY

§525   Revised from *PG* 43d; Man. 116, 11–12; Man. 109, 191. See *Z* 176; cp. §§539, 652a.

A meaningful sentence, the *Tractatus* had said, is one which can be thought, and thinking it would consist in projecting the signs, that is, mentally representing the matters described (GI 36–37). But "why do I say here: 'I can imagine . . . '? Here it means something like: I could easily fill in the picture further" (Man. 179).

(a) might perhaps be used: concerning objections raised against this way of speaking, see the commentary on §20b.

(b) See §534; *BB* 183b–184a.

§526   Revised from Man. 116, 12; *PG* 42a. Cp. §512; *PG* 163–64. In *PG* 72b and 78, W. cites other examples, e.g. puzzle pictures, in which "there occurs a familiar process of recognition, perhaps after a period of doubt. If, on the other hand, the picture is one of which we would say 'we grasp it at first glance' we find it difficult to say precisely what the understanding consists in here. Above all, what happened was not that we took the painted objects for real ones" (*PG* 78).

§527   Reworked from Man. 112, 150–51. See I, 3; quotations for §523 ("What would it mean to say"); *Z* 165; *BB* 166–67; *PG* 41e, 43a, 79a; *LC* 29; Man. 229, 291–92; Man. 133, 30–31; Man. 131, 2–3; Man. 130,

56–57, 60–62; Man. 121, May 25 (e.g. "The music of Bach resembles language more than does the music of Mozart & Haydn"); Schopenhauer, *World*, I, 256–57; cp. §22c; *Z* 157–75; 3.141; *NB* 40cf, 41ij; *PP* 313b–314a; Man. 219, 21–22; Man. 163; Schopenhauer, *World*, II, 448–49. This number is important as an explanation of Section XXXVII, on aspect-seeing. The connection with the applications to speech, and in particular with p. 214, comes out in Man. 229, §913: "Could we say that meaning-blindness would reveal itself in the man's not being able to say effectively: 'You must hear the word as . . . , then you will speak the sentence right'? That is the instruction one gives about playing a piece of music. 'Play it as though it were an answer'—and then one perhaps makes a gesture." See also *PB* 281c.

much more akin . . . : see the passage just quoted, and *BB* 167, below.

"Likewise, the expressiveness of a musical theme depends only on its situation in the whole musical language to which it belongs. Here I always think of the conclusion of the Allegretto in the seventh symphony, the final variation of the main theme, & specifically the four measures 9 to 12. They are like a concluding nod of the head, or could be accompanied by one. They are enormously expressive. As it were: unforgettable words. But naturally only in combination: first with this whole variation, but then with the whole movement, & that only for someone who understands our musical language" (Man. 130, 60). "Thus when I understand a sentence, what happens is very similar to my being able to follow a melody as a melody, in contrast with: when it is too long or too complicated and I have to say, 'I couldn't follow this part' " (*PG* 72). "The view opposed to this one is the idea that understanding a sentence means getting outside of language, that is, making the connection between language and reality" (Man. 302, 2; see ibid., 10).

theme in music: "To watch Wittgenstein listening to music was to realize that this was something very central and deep in his life. He told me that this he could not express in his writings, and yet it was so important to him that he felt without it he was sure to be misunderstood. I will never forget the emphasis with which he quoted Schopenhauer's dictum: 'Music is a world in itself' " (Drury, "Symposium", 67–68; cp. Malcolm, "Wittgenstein", 327). It is natural, therefore, that the comparison between language and music always interested W. (see the references above). Only in his later period, though, did he recognize how extensive the analogy is. All the similarities between language and games, in I, 1–10, apply to music as well.

What I mean is . . . : "I don't mean that understanding a musical theme is more like the picture which one tends to make oneself of understanding a sentence; but rather that this picture is wrong, and that understanding a sentence is much more like what really happens when we understand a tune than at first sight appears. For understanding a sentence, we say, points to a reality outside the sentence. Whereas one might say 'Understanding a sentence means getting hold of its content; and the content of the sentence is *in* the sentence' " (*BB* 167; cp. §523).

I should not be able to say: cp. p. 183b; *PG* 78. W. is not suggesting by implication that speech is as nonreferential as music, but is making with regard to a musical theme the point already made concerning propositions, in §502.

"The same strange illusion which we are under when we seem to seek the something which a face expresses whereas, in reality, we are giving ourselves up to the features before us—that same illusion possesses us even more strongly if repeating a tune to ourselves and letting it make its full impression on us, we say 'This tune says *something*,' and it is as though I had to find *what* it says. And yet I know that it doesn't say anything such that I might express in words or pictures what it says. And if, recognizing this, I resign myself to saying 'It just expresses a musical thought,' this would mean no more than saying 'It expresses itself.'—'But surely when you play it you don't play it *anyhow,* you play it in this particular way, making a crescendo here, a diminuendo there, a caesura in this place, etc.'—Precisely, and that's all I can say about it, or may be all that I can say about it" (*BB* 166).

"Could one also reply: 'I meant something by this movement, which I can only express by this movement'? (Music, musical thought)" (*Z* 30).

the same rhythm: cp. *PG* 78–79: "The familiarity consists, say, in my immediately grasping a particular rhythm of the picture and staying with it, as it were resting in it."

the same pattern: "There is a strongly musical element in verbal language. (A sigh, the intonation of voice in a question, in an announcement, in longing; all the innumerable *gestures* made with the voice.)" (*Z* 161). Cp. *BB* 178f–179b.

One says . . . : see p. 182g. "In certain cases I can justify, explain the particular expression with which I play it by a comparison, as when I say 'At this point of the theme, there is, as it were, a colon,' or 'This is, as it were, the answer to what came before,' etc." (*BB* 166). "He had said earlier that all Aesthetics is of the nature of 'giving a good simile' " (*PP* 316).

different kinds of justification: for instance, "I hear the melody entirely otherwise after I know the style of this composer. I would have described it for instance as gay, but now experience it as the expression of a great sorrow. I now describe it differently, connect it with something quite different" (Man. 138, 9A). See *PP* 314–15; cp. §533, pp. 54n, 218m; *LC* 4c.

§528 Cp. *LC* 34h; K. Bühler, *Development*, 132–33; *PG* 43e ("Do we *understand* the poems of Christian Morgenstern, or Lewis Carroll's poem 'Jabberwocky'? It is evident in these cases that the concept of understanding is fluid").

A communication medium developed and employed by Ken Feit is reported in these terms: "It's so unique and different that a written description of a soundpoem is almost impossible; you really have to hear one to believe it. But try to imagine a group of sounds, not words (well, not dictionary words anyway) that tell a story" (*National Jesuit News*, Dec. 1971). Says Feit: "How many parents have hovered over their toddler patiently coaxing, 'Say "mama, mama," ' while the child with shrieks, gurgles, hand waves, and kicks was speaking far more sophisticated language of needs and perceptions" (ibid.).

"(Words are not essential to what we call 'language', nor are samples.) Verbal language is only one of many possible kinds, and there are transitions from one to the other" (*PG* 93; see *PG* 179e).

a play of sounds: "Mightn't we imagine a man who, never having had any acquaintance with music, comes to us and hears someone playing a reflective piece of Chopin and is convinced that this is a language and people merely want to keep the meaning secret from him?" (Z 161).

'Speaking with tongues': a common phenomenon in early Christian communities, now reviving in charismatic groups. Cf. *1 Corinthians* 14 (e.g.: "He who speaks in a tongue does not speak to men but to God; for no one understands, as he is speaking mysteries in his spirit").

§529 See I, 3; cp. p. 214.

What is it in music?: see commentary on §§523, 527.

§530 See p. 218l; Man. 229, §§674, 718; cp. pp. 54n, 213–14.

"It has been said that a sentence has not only a meaning but also a soul & we mustn't let ourselves be misled by the appearance of such a soul. One could imagine a language without such souls; in fact our chemical symbolism is such a language. A language in which we would have to decode every sentence" (Man. 161; W.'s English). "The signs are e.g. written and transmitted to us, and we are able to *take notice of them*. (That is to say, the only impression that comes in here is the pattern of the sign.) If the sign is an order, we translate it into action by means of rules, tables. It does not get as far as an impression, like that of a picture; nor are stories written in this language" (Z 145; *PG* 171–72).

'soul' of the words: James's expression; see *Principles*, II, 80–81, quoted for p. 214ef.

§531 These thoughts are already quite fully developed in Man. 302, 9. See also *PG* 41–43; *LC* 34; Frege, "Thought", 295; cp. §167a; James, *Principles*, I, 261a.

"It may be that, for its effect to be achieved, a word cannot be replaced by any other, just as it may be that a gesture cannot be replaced by any other. (The word has a *soul,* and not just a meaning.) No one would suppose that a poem remains *essentially unaltered* if its words are replaced by others in accordance with an appropriate convention" (*PG* 69).

(a) See XIX, 1–2; *PG* 79a; Man. 228, §4.

Any more than . . . : "If I admire a minuet I can't say: 'Take another, it does the same thing' " (*LC* 34).

(b) Cp. Schopenhauer, *World,* II, 424, 429.

in these positions: see p. 214i ("this may, of course, depend on sentence-formation"). "What Aesthetics tries to do, he said, is to give *reasons,* e.g. for having this word rather than that in a particular place in a poem, or for having this musical phrase rather than that in a particular place in a piece of music" (*PP* 314).

Understanding a poem: see *LC* 34, e.g.: "You *could* select either of two poems to remind you of death, say. But supposing you had read a poem and admired it, could you say: 'Oh, read the other it will do the same'?

"How do we use poetry? Does it play this role—that we say such a thing as: 'Here is something just as good . . .'?

"Imagine an entirely different civilization. Here there is something you might call music, since it has notes. They treat music like this: certain music makes them walk like this. They play a record to do this. One says: 'I need this record now. Oh no, take the other, it is just as good.' "

"Do not forget that a poem, even though it is composed in the language of information, is not used in the language-game of giving information" (*Z* 160).

§532   See XIX, 1–2; Ambrose, "Universals", 345; cp. Man. 229, §1728; Man. 116, 346; Waismann, *Principles,* 360. On the double use of *meaning* and *understand,* see XXXVII, 15. "It is precisely the connection of these facets, their kinship, that here produces a *single* concept" (*PG* 77). "We cannot say either that 'game' has just several independent meanings (say like the word 'bank'). Rather, what we call 'games' are procedures related to one another in various ways" (*PG* 75). See *LC* 12. On the causal connection in cases like the present one, see XXXVII, 17.

(a) I would rather say . . . : though this answer does not say outright that there is only one meaning, it may still seem to differ from the treatment on p. 216 where, speaking of analogous cases, W. wrote: "Here one might speak of a 'primary' and 'secondary' sense of a word"—therefore of two senses, not one. However, the question in §532 asks whether there are two *different* senses, whereas p. 216 stresses the senses' close connection, and in fact says: "I want to use *these* words (with their familiar meanings) *here*." On the justification of such fluctuation and apparent inconsistency, see e.g. §§552–56, where it is evident that such verbal niceties did not have great importance in W.'s eyes. Cp. §79d.

(b) For I *want* . . . : in addition to the above explanations, see p. 204k.

§533   how can one explain . . . : not by mere translation (§§527, 531), into verbal signs or others (cp. §§449, 459), or through ostensive definition (p. 216e; cp. p. 196c).

How does one *lead* . . . : as opposed, say, to showing. Explanation may mean many things; here it does not consist in forming synonymous sentences with other familiar words, or in explaining unfamiliar terms by means of familiar ones, so that a similar revelation of sense automatically occurs (cp. p. 224l; 4.026–4.031). See p. 202k; *PP* 315 (quoted for §144); cp. §535, p. 200d.

or of a theme: see §527 and commentary.

§534   See *BB* 183b–184a; *PG* 152d, 153b; cp. §74, pp. 196g, 204l, 205e.

(a) a particular sense: in German, *Bedeutung*. See the commentary on §43a ("of a word").

How queer . . . : see p. 200ef.

(c) See §525b.

§535   See XIX, 3; p. 182g and the surrounding discussion; and the paragraph which precedes this number in *PG* 179. The word *feel* is italicized for the same reason as *hearing* is in §534; both words are here used in a similar, secondary sense which is likely to beget bewilderment in someone who has noticed only the primary sense. See p. 208cd.

§536   See XXXVII, 14; *PG* 179a; Man. 115, 26–27.

We do not mean . . . : cp. pp. 207, 208c.

an aspect of the face itself: as in the examples of Section XXXVII, for instance the duck-rabbit (p. 194), to which similar remarks apply.

§537   See *BB* 179d; *PG* 176d–177a; Man. 228, §416; Man. 115, 23; cp. *NB* 84; James, *Principles*, I, 503a.

does not seem to be . . . : cp. pp. 182h–183a.

fear is there . . . : see *Z* 220; *BB* 162b. I can be said to see it there (Man. 229, §1735).

a corresponding change in the fear: for instance, an increase or decrease.

not know how to lodge . . . : cp. §284, p. 183. More distant comparisons: §510, p. 18n.

such a question: viz., "Can you think. . . ?"

what fits what here?: see *BB* 170; cp. §§136–38, pp. 186c,

195k–196d; *PG* 180 ("For the question is: *What* do I recognize as *what?* For 'to recognize a thing as itself' is meaningless").

"One feels that what one calls the expression of the face is something that can be detached from the drawing of the face. It is as though we could say: 'This face has a particular expression: namely this' (pointing to something). But if I had to point to anything in this place it would have to be the drawing I am looking at" (*BB* 162).

§538   Like the preceding and subsequent numbers, this is already in *PG* 177 (in slightly different words).

There is a related case: here too we "work in a piece of fancy" (p. 206), seeing one thing as, or in terms of, another (cp. XXXVII, 12–13).

perhaps it will not seem so: if we confound German grammar with the rules of human thought (cp. §336), we may appear to be providing a psychological account of how Frenchmen "mean" their words (cp. §20b).

§539   W. continues to rework *PG* 177. See p. 206de; cp. §525, p. 193hi.

§540   See Man. 228, §§105–7.

(a) See p. 18n (*c*); cp. §338b, p. 208j.

"even *without*": not italicized in the German. From within W.'s former perspective, it seemed odd that thought could not anticipate the future (§437), but doubly odd that pure thought, unencumbered by the dead weight of words (§432) and unrestricted by the conventions of common language, could not fly straight to its target (Z 273). Public signs depended on thought for their sense (GI 37), but thought itself seemed self-sufficient (X, 2), reaching right out to reality (2.1511).

(b) Cp. the experience of a person who thinks he understands ordinary words but does not (§§269, 513–17), and the still closer parallel in §509. Man. 180 adds in parentheses: "Such situations occur in dreams."

Didn't he understand . . . : not in the primary sense of *understand* (§531). See *PG* 43e (quoted for §528).

§541   *later:* cp. §§342, 542, 653, 682.

§542   See *BB* 158–60; Man. 229, §1349; cp. pp. 218l–219b.

do *not* say: not so much for the reasons indicated on p. 182, but because this is a noninformative declaration. "We appear to ourselves to be on the verge of describing the way, whereas we aren't really opposing it to any other way" (*BB* 159). "Thus when I say 'red' comes in a particular way . . . , I feel that I might now give this way a name if it hasn't already got one, say 'A'. But at the same time I am not at all prepared to say that I recognize this to be the way 'red' has always come on such occasions, nor even to say that there are, say, four ways, A, B, C, D, in one of which it always comes" (ibid.). Cp. p. 66n and commentary.

What is the *expression* . . . : see Man. 180a: "For the recognition of a sensation there are characteristic *expressions*. . . . The one who gives expression to a sensation employs no criterion." Cp. XXXIV, 4–7.

§543 "I intentionally chose an example in which a man gives expression to his sensation. For in this case sounds belonging to no language are said to be full of meaning" (Z 151). So here is another use of *Bedeutung*. W. is teaching differences. On this and the next two numbers, see NL 312–13.

§544 Cp. §677.

(a) See Man. 229, §1345.

But does it give . . . : not in the ordinary sense of *meaning* (§43)—not "if meaning is what for instance I explain in a definition and reveals itself in the use of words" (Man. 180a). Cp. Z 150–54, 176–77; *EPB* 227: " 'To mean something jokingly (seriously)'.—Do you mean every word of a joke jokingly?"

(b) This recalls the question . . . : there, too, meaning and truth merge. For instance, what would it *mean* to assert that 2 plus 2 equals five? People will say "You're wrong," but is it a false hypothesis (p. 226h)?

§545 See *EPB* 226 and several pages in Man. 179.

(a) And what about . . . : the word *hope* still has meaning, but the feeling is missing or inappropriate. W. uses the same tactic in §443, p. 215g, *RFM* 143kl. Cp. §§447–48; Man. 109, 247.

means *point*: cp. §§564, 567, pp. 178g, 179e; *RFM* 8a.

But why is the feeling . . . : is the service of these words (pp. 178g, 179e) "to convey to one person how it is with another" (§317)—the precise state of his feelings? Even if we can gather something about his feelings from them (§543), is that their typical function? (Cp. §498.) For W.'s answer, see §§585–86.

(b) On hope, see §§583–84, p. 174abc. On characteristic marks of sensations and emotions, see Z 472, 488.

§546   charged with my desire . . . : cp. §329; Man. 110, 73: "The expression of the wish is not the subsequent manifestation of a wish already there but unexpressed. We wish through—or in—this expression."

Words are also deeds: "Naturally human behavior includes not only what people do without having learned a [mode of] behavior, but also what they do (so *e.g. say*) after they have received certain training" (Man. 229, §797). "Our *language-game* is behavior" (ibid., §817). See I, 7; §586.

XX. Negation (§§547–557)

(1)   Though Wittgenstein earlier judged that "the problems of negation, of disjunction, of true and false, are only reflections of the one
great problem in the variously placed great and small mirrors of philosophy" (NB 40), still negation, as the principal logical constant (5.5), had
a key role to play in the parallel structuring of language, thought, and
world (GI 31), and received corresponding attention (far more than
disjunction or conjunction). For a while he supposed that "before any
proposition can make sense at all the *logical* constants must have reference" (NB 15), but he soon changed his mind: "My fundamental
thought is that the logical constants are not proxies" (NB 37). Thus neither in an actual state of affairs nor in its logical portrayal by means of
a proposition will one discover any such thing as negation; rather negation is an operation we perform on propositions. This operation "does
not consist in, say, putting down a ~, but in the class of all negating
operations. But in that case what really are the properties of this ideal
negating operation?" (NB 43).

(2)   As §105 later put it, negation was "supposed to be something pure
and clear-cut. And we rack our brains over the nature of the *real*
sign.—Is it perhaps the *idea* of the sign? or the idea at the present
moment?" After fruitless searching, young Wittgenstein surmised: "My
mistake must lie in my wanting to use what follows from the nature of
negation, etc. in its definition" (NB 56). Nothing but the quintessence
would do. So in the *Tractatus* he could only cryptically observe: "Negation reverses the sense of a proposition" (5.2341). It is somewhat as
though one were to reverse an arrow and make it point in the opposite
direction (NB 97; Man. 228, 124; Man. 110, 107–8). In one direction
the proposition says this is how things *are*, in the other it says it is how
they are *not*. But here the word *not* stands for the whole class of negating signs (NB 42; cp. NB 43, above). "What negates in '~p' is not the
'~' in front of 'p', but is what is common to all the signs that have the
same meaning as '~p' in this notation" (NB 15; see 5.512; NB 34b).

(3)   This last quote indicates succinctly the target of the present section: the idea that there is something common to all negation
(§§547–51), that negation always has "the same meaning" (§§554–57).
For reasons which 3.11 and §36 make clear, Wittgenstein had the fol-

lowing type of essence particularly in mind: " 'The grammatical possibilities of the negation sign reveal themselves only gradually, it is true,
in the sign's use [cp. 3.262], but I *think* negation all at once [cp. §138].
The sign "not" is only a pointer to the thought "not"; it only stimulates
me to think the right thing (it is only a signal)' " (*PG* 55; Man. 109,
193). The issue of sameness or difference of meaning connects the section both with the preceding one (§532) and especially with the next
(see XXI, 1–4). The numbers treating this theme (§§552–61) form as
recognizable a unit as the sections they overlap (XX and XXI).

DETAILED COMMENTARY

§547   See XX, 1–3.

   a 'mental activity': in W.'s former theory, this aspect of a proposition's meaning, like any other, would come from the signs' being so
"thought out" (3.11; GI 36–37). The essential core of thought, however, was not something "merely psychological" (*NB* 96)—say a feeling
of dissent (Russell, *Logic,* 317; Ramsey, *Foundations,* 147c)—"but something purely logical" (Man. 108, 217). See GI 33, 39–40.

   "It seemed as though the grammatical rules were the temporal development of what we perceive in an instant when we understand a negation. And as though there were thus two representations of the essence
of negation: the very act of negation (say the mental act) & its reflection
in the system of grammar" (Man. 110, 106; see IX, 2; 5.512; commentary on §548; cp. *PG* 53c).

   Do you know . . . : see Man. 110, 105–6; cp. §§314, 316, 370–71.

§548   A reworking of Man. 108, 261, where W. added (261–62): "But
I believe it is just so in thinking, expecting, wishing. Otherwise the distinction between thought and speech—in which, it is true, we think—
would be intolerable." "Again: the expression of negation which we
employ when we use some language or other strikes us as *primitive;* as
though there were a correcter one which just isn't available to me in the
crude condition of this language" (ibid.; see XX, 1–3; commentary on
§547).

   Cp. *BB* 60b–61a.

   (b) See *PG* 108cd; Man. 110, 104; cp. commentary on §550; *BB* 106b;
PG 59a.

   cross it out: see *PB* 248a.

   and so on: "Thus one could for instance demonstrate one's understanding of the proposition 'The book is not red' by throwing away the
color red. . . . This and the like would also show how the negative
proposition has the multiplicity of the negated proposition and not of
those propositions which could perhaps be true in its stead" (*PB* 57).

   a *crude* method: cp. p. 178g. "That primitiveness of the form of expression which struck us in the case of negation, we have already met earlier; thus if we want to make clear to someone that he should go in a certain direction, we can draw the route for him & so proceed with ever greater precision. But the indication which is to show him that *he* should go that way is again of the primitive sort that we should like to improve" (Man. 108, 263; see §§433–34).

a clumsy expedient: "How can logic—all-embracing logic, which mirrors the world—use such peculiar crotchets and contrivances?" (5.511). Words like *not, relation,* and *attribute,* said Russell, by their very nature sin against the Theory of Types: "To give a meaning to these words, we have to make a detour by way of words or symbols and the different ways in which they may mean; and even then, we usually arrive, not at one meaning, but at an infinite series of different meanings" (*Logic,* 334).

"Here I think we must say that negation, disjunction, etc. are just as 'primitive' in thought as they are in our sign language. How could we think negation *in* it if it were only like ill-fitting clothing of negation?" (Man. 108, 290; see §120a; cp. 4.002). Our "crude" sign for negation "is as good as any other we can conceive & fulfils its purpose as perfectly" (Man. 108, 235–36; see *PG* 55d).

§549   See XX, 1–3; commentary on §548; *PG* 55.

"How can the word 'not' . . .": cp. 5.512; *NB* 34 ("How can the mere twiddle '$\sim$' bring it into agreement with reality?").

"The sign 'not' . . .": W. is quoting Man. 109, 92, which continued: " 'It insinuates' means that it isn't the final linguistic expression. That it isn't the picture of the thought. That there is more in the negation than that." "And this is true; it isn't the crotchet in front of the proposition that explains negation to us. That *explains* to us what we are to do. (It doesn't have the necessary multiplicity.)" (ibid., 95).

possibly something very complicated: see Man. 110, 141. "If understanding doesn't mean translating, then it means seeing the sign in the space of its grammatical rules" (Man. 110, 51; see IX, 2), and then "very simple situations will receive very complicated projections" (Man. 110, 211–12). It will be seen, for instance, that a double negative is an affirmative, that $\sim\sim\sim$p follows from $\sim$p, and so on *ad infinitum* (p. 147n; *PG* 52a; 5.43; cp. *PG* 247). And in the case of a proposition like $\sim$ [(p . q)⊃(r v s)], only a truth-table representation, filling a whole page if written out, would reveal the sense of the initial tilde.

hinted at: "In the sign '$\sim$', negation cannot reveal itself. 'Not' is only a hint as to how the proposition is to be taken. And only in the use of the sign can the nature of what is hinted at be shown" (Man. 109, 104; see 3.262; cp. *PG* 55b). "The sense would be precisely this essence which we can only hint at by means of symbols, but which we can never reach" (Man. 110, 60; see §434; commentary on §120b). "Ever and again comes the thought that what we see of a sign is only the outside of something within, in which the real operations of sense and meaning go on" (Z 140).

§550   See Man. 138, 14B; Man. 110, 119–20 ("A special something in me follows this gesture"); cp. p. 182g; PG 55c; PB 57a (quoted for §548); Man. 110, 52–53; BB 78 ("And there is no doubt that at least certain gestures are often connected with such words, as a collecting gesture with 'and', and a dismissing gesture with 'not' ").

W. had written: " 'Not' makes a gesture of rejection. No, it *is* a gesture of rejection. To understand negation is to understand a gesture of rejection" (PG 58; cp. PG 66h).

"Should we not shake our heads, though, when someone shewed us a multiplication done wrong, as we do when someone tells us it is raining, if it is not raining?—Yes; and here is a point of connexion. But we also make gestures to stop our dog, e.g. when he behaves as we do not wish" (RFM 49).

§551   See the quotation just given, which connects this number with the preceding. Cp. §251, p. 176g; Z 140; BB 79a; NB 13 f. W.'s target: "I once said that the negation in $2 + 2 \neq 5$ cannot have the same meaning as the negation of a proposition, since the negated content $2 + 2 = 5$ cannot be the picture of a non-existent logical state of affairs" (Man. 108, 297; see PB 248a; cp. PB 250 f).

what we are *thinking*: cp. §20; quotation from Moore in XXI, 1.

Insert, p. 147   See p. 230b.

(a): see PG 52abc, 53c; Man. 228, §84; cp. NB 36gh, 100b.

"must already be contained": see IX, 2–3; PG 55e. "The precedent to which we are constantly inclined to appeal must reside in the symbol itself" (5.525); the whole calculus is there (5.514). "If we are given a proposition, then *with it* we are also given the results of all truth-operations that have it as their base" (5.442).

The temptation: "In philosophy we are constantly in danger of giving a myth of symbolism or of psychology, instead of simply saying what everyone knows and must admit" (Man. 108, 104; PB 65; see PG 56). "Thus we are tempted to say: 'If we understand *this* by negation and *that* by affirmation, then a double negative gives an affirmative' " (EPB 213). The temptation was particularly evident, and evoked similar self-criticism, in Man. 109, 14, where W. had declared for instance: "The proposition couldn't be surprised that the other follows from it."

a myth of 'meaning': concerning this expression, compare Rhees, Note, 18 (quoted in the Appendix: Ernst). Number 138 brings out one aspect of the myth, PP 258 another: " 'The mere fact that we have the expression "the meaning" of a word is bound to lead us wrong: we are led to think that the rules are responsible to something not a rule, whereas they are only responsible to rules.' " See commentary on §322 ("do we fix").

It looks as if . . . : logic, as conceived in the *Tractatus*, "is not amenable to human control or manipulation; it would be the height of absurdity to speak of our making logical propositions come true. . . . The idea that logic 'takes care of itself', i.e. that logical validity is independent of human choice, decision, or convention, constantly reappears in one form or another in the text (as it does in the *Notebooks*)" (Black, *Companion*, 272–73). See GI 30–31; VI, 3; IX, 3; XXXIX, 1–3; 5.44, 5.555, 6.124; Rhees, *Discussions*, 111.

from the nature of negation: "as though negation were present first & then the rules of grammar" (Man. 110, 106); "somewhat like: iron has the property of producing iron sulphate when mixed with sulphuric acid" (Man. 110, 102; see *PG* 52). Thus for the *Tractatus*, equations such as "$p = \sim \sim p$" reveal "the logic of the world" (6.22; see 6.23). "Indeed in any symbolism $\sim\sim p$ must for instance equal p" (Man. 108, 278). "It is a property of affirmation" (6.231), as well as of negation.

***Our* nature:** see XXXIX, 5; §520 and commentary; §§569–70; *RFM* 7, 121ab; cp. *Z* 357; *PG* 94a. "If calculating looks to us like the action of a machine, it is *the human being* doing the calculation that is the machine" (*RFM* 119; cp. §§359, 492–95). "We *perform* this transition" (*RFM* 7).

(b): from Man. 110, 133. See *OC* 61–65; *RFM* 179gh; *PG* 184, 246b; *PB* 178e; *PP* 258 (quoted above); *Kreis*, 66, 71a; Man. 112, 5, 195; Man. 110, 107; cp. §§43, 136, 548b; *PG* 303d; *PB* 107c, 182b, 326a; Man. 108, 290–91 (quoted for §548b). *"It is not possible to make discoveries in syntax.*—For only the group of rules *defines* the sense of our signs and every alteration (e.g. supplementation) of the rules means an alteration of the sense" (Man. 105, 52; *PB* 182).

or none: a change in the rules, like a change in the circumstances (§142), might make our ordinary language-game lose its point (cp. 5.47321; §§520, 564). A tautological game would be the limit (*PB* 326), but whether we count it as meaningless will depend on our purpose (§499). As for clearly contradictory rules, it might be questioned whether they are rules (*PG* 304).

§552   Cp. §350, p. 175a; *PB* 130a, 133b; Man. 228, §439; Man. 106, 144; Russell, *Principles*, 46–47.

is it clear to us: cp. p. 176gh. One might wonder whether W. hits his target (*RFM* 182 f); for though the *Tractatus* would probably assert that these are two different symbols (XXI, 1–2) and would place the difference in the moment, in the mind (IX, 2), the rules are *hidden* there (§102) and easily escape our notice (3.323). However, if meaning an utterance really were a mental act accompanying it, performed now this way now that (GI 37), wouldn't we at least be aware of the difference? A person singing one tune rather than another may not know how the notes are produced (4.002), but at least he knows they are different notes. A person viewing a schematic cube now this way now that (5.5423; XXXVII, 1–8) may be equally ignorant of the mechanism (p. 212) yet is fully conscious of the fact.

"one": see *BB* 50a.

has different meanings: see XXI, 4; §553; cp. p. 225a and commentary.

one would perhaps answer: cp. Moore, *Problems*, e.g. 366; Frege, *Writings*, 195 ("the word 'one' and the sign '1' stand for the same thing, the non-sensible number one itself").

§553 See XXI, 4; cp. §350.

when it stands for . . . : as in §552.

§554 Revised from Man. 221, 260.

We can easily imagine . . . : on this approach, see GI 62.

§555 For discussion of this kindred case, see *BB* 91–95. Cp. §§19b–20.

§556 Mined from Man. 221, 259–62. See *Z* 141–42. Though W. would not argue that one of these was *the* answer (cp. §§17, 61, 499, 552–53, 561–64; *BB* 58b, 65), his preference would go to one of the first two. For the third answer conforms to neither of the ordinary uses of *meaning* (*Bedeutung*) which he recognized (see §43 and commentary). Thus the words "we could give various answers" do not mean that all the answers would be equally good ones. Cp. §551, p. 147(b).

(a): that is, they have different uses in the language; but the meaning of a word is its use in the language (§43); therefore the words, in general, have different meanings. However, the question was about their meaning in these sentences. So the argument is no more conclusive than the others; "it only specifies a way of looking at this usage" (*BB* 58). Cp. §558; *BB* 140b.

(b): "One wants to say e.g.: 'The one negation *does* the same thing with the proposition as the other, it excludes what it describes.' But that is only another way of expressing one's assimilation of the two negative propositions. (Which is valid only when the negated proposition is not itself a negative proposition.)" (*Z* 140).

just a trivial convention: cp. §§562–64, 567; *BB* 65b.

"Even the criterion of interchangeability does not force us to a decision. Let us take as an example the expressions 'to make a boat' and 'to make a key'. In the first case we can substitute 'build' for 'make', in the second 'cut'. Therefore the word should be said to have a different meaning in the two cases. Yet it seems very odd to say this, and we may instead be inclined to say 'The meaning is the same in both cases, for although the substitution rules are different, this difference is not relevant' " (Waismann, *Principles,* 190).

taught in the same way: see *BB* 138a.

(c): cp. *RFM* 7d; Man. 110, 118 (for contrast).

turns the sense through 180°: Man. 110, 107–8, connect this suggestion with W.'s earlier comparison of a proposition with an arrow (XX, 2).

§557   See *Z* 140 (quoted for §549); *PG* 52ab; Man. 228, 122; cp. Man. 108, 205.

There is no answer running . . . : cp. §36; *PG* 74b. W. is correcting Man. 221, 258, where, in the manner of *BB,* he said what meaning might consist in on a given occasion.

No one does: it is simply the normal case (§141d).

by means of words: that is, other signs, with meanings determined by normal use and not by an accompanying thought process (GI 37). See §120ab and commentary.

XXI. Word Meanings (§§558–570)

GENERAL COMMENTARY

(1) "Without philosophy," wrote Wittgenstein in the *Tractatus,* "thoughts are, as it were, cloudy and indistinct: its task is to make them clear and give them sharp boundaries" (4.112). It should not only distinguish the meaningful from the meaningless, but one meaning from another. The whole of philosophy is full of fundamental confusions arising from the fact that in ordinary language single expressions are used with different meanings, that is, not merely different referents (Tractarian *Bedeutungen*) but different "modes of signification" (3.323–3.324). Russell and Moore, too, warned about the serious errors which are occasioned by "the difficulty of seeing whether the thought, which we express by the word used as predicate in one sentence, is or is not the same as that which we express by the word we use as predicate in another" (Moore, *Problems,* 220–21).

(2)   To effect such discriminations, Wittgenstein then felt, we must distinguish between the essential and the inessential (4.465). Now "accidental features are those that result from the particular way in which the propositional sign is produced. Essential features are those without which the proposition could not express its sense" (3.34). "In general,

what is essential in a symbol is what all symbols that can serve the same purpose have in common" (3.341).

(3) The words to watch here are *could* and *can* (§497). "Is there some reality lying behind the notation, which shapes its grammar?" (§562; cp. §§559, 566). Wittgenstein had supposed that there was (XXXIX, 1–2) and that it dictated the structure not only of existing languages but of any possible language (GI 31–33). When he saw the error of this dogma, he concluded in *PB* 51 that "all that is possible and necessary is to separate what is essential in *our* language from what is inessential," in terms of the signs' purpose. In the *Investigations* he now attends to the sense of this proposal, and of its predecessors, rather than to its fulfillment. For just as no logic of the world determines our grammar, so no absolute standard dictates the viewpoint to adopt in studying grammar (§17).

(4) What shall count as "essential" features, what as "inessential"? And when, therefore, do word uses differ "essentially", when only "accidentally"? "To say that a word is used in two (or more) different ways does in itself not yet give us any idea about its use. It only specifies a way of looking at this usage by providing a schema for its description with two (or more) subdivisions. It is all right to say: 'I do *two* things with this hammer: I drive a nail into this board and one into that board.' But I could also have said: 'I am doing only one thing with this hammer; I am driving a nail into this board and one into that board.' . . . The man who says 'surely, these are two different usages' has already decided to use a two-way schema, and what he said expressed this decision," not a debatable "theory" (*BB* 58; see §17; cp. §499; *BB* 104b, 115bc, 138a; Z 143).

Recommended reading on this section as a whole: XX, 3; *EPB* 204–10; *BB* 137d–140a; *PG* 59; Man. 229, §§723–29; Waismann, *Principles,* 187–91.

DETAILED COMMENTARY

§558 The number takes shape progressively in Man. 110, 83, 100, 112. See also *PG* 53–54; Man. 302, 5–6; Man. 228, §440; Man. 138, 23A; Man. 116, 105; Man. 111, 175; Man. 110, 203, 207; Waismann, *Principles,* 155 (cp. 190, quoted for §556); cp. *PG* 336a. W. is puzzling over his own example in 3.323, of several symbols for a single term: "The word 'is' figures as the copula, as a sign for identity, and as an expression for existence." See XXI, 1–2.

for these two words: this move, like the reference to two symbols or modes of signification (3.323), "only specifies a way of looking at this usage" (XXI, 4). We can just as well speak of one word, and frequently do (cp. 3.323).

But the rule . . . : cp. p. 175c; *PG* 59c; 4.241, 6.23.

§559 See Man. 229, §§710–11 (quoted for §138). This number grew out of Man. 109, 33–36, where W. observed, for instance, that "I use the linguistic apparatus like a machine," of which words with their "bodies" are the parts. Later, after the first two sentences of p. 176g (concerning "Mr. Scot is not a Scot"), W. continued: "Each time the word functions differently in the sentence. That means comparing the word with a machine part and the *sentence* with a machine. Entirely inappropriate!" (Man. 130, 67).

One would like to speak . . . : of statements like 3.3 and 3.314 W. had written: "That a word has meaning only in a proposition means merely that it has a function only in a proposition" (Man. 110, 111; see Man. 109, 51; cp. 3.327–3.328). Cp. §138; *PG* 59c; *PB* 58d, 59d; Man. 106, 91; Ramsey, *Foundations,* 149a.

were a mechanism: or an organism (Man. 110, 144; cp. 4.002). See the quote from Man. 109, above; Man. 229, §708; cp. 3.318; *NB* 23a; Russell, "Introduction", xx.

there isn't anything hidden: cp. §102; *Z* 140; Man. 110, 113, 117: "Think how I translate negation into action. Here indeed I must use the properties of the body which lies behind the word 'not'. . . . When I translate negation, I must make use of its geometrical properties."

in operating with the word: not "by trying to see what we are *thinking* as we utter the two sentences" (§551). "We can speak of the function of a word in a sentence, in a language-game, in language. But in each of these instances 'function' means 'technique'. So refers to a *general* explanation & description" (Man. 167).

Meaning-body: this cryptic allusion to the viewpoint of Man. 109 (above) replaces a whole paragraph of Man. 228, 124, practically identical with *Z* 140. In Man. 110, 112–13, W. had written: "I want to make this comparison, that the word 'is' has a different word-body behind it. That it has the same surface both times, but belonging to a different body, as when I see a triangle in front which is the surface of a prism one time and of a tetrahedron the other." In *PG* 54, "word-body" becomes "meaning-body". See Man. 302, 5; Man. 229, §710 (quoted for §138a); cp. *NB* 70hijk.

§560 An abbreviation of Man. 116, 32. See *Z* 644; *BB* 24a; *PG* 68–69; cp. §§492, p. 225a; *PG* 131b (the sense of a sentence is what we explain when we explain its sense).

"Asking first 'What's an explanation of meaning?' has two advantages. You in a sense bring the question 'what is meaning?' down to earth. For, surely, to understand the meaning of 'meaning' you ought also to understand the meaning of 'explanation of meaning'. Roughly: 'let's ask what the explanation of meaning is, for whatever that explains will be the meaning.' Studying the grammar of the expression 'explanation of meaning' will teach you something about the grammar of the word 'meaning' and will cure you of the temptation to look about you for some object which you might call 'the meaning' " (*BB* 1).

Since "the explanation of the meaning explains the use of the word" (*PG* 59), "the use of the word in the language is its meaning" (*PG* 60).

I.e.: more directly relevant to the discussion of sameness or difference of meaning would have been a corollary: "The meaning of a particular word is indicated by the explanation of its meaning" (cp. §77b, p. 220e; *BB* 11a; *LC* 12b). From this it follows that: "As the criterion for a word's having two meanings, we may use the fact of there being two explanations given for a word" (*BB* 138). (Of course the question then arises what should count as a different explanation.)

§561 Cp. *BB* 139de; *PG* 59cde.

(a) Citing this example among others, W. had insisted in 3.323 that such like-sounding words "do not merely have different meanings: they are *different symbols*" (cp. 5.4733).

isn't it queer: for numbering depends on the concept employed (e.g. ten *copies* are not ten *books*, five *people* are not five *couples*), and in counting meanings it is clearly the use which serves as norm.

two different meanings: this was a favorite example of Russell's, to which he attached great importance. See e.g. *Logic*, 245; *History*, 831.

(b) See XXI, 2; Man. 110, 100 (quoted for §565); cp. 3.34–3.341, 4.465; *NB* 17b. "We regard understanding as the essential thing, and the sign as something inessential" (*PG* 39).

§562(a) See XXI, 2–4; §62; cp. p. 175c; *PG* 215c, 217e; Man. 106, 27.

(b) See *BB* 65b; *Kreis*, 104; Frege, *Writings*, 217: "Small and accidental differences in the form or the colour of the figures—of which the rules do not treat—need no consideration in the theory of the game."

§563 See XXI, 4; *BB* 65b.

Let us say . . . : cp. §43; see commentary on §31a.

§564 not only rules but also a point: as do language-games. See §§5 ("the aim and functioning"), 142, 567; *RFM* 8a; *PG* 69d–70a, 126b; cp. §136d; *RFM* 164 f; *PB* 51b, 229e; James, *Principles*, II, 333b–335a.

"We can imagine a variant of chess in which it is the object of each player to be checkmated, and this would be an entirely different game; but the formal description we imagined would coincide with the formal description of chess. The whole theory of chess could be formulated with reference only to the formal description; but which theorems of this theory interested us would depend upon whether we wished to play chess or the variant game" (Dummett, "Truth", 142–43; see *EPB* 134–35).

§565   Why the same word?: with varying uses, as in §§558, 561.

we make no use . . . : here the *Tractatus* speaks, with typical dogmatism. "What any picture, of whatever form, must have in common with reality, in order to be able to depict it—correctly or incorrectly—in any way at all, is logical form, i.e. the form of reality" (2.18). "The two must possess the same logical (mathematical) multiplicity" (4.04). Thus in a logical notation "identity of object I express by identity of sign" (5.53), whereas in ordinary language we make no such use of identity.

"It is essential to language that the same word occurs in different sentences, that different sentences have it in common. And also that words' sameness of sound when different grammatical rules apply to them can be replaced by different-sounding words; for then the similarity of sound is external and without significance" (Man. 110, 100).

See 3.203; *NB* 104f; cp. 3.321–3.326; Russell, *Mind,* 211c, and *Inquiry,* 57b.

For isn't it a use . . . : as things are, doesn't this sound and perhaps it alone have the desired effect?

§566 See XXI, 3, and the preceding comments, especially Man. 110, 100. Concerning the statement at the start of §558, W. had written: "If I can say that, it means I don't distinguish or identify the words just by their sound; and yet I must be able to recognize them, for only their sameness expresses sameness of sense.

"Could we use the same word for 'blue', 'red', 'green', 'yellow', as we do for '=' and '∈', albeit with the risk of confusion, yet with the *possibility* of distinguishing?" (Man. 110, 83).

had a *purpose*: cp. Frege, *Writings,* 194: "In what follows we shall understand by 'signs of similar shape' those intended by the writer to have similar shapes in order that they may designate the same thing."

"One says: *here* the use of the same word is inessential, since the sameness of shape does not serve to establish a connection" (Man. 221, 265).

should be able to recognize . . . : distinguish W.'s skepticism about the purpose from his admission that "every language-game is based on words' and objects' being recognized again" (*OC* 455). On the reasons for his skepticism and the sense of this distinction, see the next comments.

Are we talking about   . . . : said Ogden and Richards: "It is true that we can recognize a word whether it be pronounced high or low, quickly or slowly, with a rising intonation or a falling and so on. But however different two utterances of one word may be as sounds, they must yet have a common character; otherwise they could not be recognized as the same word" (*Meaning*, 211). This *could* sounds causal but is really logical; for here "common character" means simply "whatever degree of similarity does in fact result in our calling the sounds the 'same word' ". Thus the truth is that we must agree in our judgments (§242), but this agreement is not something achieved *by means of* sameness in the signs we use. Again, §654 applies.

is something to do with the game: it is not, for instance, in the class with a supply of air for both players, causally necessary but replaceable by anything else equally effective (for instance an oxygen mask).

"One can imagine a language in which the words, say names for colors, change their meanings with the days of the week; this color is called 'red' on Monday, 'blue' on Tuesday. 'A = A' might mean that in the language to which the rule applies there is no change in the meaning of the sign 'A' " (*PG* 195).

§567   But, after all . . . : this expostulation refers back to §§562–64.

defined by the rules: see §197.

then that is an essential part: see *PB* 161a.

does not see the point: see the references for §564.

§568(a) In terms of the comparison in (*b*), we might paraphrase thus: If I understand the character of this face aright—its friendliness, say— then the part in the hair isn't an essential part of it.

(b)   See XXXVII, 13; pp. 181af, 218l; *BB* 170, 174; LE 4–5; Man. 232, 682 ("A technique has a physiognomy"); Man. 229, §§989–99, 1322; Man. 228, §§251, 297; cp. p. 210f; *RFM* 25d; *PG* 69b; Man. 302, 27; Man. 229, §1002 ("Goethe's signature strikes me as Goetheisch. To this extent it is like a face, for I could say the same thing of Goethe's face").

"When I say 'I don't see mere dashes (a mere scribble) but a face (or word) with this particular physiognomy,' I don't wish to assert any general characteristic of what I see, but to assert that I see that particular physiognomy which I do see" (*BB* 174).

"When we wish to describe the use of a word—isn't it as when one wishes to paint the portrait of a face? I see it clearly; the expression of these features is *well* known to me; yet if I had to paint it, I wouldn't know where to begin" (Man. 229, §1611).

These quotations, as well as the context, suggest that the remark applies to both kinds (both senses) of meaning recognized in the *Investigations* (use in the language and the related experience).

is a: the German, lacking a copula, is more elusive.

§569   Language is an instrument: *de facto*, not by definition (XVI, 7–10; §§491–97).

Its concepts are instruments: see Z 532 ("The concept of pain is characterized by its particular function in our life"); cp. §§11–14, 23c.

As language is not just marks and sounds nor just their uses, but both together, so W. tended to view concepts as the composite sign-meaning units constituting such a system of communication (see §§384, 577, p. 183a; *RFM* 155j–156b). Thus he sometimes spoke of concepts in a way hardly applicable to word uses alone (e.g. here, and in §§282c, 316, p. 209e; *RFM* 195, below), sometimes in ways inappropriate for just signs (e.g. §§67b, 135, p. 220i), but hardly ever in a way eliminating one or the other. In particular, he did not state an equivalence between concept and meaning as he so often did between meaning and use (§43). Thus calling concepts instruments is here equivalent to calling words instruments, where *word* has its fuller sense of sign-with-meaning. (The mark or sound is, as it were, a mere handle; without its use in the language the sign would have neither weight nor edge.) Cp. references to "using" language, and the like (e.g. §§53, 120, 496).

" 'Concept' is a vague concept. . . . It is not in every language-game that there occurs something that one would call a concept. . . . Are there concepts in language-game (2)? Still, it would be easy to add to it in such a way that 'slab', 'block' etc. became concepts. For example, by means of a technique of describing or portraying those objects. There is of course no sharp dividing line between language-games which work with concepts and others. What is important is that the word 'concept' refers to one kind of expedient in the mechanism of language-games" (*RFM* 195; cp. *RFM* 155j–156a).

perhaps one thinks . . . : see *PP* 277–79 and *PG* 184–85, e.g.: " 'The reasons (if any) for fixing a unit of length do not make it "not arbitrary", in the sense in which a statement that so-and-so is the length of this object is not arbitrary' " (*PP* 279); and "the rules of grammar are arbitrary in the same sense as the choice of a unit of measurement" (*PG* 185).

even this is not true . . . : cp. XXXIX, 5; 6.341–6.342.

§570   Cp. *Z* 554; Man. 108, 135; Man. FW, 17 (similar remarks about scientific discoveries); Mauthner, *Beiträge*, I, 76–77; Ramsey, *Foundations*, 132.

"Yes: it is as if the formation of a concept guided our experience into particular channels, so that one experience is now seen together with another one in a new way. (As an optical instrument makes light come from various sources in a particular way to form a pattern.)" (*RFM* 123).

"By being educated in a technique, we are also educated to have a way of looking at the matter which is just as firmly rooted as that technique" (*RFM* 124).

"I want to say: an education quite different from ours might also be the foundation for quite different concepts. For here life would run on differently.—What interests us would not interest *them*. Here different concepts would no longer be unimaginable. In fact, this is the only way in which *essentially* different concepts are imaginable" (Z 387–88).

XXII. States: Belief, Hope, Expectation (§§571–587)

GENERAL COMMENTARY

(1)   Somewhat abruptly, §571 announces the theme of the remaining numbers in Part One. One case study after another—of believing, hoping, expecting, intending, recognizing, willing, meaning—illustrates the clash between the Wittgensteinian approach of describing language-games and the once-popular practice of introspecting "processes in the psychical sphere" so as to learn the nature of believing, hoping, expecting, and so on. The recurring target is a combination of the Reference Fallacy (GI 17–18) and the Essence Fallacy (GI 20–23), turning expressions like "I hope,' "I mean," "I intend" into reports of inner phenomena (GI 15–16; X, 20–21) which psychology must then observe more attentively and describe more precisely (GI 48; X, 22). More specifically, the chief target in this and the following section is the sort of explanation through "feelings" (§598) or "atmospheres" (§609) one finds so fully exemplified in the writings of Russell and James (see the many quotations and references in the comments on individual numbers). For Wittgenstein's own once-similar views, see GI 38.

(2)   The present section treats the kindred concepts (§574) believing (§§572–75, 577–79, 587), expecting (§§572, 574, 576–77, 581–83, 586), and hoping (§§572, 574, 585). These may be called states (§572), in contrast with thinking or deciding, on the one hand, and with sensations or feelings, on the other. However, this rough discrimination is largely a matter of grammar (§572 and commentary). If we look beneath the deceptive surface of expressions like "I hoped for a long time that she would improve" or "I was expecting him all week," we find that each such verb "describes a pattern which recurs, with different variations, in the weave of our life" (p. 174; see §583). It does not name a condition of the soul or continuous state of consciousness (pp. 59n, 191k). For the inner has need of outer criteria (§580; X, 22; GI 60); and the criteria determine the concept (§§354, 572–73); and the concept determines the "essence" (§371); and neither in first-person

(GI 15–16; §§582–86) nor in third-person uses (§573) of these terms do we generally apply inner criteria. There are indeed feelings of hope, expectation, conviction, but so are there tones of conviction, looks of expectancy, verbal expressions of hope; and the conviction is not the tone, expectancy is not the look, and hope is not the mere words. "In certain circumstances, no doubt, meaning and not meaning, believing, intending, etc. is characterized by what does or does not occur in the speaker's soul" (EPB 225; cp. GI 44). But the same might be said of other traits in the weave (GI 45). "Consider tone of voice, inflexion, gestures, as *essential* parts of our experience, not as inessential accompaniments or mere means of communication" (BB 182).

DETAILED COMMENTARY

§571 See GI 48; pp. 179–80; BB 46e–47b; Man. 229, §§948–58, 1329; cp. Man. 176, 21A; Schlick, "Psychological", 402, and "Form", 200, 213–14; Mauthner, *Beiträge*, I, 235; Köhler, *Gestalt*, 26; Stout, *Manual*, 1–4; Wisdom, *Mind*, 3, 19; Helmholtz, *Optik*, 577.

The connection with §570: Psychological concepts lead to psychological investigations (psychology) and determine the procedure followed. **(a)** See *LC* 29a; cp. *BB* 64a; Russell, *Mind*, 88b, 108–9; Spengler, *Untergang*, 424.

"What is the 'old conception'? I believe it is characterized by a *picture:* that of seeing, observing an object which does not have its place among physical objects but elsewhere" (Man. 161; see Russell, *Outline*, 19, 21, 306b; James, *Principles*, I, 185b, quoted for §416). "Here it would be as if we described something that only we and not the other saw, so something near to us and always available but hidden to others, something therefore that lies *in* us and of which we become aware by looking inside ourselves. And psychology is now the science of this inner something" (Man. 229, §1360; see ibid., §1564, quoted for p. 186c). In *Analysis of Mind*, 102, Russell listed "the place where they occur" as one of the "two ways of classifying particulars", which it is vital to note "for the understanding of the difference between psychology and physics".

This conception erred in: (1) identifying seeing, thinking, willing, and the like with an inner process (§308 and commentary); (2) supposing that a person might attentively observe an inner thought process the way he does an outer object (p. 187abc; commentary on §413).

psychology: W. did not regard the *Investigations* as a work of psychology (Man. 213, 505), any more than he considered *RFM* a book of mathematics (p. 232c). He gave an account of psychological concepts, not of the facts of human nature which underlie them (p. 230a), for instance the causal connections (GI 49) which interest psychologists (*PP* 314; p. 193f).

(b) Worked up in Man. 116, 333, and linked with Z 11. See GI 15–16; X, 22; Z 471; *PG* 82c–83a; *LC* 18abc, 21b; cp. *LC* 42bc.

"Should I call the whole realm of the psychological that of 'experience'? So call the psychological verbs, say, 'verbs of experience' ('concepts of experience')? The characteristic thing about them is this, that their third person is uttered on the basis of observations, but not the first person. These observations are observations of behavior" (Man. 229, §1504; see GI 15–16, 61).

in the same sense: (1) we see a movement but not our seeing, hear a sound but not our hearing, and so forth; (2) seeing, hearing, and the rest are not the objects of special inner "senses" (p. 187); (3) for an object which varies with observation is not an object of observation in the same sense as a physical object; (4) and the object of an inner gaze is not logically related to seeing, hearing, or the like as are drops of water to rain (§354); it is not a criterion (Man. 229, above; GI 15–16, 60). Cp. NL 302bc.

the phenomena of electricity: the appearances (*Erscheinungen*), not inferred currents or the like. Thus the remark draws a restricted contrast between physics and psychology.

observes the *external reactions*: "The psychological verbs to see, to believe, to think, to wish, do not signify phenomena. . . . But psychology observes the phenomena *of* seeing, believing, thinking, wishing" (Z 471; see XXII, 2). Contrast with James, *Principles*, I, 3 (*"the quest of the conditions* becomes the psychologist's most interesting task") and Russell, *Mind*, 299–300 ("the ultimate data of psychology are only sensations and images and their relations"). See GI 48.

the behaviour: "There is a psychology only of creatures whose *behavior* resembles that of man" (Man. 228, §694; cp. §281).

§572   grammatically, a state: see XXII, 2; commentary on p. 59n and §573b; cp. Man. 108, 249 (in GI 38). The appropriateness and necessity of calling expectation *grammatically* a state appears from *PG* 141d: "If I say 'I have been expecting him all day,' 'expect' doesn't refer to a continuous state which contains the person expected and his arrival in the way well-mixed batter contains flour, sugar, and eggs. The expectation consists rather in a series of actions, thoughts, feelings" (cp. *BB* 145a; §444, p. 174d). There might well be no verb grouping these varied strands into the enduring "state" of expecting him all day (cp. Z 473).

"as a criterion": see §354.

of fitting: see §182.

§573(a)   Of the soul?: cp. §283.

Of the mind?: cp. p. 59n (a).

that is the correct answer: see Cook, "Human Beings"; cp. §§281, 302, 360.

(b) See p. 59n and commentary. Cp. *Z* 472, on sensations, for contrast: "All have genuine duration. Possibility of giving the beginning and the end. Possibility of their being synchronized, of simultaneous occurrence." One can identify the precise moment at which a pain set in, but not for instance the precise moment at which the learner in §§145–46 began to understand. As for "genuine duration", contrast *PG* 141, quoted for §572.

in particular cases: the double thrust: "Don't generalize, *a priori*" (GI 58), but "look and see" (GI 53). The reader should not expect W. (or this commentary) to define what a state is (GI 70–71), or belief (*BB* 144–45, quoted for §574).

§574 See *Z* 51, 64; Man. 228, 72–73; cp. §317. Most of Geach's remarks in *God*, 31–32, contrasting thinking and meaning, apply here too; for instance: "Nor can we be absorbed in, or distracted by or from, meaning things [believing, expecting, hoping], as we can in regard to thinking."

In 5.542 W. had assimilated thought and belief. For Russell, too, belief was as much an event as was thinking. "If I say 'What day of the week is this?' and you say 'Tuesday', there occurs in your mind at that moment the belief that this is Tuesday" (*Logic*, 217). "I am talking of the actual occurrence of a belief in a particular person's mind at a particular moment" (ibid.; see *Problems*, 73; *Mind*, 233 and 234, quoted in GI 37).

" 'Not at all,' I should say, 'many different criteria distinguish, under different circumstances, cases of believing what you say from those of not believing what you say.' There may be cases where the presence of a sensation other than those bound up with gestures, tone of voice, etc. distinguishes meaning what you say from not meaning it. But sometimes what distinguishes these two is nothing that happens while we speak, but a variety of actions and experiences of different kinds before and after" (*BB* 144–45).

"A belief isn't like a momentary state of mind. 'At 5 o'clock he had very bad toothache' " (*LC* 54).

PG 140–41 and *BB* 41–42 are situated about halfway between the present number and W.'s earlier tendency to consider belief, expectation, and hope as so many species of thought (GI 34–38).

A proposition: see 3.12: "I call the sign with which we express a thought a propositional sign.—And a proposition is a propositional sign in its projective relation to the world."

hence in another sense: there was some foundation for asserting that "thinking and language were the same" (*NB* 82): What we can say we can also think. However, the constituents of thought do not "have the same sort of relation to reality as words" (*NB* 130). Silent thoughts do not, for example, "express" one's belief publicly, sensibly, as spoken words do.

not thinking: not thought plus attitude (GI 38), as a proposition was supposedly thought plus words (3.12, above). Cp. §693. For similar remarks on *mean*, see *EPB* 227.

A grammatical remark: see §251b and commentary; §371; *RFM* 99i.

less distantly related: cp. Man. 229, §1502. In Z 51 W. compared imperatives such as "Imagine . . . ," "Work . . . out in your head," "Consider . . . ," with others such as "Believe that it is so," "Be of the firm conviction," "Hope for his return," then commented: "Is *this* the difference, that the first are voluntary, the second involuntary mental movements? I may rather say that the verbs of the second group do not stand for actions."

§575   The number does not simply deny, but sorts out the truth and the possible falsehood in a statement like Russell's: "The question I am asking now is not whether believing is experienced, for that I take to be obvious" (*Logic*, 132; see quotations for §574). In some cases we do experience something, in others not. "But all this doesn't tell us what belief *is*. It is no definition of the word 'believe'. And I can give none, since there is none. We have here a family of cases" (Man. 228, §250).

§576   See §§442, 452–53; cp. the preceding and following numbers.

certainly a case: apply the words of Man. 228 just quoted.

§577   **does not *occupy our thoughts:*** contrast with e.g. James, *Principles*, I, 442, and Ward, *Principles*, 14: "But he cannot with propriety be said to be expecting it, unless he has actually present to his mind a series of ideas ending in that of death, a series due to previous associations, and revived at this moment in consequence of the actual recurrence as a present experience of its first member."

would mean: "In certain circumstances these words will mean (will be replaceable by) 'I believe such-and-such will occur.' Sometimes also: 'Be prepared for this to happen. . . .'" (*Z* 65).

the description of a state of mind: cp. §§585, 588, pp. 59n, 188l. There is no conflict with §572, which speaks only of a state, not of a state of mind (see §573a), and considers criteria, not criterialess avowals like "I am expecting him" (see GI 15–16, 60–61).

But we also say: see *Z* 63 (the German).

We could imagine a language: cp. p. 188i; *Z* 49.

and so on: for instance, *mean* (*BB* 146bc; *EPB* 223–24) and *understand* (§§531–32), for which a similar contrast exists, between experiential and nonexperiential uses.

would be more suitable: see GI 9ff; cp. §132; *BB* 21b, 22d, 52a.

§578   See *EPB* 222–23; *PG* 381; Man. 116, 345 (" 'But "believe" means simply: "take for true"'!—To be sure, it means to hold for true & with this definition *too* nothing of what interests us is clarified"); Man. 108, 151–52; cp. §§316, 333; Ramsey, *Foundations*, 240–41. For similar observations on the kindred concept *mean*, see p. 218e.

(a) See Ramsey, *Foundations*, 144–50.

What does it mean . . . : the answer in *PB* 204ab reflects W.'s greater emphasis at that time on verification (see the commentary on §353). Cp. *PB* 89b: "It is impossible to believe something if we can conceive no way in which it might be verified" (as is the case for Goldbach's theorem).

Goldbach's theorem: "the hypothesis that every even number can be represented as a sum of prime numbers. This property was discovered by Goldbach (1690–1764) who informed Euler of it in 1742 and said he had verified it for all the cases he knew (except for the number 2, which is itself a prime number)" (note in the Italian edition of the *Investigations*).

The example and W.'s comments are partially explained by *BB* 10–11: "The importance of investigating the diviner's answer lies in the fact that we often think we have given a meaning to a statement P if only we assert 'I *feel* (or I believe) that P is the case.' (We shall talk at a later occasion of Prof. Hardy saying that Goldbach's theorem is a proposition because he can believe that it is true.)" This promise is finally kept in the *Investigations*. Hardy had written: "I ask then, finally, whether there is anything in the proposition, as relevant to logic and as Wittgenstein seems to conceive it, which affords any justification for my belief in 'real' propositions, my invincible feeling that, if Littlewood and I both believe Goldbach's theorem, then there is something, and that the same something, in which we both believe, and that that same something will remain the same something when each of us is dead and when succeeding generations of more skilful mathematicians have proved our belief to be right or wrong" ("Proof", 24).

" 'I believe that G's theorem will come true.' How is this belief in the end verified? By a proof. By any proof? No. By this particular proof? No. By something we shall recognize as a proof" (Man. 161; W.'s English). As for the theorem itself: "What is the basis for our understanding what it says? The use of its words & word forms in other propositions, of course! Nothing else!" (ibid.; cp. Man. 123, June 4; §516).

Thus we cannot envisage a possible proof, and certainly not all the numbers referred to, and thereby provide a content for the sort of momentary belief-act W. takes as his target in these numbers. Man. 229, §1265, makes the same point by means of a similar abstract content, equally incapable of complete verification: "Compare 'The whole time, I believed in the law of gravitation' with 'The whole time, I believed I heard a slight whisper.' . . . We could also express it thus: we form a picture of someone who believes the whole time that he hears a slight noise; but not of someone who believes in the accuracy of the law of gravitation."

In a feeling of certainty: *"In its inner nature, belief, or the sense of reality, is a sort of feeling more allied to the emotions than to anything else"* (James, *Principles*, II, 283; see 287c, 295b). "Believing is an actual experienced feeling" (Russell, *Mind*, 233; see 176, 250, 252); "when we believe a proposition, we have a certain feeling which is related to the content of the proposition in the way described as 'believing that proposition' " (idem, *Logic*, 310). According to Ramsey, a person "will believe that *aRb* by having names for *a, R,* and *b* connected in his mind and accompanied by a feeling of belief" (*Foundations*, 145).

as we state, hear, or think: "All have in common the propositional form" (*NB* 96). See GI 38.

That would not interest us: a mere accompaniment would not (cp. Ramsey, above). See GI 60; X, 22; cp. pp. 181cd, 220h, 224c.

what are the characteristics . . . : cp. p. 182; Russell, in the commentary on §598.

how far the feeling may be caused . . . : which would supposedly be the reason for saying that it attaches to this rather than to some other content. "It is not enough that the content and the belief-feeling should co-exist: it is necessary that there should be a specific relation between them, of the sort expressed by saying that the content is what is believed" (Russell, *Mind*, 250). But what sort is that? "It is evident," wrote Ramsey, "that the importance of beliefs and disbeliefs lies not in their intrinsic nature, but in their causal properties, i.e. their causes and more especially their effects" (*Foundations*, 148). "Feeling belief towards the words 'not-*p*' and feeling disbelief towards the words '*p*' have then in common certain causal properties" (ibid.; see 153). Cp. *EPB* 223; *PG* 152d.

by the proposition itself: the only form the content of belief could take in this case; "it is of course impossible to make a picture of this state of affairs" (Man. 108, 152). See *EPB* 223; Russell, *Logic*, 149.

(b) See p. 225c and commentary; *Z* 471 (quoted for §571); *EPB* 219, 220, 222; *BB* 144d.

(c) See p. 225d; *RFM* 31f–32a.

how does the belief connect: see the commentary on (*a*).

what your searching really consists in: "What happens here is the planless search for the construction of a calculus" (*PB* 338; *Kreis*, 174).

what belief in the proposition amounts to: cp. §474.

"It also happens that we say: 'At the moment that I said it, I was convinced of it.' And here—one might think—there must surely be revealed what conviction consists in! But imagine such a case!—You don't find what you are looking for. This conviction, we could say, doubtless had a history" (*EPB* 223).

§579 See §578, p. 225d; *Z* 573. Number 580 suggests a connection with this other query: "What makes a feeling one of *confidence*?" The answer is: the use we make of the word *confidence*, including our behavior (§371).

§580 Cp. *Z* 206, 469, 571; NL 286e, 290g. In Section X (see X, 17–25) W. argued against "private" criteria, knowable to their possessor alone. "Inner" criteria, too, accessible through introspection to only one person, might seem to be eliminated by the very notion of criteria as ultimate evidence (§354). However, if the "inner" is knowable to all, in one way or another (§§246, 303), then descriptions might be used to establish inner criteria. Otherwise the phrase "outer criteria" would seem redundant. "But if one takes this line (which is correct) one cannot then permit a question to be raised as to whether those descriptions are in error or not—for this would be to fall back into the original difficulty. One must treat the descriptions as the *criterion* of what the inner occurrences are" (Malcolm, *Dreaming*, 55; see §§288, 344b, pp. 222h–223e). Thus "the living human being is as essential to our concepts of the mental as the chessboard is to chess" (Malcolm, *Problems*, 30; see §281). Descartes's *cogito* needs a non-Cartesian *cogitans* (Cook, "Human Beings").

'**inner process**': cp. §§305–6.

§581 Worked up in Man. 180b, 42–44. See §§576, 591; Man. 180b, 36–37; Ogden and Richards, *Meaning*, 62; cp. §337; Man. 302, 15 (quoted for §445). The expansion in Man. 228, §285 (fuller than *Z* 67), makes the connection with §580 still clearer: "The man who expects [the explosion] had heard two people whispering: 'Tomorrow at ten o'clock the fuse will be lit.' Then he thinks: perhaps someone means to blow up a house here. Towards ten o'clock he becomes uneasy, jumps at every sound, and at last answers the question why he is so tense: 'I'm expecting . . .' This answer will e.g. make his behavior intelligible. It will enable us to fill out the picture of his thoughts and feelings.

"But it is also conceivable that suddenly, without cause or preparation, someone should assume an expectant attitude and say: 'I expect an explosion any moment now.' We might then suppose he was crazy. And if he couldn't give any answer to the question why he expected an explosion and just kept expressing the expectation, we wouldn't know whether to say whether this was a genuine case of expecting. Not, however, because we can't see into his soul, but because this is a borderline case of the process of expecting." See §586; cp. §623.

imbedded in a situation: cp. §337.

is to be expected: cp. §577 and italics there.

§582 A revision of Man. 180b, 39. Cp. GI 15–16; *Z* 53; *BB* 20c–21b. To express the sense of the German *doch* (which looks forward in the sentence, not backwards) and to avoid the difficulties raised by this translation, the order of the last two clauses might be reversed, thus: "although they and their tone may be a manifestation of his feeling, still his words do not describe a feeling."

§583 **"But you talk as if . . .":** cp. §§305–6.

"hoping": cp. §545.

"*now*": see pp. 174f, 175a.

"deep significance": cp. §111.

for the space of one second: see §584 and references.

of human life: that is, behavior, including the use of language, and not just inner feelings or thoughts. "The phenomena of hope are modes of this complicated form of life" (p. 174).

only in a human face: see *EPB* 228; cp. §539; *BB* 145b. Thus W. might wish to maintain that Carroll's nonsense began when he made the Cheshire Cat "smile" and not when he had the smile linger on after the cat had disappeared.

§584 See p. 174; Man. 228, §285 (quoted for §581); cp. §§204–5, p. 217fg; Russell, *Mind*, 234a. For the thinking behind the initial objection, see also GI 38.

(a) isolated, cut out of its context: as in James, e.g. *Principles,* I, 282: "Annihilate a mind at any instant, cut its thought through whilst yet uncompleted, and examine the object present to the cross-section thus suddenly made; you will find, not the bald word in process of utterance, but that word suffused with the whole idea."

no longer part of this language: which is a condition for this hope (p. 174abc).

(b) And so on: in Man. 180a, W. did continue the development at some length.

§585 See GI 15–16; §§180, 586, pp. 187i–189e; Man. 219, 7; cp. §577, p. 174j.

"Is 'I hope . . .' a description of a state of mind? A state of mind has duration. So 'I have been hoping for the whole day' is such a description; but suppose I say to someone: 'I hope you come'—what if he asks me 'For how long have you been hoping that?' Is the answer 'For as long as I've been saying so'? Supposing I had some answer or other to that question, would it not be quite irrelevant to the purpose of the words 'I hope you'll come'?" (*Z* 78).

is this a *report*: in Man. 180b W. repeatedly suggests that it is an *act* of hope. Cp. §586, p. 187k.

this **will be called . . . :** see pp. 59n, 187i ("I keep on thinking . . ." gives a distribution in time); Z 45; cp. §§573–74, 588.

§586 Apply the remarks of p. 1880p to the present example. W. runs through varied cases.

That is a report . . . : see Man. 229, §1263; cp. Man. 228, §285, quoted for §581.

the first act: cp. §290, p. 218bc.

"I'm longing": the German uses the verb *expect* (*erwarten*). So the act is one of expecting.

an act of expecting: see §546.

The point is: see p. 1880; cp. §645a; Man. 228, §285, quoted for §581.

§587 See pp. 191–93; cp. §§676–77; Schlick, "Positivism", 99b.

(a) See p. 191hi; cp. X, 25; p. 221.

is the answer . . . : Russell thought it was: "Such things as desires and beliefs, which seem obvious to introspection, are not visible directly to external observation" (*Mind,* 44). For "what is believed, and the believing, must both consist of present occurrences in the believer" (ibid., 233). See GI 38.

(b) See p. 192e; *EPB* 225; *BB* 147ab; cp. §§441b, 586.

In *some* cases . . . : as (*c*) indicates, we should not conclude from this that belief sometimes consists of "present occurrences in the believer".

in most not: cp. §§631, 659, p. 174i.

XXIII. On Explaining Thought through Feelings (§§588–610)

GENERAL COMMENTARY

(1) The first pages of NL help to dispel the impression of aimless wandering which these numbers may produce. Why, for instance, did Wittgenstein there write that the notion of inner experience's being indescribable "plays hell with us" (NL 276, quoted for §610)? Because that is how philosophical problems about mental processes and mental states arise (*BB* 5a). "The first step is the one that altogether escapes notice. We talk of processes and states [and feelings and atmospheres and experiences and mental acts, as in these numbers] and leave their nature undecided" (§308). For, after all, the inner is intangible (§608), indescribable (§610). And if anyone questions our account, we may

readily reply, without committing ourselves to anything more specific (§594), that there *must* be something of the sort (§599); for explanation of our thinking—for instance our intending (§§588–89, 591–92), meaning (§§590, 594), recognizing (§§602–5), estimating (§§607–8), and understanding (§609)—requires it (§598).

(2)   Wittgenstein himself once thought this way (GI 38), but James and Russell are the prime examples to consider. Russell, for instance, after repeatedly invoking "feelings" to explain our thought (see commentary on §598), revealingly confessed: "I use the word 'feeling' in a popular sense, to cover a sensation or an image or a complex of sensations or images or both; I use this word because I do not wish to commit myself to any special analysis of the belief-feeling" (*Mind*, 187; see GI 38). He was sure there was one, but didn't know what it was (cp. *NB* 130b; and Russell, *Outline*, 270, quoted for §597). For after all, we do believe, hope, remember, expect, and so on, and certainly these are not external acts or occurrences (see §36). Thus, though not committed "to any specific analysis", Russell was committed to analysis in terms of sensations, images, and the like. The outer had need of the inner, not as much as a cause as to provide referents for psychological terms like *believe, remember,* and *expect* (GI 17–18; XXII, 1).

(3)   Such a doctrine is too amorphous, both in its claims and in its argumentation, for direct refutation (GI 68). "The *preconceived idea . . . can only be removed by turning our whole examination round*" (§108), in the manner described by GI 41 and 58. Citing other experiences (§596) and especially varied circumstances (§§588, 591–92, 607), Wittgenstein seeks to enrich the patient's diet (§593). For it is the refusal to take such "nonessentials", both inner and outer, into account, that leads the introspectionist to look within, then makes the inner content seem so nebulous and indefinable (§608; *BB* 149b; *PG* 75a). The artichoke has lost all its leaves (§164). (Cp. XX, 3.)

DETAILED COMMENTARY

§588   See §645. The number resembles §586; W. is teaching differences (GI 41).

   description of a state of mind: see §585 and commentary.

   But there are many . . . : for a contrasting viewpoint, see GI 38.

§589   See p. 178j; cp. §427 and commentary; *Z* 497; *EPB* 223; *PG* 106a.

   Luther: the specialists I have consulted have been unable to indicate the origin of this saying, or whether it is in fact a quotation.

§590   Cp. p. 178j.

   "How does it come out . . .": "by his use of the word, in this as in other cases" (§288a). See pp. 175, 181; Hunter, *Essays*, 195 ("presumably the interesting thing is how it does *not* come out: not by his point-ing at the heart").

§591 See *Z* 44; cp. §35. These remarks were probably occasioned by James's discussion on "Feelings of Tendency", in *Principles*, I, 249–71, e.g.: "And has the reader never asked himself what kind of a mental fact is his *intention of saying a thing* before he has said it? It is an entirely definite intention, distinct from all other intentions, an absolutely dis-tinct state of consciousness, therefore" (253). W.'s critique resembles that on pp. 181g–182e, where James is still more clearly the target.

§592 **"the mental act of meaning"**: "the word 'mental' indicating that we mustn't expect to understand how these things work" (*BB* 39; see §36). See GI 37; XXVI, 4–7.

  "gives the sentence life": see §§430–32; *Z* 143; *BB* 4d.

  it can sometimes look like that: for instance for the reasons dis-cussed in GI 15–22, and in the commentary on §413.

  will be uttered: rather: "are uttered" (cp. §489).

  "perhaps not always the *same* one": cp. *BB* 156: "Do I even re-member a set of, say, five sensations some one of which I had on every occasion when I could be said to have understood the word?"

  how is the 'undertone' to be separated: cp. §607a, pp. 182f–183c; *BB* 184d–185f.

§593 On reasons for the failing, see GI 11–12 and *BB* 18d–20a. For illustrations, see e.g. XVI, 2–3; §§2–3, 140b ("only the one case and no other occurred to us"); *BB* 149b; *PP* 315; Frege, *Foundations*, 6 ("Kant, obviously, was thinking only of small numbers"); and especially Man. 229, §706, quoted for §23c. In Man. 228 (§183) the number follows as a gloss on §305 rather than on §592. See GI 41, 50–51, 58, 62; *EPB* 229 ("It is a great help to understanding to imagine a multitude of varied cases").

§594 All but (*c*) expresses a viewpoint W. is combating. See XXIII, 1–2.

(a) "But the words . . .": Sections XXXII and XXXVII amount to a detailed examination of this claim and tendency, in an effort to see what lies behind them.

  "the dimension of depth": see §583; cp. §§111, 664; *PG* 147 ("Com-pare with this the remark: When we understand a sentence, it takes on depth for us").

  How I express this . . . : for (it has been said) we know little about these processes (§308 and commentary); and the difficulties of in-trospection are great (§456); and language is inadequate to describe what we observe (§610). See James, *Principles*, I, 472 (quoted for §436); Russell, *Mind*, 187 (quoted in XXIII, 2), and *Outline*, 270; Ramsey,

Foundations, 144: "I speak throughout as if the differences between belief, disbelief, and mere consideration lay in the presence or absence of 'feelings'; but any other word may be substituted for 'feeling' which the reader prefers, e.g. 'specific quality' or 'act of assertion' and 'act of denial'."

or that they have an atmosphere: see James's doctrine of the "fringe" (e.g. *Principles,* I, 245–46, 252, 255, 269). Cp. §§117, 173, 213, 596, 607, 609, pp. 66n, 181–83.

(b) Cp. §416 for a fuller expression of this attitude, and §§423–26 for W.'s reaction.

(c) See §§254, 299, 386b.

§595 Cp. pp. 211ab, 215h–216a; *EPB* 223–24; *BB* 146bcd. W. may have had James in mind, e.g.: "Such a vague sense as this of the words belonging together is the very minimum of fringe that can accompany them, if 'thought' at all. . . . So delicate and incessant is this recognition by the mind of the mere fitness of words to be mentioned together that the slightest misreading . . . will be corrected by a listener whose attention is so relaxed that he gets no idea of the *meaning* of the sentence at all" (*Principles,* I, 262, 263; cp. 252c, 456b–457b). The connection with §596 is suggested by Man. 229, §832: "This is like: 'Does a recognition take place when I see a familiar object//hear a familiar word?' " See §§600–603.

§596 For the point of all this, see §595 and commentary, especially the quote from James. See *EPB* 191–94; *BB* 127, 129c, 180–82 (especially 182a); Man. 229, 219–20; cp. *PG* 165def.

the feeling of 'familiarity': Russell made much of this feeling, using it to explain our belief that a memory image pictures the past (*Mind,* 161–62), much as James had before him (*Principles,* I, 223, 239). *BB* 156b–157a and 180c–181 suggest connections with W.'s present concerns.

"I think we may regard familiarity as a definite feeling, capable of existing without an object, but normally standing in a specific relation to some feature of the environment, the relation being that which we express in words by saying that the feature in question is familiar" (Russell, *Mind,* 168–69).

"Is there *one* feeling of familiarity, and do we have it, therefore, whenever we perceive familiar, well-known objects? Well, do you generally have a feeling of familiarity when you look at familiar objects in your surroundings?—When do we have such a feeling?—Yet it would have been easy to say in what circumstances we have *contrary* feelings: surprise, astonishment, strangeness" (*EPB* 191). "One could say: 'Unfamiliarity is much more of an experience than familiarity' " (*BB* 127).

We think that . . . : cp. *Z* 512.

§597 Worked up in Man. 116, 329–30. Cp. §32b; *Z* 191; Man. 228, §641.

so we often think . . . : since "just as" is repeated, we might fill out the comparison somewhat as follows, in parallel with §§335–36 and in continuity with the preceding and following numbers: So descriptive expressions creep into the speech of one who is not describing, and words elsewhere used to express feelings enter the speech of one who has no feelings (cp. §297 and commentary), thereby creating the impression that whenever the word occurs it expresses a constant mental content, for instance the "definite feeling" Russell spoke of, "which we express in words by saying that the feature in question is familiar" (*Mind*, 168–69). It then seems "as if the purpose of the proposition were to convey to one person how it is with another" (§317), and "the whole point of communication lay in this: someone else grasps the sense of my words—which is something mental" (§363). "The expression of feeling then is an indirect way of transmitting the feeling. And people have often talked of a direct transmission of feeling which would obviate the external medium of communication" (*BB* 185). Cp. Russell, *Outline*, 270: "A belief, I should say, interpreted narrowly, is a form of words related to an emotion of one of several kinds. . . . The emotion is different according as the belief embodies a reminiscence, a perception, an expectation, or something outside the experience of the believer. Moreover, a form of words is not essential."

§598 This took shape in Man. 116, 330–31. See *BB* 132gh; Man. 229, §923, quoted for §109 ("description alone"); cp. Ramsey, *Foundations*, 144, quoted for §308. W.'s criticism is directed especially at James (*EPB* 218) and Russell (see JN 82) in whose writings such thinking abounds, e.g.: "Thus when I say: 'What a wonderful man Jones is!' I am perfectly aware that I mean by man to exclude Napoleon Bonaparte or Smith. But when I say: 'What a wonderful thing Man is!' I am equally aware that I mean to *in*clude not only Jones, but Napoleon and Smith as well. This added consciousness is an absolutely positive sort of feeling, transforming what would otherwise be mere noise or vision into something *understood*" (James, *Principles*, I, 472). "*Man* meant for *mankind* is in short a different feeling from *man* as a mere noise, or from *man* meant for *that* man, to wit, John Smith alone" (ibid., 478). (See XXXII, 1–3.)

"Having elsewhere used the word 'feeling' to designate generically all states of consciousness considered subjectively, or without respect to their possible function, I shall then say that, whatever elements an act of cognition may imply besides, it at least implies the existence of a *feeling*" (James, *Meaning*, 1–2). As Lewes said: " 'Algebra cannot exist without values, nor Thought without Feelings' " (James, *Principles,* I, 270).

A paradigm illustration is Russell's account of memory (see *BB* 182c–184). First, feelings differentiate memory images from imagination images: "They differ by the fact that the images that constitute memories, unlike those that constitute imagination, are accompanied by a feeling of belief which may be expressed in the words 'this happened' " (*Mind,* 176). Second, feelings differentiate between memory and other forms of belief: "There are at least three kinds of belief, namely memory, expectation and bare assent. Each of these I regard as constituted by a certain feeling or complex of sensations, attached to the content believed" (ibid., 250). Third, "it is clear that such feelings must play an essential part in the process of dating remembered events" (ibid., 163). For instance, "in order to understand the phrase 'this morning' it is necessary that we should have a way of feeling time-intervals, and that this feeling should give what is constant in the meaning of the words 'this morning' " (ibid., 177). On the same example, see Russell's *Outline,* 196–97, 203d, 206c; and *Logic,* 309–11; James, *Principles,* II, 283. Feelings also explain, e.g., consciousness (Russell, *Mind,* 289) and negation (idem, *Logic,* 317b).

For illustrations in W.'s writings, see e.g. XXII, 1; §§170, 174, 460, 578, 588, 607, 625, 640, 645, p. 185bd; *BB* 143g–144a and *EPB* 217 (meaning, believing).

serve to explain: for W.'s attitude towards explanation, see VII, 3–5; §§109, 126, 654–55.

§599 See §128 and commentary; cp. Russell, *Mind,* 233 (quoted for §587a).

"But it must be . . .": W.'s illustration at this point in the *Brown Book:* "What is the difference between a memory image, an image that comes with expectation, and say, an image of a daydream. You may be inclined to answer, 'There is an intrinsic difference between the images.'—Did you notice that difference, or did you only say there was one because you think there must be one?" (*BB* 182; see Russell, above).

Philosophy only states . . . : to appear plausible, this too must be recognized as prescriptive, not descriptive. The trouble is that even the concluding words may have to be read: "which every one *ought* to admit". For anyone familiar with "the dogmatism into which we fall so easily in doing philosophy" (§131) knows how difficult it is to remove the prejudice which stands in the way of simply observing evident facts (§340). For possible answers to such misgivings, see the commentary on §128, where a similar claim is made.

§600 Cp. pp. 194g–195e, 213f; *BB* 178a. Doubtless the example is intended as a comparison which may help to loosen the grip of the prejudices (§§598–99) with which W. is here chiefly concerned (§§594–96, 601).

§601   See *PG* 181d–182a; Man. 228, §38, and Man. 116, 37–38 (quoted for §239); cp. *Z* 716; Schlick, "Form", 195 ("I have to recognize the colour as that particular one I was taught to call 'blue'"); James, *Principles,* I, 28–29. *BB* 182 links this number with the preceding ones: "Isn't it an experience of familiarity when on being asked 'Who is this man?' I answer straight away (or after some reflection) 'It is so and so'? . . . To [this] one might object, saying that the experience of saying the man's name was not the experience of familiarity, that he had to be familiar to us in order that we might know his name, and that we had to *know his name* in order that we might say it. . . . And this remark is certainly true if only we realize that it does not imply that knowing the name is a process accompanying or preceding saying the name." " 'But when he said "Oh, this is a pencil," how did he know that it was if he didn't recognize it as something?'—This really comes to saying 'How did he recognize "pencil" as the name of this sort of thing?' Well, how did he recognize it? He just reacted in this particular way by saying this word" (*BB* 128; cp. §§381, 384).

§§602–3   See *EPB* 191–96; *BB* 127–30; *PG* 165–66; later pages of Man. 180a; cp. §§596, 600, pp. 195d, 213f. In the *Brown Book* the discussion of recognition and feelings of familiarity opened what W. already envisaged as Part Two of the *Investigations* (GI 65). Here it is incorporated into the discussion of meaning (§594), thought (§598), and language (§601), for reasons such as those indicated in the quotations above.

an act of recognition: such as sometimes does occur: "What happens when B recognizes something as a pencil?"

"Suppose A had shown him an object looking like a stick. B handles this object, suddenly it comes apart, one of the parts being a cap, the other a pencil. B says 'Oh, this is a pencil.' He has recognized the object as a pencil" (*BB* 127).

§604   From *PG* 167, which adds: "In most cases of recognition no such comparison takes place." A similar, full critique occurs already in *Kreis,* 48b, 53–54, 86–88, and in Man. 302, 26. See also §56; *Z* 659a; *EPB* 128–29; *BB* 3abc, 87b (full, with interesting context), 88cd, 128e, 165d–166a; *PG* 78, 90a, 96b, 157f, 168d, 180; Man. 229, §1708 ("But there is no comparison of two pictures, and even if there were, we would still have to recognize one of them as the earlier"); Man. 116, 37–38 (on Frege and Ramsey; quoted for §239); Man. 115, 6–7 (already as here in §604), 9, 28–29; Man. 109, 198, 247–48; Malcolm, *Memoir,* 47 ("A man might say: 'I know this book is red, because I have a mental impression of red.' But how does he know that he remembers the impression correctly? And how does he *compare* the impression with the book?"). Cp. §§379–80; *BB* 162b–166 and *EPB* 221 (on aspect-seeing, conceived as comparison); *PB* 63de, 65a; Man. 108, 222 (similar discussion of meaning); James, *Principles*, I, 649–50, and II, 112.

It is easy . . . : W. encountered such pictures often, e.g.:

In Plato: "*Soc.*—The only possibility of erroneous opinion is, when knowing you and Theodorus, and having the seal or impression of both of you in the wax block, but seeing you both imperfectly and at a distance, I try to assign the right impression of visual memory to the right impression, and fit this into the proper mould: if I succeed, recognition will take place; but if I fail and transpose them, putting the foot into the wrong shoe—that is to say, putting the vision of either of you on to the wrong seal, or seeing you as in a mirror when the sight flows from right to left—then 'heterodoxy' and false opinion ensues" (*Theaetetus*, 193; see 194).

In Augustine: "If perchance a thing is lost from sight but not from memory (as any visible body), its image is still retained within, and it is sought until it be restored to sight; and when it is found, it is recognized by means of the image which is within" (*Confessions*, X, 18, 27).

In Russell: "The image cannot be what constitutes memory. This is easily seen by merely noticing that the image is in the present, whereas what is remembered is known to be in the past. Moreover, we are certainly able to some extent to compare our image with the object remembered, so that we often know, within somewhat wide limits, how far our image is accurate; but this would be impossible, unless the object, as opposed to the image, were in some way before the mind. Thus the essence of memory is not constituted by the image, but by having immediately before the mind an object which is recognized as past" (*Problems*, 66).

In Waismann: "But how is it when I say: 'Sing the same note'? What counts here as a criterion of identity? Comparison with memory or with a paradigm" ("Identität", 57).

In Schlick: "In order to give a name to the colour I am seeing I have to go beyond the immediacy of pure intuition, I have to think, be it ever so little. I have to recognise the colour as that particular one I was taught to call 'blue'. This involves an act of comparison, or association" ("Form", 195).

In the manuscript from which these numbers grew: " 'Is it certain that the color I now call yellow is the same color that I earlier called "yellow"?'—Of course, for it is yellow.—But how do I know that?—Because I remember it.—But can't my memory deceive me?—No. Not if its datum is precisely what I am guided by" (Man. 109, 300; cp. §389).

as if I carried a picture: for instance, "the word 'red' is used by means of a memory image" (Man. 109, 248).

or by allowing us . . . : contrast the quotation from Russell, above, with those from Plato and Augustine. See *Z* 662; cp. *PB* 82b.

§605 From Man. 115, 9. See *Z* 659a; *PG* 180c; cp. §§428, 437–39; *BB* 170a (quoted for §606); Man. 109, 228–29 (quoted for §175b); Man. 108, 220–22; James, *Principles*, I, 588 ("It instantaneously fills a socket completely moulded to its shape").

§606(a) The parallel with §605 consists in this, that one conceives of the genuine expression as somehow coinciding with the reality. For instance, if a person's tone is genuinely friendly, the friendliness does not seem to be merely associated, outwardly connected, with the voice; but friendliness is there, alive, in the tone. Here, too, one might say, friendliness *fits* this voice. But *what* fits *what* here (§537)?

"This is connected with the contrast between *saying* and *meaning*. 'Any expression can lie': but just think what you mean by 'lying'. How do you conceive a lie? Aren't you contrasting one expression with another?" (*PG* 178). And do both occur simultaneously? Does the truth hover before the speaker's mind *while* he speaks the falsehood—or the truth? (Cp. §20.) And in this latter case, are there "two the same"?

(b) See *BB* 170, e.g.: "I should like to say, 'it has one definite physiognomy.' But what is it that I am really saying about it? What is this statement, straightened out? 'The word falls,' one is tempted to explain, 'into a mould of my mind *long* prepared for it.' But as I don't perceive both the word and a mould, the metaphor of the word's fitting a mould can't allude to an experience of comparing the hollow and the solid shape before they are fitted together, but rather to an experience of seeing the solid shape accentuated by a particular background."

§607 See Man. 228, §28; Gasking, "Avowals", 160–61; cp. *BB* 11b; Man. 229, §1496; Man. 138, 24A. The quotation from JN, below, indicates the general drift of this number and its connection with the preceding discussion of memory and recognition. Here, too, we hypostatize a feeling (§598) or a picture (§604) to explain our thought. But "now remember *quite precisely*! Then the 'inner experience' . . . seems to vanish again" (§645; see §173).

(a) The five *but*'s in this paragraph belong to "the voice of temptation" (GI 55).

How does one judge . . . : see James, *Principles*, I, 623, on e.g. "the accuracy with which some men judge of the hour of day or night without looking at the clock."

"The question is: What is the method? The answer is: by no method. (It's an interesting fact; don't try to make it uninteresting by explaining it—won't anyway.) . . . Compare 'I can tell you without looking that my elbows are bent at more than 90°.' People have said 'You must have a feeling that tells you that' " (JN 20–21). On this comparison, see §§624–26, p. 185. For another, also indicated by JN, see p. 215d.

though impalpable: see §608.

a characteristic atmosphere: cp. §173.

how am I to separate it . . . : cp. §592, pp. 182f–183c; *BB* 184d–185f.

And then all at once . . . : see §20.

so long, that is . . . : cp. §§173, 645.

(b) Cp. §§477–78, pp. 215d, 225d; *Z* 513 ("One speaks of a feeling of conviction because there is a *tone* of conviction").

(c) W. is not describing his own attitude; he would be inclined to stress differences (cp. Man. 228, §692; *Z* 254).

the purpose of the picture: cp. §556c.

§608   See XXIII, 1–2; §36; *BB* 5a ("It was in fact just the occult character of the mental process which you needed for your purposes"); Man. 228, §306; Man. 128, 24–25; Malcolm, "Nature", 9–13; cp. *Z* 126.

"Don't stick the phenomenon in the wrong compartment. *There* it seems ghostlike, intangible, surprising" (Man. 229, §1047). "You looked for it among experiences" (Man. 228, §307), so were mystified. For any one phenomenon seems inessential (§§173, 175–76); so we strip off these particular coverings. In order to find the real artichoke, we divest it of its leaves (§164), so are left with a leafless, "intangible" one. See *PG* 75a.

§609(a)   Cp. §§88, 291, pp. 187–89; *BB* 184c. Whether one succeeds in describing an atmosphere must be judged from the purpose of the description. The person who declares an atmosphere ineffable (§610) has perhaps some vague notion of ideal exactness in mind, or the transfer of an experience from mind to mind, or something equally utopic. But in ordinary circumstances, the description of an atmosphere as "forlorn", "rustic", or "gay" may do quite well enough.

(b) "You notice a connection with the question about the essence of intention, of willing—of meaning and understanding" (*EPB* 187). "It is as if at first all these more or less inessential processes were shrouded in a particular atmosphere which dissipates when I look closely at them" (§173; see §§174–75; *Z* 128).

§610   See §§71b, 78, 106, 436, pp. 183b, 185h–186a, 187i, 228h; *Z* 536, 654; NL 275–76; *BB* 162b, 177d, 181c, 184d–185f; *PG* 44d, 175c; *PB* 286e; Man. 229, §§689, 1221; Man. 228, §§13, 664; Man. 213, 427–28; Man. 122, Feb. 1; Man. 110, 258–60, 269; Man. 109, 98–99, 111; Man. 107, 165, 171 ("The problem of the 'indefiniteness' of sense-data"); *Kreis*, 252 (quoted for §105); JN 78; Malcolm, *Memoir*, 47b; cp. §70b, p. 220f; *PG* 209a; *PB* 74a, 260c; Man. 108, 248.

The lesson of the number: " 'Essentially inexpressible' means that it makes no sense to speak of a fuller expression" (*PG* 45).

For sample statements about the inadequacy of language to capture the refinements of reality, see (in addition to quotes and references below): X, 12–13; Schlick, *Aufsätze*, 194, 212–13; Mauthner, *Beiträge*, I, 194, 235; Lichtenberg, "Sprachbemerkungen", 272–73; Ramsey, *Foundations*, 265c; Kraft, *Circle*, 38, 41–42; Russell, *Outline*, 276b, and *Introduction*, 61b; Waismann, in *Kreis*, 236; Spengler, *Untergang*, 422; Helmholtz, *Optik*, 583. The principal paradigm to consider is W.'s own thought, at various stages:

(1)   Early: "Objects can only be *named.* Signs are their representatives. I can only speak *about* them. I cannot *put them into words.* Propositions can only say *how* things are, not *what* they are" (3.221). Comparison with §610 is appropriate: The aroma of coffee is named, and we might say "how it is" (e.g. in this room, now), but supposedly could not say what it is, that is, could not describe it. However, it is important to notice that in 3.221 W. was speaking about ideal names and their atomic referents, whereas in the following quotations he speaks about the expressions of ordinary language (e.g. "aroma of coffee") and their shortcomings. So the background to keep in mind is W.'s vain effort (X, 8; XXXIV, 1–2) to express immediate experience in a "primary", "phenomenological" language and thereby remedy the analytic inadequacy of ordinary language.

(2)   Middle: See the commentary on §106.

"Our ordinary language lacks means for describing a specific shade of color, say the brown of my table. Thus it cannot produce a picture of this color. If I wish to inform someone what color a material is to have, I send him a sample" (*PB* 73; see 263b).

(3)   Late: "It is as though, although you can't tell me exactly what happens inside you, you can nevertheless tell me something general about it. By saying e.g. that you are having an impression which can't be described. As it were: There is something further about it, only you *can't say* it; you can only make the general statement. It is this idea which plays hell with us" (NL 276; divisions suppressed; see 275).

" 'But that is only a very rough description, for it describes the experience only in its most general traits.'—But isn't this what I *call* a description of my experience? How do I arrive at the notion of a kind of description which I can never give?" (Man. 229, §1746; see ibid., §1747; cp. *Investigations,* §§481, 483).

"If you say: 'We haven't got the technique' (I. A. Richards), what in such a case are we entitled to call such a description? You might say some such thing as: 'Well, now, if you hear this piece of music, you get certain sense impressions. Certain images, certain organic feelings, emotions, etc.,' meaning, 'we still don't know how to analyse this impression.' The mistake seems to me in the idea of description" (*LC* 37; see 38).

"What is a description of feeling at all? What is a description of pain?" (*LC* 33; see *Z* 482, below).

(a) Why can't it be done?: not because words are lacking (p. 228h). Is it, then, because "a description is a representation of a distribution in a space (in that of time, for instance)" (p. 187)? Well, I can say that a particular room is filled with the aroma of coffee, thereby giving a spatio-temporal distribution (cp. *Z* 482, below). If someone then objects that this is a description of a room filled with the aroma of coffee, but not of the aroma of coffee, it becomes evident that the limitation being set is not on the possibilities of language but on what shall count as "description" (cp. *BB* 181c). As to whether W. himself set such a limit, see the commentary on p. 187i.

for what are words lacking?: if the ineffable thing is the one mentioned, how did we manage to mention it? (Cp. Man 229, §1271; Black, *Companion*, 196.) Once again: "We destroy the outward similarity between a metaphysical proposition and an experiential one" (*BB* 55; see *Z* 458).

(b) "One would like to say for example 'I could *describe* the pain if I only had the necessary words and elementary meanings.' One feels: all that is lacking is the requisite nomenclature. (James). As if one could even paint the sensation, if only other people would understand this language.—And one really can describe pain spatially and temporally" (*Z* 482). See Man. 130, 55–57 ("Why is it difficult to describe a face precisely? Do we lack the words?"); Black, "Relations", 29c.

but I cannot . . . : see *BB* 166, quoted for §527 ("I should not be able to say").

A grave nod: see Man. 130, 60, quoted for §527 ("much more akin"); cp. p. 182g.

"Our vocabulary is inadequate": "Our psychological vocabulary is wholly inadequate to name the differences that exist, even such strong differences as these" (James, *Principles*, I, 251; see 241, 245b, 246, 252). "This absence of a special vocabulary for subjective facts hinders the study of all but the very coarsest of them" (ibid., 195).

"No words exist for describing the actual occurrence in all its particularity; all words, even proper names, are general, with the possible exception of 'this'" (Russell, *Outline*, 12). "We have no vocabulary for describing what actually takes place in us when we think or desire, except the somewhat elementary device of putting words in inverted commas. . . . We need a new vocabulary if we are to describe these occurrences otherwise than by reference to objects" (idem, *Inquiry*, 207).

"The language of psychology, owing to the primitive state of this science, is exceedingly fragmentary" (Schlick, "Form", 242).

What would have to be the case: one common answer (cp. the quote from Russell's *Outline,* above): We would need to establish names for individual experiences and their specific properties, by means of personal ostensive definition, yet in such a way that the names had public meaning (cp. X, 20). But such hypotheses do not make sense (X, 20–21). Hence there is nothing wrong—basically (§§132, 577)—with our language (§§120, 133).

XXIV. Willing (§§611–628)

GENERAL COMMENTARY

(1)   The following query provides a unifying focus for most of this section, and a point of departure for dialectical probing of the problem the section treats: "There is a strange opposition between two ideas: We would like to say 'willing is not an experience,' and—'willing is indeed merely an experience.' What in general do these two propositions mean, and why do we want to assert them *both*?" (*EPB* 235). For brief answers to these questions, *EPB* 234–35 is the place to consult; for fuller versions of the same answers, we may turn first to the Schopenhauerian viewpoint (*PG* 144) which Wittgenstein once shared (*NB* 76–89), then to the empirical approach of James (*EPB* 234). The seesaw of opinions will suggest the value of Wittgenstein's solution (§119).

(2)   Many parallels reveal Schopenhauer's influence on the *Notebooks,* both with regard to the will and with regard to its acts. "The intellect, like its objects," wrote Schopenhauer, "is mere phenomenon, the will alone is thing-in-itself" (*World,* II, 201). "The thinking subject," echoed Wittgenstein, "is surely mere illusion. But the willing subject exists" (*NB* 80). "The act of will," Schopenhauer further asserted, "and the action of the body are not two different states objectively known, connected by the bond of causality; they do not stand in the relation of cause and effect, but are one and the same thing" (*World,* I, 100; cp. 106). "The act of the will," wrote Wittgenstein, "is not the cause of the action but is the action itself" (*NB* 87). The reasons for these assertions, unclear in the *Notebooks,* are expounded by Schopenhauer as follows: " 'As perception can furnish only *phenomena,* not things-in-themselves, we too have absolutely no knowledge of things-in-themselves.' I admit this of every-

thing, but not of the knowledge everyone has of his own *willing*. This is neither a perception (for all perception is spatial), nor is it empty; on the contrary, it is more real than any other knowledge. Further, it is not *a priori*, like merely formal knowledge, but entirely *a posteriori;* hence we are unable to anticipate it in the particular case, but in this are often guilty of error concerning ourselves. In fact, our *willing* is the only opportunity we have of understanding simultaneously from within any event that outwardly manifests itself; consequently, it is the one thing known to us *immediately*, and not given to us merely in the representation, as all else is" (*World*, II, 196; see idem, *Natur*, 295, and *EPB* 235).

(3)   However, many a movement which we perform does not seem to reveal an inner, introspectable dimension. "This absence of the will act, as I shall now call it," said Wittgenstein, "was noticed by William James, and he describes the act of getting up in the morning, for example, as follows: he is lying in bed and reflecting whether it is time to get up—and all of a sudden *he finds himself getting up* [*Principles*, II, 524]. Similarly one sometimes says, 'Suddenly I heard myself saying the words. . . .' But what does it mean if I say: 'When I get up *only that* happens'? In contrast with what? What is it that does *not* occur? . . . Well, I believe that when a person lifts a heavy weight with effort, or follows a difficult path step by step, he won't say: 'I find myself. . . .' It is the feeling of muscular effort whose absence we called 'the absence of the will act' " (*EPB* 234; see *BB* 151). Here is one reason why we might be inclined to say, "Willing is merely an experience" (cp. §621b).

(4)   But how can a mere feeling constitute willing? "We say: 'Willing can't be any phenomenon, for once again [like the act itself] every phenomenon *simply happens*, is something we undergo, not what we *do*. Willing isn't *something* I see happen; it's more like being involved in our activity, our being the activity" (*PG* 144; see *NB* 88, below). It is as when we mean something: "One is oneself in motion. One is rushing ahead and so cannot also observe oneself rushing ahead" (§456). "Look at your arm and move it and you will experience this very strongly: 'You don't observe how it moves, you have no experience—or no mere experience—but you *do* something' " (*PG* 144). Thus *"doing* itself seems not to have any volume of experience" (§620).

(5)   Even a phenomenal wish, or "the *fiat,* the element of consent, or resolve that the act shall ensue", which for James constituted "the essence of the voluntariness of the act" (*Principles*, II, 501), is not willing. "Mere resolves of the will," wrote Schopenhauer, "until they are carried out, are only intentions, and therefore a matter of the intellect alone. . . . The *will itself* is active only in real action, consequently in muscular action, hence in *irritability*" (*World*, II, 248). A similar distinction ap-

pears in Wittgenstein's early notes: "Wishing is not acting. But willing is acting. . . . The fact that I will an action consists in my performing the action, not in my doing something else which causes the action. When I move something, I move. When I perform an action I am in action" (*NB* 88).

(6)   Thus the problem of intentionality did not arise in the same way for willing as it did for wishing (GI 34; §§615–16; *BB* 30; Man. 302, 18). Whereas my wish refers, for instance, to the future movement of a chair (*NB* 88), my will relates to the action I am actually performing. So there is no gap for intention to bridge. Yet willing is intentional for all that. "The will does have to have an object. Otherwise we should have no foothold and could not know what we willed. . . . My will fastens on to the world somewhere, and does not fasten on to other things" (*NB* 87–88). But where? Schopenhauer had already suggested the answer: "The nervous system exists everywhere, merely in order to make possible a *direction* of the will's action by a control thereof, to serve, so to speak, as a mirror for the will, so that it may see what it does, just as we make use of a mirror when shaving" (*World,* II, 256). Thus, "in drawing the square ⊠ in the mirror one notices that one is only able to manage it if one prescinds completely from the visual datum and relies only on muscular feeling. So here after all there are two quite different acts of the will in question. The one relates to the visual part of the world, the other to the muscular-feeling part" (*NB* 87; see Man. 111, 166; cp. *BB* 154a). Only the latter, it would seem, shows where to catch hold with the will (§617). So young Wittgenstein was inclined to draw the contrast between willing and wishing, in intentional terms, as follows: "My wish relates, e.g., to the movement of the chair, my will to a muscular feeling" (*NB* 88). (See XXXIV, 6–7.)

(7)   There is a second way in which "the will seems always to have to relate to an idea. We cannot imagine . . . having carried out an act of will without having detected that we have carried it out" (*NB* 86). Here too it seemed that feelings might provide an explanation (§§624–26, p. 185); for in Schopenhauer's view, "the whole nervous system constitutes, so to speak, the antennae of the will, which it extends and spreads inwards and outwards" (*World,* II, 256). However, "have the feelings by which I ascertain that an act of the will takes place any particular characteristic which distinguishes them from other ideas? It seems not!" (*NB* 87). But in that case, "what kind of reason is there for the assumption of a willing subject? Is not *my world* adequate for individuation?" (*NB* 89). Already the fly was buzzing loudly in the fly-bottle (§309).

(8)   These and similar buzzings are evoked in JN 41: "Suppose my head shakes. Then either it is voluntary or involuntary. If voluntary

you want to say something else happens. . . . So it looks as if the important thing was a movement in my soul; i.e., an experience. And if an experience then we want to say 'Well, it *happens;* why not say 'it wills in me' (Lichtenberg, Groddek)?' (Notice that 'I sit and will' is not English, it's philosophers' language.) And we seem to have lost the active as opposed to passive distinction. But we have gone all wrong. We get all sorts of pictures of 'mental activity', e.g. we say we decide but we rarely *decide.* Also, 'A voluntary action is one you try to do.' But 90 per cent of voluntary actions are not the ones you try to do. . . . Some will say 'A feeling of innervation is what happens.' But how do you know it's a feeling of innervation? A research would be needed. The people who say this have, in general, not done it; and if there was they'd not always find it. So 'A feeling of innervation' had another source. They felt there *must* be a *thing* to stand for the decision (a substance to correspond to the substantive). Also some say 'There is a *fiat* in me.' You scratch your head. Was it voluntary? Yes. Was there a fiat? No."

(9)   Though too much importance should not be attached to the details of rough notes, taken under adverse conditions, during discussion, this passage and subsequent paragraphs indicate clearly the general drift of Wittgenstein's thought in the present numbers. As in the two preceding sections (see XXII, 1), he is concerned with an instance of the tendency described in GI 17: "A false—falsely simplified—conception . . . seduces us into thinking that a specific, characteristic experience must correspond to the word" (*EPB* 218–19). Bewitched by a verb like *will* we look now for a feeling, now for an act, but never find anything satisfactory (§308). This is how we enter the fly-bottle, and it is also the way out. Deliverance comes when we recognize the linguistic fact (Z 590) that "there is not one common difference between so-called voluntary acts and involuntary ones, viz, the presence or absence of one element" (*BB* 151–52). "What is voluntary is certain movements with their normal *surrounding* of intention, learning, trying, acting. Movements of which it makes sense to say that they are sometimes voluntary and sometimes involuntary are movements in a special surrounding" (Z 577). Here, too, there is a family of cases (*PG* 74–75).

DETAILED COMMENTARY

§611(a) See XXIV, 1, 3; cp. *NB* 73n. The experiment described in §617, and that in *NB* 87 (see XXIV, 6), "show, we would like to say, that willing too is merely an experience (the 'will' only 'idea'). 'It comes when it comes; I cannot bring it about.'—Or: 'I cannot will when I will to. It simply happens!' " (*EPB* 236). For according to Schopenhauer and young W., his disciple (XXIV 2, 5), willing included the act, and here the act seems to be beyond my control; it cannot be foreseen *a* *priori* (§617b). "Then is the situation that I merely accompany my actions with my will?", W. had wondered. "But in that case how can I predict—as in some sense I surely can—that I shall raise my arm in five minutes' time? That I shall will this?" (*NB* 87). The answer begins in §613.

"**Willing too . . .**": as well as thought (cp. XXIV, 2; *NB* 89).

(b) As usual when he encounters a metaphysical *can* or *can't* (*BB* 55, quoted for §136b; cp. §§136b, 360), W. starts to disentangle the grammatical from the factual, the meaningful (§612) from the meaningless (§613). Insofar as the hypothesis makes sense, it is possible for us to bring about willing. But "doubtless I was trying to say: I can't will willing; that is, it makes no sense to speak of willing willing" (§613).

§612   See the preceding comments; §627; *EPB* 235.

§613   See *Z* 580; Man. 228, §§477–80.

an act of willing: better: "willing". Like those listed in *Z* 52, the verb *will* does not designate an action; and here the German has only *das Wollen*.

Doubtless I was trying to say . . . : in §611a. See the quote there from *EPB* 236.

it makes no sense . . . : as it makes no sense to speak of commanding a person to will; again, willing is not an act. Cp. Man. FW, 18: "No one would say: 'Now choose to choose so and so.'"

willing willing: see Schopenhauer, *Freiheit*, 490 ("willing one's willing, which is like talking about the self of one's self").

is not the name of an action: see XXIV, 2, 5 ("willing is acting"); *EPB* 233–34; *BB* 150c–152a; cp. *Z* 51.

an immediate non-causal bringing-about: as in Schopenhauer, e.g.: "It is not a question here of the relation between muscle and nerve, but of that between act of will and action of body. Now this does not make itself known as a causal relation. If these two presented themselves to us as cause and effect, their connexion would not be so incomprehensible to us as it actually is; for what we understand from its cause we understand in so far as there is in general for us a comprehension of things. On the other hand, the movement of our limbs by virtue of mere acts of will is indeed a miracle of such common occurrence that we no longer notice it; but if we once turn our attention to it, we become vividly conscious of the incomprehensible nature of the matter, just because we have here before us something we do *not* understand as effect of its cause" (*World*, II, 36). See *Z* 580; Schlick, "Causality", 522c; §461; Berkeley, *Dialogues*, II, 432 ("an effect *immediately* depending on the will").

the causal nexus seems . . . : see §170c; cp. *BB* 118. The viewpoint evoked is one W. had shared (XXIV, 6), not that already criticized in *NB* 84s and 5.135–5.1361.

"As we said above, if we start from the will, our own muscular movement seems to us a miracle, since certainly a strict causal chain extends from the external motive up to the muscular action; yet the will itself is not included as a link in the chain, but, as the metaphysical substratum of the possibility of the muscle's actuation through brain and nerve, it is the foundation of the muscular action in question" (Schopenhauer, *World*, II, 249).

"But the impulse to motion that we impart through the innervation of our motor nerves is something immediately perceptible. We sense that we do something in imparting such an impulse. But what it is we do, we do not know immediately. Only physiology teaches us that we excite or innervate the motor nerves, that their excitation is conveyed to the muscles, that these therefore contract and move the members" (Helmholtz, *Schriften*, 116).

The connexion may be broken . . . : e.g. "I can imagine carrying out the act of will for raising my arm, but that my arm does not move. (E.g., a sinew is torn.)" (*NB* 86). Similarly, "if, say, the motor nerve leading to my hand is severed, my will can no longer move it. But this is not because the hand has ceased to be, like every part of my body, the objectivity, the mere visibility, of my will, or in other words, because the irritability has vanished, but because the impression of the motive, in consequence of which alone I can move my hand, cannot reach it and act on its muscles as a stimulus, for the line connecting it with the brain is broken" (Schopenhauer, *World*, II, 250).

We think only . . . : cp. §193; *NB* 86d (where the words "ordinary sense of the word" are to be interpreted in the light of 5.5421, 5.631, 5.641).

§614   See Man. 116, 313.

I do not use any instrument: W. comments thus on his own former conception (XXIV, 6): "Here one is inclined to say that our real *actions*, the ones to which volition *immediately* applies, are not the movements of our hand but something further back, say, the actions of our muscles. We are inclined to compare the case with this: Imagine we had a series of levers before us, through which, by a hidden mechanism, we could direct a pencil drawing on a sheet of paper. We might then be in doubt which levers to pull in order to get the desired movement of the pencil; and we could say that *we deliberately* pulled this particular lever, although we didn't deliberately produce the wrong result that we thereby produced. But this comparison, though it easily suggests itself, is very misleading. For in the case of the levers which we saw before us, there was such a thing as deciding which one we were going to pull before pulling it. But does our volition, as it were, play on a keyboard of muscles, choosing which one it was going to use next?" (*BB* 153; see 154). Cp. Schopenhauer, *World*, II, 258; James, *Principles*, II, 493 (quoted for §621a); Berkeley, *Dialogues*, II, 432; Helmholtz, *Schriften*, 116–17, and *Optik*, 580.

My wish is not: see §616 and commentary.

"The confusion of willing with wishing is dangerous here.—For if I raise my arm, I don't first wish it would rise, after which it actually rises. (Although that too could happen in certain cases.)" (*EPB* 235).

§615 See Man. 138, 18A.

"must be the action itself": see XXIV, 4–5, and Schopenhauer, *World*, I, 100–101; II, 36; *Freiheit*, 487.

"cannot be allowed to stop . . .": cp. §§95, 428, 431, 461.

But . . . : adversative because this statement, in conjunction with the previous one, amounts to a possible refutation of the initial assertion. If the action in question is, for example, lifting an object, and I try but do not succeed, then the will does in a sense "stop short of the action".

it is also . . . : for " 'when I make an effort, I surely *do* something, I don't merely have a sensation.' And that is so; for one tells someone 'Make an effort' and he may express his intention: 'Now I will make an effort' " (*Z* 589). However, there is no contradiction between these concessions and the previous assertion that *willing* is not the name of an action (§613). For willing is no one of these things (GI 45), always (XXIV, 8), or by itself (XXIV, 9). "Let us consider various characteristics of voluntary and involuntary acts. In the case of lifting the heavy weight, the various experiences of effort are obviously most characteristic for lifting the weight voluntarily. On the other hand, compare with this the case of writing, voluntarily, where in most of the ordinary cases there will be no effort; and even if we feel that the writing tires our hands and strains their muscles, this is not the experience of 'pulling' and 'pushing' which we would call typical voluntary actions. Further compare the lifting of your hand when you lift a weight with it with lifting your hand when, e.g., you point to some object above you. This will certainly be regarded as a voluntary act, though the element of effort will most likely be entirely absent; in fact this raising of the arm to point at an object is very much like raising the eye to look at it, and here we can hardly conceive of an effort" (*BB* 152–53).

See Man. 302, 23–24; Man. 229, §721; cp. *BB* 151b; Man. 138, 18A; James, *Principles*, II, 561a; Schopenhauer, *World*, II, 202: "For not only willing and deciding in the narrowest sense, but also all striving, wishing, shunning, hoping, fearing, loving, hating, in short all that directly constitutes our own weal and woe, desire and disinclination, is obviously only affection of the will, is a stirring, a modification, of willing and not-willing, is just that which, when it operates outwards, exhibits itself as an act of will proper."

§616 I have *not* wished . . . : during the movement (see *EPB* 235, quoted for §614). "The wish precedes the event," W. had written long before, "the will accompanies it" (*NB* 88). "Then is the situation that I merely accompany my actions with my will?" (*NB* 87). No, "this is clear: it is impossible to will without already performing the act of the will" (ibid.), whereas "it is a fact of logic that wanting does not stand in any logical connexion with its own fulfilment" (*NB* 77). But how does the will effect such a sure connection? Isn't this superstition? (Cp. IX, 1.) So W. was tempted to conclude: "What does this drawing back consist in if not in wishing that the hand will draw back while it in fact does so?" (Man. 111, 166). But *NB* 88 was right at least in this, that the voluntary action excludes the wish; it makes no sense to say, at the moment my arm is rising, "I wish my arm would rise."

§617 See XXIV, 6; *BB* 153 (quoted for §614), 154; *NB* 87–88; cp. *EPB* 168; *BB* 116d; 6.374. Pages 185–86 and §§172–78 suggest what misgivings W. would have about "the absolute need of *guiding sensations* of some kind" (James, *Principles*, II, 490).

(a) One would like to say . . . : see XXIV, 6; James, *Principles*, II, 488–93; Helmholtz, *Schriften*, 116–18.

then how is it known . . . : suppose I felt all the muscles in each finger; would I know which ones to pull, in what order, so as to effect the desired movement? (See quotes from James for §621.) Here too, "we exert ourselves to find a picture and once it is found the application as it were comes about of itself" (§425). Yet nothing is solved. Cp. §§139–41; Malcolm, *Memoir*, 48.

(b) W.'s target: *a priori* requirements like James's (above), illustrative of "the dogmatism into which we fall so easily in doing philosophy" (§131).

§618(a) One imagines . . . : "For the will alone is αὐτόματος [self-moving] and therefore ἀκάματος καὶ ἀγήρατος ἤματα πάντα [untiring and not growing old for ever]. . . . It alone is active, unbidden and of its own accord, and hence often too early and too much; and it knows no weariness" (Schopenhauer, *World*, II, 211). "In consciousness everyone recognizes himself at once as the *will*, in other words, as that which, as thing-in-itself, has not the principle of sufficient reason for its form, and itself depends on nothing, but rather everything else depends on it" (ibid., I, 504; see II, 258). In this sense the will is free (idem, *Freiheit*, 478–79).

Cp. §611a.

That is: such is the grammatical ground of the picture.

Augustine: see *Confessions,* VIII, 8, 20: "Thus, if I tore my hair, beat my forehead, if locking my fingers I clasped my knee; willing it, I did it. . . . More easily did my body obey the weakest willing of my soul, in moving its limbs at its nod, than the soul obeyed itself to accomplish in the will alone this its momentous will." "The mind commands the mind, its own self, to will, and yet it does not. . . . It commands itself, I say, to will, and would not command unless it willed, and yet does not do what it commands" (ibid., 9, 21).

(b) See the commentary on §619.

§619 This would be a grammatical remark, not a description of the mind's powers. As the absence of grounds in groundless statements about one's sensations generates the idea that the grounds are fool-proof and the knowledge infallible (§§246–48), so the absence of trying in the case of this nonaction, willing, begets the notion of infallible obedience (§618). The truth is: It makes no *sense* to say I tried to will, or failed (*EPB* 236; cp. *NB* 88mn).

§620 See Man. 229, §§1434, 1568; cp. *Z* 589; *PG* 144c, 156d–157a.

Doing **itself . . . :** see XXIV, 4; *PG* 145a; *NB* 89 ("All experience is world and does not need the subject. The act of will is not an experience"); cp. Gardiner, *Schopenhauer,* 154–55, 170–71.

an extensionless point: "The I of solipsism shrinks to an extensionless point and what remains is the reality co-ordinate with it" (*NB* 82; 5.64). That is, the willing subject (XXIV, 2) lies outside all experience. "The philosophical self is not the human being, not the human body, or the human soul, with which psychology deals, but rather the metaphysical subject, the limit of the world—not a part of it" (5.641). "Indeed a composite soul would no longer be a soul" (5.5421). Notice how the drawing in 5.6331 comes to a single point, not to two, one for each eye (Man. 112, 54–55). Cp. Schopenhauer, *World,* II, 278.

seems to be the real agent: see XXIV, 2, and the commentary on §618a; cp. James, *Principles,* I, 297–98: "Probably all men would describe it in much the same way up to a certain point. They would call it the *active* element in all consciousness. . . . It is the source of effort and attention, and the place from which appear to emanate the fiats of the will."

§621 See *EPB* 235; Man. 228, §311; JN 71.

(a) *PG* 145 suggests the point of the example and relates it to the previous number: "I would like to say: 'When I will, nothing happens to me, neither the movement nor a feeling, but I am the agent.' All right, but there is no doubt that you *also* cause experiences when you move your arm voluntarily; for you surely *see* (and feel) it move whether or not you have an *observant* attitude to it. So just for once try to distinguish between *all the experiences* of acting plus the doing (which is not an experience) and *all* these experiences without the element of doing. Consider whether you still need this element, or whether it doesn't now appear redundant." These words in turn should be read in the light of James, *Principles*, II, 493: "A powerful tradition in Psychology will have it that something additional to these images of passive sensation is essential to the mental determination of a voluntary act. There must, of course, be a special current of energy going out from the brain into the appropriate muscles during the act; and this outgoing current (it is supposed) must have in each particular case a feeling *sui generis* attached to it, or else (it is said) the mind could never tell which particular current, the current to this muscle or the current to that one, was the right one to use. This feeling of the current of outgoing energy has received from Wundt the name of the *feeling of innervation*." See XXIV, 6; *EPB* 235; *PG* 145; Man. 229, §1707; Helmholtz, *Optik*, 587.

So now W. is saying: "When your arm goes up voluntarily, and you see it, and feel it, do you also detect some *sui generis* feeling which makes the whole thing active?" " 'I shall now address him' is the same kind of proposition as 'I shall now raise my hand.' It would surprise everyone if I said instead: 'My hand will now rise,' although this prediction too is fulfilled when I raise my hand. So does the statement 'I shall now . . .' say something which is very difficult to understand & which only the superficial layman thinks he understands?" (Man. 128, 29).

"The first question to consider is not 'What feeling had you?' but 'Is there any feeling?' " (JN 41). "May not rest be just as voluntary as motion? May not the cessation of movement be voluntary? What better argument against a feeling of innervation?" (Z 597; cp. §596). "Thus . . . acting voluntarily (or involuntarily) is, in many cases, characterized as such by a multitude of circumstances under which the action takes place rather than by an experience which we should call characteristic of voluntary action" (BB 157; see XXIV, 9; Z 587).

(b) Is this the consequence of rejecting "feelings of innervation" as essential to willing? "For aught we can see," wrote James, ". . . the kinaesthetic ideas, as we have defined them, or images of incoming feelings of attitude and motion, are as *likely* as any feelings of innervation are, to be the last psychic antecedents and determiners of the various currents downwards into the muscles from the brain" (*Principles*, II, 495).

For W.'s general answer, see XXIV, 9. Man. 229, §1570, applies it here: "A child stamps his feet in anger: isn't it voluntary? And do I know anything at all about his kinaesthetic sensations when he does it? *To stamp in anger is voluntary.*" See §624 and commentary; cp. §281; Man. 229, §1526; Man. 228, §§487, 489.

§§622–23   See the commentary on §624. Trying, like feelings of innervation, is another likely candidate in the search for essential traits of volition (XXIV, 8). "Think, say, of these examples: I deliberate whether to lift a certain heavyish weight, decide to do it, I then apply my force to it and lift it. Here, you might say, you have a full-fledged case of willing and intentional action. Compare with this such a case as reaching a man a lighted match after having lit with it one's own cigarette and seeing that he wishes to light his; or again the case of moving your hand while writing a letter, or moving your mouth, larynx, etc. while speaking.—Now when I called the first example a full-fledged case of willing, I deliberately used this misleading expression. For this expression indicates that one is inclined in thinking about volition to regard this sort of example as one exhibiting most clearly the typical characteristic of willing. One takes one's ideas, and one's language, about volition from this kind of example and thinks that they must apply—if not in such an obvious way—to all cases which one can properly call cases of willing" (*BB* 150; see *BB* 152–53, quoted for §615, and other references there). Such traits—deliberation, decision, effort—are " 'characteristic' because they recur often (not always)" (§35). Furthermore, trying itself is most varied (*BB* 116d; *EPB* 168).

can I try . . . : cp. *BB* 153, on raising one's eyes to look at something; "here we can hardly conceive of an effort."

§624 Cp. XXIV, 7–8; §598, p. 185; *BB* 51b ("In fact if I had the tactile and kinaesthetic sensations referred to, I might still deny the proposition 'my finger moves etc. . . .' because of what I saw"); *PG* 144d; James, *Principles*, II, 105–6, 489–90.

The number makes a case for an affirmative answer to §621b, then rejects it: If kinesthetic sensations were our reason for saying, in ordinary circumstances, that we had moved our arm (§625), then, enlightened by the experiment, we should experience little difficulty in making the supposition W. proposes. However, against this critique it might be objected that the anticipated failure of the attempt derives from the stipulated conditions: We would have to suppose on the one hand that we were moving our arm and on the other that it was motionless. And reliance on a witness would not remove the difficulty; his testimony would explain sufficiently our failure to believe what we were asked to believe.

In the laboratory . . . : cp. James, *Principles*, II, 38.

in your muscles and joints: according to James (ibid.), "our feelings of our own movement are principally due to the sensibility of our rotating *joints*."

§625 See XXIV, 7; *Z* 480 (quoted for p. 185a), 481 (quoted for p. 185c), 586 ("And of course there is no question of a feeling of each movement in writing. One feels something, but could not possibly analyse the feeling"), 595; Man. 229, §§1049, 1707; Man. 131, 213–17; Malcolm, *Memoir*, 48–49. Since the preceding number, with which this one is continuous, does not distinguish between arm-movement feelings and arm-moving feelings, we may take pp. 185–86 as providing answers to these queries.

So what you recognize . . . : it might be objected that unreflective guidance suffices for knowledge; think, for instance, of a person's unreflective conviction that a motorcycle, not a car, is passing outside. However, that case would not resemble this one unless it were asked, "How do you know it is a motorcycle?" and the person then *reflected* on his reasons and replied, "I hear it." Thus the question and implicit objection are appropriately stated in terms of recognition.

§626 See Man. 228, §173; Man. 116, 241–42; cp. James, *Principles*, II, 37–42, 195–97.

The example is intended as a comparison, not as a further example of voluntary activity. In support of the previous number, it combats the idea that a feeling has its description written into it (cp. §§379–81), e.g.: It is an arm-raising feeling, and that is why I say I have raised my arm; or it is a three-feet-under-the-ground feeling, and that is why I say there is water three feet down (*BB* 9); or it is an out-there rather than an in-here feeling, and that is why I say I have the sensation in the stick and not in my hand. But what is an "out-there" feeling? It is one I, a typical speaker of the language, so describe, while looking at the stick rather than the hand, and so on. There is no other identification, either in this or in any other language (cp. p. 186; *BB* 52).

Compare and contrast this discussion with that in *BB* 51–52.

"It is interesting here to think of the case of sucking a liquid through a tube; if asked what part of your body you sucked with, you would be inclined to say your mouth, although the work was done by the muscles by which you draw your breath" (*BB* 154).

"When I touch this object . . .": "With the point of a cane we can trace letters in the air or on a wall just as with the finger-tip; and in so doing feel the size and shape of the path described by the cane's tip just as immediately as, without a cane, we should feel the path described by the tip of our finger. Similarly the draughtsman's immediate perception seems to be of the point of his pencil, the surgeon's of the end of his knife, the duellist's of the tip of his rapier as it plunges through his enemy's skin" (James, *Principles*, II, 37–38).

§§627–28 See §612; *Z* 92, 632; *BB* 151–52. On the original stimulus of these remarks, in James, see XXIV, 3.

As the preceding numbers suggest, in many cases voluntary action is characterized by the "circumstances under which the action takes place rather than by an experience which we should call characteristic of voluntary action. And in this sense it is true to say that what happened when I got out of bed—when I should certainly not call it involuntary—was that I found myself getting up" (*BB* 157). However, there is something about this description "which tempts us to contradict it; we say: 'We don't just "find", observe, ourselves getting up, as though we were observing someone else! It isn't like, say, watching certain reflex actions' " (*BB* 151; see 152, and Man. 229, §1553). "There is, e.g. . . . . a perfect absence of what one might call surprise" (*BB* 151).

And now I do not . . . : see §§109, 126, 654–55; *Z* 586 ("But not because one had a wish").

XXV. Intention, and the Prediction of One's Own Actions (§§629–660)

GENERAL COMMENTARY

(1) *NB* 87 suggests the connection between this section and the preceding one, and the perspective of these new numbers. Having concluded from the experiment described there (see XXIV, 6) that one act of the will "relates to the visual part of the world, the other to the muscular-feeling part", Wittgenstein wondered: "Have we anything more than empirical evidence that the movement of the same part of the body is in question in both cases?" That is, is the muscular feeling somehow identifiable as an *arm-raising* feeling? (See *BB* 51–52; commentary on §§621, 625–26.) And is that why we are not surprised when our arm goes up (§627)? Mustn't the bringing about be something more than a mere accompaniment of the action (*NB* 87)? Mustn't we see the causal connection, as it were, from the inside (§631)? Otherwise, "how can I predict—as in some sense I surely can—that I shall raise my arm in five minutes' time?" (*NB* 87).

(2) "Voluntary movements," writes Strawson, summarizing Wittgenstein's answer in this and the previous section, "are characterized by a certainty of their having been made, which neither has *nor needs* a ground; though it may both have and, in another sense, need a cause. It is still far from clear that we have a sufficient condition; for this seems true of many compelled or involuntary movements of parts of the body. But for the purposes of Wittgenstein's enquiry, I do not think a sufficient condition is required. For his purpose, I think, is to throw light from 'knowing what one has done' on 'knowing what one is

going to do (intends)' and on 'knowing what one *was* going to do (intended)'. For there is no more reason to suppose that we need a *way* of knowing, of telling, in these cases than in that one. Of course, an announcement of a present intention, or a recalling of a past unexecuted intention is helped by, arises naturally from, the situation 'in which it is (or was) embedded'. But we do not read off or infer our intentions from these situations, any more than we tell what limb-movements we have just made from recognition of the accompanying sensations" ("Review", 57–58).

(3)   These clarifying remarks do not yet indicate the dichotomy which dominates the present section and explains its structure. Wittgenstein himself puts the whole discussion more sharply in focus when he asks: "Would someone who could look into your mind have been able to see that you *meant* to say *that*?" (Z 36). His italics accentuate the familiar distinction between act (GI 38) and content (GI 36) and thus reveal the combined target of the present critique (GI 41). First, as §§624–28 dealt with the idea that present movements may be known from present feelings or inner acts, in which they are somehow inscribed, so §§629–38 now consider a similar conception concerning the prediction of voluntary acts. The action, it would seem, is somehow present beforehand. For if someone says, "When you press the button I'll yell," "this is (1) a prediction (2) not done by an 'if-then' technique. So it looks as though I have an inside knowledge" (JN 67). Wittgenstein's reply (in terms of §607, which anticipates his present critique) would be: No, we do not read off our future movements from the inner clock of intention. For no inner act or feeling is intention (*Absicht* or *Willen*). This is the second theme of the section; from the notion of inferring one's future actions on the basis of inner evidence, Wittgenstein shifts to the notion of identifying one's intending as intending on the basis of inner criteria. That is, he returns to the issue which occupied him in the three previous sections. As belief, hope, expectation, meaning, recognition, and understanding are not inner acts or experiences, neither is intention (§§641–47). This conclusion is anticipated in §§588–89, 591–92.

(4)   The final numbers of the section (§§648–60) revert to the question of content, but as the object of a report rather than as the basis of a prediction. The problem thus becomes how we can remember the content so surely rather than how we can predict the future from it so confidently. If inner experience is so elusive even while it occurs, how do we manage to determine our past intentions so precisely? Wittgenstein replies as usual: "Don't always think that you read off what you say from the facts; that you portray these in words according to rules" (§292; see GI 15–16).

DETAILED COMMENTARY

§629 For the connection of this with the preceding number and with W.'s early thinking, see XXV, 1. See *Z* 583–84; cp. *OC* 380–85; *NB* 71c; 5.556.

they always forget: as W. himself did (in 5.133–5.1362); and Schlick ("Causality", 530); and especially Russell (e.g. *Logic*, 133; *Inquiry*, 123), even when he was comparing human and nonhuman actions (*Essays*, 38–41). For Russell's reasons, cp. *External World*, 229: "The desires are determined by their consequences just as much as the consequences by the desires; but as we cannot (in general) know in advance the consequences of our desires without knowing our desires, this form of inference is uninteresting as applied to our own acts, though quite vital as applied to those of others."

the fact of the prediction: see p. 224b; cp. Man. 138, 30A ("Even when I have no positive intention, I can have negative intentions; I don't know what I will do, but I am determined I *won't* do such and such"); Man. FW, 18 ("The idea that you connect predicting what a man will choose with materialism is rubbish. Prediction doesn't mean you will predict from *material* data").

§630 Cp. the preceding quotation, from Man. FW.

"It is natural," writes Anscombe, "to feel an objection both to calling commands, and to calling expressions of intention, predictions. In the case of commands, the reason lies in the superficial grammar, and just because of this is more easily disposed of" (*Intention*, 4). Her explanation: "Execution-conditions for commands correspond to truth-conditions for propositions; in fact there is no reason other than a dispensable usage why we should not call commands true and false according as they were obeyed or disobeyed" (ibid., 3). How hesitant W. might have been to accept this defense of his statement is suggested by §§21 and 24. After all, the point of a prediction differs from the point of a command (§564); thus the pupil has not sought information from the instructor concerning the future whereabouts of his limbs, as might happen prior to a prediction. However, an instructor's shouted "commands" are often such only in the sense of effecting movements; there is no exercise of authority, nor is the imperative used. And when the pupil gives himself orders, the last vestige of authority relationship disappears. Furthermore, W. may have had in mind the fact that expressions of intention, to which these commands approach, may be a source of information about one's future actions (p. 224b), especially to others (§632), so function somewhat as predictions do. Thus, though commands in general differ from predictions in general, these particular commands lie on or near the fluctuating frontier (§21) between the two categories. We might be inclined to deny that the shouted instructions are either predictions or commands, and to call them mere "signals", but the same could be said of "Now I can go on" (§180) or "Now I know" (p. 218), and we call these statements.

And here is a variation: analogous to the switch from predicting another's actions to predicting one's own (p. 224b).

§631(a) It explains nothing: "for there is no *logical* connexion between the will and the world, which would guarantee it, and the supposed physical connexion itself is surely not something that we could will" (6.374). Cp. *LC* 21c.

see the causal connexion . . . : see XXIV, 2; §§170c, 176–77, 613; *BB* 15d (quoted for p. 224k); cp. Moore, *Commonplace,* 104 ("I think you *can* know causal dependence directly, though certainly you don't always know it directly: you have to use induction to know it").

much else to the same effect: for instance: "Every voluntary act . . . should be viewed as an experiment. . . . The persuasive power of each experiment is far greater than in the case where we observe a process which takes place without our concurrence, for the principal reason that in the experiment the chain of causes runs through our self-consciousness. We know one member of the chain, our will impulse, through inner observation, and we know what motive gave rise to it" (Helmholtz, *Schriften,* 128; see idem, *Optik,* 580d). "Here the true and immediate medium in which the action takes place is not the atmosphere but cognition and it alone. We need merely perceive the object acting as motive" (Schopenhauer, *Freiheit,* 502).

(b) See the parallel treatment of action and event in 6.362–6.374. Cp. analogous remarks concerning certainty, in p. 224c.

(c) See §659b, p. 224b; *Z* 41; *BB* 154a; cp. §587, pp. 174i, 185d, 188l, 191i–192d.

"I don't see myself, usually, in a mirror and say to myself 'It looks as though I'll lose my temper soon.' This could be done, of course, but it's not (so one point is: I don't usually know the signs for *me*)" (JN 87). "Indeed, were I myself to infer my intention from the evidence, other people would be right to say that this conclusion was very uncertain" (Z 41).

it can only mislead . . . : for reasons analogous to those in §441a.

§632 I do not want to say . . . : as the recommended application of §441a might suggest (the words themselves are an act of decision, not subsequent clothing); or the sum of the preceding denials (inner causal connection, observation of behavior, decision); or a paraphrase of §441c: "Suppose it were asked 'Do I know what I intend to do before I do it?' If I have learned to talk, then I do know."

we can often predict: see p. 224b; Z 36 (quoted for §452); cp. §452; Man. 138, 16A.

§633 See p. 219e; Man. 229, §§839–40; Man. 180b, 28; Man. 112, 192; cp. §§195–96; Z 1–2. For clear expression of the view here criticized, see James's *Principles*, e.g. I, 253 (quoted for §591) or 280: "Even before we have opened our mouths to speak, the entire thought is present to our mind in the form of an intention to utter that sentence."

No: see §§197, 205, 334, 337.

Unless you take . . . : that is, unless you so define the occurrence (cp. §§184, 239b, 665b, pp. 212d, 222j).

"Interrupt a man in quite unpremeditated and fluent talk. Then ask him what he was going to say; and in many cases he will be able to continue the sentence he had begun.—'For that, what he was going to say must already have swum into view before his mind.'—Is not that phenomenon perhaps the ground [i.e. a sense-determining criterion, not a contingent clue] of our saying that the continuation had swum into his mental view?" (Z 38).

to help the continuation: cp. §§525, 534.

§634(a) See §319.

(b) I did not *choose:* cp. §§213, 219–20, pp. 195cd, 201bc, 206b.

I *remembered:* however, remembering is not contemplating a past intention (§§637, 648), just as knowing what I now intend is not perceiving a present intention (cp. §§441, 453). "The words with which I express my memory are my memory-reaction" (§343). See Z 44 (quoted for §637); cp. §682.

§635 See §§645–46; Z 41; cp. James, *Principles*, I, 253 ("and yet how much of it consists of definite sensorial images, either of words or of things? Hardly anything!").

As if I could read the darkness: see ibid., 244 (quoted in XXXII, 2).

§636 Worked up in Man. 116, 297–98. See commentary on §656a. All of this would apply equally to nonpsychological general terms, for example to the word *game*. In the light of this comparison, we see that these relevant details are "family" traits of intending (§67).

"I was going to say": W.'s own translation (Man. 116, 306).

nor need he guess them: "If I say 'I was then going to do such-and-such,' and if this statement is based on the thoughts, images etc. which I remember, then someone else to whom I tell only these thoughts, images etc. ought to be able to infer with as great certainty as mine that I was then going to do such-and-such.—But often he could not do so" (Z 41).

he *can* **'fill out the picture':** see §642.

§637 See §660; *EPB* 229–30; Man. 228, §217; Man. 116, 299–300.

(a) read it off: cp. §292.

some other process: see the commentary on §633.

" 'I had the intention of . . .' does not express the memory of an experience. (Any more than 'I was on the point of . . .') . . . Intention is neither an emotion, a mood, nor yet a sensation or image. It is not a state of consciousness. It does not have genuine duration" (Z 44–45).

"In so far as I do intend the construction of a sentence in advance, that is made [logically] possible by the fact that I can speak the language in question" (§337). But this ability is not observable through introspection.

(b) Cp. §§213, 536–37, pp. 193i, 200de; Z 27.

§638   Cp. Man. 180b, 16–24; Man. 116, 298–99.

(a) See Man. 128, 16: "The question is only whether the representation of these facts *as intention* is an interpretation. That is to say, *if* another person *interprets* what he observes in me as intention, why don't *I*? Can we say that I *know* the *essential thing*, which he merely surmises?!" Later, on p. 26: "How does it come about that in spite of this I am inclined to see an interpretation in saying 'For a moment I was going to deceive you'? Is it because I interpret what happened in that moment by means of the situation and antecedents . . . ?" The answer just given in §637 is: "No." So now W. asks, "What is the reason then?" By the end of the number it is clear that he is rejecting "the grammar which tries to force itself on us here" (§304), namely the idea that these words are the report of a past process which, if not recognizable in itself as intention (§637a) must be recognizable as such within the larger context (§637b). The strength of this notion derives in part from the fact that third-person uses of the term *willen* often are such reports based on observation (GI 15–16). Thus "the paradox disappears only if we make a radical break with the idea that language always functions in one way" (§304).

(b) See §§205, 635, 645–46.

(e) In addition to the preceding comments, see §639 and commentary, and compare §§682–84.

§639   One would like to say . . . : as W. did in Man. 116, 266 (after Z 22) and in Man. 128, 7: "Does he already know what he will say later? Should we say, 'he has an approximate idea of it'? I would like to say that an intention *develops*." See also the commentary on §640.

an opinion: better: "an intention" (see the context, and that in Man. 128).

there is a mistake . . . : see p. 219e and the quotation for §640, from James, *Principles,* I, 253. Looking at a seed, we can tell what it will become, whereas were God himself to observe that momentary process (§638) by itself, he would not know what it was the seed of (p. 217fg).

§640   Revised from Man. 128, 8. The target is James's "radical empiricism", with its stress on perceived relationships: "From our point of view both Intellectualists and Sensationalists are wrong. If there be such things as feelings at all, *then so surely as relations between objects exist in rerum naturâ, so surely, and more surely, do feelings exist to which these relations are known.* There is not a conjunction or a preposition, and hardly an adverbial phrase, syntactic form, or inflection of voice, in human speech, that does not express some shading or other of relation which we at some moment actually feel to exist between the larger objects of our thought. If we speak objectively, it is the real relations that appear revealed; if we speak subjectively, it is the stream of consciousness that matches each of them by an inward coloring of its own" (*Principles,* I, 245). For example, of "the anticipatory intention" James wrote: "As the words that replace it arrive, it welcomes them successively and calls them right if they agree with it, it rejects them and calls them wrong if they do not. It has therefore a nature of its own of the most positive sort, and yet what can we say about it without using words that belong to the later mental facts that replace it?" (ibid., 253). Thus one might want to say that the intention develops (§639); it *cannot* grow into anything else (p. 219).

Through a *feeling:* see §598.

how can a feeling . . . : cp. §169.

is very misleading: see *Z* 45 (quoted for §637), 46–48.

be unable . . . : cp. §§682–84.

that comes later: not the connection, but the ability to show it, perhaps because the connection, too, comes later (cp. §§682–84).

§641   See p. 217f; cp. §452 and commentary; §668, p. 180a. Not even in this way can intention be conceived as complete in the moment, in the mind (GI 41).

§642   See GI 44; §636, pp. 188, 219b; *EPB* 228; Man. 128, 13–14; cp. §525.

§643   Yet I would not say I was ashamed of each individual item; I would be ashamed of *hating* him, that is, of this pattern in the weave of my life (pp. 174d, 229a). Cp. *Z* 656 (quoted for p. 211k).

§644   See XXIV, 2; Man. 229, §1559; Anscombe, *Introduction,* 171–72; cp. §441a; Schopenhauer, *World,* I, 300 ("in a healthy mind only deeds, not desires and thoughts, weigh heavily on the conscience; for only our deeds hold up before us the mirror of our will").

The reader may feel more hesitant about including the action in the intention than about including "thoughts, feelings, and actions" in the hatred (§642), both because of the verbal discrimination between act and intention in a formula like "I intended to . . . ," and because a critique of psychological atomism does not seem to require such an extension into the future. "Granted," one is tempted to say, "the intention is not a mere feeling; even so, isn't it clear that we might intend the act, but not perform it. So how can the intention include the act?" W.

would point out that the same might be said of any characteristic feature of intending (§35); so let us not start plucking the artichoke (§164). Mode of verification is a principal index of meaning (§§353–54), and what single criterion indicates more surely than the act itself a person's intention to perform it?

§645 See Man. 229, §1496; cp. X, 22; §§173b, 175–77, 588, 678; *EPB* 134, 179; *BB* 92a, 125b; James, *Principles*, I, 299d–300a.

"One might say that there are two ways of looking at this matter, one as it were, at close quarters, the other as though from a distance and through the medium of a peculiar atmosphere" (*BB* 86; *EPB* 127).

(a) See GI 53; §51b.

"I meant to": note that the German verb is *willen*, as in many preceding numbers (§§633–41); the term *Absicht* (§§644, 646–48, 653, 658) predominates hereafter. The two terms come together in §653b and at the end, in §660.

an inner experience: W.'s former viewpoint. See Man. 109, 238: "Intention is a human psychological process."

and I remember it: see §634b and commentary.

§646(b) See GI 60–61; X, 22; cp. pp. 181, 231.

There is something right . . . : because some of these details are irrelevant (§636), or the impressionistic focus was better (Z 281); or (more likely) because one's gaze focused within (§647; GI 48).

§647(a) the natural expression: Miss Anscombe objects: "A cat's movements in stalking a bird are hardly to be called an expression of intention. One might as well call a car's stalling the *expression* of its being about to stop" (*Intention*, 5). However, a cat resembles a human being far more than a car does (see §281); and it is not clear why we should make the nontechnical term *expression* either more rigid or more elastic than the linguistic (§494) and psychological (§§281, 360) terms with which it is customarily associated. If we are ready to say the beast wants to escape, then we can call his behavior the expression of that desire. If we balk at saying the car intends to stop, then we shall hesitate to say it expresses its intention by stalling.

W. noted that intention, unlike an emotion such as rage (Z 488), has no characteristic expression in face, gesture, or tone of voice (Man. 138, 15B–16A); but that does not prevent us from calling a cat's crouch, or a man's atop the Golden Gate Bridge, the natural expression of *an* intention (as here).

of an intention: notice that no difficulty arises here as in §650 and p. 174b; the cat is perhaps concerned with a bird nearby, the beast with a tether which ties it.

(b) Cp. §§283ff. Paraphrasing §283a, on sensations, we might ask: "What gives us *so much as the idea* that living beings, things, have intentions and desires?" Do we observe them in ourselves and infer their presence in cats and dogs?

§648   See §634 and commentary; §§646–47, 659–60; cp. *EPB* 229.

   "I no longer remember . . .": W. is not being critical; this is the sort of thing we do say, without philosophical intentions (Man. 128, 25; §§651, 660).

   Suppose it did nothing . . . : see §343.

   which fill out the picture: see §636; cp. §642; *Z* 650.

   "I certainly remember their spirit": cp. James. *Principles*, I, 260: " '*Qu'importe le flacon, pourvu qu'on ait l'ivresse?*' . . . When we have uttered a proposition, we are rarely able a moment afterwards to recall our exact words, though we can express it in different words easily enough."

§649   See *BB* 137; *PG* 182b; Man. 115, 33; Man. 110, 89–90.

   "So if a man . . .": the question arises naturally from W.'s continued insistence that expressions of memory such as "I remember my intention precisely" (§648) are not reports based on introspection but verbal reactions—verbal memory acts, as it were, "not mere threadbare representations of the *real* experiences". (To the present paragraph, *PG* 182 adds in parentheses: "Words are deeds.") See I, 3.

   Of course: W. avoids the complex question of how closely memory, wishing, and the like approximate to imagining on the one hand and to meaning on the other (p. 18n) in their dependence on language (see GI 43).

   verbal memories, verbal wishes . . . : i.e., in language, not of language. See §650 (fear), §651 (memory), §652 (and so on).

   memories etc.: "There are cases in which we may call a particular experience 'noticing, seeing, conceiving that so and so is the case', before expressing it by word or gestures, and . . . there are other cases in which if we talk of an experience of conceiving at all, we have to apply this word to the experience of using certain words, gestures, etc." (*BB* 137).

   are not mere . . . : see *EPB* 196; *BB* 130d. "My memory-image is not evidence for that past situation, like a photograph which was taken then and convinces me now that this was how things were then. The memory-image and the memory-words stand on the *same* level" (*Z* 650). "Consider tone of voice, inflexion, gestures, as *essential* parts of our experience, not as inessential accompaniments or mere means of communication. (Compare pp. 144–6.)" (*BB* 182; see GI 44–45; commentary on §650).

   of the *real* experiences: cp. *BB* 137: "Some people are able to distinguish between fat and lean days of the week. And their experience when they conceive a day as a fat one consists in applying this word together perhaps with a gesture expressive of fatness and a certain comfort.

"But you may be tempted to say: This use of the word and gesture is not their primary experience. First of all they have to conceive the day as fat and then they express this conception by word or gesture."

§650   See GI 43; XV, 2–5; p. 174abc; cp. Z 518–20; Man. 116, 302; Man. 108, 233; Köhler, *Mentality*, 227.

W.'s move here parallels that on *BB* 137 (above); he cites another case "in which if we talk of an experience of conceiving at all, we have to apply this word to the experience of using certain words, gestures, etc.". No natural act of the mind can represent tomorrow, as no image can picture a fat day of the week. Cp. *PG* 85, 181, on remembering.

Why not?: "The answer is that the fear of a happening *tomorrow* cannot exist independently of language. It will not make sense to say of a language-less creature that it has this fear, or that it does not have it. Language provides the criterion for the existence of such a fear" (Malcolm, *Problems*, 90).

"Can you wonder if he's got a pain without words? You can be angry without using words, why not wonder? You get the idea that language is in all cases secondary, that the real thing can go on inside. But perhaps a human being who has learnt to talk has learnt to behave in a new way. Can you wonder if there are 101 people here without numerals? They say an animal is curious; can a dog be curious about what will happen tomorrow week? A dog can beg for a piece of meat; can he beg for a piece of meat in 35 minutes from now?" (JN 57).

§651   As an illustration of the theme in §649, this example is still more effective than the one in *PG* 181. The dating difficulty, for example, is doubled or tripled: (1) How picture *then*? (2) A picture which halfway resolved that problem, by means of a wall calendar turned to the appropriate date, would not picture the wish. (3) A representation timing the wish would not portray the "still longer". (In such a case, the *Tractatus* picture theory would supposedly require a picture within a picture, one of the wish, another of the wished, and each with its own timing.)

§652   Another sample of "verbal wishes or fears, and so on" (§649), to counteract the viewpoint expressed in (*b*). See *BB* 137, quoted for §649; cp. §§24, 525a, 634b.

§653   Worked up in Man. 116, 304–5. Parallels the first two paragraphs of Man. 232, 745. "In philosophy," wrote W., "we are deceived by an illusion. But the illusion too is something & I must get it clearly in view before I can say that it is only an illusion" (Man. 110, 239). For example, he had once supposed that "thought makes maps. It draws maps, of a simple or very complicated sort" (Man. 108, 255; see 256).

"The map is the picture which is interpreted. Suppose we have the order to follow a road on the map. Or the map is the picture of an expectation, showing us arriving in an hour at this and that place" (Man. 108, 233–34; see Man. 110, 67). Or intention shows us doing such and such, and memory reproduces the picture. Now, is that the way it really is? No, we have neither the makings of such a map, nor the method of interpretation; what a person sees in his memory allows no conclusion as to what he meant to do (§§638e, 651).

(a) Cp. Man. 109, 86.

a 'private' map: cp. §§269, 540–42; Man. 116, 116–17 (on "subjective" understanding).

easy to misunderstand: hence the scare quotes, here as in §269. In the ordinary sense, the following is not following and the map is not a map.

(b) **"although there is no map":** see §§638, 651.

I am now inclined to say: what I say is not testimony (§386b) or evidence for something readily intelligible to anyone who understands the individual words, but material for philosophical treatment (§254). The doctor's prescription follows.

§§654–55 See I, 4; commentary on §109; *Z* 309, 313–15; *EPB* 179; *BB* 92a, 125b.

"*This* is the unfortunate thing about the scientific way of thinking (by which the whole world is possessed these days), that it wants to resolve all disquiet with an explanation//that it takes all disquiet as a question and wonders at not being able to *answer* it" (Man. 219, 8).

Our mistake: see XXV, 1–2; commentary on §653.

language-game: see I, 1–10, and commentary on §7.

by means of our experiences: see §598 and commentary.

§656(a) Cp. p. 188l.

"We are so accustomed to communication through language," said W., that it looks as though the whole point of communication lay in the transfer of knowledge (§363); when, for instance, I tell someone I had such-and-such a wish, I make him a word picture of my wish (§§291–92) showing the exact layout of my psychic contents (4.5, 5.542). But W. has already pointed out that "if I tell someone 'For a moment I was going to say . . .' he does not learn these details from this, nor need he guess them. . . . But he *can* 'fill out the picture' in this way" (§636).

as interpretation: that is, as "filling-out", which is not usually necessary, but sometimes does occur (§§34, 396, 636, 642, 648, 663; cp. §§536, 637). See especially *BB* 146e–147d, e.g.: "What if I said 'I believe it will rain' (meaning what I say) and someone wanted to explain to a Frenchman who doesn't understand English what it was I believed.

Then, you might say, if all that happened when I believed what I did was that I said the sentence, the Frenchman ought to know what I believe if you tell him the exact words I used, or say 'Il croit "It will rain." ' Now it is clear that this will not tell him what I believe and consequently, you might say, we failed to convey just that to him which was essential, my real mental act of believing.—But the answer is that even if my words had been accompanied by all sorts of experiences, and if we could have transmitted these experiences to the Frenchman, he would still not have known what I believed. For 'knowing what I believe' just doesn't mean: feeling what I do while I say it; just as knowing what I intend with this move in our game of chess doesn't mean knowing my exact state of mind while I'm making the move. Though, at the same time, in certain cases, knowing this state of mind might furnish you with very exact information about my intention."

(b) See Z 42–43.

It would then appear how implausible is the supposition that they are transcriptions of inner experience. Are children who learn these forms of speech (III, 1–2) somehow brought to guess the proper referents for each term (X, 20–21)? Are they taught to recognize the intention feeling, and the correlation between this feeling and its object, and the criteria by which to ascertain the object? Reflection on W.'s question reveals how devastating it is for the verbal-calculus conception of speech (§§81b, 292).

§657 Cp. §§20, 24; Z 49 (quoted for p. 191efg); BB 147a (quoted for §656a).

" 'if only I . . .' ": the revised form for "I should have been glad then to stay still longer" (§651).

The purpose . . . : the hypothesis suggests most forcefully that "one cannot guess how a word functions. One has to *look at* its use and learn from that" (§340). For the surface form in this imaginary speech act strongly suggests that it functions as a report of inner speech; yet its purpose is to acquaint others with my reactions.

Compare the grammar . . . : *vouloir dire* is to *mean* as this new form is to the ordinary one; taken at face value, it suggests a desire to speak, but of course indicates no such thing. It is the equivalent of *mean* (Man. 228, 170). Once again, surface grammar is no sure guide (§664).

§658 That is the picture: W. himself had once conceived of thought—intentions, desires, and the like (GI 36)—as inner speech (GI 40), so assimilated "*A* believes that *p*," "*A* has the thought *p*," and so on, to "*A* says *p*" (5.542). The conception is natural and widespread (X, 2), but is seldom thought out in detail.

And now I want to know: the whole of §374 is applicable *ad litteram* in the present context. Cp. §§422–25.

§659   Cp. p. 222hi.

(a) Not because . . . . : "One may disturb someone in thinking—but in intending?—Certainly in planning. Also in keeping to an intention, that is in thinking or acting" (*Z* 50).

   But because . . . : cp. §§680, 686, pp. 223f–224b; *BB* 147a.

(b) of myself: *mein Inneres.*

   Not, however . . . : contrast this with *BB* 147d. See *Z* 41; cp. §§587, 631c, pp. 188l, 191i, 192, 224b; *Z* 591.

   by way of a response: see GI 15–16; p. 174i.

   an intuition: in view of W.'s negative remarks about intuition when discussing the continuation of a series (§§186, 213–14), and the connection made between that case and this, in §660, the present admission may come as a surprise. However, sureness about one's intention resembles, not the sure derivation of a series from a formula, but the assurance "that if I multiply 25 by 25 ten times I shall get 625 every time" (*RFM* 126). This "would not be a *mathematical* truth that was grasped intuitively, but a physical or psychological one." "Such a thing might be called an intuitively known *empirical* fact" (ibid.).

§660   W. has not previously discussed the expression "I could then have gone on" (cp. §187). Number 648, which this number follows in Man. 228, 63, shows how both expressions should be viewed. The similarity in W.'s treatment of "I can go on" (IX, 11–13) and "I intend" (XXV, 2–3) would make one expect such a parallel in these retrospective reports of the intention and the ability. Cp. p. 219f.

(b) Neither memory is that of an experience (*Z* 44). *Z* 45–46 connect this number with the next.

XXVI.   Meaning Something, Someone
(§§661–693)

(1)   I have already suggested why Wittgenstein himself was once inclined to say: "A person need only *mean* something by what he says, then everything essential is given" (see Man. 109, 281, quoted for §81b). The "strict and clear rules of the logical structure of propositions" may lie hidden in the understanding (§102), but it is the act of meaning which applies the rules in the particular case, projects the signs, pinpoints referents, and thereby solves the puzzle of inten-

tionality (GI 37). "The whole problem lies enclosed in the words 'to mean something'" (Man. 108, 195). Such, accordingly, is the focus of the present section, especially the final numbers (cp. III, 7; XV, 1–5).

(2)   It should not be imagined, though, that young Wittgenstein carefully distinguished between thinking, meaning, and understanding; even in the *Blue Book* they are jumbled rather indiscriminately together. Now he sorts them out. Meaning something is not an ability, like understanding (Section IX). Nor is it an act, like thinking or imagining (Sections XI, XII, XVI). It is more akin to believing, hoping, expecting, and the like (Sections XXII–XXV; see XXII, 1). These books, as it were, go together on the shelf (*BB* 44). And coming at the end of this series, meaning provides a transition to Part Two (see GI 65–66; Sections XXVIII, XXXII, XXXVII; *BB* 43–44).

(3)   The English word *meaning*, in particular, "is one of the words of which one may say that they have odd jobs in our language" (*BB* 43). Sometimes it is equivalent to *meinen* or *Meinung*, sometimes to *Bedeutung*. And each of these terms has two main modes of employment, one more situational and complex, the other experiential (GI 66; p. 216b). So it is no accident that Wittgenstein divides his treatment of *meinen*, as of *Bedeutung*, between Parts One and Two (GI 65). He is still sorting out, placing different books on different shelves (*BB* 44–45).

(4)   Leaving the secondary, experiential sense of *mean* till Section XXXVII (see especially pp. 214–18), he focuses here on the sense (or cluster of senses) which resembles and frequently overlaps that of *intend*. And he shows the same double concern—about the supposed act or process and about its supposed content—as in the preceding treatment of that concept (XXV, 3). "When you think about the essence of meaning you look for a state similar to contemplating a picture [see XXXVII, 2–8; cp. §663], or for an activity similar to speaking [cp. X, 2; p. 176]" (Man. 164, 155–56), with the difference that the meaning act, unlike the mere contemplation of a picture (§455) or speaking of words (§§430–33), seems to fix the sense unambiguously (GI 37; §§186–90; Z 236; PG 148b). As William James put it: "When I use the word *man* in two different sentences, I may have both times exactly the same sound upon my lips and the same picture in my mental eye, but I may mean, and at the very moment of uttering the word and imagining the picture, know that I mean, two entirely different things. Thus when I say: 'What a wonderful man Jones is!' I am perfectly aware that I mean by man to exclude Napoleon Bonaparte or Smith. But when I say: 'What a wonderful thing Man is!' I am equally well aware that I mean to *in*clude not only Jones, but Napoleon and Smith as well" (*Principles*, I, 472; see XXXII, 1–2; PG 103, quoted for §661).

(5)   Such conceptions of meaning illustrate what I have called the Ref-

erence Fallacy (GI 17–19). Influenced by parallels such as "say something" and "mean something" and by our general expectation of a referent to go with every word, we are prone to say: "Meaning is a mental process associated with speaking—perhaps antecedently, but especially concurrently.—If I mean something, something different goes on inside me than when I say it and don't mean it." "By and large," Wittgenstein conceded, "this last is true. *And now look and see what goes on.* And while you do so, pay no attention to what 'surely must occur' " (*EPB* 226; see XXXVII, 21). "When you imagine instances of meaning, you will see that they are endlessly varied, yet all related to one another in one way or another" (*EPB* 225; see 228).

(6) Section XXVI surveys this family of cases and concludes: "Nothing is more wrong-headed than calling meaning a mental activity!" (§693). To catch the full force of this declaration, it is necessary to contrast it not only with Wittgenstein's earliest views and those of James and Russell, but also with transitional formulations in the *Brown Book,* for example: "We use the words 'meaning', 'believing', 'intending' in such a way that they refer to certain acts, states of mind given certain circumstances; as by the expression 'checkmating somebody' we refer to the act of taking his king" (*BB* 147; see *EPB* 230). In the *Investigations,* this way of speaking disappears (cp. §687) and a new one appears: A word like *mean* indicates "a pattern which recurs, with different variations, in the weave of our life" (p. 174; see p. 229). No one strand constitutes the pattern, even in an individual case (GI 44).

(7) The point may be made in terms of sufficient and necessary conditions. Moving a chess piece, though not a sufficient condition of checkmating someone, is at least a necessary condition (in an ordinary game, not conducted by mail), whereas no inner act or experience is even a necessary condition of meaning something or someone. A chief function of Section XXVI, especially the first half, is to make this double point, stripping the artichoke (§164) of both sufficient and necessary conditions, particularly introspective ones. No experience, picture, or mental act—say of attending—is equivalent by itself to meaning something (§§663, 665, 669), any more than pointing is (§§669–70). Nor is it a necessary constituent (§§666–67, 674).

DETAILED COMMENTARY

§661   See quote from Man. 167 for p. 59n. On this and the following two numbers, see *PG* 103b.

   a process: calling it a process would suggest properties like those of sensations: "All have genuine duration. Possibility of giving the beginning and the end. Possibility of their being synchronized, of simultaneous occurrence" (Z 472; see p. 59n); whereas meaning belongs with intending: "It does not have genuine duration" (*Z* 45, quoted for §637). See p. 218e.

or state?: grammatically, perhaps (§572); but it would be misleading to call it a mental state (XXVI, 6–7; p. 59n; cp. §662).

When did it begin . . . : see the quote from *LC* 67–68 for §457; cp. GI 37; p. 59n.

" 'But when you utter the word "Napoleon" you designate just this man.'—'How then, in your view, does this act of designating occur? Instantaneously? or does it take time?'—'But after all, if someone asks you: "just now, did you mean the very man who won the battle of Austerlitz," you will say "Yes." So you meant this man *as you uttered the sentence*!'—Yes, but only in the sense, say, in which I also knew then that $6 \times 6 = 36$" (*PG* 103; cp. James in XXVI, 4).

§662   See p. 177c; cp. §682.

One can now say . . . : for I did want him to come, then; and wanting is not an act, nor a bodily state.

one may *not* say so: several of the expressions are dangerously ambiguous: (1) *describe,* since the sentence provides no picture of the events (§663); (2) *mind,* for the familiar reasons (XXVI, 6–7; see *BB* 32, quoted for §683; cp. p. 59n); (3) *at that time,* since the phrase seems to temporally locate the wanting, in the way requested at the close of §661 (cp. the quotation just given from *PG* 103).

§663   See p. 177; *Z* 236; *PG* 103b; *LC* 66c–68c; cp. §652; *Z* 14; *BB* 38b. Man. 228, §209, expands this in the manner of p. 11n.

a picture: see GI 34–37; XXVI, 4; *LC* 66–68; cp. §301 and commentary.

perhaps of how I looked at him: cp. §669, and the silent beckoning in §662.

but the picture . . . : "When one has the picture in view by itself it is suddenly dead, and it is as if something had been taken away from it, which had given it life before. It is not a thought, not an intention; whatever accompaniments we imagine for it, articulate or inarticulate processes, or any feeling whatsoever, it remains isolated, it does not point outside itself to a reality beyond" (*Z* 236; *PG* 148).

like an illustration: cp. §§396, 656a.

From it alone . . . : cp. §651.

§664   Worked over in Man. 116, 132. See GI 9–26; *Z* 111–13 (quoted for §340); *BB* 43d–44a; *LC* 2 (quoted in GI 14); Man. 232, 711; Man. 229, §1226; Man. 130, 83; cp. §182b; *Z* 462; *BB* 28b; Frege, *Funktion,* 90–91; Malcolm, *Memoir,* 55.

In GI 9–12, where the general theme of this number is treated, the distinction between surface grammar and depth grammar is equated roughly with the distinction between verbal form and use (*LC* 2), and the reader is referred to GI 13–23 for abundant illustrations. Perhaps too abundant. For the wording in this, the only passage in W.'s writings where I have noted the expressions "surface grammar" and "depth grammar" (cp. Man. 221, 187), may suggest the need for certain restrictions. In particular, the sameness of a word in its repeated appearances, though an important surface feature (GI 22), may not seem readily classifiable as a way in which the word "is used in the construction of the sentence", so may seem to be excluded from surface grammar. It would then be slightly misleading, at least as Wittgensteinian exegesis, to classify all the deceptive analogies in GI 11–23 as features of surface grammar (GI 10). In answer it may be pointed out that similarity in sound is certainly the sort of thing which is "taken in by the ear" and which "immediately impresses itself upon us"; the troublesome phrase—"used in the construction of the sentence"—need not constitute a complete account of the distinction W. had in mind; and he himself asked: "Isn't it a use, if we do in fact use the same word?" (§565).

'surface grammar': most of what has traditionally been called grammar would fall under this heading; however, the surface aspects which interest a therapeutic philosopher like W. often do not interest the grammarian, and vice versa. Cp. *RFM* 32d; commentary on §559 (on words as the "surfaces" of "meaning-bodies").

"There is a story about Wittgenstein being challenged by some dons at Trinity to say what 'surface grammar' and 'depth grammar' have in common, and of his replying, after a few moments' thought, 'Is "Should one say 'Father, Son and Holy Ghost *is* one God' or 'Father, Son and Holy Ghost *are* one God'?" a question about surface grammar or about depth grammar?' " (Vesey, "Locke", 267).

'depth': cp. §111 and commentary; Schopenhauer, *World,* II, 135c; *NB* 52 ("Words are like the film on deep water").

construction of the sentence: italicized in the German.

taken in by the ear: the features of depth grammar are equally empirical; hence the cautionary phrase, "one might say". "The use of the word 'reading'," for instance, "is, of course, extremely familiar to us in the circumstances of our ordinary life"; however, "it would be extremely difficult to describe these circumstances even roughly" (*BB* 119; *EPB* 172). Depth grammar is "something that we need to *remind* ourselves of. (And it is obviously something of which for some reason it is difficult to remind oneself.)" (§89). "Instead of looking at the *whole language,* we only look at the [verbal] contexts, the phrases of language in which a word is used" (*BB* 108; see *EPB* 157). For example, we see the past tense *meant,* note the object *him,* and imagine he must somehow have been present then in order to be meant (§689), or that meaning him was an act performed at the moment referred to (*PG* 103).

say of the word "to mean": the German does have a single word (*meinen*). See XXVI, 2–7. A synoptic account like that in Hunter, *Essays,* 5–6, cataloguing variations in the concept, forcefully illustrates W.'s point.

No wonder . . . : see §§122–23 and commentary; §182; *Z* 121 (quoted for §123).

"One must advance carefully, as if on brittle ice, always asking for the use, never trusting the appearance of the expression. For every familiar expression suggests another use, different from the actual one" (Man. 228, §159).

§665   See p. 18n; cp. *Z* 5.

(a) How can one 'mean': see §692, p. 18n.

was most important: see GI 37; §81b and commentary ("and means"); *BB* 3e.

(b) not a description . . . : see GI 15–16; XXVI, 7; §§676, 693, p. 217ak; cp. §§184, 239b, 633, pp. 205i, 212d, 222j.

§666   **what does this difference consist in?:** see XXVI 5–7; §678 and commentary; *Z* 16 ("The mistake is to say that there is anything that meaning something consists in").

direction of the attention: see §669a; cp. §33.

will correspond to: see XXVI, 6; cp. §34.

as a look often does . . . : see §669.

§667   In stripping this particular leaf (XXVI, 7), W. uses the same technique as, for instance, in §545a (see references there), citing two cases—simulated pain and past pain—where no referent is available for attention.

§668   Took shape in Man. 116, 188. Cp. §641 ("the most explicit expression of intention is by itself insufficient evidence of intention"). On varied patterns of lying, see also *BB* 146cd; *EPB* 224.

§669   Worked up in Man. 116, 189.

(a) by pointing to it: thus the demonstrative *this* often needs such help. Why, then, "does it sound wrong to say 'I spoke of him by pointing to him as I spoke those words'? 'To mean him' means, say, 'to talk of him'. Not: to point to him. And if I talk *of him,* of course there is a connexion between my talk and him, but this connexion resides in the application of the talk, not in an act of pointing. Pointing is itself only a sign, and in the language-game it may direct the application of the sentence, and so shew what is meant" (*Z* 24; see *Z* 22; Man. 228, §356).

part of the language-game: whereas directing one's attention is not. Cp. §16a and commentary.

by directing one's attention: see II, 5; end of §411; *Z* 426; *BB* 175; cp. §34.

It evidently lies . . . . : "There are *signs* of my meaning *him*. A glance could be such a sign. Even an image is no more than such a sign" (Man. 138, 15A).

by *looking:* "When I make a remark with an allusion to N., I may let this appear—given particular circumstances—in my glance, my expression, etc." (Z 26). See §§666a, 690, p. 218bc; Z 223; *PG* 81c; Man. 229, §1720; Man. 130, 17; Man. 116, 275; cp. Z 19, 35, 222; Köhler, *Gestalt*, 251; Moore, *Commonplace*, 137b, e.g.: "Not so in the demonstrative use. Here it is necessary that some gesture of some sort (possibly merely the direction of the eyes & a nod) should accompany the saying of the words."

or *listening:* in this case it is more difficult to suppose that the pointing is public. Yet §§671–72 do not sanction talk of private pointing.
(b) The next number illustrates this remark.
§670 An illustration of §669b.
§671 Cp. §448, p. 187h. W. takes a close look at the appearance mentioned in §669a, to show it is only an appearance (see Man. 110, 239, quoted for §48a). The analogy with pointing breaks down. The reason, it might be objected, is that W. has switched from listening *to* to listening *for,* and thereby falsified the *Tractatus* perspective (GI 37): A proposition, as meant, reaches right out to a *reality* (2.1511); as the eye makes contact with an object and the ear with a sound, so the mind actually *touches* the object signified (2.15121). However, W. came to recognize that the ordinary, nonatomic things we mean need not be present, nor even exist (III, 6–7).
§672 See *BB* 174–76, especially 176g.

a receptive attitude: see p. 187h.

is called a kind of 'pointing': cp. §669a, the starting point of these reflections.

then that something . . . : to spot W.'s target, see the commentary on §448; to grasp his objection, see p. 187bc. The connection with §671 appears if we ask: How can one look for something in a given place if it isn't there (§462)? Mustn't it be somehow present? In listening for a sound, say, don't I have "a shadow of the sensation" (§448) which as it were indicates what the sound must be to satisfy my search? (Cp. James, *Principles,* I, 251.) Such a shadow, W. replies, would be part of the listening, not the sound listened for. The intentional gap remains.
§673 See Man. 302, 23; cp. *BB* 35c, 148b (quoted for §329); *PG* 103 (quoted for §661). In Man. 116, 191, underlining *alone* helps to bring out the sense.

doesn't 'accompany': see XXXVII, 14; cp. pp. 217c, 218e; *BB* 169b. The point is made more fully for thinking (e.g. §§318, 329–32, 339).

a gesture: see the quotation from Moore for §669a.

As a man . . . : being accompanied by good wishes is as different from being accompanied by a person, and being full of light is as different from being full of people, as being accompanied by a gesture is different from being accompanied by meaning (or thought). If we did speak of accompaniment in this last case, the word would change its sense. Cp. §377a.

§674 **"enough for that":** cp. Frege's critique of an analogous view, in *Writings*, 84c.

"my pain and the noise": see §666.

§675 See Man. 116, 269; Man. 108, 205; cp. X, 22. Meaning is not an accompaniment (§673), as thinking the sense is not (§§329–32, 339). And that is determined in part by the fact that we do not give such an answer (§371).

§676 See GI 15–16; XXVI, 6–7; §665, p. 217a.

§677 Cp. §§544–45.

On the other hand: §§577, 587ab indicate the connection between this and the previous numbers; *BB* 146 illustrates it thus: "Compare meaning 'I shall be delighted to see you' with meaning 'The train leaves at 3.30.' Suppose you had said the first sentence to someone and were asked afterwards 'Did you mean it?', you would then probably think of the feelings, the experiences, which you had while you said it. And accordingly you would in this case be inclined to say 'Didn't you see that I meant it?' Suppose that on the other hand, after having given someone the information 'The train leaves at 3.30,' he asked you 'Did you mean it?', you might be inclined to answer 'Certainly. Why shouldn't I have meant it?' "

as a result of introspection: the details thus noted would not have constituted the meaning (cp. §§587c, 635). Yet "these 'details' are not irrelevant in the sense in which other circumstances which I remember equally well are irrelevant" (§636).

There are differences of degree here: as for the parallel sample, "I shall be delighted to see you," but not for "The train leaves at 3.30" (*BB* 146, above). The verb *mean* here shifts in the direction of sensations (Z 472g) and emotions (Z 492, 499)—"affections of the mind" (§676) —which vary in degree.

(b) Cp. §674. Though *think* differs from *mean* (Z 51; §693; cp. §574), the connection here is closer than usual (cp. §687); so the example is of interest.

§678 See Man. 130, 18–20.

What does . . . : cp. §653.

the pain, or the piano-tuning: see §§666, 674.

No answer comes: see *Z* 16 (quoted for §666), 19, 236 (quoted for §663); cp. §§175 ("*Afterwards* no description satisfies me"), 645–46; *PG* 148b.

for the answers which . . . : e.g., "Your meaning the piano-playing consisted in your *thinking* of the piano-playing" (*Z* 16; cp. §687). That answer simply delays the final reckoning (§682; cp. §687). "The mistake is to say that there is anything that meaning something consists in" (*Z* 16).

§679 *EPB* 229 suggests the same contrast for *mean* as §246 does for *pain:* As others can know I am in pain, but I simply have it, so others can know what I mean, whereas I just mean it. The question of sureness or knowledge does not arise—not because we cannot possibly err in such cases (X, 25; §681), but because the logic of the terms does not allow for error or doubt (§288), nor therefore for knowledge (§246, p. 221cde, and commentaries; cp. X, 25). However, contrast this declaration with *Z* 22; and see the commentary on p. 221 for a discussion of the problem.

§680 Developed in Man. 116, 277–78. Cp. *Z* 13.

The conclusions . . . that interest me: see §659, p. 218e.

we should not say . . . : a clearer translation: "We would not say". "That is not the usual use of 'mean' " (Man. 228, §200). See *BB* 38–39.

§681 Worked up in Man. 116, 279. A single, well-chosen sample, even a bizarre one like this (GI 62), may have great therapeutic value, as a solvent of *a priori* prejudices concerning how things are or must be (GI 58). As the essentialist has not scrutinized all general terms, of all languages, and thereby determined that they do in fact designate essences, but asks "Why else would we use the same term?", so the empiricist has not examined all indubitable assertions and found that they rest on direct, infallible evidence, but asks "Why else would doubt be excluded?" And as careful analysis of even one general term, revealing the absence of any essence, may effectively destroy the essentialist supposition and thus the whole semantic and psychological structure based on it (GI 58), so the consideration of just one indubitable assertion which is clearly not based on immediate evidence may shake the empiricist supposition concerning the foundations of knowledge and bring down the epistemological structure supported by it (X, 3, 25). Such is the significance of the present sample. For consider these three cases: (1) there is no doubt that I am (or was) in pain; (2) there is no doubt that I mean (or meant) N.; (3) there is no doubt that I am cursing (or did curse) N. In the first case, the empiricist account may seem the only plausible one: Each individual, having privileged access to his own sensations, knows for sure what they are and that they are. The fact of my being in pain seems so evident that W.'s doubts about my *knowledge* of it may appear far-fetched (§246). In the second case, the introspective evidence seems to evaporate when examined closely (§678), yet I seem as sure as ever (§679). Finally, in the third example, the nonsense is laid bare (§464); I have no doubt, I cannot doubt, yet here the notion of sure-fire, introspective evidence looks absurd.

(b) The sense of the paragraph (to which Man. 228, 58–59, add Z 7), and the point of the second example, are suggested by p. 221c.

§682   See §§187, 683–84; Z 22 (which follows this number in Man. 228, §191); Man. 116, 190–91; cp. §§633–34; Z 8, 32, 100; BB 39a, 40b.

Can't I say *both*?: consider this similar case: "I am going along a walk and stumble over a step, and say: 'I thought it continued farther.'— What happened when I thought that?" (*EPB* 227). Did my thought connect with the nonexistent stretch of path? Yet isn't my statement true? Cp. §662.

one which did not exist: i.e., the verbal one. And why should the wordless connection be the ground of the verbal one? (Cp. p. 174j.) Suppose a picture of N. floated before me when I thought of him. "Did I know that it was a picture of him, N.? I did not tell myself it was. What did its being of him consist in, then? Perhaps what I later said or did" (Z 14). "I did not *recognize* him by his appearance" (Z 31). Cp. Z 122 ("the lightning thought which I may later 'clothe in words' "); *EPB* 226–27, 230.

§683   See the quotes just given; BB 32–33; LC 66c–68c; cp. p. 177.

" 'That is supposed to be *him*' (this picture represents *him*). Herein lies the whole problem of representation.

"What is the criterion, how is it to be verified, that this picture portrays this object—i.e., is *supposed* to represent it? Similarity doesn't make the picture a portrait (it might be a striking resemblance of one person yet be the portrait of another, whom it resembles less).

"How can I know that someone means the picture as a portrait of N.?—Well, perhaps from his saying so, or writing it underneath.

"What connection does the portrait of N. have with N.? Perhaps this, that the name by which he is addressed is written beneath it" (*PG* 102).

"But it doesn't look like him": "How do I know that a picture is a picture of Lewy?—Normally by its likeness to Lewy, or, under certain circumstances, a picture of Lewy may not be like him, but like Smith. If I give up the business of being like [as a criterion], I get into an awful mess, because anything may be his portrait, given a certain method of projection" (*LC* 66; see §139; BB 36–37).

was I establishing a connexion: see GI 43; cp. BB 39: "You say: 'There's no doubt I imagine King's College and no other building.' But can't saying this be making the very connection we want? For saying it is like writing the words 'Portrait of Mr. So-and-so' under a picture."

And what connexion did exist?: better: "Then what . . . ?" "An obvious, and correct, answer to the question 'What makes a portrait the portrait of so-and-so?' is that it is the *intention*. But if we wish to know what it means 'intending this to be a portrait of so-and-so' let's see what actually happens when we intend this. Remember the occasion when we talked of what happened when we expect some one from four to four-thirty. To intend a picture to be the portrait of so-and-so (on the part of the painter, e.g.) is neither a particular state of mind nor a particular mental process. But there are a great many combinations of actions and states of mind which we should call 'intending . . .' " (*BB* 32).

§684 See the commentaries on §§682–83.

I *should have:* cp. §§187, 633–34, 693.

something about the past: not merely in the sense that the verb is in the past tense. "Most of all, it refers to a technique" (*LC* 68).

§685 See Man. 107, 257; contrast with Man. 109, 236–37 (a general rule present in the searching). Of both (*a*) and (*b*) we might say that the sense is different, but the reference the same.

§686 See Man. 116, 266–67 (the original setting), 296.

(b) points to a wider context: wider than the moment or the contents of the mind. See §§197, 337, 656, 659a; *Z* 17, 21; cp. §§338, 581, 591, p. 219f; *Z* 7, 397.

§687 See Man. 228, §356.

can . . . sometimes say: "In certain circumstances these words will mean (will be replaceable by)" those others (cp. *Z* 65), in others not (§693).

Number 685 suggests a comparison such as this: Of a single walk one might say, "I took a walk," or, "I circled the park." On that occasion, what I did could be described in either way. Similarly, to mean someone is sometimes to talk of him. But not, for instance, to point to him. Meaning him and speaking of him are more comprehensive than that (as a walk is more comprehensive than leg movements) (*Z* 24, quoted in part for §669).

"I thought of him": not merely: "He came to my mind as I spoke" (*Z* 14; Man. 138, 15A). That would be as incomplete as pointing.

sometimes even: cp. *LC* 67: "Suppose my thought consists of my *saying* 'My brother is in America'—how do I know that I *say* my brother is in America?"

Ask yourself . . . : for then you will come to the same conclusion as with regard to meaning, though perhaps more readily, the outer act being obviously insufficient by itself, whereas the inner is wont to be endowed with magic powers. This "is one way of avoiding at least partly the occult appearance of the processes of thinking" (*BB* 4; cp. §691d). Cp. §678 and commentary.

consists in: see §689. Here, too, "no answer comes" (§678), either general or particular. To speak of someone, one need not name him (§§666–67), or point to him (§670), or imagine him (§680). And when one of these things does occur, it does not constitute speaking of him (*Z* 24).

§688   From Man. 180b, 9. Cp. §596, pp. 195cd, 206b, 213f.

At best this is a characteristic feature (§35) of meaning someone.

§689   See the commentary on §687; *LC* 66c–68c; cp. Moore, *Lectures,* 29–30, and *Studies,* 217.

(a) "What connects my words with him? The situation and my thoughts. And my thoughts in just the same way as things I say out loud" (*Z* 9).

(b) Cp. *BB* 34b.

that is not enough: see *Z* 15.

(c) See *BB* 39bc.

a mental *mechanism:* "We are led astray by the idea of a mechanism which operates with special means, so can explain special movements" (*PG* 99; cp. §§95, 435). "What a remarkable process, this meaning! Can you mean someone even when he is in America and you are in Europe? And even if he no longer exists?" (*PG* 103; see Man. 112, 98).

(d) See §691b; *Z* 9, 13; *BB* 35f–36a; cp. §§462, 518; *PG* 56 ("*Bedeutung* comes from *deuten*"); Moore, *Lectures,* 26b, and *Studies,* 216b.

"Here meaning gets imagined as a kind of mental pointing, indicating" (*Z* 12).

§690   The number makes a point similar to that in §688, in similar fashion. The same references, therefore, are pertinent here.

sidelong glance: see §669a, p. 218bc; Man. 138, 15A; cp. *PG* 140d.

thinking *specially:* do I replace the perceptible glance with a mental one, pinpointing the object of thought? Page 218bc suggests an answer analogous to that in §244b: "On the contrary: the verbal expression replaces the glance."

§691   See *Z* 21 (which this number follows in Man. 228, 57); *BB* 32e–33b; cp. *PG* 140c. The whole sequence *Z* 7–22 follows much the same line of development (from meaning him to calling him) as does this single number.

(a) See §683 and commentary.

(b) he aimed at him: see §689d and commentary.

(d) *How does he call him?:* he speaks his name. It is in language that the connection is made, not in the mind (GI 43). The name used to call him is the name used to describe him, address him, point him out, and so on (XV, 2–5). Thus the present number continues the point of the last.

See Geach, *Acts,* 73; cp. §§27b, 493.

§692   Of course it is correct: see §§187, 693.
  did not mean: to think of it: see §§125d, 187, 693, pp. 33n, 217k.
  how are we to judge: see §190.
§693   Quite right: see §§187, 692.
  without necessarily even thinking . . . : see §§125d, 187.
  This shews you how different . . . : see XI, 1–4; cp. §574.
  nothing is more wrong-headed: see XXVI, 5–7; Z 19–20, 51; *BB* 3e–4a; cp. §79d; Z 645.

XXVII. Emotions (P. 174)

GENERAL COMMENTARY

(1) "Wittgenstein saw through a big mistake of his time. It was then held by most philosophers that the nature of such things as hoping and fearing, or intending, meaning, and understanding could be discovered through introspection, while others, in particular psychologists, sought to arrive at an answer by experiment, having only obscure notions as to what their results meant. Wittgenstein changed the whole approach by saying: what these words mean shows itself in the way they are used—the nature of understanding reveals itself in grammar, not in experiment" (Waismann, "How I See", 380; see GI 27; XLI, 1–5).

(2) "Consider the James-Lange theory of emotions, say of depression; the theory says that these states of the soul are feelings, not localised, so 'diffused'. (It also said 'He is sad because he cries.' And this is good, but *not* as 'part of his sadness is the feeling that he cries'—it's good as 'part of his sadness is that he cries.') People want to make depression, joy, hope, into 'sensations': the paradigm was the atom-sensation; this physics-color model dominated them. So hope, e.g. was 'the sum of feelings' " (JN 45; see Man. 232, 687–88).

(3) "I shall limit myself in the first instance," wrote James, "to what may be called the *coarser* emotions, grief, fear, rage, love, in which every one recognizes a strong organic reverberation. . . . Our natural way of thinking about these . . . is that the mental perception of some fact excites the mental affection called the emotion, and that this latter state of mind gives rise to the bodily expression. My theory, on the contrary, is that *the bodily changes follow directly the perception of the exciting fact, and that our feeling of the same changes as they occur IS the emotion*" (*Principles*, II, 449). For "what kind of an emotion of fear would be left if the feeling neither of quickened heart-beats nor of shallow breath-

ing, neither of trembling lips nor of weakened limbs, neither of goose-flesh nor of visceral stirrings, were present, it is quite impossible for me to think. Can one fancy the state of rage and picture no ebullition in the chest, no flushing of the face, no dilatation of the nostrils, no clenching of the teeth, no impulse to vigorous action, but in their stead limp muscles, calm breathing, and a placid face?" (ibid., 452). The "vital point" of the whole theory, generally stated, is this: "*If we fancy some strong emotion, and then try to abstract from our consciousness of it all the feelings of its bodily symptoms, we find we have nothing left behind,* no 'mind-stuff' out of which the emotion can be constituted, and that a cold and neutral state of intellectual perception is all that remains" (ibid., 451).

(4)   Here, "the first step is the one that altogether escapes notice" (§308). James simply supposed that emotions are constituted of "mind-stuff", so sought the most characteristic. This picture held him captive, and he could not get outside it (§115), for it lay in our language and language seemed to repeat it to him inexorably (GI 17–19). Yet the answer stared him in the face; James himself said of grief: "What would it be without its tears, its sobs, its suffocation of the heart, its pang in the breastbone?" (*Principles,* II, 452). Yet for some unnamed reason, in James's account the sobs and tears all disappear from the emotion itself, leaving only the feel of the tears as they trickle down one's cheeks, and the wracking sensation in one's heaving breast. Sobs, tears, gestures, words are mere "symptoms" of grief; the feelings constitute the emotion.

(5)   No such sundering occurs, however, in our ordinary use of the term *grief,* and it is this use which traces the nature of grief (§371; GI 60–61). Wittgenstein partially summarized his findings as follows: "Emotions. Common to them: genuine duration, a course. (Rage flares up, abates, vanishes, and likewise joy, depression, fear.)—Distinction from sensations: they are not localized (nor yet diffuse!).—Common: they have characteristic expression-behaviour. (Facial expression.) And this itself implies characteristic sensations too. Thus sorrow often goes with weeping, and characteristic sensations with the latter. (The voice heavy with tears). But these sensations are not the emotions. (In the sense in which the numeral 2 is not the number 2).—Among emotions the directed might be distinguished from the undirected. Fear *at* something, joy *over* something.—This something is the object, not the cause of the emotion" (Z 488; the dashes replace indentation). Z 484–520 are rich in further refinements, comparisons, and illustrations. However, "the treatment of all these phenomena of mental life is not of importance to me because I am keen on completeness," wrote Wittgenstein. "Rather because each one casts light on the correct treatment of *all*" (Z 465). Thus the present section treats questions not mentioned in the

summary above (dependence on language, the temporal discrimination of emotions from sensations) and omits points stressed there and in the other leftover *Zettel* (location, the distinction between target and cause). These too might have served to bring out the difference between emotions and sensations. But not as well. I leave to the reader to divine why.

DETAILED COMMENTARY

P. 174(abc) Here (*a*) notes that hope, unlike fright or anger, is specific to man; (*b*) suggests the reason, by means of a comparison; and (*c*) applies the lesson to hope. What is true of belief or fear sometimes, is true of hope regularly: Its target is distant, hence linguistically determined (GI 43; XV, 4–5; commentary on §650). So an animal can feel pain, which is never dependent on language, since it has no target; or fear, since fear may have a proximate object; but it cannot hope. Thus hope, which resembles fear or anger more than does pure ratiocination, provides an apt transition from Part One, "about the nature of thought, belief, knowledge, and the like" (*BB* 42), to Part Two in general (see GI 65–66) and to emotions in particular, which straddle the border between the domain of the greater picture theory (GI 32–38) and the varied psychological experiences and states which lie outside it.

One can imagine . . . : see Man. 229, 294–96. On this and the next two paragraphs, see Z 469; cp. Schopenhauer, *World*, II, 59–61.

unhappy: see Z 526.

happy: see Man. 228, 173; cp. Z 484–87.

why not?: see above, and below ("Only those who . . ."). "The word 'hope' refers to a phenomenon of human life" (§583), and advanced human life at that. "One does not say that a suckling hopes that . . . nor yet that he has no hope that . . . and one does say it of a grown man.—Well, bit by bit daily life becomes such that there is a place for hope in it. But now it is said: We can't be certain when a child really begins to hope, for hope is an inner process. What nonsense! For then how do we know what we are talking about at all?" (Z 469). See §§583–85; Man. 232, 604 ("Crocodiles don't hope"). For a revealing contrast between hope and fear, see p. 188mn.

A dog believes . . . : for a similar contrast, see §650 and commentary. Cp. §§250, 357; Ramsey, *Foundations*, 144.

How do I do it?: according to James, "in every proposition . . . so far as it is believed, questioned, or disbelieved, four elements are to be distinguished, the subject, the predicate, and their relation (of whatever sort it be)—these form the *object* of belief—and finally the psychic attitude in which our mind stands towards the proposition taken as a whole—and this is the belief itself" (*Principles*, II, 287). So no doubt

James would say that the dog is capable of the feeling but not of the propositional content. For Russell's similar views, see the commentary on §598; for those of W.'s youth, see GI 38. Compare his present answer in (c) with that in §25.

Only those who . . . : in general, the overall pattern of hope is missing in a dog (§§583–84). In particular, it cannot linguistically determine the object of hope (see above), nor linguistically specify it as hope, which may be equally requisite. "For if the thought that a certain delightful person may come to my party fills me all day with pleasurable feelings, there are no criteria which would decide whether these thoughts and feelings were a case of hoping, yearning, or musing. And if I later say that I have been hoping . . . , I have not *discovered* this, but have *made* what I have been doing hoping. (Cf. §§557, 653)" (Hunter, "Forms", 240). For similar remarks on remorse, see Z 518–20; on memory, see §649.

this complicated form of life: that is, language (not hope). See §§23b, 241.

(d) See Man. 232, 753–54.

"Grief": see p. 187a. Schlick's account of grief, in "Psychological Concepts", 401e–402b, sounds similar, but p. 405, quoted in X, 14, reveals the difference.

describes a pattern . . . : see GI 44–45; p. 229a; cp. §§316, 645–46; Z 486–87, 514; PG 141d; JN 45. James recognized the great variety of bodily feelings associated with emotions (*Principles,* II, 447–48); but the pattern is still broader than that, and more varied. The variations, notice, are not mere "accidentals", but constitute the pattern. "If life be seen as a weave, this pattern (pretence, say) is not always complete and is varied in a multiplicity of ways. But we, in our conceptual world, keep on seeing the same, recurring with variations. That is how our concepts take it. For concepts are not for use on a single occasion" (Z 568, translation altered).

If a man's . . . : likewise, "you can't compare 'love' with traffic-light changes" (JN 84).

alternated: or never varied (Z 526; cp. Z 527).

(e) "For a second . . .": "Consider 'amorphous' and 'definite' verbs. Would you e.g. say 'For 30 seconds I was in love'? Does this sound absurd because we've found that people aren't in love for 30 seconds? If you talk of it as a content of consciousness (a 'feeling') you *may* say 'Well, love is rounded off'—we don't find that someone is *suddenly* in love for 30 seconds and suddenly not again.' But even if it is 'rounded off' you should be able to say 'For 30 seconds, yes, for 30 seconds, no.'—You can't" (JN 83; cp. Z 504).

(f) grief *now:* see p. 175ab; cp. §§583–84.

"chess *now*": see §205; *EPB* 225; *BB* 147a.

any more like the concept of a sensation: see *Z* 488 (in XXVII, 5), 497; cp. *Z* 174, 484–85; Schlick, "Psychological", 401–2. "I should almost like to say: One no more feels sorrow in one's body than one feels seeing in one's eyes" (*Z* 495; see *Z* 510; XXVII, 5).

not the logical question: whether grief takes place in the moment, so is a feeling.

(ghi) "I am frightened": see pp. 187–89.

in a *smiling* tone of voice too: which might suggest that it is a pure report of fact, not a spontaneous *Äusserung* (GI 15–16); or that tone of voice and the like (*Z* 513) do not belong to the logical criteria of the emotion (*Z* 466) and therefore to its nature (§371). For contrast this case with *Z* 508: "Just try to think over something very sad with an expression of radiant joy!"

And do you mean . . . : the protest is that of one who takes the statement "I am frightened" for a report of observed fact, and therefore of inner fact, since the speaker does not generally observe his own expression or behavior.

he doesn't feel it?: yes, W. would answer (*Z* 487; cp. §§304–6), when he is frightened he is really frightened. And his fear is not fearful behavior, or a fearful tone of voice. But neither is it an "inward thing" (XXVII, 5).

But even when . . . : cp. §659.

as a piece of information: cp. pp. 185c, 189.

does not learn it: see GI 15–16; p. 188l; cp. §§587, 631c, 659, pp. 185abcd, 191i, 192abcd.

(j) shuddering reaction: cp. §585.

this belongs among . . . : cp. James, in XXVII, 2–3.

"Remember at this point that the personal experiences of an emotion must in part be strictly localized experiences; for if I frown in anger I feel the muscular tension of the frown in my forehead, and if I weep, the sensations around my eyes are obviously part, and an important part, of what I feel. This is, I think, what William James meant when he said that a man doesn't cry because he is sad but that he is sad because he cries. The reason why this point is often not understood, is that we think of the utterance of an emotion as though it were some artificial device to let others know that we have it" (*BB* 103 and *EPB* 149–50, quoted further for p. 189c).

Now why should . . . : see the quotation just given, and pp. 188–89; cp. p. 218c.

XXVIII. Momentary Meanings in the Mind (Pp. 175–176)

GENERAL COMMENTARY

(1)   Word meanings are a major concern of the *Investigations*, receiving repeated attention in various contexts. The critique of logical atomism in Section III focuses on the meanings of names (§§40–43). Section IX relates word meanings to the primary sense of *understand* (§§138–42, 191–97), and Section XIX links them with the secondary sense. In Sections XX and XXI, interest centers on sameness or difference of meaning. The present section initiates and Section XXXII continues a critique of Jamesean views of meaning. Finally, Section XXXVII, while adding further criticism, reveals the considerable truth such doctrines contain.

(2)   "Each word," wrote James (*Principles*, I, 265), ". . . is felt, not only as a word, but as having a *meaning*. The 'meaning' of a word taken thus dynamically in a sentence may be quite different from its meaning when taken statically or without context. The dynamic meaning is usually reduced to the bare fringe we have described, of felt suitability or unfitness to the context and conclusion. The static meaning, when the word is concrete, as 'table', 'Boston', consists of sensory images awakened." In reaction to this general conception, of momentary meanings in the mind, Wittgenstein reasserts his view that the meaning of a word is its use in the language (§43), not an atmosphere accompanying it (§117), and that there is no need to hallucinate something for every word we say (§449a). But now, in accordance with the rationale of Part Two (GI 65–66), he begins to focus on the experiential side of meaning.

DETAILED COMMENTARY

P. 175(abc) See XXVIII, 2; pp. 216i–217k; *PG* 49e (quoted for §138); cp. *BB* 117d (quoted for §193).

a *way of using:* see §20; cp. §43.

that we fail to grasp: "If someone had said 'Napoleon was crowned in 1804,' and we asked him 'Did you mean the man who won the battle of Austerlitz?' he might say 'Yes, I meant him.' And the use of the past tense 'meant' might make it appear as though the idea of Napoleon having won the battle of Austerlitz must have been present in the man's mind when he said that Napoleon was crowned in 1804" (*BB* 39; see *BB* 40b; *PG* 103b). However, "the fact that a statement refers to a point of time, but in which nothing in the external world occurs which is meant or referred to by it, does not show us that it spoke of an experience" (Man. 229, §910; see ibid., §841; *Kreis,* 167–68; cp. §36; *EPB* 215; *BB* 142a).

"I was then going to say": see §§633–38, p. 219e.

I speak of . . . : in (*a*) and (*b*) ("refers to"). This paragraph reworks Man. 229, §843.

essential *references:* cp. §§561–68; 3.34–3.341.

are the ones which would . . . : whereas, "if for an expression to convey a meaning means to be accompanied by or to produce certain experiences, our expression may have all sorts of meanings" (*BB* 65). Thus were I to say "I believe it will rain," and were a Frenchman to request an explanation of my meaning, "even if my words had been accompanied by all sorts of experiences, and if we could have transmitted these experiences to the Frenchman, he would still not have known what I believed" (*BB* 147; *EPB* 225). Cp. §§10b, 21, 558; *EPB* 148–49; *BB* 79a (quoted for p. 182bc), 102c–103a; Ogden and Richards, *Meaning,* 92; Frege, *Writings,* 60–61.

(d) See p. 181cd; *EPB* 225; *BB* 147ab; cp. §20.

"till": an appropriate English example, replacing the German one (*sondern*). Cp. p. 214f.

both a verb and a conjunction: cp. §561; 3.323.

(e) Cp. §§558–61. The first sentence is proposed for examination. It might result from a conception like that criticized in §559 (see the commentary).

(fg) this tells him . . . : cp. the commentary on §199c.

If we had chosen a senseless sequence: see *BB* 9f–10a, on "I feel in my hand that the water is three feet under the ground."

'disintegration of the sense': cp. p. 214f.

"Hail!": again, the example has been changed, to make it fit in English.

(h) As background for this paragraph, see Russell, e.g. *Mind,* 206 (quoted for §6b) and 250.

What is the content . . . : cp. p. 231cd.

The answer is a picture: not that the image is a picture (§301), but one can give the content by means of a picture or of a description (§367, p. 177e). See p. 177; commentary on §301.

And what is the content . . . : see XXXVII, 11–16.

P. 176(a) See §§73–74.

(b) Cp. p. 59n. I can keep on seeing a drawing as a cube, too (p. 193), or as a rabbit (p. 194b); but can I surround a cipher with a fiction, work a piece of fancy into it, then fix the fancy? "I should like to say that what dawns here lasts only as long as I am occupied with the object in a particular way" (p. 210e). "The aspect presents a physiognomy which then passes away" (p. 210f). "And here there is a close kinship with 'experiencing the meaning of a word' " (p. 210d).

(c) **"The whole scheme presented itself . . .":** see James, *Principles*, I, 255: "What is that shadowy scheme of the 'form' of an opera, play, or book, which remains in our mind and on which we pass judgment when the actual thing is done? What is our notion of a scientific or philosophical system? Great thinkers have vast premonitory glimpses of schemes of relation between terms, which hardly even as verbal images enter the mind, so rapid is the whole process." He then quotes Mozart to the same effect ("the best of all is the *hearing of it all at once*").

(d) Cp. §§139–41, 151–54, p. 181cd.

(ef) **not** *forgotten* **it:** not: kept it in mind (like an image). *Know* is italicized for the same reason. See §§148–50; cp. James, *Principles*, I, 265c.

(g) See Man. 130, 69; cp. §§20, 551–52, p. 181e; *PG* 47d. In Man. 130 W. compares the two *Scot*'s (*Schweizer*'s) with the two crosses on p. 207c. Can we do something like that?

"Mr. Scot": this example, too, is an English equivalent, not a translation. Cp. the similar sample in 3.323. According to young W., we would "think out" the two words differently (GI 37).

I blink with the effort: see Man. 107, 233, quoted for §436.

do I parade the meanings . . . : "How odd, if we mean something for every word, that a combination of such words can make no sense!" (*PG* 108).

(h) See *EPB* 226–27.

its sense disintegrates: see p. 175g.

but the person I am saying it to . . . : see p. 181b; *EPB* 225; *BB* 147ab.

"something *else*, quite definite": see James, *Principles*, I, 472 (quoted for §598).

not **this 'parade of the meanings':** see §329; cp. Man. 108, 209 ("A person who thinks lets pictures pass through his mind"); James, *Principles*, I, 252, 265a, 281 ("no word in an understood sentence comes to consciousness as a mere noise. We feel its meaning as it passes").

XXIX. The Reference of Images (P. 177)

(1)   Russell, who made so much of images, troubled little about the problem of their reference; the mind could take care of that. Wittgenstein's attitude had been similar (GI 37). But then he looked closer. "Supposing we asked: 'How can one *imagine* what does not exist?' The answer seems to be: 'If we do, we imagine non-existent combinations of existing elements' " (BB 31; see GI 34–37). But what are these indestructible elements, assuring reference? The doctrine does not make sense (BB 31; Section III). So the entire image must be somehow linked with its reference. However, "describe whatever process (activity) of projection we may, there is a way of reinterpreting this projection" (BB 33); so it makes no advance on the image itself (§§139–41 and commentary). Mere similarity is an equally defective solution (BB 36–37). "Someone says, he imagines King's College on fire. We ask him: 'How do you know that it's *King's College* you imagine on fire? Couldn't it be a different building, very much like it? In fact, is your imagination so absolutely exact that there might not be a dozen buildings whose representation your image could be?" (BB 39). So nothing in the image, or in the mind, makes the connection. Nor anything simultaneous with the image. True, "it might have been that *while* you imagined King's College on fire you said the words 'King's College is on fire.' But in very many cases you certainly don't speak explanatory words in your mind while you have the image. And consider, even if you do, you are not going the whole way from your image to King's College, but only to the words 'King's College'. The connection between these words and King's College was, perhaps, made at another time" (ibid.).

(2)   Like Wittgenstein in the *Blue Book* I have been linking the image with imagining. But here in the *Investigations,* in keeping with the division explained in GI 66–67, he separates them. Section XII treats imagining, Section XXIX the image. The first *Bemerkung* (that is, the first four paragraphs) rapidly evokes the points just made; the second draws the consequences: If an image is not a sort of superlikeness (§389), words or gestures may sometimes do as well. For further background to this section, see Z 31–32; PG 102abc, 147d; LC 66c–68c; Man. 229, §928; Man. 138, 17.

P. 177(abcd) What makes . . . : see Man. 109, 224; Man. 108, 201 ("I stare at the closed door and imagine that it opens. How can I imagine that *it* opens?").

Not its looking like him: see XXIX, 1; §§389, 663; *BB* 32d, 37abc, 39d; *LC* 66k; Man. 229, §849; cp. §515; *PG* 146c, 152 ("How can I recall one of two men who look exactly alike?"); Moore, *Problems,* 65–66, 240b–246a.

"I say for instance: 'I see myself walking here & there with a friend.' But—how do I know that it is *I* & my friend? Are the portraits so well done? Naturally not. But I *say* that it is myself with my friend; I make this transition from the picture (the image) to words" (Man. 116, 137).

Nothing in it or . . . : see XXIX, 1; §691; *Z* 14 (quoted for §682); cp. *Z* 25.

'behind it': see §§153–54.

ask him: see GI 43; XV, 3; the quotations just given; and (*e*); cp. §659, p. 174i.

"How do I know that this picture is my image of the *sun?*—I *call* it an image of the sun. I *use* it as a picture of the *sun*" (*RFM* 40).

But it is also . . . : cp. p. 197ghi.

(e) See XXIX, 2.

only with his finger: images, too, are often rudimentary (*Z* 25; *BB* 39, in XXIX, 1).

his answer would be decisive: "For saying it is like writing the words 'Portrait of Mr. So-and-so' under a picture" (*BB* 39; cp. p. 222hi). "But how did you know he was the one whose picture swam before you?—I didn't know it. I said it" (Man. 138, 14B; cp. §679, p. 221cde).

take the *place:* cp. §§244b, 459, pp. 174j, 178g ("it is the service which is the point"), 218bc; *PG* 140c; Man. 138, 17B.

XXX. Belief in the Soul (P. 178)

(1) This page, in which Wittgenstein returns to the themes of §§420–24, may be seen as the denouement of a dialectical process. In the *Tractatus* he rejected the soul "as it is conceived in the superficial psychology of the present day" (5.5421), replacing it with "the metaphysical subject, the limit of the world—not a part of it" (5.641). In Sec-

tion XIII of the *Investigations* he rejected this transcendent substitute too. "The idea of the human soul which is seen or not seen is very similar to that of a word meaning as a process or object which accompanies the word" (Man. 138, 32): Seeking a referent for such terms (*BB* 1), and finding none within our experience, we postulate a spiritual one (§36). But the words *self* and *soul*, like the word *meaning*, are not employed in this way; they are not names for anything. From this it does not follow, as it might have in his youth, that it is sheer nonsense to say that men have souls (cp. 6.53). Whether the statement occurs as a philosophical claim (p. 178abc) or as religious teaching (p. 178g), "all I ask is to understand the expression we use" (§423), within that specific stream of thought and life.

DETAILED COMMENTARY

P. 178(abc) See §420.

"I believe . . .": cp. §303.

Do I also *believe* . . . : see (*def*), below.

It would go against the grain: see §420; cp. *LC* 55h.

Or is it like this: is *believe* too weak to express our conviction in the latter case? Is that why it "goes against the grain"? Cp. §303a.

Nonsense!: p. 224c explains why, in terms directly applicable to this reply.

(d) "Consider how we are to state the problem of other minds. We might ask: 'Do other people have a mental life, as I do?' But this clearly won't do, for they are not people, surely, if they do not have thoughts, emotions, sensations, desires, and so on. After all, we do not mean to be asking in the ordinary way whether this or that person is in a coma or something of the sort. So we had better retreat to this formulation: 'Are the things that I take to be people really people, that is, do they have thoughts and emotions and so on?' But this, too, is unsatisfactory, for it is left unspecified what distinction we are being asked to make. If the question is whether they are people or not, we must ask: 'People as opposed to *what*?' And here the answer is not at all clear. If I look at my son playing near by and ask, 'What else might he be?', no answer readily suggests itself. He is clearly not a statue, nor is he an animated doll of the sort we sometimes see looking very lifelike. He is my own child, my own flesh and blood" (Cook, "Human Beings", 121).

(e) Malcolm explains this declaration as follows, connecting it with (*f*): "In lectures Wittgenstein imagined a tribe of people who had the idea that their slaves had no feelings, no souls—that they were automatons—despite the fact that the slaves had human bodies, behaved like their masters, and even spoke the same language. Wittgenstein undertook to try to give sense to that idea. When a slave injured himself or fell ill or complained of pains, his master would try to heal him. The master would let him rest when he was fatigued, feed him when he was hungry and thirsty, and so on. Furthermore, the masters would apply to the slaves our usual distinctions between genuine complaints and malingering. So what could it mean to say that they had the idea that the slaves were automatons? Well, they would *look* at the slaves in a peculiar way. They would observe and comment on their movements *as if* they were machines. ('Notice how smoothly his limbs move.') They would discard them when they were worn and useless, like machines. If a slave received a mortal injury and twisted and screamed in agony, no master would avert his gaze in horror or prevent his children from observing the scene, any more than he would if the ceiling fell on a printing press. Here is a difference in 'attitude' that is not a matter of believing or expecting different facts" ("Investigations", 201–2; see *LC* 68f; Man. 138, 20B).

(f) See the quotation just given; cp. Man. 116, 322–23 (on free will versus determinism); Russell, *Inquiry*, 281c–282b.

My attitude: see §284b; cp. §420; *Z* 204–5; Man. 229, §§933–34.

towards a soul: in W.'s correspondence with Malcolm, the trichotomy "soul, mind, and body" recurs (Malcolm, *Memoir*, 45, 75).

I am not of the *opinion:* cp. *LC* 55: "If you say: 'Do you believe the opposite?'—you can call it believing the opposite, but it is entirely different from what we would normally call believing the opposite. I think differently, in a different way. I say different things to myself. I have different pictures." "This is partly why one would be reluctant to say: 'These people rigorously hold the opinion (or view) that there is a Last Judgment.' 'Opinion' sounds queer" (*LC* 57). "Not only is it not reasonable, but it doesn't pretend to be" (*LC* 58). "Here believing obviously plays much more this role: suppose we said that a certain picture might play the role of constantly admonishing me, or I always think of it. Here, an enormous difference would be between those people for whom the picture is constantly in the foreground, and the others who just didn't use it at all. Those who said: 'Well, possibly it may happen and possibly not' would be on an entirely different plane" (*LC* 56).

has a soul: cp. §§283, 398a; *BB* 162b; Man. 138, 32.

(g) See §§422–25; *Z* 275; *LC* 69–71; Man. 229, §1261; cp. p. 184ef; *Z* 127; *RFM* 59b, 145a; 6.4312; Man. 113, 80.

Religion teaches: "I believe that he looked on religion as a 'form of life' (to use an expression from the *Investigations*) in which he did not participate, but with which he was sympathetic and which greatly interested him" (Malcolm, *Memoir*, 72). "True, one can compare a fixed picture in our minds to a superstition; but one can also say that it is *always* necessary to reach some firm ground, whether it be a picture or not &

that therefore a picture at the base of all thinking is to be respected & not to be treated as a superstition" (Man. 138, 32–33; cp. §144).

Now do I understand . . . : see *LC* 55kl, 58j, 65mno.

Of course I understand it: "Don't we *understand* Strachey when he surmises what Queen Victoria may have imagined just before she died? Certainly—but don't we also *understand* people who ask how many souls can fit on the head of a pin? That is: the question whether or not we understand does not help us here; we must ask *what* we can do with such a sentence.—*That* we use the sentence, is clear: *how* we use it is the question" (Man. 229, §1033; see *Investigations*, §423).

"Wittgenstein once suggested that a way in which the notion of immortality can acquire a meaning is through one's feeling that one has duties from which one cannot be released, even by death. Wittgenstein himself possessed a stern sense of duty" (Malcolm, *Memoir*, 71; see *LC* 70e).

I can imagine plenty of things . . . : see *LC* 70c–71c. Jackson's notes (p. 47) continue Malcolm's account, above ("Investigations", 201–2): "Suppose now we change our attitude to the tribe, that we feel about them as we feel about ourselves. What must change is our picture of them. We might paint their dying differently. Before when one of us died, we may have painted a bluish ghost exhaling from the head, but painted the tribe as simply lying flat with nothing from their heads; now we may give them a ghost as well. The trouble is: How can we i.e. anybody, make any use of the new techniques that the tribesmen have got souls? (Compare—an attitude to animals.)"

And haven't pictures . . . : see Man. 229, §1476, and the quote just given from Jackson.

And why should such a picture . . . : see (*i*), below; §§295b, 548b; cp. *PB* 97e; *LC* 38b.

"Take 'God created man.' Pictures of Michelangelo showing the creation of the world. In general, there is nothing which explains the meanings of words as well as a picture, and I take it that Michelangelo was as good as anyone can be and did his best, and here is the picture of the Deity creating Adam" (*LC* 63).

the *same* service: see p. 177e.

it is the service which is the point: see §397; Man. 229, §1217; cp. p. 179e. Man. 131, 70, adds: "But aren't you a pragmatist? No. For I don't say that a proposition is true if it is useful."

"It is quite clear that the rôle of pictures of Biblical subjects and rôle of the picture of God creating Adam are totally different ones. You might ask this question: 'Did Michelangelo think that Noah in the ark looked like this, and that God creating Adam looked like this?' He wouldn't have said that God or Adam looked as they look in this picture" (*LC* 63).

(h) why not much more: for thought has no location (*BB* 7–8; *Z* 606–8) and the soul is not a place; or, as some would put it, thought and the soul are spiritual whereas the head is not (§36). Cp. §454; *Z* 497.

(i) The human body is . . . : see §§357, 391; *Z* 220–23; *LC* 33; Man. 229, §§933–34, 941, 1254 (quoted in XXXI, 1); cp. p. 209g; *Z* 490; *NB* 84–85; Schopenhauer, *World*, I, 107 ("Therefore the whole body must be nothing but my will become visible, must be my will itself, in so far as this is object of perception").

On Frazer's remark, "The Malays conceive the human soul as a little man . . . who corresponds exactly in shape, proportion, and even in complexion to the man in whose body he resides," W. observed: "How much more truth there is in thus attributing to the soul the same multiplicity as to the body than there is in a modern, watered-down theory" (BUF 246).

Number 281 suggests a parallel such as: Body is to soul as behavior is to thought. Or we might add to the list and say: "Only what resembles a human being has a soul" (cp. §§284–85).

(j) See §§589–90; *Z* 497.

that we choose: cp. p. 230c, and JN 46: "Suppose one tribe says love is in the right side of the chest, and another tribe says it is in the left side of the chest; would you worry very much about which was right? But you would *worry about* 'love is in the nose.'"

XXXI.   What Psychology Treats (Pp. 179–180)

GENERAL COMMENTARY

(1)   Man. 229, §1254, links this section with the preceding: "But don't you say that everything we can express by the word 'soul' can also be expressed somehow by means of words for the bodily? I don't say it. But even were it true—what would it *indicate*? The words, as well as the things we point to in explaining them, are only instruments, and now the question is how they are used." The present answer, expanding on §571 and reworking Man. 229, §§948–58, makes the most explicit statement in the *Investigations* of Wittgenstein's middle road between behaviorism or physicalism on the one hand and introspectionism (GI 48) on the other (GI 44–45).

(2)   *PP* 307–8 reveal the solution still in embryonic form. When we say that someone has a toothache, Wittgenstein then thought, we refer to the same thing as he does when he says "I have a toothache"; but "what verifies or is a criterion for 'I have toothache' is quite different from what verifies or is a criterion for 'He has toothache.'" Verification is direct in one case, indirect in the other; we conclude to the other person's feeling from the similarity between his behavior and ours when we have toothache. "Since this is so, the *meanings* of 'I have toothache' and 'he has toothache' must be different" (ibid.; see §353 and commentary; cp. *Z* 11). To mark such differences, Wittgenstein had envisaged a "phenomenological language" which would have explicitly named the behavior along with the pain, and have separated the immediate from the merely inferred (X, 8). "We are handicapped in ordinary language," he remarked still in the *Blue Book,* "by having to describe, say, a tactile sensation by means of terms for physical objects such as the word 'eye', 'finger', etc., when what we want to say does not entail the existence of an eye or finger, etc. We have to use a roundabout description of our sensations" (*BB* 52).

(3)   By 1938 he was critical of this account. "'When we speak of an object (a table, chair, etc., etc.) we are really speaking of sense impressions, present, past, and future.' Very well, that can be said.—But when we speak in *this* way of sense impressions—what more do we want? 'But mustn't there be a directer way to speak of sense impressions, since it seems that here we are speaking of other objects, that we are naming other objects than the sense impressions?' But who says then that this isn't precisely the way '*to speak of sense impressions*'? (How does a man marry money? Isn't it by marrying a rich woman?)" (Man. 160; see NL 303c). Can one bypass the woman and marry the money directly?

(4)   Developing this comparison (see *Z* 11; Man. 116, 333), we might say that the woman's wealth or lack of it makes a considerable difference, yet forms no part of the marriage. Even when the money is truly in the bank under her name and motivates his actions, the bridegroom does not exchange vows with the bank account, or swear eternal fidelity to the money. And another bridegroom may not give it a thought. And the lady may have merely pretended to be wealthy. Yet the marriage ceremony proceeds as usual. Thus were we to conceive marriage on a single pattern (cp. §304), we would have to conclude that no one ever does marry money; the money drops out entirely (cp. §§293–308). So it is with the language-games in which psychological expressions occur, and the mental contents they are said to "refer" to. Of course it makes a difference whether a person is in pain or not (§304); but not to the performance of "He is in pain." The speaker does not supplement his observation of the sufferer's behavior by

quickly imagining a pain in his body and thereby providing a proper referent (§302). Nor does he perform any inference by analogy. Nor does he usually envisage the possibility of pretense and rule it out. Thus if we conceive "reference" according to a single model, the pain itself would seem to drop out of the language-game (cp. §293). Behaviorism would result.

(5)   And yet pain is important in this language-game, as important as the money in a marriage for money. So what *is* the connection? This, for instance, that the term used in "He is in pain" is the same one used to express pain. And the verbal expression of pain replaces and resembles the natural expression (GI 16). As it is not a matter of indifference for future use that *red* is taught by pointing to something red (§§43b, 429), so too it is decisive for the language-game with *pain* that it is taught, say, by inflicting pain (§288), or as a substitute for groaning and cries (§244). Thereafter, just as one sympathizes with a person who groans, so one sympathizes with a person who says, "I have a terrible pain." Thus already in *PP* 308 Wittgenstein "seemed quite definitely to reject the behaviourist view that 'he has toothache' means only that 'he' is behaving in a particular manner; for he said that 'toothache' doesn't in fact only mean a particular kind of behaviour, and implied that when we pity a man for having toothache, we are not pitying him for putting his hand to his cheek."

(6)   Clashes such as that between realism and idealism, or between physicalism and mentalism, Wittgenstein saw as resulting from confusions common to both sides (§402b; *BB* 57–59). It is as though one party were to assert as obvious the fact that people do marry money, whereas the other stoutly denied it. Neither realizes sufficiently that "here we have two different language-games and a complicated relation between them.—If you try to reduce their relations to a *simple* formula you go wrong" (p. 180). "One can defend common sense against the attacks of philosophers only by solving their puzzles; i.e., by curing them of the temptation to attack common sense; not by restating the views of common sense" (*BB* 58–59).

(7)   Since substantive behaviorism is rare and methodological common, one wonders whether and how Wittgenstein's position differs from that described by Russell: "The behaviourist view, as I understand it, maintains that 'mental' phenomena, though they may exist, are not amenable to scientific treatment, because each of them can only be observed by one observer—in fact, it is highly doubtful whether even one observer can be aware of anything not reducible to some bodily occurrence. Behaviourism is not a metaphysic, but a principle of method. Since language is an observable phenomenon, and since language has a property which we call 'meaning', it is essential to behaviourism to give

an account of 'meaning' which introduces nothing known only through introspection" (*Logic*, 291). As in the parallel case of mathematics (p. 232), where Wittgenstein distinguished between mathematicians' practice and their 'prose' (see commentary on §124d), he approved the switch from introspection to observation of behavior (GI 48; X, 22) but questioned much that philosophers and psychologists said about it. Russell's closing remark, for instance, may be given an acceptable sense, but smacks of reductionism like that of Schlick or Carnap (see commentary on p. 180d).

DETAILED COMMENTARY

P. 179(a) See Man. 232, 609. This *Bemerkung* and the next rework Man. 229, §§952–53. W.'s comparison should be read in the light of §§570–71, somewhat as follows. Only what behaves like a human being can be said to have sensations, see, hear, think, feel, will, and so on (§§281, 571). These expressions do not designate discrete mental acts, completely distinct from walking, talking, gesturing, and the like, but different weaves in the pattern of our lives (pp. 174, 229; GI 44) varying considerably for even a single psychological concept, still more notably from one psychological concept to another and from group to group (see e.g. §§308, 574, 693, p. 174), and more radically still between physical and psychological concepts. Thus a single utterance—this single bit of behavior—may be viewed as a flow of sounds or an assertion, libel or a reply, class warfare or morphemes, quanta or communication, temporal or Indo-European, rapid or impulsive, opinion-poll data or a rationalization, according to the perspective of the one considering it.

features: italicized in the German, no doubt to avoid the multiplication of referents, a new one for each term (GI 17–19). See the preceding comments, and the quotation from Man. 123, below.

if we were interested: see §§108c, 570.

(bc) See §571; NL 303–4; LC 18c, 21b; Man. 229, §1361; cp. PG 84bc.

Compare this question and distinction with PP 307: "He began the discussion by raising a question, which he said was connected with Behaviourism, namely, the question 'When we say "He has toothache" is it correct to say that his toothache is only his behaviour, whereas when I talk about my toothache I am not talking about my behaviour?'" It is not correct; but this much is true, that "my own relation to my words is wholly different from other people's" (p. 192). They observe my behavior and report my pain, grief, intentions, whereas I express them, without observation. But we both use the same words. Consequently pain, grief, and the like are *both* inner and outer (XXXI,

5). The criteria which establish the psychological concepts are both public and expressive. A cry of pain, for example, is an audible expression—of pain.

"The objection against a behavioristic rendering of statements of direct experience is *not* that it would not treat of experience but of something else. Rather, it is that we in fact play a different (somewhat different) game with experiences than with the description of behavior.—The objection is not that this manner of expression treats of exterior behavior, for what it 'treats' does not appear straightway from the expressions and their ostensive definitions, but from the system in which the expressions are used. If someone says concernedly: 'He is groaning frightfully,' it *can* be said that he is not speaking of the person's behavior" (Man. 123, June 3).

Then psychology treats of behaviour: under W.'s influence (see X, 6–7; commentary on §353) Waismann had written: "A proposition can say no more than is determined by its method of verification. If I say: 'My friend is angry' and verify this by the fact that he manifests certain perceptible behavior, then I *mean* only that he manifests this behavior" (*Kreis*, 244).

their utterances: their *Äusserungen* (see GI 15–16). In Man. 169 W. adds examples: "I see . . . ," "I hear . . . ," "I feel . . ." According to Waismann's account, above, if my only reason for saying "He is in pain" is his saying "I am in pain," then I mean only that he uttered this series of sounds.

***these* are not about behaviour:** for instance, "I am in pain" is not self-referring (Man. 116, 166–67). See XXXI, 1, 5, 7; §244b and commentary; the quote above from Man. 123; Stout, *Manual*, 11.

(d) See the commentary on (*bc*); §571, p. 186abc; NL 303–4; Man. 229, §954.

or the future?: see *PG* 228c, e.g.: "The proposition 'p will probably occur' says something about the future only in a sense which leaves the truth or falsehood entirely independent of what will happen in the future."

not side-by-side, however: as in W.'s earlier conception, according to which all propositional content, whether inner or outer, resulted from a similar act of intention (GI 37) and was expressed in a uniform manner (5.542). W. is warning against "the idea that language always functions in one way, always serves the same purpose: to convey thoughts—which may be about houses, pains, good and evil, or anything else you please" (§304; see GI 32).

"It is, I think, misleading to describe the genuine expression as a *sum* of the expression and something else, though it is just as misleading—we get the function of our expressions wrong—if we say that the genuine expression is a particular behavior and nothing besides" (NL 303; see NL 318-19; cp. NL 302bc).

one *via* the other: see XXXI, 5; pp. 193j-194a and commentary; *BB* 53d; cp. XXXVII, 18; p. 209de (and Man. 138, 5B, from which it grew); *BB* 66b ("via my body"); Britton, "Objects", 206. Contrast W.'s position with the early physicalism of the Vienna Circle, as described in, e.g., V. Kraft, *Circle*, 167, 172.

(e) See XXXI, 4; §363c; *Z* 537, 542; NL 290bcd, 303f-304c; *PB* 93e; cp. *RFM* 6b, 172i, 179e; Ramsey, *Foundations*, 245cd. Though there are cases where one moans and is not in pain, we should not suppose that the doctor here considers that possibility and rejects it (NL 318). "Granted," someone might say, "language does not always serve to communicate thoughts (§304). But the doctor does *learn* the person is in pain, even when he makes no explicit inference at the moment." W. would then ask what the criteria (not the mere symptoms) of this knowledge are (§363c), and the reply would be: For example, he gives him more analgesic. "Broad once said 'Perhaps nothing happens in his mind when he says he has a toothache but certainly when I sympathise with him I believe that something does.' This misunderstands, or glosses over, the totally different uses of 'believe'. When you sympathise that just is a good part of 'believing in his toothache' " (JN 47).

"The thought that behind someone's pain-behavior is the pain itself does not enter into our use of 'He's in pain,' but what does enter into it is our sympathetic, or unsympathetic, reaction to him. The fact that the latter does enter into our use of that sentence (but might not have) gives sense to saying that the sentence 'He is in pain' does not just *mean* that his behavior, words, and circumstances are such and such— although these are the criteria for its use" (Malcolm, "Investigations", 202).

"It doesn't help if anyone tells us that, though we don't know whether the other person has pains, we certainly believe it when, for instance, we pity him. Certainly we shouldn't pity him if we didn't believe that he had pains; but is this a philosophical, a metaphysical belief? Does a realist pity me more than an idealist or a solipsist?" (*BB* 48). "All psychological terms merely distract us from the thing that really matters" (*OC* 459).

without suppressing . . . : cp. *RFM* 156ef.

Isn't the point . . . : cp. p. 178g.

(f) See *OC* 153, 163, 183, 411, 477-80, 627; *Z* 540-41; NL 318c; *PG* 110c; cp. *RFM* 98g-99d; *PB* 285d; Man. 229, §901; Ramsey, *Foundations*, 245d-247.

always rests on a tacit presupposition: as every step we take would rest on the presupposition that the ground will not give way beneath us (§84; cp. §575). According to Russell, "there are many other illustrations one could take of the sort of propositions that are commonly assumed, many of them with very little justification" (*Logic*, 235–36). But "how does one assume such and such to be the case? What is an assumption that, e.g., '*A* has toothache'? Is it saying the words '*A* has toothache'? Or doesn't it consist in doing something with these words?" (NL 290). Likewise, doesn't believing the ground will hold up consist largely in walking on it?

P. 180(ab) See §652.

Should we ever . . . . : "would" would be a less ambiguous translation, and *ever* is added to the German.

Or do we not do so only . . . : cp. X, 25, and apply it to this analogous case.

(c) Cp. §§477–79; Russell, *Logic*, 180b–181a.

Doesn't a presupposition . . . : when we actually do say "I am presupposing that . . . ," isn't it to remove a possible doubt? And the nature of presupposition is determined by the grammar of the word *presuppose*, that is, its customary use (§371).

may be entirely lacking: see e.g. §84, p. 224d.

Doubting has an end: cp. I, 4; Coope, "Knowledge", 249–50.

(d) See *Z* 510; NL 316–18; *BB* 51b–52a, 60b, 64a; Man. 228, §172; Köhler, *Gestalt*, 21ff; cp. *Z* 572; *PB* 265–66; *Kreis*, 59–60; 4.002.

"This is the question to which, as it seems to me, no philosopher has hitherto suggested an answer which comes anywhere near to being *certainly* true" (Moore, *Papers*, 55; see 56–58, 129–45, and idem, *Studies*, 189–90).

two different language-games: "There are propositions of which we may say that they describe facts in the material world (external world). Roughly speaking, they treat of physical objects: bodies, fluids, etc. I am not thinking in particular of the laws of the natural sciences, but of any such proposition as 'the tulips in our garden are in full bloom,' or 'Smith will come in any moment.' There are on the other hand propositions describing personal experiences, as when the subject in a psychological experiment describes his sense-experiences; say his visual experience, independent of what bodies are actually before his eyes and, *n. b.*, independent also of any processes which might be observed to take place in his retina, his nerves, his brain, or other parts of his body. (That is, independent of both physical and physiological facts.)

"At first sight it may appear . . . that here we have two kinds of worlds, worlds built of different materials; a mental world and a physical world" (*BB* 46–47).

a *simple* formula: see XXXI, 6–7; *Z* 434. The simple formula considered at length in Man. 159 is "a picture of direct and indirect"—impressions directly named, and objects constructed (§366) or inferred (§486) from them (see XXXI, 2–3). Some others:

Man. 109, 32: "A proposition in the strict sense is related to the hypothesis as the projection of a body is to the body" (see X, 6–7).

Carnap, "Psychology", 166: "Every sentence of the protocol language of some specific person is inter-translatable with some sentence of physical language, namely, with a sentence about the physical state of the person in question" (see commentary on §244b).

Schlick, "Psychological", 403: "That in which one counts ordered coincidences in inter-subjective space, is the physical; whereas that which operates by the grouping of intensive properties is a psychological description" (see X, 13).

Russell, *Logic*, 139: " 'Ideas' of chairs and tables are identical with chairs and tables, but are considered in their mental context, not in the context of physics" (see ibid., 140, 278; §366 and commentary; *BB* 45–47, quoted above).

"When realism says that images are 'only subjective representations of things', we must reply that this is based on a false comparison between an image of a thing and a picture of it" (Man. 110, 241; see §301 and commentary).

"(We can compare an object with a picture of it, but can we compare a chair with a sense-datum of it?) Realism and idealism both present false, wrongly simplified pictures of the relation between the grammar of physical objects and that of sense data" (Waismann, *Principles*, 83–84).

"It confuses everything to say 'the one is a *different kind* of object from the other'; for those who say that a sense datum is a different kind of object from a physical object misunderstand the grammar of the word 'kind', just as those who say that a number is a different kind of object from a numeral. They think they are making such a statement as 'A railway train, a railway station, and a railway car are different kinds of objects,' whereas their statement is analogous to 'A railway train, a railway accident, and a railway law are different kinds of objects' " (*BB* 64).

XXXII. Feelings Are Not
Meanings (Pp. 181–183)

(1)   The substantive *meaning,* said Wittgenstein, "makes us look for a thing that corresponds to it" (*BB* 1). Finding no sensible correlate which qualifies, we perhaps conclude that meaning is mental (§36). And realizing that no mere image is a meaning, we perhaps have recourse to feelings, as James did, to explain our thoughts (§598). By themselves, words sound much alike, "but taken dynamically, or as significant,—as *thought,*—their fringes of relation, their affinities and repugnances, their function and meaning, are felt and understood to be absolutely opposed" (James, *Principles,* I, 265). "These feelings of relation, these psychic overtones, halos, suffusions, or fringes about the terms, may be the same in very different systems of imagery" (ibid., 269). The essential thing is "the mysterious *plus,* the understood meaning" (ibid., 478).

(2)   Mysterious it surely is, in James's account. For on the one hand, when for instance "we use a common noun, such as *man,* in a universal sense, as signifying all possible men, we are fully aware of this intention on our part, and distinguish it carefully from our intention when we mean a certain group of men, or a solitary individual before us" (ibid., 256). Yet on the other hand, unlike stable sensorial images "these bare images of logical movement . . . are psychic transitions, always on the wing, so to speak, and not to be glimpsed except in flight" (ibid., 253). "Let anyone try to cut a thought across in the middle and get a look at its section, and he will see how difficult the introspective observation of the transitive tracts is. . . . The attempt at introspective analysis in these cases is in fact like seizing a spinning top to catch its motion, or trying to turn up the gas quickly enough to see how the darkness looks" (ibid., 244). "It is as if a snapshot of a scene had been taken, but only a few scattered details of it were to be seen: here a hand, there a bit of face, or a hat—the rest is dark. And now it is as if we knew quite certainly what the whole picture represented. As if I could read the darkness" (§635).

(3)   Wittgenstein's reaction was not to claim better night vision than

James, but rather: "I cannot accept his testimony because it is not *testimony*. It only tells me what he is *inclined* to say" (§386). For James did not observe and identify all those meanings and relations in his mind, as genuine instances of negation, conclusion, universality, and the rest. How could he? The experiences bore no labels (pp. 190ab, 231e). Rather, he was already familiar with the meanings (§89) and *explained* them to himself by hypothesizing a feeling for each: "When we read such phrases as 'naught but', 'either one or the other', '*a* is *b*, but', 'although it is, nevertheless', 'it is an excluded middle, there is no *tertium quid*,' and a host of other verbal skeletons of logical relation, is it true that there is nothing more in our minds than the words themselves as they pass? What then is the meaning of the words which we think we understand as we read? What makes that meaning different in one phrase from what it is in the other? 'Who?' 'When?' 'Where?' Is the difference of felt meaning in these interrogatives nothing more than their difference of sound? And is it not (just like the difference of sound itself) known and understood in an affection of consciousness correlative to it, though so impalpable to direct examination? Is not the same true of such negatives as 'no', 'never', 'not yet'?" (James, *Principles*, I, 252).
(4)   This picture held James captive (§115). The use of a word, the system in which it functions, the speaker's mastery—these did not occur to him as possible constituents of meaning. Meaning had to be in the mind. But what good would it do if it were? If the feeling is hidden from the speaker himself, how does it help him? Even if it were patent, how *could* it guide him (p. 181cd)? And what would anyone else know about it (p. 181ab)? Furthermore, why suppose that there is any one feeling constantly associated with the word? May there not be many (p. 181g)? May there not sometimes be none (p. 216a)? Can the feeling never occur without the word (p. 182e)? And do I have any reason to suppose that others have the same as I (pp. 181b, 219a)? With such telling blows as these—Mill's methods in reverse, as it were—does Wittgenstein demolish James's myth of meanings in the mind. They were not the result of observation, so are not refuted by observation. The fly is led out by the way it entered (§309): James said there *must* be feelings, so Wittgenstein destroys the *must* (see GI 58). Towards the end of the section he hints at the kernel of truth in James's view, which he will examine at length in Section XXXVII.

DETAILED COMMENTARY

P. 181(ab) Suppose someone said: cp. §117; Frege, "Justification", 156 ("a firm new focus about which images gather"). James, named in *EPB* 218, is clearly in view. See XXXII, 1–2; James, *Principles*, I, 265 (quoted

in XXVIII, 2), 476–77, e.g.: "If each 'idea' stand for some special nascent nerve-process, then the aggregate of these nascent processes
might have for its conscious correlate a psychic 'fringe', which should
be just that universal meaning, or intention that the name or mental
picture employed should mean all the possible individuals of the class."

Just as if each figure . . . : see James, *Principles,* I, 478, e.g.: "The
generic character of either sharp image or blurred image depends on
its being felt *with its representative function.* This function is the mysterious *plus,* the understood meaning. . . . It is just that staining, fringe, or
halo of obscurely felt relation to masses of other imagery about to
come, but not yet distinctly in focus, which we have so abundantly set
forth (in Chapter IX)." "We apprehended it, in short, with a cloud of
associates" (ibid., II, 81).

in another dimension: cp. XXXVII, 2–3; commentary on §559
("meaning-body"); Man. 229, §§710–11 (quoted for §138).

Only let us . . . : see the commentary on §48a ("the method of §2").

Then we see that . . . : see §337; *Z* 236; *BB* 147; *PG* 148b.

intention: for the broad sense the word has here, see James, *Principles,* I, 256c (quoted for §138), and above ("that universal meaning, or
intention"); or GI 37, on intention as the projective act which gives
sense to signs, mental or verbal (see *PB* 63). Against this conception W.
argued: "If God had looked into our minds he would not have been
able to see there whom we were speaking of" (p. 217). "And if we are
supposed to give an account of what the 'meaning' of the word is, we
first pull out *one* from this mass of pictures—and then reject it again as
non-essential when we see that now this, now that, picture presents itself, and sometimes none at all" (*RFM* 7).

goes for *us:* see p. 219a; *Z* 179.

without knowing if . . . : see p. 176h; *BB* 79a. If we think of language as a means of communication (§242)—whether of thoughts
(§304) or of knowledge (§363) or in some broader sense (§491)—this
beetle drops out (cp. §293). James, the pragmatist, neglected prag-
matics.

"If for an expression to convey a meaning means to be accompanied
by or to produce certain experiences, our expression may have all sorts
of meanings, and I don't wish to say anything about them" (*BB* 65).

(cd) See I, 6; p. 59n; *EPB* 229–30; *BB* 147cd; Man. 302, 6; Kenny,
Wittgenstein, 142; Hallett, *Definition,* 73b; cp. pp. 175d, 176def, 218efg.

understanding was an inner process: as in Man. 110, 52–53; or in
James (e.g. *Principles,* I, 281); or in Moore (XXXVII, 21). See IX,
11–13; §§152–54, 197.

chess: see the commentary on §31.

what we are interested in: cp. Frege, *Writings*, 186a ("that train of thought which accompanied the affair for us and actually made it interesting").

criteria for the 'inner states': see XXII, 2; p. 59n.

"We might say to someone, 'Raise your finger the moment the pain stops,' but not, 'Raise your finger the moment you no longer know how to play chess.' At the very least there will be this difference: to be able to say whether the pain has stopped I need not try to do anything, whereas I might need to try reciting some rules of chess or try making a few moves in order to learn whether I could still play chess. (Contrast 'in pain' with 'sore to the touch'.) Again I could confidently plan to deceive someone into thinking that I am in pain, i.e. plan to act the part without being in pain, but I could not, by acting the part of a chess player, deceive someone who knew the game into thinking that I could play chess—or at least I could not do so without the aid of a confederate giving me signals. Or again, I might be shown by someone that I only imagined that I understood a certain word, that the explanation I would have given of it or the use I would have made of it is actually confused, whereas I could not be shown by someone that my arthritic fingers do not really hurt, that I haven't been in pain at all" (Cook, "Human Beings", 139). On this last point, see p. 53n.

Even if someone had . . . : see §179; cp. §646b; *PP* 260b (quoted for §6b).

(e) See p. 176gh; Hallett, *Definition*, 48–73.

"No word in an understood sentence comes to consciousness as a mere noise. We feel its meaning as it passes; and although our object differs from one moment to another as to its verbal kernel or nucleus, yet it is *similar* throughout the entire segment of the stream" (James, *Principles*, I, 281). "We have the idea that it is the sentence's sense, composed of the meanings of its words" (Man. 229, §993; see ibid., §988).

The meaning of a word: see §43 and commentary.

the sense of a sentence: see §20b and commentary, and Section XVII.

is not a complex: cp. §§20, 544, 559, and commentary; *BB* 78; *PG* 108 (quoted for p. 176g).

"I still haven't seen him yet": a loaded sample. Nothing comes to mind for *still* and *yet* (*noch* and *immer*); and the content for *have* and for *seen* is negated (cp. §§545, 548–49); and " 'I' is not the name of a person" (§410); and "how does he call HIM to mind?" (§691).

James had claimed that a negative, too, such as *no, never, not yet,* is "known and understood in an affection of consciousness correlative to it, though so impalpable to direct examination" (*Principles*, I, 252).

(f) See Man. 229, §§988–89.

one would like to say: "It is just like the 'overtones' in music. Different instruments give the 'same note', but each in a different voice, because each gives more than that note, namely, various upper harmonics of it which differ from one instrument to another" (James, *Principles*, I, 258). Similarly, "every definite image in the mind is steeped and dyed in the free water that flows round it . . . leaving it, it is true, an image of the same *thing* it was before, but making it an image of that thing newly taken and freshly understood" (ibid., 255). So too "we ought to say a feeling of *and*, and a feeling of *if*, a feeling of *but*, and a feeling of *by*, quite as readily as we say a feeling of *blue* or a feeling of *cold*" (ibid., 245–46); yet whenever these words occur in a sentence that is understood, "the total idea may be and usually is present not only before and after the phrase has been spoken, but also whilst each separate word is uttered. It is the overtone, halo, or fringe of the word, *as spoken in that sentence*" (ibid., 281).

a single physiognomy: see §568, pp. 210f, 218l; *BB* 174.

"Look at a written word, say 'read',—'It isn't just a scribble, it's "read",' I should like to say, 'it has one definite physiognomy.' But what is it that I am really saying about it? What is this statement, straightened out? 'The word falls,' one is tempted to explain, 'into a mould of my mind *long* prepared for it' " (*BB* 170). "The gap of one word does not feel like the gap of another, all empty of content as both might seem necessarily to be when described as gaps" (James, *Principles*, I, 251).

But a face . . . : hence the 'meaning' is not necessarily something mental, spiritual. See *BB* 4bc.

looks at us too: but does not do so constantly (p. 205jk; cp. pp. 215h–216a).

(g) "William James speaks of specific feelings accompanying the use of such words as 'and', 'if', 'or'. And there is no doubt that at least certain gestures are often connected with such words, as a collecting gesture with 'and', and a dismissing gesture with 'not'. And there obviously are visual and muscular sensations connected with these gestures. On the other hand it is clear enough that these sensations do not accompany every use of the word 'not' and 'and'. . . . Ask yourself: 'When I said, "Give me an apple *and* a pear, *and* leave the room," had I the same feeling when I pronounced the two words "and"?' " (*BB* 78–79).

"At the same time I am not at all prepared to say that I recognize this to be the way 'red' has always come on such occasions, nor even to say that there are, say, four ways, A, B, C, D, in one of which it always comes" (*BB* 159). See *BB* 156b.

if-feeling: see James, *Principles*, I, 245–46, above. The quotation just given from *BB* 78 suggests that W. may have focused on the if-feeling, rather than the and-feeling or not-feeling, as being the most ethereal of all and most clearly a fiction. There is not even an if-gesture.

P. 182(bc) See §140, p. 175d; Man. 229, §878.

"If in some language the word 'but' meant what 'not' means in English, it is clear that we should not compare the meanings of the these two words by comparing the sensations which they produce" (*BB* 79).

(d) the obvious correlate of a meaning: by which we explain our thought (§598). The word, thought James, always has "*one* character" (p. 181f), and only it has it (p. 182e). Or rather, only a word with that meaning has it. Hence it is not so much the correlate of a word as of a meaning. See the quotation for p. 181e, from James, *Principles*, I, 252.

(e) 'atmosphere': see §§117a, 594a, 609, p. 66n.

why does one regard it . . . : for one thing, because the existence of the feeling is suggested by the word (§598); to a large extent, it is a "grammatical fiction" (§307). For another thing, because the word itself is experienced in the manner examined by Section XXXVII. Both answers ground the declaration to which this question leads: "The if-feeling is not a feeling which accompanies the word 'if'."

(f) See the preceding comments.

(g) a musical phrase: see §527; cp. p. 214d.

"a gesture": cp. §§550, 610b; *BB* 78, quoted for p. 181g.

(h) See XXXVII, 14; cp. §§537, 592; *Z* 198; *BB* 184 ("Can I separate what I call this experience of pastness from the experience of hearing the tune? Or, can I separate an experience of pastness expressed by a gesture from the experience of making this gesture? Can I discover something, the essential feeling of pastness, which remains after abstracting all those experiences which we might call the experiences of expressing the feeling?").

(j) a quite special feeling: see §542, p. 66n (and commentary); cp. §165.

P. 183 See *PG* 175.

(a) that can be separated: see the references above, for p. 182h.

a different concept: different from that of an accompanying feeling. Cp. p. 196d.

A different game: see §609; cp. p. 180d.

(b) See *LC* 37–40.

is this passage: not something separate or separable, just as the rabbit aspect is not something separate or separable from the duck-rabbit sketch (p. 194).

played like *this*: cp. §534, p. 188m; *LC* 40bc.

could only *hint* at it: cp. commentary on §527; §210, pp. 186, 191d; Man. 232, 727.

"I think you would say it gives you experiences which can't be described. First of all it is, of course, not true that whenever we hear a piece of music or a line of poetry which impresses us greatly, we say: 'This is indescribable.' But it is true that again and again we do feel inclined to say: 'I can't describe my experience' " (*LC* 37).

(cde) On paragraphs (*def*) see §137; *EPB* 184; *PG* 175–79; Man. 229, §909; Man. 115, 27.

Thus the atmosphere: *thus* is misplaced. A better translation: "The atmosphere that is inseparable from its object—is therefore not an atmosphere." See *BB* 178, e.g.: "If you heard sentences spoken in a monotone, you might be tempted to say that the words were all enshrouded in a particular atmosphere. But wouldn't it be using a peculiar way of representation to say that speaking the sentence in a monotone was adding something to the mere saying of it? Couldn't we even conceive speaking in a monotone as the result of *taking away* from the sentence its inflexion?"

which we *have* associated: not which of their very nature engage with one another, like cogwheels (§136c). "A peculiarity which distinguishes such experiences, such non-separable 'halos', from 'the sensations we get from skin, muscle, viscus, eye, ear, nose, and palate' is their dependence on training, custom, or previous experience (PI 209)" (Hallett, *Definition*, 60; see James, *Principles*, I, 222c). Cp. *PG* 178c.

seem to fit: see §§171a, 537, p. 215f and commentary; Man. 229, §1010; cp. §§37, 136–38; NL 292; James, *Principles*, I, 261–63.

Do we try?: cp. *Z* 198, e.g.: "Here I am inclined to say: 'It is *very difficult* to separate the familiarity from the impression of the face.' But I also feel that this is a bad way of putting things. For I have no notion how I should so much as *try* to separate these two things. The expression 'to separate them' does not have any clear sense for me." "In this case *we* have not *determined* what thinking away the familiarity is to mean" (*PG* 175).

(f) See JN 48, quoted for p. 209g.

XXXIII. Dreaming (P. 184)

GENERAL COMMENTARY

(1) We may wonder, wrote Russell, whether "the whole outer world is nothing but a dream" (*Problems*, 7), but our dreaming we cannot doubt. "It is our particular thoughts and feelings that have primitive certainty. And this applies to dreams and hallucinations as well as to normal per-

ceptions" (ibid., 8). Wittgenstein would not doubt the dreaming. But, once again (X, 24–25), he does question this picture of "primitive certainty"—this "solid basis from which to begin our pursuit of knowledge" (Russell, *Problems*, 8; see X, 3)—and the psychologist semantics which it implies (X, 4–5).

(2)   Here too, "if I assume the abrogation of the normal language-game . . . I need a criterion of identity . . . and then the possibility of error also exists" (§288). But how would such a criterion get established (X, 20–21)? "Well, the mind confers it" (see p. 184d). To this response, the target of Section X, the whole last paragraph of p. 184 may be applied, word for word. Wittgenstein has not digressed. It is because he is dealing with just such a nebulous picture, and no definable theory, that he has employed the therapy of language-game and pointed question, rather than refutation (GI 68). His aim is to challenge and change the picture, not to replace it with a theory, even an implicit one of the kind some commentators suppose when they take therapy for refutation.

DETAILED COMMENTARY

P. 184(ab) Cp. Z 530. Man. 116, 246, discusses dream reports in the manner of §290 and p. 218bc: "The language-game begins with the dream report."

Then we teach them . . . : W. does not consider this the standard form of learning (cp. §§31b, 54b). In Man. 229, §1042, the child hears others talk of their dreams, then speaks in like manner. See the next quotation.

That is the language-game: on the reasons for this approach, avoiding the complexities of actual learning and subsequent dream-talk, see GI 56 and 62.

I have assumed here . . . : this falsifies nothing, but highlights the absence of private criteria. "The question is not precisely 'How does he learn the use of the word,' but, 'How is it shown that he uses it as we do?' " (Man. 229, §1043). And the answer is the same in this imagined language-game as in the ordinary one between people who dream: There is no way of checking to see if the learner is applying the term "correctly" to his inner experiences. Verification stops at behavior; so that is the criterion (§354). As for the dreamer, he follows no criteria when he recounts his dream (GI 15–16).

invisible presence: W. was familiar with James's pages on this topic (*Varieties*, 59–72).

whether people are deceived by their memories: with regard to the contents as well as to images. Does it make sense to ask: "Are you sure it was Hijab you dreamed of and not someone else"? (JN 62). No, "this too we cannot ask: 'How do I know that I *really* dreamed that?'—It's the content because I *say* it's the content" (Man. 229, §1030). Cp. Hunter, *Essays*, 74–86.

whether it merely seems so: Hunter formulates and discusses the question: "*Is it possible that we do not experience anything when we dream, but that something happens in our brains when we sleep, and because of this, when we awake it seems to us that we have had the experiences that we call dreams?*" (*Essays*, 67–72).

is it because we are sure . . . : cp. §265.

" 'I meant it rather as an exaggeration.' My having meant it that way consists partly in my saying so. (Compare with a dream and recounting the dream after one wakes.)" (*EPB* 226–27).

"There is no question here of trusting his memory. He 'remembered' but it was a new kind of remembering. He introduced us to a new language game. He used the past tense, words like 'remember' and so on: but we had to make a *new kind of use* of these statements" (JN 35; cp. JN 36–37; §634).

"One would like to object here that a person who is telling a dream speaks in the past tense *because* he is reporting something that took place in the past while he slept, namely, his dream. The objection rests on the idea that his report corresponds to his dream in the same way that my report of yesterday's events corresponds to them. This is wrong. It is senseless to suppose that his dream differed from his report of it unless this means that he might change, add to, or contradict his report. No one knows what it would mean to 'verify' his report. Others use his report as their criterion of what his dream was. In contrast, no one uses my report of the events of yesterday's robbery as his *criterion* of what actually happened: there are familiar ways of confirming or disconfirming my report, independently of my inclination or disinclination to amend or contradict it. . . . What I am trying to show is that *if* one thinks that a man's account of his dream is related to his dream just as my account of yesterday's happenings is related to them, one is in a hopeless difficulty: for then it *would* appear that our ostensible remembering that we dreamt such-and-such could be mistaken, not just once but all the time. If the report of the dream is 'externally' related to the dream, then it may be that we are always only under the *illusion* of having had a dream, an illusion that comes to us as we awake" (Malcolm, "Dreaming", 30–31; see XXXIII, 1–2).

suppose it were a man . . . : see pp. 222j–223a.

(c) This is expanded in Man. 229, §1036.

It will turn on the use . . . : cp. §499, p. 179e.

(d) See Man. 174, 4.

"The mind seems . . .": see XXXIII, 2; cp. II, 2–7; X, 4–17.

it is a picture: whose sense remains to be determined or explained, whereas saying that it seem to be *so* suggests clarity of sense, unsureness about the fact.

(ef) The evolution of the . . . : the connection with the preceding statement on the marvels of the mind (cp. §§110, 428) appears in *BB* 47: "It seems to us sometimes as though the phenomena of personal experience were in a way phenomena in the upper strata of the atmosphere as opposed to the material phenomena which happen on the ground. There are views according to which these phenomena in the upper strata arise when the material phenomena reach a certain degree of complexity. E.g., that the mental phenomena, sense experience, volition, etc., emerge when a type of animal body of a certain complexity has evolved. There seems to be some obvious truth in this, for the amoeba certainly doesn't speak or write or discuss, whereas we do." But see §25 and commentary.

The picture: Schopenhauer's. "Thus animals existed before men, fishes before land animals, plants before fishes, and the inorganic before that which is organic; consequently the original mass had to go through a long series of changes before the first eye could be opened" (*World*, I, 30). "As with the appearance of the sun the visible world makes its appearance, so at one stroke does the understanding through its one simple function convert the dull meaningless sensation into perception" (ibid., 12). "Thus what the eye is in space and for sensuous knowledge, reason is, to a certain extent, in time and for inner knowledge" (ibid., 84). "The will, which hitherto followed its tendency in the dark with extreme certainty and infallibility, has at this stage kindled a light for itself" (ibid., 150).

is still obscure: cp. e.g. §§352a, 374, 422–24, p. 178g.

the picture seems to spare us this work: cp. §§352b, 425–26.

XXXIV. "Kinaesthetic Sensations" (Pp. 185–186)

GENERAL COMMENTARY

(1)   When Wittgenstein returned to philosophy in 1929, his interest centered still on the logic of the world as perceived through the logic of language (GI 30). And he still dreamed of constructing a language which would lay that logic bare (X, 8). Having passed from truth-conditions in the abstract to mode of verification in the concrete as the determinant of sense (see commentary on §353), he took special interest in

the relation between statements of physical fact and the sense experiences which verify them. "We distinguish the evidence for the occurrence of a physical event according to the various kinds of such evidence: heard, seen, measured, etc., and we see that in each one of these categories there is a formal element of order, which we can call space" (*PB* 140). Thus suppose I want to know what is happening behind me, and turn around. "If I were prevented, wouldn't the idea still remain that space stretches round about me? And that I can succeed in seeing the objects which are now behind me by turning around. *Therefore* it's the possibility of turning around which leads me to that representation of space. Thus the resulting space around me is a combined visual space and *space of muscular feeling*" (*PB* 102). "Someone may say that I feel the position of my body without seeing it. But position in feeling space (as I would like for the moment to call it) has nothing to do with position in visual space; the two are independent of one another" (*PB* 257). It is the geometry of these individual spaces and their interrelations which we must discern if we would learn the structure of composite space, that is, the space of physical objects—of their shapes, movements, and locations—including our own bodies.

(2)   However, whether in stating the relation between objects and sense-data, or in formulating a notation to mirror the relation, Wittgenstein encountered enormous difficulties of expression (see commentary on §§106, 120). "It seems as though we had first to construct the whole structure of space without using propositions" (*PB* 216). For consider a proposition like "My finger moves." As evidence for this statement I might adduce, "I see it move" or "I feel it move" (*BB* 51). But now I have mentioned the finger and its movement, not just the visual or kinesthetic datum (*BB* 52). And there seems no way to express the datum more directly (*PB* 103b; XXXI, 2–4), in isolation, without bringing in the hypothesis about a physical event (see X, 6–7; Man. 176, 16A). "The reason for this peculiarity of our language is of course the regular coincidence of certain sense experiences. Thus when I feel my arm moving I mostly also can see it moving. And if I touch it with my hand, also that hand feels the motion, etc. . . . We feel in such cases a strong need for such an expression as: 'a sensation travels from my tactual cheek to my tactual eye.' I said all this because, if you are aware of the tactual and kinaesthetic environment of a pain, you may find a difficulty in imagining that one could have toothache anywhere else than in one's own teeth. But if we imagine such a case, this simply means that we imagine a correlation between visual, tactual, kinaesthetic, etc., experiences different from the ordinary correlation. Thus we can imagine a person having the sensation of toothache plus those tactual and kinaesthetic experiences which are normally bound up with

seeing his hand travelling from his tooth to his nose, to his eyes, etc., but correlated to the visual experience of his hand moving to those places in another person's face" (*BB* 52; cp. X, 13).

(3)   The present critique of these earlier views picks out kinesthetic sensations for special attention, and concentrates on two related errors: (a) the idea that there is anything which could appropriately be called a kinesthetic sensation of moving one's finger or moving one's hand to one's eye; and (b) the notion that the sensations we do have in moving our members regularly reveal to us their positions and movements. On the other hand, it would be mistaken to suppose, as some have, that Wittgenstein denied that we have any characteristic feelings (noted, correlated, or not) when we move our limbs, or that we ever learn the position of our limbs from sensations in them (characteristic or other) (p. 185e).

(4)   The point is this: The supposed parallel between "I see it move" and "I feel it move" (*BB* 51) is deceptive. "We call seeing, hearing . . . sense perceptions. There are analogies and connexions between these concepts; these are our justification for so taking them together" (*Z* 474). But the justification does not extend to "kinaesthetic sensations". For suppose we ask what is common to sense perceptions. "The answer that they give us knowledge of the external world is partly wrong and partly right" (*Z* 477). It is wrong in so far as it suggests a merely contingent connection between such sensations and physical objects (*BB* 52; §354). "It is right in so far as it is supposed to point to a *logical* criterion" (*Z* 477). Thus it is not a lesson of experience "that there is rain when we have certain sensations of wet and cold, or such-and-such visual impressions" (§354). These are (partial) criteria of rain. But is there any such connection between a muscular feeling, say, or sensation in the joint, and the bent position of one's arm or the movements of one's fingers? Is there a bent-arm feeling as there is a cold-rain feeling or green-tree look? No, here the relation is reversed. Thus if you do not know in the normal way whether your arm is stretched out, you may find out by a piercing pain in the elbow (p. 185e), but such a sensation is not a criterion of the position. And if, when subjected to an electric current with your eyes closed, you say, "I am moving my arm up and down" (§624), a feeling may account for this impression; but the logical status of the feeling, in comparison say with sight, is made clear enough by your readily accepting the testimony of those observing you, or of your own eyes when you open them and see your arm at rest (cp. §625). No conflict of criteria then arises, creating a situation like that described in §80.

(5)   With this background, Jackson's jottings (JN 21) become more readily intelligible: "Compare 'I can tell you without looking that my

elbows are bent at more than 90°.' People have said 'You must have a feeling that tells you that.' But (i) there are no such feelings; and (ii) if the *feelings* are asked for then it's a matter of remembering that you feel your cuff or a tightness of your pullover, or something like that. Again people have said 'There is a specific sense organ in your joint—there are means of getting, say kinaesthetic sensations which advise you.' The evidence is that if certain tendons around the joint, say, are cut then you can't say where your arm is. All right: no one denies this, no one denies that this may be a valuable discovery. Nor does anyone deny that sometimes there's a special feeling in, say your joint and that you may infer experientially from this that your elbow is crooked at more than 90°. But it is the case that sometimes on being asked I give the right answer and that I do not so infer the answer. I do not even have this feeling. I just know where my arm is. There is perhaps an unavoidable wish to hypostatize a feeling here." (See commentary on §598.)

(6) James still more than Wittgenstein felt this temptation. A similar doctrine of kinesthetic sensations underlay his account of voluntary action. In addition to the impressions upon remote organs of sense, he wrote, "we have, whenever we perform a movement ourselves, another set of impressions, those, namely, which come up from the parts that are actually moved. These *kinaesthetic* impressions, as Dr. Bastian has called them, are so many *resident* effects of the motion. Not only are our muscles supplied with afferent as well as with efferent nerves, but the tendons, the ligaments, the articular surfaces, and the skin about the joints are all sensitive, and, being stretched and squeezed in ways characteristic of each particular movement, give us as many distinctive feelings as there are movements possible to perform.

"It is by these resident impressions that we are made conscious of *passive movements*—movements communicated to our limbs by others. If you lie with closed eyes, and another person noiselessly places your arm or leg in any arbitrarily chosen attitude, you receive an accurate feeling of what attitude it is, and can immediately reproduce it yourself in the arm or leg of the opposite side. Similarly a man waked suddenly from sleep in the dark is aware of how he finds himself lying" (*Principles*, II, 488). "All these cases," he remarks two pages later, "whether spontaneous or experimental, show the absolute need of *guiding sensations* of some kind for the successful carrying out of a concatenated series of movements. It is, in fact, easy to see that, just as where the chain of movements is automatic . . . , each later movement of the chain has to be discharged by the impression which the next earlier one makes in being executed, so also, where the chain is voluntary, we need to know at each movement just *where we are in it,* if we are to will intelligently what the next link shall be." "We may consequently set it down as certain that, *whether or no there be anything else in the mind at the moment when we consciously will a certain act, a mental conception made up of memory-images of these sensations, defining which special act it is, must be there*" (ibid., 492).

(7) Malcolm's notes make explicit the connection between the present section and this Jamesean conception of willing, similar to one Wittgenstein himself had once held (see XXIV, 6–7): "In order to move my arm voluntarily I must know what position it is in and whether I have moved it. Now how do I know what the position of my hand is, when I am not looking at it or feeling it with the other hand? How do I know, e.g., that my fingers are bent? There is a temptation to say 'I feel that they are bent.' This is a peculiar reply. For do you always have a certain feeling when your fingers are bent in that way; have you always noticed that feeling; and what feeling is it?

"The feeling that my fingers are bent: is it subject to more and less, to *degrees*, as are feelings of temperature and pressure? No. This may show that 'I feel that my fingers are bent' means nothing different from 'I know that they are bent.' If we try to say what feelings of temperature, pressure, etc. go to make up this feeling that my fingers are bent, we shall see that it is not easy to say what they are, and furthermore we see that we rarely have them" (*Memoir*, 48–49; see §625).

DETAILED COMMENTARY

P. 185(ab) See XXIV, 6–7; XXXIV, 1–2, 6; §§624–25; end of Man. 131 and start of Man. 132.

"I feel my arm and in a queer way I should now like to say: I feel it in a definite position in space; as if the feeling of my body in a space were disposed in the shape of an arm, so that in order to represent it I should have to model my arm, in plaster say, in the right position" (Z 480). In *BB* 63–64 W. had written: "If, e.g., my eyes are shut, I can still have the characteristic kinaesthetic experience in my arm which I should call the kinaesthetic experience of raising my hand to my eye. That I had succeeded in doing so, I shall recognize by the peculiar tactile sensation of touching my eye. But if my eye were behind a glass plate fastened in such a way that it prevented me from exerting a pressure on my eye with my finger, there would still be a criterion of muscular sensation which would make me say that now my finger was in front of my eye." Such is the conception here criticized.

Not at all in the joint: "If sensations are characteristic of the position and movements of the limbs, at any rate their place is not the joint" (Z 483).

James had written: "Our feelings of our own movement are principally due to the sensibility of our rotating *joints*. Sometimes by fixing the attention, say on our elbow-joint, we can feel the movement in the joint itself; but we always are simultaneously conscious of the path which during the movement our finger-tips describe through the air, and yet these same finger-tips themselves are in no way physically modified by the motion" (*Principles*, II, 38). "*We indubitably localize the finger-tip at the successive points of its path by means of the sensations which we receive from our joints*" (ibid., 193; see 189–97). "Thus the sensations to which our joints give rise when they rotate are signs of what, through a large number of other sensations, tactile and optical, we have come to know as the movement of the whole limb" (ibid., 41).

And this sensation advises me . . . : "Make the same movement with the right and left thumb, and judge whether the kinesthetic sensations are the same!—Do you have a memory-image of the kinesthetic sensation while walking?—When you are tired, or in pain, or have sore muscles, or smarting skin—are the sensations during the limb's movement the same as in *another* situation? But are you sometimes in doubt then whether you have really raised your leg yet, since the feeling is so different?" (Man. 229, §1049; see §1055).

describe the movement exactly: without looking.

(c) "So it is not really as if I felt the position of my arm, but as if I felt my *arm*, and the feeling had such-and-such a *position*. But that means only: I simply *know* how it is—without knowing it *because*. . . . Just as I also know where I feel pain—but do not know it because. . . ." (Z 481). For this comparison, see (*d*).

"But after all . . .": this is clearly James's reasoning, for instance in *Principles*, II, 488 (see XXXIV, 6). The fact that "a man waked suddenly from sleep in the dark is aware of how he finds himself lying" is taken as proof that he has a feeling of his position.

"knowing" it only means: the remark stresses "the difference between 'knowing' and 'being aware of' " (Z 85); it does not exclude other acts of knowledge ("for instance, I look in that direction"). "We are tempted to think that there is one particular psychical state or event, the knowledge of the place, which must precede every deliberate act of pointing, moving towards, etc." (*BB* 50).

being able to describe it: "One *knows* the position of one's limbs and their movements. One can give them if asked, for example" (Z 483).

"If I point to the painful spot on my arm, in what sense can I be said to have known where the pain was before I pointed to the place? Before I pointed I could have said 'The pain is in my left arm' " (*BB* 50).

for instance, I look: and this is not a mere consequence or symptom of knowing, but a characteristic criterion.

(d) "No local sign about the sensation. Any more than a temporal sign about a memory-image. (Temporal signs in a photograph.)" (Z 483).

some feature of our pain: see Z 481 (quoted above); OC 417; BB 50;

cp. Z 498, 510–11. James opens his discussion of "Local Signs" with the remark: "Every sensation of the skin and every visceral sensation seems to derive from its topographic seat a peculiar shade of feeling, which it would not have in another place" (*Principles*, II, 155). After illustrating these "local colorings" in the case of pain (ibid., 156), he offers an explanation of how a pain at a single point may reveal its location: "*The peculiar feeling of the first point* SUGGESTS *the feeling of the entire region with whose stimulation its own excitement has been habitually* ASSOCIATED" (ibid., 158).

and some feature of our memory image: cp. §166b; see Russell, *Mind*, 163, 177 (both quoted for §598); and James, *Principles*, I, 605: "What is the *original* of our experience of pastness, from whence we get the meaning of the term? It is this question which the reader is invited to consider in the present chapter. We shall see that we have a constant feeling *sui generis* of pastness, to which every one of our experiences in turn falls a prey. To think a thing as past is to think it amongst the objects or in the direction of the objects which at the present moment appear affected by this quality. This is the original of our notion of past time, upon which memory and history build their systems."

(e) A sensation *can* advise us . . . : "For naturally we do have movement feelings and *can* reproduce them too" (Man. 229, §1056; see Z 478–79).

"There *could* be cases in which I knew the position of my hand by a certain feeling. Also it may be true that if my hand were anaesthetized I should *not* know its position. But from this it does not follow that normally I know the position of my hand by certain sensations" (Malcolm's notes, *Memoir*, 49). And the sensations in question would not be the sensation "of having my hand open" or "of having my arm stretched out", but e.g. "a piercing pain in the elbow".

(f) What is the criterion . . . : it is, for instance, my ability to describe the shape and color after having the impression; I need not be able to state any "correlation between visual, tactual, kinaesthetic, etc., experiences" (*BB* 52) as evidence that I really derived the description from the impression (cp. §§380, 486). And the same is true of the sensations which inform me of the movement or position of a limb.

(gh) I use words . . . : e.g. "a piercing pain in the elbow". But can we give a similar description of a "finger-movement feeling"?

And now: what do you . . . : can you say "I have an *intense* feeling of my fingers being crossed," or, "The feeling of their being crossed is in the joints," as you might speak of an intense pain in the joints? (Cp. p. 186c.) Consider too "the duration of sensation. Compare the duration of a sense-experience of sound with the duration of the sensation of touch which informs you that you have a ball in your hand; and with the 'feeling' that informs you that your knees are bent" (Z 478). The word *feeling* is in scare quotes because sensations, feelings, "all have genuine duration. Possibility of giving the beginning and the end. Possibility of their being synchronized, of simultaneous occurrence" (Z 472).

"something special and indefinable": see the commentary on p. 66n and §610; cp. Helmholtz, *Optik*, 583. "At most," wrote James, "I can say to my friends, Go to certain places and act in certain ways, and these objects will probably come" (*Principles*, I, 221).

it must be possible . . . : see the comments on §182c (Wittgenstein's reply to Moore); Man. 138, 31B–32A; cp. §208a. "Once as a child I asked someone what the word 'etwas' meant. The answer was: 'You don't understand it yet.' But how should it have been explained? By a definition? Or should he have said the word was indefinable? I don't know how I later learned it, but probably I learned to use phrases in which the word occurs. I listened & observed how adults spoke & imitated them" (Man. 116, 34). "Whoever has not mastered a language, I can train to mastery; whoever has mastered it, I can remind of the manner of the training, or describe it" (Man. 164, 90–91).

(i) the grammatical difference: between the grammar of sensations and this talk about "feelings" of position and movement. See XXXIV, 4; and the comments on (*gh*). Z 472 continues thus on sensations: "All have degrees and qualitative mixtures. Degree: scarcely perceptible— unendurable. In this sense there is not a sensation of position or movement."

P. 186(a) Cp. commentary on p. 185gh; §378, pp. 183b, 193j–194a; *PB* 200c; *LC* 38b.

is this a description of a feeling?: is the feeling thus distributed in space or time (p. 187i)? "If someone told me, 'Bend your arm and call forth the characteristic feeling for it,' and I bent my arm, wouldn't I now have to ask: 'What feeling did you mean? A slight tension in the biceps, or a feeling in the skin on the inner side of the elbow joint? . . . And I would often have to say, too, that I felt *nothing*" (Man. 229, §1426; see p. 185b).

And what kind . . . must it be?: e.g. "slight tension in the biceps", "cutaneous feeling on the inner side of the elbow joint" (above), "a slight tension in the tip of the finger" (p. 185b). And now it no longer seems *the* elbow-bending feeling, or *the* finger-moving feeling. Instead one notes pains, pressures, tensions, and the like (cp. §645).

(b) "Do *this*, and . . .": see James, *Principles*, I, 221, quoted above.

Mustn't there be one . . . ?: see Man. 229, §1426 (quoted above), and *LC* 39: "Suppose I make a gesture and I think the gesture characteristic for the impression I get. Suppose I gave the gesture by co-ordinates and I wish to make it clear to Mr. Lewy. He might have to make an analogous gesture. His muscles, hands, etc., are differently shaped. So in one sense, he can't copy and in another sense he can. What are we to regard as the copy? 'It will depend on how such muscles contract.' But how on earth are you to know? If I make a gesture, and you are good imitators, these gestures will have to be similar, but different; the shape of the fingers, etc., is different."

(c) See §379 and commentary; NL 287bc, 288b, 301f; *Kreis,* 108a; cp. §380 and commentary; pp. 183b, 194a, 200cd, 207e (and references there); *RFM* 27f; *PG* 180d; Man. 164, 85; Man. 108, 164. "The *content* of experiences. We would like to say, 'I see red *so,*' 'I hear the note you strike *so,*' 'I feel pleasure *so,*' 'I experience sorrow *so,*' or even, 'This is what a person experiences when he is sorrowful, when he is happy,' etc. We would like to people a world, similar to the physical one, with these *this*'s and *so*'s. But this is meaningful only when there is a picture of what is *experienced* to which one can point when *saying* such things" (Man. 229, §1564).

"We could describe our trouble by saying that we feel as though we could give an experience a name without at the same time committing ourselves about its use, and in fact without any intention to use it at all" (*BB* 159).

This **looks** *so:* e.g. "This photograph looks old" (p. 185e), but not: "This photograph looks the way photographs do (be they old or new)."

this **feels** *so:* e.g. "My arm feels bent," but not: "A bent arm has a bent feeling." This latter is what the suggested "description" amounts to. "Bend your arm," it says, "and you will get the feeling." "What feeling?" "The feeling you get when you bend your arm—whatever that may be."

must be differently explained: "That is, what I refer to by the word 'this' must be independent of what is said about it" (*PB* 121). Otherwise (as in the examples just given) "my expression is moving in a circle" (*BB* 174). W.'s inveterate opposition to veiled tautology took many forms, e.g.: "All that I am saying comes to this, that Φ(x) must be an *external* description of x" (*PG* 207; *PB* 122b; see *PG* 206–8; *PB* 119d). More general still was his concern about philosophers' idle use of words. Here, "what I see, or feel, enters my sentence as a sample does; but no use is made of this sample" (*BB* 175). "What was it that happened? You concentrated on, as it were stared at, your sensations" (*BB* 159).

For examples of "external description" in analogous cases, see *BB* 179c; and for the general distinction between "transitive" and "intransitive" expressions (the principal background for the present remark), see *BB* 158–59, 162–63, 175–79.

(d) See the comments on p. 185ghi.

Our interest: see §570.

a quite *particular* kind: the italics are explained by p. 185i and commentary ("What I am looking for . . .").

It includes, for instance . . . : see the examples above, in p. 185b (a slight tension in the tip of the finger), p. 185e (a piercing pain in the elbow), and the commentary on p. 186a.

its 'place': "Place of feeling in the body: differentiates seeing and hearing from sense of pressure, temperature, taste and pain" (Z 472).

does this make it uncertain . . . : see p. 185abc and commentary.

XXXV. Expressions of Emotion (Pp. 187–189)

GENERAL COMMENTARY

(1)   The contrast between avowals and descriptions (GI 15–16) receives its fullest, most explicit treatment in this second section (see XXVII) on emotions (particularly grief and fear). Wittgenstein focuses first on the apparent parallel between inner and outer objects, which makes it plausible to suppose that a statement such as "I am afraid" reports something observed within, whereas a statement such as "There is a tree" reports something observed without. Doubtless in that supposition "I feel fear" would parallel "I see a tree," and "I observe my fear" would parallel "I observe the tree." However, the tree may exist without my seeing it, whereas grief, anger, and fear cease to exist if not "felt". And I may observe the tree as attentively as I please without producing, destroying, or altering it, whereas if I interrupt my sorrowful reflections on a loss or my angry ruminations on an injury, and, recalling the interest of such specimens, start to examine closely the state of my feelings, I surely modify them somewhat by this shift in my attitude and activity.

(2)   "So where is the science of mental phenomena? Answer: You observe your own mental happenings. How? By introspection. But if you observe, i.e., if you go about to observe your own mental happenings you alter them and create new ones; and the whole point of *observing* is that you should not do this—observing is supposed to be just the thing that avoids this. Then the science of mental phenomena has this puzzle: I can't observe the mental phenomena of others and I can't observe my own, in the proper sense of 'observe'. So where are we?" (JN 1).

(3)   No doubt James is a principal target here, for he had declared: "*Introspective Observation is what we have to rely on first and foremost and*

always. The word introspection need hardly be defined—it means, of course, the looking into our own minds and reporting what we there discover" (*Principles,* I, 185). "If to *have* feelings or thoughts in their immediacy were enough, babies in the cradle would be psychologists, and infallible ones. But the psychologist must not only *have* his mental states in their absolute veritableness, he must report them and write about them, name them, classify and compare them and trace their relations to other things. Whilst alive they are their own property; it is only *post-mortem* that they become his prey. And as in the naming, classing, and knowing of things in general we are notoriously fallible, why not also here? Comte is quite right in laying stress on the fact that a feeling, to be named, judged, or perceived, must be already past. No subjective state, whilst present, is its own object; its object is always something else" (ibid., 189–90). It would seem to follow that in order for there to be genuine "discovery" there can be no "looking" at all, but only accurate memory of something never attended to. James concluded instead that introspection is indeed difficult and fallible, but *"that the difficulty is simply that of all observation of whatever kind"* (ibid., 191). Wittgenstein denies this parity (p. 187; *BB* 171).

(4)   His target in the rest of the section can be found perfectly expressed in Stout (*Manual,* 20): "Thus when a man clenches his fist, stamps, etc., we infer that he is angry. When a dog wags its tail, we infer that it is pleased. The knowledge acquired in this way must be carefully distinguished from that which is obtained through intercommunication by means of language. When a man tells us that he is or was angry, he is not directly expressing his anger, but his knowledge of his anger. He is conveying to us the result of his own introspection." His telling results in our knowing. "It produces this mental phenomenon; everything else is inessential to the telling" (§363). Language, as usual (§304), serves to picture (GI 32) or describe (§24) reality.

(5)   So "are the words 'I am afraid' a description of a state of mind?" (p. 187k). In answer Wittgenstein notes that these words do not always serve the same purpose (p. 187l), nor necessarily any precise purpose at all (p. 188q). "Describing my state of mind . . . is something I do in a particular context" (p. 188o), and we can imagine widely varied contexts for such an expression as "I am afraid" (p. 188h). So "why should it *always* be a description of a state of mind?" (p. 189e). Besides, whether the utterance be description or avowal, "it is misleading to say that the word 'fright' signifies something which goes along with the experience of expressing fright" (NL 275; see p. 188lm; X, 20–22). Doubtless it is to avoid giving any contrary impression that Wittgenstein leaves implicit the admission that "I am afraid" might sometimes describe one's state of mind. "Description" means such varying things (§§290–91).

DETAILED COMMENTARY

P. 187(abc) See XXXV, 1–3; §672; *EPB* 204; *BB* 136fg, 177f; *PB* 88; cp. §413 and commentary; p. 193abc; Ramsey, *Foundations,* 265d–266a; Russell, *Logic,* 119a, and *Mind,* 111a.

"It seems that I am pointing out to myself what I am feeling,—as though my act of concentration was an 'inward' act of pointing, one which no one else but me is aware of, this however is unimportant. But I don't point to the feeling by attending to it. Rather, attending to the feeling means producing or modifying it. (On the other hand, observing a chair does not mean producing or modifying the chair.)" (*BB* 174).

"When we obey the order, 'Observe the colour . . . ,' what we do is to open our eyes to colour. 'Observe the colour . . .' doesn't mean 'See the colour you see.' The order, 'Look at so and so,' is of the kind, 'Turn your head in this direction'; what you will see when you do so does not enter this order. By attending, looking, you produce the impression; you can't look at the impression" (*BB* 176).

grief: see p. 174def.

which senses do you use: "I should almost like to say: One no more feels sorrow in one's body than one feels seeing in one's eyes" (*Z* 495; see *Z* 510–11). On the other hand, "could a person say: 'It seems to me that I am sad, I let my head hang so'?" (*PB* 90).

A particular sense: as in Locke (*Essay,* Bk. II, ch. 1, sec. 4; quoted by Malcolm, *Problems,* 8–9): "Such are *perception, thinking, doubting, believing, reasoning, knowing, willing,* and all the different actings of our own minds;—which we being conscious of, and observing in ourselves, do from these receive into our understandings as distinct ideas as we do from bodies affecting our senses. This source of ideas every man has wholly in himself: and though it be not sense, as having nothing to do with external objects, yet it is very like it, and might properly enough be called *internal sense.*"

See Man. 229, §778 (quoted for p. 231cd); Schopenhauer, *Freiheit,* 480; Helmholtz, *Optik,* 577.

Then do you feel it *differently*: was it somehow there before, in the organism, but felt only now (cp. §171b), by this sense which *feels* grief? James expresses (and later criticizes) such a view: "Consider, too, the difference between a sensation which we simply *have* and one which we *attend to.* Attention gives results that seem like fresh creations; and yet the feelings and elements of feeling which it reveals must have been already there—in an unconscious state" (*Principles,* I, 171).

Compare the remark in §246a, about "knowing" I am in pain: "What is it supposed to mean—except perhaps that I *am* in pain?"

is it one which . . . : the James-Lange theory asserted "that the bodily changes follow directly the perception of the exciting fact, and that our feeling of the same changes as they occur IS the emotion" (see XXVII, 3). So if being felt means being observed, it would follow that grief "is there only while it is being observed". To this W. replied: "If someone acts grief in the study, he will indeed readily become aware of the tensions in his face. But be really sad, or follow a sorrowful action in a film, and ask yourself if you were aware of your face" (Z 503).

a conceptual statement: that is, one concerning the way we use the word *observe,* though expressed in the material mode. See §371.

(defg) That is a result of observation: the statements are, not the things reported. The latter illustrate the remark, "The object of observation is something *else.*" Notice that here, where there is observation, there is also description, that is, "a representation of a distribution in a space (in that of time, for instance)" (p. 187i).

(h) See *BB* 176g, quoted above; cp. §§666 ("a way of shutting one's eyes which might be called 'looking into oneself' "), 671–72. This does not mean that the observer awaits an object of observation. Distinguish between the object and the impressions (for instance between the thicket a person watches and the movement he then detects).

(i) See the commentary on §610.

If you trained someone . . . : see Cook, "Solipsism", 58–60, for full discussion and illustration of this statement.

a particular sound: cp. §261.

A description is a representation . . . : see *Z* 482 ("And one really can describe pain spatially and temporally"); *BB* 181c; *PB* 97; *LC* 38c–39a.

"And at one place the voice of the author of the *Tractatus* is heard, like that of the drowned ghost in the song: 'A description is a projection of a distribution in a space' " (Anscombe, *Introduction,* 78).

"A description of a pain as waxing and waning would precisely be a description of the distribution of pain in the space of time; and this could not plausibly be regarded as, say, a civilized substitute for now yelling loudly and now giving only a low moan. Here one does have to bring in the idea of description as opposed to *Äusserung*" (Geach, lecture notes). To mark the distinction more sharply, "you'd choose to give a complex or a patchwork, e.g. 'first I felt a sharp pain, then it became nagging, five minutes later it stopped, two and a half minutes later it came on again but not so bad.' A really full-blown case would be a list of dinner places. Mr. A. just on the left, Mrs. B. next. . . ." (JN 30).

Objection: "But can't we describe a pain as sharp, or throbbing? And that doesn't distribute it in a space." Reply: "In my old terminology it does. It locates it in pain space, that is, in the realm of possibilities for a pain (see 2.013–2.0131). Besides, 'throbbing pain' is not a description.

But 'I have a throbbing headache' is, and that distributes the pain both in space and in time."

   in a space: for a similar echo of W.'s former terminology, see p. 200f.

   in that of time, for instance: an important addition, in this discussion of grief and fear. See Z 488 (quoted in XXVII, 5).

(j) Cp. p. 197cd.

(k) Are the words . . . : see XXXV, 5.

(l) "**A cry of fear**": as in the first sample on p. 188.

   Could I never . . . : doubtless I sometimes could (p. 188l), but that does not indicate what the answer would be. Nor do the subsequent samples, for in only three do these exact words ("I am afraid") occur, and it is not clear which expressions we should qualify as an account of how one feels, or a reflection on one's state.

P. 188(a–i) a special tone of voice: *may* be a manifestation of feeling (§582) or of a special application (§21).

   a different context: the connection with the questions in p. 187kl is indicated by p. 188o: "Describing my state of mind (of fear, say) is something I do in a particular context." Hence these are not all such descriptions.

   It would be possible . . . : and then there would be no inclination to suppose uniformity of use. Cp. §577.

(jk) we find no answer: for of course (to paraphrase Z 487), fear is not fearful behavior, nor yet a cold sweat or palpitation of the heart. "But *fear* surely designates an inward thing." No. *Fear* designates nothing at all. Neither any inward nor any outward thing. See GI 17–23; cp. Hallett, "Happiness".

   The question is: see §§117, 349; cp. §164b.

(l) I can find no answer . . . : "The experience of fright appears to us (when we philosophize) to be an amorphous experience behind the experience of starting" (NL 275)—amorphous "because we refuse to count what is tangible about our state [e.g. the start itself] as part of the specific state which we are postulating" (§608).

   attending to myself: cp. §§314, 316, p. 219ab.

   out of the corner of my eye: cp. §274.

   not on the ground of observing . . . : see p. 174i; cp. §§587, 631, 659b, pp. 191hi, 192ab.

(m) to define it: "explain" would seem a preferable translation here.

   I should *play-act* fear: by means of gestures, faces, tones of voice, and the like (p. 219b; §642; Man. 128, 13–14). Cp. §393b; and Z 488 on emotions: "Common: they have characteristic expression-behaviour." "The characteristic mark of all 'feelings' is that there is expression of them, i.e. facial expression, gestures, of feeling" (Z 513).

(n) Rather than generalizations like the preceding from Z, in this finer-grained treatment W. provides intermediate cases (§122) suggesting differences. Though hope would generally be classed as an emotion, in this respect it resembles intention more than it does fear: "Intention has no expression in face, gesture, or tone" (Man. 138, 15B–16A).

And what about belief?: "Well, there is a tone of belief, as of doubt" (§578). "It would also be possible to describe a kind of average physiognomy of belief" (Z 514)—but in a sense which would apply equally to hope and expectation (§§444, 579, 584).

(op) is something I do in a particular context: hence the differing contexts suggested by the sample statements at the top of the page furnish an answer to the question whether "I am afraid" is such a description. The answer: Sometimes it is, sometimes it isn't (p. 189e).

an experiment: see p. 180a, and the early pages of Man. 163.

Is it, then, so surprising . . . : only because they ignored particular contexts could philosophers like the author of the *Tractatus* suppose that expressions function uniformly.

between the games: as a boy does not run just in football and in tag, but sometimes between the games—without any definite purpose. See §§83a, 122a and commentary ("intermediate cases").

(q) And do I always . . . : cp. §§83, 467.

P. 189 See Man. 229, §§1128–29.

(a) But in a prayer . . . : "For when we speak of God and that he sees everything and when we kneel and pray to him all our terms and actions seem to be parts of a great and elaborate allegory which represents him as a human being of great power whose grace we try to win, etc., etc." (LE 9).

(b) See NL 302d; cp. Man. 229, §1132: "Is the cry 'Help' a description of my state of mind? And *isn't* it the expression of a wish? Isn't it one as much as any other"—for instance "I want someone to help me"? Likewise, sometimes "the statement 'I want to drink wine' has practically the same sense as 'Wine, please!' And no one will call the *latter* a description" (ibid., §1137). Cp. §24.

which cannot be called a description: cp. pp. 187ij, 197cd.

serves as a description: does the job of a description (Man. 232, 771). Cp. §404a and Wisdom, "Constructions", 461–62 ("We may express this by saying that the cry during any period echoes the pain during that period").

(c) See NL 302abcd, 319b; Man. 232, 771; cp. Russell, *Inquiry*, 214d.

there are transitions: for cries as well as for words, and from one to the other (for a cry may be forced from us, or may be used to win sympathy, get help, warn, alarm). See p. 188p; commentary on §122a ("intermediate cases").

"We think of the utterance of an emotion as though it were some artificial device to let others know that we have it. Now there is no sharp line between such 'artificial devices' and what one might call the natural expressions of emotion. Cf. in this respect: *a*) weeping, *b*) raising one's voice when one is angry, *c*) writing an angry letter, *d*) ringing the bell for a servant you wish to scold" (*BB* 103; *EPB* 149–50).

may approximate more, or less: cp. §244, p. 198a; and see the examples at the top of p. 188. The first approximates more to a cry, others less. "There are certainly cases in which we say, 'I feel a longing, though I don't know what I'm longing for' or, 'I feel fear, but I don't know what I'm afraid of'" (*BB* 22). Here the words are not "forced from us" (p. 197d).

(d) may be something else: "'Is "I believe . . ." a description of my state of mind?'—Well, what *is* such a description? Say: 'I am sad,' 'I am in good humor,' perhaps 'I am in pain'" (Man. 229, §1138).

Geach asked W. in class about first-person pain expressions in the past tense, which would not seem to be mere *Äusserungen*. W. said he had a point and that he would return to it, but didn't.

(e) why should it *always* . . . : see XXXV, 5; cp. §180; Man. 128, 8 ("Is 'I meant . . .' always a report?"). Consider a cry of pain: Does the person always mean to inform you of his pain, or to gain your sympathy, or to have you help him? Yet even if he intended all three, the cry would not be a description. Cp. p. 14n.

description of a state of mind: cp. §§180, 577, 585, p. 59n.

XXXVI. Moore's Paradox (Pp. 190–192)

GENERAL COMMENTARY

(1)   Though this section does not fit naturally into the scheme for Part Two described in GI 65–66, it does connect smoothly with the preceding section, on expressions of emotion. As "I am afraid" is not generally a description, neither is "I believe" (GI 15–16). Nor therefore is belief some introspectible state. This last point has already appeared in Section XXII, on belief, expectation, and hope. But the expression "I believe" is not considered there, though "I am expecting him" (§577) and "I hope he'll come" (§585) are. Wittgenstein has left "I believe" till now, apparently because "Moore's paradox" suggested the possibility of a fuller, more complex development, one which could not conveniently

be incorporated in the earlier section. (On this development, see Man. 229, pp. 299–304; Hintikka, *Belief*, 64–67.)

(2)   A letter to Moore in 1944 reveals the section's origin and general drift: "I should like to tell you how glad I am that you read us a paper yesterday. It seems to me that the most important point was the 'absurdity' of the assertion 'There is a fire in this room and I don't believe there is.' To call this, as I think you did, 'an absurdity for *psychological* reasons' seems to me to be wrong, or *highly* misleading. (If I ask someone 'Is there a fire in the next room?' and he answers 'I believe there is' I can't say: 'Don't be irrelevant. I asked you about the fire, not about your state of mind!') But what I wanted to say was this. Pointing out that 'absurdity' which is in fact something *similar* to a contradiction, though it isn't one, is so important that I *hope you'll publish* your paper. By the way, don't be shocked at my saying it's something 'similar' to a contradiction. This means roughly: it plays a similar role in logic. You have said something about the *logic* of assertion. Viz.: It makes sense to say 'Let's suppose: p is the case and I don't believe that p is the case,' whereas it makes *no* sense to assert ' $\vdash$ p is the case and I don't believe that p is the case.' This *assertion* has to be ruled out and *is* ruled out by 'common sense', just as a contradiction is. And this just shows that logic isn't as simple as logicians think it is. In particular: that contradiction isn't the *unique* thing people think it is. It isn't the *only* logically inadmissible form and it is, under certain circumstances, admissible. And to show this seems to me the chief merit of your paper" (*LR* 177).

(3)   Other implications, however, also merit notice. To preserve the unity of language and logic, the *Tractatus* had argued that all propositions, whether first-person or third-person, describe states of affairs (GI 32), and that "propositions occur in other propositions only as bases of truth-operations" (5.54). Thus "A believes that *p*," whether A be the speaker or someone else, reports that certain psychic contents are correlated in a specific way with the objects named in "*p*", just as "A says *p*" asserts a specific correlation between spoken words and those same objects (5.542). If, for example, a person believes that it is raining, he forms a logical picture of that state of affairs (GI 36), and assumes towards this content an attitude of belief (GI 37–38); and when he says "I believe it is raining," such is the mental state he reports. Thus what occurs in the proposition "I believe *p*" is the propositional sign "*p*", not the proposition *p*, as the mere look of the sentence suggests.

(4)   However, if language really functioned in this way, there should be no oddity in declaring, "I believe it is raining but it isn't." The two clauses (as Wittgenstein still asserted in Man. 109, 215–16) would describe entirely different facts, one the state of the weather, the other

the state of my mind. Thus the actual conflict, noted by Moore, continues the lesson begun in LF, where Wittgenstein was forced to recognize another "sort of contradiction"—though he preferred to call it an "exclusion"—which clashed with his uniform picture theory (LF 35). There are more things in language than logicians dream of.

DETAILED COMMENTARY

P. 190(ab) Cp. p. 231ef.

How did we ever come to use . . . : on the significance of this question about learning, see III, 1–2. Concerning the use of "I believe" insinuated by W.'s questions, see XXXVI, 3; High, *Belief*, 149.

Did we at some time . . . : the answer to this and the next question is, of course, negative. For what would identify the phenomenon as belief? (See X, 20–21; §371 and commentary.) How could a mere feeling direct us to *say* "I believe" (cp. §486)? Cp. p. 231ef; *OC* 589; Man. 229, §1146: "Can a person understand the hypothesis that I wish something before he understands the expression of a wish?—A child first learns to express a wish and only later to suppose it wishes this or that."

There is no indication that W. thought that belief comes into existence through language, for instance through the use of "I believe" in linguistic acts of belief, and *therefore* could not be introspectively identified prior to the use of "I believe". See §§473–74.

(c) See XXXVI, 2; Man. 232, 677–78, 712; Man. 132, 103ff.

Moore's paradox: "To say such a thing as 'I went to the pictures last Tuesday, but I don't believe that I did' is a perfectly absurd thing to say, although *what* is asserted is something which is perfectly possible logically: it is perfectly possible that you did go to the pictures and yet you do not believe that you did" (Moore, "Reply", 543; see 541–43). "The absurdity I mean arises from the fact that when we use expressions to make an assertion, we *imply* by the mere fact of using them, that we are using them in accordance with established usage. . . . And this which we *imply* is, of course, the contradictory of what we are asserting" (idem, *Papers*, 175–76). See *LR* 178; Hintikka, *Belief*, 64.

is used like: "since the effect of my saying so will, in general, be to make people believe it, and since I know quite well that my saying it will have this effect" (Moore, *Papers*, 176; cp. p. 191d) and in neither case do I give a description of myself (XXXVI, 2; cp. *OC* 587). Thus to either assertion one might reply "You are wrong" (or "You are right") for the same reason. However, W. does not assert complete equivalence (see Man. 132, 103, below).

the *hypothesis*: the *Annahme* or "unasserted proposition" (*NB* 96). Thus "assumption" or "supposition" seems a preferable translation, to bring out the connection with §22 (see Man. 229, §1168; Man. 116,

321) and to avoid confusion with what W. once called "hypotheses" (X, 6). See XXXVI, 2, and an earlier version of this paragraph: "Moore's paradox can also be put like this: 'I believe p' says roughly the same as '⊦p'; but 'Suppose that I believe p' does not say roughly the same as 'Suppose that p' " (Man. 132, 103; see ibid., 121).

is not used . . . : see the preceding quotation.

(d) W.'s distinction between avowal (GI 15–16) and description might create a similar impression, that if a person says, "I believe *p*," and I reply, "You do not believe *p*," I do not contradict him. Cp. §444 for a similar appearance and W.'s answer, applicable here.

(ef) has a meaning like: see commentary on (*c*).

that is to say a use like: see commentary on §20b.

is not like: there is no paradox in a person's saying "I believed it was going to rain but it didn't," whereas there is in saying, "I believe it's going to rain but it won't."

This means nothing: it is not merely false. For the speaker has no idea what relation he is asserting (cp. §§13, 47a, 227, 509a), and no general agreement exists concerning criteria for sameness of meaning (§§61, 556).

(gh) "At bottom . . .": this analysis proposes an alternative explanation of the contradiction in "I believe it is raining, but it isn't."

"describing my own state of mind": cp. §§24, 180, 573, 585, 588, 662, p. 189e; *PG* 104b.

"is indirectly an assertion": hence the contradiction in denying *p* and saying you believe it. Cp. p. 193j.

The claim would be more plausible with respect to "I know. . . ."

But then I must . . . : this amounts to a rejection of the proposed explanation. There is no paradox in saying, "This photo makes his hair look red, but it is really brown," nor would there be in saying, "In my belief it appears to be raining, but it isn't."

would be a kind of sense-impression: see *Z* 477, quoted in XXXIV, 4.

(i) one's own senses: see §354.

but not: why can't I? Because "belief is 'in my soul' here and rain is out there" (JN 65)? No, this *can* is grammatical; it indicates a rule of the game (*BB* 55c). Cp. §§246–47, 441, p. 221de; *BB* 21d, 30c.

(j) meaning 'to believe falsely': that is, substituting for this expression as actually employed (not in any variant language-game we might envisage). Since it has no use in the first-person present indicative, neither would its replacement.

(k) Don't look at it . . . : see Man. 229, §1419; cp. §524, p. 191efg.

but as a most remarkable thing: as though Eskimos and Hottentots, humans and lemurs all parted their hair in the middle. "We must tell ourselves that there could very well be the first person 'I believe' without a third person. Why shouldn't a verb get formed in language which has only the first person present? It is irrelevant what led to this development, what images" (Man. 232, 677).

"chew": cp. *BB* 21b.

(l) Cp. §§24, 317, p. 189b.

P. 191(a) You can measure . . . : Man. 229, §1152, is fuller. You already know the length of the object, as you know the answer to the question, and use each as a norm whereby to judge, rather than learning the length from the ruler or the answer from the statement, as on other occasions.

(b) So the expression need not . . . : for a person may be sure he believes *p*, even though he is not sure about *p*.

Remember that . . . : here too one may be sure of the probability, though not of his coming.

would be a contradiction: for the information conveyed about the reporter would concern what he *believed* (not an inner photograph), and the second clause would indicate a different belief. Thus (to reapply p. 192g) "even in the *hypothesis* the pattern is not what you think": Even if "I believe" were indeed a self-report, as W. had once supposed (5.542), it would not be possible to apply truth tables. Moore's paradox would remain.

(c) on my state: cp. p. 189b.

So there is . . . : cp. p. 188m.

(d) hint at it: apparently meant seriously here; cp. §636, p. 183b; *PG* 104b; Man. 232, 678; Man. 116, 197; Man. 109, 215–16. "The accompanying feeling is of course a matter of indifference to us, and equally we have no need to bother about the words 'I am sure that' either.— What is important is whether they go with a difference in the *practice* of the language" (*OC* 524).

(efg) See Man. 116, 320.

Moore's paradox would not exist: a contradiction like "I believe it is raining but it isn't" can be achieved neither in word (by saying "I am inclined to say *p*" and omitting the asserting tone for "*p*") nor in tone (by saying just "*p*" but in two tones at once).

a verb lacking one inflexion: i.e., the first-person present indicative of "be inclined to say". Cp. p. 190j.

ought not to surprise us: see §524. More surprising are verbal similarities despite diversity of use (see the next sentence; p. 190k; cp. §577).

one can predict . . . by an expression of intention: see XXV, 3; §629, p. 224b.

"There might be a verb which meant: to formulate an intention in words or other signs, out loud or in one's thoughts. This word would not mean the same as our 'intend'. There might be a verb which meant: to act according to an intention; and neither would this word mean the same as our 'intend' " (Z 49). Viewed in this perspective, our *intend* may seem an exotic hybrid, quite as strange as that verb without an inflexion.

one's *own:* in contrast with a simple prediction of another's actions, without reference to his intention; or with predictions based on observation, as when predicting others' actions (p. 224b); or with pure expressions of attitude. In comparison with these paradigms, first-person predictions may appear odd.

(i) See §607b and commentary; cp. §§587, 631, 659b.

(j) "Here it *looks* . . .": see p. 190d.

"in the hypothesis": or assumption, that I believe (cp. p. 190c).

look for a different development: in the manner of §577, Z 49, or *BB* 60b. For one might say that "I believe" is not a value of the function "believing *p*", as "I eat a chair" is of "eating x" (*BB* 21b), so seek to provide the missing form (cp. 192c).

(k) how I think of it: an inoffensive way of stating the view to be probed.

a state of mind: see XXII, 2; §149; cp. p. 59n.

has a duration: cp. §573; Z 81–83, 472.

P. 192(a) And under this head . . . : see p. 191d.

Here it will have been necessary . . . : the shortcut of introspection (§587) would not be available, for when the state of mind in question is called a disposition, "one is thinking of a state of a mental apparatus (perhaps of the brain) by means of which we explain the *manifestations*" of the disposition (§149). And to designate consistently the same inner state, I would need to note the same phenomena in my own case as in others'. The fact that I do no such thing reveals that this model of inner designation is mistaken.

(bc) is wholly different: "I don't listen to them & thereby learn something about myself" (Man. 169; see p. 191i). "Why do I never infer my probable actions from my words? For the same reason as I do not infer my probable behaviour from my facial expression.—For the interesting thing is not that I do not infer my emotion from my expression of emotion, but that I also do not infer my later behaviour from that expression, as other people do, who observe me" (Z 576). See pp. 188l, 191hi; cp. §357, p. 174i; *OC* 629; Z 540; *PB* 89, 93b; *Kreis*, 50n; Man. 229, §§1371–73, 1378–80, 1412; Man. 138, 23B; Hintikka, *Belief*, 94.

That different development: "in the first person present indicative" (p. 191j).

if only I could say . . . : cp. §288c; *PB* 89–90: "When I say I believe someone is sad, I view his behavior as it were through the medium, from the standpoint, of sadness. Could one say though: 'It seems to me I am sad, I hang my head so'?"

(d) I might say that someone else . . . : towards my own voluntary actions, including speech, my attitude is not: "Look, that same turn of phrase! And note the tone of conviction!" (See §627; *BB* 153a.)

(ef) to think out circumstances: suppose, for instance, that Moore proposed his several analytic versions of "Esse est percipi" to an idealist, and inquired: "Which of these expresses your belief?" The idealist, had he never contemplated these alternatives, might perhaps reply, "Judging from what I say. . . ." However, the whole of (*f*) suggests that W. envisaged a different setting. Cp. §587b.

And then it would also be possible: the illustration just given suggests that this inference is questionable if generalized.

(gh) Even in . . . : Tractarian views misrepresent not only the assertion that I believe *p*, in the way revealed by Moore's paradox (XXXVI, 4), but also the so-called *Annahme*, in the manner now described.

the *hypothesis:* better: "the supposition". This translation, preferable throughout for other reasons (see the commentary on p. 190c), also indicates more clearly the connection with what follows (" 'Suppose I believe' ").

the whole grammar: for instance (according to Man. 232, 678): "One can say 'I believe he believes . . . ,' 'I believe I believed . . . ,' but not 'I believe I believe.' "

a picture presents unambiguously: cp. §§352, 425–26.

so that you can tack . . . : literally: "so that you can tack on to this supposition ["Suppose I believe . . ."] some assertion other than the ordinary one."

Let the model of belief be that discussed in (*a*). Then you might for instance continue the supposition thus: "and suppose that being asked what I believe, I truthfully reply I don't know"; or: "I reply mistakenly that I believe . . ."

You would not know at all . . . : the sound *believe* "is an expression only as it occurs in a particular language-game, which should now be described" (§261).

what, for example, would follow: cp. p. 191c.

(i) Note the parallel with p. 190c.

comes to the same thing: cp. commentary on p. 190c ("is used like").

(j) Different concepts: though the expression refers most naturally to the limited equivalence just noted between *say* and *believe*, doubtless W. has the others in mind too.

touch here: on certain occasions in certain contexts, the expressions are equivalent. Cp. p. 220a.

are *circles:* so that if they coincide over a stretch they coincide completely.

(kl) Consider: here, though the example is similar, Moore would be less inclined to adduce psychological reasons for the absurdity (XXXVI, 2).

"It may be raining": rather: "It's probably raining" in (*k*) (*hence* the conflict with "but it isn't") and "It will probably rain" in (*l*) (hence the rough equivalence with "I think it will rain"). The German permits both senses, and is stronger than "it may".

For why not . . . : cp. §§19, 24.

(m) Someone might be tempted to say that "It may rain" really means "I'm not sure whether it will rain" (cp. *l*), thus turning a statement about the weather into a description of the speaker (§24d and commentary).

XXXVII. Aspect Seeing and the Second Sense of *Meaning* (Pp. 193–219)

(1)   Two sentences summarize this section and introduce its two main parts. At the beginning of a long discussion on "seeing an aspect" (pp. 193–214), Wittgenstein explains: "We are interested in the concept and its place among the concepts of experience" (p. 193). The reason for his special interest appears clearly later: "The importance of this concept lies in the connexion between the concepts of 'seeing an aspect' and 'experiencing the meaning of a word' " (p. 214). This correlation with aspect-seeing adds an important dimension to his treatment not only of meaning but also of language and thought in general (pp. 214–19).

(2)   Examination of 5.5423 shows the connection to be an old one (cp. Man. 123, May 20), and helps to explain the sequence here in Part Two of the *Investigations*. In the preceding section Wittgenstein criticized the account of belief (and thought, judgment, and so on) proposed in 5.541–5.5422 (see XXXVI, 3–4). Now he passes to a concrete illustration in the next number of the *Tractatus* (5.5423), with which he sought to explain and defend that account. It is the same illustration as reappears in the transitional manuscripts (e.g. Man. 110, 104–5), in *PG* 165, *BB* 169, and here on p. 193: the sketch of a cube, seen three-dimen-

sionally, now this way, now that (cp. §§139–41). Reflection on the example and on its context in the *Tractatus* suggests why Wittgenstein made much of it and of aspect-seeing in general. The phenomenon might be used to illustrate all the main points in the broad picture theory which underlay the *Tractatus* (GI 32–42).

(3)   The number immediately preceding 5.5423 provides a first lead: "The correct explanation of the form of the proposition '*A* makes the judgement *p*,' must show that it is impossible for a judgement to be a piece of nonsense. (Russell's theory does not satisfy this requirement)" (5.5422). Wittgenstein's explanation, in general terms, was that "a thought contains the possibility of the situation of which it is the thought. What is thinkable is possible too" (3.02). The cube example aptly illustrates this suggestion. For when we view the sketch now this way, now that, "we really see two different facts" (5.5423; see *Z* 208). How could either cube be impossible if I actually *see* it there? (Cp. §512.) And how could I *see* an impossible configuration? As Wittgenstein had observed, the picture—that is, these lines, so projected—"contains the possibility of the situation that it represents" (2.203; see *PG* 154b; Man. 110, 104).

(4)   With this insight into "the correct explanation of the form of the proposition '*A* makes the judgment *p*'" (5.5422), we see more clearly the truth of the preceding remark, that such a proposition "does not involve a correlation of a fact with an object, but rather the correlation of facts by means of the correlation of their objects" (5.542). No object A—no self—enters the experience of a cube seen now this way, now that. But a fact—the corners and edges in this or that position—does. And in the judgment or belief that such a figure exists, the psychic fact would be correlated with the physical, the one cube with the other, via the projective pairing of their corners and edges. If the position of the real cube corresponded to that of the mental, the judgment or belief would be true, otherwise false.

(5)   Thus, though this account is not fully analytic—the corners and edges are not true atomic objects, since the cube, and therefore they, might not exist (GI 35)—we can understand how the model might seem to illustrate and clarify the great problem of falsehood (GI 34–36). For one thing, the corners and edges remain, no matter how the cube is projected, in its actual position or in another; in either case, therefore, the picture retains its reference to reality. Furthermore, not only does it possess the same "logical multiplicity" as the pictured state of affairs (Man. 110, 49) but, when so interpreted, it unequivocally represents just that one; we really see the pictured fact (5.5423). Were God to inspect our minds at the moment of judgment or belief, he would see precisely what we were thinking: these corners in front, those in back

(GI 37; commentary on §141a; Man. 110, 66; Man. 108, 238, quoted for §140a; cp. p. 217g). However, the thought-out version of the sketch, with the corners and edges in this position rather than that, does not actually include the pictured cube (3.13); and seeing a cube so situated (in this sense of *see*) does not entail that any cube actually has that position. Hence what the picture represents it represents independently of its truth or falsehood.

(6)   In this and other respects, aspect-seeing seemed to illuminate the central notion of the greater picture theory: intention (GI 37). "By 'intention' I mean here what uses a sign in a thought. The intention seems to interpret, to give the final interpretation; which is not a further sign or picture, but something else—the thing that cannot be further interpreted" (Z 231; *PG* 145–46; see *BB* 34). Thus consider the pictured cube: It makes sense to ask how a person sees the picture, or even how he sees a pictured projection of the picture (§141), but not how he sees his seeing-as. So too, one can interpret signs, but not the interpreting; one can "think them out" (3.11), but not the thinking out. (See *PG* 144; Man. 110, 81.)

(7)   Furthermore, "think of a sign language, an 'abstract' one, I mean one that is strange to us, in which we do not feel at home, in which, as we should say, we do not *think;* and let us imagine this language interpreted by a translation into—as we should like to say—an unambiguous picture-language, a language consisting of pictures painted in perspective. It is quite clear that it is much easier to imagine different *interpretations* of the written language than of a picture painted in the usual way. Here we shall also be inclined to think that there is no further possibility of interpretation" (Z 231; see Man. 110, 47–48; cp. §140). Not only is the interpreting not interpreted, but only one interpretation seems possible.

(8)   Thus, whereas the views of many others besides the early Wittgenstein can be characterized by saying "there are *certain definite* mental processes bound up with the working of language . . . which we may call understanding these signs, meaning them, interpreting them, thinking" (*BB* 3), it could be said with special truth of him that "when you think about the essence of meaning you look for a state similar to contemplating a picture" (Man. 164, 155; Man. 111, 4–5; see NL 309h; cp. §139c). And from GI 36–37 it is clear that he extended this viewpoint far beyond language. All thought, of whatever variety, required such projective meaning. Thus shortly before the passing of the picture theory, Wittgenstein wrote: "The expression of a wish is not the subsequent manifestation of a wish already there but unexpressed. We wish through—or in—this expression as we see a face in [here he made a sketch like that on p. 194]" (Man. 110, 73; cp. ibid., 5, 53, 75). The

same would hold equally for expectation, hope, regret, and all the rest (GI 36; Man. 111, 4–5).

(9)   It made little difference to Wittgenstein, then (GI 40; I, 1; X, 2) or later (Man. 138, 14B), whether the representation came before a person's mind or before his eyes (§141b), for instance as a sketch (§319). So without unfairness to his former view he could propose: "There is one way of avoiding at least partly the occult appearance of the processes of thinking, and it is, to replace in these processes any working of the imagination by acts of looking at real objects" (*BB* 4). It is abundantly clear, then, why in Section XXXVII he lingers so long over aspect-seeing.

(10)   The procedure resembles closely that in Section IX. As Wittgenstein there digresses at length on reading (§§156–71) and being guided (§§172–78) so as to indirectly illuminate the concept of understanding, so here he devotes many pages to aspect-seeing, for the light it throws on meaning, intending, thinking. And in both places he focuses on samples which most favor a mistaken notion about which he was specially concerned: the mental *act* of meaning or understanding. As there is such a thing as suddenly understanding and exclaiming "Now I understand!" (§151), so there is an experience of contemplating a face, then suddenly noticing its likeness to another, or seeing a sketch now as this, now as that (p. 193). "In the relevant text something different is in question every time: here a glass cube, there an inverted open box, there a wire frame of that shape, there three boards forming a solid angle. Each time the text supplies the interpretation" (ibid.). And isn't it the same with words (§20 and commentary)? Isn't every one somehow interpreted (§§138–41 and commentary), much as an interpretation is said to accompany every sensation, turning it into a perception? (See XXXVII; 22; Frege, *Writings*, 186; Köhler, *Gestalt*, 81.)

(11)   First we should notice the difference between seeing Jastrow's duck-rabbit, say, and seeing a knife and fork: "One doesn't 'take' what one knows as the cutlery at a meal *for* cutlery; any more than one ordinarily tries to move one's mouth as one eats, or aims at moving it" (p. 195). "Seeing an aspect and imagining are subject to the will. There is such an order as 'Imagine *this*,' and also: 'Now see the figure like *this*'; but not: 'Now see this leaf green'" (p. 213). Similarly, it would make little sense to point to the picture of a face and say, "See this picture as a face." We wouldn't know how else to see it, and seeing it so is not a voluntary act (pp. 194–95, 206b). Even pictures which by themselves we might see in a variety of ways—for instance the sketch of a triangle (p. 200)—may be permanently fixed within a given setting (p. 201). Furthermore, even outside such a context, a duck-rabbit, say, might be seen simply as a picture-rabbit from the start (p. 194), with no more

"interpretation" than when a person declares: "I see a red circle over there" (p. 195). In short, active aspect-seeing is a relatively rare phenomenon, even in this family of cases—as rare as meaning a single word this way then that, inside (p. 176) or outside (p. 215) a context.

(12)   The phenomenon is frequently encountered, it is true, in art and music, "where, for example, there is a question of phrasing by eye or ear" (Z 208). And between these and language there is more analogy than is generally recognized, precisely with respect to such "meaning" and "understanding" (I, 3): "We say 'You have to hear these bars as an introduction,' 'You must hear it as in this key.' 'Once you have seen this figure as . . . it is difficult to see it otherwise,' 'I hear the French "ne . . . pas" as a negation in two parts, not as "not a step" ' etc., etc." (Z 208; see p. 202k). Even so, for the reasons indicated (see Z 208), it would be misleading, not only conceptually (XXVI, 2) but also factually, to call meaning an *activity* (§693) by which we projectively think out the sense of signs.

(13)   The same investigation which reveals the inadequacy of the single, too-active Tractarian model (EPB 207) suggests how extensive, nonetheless, are the similarities between meaning and seeing; both form a "family", and between the varied members of each family multiple parallels appear. (Compare Wittgenstein's tactics here with those in XVIII, 1–2.) Thus, as one can voluntarily see a cube now one way, now another, so too "you can say the word 'March' to yourself and mean it at one time as an imperative at another as the name of a month" (p. 215). And as one can say of an unambiguous sketch, "This is a *face*, and not mere strokes" (BB 163), so too one can say of a written word, for instance *read:* "It isn't just a scribble, it's 'read' " (BB 170). " 'I don't see mere dashes (a mere scribble) but a face (or word) with this particular physiognomy' " (BB 174). And yet just as "a picture does not always *live* for me while I am seeing it" (p. 205), so I often do not have *any* experience of a word in the course of talking (p. 216; Man. 229, §832). In some cases, "I should like to say that what dawns here lasts only as long as I am occupied with the object in a particular way" (p. 210; see pp. 204c, 205, 211, 215h; BB 156, 159c, 167f; Man. 229, §§1687–89, 1700, 1716; cp. BB 181a). For instance, "someone makes up a pun for the first time. He 'plays with the meaning of two words'; making the pun seems to consist of . . . seeing *two* meanings before you and *one* word" (JN 59). However, consider this case too: "You are not listening particularly to a sentence when suddenly 'the meaning of a word dawns upon you' " (ibid.)—much as an aspect may "dawn upon" the beholder (pp. 194b, 206hk).

(14)   "Now although the expression that seeing a drawing as a face is not merely seeing strokes seems to point to some kind of addition of

experiences, we certainly should not say that when we see the drawing as a face we also have the experience of seeing it as mere strokes and some other experience *besides*. And this becomes still clearer when we imagine that someone said that seeing the drawing . . . as a cube consisted in seeing it as a plane figure plus having an experience of depth" (*BB* 168–69; cp. Russell, *Mind*, 131, 140, 237). "Thus also we may think that when we look at our drawing and see it as a face, we compare it with some paradigm, and it agrees with it, or it fits into a mould ready for it in our mind. But no such mould or comparison enters into our experience, there is only this shape, not any other to compare it with" (*BB* 166; see *BB* 162, 165; cp. §§604–5). The same holds true of words, when in reading or conversing we experience them in characteristic ways (p. 182; *BB* 148b, quoted for §329). Thus Wittgenstein had been mistaken when he supposed that there was a sense of the word *mean* (*meinen*) "in which it is used 'as a name for a process accompanying our use of a word and our hearing of a word' " (*PP* 257), or a sense of the verb *think* in which "we mean a particular psychic process which e.g. accompanies the utterance of a sentence" (*PG* 51; see §329). He would no longer say that in a secondary sense of the word, "understanding the sentence is something that happens to me, as is hearing it, and accompanies the hearing" (*PG* 41; cp. *BB* 35c, 78). In no sense is understanding (§§527–37), meaning (§22c; p. 176h), intending (p. 217c), or thinking (§339) a process which *accompanies* a word (p. 218e). (Cp. p. 183; *Z* 198–200.)

(15)   The point was especially urgent. For Wittgenstein admitted that in addition to the "large class of cases" in which *meaning* refers to a word's use in the language (§43), there are occasions on which, for instance, "we say we pronounced the word with *this* meaning and take the expression over from that other language-game" (p. 216; see XIX, 2; *BB* 78; *PP* 257–58). And he knew the inclination to hunt up a referent for the substantive *meaning* (*BB* 1), so to "think of the meaning as a thing of the same kind as the word, though also different from the word" (§120). This underlying concern helps to explain not only his attention to the "two uses of the word 'see' " (p. 193), analogous to those of *meaning*, but his stress on "the difference of category between the two 'objects' of sight" (ibid.), and his emphatic warning (note the parallel with §120, above): "Above all do *not* say 'After all my visual impression isn't the *drawing*; it is *this*—which I can't shew to anyone.'—Of course it is not the drawing, but neither is it anything of the same category, which I carry within myself" (p. 196).

(16)   Like pain, when conceived as an inner object reported by "I have a pain" (§293c), so too the visual impression, when conceived as an inner object reported by "I see it as *this*," becomes "a chimera; a queerly

shifting construction" (p. 196f; see p. 202de). So Wittgenstein proposes (cp. §293b) that we "get rid of the idea of the private object in this way: assume that it constantly changes, but that you do not notice the change because your memory constantly deceives you" (p. 207). You will then come to recognize that the criteria for having this experience are not and cannot be private (X, 20–21); they are what we say (pp. 195l, 202b, 206i) and do (p. 203b). For in what alternative manner could common criteria be established? Not by the hidden workings of the eyes or brain (p. 211f; GI 60–61). Nor by each one's scrutinizing the contents of his consciousness and describing them to others (pp. 204g, 206c, 211a; X, 20–21). How would the description go? If we are to avoid tautology (see *BB* 174–75), we must give a different explanation for *this* and *so* in "*This* looks *so*" or "I see *this so*" (p. 186). But after a change in aspect, the lines remain just as before (pp. 195i, 196bc) and no second experience is added (XXXVII, 14) which might permit an internal analysis of *so*, without reference to external objects. Accordingly, we *have* to use terms such as *rabbit* and *box*, no alternative description being available or conceivable (pp. 196h, 200d; Man. 229, §1540). When, for instance, we say "I see the figure as a box," this is not a roundabout manner of saying something we might state more directly, by describing some characteristic experience correlated with seeing boxes or with interpreting such figures as boxes (pp. 193–94; cp. *LC* 39, quoted for p. 186b). This is the word that forces itself on us (p. 204k), not a metaphor which might be replaced by another or by a more straightforward mode of expression (cp. p. 216h). Similarly, if asked to explain the statement "It's a picture-rabbit," I should have to point to pictures of rabbits or to real rabbits, describe their habits, give an imitation, or the like (p. 194f). That is, the nontautological account of the *this* and the *so* (p. 186) would be: "If I saw the duck-rabbit as a rabbit, then I saw: these shapes and colours (I give them in detail)—and I saw besides something like this: and here I point to a number of different pictures of rabbits" (pp. 196–97; cp. §571).

(17) "But the question now remains why, in connexion with this *game* of experiencing a word, we also speak of 'the meaning' and of 'meaning it' " (p. 216). Why, if the uses of *understand* are equally diverse, do "I *want* to apply the word 'understanding' to all this" (§532)? Why, too, do such disparate uses of *see* force themselves on us (pp. 197k, 204k)? Why do "I want to use *these* words (with their familiar meanings) *here*" (p. 216)? Earlier, Wittgenstein suggested a causal explanation: "The mental experiences which accompany the use of a sign undoubtedly are caused by our usage of the sign in a particular system of language" (*BB* 78; see *PP* 258a; *BB* 20e), that is, by meaning in the primary sense of the term (§43). If you have learned the language-game, then you react

to the words in this way (*PG* 41c; cp. *Z* 201). Likewise, you only "see" the duck-rabbit aspects if you have previously seen these animals or pictures of them, in the primary sense of *see* (p. 207; see *PG* 42a). However, even were we to satisfactorily trace the present experience to an antecedent practice or experience, that would not explain the extension of these terms. For relatively few effects take over the names of their causes. And think of a word like *deep:* "deep well", "deep grief", "deep blue", "deep thought", "deep notes", "deep meaning", and so forth (*BB* 137a). Who is to say what the connections are here, or why we stretch the word as we do? So Wittgenstein disavowed any intention to determine the origin either of aspect-experiences (pp. 193f, 201j, 203gh, 208g) or of our extended application of terms (p. 216d). He was interested in concepts and their connections—in the existing language-game and not in its history (*PG* 90, 119, 166; *BB* 14b). (See GI 49–50; *PG* 66c; cp. 4.1121.)

(18)   However, that interest forced him to reintroduce the "historical", in a nonscientific way. For often a conceptual connection parallels a causal one (*Z* 570). Thus the practice of going by signposts perpetuates itself causally, the regular practice bringing it about that this or that individual goes by a signpost; but it is also a conceptual fact, concerning the grammar of the expression "go by", that "a person goes by a signpost only in so far as there exists a regular use of sign-posts" (§198). It is conceivable that the signpost might not affect a person in the ordinary way, but not that what he then did would be "going by the signpost". Such cases (see also *EPB* 229) provide a stepping stone to others, where once again both a causal and a conceptual tie connect the effect with the previous practice but where the effect is now a notably different practice (§364). Thus there is a more than causal difficulty in supposing that a child who had never dealt with people should treat a doll as a person (§282); or that children who had no knowledge of trains should play at trains (ibid.); or that someone might learn to do sums in his head without ever doing written or oral ones (§385; pp. 216g, 220f). For here too the history belongs to the concept; previous ability to do sums publicly is a logical condition for being able to do them in one's head. Another step along the continuum (§122) brings us to cases where previous practice is both cause and criterion not of a similar or related practice, but of an experience. Doubtless an example would be the connection between language-game and word-experience: Only of someone familiar with the substantive and imperative uses would we say that he "meant" the word *March* now as a name, now as a command (p. 215). Similarly, "the words 'Now I am seeing *this* as the apex' cannot so far mean anything to a learner who has only just met the concepts of apex, base, and so on. . . . . 'Now he's seeing it like

this,' 'now like *that*' would only be said of someone *capable* of making certain applications of the figure quite freely" (p. 208; see p. 209ab).

(19) However, consequences interested Wittgenstein more than causes. He wanted to know: "What would you be missing if you did not *experience* the meaning of a word?" (p. 214). So he asked in the parallel case of seeing: What would it entail, and "what sort of consequences would it have" if human beings lacked the capacity to see something as something (p. 213)? Doubtless both our verbal and our nonverbal behavior would be affected. For a person who sees an appearance which he does not recognize will generally describe it differently from one who recognizes it (p. 197gh; see p. 203i). And the way we see a figure determines how we copy it (p. 204a), how we treat it (pp. 204, 205a). "What tells us that someone is seeing the drawing three-dimensionally is a certain kind of 'knowing one's way about'. Certain gestures, for instance, which indicate the three-dimensional relations: fine shades of behaviour" (p. 203). These are important, for they have important consequences (p. 204). "For example, if you see the schematic drawing of a cube as a plane figure consisting of a square and two rhombi you will, perhaps, carry out the order 'Bring me something like this' differently from someone who sees the picture three-dimensionally" (§74). Likewise, "if you see the drawing as such-and-such an animal, what I expect from you will be pretty different from what I expect when you merely know what it is meant to be" (p. 205). Notice that Wittgenstein does not indulge here in precise, debatable hypotheses, but simply notes things everyone would agree to (§128). Similarly he felt safe in saying that the way we experience words has something to do with the way we choose and value them (p. 218lm). And of course if a person takes a word or other sign one way rather than another it may affect what he does (§534; *PG* 438e).

(20) Still, if the meaning of the sign is, "roughly, that which is of importance about the sign" (*BB* 5), the meaning-experience is not the meaning. For "we communicate with other people without knowing if they have this experience too" (p. 181); and were someone to alter the usual experiences and "mean" his words in unusual ways, communication would continue as before (p. 176h). As for his capacity to talk as usual without the usual experiences, we often note no experience of a word in the course of speaking (p. 216a). And if one person agrees on a code with another, the system does not stutter along until the signs "take on" the meaning (p. 214h; cp. p. 175d). Thus "meaning it is not a process which accompanies a word. For no *process* could have the consequences of meaning" (p. 218).

(21) Like the section itself, I have ended on a negative note. After

insisting in Part One that the meaning of a word is its use in the language, and that meaning, thinking, intending are not introspectible acts or experiences, Wittgenstein would not now give the impression that "all we have said . . . may have to go into the melting-pot" (*BB* 44). Those findings stand firm, and those criticisms of introspective psychology. Still, "one cannot take too much care in handling philosophical mistakes, they contain so much truth" (*Z* 460). Surely Moore, for example, was not completely mistaken when he wrote: "It is quite plain, I think, that when we understand the meaning of a sentence, something else does happen in our minds *besides* the mere hearing of the words of which the sentence is composed. You can easily satisfy yourselves of this by contrasting what happens when you hear a sentence, which you *do* understand, from what happens when you hear a sentence which you do *not* understand: for instance, when you hear words spoken in a foreign language, which you do not understand at all. Certainly in the first case, there occurs, beside the mere hearing of the words, another act of consciousness—an apprehension of their meaning, which is absent in the second case" (*Problems,* 58–59; see James, *Meaning,* 31; XXXII, 3; *BB* 157b; Man. 110, 117–18, 187). "By and large this last is true," Wittgenstein commented. *"And now look and see what goes on"* (*EPB* 226, in XXVI, 5). Such, briefly, seems to be the chief rationale of Section XXXVII.

(22)   Another perspective should at least be mentioned, however, since it accounts more naturally for some of Wittgenstein's remarks (e.g. pp. 199hi, 200b). "There is a philosophical question as to what one *really sees.* Does one really see depth, or physical objects, or sadness, or a face, etc.? There is a temptation to say that all of this is 'interpretation', 'hypothesis', etc., and that what one *really* sees is a flat surface of coloured patches" (Malcolm's notes, *Memoir,* 49). "In order, therefore, to arrive at what really is sensation in an occurrence which, at first sight, seems to contain nothing else, we have to pare away all that is due to habit or expectation or interpretation" (Russell, *Mind,* 140). Wittgenstein once envisaged a "phenomenological language" which would express this residue directly without employing physical-object terms (X, 8). But the enterprise led him into "a bewitched morass in which everything disappeared" (Man. 105, 116). The present section helps to indicate why (see e.g. XXXVII, 16).

Some closely related background reading: Sections XIX, XXXII; *Z* 143–49; 198–223, 231–43; *RFM* 85–87; *BB* 127–41, 148–50, 155–85; *PG* 143–48, 163–80, 437–45; Man. 232, 609–11, 620–36, 696–705, 716–40; Man. 229, §§670–702, 1172–1214, 1627–1759; Man. 135; Man. 134; Man. 132; Man. 130, 9off; Man. 115, 19–23; Man. 110, 5–105; Geach's, Shah's, and Jackson's notes on the lectures of 1946–1947;

James, *Principles,* I, 442–43, II, 76–84, 253–66; Köhler, *Gestalt;* Malcolm, *Memoir,* 49–50.

DETAILED COMMENTARY

P. 193(abc) Two uses: W. does not say there are only two, covering all the varied cases that follow. On the other hand, it becomes clear in (*e*) that seeing a likeness is representative of a large and varied group (XXXVII, 11–12). "Later we shall speak of taking (or seeing) something as something. Very diverse processes are so called, and not *one* simple, fundamental process, as our form of expression leads us to suppose" (*EPB* 207; see *PB* 281a).

"I see a likeness": so an internal relation (p. 212a). See pp. 210gh, 211gh, 213h.

let the man I tell . . . : so that in most circumstances it would be pointless to say what I see in the first sense of *see,* but not in the second. See (*d*).

difference of category . . . : see XXXVII, 15; p. 196def; NL 279; *BB* 64a.

(e) See XXXVII, 10, 11, 14.

it has not changed: see pp. 195i, 196bc.

(f) Its *causes* . . . : see GI 49; XXXVII, 17; cp. *PB* 273a.

"I do not say (as Gestalt psychologists do) that the impression of whiteness comes about in this or that way. Rather the question is just this: what the impression of whiteness is. What the meaning of this expression is, what the logic of the concept" (Man. 176, 11A; cp. Köhler, *Gestalt,* 190; Koffka, *Principles,* e.g. 112–13, 244–45).

to psychologists: for instance to James, as well as to Gestalt psychologists. See *Principles,* II, 82–83.

(g) concepts of experience: see GI 65–66.

(hi) On the cube illustration and its history, see XXXVII, 2–5.

In the relevant text . . . : note the analogy with a word or proposition, which may receive varying senses from the text, but which we can also take this way or that. See §525.

So we interpret it . . . : see pp. 200e, 212ef and commentary.

(j) Precipitate from Man. 130, 92–94. Cp. §§179a, 197 ("Is it experience that tells me . . ."); Z 53; NL 320f; *BB* 114a, 159b; *PG* 158b; *PB* 68b; *Kreis,* 250 (quoted in II, 8); Man. 228, 189; Berkeley, *Dialogues,* I, 413: "From the ideas you actually perceive by sight, you have by experience learned to collect what other ideas you will (according to the standing order of nature) be affected with."

is an indirect description: W.'s former tendency (XXXIV, 2; XXXVII, 22). For his viewpoint here, see XXXVII, 16; *BB* 181c, 185b (quoted for §597).

Such experiences, wrote Helmholtz (*Schriften,* 124–25), "in my earlier works I called unconscious inferences: unconscious, inasmuch as the major premise consists of a series of experiences which have long since vanished from memory and which, furthermore, entered our consciousness merely as sensible observations, not necessarily as verbal propositions. The new sense impression occurring in present perception forms the minor premise, to which the rule imprinted by the earlier observations is applied."

I have a particular experience which . . . : "When I said to myself 'What at one time appears to me like this, at another . . . ,' did I recognize the two aspects, this and that, as the same which I got on previous occasions? Or were they new to me and I tried to remember them for future occasions? Or was all that I meant to say 'I can change the aspect of this figure'?" (*BB* 171).

"The present picture," wrote Helmholtz of kindred examples (*Optik,* 777), "evokes in us a weak recollection of all that was similar in earlier visual images, as well as of everything in other experiences that was regularly linked with these former images."

P. 194(a)   See XXXIV, 2; XXXVII, 16; cp. X, 13; XXXIV, 4, 7; *BB* 181; *PB* 208d; Man. 180b, 2–3.

I ought to know it: see GI 60.

I ought to be able . . . : otherwise the talk about *indirect* description lacks a possible contrast, so is senseless (NL 319a).

(bc) And I must distinguish . . . : see XXXVII, 10–11.

and I never have seen . . . : see (*f*).

(de)   For discussion of picture-faces and their expressions, see *EPB* 221; *BB* 162b–163b, 164c, 165b, 168d, 174a, 179d–180b. For their relevance to W.'s earlier picture theory (GI 32–36), see for instance Man. 110, 6 ("Think of the remarkable method of projection by which the drawing . . . is projected into a human face") and 73 (in XXXVII, 8).

Here it is useful: to illustrate the point to which W. returns in (*f*), i.e. the possibility of seeing a picture just one way from the start. As I do not actively "take" a person's face for a face, so I do not generally "take" a picture-face as the picture of a face (cp. p. 206b).

as I do towards a human face: cp. p. 205.

A child can talk . . . : cp. p. 206efgh.

(f) I should have explained by . . . : see XXXVII, 16.

(g) I should not have answered . . . : as I might had I noted the two possibilities. *Now* and *see as* reflect awareness of an alternative. See p. 195ce.

P. 195(ab) someone else: "if, that is, we know that it can also be seen differently" (*Z* 208; cp. §20).

(c) Contrast this with Moore, "Cognitive", 135–37. See Man. 232, 733–34 (other examples); cp. §688; *RFM* 15e–16a.

(d) One doesn't '*take*' . . . : see pp. 206b, 213f; Man. 115, 4; cp. §§602–3. Apropos of the notion that "I always see something also as something" (Man. 180a), adding an interpretation, see the references at the end of XXXVII, 10.

(f) Does it *follow* . . . : see pp. 197g, 212e; Man. 229, §1545. In one case, asked what I saw, I would probably reply "A rabbit" or "A picture-rabbit," in the other "A duck" or "A picture-duck" (p. 194f). So the conclusion might seem to follow rigorously. However, there is another sense of *see*, and in that sense I didn't see anything different (pp. 193e, 196bc). Besides, "I may also react to the question quite differently" (p. 195j).

"If, with different coloring, a person does not note the Mediterranean on a map, that does not show that here there *really* is another visual object. (Köhler's example) At most it could offer a good ground for a certain *form of expression*. But it is not one and the same thing to say 'That shows that in fact different things are seen here'—and 'Under these circumstances it would be better to speak of 'two different visual objects' " (Man. 229, §1702; see Köhler, *Gestalt*, 196).

"It won't do to ask people. Köhler never says it will; but he says 'If you're not blinded by a theory you'll admit there are two visual realities.' But of course, he can't mean only that those who don't hold a certain theory will say 'There are two visual realities.' He must intend to say that whether or not you're (1) blinded by a theory, or (2) whether or not you do say one thing or the other, you must, to be right, say 'there are two visual realities' " (JN 90; see Man. 134, March 21; Köhler, *Gestalt*, 200).

It gives us a reason . . . : "*But why?* Well, interpreting is a procedure" (Z 208). Had I noticed the two possibilities and opted for one, that would be a voluntary act on my part (XXXVII, 13), whereas "seeing is not an action but a state" (Z 208; cp. *NB* 77j). See (*j*).

"Köhler said: 'You see two visual realities.' As opposed to what? To interpreting, presumably" (JN 90).

(g) See p. 201k.

that is an exclamation: not a sure report by a privileged observer. See §386; cp. Man. 229, §1202.

there is also a justification for it: e.g. of the sort just suggested in the comments on (*f*); not an introspective one (§289). See p. 198f and commentary. Cp. the dubious justification in JN 90.

(hi) a different mode of comparison: one which leads to the declaration that they are entirely different, not that they are congruent (p. 195ik).

Nor has the head . . . : see p. 196b.

(j) **reporting my perception:** see (a).

quite differently: cp. p. 201gh.

is not: cp. pp. 194g–195a, 197b. The *now*, one might say, relates to me, not to the object. Compare, for instance, reports of attention or visual fixation ("Now the top is prominent, now the bottom").

(kl) See p. 212a; Man. 229, §1545.

"But surely you . . .": see (g).

my impression?: see XXXVII, 14; p. 196cd.

I *describe* **the alteration . . . :** see XXXVII, 16.

like a perception: see (j) and p. 196a.

P. 196(ab) See Man. 232, 723; Man. 115, 9; cp. p. 198gh.

This has the form . . . : so here is one answer to the question "What is different?" (p. 195l), and one reason for saying that the perception has changed (p. 195f; cp. p. 198f; *BB* 128b). Paraphrasing §134b, we might say: "*One* feature of our concept of a new perception is being expressed like a new perception." For counterremarks, see (b) and p. 197ab.

(c) Cp. *BB* 163b.

a quite particular 'organization': see Man. 229, §§1201–4. Köhler, who has a chapter in *Gestalt Psychology* on "Sensory Organization", would speak of the picture's "natural organization" prior to the "meaning" (p. 152). JN 94 criticizes saying "The organization has changed," but for reasons which do not seem valid; and indeed p. 208f is less critical (cp. Man. 229, §1202). However, talk of new organization is more appropriate in some cases than in others. "Someone said 'The dot case.' W: Yes, and does it readily apply to the hanging case?" (JN 91; see p. 200c and comments on p. 208f).

no change is shewn: see (b); cp. pp. 195i, 198h.

(d) See XXXVII, 14–15; §§280, 300–301, 374, 401a, pp. 199g, 212a; Z 638–40; NL 279; *BB* 168bc; Man. 229, §§778 (quoted for p. 231d), 1748; cp. p. 183a; Man. 109, 229–30 (quoted for §175b).

above all do *not* **say . . . :** as sense-data theorists like Russell and Moore would be inclined to, and the long tradition which they represent. Cp. §§275–80.

(e) See §§280, 300–301, 374, 401a; NL 279.

'inner picture': see §294, p. 199hi. "It seems that the visual image which I'm having . . . is almost like something painted on a screen which surrounds me" (NL 311), distinct from the objects themselves (§276). " 'I have *got* something which my neighbour has not' " (§398). See commentary on §280.

is misleading: cp. §§300–301, 386, p. 220cdef; Z 637.

"One might think the whole difference between the two cases is this, that in the first the pictures are mental, in the second, real drawings. We should here ask ourselves in what sense we can call mental images pictures, for in some ways they are comparable to drawn or painted pictures, and in others not" (*BB* 171; a quotation for §301 gives some of the differences then cited).

" 'Yes, but the image itself, like the visual impression, is surely the inner picture, and *you* are talking only of differences in the production, the coming to be, and in the treatment of the picture.' The image is not a picture, nor is the visual impression one. Neither 'image' nor 'impression' is the concept of a picture, although in both cases there is a tie-up with a picture, and a different one in either case" (*Z* 638).

uses the '*outer* picture' . . . : "We are thinking of a game in which there is an inside in the normal sense" (NL 280).

'numeral' and 'number': see *BB* 27c, 64a; *Kreis,* 105; JN 6–8; cp. commentary on §108c. "Frege shows with many examples that the formalists persistently confuse numbers with numerals. Some of them explicitly identify numbers with sensible signs, and others give the same impression without committing themselves to a clear declaration" (Kneale, *Development,* 454).

'ideal numerals': cp. §§105, 120f, 339b; *Z* 106; *RFM* 16b, 22e, 116; *PB* 129 ("Numbers must always be the same sort of thing as what represents them"), 207 ("The notation of the number system mirrors the nature of number"); *PP* 291; Plato, *Republic,* 526A; Frege, *Foundations,* 31 (" 'number is, as it were, a kind of metaphysical figure' "); idem, *Writings,* 195, 219 ("the members of Cantor's fundamental series are not visible, tangible figures, but rather seem to be of a non-sensible kind").

a similar confusion: paraphrasing *RFM* 136e, we might say: "It means that the word 'number' has a use which is somewhat similar to the use of 'numeral' but that it does not designate any numeral." So, too, the expression "inner picture" has a use somewhat similar to that of *picture,* yet does not designate a picture (§301).

(f) If you put the . . . : "The claim for the gestalt psychological 'organization' is most generally put as 'It's on the same level as shape, color, etc.' " (JN 91). "We say perhaps: 'In my visual room the objects are arranged as follows" (Man. 116, 237). Cp. Man. 135, in XLI, 5.

an inner object: see pp. 199h, 202d; NL 311ef, 316a.

a queerly shifting construction: see XXXVII, 14, and the next paragraph. It flickers from rabbit to duck, from open box to wire frame, from flat thing to three-dimensional, in a way no physical object does (p. 195l; Man. 130). Cp. §293, p. 187c.

is now impaired: the inner object is, for instance, three-dimensional, whereas the drawing is two-dimensional; and its lines move back and forth (the cube) or perhaps even pass in and out of existence (the duck-rabbit) whereas those of the picture do not budge.

(gh) a model . . . in addition to a copy: as one might do for a knife and fork (p. 195c), the model showing what is seen (knife and fork), the drawing indicating the sensible appearance from where the person stands. See (*j*).

   the case is altered: it is "quite as if the object had altered before my eyes" (p. 195l); and this experience cannot be expressed by a drawing, or even by a drawing plus a model, but for instance by saying "Now I see it as *this*," and pointing to a model (pp. 194g–195c, 196ab).

   the only possible expression . . . : cp. XXXVII, 16; p. 200d.

   or even was: for instance, a person for whom the duck-rabbit was simply a picture-rabbit would often reveal this fact by the way he made a copy (cp. pp. 197hi, 204a).

(i) And this by itself . . . : for color and shape, a faithful copy suffices, there being no comparable fluctuation in their regard.

(j) A distinct contrast from that just noted, though closely related. See XXXVII, 16.

   I give them: the colors and shapes themselves, not something I didn't see (e.g. pictures of rabbits).

   in detail: faithfully, exactly, not allusively.

P. 197(ab) and here I point . . . : to other pictures rather than to a feature of the duck-rabbit drawing (its 'organization').

   between the concepts: i.e. the sense of the second "I saw" in the preceding sentence and that of the third. See XXXVII, 16.

   is not part of perception: as Russell's words would suggest: "Theoretically, though often not practically, we can, in our perception of an object, separate the part which is due to past experience from the part which proceeds without mnemic influences out of the character of the object" (*Mind*, 131; see XXXVII, 22).

   for that reason it is like seeing: for neither is seeing a *part* of perception, as it is in Russellian doctrines of "what is really seen" (XXXVII, 22).

   and again not like: seeing-as is not a parallel component of perception, contributing organization to the total picture while seeing provides the color and lines. See p. 196f.

(cd) I exclaim: see Man. 229, §1542.

   the report and the exclamation: see GI 15–16.

   as a cry is to pain: see §244, p. 189; cp. NL 312h.

(e) since it is the description: i.e. "serves as a description" (p. 189b). Cp. p. 199f.

   of a perception: and not merely of a sensation ("looking at the object").

you are also *thinking:* not, however, in the sense Schlick claimed (see "Form", 195, quoted for §604). "Let us imagine that German were altered in such a way that the order of the words in a sentence is the reverse of the present correct one. The result would thus be word sequences such as we get if we read the sentences of a German book from right to left. It is clear that the multiplicity of possible modes of expression in this language must be exactly the same as in German; but we would find it extremely difficult to understand a fairly long sentence when read this way, and might never learn 'to think in this language'. (The example of such a language can throw some light on the nature of what we call 'thought')" (*PG* 122–23). So can the present example. See p. 204c; *PG* 145b; Man. 232, 697; Man. 110, 57; cp. XXXVII, 14, 21; §332, pp. 210e, 212, and the commentary on p. 212e.

(f) half visual experience, half thought: but not visual experience plus thought (p. 211j). See pp. 197jk, 212bc.

(g) Someone suddenly sees . . . : cp. *BB* 127k–128g.

Is it correct . . . : in the next two paragraphs, W. gives no verdict, but first suggests a reason against, then one in favor. "The question is: *Why* does one want to say this?" (p. 197k).

different visual experience: cp. pp. 195fg, 212e.

(h) For might not . . . : or: "Then might not". Either way, the correctness of the preceding assertion is being questioned, not confirmed.

(i) See *PG* 167e; cp. Man. 115, 7.

I should do a different portrait: cp. p. 198f; Malcolm, *Memoir,* 49 ("I can hardly paint at all unless I know what physical *objects* I am painting").

(jk) both seeing and thinking?: See (*ef*).

or an amalgam: cp. XXXVII, 14; pp. 211j, 212abc.

The question is: not what is "correct", or "follows" from the facts (p. 195f). Language is not a calculus with all the steps predetermined (IX, 3). See the quotation for p. 198d.

Why does one . . . : contrast this *why,* evoking familiar features of the language-game which elicit this reaction and which interested W. (§§127–29), with the sort of *why* he avoided (§471 and commentary). Cp. commentary on (*g*).

P. 198(a) See p. 197cd.

(bc) See XXXVII, 16; cp. X, 20–22. On criteria in general, see GI 60–61; §354 and commentary.

What do you suppose?: "the other person's behavior (e.g., what he tells us)" (NL 316).

(d) See Man. 229, §1590.

is very elastic: "We have the idea of an *ideal* model or an *ideal* description of what one sees at any time. But no such ideal description exists. There are numerous sorts of things which we call 'descriptions' of what we see. They are all *rough*. And 'rough' here does *not* mean 'approximation'. We have the mistaken idea that there is a certain exact description of what one sees at any given moment" (Malcolm's notes, *Memoir*, 50). See p. 200a; cp. §24b.

and so *together with it*: for, as (*c*) notes, the representation of what is seen is the criterion of what is seen, and the criterion determines the concept. Cp. p. 225a.

intimately connected: cp. §§150, 225, pp. 209g, 217d; *Z* 625.

that they are alike: e.g., that the concepts overlap as do the members of a "family" (§66b). Cp. p. 209g; *Z* 625, 646.

(e) How does one tell . . . : what is the criterion, not merely the symptom (§354)? W. is illustrating (*c*).

He does not give reasons: so is not reporting an inference from clues (shading, foreshortening, and the like) but what he *sees*. Cp. pp. 193j–194a.

surmise: italicized in the German. Cp. Helmholtz, e.g. *Optik*, 769: "In many cases it suffices to know or surmise that a seen object has a figure of a certain regularity, in order to correctly interpret its likeness, presented to us in perspective by the eye or a skillful drawing, as the figure of a body. If a house, a table, or some other human artifact is represented, we may assume that its angles are right angles and its surfaces flat, or that its surfaces are cylindrical, or spherical."

The only thing . . . : cp. p. 213a.

to us: normal adults. See Helmholtz, *Schriften*, 126.

children's drawings: e.g. young Klecksel's two-eyed profiles (*PG* 80a; *EPB* 226).

(f) does he see it differently . . . : cp. p. 195fgh.

He mimics it differently: in view of (*c*), this constitutes a reason for saying he sees it differently. Cp. p. 197i.

(gh) See *EPB* 192–93; *BB* 127 (end), 128b; Man. 125; cp. *Z* 149; *RFM* 128e–129d; *PG* 122–23 (quoted for p. 197e).

Hold the drawing of a face . . . : "Another well-known change is when we look at a landscape with our head upside down. Perception is to a certain extent baffled by this manoeuvre. . . . The same thing occurs when we turn a painting bottom upward. We lose much of its meaning" (James, *Principles*, II, 81).

You cannot imitate . . . : this remark too (cp. pp. 197i, 198f) is to be read in the light of (*bc*).

And yet the picture . . . : cp. pp. 195i, 196bc; Köhler, *Dynamics*, 15.

(i) See Man. 232, 696.

a different difference: neither of the following observations about (c) and (d) applies to (a) and (b).

P. 199e suggests the motivation of this paragraph. It is not enough to say, "A word in reverse has a *new* face" (*RFM* 128). So does the figure (b).

Compare a remark of Lewis Carroll's: probably not Humpty Dumpty's when Alice pointed out that the book he was examining so attentively was upside down ("I thought it looked a little queer"), but possibly Bruno's in the first chapter of *Sylvie and Bruno Concluded.* "I just twiddled my eyes," he explained, and directly he saw the letters E-V-I-L as "LIVE" spelled backwards.

P. 199(ab) No: for my representation of what I see remains the same (see p. 198bc; cp. pp. 194f, 196j–197a).

(c) in a new way: for here, unlike (*a*), "you give a new kind of description."

a new visual experience: cp. "Köhler's insistence that the figure seen now this way now that is each time really a different *experience*" (Man. 131, 128; see Köhler, *Gestalt,* 106). The progress from p. 196g to 196h, from "what he sees" to "our experience", parallels that in the present paragraph.

(d) you would not necessarily want to say: as in p. 195i, where the contrast is between the picture seen as a duck and seen as a rabbit. This implicit reference helps to explain the remark in (*e*).

(e) There are hugely many . . . : see the commentary on p. 193a.

"These days the danger incurred by the desire to conceive things as simpler than they really are is often much exaggerated. But the danger is indeed extremely great in the phenomenological study of sense impressions. These are always taken to be *much* simpler than they are" (*PB* 281).

and possible concepts: "If I tell him: 'Now I see the figure as . . . ,' in many respects my communication *resembles* that of a visual perception, but also that of a conception, or of an interpretation, or of a comparison, or of knowledge" (Man. 232, 701).

(f) Then is the copy . . . : see pp. 196gh, 199c.

an *incomplete* description: cp. the quotation for p. 198d. W.'s remarks on exactness, in §88, are applicable here. No single ideal of completeness has been laid down. The point is, what is our goal?

(g) W. is making the same point as in p. 196d: The impression is not anything of the same category as the drawing. For the drawing is simultaneously picture-duck and picture-rabbit, whereas the impression is not.

(hi) See XXXVII, 22; p. 196ef; NL 311def; Man. 229, §§1362, 1564 (quoted for p. 186c); cp. §280.

"What I really *see* . . . ": cp. *PB* 259b, and Köhler's full formulation of this viewpoint, then criticism of it, in Chapter 3 of *Gestalt Psychology.*

"by the influence of the object": "Professor Stout . . . says: 'One characteristic mark of what we agree in calling sensation is its mode of production. It is caused by what we call a *stimulus*. A stimulus is always some condition external to the nervous system itself and operating upon it.' I think that this is the correct view" (Russell, *Mind*, 149; see 139–40). "What is called perception differs from sensation by the fact that the sensational ingredients bring up habitual associates—images and expectations of their usual correlates—all of which are subjectively indistinguishable from the sensation" (ibid., 157).

like a *materialization*: an inner picture (p. 196e) or inner object (p. 196f). "With the schematic cube, for instance, it is a cube" (p. 202). "Indeed," W. had written, "I could e.g. represent the visual images plastically, say in reduced scale by means of plaster figures, which I carry out only as far as I have actually seen them" (*PB* 97).

in purely spatial terms: "It is clear," W. had said in *PB* 98, "that we need a form of expression in which we can represent the phenomena of visual space as such, in isolation." See X, 8. On purely visual concepts, see Man. 138, 5B–6A.

can smile: can have that shape (p. 209g).

the concept of friendliness, however . . . : cp. XXXVII, 14; p. 209g; NL 282f; *BB* 162: "One feels that what one calls the expression of the face is something that can be detached from the drawing of the face."

it may subserve it: the primary language (X, 8; XXXVII, 22) might have to be introduced by means of the secondary, physical one. Cp. §120.

(j) See p. 212d; Man. 229, §1698; cp. *PP* 308–9.

I shall mostly have no recollection . . . : hence (GI 60) "this *explanation* of the phenomenon of seeing" (*BB* 164) does not determine the concept *seeing* (p. 212d).

P. 200(a) See p. 198d; Malcolm, *Memoir*, 50 (quoted for p. 198d).

it is tangled: see Man. 232, 700.

And now look at all . . . : see e.g. pp. 193b, 194f, 196a, 196j–197a, 198efg, 199c; cp. §§24, 291.

not *one genuine* proper . . . : the attitude criticized appears for instance in James's remark concerning a number of figures like the picture-cube: "The real object, lines meeting or crossing each other on a plane, is replaced by an *imagined solid which we describe as seen. Really it is not seen but only so vividly conceived as to approach a vision of reality.* . . . In these changes the actual retinal image receives different *complements from the mind*" (*Principles*, II, 257–58). Since there is always development between retinal image and sight, James has not yet provided an intelligible contrast, nor a reason for restricting the verb *see* as he does. W.

would bring back this word from its metaphysical to its everyday use (§116).

(b) fine distinctions: cp. §254 and commentary. In pp. 203b, 204l, 207a, W. mentions fine distinctions, but does not make them. They are not necessary for conceptual clarification, since the concept has no sharp edge to determine by their means. James, however, when he made the remark above, or Russell, when he spoke of paring away all but the true sensation (XXXVII, 22), apparently presupposed the existence of a perfectly definite concept of sight or sensation, distinct from the vague and fluctuating one of everyday speech.

Cp. Man. 232, 613–14: "If I play the language-games with a stop-watch, say, so as to show myself the difference between the *concepts* know and see, of course it looks as though I am demonstrating an extremely fine distinction where the real one is *enormous*. But this enormous distinction consists (I would always like to say) in the fact that the two concepts are imbedded quite differently in our language-games."

tries to define the concept . . . : thus W. is not referring to solipsistic claims concerning what is "really seen" (*BB* 61, 66, 71). See X, 6–8; *PG* 219–23.

'what is really seen': see XXXVII, 22; p. 199h.

is to *accept* . . . : Russell, for instance, was wont to deny that we ever see a table or a sunrise. See the commentaries on §§241–42.

needs no justification: for it is not a "theory", which might be right or wrong (§241; *Z* 223; *BB* 61b); nor must it satisfy *a priori* requirements, imposed by reality (p. 230b). On W.'s former attitude, see for instance XXXIX, 1; Man. 105, 19 (quoted for §1d); *NB* 70 ("I only want to justify the vagueness of ordinary sentences, for it *can* be justified"). See I, 4–5; §402; *Z* 319–20, 331; *BB* 73a; *PP* 277 ("He first tried to express his view by saying that it is impossible to 'justify' any grammatical rule"); *Kreis,* 104–5; Man. 109, 63–64 (in what words might one talk about pains, colors, and the like so as to justify the way we speak of them?), 225 ("For to justify means to justify with words"); Cook, "Human Beings", 144; cp. *RFM* 165j; *PG* 267b; Man. 112, 139 ("Lichtenberg: 'Our whole philosophy is a justification of linguistic usage, so the justification of a philosophy and indeed of the most universal' ").

(c) on its base . . . from its apex: see p. 208ghi.

as hanging: see JN 91, quoted for p. 196c.

as an arrow or pointer: see p. 206d.

as an overturned object: see p. 207j.

(d) *What* way?: "Are the different ways of seeing the drawing different ways which might also be described *otherwise*? So not via physical objects with which we associate them? Or is precisely this mode of description essential? Thus could we say: a person who sees the drawing 'as a box with slits' [James, *Principles*, II, 254], sees it *this* way: . . . and now there follows, say, a description of the way our glance travels over the picture, how we direct our attention, etc.?" (Man. 123, May 18). See Man. 229, §1564, quoted for p. 186c; cp. p. 212d.

There *is* no further qualification: see XXXI, 2–5; XXXVII, 16; §285, pp. 193j–194a; Man. 229, §§1586, 1621–22, 1657, 1713, 1754; JN 33; Malcolm, *Memoir*, 49; cp. XXXIV, 2–7; commentary on §571; *BB* 166b, 184c; *LC* 71c ("Why should you be able to substitute anything else?"); Man. 229, §§1611, 1697; Man. 110, 86 ("If I say: I imagine a red patch on this wall, that is at any rate the description of a process, a fact, which is independent of the facts described by the proposition 'There is a red patch on this wall,' but I can't describe that fact without using the expressions 'red', 'patch', etc."), 89 ("How does language describe the process of understanding the sentence 'p'? Can it do so otherwise than by saying I understand 'p'?").

" 'For me it is now *this* ornament.' The 'this' must be explained through reference to a *class* of ornaments. One can say, for instance, 'They are white bands on something black.' Yes—it cannot be described otherwise. Although one would like to say: 'But there must be a simpler expression for what I see!' And perhaps there really is one. For above all one might use the expression 'stand out'. One could say, 'These parts stand out.' And now we could imagine a primitive human reaction which does not express this in words, but for example indicates with the finger and *a special gesture* the parts which stand out. Yet even so this primitive expression would not yet be *equivalent* to the verbal expression 'white border decoration' " (Man. 229, §1713).

(e) See p. 193i; cp. Man. 229, §1665: "But how strange!—one would like to say—if a person can discover a certain structure—how is it possible to also *see* it!—How is it possible to know all of a sudden what one wants to say? Isn't this equally remarkable?" (Cp. §524b.)

(f) See pp. 201a, 215a; *RFM* 17cdef; Janik and Toulmin, *Vienna*, 144 ("It is worth pointing out that this notion of a 'space of theoretical possibilities', which plays the key part in Boltzmann's method of analysis, can be summarized concisely in words from Wittgenstein's *Tractatus*"); cp. *Z* 710; *NB* 56f; *Kreis*, 260b, 261a; Man. 106, 93.

When it looks as if . . . : cp. e.g. Russell, *Inquiry*, 110: "Is 'this' a name, or a description, or a general concept? To any answer there are objections." (Why need it be any of these?)

in another dimension: see *Z* 180; *RFM* 140b; JN 48; Man. 229, §1184.

"The notion of mutually independent components of description as 'dimensions' is not an uncommon metaphor in ordinary language" (Stenius, *Tractatus*, 41).

"All that is required is that we should construct a system of signs with a particular number of dimensions—with a particular mathematical multiplicity" (5.475).

"The number of constants occurring in a proposition equals the number of dimensions in which it is variable. The space in which the proposition is situated has that number of dimensions" (*Kreis*, 91).

"Every higher system is a world with more dimensions than the lower" (Man. 105, 30).

" 'Here I cannot . . .'—Where *can* I then? In a different game. (Here—in tennis—I cannot score a goal.)" (Man. 229, §1235).

"Couldn't the sentence, once again, fall 'between several games'?" (Man. 138, 8A; see p. 188p).

"What I give is the morphology of the use of an expression. I show that it has kinds of uses of which you had not dreamed. In philosophy one feels *forced* to look at a concept in a certain way. What I do is to suggest, or even invent, other ways of looking at it. I suggest possibilities of which you had not previously thought. You thought that there was one possibility, or only two at most. But I made you think of others. Furthermore, I made you see that it was absurd to expect the concept to conform to those narrow possibilities. Thus your mental cramp is relieved, and you are free to look around the field of use of the expression and to describe the different kinds of uses of it" (Malcolm, *Memoir*, 50).

P. 201(a) Cp. Frege, *Foundations*, 107c.

one never dreamed of: cp. *PG* 444d: "Only when something is viewed a certain way does a person realize that it can be viewed that way. Only when an aspect is there does a person see that it is possible."

(bc) might sometimes have *permanently*: as the duck-rabbit, for example, surrounded by rabbits is the picture of a rabbit or surrounded by ducks is the picture of a duck (p. 195f), so the triangle of p. 200c "can really be *standing up* in one picture, be hanging in another, and can in a third be something that has fallen over" (p. 201d). See Man. 232, 684.

(e) See XXXVII, 17.

(fghi) be the conventional description: as *duck-rabbit* is a conventional name, and in "It's a duck-rabbit" does not report the aspect one is seeing. See p. 195j.

But not being . . . : rather: "But not used as such," that is, to inform others how it is with me (cp. §§24, 179b, 317, p. 189b).

(j) Here we are not asking . . . : see XXXVII, 17.

what are the causes: e.g. eye movements (Man. 229, §§690—91).

(k) "Surely I see . . .": see p. 212e and commentary.

This really means . . . : see p. 195fg; cp. p. 197g.

a repetition: in general terms ("something different") and specific ("floating" and "lying there").

P. 202(a) See p. 213a.

(b) "really a different impression?": to W., this recurring question (cp. pp. 195, 199ad, 201k) appeared as ill-defined as the question about sameness or difference of meaning (XXI, 4).

how can I find out?: can I view the picture in the appropriate way and at the same time attentively observe my viewing? And would the viewing be unaltered by the observing? And even if it were, how could I tell? Can I compare unobserved viewing with observed? And even if that were possible, would the observed difference in that particular case be typical of other people, or even of me? And none of this yet connects the inner phenomenon with the *expression* "different impression" (see GI 60–61; X, 20–22).

I *describe* . . . **differently:** see XXXVII, 16.

(cd) Here one would now like to say . . . : 5.542 and 5.5423 together suggest such a view. See XXXVII, 3–4; pp. 196de, 199hi.

is three-dimensional: see p. 199h and commentary ("like a *materialization*").

(e) then it seems queer: in the inner world of the sense-datum theorist (§§398–400 and commentary), some of the objects (§§374, 401, pp. 196f, 199hi, 207e) would have three dimensions and others only two!

(f) See Man. 232, 702–3; Man. 229, §1541; cp. p. 54n.

do I merely *know* . . . : as Berkeley would maintain (*Dialogues*, I, 415). See pp. 200ab, 203bcde, 204l; cp. p. 212ef.

And does my visual impression . . . : this evident nonsense is meant to reveal the veiled nonsense in (*de*); for it would follow equally from accepting the description of the impression as an indication of its intrinsic properties.

(g) See XXXVII, 19; cp. §363.

(hij) associate colours with vowels: see p. 216h; *Z* 185; *EPB* 203–4; *BB* 136–37, 138b–140b, 148cd; cp. *PG* 92ab.

when it was repeated . . . : cp. p. 214f.

might have no more significance . . . : these words suggest the reason for (*hij*), and their connection with (*g*).

(k) See §527; *Z* 208 (quoted in XXXVII, 12); *BB* 167ab; cp. *BB* 166b.

Here it occurs to me . . . : for the question in (*g*) requires that we locate the stream of thought and life in which the expression "see as" occurs (§§117b, 520). "On what occasions does it get formed, when is there need of it? (Very frequently in art)" (*Z* 208).

P. 203(a) This figure: cp. Man. 110, 49, 52.

that is just as if . . . : thus in answer to (*g*) on p. 202, (*hi*) first give a case where aspect-seeing (or the like) has little significance; then (*j*) suggests how it might have importance even there; (*k*) indicates an entirely different way; and p. 203a now adds a third. See XXXVII, 19.

(bcd) What tells us that . . . : not only as symptom (§74) but as criterion (XXXVII, 16).

fine shades of behaviour: see pp. 204l, 207a.

or do you merely *know:* see pp. 202f, 203bde, 204l; cp. p. 212ef.

Compare Köhler's figure: perhaps a reference to figure 11, p. 189, of *Gestalt Psychology,* where the hexagons, though "geometrically present", are not noted. However, cp. (*i*) and p. 204bc, which better describe Koffka's figure in *Principles,* 154.

(e) See Man. 229, §§1768–71.

It must be possible . . . : "The introspective theorem that changes of attitude cannot influence 'true' sensory experience," wrote Köhler (*Gestalt,* 123), ". . . seems rather to be an arbitrary definition of 'true' sensory experience." W. would agree that the definition is unwarranted (p. 193; cp. 200a), but not that it is arbitrary. Both inclinations are motivated (cp. p. 195g). Consider the questions "Did she really marry money?", "Are people really murdered in plays?" That's what we say—in a secondary sense (Man. 166). See (*f*).

Cp. Man. 138, 5A: "So *is* noting a likeness seeing or not? How am I to decide? There are here dissimilar, but related concepts."

(f) See the preceding comments; and p. 204i.

(gh) See p. 193fg and commentary.

a physiological explanation: see p. 212d.

Our problem: that in (*f*).

not a causal: see XXXVII, 17.

(i) See p. 204ef.

that **would be my description:** here, then, is a "conceptual justification" (see p. 198bc) for saying "This is seeing" (*e*). For the picture is shown me "just for a moment"; I do not examine it and conclude that "These two bits are supposed to represent part of an arrow" (*c*). See p. 204b.

P. 204(a) See XXXVII, 19; cp. Man. 229, §1650; Malcolm, *Memoir,* 49.

(bc) The first thing . . . : see the comments on p. 203i.

and for the whole time . . . : now comes a justification for saying "This isn't seeing" (p. 203e)—in the primary sense of seeing. Cp. p. 197ef.

I should like to reply . . . : see XXXVII, 13.

(d) "*what* I saw": cp. p. 193abc.

(ef) See p. 203i; cp. p. 209jkl.

Was it *seeing:* see p. 198abcd.

or was it a thought?: see p. 197ef.

(g) Do not try . . . : see XXXVII, 16; p. 202b and commentary; p. 206c.

(h) does this prove: cp. p. 195f.

saw it as something definite?: "when should I call it a mere case of knowing, not seeing?" (*l;* cp. pp. 202f, 203b). "Or was it a thought?" (*f;* cp. p. 197ef).

(i) The question is . . . : W. is quoting the question he asked and wrestled with in Man. 130. See p. 203f; Man. 229, §1046; cp. §570.

(jk) it is *difficult:* cp. §§369–70. "It is as though we expressed an experience and then couldn't recall what the experience really was" (Man. 130).

the fixing of concepts: that is, noting and accepting their actual contours, the words' "field of force" (p. 219c), rather than making subtle discriminations by means of supposedly sharp categories (*see, think, imagine, interpret,* and so forth). See GI 70; p. 200ab.

A *concept* . . . : i.e., this way of seeing things (Man. FW, 11), the use of this word (§532, p. 216d).

forces itself on one: see references at start of XXXVII, 17; §178b, pp. 215a, 230c; *RFM* 35e; *BB* 136–37; cp. §219, p. 178h; *RFM* 7k, 121jkl; *Kreis,* 166a; Man. 163 (quoted for §524a).

"What right has he to use the word 'see'? Or does he have no justification, and is it only a piece of linguistic stupidity? Or does the only justification lie in my being inclined to say: 'now I see it as this,' 'now I see it as that'? Perhaps. But I am most reluctant to admit it; I feel I *have* to say 'I see something.' But what does that mean?—Well, I have *learned* the word 'see'. What fits is not the *word,* the sound or written figure. The use of the word is what forces the idea on me that I *see* this" (Man. 232, 699).

This is what you must not forget: if, for example, you would avoid the Description Fallacy (GI 15–16) and the model on which it is based (§292), or fruitless "attempts at justification" (p. 200b; see the preceding quote), Russellian skepticism (X, 3–4), and the like (see X, 20–21), to which it also gives rise. Sometimes we can give a reason for what we say, sometimes not. "The second alternative is the one we find important" (JN 23, quoted for p. 215d).

"One might be inclined to say 'Surely a similarity must strike us, or we shouldn't be moved to use the same word.'—Compare that statement with this: 'A similarity between these cases must strike us in order that we should be inclined to use the same picture to represent both.' This says that some act must precede the act of using this picture. But why shouldn't what we call 'the similarity striking us' consist partially or wholly in our using the same picture? And why shouldn't it consist partially or wholly in our being prompted to use the same phrase?" (*BB* 130).

"It is easier to see this when we speak of a *deep* sorrow, a *deep* sound, a *deep* well" (*BB* 137). It would go against the grain to call the sound "high" or the sorrow "thick"; yet we have no *reason* for using the word *deep* (BB 136). (We do not, for instance, note a similarity between grief at the death of a loved one and the impression made on us by staring into a deep well.)

"All the questions considered here link up with this problem: Suppose you had taught someone to write down series of numbers according to rules. . . . How and when is it to be decided which at a particular point is the correct step to take? . . . *We need have no reason to follow the rule as we do*" (*BB* 141–43). See IX, 5–6.

A secondary motive for W.'s insistence may be the fact that the philosopher, for instance the solipsist, is often "irresistibly tempted to use a certain form of expression" (*BB* 60; see §§178, 299; Man. 116, 152).

(l) For when . . . : this translation obscures the connection, which might be suggested thus: "In what circumstances, then, if it is a conceptual distinction we wish to fix, and that largely in terms of our inclinations (not predetermined criteria), would we feel inclined to call it a mere case of knowing, not seeing?"

Perhaps when someone treats . . . : for "the grammar of the word 'knows' is evidently closely related to that of 'can', 'is able to' " (§150), whereas that of *see* is not.

as a working drawing: cp. pp. 205cd, 213i.

reads it: as §§156–78 stress, *knowing how* to read is a logical condition of reading, but a special "seeing" of the signs is not. A practiced reader may "function as a mere reading-machine" (§156).

Fine shades of behaviour: see pp. 203b, 207a; *LC* 35c.

important consequences: see XXXVII, 19.

"This reminds me of certain remarks of Köhler, when he is describing the behavior of his apes. He makes evidently correct psychological observations, without however emphasizing that one must attend to the *finer* differences of behavior" (Man. 130).

P. 205(a) "To me . . .": the same phrase, in *PG* 154, recalls the intended application (XXXVII, 2–9) of this whole discussion: " 'Thinking, this remarkable thing' . . . for *to me* what I think then *really* occurs." "The attitude we take toward the picture (the thought)—the way we experience it, makes it real for us. That is, it connects it with reality" (*PG* 183).

my *attitude:* "The concept of an attitude. Our attitude to the visual field, says Köhler, alters our visual impression. And naturally he surrounds the assertion with vague physiological hypotheses. But if we now leave aside all these hypotheses as unsure & unessential, *what* remains of that assertion?—When do we speak of a certain attitude of a person toward what he sees? When do we say that the attitude changes? Is the attitude an experience? or is it a physiological fact?

"I tell someone: 'Now treat the drawing as the picture of a . . . !'—Thereupon his attitude alters. Was it an experience? Do I know anything about a physiological process in him?—'Attitude' is a different *category*" (Man. 135, August 2; see Köhler, *Gestalt*, 183–84).

This is one meaning . . . : "What is the description of an 'attitude' like? One says e.g. 'Disregard these spots and this little irregularity, and look at it as a picture of a. . . .' 'Think *that* away. Would you dislike the thing even without this. . . .' Of course it will be said that I alter my visual image—as by blinking or blocking out a detail. This 'Disregarding . . .' does indeed play a part quite like, say, the production of a new picture.

"Very well—that is good reason to say that we altered our visual impression through our attitude. That is to say, there are good reasons to delimit the concept 'visual impression' in this way" (Z 204–5). See p. 206fg; *LC* 35c; cp. p. 178f.

(b) Not in the same sense: for instance, it is not evident that you might see the pierced animal as something different, as you can the two hexagons (p. 204h). Besides, you need to think of the role these pictures play in our lives (*c*), in order to discover the sense of "what I treat it as" (*a*).

(cd) On these and subsequent paragraphs, see Man. 229, §1685. Cp. §§291, 522.

(e) See XXXVII, 19.

will be pretty different: if, for instance, you are a lover of animals, you may be pained or revolted by the picture in (*a*), and have it removed.

(f) See p. 194e; *PG* 183, quoted for (*a*); Man. 232, 733.

(g) See Man. 229, §1686; cp. §524; *PG* 171e.

(hi) I say: literally, "if I now say" (in accorance with *f*, and as W. had in *PG* 155c).

determine the concept: cp. p. 204j.

while I am actually concerning myself: for the significance of this consideration, and for references, see XXXVII, 13, and §432. See also Man. 232, 721.

(jk) See XXXVII, 13; Z 232–33; *PG* 146bd; cp. p. 181f and commentary.

does not always: cp. pp. 215h–216a.

live **for me:** cp. §§430–32, 537; *BB* 4–5.

(l) Cp. Z 222–23.

The duck-rabbit: see p. 194.

But one does not . . . : see p. 206i; Man. 232, 720.

does it express a sensation?: that is, does this count as a sensation? Cp. pp. 204j, 205i; Z 223 ("I have not *made any admissions* by using that manner of speaking, and I should contradict anyone who told me I saw the glance 'just the way' I see the shape and colour of the eye"). Cp. p. 196hi.

The quotation for p. 206a, from Man. 229, §1783, reveals the import of this question.

P. 206(a) See Man. 138, 30B–31A.

at some kind of completeness: "The treatment of all these phenomena of mental life is not of importance to me because I am keen on completeness. Rather because each one casts light on the correct treatment of *all*" (Z 465).

"Can Gestalt psychology classify the various organizations which can enter the unorganized visual image? Can it list, once for all, the possible *kinds* of modification which the organizing power of our nervous system can bring about? If I see the dot as an eye which looks in *this* direction,—in what system of modifications does this aspect belong?" (Man. 229, §1783).

some classification: see the quotation above, and cp. Z 472, 488.

They are only meant . . . : "He went on to say that, though philosophy had now been 'reduced to a matter of skill', yet this skill, like other skills, is very difficult to acquire. One difficulty was that it required a 'sort of thinking' to which we are not accustomed and to which we have not been trained—a sort of thinking very different from what is required in the sciences" (*PP* 322; see GI 8, 71). See Man. 108, 248.

(b) goes with: for seeing an aspect is subject to the will (p. 213f), and willing "is also trying, attempting, making an effort" (§615; see §§618–19)—though frequently there is no trying when one acts voluntarily (§§622–23).

But I cannot try . . . : so it would be misleading to classify such seeing as a voluntary act (see XXXVII, 11); for here the reason is not the ease with which the deed is done, or the absence of obstacles (§623).

an F: cp. Z 208.

(c) Do not ask . . . : see GI 48, 60; X, 22; XXXVII, 16; pp. 204g, 211a.

"This is a personal report. It is, therefore, for us, not interesting. It records what is the case (1) so far, (2) now, (3) for me" (JN 84).

(d) not simply another figure: like that on the right; but, for instance, a pointer (see §454) or an object streaking through space ("very different things", therefore).

(e) See Man. 232, 735; cp. §282c; Man. 232, 732.

A piece of fancy . . . : cp. §539, pp. 207j, 208cd, 210d.

(fg) See Man. 232, 735–36; Man. 132, 12–13.

to say he *sees* it: since seeing, unlike intending or thinking, "is not an action but a state" (Z 208); and here the chest simply *is* a house for the child, without any effort on his part (see pp. 205a, 212e). Or the justification might go as follows: Sight gives us knowledge of what things are, not what they seem to be (Z 477); and for the child the chest *is* a house. W. no longer suggests, as in Man. 232, that he might say, "*Now* I see it as a house" (cp. p. 195j).

(h) **to the dawning of an aspect:** see pp. 194b, 195j, 206k, 212a.

(i) See p. 195b.

and *now* he spoke: see p. 205l ("One does not say and do this the whole time").

(jk) the expression in one's voice and gestures: an example of "fine shades of behaviour" (cp. p. 207a) which "have important consequences" (p. 204l).

ended by *becoming* . . . : see pp. 195l, 205afh, 206g; cp. pp. 194e, 201d.

I have a theme played . . . : cp. p. 202k.

P. 207(a) 'Fine shades of behaviour': see pp. 203b, 204l.

(b) See Man. 232, 718 (different example).

The aspects of the triangle: it is apparently not necessary, for W.'s present purposes (cp. *h*), to distinguish between permanent aspects, in a picture (p. 201cd), and aspects of a bare triangle (p. 200c), demanding imagination (p. 207j).

it is as if: but see XXXVII, 14.

an *image:* though in general "the concept of an aspect is akin to the concept of an image" (p. 213), the present remark does not apply to aspects in general. See (*c*).

(c) Cp. (*h*); Köhler, *Gestalt,* 219–20. Man. 130 considers the relation of this case to that in p. 176g.

of the step: on p. 203.

"double cross": Koffka's figure (*Principles,* 83).

(d) You must remember . . . : for such representations of what is seen are the criteria of the visual experience (p. 198bc); the impression is different if I describe it differently (p. 202b).

(e) See XXXVII, 16.

The temptation . . . : see Man. 229, §1531. This temptation is correlative to that discussed in XXXVII, 14 ("some kind of addition of experiences").

"I am tempted to say, 'This isn't just a scribble, but it's *this* particular face.'—But I can't say, 'I see *this* as *this* face,' but ought to say 'I see this as *a* face.' But I feel I want to say, 'I don't see this as *a* face, I see it as *this* face.' But in the second half of this sentence the word 'face' is redundant, and it should have run, 'I don't see this as a face, I see it like *this* ' " (*BB* 170). See p. 186c and commentary.

   pointing to the same thing: rather than as in, e.g., pp. 196j–197a.
   the private object: see §§374, 401, pp. 196f, 199hi.
   in this way: cp. Man. 229, §1730, quoted for p. 212d ("this can screen").
   assume that it constantly changes: as in §§270–71, 293, p. 222h. "We are meant to see the *senselessness* of this supposition: for what in the world would *show* that I was deceived constantly or even once? Do I look again—and why can't I be deceived that time, too?" (Malcolm, "Investigations", 211; see commentary on §258, and X, 20–21, in addition to XXXVII, 16). "Where what is remembered is a private object, we have no way of distinguishing between an accurate memory of an unchanging object and a deceptive memory of a changing one" (Kenny, "Criterion", 260).

   A helpful comparison: "To get rid of the notion of absolute size, assume that the size of your desk constantly changes, but that you do not notice the change because the size of everything else changes correspondingly." Closer: "To get rid of the Russellian idea that you see only your visual impressions, assume that the desk constantly changes color but that people do not notice the change since their sight is defective" (see NL 316b). Or "what if someone asked: 'How do I know that what I call seeing red isn't an *entirely* different experience very time? and that I am not deluded into thinking that it is the same or nearly the same?' Here again the answer 'I can't know' and the subsequent removal of the question" (NL 279).

(fgh) Revised from Man. 232, 728.
   before it could talk: or had even seen white or black crosses (*i*).
   could not be described . . . : see pp. 194f, 196a, 196j–197a.
(i) Cp. Köhler, *Gestalt*, 208.
   conversant with the shapes: see Man. 229, §740. W. does not say, as in Man. 229, §1540: "Don't you have need of *these concepts*?" Notice the parallel that emerges, therefore, with imagination (a theme of this page and of p. 213): Imagining and aspect-seeing are sometimes dependent on concepts (compare §517 with p. 208; XXXVII, 18), sometimes not (compare Man. 179, in GI 43, with the duck-rabbit and the aspects A).
   analogous condition: e.g. needing to have seen "an isolated white and an isolated black cross" (*f*) or (still closer) three-dimensional crosses (p. 208a).
(j) the bare triangular figure: as in p. 200c, and not in p. 201d.
   demands *imagination*: cp. (*b*); §539; Z 201; PG 176c.

P. 208(ab) See p. 207i.

not essentially three-dimensional: one may see "a white cross on a black ground" (p. 207c) either as standing out from the ground or as in the same plane, much as one may see a single drawing "either as a cube or as a plane figure consisting of a square and two rhombuses" (*BB* 163). And defining the aspects A in these terms does not specify just one of the two possibilities, as the expression "see as a cube" does.

as are the three-dimensional aspects: this may sound tautological ("Of course," one might say, "if you mention just three-dimensional aspects, then the aspects A, which may be either flat or three-dimensional, differ from them"). But note that though one may see the cube drawing as a plane figure, it does not have plane aspects—that is, alternate ways of seeing it flat, analogous to those of seeing the double cross. Cp. p. 207bc and Man. 229, §1780, quoted for (*f*).

(cd) Considerably revised from Man. 232, 727.

as a box: see XXXVII, 2–5.

now as a paper, now as a tin: cp. p. 193h ("here a glass cube . . . there a wire frame").

I can set a limit . . . : "one will have to depict it as a limiting case" (§385), not simply exclude it (pp. 193i, 208d). Even so, the following series of possibilities emerges: aspect-seeing without imagination (e.g. the aspects A); aspect-seeing with imagination (e.g. p. 207j); imagination without aspect-seeing (e.g. §517b).

Knowing in dreams: see the commentary on p. 216c ("Call it a dream").

(e) See (*ghi*) and XXXVII, 18.

" 'But in seeing I can obviously *take elements together* (lines for example).' But why does one call it 'taking together'? Why does one here—*essentially*—need a word that already has another meaning? (This is of course like the case of the phrase '*calculating* in one's head'.)" (*Z* 206).

"*these* things": rather, these dots (*Punkte*). See JN 91 (quoted for p. 196c) and *BB* 164 (quoted for *f,* below).

(f) See Man. 229, 453–55, and the quotation from Man. 229, §1783, for p. 206a.

One *kind:* "The word 'organization' goes very well with the concept 'go together'. There seem here to be a number of simple modifications of the visual impression which are genuinely 'optical'. However, in different aspects one may do entirely different things than separate parts and take them together, or repress them and bring them out" (Man. 229, §1780). See JN 91, quoted for p. 196c.

'aspects of organization': see p. 196ci.

parts of the picture go together: for instance, the head, torso, and arms of a human shape where before one saw only branches (p. 196c). Cp. "seeing these four dots . . . . as two pairs of dots side by side with each other, or as two interlocking pairs, or as one pair inside the other, etc." (*BB* 164).

(ghi) Revised from Man. 232, 725. See (*e*); XXXVII, 18; §508, p. 209ab.

cannot so far mean anything: the words evoke a situation like this: A parent points out a train, station, and passengers to a child for the first time, then tells him: "Now play trains with these blocks—see them as trains" (cp. §282c).

only just met . . . : cp. the analogous case in p. 214h.

as an empirical proposition: but rather as a remark about the concept *see as*. Cp. §§251b, 360; *BB* 55c.

mastery of a technique: cp. §§199, 692.

(j) the logical condition: not merely *a* criterion. Cp. *Z* 124.

different though related concept: compare this modified concept of experience with the similarly modified concepts of seeing (p. 209b) and of sensation (p. 209m).

P. 209(abc) See XXXVII, 16, 18; p. 208ghij.

the *concept* of seeing is modified: cp. pp. 208j, 209m.

dizziness in mathematics: for instance over minus one interpreted as a cardinal number (p. 219e) or imaginary numbers in comparison with real.

and only *later:* see GI 10–11; I, 5; §122; *Z* 114–21, 525; *PG* 62d–63a; cp. 4.002.

of their life: see §432; *BB* 4d–5a.

(de) For how could I . . . : "for" (not required by *denn*) makes too strong a connection; W. is not providing an illustration of (*a*), but an analogous case.

But surely that only means: the objection provides an alternative explanation of why the sensation alone does not suffice: The description adds to what I see—as does *sad* when applied to a human being (*g*).

to describe the object of sight: that is, just the object of sight; difficulties arise of the kind W. encountered (XXXIV, 2) when he attempted to construct a purely phenomenological language (X, 8).

a purely visual concept: stripped of "hypotheses" (X, 6). See (*g*); cp. quote for p. 210c.

(g) Cp. p. 199i.

this does *not* mean . . . : see commentary on p. 204jk; pp. 198d, 217d; *Z* 625, 646; cp. Augustine, *Confessions*, I, 6, 8 ("So I flung out limbs and sounds, making signs similar to my desires").

"Such an association may be due to a similarity but it is *not noticing a similarity.* Koehler said that the truth that the 'sea-gulls looked as if they were called Emma' proves that there is a fundamental similarity between different sense experiences. This is wrong. The common limpness among some seagulls and some of the bourgeoisie at the sea side may be the cause of the remark. But there is no resemblance between the 'appearance' and the 'sound'. There is no similarity between Beethoven's music and his name. You may feel 'that the music goes rightfully with the name' but there is not involved any similarity" (JN 48; see Köhler, *Gestalt*, 242; cp. *BB* 132–34, 137).

(jkl) See p. 203ef.

One cannot mention . . . : cp. p. 187a.

Others: for instance Berkeley, in *Dialogues,* I, 383–84, 416 ("in truth and strictness, nothing can be *heard* but *sound*").

differences of concept: "What does it mean to say I 'hear' *in a different sense* the piano, its sound, the piece, the player, his fluency? I 'marry', in one sense a woman, in another her money" (Z 11).

(m) in the *full* sense: not a purely visual one; cp. (*efg*).

in our muscles and joints: where James localized much sensing. See the commentary on p. 185b.

modified concept: see pp. 208j, 209b.

**P. 210(ab) blind to the *expression:* cp. pp. 213g–214d.

not simply a question for physiology: cp. p. 213g ("A conceptual investigation"). The words "on that account" could be understood as a logical inference or as a scientific one. The conceptual question can be studied without determining whether certain eye movements, say, are a causal condition for having the experience in question (cp. p. 212d).

the physiological: that is, this talk of blindness or defective eyesight. Man. 138, 8A, adds: " 'He has the eye of a painter,' 'the ear of a musician'."

(c) Cp. pp. 196j–197a; Man. 138, 6B: "But the truth is: 'Plaint' is a concept which is not purely auditory."

seriousness: cp. *Kreis,* 170.

(d) here there is a close kinship: see XXXVII, 13; p. 214e; Man. 229, §1731; cp. p. 181f; *BB* 165bc. P. 193h provides an intermediate case between this one and that, say, of §652.

'experiencing the meaning': see pp. 175–76, 216ab.

(e) Comparison with p. 176bc shows that the observations which start here and continue to the end of p. 211 illustrate the preceding remark about "close kinship with 'experiencing the meaning of a word' ", and are therefore relevant to the central question of this section discussed in XXXVII, 11–13.

only as long as I am occupied . . . : see pp. 204c, 205i.

"See, it's looking!": see pp. 181f (for connection with experiencing a word), 205l.

"**For how long . . .**": see XXXVII, 11; Man. 229, §1528.

(**f**) **a physiognomy:** another connection with experiencing words. See §568, p. 181f.

which at first I imitate: cp. p. 205l ("And one 'looks' oneself as one says this").

isn't it too much?: e.g. *imitate* suggests a voluntary act, and *accept* suggests another, whereas what follows may be the mere absence of the initial experience (cp. §596). Such misgivings arise naturally from e.g. p. 205jk. Like much of what follows, they are relevant to p. 212e.

(**g**) "**I observed the likeness**": see p. 193be.

P. 211(ab)   the whole time?: see XXXVII, 11; cp. §§595–96, p. 59n.

in the third person: see pp. 204g, 206c.

When would you say of someone . . . : see XXXVII, 16.

how did he learn . . . : cp. (*i*) and e.g. §646, p. 231ef.

do I believe him?: cp. §386.

a false foundation: for the false foundation in the first case, see e.g. §148 ("a state of consciousness or a process") and §596 ("The place for this kind of atmosphere is there . . ."); for that in the second, see James, *Principles*, I, 472 (quoted for §598).

(**cde**) **I can imagine a significant context . . . :** the word *conscious* does not have one clear meaning (*e*) which it carries with it into every kind of application (§§117, 520).

(**f**) **Above all . . . :** see GI 60; XLI, 5; pp. 210ab, 212d.

(**ghi**) **The likeness . . . :** see pp. 193be, 210gh.

What can I recall?: cp. §§645–46. The avowal "I was struck by the likeness" is no more based on these "phenomena of being struck" than it is on what goes on in the eyes or brain (*f*).

had seen my face . . . : such are the criteria of being struck (XXXVII, 16).

No. These are the phenomena . . . : not the criteria, nor therefore the "essence" (§§370–71).

(**j**) **No:** "Being struck is related to thinking" (Man. 138, 3), and "the flashing of an aspect on us seems half visual experience, half thought" (p. 197f), but there is here no "addition of experiences" (XXXVII, 14), visual and mental. See pp. 197jk, 212bc.

cross **here:** see Z 569 and Man. 228, §160 (quoted for Preface, *c*). On one and the same occasion (e.g. p. 210g), following similar or partly identical criteria, one might say: "You *saw* the similarity between him and his father," "You *thought* of his father," "He *reminded* you of his father," "You were *struck* by his resemblance to his father," and so on (cp. p. 197de). For aspect-seeing in general the connections are far broader: with meaning, understanding, intending, imagining, interpreting, recognizing, perceiving, and so forth.

(**k**) Before exploring further the relation between thinking and the dawning of an aspect, W. sets aside a conception which would make the connection appear more distant than it is. Herder, for instance, wrote in *Metakritik der reinen Vernunft:* "What does thinking mean? Speaking internally. Speaking is thinking aloud" (Brann, Review, 666). *"Thought* and *discourse,* then," wrote Plato, "are one and the same thing, only that it is the interior voiceless converse of a soul with itself to which we have given this particular name, *thought"* (*Sophist,* 263E). Russell was slightly more guarded: "What is called 'thought' consists mainly (though I think not wholly) of inner speech" (*Mind,* 152). For further samples, see the commentary on §32.

I do not say 'to oneself': W. is both clarifying his meaning and eliminating an error. And he clarifies his meaning so as to eliminate a second, more fundamental mistake: the identification of thought with inner speech (see above). The latter differs from speaking to oneself, first because "when one says 'I talk to myself' one generally means just that one speaks and is the only person listening" (NL 276), not that the speech is silent, and second because "a person can speak silently without speaking to himself" (Man. 138, 18B; see Man. 228, §116). For "can't I say something to nobody, neither to anybody else *nor* to myself?" (NL 299). Sometimes, it is true, when we speak of silent talk to oneself we mean no more than silent talk (see p. 223b; cp. §357); but one may wonder whether that was all that Plato meant, or whether he had even considered the difference, when he spoke (above) about "the interior voiceless converse of a soul with itself". In this vein, see also GI 40; X, 5, 10 (final quotation), 15–16; commentary on §32b (" 'talk to itself' "). One may also speculate whether private language theories, naive (X, 2) or refined, would have survived the distinction W. here makes (cp. §280 and commentary); for language has typically been conceived as a system of communication (§§363, 491).

different concepts: "sometimes, when I say 'I thought . . .' I can recount that I then said just these words, silently or aloud; or that I did not then use these precise words but others, of which the present ones are an equivalent rendering" (Man. 229, §904). This is what happens, sometimes, but it does not determine the concept *thought* (p. 217cdef; §316). "To be ashamed of a thought. Is one ashamed at the fact that one has spoken such-and-such a sentence in one's imagination?" (Z 656; cp. §§643–44).

P. 212(a) is not a property of the object: see XXXVII, 14; p. 196d ("neither is it anything of the same category"); Man. 109, 291; cp. p. 196i.

but an internal relation: see *RFM* 30; cp. *PG* 445a; *PB* 63e; Man. 138, 5A ("In noting an aspect one perceives an internal relation and accordingly I related it to *imagination*").

"A property is internal," said W. in the *Tractatus,* "if it is unthinkable that its object should not possess it" (4.123). Thus if a relation is internal, "it is unthinkable that *these* two objects should not stand in this relation" (ibid.; see *Kreis,* 54–55; *PP* 294; Man. 176, 1). Likeness between two things (as opposed, say, to their spatial proximity) is a paradigm example; change the terms of the relation and the relation changes. And the example W. used to illustrate "noting an aspect" was: "I see the likeness between these two faces" (p. 193; see pp. 210gh, 211ghi). "Seeing the likeness of one face with another, the analogy of one mathematical form with another, a human form in the lines of a picture-puzzle, a spatial form in a schematic drawing, hearing or saying the 'pas' in 'ne . . . pas' in the sense of 'step' " (Man. 229, §982)—"in *all those* cases it may be said that we experience a *comparison.* For the expression of the experience is that we are inclined to make a comparison" (ibid., §983). Though we do not, for instance, call a rabbit to mind when we see the duck-rabbit figure as a rabbit, nor make a comparison (XXXVII, 14), we explain our experience by pointing to rabbits or pictures of rabbits (pp. 194f, 196j–197a).

(bc) echo of a thought: see pp. 197efjk, 211j; Man. 229, §1703; cp. p. 207b. On the one hand, no comparison takes place (see above and below); on the other hand, the object responsible for the experience—for instance the person whom I have not seen for years (p. 197i)—is not merely a causal antecedent. "I see the old face in the altered one" (ibid.).

(d) See Man. 229, §§690, 1097–1100, 1656, 1679; cp. *BB* 6; Köhler, *Gestalt,* 212; Helmholtz, *Schriften,* 125–26 ("In my works on physiological optics I sought to explain our knowledge of the visual field through observation of likenesses while we move our eyes"). *BB* 164 anticipates this paragraph and suggests a connection with the preceding one. "This *explanation* of the phenomenon of seeing the figure as a swastika is of no fundamental interest to us. It is of interest to us only in so far as it helps one to see that the expression 'seeing the figure as a swastika' did not mean seeing *this* or *that,* seeing one thing as something else, when, essentially, *two* visual objects entered the process of doing so. . . . And in this way 'seeing dashes as a face' does not involve a comparison between a group of dashes and a real human face." Now, however, W. rejects more resolutely the idea that such observations would have *any* relevance for the conceptual problem. With what right could we infer from eye movements that no comparison takes place?

Aspects A: see p. 207f.

"Yes, that shews . . .": see Man. 229, §1679; cp. Helmholtz, *Optik,* 611.

You have now introduced a new . . . : cp. §§184, 239b, 633, 665, pp. 205i, 222j.

this can screen . . . : "Thinking in terms of physiological processes is extremely dangerous for the clarification of conceptual problems in psychology. Thinking in physiological hypotheses sometimes suggests false difficulties, and sometimes false solutions. The best antidote is the thought that I don't know at all whether my acquaintances really have a nervous system" (Man. 229, §1730; see *Z* 608–9; cp. GI 60; p. 207e).

Russell exemplifies the approach here criticized when, for example, he distinguishes images from sensations "by the fact that their causes and effects are different from those of sensations" (*Mind*, 145; see also 152b). Were this presented as an account of the concept *image*, the question would be whether we know anything about these causal differences (GI 60). If it is meant as a scientific hypothesis, then the question becomes: What class of things does the hypothesis cover, if not the class called "images", and how is that class to be determined if not by consulting the word's use, and what reason is there to suppose that its use is such as to permit such a scientific hypothesis (GI 70)? Besides, what need is there in philosophy of causal hypotheses if our unclarity is conceptual (§122)?

the old problem: that is, conceptual puzzlement such as that expressed in p. 197j (connecting with the preceding paragraph here on p. 212), and more particularly (as indicated by this and the subsequent paragraphs) the question whether aspect-seeing is really seeing (pp. 203ef, 206fg) and therefore whether I really *see* something different each time (*e*).

but not solve it: the method of §370 is required for that. See p. 220b.

when a physiological explanation is offered: "The whole show could be described without physiological facts; but as the Gestalt men make great play with these facts, their opponents, and ordinary men, naturally give them weight: at the very least the Gestalt psychologists treat the retinal point as something to be explained away, or considered as prima facie telling against them" (JN 90). See Köhler, *Gestalt,* chapter on "Dynamics opposed to Machine Theory", e.g. 168. For full illustration of W.'s viewpoint, see Malcolm, "Nature", 25–28.

hangs out of reach: see GI 60; p. 232b; Man. 229, §981; Hunter, *Essays,* 164–67, 197–98; cp. *Z* 66; *PB* 69f.

And this makes . . . : see Man. 232, 609–10. Once we realize that anything or nothing may happen in the eyes, brain, and so forth (p. 211f; *Z* 608–9; cp. p. 207e), then we know that seeing cannot be defined in physiological terms (§§370–71), and are ready to let the use of the word *see* teach us its meaning (*f*). That is, (*d*) is a remedy for the kind of situation described in §308.

(e) See commentary on p. 195f; *Z* 208; cp. *PG* 147bc.

Do I really see something different: see XXXVII, 22; pp. 195fg, 201k; cp. p. 197g.

do I only interpret . . . : cp. pp. 193ij, 200e.

I am inclined to say: as W. did in 5.5423 and *PG* 78. Cp. pp. 195f, 205a, 206g. P. 213f suggests one reason why it is a mere inclination.

is to think: see §201c, and (*f*). Cp. Man. 123 (17.5): "Interpreting is an articulated process, like translating, decoding; seeing a drawing as this or that is amorphous." "An *interpretation* is something that is given in signs" (*Z* 229)—say, "the substitution of one expression of the rule for another" (§201)—whereas aspect-seeing is not.

to do something: "When I interpret, I step from one level of thought to another" (*Z* 234; *PG* 147). Cp. *PG* 172: "Thinking is an activity, as is calculating. No one would call calculating a state, or playing chess."

is a state: see Berkeley, *Dialogues*, I, 407. "Seeing is not an action but a state. (A grammatical remark)" (*Z* 208). For instance, seeing has duration (cp. p. 59n), and so does aspect-seeing (Man. 229, §1550). True, in the cases W. has just been discussing, "what dawns here lasts only as long as I am occupied with the object in a particular way" (p. 210); but it does last that long, and it is not the operation. See (*f*).

(f) Took form in Man. 130, 90–91.

we form hypotheses: interpretation "may for example consist in somebody's saying 'That is *supposed* to be an F'; or not saying it, but replacing the sign with an F in copying; or again considering: 'What can that be? It'll be an F that the writer did not hit off' " (*Z* 208). See §539.

or in the same sense as: that is, by "a confession whose truth is guaranteed by the special criteria of *truthfulness*" (p. 222). See pp. 198bc, 202b.

So there is a similarity: in addition to that just pointed out for (*e*).

do not think you knew in advance: or else you may, for instance, overlook the fact that unlike many states and like many acts, seeing an aspect is subject to the will (p. 213f). See §308.

Let the use *teach* you . . . : see §340, p. 220e.

(g) we find certain things . . . puzzling: see e.g. pp. 200e, 203efg, 208j, 209b; cp. p. 215e.

because we do not find . . . : see §524, pp. 200a (and commentary), 213b; cp. §§308, 363b, p. 205g; Malcolm, *Memoir*, 50 (quoted for p. 198d).

P. 213(a)   See p. 202a. This paragraph and the next continue p. 212g, suggesting aspects of seeing we might find surprising.

(b) See Man. 229, §1759; cp. James, *Principles*, II, 222ff.

(cd) is akin to: for "another expression would be: 'Imagine the drawing as something.' But that does *not* mean, so to say, hallucinating something onto the drawing" (Man. 123 [17.5]). "A chief characteristic which distinguishes imagination from a sense impression or hallucination is this, that one who imagines does not take an observant attitude towards the image, and that the image is thus voluntary" (Man. 229, §1553; see §1567 below), as an aspect is (*f*). Thus neither is like a picture (Z 621; see Köhler, *Gestalt,* 180–81), or like a sensation. "It is just because forming images is a voluntary activity that it does not instruct us about the external world" (Z 627). "Images," like aspects (XXXVII, 5; Man. 229, §1567, below), "tell us nothing, either right or wrong, about the external world" (Z 621). In fact, I cannot imagine an object while I am actually looking at it (ibid.), much as I cannot take the cutlery itself as cutlery (p. 195d), nor see the old face in the *old* face (p. 197i). In neither case, though, does a mental comparison take place with the absent object (XXXVII, 14; Z 621). Yet in both cases we are dependent on the object and on sense-concepts to express the aspect or what we have imagined (XXXVII, 16; Man. 229, §1553). For further observations on this kinship, see the following parapraphs, and Man. 229, §§1659, 1668.

'having *this* image': a better translation: "imagining *this*".

Doesn't it take imagination . . . : cp. p. 207bj.

And yet one is perceiving . . . : cp. p. 197e.

(e) "you have this other thing": to sense the connection with the preceding sentence, and the point of the subsequent remark about proof, stress the word *have* (cp. pp. 205f, 206efg). We perceive, as we prove, what is. Cp. *RFM* 16: "I should like to say that it is not merely these individual figures that are correlated in the proof, but the *shapes themselves*."

One can use imagining . . . : rather: "In the medium of imagination one can prove something." One can arrive at what *is*. Cp. *RFM* 29, e.g.: "I can *calculate* in the medium of imagination, but not experiment."

(f) Cp. Man. 232, 737: "One would like to ask about aspect-seeing: 'Is it seeing? Is it thinking?' The aspect is subject to the will: that makes it akin to thinking."

are subject to the will: see XXXVII, 11; p. 206b; Z 51–52, 632–33, 637, 640–43; Man. 232, 620–36 ("The proposition 'The imagination is subject to the will' is not a proposition of psychology"); Man. 112, 98; James, *Principles,* II, 257a; Helmholtz, *Optik,* 771.

"What Köhler doesn't treat is the fact that a person can *view* the figure . . . thus and so, that the aspect is subject to the will, at least to a certain degree" (Man. 229, §1638). "The fact that the aspect is voluntary (at least to a certain extent) seems essential to it, as also to imagination. I mean: voluntariness seems to me (but why?) not to be a trimming, as though one were to say, 'As a matter of experience, this movement can also be brought about *thus.*' That is: it is essential that a person can say 'See it thus!' and 'Imagine. . . .' For this is connected with the fact that the aspect 'teaches us nothing about the external world' " (Man. 229, §1567; cp. Z 593).

but not: see p. 195cd.

(gh) See XXXVII, 19. Revised from Man. 232, 723–24.

The question now arises: see Man. 229, §§690, 736, 834. For an analogous investigation, cp. *RFM* 118–19. On W.'s motivation, see Man. 232, 745: "*We* are not interested in what forms of mental deficiency actually exist, but in the possibility of such forms. . . . Where does this concept lead us?"

What sort of consequences . . . : this question differs from, but is dependent on, the "conceptual investigation" ("what would that be like?").

"aspect-blindness": cp. Köhler, *Gestalt,* 169–72; James, *Principles,* I, 48c–50, e.g.: "A most interesting effect of cortical disorder is *mental blindness.* This consists not so much in insensibility to optical impressions, as in *inability to understand* them. Psychologically it is interpretable as *loss of associations* between optical sensations and what they signify." W.'s question is: Would the loss of "associations" such as he has been studying result in loss of understanding? Would our words, for instance, cease to have meaning (XXXVII, 19; p. 214)?

A conceptual investigation: cp. Z 267.

the aspects A: the two aspects of the double cross, on p. 207.

I do not want to settle this: for he does not strive for completeness (p. 206a) or fine distinctions (p. 200b) but for a synoptic view (Z 464). The decision would be verbal (cp. §68a), adding little or nothing to our understanding of the case.

(i) It would not follow . . . : cp. pp. 195j, 201h, 214h.

a working drawing: see p. 204l.

P. 214(ab) see Man. 232, 724.

take **it:** this term (*halten*) is much discussed in Man. 130, for instance: "Let us consider the case of the picture of wheels rotating against one another [cp. drawing in Man. 166]. First I can see the movement in the picture as *one* or the *other*. Second, I can also *take* it for one or the other."

"Isn't what Köhler says roughly this: 'We couldn't *take* something for this or that if we couldn't *see* it as this or that'? But what does that mean? Does a child start by seeing a thing this or that way before it learns to take it as this or that?" (Man. 134, May 10; see Köhler, *Gestalt,* 151–52).

this could not very well . . . : thus, as the words "in certain circumstances" and the contrast with seeing the cube as a cube already indicate, the sense of *take* is not the same here as in pp. 195d and 201i, but one suggested, for instance, by p. 204l or p. 206e. Though we might *also* say that the children see the chest as a house (p. 206fg), inability to play house or to play trains (§282c) would hardly be called a sort of blindness. Cp. Man. 229, §1770.

    an altogether different relationship: see p. 205cd.

    to pictures: cp. *Z* 233; *PG* 146d.

(c) Anomalies of *this* kind: see Man. 232, 724–26 (e.g.: "He shouldn't be able to see the picture of someone running as a picture of movement"). After examples like those in p. 205g and *PG* 42a, Man. 130 adds: "There could be people who in a photograph saw no more than a sort of diagram, as we for instance regard a map. We could gather various things about the landscape from it, but could not admire the scenery as we looked at the map, or exclaim 'What a marvellous view!'"

(d) will be *akin* to: cp. §67b, p. 213.

    a 'musical ear': see §534; *Z* 208c (quoted in XXXVII, 12).

(ef) See Man. 229, §§718, 916; Man. 131, 24ff.

    the connexion between the concepts . . . : see XXXVII, 13–19; Man. 110, 44; *PG* 42 ("The various experiences I have when I see a picture first one way and then another are comparable to the experience I have when I read a sentence with understanding and without"). Cp. Helmholtz, *Schriften*, 124.

    "What would you be missing . . . ?": see XXXVII, 19; *PG* 64b; Man. 229, §868; JN 60; cp. Man. 115, 19–23.

In answer to the impression "that there are *certain definite* mental processes bound up with the working of language, processes through which alone language can function" (*BB* 3; see *BB* 42a), W. has already pointed out the possibility of a language without such characteristic experiences (§530); now he would like to know just how radically such a language would differ from ours.

The queries and suggestions in Man. 130 are fuller. For instance: "How can the lack of an experience in hearing the word hinder or influence calculating with words?" (Cp. §449.) Again: "Should the 'meaning-blind' be unable to say: 'As I started the sentence, I was going to say . . . then I thought better of it & said . . .'?" "So is the meaning-blind person the one who *doesn't* say: 'The whole train of thought stood before me in a flash'? But does that mean he cannot say, 'Now I have it!'?" "If someone were what we would call 'meaning-blind', we would imagine that he had to make a less lively impression than we, that he would have to act more 'like an automaton'. . . . In the experiment where one speaks an isolated word, our 'meaning-blind' people could not say which of its meanings it had had for them. But if we speak the word in a context where it has a meaning, even though not in a sentence, they react to it according to *one* of its meanings."

    "did not *experience* the meaning": see §530 and references, commentary; §432, p. 210d; *PG* 58c; cp. *Z* 233; *PG* 146de.

    if it was repeated: see JN 57; cp. p. 202h.

"If we look at an isolated printed word and repeat it long enough, it ends by assuming an entirely unnatural aspect. Let the reader try this with any word on this page. He will soon begin to wonder if it can possibly be the word he has been using all his life with that meaning. It stares at him from the paper like a glass eye, with no speculation in it. Its body is indeed there, but its soul is fled" (James, *Principles,* II, 80–81).

(g) from certain facts: not introspectible or physiological ones (cp. *LC* 21c).

It is a question of *intention*: see p. 216i.

But could how . . . : pp. 217c and 218e give the answer.

the word "bank": see p. 216i; *Z* 183.

(h) Revised from Man. 232, 726 (different examples).

Suppose I had agreed: See JN 59.

he understands me: so once again, experiencing the meaning is not a process "through which alone language can function" (*BB* 3).

and acts accordingly: this, too, belongs to the functioning of language. The idea that language cannot operate without a flow of meanings through the mind stems largely from the narrow conception criticized in §363 ("someone else grasps the sense of my words . . . everything else is inessential").

to be strange: see *Z* 231; *PG* 145b; cp. p. 208g.

(i) See §531; *Z* 170; cp. p. 206k; *LC* 4c.

"When I read a poem . . .": as W. frequently did, aloud, very effectively.

a different *ring*: see §545.

I can also . . . : cp. §534.

And this may, of course . . . : a concession, perhaps, to the viewpoint treated in §559. Cp. *Z* 233; *PG* 146d.

p. 215(a) filled with its meaning: cp. §543; *Z* 176.

"meaning is the use": see §43.

intended figuratively: yet was not a metaphor (p. 216h).

it forced itself: see p. 204k.

can't get into conflict: see p. 200f.

(b) Perhaps it could be explained: see XXXVII, 17; cp. p. 216d.

***this* picture:** of the word "filled with its meaning".

(c) can strike me as like a painting: see GI 32; I, 1; *Z* 241 ("a sentence of our word-language approximates to a picture in this picture-language much more closely than we think"); *PG* 169e–170b, 171def.

"It is obvious that a proposition of the form '*aRb*' strikes us as a picture. In this case the sign is obviously a likeness of what is signified" (4.012).

and the very individual word . . . : as in a hieroglyphic script, which according to 4.016 reveals "the essential nature of a proposition".

" 'The picture tells me something': it uses *words,* so to speak: here are eyes, mouth, nose, hands, etc., etc. I am comparing the picture to a combination of linguistic forms" (*PG* 170).

in itself: see I, 3.

(d) Cp. §607; James, *Principles,* II, 85–103.

throws light on these matters: that is, on the application of a term for no reason (pp. 215a, 216), though as a result of causes which might perhaps be detected or surmised (XXXVII, 17; pp. 215c, 216d).

"You may think it's like the case where you are forced to answer 'which composer would you say was thin soup and which was thick soup?' Everyone might say the same. Sometimes they give a reason, sometimes not. The second alternative is the one we find important" (JN 23; see *BB* 88, quoted for p. 216b).

(e) Cp. §524, p. 212g.

our sense impressions for instance: whereas we (often) say a thing is red because we have seen it is, here we have not observed the city on our right.

(f) "as if the name . . . fitted": not because I have made a comparison, or even know how one might be attempted (*BB* 166a, 170a); yet here too we sense at least a causal explanation: "Closely associated things, things which we *have* associated, seem to fit one another" (p. 183; see XXXVII, 17).

See p. 183def; *EPB* 184; *PG* 179b; JN 48 (quoted for p. 209g); cp. §171a; NL 292a; *BB* 148c. W. often cited Goethe in this connection (see the Appendix).

(g) "March": chosen in place of *Weiche,* which can be either an imperative ("Away!") or an adjective ("soft", etc.). The example was suggested by a pun (Man. 131, 165; Man. 135, July 22).

"March *no further!*": the action is prohibited rather than commanded (as also in the German example); hence the feeling would doubtless differ. W. uses this tactic repeatedly (e.g. §§443, 545; *RFM* 143kl).

Does the *same* experience: see XXXII, 4; pp. 181f–182a; *Z* 177.

(h) If a sensitive ear shews me . . . : see §595; *EPB* 218; *BB* 78–79a, 156a–157a, 159bc; Man. 229, §§832–33, 857, 860, 1720; cp. §§596, 602–4, pp. 205jkl, 210d–211b; *BB* 127a.

P. 216(a) is, of course, not in question: see pp. 181, 216i–217c.

(bc) experiencing a word: as opposed to its customary use in the language, which is ordinarily called its meaning (§43). See p. 216a; *BB* 156–57, 159bc.

a different kind of question: not experiential, as in (*a*), but apparently an "attempt at justification". Apply §§654–55 and p. 200ab.

"If you ask 'why', do you ask for the cause or for the reason? If for the cause, it is easy enough to think up a physiological or psychological hypothesis which explains this choice under the given conditions. It is the task of the experimental sciences to test such hypotheses. If on the other hand you ask for a reason the answer is, 'There need not have been a reason'" (*BB* 88).

in *this* situation: see §441; Man. 180b, 5–6.

take this expression over: the expression *meaning* (*Bedeutung*). Cp. *Z* 506.

Call it a dream: "Indeed I could dream of a chess game, but the dream perhaps showed me only one move of the game. Nevertheless I would have dreamed that I played a game of chess. Someone will say, 'You didn't really play, you only dreamed it.' Why shouldn't we also say 'You didn't really mean the word that way, you only dreamed it'?" (Man. 229, §1724). "Remember especially the expression used in recounting a dream: 'And I knew that. . . .' We might think: It is remarkable that man can dream that he *knew*" (ibid., §889; cp. §898). Cp. *LC* 43c.

(d) For similar remarks on *meaning* (*Bedeutung*), see Man. 229, §1728.

"fat" and "lean": see *EPB* 204; *BB* 137.

Certainly not: however, cp. §577.

I want to use *these* words: see §532b, pp. 204k (and commentary), 215a; *BB* 136.

They *might* be . . . : see Man. 131, 173–74: "Each of the days of the week has a special character for me, almost a special coloring. Monday, Wednesday, and Friday are fat, the others (except Sunday) are lean; there is something black and yellowish about Thursday. Now I think I know the origin of these feelings. They derive from two teachers who came to me alternately on these days. However, though I offer this explanation of the matter, I had the feelings before the explanation occurred to me."

(e) Cp. XXXVII, 16; §533.

I could *not*: cp. pp. 194f, 197a.

(f) 'secondary' sense: see (*h*); §282c; *EPB* 211–12; Man. 229, §§791–92, 799–800, 821, 1540–41; JN 60; Diamond, "Secondary", 189–200; cp. *PG* 178c.

of a word: *expectation* (*BB* 20e), *see, understand, mean,* and others (XXXVII, 15, 17–18).

(g) Only if you have learnt . . . : see XXXVII, 18; p. 208e and commentary; cp. Man. 138, 18B–19A (does playing tennis without a ball require that one play it first with one?).

(h) Cp. *RFM* 87ef; *BB* 117d; LE 10; NT 16; Man. 232, 610; Man. 138,

13B (on *good* and "good God", *punishment* and "punishments of Hell"); Man. 130 (similar discussion of the expression "feeling of unreality"); James, *Principles*, I, 582.

not a 'metaphorical' sense: cp. *BB* 6e; Frege, *Writings*, 115 ("I must confine myself to hinting at what I have in mind by means of a metaphorical expression, and here I rely on my reader's agreeing to meet me half-way").

Concerning, say, the use of *lighter* and *darker* for vowels as well as for colored objects, one may feel inclined to say: " 'What I mean by "darker" is not found in the relation between the sounds; I say it of the sounds only in a metaphorical sense, that is, only by way of comparison' " (*EPB* 231); or: " 'We don't think that the words "darker", "lighter" actually fit the relation between the vowels, we only feel a resemblance between the relation of the sounds and the darker and lighter colours' " (*BB* 148). "Again we might be inclined to say 'He must have seen something that was in common both to the relation between two colours and to the relation between two vowels.' But if he isn't capable of specifying what this common element was, this leaves us just with the fact that he was prompted to use the words 'darker', 'lighter' in both these cases" (*BB* 136).

"the vowel *e* is yellow": see p. 202h; Z 185; Man. 229, §1674; cp. James, *Principles*, II, 29b; Köhler, *Gestalt*, 242–43. In *Principles,* 266, Waismann refers to: "Rimbaud's poem 'Voyelles': 'A noir, E blanc, I rouge, U vert, O bleu, voyelles. . . .' " In *BB* and *EPB* W. discussed the arrangement of vowels in the order of their darkness (see the quotation above, and *EPB* 203–4, 210–12, 216, 231; *BB* 136–40, 143e, 148cd).

W.'s example may seem less suspect if put in series with others: (1) "When someone asks me 'What colour is the book over there?', and I say 'Red', and then he asks 'What made you call this colour "red"?', I shall in most cases have to say: 'Nothing *makes* me call it red; that is, *no reason*" (*BB* 148). (2) "Suppose we had taught a man to use the words 'green', 'red', 'blue' by pointing to patches of these colours. . . . Suppose we now show him a heap of leaves, some of which are slightly reddish brown, others a slightly greenish yellow, and give him the order 'Put the red leaves and the green leaves on separate heaps.' . . ." (*BB* 137). (3) "Now to the question 'What made you use the word "darker" . . . ?' the answer may be 'Nothing made me use the word "darker",— that is, if you ask me for a *reason* why I use it.' . . . It is easier to see this when we speak of a *deep* sorrow, a *deep* sound, a *deep* well" (*BB* 136–37).

for I could not express . . . : cp. XXXVII, 16; §§356, 439.

"It is not simply that words are lacking for a feature which I see in Tuesday, and to which I want to draw attention. It is not that I am aware of something in Tuesday, and then I see that the metaphorical use of 'lean' is appropriate" (Diamond, "Secondary", 191). And "the connection here is not like that between 'break off the thread' and 'break off the conversation', for in this case we *need* not use the figurative expression" (Man. 138, 13). Thus the difficulty of finding another, equally effective expression does not derive from my limited powers of expression as compared with those of a gifted poet.

"All he can say is 'I multiplied 16 × 17 in my head.' How do we use this phrase which sounds like a description or report? An obvious thing to begin with is to say 'in his head' is a metaphor, the multiplying is not localized in that way. But actually this business of localization is serious" (JN 33; cp. §427).

(i)   See Man. 232, 666, 669–71.

It refers to a definite time . . . : cp. pp. 175ab, 217i.

not to an *experience*: as James, for instance, maintained (e.g. *Principles*, I, 256 and 472, quoted for §138 and in XXVI, 4), and Moore (XXXVII, 21). See §§673–76.

P. 217(ab) See Man. 232, 667.

Meaning is as little an experience: see XXVI, 3–5; §676; *EPB* 223–30; *BB* 146–47.

as intending: see XXV, 2–4.

They have no . . . : see §§645–46; cp. pp. 218e, 231c; Man. 229, §774.

experience-content: see p. 231cd and commentary; Man. 229, §§1362, 1564 (quoted for p. 186c).

These references suggest the relevance of pp. 196de, 199hi, 207e as preparation for the present remarks.

are not the meaning: see §646; cp. §§314, 316, p. 181cd.

(c) does not 'accompany' the action: cp. §673; p. 218e and commentary.

any more than the thought . . . : see XI, 2; §330, p. 218g; *Z* 93–96, 100–101.

neither 'articulated': here W. corrects not only his earliest thought (e.g. 3.141) but also *PB* 70a and *BB* 6e, 16c. Cp. *BB* 35a.

nor 'non-articulated': to call it "amorphous" as in Man. 123 (17.5) would suggest that it is an amorphous process, running through the mind.

nor with a tune: see *BB* 42e, quoted for §330a; cp. *BB* 35: "A process accompanying our words which one might call the 'process of meaning them' is the modulation of the voice in which we speak the words; or one of the processes similar to this, like the play of facial expression. These accompany the spoken words not in the way a German sentence might accompany an English sentence, or writing a sentence accompany speaking a sentence; but in the sense in which the tune of a song accompanies its words." This too W. now rejects.

(d) Cp. pp. 198d, 209g, 211k, 223b (*"I* need not be talking"); *Z* 265; Man. 130 ("Plato said thought is speech").

   are not concepts of the same kind: as late as *BB* 6e and 16c W. thought they were. See also GI 40; X, 2; the references for §32b and p. 211k; *PG* 106b; Frege, *Funktion,* 90. For a similar denial, see p. 211k.

   in closest connexion: see §329 and commentary; cp. §§150, 225, pp. 198d, 209g; *Z* 625.

(e) The *interest . . .* **:** cp. pp. 181cd, 218efg.

   'unconscious' **intention:** see *BB* 23a; cp. §441b; *BB* 57–58.

   "Suppose Taylor and I are walking along the river and Taylor stretches out his hand and pushes me in the river. When I ask why he did this he says: 'I was pointing out something to you,' whereas the psycho-analyst says that Taylor subconsciously hated me. . . . Both explanations may be correct" (*LC* 22–23).

(f) Cp. §584; *Z* 31–32, and especially 36 (quoted in part for §452).

   how can it mean MORE: see GI 41, 43; XV, 1–5; cp. §§452–53.

   only a *germ:* see §641; *Z* 656; Man. 229, §§922, 1057; Man. 138, 15A, 17 (quoted for p. 219e). "The germ could be a word or a picture in the imagination, or various other things" (Man. 138, 15B).

(g) If God: "someone who could look into your mind" (*Z* 36).

   would not have been able to see there: see GI 43–44; XV, 1–4; *LC* 67d (quoted for §389). Contrast this with W.'s earlier view (GI 36–37) or Russell's (GI 37) or James's (e.g. *Principles,* I, 279c, or 282, quoted for §584).

(ij) you refer to that moment: cp. pp. 175ab, 216i.

   Mere explanation of a word: for instance of "the references that are essential to an utterance" and "which would make us translate some otherwise alien form of expression into this, our customary form" (p. 175c); as opposed here to reporting what one thought (*ik*).

(k) subsequent explanation of a word: e.g. "By 'Slab!' I meant 'Bring me a slab' " (see §19) or "When I said 'It'll get better soon' I meant the pain" (see §667).

   is quite different: see XI, 1; XXVI, 4–5; §§687, 693; Man. 138, 15A.

   is akin to: see (*h*).

(l) Of what importance . . . : the point parallels (*e*): The interest of the experience one had and of the remembering is not the same (see §305, p. 231).

P. 218(a) of the statement itself: "I don't read it off from some other process which took place then" (§637; see p. 231a), nor does it simply inform the hearer that this process took place (§363).

   It permits certain conclusions: cp. p. 189b and commentary.

(bc) See the commentary on p. 217f ("only a *germ*"); cp. §§290, 343, 379–82, p. 231a; Man. 138, 15A.

primitive reaction: to the words.

can then be translated: a loose way of speaking (see §§386a, 449, 459), about a relationship still to be discerned (cp. Z 191). Someone might say, as in §290: "But isn't the beginning my thought of him, which I now translate with the verbal expression *he*?" But, W. would ask, how did you think of *him* (§689)? If you had an image, was it such a faithful representation that you instantly recognized it was of him (§382, p. 177)?

How do people get to . . . : do they learn, for instance, that this is the process called "occurring to someone", or that a person is said to occur to one when this much of him appears, or these thoughts flash through one's mind? Cp. §§379–82, p. 231ef.

a glance or a gesture: cp. (*d*) and §669.

it may also have been a word: for instance his name; for what better sign is there of him? See p. 217f; cp. §§245, 669, pp. 174j, 177e; *BB* 128g.

(d) "look at me and shake your head": cp. "a glance or a gesture", in (*c*).

not a symbolic convention: establishing an equivalence between "primary signs" (*PG* 88–90)—e.g. the look and the shake of the head—and verbal ones (indicated by the dots). For W.'s target, see the quotation from *BB* 35 for (*f*).

but the purpose of my action: I state it confidently, yet could not give any rule (§653) by which I read off my intention from what went before (cp. §386). Intention—or meaning (see p. 214g)—cannot be identified with this antecedent process. "What sort of process—even if you could dream one up [as here]—could satisfy our requirements about purpose?" (Z 192; cp. *f*).

(ef) Meaning is not a process . . . : see the preceding comments; XXVI, 5–7; §329, p. 176h; *BB* 35; *PG* 152d–154a; cp. §34, pp. 181cd, 217bc; *PG* 271a; Man. 180b, 8.

In the *Investigations* W. no longer concedes that "there are, of course, real cases in which what we call meaning is a definite conscious process accompanying, preceding, or following the verbal expression and itself a verbal expression of some sort or translatable into one" (*BB* 35).

For no *process* . . . : cp. XXXVII, 19; §680, p. 176ef; James, *Principles*, I, 477 ("nor will swarms of copies of the same 'idea', recurring in stereotyped form, or 'by the irresistible laws of association formed into one idea', ever be the same thing as a thought of '*all the possible members*' of a class").

On the one hand, the process could not have the conceptual ramifications of meaning (*BB* 43a). On the other hand, it could not have the causal consequences; for "the 'specific experience' we had been looking for was meant to have played the role which has been assumed by the mass of experiences revealed to us by our scrutiny" (*BB* 86; *EPB* 127).

a calculation is not an experiment: see *RFM* 46, 95–96, 172; cp. *RFM* 32d. "I am . . . curious about the result. Not, however, as what I am *going* to say, but as what I *ought* to say" (*RFM* 95). "This might be expressed like this: if calculation reveals a causal connexion to you, then you are not calculating" (*RFM* 190).

for no experiment could have the . . . : this, too, is not a purely causal observation. "Do we forget that a particular *application* is part of a procedure's being an experiment?" (*RFM* 172). And even "if a proof is conceived as an experiment, at any rate the result of the experiment is not what is called the result of the proof. The result of the calculation is the proposition with which it concludes; the result of the experiment is that from these propositions, by means of these rules, I was led to this proposition" (*RFM* 46).

(g) *they* **are not the thinking:** see §§327–39, pp. 217bc, 219b; *Z* 93–101; *EPB* 230–31; *BB* 42–43, 148ab (quoted for §329).

"If a normal human is holding a normal conversation under normal circumstances, and I were to be asked what distinguishes thinking from not-thinking in such a case,—I should not know what answer to give. And I could *certainly not* say that the difference lay in something that goes on or fails to go on while he is speaking" (*Z* 93).

(hijk) Compare this treatment of knowledge with the parallel one of intention, in (*bcd*).

So did I *not* **know:** when I attend quite precisely to the events of that moment I find only "thoughts, feelings, movements", and so on (§645), but nothing I could call knowledge (cp. §§632–33, 638). So it seems I "have to deny the yet uncomprehended process in the yet unexplored medium" (§308).

You are looking at it wrong: see GI 15–16 (Description Fallacy), 17–19 (Reference Fallacy); cp. §§179, 184.

What is the signal for?: cp. (*a*), and 6.211. On the significance of the term *signal*, see GI 15–16, §§179–80. For that of the question, see §§292, 363.

could the 'knowing' be called an accompaniment: see §363, p. 219f; *BB* 40b (quoted for p. 59n).

(l) Worked up in Man. 130, 88–89, and followed by the jottings: "(Goethe on proper names) (if-feeling)".

The familiar physiognomy: see §568, pp. 181f, 210f; *BB* 170a, 174a.

into itself: see p. 215a.

an actual likeness: see p. 181a and commentary; *BB* 170a.

there could be human beings . . . : see p. 214ef; cp. §530, p. 213g.

attachment to their words: see §§530–31; Z 184.

By the way we choose . . . : see (m); XXXVII, 19; p. 54n.

(m) See p. 54n; cp. LC 5b, 7, 13.

what searching: cp. BB 129g–130d.

P. 219(ab) See BB 155d–156a.

'come' in a special way: see NL 319b; EPB 180, 231–33; BB 149ab, 167e.

is no use to me: see GI 48, 60.

what is *now:* momentarily, and on this one occasion—when I am paying careful attention. See pp. 215h–216a; Z 567; EPB 220.

in *me:* see pp. 181b, 206c; BB 79a ("Ask yourself what means we have of finding out the feelings which they produce in different people and on different occasions"). Concerning (e) W. wrote: "Here too James makes what sounds like a psychological assertion & is none. For whether the thought is already complete at the start would have to be shown from the experience of individual people" (Man. 130). "Introspection can never lead to a definition. It can only lead to a psychological account of the one who introspects. If someone says for instance: 'I believe that when I hear a word I understand, I always feel something which I don't feel when I don't understand the word,' that is an account of *his* particular experience" (ibid.).

And how can I . . . : cp. p. 188l.

I ought to have to . . . : for if I actively recall the word, the observation will be falsified (p. 187abc). Cp. EPB 194.

could give myself an exhibition: see §311.

I *act* it: cp. §§178, 391, 642, p. 188m.

Characteristic: because they occur often, not always (§35).

accompaniments: one wonders why here and in Z 97 (below) W. reverses his judgment in BB 148b (quoted for §329) that nobody would describe things like tone and accent as accompaniments of the words. Cp. BB 35, quoted for p. 217c.

Primarily: "What one mimics is, say, a man's tone in speaking, his expression and similar things; and that suffices us. This proves that the important accompanying phenomena of talking are found *here*" (Z 97), not in the mind. "Consider tone of voice, inflexion, gestures, as *essential* parts of our experience, not as inessential accompaniments or mere means of communication" (BB 182). See Man. 138, 18A.

gestures, faces, tones of voice: in addition to Z 97 and BB 182, above, see §1a (Augustine's list); EPB 211, 218–19, 231; BB 144cd, 148b; PG 66. Cp. §332; BB 103: "You will find that the justifications for calling something an expression of doubt, conviction, etc., largely, though of course not wholly, consist in descriptions of gestures, the play of facial expressions, and even the tone of voice."

(c) *"This* **word fits":** cp. §§136–38, 537, p. 183d; *LC* 19.

the extensive ramifications: cp. §§525b, 534. "The words we call expressions of aesthetic judgment play a very complicated rôle, but a very definite rôle, in what we call a culture of a period. To describe their use . . . you have to describe a culture" (*LC* 8).

not **the end of the matter:** as it might be were the term *fits* motivated by a conscious comparison, as of a mould and a form which fits into it (*BB* 166a, 170a).

(d) Revised from Man. 138, 15B.

That is not the point: see (*f*).

certain wordless behaviour: see §591; cp. §636.

(e) See commentary on (*ab*) ("in *me*"); *Z* 1; Man. 229, §§839, 885, 920; cp. §§633–38; Man. 138, 16B (an earlier version).

James: see *Principles*, I, 251; cp. ibid., 253, 255–56.

"which *cannot* grow": see Man. 138, 17.

this is not an experience: cp. §640. "Where does the idea of the logical germ come from? That is: whence comes the idea 'Everything was there already at the start & contained in the initial experience'?" (Man. 138, 17B). "This is a case where people invent; e.g. James said that before you say a sentence you have a thought of the sentence. He did no experiments. . . ." (*JN* 71).

As does intention . . . : "James's assertion that the thought is complete at the start of the sentence . . . treats intention as an experience" (Man. 138, 17B). "The *intention* of uttering the thought may already exist before the first word has been said. For if you ask someone: 'Do you know what you mean to say?' he will often say yes" (*Z* 1).

(f) See Man. 138, 17A, for an earlier version.

are no more the expression . . . : lest this appear to contradict common experience, notice that "Now I know how to go on!" may sometimes be triggered by, e.g., thinking of a formula (§151); yet even then the words do not mean "The formula occurred to me" (§§152–53, p. 181cd). If it seems that a word on the tip of one's tongue is like a ship on the horizon at night, glimpsed with peripheral vision, we may ask: "How do we know it is a *ship?*" The answer is: "Particular circumstances" (§154)—sea, horizon, and so on. To complete the (partial) parallel we might also ask: "What would it be like if people never found and observed the ship thus glimpsed in peripheral vision?"

certain situations: cp. §§154–55, 337, 581, 591–92.

"What would it be like . . .": cp. §§269, 323b, 581; NL 304d.

"never": cp. §§344–45.

XXXVIII. The Picture of Complete Seclusion (Pp. 220–229)

GENERAL COMMENTARY

(1) This section requires closer attention than most to detect its inner unity. The immediate connection with the previous section, however, is not difficult to discern. There, concerned with the notion of meaning as a personal experience, Wittgenstein countered by stressing the difference between two senses of *meaning* and the dependence of the secondary, experiential sense on the primary, more public one. Meaning experiences, too, have outer criteria (XXXVII, 16, 18). Indeed, the experiences most characteristic of thoughtful speech are primarily public: gestures, faces, tones of voice (p. 219). Our impression that the inner stream of thought is "hidden", Wittgenstein now observes, reflects confusion (p. 220). The doubt which may exist for me concerning another's thought does not exist for him (p. 221), but this grammatical fact indicates no insuperable barrier in nature, preventing me from ever knowing his inner states (X, 18). I can know, and not merely believe, what another is thinking, or that he is in pain (p. 223). Indeed, "I can be as *certain* of someone else's sensations as of any fact" (p. 224).

(2) "Granted," someone may reply, "it is . . . possible to be convinced by evidence that someone is in such-and-such a state of mind, that, for instance, he is not pretending" (p. 228); "still it is always merely subjective, not objective, certainty" (p. 225). The person *feels* sure, but for no adequate reason (*OC* 194). To this Wittgenstein replies that the words *subjective* and *objective* here "betoken a difference between language-games" (p. 225) and not a psychological contrast or disparate legitimacy. The rest of the section, dealing first with "mathematical certainty" (pp. 225–27), then with the "subjective" variety (pp. 227–29), illustrates the differences between the games. On the one hand, people generally agree in their mathematical judgments, as they agree in their judgments of colors (pp. 225–27), whereas "there is in general no such agreement over the question whether an expression of feeling is genuine or not" (p. 227). And though in this latter case there is "evidence", it includes "imponderable evidence" (p. 228); and although "there are also rules, . . . they do not form a system, and only experienced peo-

714

ple can apply them right. Unlike calculating-rules" (p. 227; see *OC* 563).

(3) These differences justify neither the word *hidden*, nor biased contrasts such as "know"/"merely believe" or "objective"/"merely subjective". We might say of the future, too, that it is hidden from us (p. 223d), but not because the evidence falls short of that required for knowledge (§481; Malcolm, *Memoir*, 88a). "For the question here is not one of an approximation to logical inference" (§481). Nor is it in the case of psychological judgments. Here too one might ask: "If *these* are not grounds, then what are grounds?" (ibid.). A good ground for judging the genuineness of an expression or the truth of an avowal "looks *like this*" (§483). "What has to be accepted, the given, is—so one could say—*forms of life*" (p. 226).

(4) Mathematics is no exception (p. 226g; cp. *OC* 447–48). We ought not to take agreement in mathematics as a sign that mathematicians succeed better than others in discovering what is so (*RFM* 135e)—as though the "correct" results would remain unaffected, though known to God alone, if human calculators ceased to agree (p. 226; cp. §§344–45). The corresponding notion in psychology is that the individual who expresses his inner states is alone omniscient and infallible, and that less privileged observers might disagree still more than they do in their judgments without altering the facts in the least. As "2 + 2 = 4" would still be the correct answer even if mathematicians failed to agree on it (p. 226h), so "I meant it" or "I dreamt it" might still be an accurate report even if the population as a whole grew skeptical about such avowals. In Section X, using simple paradigms, Wittgenstein dealt with the fallacies underlying this point of view; now, after long discussions of meaning, thought, intention, and the like in Parts One and Two, he is ready to mount a broader attack on the philosophical conception of privacy.

DETAILED COMMENTARY

P. 220 See Squires, "Soliloquy".

(ab) not a half hidden: to the person himself. When introspection fails to reveal a full inner replica of outer speech, we may suppose that it is there after all (for otherwise why do we mention "speech"?) but is hard to get hold of, slips quickly by, or something of the kind (§436). Cp. §364.

cheek by jowl: see (*c*); cp. p. 192j; NL 285a.

"We can call it an articulated process: for it takes place during a *period of time*, and can *accompany* an 'outer' process" (Man. 138, 18B).

but not in our investigation: see (*h*); GI 49, 60; pp. 212d, 230a; Man. 138, 32A.

(c) in the possibility of telling . . . : cp. §§301, 367.

accompanying **inward speech:** see Man. 138, 18B (above).

(de) "which I have to learn": presumably by saying things out loud, then doing the "same thing" silently (cp. the critique of a similar attitude in §386).

but what is 'doing' . . . : see XXXVII, 18; cp. p. 224l; *Z* 434 ("Don't we have to learn something new here?").

Let the use . . . : see GI 53; §340, p. 212f; cp. 3.262, 3.326–3.327, 6.211.

can often say: W. speaks with caution, for reasons which appear in *RFM* 165, where he criticizes his former, more dogmatic way of speaking, for instance in *PB* 193d and *Kreis*, 33; cp. Man. 105, 46 ("A mathematical proposition always says that which its proof proves. That is, it never says more than its proof proves").

let the *proof* teach you . . . : see *RFM* 26–27, 33, 52, 54f, 76k, 146, 153i–154l; *PG* 350, 369–76, 455, 458, 462, 484b; *PB* 144 (note), 181e, 183b, 192, 198g, 201ef, 202f, 204c; 6.1261; *NB* 42k; *Kreis*, 109; Man. 219, 9, 12; Man. 123 (June 4); Malcolm, Review of *PB*, 228; cp. §516; *PB* 145b; *LC* 70e.

"Tell me *how* you seek and I will tell you *what* you seek" (*PG* 370). If this is true of looking for books in bookstores or for birds with binoculars, it is truer still in mathematics. "For the proof belongs to the grammar of the proposition" (*PG* 370; cp. §353, p. 225a).

(f) "So I don't *really* calculate . . .": a reaction to the point implicit in (*d*). See §364a.

you yourself distinguish . . . : see §364b.

But you can only learn . . . : see XXXVII, 18; §385, p. 216g.

(g) See Man. 138, 19B.

(h) is only of interest to us . . . : see p. 230a.

to a possible use: similar to that in §270a.

(i) is part of the *concept* . . . : see §§247–48.

is the wrong word: see XXXVIII, 3.

P. 221 Most of this page (*abcdef*) originated in Man. 138, 21.

(a) *he* would have to *know* it: not so much, perhaps, because *hidden* requires intelligible contrast (see §251 and commentary), as because the other's silent talk is said to be hidden *from me;* were it hidden to everyone the phrase would be redundant. The use of *hidden* which W. is criticizing arises from a contrast between privileged and unprivileged observers (§246a).

he does not 'know' it: see X, 25; cp. §679, p. 222bcd; *OC* 504.

does not exist for him: cp. §§246c, 288. "We interpret the absence of doubt as *knowledge*" (Man. 228, §245), somewhat as we interpret the absence of surprise as an experience of familiarity (§596).

"The prop. is not unquestionable because it rests so securely on something but there is no question of its resting on anything. To say that we are *certain* that we have this impression is like saying the earth rests on something that is firm in itself. . . . 'You can't go on having one thing resting on another; in the end there must be something resting on itself.' (The a priori) Something firm in itself. I propose to drop this mode of speech as it leads to puzzlements" (Man. 159; W.'s English).

(b) "There are quite *special* cases in which the inner seems hidden. And the uncertainty thus expressed is not philosophical, but practical and primitive" (Man. 232, 740).

" 'He is hiding something from me, and can hide it so that I not only never will find it, but could not conceivably find it.'—That would be a metaphysical hiding" (Man. 232, 746).

might of course also mean: but doesn't (p. 223c). Man. 138, 32B, adds: "but not that he can't perceive it, since it is in my soul".

the movements of his throat: cp. p. 220g.

which would be a possibility: whereas introspecting his soul would not be (see Man. 138, above). Cp. *PP* 263: "His object was to give us some 'firm ground' such as 'If a proposition has a meaning, its negation must have a meaning.' "

(c) See *OC* 467–68; NL 284fg, 304d–305d, 319a; cp. X, 3; §409; Russell, *Outline*, 20a, 132–33, 139a; Moore, *Commonplace*, 182, 356b.

"what I want": or will. Cp. *NB* 86m, 87q–88a. Distinguish this form of expression from others to which W. was similarly opposed, e.g.: "I know where I am feeling pain," "I know that I am in pain" (*OC* 41; §§246, 408). Kindred difficulties would arise for "I *knew* what I wanted, wished, etc." However, a person does remember having meant so-and-so (§661), and does know he intended to say such-and-such (§634). "It would seem from this that it is not the present tense that is essential but that the time of the instantiation of the psychological verb be the same as the time at which knowledge is ascribed" (Hacker, *Insight*, 255; he cites NL 309).

through all the psychological verbs: e.g. *see* (Man. 176, 21B; NL 278, 283a); cp. §281. Z 22, on *mean*, causes some difficulty.

is either: for similar contrasts see §§408 and 409, 587, p. 223j.

philosophers' nonsense: see *OC* 564; Man. 159, quoted for (*a*); Hallett, "Contrast", 686–91; Malcolm, *Memoir*, 90b, 91c (quoted for §246a); cp. *OC* 569, 589; *PB* 94b. See X, 25, for various lines of explanation, for instance: that suggested by §486 (the tendency to confuse immediate experience with knowledge, or with the sense of a proposition in which knowledge is expressed); by §520 (what is the application of the statement?); and by Z 458 (the essential thing about metaphysics is that it obliterates the distinction between the factual and the conceptual). Joining these last two, we might ask: What fact could anyone *learn* from this apparently factual statement?

"When the sceptical philosophers say 'You don't know' and Moore replies 'I do know,' his reply is quite useless, unless it is to assure them that he, Moore, doesn't feel any doubt whatever. But that is not what is at issue" (Malcolm's notes, *Memoir*, 91). "Moore himself isn't clear what he means by it. It isn't even clear to him that he is not giving it an ordinary usage. He is confused by the difference between using it in some ordinary sense and using it to make a philosophical point" (ibid., 89).

or at any rate *not* . . . : see Malcolm, *Memoir*, 91 (above), and *Knowledge*, 239; Russell, *Mind*, 43b; James, *Principles*, I, 190; cp. *Z* 22. The main alternatives: (1) " 'Of course I know what I wish' can be interpreted to be a grammatical statement" (*BB* 30). See §247; *OC* 58, 371, 412, 433; NL 305a; *BB* 15c; *PP* 268; Malcolm, *Memoir*, 89b; Hallett, "Contrast", 692–95. (2) There is a use of psychological verbs which permits one to say: "Ah, now I know what I want" (cp. §441; *BB* 22b). (3) Such declarations might perhaps be used "to express just my subjective certainty" (*OC* 245), my not feeling "any doubt whatever" (Malcolm, *Memoir*, 91, above). Notice that the first two of these three possibilities do not apply to, e.g., "I know that I am in pain," and that the possible interpretation of that statement mentioned in §246a ("except perhaps that I *am* in pain") does not apply here.

(d) See *OC* 2–4, 10, 58; *RFM* 37 ("The question here is not really one of certainty but of something stipulated by us"); Man. 108, 185; cp. *OC* 355–56; NL 305a; *PG* 220c; Man. 109, 21.

does not mean: in typical circumstances, though it might in explaining the term *know* (§247) or in philosophical discourse (see the commentary on the preceding sentence, and *OC* 325).

are *senseless*: Moore did not notice the grammatical nature of his assertion when he exclaimed: "How absurd it would be to suggest that I did not know it, but only believed it, and that perhaps it was not the case!" (*Papers*, 146). " 'Nonsense!' one will say. 'How should all these people be wrong?'—But is that an argument? Is it not simply the rejection of an idea? And perhaps the determination of a concept? For if I speak of a possible mistake here, this changes the role of 'mistake' and 'truth' in our lives" (*OC* 138). "If Moore were to pronounce the opposite of those propositions which he declares certain, we should not just not share his opinion: we should regard him as demented" (*OC* 155).

is logically excluded: as it is in the cases under discussion (*c*). The inclusion of possible doubt as a logical condition of knowledge is implicit in the condition that we be able to make sure (*e*), but becomes explicit in Man. 138, 16A: "We say 'I know . . .' where it is possible to doubt, whereas philosophers say we know something precisely where there is no doubt, and where accordingly the words 'I know' are a superfluous preamble."

(**e**) See Man. 109, 57; Malcolm, *Memoir*, 88–92; cp. Ramsey, *Foundations*, 72b.

"I believe": "What I know, I believe" (*OC* 177)—though it does not always make sense to say I do (see below). Cp. Man. 232, 683.

or "I suspect": cp. *PB* 310.

where one can: an important ambiguity lurks here. Concerning conversations in 1949 Malcolm writes: "At this stage of our discussion Wittgenstein came to the conclusion that, contrary to what he had previously said, it is *false* that 'In the ordinary use of "know" it is always sensible to speak of "making sure" ': There is an ordinary use of 'I know' when there isn't any *making sure*. E.g. a sighted person could say it to a blind man who asks 'Are you sure that it's a tree?' And also when we have *completed* an investigation we can say, 'I know now that it's a tree.' Another example: if you and I were coming through woods toward a house and I broke out into the clearing and there was the house right before me, I might exclaim 'There's the house.' You, back in the bushes, might ask doubtfully 'Are you sure?', and I should reply 'I *know* it' " (*Memoir*, 89–90; cp. *OC* 520). The words here on p. 221 do not indicate another reversal, for the perspective is different. The words "where one can also say" clearly refer to a type of content, not a type of situation (see Buck, "Non-other Minds", 207). The presence of the house is something that could be doubted, suspected, believed, known; but not all in the same instant. The person with the house before his eyes could not say "I believe there's a house," or "I suspect that there's a house over there."

find out: so where a mistake is conceivable, whereas Moore's truisms often exclude error (*OC* 660–63, 667, 671, 674–76).

"Make sure" seems a preferable translation (cp. *OC* 23). In the cases mentioned in (*c*) one generally cannot make sure (nor find out). Thus "the question 'How do you know that you have toothache?' is nonsensical" (*PP* 307). Moore adds: "I think that he here meant what he said of 'I've got a toothache' to apply to all those propositions which he had originally distinguished from 'hypotheses' as 'what I call propositions' " (*PP* 266). That earlier distinction, notice, reveals the very viewpoint W. is here criticizing (X, 6–7). In illustration of his later view, see e.g. GI 15–16 (avowals); commentary on §353 (verification); §587 (belief); §§631, 659 (intention); p. 174i (fright). On the present criterion of knowledge, see *OC* 23, 137–38, 438, 483–84, 504, 550, 574; *BB* 23a–24a (quoted in part for §370); Man. 232, 678; Man. 138, 16A; cp. Man. 176, 58B; *Theaetetus*, 201–2; Ramsey, *Foundations*, 258.

Notice that W.'s difficulties are not skeptical, but conceptual: "If Moore says he knows the earth existed etc., most of us will grant him that it has existed all that time, and also believe him when he says he is convinced of it. But has he also got the right *ground* for his conviction? For if not, then after all he doesn't *know* (Russell)" (*OC* 91). If, for instance, what a person believes "is of such a kind that the grounds that he can give are no surer than his assertion, then he cannot say that he knows what he believes" (*OC* 243; cp. *OC* 250). Thus suppose that Moore really could deduce the fact that he perceives a hand "from a pair of propositions simpler still" (*Papers,* 53, quoted for §486), or that he succeeded in producing a proposition "which is both true itself and is also such that it would not be true, unless other people existed" (*Studies,* 34–36); this would not establish his knowledge that other people exist or that he is perceiving a hand: He would not thereby ground, discover, or confirm these truths.

and similar things: for instance, "You must know if it seems that way to you" (discussed in Man. 109, 21–22), or "the case in which we should be inclined to answer the question 'Are you sure that it is this you wish?' by saying: 'Surely I must know what I wish.' Now compare this answer to the one which most of us would give to the question: 'Do you know the ABC?' Has the emphatic assertion that you know it a sense analogous to that of the former assertion? Both assertions in a way brush aside the question. But the former doesn't wish to say 'Surely I know such a simple thing as this' but rather: 'The question which you asked me makes no sense' " (*BB* 30).

"War is war": cp. *RFM* 7k; *BB* 161ac.

(f) See *OC* 125, 444–46; cp. *OC* 255, 460.

"If I don't know whether someone has two hands (say, whether they have been amputated or not) I shall believe his assurance that he has two hands, if he is trustworthy. And if he says he *knows* it, that can only signify to me that he has been able to make sure, and hence that his arms are e.g. not still concealed by coverings and bandages, etc. etc. My believing the trustworthy man stems from my admitting that it is possible for him to make sure. But someone who says that perhaps there are no physical objects makes no such admission" (*OC* 23).

It is possible . . . . : see *OC* 23 (above), 412; cp. Malcolm, *Memoir,* 92c.

I had two hands: see Moore's famous defense of common sense, establishing the existence of physical objects: "I can prove now, for instance, that two human hands exist. How? By holding up my two hands, and saying, as I make a certain gesture with the right hand, 'Here is one hand,' and adding, as I make a certain gesture with the left, 'and here is another' " (*Papers*, 145–46). For W.'s handling of idealism and radical skepticism, see X, 24.

I *cannot* do so: "Under ordinary circumstances I do not satisfy myself that I have two hands by seeing how it looks. *Why* not? Has experience shown it to be unnecessary? Or (again): Have we in some way learnt a universal law of induction, and do we trust it here too?" (*OC* 133).

"What would it be like to doubt now whether I have two hands? Why can't I imagine it at all? What would I believe if I didn't believe that? So far I have no system at all within which this doubt might exist" (*OC* 247).

"But all you need . . . ": W.'s answer: "There is no common sense answer to a philosophical problem" (*BB* 58). The skeptic or idealist has not overlooked this evidence. His problems are conceptual.

I need not believe my eyes: "For why shouldn't I test my *eyes* by looking to find out whether I see my two hands? *What* is to be tested by *what*?" (*OC* 125). "My having two hands is, in normal circumstances, as certain as anything that I could produce in evidence for it. That is why I am not in a position to take the sight of my hand as evidence for it" (*OC* 250).

(g) See *OC* 17, 24, 84–85, 185–88, 261, 301; *PP* 319c–322a; Russell, *Mind*, 159b; cp. Ramsey, *Foundations*, 197b.

With this is connected . . . : *OC* 24 indicates the link: "The idealist's question would be something like: 'What right have I not to doubt the existence of my hands?' (And to that the answer can't be: I *know* that they exist.) But someone who asks such a question is overlooking the fact that a doubt about existence only works in a language-game. Hence, that we should first have to ask: what would such a doubt be like?, and don't understand this straight off."

"for millions of years": note the difference between this and a vaguer form. "Such an expression as 'The earth has existed for many years past,' " wrote Moore, "is the very type of an unambiguous expression, the meaning of which we all understand" (*Papers*, 37; see *OC* 84). But on what occasion do we understand it? In the abstract it contrasts with "The earth has not existed for many years past," and that is already problematic.

makes clearer sense: see *OC* 52, 54 ("at some point it has ceased to be conceivable"), 236–37; Malcolm, *Memoir*, 90de; cp. Moore, *Papers*, 53.

"in the last five minutes": Russell had written: "Remembering, which occurs now, cannot possibly—he may say—prove that what is remembered occurred at some other time, because the world might have sprung into being five minutes ago, exactly as it then was, full of acts of remembering which were entirely misleading. Opponents of Darwin, such as Edmund Gosse's father, urged a very similar argument against evolution. The world, they said, was created in 4004 B.C., complete with fossils, which were inserted to try our faith. The world was created suddenly, but was made such as it would have been if it had evolved. There is no logical impossibility about this view. And similarly there is no logical impossibility in the view that the world was created five minutes ago, complete with memories and records. This may seem an improbable hypothesis, but it is not logically refutable" (*Outline,* 7). "There is no logical impossibility in the hypothesis that the world sprang into being five minutes ago, exactly as it then was, with a population that 'remembered' a wholly unreal past" (*Mind,* 159).

"To say (as Russell does): 'The world could have been created five minutes ago exactly as it actually was five minutes ago, with all the memories and documents, which in that case would be completely deceptive,' is meaningless, since admittedly there would be no way of verifying the proposition. It is a picture . . ." (Man. 219, 18–19; see Ambrose, "Metamorphoses", 68).

"What observations": see commentary on §§353–54; *OC* 138, 231; Malcolm, *Memoir,* 91b, 92: "Certain propositions belong to my 'frame of reference'. If I had to give *them* up, I shouldn't be able to judge *any-thing.* Take the example of the earth's having existed for many years before I was born. What evidence against it could there be? A document?"

(h) See *OC* 454; Hallett, "Contrast", 690–92.

Here, too, at some indefinite point the claim ceases to be intelligible (*OC* 52, 54); for we no longer know "what ideas and observations the . . . proposition goes with".

is obviously true: like the existence of the Earth for the last five minutes, which is surer still (it might be said) than its existence for many years past.

It is even surer . . . : " 'A goose has no teeth' seems just a very sure biological fact, for we can imagine finding geese with teeth in their mouths. But 'A rose has no teeth' appears not merely certain, but foolproof. For the opposite [it might be said] is *inconceivable,* and therefore logically, metaphysically impossible" (Hallett, "Contrast", 691).

where should a rose's teeth have been?: cp. §361. "When I tell you I have just bought a house," it might be objected, "I am not obliged to tell you where it is, under pain of speaking nonsense. And when I say I own *no* house, it is clearer still that I need not designate a particular place. The negation covers them all." "Very well," says W.; "if you don't mind where the rose has its teeth, let us suppose they are in the mouth of the cow that dunged it. Now where is your necessary truth?"

P. 222(a) suppose one were to say: see the preceding comments.

one has no notion in advance . . . : "We easily forget that the word 'locality' is used in many different senses" (*BB* 8); "the word 'where' can refer to localities in many different senses" (*BB* 50); and so can *in* (one puts one's thoughts in print, one's money in bonds, one's car in second gear, and a bug in somebody's ear!). See *BB* 49.

Connexion with . . . : see §253. "An innumerable variety of cases can be thought of in which we should say that someone has pains in another person's body; or, say, in a piece of furniture, or in any empty spot" (*BB* 50–51). "If, for example, the person concerned always felt a pain when a certain object, for example the candlestick on the table, was violently disturbed, and, should the candlestick move, perceived a sensation akin to the kinaesthetic sensation which normally accompanies the movement of his hand, such experience could lead him to coordinate the space of the 'handache' with that of the candlestick. . . . He could thus meaningfully say, 'I have a pain in the candlestick' " (Schlick, "Psychological", 395–96).

(bcd) I can know . . . : "This and similar remarks are made within the context of the knowledge and doubt contrast, directed against opponents who misuse this contrast to say the exact opposite" (Matthews, "Meaning", 107). See X, 24–25; p. 221cde; cp. §§246, 288, pp. 184ab, 221a.

A whole cloud of philosophy . . . : reversing, for instance, "the familiar solipsistic doctrine that a person can know only what he himself, and not anyone else, is thinking" (Malcolm, "Symposium", 72); the Cartesian solution to skeptical doubt (X, 24–25); and empiricist theory about the foundations of knowledge (X, 3).

(ef) See Man. 229, §§1232–53.

"A man's thinking . . .": still more than, for instance, his pains (JN 88).

"in comparison with which . . .": see *PG* 106c; James, *Principles*, I, 226: "No thought even comes into direct *sight* of a thought in another personal consciousness than its own. Absolute insulation, irreducible pluralism, is the law. . . . Neither contemporaneity, nor proximity in space, nor similarity of quality and content are able to fuse thoughts together which are sundered by this barrier of belonging to different personal minds. The breaches between such thoughts are the most absolute breaches in nature."

If there were people . . . : for the point of this remark, see X, 18. For an analogous suggestion, see §312b. What confuses us here is the distinction between logical and physical possibility (Man. 229, §1249).

who always read . . . : and therefore succeed regularly where we (who rely chiefly on truthful confessions) succeed only rarely (*LC* 18ab; cp. p. 221b). Cp. Man. 109, 176.

say by observing the larynx: see p. 221b; cp. §376, p. 220g.

(g) See Man. 232, 741 (much fuller); cp. NL 314hj. This observation, like the preceding one, is meant to indicate the contingent, nonconceptual nature of the seclusion, and to dissipate the notion that the "mental" character of thoughts hides them *ipso facto* from all save the thinker (*e*). Laryngeal motions might reveal them, and spoken words might conceal them. See p. 223c.

(h) saying to myself: i.e. my "silent internal discourse" (*f*). Cp. §32b, p. 211k.

can my memory not deceive me?: "He is not declaring, as Strawson thinks, that I cannot report what words went through my mind. He is saying that it is a report 'whose truth is guaranteed by the special criteria of truthfulness' (p. 222)" (Malcolm, "Investigations", 211; cp. *j*). "Think" and "say to myself" differ in this respect from "understand" (p. 53n; cp. *OC* 179–80). Yet the reason is not that here I introspect more surely, or that the inner event alone is an adequate criterion (X, 20–21). Even were the words ever so distinct, what criteria would I have for their being my silent discourse rather than words I imagine myself or another saying, or which I remember, or which simply "run through my mind"? On such avowals as "I thought . . . ," or, "I said to myself . . . ," see GI 15–16 and XXXVII, 18; and cp. XXXVII, 16.

might it not always do so: see p. 207e and commentary. Cp. §§258, 270, 288c, 344–45.

is not the point at all: it "drops out of consideration as irrelevant" (§293) in the search for criteria of truth (*i*). "The criterion for it being the one that was in your mind is that when I tell you, you agree" (*LC* 18).

a construction-line: the one stated in the next sentence.

(i) are not the criteria: in the first case one considers the speaker (his character, motives, wakefulness, background, occupation at the moment, other statements, and so on); in the second one considers the process described. Cp. §§374–76, p. 186abc.

does not reside in . . . : pp. 217l–218a suggest a double reason. Cp. pp. 181c, 218ef.

its being a correct . . . : though of course it does matter *what* he confesses (a wish or a thought, this thought or that).

in the special consequences: cp. §270, p. 224b.

is guaranteed by . . . : see *Z* 558; cp. p. 224g.

special criteria of *truthfulness:* " 'I didn't know that I was lying.'—

'You *must* have known!' " (NL 315). "It is important here that I exclude the case of saying the untruth by mistake" (NL 294).

"In what circumstances is it impossible to doubt his credibility? Can I indicate them? No" (Man. 232, 760).

(j) See p. 184abc (and commentary); Malcolm, *Dreaming*, especially chap. 12; cp. §288c; Man. 176, 48B–49A (similar treatment of pain); Man. 138, 30 (hallucinations).

Assuming that dreams . . . : cp. §270.

cannot arise: consider the fact that a person reports spontaneously that he spent a dreamless night, or, when asked if he had any dreams, replies without hesitation, "No." He does not say, "Perhaps I had a great many but forgot them completely." If he did so reply, he would be altering the concept *dream*. Now the same holds true for the content of dreams: The dreamer's memory (cp. §§634b, 660–61) is decisive (p. 184b). "If someone questioned whether there really are dreams corresponding to peoples' reports of dreams presumably he would have some idea of what would settle the question. He would not be using the report of a dream as the criterion of what the dream was, and so he would have to mean something different by 'dreaming' " (Malcolm, *Dreaming*, 56). "Considering this, one may be inclined to think that there cannot be a *criterion* (something that settles a question with certainty) of someone's . . . having dreamt, but merely various 'outer' phenomena that are empirically correlated with . . . dreams. This view, however, is self-contradictory: without criteria for the occurrence of these things the correlations could not be established" (ibid., 60–61).

unless indeed we . . . : cp. §§184, 239b, 633, 665, pp. 205i, 212d.

P. 223(a) a concept of: this is an addition to the German.

(b) See NL 282hi; (*c*) applies this paragraph, in reply to p. 222e.

'guessing thoughts': see Z 35; cp. pp. 221b, 222h.

in a language that B . . . : see p. 222g.

I write down: say in a diary; for the writing must qualify as thought (*c*).

Yet another: see Man. 138, 23A.

***I* need not be talking . . . :** see §330, pp. 211k, 217d; Z 100, 122; Malcolm, *Memoir*, 55 (below).

to myself: see commentary on p. 211k.

(c) See NL 314j; Man. 138, 23A (the original version).

any more hidden: but of course there is a contingent sense in which the *unperceived* physical proceedings are hidden. W. himself "had an extraordinary gift for divining the thoughts of the person with whom he was engaged in discussion. While the other struggled to put his thought into words Wittgenstein would perceive what it was and state it for him" (Malcolm *Memoir,* 55). "But there is something 'private'; we don't often guess Smith's thoughts. Suppose a tribe which always murmured and read each other's murmurs. That (1) it might happen but (2) does not happen is very important in this matter" (JN 39).

(d) See Man. 229, §§1232–53.

"**What is** *internal* . . . ": "Isn't that as vague as the concept 'internal'? (For think: the internal is sensations & thoughts & images & mood & intention and so on)" (Man. 138, 29–30). "In certain circumstances 'The inner is hidden' would be like saying 'You *see* only the outer manipulation of the numbers in a multiplication; the multiplication itself is hidden from us" (Man. 169). " '*His* pains are hidden from me' would be like saying: 'These sounds are hidden from my eye' " (Man. 138, 21B). See X, 18–19.

The future is hidden . . . : "We cannot see it," we might say, in continuation of the series above, thereby expressing confusion similar to that which begets talk about mental privacy. On the one hand, people cannot, in fact, foresee the course of events for years ahead (*LC* 56e); on the other hand they cannot, as a matter of logic, *see* future events. Similarly, "what confuses us is that, seen from one angle, it is logically impossible to be acquainted with another's thoughts, and seen from another angle, it is psychologically and physiologically impossible" (Man. 229, §1249). The truth is: grammar precludes our observing others' thoughts, but not our knowing them; for knowledge is not restricted, as many have thought, to immediate intuition and what is deduced from it.

(e) If I see someone . . . : see §303, p. 224c.

(f) See Man. 232, 742.

with entirely strange traditions: see *RFM* 44; BUF 247c; Malcolm, *Memoir,* 48.

even given a mastery . . . : thus in his chance remarks on religion, W. spoke English or German; yet Miss Anscombe sensed that long explanations would be necessary before she "found her feet" with him. "I think differently, in a different way. I say different things to myself. I have different pictures. . . . The expression of belief may play an absolutely minor role" (*LC* 55; cp. GI 54). Cp. (*h*).

We do not *understand* . . . : see *OC* 108, 332.

what they are saying to themselves: in mentalese (§32b). Cp. p. 217cd.

(g) See Man. 232, 741, 762.

a *picture:* see p. 222ef and commentary. Cp. the italics in §115.

the reasons for the conviction: see X, 18, and the commentary on (*d*).

(h) See Waismann, *Principles*, 259; cp. *Z* 390; Mauthner, *Beiträge*, I, 232; James, *Principles*, I, 289.

If a lion could talk . . . : using a language we know, he might still be a complete enigma to us (*f*).

we could not understand him: as we do not understand the people in (*f*). If anything, the breakdown in communication would be more complete. For the lion's interests differ more radically from ours (§570), and so do his forms of life (§§241–42; *Z* 173). "He is made a puzzle to us by a certain behavior" (Man. 167). "For example, suppose a lion says 'It is now three o'clock,' but without looking at a clock or his wrist-watch—and we may imagine that it would be merely a stroke of luck if he should say this when it actually *is* three o'clock. Or suppose he says 'Goodness, it is three o'clock; I must hurry to make that appointment,' but that he continues to lie there, yawning, making no effort to move, as lions are wont to do. In these circumstances—assuming that the lion's general behavior is in every respect exactly like that of an ordinary lion, save for his amazing ability to utter English sentences— we could not say that he has *asserted* or *stated* that it is three o'clock, even though he has uttered suitable words. We could not tell what, if anything, he has asserted, for the modes of behavior into which his use of words is woven are too radically different from our own" (Pitcher, *Philosophy*, 243; see Malcolm, *Problems*, 89).

"On the other hand, it is not hard to imagine a lion talking as we do, and Lewis Carroll has presented us one in *Through the Looking-Glass*. Alice understands the lion, as well as she understands anyone in Looking-Glass Land, and so do we, but this is a lion who mops his brow from the work of chasing the unicorn all around the town, who stops for tea, who in fact acts as human beings do, including that special way that is speaking" (van Buren, *Edges*, 48).

(ij) Revised from Man. 138, 23.

is actually *going to do*: and that, like motions of the larynx (p. 222f), words of an unknown language (p. 222g), or concealed writing or actions (p. 223b), is probably a physical proceeding (p. 223c), not "internal" (p. 223d); yet like the future in general (ibid.), it is in a sense hidden from us. To dispel the notion of an absolute dichotomy between the "mental" and the physical, and the mysteriousness of the former, W. keeps suggesting parallels between the two, and treats them alike (*BB* 4).

To say . . . : this double negation parallels that in §246, and the double affirmation in p. 222bc.

is nonsense: see p. 221cde.

wrong: not because he cannot know (§629) but because others can (just as they can know that he is in pain, or what he is thinking).

prediction contained in my expression: the words at least "serve as" a prediction (cp. p. 189b); "we can often predict a man's actions from his expression of a decision" (§632). See §631, p. 224b.

P. 224(b) See Man. 138, 23B.

Two points: really three, but the last two are closely related.

are important: with regard to the issue of seclusion, both as an explanation of the picture (p. 223g) and an element of truth in the claims. Cp. JN 39 (quoted for p. 223c).

that in many cases . . . : cp. pp. 221b, 223c.

I foresee them in my intentions: that is, I know what I intend to do; but not on the basis of self-observation (§631).

has not the same foundation: I do not observe my own behavior (§631c) or listen to my own words (§632), whereas he does observe them.

are quite different: from what he says about my future actions I may surmise his opinion of my character, what he will do, what information he has received or already possessed.

(c) Revised from Man. 232, 742. See *OC* 563, 651; *RFM* 114kl; Hacker, "Frege", 283–84; Malcolm, "Certainty", 25–26.

I can be as *certain* . . . : see (*e*); §303; cp. *OC* 657–58. Notice the absence of such truths in Russell's list: "Self-evidence has degrees: it is not a quality which is simply present or absent, but a quality which may be more or less present, in gradations ranging from absolute certainty down to an almost imperceptible faintness. Truths of perception and some of the principles of logic have the very highest degree of self-evidence; truths of immediate memory have an almost equally high degree" (*Problems*, 67).

"*Certainty* also has degrees, e.g. 'How certain are you?' Since certainty has degrees we are helped to have the idea that knowledge is a mental state" (Malcolm's notes, *Memoir*, 87). "The sceptical philosophers . . . think that degree of *certainty* is degree of *conviction*. They interpret Moore's 'I know it with absolute certainty' as an expression of extreme conviction. What is needed is to show them that the highest degree of certainty is nothing psychological but something logical: that there is a point at which there is neither any 'making more certain' nor any 'turning out to be false'. Some experiential statements have this property. Some others are related in various ways to those that have this property" (ibid., 91).

"The puzzling problem now presents itself: if it does not *follow* from his behavior and circumstances that he is in pain, then how can it ever be *certain* that he is in pain? 'I can be as *certain* of someone else's sensations as of any fact,' says Wittgenstein (p. 224). How can this be so, since there is not a definite set of six or eight conditions (each of which would nullify his pain-behavior) to be checked off as not fulfilled? It *looks* as if the conclusion ought to be that we cannot 'completely verify' that he is in pain. This conclusion is wrong, but it is not easy to see why" (Malcolm, "Investigations", 199).

similar instruments: cp. §§11–14, 23.

a different *kind*: rather than degree. People have in fact classified certainty as "metaphysical", "physical", "moral", and so on without clear insight into the basis of the classifications. See (*f*), and Malcolm, "Certainty", 36, quoted for (*e*); cp. *OC* 567; Man. 229, §777 (quoted for p. 231cd).

to a psychological difference: say a feeling of conviction (p. 225c), which differs when it results from mathematical reasoning and when it has no such basis. In one case, it might be said, the person shuts his eyes (*d*), whereas in the other the evidence shuts them for him (cp. p. 225e, and Russell, above). Thus here too we should like to explain the difference by hypostatizing feelings where there are none (§598).

But the difference is logical: that is, grammatical (*Z* 590), as is the difference in uncertainty (Man. 138, 29A) and the similarity in certainty: "I want to say: The physical game is just as certain as the arithmetical. But this can be misunderstood. My remark is a logical and not a psychological one" (*OC* 447).

"The strength of a belief is not comparable with the intensity of a pain. An entirely different way of comparing beliefs is seeing what sorts of grounds he will give" (*LC* 54). In the case of another's pain, "There is no such thing as a proof, based on (generally) accepted principles" (Man. 176, 47B), as Russell, for instance, required (*Problems*, 33–34).

See *OC* 655–56; Man. 232, 767; Man. 176, 47B; Man. 108, 10; cp. *RFM* 25a, 177f; *PG* 379b.

(d) See §84, p. 180c; *OC* 87–88, 148, 220 ("The reasonable man does *not have* certain doubts"), 651; *RFM* 3g, 45e, 101 ("We went sleepwalking along the road between abysses").

They are shut: "But that does not mean that one takes certain presuppositions on trust" (*OC* 337). "It isn't that the situation is like this: We just *can't* investigate everything, and for that reason we are forced to rest content with assumption" (*OC* 343; see *OC* 150). Thus our not doubting is not the result of explicit exclusion, but "is simply our manner of judging, and therefore of acting" (*OC* 232; see I, 4–5). "Here one must realize that complete absence of doubt at some point, even where we would say that 'legitimate' doubt can exist, need not falsify a language-game. For there is also something like *another* arithmetic. I believe that this admission must underlie any understanding of logic" (*OC* 375).

(ef) See Man. 232, 764.

Am I less certain . . . : Russell, for one, would say we were (e.g. *Problems,* 79–80). "Some philosophers, who admit that there is a perfectly proper sense of 'certain', in which empirical statements can be certain, are inclined, nevertheless, to talk as if sense-statements or *a priori* statements have a *superior* kind of certainty" (Malcolm, "Certainty", 36). See idem, *Memoir,* 91d, quoted for (*c*); cp. ibid., 88a.

this man: "writhing in pain with evident cause" (p. 223e).

Does this shew . . . : so it would appear, if we conceive the degree of certainty as a degree of intensity (Malcolm, *Memoir,* 91, above), like the intensity of a pain (*LC* 54, above), and regard mathematical certainty as the highest degree.

is not a psychological concept: to continue the preceding comparison: Even if some other cause produced a pain as intense as that of toothache, it would not therefore be toothache. *Toothache* is not a concept of degree. Similarly, "mathematical certainty" is not the name for a certain fullness of conviction. See *OC* 38–39; cp. 6.1271.

The kind of certainty . . . : see the comments on (*c*) ("a different kind"); cp. *OC* 151.

(g) "He alone knows . . .": see *BB* 15c; cp. §§246–47.

he will tell us them: and his sincerity will guarantee truth. See *LC* 21–23 and the quotation for (*k*); cp. p. 222ij; Malcolm, *Memoir,* 87c.

This is where: cp. GI 61.

there is a kinship: for the negative side, see p. 221c and commentary.

(h) Let yourself be *struck* . . . : see §524. "W. said the other night that it is remarkable that you *give motives.* Someone then asked what is remarkable about that; wouldn't it be remarkable if they didn't? And of course it would be remarkable if they didn't: It would be remarkable to us. But it is also remarkable that motives *are* given, you could not have foreseen it were you not on earth" (JN 28). You could not, for instance, have deduced it from the language-game of reporting others' motives, or from the first-person practice of reporting one's income, size of shoe, number of fillings, and so on. These and other apparent parallels suggest that a person must *know* his own motives, as he knows these other things he reports. But this inference, too, is illegitimate, for the parallels are illusory (*i*).

(ij) The connection between (*i*) and (*j*) is clarified by analogous passages, e.g. *PG* 441a or Man. 229, §1140: "From this we only see clearly that the grammar of 'I believe' differs greatly from that of 'I write'. . . . . Consider that the resemblances and differences in question are of concepts not of phenomena."

We remain unconscious . . . : see GI 11–13; §§11–12; LF 33a; 3.323, 4.002; Man. 138, 24A.

Something new: some examples:

"Someone makes an addition to mathematics, gives new definitions and discovers new theorems—and in a *certain* respect he can be said not to know what he is doing.—He has a vague imagination of having *discovered* something like a space (at which point he thinks of a room), of having opened up a kingdom, and when asked about it he would talk a great deal of nonsense" (*RFM* 136).

"The mathematician is an inventor, not a discoverer" (*RFM* 47). "The discoverer of periodicity discovers a new calculus" (*PG* 445).

"W. wants you to regard 'telling what you thought' as a 'completely new game' " (JN 38).

"And calculating in my head seems something new—a break in the natural development (the *phrase* is spontaneous)" (JN 36; see JN 19).

"The objectors to unconscious thought did not see that they were not objecting to the newly discovered psychological reactions, but to the way in which they were described. The psychoanalysts on the other hand were misled by their own way of expression into thinking that they had done more than discover new psychological reactions; that they had, in a sense, discovered conscious thoughts which were unconscious" (*BB* 57).

"Thus, by the expression 'unconscious toothache' you may either be misled into thinking that a stupendous discovery has been made, a discovery which in a sense altogether bewilders our understanding; or else you may be extremely puzzled by the expression" (*BB* 23).

For other examples, see §§400–401; *Z* 215; *RFM* 17; *BB* 45d, 70c; *PG* 238, 466a; *PB* 183, 338–39. See *RFM* 184–87; *PB* 186b; *Kreis,* 175a; Man. 228, §172; Man. 112, 83; Man. 108, 18; Malcolm, "Wittgenstein", 335; Cook, "Privacy", 310; Waismann, *Introduction,* 93–99 and last chapter; cp. §284; *Z* 388; *PB* 120b; NB 75l, 89gh; Man. 228, §87; Man. 106, 153.

spontaneous: " 'We decide *spontaneously*' (I should like to say) 'on a new language-game' " (*RFM* 120; see JN 36, above).

'specific': "We ask the man who says this 'What happens in you?' and he replies 'I did a sum in my head'; 'I can't say anything more about it, but I did do that,' so this is a strong case of wanting to say 'a specific experience', because it's the case where you naturally say that it's describable only by those words" (JN 33; see Man. 229, §§825–26, 866, 880; cp. §610, p. 66n, and commentary).

is always . . . : it is not, for instance, something brought to light by logical analysis (*Kreis,* 182–83; cp. Man. 224, 3–4). We do, of course, discover new scientific facts (Man. FW, 17). But not radically new natures (§371). "I agree with the views of contemporary physicists," W. wrote in *PG* 223, "when they say that the signs in their equations no longer have any 'meanings', and that physics cannot arrive at any such meanings, but must rest content with the signs: however, they do not see that the signs have meaning insofar—and only insofar—as observed phenomena do or do not correspond to them, in however circuitous a manner." But what of the phenomena? Mightn't we have, not merely new tastes, say, when we eat new things, but new *kinds* of sensations? "Ramsey used to reply to such questions: 'But it *just is* possible to think of such a thing.' As, perhaps, one says: 'Technology achieves things nowadays which you can't imagine at all' " (*Z* 272). However, such a revelation would have to consist, say, in the gift of a new sense (*PB* 172e)—a new sense-*organ* (Man. 228, §42).

See Man. 176, 5B; cp. 2.0123–2.01231.

(k)   See §§353–54, pp. 224g, 225a; *EPB* 161–62; *BB* 15cd, 88b, 110–11; Man. 302, 13; Man. 138, 22A, 23B; JN 76; Waismann, *Principles*, 119–22; cp. Man. 110, 94 ("Thus Ogden & Richards' & Russell's theory of meaning rests on a confusion, or equation, of motive and cause"); Gardiner, *Schopenhauer*, 76 ("Schopenhauer regards both these concepts as being basically causal in character").

"The double use of the word 'why', asking for the cause and asking for the motive, together with the idea that we can know, and not only conjecture, our motives, gives rise to the confusion that a motive is a cause of which we are immediately aware, a cause 'seen from the inside', or a cause experienced" (*BB* 15). See *LC* 21c; Russell, *Inquiry*, 61b.

"This is also connected with the fact that we say that anyone can know the motive of his action with certainty, but not its cause" (*EPB* 189).

"We judge the motive of a deed by what the person who did it tells us, the account of witnesses, the antecedents" (Man. 229, §1299). As for the person himself, "this game of giving the reason why one acts in a particular way does not involve finding the causes of one's actions (by frequent observations of the conditions under which they arise)" (*BB* 110).

"In support of this statement he asserted that a psycho-analysis is successful only if the patient agrees to the explanation offered by the analyst. He said there is nothing analogous to this in Physics; and that what a patient agrees to can't be a *hypothesis* as to the *cause* of his laughter, but only that so-and-so was the *reason* why he laughed. He explained that the patient who agrees did not think of this reason at the moment when he laughed, and that to say that he thought of it 'subconsciously' 'tells you nothing as to what was happening at the moment when he laughed' " (*PP* 317).

(l) See Man. 229, §1299.

and we do not learn this . . . : see *PG* 483 (quoted for §117); cp. §§117, 350, 377, p. 225a; *Z* 434; NL 312e; *BB* 23d–24a, 9 ("But the diviner would say: 'Surely you know what it means. You know what "three feet under the ground" means, and you know what "I feel" means.' But I should answer him: I know what a word means *in certain contexts*"); *PP* 304–5 (quoted for §334).

P. 225(ab) See *RFM* 45f, 174b; NL 305f, 306; Man. 302, 16–17; Man. 111, 7–8; Bensch, *Wittgenstein*, 66–67; cp. §373, p. 220e; *RFM* 43–44d, 80e; *EPB* 154; *BB* 106b; *PG* 353b; *PB* 217–18; *PP* 282–83; Man. 219, 3; JN 64–65; Russell, *Matter*, 92–96, 100; Waismann, "Analyse", 229–30. The paragraph resorts to a simpler case to clarify the preceding assertion (p. 224l). As we do not learn what "determining the length" means by learning what determining and length are, so we do not learn what "judging a motive" means by being told what judging and motives are.

One judges the length . . . : cp. *BB* 1.

is to make a mistake: see *RFM* 4c–5b; cp. *Kreis*, 89.

"Einstein: how size is measured is what it is" (*PB* 200; *PG* 459). "Physical properties are *measurable* properties. They are defined by the methods of measurement. (Bridgman's book, *The Logic of Modern Physics*, carries this thought through for physics as a whole.)" (Schlick, "Psychological", 396–97). "The most famous example of this sort . . . is Einstein's analysis of the concept of time. . . . Einstein said . . . you must first state what you *mean* by simultaneity, and you can do this only by showing how the proposition 'two events are simultaneous' is verified" (Schlick, "Positivism", 89–90; see idem, "Meaning", 149b; Man. 119, quoted for §350a).

"It may be objected to our method as follows: 'If someone asks what *time* is, you ask in return, "How do we measure time?" But time and the measurement of time are two different things. It is as if someone asked "What is a book?" and you replied, "How does one obtain a book?" '

"This objection conceives that we know what *time* is, and we know what *measuring* is, *so* we know what measuring time is. But this is not true. If I have taught you to measure lengths, and then say, 'Now go ahead and measure time,' this will mean nothing" (Malcolm's notes, *Memoir*, 47–48; see the rest).

To say "The height . . .": "W. has often talked in a way that has been criticized. For instance, he has taken 'What is length?' as answerable by 'How do you measure length?' This has been criticized as though to 'Where is London?' the answer were given 'It depends on how you go' " (JN 28). Cp. *PP* 304b.

in certain cases it is *not*: "Empirical studies of dreaming have produced the most divergent estimates of the duration of dreams, some investigators holding that dreams rarely last more than 1 or 2 seconds: others believe that it is 1 to 10 minutes. Dement and Kleitman . . . think that dreams last as long as 50 minutes and that the average length is 20 minutes. These different estimates arise solely from the employment of different criteria of measurement" (Malcolm, *Dreaming*, 79).

is not learned by . . . : see the references for p. 224l; cp. *BB* 9–11.

has a double meaning: W.'s writings are full of methodology in the second sense, for instance of remarks about calculation, experiment, and proof in mathematics (*RFM* 94–96 and *passim*); about correctness (*LC* 5, 7–8) and explanation (*LC* 18–21) in aesthetics; and about verification (§353), criteria (§354), exactness (§88), description (§§24, 291, pp. 187i, 200a), and explanation (§§5, 71, 87, 288, 533) here in the *Investigations*. Cp. *Kreis*, 162–63, on geometry as hypothesis and as syntax.

" 'Methodology' can be the name for two sorts of things: the description of activities which (e.g.) we call 'measuring', of a sector of human natural history, which will give understanding of the concepts of measuring, exactness, etc., in their various forms; but also a sector of applied physics, teaching how we can best (most exactly, conveniently, etc.) measure this or that in these or those circumstances. (Popper)" (Man. 135, August 1; see Man. 229, §1776).

"There are propositions which describe the calculating of human beings. They say how people learn and teach to calculate (I am thinking of purely behavioristic description), how in certain circumstances they then calculate in writing, etc. A description is also given of how the word 'calculate' (etc.) is used. In this description there is naturally mention as well of mathematical propositions and their function" (Man. 163).

"Words like 'description' or 'report' are on the same level of generality. Suppose it were asked 'Is that which you have given, a description?' You have to ask 'Well, what is a description?' And you could only begin with examples" (JN 30). "The thing is: We have to get down to 'What *is* reporting?' What is describing?" (JN 16). "The concept of an experience: similar to that of an event, process, state, thing, fact, description, report. Here, I mean, we stand on the hard bedrock, which lies deeper than all special methods and language-games" (Man. 229, §1316).

"We may say of some philosophizing mathematicians that they are obviously not aware of the difference between the many different usages of the word 'proof'; and that they are not clear about the dif-

ference between the uses of the word 'kind', when they talk of kinds of numbers, kinds of proofs, as though the word 'kind' here meant the same thing as in the context 'kinds of apples'. Or, we may say, they are not aware of the different *meanings* of the word 'discovery', when in one case we talk of the discovery of the construction of the pentagon and in the other case of the discovery of the South Pole" (*BB* 28–29).
(cd) From Man. 169 and Man. 138, 23B. *BB* 144cd is fuller, and *EPB* 217–20 fuller still. See *OC* 42; Man. 302, 21.

in the *tone* of voice: see *OC* 30; *BB* 103a (quoted for p. 219b); Malcolm, *Memoir*, 92. "One speaks of a feeling of conviction because there is a *tone* of conviction. For the characteristic mark of all 'feelings' is that there is expression of them, i.e. facial expression, gestures, of feeling" (*Z* 513; see §578b). "Let us also recall how, for instance, someone teaches a child the word 'sure' or 'certain'; he tells him, say, 'He is quite sure to come!' and here the tone of voice plays the largest role—and also gestures and facial expressions. The word is above all the bearer of this tone of voice" (*EPB* 220).

The temptation also arises from the fact that feelings such as anxiety and pain have degrees, and so does certainty (Malcolm, *Memoir*, 87d, 91d).

But do not think . . . : as James and Russell did (see commentary on §578a). Terms like *feeling* "merely distract us from the thing that really matters" (*OC* 459). See p. 224c and commentary.

Ask, not . . . : "The accompanying feeling is of course a matter of indifference, and equally we have no need to bother about the words 'I am sure that' either.—What is important is whether they go with a difference in the *practice* of the language" (*OC* 524). Cp. §§314, 316, 370, 645–46, p. 181.

but: How . . . : see §§578–79 and commentary; *OC* 7, 89, 337–38; *RFM* 76hi.
(e) See XXXVIII, 2; p. 224c and commentary; cp. §149 ("nothing would be more confusing . . ."); *OC* 404; *RFM* 179f; Man. 138, 28B.

"merely subjective": " 'subjective' is used derogatorily, as when we say that an opinion is *merely* subjective, a matter of taste" (*BB* 48). "It is an odd fact," wrote Russell, "that subjective certainty is inversely proportional to objective certainty" (*Scientific Outlook*, 64).

a difference between language-games: "With the word 'certain' we express complete conviction, the total absence of doubt, and thereby we seek to convince other people. That is *subjective* certainty. But when is something objectively certain? When a mistake is not possible. But what kind of possibility is that? Mustn't mistake be *logically* excluded?" (*OC* 194). " 'I have compelling grounds for my certitude.' These grounds make the certitude objective" (*OC* 270). " 'Objective uncertainty' is an indefiniteness in the nature of the game, the rules of evidence" (Man. 138, 21B; see p. 227k). See *OC* 174, 245, 273, 563.

(fg) See §240; *OC* 651–58; cp. *RFM* 97fg.

This is an important fact: to which the whole of §129 applies. Think, for instance, of the influence mathematics has exercised as a paradigm of knowledge, and of the reasons for this influence, as revealed, for example, in the explicit statements of Russell or Descartes. Consider, too, the role of mathematics in science and technology, and how these would be affected by disagreement (*RFM* 101; §240). See p. 226gh; *RFM* 3h, 13f, 129jkl; cp. §§241–42; *OC* 375.

If it were otherwise . . . : see *RFM* 120ijk; Man. 232, 750; cp. p. 226c; *OC* 651; *RFM* 14ab, 98fg, 119cd. "Proofs in mathematics involve the writing of equations on paper and seeing that one expression is contained in another. But if it is always to be doubted what expressions appear on a paper, then there can't be any proofs or any mathematics" (Malcolm's notes, *Memoir*, 92).

someone else's memory: see *OC* 632.

and so on: other doubts *may* be added, other mathematicians *must*. (The doubts of one would not destroy all mathematical certainty.)

would not exist: a clear indication that " 'mathematical certainty' is not a psychological concept" (p. 224e) and that "the kind of certainty is the kind of language-game" (p. 224f). See XXXVIII, 2; *Z* 393 ("there isn't any sharp line between such a condition and the normal one").

(h) See XXXVIII, 4; p. 226h; *OC* 43–46; *RFM* 35e, 72–73; *PB* 237b; JN 32; Baker and Hacker, Notice, 285–86; cp. §§193–95 and commentary; *RFM* 129f, 162; Frege, *Foundations*, ix.

Even then: i.e., if there were disagreement among mathematicians about the result, as there was among psychologists concerning the length of dreams. For notice that the disputants in that actual debate supposed that the dreams had one definite duration, though known perhaps to God alone. See the commentary on "in certain cases it is *not*", in (*a*).

it might always be said: rather: might still be said (*noch immer*), as it is now. "We say, not: 'So *that's* how we go!', but: 'So *that's* how it goes!' " (*RFM* 96; see *RFM* 162). For example:

"T. said that the best he could get is the result that *he* had obtained such & such a number. Does God know more about it?" (Man. 161; W.'s English).

"It seems to me that no philosophy can possibly be sympathetic to a mathematician which does not admit, in one manner or other, the immutable and unconditional validity of mathematical truth. Mathematical theorems are true or false; their truth or falsity is absolute and independent of our knowledge of them" (Hardy, "Proof", 4).

"That one proposition follows from certain others is something objective, something independent of the laws that govern the movements of our attention, and something to which it is immaterial whether we actually draw the conclusion or not" (Frege, *Foundations*, 93).

"The complete certainty of the *a priori* sciences, logic and mathematics, depends mainly on the fact that in them the path from ground to consequent is open to us, and is always certain. This endows them with the character of purely *objective* sciences, in other words, of sciences about whose truths all must judge in common, when they understand them" (Schopenhauer, *World*, II, 89).

"Although there is something arbitrary in our notations, *this* much is not arbitrary—that *when* we have determined one thing arbitrarily, something else is necessarily the case" (3.342). "Generality consists in the generality of use. And this subsists as it were regardless of whether we wish it or not—simply through the inner relation of the individual case to the paradigm" (Man. 108, 161), "as a searchlight casts its light as far as it does no matter how far we want it to" (ibid., 165). See IX, 1–4; *RFM* 127; Man. 123 (June 5), quoted for §193; cp. *Z* 299.

The truth: "Mathematical propositions seem to treat neither of signs nor of human beings, and therefore they *do* not" (*RFM* 124). The misunderstanding: "If a calculation is checked countless times, we cannot then say: 'Its correctness is nevertheless just *very probable*—since it is always possible that an error has crept in.' For let us suppose that an error is finally discovered—why shouldn't we suppose an error *here?*" (Man. 177, 4B).

"a quite definite result": cp. *PG* 115b.

P. 226(a) See preceding commentary; V, 3; IX, 5; §426a; *RFM* 6b, 9c, 185; cp. §§193–94; *RFM* 22g, 36; Man. FW, 3 (a like treatment of natural law).

God knows it: "The distribution of prime numbers would then for once provide us with something in logic that a god could know but not we. That is, there would be something in logic that we could not know but which could be known. (This is what I cannot believe.)" (Man. 106, 260, 262; cp. *PB* 212).

Mathematics is indeed . . . . : "Might it not be said that the *rules* lead this way, even if no one went it? For that is what one would like to say" (*RFM* 127).

though we . . . . : better: "even if we".

(b) See *RFM* 47bc; cp. *RFM* 124j; *PB* 161de; Man. 105, 55, 57; Waismann, "Analyse", 233–34. On this and the next two paragraphs, see *OC* 341–46; *Z* 309; *RFM* 36a.

But am I trying to say . . . . : in p. 225g or in *RFM* 81h ("it is not our conviction of the truth of logic that is responsible"). Cp. §242; *Kreis*, 106.

is based on the reliability: in a sense analogous to that in §482, that is: "These calculations are sure, for the ink and paper are reliable." Mathematicians would not necessarily advert to this underlying fact, but it could be cited in justification of their certainty.

"A delightful example of the way in which even mathematicians can confuse the grounds of proof with the mental or physical conditions to be satisfied if the proof is to be given is to be found in E. Schröder. Under the heading 'Special Axiom' he produces the following: 'The principle I have in mind might well be called the Axiom of Symbolic Stability. It guarantees us that throughout all our arguments and deductions the symbols remain constant in our memory—or preferably on paper,' and so on" (Frege, *Foundations*, viii).

No: yet this is true: "If the proposition $12 \times 12 = 144$ is exempt from doubt, then so too must non-mathematical propositions be" (*OC* 653). Cp. *PB* 155f.

That would be a vicious circle: for here reliability does not mean merely constancy, nor even such constancy as assures constant results, but rather: *whatever* behavior of ink and paper assures *correct* results (*RFM* 189d–190a). And by what other criterion than presently accepted correctness could the fulfillment of this condition be tested? "We judge identity and agreement by the results of our calculating; that is why we cannot use agreement to explain calculating" (*RFM* 115). Cp. Ramsey, *Foundations*, 251cd.

I have not said *why:* see GI 49; cp. *Kreis*, 193b.

(c) The point of the paragraph: Justification, like doubt, comes to an end; if it did not, it would not be justification (cp. §§217, 485; I, 4). "But the end is not an ungrounded presupposition: it is an ungrounded way of acting" (*OC* 110). See (*d*); cp. *OC* 34.

(d) See I, 4, 6.

What has to be . . . : see I, 4; *OC* 47, 189 ("At some point one has to pass from explanation to mere description"), 217, 375; *RFM* 20k, 133a; *BB* 73a.

"The danger here, I believe, is one of giving a justification of our procedure where there is no such thing as a justification and we ought simply to have said: *that's how we do it*" (*RFM* 98; see p. 200b). The thoughts of (*c*) and (*d*) are similarly joined in *OC* 110 (above), 203–4, 212.

the given: for an empiricist like Russell the "given" is an évident item of present experience, or "sense-datum", whereas for W. "the limit of the empirical—is *concept-formation*" (*RFM* 121; see 96, 171; X, 25). "The limits of empiricism are not assumptions unguaranteed, or intuitively known to be correct: they are ways in which we make comparisons and in which we act" (*RFM* 176; see *OC* 204). " 'In the beginning was the deed' " (*OC* 402).

forms of life: see *OC* 358 and the commentary on §19a; cp. *Z* 545.

(ef) Does it make sense . . . : it would have to be an observation about the concept "judgment of colour" (p. 227cd), so resemble §242, whereas *generally* suggests an empirical truth. Cp. §491 and commentary.

What would it be like . . . : only if we can imagine the opposite is the proposition empirical (*RFM* 114). See the commentary on §251.

But what right . . . : and how would what they did constitute disagreement in judgments of color, if by "judgment of color" is meant the type of linguistic activity we ordinarily engage in?

How would they learn . . . : see III, 1–2; cp. p. 227c.

And is the language-game . . . : where considerable disagreement does exist—e.g. in the use of *beautiful* and *good,* in the cheers of opposed factions at a game, and so on—the expressions differ notably from color predicates.

There are evidently . . . : for we may imagine differing degrees of disagreement, affecting various proportions of the population. See *(g).*

(g) See *RFM* 94, 97–98.

(h) See pp. 225h–226a and commentary; *OC* 303–5; *RFM* 31e–33e; Man. 138, 26–27; cp. *RFM* 3i–4a; 186h–187a. Number 241 spells out the message of this paragraph in more general terms.

do not mean the same: cp. *OC* 43; *Z* 406; *RFM* 94b, 124f, 172g, 173h, 184gh.

if it makes sense at all: see *Z* 407; *RFM* 33 (the quote for p. 227b); cp. *Z* 701. A mathematical proposition functions as a rule (Hallett, "Contrast", 695–97), and one does not believe a rule. "Compare: 'If you say: "I believe that castling takes place in such and such a way," then you are not believing the rule of chess, but believing e.g. that a rule of chess runs like *that'* " (*RFM* 33).

have *arrived* at: for instance as in 6.241. See §578c.

different *uses:* "Something is an axiom, *not* because we accept it as extremely probable, nay certain, but because we assign it a particular function, and one that conflicts with that of an empirical proposition" (*RFM* 114).

a different calculus: see *RFM* 166d; Hunter, *Essays,* 177–78.

or a technique: "Another game could quite well be imagined, in which people were prompted by expressions (similar perhaps to general rules) to let sequences of signs come to them for particular purposes, i.e. *ad hoc;* and that this even proved to pay. And here the 'calculations', if we choose to call them that, do not have to agree with one another" (*RFM* 164).

we should not call "calculating": "If there is confusion in our operations, if everyone calculates differently, and each one differently at different times, then there isn't any calculating yet" (*RFM* 160; cp. *RFM* 187bc). For a borderline case, see *RFM* 144e.

P. 227(a) would it be *wrong*?: see *OC* 188, 217, 497; *RFM* 41de, 43–44, 98efg, 102a, 106, 120l, 166h, 169, 170n, 179g–180a, 181bc; Rhees, *Discussions*, 117–22; cp. *OC* 284, 609; *PP* 279–80. "If you follow other rules than those of chess you are *playing another game;* and if you follow grammatical rules other than such-and-such ones, that does not mean you say something wrong, no, you are speaking of something else" (*Z* 320; cp. §136d).

Is a coronation *wrong*?: see *RFM* 45a. Man. 138, 27A, answers: "At most useless. And perhaps not even that." An intermediate case in *RFM* 137 clarifies the connection between this question and the preceding: "Calculation that belongs to the performance of a ceremony. For example, let the number of words in a form of blessing that is to be applied to a home be derived by a particular technique from the ages of the father and mother and the number of their children. We could imagine procedures of calculating described in such a law as the Mosaic law. And couldn't we imagine that the nation with these ceremonial prescriptions for calculating never calculated in practical life?"

To beings . . . : the punctuation in the German is wrong.

(b) Revised from Man. 138, 27A.

in one sense: "One says 'I know' where one can also say 'I believe' " (p. 221). " 'But you surely don't believe a mathematical proposition.'—That means: 'Mathematical proposition' signifies a role for the proposition, a function, in which believing does not occur" (*RFM* 33; see p. 226h). However, there is also knowing how, and mathematics might be characterized as largely knowing-how, in the garb of knowledge-that. "If you know a mathematical proposition, that's not to say you yet know *anything.* I.e., the mathematical proposition is only supposed to supply a framework for a description" (*RFM* 160; see *RFM* 163).

only exist as the exception: cp. §345; *OC* 34.

would have been abrogated: see *RFM* 160c, 164; cp. §142.

(c) an observation about the concept: if it were not generally true that people learn the same multiplication table, the expression "multiplication table" would not have the meaning it does. Cp. (*d*) and pp. 225g, 226g.

(d) Cp. *Z* 351.

judgments of colours . . . judgment of colour: "colour predications" seems a preferable translation of *Farbaussagen.* "*Colour-words* are explained like *this:* 'That's red' e.g.—Our language-game only works, of course, when a certain agreement prevails, but the concept of agreement does not enter into the language-game" (*Z* 430; see *Z* 428–32).

(e) an expression of feeling: e.g. "I'm sorry," "I'm frightened," "I hope he does."

(f) Revised from Man. 232, 765.

is there some mistake . . . : see (*ij*).

(g) we cannot prove anything: much as we might be unable to prove that a painting is (or is not) by a certain artist, though we are sure it is, simply by looking at it (Man. 138, 25B; p. 228f). In both cases it is helpful to ask: "What would it be like if there were a proof?" (Man. 138, 25A).

(hij) See Man. 232, 750–52.

'expert judgment': that is, does the comparison with assigning a work of art really hold? Is a "judge of men" comparable to a "connoisseur of art", who, in virtue of long experience and accumulated knowledge, judges that a given work of art is or is not by a given artist? The following remarks suggest that the parallel is close. See Man. 138, 25.

Not, however . . . : as the would-be art expert must examine works of art, not just hear or read about them, so the would-be judge of men must observe their gestures, actions, expressions, tones of voice (p. 228gh). There is no doctrine of these things (p. 228b).

is not a technique . . . : again, think of the comparison with the judgment of paintings.

but they do not form a system: see Man. 138, 29A; cp. p. 228b.

(k) What is most difficult . . . : see p. 228h; Man. 229, §1611 (quoted for §568b). "What shows that a person has the correct judgment? That is *difficult* to say. I could mention many things, but they would be shreds of a description" (Man. 138, 25A; see ibid., 7A).

this indefiniteness: see Man. 138, 21B (quoted for p. 225e).

P. 228(ab) Revised from Man. 232, 766.

"cannot be proved": see p. 227g; cp. commentary on p. 227k.

what does one go on to do: the movement here parallels that in p. 225cd; W. questions the notion that recognition of genuineness amounts simply to the alleged feeling.

and does the game *end* . . . : cp. p. 218bc.

and they too: see p. 227j.

the fragments of a system: the remark reflects W.'s general viewpoint. See GI 43–44; Man. 229, §1225.

(c) See Man. 232, 747; Man. 138, 25.

(def) The question is . . . : concerning the fine shades of behavior which largely constitute such evidence (*h*), W. asked: "Why are they *important*? They have important consequences" (p. 204), in subsequent behavior. And this behavior sometimes "*can* be weighed" (*e*). It may decisively corroborate one's judgment that, e.g., a loving look was genuine (*h*). Indeed, only through such corroboration can imponderable evidence prove itself to be evidence (*e*).

that a picture was a . . . : see Man. 138, 25B. Another comparison, suggested by Man. 138, 24A: judging the weather by present impression and by subsequent observation.

(gh) See Man. 138, 25B, 27.

I may be quite incapable . . . : see p. 227k and commentary.

And this not . . . : see §§78, 610. The person who cannot capture an expression on canvas does not lack the right paints (Man. 229, §1611, quoted for §568b).

(i) how can this nose be used?: a farmer with a "nose" for the weather plows, plants, brings in the hay; a man with a "nose" for sincerity entrusts a task or doesn't, loans or refuses money, and so on. The game does not end with the recognition of genuineness (*a*). See (*b*).

(j) On pretending, see §§249–50; *Z* 383–88; Man. 138, 19B–20A.

a special case: others: couvade (Man. 232, 769); crying out in one's sleep (ibid.); "it is a scene in a play" (p. 180a).

P. 229(a) Revised from Man. 232, 751.

this very special pattern: see *Z* 568–69; cp. p. 174d. "Only in a complicated *expression-game* is there pretense and its opposite. (As only *in a game* is there a false move or a correct one.)" (Man. 138, 28B). See the commentary on §§249–50.

(b) has much to learn: see §249 and commentary. "Nor can the newborn child be naughty, friendly, thankful. Only in a complicated pattern of behavior is there thankfulness" (Man. 138, 27B). "Granted, an adult can pretend without speaking a word, by means of facial expressions, gestures, and inarticulate sounds" (ibid., 28A).

A dog cannot . . . : see §250; cp. §650, p. 174bc.

neither can he be sincere: "Only of someone who can speak do we normally say that he is sincere" (Man. 138, 28A).

(c) "*believes* he is pretending": but is not, since (for example) he has not learned enough (*b*). Thus were a person to mistakenly clutch his left side instead of the right, we might say: "He believes he is pretending to have appendicitis, but he doesn't know how." In this respect pretending resembles understanding; a person may believe he understands a word when he doesn't (p. 53n). Cp. *RFM* 169c; Man. 138, 19B.

Man. 232, 752, suggests a different form of failure when it adds: "Pilgrim's Progress: he *believes* he utters the oaths the devil utters." (The passage: "Just when he was come over against the mouth of the burning pit, one of the wicked ones got behind him, and stepped up softly to him, and whisperingly, suggested many grievous blasphemies to him, which he verily thought had proceeded from his own mind.")

XXXIX. Wittgenstein's Middle Way between Conventionalism and Essentialism (P. 230)

(1)   Opposed like his mentors, Frege and Russell, to sheer formalism or conventionalism, young Wittgenstein showed appropriate interest in the conditions of possibility of any language (GI 30). Stressing their *a priori* character still more strongly than Russell, he judged it misleading to say that "logic is concerned with the real world just as truly as zoology, though with its more abstract and general features" (Russell, *Introduction*, 169). For "all theories that make a proposition of logic appear to have content are false" (6.111). The same holds, he thought, of philosophy as a whole (GI 8): "Philosophy gives no pictures of reality, and can neither confirm nor confute scientific investigations. It consists of logic and metaphysics, the former its basis" (*NB* 93). From the metaphysics of the *Tractatus* we learn about the unalterable form—the "essence" (3.3421)—shared by all imaginable worlds (2.022–2.023) and mirrored in the propositions of any conceivable language (2.18; GI 31). "Some things are arbitrary in the symbols that we use" (6.124), and some things are a matter of convenience (6.341–6.342); but others are neither arbitrary nor merely convenient, and only these interest the logician (6.124). "Logic is not a field in which *we* express what we wish with the help of signs, but rather one in which the nature of the natural and inevitable signs speaks for itself" (ibid.).

(2)   The therapeutic philosopher who would reformulate contingent propositions in "a sign-language that is governed by *logical* grammar—by logical syntax" (3.325; see GI 25)—is similarly bound. As the tautologies of logic must mirror the form of the world, common to all facts, so the analytic translations of particular propositions must mirror the forms of the pictured states of affairs. It makes little difference what names are used, but names there must be, just one for each object (*NB* 53). Again, it makes little difference how the names are related, but relations they must of course have, and a distinct kind for each type of relation between objects (Hallett, *Definition*, 19–25). In this sense, there is only one correct analysis, as there is only one correct logic (3.25).

(3)   The logical forms of reality not only dictate what forms logical and fully analyzed propositions shall take, but they thereby determine as

well what forms they shall not take. Hence logic and analysis together, it seemed, might realize the chief goal of the *Tractatus:* "to set a limit to thought, or rather—not to thought, but to the expression of thoughts: for in order to be able to set a limit to thought, we should have to find both sides of the limit thinkable (i.e. we should have to be able to think what cannot be thought). It will therefore only be in language that the limit can be set, and what lies on the other side of the limit will simply be nonsense" (Preface; division omitted; see GI 6). "Where ordinary language disguises logical structure," Wittgenstein still wrote in 1929, "where it allows the formation of pseudopropositions" (LF 32), "a perfect notation will have to exclude such structures by definite rules of syntax. These will have to tell us that in the case of certain kinds of atomic propositions described in terms of definite symbolic features certain combinations of the T's and F's must be left out. Such rules, however, cannot be laid down until we have actually reached the ultimate analysis of the phenomena in question" (LF 37). Of this "false concept that Russell, Ramsey, and I had," Wittgenstein later wrote: "One waits for an ultimate logical analysis of facts, as for a chemical analysis of compounds. An analysis by which one really discovers a 7-place relation, say, like an element that really has the specific weight 7" (*PG* 311–12; see *Kreis,* 182–83).

(4)   Section xi of Part Two, which the present page appropriately follows, reveals Wittgenstein's altered viewpoint. Secondary senses such as those of *see* and *meaning* bud spontaneously in the thickets of language, without regard for *a priori* rules or limits. And the realities which beget and underlie these uses are not ineluctable structures of this or any world, but facts of our natural history which might conceivably be otherwise. Were we aspect-blind or meaning-blind (pp. 213–14), not only these but many other expressions would be affected. Similarly, in mathematics no set of answers in the divine mind dictates the rules of the game (pp. 225–26); we simply do agree in the results we reach. If we didn't, the whole game would alter, and the sense of mathematical terms.

(5)   In reaction against his former view, Wittgenstein declared: "Not only the axioms of mathematics but all syntax is arbitrary" (*Kreis,* 103; see *PG* 184b). "When I say the rules are arbitrary I mean that they are not determined by reality, as the description of reality is. And that means: It is nonsense to say of them that they agree with reality; that the rules for the words 'blue' and 'red', say, agree with the facts concerning these colors (*PG* 246; see *Z* 331; *BB* 134–35; *PG* 186). "If you talk about *essence*—, you are merely noting a convention. But here one would like to retort: there is no greater difference than that between a proposition about the depth of the essence and one about—a mere con-

vention. But what if I reply: to the *depth* that we see in the essence there corresponds the *deep* need for the convention" (*RFM* 23). In such terms may a synthetic balance be struck, between conventionalism and essentialism. In the case of mathematics, for example, "isn't it the *application* of the calculation that produces this conception of its being the calculation, not ourselves, that takes this course?" (*RFM* 163). Just as having once been burnt a person would do anything rather than put his hand into a fire, "so he would do anything rather than not calculate for a boiler" (§466; see *RFM* 4a; *PG* 110c). Here, then, is the kernel of truth in Frege's contention that logical distinctions are not made arbitrarily, "but founded deep in the nature of things" (*Writings*, 41): They are founded deep in *our* nature (p. 147n and commentary), in our needs and tendencies and ways of life. (Cp. XVI, 7–10.)

(6)   In a sense, therefore, Russell too was right when he related logic to general features of the world (XXXIX, 1); but the general features just mentioned are not the ones he had in mind, nor does logic study them. It is not concerned, for example, with the fact that people agree in their judgments (§242); it is not sociology or psychology. Nor is the philosophy of logic, even as practiced by Wittgenstein in the *Investigations*, to be confused with empirical science (VII, 6–7). True, in order to solve philosophical problems he had to look into the workings of our language (§109); but he described them as one does when stating the rules of a game (§108). And "a rule *qua* rule is detached, it stands as it were alone in its glory; although what gives it importance is the facts of daily experience" (*RFM* 160, continued in XVI, 2).

DETAILED COMMENTARY

P. 230(a) Worked up in Man. 130, 71–73. See commentary on (*b*); references for p. 204k; *OC* 617; *RFM* 156ei, 159bcd; NL 306; *PG* 204b; Man. 229, §§714, 1776 (quoted for p. 225b); Schlick, "Psychological", 402–7; Specht, "Problem", 169–77; cp. 4.112; Man. 109, 38–39.

explained by facts of nature: see XXXIX, 3–4; *Z* 350–55; *RFM* 161f; Strawson, "Review", 47–49; cp. §492a. For examples, see e.g.: §80 (chair); *BB* 62b (bodily appearance); §§142 and 257 (natural expressions of pain); §§253 and 312 (patterns of pain); p. 225g (agreement in mathematics); Malcolm, *Memoir*, 92c (several of the preceding); Man. 229, 201 (drawing with pencil, pen); *PB* 76c (possibilities of movement); *RFM* 174a (measuring time); and the commentary on (*b*) ("then let him imagine"). "There correspond to our laws of logic very general facts of daily experience. They are the ones that make it possible for us to keep on demonstrating those laws in a very simple way (with ink on paper for example). They are to be compared with the facts that make measurement with a yardstick easy and useful" (*RFM* 36). Our calculating too is founded on empirical facts (pp. 225g, 226bc). "But what empirical facts are you now thinking of? The psychological and physiological ones that make it possible, or those that make it a useful activity?" (*RFM* 173).

Our interest certainly includes . . . : see XXXIX, 4; §129, pp. 56n, 220h; Man. 229, §715 (quoted below). W.'s attitude is no longer that of, e.g., Man. 108, 217 and 242 (both quoted for §108bcd).

because of their generality: see §129, p. 56n.

our interest does not fall back . . . : so that we are interested in these connections in and for themselves. See GI 8, 47–51; XXXIX, 6.

we are not doing natural science . . . : see GI 49; VII, 1–7.

we can also invent . . . : see GI 62; cp. 5.555.

fictitious natural history: see e.g. §§80, 142, 253b, 257, 312b, pp. 213–14, 220gh, 221b, 222f; *RFM* 118, 136–37.

for our purposes: e.g. that in (*b*); but see also GI 62.

(b) See I, 3; *OC* 191; *Z* 331–32, 380–81, 430, 439; *RFM* 14ab, 15a, 156c, 189a; NL 287n; *Kreis*, 65, 77; Man. 130, 73–77 (where this paragraph took shape); Waismann, *Principles*, 201–3; Mauthner, *Beiträge*, II, 66–69; Hacker, *Insight*, 100–102, 156–63, 166–70; cp. §562a; *RFM* 98; *PB* 107a; 3.315; Man. 109, 228; Russell, *Logic*, 270b; Rhees, *Discussions*, 123–24 (like remarks on mathematics).

I am not saying: this remark is more readily intelligible in Man. 229, 201, where it follows many imagined changes, and corresponding conceptual shifts. Cp. *OC* 492 ("I do not intend this as a *prophecy*"), 559 ("the language-game is so to say something unpredictable"); commentary below on "will become intelligible".

if anyone believes . . . : see XXXIX, 1–3; p. 147n and commentary; *OC* 130; *RFM* 7h, 121g ("We only seem always to be fitting our thinking to experience"), 171d; *PG* 185e–186b; *PB* 53d; LF 36 ("Our symbolism . . . gives here no correct picture of reality"); *PP* 278; *Kreis*, 184; Man. 229, §§1290–92; Man. 228, §386; Man. 116, 134 (quoted for §497b); Man. 112, 171–72; Frege, *Laws*, 13 ("boundary stones set in an eternal foundation, which our thought can overflow, but never displace"); Ogden and Richards, *Meaning*, 207; cp. §63, p. 224j (the other side of the coin); *PG* 111b; *PB* 85c; 14j, 35–36.

"Every *real* proposition," wrote the early W., ". . . mirrors some logical property of the Universe" (*NB* 107); otherwise it is a mere pseudo-proposition. "The error here always consists in my forgetting that it is just the *totality* of its rules which characterize the game, the language, & that the rules are not answerable to any reality, so that they are governed by it & we could doubt that a rule is necessary or correct (compare the problem of non-contradiction in non-Euclidean geometry). Grammar is answerable to no reality" (Man. 110, 215–16; see Man. 302, 17).

"We are tempted to say that some concepts can't be changed. We support this perhaps by saying that e.g. material objects are *given in nature*. . . . But that won't do. . . . The *concept* isn't given" (JN 55).

then let him imagine . . . : see *OC* 63, 617; *Z* 350, 376, 383–88; *RFM* 104f; *EPB* 202–3; *BB* 61d–62c, 134d, 135d; Man. 302, 17; Man. 232, 760–61; cp. Schlick, "Meaning", 168b.

"It interests us, for instance, to ascertain that in our surroundings certain shapes are not connected with certain colors, that for instance we do not see green always associated with circularity and red with squareness. Were we to imagine a world in which colors and shapes were joined in this fashion, we would find intelligible a conceptual system in which the basic *division*—shape and color—would not exist" (Man. 229, §715; cp. *BB* 134d). "Or think of a world in which colors were almost always distributed as in a rainbow, so that if, by way of exception, there occurred a green patch, we would view it as the *modification of a rainbow*" (Man. 229, §1310). Similarly, "let us imagine a color-blind *population* (and such there could easily be). They would not have the same color concepts as we. For even if they spoke e.g. German, so had all the German color terms, they would use them differently than we and would *learn* their use differently" (Man. 176, 5). Again, if "human beings could really observe the functioning of others' nervous systems . . . and regulated their dealings with others accordingly, I believe they would not have our concept of pain (e.g.), although it might be a related one. Their life would *look entirely different* from ours" (Man. 169, 65).

will become intelligible: not predictable (§340, p. 230a; JN 28). In Man. 229, 202, W. uses the word *natural* instead of *intelligible,* and contrasts it with *necessary;* see also Man. 130, 76–77.

(c) Revised from Man. 232, 715. See XXXIX, 5; §§520, 569–70, pp. 147n, 204k; *Z* 358, 700; *RFM* 23f, 34d, 129; Man. 302, 30; Man. 229, §1313; Man. 108, 96–99; Pitcher, "Same", 124–34; cp. *OC* 317; *RFM* 17h, 18c.

"It is true, however, that we may be irresistibly attracted or repelled by a notation. (We easily forget how much a notation, a form of expression, may mean to us, and that changing it isn't always as easy as it often is in mathematics or in the sciences. A change of clothes or of names may mean very little and it may mean a great deal.)" (*BB* 57).

Compare a concept . . . : see §401b.

a style: see Man. 302, 30; Spengler, *Untergang,* 284: "Style, an unwilled and unavoidable tendency (this needs to be stressed today) in all production".

Can we choose one . . . : think, for instance, of "a painting in which the light side of a body is always green and the shaded side is always red" (Man. 167). "A stylistic expedient may be practical, yet be denied one. For instance, the Schopenhauerian *'als welcher'*. It would often facilitate, clarify expression, but cannot be used by a person who finds it old-fashioned; and he has no right to disregard this feeling. . . . Tradition is not something a person can learn, it isn't a garment he can take off when he pleases; any more than a person can choose his own ancestors" (Man. 168, 2, 4).

XL. Remembering Has No Experiential Content (P. 231)

GENERAL COMMENTARY

(1)   This discussion of memory concluded the *Investigations* in Wittgenstein's own arrangement, as an earlier treatment of the topic terminated the *Brown Book*. The focus fixed by the first sentence there reveals clearly why the discussion was left till Part Two (GI 65–66): "What is the difference," Wittgenstein asked, "between a memory image, an image that comes with expectation, and say, an image of a daydream?" (*BB* 182). Here in the *Investigations* a slightly broader focus, on memory "experiences", suggests (and may be explained by) other comparisons.

(2)   The puzzle of memory is closely related to that of imagining (XXIX), aspect-seeing, or meaning (XXXVII). Looking at a man, we suddenly *see* his likeness to his father (p. 210); yet his father is perhaps not present, even in our minds (XXXVII, 14). Uttering a name, we at that moment *mean* a man long dead, or halfway round the world (*LC* 67); once again, he is not there, yet the connection is unmistakable. Likewise, in memory we *know* what happened yesterday or the day before, though the events we recall are irretrievably lost to inspection. "So is the appearance of an aspect any stranger than my remembrance of a specific real person of whom I have a memory-image? There is indeed a similarity between the two cases. For here too one asks: How is it *possible* for me to have an image of *him* and for there to be no doubt that it is *of him*?" (Man. 229, §1666; see GI 34). "You certainly . . . are not now directly perceiving the original sense-datum," wrote Moore

(*Problems*, 246). "But in what sense, then, are you now conscious of it? All that can be said, I think, with certainty, is that you are conscious of it, in the obscure sense in which it is necessary that you should be conscious of it, in order to know that it was different from the image—different, therefore, from anything which you are directly perceiving. This obscure sort of consciousness is what I said that even those who admit its existence seem unable to give a clear account of. And I confess I can't give any clear account of it myself." In such a situation, one is inclined to say that the "obscure sort of consciousness"—the memory sort—is too "specific" to be expressed in other words, that it is therefore "intangible", "indescribable" (§608).

(3) "Remembering," Wittgenstein tersely counters, "has no experiential content" (p. 231c). The sense of this denial is revealed by his reasons, of which the first and simplest is the paucity of images when we remember the past (*PG* 181c). "When," for instance, "someone asks me what I have done during the last two hours, I answer straight off and do not read the answer off from an experience" (Man. 229, §774). But if this is so—if a memory-image is no more necessary for memory than a meaning-experience is for meaning (XXXII)—why does the experience seem so important? "Doesn't it come from the fact that this phenomenon conflicts with a certain primitive interpretation of our grammar (logic of language)? Thus people often suppose that remembering an event must consist in an inner picture, and indeed such a picture sometimes actually exists" (Man. 229, §1717), as does a meaning experience (XXXVII, 11, 13).

(4) Effective therapy required Wittgenstein to show that even when an image does occur, it is not the remembering, nor an indispensable means of remembering. Only in this way could the philosophical *must*, requiring a picture, be weakened (cp. §§305–6; *BB* 12a). Here in XL he dwells on the first point (the experience is not memory), whereas elsewhere he stressed the second: We need not, indeed often cannot, read off the past from our images. Suppose, for example, that someone asks me, "Were you in your room yesterday?" and I reply "Yes." "For that I needn't see myself, even for a moment, in memory there in my room. But let us suppose that when I said that, I did see myself standing by the window in my room. How does the picture show me it was yesterday? Granted, the picture could show that too, if it had me looking at a wall calendar, say, with yesterday's date on it. But if that was not the case, how did I read off from the memory-image, or from the memory, that I stood thus at the window *yesterday*? How do I translate the experience of remembering into words?—But did I translate an experience into words? Didn't I simply utter the words, in a certain tone of voice

and with other experiences of certitude? . . . But what made you so certain when you spoke these words? Nothing: I *was* certain" (*PG* 181; see *PG* 85).

(5)   If I gave this report of my whereabouts and others corroborated it, people would not hesitate: They would say I had remembered. But is that because they would be so sure I had performed an inner act, called remembering? And as for myself, how would I know that I truly *remembered*? By introspection? "But surely I recognize a memory image as a memory image, an image of a daydream as an image of a daydream, etc.!" (*BB* 182). Very well, but "what do you mean by 'recognizing an image as a memory image'? I agree that (at least in most cases) while an image is before your mind's eye you are not in a state of doubt as to whether it is a memory image, etc. Also, if asked whether your image was a memory image, you would (in most cases) answer the question without hesitation" (*BB* 183). However, "if you answer the question what sort of image it was you had, do you do so by, as it were, looking at the image and discovering a certain characteristic in it (as though you had been asked by whom a picture was painted, looked at it, recognized the style, and said it was a Rembrandt)?" (ibid.). How could this hidden trait become the defining characteristic of memory (p. 231e; X, 20–21)?

(6)   "It is easy, on the other hand, to point out experiences characteristic of remembering, expecting, etc., accompanying the images, and further differences in the immediate or more remote surrounding of them. Thus we certainly *say* different things in the different cases, e.g., 'I remember his coming into my room,' 'I expect his coming into my room,' 'I imagine his coming into my room.'—'But surely this can't be all the difference there is!' It isn't all: There are the three different games played with these three words surrounding these statements" (*BB* 183).

DETAILED COMMENTARY

P. 231(ab) Cp. Russell, *Outline*, 206b.

   "half an hour ago": *PG* 85 and 181 (see XL, 3) suggest W.'s reason for using this phrase. Even if some memory-image accompanied the words, it would hardly contain a clock with the hands clearly pointing to the minute and the hour. And even if it did, the clock would not show whether it was morning or evening, or the day of the week, or whether the clock was going and correct.

   of a present experience: as Russell asserted: "It is clear that, in so far as the child is genuinely remembering, he has a picture of the past occurrence, and his words are chosen so as to describe the picture" (*Logic*,

302; cp. 132–33). Or as W. once put it: "When I describe the past which is immediately given I describe my memory, not something that this memory intimates to me (for which the memory would be just a symptom)" (Man. 110, 9). See GI 15–16; XL, 3; Z 650; Man. 115, 31.

are accompaniments of remembering: not the content (*c*), as the claim just rejected (*a*) would suggest.

(cd) has no experiential content: see XL, 2–5; p. 217b and commentary; OC 417; cp. PB 81b, 82a; Man. 229, §774.

Russell expounded a theory of acquaintance according to which "between subject and object there is a third entity, the 'content', which is mental, and is that thought or state of mind by means of which the subject apprehends the object" (*Logic*, 127). "The content of a belief [for instance a memory belief] may consist of words only, or of images only, or of a mixture of the two, or of either or both together with one or more sensations. It must contain at least one constituent which is a word or an image, and it may or may not contain one or more sensations as constituents" (*Mind*, 236–37). "What, if we followed Meinong's terminology, we should call the 'object' in memory, i.e. the past event which we are said to be remembering, is unpleasantly remote from the 'content', i.e. the present mental occurrence in remembering" (ibid., 164). See commentary on §598.

"You should avoid 'experience'. It suggests 'contents' which suggests 'descriptions' which suggests 'introspection' which suggests 'private' which suggests 'he's got something I haven't got' " (JN 62).

Surely this . . . : the implicit opposition to §§370–71 appears more clearly if we translate: "Isn't it through introspection, though, that this is to be seen?" Doesn't *it*, and it alone, warrant the claim? See Z 86; cp. EPB 235 ("Have we observed ourselves when willing, and observed that willing is not an experience?").

in this case or that: cp. commentary on p. 219a; Z 653.

where **to look:** cp. §448; however, here W. is not speaking of a location (cp. RFM 146c). The sense is: Which of all my innumerable experiences is a memory-experience? How am I to know? See X, 22; XL, 5.

I get the *idea* . . . : "That is no experience, that is an 'idea' (Schiller)" (Man. 110, 256; see the Appendix: Goethe).

"Whence do we get the concept of the 'content' of an experience? Well, the experience-content is the private object, the sense-datum, the 'Gegenstand' which I directly perceive with the mental eye, ear, etc. etc. The inner picture" (Man. 229, §778).

I assimilate psychological concepts: again, see Russell, in the commentary on §598. Of his own memory-content account, Stout remarked: "This analysis of remembrance is important for the purpose of the present paper because, as I shall try to show, it applies also, *mutatis mutandis*, to the sense-perception through which we are primarily cognisant of material objects" (Phenomenalism", 5).

"Look not at 'the content of consciousness'. Some psychological verbs seem to have it, e.g. 'I've got a pain' and 'I am feeling ill'; these contrast with 'I know the ABC,' 'I believe he'll come this afternoon.' There is, of course, something in this" (JN 83).

"If I now say that the experience of remembering and the experience of pain, say, are of different kinds, this is misleading, since the words 'different kinds of experience' perhaps make us think of a difference like that between a pain, a tickle, and a feeling of nausea, whereas the distinction we are talking of is comparable to that between 1 and i" (Man. 229, §777).

like assimilating two *games*: cp. §248; *RFM* 61ce; *BB* 19b; *PG* 82c.
(efg) See X, 22; Man. 138, 16B; Man. 121, May 17–19; Man. 116, 203–4; cp. p. 190ab; Man. 138, 20A (similar treatment of believing); James, *Principles*, I, 272b.

Would this situation . . . : see Man. 229, §781; cp. *PB* 72a.

"What it *feels like*": Russell's statements provide pointed contrast for the present paragraph: "I think the characteristic by which we distinguish the images we trust is the feeling of *familiarity* that accompanies them" (*Mind*, 161). "We may say, then, that images are regarded by us as more or less accurate copies of past occurrences because they come to us with two sorts of feelings: (1) Those that may be called feelings of familiarity; (2) those that may be collected together as feelings giving a sense of pastness. The first lead us to trust our memories, the second to assign places to them in the time-order" (ibid., 163). See commentary on §598.

Compare: Man. 130 discusses this comparison, and draws a contrast with §288a.

by remembering: cp. Man. 121, May 19: "Above all it is *correct* recollection that we call remembering. But naturally we don't learn the memory signal 'I remember . . .' as a description of a correct recollection."

Implicit in these words is an antiskeptical argument like that in X, 24, and §293. "He was trying to show what was wrong with the following statement which Russell made in his *Outline of Philosophy*: 'Remembering, which occurs now, cannot possibly prove that what is remembered occurred at some other time'" (*PP* 319). Just as many have supposed that the truths of mathematics are independent of human calculations (XXXVIII, 4; pp. 225h, 226ah, 227a and commentary), so Russell supposed we might all be mistaken in our memories (cp. §345):

"The occurrences which are *called* knowledge of the past are logically independent of the past; they are wholly analysable into present contents, which might, theoretically, be just what they are even if no past had existed" (*Mind*, 160; cp. p. 221g and commentary). But if present experience is at best a symptom of the past, what counts as a sure *criterion* (§354)? Whence does the word get its *sense*? From remembering, W. answered—from this form of agreement in judgments (§§241–42). Much as measurements determine both individual lengths and the meaning of the measures (p. 225a and commentary), so "we can conceive recognition, like memory, in two different ways: as source of the concepts past and sameness, or as a test of sameness and of what is past" (*PB* 62).

See Z 662–64; *PG* 181b; *PB* 82b, 104b (not *just* by remembering); *Kreis*, 98; Man. 138, 16B; Man. 109, 47; Man. 105, 96, 98; cp. §378; *OC* 45; *RFM* 184 (quoted for §206a); *PB* 61e, 81b; *Kreis*, 53b, 55a; Russell, *Logic*, 133 ("'Present' and 'past' are given in experience, and 'future' is defined in terms of them"). Note the clear contrast with James, *Principles*, I, 605 (quoted for p. 185d).

And how will he know . . . : see Z 666–67.

On the other hand . . . : see Man. 229, §783; *BB* 184–85 (a sampling: "But isn't there also a peculiar feeling of pastness characteristic of images as memory images? There certainly are experiences which I should be inclined to call feelings of pastness, although not always when I remember something is one of these feelings present.—To get clear about the nature of these feelings it is again very useful to remember that there are gestures of pastness and inflexions of pastness which we can regard as representing the experiences of pastness").

one might, perhaps: W.'s hesitancy is explained by "the idea that the feeling, say, of pastness, is an amorphous something in a place, the mind, and that this something is the cause or effect of what we call the expression of feeling" (*BB* 185). He asked: "Can I discover something, the essential feeling of pastness, which remains after abstracting all those experiences which we might call the experiences of expressing the feeling?" (*BB* 184). "In a sense it seems just as elusive as any other feeling of memory. ('Far away look in his eyes.')" (NL 272).

for there is a tone, a gesture: and not only does the "inner" have need of such outer criteria (X, 22), but gestures and the like have their own experiential dimension. "The mental states usually distinguished as feelings," wrote James (*Principles*, I, 222), include "the *sensations* we get from skin, muscle, viscus, eye, ear, nose, and palate." See *BB* 184, above; cp. p. 225c; *RFM* 10c.

XLI. Conceptual Confusion in Psychology and Mathematics (P. 232)

(1)   Relocated by the editors from after Section XXXVIII to the end of the book, this page gave notice of material still to come (in *RFM*). Another possible motive for the shift appears in von Wright's remark that an earlier version of the *Investigations* had existed (*PG,* then Man. 220), "the second half of which dealt with the philosophy of mathematics. This second half Wittgenstein had later 'laid aside' and it formed no part of the book in the final form he gave it. Yet it somehow belonged there, perhaps after the discussion of the philosophy of psychology in Part II of the *Investigations*" ("Papers", 501). Man. 108, 134, the remote ancestor of this section, indicates in a rough, general way how Wittgenstein had conceived the connection: "The method of recent mathematical logicians recalls, I believe, that of contemporary experimental psychology. In both, it is true, there is a specific task, but error in both cases concerning the meaning and import of the task. Tests of intelligence, of presence of mind, etc. show something, no doubt, but not what we call presence of mind, intelligence, etc. & proofs of non-contradiction may show something, but nothing important. At least so I believe. They are always scuttling around on the surface of the questions & do not generally see the really essential thing. When, however, the real task is accomplished, many of those superficial games become obsolete or have to be completely reinterpreted. (Here, once again, there is much technique and no intelligence.)" (See *Z* 66; *PB* 69f.)

(2)   Reference to tests of intelligence, by Wittengenstein, brings Wolfgang Köhler to mind, who in *The Mentality of Apes* described his "specific task" as follows: "I am by no means trying in this work to prove that the chimpanzee is a marvel of intelligence: on the contrary, the narrow limit of his powers (as compared to man's) has often been demonstrated. All that has to be decided is whether *any* of his actions have ever the characteristics of insight, and the answer to this question of principle is at present far more important than an exact determination of *degrees* of intelligence" (176). This statement of the question, and the ensuing argumentation in favor of an affirmative answer, are

rather puzzling in view of Köhler's initial suggestion that precisely these contested cases be treated "as the logical starting-point of theoretical speculation" concerning intelligence (ibid., 9).

(3)   Up to this crucial phrase, Köhler's methodological proposal resembles so strikingly the one in §5a and especially *BB* 17a (see GI 56) that it merits fuller quotation: "Even assuming that the anthropoid ape behaves intelligently in the sense in which the word is applied to man, there is yet from the very start no doubt that he remains in this respect far behind man, becoming perplexed and making mistakes in relatively simple situations; but it is precisely for this reason that we may, under the simplest conditions, gain knowledge of the nature of intelligent acts. The human adult seldom performs for the *first* time in his life tasks involving intelligence of so simple a nature that they can be easily investigated; and when in more complicated tasks adult men really find a solution, they can only with difficulty observe their own procedure. So one may be allowed the expectation that in the intelligent performances of anthropoid apes we may see once more in their plastic state processes with which we have become so familiar that we can no longer immediately recognize their original form: but which, because of their very simplicity, we should treat as the logical starting-point of theoretical speculation."

(4)   The *logical* starting-point, Wittenstein might say, is the concept, and that is determined by the word's use in the language (§371). Thus, for instance, "it is *primarily* the apparatus of our ordinary language, of our word-language, that we call language; and then other things by analogy or comparability with this" (§494). Since the degree of comparability is not fixed in advance (§§68–69), it would be futile to *argue* (as Köhler does, in analogous cases) whether the language-game of §2 is a "genuine" language. The study of primitive activities may indeed give insight into the *workings* of language or of intelligence (see §5a), but these examples are not *conceptual* paradigms. Thus Köhler missed the methodological significance of his observation: "The experiments in which we tested these animals brought them into situations in which all essential conditions were actually visible, and the solution could be achieved immediately. This method of experimentation is as well adapted to the chief problem of insight as are any which can bring about the decision 'yes' or 'no'; in fact, it may be the very best method possible at present, as it yields very many, and very clear, results. But we must not forget that it is just in these experimental circumstances that certain factors hardly appear, or appear not at all, which are rightly considered to be of the greatest importance for *human* intelligence" (*Mentality*, 227).

(5)   One is reminded of the manner in which James, while admitting

that introspection differs greatly from ordinary observation and that its
findings are therefore more problematic (XXXII, 2), maintained nevertheless that *"introspective observation is what we have to rely on first and
foremost and always"* (XXXV, 3; cp. Köhler, *Mentality*, 21). Here too,
problem and method pass one another by (p. 232b), for the linguistic
parameter is similarly ignored (XXVII, 1). However, though doubtless
Wittenstein had James too within his sights (X, 22; XXXII, 3–4;
XXXV, 1–2), in the penultimate version of the present section he singled out Köhler (Man. 135, July 20), after criticism similar to that in p.
212d (and commentary): "Köhler thinks in terms of processes in the
retina & nervous system [e.g. *Gestalt*, 54–55]. He says that a contour can
be directed this way or that & explains this fact through currents, say,
which are directed thus or so [ibid., 184–85]. And as long as one thinks
physiologically, then color, shape, and aspect really are on a par" (Man.
135, July 18; see quote for p. 205a). For Wittgenstein's contrasting
treatment of this particular point, see p. 196; as background, see for instance GI 27, 60–61.

DETAILED COMMENTARY

P. 232(ab) See XLI, 1–5; Drury, *Danger*, 25–35.

The confusion and barrenness: see Köhler, *Mentality*, 160.

by calling it a "young science": as Köhler did: "Why does this difficulty beset behavioristic psychology, and not occur in physics? The answer is simple enough: Physics is an old science and psychology is in its
infancy" (*Gestalt*, 41, in a chapter entitled "Psychology as a Young
Science").

"Köhler himself is unclear as to what the *nature* of such discoveries,
say, might be. As I said, the difficulty in psychology resembles most
closely that regarding the 'foundations' of mathematics" (Man. 135,
July 20; see ibid., July 18).

certain branches: see e.g. *RFM* 148–51 on Dedekind's theorem.

Set theory: see §§412a; 426a; *RFM* 56d, 137; *PG* 460–70; *PB* 165a,
211; *Kreis*, 102–3, 228. "The error in the set-theoretical approach continually consists in treating laws & reports (lists) as basically one and the
same" (Man. 108, 180; see ibid., 172; *RFM* 57b; Man. 106, 145). "The
law is not another way of giving what the list gives. What the law gives,
the list *cannot* give. A list is no longer conceivable" (*Kreis*, 103). Thus "in
set theory, one is doing a branch of mathematics of whose application
one forms an entirely false idea" (*RFM* 134). "One always conceives
analysis and set theory as a theory which describes something, and not
as a calculus" (*Kreis*, 141; see *PB* 188).

pass one another by: see p. 212d; Man. 229, §1706.

" 'Thought is a puzzling process, which we are still far from understanding fully.' And now one undertakes experiments. Obviously without realizing *in what* the puzzling aspect of thought consists for us.

"The experimental method does *something*; the fact that it does not resolve the problem is attributed to its being still in its infancy. It is as though one wanted to determine through chemical experiments what matter and mind are" (Man. 229, §1760).

"The connexion of our main problem with the epistemological problem of willing has occurred to me before. When such an obstinate problem makes its appearance in psychology, it is never a question about facts of experience (such a problem is always much more tractable), but a logical, and hence properly a grammatical question" (Z 590).

(c) **entirely analogous:** compare §§109, 120, 122, 126 with §§124–25, or §108c with *RFM* 160hi. In both inquiries, "what we want is to *describe,* not to explain" (*RFM* 101; cp. §109); and "our task is, not to discover calculi, but to describe the *present* situation" (*RFM* 104; cp. §§132–33). "What mathematical propositions do stand in need of is a clarification of their grammar, just as do those other propositions" (*RFM* 171; see GI 8–10). The parallel is illustrated in Section XXXVIII (see XXXVIII, 2, 4) and in §§65–67.

as little a *mathematical* investigation: see §§124–25; *RFM* 157. Commentators on *RFM* have sometimes overlooked or failed to grasp this proposal, so have misjudged the significance of W.'s efforts there.

as the other is a psychological one: see commentary on §571a ("Psychology").

It might deserve the name: much as W.'s investigations in general deserve to be called philosophy. It would provide no foundation of mathematics (§125), just as the inquiries of the *Investigations* provide none for language (§124), nor any of the theories, definitions, constructions, and explanations which philosophers have sought; but it would resolve the same problems, and put an end to the search. "People might feel that it 'takes the place' of what they had done—might be inclined to say 'This is what I really wanted' and to identify it with what they had done, though it is really different" (*PP* 322).

APPENDIX: AUTHORS
WITTGENSTEIN KNEW OR READ

The following list, providing information on authors of W.'s generation or before, whom he knew or read, and who are cited in this commentary, permits me to say just once things I would otherwise need to say repeatedly in order to explain, in each instance, why I have cited or quoted a given author or work rather than others on the same topic, and what importance should be attributed to the citation or quotation.

It should also permit a balanced, realistic interpretation of remarks by acquaintances and by W. himself concerning the meagerness of his philosophical background. W., laughing, assured Karl Britton "that no assistant lecturer in philosophy in the country had read fewer books on philosophy than he had" (Britton, "Portrait", 60–61). He actually warned his students against reading philosophical works. "If we took a book seriously, he would say, it ought to puzzle us so much that we would throw it across the room and think about the problem for ourselves. Wittgenstein almost never referred to boooks in his lectures; seldom to the views of any philosopher not actually present" (ibid., 58; see Gasking and Jackson, "Wittgenstein", 54). He thus shared, and perhaps was early influenced by, Schopenhauer's attitude: "The constant influx of other people's ideas must certainly stop and stifle our own, and indeed, in the long run, paralyse the power of thought, unless it has a high degree of elasticity able to withstand that unnatural flow. Therefore incessant reading and study positively ruin the mind" (*World*, II, 78). Schopenhauer's abundant reading shows, however, that a man's practice cannot be surely inferred from his words. The present appendix indicates W.'s actual practice.

Yet only partially. For the criteria of selection, dictated by the primary purpose of the list, exclude a great many authors, for instance: (1) favorites like Bismarck (Malcolm, *Memoir,* 75); Buffon (*LC* 8); George Fox (Malcolm, *Memoir,* 71–72); Franz Grillparzer (Man. 135, July 28; Man. 133, 30–31; Man. 232, 667–68); the Grimm brothers (Malcolm, *Memoir,* 75; Rhees, Note, 18); Johann Hebel (Man. 229, §1375; Man. 117, 270); Ibsen and Björnson (von Wright, in a letter: "W., incidentally, knew Norwegian *very well* and was familiar with the great literature in that language. He often in conversations referred both to Ibsen and to Björnson"); Eduard Mörike (*LR* 47–48); Johann Nestroy (motto); Friedrich Nietzsche (*EPB* 207; *BB* 104; Man. 302, 5; Man. 131, 69; Man. 110,

12); A. Silesius (*LR* 82; Colombo, "Introduzione", 27); Rabindranath Tagore (*Kreis*, 15; Feigl, "Kreis", 638); Otto Weininger (von Wright, "Sketch", 21; *PG* 176d; *LR* 159; Man. 228, §416; Man. 111, 196); (2) others whom he knew or referred to, and sometimes evidently read: S. Alexander (Goodstein, "Mathematics", 272); J. Austin (*LR* 186); A. Ayer (Man. 138, 17A); N. Bachtin (von Wright, "Papers", 497); F. Bacon (Man. 132, Oct. 21); E. Barnes (Man. FW, 18); K. Barth (Man. 130, 9; Man. 173, 93); H. Bergson (Man. 109, 197; Man. 110, 47); J. Calvin (Drury, *Danger*, xiii; Man. 133, Nov. 19); G. Cantor (*RFM* 56, 58; *PG* 468; *PB* 208; *LC* 27–28; Man. 229, §1764); M. Claudius (Man. 134, April 4); C. Dallago (*Briefe*, 38, 45, 51–52); R. Descartes (*BB* 69; Coope et al., *Workbook*, 21; Man. 219, 19; Man. 134, April 2; JN 49); C. Dickens (Malcolm, *Memoir*, 72); P. Dirichlet (*Z* 705; *PG* 315); F. Dobson (*LC* 8–9); Euclid (*RFM* 8, 30, 50, 90); L. Euler (*PG* 383; *Kreis*, 108); B. Farrell (Malcolm, *Memoir*, 59); F. Fénelon (Man. 133, Nov. 19); F. Galton (*PB* 293; *PG* 229); K. Gödel (Man. 163; *RFM* 50–54, 174, 176–77); C. Grabbe (Man. 119, 36); T. Haecker (*Briefe*, 38, 46); M. Heidegger (*Kreis*, 68; Murray, "Note"; Man. 302, 28–30); G. Hegel (Man. 131, 154); E. Heine (*PB* 321); J. Hjelmslev (*Kreis*, 56–57); E. Husserl (*Kreis*, 67–68; cp. Man. 172, 1–4); J. Jastrow (p. 194); H. Jeffreys (one of the few offprints in W.'s possession at his death was Jeffreys' "The Nature of Mathematics", *Philosophy of Science*, October 1938); F. Kaufmann (*Kreis*, 84); F. Klein (*Kreis*, 57); F. Klopstock (*LC* 4); K. Koffka (JN 92); L. Kronecker (Man. 213, 497); N. Lenau (Man. 132, Oct. 19, 20); G. Lessing (*RFM* 182; Man. 229, §1160; Man. 110, 5); M. Luther (§589; JN 33); T. Macaulay (Man. 229, §1223; Man. 132, Oct. 20; and elsewhere); J. Maxwell (*PB* 323; *NB* 30); A. Meinong (Man. 109, 26); E. Meyer (whose history of the Mormons fascinated W.); J. Milton (Man. 131, 46); T. Mommsen (Malcolm, *Memoir*, 57); C. Morgenstern (*PG* 43); J. Morley (Drury, "Symposium", 67); C. Myers (*LR* 10); I. Newton (*PB* 322); Occam (3.328, 5.47321); C. O'Hara (*LC* 57–58); B. Pascal (Man. 138, 3A; Man. 125, 3); St. Paul (Man. 119, 71–73); Pliny (Man. 221, 145; Man. 131, 181; Man. 117, 11); J. H. Poincaré (*Kreis*, 211); W. Prescott (Malcolm, *Memoir*, 75; Drury, "Symposium", 67); H. Price (*LR* 186); K. Reach (another offprint in W.'s possession at his death was Reach's "The Name Relation and the Logical Antinomies"); G. Riemann (*PG* 362; *PB* 334–35); R. Rilke (*Briefe*, 16, 45–46); C. Runge (Man. 173, 24A, 26B; Man. 176, 6A, 7B); G. Ryle; Shakespeare (Man. 173, 36, 76; Man. 168, 1–2; Man. 131, 46, 163–64; Man. 174, 5); H. Sheffer (*PG* 361, 441, 443; *PB* 182, 191, 336; *NB* 102; *Kreis*, 122–23); T. Skolem (*PG* 397–99, 418, 420, 423, 448; *PB* 194–95; *PP* 301–2; W. owned and wrote comments in a copy of Skolem's *Begründung der Elementaren Arithmetik*); Spinoza (von Wright, "Sketch", 9, 21); E. Spranger (Toulmin, "Wittgenstein", 71); J. Thomae (*PB* 321); G. Trakl (*Briefe*, 15, 17, 20–22, 26–27, 45–47); A. Turing (who attended W.'s lectures; found among W.'s belongings was Turing's "On Computable Numbers", *Proceedings of the London Mathematical Society*, 1937; see Man. 229, §1763; Man. 135, July 30; and the quotation from Man. 161 for p. 225h); L. Uhland (GI 7); A. Watson (Man. 229, §1763; Man. 135, July 30; Man. 131, 173); H. G. Wells (Man. 113, 87; *Z* 456).

I am more likely to have overlooked references in unpublished works of W. than in published works by or about him, and in unpublished writings not included in the List of Manuscripts than in those included. The amount of space accorded an author here is no sure indication of the extent or importance of W.'s contact with him, since it depends as well on the amount of information I have found and on the amount already provided in the commentary. Fuller information can sometimes be had by consulting the index.

I am specially grateful to Peter Geach, A. C. Jackson, Brian McGuinness, Rush Rhees, and G. H. von Wright for enriching my store of information in various ways: Rhees, for instance, by indicating works in W.'s possession when he died, Jackson by distinguishing carefully between his own references and W.'s in JN.

AQUINAS, ST. THOMAS. Among the few philosophical works in W.'s possession when he died Rush Rhees lists two volumes of the *Summa Theologica*, in the Pustet edition (Salzburg and Leipzig, 1934), which gives the German on the top half and the Latin on the lower half of the page. The first volume, given to W. by Ludwig Hänsel in 1938, contains Part One, Articles 1 to 13; the second, which Hänsel gave him a year later, contains Articles 14 to 26. "The only remark of Wittgenstein's about Aquinas that I can remember," adds Rhees, "was that he found him extremely good in his formulation of questions but less satisfactory in his discussion of them."

AUGUSTINE, SAINT. Augustine was one of W.'s favorite authors (see von Wright, "Sketch", 21; the commentary on §1a), though I have found no evidence of his having read anything but the *Confessions*. Among the few books in his possession when he died there was both a Latin edition (Teubner's, 1898) and a German translation by O. F. Lachmann (Reklam edition, 1888). Rush Rhees believes W. almost always used the Latin.

Augustine is one of the handful of authors to whom W. frequently referred by name. The explicit citations deal mainly with language (§§1–3, 32; *BB* 77; *PG* 56) and with time (§§89–90; *BB* 26; *PG* 50, 471; Man. 302, 24). *PB* 83–86 may also reflect familiarity with Book XI of the *Confessions*. For other references to Augustine, see §§436, 618; *Z* 457; *BUF* 234. The absence of citations in the *Notebooks* and the *Tractatus* suggest that W. came to know and appreciate Augustine some time after World War I, when his attitude towards Christianity had become more favorable.

BERKELEY, GEORGE. It is reported (Drury, via McGuinness) that W. thought Berkeley a very profound writer, whereas Schopenhauer "was so clear one could see to the bottom". More than once (e.g. Man. 130) W. remarked: "How would we note it if people could not *see* depth? If they were as Berkeley thought we are." The citations reported by Moore (*PP* 305, 311, 322) are more general. Those in JN are not W.'s.

BOLTZMANN, LUDWIG. "Boltzmann's suicide frustrated Wittgenstein's hope of studying with him, but the pages of the *Tractatus* echo with phrases—'logical spaces', comprising 'ensembles of possibilities' etc.—which have roots in Boltzmann's generalised thermodynamics" (Toulmin, "Wittgenstein", 66; see von Wright, "Sketch", 3). An explicit connection is made in Man. 111, 120: "What I am saying here is what Boltzmann said about the place of a mechanical model, for instance in the theory of electricity."

BRAITHWAITE, R. B. Of chief interest is an article by Braithwaite, a fellow

Cambridge professor (see *LR* 159), which W. read and took exception to. In addition to W.'s letter to *Mind*—Vol. 42 (1933), 415–16—see the quotation from Man. 116, 43, for §17.

BROAD, C. D. Between W. and Broad, contemporaries at Cambridge, there was apparently such incompatibility, both of temperament and of thought, that W. avoided a meeting even in print (see *LR* 103). References in the *Nachlass* are rare, and critical, e.g. Man. 132, 75–76 ("Broad's thoughts all cost *very* little"); Man. 111, 138, and Man. 213, 78 ("False ideas about the functioning of language; Dr. Broad, who says the assertion 'something *will* happen' is not a proposition"). See also the quotation from JN 47, for p. 179e, and the commentary on §352a.

BROUWER, L. E. J. W. was stirred to take up philosophy again, after an absence of ten years, when, in March 1928, he attended two lectures which Brouwer gave in Vienna (von Wright, "Sketch", 13; Feigl, "Kreis", 639). Of these C. van Peursen has written me: "Brouwer told me, only one year before his death, about his encounter with L. W. His first, more general lecture [was] published afterwards: 'Mathematik, Wissenschaft, und Sprache', in: *Monatshefte für Mathematik und Physik* 36 (1929); his second lecture, also attended by L. W., was on technical problems of intuitionist mathematics and has not been published, as far as I know." (See van Peursen, *Wittgenstein*, 96.) W. subsequently showed intense interest in these same areas—excluded middle, set theory, the nature of infinity and of mathematics in general, and so on—and took positions similar to those of Brouwer. The resemblance was strongest when he still held that insight guides each step in mathematics (contrast *PB* 198c and 212e with §186). However, since he was stirred to efforts of his own by Brouwer's talks, it is not surprising to find that his explicit references to the Dutch mathematician contain more disagreement than agreement (*PB* 176, 210, 212; Man. 113, 198–99; *Kreis*, 73; *PG* 238, 458). Cp. *PP* 302–3.

BÜHLER, KARL and CHARLOTTE. In view of their prominence and interests (Toulmin, "Wittgenstein", 71), one might be inclined to make much of W.'s encounter with the Bühlers at his sister's house (Engelmann, *Letters*, 118). However, he never cites them, and according to Anscombe he considered Karl Bühler a charlatan. See Kaplan, "Considerations", 82–86.

BUNYAN, JOHN. See the commentary on p. 229c. A reference to "B's allegory" opens a long discussion in Man. 118.

BUSCH, WILHELM. A favorite of W.'s. See *PG* 80a, 379a; *EPB* 226 (quoted for §66a, with reference); Man. 229, §1650; Man. 134, May 10; Man. 113, 227; and the comments in Man. 168, 3, which start: "It is remarkable that Busch's drawings can sometimes be called 'metaphysical'."

CARNAP, RUDOLF. Though W. knew Carnap and met with him several times during the summer of 1927, it seems unlikely that Carnap influenced W.'s thought very much, one way or the other; he and Schlick (at Schlick's suggestion) said little during the meetings (Carnap, "Autobiography", 34), and W.'s rare references to Carnap (Man. 229, §1587; *Kreis*, 182; Man. 213, 100; cp. *RFM* 6, quoted for §89a; Man. 117, 11, and Man. 159, quoted for §23c) suggest only limited reading of his works, for instance of "Die physikalische Sprache als Universalsprache der Wissenschaft" (see *Kreis*, 25, 209). "The fact is," writes McGuinness, "there was a *Prioritätsstreit* between them" (cp. Feigl, "Kreis", 638–39).

CARROLL, LEWIS (Charles Dodgson). George Pitcher writes ("Carroll", 316): "Quite apart from the fact that anyone who lived in England, and particularly Cambridge, during the time that Wittgenstien did, could not fail to have read Lewis Carroll—especially the *Alice* books—it is known with certainty that Wittgenstein did read and admire Carroll. . . . Mr. Rhees recalls a conversation in 1938 in which Wittgenstein referred admiringly to a passage in *Sylvie and Bruno;* but he adds that in the last eight or ten years of his life, Wittgenstein no longer thought as highly of Carroll as he had earlier. Carroll is mentioned by name in *PI,* §13 and p. 198; and it is a safe bet that the nonsense poems referred to in *PI* §282 are those of Carroll." The remark on p. 198 suggests familiarity with *Sylvie and Bruno Concluded,* while BUF 239 refers to a passage in chapter 3 of *Alice in Wonderland.*

CHAMISSO, ADELBERT VON. Man. 111, 77, contains comments on von Chamisso's tales of "Peter Schlemihl", referred to in §339a.

DEDEKIND, RICHARD. W. frequently criticized Dedekind's explanation of infinity (*PB* 151, 208, 211; *PG* 460, 464; *RFM* 148–51, 153, 186; *Kreis,* 69ff, 103, 232).

DOSTOIEVSKI, FĔDOR. "Wittgenstein also admired the writings of Dostoievsky. He had read *The Brothers Karamazov* an extraordinary number of times; but he once said that *The House of the Dead* was Dostoievsky's greatest work" (Malcolm, *Memoir,* 52). A precise reference to Dostoievski appears already in *NB* 73; and in 1919 Russell wrote that despite W.'s attachment to Tolstoi's book on the gospels, "on the whole he likes Tolstoy less than Dostoewski (especially Karamazov)" (*LR* 82). See *Z* 499; BUF 253.

DRIESCH, HANS. With W.'s knowledge of Driesch established by an explicit citation (Man. 133, Feb. 12, and Man. 229, §1389, quoted for §261) and a quotation (Man. 302, 30; Man. 113, 247; and Man. 213, 492, quoted for §261), other less explicit connections appear, for instance with §304 and §398, in addition to §261. See the index.

EDDINGTON, ARTHUR. In *PB* 282 W. discusses a view of modern physicists concerning the meaning of their equations and cites Eddington as representative of the view. Pupils say he detested Eddington's work, at least his popular science.

EINSTEIN, ALBERT. References in *PB* 200, *PG* 459 and *Kreis,* 38 and 71, indicate that W. read at least Einstein's *Geometrie und Erfahrung* and/or *Über die spezielle und die allgemeine Relativitätstheorie.* For a remark in Man. 130 see this Appendix: Freud.

ENGELMANN, PAUL. Of Engelmann's varied literary output, W. read at least a poem (Engelmann, *Letters,* 8, 75–76). In Man. 111, 196–200, there are long remarks on "Engelmann's Orpheus". Doubtless their close friendship exercised greater influence on W.

ERNST, PAUL. Of the expression "mythology in our language", Rush Rhees writes: "Wittgenstein said he took this phrase from a preface to Grimm's *Märchen* by the Austrian story writer and critic Paul Ernst [see Man. 213, 433]. The same preface gave him the expression 'a misunderstanding of the logic of language' ('*Missverstehen der Sprachlogik*') which the *Tractatus* uses (or a variant of it) to explain the thinking that leads to metaphysical problems; 4.003, for instance. Wittgenstein said repeatedly that he ought to have acknowledged this when the *Tractatus* was first printed" (Note, 18; see McGuinness, "Philosophy of Science", 9). (McGuinness informs me that the edition in question—Munich, 1910—has a postface by Ernst.)

EWING, A. C. "I believe he had a grudging respect for Ewing," says McGuinness, "though he no doubt expressed himself differently at different times." (Geach has an anecdote about W.'s drawing up a list of speakers for the Moral Science Club and remarking that it would be "scraping the bottom of the barrel" if they had to invite Ewing to fill the final slot.) There is a rare reference to Ewing (W.'s colleague at Cambridge) in JN 84.

FARADAY, MICHAEL. Malcolm recounts that W. "thought that perhaps the most useful work a man trained in philosophy could do nowadays would be to present a popular but clear and decent account of some science, and he mentioned as an example of such a work, Faraday's *The Chemical History of a Candle*" ("Symposium", 73). See p. 46n and commentary.

FEIGL, HERBERT. Between 1927 and 1929, Feigl was among the members of the Vienna Circle who met with W. to hear him expound his ideas (Carnap, "Autobiography", 36; Feigl, "Kreis", 638).

FRAZER, SIR JAMES. "Wittgenstein wrote two sets of remarks on *The Golden Bough;* the first in a manuscript book in 1931, the second on separate sheets at least five years later, I think" (Rhees, Note, 18). The latter (BUF) may have been stimulated by Raymond Townsend's gift of an abridged edition in July 1936; but *PP* 312, 315–16, and scattered jottings in contemporary notebooks (e.g. Man. 213, 433; Man. 110, 195–99, 204, 256, 297) show what close (and consistently critical) attention W. had already given the work. "At one time for a short period," reports Drury, "Wittgenstein got me to read aloud to him the opening chapters of Frazer's *Golden Bough*" (*Danger,* x).

FREGE, GOTTLOB. Frege was a major influence on W.—some would say the most important influence (Coope et al., *Workbook,* 5–6)—especially at the start, when his conceptual realism made W. abandon the Schopenhauerian epistemological idealism which had been his first philosophy (von Wright, "Sketch", 5). When W. decided to give up his studies in engineering, he went to Jena to discuss his plans with Frege, and it was apparently Frege who advised him to go to Cambridge and study with Russell (ibid.). Thereafter W. corresponded with Frege (ibid., 9; *LR* 77) and read widely in his works, as is attested by numerous citations in the *Notebooks* (2, 10, 29, 95–96, 100, 104, 120), *Tractatus* (see the index), *Philosophische Bemerkungen* (119–20, 127, 137, 141, 182, 302, 318, 320, 325), *Philosophische Grammatik* (40, 106, 200, 202, 205, 265, 281, 307, 355, 444, 464, 468–69), lectures (*PP* 261, 291, 300), *LR* 9, and transitional manuscripts (e.g. Man. 105, 54; Man. 107, 7; Man. 111, 182; and especially Man. 106, 120). For some piquant details on their relationship, see Goodstein, "Mathematics", 271–72.

The somewhat smaller number of citations in W.'s later works (see §§22, 49, 71, p. 11; *Z* 684, 704, 712; *OC* 494; *EPB* 236; index of *RFM;* Man. 232, 749; Man. 220, 86; Man. 134, 6; Man. 122, Jan. 19) does not indicate declining interest. Malcolm recounts that in 1949 "with Oets Bouwsma and me he began to read Frege's paper 'Über Sinn und Bedeutung'; and this led to two or three meetings in which Wittgenstein expounded his divergence from Frege" (*Memoir*, 86). Despite the divergence of their views, which increased with time, W.'s admiration for Frege never flagged. Professor Geach recalls that only a few weeks before his death, W. took Frege's "On Concept and Object" in his hands and after reading it silently for a little said, "How I envy Frege! How I wish I could have written like that!" (See the quote from Man. 176, in this Appendix: Freud.) He felt that his long reading of Frege had in fact influenced his own style far more strongly than anyone but himself would suspect (Man. 112, 20; *Z* 712). At his death, Frege's *Grundlagen der Arithmetik* was one of the few philosophical works in W.'s possession.

FREUD, SIGMUND. W. told Rush Rhees (*LC* 41) "that when he was in Cambridge before 1914 he had thought psychology a waste of time" (though he spent some time himself in C. S. Myers' laboratory working on rhythms). " 'Then some years later I happened to read something by Freud, and I sat up in surprise. Here was someone who had something to say.' I think this was soon after 1919. And for the rest of his life Freud was one of the few authors he thought worth reading. He would speak of himself—at the period of these discussions—as 'a disciple of Freud' and 'a follower of Freud' " (*LC* 41). Yet with such "followers", one may ask, who has need of critics? "Freud has done a disservice," wrote W., "through his fantastic pseudo-explanations (precisely because they are ingenious)" (Man. 133, 21; see *LC* 41, 51–52; Malcolm, *Memoir*, 44–45). Concerning the man, as distinct from the work, W. remarked: "The less a person knows and understands himself, the less great he is, no matter how great his talent may be. Hence our scientists are not great. Hence Freud, Spengler, Kraus, Einstein are not great" (Man. 130). As for style, "Frege's is sometimes *great;* Freud's is excellent, & it is a pleasure to read him, but he is never *great* in his writing" (Man. 176, 56A). The abundance of comment on Freud reported by Moore (*PP* 310–12, 316–17) and in *LC*, even in the section on aesthetics (18, 23–27), revealing acquaintance with such works as *Wit and Its Relation to the Unconscious* (*LC* 18) and *The Interpretation of Dreams* (*LC* 23, 50), contrasts strangely with the paucity of references to Freud in W.'s writings (e.g. Man. 173, 72; *PG* 382). I know of no evidence that W. himself ever met Freud, though his sister did (*LC* 43).

GOETHE, J. W. As a highly educated person with a singularly cultured background, W. was of course acquainted with such works as Goethe's *Faust* (*LR* 10; Man. 174, 2; Man. 116, 56), *Götz* (§356), *Wilhelm Meister* (*OC* 8), and *Iphigenie* (*LR* 48). And the dictum of Schiller quoted for p. 231d suggests acquaintance with Goethe's "Biographische Einzelheiten" ("Erste Bekanntschaft mit Schiller"). In addition, W. wrote to Malcolm in 1950: "I'm reading various odds & ends, e.g. Goethe's Theory of colour which, with all its absurdities, has very interesting points, & stimulates me to think" (*Memoir*, 96; see *Z* 347). Though his references to Goethe on colors are most plentiful in notebooks of that year (e.g. Man. 172, 4; Man. 173, 29, 49; Man. 174, 10; Man. 176, 2A, 6A, 14A, 18AB, 19A; this Appendix: James), others occur already in, for instance, Man. 112, 254, and Man. 133, 32. The topic had long engaged W.'s attention (see X, 8).

A number of passages in W.'s later writings (e.g. §171a, pp. 183def, 215; *EPB* 184; *PG* 179b) echo a remark of Goethe's on proper names, which W. often cited (*Z* 184; Man. 229, §§718, 992; Man. 131, 141; Man. 130, 89) and which Xavier Tilliette, S.J., has located for me in *Dichtung und Wahrheit* II, 10. It was not very gentlemanly of Herder, observed Goethe, to take liberties with his name, "for a man's name is not, for instance, like a cloak, which simply hangs about him and which can be tugged this way and that, if need be, but a garment which perfectly fits him, indeed like his very skin which has completely grown onto him and which may not be scraped and flayed without injuring the man himself."

For further references to Goethe, see *LR* 47–48; Man. 229, §1557; Man. 134, April 27; Man. 110, 12, 257.

HALDANE, J. B. S. W. heard Haldane say the words quoted in JN 38.

HARDY, G. H. W. knew Hardy from his first stay in Cambridge (von Wright, "Sketch", 6). The quotation on which he comments in Man. 228, §45, and in *Z* 273 is from Hardy's "Mathematical Proof", *Mind*, 38 (1929), 5. An offprint of this article, and Hardy's *Pure Mathematics*, with numerous marginal comments by W. in one section, were found among W.'s belongings at his death. See Man. 134, 4.

HELMHOLTZ, H. L. F. VON. Concerning a remark on Helmholtz in JN 96, Jackson observes: "No reference was given. But it was clear that Wittgenstein had read and knew Helmholtz's works on sight and hearing. He referred (on other occasions) to Helmholtz's view that seeing involves inference and interpretation because the actual retinal image is flat and upside down." In *PP* 265 and 270–71 there are comments concerning Helmholtz's reputed statement that he could imagine four-dimensional space.

HERTZ, HEINRICH. Of Hertz's *Die Prinzipien der Mechanik*, von Wright says ("Sketch", 7): "Wittgenstein knew this work and held it in high esteem. There are traces of the impression that it made on him both in the *Tractatus* and in his later writings." For instance, an earlier version of the *Investigations* had as its motto a quotation from Hertz. For explicit references to Hertz, see *BB* 26, 169; 4.04, 6.361; *NB* 36; Man. 213, 421: "In my way of doing philosophy, its whole aim is to give an expression such a form that certain disquietudes disappear. (Hertz)." On the nature of his influence, see also Hallett, *Definition*, 19, 175, 178, and Toulmin, "From Logical Analysis". According to von Wright, W. was especially impressed by Hertz's remarks about the nature of a philosopher's inquiry into the foundations of a science.

HILBERT, DAVID. "I have read a work of Hilbert on avoidance of contradiction," said W. at the start of a discussion reported in *Kreis*, 119. According to the editor, "the reference is probably to 'Neubegründung der Mathematik' (1922)". A later remark (*Kreis*, 147) suggests acquaintance with Hilbert's *Grundlagen der Geometrie*. Found among W.'s possessions was a copy of Hilbert's "Die Grundlagen der Mathematik" (1928), with some underscorings and a comment. For lengthy discussion of Hilbert's views, see *Kreis*, 147–49; *PB* 318–40; *PG* 297.

HUME, DAVID. "From Spinoza, Hume and Kant he said that he could get only occasional glimpses of understanding" (von Wright, "Sketch", 21). He told

Britton ("Portrait", 61) that "he could not sit down and read Hume—he knew far too much about the subject of Hume's writings to find this anything but a torture." So Anscombe is doubtless right when she says he never read more than a few pages of Hume (*Introduction*, 12). One or two of the references in Jackson's notes are by W. himself.

JAMES, WILLIAM. A work of special importance for understanding the *Investigations* is James's *Principles of Psychology*, particularly the first volume. At one time the *Principles*, one of the standard readings in psychology at Cambridge when W. studied there (Moore, "Autobiography", 29), was the only philosophical work visible on his bookshelves (Passmore, *Hundred Years*, 428), and it was still in his possession when he died. W. also read and valued James's *Varieties of Religious Experience*, which Drury recalls was one of the few works that W. insisted he should read ("Symposium", 68). "This book," he wrote to Russell in 1912, "does me a *lot* of good" (*LR* 10; see *LR* 82). W.'s admiration for James, both as a thinker and as a human being (Drury, "Symposium", 68), was reflected in his frequent references to him, both in class (Passmore, *Hundred Years*, 428) and in his writings. Topics treated (usually critically) in W.'s explicit references to James are the following: word feelings (*PG* 58; *EPB* 218; *BB* 78; Man. 302, 6; Man. 229, §1001); the experience of tending (*Z* 33; Man. 133, Feb. 12; Man. 229, §§885, 1445); anticipation in thought (p. 219; *Z* 1; Man. 229, §§839, 920; Man. 138, 17B; *JN* 71, 103); the process of thinking (Man. 229, §859; Man. 116, 203); thought without words (§342; *Z* 109; *JN* 49); the introspected self (§413; *JN* 64); inadequate terminology (§610; *Z* 482; Man. 229, §1363); the James-Lange theory of emotions (*BB* 103; Man. 302, 23; Man. 232, 687; Man. 229, §§1395, 2019; Man. 133, Feb. 12; Man. 110, 73; *JN* 45–46); voluntary acts (*EPB* 188; Man. 133, Feb. 12); trying to remember a word (Man. 134, March 18). For further correlations, of passages in which James is not actually named, see Coope et al., *Workbook*, 48; Hallett, *Definition*, 186; or the index of this commentary. In Man. 176, 18 (worked up in Man. 173, 29), W. wrote: "Goethe's doctrine on the origin of spectral colors is not a theory which has proved inadequate, but is in fact no theory. It permits no predictions. It is just a vague thought-schema, of the kind one finds in James's psychology. There is no *experimentum crucis* which could decide for or against this doctrine." (See *JN* 52.)

JEANS, SIR JAMES. "Jeans has written a book called *The Mysterious Universe*," *LC* 27 quotes W. as saying, "and I loathe it and call it misleading."

JOHNSON, SAMUEL. According to Drury ("Symposium", 67), W. "loved and revered old Dr. Johnson". In a letter to Malcolm (*Memoir*, 44) he wrote: "The other day I read Johnson's 'Life of Pope' & I liked it very much. As soon as I get to Cambridge I'm going to send you a little book 'Prayers & Meditations' by Johnson. You may not like it at all,—on the other hand you may. I do." Of the latter work W. said in a subsequent letter: "I wish to say that normally I can't read any printed prayers but that Johnson's impressed me by being *human*" (ibid.). There are references to Johnson in *PP* 311 and Man. 111, 138.

JOHNSON, W. E. W. described to Karl Britton ("Portrait", 61; see *LR* 65) "how, when he first came to Cambridge from Manchester, puzzled about logical questions, he had W. E. Johnson as a supervisor: so he went and fired off all his questions at Johnson. This produced nothing but frustration on both sides, and they soon had to agree that Wittgenstein should not attend any more supervisions. But (to his surprise and pleasure) Johnson asked him to come to his Sunday tea-parties, which he did regularly. He said how very much he liked and admired Johnson and how well they got on as soon as they had decided to give up the philosophical questions." As token of his esteem (*LR* 110, 121), "Wittgenstein gave a grant of £200 a year in order to enable . . . Johnson to cut down his teaching and have more time for research" (*LR* 108). For references to Johnson, see *PP* 265 and *LO* 18, 47, 55, 68. Though W. expressed a desire "to see his book" (*LO* 47), von Wright comments: "There is no evidence that Wittgenstein ever studied Johnson's *Logic.*"

KANT, IMMANUEL. W. thought Kant a profound philosopher (Drury); considered the *Critique of Pure Reason* "a work of the first rank" (McGuinness); mentioned Kant with some frequency, for him (*NB* 15; 6.36111; *PB* 129; *PG* 404); and sometimes revealed a Kantian trace in his own thinking. See, for instance, Malcolm's *Memoir*, 71; the commentary on §119; and Man. 110, 61: "The boundary of language reveals itself in the impossibility of describing the fact which corresponds to a proposition (is its translation) without repeating just that proposition. We have to do here with the Kantian solution of the problem of philosophy." However, I cannot agree with Engel that the references and parallels listed in his article, "Wittgenstein and Kant", "make clear that Wittgenstein had obviously read much more of Kant than has been supposed and read him much more closely too" (p. 497). Kant was one of those authors from whom W. said "he could get only occasional glimpses of understanding" (von Wright, "Sketch", 21), and such writers he was not wont to read very much or very attentively. Furthermore, as Stenius remarks (*Tractatus*, 214): "One did not need to have read Kant to be influenced by a more or less clearly stated Kantianism; it belonged to the intellectual atmosphere in the German speaking world. Moreover we know that Wittgenstein read and appreciated Schopenhauer, who was in his way a Kantian of a peculiar kind." Schopenhauer's *World as Will and Representation*, which W. read, is full of lengthy comments on Kant. So is Frege's *Grundlagen*, another W. favorite. And Lichtenberg, whom W. admired, was strongly influenced by Kant.

KELLER, GOTTFRIED. "Wisdom was something he did admire in his favourite story writers—in Gottfried Keller, for instance" (*LC* 41). W. used to read aloud from Keller, both his prose and his poetry. And Malcolm reports that "once he sent me a paper-bound copy of Gottfried Keller's *Hadlaub*, saying: 'I enclose a foul copy of a very wonderful German novel' " (*Memoir*, 37). There is a reference to *Der grüne Heinrich* in Man. 219, 6 (quoted for §373), and to *Romeo und Julia auf dem Dorfe* in *LC* 25. See also *LC* 32.

KEYNES, JOHN MAYNARD. The correspondence between W. and Keynes (the letters in *LR* 107–41 stretch from 1913 to 1939) and Keynes's repeated efforts on W.'s behalf (*LR* 1–3, 120–21, 132–38, 141) attest to the closeness of their relations. W. read at least some of the various writings Keynes sent him (*LR* 114–17, 123), but it is not clear whether he read the book on probability (*LR* 116).

KIERKEGAARD, SÖREN. "Wittgenstein received deeper impressions from some writers in the borderland between philosophy, religion, and poetry than from the philosophers, in the restricted sense of the word. Among the former are . . . Kierkegaard" (von Wright, "Sketch", 21), whom W. was reading already in 1919 (LR 82). "He referred to him," recalls Malcolm, "with something of awe in his expression, as a 'really religious' man. He had read the *Concluding Unscientific Postscript*—but found it 'too deep' for him" (*Memoir*, 71). In a letter, W. himself remarked: "I've never read 'The Works of Love.' Kierkegaard is far too deep for me, any how. He bewilders me without working the good effects which he would in *deeper* souls" (ibid., 75). W. went so far as to call Kierkegaard not merely "a great writer" (compare *LC* 70 with the autobiographical account Kierkegaard put in the mouth of Judge William) but "by far the greatest philosopher of the nineteenth century" (Drury, "Symposium", 70). Malcolm indicates one area of agreement: "Any cosmological conception of a Deity, derived from the notions of cause or of infinity, would be repugnant to him. He was impatient with 'proofs' of the existence of God, and with attempts to give religion a *rational* foundation. When I once quoted to him a remark of Kierkegaard's to this effect: 'How can it be that Christ does not exist, since I know that He has saved me?', Wittgenstein exclaimed: 'You see! It isn't a question of *proving* anything!'" (*Memoir*, 71). Thus, "in a letter to a friend Wittgenstein seemed to suggest that what he himself had been trying to say had already been said by Kierkegaard (in his emphasis on the individual's relation to God in the life of tension and paradox)" (van Peursen, *Wittgenstein*, 22; cp. *Kreis*, 68, and NT 13). However, references to Kierkegaard in W.'s writings are rare (Man. 132, 168; Man. 119, 151–54). Kierkegaard's influence, or at least the deep affinity of their views, probably had more to do with the topics which W. did not treat and his reasons for not doing so (see GI 5–7).

KLEIST, HEINRICH VON. For a reference to Kleist, apparently based on reading, see the commentary on §363c. *Michael Kohlhaas* was a favorite of W.'s.

KÖHLER, WOLFGANG. The single reference to Köhler on page 203 of the *Investigations* gives no true indication of how closely W. studied Köhler's *Gestalt Psychology*, especially the chapter on "Sensory Organization". However, the abundant references to Köhler in Jackson's notes (JN 48, 89–92, 100, 105) and unpublished manuscripts (e.g. Man. 232, 691; Man. 229, §§1537, 1638, 1644, 1649, 1690, 1702, 1784; Man. 135, July 18, 20, and 27, Aug. 2; Man. 134, March 21, May 10; Man. 131, 128) reveal how important Köhler is for Part Two of the *Investigations*, especially Sections XXXVII and XLI, (see the index). Jackson reports that "Wittgenstein began lecturing on seeing-as by reading a short passage from Köhler's *Gestalt Psychology*—a rare procedure for him." Man. 232, 661; Man. 229, §1229; Man. 132, Oct. 21; and the quote from Man. 130 for p. 204l indicate acquaintance with Köhler's *The Mentality of Apes*.

KRAUS, KARL. "He told me that he had Karl Kraus's *Die Fackel* sent to his address in Norway," writes Engelmann (*Memoir*, 123), "which indicates that he had been a keen reader of that journal before leaving Vienna [cp. *Briefe*, 12]. I am convinced that the way of thinking which he found in Kraus's writings exercised a decisive and lasting influence on the objectives of his philosophical activity." In this connection, see W. Kraft's article. W.'s judgment on Kraus: "Genius is talent in which character finds expression. So I would say that Kraus had talent, extraordinary talent, but not genius" (Man. 168, 5; see the quotation from Man. 130 in this Appendix: Freud).

LICHTENBERG, GEORG CHRISTOPH. "An author . . . who reminds one, often astonishingly, of Wittgenstein," observes von Wright, "is Lichtenberg. Wittgenstein esteemed him highly. To what extent, if any, he can be said to have learned from him I do not know. It is deserving of mention that some of Lichtenberg's thoughts on philosophic questions show a striking resemblance to Wittgenstein's" ("Sketch", 22). On this topic, see von Wright's "Georg Christoph Lichtenberg als Philosoph". Though W. did not cite Lichtenberg very frequently (e.g. Man. 112, 139; Man. 176, 2A; Man. 213, 422–23; *PP* 309; *PG* 461), both Geach and von Wright recount that he read him a great deal—and not just the aphorisms (Man. 220, 78, cites "Briefen von Mägden über Literatur")—and McGuinness reports that W. gave Russell a book by Lichtenberg before World War I. W. often referred to Lichtenberg in conversation, and once said to von Wright: "Lichtenberg is terrific!"

MACH, ERNST. Citations in *PB* suggest acquaintance with Mach's *Erkenntnis und Irrtum*, in particular the chapter entitled "Gedankenexperimente" (*PB* 52), and chapter 1 of Mach's *Analyse der Empfindungen* (*PB* 267). However, W. told Russell: "Mach writes such a horrid style that it makes me nearly sick to read him" (*LR* 20). See Man. 131, 96.

MAUTHNER, FRITZ. Though G. Weiler's section on W. and Mauthner in *Mauthner's Critique of Language* is not a very safe guide to the relation between the two men, he seems right in asserting W.'s familiarity with Mauthner's *Beiträge zu einer Kritik der Sprache* and pointing out multiple analogies in thought, both with the *Tractatus* and with the *Investigations,* and W.'s indebtedness for this or that figure (e.g. the ladder image in 6.54, which may come from *Beiträge,* I, 2) or an occasional expression (e.g. the famous concluding sentence of the *Tractatus,* which echoes *Beiträge,* I, 230). W. mentions Mauthner in 4.0031. For further connections, see this commentary, *passim.*

MOORE, G. E. For years, first as a student at Cambridge, then as a professor, W. was in close contact with Moore. "Wittgenstein respected Moore's honesty and seriousness, and once he said that Moore was 'deep' " (Malcolm, *Memoir,* 66). However, he meant Moore's character, not his thought (see e.g. GI 14, 17; XXXVII, 21; *LC* 64; JN 99; 5.541). "He once remarked that the only work of Moore's that greatly impressed him was his discovery of the peculiar kind of nonsense involved in such a sentence as, e.g. 'It is raining but I don't believe it.' (This is referred to as 'Moore's paradox' in Sec. x, Part II, of the *Investigations.*) But he admitted that Moore's 'defence of common sense' was an important idea" (Malcolm, *Memoir,* 66–67; see XXXVI, 2)—despite grave faults in the execution (p. 221f; X, 25). Moore dominates *On Certainty,* where he is mentioned by name more than two dozen times, much as the former W. does the *Investigations,* that is, as the chief single adversary. For his relation to the *Investigations,* see the index to this commentary. For further connections, both personal and philosophical, see (in addition to those already cited) pages 6, 33–34, 73, 79–80, 87–92 in Malcolm's *Memoir;* and *LR* 9 ("I have just been reading part of Moore's Principia Ethica . . . I do not like it at all"), 31 ("send me *two* copies of Moore's paper: 'The Nature and Reality of Objects of Perception' ").

NEWMAN, JOHN CARDINAL. As might be expected (see this Appendix:

Kierkegaard), W. "disliked the theological writings of Cardinal Newman, which he read with care during his last year at Cambridge" (Malcolm, *Memoir*, 71). *OC* 1 may indicate acquaintance with *The Present Position of Catholics in England* (see Coope, "Knowledge", 249). See also Man. 117, 209: "Here a description, not an explanation (Newman), leads to clarity."

NICOD, JEAN. Man. 105, 43–45, and *PB* 252–53, reveal acquaintance with Nicod's *Foundations of Geometry and Induction* (for instance pages 59–60). Man. 213, 202 (quoted in BB viii) contrasts W.'s use of language-games with Nicod's similar technique.

OGDEN, C. K. In a letter to Ogden, W. wrote: " 'The meaning of meaning' reached me a few days ago . . . I have not yet been able to read your book thoroughly. I have however read in it and I think I ought to confess to you frankly that I believe you have not quite *caught the problems* which—for instance—I was at in my book" (*LO* 69). "Indeed it is 'the meaning of meaning' that we are looking for," W. wrote later, "namely, the grammar of the word 'meaning' " (Man. 110, 157). "Ogden and Richards are correct in their causal approach, only they don't see the other aspect" (Man. 109, 210). And even in their attempts at explanation, he felt they confused motive and cause (Man. 110, 94, quoted for p. 224k). Concerning their treatment of recognition, see *PB* 63.

PLATO. W. did not read Aristotle (Britton, "Portrait", 61), "but it is significant that he did read and enjoy Plato. He must have recognized congenial features, both in Plato's literary and philosophic method and in the temperament behind the thoughts" (von Wright, "Sketch", 21). In 1946 he said he was deriving much profit from his reading of Plato (Britton, "Portrait", 61); yet no doubt he still agreed with what he had said earlier: "I cannot characterize my standpoint better than by saying that it is opposed to that which Socrates represents in the Platonic dialogues" (Man. 302, 14; see *PP* 305, 322). Man. 111, 55, is still more negative.

W. owned all the dialogues (a German translation by Preisendanz in five volumes) when he died. Most of his allusions are to the *Theaetetus* (Man. 228, §514; Man. 229, §846; Man. 302, 14; Man. 213, 66, 69, 434; Man. 111, 26–27; *BB* 20, 26–27; *PG* 120, 137, 164, 208; *Z* 69; §§46, 48, 518), but there are also indications of his having read the *Philebus* (Man. 213, 223; and compare 40A with *PG* 141); the *Cratylus* (Man. 213, 40); the *Sophist* (compare 261E and 262A and *PG* 56); and the *Charmides* (compare 174–75 with *Z* 454). There are more general references in *RFM* 22; Man. 219, 6; Man. 169; Man. 133, Feb. 27; Man. 111, 134, 192–93; and a specific one in Man. 220, 53.

POPPER, KARL. For Popper's account of a famous encounter, at which he and W. debated the nature and possibility of philosophical problems, see his "Autobiography", 97–99. For a reference to Popper, see the quotation from Man. 135 for p. 225b.

PRICHARD, HAROLD. W.'s main encounter with Prichard occurred when W. agreed to comment on an Oxford undergraduate's paper on Descartes and the *cogito*. Geach reports that Prichard disliked W. intensely and showed it. For an interesting excerpt from the debate, see Coope et al., *Workbook*, 21. Concerning Prichard on " 'Ought' implies 'can'," see JN 71.

RAMSEY, FRANK. Ramsey was an important stimulus to W.'s thinking. Their conversations began in 1923, when Ramsey visited W. at Puchberg (von Wright, "Sketch", 12) and, for a fortnight or more (*PP* 253), questioned him about the *Tractatus*. They were continued in 1924 (von Wright, ibid.) and supplemented by correspondence (*LO* 75–87), but became especially numerous and fruitful (*Investigations*, Preface) during 1929, prior to Ramsey's death in January 1930. Moore surmises that it may have been Ramsey's presence there which drew W. to Cambridge early in 1929 (*PP* 252). Already in 1927 and 1928 W. was discussing Ramsey's "Foundations of Mathematics" with members of the Vienna Circle (*Kreis*, 16, 189–92; *LR* 2–3). Ramsey's widow gave W. a copy of the book by the same title. Rush Rhees thinks Ramsey himself gave W. a copy of "On a Problem of Formal Logic", which W. also read (Man. 110, 189; §124d). Both works were in his possession when he died. W.'s explicit references to Ramsey are numerous, and cover a wide range of topics (§81; *Z* 272; *PG* 311; Man. 228, §§38, 42; Man. 163; Man. 105, 23), though mathematics and mathematical logic predominate (*PG* 308–9, 315–18, 453; *PB* 141–43, 155, 163, 180, 209, 304; Man. 213, 550–64; Man. 134, April 7; Man. 132, 7; Man. 113, 117–18; Man. 106, 13, 115; Man. 105, 131). He sketches an intellectual portrait of his friend in Man. 112, 139–40.

RENAN, J. E. In Man. 109, 200–202, W. comments at length on Renan's *Histoire du peuple d'Israël*.

RICHARDS, I. A. See OGDEN. Several citations (Man. 229, §1467; *JN* 71, 74) show W.'s familiarity with the chapter on "Pleasure" in Richards' *Principles of Criticism*. See also *LC* 37.

RUSSELL, BERTRAND. Mathematical logic was the gateway through which W. entered philosophy, and Russell the teacher who ushered him in. Soon after W. arrived in Cambridge, in 1912, he became intimate with Russell (von Wright, "Sketch", 6) and was influenced by him far more than by any of his other professors (see e.g. Preface to the *Tractatus*). When W. was at Cambridge, they talked endlessly of logic; when he was away they corresponded (*LR*; von Wright, "Sketch", 7; *NB* 119–31). "Wittgenstein more than once expressed admiration of the keenness of Bertrand Russell's intellect when the two of them worked together on problems of logic before the First World War. Russell was extremely 'bright', is how he put it. . . . Wittgenstein believed that the Theory of Descriptions was Russell's most important production, and he once remarked that it must have been an enormously difficult undertaking for him. But in 1946 Wittgenstein had a poor opinion of Russell's contemporary philosophical writings" (Malcolm, *Memoir*, 68; see Drury, *Danger*, xiii; *LR* 186). Yet Russell continued to influence W.'s thought even then; the old Russellian doctrines, both those he had once accepted and those he never had, formed the background of his thinking on one question after another (see GI 4, 27). Not only are there innumerable references in W.'s writings to Russell's mathematical logic, but many also on psychological topics (e.g. Man. 163; Man. 229, §1465; Man. 302, 31; *NB* 96; *PB* 63–65; *BB* 21–22) and on language (e.g. *NB* 21, 98, 103; 3.318, 4.0031; *PB* 120, 200; *PG* 131, 202, 211, 309, 311; §§46, 79; *Z* 704). For less explicit but often important connections see the index.

It is difficult (and perhaps not too important) to determine precisely which of Russell's writings W. read. It seems clear that *The Principles of Mathematics* profoundly affected his development (von Wright, "Sketch", 4; see Coope et al., *Workbook*, 47), and he often cited *Principia Mathematica*. Russell's own course was radically altered by W.'s criticism of the work on theory of knowledge of which six chapters appeared in *The Monist*, 1914–1915 (see *LR* 23–24) and three later in *Logic and Knowledge* (pp. 125–74). *LR* 103–4 suggest that W. probably became acquainted with the contents of Russell's paper on "The Limits of Empiricism"; he frequently cited or evoked the title, as in *RFM* 121d. Jackson's lecture notes (*NB* 32, 82, 88) and internal evidence indicate he knew Russell's *Analysis of Mind* and *Our Knowledge of the External World*. Russell apparently sent him copies of the latter and of *Mysticism and Logic* (*LR* 83), as also of *An Introduction to Mathematical Philosophy*, which W. seems to have looked at (*LR* 70). Moore's notes (*PP* 319–20) report criticism of a statement in *An Outline of Philosophy*. W. once remarked that Russell's "What I Believe" was by no means "harmless" (*Kreis*, 142). A comment in *NB* 44 about Russell's "On Scientific Method in Philosophy" may be based on reading.

SCHILLER, F. C. "Wittgenstein got hold of me and showed me an article in *Mind* by Schiller on 'The Value of Formal Logic'. He said I ought to look at it because it was a good illustration of what he had been talking about that same afternoon—that is, 'Nonsense' in the philosophical sense. And he insisted that his remark was meant seriously" (Britton, "Portrait", 58). See the bibliography.

SCHILLER, J. C. F. VON. See *NB* 86; *Z* 15; Man. 110, 256 (quoted for p. 231d); Man. 168, 5: "Schiller speaks, in a letter, of a 'poetische Stimmung'."

SCHLICK, MORITZ. Impressed already by the *Tractatus* (von Wright, "Sketch", 12), Schlick was still more strongly influenced (Carnap, "Autobiography", 36; Feigl, "Kreis", 638) by the close personal contact he had with W. starting in 1927 (*Kreis*, 13–27). "I can hardly exaggerate," he declared, "my indebtedness to this philosopher" ("Meaning", 148). Therein lies much of the interest of his works for the study of W.; in them one often catches glimpses of W.'s thinking at the time he talked with Schlick—thoughts never published or polished by W. himself, and often later criticized (see especially X, 13–14). It is not clear, nor perhaps important to determine, how well W. knew Schlick's writings. For a time he owned a copy of *Gesammelte Aufsätze*, and at his death he still had his *Fragen der Ethik;* this latter he discussed with Waismann (*Kreis*, 23, 115), and wrote interesting remarks in the margins, but less than a quarter of the pages were cut.

SCHOPENHAUER, ARTHUR. "As a boy of sixteen Wittgenstein had read Schopenhauer and had been greatly impressed by Schopenhauer's theory of the 'world as idea' (though not of the 'world as will'); Schopenhauer then struck him as fundamentally right, if only a few adjustments and clarifications were made" (Anscombe, *Introduction*, 11). Thus, "if we look for Wittgenstein's philosophical ancestry, we should rather look to Schopenhauer; specifically, his 'solipsism', his conception of 'the limit' and his ideas on value will be better understood in the light of Schopenhauer than of any other philosopher" (ibid., 12; see Hacker, "Soul", 166–71). One thinks also of W.'s profound pessimism, his early antipathy to Christianity, his negative attitude towards metaphysics and distrust of professional philosophy, and wonders if such resemblances are merely a matter of natural affinity. W. read Schopenhauer's *Die Welt als Wille und Vorstellung* (von Wright, "Sketch", 5) and perhaps his *Über den Willen der Natur* (*Kreis*, 118). Though W. cites him only rarely (*PG* 144; Man. 168; Man. 121, May 25; Man. 143) and in the *Investigations* not at all, one can frequently detect Schopenhauer's influence even there (see the index). Acquaintance with his views on the will is important for Section XXIV (see XXIV, 2, 5–7).

SPENGLER, OSWALD. Remarks in Man. 110, 13, 257; Man. 111, 118–19, 196; Man. 220, 85 (quoted for §131); BUF 241; Man. 213, 417; and *PG* 299 indicate that W. had read Spengler's *Untergang des Abendlandes* attentively and appreciatively. "The strength of Spengler's impact on Wittgenstein," says von Wright, "should not be underrated. Wittgenstein was much interested in the Spenglerian conception of a morphology of history and in Spengler's attack on causality in history. I should not regard it as excluded that Spengler's remarks on various historical categories contributed to Wittgenstein's notion of family-resemblance." Such a connection in fact appears in Man. 111, 119, and Man. 213, 259.

STOUT, G. F. Malcolm recounts that when Stout came to Cambridge for a brief visit, apparently in the early thirties, W. invited him to tea and was impressed by his seriousness and genuine desire to understand (*Memoir*, 65–66). In JN 51 there is a reference to Stout's view on universals. His *Manual of Psychology* and *Analytic Psychology* are listed by Moore ("Autobiography", 29) as two of the standard texts in psychology used at Cambridge when W. studied there, and W. may have attended some lectures in which Moore discussed them (ibid., 33; Malcolm, *Memoir*, 66).

STRACHEY, LYTTON. In JN 37–38 and Man. 229, §1033 (quoted for p. 178g) W. discusses a passage from Strachey on the death of Queen Victoria (see Geach, *Mental Acts*, 3, quoted for §243b). McGuinness says W. knew Strachey quite well personally.

TOLSTOI, COUNT LEV N. Russell recounts of W. that "he had been dogmatically anti-Christian, but in this respect he changed completely. The only thing he ever told me about this was that once in a village in Galicia during the war he found a bookshop containing only one book, which was Tolstoy on the Gospels. He bought the book, and, according to him, it influenced him profoundly" ("Wittgenstein", 31; see *LR* 82; Malcolm, *Memoir*, 70). "If you aren't acquainted with it, you can't even imagine the effect it can have on people," he wrote to von Ficker (*Briefe*, 28). It was, he said, the book which "saved my life" (ibid.), and accompanied him so constantly that "his fellow soldiers nicknamed him 'the man with the Gospels' " (Janik and Toulmin, *Vienna*, 200–201). W. also had a very high opinion of Tolstoi's *Twenty-Three Tales* (Malcolm, *Memoir*, 52), of his short novel *Hadshi Murat* (ibid., 41; *LR* 16), and of Tolstoi in general (Malcolm, *Memoir*, 42); but he couldn't read *Resurrection*: "You see," he explained, "when Tolstoy just tells a story he impresses me infinitely more than when he addresses the reader. When he turns his back to the reader then he seems to me *most* impressive. . . . It seems to me his philosophy is most true when it's *latent* in the story" (ibid., 43). This helps to explain (GI 7) why W. so seldom cited Tolstoi (e.g. Man. 213, 406; Man. 112, 220).

WAISMANN, FRIEDRICH. Given the extent of Waismann's contact with W., from 1927 through the thirties (Carnap, "Autobiography", 34, 36–37; *Kreis*,

15–26), it is strange that W. never mentions him. Waismann sometimes acknowledged his great debts to W. (e.g. "Relevance", 211), but apparently not fully enough to suit W. (compare Malcolm, *Memoir*, 58–59, with Waismann's "Über den Begriff der Identität"). I frequently cite his writings, because they often amount to a popularized version of W.'s thought (see Carnap, "Autobiography", 37).

WEYL, HERMANN. W. read and discussed Weyl's "Die heutige Erkenntnislage in der Mathematik" (see *Kreis*, 81–84) and his "Philosophie der Mathematik und Naturwissenschaft" (see *Kreis*, 37, 84), and showed special interest in Weyl's remark that the formalists conceive the axioms of mathematics as analogous to rules of chess (*Kreis*, 103–5). For further allusions to Weyl, see *PB* 170, 176; Man. 228, §121; Man. 106, 287.

WHITEHEAD, ALFRED N. During W.'s student days, he saw a good deal of Whitehead (von Wright, "Sketch", 6) and liked him (*LR* 29), but he knew only the Whitehead of *Principia Mathematica*, and refers to him infrequently (*NB* 70, 96; 5.252, 5.452; *PB* 144, 192; *PG* 296).

WISDOM, JOHN. After returning to Cambridge in 1934, Wisdom attended W.'s lectures and discussed philosophical questions with him for several years (Wisdom, "Wittgenstein", 46). In *LR* 173 W. expresses affection for Wisdom, but the more philosophical remark in Man. 138, 17A, is critical.

BIBLIOGRAPHY

Only works cited are included. For Wittgenstein's published writings, lectures, conversations, and correspondence, see the List of Abbreviations.

Ambrose, Alice. "Metamorphoses of the Principle of Verifiability". In F. Dommeyer, ed., *Current Philosophical Issues*, pp. 54–78. Springfield, Ill., 1966.

——. "Wittgenstein on Universals". In K. T. Fann, ed., *Ludwig Wittgenstein: The Man and His Philosophy*, pp. 336–52. New York, 1967.

Anscombe, G. E. M. *Intention*. Oxford, 1957.

——. "Intention". *Proceedings of the Aristotelian Society*, 57 (1956–1957), 321–32.

——. *An Introduction to Wittgenstein's Tractatus*. London, 1959.

——. "On the Form of Wittgenstein's Writing". In R. Klibansky, ed., *Contemporary Philosophy. A Survey*, III, 373–78. Florence, 1969.

——. "Pretending". In S. Hampshire, ed., *Philosophy of Mind*, pp. 294–310. New York, 1966.

Ayer, A. J. *The Problem of Knowledge*. London, 1956.

——. "The Vienna Circle". In A. Ayer et al., *The Revolution in Philosophy*, pp. 70–87. London, 1956.

Baker, G. P., and Hacker, P. M. S. Critical Notice of *Philosophical Grammar*. *Mind*, 85 (1976), 269–94.

Bambrough, Renford. "Universals and Family Resemblance". In G. Pitcher, ed., *Wittgenstein: The Philosophical Investigations*, pp. 186–204. London, 1968.

Bensch, Rudolf. *Ludwig Wittgenstein. Die apriorischen und mathematischen Sätze in seinem Spätwerk*. Bonn, 1973.

Berkeley, George. *Three Dialogues between Hylas and Philonous*. In *The Works of George Berkeley*. Edited by A. Fraser, I, 373–485. Oxford, 1901.

Binkley, Timothy. *Wittgenstein's Language*. The Hague, 1973.

Bird, Graham. *Philosophical Tasks. An Introduction to Some Aims and Methods in Recent Philosophy*. London, 1972.

Black, Max. *A Companion to Wittgenstein's 'Tractatus'*. Ithaca, 1964.

——. "Relations between Logical Positivism and the Cambridge School of Analysis". *Erkenntnis*, 8 (1939–1940), 24–35.

Bogen, James. *Wittgenstein's Philosophy of Language: Some Aspects of Its Development*. London, 1972.

Bradley, F. H. *The Principles of Logic*, Vol. I. 2d ed. London, 1922.

Brann, Henry W. Review of A. Schopenhauer, *Der handschriftliche Nachlass*. *International Philosophical Quarterly*, 10 (1970), 664–67.

Bridgman, Percy. *The Way Things Are.* Cambridge, Mass., 1959.

Britton, Karl. *Communication: A Philosophical Study of Language.* London, 1939.

——. "Language: Public and Private". *The Monist*, 45 (1935), 1–59.

——. "On Public Objects and Private Objects". *The Monist*, 46 (1936), 190–210.

——. "Portrait of a Philosopher". In K. Fann, ed., *Ludwig Wittgenstein: The Man and His Philosophy*, pp. 56–63. New York, 1967.

Broad, C. D. *Examination of McTaggart's Philosophy.* 2 vols. Cambridge, 1933–1938.

——. *Induction, Probability, and Causation. Selected Papers.* Dordrecht, 1968.

——. "Two Lectures on the Nature of Philosophy". In H. D. Lewis, ed., *Clarity Is Not Enough*, pp. 42–75. London, 1963.

Brouwer, L. E. J. "Mathematik, Wissenschaft und Sprache". *Monatshefte für Mathematik und Physik*, 36 (1929), 153–64.

Buck, Roger C. "Non-other Minds". In R. J. Butler, ed., *Analytical Philosophy*, pp. 187–210. Oxford, 1962.

Bühler, Karl. *The Mental Development of the Child.* Translated by O. Oeser. New York, 1930.

Busch, Wilhelm. *Das Gesamtwerk des Zeichners und Dichters*, Vol. V. Stuttgart, 1959.

Carnap, Rudolf. Excerpt from his "Autobiography". In K. Fann, ed., *Ludwig Wittgenstein: The Man and His Philosophy*, pp. 33–39. New York, 1967.

——. *Der logische Aufbau der Welt. Scheinprobleme in der Philosophie.* 2d ed. Hamburg, 1961.

——. "Psychology in Physical Language". In A. Ayer, ed., *Logical Positivism*, pp. 165–98. Glencoe, Ill., 1959.

——. "Über Protokollsätze". *Erkenntnis*, 3 (1932–1933), 215–28.

Cavell, Stanley. "The Availability of Wittgenstein's Later Philosophy". In G. Pitcher, ed., *Wittgenstein: The Philosophical Investigations*, pp. 151–85. London, 1968.

Chappell, Vere C. "The Concept of Dreaming". *Philosophical Quarterly*, 13 (1963), 193–213.

Chihara, Charles S., and Fodor, Jerry A. "Operationalism and Ordinary Language: A Critique of Wittgenstein". In G. Pitcher, ed., *Wittgenstein: The Philosophical Investigations*, pp. 384–419. London, 1968.

Chomsky, Noam. *Language and Mind.* New York, 1968.

Colombo, Gian Carlo. "Introduzione critica". In his Italian translation of the *Tractatus*, pp. 13–35. Rome, 1954.

Cook, John W. "Human Beings". In P. Winch, ed., *Studies in the Philosophy of Wittgenstein*, pp. 117–51. London, 1969.

——. "Solipsism and Language". In A. Ambrose and M. Lazerowitz, eds., *Ludwig Wittgenstein: Philosophy and Language*, pp. 37–72. London, 1972.

——. "Wittgenstein on Privacy". In G. Pitcher, ed., *Wittgenstein: The Philosophical Investigations*, pp. 286–323. London, 1968.

Cooke, Vincent M. "Wittgenstein's Use of the Private Language Discussion". *International Philosophical Quarterly*, 14 (1974), 25–49.

Coope, Christopher. "Wittgenstein's Theory of Knowledge". In G. Vesey, ed., *Understanding Wittgenstein*, pp. 246–67. London, 1974.

——, Geach, Peter, Potts, Timothy, and White, Roger. *A Wittgenstein Workbook.* Oxford, 1970.

Copleston, Frederick. *A History of Philosophy,* Vol. VII. Westminster, Md., 1963.

Diamond, Cora. "Secondary Sense". *Proceedings of the Aristotelian Society,* 67 (1966–1967), 189–208.

Dilman, Ilham. "Wittgenstein, Philosophy and Logic". *Analysis,* 31 (1970–1971), 33–42.

Donagan, Alan. "Wittgenstein on Sensation". In G. Pitcher, ed., *Wittgenstein: The Philosophical Investigations,* pp. 324–51. London, 1968.

Driesch, Hans. *Ordnungslehre. Ein System des nichtmetaphysischen Teiles der Philosophie.* 2d ed. Jena, 1923.

——. *Wirklichkeitslehre. Ein metaphysischer Versuch.* Leipzig, 1922.

——. *Wissen und Denken. Ein Prolegomenon zu aller Philosophie.* Leipzig, 1919.

Drury, M. O'C. *The Danger of Words.* London, 1973.

——. "A Symposium: Assessments of the Man and the Philosopher". In K. Fann, ed., *Ludwig Wittgenstein: The Man and His Philosophy,* pp. 67–71. New York, 1967.

Dummett, Michael. "Truth". *Proceedings of the Aristotelian Society,* 59 (1958–1959), 141–62.

Engel, S. Morris. "Wittgenstein and Kant". *Philosophy and Phenomenological Research,* 30 (1970), 483–513.

Engelmann, Paul. *Letters from Ludwig Wittgenstein, with a Memoir.* Translated by L. Furtmüller, edited by B. McGuinness. Oxford, 1967.

Ewing, A. C. "Pseudo-Solutions". *Proceedings of the Aristotelian Society,* 57 (1956–1957), 31–52.

——. *Second Thoughts in Moral Philosophy.* London, 1959.

Faraday, Michael. *The Chemical History of a Candle.* Put into basic English by P. Rossiter. London, 1933.

Farrell, B. "An Appraisal of Therapeutic Positivism". *Mind,* 55 (1946), 25–48, 133–50.

Feigl, Herbert. "The Wiener Kreis in America". In *Perspectives in American History,* II, 630–73. Cambridge, Mass., 1968.

Fischer, Heinrich. "Nachwort". In K. Kraus, *Die Sprache,* pp. 441–45. Munich, 1954.

Frege, Gottlob. *The Basic Laws of Arithmetic.* Edited and translated by M. Furth. Berkeley and Los Angeles, 1964.

——. "Compound Thoughts". Translated by R. Stoothoff. *Mind,* 72 (1963), 1–17.

——. *The Foundations of Arithmetic.* Translated by J. Austin. 2d ed. Oxford, 1959.

——. *Funktion, Begriff, Bedeutung: Fünf logische Studien.* Edited by G. Patzig. Göttingen, 1962.

——. *Grundgesetze der Arithmetik.* 2 vols. Darmstadt, 1962.

——. "On the Foundations of Geometry". Translated by M. Szabo. *Philosophical Review,* 69 (1960), 3–17.

——. "On the Scientific Justification of a Concept-script". Translated by J. Bartlett. *Mind,* 73 (1964), 155–60.

——. "The Thought: A Logical Inquiry". Translated by A. M. and Marcelle Quinton. *Mind*, 65 (1956), 289–311.

——. *Translations from the Philosophical Writings of Gottlob Frege*. Edited by P. Geach and M. Black. 2d ed. Oxford, 1970.

——. "The Whole Number". Translated by V. Dudman. *Mind*, 79 (1970), 481–86.

Gardiner, Patrick. *Schopenhauer*. Harmondsworth, 1963.

Garver, Newton. "Wittgenstein on Private Language". *Philosophy and Phenomenological Research*, 20 (1959–1960), 389–96.

Gasking, D.A.T. "Avowals". In R. Butler, ed., *Analytical Philosophy*, pp. 154–69. Oxford, 1962.

——, and Jackson, A. C. "Wittgenstein as a Teacher". In K. Fann, ed., *Ludwig Wittgenstein: The Man and His Philosophy*, pp. 49–55. New York, 1967.

Gätschenberger, Richard. *Symbola*. Karlsruhe, 1920.

Geach, Peter. *God and the Soul*. London, 1969.

——. "Identity". *Review of Metaphysics*, 21 (1967–1968), 3–12.

——. *Mental Acts, Their Content and Their Objects*. London, 1957.

——. "A Reply". *Review of Metaphysics*, 22 (1968–1969), 556–59.

Goodstein, R. L. "Wittgenstein's Philosophy of Mathematics". In A. Ambrose and M. Lazerowitz, eds., *Ludwig Wittgenstein: Philosophy and Language*, pp. 271–86. London, 1972.

Gosling, Justin. "Mental Causes and Fear". *Mind*, 71 (1962), 289–306.

Griffiths, A. Phillips. "Wittgenstein, Schopenhauer, and Ethics". In G. Vesey, ed., *Understanding Wittgenstein*, pp. 96–116. London, 1974.

Gustafson, Donald. "A Note on a Misreading of Wittgenstein". *Analysis*, 28 (1967–1968), 143–44.

Hacker, P. M. S. "Frege and the Private Language Argument". *Idealistic Studies*, 2 (1972), 264–87.

——. *Insight and Illusion. Wittgenstein on Philosophy and the Metaphysics of Experience*. Oxford, 1972.

——. "Wittgenstein's Doctrines of the Soul in the Tractatus". *Kant-Studien*, 62 (1971), 162–71.

Hahn, Hans. "Logic, Mathematics and Knowledge of Nature". In A. Ayer, ed., *Logical Positivism*, pp. 147–61. London, 1959.

Haller, Rudolf. "Ludwig Wittgenstein und die Österreichische Philosophie". *Wissenschaft und Weltbild*, 21 (1968), 77–87.

Hallett, Garth. "The Bottle and the Fly". *Thought*, 46 (1971), 83–104.

——. *Darkness and Light: The Analysis of Doctrinal Statements*. New York, 1975.

——. "Did Wittgenstein Really *Define* 'Meaning'?" *Heythrop Journal*, 11 (1970), 294–98.

——. "Happiness". *Heythrop Journal*, 12 (1971), 301–3.

——. "Is There a Picture Theory of *Language* in the *Tractatus*?" *Heythrop Journal*, 14 (1973), 314–21.

——. "The Theoretical Content of Language". *Gregorianum*, 54 (1973), 307–37.

——. "Wittgenstein and the 'Contrast Theory of Meaning' ". *Gregorianum*, 51 (1970), 679–710.

Hallett, Garth. *Wittgenstein's Definition of Meaning as Use.* New York, 1967.

Hampshire, Stuart, ed. *Philosophy of Mind.* New York, 1966.

Hardy, Godfrey. "Mathematical Proof". *Mind,* 38 (1929), 1–25.

Harnack, Adolf von. *Das Wesen des Christentums.* Leipzig, 1920.

Hartnack, Justus. "Kant and Wittgenstein". *Kant-Studien,* 60 (1969), 131–34.

Hawkins, D. J. B. *Wittgenstein and the Cult of Language.* London, 1957.

Heijenoort, Jean van, ed. *From Frege to Gödel. A Source Book in Mathematical Logic, 1879–1931.* Cambridge, Mass., 1967.

Helmholtz, Hermann von. *Handbuch der physiologischen Optik.* 2d ed. Hamburg, 1896.

——. *Schriften zur Erkenntnistheorie.* Edited by P. Hertz and M. Schlick. Berlin, 1921.

Hempel, Carl. "On the Logical Positivists' Theory of Truth". *Analysis,* 2 (1935), 49–59.

Hertz, Heinrich. *The Principles of Mechanics.* Translated by D. Jones and J. Walley. London–New York, 1899.

High, Dallas. *Language, Persons, and Belief. Studies in Wittgenstein's Philosophical Investigations and Religious Uses of Language.* New York, 1967.

Hintikka, Jaakko. *Knowledge and Belief. An Introduction to the Logic of the Two Notions.* Ithaca, 1962.

——. "Wittgenstein on Private Language: Some Sources of Misunderstanding". *Mind,* 78 (1969), 423–25.

Holborow, Les. "Wittgenstein's Kind of Behaviourism?" *Philosophical Quarterly,* 17 (1967), 345–57.

Hume, David. *A Treatise of Human Nature.* Edited by L. A. Selby-Bigge. Oxford, 1928.

Hunter, J. F. M. *Essays after Wittgenstein.* London, 1973.

——. "'Forms of Life' in Wittgenstein's *Philosophical Investigations*". *American Philosophical Quarterly,* 5 (1968), 233–43.

James, William. *Essays in Radical Empiricism.* New York, 1912.

——. *The Meaning of Truth.* London, 1909.

——. *Pragmatism. A New Name for Some Old Ways of Thinking.* New York, 1928.

——. *The Principles of Psychology.* 2 vols. London, 1901.

——. *The Varieties of Religious Experience.* New York, 1902.

Janik, Allan, and Toulmin, Stephen. *Wittgenstein's Vienna.* New York, 1973.

Jeans, Sir James. *The Mysterious Universe.* London, 1930.

Kaplan, Bernard. "Some Considerations of Influences on Wittgenstein". *Idealistic Studies,* 1 (1971), 73–88.

Kenny, Anthony. "Aquinas and Wittgenstein". *Downside Review,* 77 (1959), 217–35.

——. "Cartesian Privacy". In G. Pitcher, ed., *Wittgenstein: The Philosophical Investigations,* pp. 352–70. London, 1968.

——. "Criterion". In P. Edwards, ed., *The Encyclopedia of Philosophy,* II, 258–61. New York–London, 1967.

——. *Wittgenstein.* London, 1973.

King-Farlow, John. "Constructor Reconstructus: A Symposium on Wittgenstein's Primitive Languages: 1. Wittgenstein's Primitive Languages". *Philosophical Studies* (Maynooth), 18 (1969), 100–110.

Kneale, William, and Kneale, Martha. *The Development of Logic*. Oxford, 1964.

Köhler, Wolfgang. *Dynamics in Psychology*. New York, 1940.

——. *Gestalt Psychology*. New York, 1929.

——. *Gestaltprobleme und Anfänge einer Gestalttheorie*. 1924. Mimeographed.

——. *The Mentality of Apes*. Translated from 2d ed. by E. Winter. London, 1957.

——. *Die physischen Gestalten in Ruhe und im stationären Zustand*. Erlangen, 1924.

Koffka, Kurt. *Principles of Gestalt Psychology*. London, 1935.

Kraft, Viktor. *The Vienna Circle*. Translated by A. Pap. New York, 1953.

Kraft, Werner. "Ludwig Wittgenstein und Karl Kraus". *Die neue Rundschau*, 72 (1961), 812–44.

Kretzmann, Norman. "Semantics, History of". In P. Edwards, ed., *The Encyclopedia of Philosophy*, VII, 358–406. New York–London, 1967.

Lakatos, Imre. "Changes in the Problem of Inductive Logic". In I. Lakatos, ed., *The Problem of Inductive Logic*, pp. 315–417. Amsterdam, 1968.

Langacker, Ronald. *Language and Its Structure. Some Fundamental Linguistic Concepts*. New York, 1967.

Lazerowitz, Morris. "Necessity and Language". In A. Ambrose and M. Lazerowitz, eds., *Ludwig Wittgenstein: Philosophy and Language*, pp. 233–70. London 1972.

Levi, Albert W. *Philosophy and the Modern World*. Bloomington, 1959.

Levison, Arnold B. "Wittgenstein and Logical Laws". In K. Fann, ed., *Ludwig Wittgenstein: The Man and His Philosophy*, pp. 297–314. New York, 1967.

Lewy, Casimir. "*Mind* under G. E. Moore (1921–1947)". *Mind*, 85 (1976), 37–46.

Lichtenberg, Georg Christoph. "Sprachbemerkungen". In his *Vermischte Schriften*. Edited by L. Lichtenberg and F. Kries, pp. 272–86. Göttingen, 1800.

Linsky, Leonard. "Wittgenstein on Language and Some Problems of Philosophy". In K. Fann, ed., *Ludwig Wittgenstein: The Man and His Philosophy*, pp. 171–80. New York, 1967.

Llewellyn, J. E. "Family Resemblance". *Philosophical Quarterly*, 18 (1968), 344–46.

Locke, Don. "The Privacy of Pains". *Analysis*, 24 (1963–1964), 147–52.

Lübbe, Hermann. " 'Sprachspiele' und 'Geschichten', Neopositivismus und Phänomenologie im Spätstadium, zu Ludwig Wittgenstein, *Philosophische Untersuchungen*, und Wilhelm Schapp, *Philosophie der Geschichten*". *Kant-Studien*, 52 (1960–1961), 220–43.

McGuinness, Brian. "Philosophy of Science in the Tractatus". In G. Granger, ed., *Wittgenstein et le problème d'une philosophie de la science*, pp. 9–18. Paris, 1971.

Mach, Ernst. *Die Analyse der Empfindungen und das Verhältnis des Physischen zum Psychischen*. 5th ed. Jena, 1906.

Malcolm, Norman. "Certainty and Empirical Statements". *Mind*, 51 (1942), 18–46.

——. "Defending Common Sense". *Philosophical Review*, 58 (1949), 201–20.

Malcolm, Norman. *Dreaming*. London, 1959.

——. "Dreaming and Scepticism". *Philosophical Review*, 65 (1956), 14–37.

——. *Knowledge and Certainty. Essays and Lectures*. Englewood Cliffs, 1963.

——. "Knowledge of Other Minds". In G. Pitcher, ed., *Wittgenstein: The* Philosophical Investigations, pp. 371–83. London, 1968.

——. *Ludwig Wittgenstein: A Memoir*. London, 1962.

——. "Philosophy for Philosophers". *Philosophical Review*, 60 (1951), 329–40.

——. *Problems of Mind: Descartes to Wittgenstein*. New York, 1971.

——. Review of Wittgenstein's *Philosophische Bemerkungen*. *Philosophical Review*, 76 (1967), 220–29.

——. "A Symposium: Assessments of the Man and the Philosopher". In K. Fann, ed., *Ludwig Wittgenstein: The Man and His Philosophy*, pp. 71–74. New York, 1967.

——. "Wittgenstein". In P. Edwards, ed., *The Encyclopedia of Philosophy*, VIII, 327–40. New York–London, 1967.

——. "Wittgenstein on the Nature of the Mind". In N. Rescher, ed., *Studies in the Theory of Knowledge*, pp. 9–29. Oxford, 1970.

——."Wittgenstein's *Philosophical Investigations*". In K. Fann, ed., *Ludwig Wittgenstein: The Man and His Philosophy*, pp. 181–213. New York, 1967.

Manser, Anthony R. "Pain and Private Language". In P. Winch, ed., *Studies in the Philosophy of Wittgenstein*, pp. 166–83. London, 1969.

Maslow, Alexander. *A Study in Wittgenstein's Tractatus*. Berkeley, 1961.

Matthews, Gareth B. "Meaning and Contrast" (symposium). *Proceedings of the Aristotelian Society*, Supplementary Vol. 43 (1969), 97–108.

Mauthner, Fritz. *Beiträge zu einer Kritik der Sprache*. 3 vols. 3d ed. Leipzig, 1923.

Moore, G. E. "The Character of Cognitive Acts" (symposium). *Proceedings of the Aristotelian Society*, 21 (1920–1921), 132–40.

——. *Commonplace Book 1919–1953*. Edited by C. Lewy. London, 1962.

——. *Ethics*. London, 1912.

——. Excerpt from his "Autobiography". In K. Fann, ed., *Ludwig Wittgenstein: The Man and His Philosophy*, pp. 39–40. New York, 1967.

——. *Lectures on Philosophy*. Edited by C. Lewy. London, 1966.

——. *Philosophical Papers*. London, 1959.

——. *Philosophical Studies*. London, 1922.

——. *Principia Ethica*. Cambridge, 1959.

——. "Reply to My Critics". In P. Schilpp, ed., *The Philosophy of G. E. Moore*, pp. 535–677. 2d ed. New York, 1952.

——. *Some Main Problems of Philosophy*. London, 1953.

Morick, Harold, ed. *Wittgenstein and the Problem of Other Minds*. New York, 1967.

Mounce, H. O. Review of E. Klemke, ed., *Essays on Wittgenstein*. *Mind*, 81 (1972), 618–20.

Mundle, Clement. *A Critique of Linguistic Philosophy*. Oxford, 1970.

Murphy, John P. "Another Note on a Misreading of Wittgenstein". *Analysis*, 29 (1968–1969), 62–64.

Murray, Michael. "A Note on Wittgenstein and Heidegger". *Philosophical Review*, 83 (1974), 501–3.

Naess, Arne. *Four Modern Philosophers: Carnap, Wittgenstein, Heidegger, Sartre*. Translated by A. Hannay. Chicago, 1968.

Nell, Edward J. "The Hardness of the Logical 'Must'". *Analysis*, 21 (1960–1961), 68–72.

Nestroy, Johann. *Ausgewählte Werke*. Edited by H. Weigel. Gütersloh, no date.

Neurath, Otto. "Protokollsätze". *Erkenntnis*, 3 (1932–1933), 204–14.

——. "Wege der wissenschaftlichen Weltauffassung". *Erkenntnis*, 1 (1930–1931), 106–25.

Nicod, Jean. *Foundations of Geometry and Induction*. Translated by P. Wiener. New York, 1950.

Ogden, C. K., and Richards, I. A. *The Meaning of Meaning*. 5th ed. London, 1938.

Passmore, John. *A Hundred Years of Philosophy*. London, 1957.

Pedersen, Johannes. *Israel. Its Life and Culture*. 2 vols. London, 1926.

Pitcher, George. "About the Same". In A. Ambrose and M. Lazerowitz, eds., *Ludwig Wittgenstein: Philosophy and Language*, pp. 120–39. London, 1972.

——. *The Philosophy of Wittgenstein*. Englewood Cliffs, 1964.

——. "Wittgenstein, Nonsense and Lewis Carroll". In K. Fann, ed., *Ludwig Wittgenstein: The Man and His Philosophy*, pp. 315–35. New York, 1967.

Pole, David. *The Later Philosophy of Wittgenstein*. London, 1958.

Popper, Karl. "Autobiography". In P. Schilpp, ed., *The Philosophy of Karl Popper*, I, 3–181. La Salle, Ill., 1974.

Prior, Arthur N. "Correspondence Theory of Truth". In P. Edwards, ed., *The Encyclopedia of Philosophy*, II, 223–32. New York–London, 1967.

Quine, Willard van Orman. *Word and Object*. New York, 1960.

Quinton, Anthony. "Excerpt from 'Contemporary British Philosophy'". In G. Pitcher, ed., *Wittgenstein: The Philosophical Investigations*, pp. 1–21. London, 1968.

Ramsey, Frank. *The Foundations of Mathematics and Other Logical Essays*. Edited by R. Braithwaite. London, 1931.

Reach, K. "The Name Relation and the Logical Antinomies". *Journal of Symbolic Logic*, 3 (1938), 97–111.

Rhees, Rush. *Discussions of Wittgenstein*. London, 1970.

——. Introductory Note to the English translation of Wittgenstein's remarks on Frazer's *Golden Bough*. *The Human World*, May 1971, 18–28.

——. "A Symposium: Assessments of the Man and the Philosopher". In K. Fann, ed., *Ludwig Wittgenstein: The Man and His Philosophy*, pp. 74–78. New York, 1967.

Richards, I. A. *Principles of Criticism*. 3d ed. London, 1947.

Russell, Bertrand. *The Analysis of Matter*. 2d ed. London, 1954.

——. *The Analysis of Mind*. London, 1933.

——. *The Autobiography of Bertrand Russell*, Vol. II. London, 1968.

——. *A History of Western Philosophy*. London–New York, 1945.

——. *An Inquiry into Meaning and Truth*. London, 1940.

——. *Introduction to Mathematical Philosophy*. London, 1948.

——. "Introduction". In Wittgenstein's *Tractatus* (see List of Abbreviations), pp. ix–xxii.

Russell, Bertrand. "The Limits of Empiricism". *Proceedings of the Aristotelian Society*, 36 (1935–1936), 131–50.

——. *Logic and Knowledge, Essays 1901–1950*. Edited by R. Marsh. London, 1956.

——. "Ludwig Wittgenstein". In K. Fann, ed., *Ludwig Wittgenstein: The Man and His Philosophy*, pp. 30–31. New York, 1967.

——. "Meinong's Theory of Complexes and Assumptions". *Mind*, 13 (1904), 204–19, 336–54, 509–24.

——. *My Philosophical Development*. London, 1959.

——. "On Propositions: What They Are and How They Mean". *Proceedings of the Aristotelian Society*, Supplementary Vol. 2 (1919), 1–43.

——. "On Scientific Method in Philosophy". In his *Mysticism and Logic*, pp. 75–93. London, 1963.

——. "On Verification". *Proceedings of the Aristotelian Society*, 38 (1937–1938), 1–20.

——. *Our Knowledge of the External World as a Field for Scientific Method in Philosophy*. London, 1926.

——. *An Outline of Philosophy*. London, 1927.

——. *Philosophical Essays*. London, 1910.

——. *Philosophy*. New York, 1927.

——. *The Principles of Mathematics*. 2d ed. London, 1927.

——. *The Problems of Philosophy*. Oxford, 1970.

——. "The Relevance of Psychology to Logic" (symposium). *Proceedings of the Aristotelian Society*, Supplementary Vol. 17 (1938), 42–53.

——. *The Scientific Outlook*. New York, 1931.

——, and Whitehead, Alfred N. *Principia Mathematica*. 3 vols. 2d ed. Cambridge, 1927.

Ryle, Gilbert. "The Theory of Meaning". In C. Mace, ed., *British Philosophy in Mid-Century*, pp. 239–64. London, 1957.

Schiller, F. C. S. "The Value of Formal Logic". *Mind*, 41 (1932), 53–71.

Schlick, Moritz. *Allgemeine Erkenntnislehre*. Berlin, 1918.

——. "Causality in Everyday Life and in Recent Science". In H. Feigl and W. Sellars, eds., *Readings in Philosophical Analysis*, pp. 515–33. New York, 1949.

——. "Form and Content, an Introduction to Philosophical Thinking". In his *Gesammelte Aufsätze* (below), pp. 151–250.

——. "The Foundations of Knowledge". In A. Ayer, ed., *Logical Positivism*, pp. 209–27. Glencoe, Ill., 1959.

——. "The Future of Philosophy". In R. Rorty, ed., *The Linguistic Turn*, pp. 43–53. Chicago, 1967.

——. *Gesammelte Aufsätze, 1926–1936*. Vienna, 1938.

——. "Meaning and Verification". In H. Feigl and W. Sellars, eds., *Readings in Philosophical Analysis*, pp. 146–70. New York, 1949.

——. "On the Relation between Psychological and Physical Concepts". In H. Feigl and W. Sellars, eds., *Readings in Philosophical Analysis*, pp. 393–407. New York, 1949.

——. "Positivism and Realism". In A. Ayer, ed., *Logical Positivism*, pp. 82–107. Glencoe, Ill., 1959.

——. "Vom Sinn des Lebens". *Symposion*, 1 (1927), 331–54.

Schopenhauer, Arthur. *Preisschrift über die Freiheit des Willens*. In *Arthur Schopenhauers sämtliche Werke*, III, 471–572. Munich, 1912.

——. *Über den Willen in der Natur*. In *Arthur Schopenhauers sämtliche Werke*, III, 271–427. Munich, 1912.

——. *The World as Will and Representation*. Translated by E. Payne. 2 vols. New York, 1966.

Searle, John. *Speech Acts: An Essay in the Philosophy of Language*. London, 1969.

Sellars, Wilfrid. *Science, Perception and Reality*. London, 1968.

Simon, Michael A. "When is a Resemblance a Family Resemblance?" *Mind*, 78 (1969), 408–16.

Smokler, Howard. Review of C. D. Broad, *Induction, Probability, and Causation*. *Journal of Philosophy*, 67 (1970), 45–49.

Specht, Ernst K. *The Foundations of Wittgenstein's Late Philosophy*. Translated by D. Walford. Manchester–New York, 1969.

——. "Wittgenstein und das Problem des *a priori*". *Revue internationale de philosophie*, 23 (1969), 167–82.

Spengler, Oswald. *Der Untergang des Abendlandes*, Vol. I. Vienna and Leipzig, 1918.

Spranger, Eduard. *Lebensformen*. Halle, 1930.

Squires, Roger. "Silent Soliloquy". In G. Vesey, ed., *Understanding Wittgenstein*, pp. 208–25. London, 1974.

Stegmüller, Wolfgang. *Hauptströmungen der Gegenwartsphilosophie*. Stuttgart, 1965.

Stenius, Erik. *Wittgenstein's 'Tractatus'. A Critical Exposition of Its Main Lines of Thought*. Oxford, 1960.

Stout, George F. *Analytic Psychology*. 2 vols. London, 1896.

——. *A Manual of Psychology*. New York, 1899.

——. "Phenomenalism". *Proceedings of the Aristotelian Society*, 39 (1938–1939), 1–18.

Strawson, Peter. "Review of Wittgenstein's *Philosophical Investigations*". In G. Pitcher, ed., *Wittgenstein: The Philosophical Investigations*, pp. 22–64. London, 1968.

——. *Introduction to Logical Theory*. London, 1952.

Teichman, Jenny. "Wittgenstein on Persons and Human Beings". In G. Vesey, ed., *Understanding Wittgenstein*, pp. 133–48. London, 1974.

Thornton, M. T. "Locke's Criticism of Wittgenstein". *Philosophical Quarterly*, 19 (1969), 266–71.

Toulmin, Stephen. "From Logical Analysis to Conceptual History". In P. Achinstein and S. Barker, eds., *The Legacy of Logical Positivism for the Philosophy of Science*, pp. 25–53. Baltimore, 1969.

——. "Ludwig Wittgenstein". *Encounter*, 32 (1969), 58–71.

Ullmann, Stephen. *Semantics, An Introduction to the Science of Meaning*. Oxford, 1962.

van Buren, Paul M. *The Edges of Language. An Essay in the Logic of a Religion*. New York, 1972.

van Peursen, Cornelis A. *Ludwig Wittgenstein: An Introduction to His Philosophy*. Translated by R. Ambler. New York, 1970.

Vesey, Godfrey. "Locke and Wittgenstein on Language and Reality". In H.

Lewis, ed., *Contemporary British Philosophy*, pp. 253–73. 4th ser. London, 1976.

Vesey, Godfrey. "Other Minds". In G. Vesey, ed., *Understanding Wittgenstein*, pp. 149–61. London, 1974.

von Wright, Georg Henrik. "Biographical Sketch". In N. Malcolm, *Ludwig Wittgenstein. A Memoir*, pp. 1–22. London, 1962.

——. "Georg Christoph Lichtenberg als Philosoph". *Theoria*, 8 (1942), 201–17.

——. "The Wittgenstein Papers". *Philosophical Review*, 78 (1969), 483–503.

——. "Wittgenstein's Views on Probability". *Revue internationale de philosophie*, 23 (1969), 259–83.

Waismann, Friedrich. "How I See Philosophy". In A. Ayer, ed., *Logical Positivism*, pp. 345–80. Glencoe, Ill., 1959.

——. *Introduction to Mathematical Thinking*. New York, 1951.

——. "Logische Analyse des Wahrscheinlichkeitsbegriffes". *Erkenntnis*, 1 (1930–1931), 228–48.

——. *The Principles of Linguistic Philosophy*. London, 1965.

——. "The Relevance of Psychology to Logic". In H. Feigl and W. Sellars, eds., *Readings in Philosophical Analysis*, pp. 211–21. New York, 1949.

——. "Über den Begriff der Identität". *Erkenntnis*, 6 (1936), 56–64.

——. "Verifiability" (symposium). *Proceedings of the Aristotelian Society*, Supplementary Vol. 19 (1945), 119–50.

Ward, James. *Psychological Principles*. 2d ed. Cambridge, 1920.

Warnock, G. J. *English Philosophy Since 1900*. 2d ed. Oxford, 1969.

Weiler, Gershon. *Mauthner's Critique of Language*. Cambridge, 1970.

Weyl, Hermann. "Die heutige Erkenntnislage in der Mathematik". *Symposion*, 3 (1926), 1–32.

Whittaker, James O. *Introduction to Psychology*. Philadelphia, 1965.

Wiedmann, Franz. *Philosophische Strömungen der Gegenwart*. Zurich, 1972.

Williams, Bernard, and Montefiore, Alan, eds. *British Analytical Philosophy*. London, 1966.

Wisdom, John. "A Feature of Wittgenstein's Technique". In K. Fann, ed., *Ludwig Wittgenstein: The Man and His Philosophy*, pp. 353–65. New York, 1967.

——. "Logical Constructions, II". *Mind*, 40 (1931), 460–75.

——. "Ludwig Wittgenstein, 1934–1937". In K. Fann, ed., *Ludwig Wittgenstein: The Man and His Philosophy*, pp. 46–48. New York, 1967.

——. *Problems of Mind and Matter*. Cambridge, 1934.

Zemach, Eddy. "The Nature of Consciousness". *Dialectica*, 27 (1973), 43–65.

——. "The Reference of 'I' ". *Philosophical Studies*, 23 (1972), 68–75.

GENERAL INDEX

The index, like the commentary, is intended to be used with the *Philosophical Investigations* close at hand, for some entries will lead the reader through the commentary to the relevant section or page of the *Investigations*.

A Companion to Wittgenstein's
"Philosophical Investigations"

Designed by R. E. Rosenbaum.
Composed by Vail-Ballou Press, Inc.,
in 10 point VIP Baskerville, 2 points leaded,
with display lines in Baskerville.
Printed offset by Vail-Ballou Press
Warren's Olde Style Wove, 50 pound basis.
Bound by Vail-Ballou Press
in Joanna book cloth
and stamped in All Purpose foil.

Library of Congress Cataloging in Publication Data
(For library cataloging purposes only)

Hallett, Garth.
  A companion to Wittgenstein's "Philosophical investigations"

  Bibliography: p.
  Includes index.
    1. Wittgenstein, Ludwig, 1889–1951. Philoso-
phische Untersuchungen.   I. Wittgenstein, Ludwig,
1889–1951. Philosophische Untersuchungen.   II. Title.
B3376.W563P5325   192   76-28014
ISBN 0-8014-0997-7